P9-CSF-259

Economics

FOR TODAY

8TH EDITION

Irvin B. Tucker
University of North Carolina Charlotte

SOUTH-WESTERN
CENGAGE Learning·

Australia • Brazil • Japan • Korea • Mexico • Singapore • Spain • United Kingdom • United States

SOUTH-WESTERN
CENGAGE Learning·

Economics for Today, Eighth Edition
Irvin B. Tucker

Senior Vice President, LRS/Acquisitions & Solutions Planning: Jack W. Calhoun

Editorial Director, Business & Economics: Erin Joyner

Editor-in-Chief: Joe Sabatino

Senior Acquisitions Editor: Steven Scoble

Developmental Editor: Clara Goosman

Editorial Assistant: Elizabeth Beiting-Lipps

Content Project Manager: Darrell E. Frye

Senior Market Development Manager: John Carey

Senior Brand Manager: Robin LeFevre

Marketing Coordinator: Chris Walz

Media Editor: Anita Verma

Senior Art Director: Michelle Kunkler

Senior Manufacturing Planner: Kevin Kluck

Rights Acquisition Director: Audrey Pettengill

Senior Rights Acquisition Specialist, Image: Deanna Ettinger

Senior Rights Acquisition Specialist, Text: John Hill

Cover and Internal Designer: Lou Ann Thesing

Cover Image: © Biddiboo/Taxi/Getty Images, Inc.

© 2014, 2011 South-Western, Cengage Learning

ALL RIGHTS RESERVED. No part of this work covered by the copyright herein may be reproduced, transmitted, stored, or used in any form or by any means graphic, electronic, or mechanical, including but not limited to photocopying, recording, scanning, digitizing, taping, web distribution, information networks, or information storage and retrieval systems, except as permitted under Section 107 or 108 of the 1976 United States Copyright Act, without the prior written permission of the publisher.

For product information and technology assistance, contact us at
Cengage Learning Customer & Sales Support, 1-800-354-9706
For permission to use material from this text or product,
submit all requests online at **www.cengage.com/permissions**
Further permissions questions can be emailed to
permissionrequest@cengage.com

Library of Congress Control Number: 2012949204

ISBN-13: 978-1-133-19010-3

ISBN-10: 1-133-19010-3

South-Western
5191 Natorp Boulevard
Mason, OH 45040
USA

Cengage Learning is a leading provider of customized learning solutions with office locations around the globe, including Singapore, the United Kingdom, Australia, Mexico, Brazil, and Japan. Locate your local office at: **www.cengage.com/global**

Cengage Learning products are represented in Canada by Nelson Education, Ltd.

For your course and learning solutions, visit **www.cengage.com**

Purchase any of our products at your local college store or at our preferred online store **www.cengagebrain.com**

Printed in Canada
1 2 3 4 5 6 7 16 15 14 13 12

Irvin B. Tucker

Irvin B. Tucker has over 30 years of experience teaching introductory economics at the University of North Carolina Charlotte. He earned his B.S. in economics at N.C. State University and his M.A. and Ph.D. in economics from the University of South Carolina. Dr. Tucker is former director of the Center for Economic Education at the University of North Carolina Charlotte and was a longtime member of the National Council on Economic Education. He is recognized for his ability to relate basic principles to economic issues and public policy. His work has received national recognition by being awarded the Meritorious Levy Award for Excellence in Private Enterprise Education, the Federation of Independent Business Award for Postsecondary Educator of the Year in Entrepreneurship and Economic Education, and the Freedom Foundation's George Washington Medal for Excellence in Economic Education. In addition, his research has been published in numerous professional journal articles on a wide range of topics including industrial organization, entrepreneurship, and economics of education. Dr. Tucker is also the author of the highly successful *Survey of Economics*, Eighth Edition, a text for the one-semester principles of economics courses published by Cengage South-Western Publishing.

Brief Contents

PART 1   **Introduction to Economics**   1

     Chapter   1   Introducing the Economic Way of Thinking   2

                     Appendix to Chapter 1: Applying Graphs to Economics   21

     Chapter   2   Production Possibilities, Opportunity Cost, and Economic Growth   34

PART 2   **Microeconomic Fundamentals**   57

     Chapter   3   Market Demand and Supply   58

                     Appendix to Chapter 3: Consumer Surplus, Producer Surplus, and Market Efficiency   91

     Chapter   4   Markets in Action   100

                     Appendix to Chapter 4: Applying Supply and Demand Analysis to Health Care   125

     Chapter   5   Price Elasticity of Demand and Supply   129

     Chapter   6   Consumer Choice Theory   154

                     Appendix to Chapter 6: Indifference Curve Analysis   169

     Chapter   7   Production Costs   181

PART 3   **Market Structures**   211

     Chapter   8   Perfect Competition   212

     Chapter   9   Monopoly   241

     Chapter   10   Monopolistic Competition and Oligopoly   267

     Chapter   11   Labor Markets   293

PART 4   **Microeconomics Policy Issues**   319

     Chapter   12   Income Distribution, Poverty, and Discrimination   320

     Chapter   13   Antitrust and Regulation   346

     Chapter   14   Environmental Economics   371

PART 5   **Macroeconomics Fundamentals**   401

     Chapter 15   Gross Domestic Product   402

                 Appendix to Chapter 15: A Four-Sector Circular Flow Model   429

     Chapter 16   Business Cycles and Unemployment   431

     Chapter 17   Inflation   457

PART 6   **Macroeconomic Theory and Policy**   483

     Chapter 18   The Keynesian Model   484

     Chapter 19   The Keynesian Model in Action   506

     Chapter 20   Aggregate Demand and Supply   530

                 Appendix to Chapter 20: The Self-Correcting Aggregate Demand and Supply Model   560

     Chapter 21   Fiscal Policy   576

     Chapter 22   The Public Sector   602

     Chapter 23   Federal Deficits, Surpluses, and the National Debt   626

PART 7   **Money, Banking, and Monetary Policy**   657

     Chapter 24   Money and the Federal Reserve System   658

     Chapter 25   Money Creation   680

     Chapter 26   Monetary Policy   704

                 Appendix to Chapter 26: Policy Disputes Using the Self-Correcting Aggregate Demand and Supply Model   732

     Chapter 27   The Phillips Curve and Expectations Theory   739

PART 8   **The International Economy**   769

     Chapter 28   International Trade and Finance   770

     Chapter 29   Economies in Transition   804

     Chapter 30   Growth and the Less-Developed Countries   825

Appendix A   Answers to Odd-Numbered Study Questions and
              Problems   849

Appendix B   Answers to Sample Quizzes   871

Appendix C   Answers to Road Map Questions   875

Appendix D   U.S. Gross Domestic Product and Related Statistics   876

Glossary   886

Index   900

Contents

ABOUT THE AUTHOR   iii

PREFACE   xxi

PART 1   Introduction to Economics   1

CHAPTER 1

Introducing the Economic Way of Thinking   2

1-1   The Problem of Scarcity   3

1-2   Scarce Resources and Production   3

1-3   Economics: The Study of Scarcity and Choice   5

1-4   The Methodology of Economics   6

CHECKPOINT   Can You Prove There Is No Trillion-Dollar Person?   9

1-5   Hazards of the Economic Way of Thinking   9

CHECKPOINT   Should Nebraska State Join a Big-Time Athletic Conference?   10

YOU'RE THE ECONOMIST   Mops and Brooms, the Boston Snow Index, the Super Bowl, and Other Economic Indicators   11

1-6   Why Do Economists Disagree?   12

YOU'RE THE ECONOMIST   Does the Minimum Wage Really Help the Working Poor?   13

1-7   Careers in Economics   14

Appendix to Chapter 1
Applying Graphs to Economics   21

A-1   A Direct Relationship   21

A-2   An Inverse Relationship   23

A-3   The Slope of a Straight Line   23

A-4   The Slope of a Curve   26

A-5   A Three-Variable Relationship in One Graph   27

A-6   A Helpful Study Hint for Using Graphs   29

CHAPTER 2

Production Possibilities, Opportunity Cost, and Economic Growth   34

2-1   Three Fundamental Economic Questions   35

2-2   Opportunity Cost   36

2-3 Marginal Analysis 37

2-4 The Production Possibilities Curve 38

2-5 The Law of Increasing Opportunity Costs 40

2-6 Sources of Economic Growth 42

CHECKPOINT What Does a War on Terrorism Really Mean? 44

YOU'RE THE ECONOMIST FedEx Wasn't an Overnight Success 45

2-7 Present Investment and the Future Production Possibilities Curve 45

GLOBAL ECONOMICS How Does Public Capital Affect a Nation's Curve? 47

Part 1: Road Map 54

PART 2 Microeconomic Fundamentals
57

CHAPTER 3
Market Demand and Supply 58

3-1 The Law of Demand 59

3-2 The Distinction between Changes in Quantity Demanded and Changes in Demand 60

3-3 Nonprice Determinants of Demand 63

CHECKPOINT Can Gasoline Become an Exception to the Law of Demand? 66

3-4 The Law of Supply 68

CHECKPOINT Can the Law of Supply Be Repealed for the Oil Market? 70

3-5 The Distinction between Changes in Quantity Supplied and Changes in Supply 71

3-6 Nonprice Determinants of Supply 72

YOU'RE THE ECONOMIST PC Prices: How Low Can They Go? 76

3-7 A Market Supply and Demand Analysis 78

3-8 Rationing Function of the Price System 80

GLOBAL ECONOMICS The Market Approach to Organ Shortages 82

CHECKPOINT Can the Price System Eliminate Scarcity? 83

Appendix to Chapter 3
Consumer Surplus, Producer Surplus, and Market Efficiency 91

CHAPTER 4

Markets in Action   100

4-1   Changes in Market Equilibrium   101

CHECKPOINT Why the Higher Price for Ethanol Fuel?   104

4-2   Can the Laws of Supply and Demand Be Repealed?   105

YOU'RE THE ECONOMIST Rigging the Market for Milk   110

CHECKPOINT Is There Price Fixing at the Ticket Window?   110

YOU'RE THE ECONOMIST Can Vouchers Fix Our Schools?   116

CHECKPOINT Should There Be a War on Drugs?   118

Appendix to Chapter 4
Applying Supply and Demand Analysis to Health Care   125

4A-1   The Impact of Health Insurance   125

4A-2   Shifts in the Demand for Health Care   127

4A-3   Shifts in the Supply of Health Care   128

CHAPTER 5

Price Elasticity of Demand and Supply   129

5-1   Price Elasticity of Demand   130

5-2   Price Elasticity of Demand Variations along a Demand Curve   136

CHECKPOINT Will Fliers Flock to Low Summer Fares?   136

5-3   Determinants of Price Elasticity of Demand   138

CHECKPOINT Can Trade Sanctions Affect Elasticity of Demand for Cars?   139

5-4   Other Elasticity Measures   140

YOU'RE THE ECONOMIST Cigarette Smoking Price Elasticity of Demand   141

CHECKPOINT Can Honda Compete with Itself?   147

CHAPTER 6

Consumer Choice Theory   154

6-1   From Utility to the Law of Demand   155

YOU'RE THE ECONOMIST Why Is Water Less Expensive than Diamonds?   157

CHECKPOINT When Dining Out, Do You Eat Smart?   160

6-2   Income and Substitution Effects and the Law of Demand   160

YOU'RE THE ECONOMIST Testing the Law of Demand with White Rats   162

CHECKPOINT Does the Substitution Effect Apply to Buying a Car?   163

Appendix to Chapter 6
Indifference Curve Analysis   169

   6A-1   Constructing an Indifference Curve   169

CHAPTER 7

Production Costs   181

   7-1   Costs and Profit   182

   CHECKPOINT   Should the Professor Go or Stay?   184

   7-2   Short-Run Production Costs   184

   7-3   Short-Run Cost Formulas   187

   7-4   Marginal Cost Relationships   190

   CHECKPOINT   Did Michael Jordan Beat the Marginal-Average Rule?   192

   7-5   Long-Run Production Costs   193

   7-6   Different Scales of Production   196

   YOU'RE THE ECONOMIST   Why Is That Web Site You're Using Free?   198

Part 2: Road Map   206

PART 3 Market Structures   211

CHAPTER 8

Perfect Competition   212

   8-1   Perfect Competition   213

   8-2   Short-Run Profit Maximization for a Perfectly Competitive Firm   215

   8-3   Short-Run Loss Minimization for a Perfectly Competitive Firm   220

   CHECKPOINT   Should Motels Offer Rooms at the Beach for Only $50 a Night?   223

   8-4   Short-Run Supply Curves under Perfect Competition   223

   8-5   Long-Run Supply Curves under Perfect Competition   226

   CHECKPOINT   Are You in Business for the Long Run?   228

   8-6   Three Types of Long-Run Supply Curves   228

   YOU'RE THE ECONOMIST   Recession Takes a Bite out of Gator Profits   232

CHAPTER 9

Monopoly   241

   9-1   The Monopoly Market Structure   242

GLOBAL ECONOMICS   Monopolies around the World   245

9-2   Price and Output Decisions for a Monopolist   246

YOU'RE THE ECONOMIST   The Standard Oil Monopoly   254

9-3   Price Discrimination   255

CHECKPOINT   Why Don't Adults Pay More for Popcorn at the Movies?   257

9-4   Comparing Monopoly and Perfect Competition   257

9-5   The Case against and for Monopoly   259

YOU'RE THE ECONOMIST   New York Taxicabs: Where Have All
the Fare Flags Gone?   260

CHAPTER 10
Monopolistic Competition and Oligopoly   267

10-1 The Monopolistic Competition Market Structure   268

10-2 The Monopolistically Competitive Firm as a Price Maker   269

YOU'RE THE ECONOMIST   Social Networking Sites: The New
Advertising Game   272

10-3 Price and Output Decisions for a Monopolistically Competitive Firm   272

10-4 Comparing Monopolistic Competition and Perfect Competition   274

10-5 Oligopoly—Competition among the Few   277

10-6 Price and Output Decisions for an Oligopolist   278

GLOBAL ECONOMICS   Major Cartels in Global Markets   282

10-7 An Evaluation of Oligopoly   285

CHECKPOINT   Which Model Fits the Cereal Aisle?   285

10-8 Review of the Four Market Structures   285

YOU'RE THE ECONOMIST   How Oligopolists Compete at the Final Four   286

CHAPTER 11
Labor Markets   293

11-1 The Labor Market under Perfect Competition   294

11-2 Labor Unions: Employee Power   299

11-3 Unions Use Collective Bargaining to Boost Wages   302

11-4 Union Membership around the World   302

11-5 Employer Power   304

CHECKPOINT   Can the Minimum Wage Create Jobs?   308

CHECKPOINT If You Don't Like It, Mickey, Take Your Bat and Go Home   308

YOU'RE THE ECONOMIST Should College Athletes Be Paid?   309

Part 3: Road Map   316

PART 4   Microeconomics Policy Issues   319

CHAPTER 12
Income Distribution, Poverty, and Discrimination   320

12-1 The Distribution of Income   321

12-2 Global Comparisons of Income Distribution   327

12-3 Poverty   327

12-4 Antipoverty Programs   330

Social Security: Past, Present, and Future   332

12-5 Reform Proposals   333

CHECKPOINT Does a Negative Income Tax Discourage Work?   335

YOU'RE THE ECONOMIST Pulling on the Strings of the Welfare
Safety Net   336

12-6 Discrimination   336

YOU'RE THE ECONOMIST Is Pay for Females Fair?   339

CHECKPOINT Should the Law Protect Women?   340

CHAPTER 13
Antitrust and Regulation   346

13-1 Antitrust   347

YOU'RE THE ECONOMIST Is Utah Pie's Slice of the Pie Too Small?   351

13-2 Key Antitrust Cases   352

CHECKPOINT Does Price-Fixing Improve Your Education?   355

13-3 Mergers and Global Antitrust Policy   356

13-4 Regulation   357

13-5 Three Cases for Government Regulation   359

YOU'RE THE ECONOMIST Who Turned Out the Lights in California?   362

CHECKPOINT Why Doesn't the Water Company Compete?   363

YOU'RE THE ECONOMIST Does Airline Deregulation Mean
Friendlier Skies?   365

CHAPTER 14
Environmental Economics   371

14-1 Competitive Markets and Environmental Efficiency   372

14-2 Achieving Environmental Efficiency   378

GLOBAL ECONOMICS How Should Carbon Emissions Be Reduced:
Cap and Trade or Carbon Taxes?   388

GLOBAL ECONOMICS Why Is the Climate Change Problem So Hard to Solve?   390

CHECKPOINT Is It Efficient to Buy Odor-Reducing Technology
if You Live Next to a Hog Farm?   393

Part 4: Road Map   399

PART 5 Macroeconomics Fundamentals   401

CHAPTER 15
Gross Domestic Product   402

15-1 Gross Domestic Product   403

15-2 Measuring GDP   404

15-3 The Expenditure Approach   406

15-4 The Income Approach   409

15-5 Compensation of Employees   409

CHECKPOINT How Much Does Mario Add to GDP?   411

15-6 GDP in Other Countries   412

15-7 GDP Shortcomings   412

15-8 Other National Income Accounts   415

YOU'RE THE ECONOMIST Is GDP a False Beacon Steering Us into the Rocks?   416

15-9 Changing Nominal GDP to Real GDP   419

CHECKPOINT Is the Economy Up or Down?   422

Appendix to Chapter 15
A Four-Sector Circular Flow Model   429

CHAPTER 16
Business Cycles and Unemployment   431

16-1 The Business-Cycle Roller Coaster   432

CHECKPOINT Where Are We on the Business-Cycle Roller Coaster?   436

16-2 Total Spending and the Business Cycle   438

16-3 Unemployment   439

16-4 Types of Unemployment   443

CHECKPOINT What Kind of Unemployment Did the Invention of the Wheel Cause?   446

16-5 The Goal of Full Employment   446

ECONOMICS IN PRACTICE What Kind of Unemployment Do Robot Musicians Cause?   447

16-6 The GDP Gap   448

YOU'RE THE ECONOMIST Brother Can You Spare a Dime?   451

CHAPTER 17

Inflation   457

17-1 Meaning and Measurement of Inflation   458

CHECKPOINT The College Education Price Index   461

YOU'RE THE ECONOMIST How Much More Does It Cost to Laugh?   462

17-2 Consequences of Inflation   465

CHECKPOINT What Is the Real Price of Gasoline?   467

17-3 Demand-Pull and Cost-Push Inflation   469

17-4 Inflation in Other Countries   470

GLOBAL ECONOMICS Who Wants to Be a Trillionaire?   472

Part 5: Road Map   479

PART 6   Macroeconomic Theory and Policy   483

CHAPTER 18

The Keynesian Model   484

18-1 Introducing Classical Theory and the Keynesian Revolution   485

CHECKPOINT What's Your MPC?   492

18-2 Reasons the Consumption Function Shifts   492

18-3 Investment Expenditures   494

18-4 Why Investment Demand Is Unstable   496

YOU'RE THE ECONOMIST Does a Stock Market Crash Cause Recession?   498

CHAPTER 19

The Keynesian Model in Action   506

19-1 Adding Government and Global Trade to the Keynesian Model   507

19-2 The Aggregate Expenditures Model   508

19-3 The Spending Multiplier Effect   513

19-4 Recessionary and Inflationary Gaps   517

CHECKPOINT Full-Employment Output, Where Are You?   520

CHECKPOINT How Much Spending Must Uncle Sam Cut?   520

GLOBAL ECONOMICS The Great Ice Cream War   522

CHAPTER 20

Aggregate Demand and Supply   530

20-1 The Aggregate Demand Curve   531

20-2 Reasons for the Aggregate Demand Curve's Shape   532

20-3 Nonprice-Level Determinants of Aggregate Demand   533

20-4 The Aggregate Supply Curve   534

20-5 Three Ranges of the Aggregate Supply Curve   539

20-6 Changes in the AD-AS Macroeconomic Equilibrium   542

20-7 Nonprice-Level Determinants of Aggregate Supply   546

20-8 Cost-Push and Demand-Pull Inflation Revisited   547

YOU'RE THE ECONOMIST Was John Maynard Keynes Right?   550

20-9 Increase in Both Aggregate Demand and Aggregate Supply Curves   551

CHECKPOINT Would the Greenhouse Effect Cause Inflation,
Unemployment, or Both?   551

Appendix to Chapter 20
The Self-Correcting Aggregate Demand and Supply Model   560

20A-1 Why the Short-Run Aggregate Supply Curve Is Upward Sloping   560

20A-2 Why the Long-Run Aggregate Supply Curve Is Vertical   562

20A-3 Equilibrium in the Self-Correcting AD-AS Model   563

20A-4 The Impact of an Increase in Aggregate Demand   563

20A-5 The Impact of a Decrease in Aggregate Demand   565

20A-6 Changes in Potential Real GDP   567

20A-7 Increase in the Aggregate Demand and Long-Run Aggregate Supply Curves 568

CHAPTER 21

Fiscal Policy   576

21-1 Discretionary Fiscal Policy   577
CHECKPOINT What Is the MPC for Uncle Sam's Stimulus Package?   581
CHECKPOINT Walking the Balanced Budget Tightrope   587
21-2 Automatic Stabilizers   587
21-3 Supply-Side Fiscal Policy   589
YOU'RE THE ECONOMIST The Laffer Curve   594

CHAPTER 22

The Public Sector   602

22-1 Government Size and Growth   603
22-2 Financing Government Budgets   605
22-3 The Art of Taxation   607
YOU'RE THE ECONOMIST Is It Time to Trash the 1040s?   614
22-4 Public Choice Theory   616
CHECKPOINT What Does Public Choice Say about a Budget Deficit?   620

CHAPTER 23

Federal Deficits, Surpluses, and the National Debt   626

23-1 The Federal Budget Balancing Act   627
YOU'RE THE ECONOMIST The Great Federal Budget Surplus Debate   633
23-2 Why Worry over the National Debt?   634
CHECKPOINT What's Behind the National Debt?   639
YOU'RE THE ECONOMIST How Real Is Uncle Sam's Debt?   644

Part 6: Road Map   651

PART 7   Money, Banking, and Monetary Policy   657

CHAPTER 24

Money and the Federal Reserve System   658

24-1 What Makes Money *Money*?   659
CHECKPOINT Are Debit Cards Money?   661
24-2 Other Desirable Properties of Money   661

GLOBAL ECONOMICS   Why a Loan in Yap Is Hard to Roll Over   662

24-3 What Stands behind Our Money?   663

24-4 Money Supply Definitions   663

History of Money in the Colonies   664

24-5 The Federal Reserve System   667

24-6 What a Federal Reserve Bank Does   670

24-7 The U.S. Banking Revolution   673

YOU'RE THE ECONOMIST   The Wreck of Lincoln Savings and Loan   674

CHAPTER 25

Money Creation   680

25-1 Money Creation Begins   681

25-2 How a Single Bank Creates Money   681

25-3 Multiplier Expansion of Money by the Banking System   686

25-4 How Monetary Policy Creates Money   688

CHECKPOINT   Who Has More Dollar Creation Power?   691

YOU'RE THE ECONOMIST   How Does the FOMC Really Work?   694

25-5 Monetary Policy Shortcomings   696

CHAPTER 26

Monetary Policy   704

26-1 The Keynesian View of the Role of Money   705

CHECKPOINT   What Does the Money Supply Curve Look Like When
the Fed Targets the Federal Funds Rate?   711

26-2 The Monetarist View of the Role of Money   714

CHECKPOINT   A Horse of Which Color?   718

26-3 A Comparison of Macroeconomic Views   719

YOU'RE THE ECONOMIST   Did the Fed Cause the Great Recession?   720

YOU'RE THE ECONOMIST   Monetary Policy during the Great Depression   723

Appendix to Chapter 26
Policy Disputes Using the Self-Correcting Aggregate
Demand and Supply Model   732

26A-1 The Classical versus Keynesian Views of Expansionary Policy   732

26A-2 Classical versus Keynesian Views of Contractionary Policy   733

CHAPTER 27

The Phillips Curve and Expectations Theory   739

27-1 The Phillips Curve   740

27-2 The Long-Run Phillips Curve   742

YOU'RE THE ECONOMIST   The Political Business Cycle   747

27-3 The Theory of Rational Expectations   748

CHECKPOINT   Does Rational Expectations Theory Work in the Classroom?   750

27-4 Applying the AD-AS Model to the Great Expectations Debate   750

27-5 Incomes Policy   752

CHECKPOINT   Can Wage and Price Controls Cure Stagflation?   754

27-6 How Different Macroeconomic Theories Attack Inflation   754

YOU'RE THE ECONOMIST   Ford's Whip Inflation Now (WIN) Button   756

Part 7: Road Map   764

PART 8   The International Economy   769

CHAPTER 28

International Trade and Finance   770

28-1 Why Nations Need Trade   771

28-2 Absolute and Comparative Advantage   774

CHECKPOINT   Do Nations with an Advantage Always Trade?   776

28-3 Free Trade versus Protectionism   776

28-4 Arguments for Protection   778

GLOBAL ECONOMICS   World Trade Slips on Banana Peel   780

28-5 Free Trade Agreements   781

Birth of the Euro   782

28-6 The Balance of Payments   782

CHECKPOINT   Should Everyone Keep a Balance of Payments?   788

28-7 Exchange Rates   788

GLOBAL ECONOMICS   Return to the Yellow Brick Road?   796

CHAPTER 29

Economies in Transition   804

29-1 Basic Types of Economic Systems   805

29-2 The "ISMS"   811

CHECKPOINT To Plan or Not to Plan—That Is the Question   815

29-3 Comparing Economic Systems   815

29-4 Economies in Transition   816

GLOBAL ECONOMICS China's Quest for Free Market Reform   818

29-5 Privatization versus Nationalization   820

CHAPTER 30

Growth and the Less-Developed Countries   825

30-1 Comparing Developed and Less-Developed Countries   826

30-2 Economic Growth and Development around the World   830

CHECKPOINT Does Rapid Growth Mean a Country Is Catching Up?   833

30-3 The Helping Hand of Advanced Countries   837

GLOBAL ECONOMICS Hong Kong: A Leaping Pacific Rim Tiger   838

CHECKPOINT Is the Minimum Wage an Antipoverty Solution
for Poor Countries?   842

Part 8: Road Map   847

Appendix A:
Answers to Odd-Numbered Study Questions and Problems   849

Appendix B:
Answers to Sample Quizzes   871

Appendix C:
Answers to Road Map Questions   875

Appendix D:
U.S. Gross Domestic Product and Related Statistics   876

GLOSSARY   886

INDEX   900

Available Versions

Conversion Table for the Four Versions of This Text

Economics for Today	Economics for Today	Macroeconomics for Today	Microeconomics for Today	Survey of Economics
1 Introducing the Economic Way of Thinking	X	X	X	X
2 Production Possibilities, Opportunity Cost, and Economic Growth	X	X	X	X
3 Market Demand and Supply	X	X	X	X
4 Markets in Action	X	X	X	X
5 Price Elasticity of Demand and Supply	X		X	X
6 Consumer Choice Theory	X		X	
7 Production Costs	X		X	X
8 Perfect Competition	X		X	X
9 Monopoly	X		X	X
10 Monopolistic Competition and Oligopoly	X		X	X
11 Labor Markets	X		X	X
12 Income Distribution, Poverty, and Discrimination	X		X	X
13 Antitrust and Regulation	X		X	
14 Environmental Economics	X		X	
15 Gross Domestic Product	X	X		X
16 Business Cycles and Unemployment	X	X		X
17 Inflation	X	X		X
18 The Keynesian Model	X	X		
19 The Keynesian Model in Action	X	X		
20 Aggregate Demand and Supply	X	X		X
21 Fiscal Policy	X	X		X
22 The Public Sector	X	X		X
23 Federal Deficits, Surpluses, and the National Debt	X	X		X
24 Money and the Federal Reserve System	X	X		X
25 Money Creation	X	X		X
26 Monetary Policy	X	X		X
27 The Phillips Curve and Expectations Theory	X	X		
28 International Trade and Finance	X	X	X	X
29 Economies in Transition	X	X	X	X
30 Growth and the Less-Developed Countries	X	X	X	X

Note: Chapter numbers refer to the complete book, *Economics for Today.*

Text with a Mission

The purpose of *Economics for Today*, eighth edition, is to teach, in an engaging style, the basic operations of the U.S. economy to students who will take a two-term economics course. Rather than taking an encyclopedic approach to economic concepts, *Economics for Today* focuses on the most important tool in economics—supply and demand analysis—and applies it to clearly explained real-world economic issues.

Every effort has been made to ensure that *Economics for Today* is the most "student-friendly" text on the market. This text was written because so many other economics textbooks expose students to a confusing array of analyses that force students to memorize facts to pass the course. Instead, *Economics for Today* presents a straightforward and unbiased approach that effectively teaches the application of basic economic principles. After reading this text, students should be able to say "now that economics stuff in the news makes sense."

How It Fits Together

This text presents the core principles of microeconomics, macroeconomics, and international economics. The first 14 chapters introduce the logic of economic analysis and develop the core of microeconomic analysis. Here students learn the role of demand and supply in determining prices in competitive versus monopolistic markets. This part of the book explores issues such as minimum wage laws, rent control, and pollution. The next 13 chapters develop the macroeconomics part of the text. Using the modern yet simple aggregate demand and aggregate supply model, the text explains measurement of and changes in price level, national output, and employment in the economy. The study of macroeconomics also includes how the supply of and demand for money influence the economy. Finally, this text concludes with three chapters devoted entirely to global issues. For example, students will learn how the supply of and demand for currencies determine exchange rates and what the complications of a strong or a weak dollar are.

Text Flexibility

The full version of *Economics for Today* is easily adapted to an instructor's preference for the sequencing of microeconomics and macroeconomics topics. This text can be used in a macroeconomic-microeconomic sequence by teaching the first four chapters and then Parts 5 through 7. Microeconomics is then covered in Parts 2 through 4. Finally, the course can be completed using Part 8, consisting of three chapters devoted to international economics.

An important design of this text is that it accommodates the two camps for teaching principles of macroeconomics: (1) those who cover both the Keynesian Cross and AD/AS models and (2) those who skip the Keynesian model and cover only the AD/AS model. For instructors who prefer the former model sequence, *Economics for Today* moves smoothly in Chapters 18 and 19 (8 and 9) from the Keynesian model (based on the Great Depression) to the AD/AS model in

Chapter 20 (10). For instructors using the latter approach, this text is written so that they can skip the Keynesian model in Chapters 18 and 19 (8 and 9) and proceed from Chapter 17 (7) to Chapter 20 (10) without losing any content. For example, the spending multiplier is covered in both the Keynesian and AD/AS model chapters.

For instructors who want to teach the self-correcting AD/AS model, they can emphasize the appendixes to Chapters 20 (10) and 26 (16). Instructors who choose not to cover this model can skip these appendixes. In short, *Economics for Today* provides more comprehensive and flexible coverage of macroeconomics models than is available in other texts. Also, a customized text might meet your needs. If so, contact your Cengage South Western sales representative for information.

How Not to Study Economics

To some students, studying economics is a little frightening because many chapters are full of graphs. Students often make the mistake of preparing for tests by trying to memorize the lines of graphs. When their graded tests are returned, students using this strategy may wonder what happened. The answer is that they should have learned the economic concepts *first;* then they would have understood the graphs as *illustrations* of the underlying concepts. Stated simply, superficial cramming for economics quizzes does not work.

For students who are anxious about using graphs, the appendix to Chapter 1 provides a brief review of graphical analysis. In addition, *The Graphing Workshop* on the Tucker Web site and the *Study Guide* contain step-by-step features on how to interpret graphs.

Changes to the Eighth Edition

The basic layout of the eighth edition remains the same. The following changes have been made:

- Chapter 1 recognizes that students taking introductory college-level economics courses are considering their major. One reason to select economics is that the average starting salary for an undergraduate economics major is higher compared to many other majors. To aid in their decision, current average starting salary figures for selected majors have been updated.

- Chapter 12 on income distribution, poverty, and discrimination has been updated with the latest figures on family income distribution and poverty rates. In addition, the feature article on fair pay for females has been updated. This feature generates great interest for students.

- Chapter 14 on environmental economics is one of today's highly controversial issues. This chapter has been updated and a new concept of sustainability added.

- Chapter 16 (6) on business cycles and unemployment includes updated business cycles and unemployment data. A new section on globalization discusses the differences between outsourcing and offshoring.

- Chapter 17 (7) on inflation updates data on inflation, including a global comparison of annual inflation rates. In addition, the Checkpoint titled "What Is the Real Price of Gasoline?" provides an application for adjusting the price of gasoline for inflation over time. In addition, students enjoy learning how Babe Ruth's 1932 salary is converted into today's dollars.

- Chapter 18 (8) on the Keynesian model now ends with a discussion of the investment function. Instead of the aggregate expenditures function being introduced here with only consumption and investment components, the aggregate expenditure model is presented after all components $(C + I + G + (X - M))$ are explained in Chapter 19 (9) on the Keynesian model in action. The complete aggregate expenditures model is now presented in a new Exhibit 2 in Chapter 19 (9). The objective is to make these two chapters more equal in length and provide a smoother progression in the development of the model.

- Chapter 21 (11) on fiscal policy uses realism as its hallmark by explaining the stimulus package and the spending multiplier process with real-world updated numbers.

- Chapter 22 (12) on the public sector highlights the important current issue of the changing economic character of the United States with global comparisons to other countries. Here, for example, updated data and exhibits trace the growth of U.S. government expenditures and taxes since the Great Depression. In addition, global comparison of spending and taxation exhibits have been revised.

- Chapter 23 (13) on federal deficits, surpluses, and the national debt focuses on the current "hot button" issue of federal deficits and the national debt by using updated data and exhibits. This chapter includes global comparisons of the deficit and national debt as a percentage of GDP.

- Chapter 24 (14) on money and the Federal Reserve System has updated money supply figures and Exhibit 4 showing the current listing of the ten top U.S. banks by asset size.

- Chapter 26 (16) on monetary policy has been updated using actual data in the model that link changes in the money supply and changes in the aggregate demand curve required to restore the economy to full employment. Student interest is enhanced by Exhibit 9 that compares monetary policy during the Great Depression to monetary policy during the current Great Recession.

- Each of the final three chapters of the text, the international chapters, has been updated. For example, the chapter on international trade and finance explains the recent U.S. balance of trade. The difference between absolute advantage and comparative advantage has been rewritten, with the discussion of absolute advantage now preceding the explanation of comparative advantage. The chapter on economies in transition contrasts privatization in Cuba, Russia, and China to recent nationalization in the United States. And the chapter on growth and the less-developed countries presents updated data used to explain, for example, the link between economic freedom and quality-of-life indicators.

- The lecture PowerPoint® slides have been updated and revised by the author.

- Each chapter includes a new sample quiz with new free corresponding tutorial quizzes that explain the answers on the Tucker Web site.

- New questions have been written by the author and added to the test bank.
- New Appendix D presents U.S. Gross Domestic Product and Related Statistics.
- With the growth in eReader usage among students, this edition features a new numbering system for major headings that we recommend instructors use instead of page numbers when creating assignments. For more information or to purchase an eReader for *Economics for Today,* please visit www.cengage brain.com.

Alternate Versions of the Book

For instructors who want to spend different amounts of time on their courses and offer different topics of this text:

- *Economics for Today.* This complete version of the book contains all 30 chapters. It is designed for two-semester introductory courses that cover both microeconomics and macroeconomics.
- *Microeconomics for Today.* This version contains 17 chapters and is designed for one-semester courses in introductory microeconomics.
- *Macroeconomics for Today.* This version contains 20 chapters and is designed for one-semester courses in introductory macroeconomics.
- *Survey of Economics for Today.* This version of the book contains 23 chapters. It is designed for one-semester courses that cover the basics of both microeconomics and macroeconomics.

The accompanying table shows which chapters are included in each book.

Instructors who want more information about these alternative versions should contact their local Cengage South-Western representative or visit www.cengage brain.com.

Motivational Pedagogical Features

Economics for Today strives to motivate and advance the boundaries of pedagogy with the following features:

PART OPENERS

Each part begins with a statement of the overall mission of the chapters in the part. In addition, there is a nutshell introduction of each chapter in relation to the part's learning objective.

CHAPTER PREVIEWS

Each chapter begins with a preview designed to pique student interest and reinforce how the chapter fits into the overall scheme of the book. Each preview appeals to students' "Sherlock Holmes" impulses by posing several economics puzzles that can be solved by understanding the material presented in the chapter.

Margin Definitions and Flashcards

Key concepts introduced in the chapter are highlighted in bold type and then defined with the definitions again in the margins. Therefore, this feature serves as a quick reference. Key terms are also defined on the Tucker Web site with a Flashcard feature that is useful for learning terms.

You're the Economist

Each chapter includes boxed inserts that provide the acid test of "relevance to everyday life." This feature gives students an opportunity to encounter timely, real-world extensions of economic theory. For example, students read about Fred Smith as he writes an economics term paper explaining his plan to create FedEx. To ensure that students waste no time figuring out which concepts apply to the article, applicable concepts are listed after each title. Many of these boxed features include quotes from newspaper articles over a period of years, demonstrating that economic concepts remain relevant over time.

Conclusion Statements

Throughout the chapters, highlighted conclusion statements of key concepts appear at the end of sections and tie together the material just presented. Students will be able to see quickly whether they understand the main points of the section. A summary of these conclusion statements is provided at the end of each chapter.

Global Economics

Today's economic environment is global. *Economics for Today* carefully integrates international topics throughout the text and presents the material using a highly readable and accessible approach designed for students with no training in international economics. All sections of the text that present global economics are identified by a special global icon in the margin and in the Global Economics boxes. In addition, the final three chapters of the book are devoted entirely to international economics.

Analyze the Issue

This feature follows each *You're the Economist* and *Global Economics* feature and asks specific questions that require students to test their knowledge of how the material in the boxed insert is relevant to the applicable concept. So that these questions can be used in classroom discussions or homework assignments, answers are provided in the *Instructor's Manual* rather than the text.

Checkpoint

Watch for these! Who said learning economics can't be fun? This feature is a unique approach to generating interest and critical thinking. These questions spark students to check their progress through challenging economics puzzles in gamelike style. Students enjoy thinking through and answering the questions then checking the answers at the end of the chapter. Students who answer correctly earn the satisfaction of knowing they have mastered the concepts.

ILLUSTRATIONS

Attractive large graphical presentations with grid lines and real-world numbers are essential for any successful economics textbook. Each exhibit has been carefully analyzed to ensure that the key concepts stand out clearly. Brief descriptions are included with graphs to provide guidance as students study the graphs. When actual data are used, the Web site reference is provided so that students can easily locate the data source.

CAUSATION CHAINS GAME

This will be one of your favorites. The highly successful causation chains are included under many graphs throughout the text. This pedagogical device helps students visualize complex economic relationships in terms of simple box diagrams that illustrate how one change causes another change. Each exhibit having a causation chain in the text is included in the Animated Causation Chains game on the Tucker Web site. This game makes it fun to learn. Arrange the blocks correctly and hear the cheers.

KEY CONCEPTS

Key concepts introduced in the chapters are listed at the end of each chapter and on the Tucker Web site. As a study aid, students can use the key concepts as flashcards to test their knowledge. First state the definition and then click on the term to check for correctness.

VISUAL SUMMARIES

Each chapter ends with a brief point-by-point summary of the key concepts. Many of these summarized points include miniaturized versions of the important graphs and causation chains that illustrate key concepts. These are intended to serve as visual reminders for students as they finish the chapters and are useful in reviewing and studying for quizzes and exams.

STUDY QUESTIONS AND PROBLEMS

The end-of-chapter questions and problems offer a variety of levels ranging from straightforward recall to deeply thought-provoking applications. The answers to odd-numbered questions and problems are in the back of the text. This feature gives students immediate feedback without requiring the instructor to check their work.

END-OF-CHAPTER SAMPLE QUIZZES

A great help before quizzes. Many instructors test students using multiple-choice questions. For this reason, the final section of each chapter provides the type of multiple-choice questions given in the instructor's Test Bank. The answers to all of these questions are given in the back of the text. In addition, students may visit the Tucker Web site and answer the questions in the online sample quizzes for free. In addition, students can email themselves and/or their instructor the quiz results with a list of correct and incorrect answers. The Web site is a tutorial because it provides explanations for why answers are correct.

PART ROAD MAP

This feature concludes each part and includes review questions listed by chapter from the previous part. To reinforce the concepts, each set of questions relates to the interactive causation chain game. Click on the Tucker Web site and make learning fun by listening to the cheers when correct and the jeers for a wrong answer. Answers to the questions are in the back of the text.

INTERACTIVE QUIZZES

In addition to the end-of-chapter sample quizzes, additional multiple-choice questions written by the author are available on the Tucker CourseMate Web site. Each quiz contains multiple questions like those found on a typical exam. Feedback is included for each answer so that students know instantly why they answered correctly or incorrectly. In addition, students can email themselves and/or their instructor the quiz results with a listi of correct and incorrect answers. Between this feature and the end-of-chapter sample quizzes, students are well prepared for tests.

ONLINE EXERCISES

These exercises for each chapter are designed to spark student excitement about researching on the Internet by asking them to access online economic data and then answer questions related to the content of the chapter. All Internet exercises are on the Tucker CourseMate site with direct links to the addresses so that students do not have the tedious and error-prone task of entering long Web site addresses.

LEARNING OBJECTIVES

Learning objectives link sections in the text and steps to achieve learning objectives. The steps include reference to "Ask the Instructor Video Clips" and the "Graphing Workshop" that are available through CourseMate on the Tucker Web site.

A Supplements Package Designed for Success

To access additional course materials for *Economics for Today,* [including Course-Mate], please visit www.cengagebrain.com. At the CengageBrain.com home page, search for the ISBN of your title (from the back cover of your book) using the search box at the top of the page. This will take you to the product page where these resources can be found. Or visit the Tucker Web site, www.cengage.com/economics/tucker. For additional information, contact your Cengage South-Western sales representative.

Instructor Resources

APLIA™

Aplia™, www.aplia.com, has joined forces with Cengage South-Western, the leading publisher for principles of economics and finance, to create the Aplia Integrated Textbook Solution. More students are currently using an Aplia™ product for principles of economics than those who are using all other Web-based learning programs combined. Because the homework in Aplia™ is automatically graded, you can assign homework more frequently to ensure that students are putting forth their full effort and getting the most out of your class.

INSTRUCTOR'S MANUAL

This manual, prepared by Douglas Copeland of Johnson County Community College, provides valuable course assistance to instructors. It includes chapter outlines, instructional objectives, critical-thinking/group discussion questions, hints for effective teaching, answers to the Analyze the Issue questions, answers to even-numbered questions and problems, summary quizzes with answers, and classroom games.

Instructor's Manual ISBN: 9781133562368

TEST BANK

Too often, Test Banks are not written by the author and the questions do not really fit the text. Not so here. This Test Bank was prepared by the text author to match the text. The Test Bank includes over 7,000 multiple-choice, true/false, and short essay questions arranged in the order presented in the chapter and grouped with concept headings that make it easy to select questions. Most questions have been thoroughly tested in the classroom by the author and are classified by topic and degree of difficulty.

Test Bank ISBN: 9781285184395 (Macroeconomics split), 9781285184401 (Microeconomics split), or on the IRCD: 9781285074269

ExamView®

ExamView® Computerized Testing Software contains all of the questions in the printed Test Bank. ExamView® is easy-to-use test creation software that is compatible with both Microsoft Windows® and Apple Macintosh®. You can add or edit questions, instructions, and answers; select questions by previewing them on the screen; or select questions randomly or by number. You can also create and administer quizzes online, whether over the Internet, a local area network (LAN), or a wide area network (WAN).

ExamView® available on Instructor's Resource CD: ISBN: 9781285074269

PowerPoint® Lecture Slides

This state-of-the-art slide presentation written and prepared by the text author provides you with visual support in the classroom for each chapter. Lecture slides contain vivid automated highlights of important concepts and exhibits. You can edit the PowerPoint® presentations or create your own exciting in-class presentations. These slides are available on the Instructor's Resource CD (9781285074269) as well as the Tucker Web site.

PowerPoint® Exhibit Slides

These slides contain the exhibits, charts, and tables from the text. You can easily incorporate them into your own PowerPoint® presentations by downloading them from the Instructor's Resource CD (9781285074269) as well as the Tucker Web site.

Instructor's Resource CD

Get quick access to all instructor ancillaries from your desktop. This easy-to-use CD lets you review, edit, and copy exactly what you need in the format you want. This supplement contains the *Instructor's Manual*, Test Bank, ExamView® Testing software, and PowerPoint® presentation slides.

IRCD ISBN: 9781285074269

Student Resources
The Tucker CourseMate Web Site

Available for purchase, the CourseMate Web site (www.cengagebrain.com) features a content-rich, robust set of interactive learning, study, and exam preparation tools to support the textbook. CourseMate includes an integrated eBook, interactive teaching and learning tools, quizzes, flashcards, videos, and more. It also includes Engagement Tracer, a first-of-its kind resource that monitors student engagement in the course.

Following are some of the CourseMate features that have been specifically developed with the student in mind:

- **Study Guide.** *The Study Guide*, available on the Cengage CourseMate site, is recommended for each student using the text. It is perhaps the best way to prepare for quizzes. The *Study Guide* was prepared by the text author to prepare students before they take tests in class. The *Study Guide* contains student-friendly features such as "Chapter in a Nutshell," key concepts review, learning objectives, fill-in-the-blank questions, step-by-step interpretation of the graph boxes, multiple-choice questions, true/false questions, and crossword puzzles.
  Study Guide ISBN: 9781285184371 (CourseMate ISBN)
- **News Videos.** This supplement consists of high-interest clips from current news events as well as historic raw footage going back 40 years. Perfect to use as discussion starters or to enrich your lectures and spark interest in the material in the text, these brief videos provide students with a new lens through which to view the past and present, one that will greatly enhance their knowledge and understanding of significant events and open up new dimension in learning. Clips are drawn from such programs as *World News Tonight, Good Morning America, This Week, PrimeTime Live, 20/20,* and *Nightline,* as well as numerous British Movietone News collections. Your Cengage South-Western representative will be happy to provide a complete list of the videos and policies addressed.
- **The Graphing Workshop.** The Graphing Workshop is a one-stop learning resource for help in mastering the language of graphs, one of the more difficult aspects of an economics course for many students. It enables students to explore important economic concepts through a unique learning system made up of tutorials; interactive drawing tools; and exercises that teach how to interpret, reproduce, and explain graphs.
- **Ask the Instructor Video Clips.** Via streaming video, difficult concepts are explained and illustrated. These video clips are extremely helpful review and clarification tools if a student has trouble understanding an in-class lecture or is a visual learner.

For Students and Instructors
CENGAGE LEARNING'S GLOBAL
ECONOMIC WATCH

Lessons from real life right now

The credit collapse. Tumbling markets. Bailouts and bankruptcies. Surging unemployment. Political debate. Today's financial turmoil transforms academic theory into intense real-life challenges that affect every family and business sector, making it one of the most teachable moments in modern history.

Cengage Learning's Global Economic Watch helps instructors bring these pivotal current events into the classroom through a powerful, continuously updated online suite of content, discussion forums, testing tools, and more.

The Watch, a first-of-its kind resource, stimulates discussion and understanding of the global downturn with easy-to-integrate teaching solutions:

- A content-rich blog of breaking news, expert analysis, and commentary updated multiple times daily, in addition to links to other blogs
- A powerful real-time database of hundreds of relevant and vetted journal, newspaper, and periodical articles; videos; and podcasts updated four times every day
- A thorough overview and timeline of events leading up to the global economic crisis
- Discussion and testing content, PowerPoint® slides on key topics, sample syllabi, and other teaching resources
- Instructor and student forums for sharing questions, ideas, and opinions

History is happening now. Bring it into your classroom. For more information on how you can enrich your course with The Watch, please visit www.cengage .com/thewatch.

TUCKER WEB SITE

The Tucker Web site at www.cengage.com/economics/tucker provides open access to PowerPoint® chapter review slides, flashcards, animated causation chains, tutorials for the text's end-of-chapter sample quizzes, and other downloadable teaching and learning resources.

Acknowledgments

A deep debt of gratitude is owed to the reviewers for their expert assistance. All comments and suggestions were carefully evaluated and served to improve the final product. To each of the reviewers of all eight editions, I give my sincerest thanks.

Special Thanks

My appreciation goes to Steve Scoble, Acquisitions Editor for Cengage South-Western. My thanks also to Clara Goosman, Developmental Editor; Darrell Frye, Content Project Manager; Elizabeth Beiting-Lipps, Editorial Assistant; and Iyssa Harbatkin, Marketing Coordinator who put all the pieces of the puzzle together and brought their creative talent to this text. I especially wish to express my deepest appreciation to Douglas Copeland of Johnson County Community College for preparing the *Instructor's Manual*. I am also grateful to John Carey and Robin LeFevre for their skillful marketing. Finally, I give my sincere thanks for a job well done to the entire team at Cengage South-Western.

Introduction to Economics

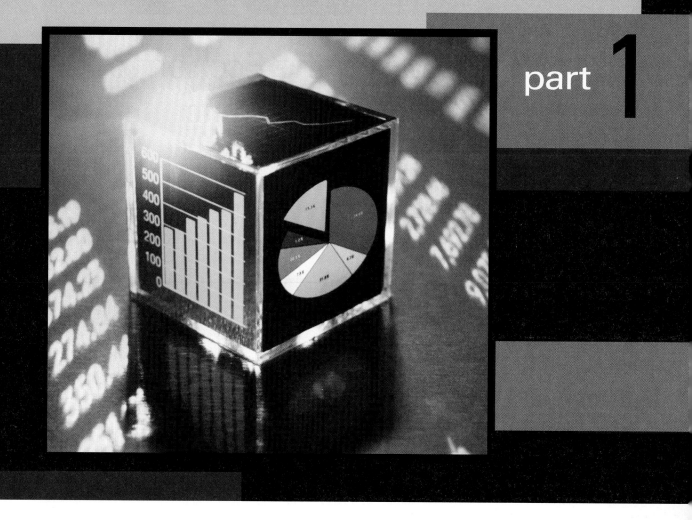

part 1

Jean Louis Batt/Getty Images

T he first two chapters introduce you to a foundation of economic knowledge vital to understanding the other chapters in the text. In these introductory chapters, you will begin to learn a valuable reasoning approach to solving economics puzzles that economists call "the economic way of thinking." Part 1 develops the cornerstone of this type of logical analysis by presenting basic economic models that explain such important topics as scarcity, opportunity cost, production possibilities, and economic growth.

chapter 1

Introducing the Economic Way of Thinking

Welcome to an exciting and useful subject economists call "the economic way of thinking." As you learn this reasoning technique, it will become infectious. You will discover that the world is full of economics problems requiring more powerful tools than just common sense. As you master the methods explained in this book, you will appreciate economics as a valuable reasoning approach to solving economics puzzles. Stated differently, the economic way of thinking is important because it provides a logical framework for organizing your thoughts and understanding an economic issue or event. Just to give a sneak preview, in later chapters, you will study the perils of government price fixing for gasoline and health care. You will also find out why colleges and universities charge students different tuitions for the same education. You will investigate whether you should worry if the federal government fails to balance its budget.

You will learn that the island of Yap uses large stones with holes in the center as money. In the final chapter, you will study why some countries grow rich while others remain poor and less developed. And the list of fascinating and relevant topics continues throughout each chapter. As you read these pages, your efforts will be rewarded by an understanding of just how economic theories and policies affect our daily lives—past, present, and future.

Chapter 1 acquaints you with the foundation of the economic way of thinking. The first building blocks joined are the concepts of scarcity and choice. The next building blocks are the steps in the model-building process that economists use to study the choices people make. Then we look at some pitfalls of economic reasoning and explain why economists might disagree with one another. The chapter concludes with a discussion of why you may want to be an economics major.

In this chapter, you will learn to solve these economics puzzles:

- Can you prove there is no person worth a trillion dollars?

- Why would you purchase more Coca-Cola when the price increases?

- How can we explain the relationship between the Super Bowl winner and changes in the stock market?

1-1 The Problem of Scarcity

Our world is a finite place where people, both individually and collectively, face the problem of scarcity. Scarcity is the condition in which human wants are forever greater than the available supply of time, goods, and resources. Because of scarcity, it is impossible to satisfy every desire. Pause for a moment to list some of your unsatisfied wants. Perhaps you would like a big home, gourmet meals, designer clothes, clean air, better health care, shelter for the homeless, and more leisure time. Unfortunately, nature does not offer the Garden of Eden, where every desire is fulfilled. Instead, there are always limits on the economy's ability to satisfy unlimited wants. Alas, scarcity is pervasive, so "You can't have it all."

> **Scarcity**
>
> The condition in which human wants are forever greater than the available supply of time, goods, and resources.

You may think your scarcity problem would disappear if you were rich, but wealth does not solve the problem. No matter how affluent an individual is, the wish list continues to grow. We are familiar with the "rich and famous" who never seem to have enough. Although they live well, they still desire finer homes, faster planes, and larger yachts. In short, the condition of scarcity means all individuals, whether rich or poor, are dissatisfied with their material well-being and would like more. What is true for individuals also applies to society. Even Uncle Sam can't escape the problem of scarcity because the federal government never has enough money to spend for the poor, education, highways, police, national defense, Social Security, and all the other programs it wishes to fund.

Scarcity is a fact of life throughout the world. In much of South America, Africa, and Asia, the problem of scarcity is often life-threatening. On the other hand, North America, Western Europe, and some parts of Asia have achieved substantial economic growth and development. Although life is much less grueling in the more developed countries, the problem of scarcity still exists because individuals and countries never have as much of all the goods and services as they would like to have.

> **CONCLUSION:** *The problem of scarcity and choice are basic economic problems faced by every society.*

1-2 Scarce Resources and Production

Because of the economic problem of scarcity, no society has enough resources to produce all the goods and services necessary to satisfy all human wants. Resources are the basic categories of inputs used to produce goods and services. Resources are also called *factors of production*. Economists divide resources into three categories: *land*, *labor*, and *capital* (see Exhibit 1).

> **Resources**
>
> The basic categories of inputs used to produce goods and services. Resources are also called *factors of production*. Economists divide resources into three categories: land, labor, and capital.

3

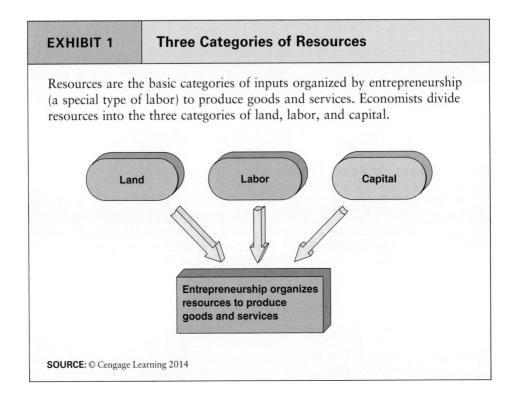

EXHIBIT 1	Three Categories of Resources

Resources are the basic categories of inputs organized by entrepreneurship (a special type of labor) to produce goods and services. Economists divide resources into the three categories of land, labor, and capital.

Land   Labor   Capital

Entrepreneurship organizes resources to produce goods and services

SOURCE: © Cengage Learning 2014

1-2a LAND

Land

Any natural resource provided by nature that is used to produce a good or service.

Land is a shorthand expression for any natural resource provided by nature that is used to produce a good or service. *Land* includes those resources that are gifts of nature available for use in the production process. Farming, building factories, and constructing oil refineries would be impossible without land. Land includes anything natural above or below the ground, such as forests, gold, diamonds, oil, coal, wind, and the ocean. Two broad categories of natural resources are *renewable resources* and *nonrenewable resources*. Renewable resources are basic inputs that nature can automatically replace. Examples include lakes, crops, and clean air. Nonrenewable resources are basic inputs that nature cannot automatically replace. There is only so much coal, oil, and natural gas in the world. If these fossil fuels disappear, we must use substitutes.

1-2b LABOR

Labor

The mental and physical capacity of workers to produce goods and services.

Labor is the mental and physical capacity of workers to produce goods and services. The services of farmers, assembly-line workers, lawyers, professional football players, and economists are all *labor*. The labor resource is measured both by the number of people available for work and by the skills or quality of workers. One reason nations differ in their ability to produce is that human characteristics, such as the education, experience, health, and motivation of workers, differ among nations.

Entrepreneurship

The creative ability of individuals to seek profits by taking risks and combining resources to produce innovative products.

Entrepreneurship is a special type of labor. Entrepreneurship is the creative ability of individuals to seek profits by taking risks and combining resources to produce innovative products. An *entrepreneur* is a motivated person who seeks profits by undertaking such risky activities as starting new businesses, creating new products, or inventing new ways of accomplishing tasks. Entrepreneurship is a scarce human resource because relatively few people are willing or able to innovate and make decisions involving greater-than-normal chances for failure. An important benefit of entrepreneurship is that it creates a growing economy.

Entrepreneurs are the agents of change who bring material progress to society. The birth of the Levi Strauss Company is a classic entrepreneurial success story. In 1853, at the age of 24, Levi Strauss, who was born in Bavaria, sailed from New York to join the California Gold Rush. His intent was not to dig for gold, but to sell cloth. By the time he arrived in San Francisco, he had sold most of his cloth to other people on the ship. The only cloth he had left was a roll of canvas for tents and covered wagons. On the dock, he met a miner who wanted sturdy pants that would last while digging for gold, so Levi made a pair from the canvas. Later, a customer gave Levi the idea of using little copper rivets to strengthen the seams. Presto! Strauss knew a good thing when he saw it, so he hired workers, built factories, and became one of the largest pants makers in the world. As a reward for taking business risks, organizing production, and introducing a product, the Levi Strauss Company earned profits, and Strauss became rich and famous.

1-2c CAPITAL

Capital is a human-made good used to produce other goods and services. Capital includes the physical plants, machinery, and equipment used to produce other goods. Capital goods are human-made goods that do not directly satisfy human wants. Before the Industrial Revolution, *capital* meant a tool, such as a hoe, an axe, or a bow and arrow. In those days, these items served as capital to build a house or provide food for the dinner table. Today, capital also consists of factories, office buildings, warehouses, robots, trucks, roads, and distribution facilities. College buildings, the printing presses used to produce this textbook, and iPhones are also examples of capital. The term *capital* as it is used in the study of economics can be confusing. Economists know that capital in everyday conversations means money or the money value of paper assets, such as stocks, bonds, or a deed to a house. This is actually *financial* capital. In the study of economics, capital does not refer to money assets. Capital in economics means a factor of production, such as a factory or machinery. Stated simply, you must pay special attention to this point: Money is not capital and is therefore not a resource. Instead, money is used to purchase land, labor, or capital.

Capital
A human-made good used to produce other goods and services.

> **CONCLUSION:** *Money by itself does not produce goods and services; instead, it is only a means of buying capital.*

1-3 Economics: The Study of Scarcity and Choice

The perpetual problem of scarcity forcing people to make choices is the basis for the definition of economics. Economics is the study of how society chooses to allocate its scarce resources to the production of goods and services to satisfy

Economics
The study of how society chooses to allocate its scarce resources to the production of goods and services to satisfy unlimited wants.

unlimited wants. You may be surprised by this definition. People often think economics means studying supply and demand, the stock market, money, and banking. In fact, there are many ways one could define *economics*, but economists accept the definition given here because it includes the link between *scarcity* and *choices*.

Society makes two kinds of choices: economy-wide, or macro choices, and individual, or micro, choices. The prefixes *macro* and *micro* come from the Greek words meaning "large" and "small," respectively. Reflecting the macro and micro perspectives, economics consists of two main branches: *macroeconomics* and *microeconomics*.

1-3a MACROECONOMICS

Macroeconomics

The branch of economics that studies decision making for the economy as a whole.

The old saying "Looking at the forest rather than the trees" describes macroeconomics. Macroeconomics is the branch of economics that studies decision making for the economy as a whole. Macroeconomics applies an overview perspective to an economy by examining economy-wide variables, such as inflation, unemployment, growth of the economy, the money supply, and the national incomes of developing countries. Macroeconomic decision making considers such "big picture" policies as the effect that federal tax cuts will have on unemployment and the effect that changing the money supply will have on prices.

1-3b MICROECONOMICS

Microeconomics

The branch of economics that studies decision making by a single individual, household, firm, industry, or level of government.

Examining individual trees, leaves, and pieces of bark, rather than surveying the forest, illustrates microeconomics. Microeconomics is the branch of economics that studies decision making by a single individual, household, firm, industry, or level of government. Microeconomics applies a microscope to study specific parts of an economy, as one would examine cells in the body. The focus is on small economic units, such as economic decisions of particular groups of consumers and businesses. An example of microeconomic analysis would be to study economic units involved in the market for ostrich eggs. Will suppliers decide to supply more, less, or the same quantity of ostrich eggs to the market in response to price changes? Will individual consumers of these eggs decide to buy more, less, or the same quantity at a new price?

We have described macroeconomics and microeconomics as two separate branches, but they are related. Because the overall economy is the sum, or aggregation, of its parts, micro changes affect the macro economy, and macro changes produce micro changes.

1-4 The Methodology of Economics

As used by other disciplines, such as criminology, biology, chemistry, and physics, economists employ a step-by-step procedure for solving problems by identifying the problem, developing a model, gathering data, and testing whether the data are consistent with the theory. Based on this analysis, economists formulate a conclusion. Exhibit 2 summarizes the model-building process.

EXHIBIT 2	The Steps in the Model-Building Process

The first step in developing a model is to identify the problem. The second step is to select the critical variables necessary to formulate a model that explains the problem under study. Eliminating other variables that complicate the analysis requires simplifying assumptions. In the third step, the researcher collects data and tests the model. If the evidence supports the model, the conclusion is to accept the model. If the evidence doesn't support the model, the model is rejected.

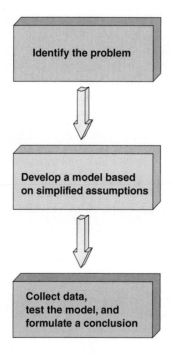

SOURCE: © Cengage Learning 2014

1-4a PROBLEM IDENTIFICATION

The first step in applying the economic method is to define the issue. Suppose an economist wishes to investigate the microeconomic problem of why U.S. motorists cut back on gasoline consumption in a given year from, for example, 400 million gallons per day in May to 300 million gallons per day in December.

1-4b MODEL DEVELOPMENT

The second step in our hypothetical example toward finding an explanation is for the economist to build a model. A model is a simplified description of reality used to understand and predict the relationship between variables. The terms *model* and *theory* are interchangeable. A model emphasizes only those variables that

Model

A simplified description of reality used to understand and predict the relationship between variables.

A map is a model because it is an abstraction from reality.

are most important to explaining an event. As Albert Einstein said, "Theories should be as simple as possible, but not more so." The purpose of a model is to construct an abstraction from real-world complexities and make events understandable. Consider a model airplane that is placed in a wind tunnel to test the aerodynamics of a new design. For this purpose, the model must represent only the shapes of the wings and fuselage, but it does not need to include tiny seats, electrical wiring, or other interior design details. A highway map is another example. To find the best route to drive between two distant cities, you do not want extraneous information on the location of all roads, streets, potholes, telephone lines, trees, stoplights, schools, hospitals, and firehouses. This would be too much detail, and the complexity would make it difficult to choose the best route.

To be useful, a model requires simplified assumptions. Someone must decide, for example, whether a map will include only symbols for the major highways or the details of hiking trails through mountains. In our gasoline consumption example, several variables might be related to the quantity of gasoline consumed, including consumer incomes, the prices of substitutes for gasoline, the price of gasoline, the fuel economy of cars, and weather conditions. Because a theory focuses only on the main or critical variables, the economist must be a "Sherlock Holmes" and use a keen sense of observation to form a model. Using his or her expertise, the economist must select the variables that are related to gasoline consumption and reject variables that have only a slight or no relationship to gasoline consumption. In this simple case, the economist removes the cloud of complexity by formulating the theory that increases in the price of gasoline *cause* the quantity of gasoline consumed to decrease during the time period.

1-4c TESTING A THEORY

An economic model can be stated as a verbal argument, numerical table, graph, or mathematical equation. You will soon discover that a major part of this book is devoted to building and using economic models. The purpose of an economic model is to *forecast* or *predict* the results of various changes in variables. Note that the appendix to this chapter provides a review of graphical analysis. An economic theory can be expressed in the form "If *A*, then *B*, other things held constant." An economic model is useful only if it yields accurate predictions. When the evidence is consistent with the theory that *A* causes outcome *B*, there is confidence in the theory's validity. When the evidence is inconsistent with the theory that *A* causes outcome *B*, the researcher rejects this theory.

In the third step, the economist gathers data to test the theory that if the price of gasoline rises, then gasoline purchases fall—all other relevant factors held constant. Suppose the investigation reveals that the price of gasoline rose sharply between May and December of the given year. The data are therefore consistent with the theory that the quantity of gasoline consumed per month falls when its price rises, assuming no other relevant factors change. Thus, the conclusion is that the theory is valid if, for example, consumer incomes or population size does not change at the same time that gasoline prices rise.

✔ CHECKPOINT

Can You Prove There Is No Trillion-Dollar Person?

Suppose a theory says that no U.S. citizen is worth $1 trillion. You decide to test this theory and send researchers to all corners of the nation to check financial records to see whether someone qualifies by owning assets valued at $1 trillion or more. After years of checking, the researchers return and report that not a single person is worth at least $1 trillion. Do you conclude that the evidence proves the theory? Explain.

1-5 Hazards of the Economic Way of Thinking

Models help us understand and predict the impact of changes in economic variables. A model is an important tool in the economist's toolkit, but it must be handled with care. The economic way of thinking seeks to avoid reasoning mistakes. Two of the most common pitfalls to clear thinking are (1) failing to understand the *ceteris paribus assumption* and (2) confusing *association* and *causation*.

1-5a THE CETERIS PARIBUS ASSUMPTION

As you work through a model, try to think of a host of relevant variables assumed to be "standing still," or "held constant." Ceteris paribus is a Latin phrase that means while certain variables change, "all other things remain unchanged." In short, the ceteris paribus assumption allows us to isolate or focus attention on selected variables. In the gasoline example discussed earlier, a key simplifying assumption of the model is that changes in consumer incomes and certain other variables do not occur and complicate the analysis. The ceteris paribus assumption holds everything else constant, and therefore allows us to concentrate on the relationship between two key variables: changes in the price of gasoline and the quantity of gasoline purchased per month.

> **Ceteris paribus**
>
> A Latin phrase that means while certain variables change, "all other things remain unchanged"

Now suppose an economist examines a model explaining the relationship between the price and quantity purchased of Coca-Cola. The theory is "If the price increases, then the quantity of Coca-Cola purchased decreases, ceteris paribus." Now assume you observe that the price of Coca-Cola increased one summer and some people actually bought more, not less. Based on this real-world observation, you declare the theory is incorrect. Think again! The economist responds that this is a reasoning pitfall because the model is valid based on the assumption of ceteris paribus, and your observation gives us no reason to reject the model. The reason the model appeared flawed is because another factor, a sharp rise in the temperature, *caused* people to buy more Coca-Cola in spite of its higher price. If the temperature and all other factors are held constant as the price of Coca-Cola rises, then people will indeed buy less Coca-Cola, as the model predicts.

> **CONCLUSION:** *A theory cannot be tested legitimately unless its ceteris paribus assumption is satisfied.*

1-5b ASSOCIATION VERSUS CAUSATION

Another common error in reasoning is confusing *association* (or correlation) and *causation* between variables. Stated differently, you err when you read more into a relationship between variables than is actually there. A model is valid only when a cause-and-effect relationship is stable or dependable over time, rather than being an association that occurs by chance and eventually disappears. Suppose a witch doctor performs a voodoo dance during three different months and stock market prices skyrocket during each of these months. The voodoo dance is *associated* with the increase in stock prices, but this does not mean the dance *caused* the event. Even though there is a statistical relationship between these two variables in a number of observations, eventually the voodoo dance will be performed, and stock prices will fall or remain unchanged. The reason is that there is no true systematic economic relationship between voodoo dances and stock prices.

Further investigation may reveal that stock prices actually responded to changes in interest rates during the months that the voodoo dances were performed. Changes in interest rates affect borrowing and, in turn, profits and stock prices. In contrast, there is no real economic relationship between voodoo dances and stock prices, and, therefore, the voodoo model is not valid.

CONCLUSION: *The fact that one event follows another does not necessarily mean that the first event caused the second event.*

✔ CHECKPOINT

Should Nebraska State Join a Big-Time Athletic Conference?

Nebraska State (a mythical university) stood by while Penn State, Florida State, the University of Miami, and the University of South Carolina joined big-time athletic conferences. Now Nebraska State officials are pondering whether to remain independent or to pursue membership in a conference noted for high-quality football and basketball programs. An editorial in the newspaper advocates joining and cites a study showing that universities belonging to major athletic conferences have higher graduation rates than nonmembers. Because educating its students is the number one goal of Nebraska State, will this evidence persuade Nebraska State officials to join a big-time conference? Why or why not?

Throughout this book, you will study economic models or theories that include variables linked by stable cause-and-effect relationships. For example, the theory that a change in the price of a good *causes* a change in the quantity purchased is a valid microeconomic model. The theory that a change in the money supply *causes* a change in interest rates is an example of a valid macroeconomic model. The You're the Economist gives some amusing examples of the "association means causation" reasoning pitfall.

Mops and Brooms, the Boston Snow Index, the Super Bowl, and Other Economic Indicators

Applicable Concept: association versus causation

Although the Commerce Department, the Wharton School, the Federal Reserve Board, and other organizations publish economic forecasts and data on key economic indicators, they are not without armchair competition. For example, the chief executive of Standex International Corporation, Daniel E. Hogan, reported that his company can predict economic downturns and recoveries from sales reports of its National Metal Industries subsidiary in Springfield, Massachusetts. National makes metal parts for about 300 U.S. manufacturers of mops and brooms. A drop in National's sales always precedes a proportional fall in consumer spending. The company's sales always pick up slightly before consumer spending does.[1]

The Boston Snow Index (BSI) is the brainchild of a vice president of a New York securities firm. It predicts a rising economy for the next year if there is snow on the ground in Boston on Christmas Day. The BSI predicted correctly about 73 percent of the time over a 30-year period. However, its creator, David L. Upshaw, did not take it too seriously and views it as a spoof of other forecasters' methods.

Greeting card sales are another tried and true indicator, according to a vice president of American Greetings. Before a recession sets in, sales of higher-priced greeting cards rise. It seems that people substitute the cards for gifts, and since there is no gift, the card must be fancier.

A Super Bowl win by an NFC team predicts that in the following December, the stock market will be higher than the year before. A win by an old AFL team predicts a dip in the stock market.

Several other less well-known indicators have also been proposed. For example, one economist suggested that the surliness of waiters is a countercyclical indicator. If they are nice, expect that bad times are coming, but if they are rude, expect an upturn. Waiters, on the other hand, counter that a fall in the average tip usually precedes a downturn in the economy.

Finally, Anthony Chan, chief economist for Bank One Investment Advisors, studied marriage trends

over a 34-year period. He discovered that when the number of marriages increases, the economy rises significantly, and a slowdown in marriages is followed by a decline in the economy. Chan explains that there is usually about a one-year lag between a change in the marriage rate and the economy.[2]

Analyze the Issue

Which of the above indicators are examples of causation? Explain.

---

1. "Economic Indicators, Turtles, Butterflies, Monks, and Waiters," *The Wall Street Journal*, Aug. 27, 1979, pp. 1, 16.
2. Sandra Block, "Worried? Look at Wedding Bell Indicator," *The Charlotte Observer*, Apr. 15, 1995, p. 8A.

Source: © Cengage Learning 2014

1-6 Why Do Economists Disagree?

Why might one economist say a clean environment should be our most important priority and another economist say economic growth should be our most important goal? If economists share the economic way of thinking and carefully avoid reasoning pitfalls, then why do they disagree? Why are economists known for giving advice by saying, "On the one hand, if you do this, then *A* results, and on the other hand, doing this causes result *B*?" In fact, President Harry Truman once jokingly exclaimed, "Find me an economist with only one hand." George Bernard Shaw offered another famous line in the same vein: "If you took all the economists in the world and laid them end to end, they would never reach a conclusion." These famous quotes imply that economists should agree, but the quotes ignore the fact that physicists, doctors, business executives, lawyers, and other professionals often disagree.

Economists may appear to disagree more than other professionals partly because it is more interesting to report disagreements than agreements. Actually, economists agree on a wide range of issues. Many economists, for example, agree on free trade among nations, the elimination of farm subsidies and rent ceilings, government deficit spending to recover from a recession, and many other issues. When disagreements do exist, the reason can often be explained by the difference between *positive economics* and *normative economics*.

1-6a POSITIVE ECONOMICS

Positive economics

An analysis limited to statements that are verifiable.

Positive economics deals with facts and therefore addresses "what is" or "verifiable" questions. Positive economics is an analysis limited to statements that are verifiable. Positive statements can be proven either true or false. Often a positive statement is expressed: "If *A*, then *B*." For example, if the national unemployment rate rises to 9 percent, then teenage unemployment exceeds 80 percent. This is a positive "if-then" prediction, which may or may not be correct. Accuracy is not the criterion for a statement to be positive. The key consideration is whether the statement is *testable* and not whether it is true or false. Suppose the data show that when the nation's overall unemployment rate is close to 9 percent, the unemployment rate for teenagers never reaches 80 percent. For example, the overall unemployment rate was 9.3 percent in 2011, and the rate for teenagers was 24.3 percent—far short of 80 percent. Based on the facts, we would conclude that this positive statement is false.

Now we can explain one reason why economists' forecasts can diverge. The statement "If event *A* occurs, then event *B* follows" can be thought of as a *conditional* positive statement. For example, two economists may agree that if the federal government cuts spending by 10 percent this year, prices will fall about 2 percent next year. However, their predictions about the fall in prices may differ because one economist assumes Congress will not cut spending, while the other economist assumes Congress will cut spending by 10 percent.

CONCLUSION: *Economists' forecasts can differ because using the same methodology, economists can agree that event A causes event B, but disagree over the assumption that event A will occur.*

Does the Minimum Wage Really Help the Working Poor?

Applicable Concepts: positive and normative analyses

Minimum wages exist in more than 100 countries. In 1938, Congress enacted the federal Fair Labor Standards Act, commonly known as the "minimum-wage law." Today, a minimum wage worker who works full-time still earns a deplorably low annual income. One approach to help the working poor earn a living wage might be to raise the minimum wage.

The dilemma for Congress is that a higher minimum wage for the employed is enacted at the expense of jobs for unskilled workers. Opponents forecast that the increased labor cost from a large minimum wage hike would jeopardize hundreds of thousands of unskilled jobs. For example, employers may opt to purchase more capital and less expensive labor. The fear of such sizable job losses forces Congress to perform a difficult balancing act to ensure that a minimum wage increase is large enough to help the working poor, but not so large as to threaten their jobs.

Some politicians claim that raising the minimum wage is a way to help the working poor without cost to taxpayers. Others believe the cost is hidden in inflation and lost employment opportunities for marginal workers, such as teenagers, the elderly, and minorities. One study by economists, for example, examined 60 years of data and concluded that minimum wage increases resulted in reduced employment and hours of work for low-skilled workers.[1]

Another problem with raising the minimum wage to aid the working poor is that minimum wage is a blunt weapon for redistributing wealth. Studies show that only a small percentage of minimum wage earners are full-time workers whose family income falls below the poverty line. This means that most increases in the minimum wage go to workers who are not poor. For example, many minimum wage workers are students living at home or workers whose spouse earns a much higher income. To help only the working poor, some economists argue that the government should target only those people who need assistance, rather than using the "shotgun" approach of raising the minimum wage.

Supporters of raising the minimum wage are not convinced by these arguments. They say it is outrageous that a worker can work full-time and still live in poverty. Moreover, people on this side of the debate believe that opponents exaggerate the dangers to the economy from a higher minimum wage. For example, one could argue that a higher minimum wage will force employers to upgrade the skills and productivity of their workers. Increasing the minimum wage may therefore be a win-win proposition rather than a win-lose proposition. Finally, across the United States, 32 states and numerous localities have implemented minimum wage laws. At least 17 states recently raised the minimum wage or are considering doing so in 2012, the most in at least six years. The Republican presidential candidate Mitt Romney and President Obama

iStockphoto.com/Tomislav Stajduhar

support automatic federal minimum wage increases to keep up with inflation. Note that we return to this issue in Chapter 4 as an application of supply and demand analysis.

Analyze the Issue

1. Identify two positive and two normative statements given above concerning raising the minimum wage. List other minimum wage arguments not discussed in this You're the Economist, and classify them as either positive or normative economics.

2. Give a positive and a normative argument why a business leader would oppose raising the minimum wage. Give a positive and a normative argument why a labor leader would favor raising the minimum wage.

3. Explain your position on this issue. Identify positive and normative reasons for your decision. Are there alternative ways to aid the working poor? Explain.

1. David Neumark and William Wascher, *Minimum Wages*, Cambridge, MA: *The MIT Press*, 2008.
Source: © Cengage Learning 2014

1-6b NORMATIVE ECONOMICS

Normative economics

An analysis based on value judgment.

Instead of using objective statements, an argument can be phrased subjectively. Normative economics attempts to determine "what should be." Normative economics is an analysis based on value judgments. Normative statements express an individual or collective opinion on a subject and cannot be proven by facts to be true or false. Certain words or phrases, such as *good, bad, need, should*, and *ought to*, tell us clearly that we have entered the realm of normative economics.

The point here is that people wearing "different-colored glasses" see the same facts differently. Each of us has individual subjective preferences that we apply to a particular subject. An animal rights activist says that no one *should* purchase a fur coat. Or one senator argues, "We *ought to* ensure that every teenager who wants a job has one." Another senator counters by saying, "Maintaining the purchasing power of the dollar is *more important* than teenage unemployment."

> **CONCLUSION:** *When opinions or points of view are not based on facts, they are scientifically untestable.*

When considering a debate, make sure to separate the arguments into their positive and normative components. This distinction allows you to determine whether you are choosing a course of action based on factual evidence or on opinion. The material presented in this textbook, like most of economics, takes pains to stay within the boundaries of positive economic analysis. In our everyday lives, however, politicians, business executives, relatives, and friends use mostly normative statements to discuss economic issues. Economists also may associate themselves with a political position and use normative arguments for or against some economic policy. When using value judgments, an economist's normative arguments may have no greater validity than those of other people. Biases or preconceptions can cloud an economist's thinking about deficit spending or whether to increase taxes on gasoline. Like beginning economics students, economists are human.

1-7 Careers in Economics

The author of this text entered college more years ago than I would like to admit. In those days, economics was not taught in high school, so I knew nothing of the subject. Like many students taking this course, I was uncertain about which major to pursue, but selected electrical engineering because I was an amateur radio operator and enjoyed building radio receivers and transmitters. My engineering curriculum required a course in economics. I signed up thinking that "econ is boring." Instead, it was an eye-opening experience that inspired me to change my major to economics and pursue an economics teaching career.

The study of economics has attracted a number of well-known people. For example, The Rolling Stones' Mick Jagger attended the London School of Economics, and other famous people who majored in economics include former Supreme Court Justice Sandra Day O'Connor, and three former presidents—George H. W. Bush, Ronald Reagan, and Gerald Ford.

An economics major can choose many career paths. Most economics majors work for business firms. Because economists are trained in analyzing financial matters, they find good jobs in management, sales, or as a market analyst interpreting economic conditions relevant to a firm's market. For those with an undergraduate degree, private-sector job opportunities exist in banking, securities brokering, management consulting, computer and data processing firms, the power industry, market research, finance, health care, and many other industries. Other economics majors work for government agencies and in colleges and universities.

Government economists work for federal, state, and local governments. For example, a government economist might compile and report national statistics for economic growth or work on projects such as how to improve indexes to measure trends in consumer prices. Economists in academe not only enjoy the challenge of teaching economics, but also have great freedom in selecting research projects.

Studying economics is also an essential preparation for other careers. Those preparing for law school, for example, find economics an excellent major because of its emphasis on a logical approach to problem solving. Economics is also great preparation for an MBA. In fact, students majoring in any field will benefit throughout their lives from learning how to apply the economic way of thinking to analyze real-world economic issues.

Finally, economics majors shine in salary offers upon graduation. Exhibit 3 shows average yearly salary offers for bachelor's degree candidates for April 2011.

EXHIBIT 3	Average Yearly Salary Offers for Selected Majors
Undergraduate Major	**Average Offer, April 2011**
Computer science	$63,017
Electrical engineering	60,646
Computer engineering	60,112
Nursing	55,774
Mathematics	55,300
Economics	54,634
Management information systems	54,372
Accounting	50,316
Liberal arts and sciences	50,313
Political sciences	48,129
Business administration	46,832
Marketing	44,432
Psychology	40,611
Environmental science	40,093
Criminal justice	38,741
Foreign languages	37,743
Sociology	37,464
Animal Science	34,324
Visual and performing arts	32,371
Journalism	31,591
Social work	31,397

SOURCE: National Association of Colleges and Employers, *Salary Survey*, Spring 2011.

Key Concepts

Scarcity
Resources
Land
Labor
Entrepreneurship

Capital
Economics
Macroeconomics
Microeconomics
Model

Ceteris paribus
Positive economics
Normative economics

Summary

- **Scarcity** is the fundamental economic problem that human wants exceed the availability of time, goods, and resources. Individuals and society therefore can never have everything they desire.
- **Resources** are factors of production classified as land, labor, and capital. Entrepreneurship is a special type of labor. An entrepreneur seeks profits by taking risks and combining resources to produce innovative products.
- **Economics** is the study of how individuals and society choose to allocate scarce resources to satisfy unlimited wants. Faced with unlimited wants and scarce resources, we must make choices among alternatives.

SOURCE: © Cengage Learning 2014

- **Macroeconomics** applies an economy-wide perspective that focuses on such issues as inflation, unemployment, and the growth rate of the economy.
- **Microeconomics** examines individual decision-making units within an economy, such as a

consumer's response to changes in the price of coffee and the reasons for changes in the market price of personal computers.
- **Models** are simplified descriptions of reality used to understand and predict economic events. An economic model can be stated verbally or in a table, a graph, or an equation. If the event is not consistent with the model, the model is rejected.

- **Ceteris paribus** holds "all other factors unchanged" that might affect a particular relationship. If this assumption is violated, a model cannot be tested. Another reasoning pitfall is to think that *association* means *causation*.
- Use of positive versus normative economic analysis is a major reason for disagreements among economists. **Positive economics** uses testable statements. Often a positive argument is expressed as an *if-then* statement. **Normative economics** is based on value judgments or opinions and uses words such as *good, bad, ought to,* and *should.*

Summary of Conclusion Statements

- The problem of scarcity and choice are basic economic problems faced by every society.

- Money by itself does not produce goods and services; instead, it is only a means of buying capital.

- A theory cannot be tested legitimately unless its ceteris paribus assumption is satisfied.
- The fact that one event follows another does not necessarily mean that the first event caused the second event.
- Economists' forecasts can differ because using the same methodology, economists can agree that event *A* causes event *B*, but disagree over the assumption that event *A* will occur.
- When opinions or points of view are not based on facts, they are scientifically untestable.

Study Questions and Problems

1. Explain why both nations with high living standards and nations with low living standards face the problem of scarcity. If you won $1 million in a lottery, would you escape the scarcity problem?

2. Why isn't money considered capital in economics?

3. Explain the difference between macroeconomics and microeconomics. Give examples of the areas of concern to each branch of economics.

4. Which of the following are microeconomic issues? Which are macroeconomic issues?
   a. How will an increase in the price of Coca-Cola affect the quantity of Pepsi-Cola sold?
   b. What will cause the nation's inflation rate to fall?
   c. How does a quota on textile imports affect the textile industry?
   d. Does a large federal budget deficit reduce the rate of unemployment in the economy?

5. Explain why it is important for an economic model to be an abstraction from the real world.

6. Explain the importance of the ceteris paribus assumption for an economic model.

7. Suppose Congress cuts spending for the military, and then unemployment rises in the U.S. defense industry. Is there causation in this situation, or are we observing an association between events?

8. Analyze the positive versus normative arguments in the following case. What statements of positive economics are used to support requiring air bags? What normative reasoning is used?

Should the Government Require Air Bags?

Air bag advocates say air bags will save lives and the government should require them in all cars. Air bags add an estimated $600 to the cost of a car, compared to about $100 for a set of regular seat belts. Opponents argue that air bags are electronic devices subject to failure and have produced injuries and death. For example, air bags have killed both adults and children whose heads were within the inflation zone at the time of deployment. Opponents therefore believe the government should leave the decision of whether to spend an extra $600 or so for an air bag to the consumer. The role of the government should be limited to providing information on the risks of having versus not having air bags.

For Online Exercises, go the Tucker Web site at www.cengage.com/economics/tucker.

✓ CHECKPOINT ANSWERS

Can You Prove There Is No Trillion-Dollar Person?

How can researchers ever be certain they have found all the rich people in the United States? There is always the possibility that somewhere there is a person who qualifies. If the researchers had found one, you could have rejected the theory. Because they did not, you cannot reject the theory. If you said that the evidence can support, but never prove the theory, **YOU ARE CORRECT.**

Should Nebraska State Join a Big-Time Athletic Conference?

Suppose universities that belong to big-time athletic conferences do indeed have higher graduation rates than nonmembers. This is not the only possible explanation for the statistical correlation (or association) between the graduation rate and membership in a big-time athletic conference. A more plausible explanation is that improving academic variables, such as tuition, quality of faculty, and student-faculty ratios, and not athletic conference membership, increase the graduation rate. If you said correlation, does not mean causation, and therefore Nebraska State officials will not necessarily accept the graduation rate evidence, **YOU ARE CORRECT.**

Sample Quiz

For an explanation of the correct answers, visit the Tucker Web site at www.cengage.com/economics/tucker.

1. Which of the following illustrates the concept of scarcity?
   a. More clean air is wanted than is available in large polluted metropolitan areas such as Mexico City.
   b. There is usually more than one use of your "free" time in the evening.
   c. There are many competing uses for the annual budget of your city, county, or state.
   d. All of the above are correct.

2. Which of the following are factors of production?
   a. The outputs generated by the production process transforming land, labor, and capital into goods and services
   b. Resources restricted to the land, such as natural resources that are unimproved by human economic activity
   c. Land (natural resources), labor (human capital, entrepreneurship), and capital (constructed inputs such as factories).
   d. Just labor and capital in industrialized countries, where natural resources are no longer used to produce goods and services

3. Which of the following is *not* an example of a capital input?
   a. A person's skills and abilities, which can be employed to produce valuable goods and services
   b. Factories and offices where goods and services are produced
   c. Tools and equipment
   d. Computers used by a company to record inventory, sales, and payroll

Sample Quiz *continued*

4. Which of the following is the best definition of economics?
   a. Economics is the study of how to manage corporations to generate the greatest return on shareholder investment.
   b. Economics is the study of how to manage city and county government to generate the greatest good to its citizens.
   c. Economics is the study of how society chooses to allocate its scarce resources.
   d. Economics is the study of how to track revenues and costs in a business.

5. Which of the following *best* illustrates the application of the model-building process to economics?
   a. On a Sunday morning talk show, two economists with differing political agendas argue about the best way to solve the Social Security problem.
   b. A labor economist notices that unemployment tends to be higher among teenagers than more experienced workers, develops a model, and gathers data to test the hypotheses in the model.
   c. A Ph.D. student in economics makes up data on the lumber market and develops a model for his dissertation that seems to be consistent with the data.
   d. Economists come to believe that some economic models are true simply because prominent leading economists say they are true.

6. Which of the following represents causality rather than association?
   a. In years that fashion dictates wider lapels on men's jackets, the stock market grows by at least 5 percent.
   b. Interest rates are higher in years ending with a 1 or a 6.
   c. Unemployment falls when the AFC champion wins the Super Bowl.
   d. Quantity demanded goes up when price falls because lower prices increase consumer purchasing power and because some consumers of substitute goods switch.

7. Which of the following describes the ceteris paribus assumption?
   a. If we increase the price of a good, reduce consumer income, and lower the price of substitutes and if quantity demanded is observed to fall, we know that the price increase caused the decline in quantity demanded.
   b. If the federal government increases government spending and the Federal Reserve Bank lowers interest rates, we know that the increase in government spending caused unemployment to fall.
   c. If a company reduces its labor costs, negotiates lower materials costs from its vendors, and advertises, we know that the reduced labor costs are why the company's profits are higher.
   d. If we decrease the price of a good and observe that there is an increase in the quantity demanded, holding all other factors that influence this relationship constant.

8. The condition of scarcity
   a. cannot be eliminated.
   b. prevails in poor economies.
   c. prevails in rich economies.
   d. all of the above are correct.

9. Which of the following *best* describes an entrepreneur?
   a. A person who works as an office clerk at a major corporation
   b. A person who combines the factors of production to produce innovative products
   c. A special type of capital
   d. Wealthy individuals who provide savings that stimulates the economy

10. Which of the following is *true* about renewable natural resources?
    a. They are a type of land resource (for example, oil, coal, and natural gas) that has a fixed stock.
    b. They are a type of capital resource (for example, irrigation networks and wastewater treatment plants) that utilize water.
    c. They are a type of capital resource (for example, air filtration systems in buildings)

Sample Quiz *continued*

that renew and refresh polluted air from the outside.

d. They are a type of land resource (for example, forests, rangelands, and marine fisheries) that naturally regenerate and thus can tolerate a sustained harvest but can be depleted from excessive harvest.

11. Because of scarcity,
    a. it is impossible to satisfy every desire and choices must be made.
    b. the available supply of time, goods, and resources is greater than human wants.
    c. every desire is fulfilled.
    d. there are no limits on the economy's ability to satisfy unlimited wants.

12. Which of the following represents positive economics?
    a. Policy A is fair.
    b. Outcome B is the best objective to achieve.
    c. If policy A is followed, then outcome B results.
    d. All of the above are positive economic analyses.

13. Which of the following is the last step in the model-building process?
    a. Collect data and test the model.
    b. Develop a model based on simplified assumptions.
    c. Identify the problem.
    d. Formulate an assumption.

14. Which of the following is *not* a type of economic analysis?
    a. Positive
    b. Resources
    c. Normative
    d. None of the above

15. Which word indicates that an economist is using positive economics?

a. Good
b. Bad
c. If-then
d. Should

16. Which of the following would eliminate scarcity as an economic problem?
    a. Moderation of people's competitive instincts
    b. Discovery of new, sufficiently large energy reserves
    c. Resumption of steady productivity growth
    d. None of the above is correct

17. Which resource is *not* an example of capital?
    a. Equipment
    b. Machinery
    c. Physical plants
    d. Stocks and bonds

18. Which of the following is the second step in the model-building process?
    a. Collect data and test the model.
    b. Develop a model based on simplified assumptions.
    c. Identify the problem.
    d. Include all possible variables that affect the model.

19. Which of the following is a type of economic analysis?
    a. Positive
    b. Resources
    c. Association
    d. None of the above is correct.

20. Which of the following careers could result from majoring in economics?
    a. Management
    b. Banking
    c. Government
    d. All of the above is correct.

Applying Graphs to Economics

Economists are famous for their use of graphs. The reason is that "a picture is worth a thousand words." Graphs are used throughout this text to present economics models. By drawing a line, you can use a two-dimensional illustration to analyze the effects of a change in one variable on another. You could describe the same information using other model forms, such as verbal statements, tables, or equations, but a graph is the simplest way to present and understand the relationship between economic variables.

Don't be worried that graphs will "throw you for a loop." Relax! This appendix explains all of the basic graphical language you will need. The following illustrates the simplest use of graphs for economic analysis.

A-1 A Direct Relationship

Basic economic analysis typically concerns the relationship between two variables, both having positive values. Hence, we can confine our graphs to the upper-right (northeast) quadrant of the coordinate number system. In Exhibit A-1, notice that the scales on the horizontal axis (x-axis) and the vertical axis (y-axis) do not necessarily measure the same numerical values.

The horizontal axis in Exhibit A-1 measures annual income, and the vertical axis shows the amount spent per year for a personal computer (PC). In the absence of any established traditions, we could decide to measure income on the vertical axis and expenditure on the horizontal axis. The intersection of the horizontal and vertical axes is the *origin*—and the point at which both income and expenditure are zero. In Exhibit A-1, each point is a coordinate that matches the dollar value of income and the corresponding expenditure for a PC. For example, point A on the graph shows that people with an annual income of $10,000 spent $1,000 per year for a PC. Other incomes are associated with different expenditure levels. For example, at $30,000 per year (point C), $3,000 will be spent annually for a PC.

The straight line in Exhibit A-1 allows us to determine the direction of change in PC expenditure as annual income changes. This relationship is *positive* because PC expenditure, measured along the vertical axis, and annual income, measured along the horizontal axis, move in the same direction. PC expenditure increases as annual income increases. As income declines, so does the amount spent on a PC. Thus, the straight line representing the relationship between income and PC expenditure is a direct relationship. A direct relationship is a positive association between two variables. When one variable increases, the other variable increases, and when one variable decreases, the other variable decreases. In short, both variables change in the *same* direction.

Finally, an important point to remember: A two-variable graph, like any model, isolates the relationship between two variables and holds all other variables

Direct relationship
A positive association between two variables. When one variable increases, the other variable increases, and when one variable decreases, the other variable decreases.

21

EXHIBIT A-1	A Direct Relationship between Variables

The line with a positive slope shows that the expenditure per year for a personal computer has a direct relationship to annual income, ceteris paribus. As annual income increases along the horizontal axis, the amount spent on a PC also increases, as measured by the vertical axis. Along the line, each 10-unit increase in annual income results in a 1-unit increase in expenditure for a PC. Because the slope is constant along a straight line, we can measure the same slope between any two points. Between points *B* and *C* or between points *A* and *D*, the slope $= \Delta Y / \Delta X = +3/+30 = +1/+10 = 1/10$.

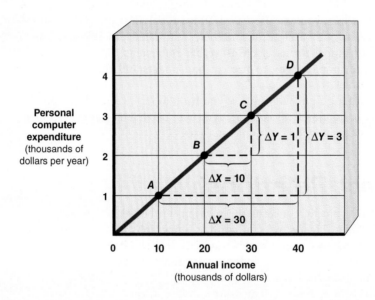

Expenditure for a Personal Computer at Different Annual Incomes		
Point	Personal computer expenditure (thousands of dollars per year)	Annual income (thousands of dollars)
A	$1	$10
B	2	20
C	3	30
D	4	40

SOURCE: © Cengage Learning 2014

constant under the ceteris paribus assumption. In Exhibit A-1, for example, factors such as the prices of PCs and education are held constant by assumption. In Chapter 3, you will learn that allowing variables not shown in the graph to change can shift the position of the curve.

A-2 An Inverse Relationship

Now consider the relationship between the price of compact discs (CDs) and the quantity consumers will buy per year, shown in Exhibit A-2. These data indicate a *negative* relationship between the price and quantity variables. When the price is low, consumers purchase a greater quantity of CDs than when the price is high.

In Exhibit A-2, there is an inverse relationship between the price per CD and the quantity consumers buy. An inverse relationship is a negative association between two variables. When one variable increases, the other variable decreases, and when one variable decreases, the other variable increases. Stated simply, the variables move in *opposite* directions.

The line drawn in Exhibit A-2 is an inverse relationship. By long-established tradition, economists put price on the vertical axis and quantity on the horizontal axis. In Chapter 3, we will study in more detail the relationship between price and quantity called the *law of demand*.

In addition to observing the inverse relationship (slope), you must interpret the *intercept* at point *A* in the exhibit. The intercept in this case means that at a price of $25 no consumer is willing to buy a single CD.

Inverse relationship

A negative association between two variables. When one variable increases, the other variable decreases, and when one variable decreases, the other variable increases.

A-3 The Slope of a Straight Line

Plotting numbers provides a clear visual expression of the relationship between two variables, but it is also important to know how much one variable changes as another variable changes. To find out, we calculate the slope. The slope is the ratio of the change in the variable on the vertical axis (the rise or fall) to the change in the variable on the horizontal axis (the run). Algebraically, if *Y* is on the vertical axis and *X* is on the horizontal axis, the slope is expressed as follows (the delta symbol, Δ, means "change in"):

Slope

The ratio of the change in the variable on the vertical axis (the rise or fall) to the change in the variable on the horizontal axis (the run).

$$\text{Slope} = \frac{\text{rise}}{\text{run}} = \frac{\text{change in vertical axis}}{\text{change in horizontal axis}} = \frac{\Delta Y}{\Delta X}$$

Consider the slope between points *B* and *C* in Exhibit A-1. The change in expenditure for a PC, *Y*, is equal to +1 (from $2,000 to $3,000 per year), and the change in annual income, *X*, is equal to +10 (from $20,000 to $30,000 per year). The slope is therefore +1/+10. The sign is positive because computer expenditure is directly, or positively, related to annual income. The steeper the line, the greater the slope because the ratio of ΔY to ΔX rises. Conversely, the flatter the line, the smaller the slope. Exhibit A-1 also illustrates that the slope of a straight line is constant. That is, the slope between any two points along the line, such as between points *A* and *D*, is equal to +3/+30 = 1/10.

What does the slope of 1/10 mean? It tells you that a $1,000 increase (decrease) in PC expenditure each year occurs for each $10,000 increase (decrease) in annual income. The line plotted in Exhibit A-1 has a *positive slope*, and we describe the line as "upward-sloping."

On the other hand, the line in Exhibit A-2 has a *negative slope*. The change in *Y* between points *C* and *D* is equal to −5 (from $15 down to $10), and the change in *X* is equal to +25 (from 50 million up to 75 million CDs purchased

EXHIBIT A-2	An Inverse Relationship between Variables

The line with a negative slope shows an inverse relationship between the price per compact disc and the quantity of CDs consumers purchase, ceteris paribus. As the price of a CD rises, the quantity of CDs purchased falls. A lower price for CDs is associated with more CDs purchased by consumers. Along the line, with each $5 decrease in the price of CDs, consumers increase the quantity purchased by 25 units. The slope $= \Delta Y/\Delta X = -5/+25 = -1/5$.

The Quantity of Compact Discs Consumers Purchase at Different Prices

Point	Price per compact disc	Quantity of compact discs purchased (millions per year)
A	$25	0
B	20	25
C	15	50
D	10	75
E	5	100

SOURCE: © Cengage Learning 2014

per year). The slope is therefore $-5/+25 = -1/5$, and this line is described as "downward-sloping."

What does this slope of $-1/5$ mean? It means that raising (lowering) the price per CD by $1 decreases (increases) the quantity of CDs purchased by 5 million per year.

Suppose we calculate the slope between any two points on a flat line—for example, points *B* and *C* in Exhibit A-3. In this case, there is no change in *Y* (expenditure for toothpaste) as *X* (annual income) increases. Consumers spend $20 per year on toothpaste regardless of annual income. It follows that $\Delta Y = 0$ for any ΔX, so the slope is equal to 0. The two variables along a flat line (horizontal or vertical) have an independent relationship. An independent relationship is a zero association between two variables. When one variable changes, the other variable remains unchanged.

Independent relationship

A zero association between two variables. When one variable changes, the other variable remains unchanged.

EXHIBIT A-3	**An Independent Relationship between Variables**

The flat line with a zero slope shows that the expenditure per year for toothpaste is unrelated to annual income. As annual income increases along the horizontal axis, the amount spent each year for toothpaste remains unchanged at 20 units. If annual income increases 10 units, the corresponding change in expenditure is zero. The slope $= \Delta Y/\Delta X = 0/+10 = 0$.

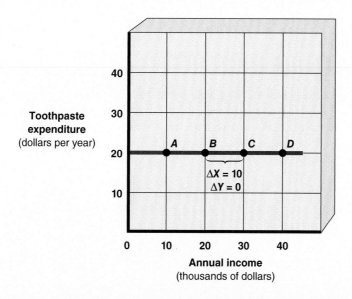

Expenditure for Toothpaste at Different Annual Incomes		
Point	**Toothpaste expenditure (dollars per year)**	**Annual income (thousands of dollars)**
A	$20	$10
B	20	20
C	20	30
D	20	40

SOURCE: © Cengage Learning 2014

A-4 The Slope of a Curve

The slope of a curve changes from one point to another. Suppose the relationship between the expenditure for a PC per year and annual income is not a straight line, but an upward-sloping curve, as drawn in Exhibit A-4. This means that the slope of the curve is *positive* as we move along the curve. To calculate the slope of a given point on the curve requires two steps. For example, at point *A*, the first step is to draw a tangent line that just touches the curve at this point without crossing it. The second step is to determine the slope of the tangent line. In Exhibit A-4, the slope of the tangent line, and therefore the slope of the curve at point *A*, is +2/+30 = 1/15. What does this slope of 1/15 mean? It means that at point *A*, there will be a $1,000 increase (decrease) in PC expenditure each year for each $15,000 increase (decrease) in annual income.

Now consider that the relationship between the price per CD and the quantity demanded by consumers per year is the downward-sloping curve shown in Exhibit A-5. In this case, the slope of the curve is *negative* as we move along the curve. To calculate the slope at point *A*, draw a line tangent to the curve at point *A*. Thus, the slope of the curve at point *A* is −10/+50 = −1/+5 = −1/5.

EXHIBIT A-4	The Slope of an Upward-Sloping Curve

The slope of a curve at any given point, such as point *A*, is equal to the slope of the straight line drawn tangent to the curve at that point. The tangent line just touches the curve at point *A* without crossing it. The slope of the upward-sloping curve at point *A* is +2/+30 = +1/+15 = 1/15.

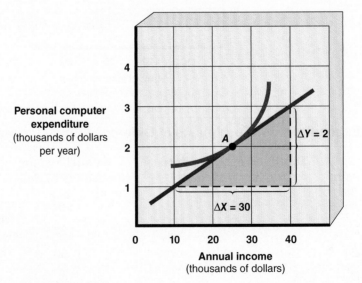

SOURCE: © Cengage Learning 2014

EXHIBIT A-5	The Slope of a Downward-Sloping Curve

In this exhibit, the negative slope changes as one moves from point to point along the curve. The slope at any given point, such as point A, can be determined by the slope of the straight line tangent to that point. The slope of the downward-sloping curve at point A is $-10/+50 = -1/+5 = -1/5$.

Quantity of compact discs purchased
(millions per year)

SOURCE: © Cengage Learning 2014

A-5 A Three-Variable Relationship in One Graph

The two-variable relationships drawn so far conform to a two-dimensional flat piece of paper. For example, the vertical axis measures the price per CD variable and the horizontal axis measures the quantity of CDs purchased variable. All other factors, such as consumer income, that may affect the relationship between the price and quantity variables are held constant by the ceteris paribus assumption. But reality is frequently not so accommodating. Often a model must take into account the impact of changes in a third variable (consumer income) drawn on a two-dimensional piece of graph paper.

Economists' favorite method of depicting a three-variable relationship is shown in Exhibit A-6. As explained earlier, the cause-and-effect relationship between price and quantity of CDs determines the downward-sloping curve. A change in the price per CD causes a movement downward along either of the two separate curves. As the price falls, consumers increase the quantity of CDs demanded. The location of each curve on the graph, however, depends on the annual income of consumers. As the annual income variable increases from $30,000 to $60,000 and consumers can afford to pay more, the price-quantity

EXHIBIT A-6	**Changes in Price, Quantity, and Income in Two Dimensions**

Economists use a multicurve graph to represent a three-variable relationship in a two-dimensional graph. A decrease in the price per CD causes a movement downward along each curve. As the annual income of consumers rises, there is a shift rightward in the position of the demand curve.

demanded curve shifts rightward. Conversely, as the annual income variable decreases and consumers have less to spend, the price-quantity demanded curve shifts leftward.

This is an extremely important concept that you must understand: Throughout this book, you must distinguish between *movements along* and *shifts in* a curve. Here's how to tell the difference. A change in one of the variables shown on either of the coordinate axes of the graph causes *movement along* a curve. On the other hand, a change in a variable not shown on one of the coordinate axes of the graph causes a *shift in* a curve's position on the graph.

> **CONCLUSION:** *A shift in a curve occurs only when the ceteris paribus assumption is relaxed and a third variable not shown on either axis of the graph is allowed to change.*

SOURCE: © Cengage Learning 2014

A-6 A Helpful Study Hint for Using Graphs

To some students, studying economics is a little frightening because many chapters are full of graphs. An often-repeated mistake is to prepare for tests by trying to memorize the lines of graphs. When their graded tests are returned, the students using this strategy will probably exclaim, "What happened?" The answer is that if you learn the economic concepts first, you will understand the graphs as illustrations of these underlying concepts. Stated simply, superficial cramming for economics quizzes does not work. For students who are anxious about using graphs, in addition to the brief review of graphical analysis in this appendix, the Graphing Workshop on the EconCentral link of the Tucker Web site and the Study Guide contain step-by-step features on how to interpret graphs.

Key Concepts

Direct relationship   Slope
Inverse relationship   Independent relationship

Summary

- **Graphs** provide a means to clearly show economic relationships in two-dimensional space. Economic analysis is often concerned with two variables confined to the upper-right (northeast) quadrant of the coordinate number system.
- A **direct relationship** occurs when two variables change in the *same* direction.

Direct Relationship

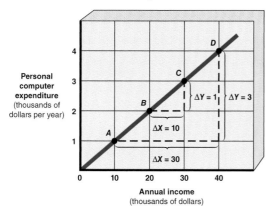

SOURCE: © Cengage Learning 2014

- An **inverse relationship** occurs when two variables change in *opposite* directions.

Inverse Relationship

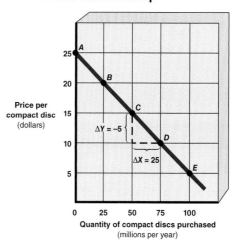

SOURCE: © Cengage Learning 2014

- An **independent relationship** occurs when two variables are unrelated.

Independent Relationship

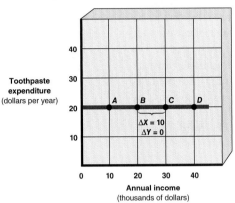

SOURCE: © Cengage Learning 2014

- **Slope** is the ratio of the vertical change (the rise or fall) to the horizontal change (the run). The slope of an *upward-sloping* line is *positive*, and the slope of a *downward-sloping* line is *negative*.

Positive Slope of an Upward-Sloping Curve

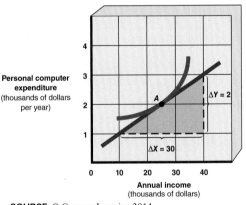

SOURCE: © Cengage Learning 2014

Negative Slope of a Downward-Sloping Curve

SOURCE: © Cengage Learning 2014

- A **three-variable relationship** is depicted by a graph showing a shift in a curve when the ceteris paribus assumption is relaxed and a third variable (such as annual income) not on either axis of the graph is allowed to change.

Three-Variable Relationship

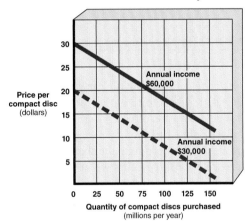

SOURCE: © Cengage Learning 2014

Summary of Conclusion Statement

- A shift in a curve occurs only when the ceteris paribus assumption is relaxed and a third variable not shown on either axis of the graph is allowed to change.

Study Questions and Problems

1. Draw a graph without specific data for the expected relationship between the following variables:
   a. The probability of living and age
   b. Annual income and years of education
   c. Inches of snow and sales of bathing suits
   d. Number of football games won and the athletic budget

In each case, state whether the expected relationship is *direct* or *inverse*. Explain an additional factor that would be included in the *ceteris paribus* assumption because it might change and influence your theory.

2. Assume that a research firm collects survey sales data that reveal the relationship between the possible selling prices of hamburgers and the quantity of hamburgers consumers would purchase per year at alternative prices. The report states that if the price of a hamburger is $4, 20,000 will be bought. However, at a price of $3, 40,000 hamburgers will be bought. At $2, 60,000 hamburgers will be bought, and at $1, 80,000 hamburgers will be purchased.

Based on these data, describe the relevant relationship between the price of a hamburger and the quantity consumers are willing to purchase, using a verbal statement, a numerical table, and a graph. Which model do you prefer? Why?

Sample Quiz

For an explanation of the correct answers, visit the Tucker Web site at www.cengage.com/economics/tucker.

1. What is used to illustrate an independent relationship between two variables?
   a. An upward-sloping curve
   b. A downward-sloping curve
   c. A hill-shaped curve
   d. A horizontal or vertical line

2. Which of the following pairs is *most* likely to exhibit an inverse relationship?
   a. The amount of time you study and your grade point average
   b. People's annual income and their expenditure on personal computers
   c. Baseball players' salaries and their batting averages
   d. The price of a concert and the number of tickets that people purchase

3. According to Exhibit A-7, what is the relationship between the price per pizza and the quantity of pizzas purchased?
   a. Direct
   b. Inverse
   c. Complex
   d. Independent

4. What is the slope of the line shown in Exhibit A-7?
   a. −1
   b. −1/2
   c. −1/4
   d. 0

5. Which of the following would cause a leftward shift in the relationship shown in Exhibit A-7?
   a. A fall in household incomes
   b. A fall in the price of pizza
   c. A fall in the quantity of pizza that people want to purchase
   d. All of the above would shift the line in the graph

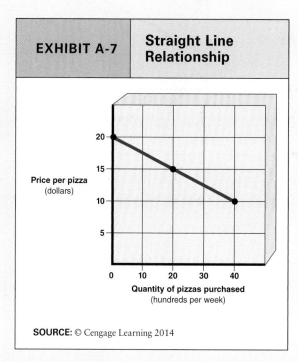

EXHIBIT A-7   **Straight Line Relationship**

SOURCE: © Cengage Learning 2014

Sample Quiz *continued*

6. Suppose two variables are directly related. If one variable rises, the other variable
   a. also rises.
   b. falls.
   c. remains unchanged.
   d. reacts unpredictably.

7. When an inverse relationship is graphed, the resulting line or curve is
   a. horizontal.
   b. vertical.
   c. upward-sloping.
   d. downward-sloping.

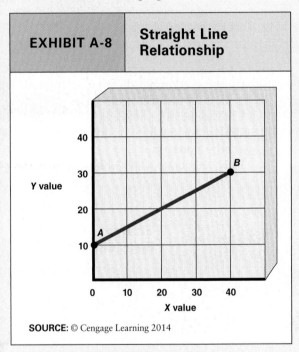

EXHIBIT A-8	Straight Line Relationship

SOURCE: © Cengage Learning 2014

8. Straight line AB in Exhibit A-8 shows that
   a. increasing values for X decreases the values of Y.
   b. decreasing values for X increases the values of Y.
   c. there is a direct relationship between X and Y.
   d. all of the above are true.

9. In Exhibit A-8, what is the slope of straight line AB?
   a. Positive
   b. Zero
   c. Negative
   d. Variable

10. In Exhibit A-8, what is the slope of straight line AB?
    a. 1
    b. 5
    c. 1/2
    d. −1

11. As shown in Exhibit A-8, the slope of straight line AB
    a. decreases with increases in X.
    b. increases with increases in X.
    c. increases with decreases in X.
    d. remains constant with changes in X.

12. In Exhibit A-8, as X increases along the horizontal axis, the Y values increase. What is the relationship between the X and Y variables?
    a. Direct
    b. Inverse
    c. Independent
    d. Variable

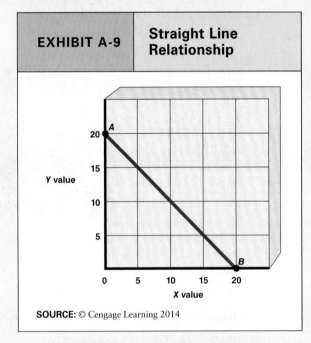

EXHIBIT A-9	Straight Line Relationship

SOURCE: © Cengage Learning 2014

13. In Exhibit A-9, as X increases along the horizontal axis, the Y values decrease. What is the relationship between the X and Y variables?
    a. Direct
    b. Inverse
    c. Independent
    d. Variable

Sample Quiz *continued*

14. Straight line AB in Exhibit A-9 shows that
    a. increasing values for X reduces the value of Y.
    b. decreasing values for X increases the value of Y.
    c. there is an inverse relationship between X and Y.
    d. all of the above are true.

15. As shown in Exhibit A-9, the slope of straight line AB
    a. decreases with increases in X.
    b. increases with increases in X.
    c. increases with decreases in X.
    d. remains constant with changes in X.

16. In Exhibit A-9, what is the slope for straight line AB?
    a. 3
    b. 1
    c. −1
    d. −5

17. In Exhibit A-9, what is the slope of straight line AB?
    a. Positive
    b. Zero
    c. Negative
    d. Variable

18. In Exhibit A-10, as X increases along the horizontal axis, corresponding to points A–D on the line, the Y values remain unchanged at 20 units. What is the relationship between the X and Y variables?
    a. Direct
    b. Inverse
    c. Independent
    d. Undefined

19. In Exhibit A-10, what is the slope of straight line A–D?
    a. Greater than 1
    b. Equal to 1
    c. Less than 1
    d. Zero

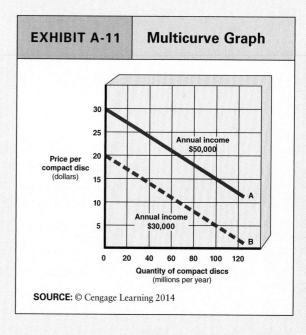

EXHIBIT A-11   Multicurve Graph

Price per compact disc (dollars)

Annual income $50,000

Annual income $30,000

Quantity of compact discs (millions per year)

SOURCE: © Cengage Learning 2014

EXHIBIT A-10   Straight Line Relationship

Y value

X value

SOURCE: © Cengage Learning 2014

---

20. Exhibit A-11 represents a three-variable relationship. As the annual income of consumers falls from $50,000 (line A) to $30,000 (line B), the result is a(n)
    a. upward movement along each curve.
    b. downward movement along each curve.
    c. leftward shift in curve A to curve B.
    d. rightward shift in curve A to curve B.

chapter 2

Production Possibilities, Opportunity Cost, and Economic Growth

This chapter continues building on the foundation laid in the preceding chapter. Having learned that *scarcity* forces *choices*, here you will study the choices people make in more detail. This chapter begins by examining the three basic choices: *What, How,* and *For Whom* to produce. The process of answering these basic questions introduces two other key building blocks in the economic way of thinking: *opportunity cost* and *marginal analysis*. Once you understand these important concepts stated in words, it will be easier to interpret our first formal economic model, the *production possibilities curve*. This model illustrates how economists use graphs as a powerful tool to supplement words and develop an understanding of basic economic principles. You will discover that the production possibilities model teaches many of the most important concepts in economics, including scarcity, the law of increasing opportunity costs, efficiency, investment, and economic growth. For example, the chapter concludes by using the production possibilities curve to explain why underdeveloped countries do not achieve economic growth and thereby improve their standard of living.

In this chapter, you will learn to solve these economics puzzles:

- Why do so few rock stars and movie stars go to college?
- Why would you spend an extra hour reading this text rather than going to a movie or sleeping?
- Why are investment and economic growth so important?
- What does a war on terrorism really mean?

2-1 Three Fundamental Economic Questions

Because of the problem of scarcity, whether rich or poor, every nation must answer the same three fundamental economic questions: (1) *What* products will be produced? (2) *How* will they be produced? (3) *For Whom* will they be produced? Later, the chapter on economies in transition introduces various types of economic systems and describes how each deals with these three economic choices.

2-1a WHAT TO PRODUCE?

The *What* question requires an economy to decide the mix and quantity of goods and services it will produce. Should society devote its limited resources to producing more health care and fewer military goods? Should society produce more iPods and fewer CDs? Should more capital goods be produced instead of consumer goods, or should small hybrid cars and fewer SUVs be produced? The problem of scarcity restricts our ability to produce everything we want during a given period, so the choice to produce "more" of one good requires producing "less" of another good. In the United States, consumer sovereignty answers the *What* question. In Cuba and North Korea, for example, the government and not the consumer answers this question.

2-1b HOW TO PRODUCE?

After deciding which products to make, the second question for society to decide is *how* to mix technology and scarce resources in order to produce these goods. For instance, a towel can be sewn primarily by hand (labor), partially by hand and partially by machine (labor and capital), or primarily by machine (capital). In short, the *How* question asks whether a production technique will be more or less capital-intensive. The *How* question also concerns choices among resources for production. Should electricity be produced from oil, solar power, or nuclear power?

Education plays an important role in answering the *How* question. Education improves the ability of workers to perform their work. Variation in the quality and quantity of education among nations is one reason economies differ in their capacities to apply resources and technology to answer the *How* question. For example, the United States is striving to catch up with Japan in the use of robotics. Answering the question *How do we improve our robotics?* requires engineers and employees with the proper training in the installation and operation of robots.

2-1c FOR WHOM TO PRODUCE?

Once the *What* and *How* questions are resolved, the third question is *For Whom*. Among all those desiring the produced goods, who actually receives them? This question concerns how the economic pie is divided. Who is fed well? Who drives a Mercedes? Who receives organ transplants? Should economics professors earn a salary of $1 million a year and others pay higher taxes to support economists? The *For Whom* question means that society must have a method to decide who will be "rich and famous" and who will be "poor and unknown." Chapter 10 returns to the *For Whom* question and discusses it in more detail.

2-2 Opportunity Cost

Because of scarcity, the three basic questions cannot be answered without sacrifice or cost. But what does the term *cost* really mean? The common response would be to say that the purchase price is the cost. A movie ticket *costs* $8, or a shirt *costs* $50. Applying the economic way of thinking, however, *cost* is defined differently. A well-known phrase from Nobel Prize-winning economist Milton Friedman says, "There is no such thing as a free lunch." This expression captures the links among the concepts of scarcity, choice, and cost. Because of scarcity, people must make choices, and each choice incurs a cost (sacrifice). Once one option is chosen, another option is given up. The money you spend on a movie ticket cannot also buy a Blu-ray. A business may purchase a new textile machine to manufacture towels, but this same money cannot be used to buy a new recreation facility for employees.

The Blu-ray and recreation facility examples illustrate that the true cost of these decisions is the opportunity cost of a choice, not the purchase price. Opportunity cost is the best alternative sacrificed for a chosen alternative. Stated differently, it is the cost of not choosing the next best alternative. This principle states that some highly valued opportunity must be forgone in all economic decisions. The actual good or use of time given up for the chosen good or use of time measures the opportunity cost. We may omit the word *opportunity* before the word *cost*, but the concept remains the same. Exhibit 1 illustrates the causation chain linking scarcity, choice, and opportunity cost.

Examples are endless, but let's consider a few. Suppose your economics professor decides to become a rock star in the Rolling in Dough band. Now all his or

Opportunity cost

The best alternative sacrificed for a chosen alternative.

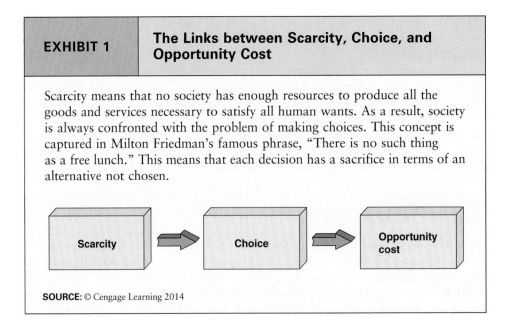

EXHIBIT 1   **The Links between Scarcity, Choice, and Opportunity Cost**

Scarcity means that no society has enough resources to produce all the goods and services necessary to satisfy all human wants. As a result, society is always confronted with the problem of making choices. This concept is captured in Milton Friedman's famous phrase, "There is no such thing as a free lunch." This means that each decision has a sacrifice in terms of an alternative not chosen.

Scarcity → Choice → Opportunity cost

SOURCE: © Cengage Learning 2014

her working hours are devoted to creating hit music, and the opportunity cost is the educational services no longer provided. Now a personal example: The opportunity cost of dating a famous model or movie star (name your favorite) might be the loss of your current girlfriend or boyfriend. Opportunity cost also applies to national economic decisions. Suppose the federal government decides to spend tax revenues on a space station. The opportunity cost depends on the next best program *not* funded. Assume roads and bridges are the highest-valued projects not built as a result of the decision to construct the space station. Then the opportunity cost of the decision to devote resources to the space station is the forgone roads and bridges and not the money actually spent to build the space station.

To personalize the relationship between time and opportunity cost, ask yourself what you would be doing if you were not reading this book. Your answer might be watching television or sleeping. If sleeping is your choice, the opportunity cost of studying this text is the sleep you sacrifice. Rock stars and movie stars, on the other hand, must forfeit a large amount of income to attend college. Now you know why you see so few of these stars in class.

Decisions often involve sacrifice of *both* goods and time. Suppose you decide to see a movie at a theater located 15 minutes from campus. If you had not spent the money at the movie theater, you could have purchased a Blu-ray and watched a movie at home. And the time spent traveling to and from the movie and sitting through it could have been devoted to studying for your economics exam. The opportunity cost of the movie consists of giving up (1) a Blu-ray and (2) study time needed to score higher on the economics exam.

2-3 Marginal Analysis

At the heart of many important decision-making techniques used throughout this text is marginal analysis. Marginal analysis examines the effects of additions to or subtractions from a current situation. This is a very valuable tool in the economic-way-of-thinking toolkit because it considers the "marginal" effects of change. The rational decision maker decides on an option only if the marginal benefit exceeds the marginal cost. For example, you must decide how to use your scarce time. Should you devote an extra hour to reading this book, going to a movie, watching television, texting, or sleeping? Which of your many options do you choose? The answer depends on marginal analysis. If you decide the benefit of a higher grade in economics exceeds the opportunity cost of, say, sleep, then you allocate the extra hour to studying economics. Excellent choice!

Businesses use marginal analysis. Hotels, for example, rent space to student groups for dances and other events. Assume you are the hotel manager and a student group offers to pay $400 to use the ballroom for a party. To decide whether to accept the offer requires marginal analysis. The marginal benefit of renting otherwise vacant space is $400, and the marginal cost is $300 for extra electricity and cleaning services. Since the marginal benefit exceeds the marginal cost, the manager sensibly accepts the offer.

Similarly, farmers use marginal analysis. For example, a farmer must decide whether to add fertilizer when planting corn. Using marginal analysis, the farmer estimates that the corn revenue yield will be about $75 per acre without fertilizer and about $100 per acre using fertilizer. If the cost of fertilizer is $20 per acre,

Marginal analysis
An examination of the effects of additions to or subtractions from a current situation.

marginal analysis tells the farmer to fertilize. The addition of fertilizer will increase profit by $5 per acre because fertilizing adds $25 to the value of each acre at a cost of $20 per acre.

Marginal analysis is an important concept when the government considers changes in various programs. For example, as demonstrated in the next section, it is useful to know that an increase in the production of military goods will result in an opportunity cost of fewer consumer goods produced.

2-4 The Production Possibilities Curve

Production possibilities curve

A curve that shows the maximum combinations of two outputs an economy can produce in a given period of time with its available resources and technology.

The economic problem of scarcity means that society's capacity to produce combinations of goods is constrained by its limited resources. This condition can be represented in a model called the production possibilities curve. The production possibilities curve shows the maximum combinations of two outputs that an economy can produce in a given period of time with its available resources and technology. Three basic assumptions underlie the production possibilities curve model:

1. **Fixed Resources.** The quantities and qualities of all resource inputs remain unchanged during the time period. But the "rules of the game" do allow an economy to shift any resource from the production of one output to the production of another output. For example, an economy might shift workers from producing consumer goods to producing capital goods. Although the number of workers remains unchanged, this transfer of labor will produce fewer consumer goods and more capital goods.
2. **Fully Employed Resources.** The economy operates with all its factors of production fully employed and producing the greatest output possible without waste or mismanagement.
3. **Technology Unchanged.** Holding existing technology fixed creates limits, or constraints, on the amounts and types of goods any economy can produce. Technology is the body of knowledge applied to how goods are produced.

Technology

The body of knowledge applied to how goods are produced.

Exhibit 2 shows a hypothetical economy that has the capacity to manufacture any combination of military goods ("guns") and consumer goods ("butter") per year along its production possibilities curve (*PPC*), including points *A*, *B*, *C*, and *D*. For example, if this economy uses all its resources to make military goods, it can produce a *maximum* of 160 billion units of military goods and zero units of consumer goods (combination *A*). Another possibility is for the economy to use all its resources to produce a *maximum* of 100 billion units of consumer goods and zero units of military goods (point *D*). Between the extremes of points *A* and *D* lie other production possibilities for combinations of military and consumer goods. If combination *B* is chosen, the economy will produce 140 billion units of military goods and 40 billion units of consumer goods. Another possibility (point *C*) is to produce 80 billion units of military goods and 80 billion units of consumer goods.

What happens if the economy does not use all its resources to their capacity? For example, some workers may not find work, or plants and equipment may be idle for any number of reasons. The result is that our hypothetical economy fails to reach any of the combinations along the *PPC*. In Exhibit 2, point *U* illustrates an *inefficient* output level for any economy operating without all its resources fully employed. At point *U*, our model economy is producing 80 billion units of military

EXHIBIT 2	The Production Possibilities Curve for Military Goods and Consumer Goods

All points along the production possibilities curve (*PPC*) are maximum possible combinations of military goods and consumer goods. One possibility, point *A*, would be to produce 160 billion units of military goods and zero units of consumer goods each year. At the other extreme, point *D*, the economy uses all its resources to produce 100 billion units of consumer goods and zero units of military goods each year. Points *B* and *C* are obtained by using some resources to produce each of the two outputs. If the economy fails to utilize its resources fully, the result is the inefficient point *U*. Point *Z* lies beyond the economy's present production capabilities and is unattainable.

Production Possibilities Schedule for Military and Consumer Goods per Year

Output (billions of units per year)	Production possibilities			
	A	**B**	**C**	**D**
Military goods	160	140	80	0
Consumer goods	0	40	80	100

SOURCE: © Cengage Learning 2014

goods and 40 billion units of consumer goods per year. Such an economy is under-producing because it could satisfy more of society's wants if it were producing at some point along the *PPC*.

Even if an economy fully employs all its resources, it is impossible to produce certain output quantities. Any point outside the production possibilities curve is *unattainable* because it is beyond the economy's present production capabilities. Point Z, for example, represents an unattainable output of 140 billion units of military goods and 80 billion units of consumer goods. Society would prefer this combination to any combination along, or inside, the *PPC*, but the economy cannot reach this point with its existing resources and technology.

> **CONCLUSION:** *Scarcity limits an economy to points on or below its production possibilities curve.*

Because all the points along the curve are *maximum* output levels with the given resources and technology, they are all called *efficient* points. A movement between any two efficient points on the curve means that *more* of one product is produced only by producing *less* of the other product. In Exhibit 2, moving from point A to point B produces 40 billion additional units of consumer goods per year, but only at a cost of sacrificing 20 billion units of military goods. Thus, a movement between any two efficient points graphically illustrates that "There is no such thing as a free lunch."

> **CONCLUSION:** *The production possibilities curve consists of all efficient output combinations at which an economy can produce more of one good only by producing less of the other good.*

2-5 The Law of Increasing Opportunity Costs

Why is the production possibilities curve shaped the way it is? Exhibit 3 will help us answer this question. It presents a production possibilities curve for a hypothetical economy that must choose between producing tanks and producing sailboats. Consider expanding the production of sailboats in 20,000-unit increments. Moving from point A to point B, the *opportunity cost* is 10,000 tanks; between point B and point C, the *opportunity cost* is 20,000 tanks; and the *opportunity cost* of producing at point D, rather than point C, is 50,000 tanks.

Law of increasing opportunity costs

The principle that the opportunity cost increases as production of one output expands.

Exhibit 3 illustrates the law of increasing opportunity costs, which states that the opportunity cost increases as production of one output expands. Holding the stock of resources and technology constant (ceteris paribus), the law of increasing opportunity costs causes the production possibilities curve to display a *bowed-out* shape.

Why must our hypothetical economy sacrifice larger and larger amounts of tank output in order to produce each additional 20,000 sailboats? The reason is that all workers are not equally suited to producing one good compared to another good.

EXHIBIT 3	The Law of Increasing Opportunity Costs

A hypothetical economy produces equal increments of 20,000 sailboats per year as we move from point *A* through point *D* on the production possibilities curve (*PPC*). If the economy moves from point *A* to point *B*, the opportunity cost of 20,000 sailboats is a reduction in tank output of 10,000 per year. This opportunity cost rises to 20,000 tanks if the economy moves from point *B* to point *C*. Finally, production at point *D*, rather than point *C*, results in an opportunity cost of 50,000 tanks per year. The opportunity cost rises because workers are not equally suited to making tanks and sailboats.

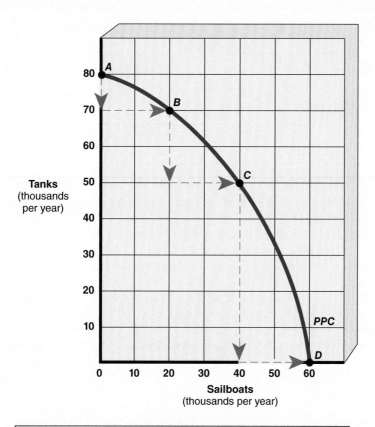

Production Possibilities Schedule for Tanks and Sailboats per Year

Output (thousands per year)	Production possibilities			
	A	B	C	D
Tanks	80	70	50	0
Sailboats	0	20	40	60

SOURCE: © Cengage Learning 2014

Expanding the output of sailboats requires the use of workers who are less suited to producing sailboats than producing tanks. Suppose our hypothetical economy produces no sailboats (point *A*) and then decides to produce them. At first, the least-skilled tank workers are transferred to making sailboats, and 10,000 tanks are sacrificed at point *B*. As the economy moves from point *B* to point *C*, more highly skilled tank makers become sailboat makers, and the opportunity cost rises to 20,000 tanks. Finally, the economy can decide to move from point *C* to point *D*, and the opportunity cost increases even more—to 50,000 tanks. Now the remaining tank workers, who are superb tank makers, but poor sailboat makers, must adapt to the techniques of sailboat production.

Finally, it should be noted that the production possibilities curve model could assume that resources can be substituted and the opportunity cost remains constant. In this case, the production possibilities curve would be a straight line, which is the model employed in the chapter on international trade and finance.

> **CONCLUSION:** *The lack of interchangeability between workers is the cause of increasing opportunity costs and the bowed-out shape of the production possibilities curve.*

2-6 Sources of Economic Growth

Economic growth

The ability of an economy to produce greater levels of output, represented by an outward shift of its production possibilities curve.

The economy's production capacity is not permanently fixed. If either the resource base increases or technology advances, the economy experiences economic growth, and the production possibilities curve shifts outward. Economic growth is the ability of an economy to produce greater levels of output, represented by an outward shift of its production possibilities curve. Exhibit 4 illustrates the importance of an outward shift. (Note the causation chain, which is often used in this text to focus on a model's cause-and-effect relationship.) At point *A* on PPC_1, a hypothetical full-employment economy produces 40,000 computers and 200 million pizzas per year. If the curve shifts outward to the new curve PPC_2, the economy can expand its full-employment output options. One option is to produce at point *B* and increase computer output to 70,000 per year. Another possibility is to increase pizza output to 400 million per year. Yet another choice is to produce more of both at some point between points *B* and *C*.

2-6a CHANGES IN RESOURCES

One way to accelerate economic growth is to gain additional resources. Any increase in resources, for example, more natural resources, a baby boom, or more factories will shift the production possibilities curve outward. In Exhibit 4, assume curve PPC_1 represents Japan's production possibilities for clothing and food in a given year. Suddenly, Japan discovers within its borders new sources of labor and other resources. As a result of the new resources, Japan will have an expanded capacity to produce any combination along an expanded curve, such as curve PPC_2.

Reductions in resources will cause the production possibilities curve to shift inward. Assume curve PPC_2 describes Japan's economy before World War II and the destruction of its factors of production during the war caused

EXHIBIT 4	An Outward Shift of the Production Possibilities Curve for Computers and Pizzas

The economy begins with the capacity to produce combinations along the first production possibilities curve PPC_1. Growth in the resource base or technological advances can shift the production possibilities curve outward from PPC_1 to PPC_2. Points along PPC_2 represent new production possibilities that were previously impossible. This outward shift permits the economy to produce greater quantities of output. Instead of producing combination A, the economy can produce, for example, more computers at point B or more pizzas at point C. If the economy produces at a point between B and C, more of both pizzas and computers can be produced, compared to point A.

SOURCE: © Cengage Learning 2014

Japan's curve to shift leftward to curve PPC_1. Over the years, Japan trained its workforce, built new factories and equipment, and used new technology to shift its curve outward and surpass its original production capacity at curve PPC_2.

2-6b TECHNOLOGICAL CHANGE

Another way to achieve economic growth is through research and development of new technologies. The knowledge of how to transform a stone into a wheel vastly improved the prehistoric standard of living. Technological change also makes it possible to shift the production possibilities curve outward by producing more from the same resources base. One source of technological change is *invention*. Computer chips, satellites, and the Internet are all examples of technological advances resulting from the use of science and engineering knowledge.

Technological change also results from the innovations of entrepreneurship, introduced in the previous chapter. Innovation involves creating and developing new products or productive processes. Seeking profits, entrepreneurs create new, better, or less expensive products. This requires organizing an improved mix of resources, which expands the production possibilities curve.

One entrepreneur, Henry Ford, changed auto industry technology by pioneering the use of the assembly line for making cars. Another entrepreneur, Chester Carlson, a law student, became so frustrated copying documents that he worked on his own to develop photocopying. After years of disappointment, a small firm named Xerox Corporation accepted Carlson's invention and transformed a good idea into a revolutionary product. These and a myriad of other business success stories illustrate that entrepreneurs are important because they transform their new ideas into production and practical use. Throughout history, technological advances have fostered economic growth by increasing our nation's productive power. Today, the Internet and computers are "new" technologies, but railroads, electricity, and automobiles, for example, were also "new" technologies in their time.

✔ CHECKPOINT

What Does a War on Terrorism Really Mean?

With the disappearance of the former Soviet Union and the end of the Cold War, the United States became the world's only superpower and no longer engaged in an intense competition to build up its military. As a result, in the 1990s, Congress and the White House had the opportunity to reduce the military's share of the budget and spend more funds for nondefense goods. This situation was referred to as the "peace dividend." Now consider that the need to combat terrorism diverts resources back to military and security output. Does the peace dividend or a reversal to more military spending represent a possible shift of the production possibilities curve or a movement along it?

FedEx Wasn't an Overnight Success

Applicable Concept: entrepreneurship

Frederick W. Smith is a classic entrepreneurial success story. Young Fred went to Yale University, had a good new idea, secured venture capital, worked like crazy, and made a fortune, and the Smithsonian Institution rendered its ultimate accolade. It snapped up an early Federal Express jet for its collection, displaying it for a time in the National Air and Space Museum in Washington, D.C., not far from the Wright brothers' first airplane.

Smith's saga began with a college economics term paper that spelled out a nationwide overnight parcel delivery system that would be guaranteed to "absolutely, positively" beat the pants off the U.S. Postal Service. People, he said, would pay much more if their packages arrived at their destination the next morning. To accomplish his plan, planes would converge nightly on Memphis, Tennessee, carrying packages accepted at any location throughout the nation. Smith chose this city for its central U.S. location and because its airport has little bad weather to cause landing delays. In the morning hours, all items would be unloaded, sorted, and rerouted to other airports, where vans would battle rush-hour traffic to make deliveries before the noon deadline.

Smith's college term paper only got a C grade. Perhaps the professor thought the idea was too risky, and lots of others certainly agreed. In 1969, after college and a tour as a Marine pilot in Vietnam, the 24-year-old Smith began pitching his parcel delivery plan to mostly skeptical financiers. Nevertheless, with $4 million of his family's money, he persuaded a few venture capitalists to put up $80 million. At the time, this was the largest venture capital package ever assembled. In 1973, delivery service began with 33 jets connecting 25 cities, but on the first night, only 86 packages showed up.

It was years before Smith looked like a genius. The company posted a $27 million loss the first

Daryl Lang / Shutterstock.com

year; turned the corner in 1976; and then took off, helped by a 1981 decision to add letters to its basic package delivery service. Today, Smith's basic strategy hasn't changed, but the scale of the operation has exploded. FedEx is the world's largest express transportation company serving over 200 countries.

Analyze the Issue

Draw a production possibilities curve for an economy producing only pizzas and computers. Explain how Fred Smith and other entrepreneurs affect the curve.

Source: © Cengage Learning 2014

2-7 Present Investment and the Future Production Possibilities Curve

GLOBAL ECONOMICS

When the decision for an economy involves choosing between capital goods and consumer goods, the output combination for the present period can determine future production capacity.

Exhibit 5 compares two countries producing different combinations of capital and consumer goods. Part (a) shows the production possibilities curve for the low-investment economy of Alpha. This economy was producing combination A in 2000, which is an output of C_a of consumer goods and an output of K_a of capital goods per year. Let's assume K_a is just enough capital output to replace the capital being worn out each year (depreciation). As a result, Alpha fails to accumulate the net gain of

iStockphoto.com/evirgen

EXHIBIT 5	Alpha's and Beta's Present and Future Production Possibilities Curves

In part (a), each year Alpha produces only enough capital (K_a) to replace existing capital that has worn out. Without greater capital and assuming other resources remain fixed, Alpha is unable to shift its production possibilities curve outward. In part (b), each year Beta produces K_b capital, which is more than the amount required to replenish its depreciated capital. In 2010, this expanded capital provides Beta with the extra production capacity to shift its production possibilities curve to the right (outward). If Beta chooses point B on its curve, it has the production capacity to increase the amount of consumer goods from C_b to C_c without producing fewer capital goods.

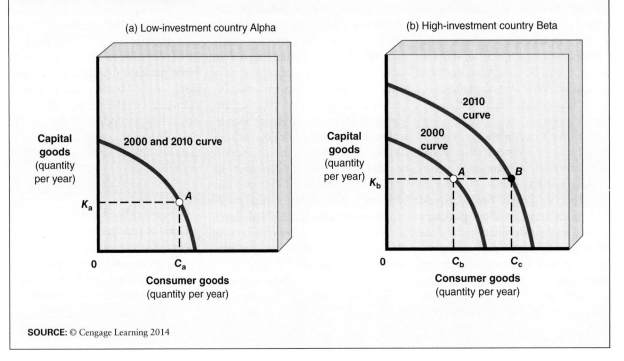

SOURCE: © Cengage Learning 2014

factories and equipment required to expand its production possibilities curve outward in future years.[1] Why wouldn't Alpha simply move up along its production curve by shifting more resources to capital goods production? The problem is that sacrificing consumer goods for capital formation causes the standard of living to fall.

Comparing Alpha to Beta illustrates the importance of being able to do more than just replace worn-out capital. Beta operated in 2000 at point A in part (b), which is an output of C_b of consumer goods and K_b of capital goods. Assuming K_b is more than enough to replenish worn-out capital, Beta is a high-investment economy, adding to its capital stock and creating extra production capacity. This process of accumulating capital *(capital formation)* is investment. Investment is the accumulation of capital, such as factories, machines, and inventories, used to produce goods and services. Newly built factories and machines in the present provide an economy

Investment

The accumulation of capital, such as factories, machines, and inventories used to produce goods and services.

---

[1]Recall from the appendix to Chapter 1 that a third variable can affect the variables measured on the vertical and horizontal axes. In this case, the third variable is the quantity of capital worn out per year.

How Does Public Capital Affect a Nation's Curve?

Applicable Concept: economic growth

Robert Hackett/iStockphoto.com

The discussion of low-investment country Alpha versus high-investment country Beta explained that sacrificing production of consumer goods for an increase in capital goods output can result in economic growth and a higher standard of living. Stated differently, there was a long-run benefit from the accumulation of capital that offset the short-run opportunity cost in terms of consumer goods. Here the analysis was in terms of investment in private capital such as factories, machines, and inventories. However, public or government capital can also influence the production of both capital goods and consumption goods. For example, the government provides infrastructure such as roads, schools, bridges, ports, dams, and sanitation that makes the accumulation process for private capital more efficient, and in turn, an economy grows at a greater rate.

Using data from 21 high-investment countries, a recent study by economists investigated how government investment policy affected the productivity of new private capital goods.[1] Countries included in the research were, for example, Canada, Japan, New Zealand, Spain, and the United States. A key finding was that a 1 percent increase in public investment increased the productivity of private investment by 27 percent. As a result, public capital caused the stock of private capital to rise more quickly over time.

Finally, economic growth and development is a major goal of countries throughout the world, and there are numerous factors that cause some countries to experience greater economic growth compared to other countries. Note that this topic is discussed in more depth in the last chapter of the text.

Analyze the Issue

Construct a production possibilities curve for a hypothetical country. Put public capital goods per year on the vertical axis and consumer goods per year on the horizontal axis. Not shown directly in your graph, assume that this country produces just enough private capital per year to replace its depreciated capital. Assume further that this country is without public capital and is operating at point *A*, where consumer goods are at a maximum. Based on the above research and using a production possibilities curve, show and explain what happens to this country's private capital, production possibilities curve, and standard of living if it increases its output of public capital.

---

1. Stuart Fowler and Bichaka Fayissa, "Public Capital Spending Shocks and the Price of Investment: Evidence from a Panel of Countries," The 2007 Missouri Economics Conference.

Source: © Cengage Learning 2014

with the capacity to expand its production options in the future. For example, the outward shift of its curve allows Beta to produce C_c consumer goods at point *B* in 2010. This means Beta will be able to improve its standard of living by producing $C_c - C_b$ extra consumer goods, while Alpha's standard of living remains unchanged because the production of consumer goods remains unchanged.

CONCLUSION: *A nation can accelerate economic growth by increasing its production of capital goods in excess of the capital being worn out in the production process.*

Key Concepts

What, How, and *For Whom*
   questions
Opportunity cost
Marginal analysis

Production possibilities curve
Technology
Law of increasing opportunity
   costs

Economic growth
Investment

Summary

- **Three fundamental economic questions** facing any economy are *What, How,* and *For Whom* to produce goods. The *What* question asks exactly which goods are to be produced and in what quantities. The *How* question requires society to decide the resource mix used to produce goods. The *For Whom* problem concerns the division of output among society's citizens.

- **Opportunity cost** is the best alternative forgone for a chosen option. This means no decision can be made without cost.

SOURCE: © Cengage Learning 2014

- **Marginal analysis** examines the impact of changes from a current situation and is a technique used extensively in economics. The basic approach is to compare the additional benefits of a change with the additional costs of the change.

- A **production possibilities curve** illustrates an economy's capacity to produce goods, subject to the constraint of scarcity. The production possibilities curve is a graph of the maximum possible combinations of two outputs that can be produced in a given period of time, subject to three conditions: (1) All resources are fully employed. (2) The resource base is not allowed to vary during the time period. (3) **Technology**, which is the body of knowledge applied to the production of goods, remains constant. **Inefficient** production occurs at any point inside the production possibilities curve. All points along the curve are **efficient** points because each point represents a maximum output possibility.

Production Possibilities Curve

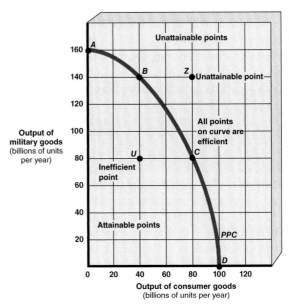

SOURCE: © Cengage Learning 2014

- The **law of increasing opportunity costs** states that the opportunity cost increases as the production of an output expands. The explanation for this law is that the suitability of resources declines sharply as greater amounts are transferred from producing one output to producing another output.

- **Economic growth** is represented by the production possibilities curve shifting outward as the result of an increase in resources or an advance in technology.

Economic Growth

CAUSATION CHAIN

Increase in resources or technological advances ⟹ Economic growth

SOURCE: © Cengage Learning 2014

- **Investment** means that an economy is producing and accumulating capital. Investment consists of factories, machines, and inventories (capital) produced in the present that are used to shift the production possibilities curve outward in the future.

Summary of Conclusion Statements

- Scarcity limits an economy to points on or below its production possibilities curve.
- The production possibilities curve consists of all efficient output combinations at which an economy can produce more of one good only by producing less of the other good.

- The lack of perfect interchangeability between workers is the cause of increasing opportunity costs and the bowed-out shape of the production possibilities curve.
- A nation can accelerate economic growth by increasing its production of capital goods in excess of the capital being worn out in the production process.

Study Questions and Problems

1. Explain why scarcity forces individuals and society to incur opportunity costs. Give specific examples.

2. Suppose a retailer promotes its store by advertising a drawing for a "free car." Is this car *free* because the winner pays *zero* for it?

3. Explain verbally the statement "There is no such thing as a free lunch" in relation to scarce resources.

4. Which of the following decisions has the greater opportunity cost? Why?
   a. A decision to use an undeveloped lot in Tokyo's financial district for an apartment building.
   b. A decision to use a square mile in the desert for a gas station.

5. Attending college is expensive, time-consuming, and requires effort. So why do people decide to attend college?

6. The following is a set of hypothetical production possibilities for a nation.

Combination	Automobiles (thousands)	Beef (thousands of tons)
A	0	10
B	2	9
C	4	7
D	6	4
E	8	0

  a. Plot these production possibilities data. What is the opportunity cost of the first 2,000 automobiles produced? Between which points is the opportunity cost per thousand automobiles highest? Between which points is the opportunity cost per thousand tons of beef highest?

  b. Label a point F inside the curve. Why is this an inefficient point? Label a point G outside the curve. Why is this point unattainable? Why are points A through E all efficient points?

  c. Does this production possibilities curve reflect the law of increasing opportunity costs? Explain.

  d. What assumptions could be changed to shift the production possibilities curve?

7. The following table shows the production possibilities for pies and flower boxes. Fill in the opportunity cost (pies forgone) of producing the first through the fifth flower box.

Combination	Pies	Flower boxes	Opportunity cost
A	30	0	_____
B	26	1	_____
C	21	2	_____
D	15	3	_____
E	8	4	_____
F	0	5	_____

8. Why does a production possibilities curve have a bowed-out shape?

9. Interpret the phrases "There is no such thing as a free lunch" and "A free lunch is possible" in terms of the production possibilities curve.

10. Suppose, unfortunately, your mathematics and economics professors have decided to give tests two days from now and you can spend a total of only 12 hours studying for both exams. After some thought, you conclude that dividing your study time equally between each subject will give you an expected grade of C in each course. For each additional three hours of study time for one of the subjects, your grade will increase one letter for that subject, and your grade will fall one letter for the other subject.

  a. Construct a table for the production possibilities and corresponding number of hours of study in this case.

  b. Plot these production possibilities data in a graph.

  c. Does this production possibilities curve reflect the law of increasing opportunity costs? Explain.

11. Draw a production possibilities curve for a hypothetical economy producing capital goods and consumer goods. Suppose a major technological breakthrough occurs in the capital goods industry and the new technology is widely adopted only in this industry. Draw the new production possibilities curve. Now assume that a technological advance occurs in consumer goods production, but not in capital goods production. Draw the new production possibilities curve.

12. The present choice between investing in capital goods and producing consumer goods now affects the ability of an economy to produce in the future. Explain.

✓ CHECKPOINT ANSWERS

What Does a War on Terrorism Really Mean?

A "peace dividend" suggests resources are allocated away from military production and used for greater nonmilitary production. The war on terrorism arguably shifts resources in the opposite direction. If you said that this phrase represents a movement along the production possibilities curve, **YOU ARE CORRECT.**

Sample Quiz

For an explanation of the correct answers, visit the Tucker Web site at www.cengage.com/economics/tucker.

1. Which of the following *best* describes the three fundamental economic questions?
   a. What to produce, when to produce, and where to produce
   b. What time to produce, what place to produce, and how to produce
   c. What to produce, when to produce, and for whom to produce
   d. What to produce, how to produce, and for whom to produce

2. Suppose the alternative uses of an hour of your time in the evening, ranked from best to worst, are (1) study economics, (2) watch two half-hour sitcoms, (3) play video games, and (4) jog around town. You can choose only one activity. What is the opportunity cost of studying economics for one hour given this information?
   a. Jogging around town
   b. Watching two half-hour TV sitcoms
   c. Playing video games
   d. The sum of watching two half-hour TV sitcoms, playing pool, and doing your laundry

3. Which word or phrase *best* completes the following sentence? Marginal analysis means evaluating _____ changes from a current situation.
   a. positive or negative
   b. infinite
   c. no
   d. maximum

4. Which of the following is an example of an organization using marginal analysis?
   a. A hotel manager calculating the average cost per guest for the past year
   b. A farmer hoping for rain
   c. A government official considering the effect an increase in military goods production will have on the production of consumer goods
   d. A businessperson calculating economic profits

5. A production possibilities curve shows the various combinations of two outputs that
   a. consumers would like to consume.
   b. producers would like to produce.
   c. an economy can produce.
   d. an economy should produce.

6. A production possibilities curve is drawn based on which of the following assumptions?
   a. Resources are fixed and fully employed, and technology advances at the rate of growth of the economy overall.
   b. Resources such as nonrenewable resources will decline, but labor remains fully employed and technology is unchanged.
   c. Resources can vary; most resources experience times of unemployment; and technology advances, particularly during wartime.

Sample Quiz *continued*

d. Resources such as labor and capital will grow and are fully employed, and technology is unchanged.

e. None of the above answers is correct.

7. If an economy can produce various combinations of food and shelter along a production possibilities curve (PPC), then if we increase the production of shelter along the PPC, which of the following is *true*?

a. We also increase the production of food.

b. We must decrease the production of food. This forgone food production represents the opportunity cost of the increase in shelter.

c. We cannot change the production of food.

d. The concept of opportunity cost does not apply along PPC.

8. An economy can produce various combinations of food and shelter along a production possibilities curve (PPC). We first increase the production of shelter along the PPC. If we then continue to shift more and more production to shelter, which of the following will *most* likely happen to the opportunity cost of a unit of shelter?

a. Opportunity cost will increase because as more and more shelter is produced, labor and capital that is highly productive at producing food is being shifted to shelter production, and so more and more food is being given up to produce a unit of shelter.

b. Opportunity cost is the amount of labor (but not capital) that is used to produce the extra shelter.

c. Opportunity cost must stay constant if we are to stay on the production possibilities curve (PPC).

d. Opportunity cost includes all options given up to produce shelter.

9. An economy can produce various combinations of food and shelter along a production possibilities curve (PPC). Suppose a technological innovation resulted in a new, higher-yielding crop that generated more bushels of grain for a given set of land, labor, and capital resources. If this innovation did not affect the productivity of shelter production, which of the following would be *true*?

a. The PPC will shift outward equally along both axes of the graph.

b. The PPC will rotate inward along the food axis, but will not shift on the shelter axis.

c. The PPC will rotate outward along the food axis, but will not shift on the shelter axis.

d. The PPC will not change.

10. If a production possibilities curve (PPC) has capital on the vertical axis and consumer goods on the horizontal axis, which of the following is true?

a. There is a trade-off between emphasizing the production of capital today to benefit people today versus emphasizing the production of consumer goods today that will generate benefits in the future.

b. Greater emphasis on the production of capital today leads to future inward shifts in the PPC, thus decreasing the wealth of people in the future.

c. Greater emphasis on the production of consumer goods today leads to greater outward shifts in the PPC, thus increasing the wealth of people in the future.

d. Greater emphasis on the production of capital today leads to greater outward shifts in the PPC, thus increasing the wealth of people in the future.

11. Which of the following reasons could explain why an economy would be operating inside its production possibilities curve (PPC)?

a. Because shrinking population has reduced the number of productive workers in the economy

b. Because technological innovations have increased the productivity of labor and capital

c. Because damage to natural resources, such as damage caused by deforestation leading to erosion of topsoil, has shrunk the land resource

d. Because of unemployment or underemployment of labor, perhaps due to discrimination against employing workers of a certain race or gender

Sample Quiz *continued*

12. Combinations of goods outside the production possibilities curve (PPC) have which of the following characteristics?
    a. They are attainable today only if we employ all unemployed or underemployed resources.
    b. They are not attainable given our existing stock of resources and technology.
    c. They imply that some resources, such as labor, are unemployed or underemployed.
    d. None of the above answers is correct.

13. Suppose an economy can produce various combinations of fish and bread. If more people with strong fishing skills became employed in this economy, how would the production possibilities curve (PPC) change?
    a. The PPC would shift outward on the fish axis, but would not change on the bread axis.
    b. The PPC would shift outward equally along both the fish and bread axes.
    c. The PPC would shift inward on the bread axis, but would not change on the fish axis.
    d. The PPC would shift inward equally along both the fish and bread axes.

14. Three different economies have made choices about the production of capital goods. Which of the following is *most* likely to produce the greatest growth in the production possibilities curve (PPC)?
    a. Capital goods produced at the exact rate needed to replace worn-out capital.
    b. Greater production of capital goods than what is needed to replace worn-out capital.
    c. Less production of capital goods than what is needed to replace worn-out capital.
    d. More production of consumption goods that replace worn-out capital.

15. In the study of economics, investment means
    a. the accumulation of capital that is used to produce goods and services.
    b. owning stocks and bonds.

    c. the principle that the opportunity cost increases as the production of one output expands.
    d. the effect of stock prices on the production possibilities curve.

16. Which of the following is *not* one of the three fundamental economic questions?
    a. What happens when you add to or subtract from a current situation?
    b. For whom to produce?
    c. How to produce?
    d. What to produce?

17. Opportunity cost
    a. represents the best alternative sacrificed for a chosen alternative.
    b. has no relationship to the various alternatives that must be given up when a choice is made in the context of scarcity.
    c. represents the worst alternative sacrificed for a chosen alternative.
    d. represents all alternatives not chosen.

18. Which words best complete the following sentence? A rational decision maker always chooses the option for which marginal benefit is _____ marginal cost.
    a. less than
    b. equal to
    c. unrelated to
    d. more than

19. The principle that the opportunity cost increases as the production of one output expands is the
    a. law of increasing opportunity costs.
    b. law of demand.
    c. law of supply.
    d. law of increasing returns to scale.

20. The ability of an economy to produce greater levels of output per time period is called
    a. positive economics.
    b. negative economics.
    c. economic growth.
    d. the law of specialization.

Road Map
Introduction to Economics

This road map feature helps you tie together material in the part as you travel the Economic Way of Thinking Highway. The following are review questions listed by chapter from the previous part. The key concept in each question is given for emphasis, and each question or set of questions concludes with an interactive game to reinforce the concepts. Click on the Tucker Web site at www.cengage.com/economics/tucker, select the chapter, and play the visual causation chain game designed to make learning fun. Enjoy the cheers when correct and suffer the jeers if you miss. The correct answers to the multiple choice questions are given in Appendix C of the text.

CHAPTER 1. INTRODUCING THE ECONOMIC WAY OF THINKING

1. **Key Concept: Scarcity**
   Economists believe that scarcity forces everyone to
   a. satisfy all wants.
   b. abandon consumer sovereignty.
   c. lie about their wants.
   d. create unlimited resources.
   e. make choices.

2. **Key Concept: Economics**
   The subject of economics is primarily the study of
   a. the government decision-making process.
   b. how to operate a business successfully.
   c. decision making because of the problem of scarcity.
   d. how to make money in the stock market.

 Causation Chain Game
The Relationship between Scarcity and Decision Making

3. **Key Concept: Model**
   When building a model, an economist must
   a. adjust for exceptional situations.
   b. provide a complete description of reality.
   c. make simplifying assumptions.
   d. develop a set of behavioral equations.

4. **Key Concept: Ceteris paribus**
   If the price of a textbook rises and students purchase fewer textbooks, an economic model can show a cause-and-effect relationship only if which of the following conditions holds?

Top image: GSK/Shutterstock.com/Image for chain icon: IMAGEMORE Co, Ltd./Getty Images

a. Students' incomes fall.
b. Tuition decreases.
c. The number of students increases.
d. Everything else is constant.
e. The bookstore no longer accepts used book trade-ins.

5. **Key Concept: Association versus causation**

Someone notices that sunspot activity is high just prior to recessions and concludes that sunspots cause recessions. This person has
a. confused association and causation.
b. misunderstood the ceteris paribus assumption.
c. used normative economics to answer a positive question.
d. built an untestable model.

Causation Chain Game
The Steps in the Model-Building Process—Exhibit 2

CHAPTER 2. PRODUCTION POSSIBILITIES, OPPORTUNITY COST, AND ECONOMIC GROWTH

6. **Key Concept: Production possibilities curve**

Which of the following is *not* true about a production possibilities curve? The curve
a. indicates the combinations of goods and services that can be produced with a given technology.
b. indicates the efficient production points.
c. indicates the nonefficient production points.
d. indicates the feasible (attainable) and nonfeasible production points.
e. indicates which production point will be chosen.

7. **Key Concept: Production possibilities curve**

Which of the following is *true* about the production possibilities curve when a technological progress occurs?
a. Shifts inward to the left
b. Becomes flatter at one end and steeper at the other end
c. Becomes steeper
d. Shifts outward to the right
e. Does not change

8. **Key Concept: Shifting the production possibilities curve**

An outward shift of an economy's production possibilities curve is caused by
a. entrepreneurship.
b. an increase in labor.
c. an advance in technology.
d. all of the above.

9. **Key Concept: Shifting the production possibilities curve**
   Which would be *least* likely to cause the production possibilities curve to shift to the right?
   a. An increase in the labor force
   b. Improved methods of production
   c. An increase in the education and training of the labor force
   d. A decrease in unemployment

10. **Key Concept: Investment**
    A nation can accelerate its economic growth by
    a. reducing the number of immigrants allowed into the country.
    b. adding to its stock of capital.
    c. printing more money.
    d. imposing tariffs and quotas on imported goods.

Causation Chain Game
Economic Growth and Technology—Exhibit 4

Microeconomic Fundamentals

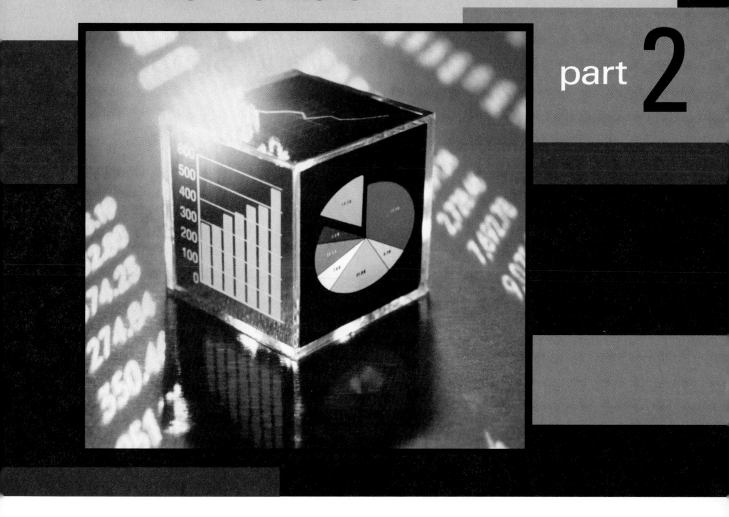

part 2

In your study of the microeconomy, the chapters in Part 2 build on the basic concepts you learned in Part 1. Chapters 3 and 4 explain the market demand and supply model, which has a wide range of real-world applications. Chapter 5 takes a closer look at movements along the demand curve introduced in Chapter 3. Chapter 6 returns to the law of demand and explores in more detail exactly why consumers make their choices among goods and services. Part 2 concludes in Chapter 7 with an extension of the concept of supply that explains how various costs of production change as output varies.

Market Demand and Supply

A cornerstone of the U.S. economy is the use of markets to answer the basic economic questions discussed in the previous chapter. Consider baseball cards, Blu-rays, physical fitness, gasoline, soft drinks, and sneakers. In a *market economy*, each is bought and sold by individuals coming together as buyers and sellers in markets. This chapter is extremely important because it introduces basic supply and demand analysis. This technique will prove to be valuable because it is applicable to a multitude of real-world choices of buyers and sellers facing the problem of scarcity. For example, the Global

Economics feature asks you to consider the highly controversial issue of international trade in human organs.

Demand represents the choice-making behavior of consumers, while supply represents the choices of producers. The chapter begins by looking closely at demand and then supply. Finally, it combines these forces to see how prices and quantities are determined in the marketplace. Market demand and supply analysis is the basic tool of microeconomic analysis.

In this chapter, you will learn to solve these economics puzzles:

- What is the difference between a "change in quantity demanded" and a "change in demand"?
- Can Congress repeal the law of supply to control oil prices?
- Does the price system eliminate scarcity?

3-1 The Law of Demand

Economics might be referred to as "graphs and laughs" because economists are so fond of using graphs to illustrate demand, supply, and many other economic concepts. Unfortunately, some students taking economics courses say they miss the laughs.

Exhibit 1 reveals an important "law" in economics called the law of demand. The law of demand states there is an inverse relationship between the price of a good and the quantity buyers are willing to purchase in a defined time period, ceteris paribus. The law of demand makes good sense. At a "sale," consumers buy more when the price of merchandise is cut.

Law of demand

The principle that there is an inverse relationship between the price of a good and the quantity buyers are willing to purchase in a defined time period, ceteris paribus.

EXHIBIT 1	An Individual Buyer's Demand Curve for Blu-rays

Bob's demand curve shows how many Blu-rays he is willing to purchase at different possible prices. As the price of Blu-rays declines, the quantity demanded increases, and Bob purchases more Blu-rays. The inverse relationship between price and quantity demanded conforms to the law of demand.

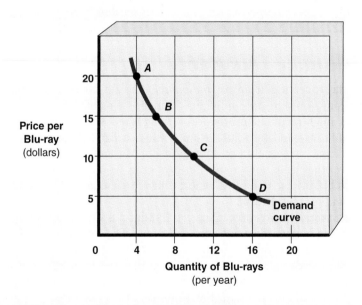

An Individual Buyer's Demand Schedule for Blu-rays

Point	Price per Blu-ray	Quantity demanded (per year)
A	$20	4
B	15	6
C	10	10
D	5	16

SOURCE: © Cengage Learning 2014

In Exhibit 1, the *demand curve* is formed by the line connecting the possible price and quantity purchased responses of an individual consumer. The demand curve therefore allows you to find the quantity demanded by a buyer at any possible selling price by moving along the curve. For example, Bob, a sophomore at Marketplace College, enjoys watching Blu-ray movies. Bob's demand curve shows that at a price of $15 per Blu-ray, his quantity demanded is 6 Blu-rays purchased annually (point *B*). At the lower price of $10, Bob's quantity demanded increases to 10 Blu-rays per year (point *C*). Following this procedure, other price and quantity possibilities for Bob are read along the demand curve.

Note that until we know the actual price determined by both demand and supply, we do not know how many Blu-rays Bob will actually purchase annually. The demand curve is simply a summary of Bob's buying intentions. Once we know the market price, a quick look at the demand curve tells us how many Blu-rays Bob will buy.

Demand

A curve or schedule showing the various quantities of product consumers are willing to purchase at possible prices during a specified period of time, ceteris paribus.

> **CONCLUSION:** *Demand is a curve or schedule showing the various quantities of a product consumers are willing to purchase at possible prices during a specified period of time, ceteris paribus.*

3-1a MARKET DEMAND

To make the transition from an *individual* demand curve to a *market* demand curve, we total, or sum, the individual demand schedules. Suppose the owner of ZapMart, a small retail chain of stores serving a few states, tries to decide what to charge for Blu-rays and hires a consumer research firm. For simplicity, we assume Fred and Mary are the only two buyers in ZapMart's market, and they are sent a questionnaire that asks how many Blu-rays each would be willing to purchase at several possible prices. Exhibit 2 reports their price-quantity demanded responses in tabular and graphical form.

The market demand curve, D_{total}, in Exhibit 2 is derived by summing *horizontally* the two individual demand curves, D_1 and D_2, for each possible price. At a price of $20, for example, we sum Fred's 2 Blu-rays demanded per year and Mary's 1 Blu-ray demanded per year to find that the total quantity demanded at $20 is 3 Blu-rays per year. Repeating the same process for other prices generates the market demand curve, D_{total}. For example, at a price of $5, the total quantity demanded is 12 Blu-rays.

3-2 The Distinction between Changes in Quantity Demanded and Changes in Demand

Price is not the only variable that determines how much of a good or service consumers will buy. Recall from Exhibit A-6 of Appendix 1 that the price and quantity variables in our model are subject to the ceteris paribus assumption. If we relax this assumption and allow other variables held constant to change, a variety

EXHIBIT 2	The Market Demand Curve for Blu-rays

Individual demand curves differ for consumers Fred and Mary. Assuming they are the only buyers in the market, the market demand curve, D_{total}, is derived by summing horizontally the individual demand curves, D_1 and D_2.

Market Demand Schedule for Blu-rays

	Quantity Demanded per Year			
Price per Blu-ray	Fred	+	Mary	=	Total Demand
$25	1		0		1
20	2		1		3
15	3		3		6
10	4		5		9
5	5		7		12

SOURCE: © Cengage Learning 2014

of factors can influence the position of the demand curve. Because these factors are not the price of the good itself, these variables are called *nonprice determinants,* or simply, *demand shifters.* The major nonprice determinants include (1) the number of buyers; (2) tastes and preferences; (3) income; (4) expectations of future changes in prices, income, and availability of goods; and (5) prices of related goods.

Before discussing these nonprice determinants of demand, we must pause to explain an important and possibly confusing distinction in terminology. We have been referring to a change in quantity demanded, which results solely from a change in the price. A change in quantity demanded is a movement between points along a stationary demand curve, ceteris paribus. In Exhibit 3(a), at the price of $15, the quantity demanded is 20 million Blu-rays per year. This is shown as

Change in quantity demanded

A movement between points along a stationary demand curve, ceteris paribus.

EXHIBIT 3 — Movement along a Demand Curve versus a Shift in Demand

Part (a) shows the demand curve, D, for Blu-rays per year. If the price is $15 at point A, the quantity demanded by consumers is 20 million Blu-rays. If the price decreases to $10 at point B, the quantity demanded increases from 20 million to 30 million Blu-rays.

Part (b) illustrates an increase in demand. A change in some nonprice determinant can cause an increase in demand from D_1 to D_2. At a price of $15 on D_1 (point A), 20 million Blu-rays is the quantity demanded per year. At this price on D_2 (point B), the quantity demanded increases to 30 million.

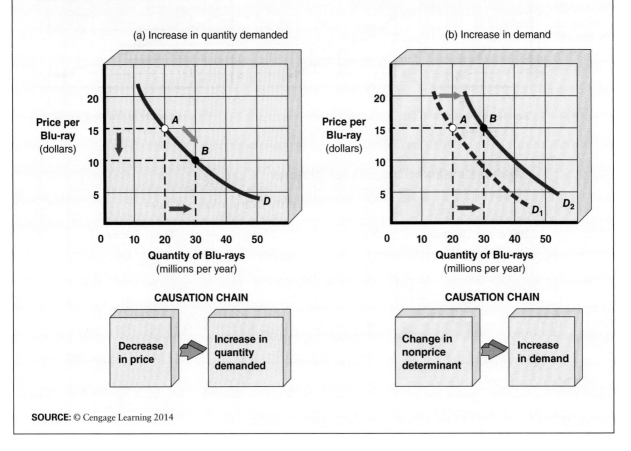

SOURCE: © Cengage Learning 2014

point A on the demand curve, D. At a lower price of, say, $10, the quantity demanded increases to 30 million Blu-rays per year, shown as point B. Verbally, we describe the impact of the price decrease as an increase in the quantity demanded of 10 million Blu-rays per year. We show this relationship on the demand curve as a movement down along the curve from point A to point B.

CONCLUSION: *Under the law of demand, any decrease in price along the vertical axis will cause an increase in quantity demanded, measured along the horizontal axis.*

A change in demand is an increase (rightward shift) or a decrease (leftward shift) in the quantity demanded at each possible price. If ceteris paribus no longer applies and if one of the five nonprice factors changes, the location of the demand curve shifts.

Change in demand

An increase or a decrease in the quantity demanded at each possible price. An increase in demand is a rightward shift in the entire demand curve. A decrease in demand is a leftward shift in the entire demand curve.

> **CONCLUSION:** *Changes in nonprice determinants can produce only a shift in the demand curve and not a movement along the demand curve, which is caused by a change in the price.*

Comparing parts (a) and (b) of Exhibit 3 is helpful in distinguishing between a change in quantity demanded and a change in demand. In part (b), suppose the market demand curve for Blu-rays is initially at D_1 and there is a shift to the right (an increase in demand) from D_1 to D_2. This means that at *all* possible prices, consumers wish to purchase a larger quantity than before the shift occurred. At \$15 per Blu-ray, for example, 30 million Blu-rays (point *B*) will be purchased each year, rather than 20 million Blu-rays (point *A*).

Now suppose a change in some nonprice factor causes demand curve D_1 to shift leftward (a decrease in demand). The interpretation in this case is that at *all* possible prices, consumers will buy a smaller quantity than before the shift occurred.

Exhibit 4 summarizes the terminology for the effects of changes in price and nonprice determinants on the demand curve.

3-3 Nonprice Determinants of Demand

Distinguishing between a change in quantity demanded and a change in demand requires some patience and practice. The following discussion of specific changes in nonprice factors, or demand shifters, will clarify how each nonprice variable affects demand.

3-3a NUMBER OF BUYERS

Look back at Exhibit 2 and imagine the impact of adding more individual demand curves to the individual demand curves of Fred and Mary. At all possible prices, there is extra quantity demanded by the new customers, and the market demand curve for Blu-rays shifts rightward (an increase in demand). Population growth therefore tends to increase the number of buyers, which shifts the market demand curve for a good or service rightward. Conversely, a population decline shifts most market demand curves leftward (a decrease in demand).

The number of buyers can be specified to include both foreign and domestic buyers. Suppose the market demand curve D_1 in Exhibit 3(b) is for Blu-rays purchased in the United States by customers at home and abroad. Also assume Japan

EXHIBIT 4	Terminology for Changes in Price and Nonprice Determinants of Demand

Caution! It is important to distinguish between a change in quantity demanded, which is a movement along a demand curve (D_1) caused by a change in price, and a change in demand, which is a shift in the demand curve. An increase in demand (shift to D_2) or a decrease in demand (shift to D_3) is not caused by a change in price. Instead, a shift is caused by a change in one of the nonprice determinants.

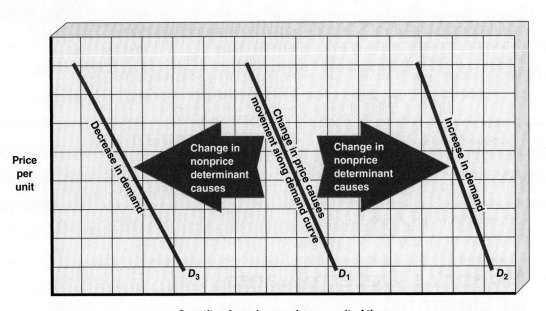

Quantity of good or service per unit of time

Change	Effect	Terminology
Price increases	Upward movement along the demand curve	Decrease in the quantity demanded
Price decreases	Downward movement along the demand curve	Increase in the quantity demanded
Nonprice determinant	Leftward or rightward shift in the demand curve	Decrease or increase in demand

SOURCE: © Cengage Learning 2014

restricts the import of Blu-rays into Japan. What would be the effect of Japan removing this trade restriction? The answer is that the demand curve shifts rightward from D_1 to D_2 when Japanese consumers add their individual demand curves to the U.S. market demand for Blu-rays.

3-3b TASTES AND PREFERENCES

A favorable or unfavorable change in consumer tastes or preferences means more or less of a product is demanded at each possible price. Fads, fashions, advertising, and new products can influence consumer preferences to buy a particular good or service. Beanie Babies, for example, became the rage in the 1990s, and the demand curve for these products shifted to the right. When people tire of a product, the demand curve will shift leftward. The physical fitness trend has increased the demand for health clubs and exercise equipment. On the other hand, have you noticed many stores selling hula hoops? Advertising can also influence consumers' taste for a product. As a result, consumers are more likely to buy more at every price, and the demand curve for the product will shift to the right. Concern for global climate change has increased the demand for hybrid cars and recycling.

3-3c INCOME

Most students are all too familiar with how changes in income affect demand. There are two possible categories for the relationship between changes in income and changes in demand: (1) normal goods and (2) inferior goods.

A normal good is any good for which there is a direct relationship between changes in income and its demand curve. For many goods and services, an increase in income causes buyers to purchase more at any possible price. As buyers receive higher incomes, the demand curve shifts rightward for such *normal goods* as cars, steaks, vintage wine, cleaning services, and Blu-rays. A decline in income has the opposite effect, and the demand curve shifts leftward.

An inferior good is any good for which there is an inverse relationship between changes in income and its demand curve. A rise in income can result in reduced purchases of a good or service at any possible price. This might happen with such *inferior goods* as generic brands, Spam, discount clothes, and used cars. Instead of buying these inferior goods, higher incomes allow consumers to buy brand-name products, steaks, designer clothes, or new cars. Conversely, a fall in income causes the demand curve for inferior goods to shift rightward.

Normal good

Any good for which there is a direct relationship between changes in income and its demand curve.

Inferior good

Any good for which there is an inverse relationship between changes in income and its demand curve.

3-3d EXPECTATIONS OF BUYERS

What is the effect on demand in the present when consumers anticipate future changes in prices, incomes, or availability? What happens when a war breaks out in the Middle East? Expectations that there will be a shortage of gasoline induce consumers to say "fill 'er up" at every opportunity, and demand increases. Suppose students learn that the prices of the textbooks for several courses they plan to take next semester will double soon. Their likely response is to buy now, which causes an increase in the demand curve for these textbooks. Another example is a change in the weather, which can indirectly cause expectations to shift demand for some products. Suppose severe weather destroys a substantial portion of the peach crop. Consumers reason that the reduction in available supply will soon drive up prices, and they dash to stock up before it is too late. This change in expectations causes the demand curve for peaches to increase. Prior to Hurricane Katrina hitting New Orleans, sales of batteries and flashlights soared.

3-3e PRICES OF RELATED GOODS

Possibly the most confusing nonprice factor is the influence of other prices on the demand for a particular good or service. The term *nonprice* seems to forbid any shift in demand resulting from a change in the price of *any* product. This confusion exists when one fails to distinguish between changes in quantity demanded and changes in demand. Remember that ceteris paribus holds all prices of other goods constant. Therefore, movement along a demand curve occurs solely in response to changes in the price of a product, that is, its "own" price. When we draw the demand curve for Coca-Cola, for example, we assume that the prices of Pepsi-Cola and other colas remain unchanged. What happens if we relax the ceteris paribus assumption and the price of Pepsi rises? Many Pepsi buyers switch to Coca-Cola, and the demand curve for Coca-Cola shifts rightward (an increase in demand). Coca-Cola and Pepsi-Cola are one type of related goods called substitute goods. A substitute good competes with another good for consumer purchases. As a result, there is a direct relationship between a price change for one good and the demand for its "competitor" good. Other examples of substitutes include margarine and butter, domestic cars and foreign cars, and Blu-rays and Internet movie downloads.

Blu-rays and Blu-ray players illustrate a second type of related goods called complementary goods. A complementary good is jointly consumed with another good. As a result, there is an inverse relationship between a price change for one good and the demand for its "go together" good. Although buying a Blu-ray and buying a Blu-ray player can be separate decisions, these two purchases are related. The more Blu-ray players consumers buy, the greater the demand for Blu-rays. What happens when the price of Blu-ray players falls sharply? The market demand curve for Blu-rays shifts rightward (an increase in demand) because new owners of players add their individual demand curves to those of people already owning players and buying Blu-rays. Conversely, a sharp rise in the price of deskjet printers would decrease the demand for ink cartridges.

Exhibit 5 summarizes the relationship between changes in the nonprice determinants of demand and the demand curve, accompanied by examples for each type of nonprice factor change.

Substitute good

A good that competes with another good for consumer purchases. As a result, there is a direct relationship between a price change for one good and the demand for its "competitor" good.

Complementary good

A good that is jointly consumed with another good. As a result, there is an inverse relationship between a price change for one good and the demand for its "go together" good.

✔ CHECKPOINT

Can Gasoline Become an Exception to the Law of Demand?

Suppose war in the Middle East threatened oil supplies, and gasoline prices began rising. Consumers feared future oil shortages, so they rushed to fill up their gas tanks. In this case, as the price of gas increased, consumers bought more, not less. Is this an exception to the law of demand?

EXHIBIT 5	Summary of the Impact of Changes in Nonprice Determinants of Demand on the Demand Curve		
Nonprice Determinant of Demand	**Relationship to Changes in Demand Curve**	**Shift in the Demand Curve**	**Examples**
1. Number of buyers	Direct		• Immigration from Mexico increases the demand for Mexican food products in grocery stores.
			• A decline in the birthrate reduces the demand for baby clothes.
2. Tastes and preferences	Direct		• For no apparent reason, consumers want Beanie Babies and demand increases.
			• After a while, the fad dies and demand declines.
3. Income a. Normal goods	Direct		• Consumers' incomes increase, and the demand for steaks increases.
			• A decline in income decreases the demand for air travel.
b. Inferior goods	Inverse		• Consumers' incomes increase, and the demand for hamburger decreases.
			• A decline in income increases the demand for bus service.

Continued

Continued from previous page

Nonprice Determinant of Demand	Relationship to Changes in Demand Curve	Shift in the Demand Curve	Examples
4. Expectations of buyers	Direct	*(graph: Price vs Quantity, D_1 shifting right to D_2)*	• Consumers expect that gasoline will be in short supply next month and that prices will rise sharply. Consequently, consumers fill the tanks in their cars this month, and there is an increase in demand for gasoline.
		(graph: Price vs Quantity, D_2 shifted left from D_1)	• Months later, consumers expect the price of gasoline to fall soon, and the demand for gasoline decreases.
5. Prices of related Goods			
a. Substitute goods	Direct	*(graph: Price vs Quantity, D_2 shifted left from D_1)*	• A reduction in the price of tea decreases the demand for coffee.
		(graph: Price vs Quantity, D_1 shifting right to D_2)	• An increase in the price of airfares causes higher demand for bus transportation.
b. Complementary goods	Inverse	*(graph: Price vs Quantity, D_1 shifting right to D_2)*	• A decline in the price of cellular service increases the demand for cell phones.
		(graph: Price vs Quantity, D_2 shifted left from D_1)	• A higher price for peanut butter decreases the demand for jelly.

SOURCE: © Cengage Learning 2014

3-4 The Law of Supply

Law of supply

The principle that there is a direct relationship between the price of a good and the quantity sellers are willing to offer for sale in a defined time period, ceteris paribus.

In everyday conversations, the term *supply* refers to a specific quantity. A "limited supply" of golf clubs at a sporting goods store means there are only so many clubs for sale and that's all. This interpretation of supply is *not* the economist's definition. To economists, supply is the relationship between ranges of possible prices and quantities supplied, which is stated as the law of supply. The law of supply states there is a direct relationship between the price of a good and the quantity sellers are willing to offer for sale in a defined time period, ceteris paribus. Interpreting the individual *supply curve* for ZapMart shown in Exhibit 6 is basically the same

EXHIBIT 6	An Individual Seller's Supply Curve for Blu-rays

The supply curve for an individual seller, such as ZapMart, shows the quantity of Blu-rays offered for sale at different possible prices. As the price of Blu-rays rises, a retail store has an incentive to increase the quantity of Blu-rays supplied per year. The direct relationship between price and quantity supplied conforms to the law of supply.

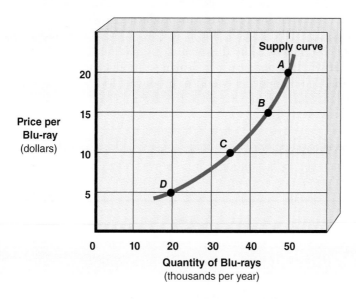

An Individual Seller's Supply Schedule for Blu-rays

Point	Price per Blu-ray	Quantity supplied (thousands per year)
A	$20	50
B	15	45
C	10	35
D	5	20

SOURCE: © Cengage Learning 2014

as interpreting Bob's demand curve shown in Exhibit 1. Each point on the curve represents a quantity supplied (measured along the horizontal axis) at a particular price (measured along the vertical axis). For example, at a price of $10 per Blu-ray (point C), the quantity supplied by the seller, ZapMart, is 35,000 Blu-rays per year. At the higher price of $15, the quantity supplied increases to 45,000 Blu-rays per year (point B).

Supply

A curve or schedule showing the various quantities of a product sellers are willing to produce and offer for sale at possible prices during a specified period of time, ceteris paribus.

> **CONCLUSION:** *Supply is a curve or schedule showing the various quantities of a product sellers are willing to produce and offer for sale at possible prices during a specified period of time, ceteris paribus.*

Why are sellers willing to sell more at a higher price? Suppose Farmer Brown is trying to decide whether to devote more of his land, labor, and barn space to the production of soybeans. Recall from Chapter 2 the production possibilities curve and the concept of increasing opportunity cost developed in Exhibit 3. If Farmer Brown devotes few of his resources to producing soybeans, the opportunity cost of, say, producing milk is small. But increasing soybean production means a higher opportunity cost, measured by the quantity of milk not produced. The logical question is: What would induce Farmer Brown to produce more soybeans for sale and overcome the higher opportunity cost of producing less milk? You guessed it! There must be the *incentive* of a higher price for soybeans.

> **CONCLUSION:** *Only at a higher price will it be profitable for sellers to incur the higher opportunity cost associated with producing and supplying a larger quantity.*

✓ CHECKPOINT

Can the Law of Supply Be Repealed for the Oil Market?

The United States experienced two oil shocks during the 1970s in the aftermath of Middle East tensions. Congress said no to high oil prices by passing a law prohibiting prices above a legal limit. Supporters of such price controls said this was a way to ensure adequate supply without allowing oil producers to earn excess profits. Did price controls increase, decrease, or have no effect on U.S. oil production during the 1970s?

3-4a MARKET SUPPLY

To construct a *market* supply curve, we follow the same procedure used to derive a market demand curve. That is, we *horizontally* sum all the quantities supplied at various prices that might prevail in the market.

Let's assume that Entertain City and High Vibes are the only two firms selling Blu-rays in a given market. As you can see in Exhibit 7, the market supply curve, S_{total}, slopes upward to the right. At a price of $25, Entertain City will supply 25,000 Blu-rays per year, and High Vibes will supply 35,000 Blu-rays per year. Thus, summing the two individual supply curves, S_1 and S_2, *horizontally*, the total of 60,000 Blu-rays is plotted at this price on the market supply curve, S_{total}. Similar calculations at other prices along the price axis generate a market supply curve, telling us the total amount of Blu-rays these businesses offer for sale at different selling prices.

EXHIBIT 7	The Market Supply Curve for Blu-rays

Entertain City and High Vibes are two businesses selling Blu-rays. If these are the only two firms in the Blu-ray market, the market supply curve, S_{total}, can be derived by summing horizontally the individual supply curves, S_1 and S_2.

The Market Supply Schedule for Blu-rays

	Quantity supplied (thousands per year)				
Price per Blu-ray	Entertain City	+	High Vibes	=	Total Supply
$25	25		35		60
20	20		30		50
15	15		25		40
10	10		20		30
5	5		15		20

SOURCE: © Cengage Learning 2014

3-5 The Distinction between Changes in Quantity Supplied and Changes in Supply

As in demand theory, the price of a product is not the only factor that influences how much sellers offer for sale. Once we relax the ceteris paribus assumption, there are six principal *nonprice determinants* (also called *supply shifters)* that can shift the supply curve's position: (1) the number of sellers, (2) technology, (3) resource prices, (4) taxes and subsidies, (5) expectations, and (6) prices of other goods. We will discuss these nonprice determinants in more detail momentarily,

Change in quantity supplied

A movement between points along a stationary supply curve, ceteris paribus.

Change in supply

An increase or a decrease in the quantity supplied at each possible price. An increase in supply is a rightward shift in the entire supply curve. A decrease in supply is a leftward shift in the entire supply curve.

but first we must distinguish between a change in quantity supplied and a change in supply.

A change in quantity supplied is a movement between points along a stationary supply curve, ceteris paribus. In Exhibit 8(a), at the price of $10, the quantity supplied is 30 million Blu-rays per year (point A). At the higher price of $15, sellers offer a larger "quantity supplied" of 40 million Blu-rays per year (point B). Economists describe the effect of the rise in price as an increase in the quantity supplied of 10 million Blu-rays per year.

> **CONCLUSION:** *Under the law of supply, any increase in price along the vertical axis will cause an increase in the quantity supplied, measured along the horizontal axis.*

A change in supply is an increase (rightward shift) or a decrease (leftward shift) in the quantity supplied at each possible price. If ceteris paribus no longer applies and if one of the six nonprice factors changes, the impact is to alter the supply curve's location.

> **CONCLUSION:** *Changes in nonprice determinants can produce only a shift in the supply curve and not a movement along the supply curve.*

In Exhibit 8(b), the rightward shift (an increase in supply) from S_1 to S_2 means that at all possible prices, sellers offer a greater quantity for sale. At $15 per Blu-ray, for instance, sellers provide 40 million for sale annually (point B), rather than 30 million (point A).

Another case is that some nonprice factor changes and causes a leftward shift (a decrease in supply) from supply curve S_1. As a result, a smaller quantity will be offered for sale at any price.

Exhibit 9 summarizes the terminology for the effects of changes in price and nonprice determinants on the supply curve.

3-6 Nonprice Determinants of Supply

Now we turn to how each of the six basic nonprice factors affects supply.

3-6a NUMBER OF SELLERS

What happens when a severe drought destroys wheat or a frost ruins the orange crop? The damaging effect of the weather may force orange growers out of business, and supply decreases. When the government eases restrictions on hunting alligators, the number of alligator hunters increases, and the supply curve for alligator meat and skins increases. Internationally, the United States may decide to lower trade barriers on textile imports, and this action increases supply by allowing new

EXHIBIT 8	Movement along a Supply Curve versus a Shift in Supply

Part (a) presents the market supply curve, *S*, for Blu-rays per year. If the price is $10 at point *A*, the quantity supplied by firms will be 30 million Blu-rays. If the price increases to $15 at point *B*, the quantity supplied will increase from 30 million to 40 million Blu-rays.

Part (b) illustrates an increase in supply. A change in some nonprice determinant can cause an increase in supply from S_1 to S_2. At a price of $15 on S_1 (point *A*), the quantity supplied per year is 30 million Blu-rays. At this same price on S_2 (point *B*), the quantity supplied increases to 40 million.

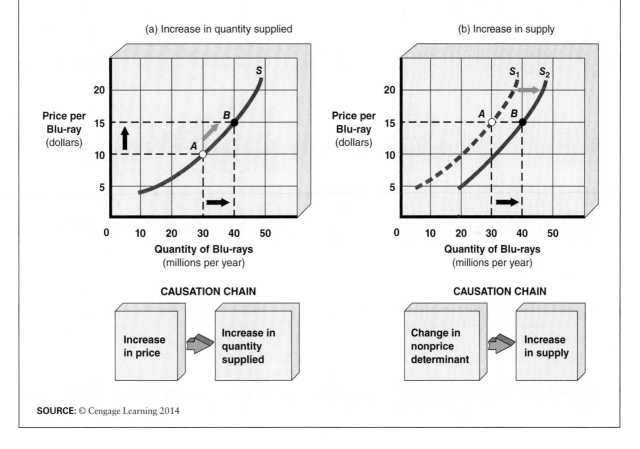

SOURCE: © Cengage Learning 2014

foreign firms to add their individual supply curves to the U.S. market supply curve for textiles. Conversely, higher U.S. trade barriers on textile imports shift the U.S. market supply curve for textiles leftward.

3-6b TECHNOLOGY

Never has society experienced such an explosion of new production techniques. Throughout the world, new and more efficient technology is making it possible to manufacture more products at any possible selling price. New, more powerful personal computers (PCs) reduce production costs and increase the supply of all sorts of goods and services. For example, computers are now milking cows. Computers

EXHIBIT 9	**Terminology for Changes in Price and Nonprice Determinants of Supply**

Caution! As with demand curves, you must distinguish between a change in quantity supplied, which is a movement along a supply curve (S_1) in response to a change in price, and a shift in the supply curve. An increase in supply (shift to S_2) or a decrease in supply occurs (shift to S_3) is caused by a change in some nonprice determinant and not by a change in the price.

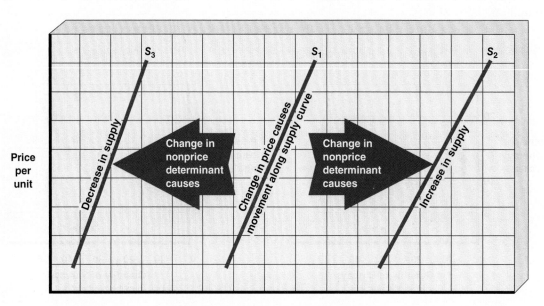

Quantity of good or service per unit of time

Change	Effect	Terminology
Price increases	Upward movement along the supply curve	Increase in the quantity supplied
Price decreases	Downward movement along the supply curve	Decrease in the quantity supplied
Nonprice determinant	Leftward or rightward shift in the supply curve	Decrease or increase in supply

SOURCE: © Cengage Learning 2014

admit the cows into the milking area and then activate lasers to guide milking cups into place. Dairy farmers no longer must wake up at 5:30 a.m., and cows get milked whenever they wish, day or night. As this technology spreads across the United States, it will be possible to offer more milk for sale at each possible price, and the entire supply curve for milk shifts to the right.

3-6c RESOURCE PRICES

Natural resources, labor, capital, and entrepreneurship are all required to produce products, and the prices of these resources affect supply. Suppose many firms are competing for computer programmers to design their software, and the salaries of these highly skilled workers increase. This increase in the price of labor adds to the cost of production. Along the original supply curve, extra costs must be added to each possible price. As a result, the supply of computer software shifts leftward (decreases) because sellers must charge more than before for any quantity supplied. Any reduction in production cost caused by a decline in the price of resources will have an opposite effect on the supply curve and it shifts rightward (increases). Along the original supply curve, cost declines, so the price can be reduced at each possible price.

3-6d TAXES AND SUBSIDIES

Certain taxes, such as sales taxes, have the same effect on supply as does an increase in the price of a resource. The impact of an increase in the sales tax is similar to a rise in the salaries of computer programmers. The higher sales tax imposes an additional production cost on, for example, Blu-rays, and the supply curve shifts leftward. Conversely, a payment from the government for each Blu-ray produced (an unlikely subsidy) would have the same effect as lower prices for resources or a technological advance. That is, the supply curve for Blu-rays shifts rightward.

3-6e EXPECTATIONS OF PRODUCERS

Expectations affect both current demand and current supply. Suppose a war in the Middle East causes oil producers to believe that oil prices will rise dramatically. Their initial response could be to hold back a portion of the oil in their storage tanks so that they can sell more and make greater profits later when oil prices rise. One approach used by the major oil companies might be to limit the amount of gasoline delivered to independent distributors. This response by the oil industry shifts the current supply curve to the left. Now suppose farmers anticipate that the price of wheat will soon fall sharply. The reaction is to sell their inventories stored in silos today before the price declines tomorrow. Such a response shifts the supply curve for wheat to the right.

3-6f PRICES OF OTHER GOODS THE FIRM COULD PRODUCE

Businesses are always considering shifting resources from producing one good to producing another good. A rise in the price of one product relative to the prices of other products signals to suppliers that switching production to the product with the higher relative price yields higher profit. Suppose the price of corn rises because of government incentives to grow corn for ethanol while the price of wheat remains the same; then many farmers will divert more of their land to corn and less to wheat. The result is an increase in the supply of corn and a decrease in the supply

PC Prices: How Low Can They Go?

Applicable Concept: nonprice determinants of demand and supply

Radio was in existence for 38 years before 50 million people tuned in. Television took 13 years to reach that benchmark. Sixteen years after the first PC kit was introduced, 50 million people were using one. Once available to the public, the Internet crossed that line in four years.[1] Before 1999, there were no blogs, and now there are millions. Today, over 80 percent of U.S. households have a computer. Following are quotes from articles that illustrate changes in supply and demand for computers over time.

An Associated Press article reported in 1998:

Personal computers, which tumbled below the $1,000-price barrier just 18 months ago, now are breaking through the $400 price mark—putting them within reach of the average U.S. family. The plunge in PC prices reflects declining wholesale prices for computer parts, such as microprocessors, memory chips, and hard drives. "We've seen a massive transformation in the PC business," said Andrew Peck, an analyst with Cowen & Co., based in Boston.[2]

In 1999, an article in *The Wall Street Journal* reported that PC makers and distributors smashed their industry's time-honored sales channels. PC makers such as Hewlett-Packard Company began using the Internet to sell directly to consumers.

In doing so, they are following the successful strategy of Dell, which for years bypassed storefront retailers and the PC distributors who traditionally keep them stocked, going instead straight to the consumer with catalogs, an 800 number, and Web sites.[3]

In 2001, an article in *The New York Times* described a computer price war:

We reached a situation where the market was saturated in 2000. People who needed computers had them. Vendors are living on sales of replacements, at least in the United States. But that doesn't give you the kind of growth these companies were used to. In the past, most price cuts came from falling prices for processors and other components. In addition, manufacturers have been narrowing profit margins for the last couple years. But when demand dried up last fall, the more aggressive manufacturers decided to try to gain market share by cutting prices to the bone. This is an all-out battle for market share.[4]

In 2012, an analyst in *USA Today* observed the following:

The TV market has been flat for the past two years, while PC sales—despite the enthusiasm for next generation products such as tablets and smartphones—are growing. The

Mircea BEZERGHEANU/Shutterstock.com

way consumers are actually using PCs "is expanding, not contracting," says Matt McRae, Vizio's chief technology officer. "They come home and use their PC for e-mail, but they're also using it for entertainments experiences."[5]

Finally, Wikipedia reports that over time, changes in supply and demand have continued to reduce PC prices. In 1982, for example, Dell offered a $3,000 PC. By 1998, the average selling price was below $1,000. Today, computers selling for less than $300 outperform computers from only a few years previously.

Analyze the Issue

Identify changes in quantity demanded, changes in demand, changes in quantity supplied, and changes in supply described in the article. For any change in demand or supply, also identify the nonprice determinant causing the change.

1. The Emerging Digital Economy (U.S. Department of Commerce, 1998), Chap. 1, p. 1.
2. David E. Kalish, "PC Prices Fall Below $400, Luring Bargain-Hunters," Associated Press/*Charlotte Observer*, Aug. 25, 1998, p. 3D.
3. George Anders, "Online Web Seller Asks: How Low Can PC Prices Go?" *The Wall Street Journal*, Jan. 19, 1999, p. B1.
4. Barnaby J. Feder, "Five Questions for Martin Reynolds: A Computer Price War Leaves Buyers Smiling," *The New York Times*, May 13, 2001.
5. Jefferson Graham, "Plans to Sell Budget, High-Performance PCs," *USA Today*, Jan. 9, 2012, p. 1B.

of wheat. This happens because the opportunity cost of growing wheat, measured in forgone corn profits, increases.

Exhibit 10 summarizes the relationship between changes in the nonprice determinants of supply and the supply curve, accompanied by examples for each type of nonprice factor change.

EXHIBIT 10	Summary of the Impact of Changes in Nonprice Determinants of Supply on the Supply Curve		
Nonprice Determinant of Supply	**Relationship to Changes in Supply Curve**	**Shift in the Supply Curve**	**Examples**
1. Number of sellers	Direct		• The United States lowers trade restrictions on foreign textiles, and the supply of textiles in the United States increases.
			• A severe drought destroys the orange crop, and the supply of oranges decreases.
2. Technology	Direct		• New methods of producing automobiles reduce production costs, and the supply of automobiles increases.
			• Technology is destroyed in war, and production costs increase; the result is a decrease in the supply of good *X*.
3. Resource prices	Inverse		• A decline in the price of computer chips increases the supply of computers.
			• An increase in the cost of farm equipment decreases the supply of soybeans.
4. Taxes and subsidies	Inverse		• An increase in the per-pack tax on cigarettes reduces the supply of cigarettes.
	Direct		• A government payment to dairy farmers based on the number of gallons produced increases the supply of milk.

Continued

Continued from previous page

Nonprice Determinant of Supply	Relationship to Changes in Supply Curve	Shift in the Supply Curve	Examples
5. Expectations	Inverse		• Oil companies anticipate a substantial rise in future oil prices, and this expectation causes these companies to decrease their current supply of oil.
			• Farmers expect the future price of wheat to decline, so they increase the present supply of wheat.
6. Prices of other goods and services	Inverse		• A rise in the price of brand-name drugs causes drug companies to decrease the supply of generic drugs.
			• A decline in the price of tomatoes causes farmers to increase the supply of cucumbers.

SOURCE: © Cengage Learning 2014

3-7 A Market Supply and Demand Analysis

"Teach a parrot to say 'supply and demand' and you've got an economist." Drumroll please! Buyer and seller actors are on center stage to perform a balancing act in a market. A market is any arrangement in which buyers and sellers interact to determine the price and quantity of goods and services exchanged. Let's consider the retail market for sneakers. Exhibit 11 displays hypothetical market demand and supply data for this product. Notice in column 1 of the exhibit that price serves as a common variable for both supply and demand relationships. Columns 2 and 3 list the quantity demanded and the quantity supplied for pairs of sneakers per year.

The important question for market supply and demand analysis is this: Which selling price and quantity will prevail in the market? Let's start by asking what will happen if retail stores supply 75,000 pairs of sneakers and charge $105 a pair. At this relatively high price for sneakers, consumers are willing and able to purchase only 25,000 pairs. As a result, 50,000 pairs of sneakers remain as unsold inventory on the shelves of sellers (column 4), and the market condition is a surplus (column 5). A surplus is a market condition existing at any price where the quantity supplied is greater than the quantity demanded.

How will retailers react to a surplus? Competition forces sellers to bid down their selling price to attract more sales (column 6). If they cut the selling price to $90, there will still be a surplus of 40,000 pairs of sneakers, and pressure on sellers

Market

Any arrangement in which buyers and sellers interact to determine the price and quantity of goods and services exchanged.

Surplus

A market condition existing at any price where the quantity supplied is greater than the quantity demanded.

EXHIBIT 11	Demand, Supply, and Equilibrium for Sneakers (pairs per year)				
(1) Price per pair	(2) Quantity demanded	(3) Quantity supplied	(4) Difference (3) – (2)	(5) Market condition	(6) Pressure on price
$105	25,000	75,000	+50,000	Surplus	Downward
90	30,000	70,000	+40,000	Surplus	Downward
75	40,000	60,000	+20,000	Surplus	Downward
60	50,000	50,000	0	Equilibrium	Stationary
45	60,000	35,000	–25,000	Shortage	Upward
30	80,000	20,000	–60,000	Shortage	Upward
15	100,000	5,000	–95,000	Shortage	Upward

SOURCE: © Cengage Learning 2014

to cut their selling price will continue. If the price falls to $75, there will still be an unwanted surplus of 20,000 pairs of sneakers remaining as inventory, and pressure to charge a lower price will persist.

Now let's assume sellers slash the price of sneakers to $15 per pair. This price is very attractive to consumers, and the quantity demanded is 100,000 pairs of sneakers each year. However, sellers are willing and able to provide only 5,000 pairs at this price. The good news is that some consumers buy these 5,000 pairs of sneakers at $15. The bad news is that potential buyers are willing to purchase 95,000 more pairs at that price, but cannot because the shoes are not on the shelves for sale. This out-of-stock condition signals the existence of a shortage. A shortage is a market condition existing at any price where the quantity supplied is less than the quantity demanded.

Shortage
A market condition existing at any price at where the quantity supplied is less than the quantity demanded.

In the case of a shortage, unsatisfied consumers compete to obtain the product by bidding to pay a higher price. Because sellers are seeking the higher profits that higher prices make possible, they gladly respond by setting a higher price of, say, $30 and increasing the quantity supplied to 20,000 pairs annually. At the price of $30, the shortage persists because the quantity demanded still exceeds the quantity supplied. Thus, a price of $30 will also be temporary because the unfulfilled quantity demanded provides an incentive for sellers to raise their selling price further and offer more sneakers for sale. Suppose the price of sneakers rises to $45 a pair. At this price, the shortage falls to 25,000 pairs, and the market still gives sellers the message to move upward along their market supply curve and sell for a higher price.

3-7a EQUILIBRIUM PRICE AND QUANTITY

Assuming sellers are free to sell their products at any price, trial and error will make all possible price-quantity combinations unstable except at equilibrium. Equilibrium occurs at any price and quantity where the quantity demanded and the quantity supplied are equal. Economists also refer to *equilibrium* as *market clearing*.

In Exhibit 11, $60 is the *equilibrium* price, and 50,000 pairs of sneakers is the *equilibrium* quantity per year. Equilibrium means that the forces of

Equilibrium
A market condition that occurs at any price and quantity at which the quantity demanded and the quantity supplied are equal.

supply and demand are "in balance" or "at rest" and there is no reason for price or quantity to change, ceteris paribus. In short, all prices and quantities except a unique equilibrium price and quantity are temporary. Once the price of sneakers is $60, this price will not change unless a nonprice factor changes demand or supply.

English economist Alfred Marshall (1842–1924) compared supply and demand to a pair of scissor blades. He wrote, "We might as reasonably dispute whether it is the upper or the under blade of a pair of scissors that cuts a piece of paper, as whether value is governed by utility [demand] or cost of production [supply]."[1] Joining market supply and market demand in Exhibit 12 allows us to clearly see the "two blades," that is, the demand curve, D, and the supply curve, S. We can measure the amount of any surplus or shortage by the horizontal distance between the demand and supply curves. At any price *above* equilibrium—say, $90—there is an *excess quantity supplied* (surplus) of 40,000 pairs of sneakers. For any price *below* equilibrium—$30, for example—the horizontal distance between the curves tells us there is an *excess quantity demanded* (shortage) of 60,000 pairs. When the price per pair is $60, the market supply curve and the market demand curve intersect at point E and the quantity demanded equals the quantity supplied at 50,000 pairs per year.

> **CONCLUSION:** *Graphically, the intersection of the supply curve and the demand curve is the market equilibrium price-quantity point. When all other nonprice factors are held constant, this is the only stable coordinate on the graph.*

3-8 Rationing Function of the Price System

Our analysis leads to an important conclusion. The predictable or stable outcome in the sneakers example is that the price will eventually come to rest at $60 per pair. All other factors held constant, the price may be above or below $60, but the forces of surplus or shortage guarantee that any price other than the equilibrium price is temporary. This is the theory of how the price system operates, and it is the cornerstone of microeconomic analysis. The price system is a mechanism that uses the forces of supply and demand to create an equilibrium through rising and falling prices. Stated simply, price plays a *rationing* role. The price system is important because it is a mechanism for distributing scarce goods and services. At the equilibrium price of $60, only those consumers willing to pay $60 per pair get sneakers, and there are no shoes for buyers unwilling to pay that price.

Price system

A mechanism that uses the forces of supply and demand to create an equilibrium through rising and falling prices.

Why would you prefer a world with all markets in equilibrium? If all markets were in equilibrium, there would be no shortages or surpluses for any good or service. In this world, consumers are not frustrated because they want to buy something and it is not on the shelf. Sellers are not upset because unsold merchandise is piling up unsold in their storerooms. Everyone is happy!

---

[1]Alfred Marshall, *Principles of Economics*, 8th ed. (New York: Macmillan, 1982), p. 348.

EXHIBIT 12	The Supply and Demand for Sneakers

The supply and demand curves represent a market for sneakers. The intersection of the demand curve, *D*, and the supply curve, *S*, at point *E* indicates the equilibrium price of $60 and the equilibrium quantity of 50,000 pairs bought and sold per year. At any price above $60, a surplus prevails and pressure exists to push the price downward. At $90, for example, the excess quantity supplied of 40,000 pairs remains unsold. At any price below $60, a shortage provides pressure to push the price upward. At $30, for example, the excess quantity demanded of 60,000 pairs encourages consumers to bid up the price.

CAUSATION CHAINS

SOURCE: © Cengage Learning 2014

The Market Approach to Organ Shortages

Applicable concept: price system

There is a global market in human organs in spite of attempts to prevent these transactions. For example, China banned organ sales in 2006, and India did the same in 1994. The National Transplant Organ Act of 1984 made sale of organs illegal in the United States. Economist James R. Rinehart wrote the following on this subject:

> If you were in charge of a kidney transplant program with more potential recipients than donors, how would you allocate the organs under your control? Life and death decisions cannot be avoided. Some individuals are not going to get kidneys regardless of how the organs are distributed because there simply are not enough to go around. Persons who run such programs are influenced in a variety of ways. It would be difficult not to favor friends, relatives, influential people, and those who are championed by the press. Dr. John la Puma, at the Center for Clinical Medical Ethics, University of Chicago, suggested that we use a lottery system for selecting transplant patients. He feels that the present rationing system is unfair.
>
> The selection process frequently takes the form of having the patient wait at home until a suitable donor is found. What this means is that, at any given point in time, many potential recipients are just waiting for an organ to be made available. In essence, the organs are rationed to those who are able to survive the wait. In many situations, patients are simply screened out because they are not considered to be suitable candidates for a transplant. For instance, patients with heart disease and overt psychosis often are excluded. Others with end-stage liver disorders are denied new organs on the grounds that the habits that produced the disease may remain to jeopardize recovery....
>
> Under the present arrangements, owners receive no monetary compensation; therefore, suppliers are willing to supply fewer organs than potential recipients want. Compensating a supplier monetarily would encourage more people to offer their organs for sale. It also would be an excellent incentive for us to take better care of our organs. After all, who would want an enlarged liver or a weak heart ...?[1]

The following excerpt from a newspaper article illustrates the controversy:

> Mickey Mantle's temporary deliverance from death, thanks to a liver transplant, illustrated how the organ-donations system is heavily weighted against poor potential recipients who cannot pass what University of Pennsylvania medical ethicist Arthur Caplan calls the "wallet biopsy."... Thus, affluent patients like Mickey Mantle may get evaluated and listed simultaneously in different regions to increase their odds of finding a donor. The New Yorker found his organ donor in Texas' Region 4. Such a system is not only highly unfair, but it leads to other kinds of abuses.[2]

Based on altruism, the organ donor distribution system continues to result in shortages. In 2012, over 122,000 patients were on the waiting list for organs. To address the shortage of organ donation, some European countries such as Spain, Belgium, and Austria have implemented an "opt-out" organ donation system. In the "opt-out" system, people are automatically considered to be organ donors unless they officially declare that they do not wish to be donors. Also, Facebook encourages everyone to advertise their donor status on their pages.

Analyze the Issue

1. Draw supply and demand curves for the U.S. organ market and compare the U.S. market to the market in a country where selling organs is legal.
2. What are some arguments against using the price system to allocate organs?
3. Should foreigners have the right to buy U.S. organs and U.S. citizens have the right to buy foreign organs?

---

1. James R. Rinehart, "The Market Approach to Organ Shortages," *Journal of Health Care Marketing* 8, no. 1, March 1988, pp. 72–75.
2. Carl Senna, "The Wallet Biopsy," *Providence Journal*, June 13, 1995, p. B7.

✓ CHECKPOINT

Can the Price System Eliminate Scarcity?

You visit Cuba and observe that at "official" prices, there is a constant shortage of consumer goods in government stores. People explain that in Cuba, scarcity is caused by low prices combined with low production quotas set by the government. Many Cuban citizens say that the condition of scarcity would be eliminated if the government would allow markets to respond to supply and demand. Can the price system eliminate scarcity?

Key Concepts

Law of demand	Substitute good	Market
Demand	Complementary good	Surplus
Change in quantity demanded	Law of supply	Shortage
Change in demand	Supply	Equilibrium
Normal good	Change in quantity supplied	Price system
Inferior good	Change in supply	

Summary

- The **law of demand** states there is an inverse relationship between the price and the quantity demanded, ceteris paribus. A market demand curve is the horizontal summation of individual demand curves.

- A **change in quantity demanded** is a movement along a stationary demand curve caused by a change in price. When any of the nonprice determinants of demand change, the demand curve responds by shifting. An *increase in demand* (rightward shift) or a *decrease in demand* (leftward shift) is caused by a change in one of the nonprice determinants.

Change in Quantity Demanded

(a) Increase in quantity demanded

SOURCE: © Cengage Learning 2014

Change in Demand

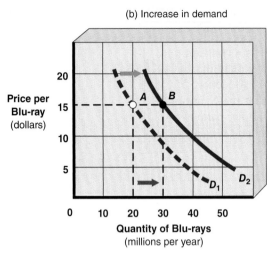

(b) Increase in demand

SOURCE: © Cengage Learning 2014

- **Nonprice determinants of demand** are as follows:
  a. Number of buyers
  b. Tastes and preferences
  c. Income (normal and inferior goods)
  d. Expectations of future price and income changes
  e. Prices of related goods (substitutes and complements)
- The **law of supply** states there is a direct relationship between the price and the quantity supplied, ceteris paribus. The market supply curve is the horizontal summation of individual supply curves.
- A **change in quantity supplied** is a movement along a stationary supply curve caused by a change in price. When any of the nonprice determinants of supply change, the supply curve responds by shifting. An *increase in supply* (rightward shift) or a *decrease in supply* (leftward shift) is caused by a change in one of the nonprice determinants.

Change in Quantity Supplied

(a) Increase in quantity supplied

SOURCE: © Cengage Learning 2014

Change in Supply

(b) Increase in supply

SOURCE: © Cengage Learning 2014

- **Nonprice determinants of supply** are as follows:
  a. Number of sellers
  b. Technology

c. Resource prices

d. Taxes and subsidies

e. Expectations of future price changes

f. Prices of other goods and services

- A **surplus** or **shortage** exists at any price where the quantity demanded and the quantity supplied are not equal. When the price of a good is higher than the equilibrium price, there is an excess quantity supplied, or *surplus*. When the price is less than the equilibrium price, there is an excess quantity demanded, or *shortage*.

- **Equilibrium** is the unique price and quantity established at the intersection of the supply and demand curves. Only at equilibrium does quantity demanded equal quantity supplied.

Equilibrium

SOURCE: © Cengage Learning 2014

- The **price system** is the supply and demand mechanism that establishes equilibrium through the ability of prices to rise and fall.

Study Questions and Problems

1. Some people will pay a higher price for brand-name goods. For example, some people buy Rolls Royces and Rolex watches to impress others. Does knowingly paying higher prices for certain items just to be a "snob" violate the law of demand?

2. Draw graphs to illustrate the difference between a decrease in the quantity demanded and a decrease in demand for Mickey Mantle baseball cards. Give a possible reason for change in each graph.

3. Suppose oil prices rise sharply for years as a result of war in the Persian Gulf region. What happens and why to the demand for each of the following?
   a. Cars
   b. Home insulation
   c. Coal
   d. Tires

4. Draw graphs to illustrate the difference between a decrease in quantity supplied and a decrease in supply for condominiums. Give a possible reason for change in each graph.

5. Use supply and demand analysis to explain why the quantity of word processing software exchanged increases from one year to the next.

6. Predict the direction of change for either supply or demand in the following situations:
   a. Several new companies enter the cell phone industry.
   b. Consumers suddenly decide SUVs are unfashionable.
   c. The U.S. Surgeon General issues a report stating that tomatoes prevent colds.
   d. Frost threatens to damage the coffee crop, and consumers expect the price to rise sharply in the future.
   e. The price of tea falls. What is the effect on the coffee market?
   f. The price of sugar rises. What is the effect on the coffee market?
   g. Tobacco lobbyists convince Congress to remove the tax paid by sellers on each carton of cigarettes sold.
   h. A new type of robot is invented that will pick peaches.
   i. Nintendo anticipates that the future price of its games will fall much lower than the current price.

7. Explain the effect of the following situations:
   a. Population growth surges rapidly.
   b. The prices of resources used in the production of good X increase.
   c. The government is paying a $1-per-unit subsidy for each unit of a good produced.
   d. The incomes of consumers of normal good X increase.
   e. The incomes of consumers of inferior good Y decrease.
   f. Farmers are deciding what crop to plant and learn that the price of corn has fallen relative to the price of cotton.

8. Explain why the market price may not be the same as the equilibrium price.

9. If a new breakthrough in manufacturing technology reduces the cost of producing Blu-ray players by half, what will happen to the each of the following?
   a. Supply of Blu-ray players
   b. Demand for Blu-ray players

   c. Equilibrium price and quantity of Blu-ray players
   d. Demand for Blu-rays

10. The U.S. Postal Service is facing increased competition from firms providing overnight delivery of packages and letters. Additional competition has emerged because communications can be sent by emails, fax machine, and text messaging. What will be the effect of this competition on the market demand for mail delivered by the post office?

11. There is a shortage of college basketball and football tickets for some games, and a surplus occurs for other games. Why do shortages and surpluses exist for different games?

12. Explain the statement "People respond to incentives and disincentives" in relation to the demand curve and supply curve for good X.

For Online Exercises, go to the Tucker Web site at www.cengage.com/economics/tucker.

✔ CHECKPOINT ANSWERS

Can Gasoline Become an Exception to the Law of Demand?

As the price of gasoline began to rise, the expectation of still higher prices caused buyers to buy more now, and therefore, demand increased. As shown in Exhibit 13, suppose the price per gallon of gasoline was initially at P_1 and the quantity demanded was Q_1 on demand curve D_1 (point A). Then war in the Middle East caused the demand curve to shift rightward to D_2. Along the new demand curve, D_2, consumers increased their quantity demanded to Q_2 at the higher price of P_2 per gallon of gasoline (point B).

The expectation of rising gasoline prices in the future caused "an increase in demand," rather than "an increase in quantity demanded" in response to a higher price. If you said that there are no exceptions to the law of demand, **YOU ARE CORRECT.**

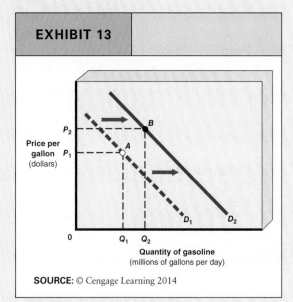

EXHIBIT 13

SOURCE: © Cengage Learning 2014

Can the Law of Supply Be Repealed for the Oil Market?

There is not a single quantity of oil—say, 3 million barrels—for sale in the world on a given day. The supply curve for oil is not vertical. As the law of supply states, higher oil prices will cause greater quantities of oil to be offered for sale. At lower prices, oil producers have less incentive to drill deeper for oil that is more expensive to discover.

The government cannot repeal the law of supply. Price controls discourage producers from oil exploration and production, which causes a reduction in the quantity supplied. If you said U.S. oil production decreased in the 1970s when the government put a lid on oil prices, **YOU ARE CORRECT.**

Can the Price System Eliminate Scarcity?

Recall from Chapter 1 that scarcity is the condition in which human wants are forever greater than the resources available to satisfy those wants. Using markets free from government interference will not solve the scarcity problem. Scarcity exists at any price for a good or service. This means scarcity occurs at any disequilibrium price at which a shortage or surplus exists, and scarcity remains at any equilibrium price at which no shortage or surplus exists.

Although the price system can eliminate shortages (or surpluses), if you said it cannot eliminate scarcity, **YOU ARE CORRECT.**

Sample Quiz

For an explanation of the correct answers, visit the Tucker website at www.cengage.com/economics/tucker.

1. Which of the following causes the demand for veggie burgers to increase?
   a. A decline in the price of veggie burgers
   b. An increase in the price of tofu burgers, perceived as a substitute by veggie burger consumers
   c. An increase in the price of burger buns
   d. A technological innovation that lowers the cost of producing veggie burgers

2. Which of the following would *not* cause market demand for a normal good to decline?
   a. An increase in the price of a substitute
   b. An increase in the price of a complement
   c. A decline in consumer income
   d. Consumer expectations that the good will go on sale in the near future
   e. An announcement by the Surgeon General that the product contributes to premature death

3. Low-income families consume proportionately more of which of the following kinds of goods?
   a. Luxury goods
   b. Substitute goods
   c. Normal goods
   d. Inferior goods

4. Suppose each of the seven dwarfs buys four mugs of ginger ale per week from Snow White's café when the price per mug is $2. If the seven dwarfs are the entire market demand for Snow White's ginger ale, which of the following is the correct value for market quantity demanded of ginger ale at a price of $2?
   a. 4
   b. 8
   c. 28
   d. 7

Sample Quiz *continued*

5. Which of the following increases the supply of corn?
   a. The farm worker's union successfully negotiates a pay increase for corn harvest workers.
   b. The Surgeon General announces that eating corn bread contributes to baldness in men.
   c. Congress and the President eliminate subsidies formerly paid to corn farmers.
   d. Farmers who grow soybeans can also grow corn, and the price of soybeans drops by 75 percent.

6. With an upward-sloping supply curve, which of the following is *true*?
   a. An increase in price results in a decrease in quantity supplied.
   b. An increase in price results in an increase in supply.
   c. A decrease in price results in a decrease in quantity supplied.
   d. A decrease in price results in an increase in supply.

7. A rightward shift in the demand curve is called a(an)
   a. decrease in output.
   b. decrease in demand.
   c. increase in demand.
   d. increase in income.

8. A surplus occurs when
   a. the quantity demanded exceeds the quantity supplied.
   b. price is below the equilibrium price.
   c. price is at the equilibrium.
   d. price is above the equilibrium.

9. A shortage occurs when
   a. the quantity supplied exceeds the quantity demanded.
   b. price is below the equilibrium price.
   c. price is at the equilibrium.
   d. price is above the equilibrium.

10. Which of the following decreases supply in the market for pizza?
    a. Pizza shop employees successfully organize a union and negotiate a pay increase.
    b. The Surgeon General announces that eating pizza reduces the incidence of stomach cancer.

c. Cheese prices drop because price supports for dairy farmers are removed.
d. Some hot sandwich shops can also make and sell pizzas, and consumer demand for hot sandwiches declines sharply, reducing the profitability of producing hot sandwiches.

11. Which of the following results from an increase in the price of a one-week vacation at beach resorts on the coast of Mexico?
    a. An increase in the supply of bicycle tires in Toledo, Ohio
    b. An increase in the demand for vacations at resorts on Caribbean islands
    c. An increase in the supply of vacation opportunities at resorts on the coast of Mexico
    d. A decrease in the demand for vacations at resorts on Caribbean islands

12. There is news that the price of Tucker's Root Beer will increase significantly next week. If the demand for Tucker's Root Beer reacts *only* to this factor and shifts to the right, the position of this demand curve has reacted to a change in
    a. tastes.
    b. income levels.
    c. the prices of related goods.
    d. the number of buyers.
    e. expectations.

13. Which of the following causes a shortage to become larger?
    a. An increase in market price
    b. An increase in supply
    c. A decrease in demand
    d. A decrease in price

14. Which of the following is *true* in ski towns such as Crested Butte, Colorado, and Whistler, British Columbia, during the peak winter ski season as compared to May and June?
    a. Demand for motel rooms is higher.
    b. Demand for motel rooms is lower.
    c. There is a surplus of motel rooms.
    d. The price of motel rooms will be lower.

15. In moving from a shortage toward the market equilibrium, which of the following is *true*?
    a. Price falls.
    b. Price rises.

Sample Quiz *continued*

c. Quantity demanded increases.

d. Quantity supplied decreases.

16. The law of demand is the principle that there is _____ relationship between the price of a good and the quantity buyers are willing to purchase in a defined time period, ceteris paribus.
   a. a direct
   b. no
   c. an inverse
   d. an independent

17. A curve that is derived by summing horizontally individual demand curves is called
   a. aggregate supply.
   b. market supply.
   c. aggregate demand.
   d. market demand.

18. A leftward shift in the demand curve is called a(an)
   a. decrease in demand.
   b. decrease in output.
   c. increase in demand.
   d. increase in income.

19. Under the law of demand, any increase in price will cause _____ in quantity demanded.
   a. a decrease
   b. an increase
   c. no change
   d. constant change

20. The law of supply is the principle that there is _____ relationship between the price of a good and the quantity sellers are willing to offer for sale in a defined time period, ceteris paribus.
   a. an inverse
   b. a direct
   c. no
   d. an independent

EXHIBIT 14	Demand and Supply Data for Video Games	
Price	Quantity demanded of video games	Quantity supplied of video games
$75	400	900
70	450	850
65	500	800
60	550	750
55	600	700
50	650	650
45	700	600
40	750	550

SOURCE: © Cengage Learning 2014

21. Exhibit 14 presents supply and demand data for the video game market. If the price of video games was currently $70, there would be an _____ of _____ video games in this market.
   a. excess demand; 450
   b. excess demand; 500
   c. excess supply; 400
   d. excess supply; 850
   e. excess demand; 400

22. In Exhibit 14, if the price of video games was currently $45, there would be an _____ of _____ video games in this market.
   a. excess demand; 700
   b. excess demand; 500
   c. excess supply; 100
   d. excess supply; 600
   e. excess demand; 100

Sample Quiz *continued*

23. In Exhibit 14, at any market price of video games above $50, a (an) _____ would result, causing price to _____.
    a. excess demand; rise
    b. excess supply; rise
    c. excess demand; fall
    d. excess supply; fall
    e. shortage; rise

24. In Exhibit 14, at any market price of video games below $50, a (an) _____ would result, causing price to _____.
    a. excess demand; rise
    b. excess supply; rise
    c. excess demand; fall
    d. excess supply; fall
    e. surplus; rise

25. In Exhibit 14, if there is a shortage of video games of 200 units, the current price of video games must be
    a. $60.
    b. $55.
    c. $50.
    d. $45.
    e. $40.

Consumer Surplus, Producer Surplus, and Market Efficiency

This chapter explained how the market forces of demand and supply establish the equilibrium price and output. Here it will be demonstrated that the equilibrium price and quantity determined in a competitive market are desirable because the result is *market efficiency*. To understand this concept, we use the area between the market price and the demand and supply curves to measure gains or losses from market transactions for consumers and producers.

3A-1a CONSUMER SURPLUS

Consider the market demand curve shown in Exhibit A-1(a). The height of this demand curve shows the maximum willingness of consumers to purchase ground beef at various prices per pound. At a price of $4.00 (point X), no one will purchase ground beef. But if the price drops to $3.50 at point A, consumers will purchase 1 million pounds of ground beef per year. Moving downward along the demand curve to point B, consumers will purchase an additional million pounds of ground beef per year at a lower price of $3.00 per pound. If the price continues to drop to $2.50 per pound at point C and lower, consumers are willing to purchase more pounds of ground beef consistent with the law of demand.

Assuming the market equilibrium price for ground beef is $2.00 per pound, we can use the demand curve to measure the net benefit, or *consumer surplus*, in this market. Consumer surplus is the value of the difference between the price consumers are willing to pay for a product on the demand curve and the price actually paid for it. At point A, consumers are willing to pay $3.50 per pound, but they actually pay the equilibrium price of $2.00. Thus, consumers earn a surplus of $1.50 ($3.50 − $2.00) per pound multiplied by 1 million pounds purchased, which is a $15 million consumer surplus. This value is represented by the shaded vertical rectangle formed at point A on the demand curve. At point B, consumers who purchase an additional million pounds of ground beef at $3.00 per pound receive a lower extra consumer surplus than at point A, represented by a rectangle of lower height. At point C, the marginal consumer surplus continues to fall until at equilibrium point E, where there is no consumer surplus.

The total value of consumer surplus can be interpreted from the explanation given above. As shown in Exhibit A-1(b), begin at point X and instead of selected prices, now imagine offering ground beef to consumers at each possible price downward along the demand curve until the equilibrium price of $2.00 is reached at point E. The result is that the entire green triangular area between the demand curve and the horizontal line at the equilibrium price represents total consumer surplus. Note that a rise in the equilibrium price decreases total consumer surplus and a fall in the equilibrium price increases total consumer surplus.

Consumer surplus
The value of the difference between the price consumers are willing to pay for a product on the demand curve and the price actually paid for it.

EXHIBIT A-1	**Market Demand Curve and Consumer Surplus**

As illustrated in part (a), consumers are willing at point A on the market demand curve to pay $3.50 per pound to purchase 1 million pounds of ground beef per year. Because the equilibrium price is $2.00, consumers receive a surplus of $1.50 for each pound of ground beef and the vertical shaded rectangular area is the consumer surplus earned only at point A. Others who pay less at points B, C, and E receive less consumer surplus and the height of the corresponding rectangles falls at each of these prices. In part (b), moving downward along all possible prices on the demand curve yields the green shaded triangle, which is equal to total consumer surplus (net benefit).

SOURCE: © Cengage Learning 2014

CONCLUSION: *Total consumer surplus measured in dollars is represented by the total area under the market demand curve and above the equilibrium price.*

3A-1b PRODUCER SURPLUS

Similar to the concept of consumer surplus, the height of the market supply curve in Exhibit A-2(a) shows the producers' minimum willingness to accept payment for ground beef offered for sale at various prices per pound. At point X, firms offer no ground beef for sale at a price of zero and they divert their resources to an alternate use. At a price of $0.50 per pound (point A), the supply curve tells us that 1 million pounds will be offered for sale. Moving upward along the supply curve to point *B*, firms will offer an additional million pounds of ground beef for sale at the higher price of $1.00 per pound. If the price rises to $1.50 at point *C* and higher, firms allocate more resources to ground beef production and another million pounds will be supplied along the supply curve.

Again, we will assume the equilibrium price is $2.00 per pound, and the supply curve can be used to measure the net benefit, or *producer surplus*. Producer surplus is the value of the difference between the actual selling price of a product and the price producers are willing to sell it for on the supply curve. Now assume the first million pounds of ground beef is sold at point *A* on the supply curve. In this case, producer surplus is the difference between the equilibrium selling price of $2.00 and the $0.50 minimum price producers will accept to supply this quantity of ground beef. Thus, producer surplus is equal to $1.50 ($2.00 – $0.50) per pound multiplied by 1 million pounds sold, which is a $1.5 million producer surplus. This value is represented by the vertical shaded rectangle formed at point *A* on the supply curve. The second million pounds of ground beef offered for sale at point *B* also generates a producer surplus because the selling price of $2.00 exceeds the

Producer surplus

The value of the difference between the actual selling price of a product and the price producers are willing to sell it for on the supply curve.

EXHIBIT A-2   Market Supply Curve and Producer Surplus

In part (a), firms are willing at $0.50 (point *A*) to supply 1 million pounds of ground beef per year. Because $2.00 is the equilibrium price, the sellers earn a producer surplus of $1.50 per pound of ground beef sold. The first vertical shaded rectangle is the producer surplus earned only at point *A*. At points *B*, *C*, and *E*, sellers receive less producer surplus at each of these higher prices and the sizes of the rectangles fall. In part (b), moving upward along all possible selling prices on the supply curve yields the red-shaded triangle that is equal to total producer surplus (net benefit).

SOURCE: © Cengage Learning 2014

$1.00 price at which firms are willing to supply this additional quantity of ground beef. Note that producer surplus is lower at point *B* compared to point *A* and marginal producer surplus continues to fall at point *C* until it reaches zero at the equilibrium point *E*.

The total value of producer surplus is represented in Exhibit A-2(b). Start at point *X*, where none of the product will be supplied at the price of zero. Now consider the quantities of ground beef producers are willing to offer for sale at each possible price upward along the supply curve until the equilibrium price of $2.00 is reached at point *E*. The result is that the entire red triangular area between the horizontal line at the equilibrium price and the supply curve represents total producer surplus.

CONCLUSION: *Total producer surplus measured in dollars is represented by the total area under the equilibrium price and above the supply curve.*

3A-1c MARKET EFFICIENCY

In this section, the equilibrium price and quantity will be shown to achieve market efficiency because at any other market price, the total net benefits to consumers and producers will be less. Stated differently, competitive markets are efficient when they maximize the sum of consumer and producer surplus. The analysis continues in Exhibit A-3(a), which combines part (b) from each of the two previous exhibits. The green triangle represents consumer surplus earned in excess of the $2.00 equilibrium price consumers pay for ground beef. The red triangle represents producer surplus producers receive by selling ground beef at $2.00 per pound in excess of the minimum price at which they are willing to supply it. The total net benefit (total surplus) is therefore the entire triangular area consisting of both the green consumer surplus and red producer surplus triangles.

Now consider in Exhibit A-3(b) the consequences to market efficiency of producers devoting fewer resources to ground beef production and only 2 million pounds being bought and sold per year compared with 4 million pounds at the equilibrium price of $2.00. The result is a deadweight loss. Deadweight loss is the net loss of consumer and producer surplus from underproduction or overproduction of a product. In Exhibit A-3(b), the deadweight loss is equal to the gray triangle *ABE*, which represents the total surplus of green and red triangles in part (a) that is not obtained because the market is operating below equilibrium point *E*.

Exhibit A-3(c) illustrates that a deadweight loss of consumer and producer surplus can also result from overproduction. Now suppose more resources are devoted to production and 6 million pounds of ground beef are bought and sold at the equilibrium price. However, from the producers' side of the market, the equilibrium selling price is only $2.00 and is below any possible selling price on the supply curve between points *E* and *C*. Therefore, firms have a net loss for each pound sold, represented by the area under the supply curve and bounded below by the horizontal equilibrium price line. Similarly, consumers pay the equilibrium price of $2.00, but this price exceeds any price consumers are willing to pay between points *E* and *D* on the demand curve. This means consumers

Deadweight loss

The net loss of consumer and producer surplus from underproduction or overproduction of a product.

EXHIBIT A-3 **Comparison of Market Efficiency and Deadweight Loss**

In part (a), the green triangle represents consumer surplus and the red triangle represents producer surplus. The total net benefit, or total surplus, is the entire triangle consisting of the consumer and producer surplus triangles.

In part (b), too few resources are used to produce 2 million pounds of ground beef compared to 4 million pounds at equilibrium point E. The market is inefficient because the deadweight loss gray triangle *ABE* is no longer earned by either consumers or producers. As shown in part (c), overproduction at the equilibrium price of $2.00 can also be inefficient. If 6 million pounds of ground beef are offered for sale, too many resources are devoted to this product and a deadweight loss of area *EDC* occurs.

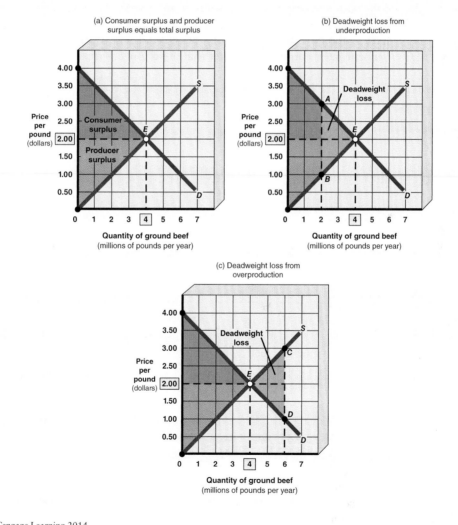

SOURCE: © Cengage Learning 2014

experience a total net benefit loss for each pound purchased, represented by the rectangular area between the horizontal equilibrium price line above and the demand curve below. The total net loss of consumer and producer surplus (deadweight loss) is equal to the gray shaded area *EDC*.

> **CONCLUSION:** *The total dollar value of potential benefits not achieved is the deadweight loss resulting from too few or too many resources used in a given market.*

Looking ahead, the conclusion drawn from this appendix is that market equilibrium is efficient, but this conclusion is not always the case. In the next chapter, the topic of *market failure* will be discussed, in which market equilibrium under certain conditions can result in too few or too many resources being used to produce goods and services. For example, the absence of a competitive market, the existence of pollution, or vaccinations to prevent a disease can establish equilibrium conditions with misallocations of resources. In these cases, government intervention may be preferable in order to achieve optimal allocation of resources. In other cases, such as the government imposing price ceilings and price floors, the result of government intervention is a market that is no longer efficient.

Key Concepts

Consumer surplus   Producer surplus   Deadweight loss

Summary

- **Consumer surplus** measures the value between the price consumers are willing to pay for a product along the demand curve and the price they actually pay.
- **Producer surplus** measures the value between the actual selling price of a product and the price along the supply curve at which sellers are willing to sell the product. Total surplus is the sum of consumer surplus and producer surplus.
- **Deadweight loss** is the result of a market that operates in disequilibrium. It is the net loss of both consumer and producer surplus resulting from underproduction or overproduction of a product.

Summary of Conclusion Statements

- Total consumer surplus measured in dollars is represented by the total area under the market demand curve and above the equilibrium price.
- Total producer surplus measured in dollars is represented by the total area under the equilibrium price and above the supply curve.
- The total dollar value of potential benefits not achieved is the deadweight loss resulting from too few or too many resources used in a given market.

Study Questions and Problems

1. Consider the market for used textbooks. Use Exhibit A-4 to calculate the total consumer surplus.

EXHIBIT A-4	Used Textbook Market	
Potential buyer	Willingness to pay	Market price
Brad	$60	$30
Juan	45	30
Sue	35	30
Jamie	25	30
Frank	10	30
SOURCE: © Cengage Learning 2014		

2. Consider the market for used textbooks. Use Exhibit A-5 to calculate the total producer surplus.

EXHIBIT A-5	Used Textbook Market	
Potential seller	Willingness to sell	Market price
Forest	$60	$30
Betty	45	30
Alan	35	30
Paul	25	30
Alice	10	30
SOURCE: © Cengage Learning 2014		

3. Using Exhibits A-4 and A-5 above, calculate the total surplus. Then calculate the effect on consumer surplus, producer surplus, and total surplus of a fall in the equilibrium price of textbooks from $30 to $15 each. Explain the meaning of your calculations.

4. Using Exhibit A-6 and assuming the market is in equilibrium at Q_E, identify areas ACD, DCE, and ACE. Then explain the result of underproduction at Q in terms of areas BCG, GCF, and BCF.

EXHIBIT A-6	Used Textbook Market

SOURCE: © Cengage Learning 2014

Sample Quiz

For an explanation of the correct answers, visit the Tucker Web site at www.cengage.com/economics/tucker.

1. Consumer surplus measures the value between the price consumers are willing to pay and the:
   a. producer surplus price.
   b. deadweight gain price.
   c. actual price paid.
   d. preference price.

2. If Sam is willing to pay $50 for one good X, $30 for a second, $20 for a third, $8 for a fourth, and the market price is $10. What is Sam's consumer surplus?
   a. $10
   b. $40
   c. $70
   d. $100

3. Suppose Tucker Inc. is willing to sell one gizmo for $10, a second gizmo for $15, a third for $20 and the market price is $25. What is Tucker Inc.'s producer surplus?
   a. $10
   b. $15
   c. $30
   d. $50

4. In an efficient market, deadweight loss is
   a. maximum
   b. minimum
   c. constant
   d. zero

5. Deadweight loss results from
   a. equilibrium.
   b. underproduction.
   c. overproduction.
   d. none of the above.
   e. either b or c.

6. Deadweight loss is the net loss of
   a. consumer surplus.
   b. producer surplus.
   c. disequilibrium surplus.
   d. both a and b.

7. If the quantity supplied exceeds the quantity demanded in a market, what is the result?
   a. Deadweight loss
   b. Inefficiency

c. Overproduction
d. All of the above answers are correct

8. Suppose a consumer is willing to pay $20 for one good X, $10 for a second, and $5 for a third and the market price is $4. What is the consumer surplus?
   a. $16
   b. $6
   c. $1
   d. $23

9. Producer surplus measures the value between the actual selling price and the
   a. price at which sellers are willing to sell the product.
   b. deadweight loss price.
   c. lowest price at which sellers are willing to sell the product.
   d. profit-maximization price.

10. Suppose seller X is willing to sell one good X for $5, a second good X for $10, a third for $16, a fourth for $25 and the market price is $20. What is seller X's producer surplus?
    a. $15
    b. $20
    c. $22
    d. $29

11. Deadweight loss is the result of
    a. disequilibrium.
    b. underproduction.
    c. overproduction.
    d. all of the above.

12. Deadweight loss is computed as the net of
    a. consumer surplus minus producer surplus.
    b. disequilibrium surplus plus consumer surplus.
    c. producer surplus minus disequilibrium surplus.
    d. consumer surplus plus producer surplus.

13. Deadweight loss is *not* the result of
    a. an efficient market.
    b. an inefficient market.
    c. zero consumer surplus.
    d. zero producer surplus.

Sample Quiz *continued*

14. At the equilibrium price, deadweight loss is
    a. minimized.
    b. zero.
    c. maximized.
    d. equal to the equilibrium price multiplied by the quantity exchanged.

15. If the quantity supplied exceeds the quantity demanded in a market, what is the result?
    a. Deadweight loss
    b. Inefficiency
    c. Overproduction
    d. None of the above answers are correct

EXHIBIT A-7	Comparison of Market Efficiency and Deadweight Loss

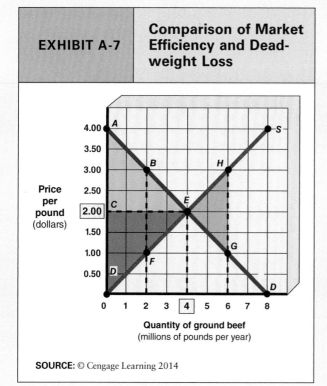

Quantity of ground beef
(millions of pounds per year)

SOURCE: © Cengage Learning 2014

16. As shown in Exhibit A-7, if the market is in equilibrium, _____ represents consumer surplus.
    a. *ABEC*
    b. *AED*
    c. *EGH*
    d. *BEF*

17. As shown in Exhibit A-7, if the market is in equilibrium, _____ represents producer surplus.
    a. *ADFB*
    b. *CEFD*
    c. *EGH*
    d. *BEF*

18. As shown in Exhibit A-7, if the quantity supplied is 2 million pounds of ground beef per year, what is the result?
    a. Deadweight loss
    b. Inefficiency
    c. Underproduction
    d. All of the above
    e. None of the above

19. As shown in Exhibit A-7, if the quantity supplied is 6 million pounds of ground beef per year, what is the result?
    a. Deadweight loss
    b. Inefficiency
    c. Overproduction
    d. All of the above
    e. None of the above

20. As shown in Exhibit A-7, if the quantity supplied is 2 million pounds of ground beef per year, the result is a deadweight loss represented by area
    a. *ABEC*.
    b. *CEFD*.
    c. *EGH*.
    d. *BEF*.

chapter 4

Markets in Action

Once you understand how buyers and sellers respond to changes in equilibrium prices, you are progressing well in your quest to understand the economic way of thinking. This chapter begins by showing that changes in supply and demand influence the equilibrium price and quantity of goods and services exchanged around you every day. For example, you will study the impact of changes in supply and demand curves on the markets for Caribbean cruises, new homes, and AIDS vaccinations. Then you will see why the laws of supply and demand cannot be repealed. Using market supply and demand analysis, you will learn that government policies to control markets have predictable consequences. For example, you will understand what happens when the government limits the maximum rent landlords can charge and who benefits and who loses from the federal minimum wage law.

In this chapter, you will also study situations in which the market mechanism fails. Have you visited a city and lamented the smog that blankets the beautiful surroundings? Or have you ever wanted to swim or fish in a stream, but could not because of industrial waste? These are obvious cases in which market system magic failed and the government must consider cures to reach socially desirable results.

In this chapter, you will learn to solve these economics puzzles:

- How can a spotted owl affect the price of homes?
- How do demand and supply affect the price of ethanol fuel?
- Why might government warehouses overflow with cheese and milk?
- What do ticket scalping and rent controls have in common?
- Can vouchers fix our schools?

4-1 Changes in Market Equilibrium

Using market supply and demand analysis is like putting on glasses if you are nearsighted. Suddenly, the fuzzy world around you comes into clear focus. Many people believe that prices are set by sellers adding a certain percentage to their costs. If costs rise, sellers simply raise their prices by that percentage. In free markets, there is more to the story. In the following examples, you will open your eyes and see that economic theory has something important to say about so many things in the real world.

4-1a CHANGES IN DEMAND

The Caribbean cruise market shown in Exhibit 1(a) assumes market supply, S, is constant and market demand increases from D_1 to D_2. Why has the demand curve shifted rightward in the figure? We will assume the popularity of cruises to these vacation islands has suddenly risen sharply due to extensive advertising that influenced tastes and preferences. Given supply curve S and demand curve D_1, the initial equilibrium price is $600 per cruise, and the initial equilibrium quantity is 8,000 cruises per year, shown as point E_1. After the impact of advertising, the new equilibrium point, E_2, becomes 12,000 cruises per year at a price of $900 each. Thus, the increase in demand causes both the equilibrium price and the equilibrium quantity to increase.

It is important to understand the force that caused the equilibrium to shift from E_1 to E_2. When demand initially increased from D_1 to D_2, there was a temporary shortage of 8,000 cruises at $600 per cruise. Firms in the cruise business responded to the excess demand by hiring more workers, offering more cruises to the Caribbean, and raising the price. The cruise lines therefore move upward along the supply curve (increasing quantity supplied, but not changing supply). During some period of trial and error, Caribbean cruise sellers increase their price and quantity supplied until a shortage no longer exists at point E_2. Therefore, the increase in demand causes both the equilibrium price and the equilibrium quantity to increase.

What will happen to the demand for gas-guzzling automobiles (for example, SUVs) if the price of gasoline triples? Because gasoline and automobiles are complements, a rise in the price of gasoline decreases the demand for gas guzzlers from D_1 to D_2 in Exhibit 1(b). At the initial equilibrium price of $30,000 per gas guzzler ($E_1$), the quantity supplied now exceeds the quantity demanded by 20,000 automobiles per month. This unwanted inventory forces automakers to reduce the price and quantity supplied. As a result of this movement downward on the supply curve, market equilibrium changes from E_1 to E_2. The equilibrium price falls from $30,000 to $20,000, and the equilibrium quantity falls from 30,000 to 20,000 gas guzzlers per month.

4-1b CHANGES IN SUPPLY

Now reverse the analysis by assuming demand remains constant and allow some nonprice determinant to shift the supply curve. In Exhibit 2(a), begin at point E_1 in a market for babysitting services at an equilibrium price of $9 per hour and

EXHIBIT 1 — The Effects of Shifts in Demand on Market Equilibrium

In part (a), demand for Caribbean cruises increases because of extensive advertising and the demand curve shifts rightward from D_1 to D_2. This shift in demand causes a temporary shortage of 8,000 cruises per year at the initial equilibrium of E_1. This disequilibrium condition encourages firms in the cruise business to move upward along the supply curve to a new equilibrium at E_2.

Part (b) illustrates a decrease in the demand for gas-guzzling automobiles (SUVs) caused by a sharp rise in the price of gasoline (a complement). This leftward shift in demand from D_1 to D_2 results in a temporary surplus of 20,000 gas guzzlers per month at the initial equilibrium of E_1. This disequilibrium condition forces sellers of these cars to move downward along the supply curve to a new equilibrium at E_2.

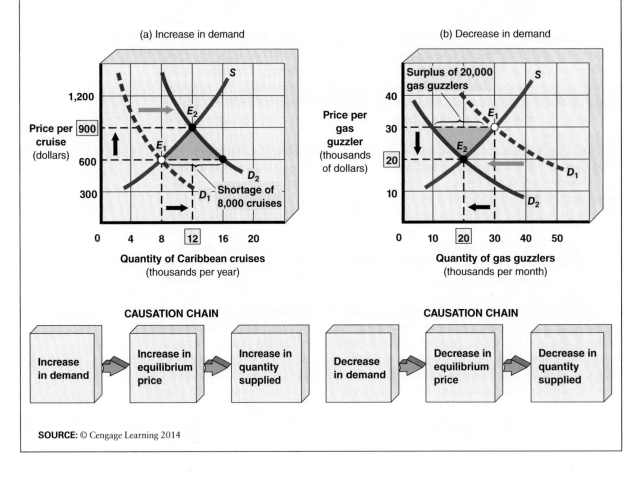

(a) Increase in demand

(b) Decrease in demand

SOURCE: © Cengage Learning 2014

4,000 babysitters hired per month. Then assume there is a population shift and the number of people available to babysit rises. This increase in the number of sellers shifts the market supply curve rightward from S_1 to S_2 and creates a temporary surplus of 4,000 babysitters at point E_1 who offer their services but are not hired. The unemployed babysitters respond by reducing the price and the number of babysitters available for hire, which is a movement downward along S_2. As the price falls, buyers move down along their demand curve and hire more babysitters per month. When the price falls to $6 per hour, the market is in equilibrium again at point E_2, instead of E_1, and consumers hire 6,000 babysitters per month.

Exhibit 2(b) illustrates the market for lumber. Suppose this market is at equilibrium at point E_1, where the going price is $400 per thousand board

---

EXHIBIT 2   **The Effects of Shifts in Supply on Market Equilibrium**

In part (a), begin at equilibrium E_1 in the market for babysitters and assume an increase in the number of babysitters shifts the supply curve rightward from S_1 to S_2. This shift in supply causes a temporary surplus of 4,000 unemployed babysitters per month. This disequilibrium condition causes a movement downward along the demand curve to a new equilibrium at E_2. At E_2, the equilibrium price declines and the equilibrium quantity rises.

In part (b), steps to protect the environment cause the supply curve for lumber to shift leftward from S_1 to S_2. This shift in supply results in a temporary shortage of 4 billion board feet per year. Customer bidding for the available lumber raises the price. As a result, the market moves upward along the demand curve to a new equilibrium at E_2, and the quantity demanded falls.

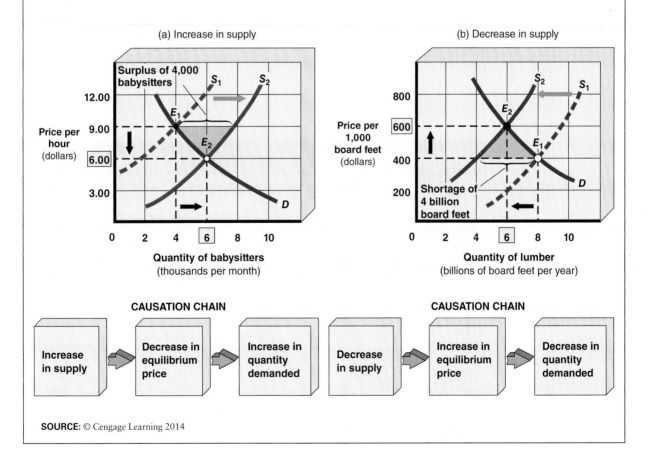

SOURCE: © Cengage Learning 2014

EXHIBIT 3	Effect of Shifts in Demand or Supply on Market Equilibrium	
Change	**Effect on equilibrium price**	**Effect on equilibrium quantity**
Demand increases	Increases	Increases
Demand decreases	Decreases	Decreases
Supply increases	Decreases	Increases
Supply decreases	Increases	Decreases

SOURCE: © Cengage Learning 2014

feet, and 8 billion board feet are bought and sold per year. Now suppose a new Endangered Species Act is passed, and the federal government sets aside huge forest resources to protect the spotted owl and other wildlife. This means the market supply curve shifts leftward from S_1 to S_2, and a temporary shortage of 4 billion board feet of lumber exists at point E_1. Suppliers respond by hiking their price from $400 to $600 per thousand board feet, and a new equilibrium is established at E_2, where the quantity is 6 billion board feet per year. This higher cost of lumber, in turn, raises the price of a new home.

Exhibit 3 gives a concise summary of the impact of changes in demand or supply on market equilibrium.

✓ CHECKPOINT

Why the Higher Price for Ethanol Fuel?

Suppose more consumers purchased ethanol fuel for their cars, and at the same time, producers switched to ethanol fuel production. Within a year, the price of ethanol fuel shot up $2 per gallon. During this period, which increased more—demand, supply, or neither?

4-1c TREND OF EQUILIBRIUM PRICES OVER TIME

Basic demand and supply analysis allows us to explain a trend in prices over a number of years. Exhibit 4 shows the effect of changes in nonprice determinants that increase both the demand and supply curves for good X between 2000, 2005, and 2010. A line connects the equilibrium prices for each year in order to summarize the trend of equilibrium price and quantity changes over this time period. In this case, the observed prices trace an upward-sloping trend line.

EXHIBIT 4	Trend of Equilibrium Prices over Time

Nonprice determinants of demand and supply for good X have caused both the demand and supply curves to shift rightward between 2000 and 2010. As a result, the equilibrium price and quantity in this example rise along the upward-sloping trend line, connecting each observed equilibrium price.

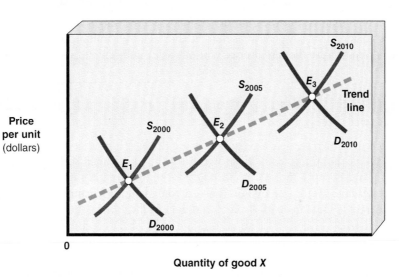

SOURCE: © Cengage Learning 2014

4-2 Can the Laws of Supply and Demand Be Repealed?

The government intervenes in some markets with the objective of preventing prices from rising to the equilibrium price. In other markets, the government's goal is to intervene and maintain a price higher than the equilibrium price. Market supply and demand analysis is a valuable tool for understanding what happens when the government fixes prices. There are two types of price controls: *price ceilings* and *price floors*.

4-2a PRICE CEILINGS

Case 1: Rent Controls   What happens if the government prevents the price system from setting a market price "too high" by mandating a price ceiling? A price ceiling is a legally established maximum price a seller can charge. Rent controls are an example of the imposition of a price ceiling in the market for rental units. New York City, Washington, D.C., Los Angeles, San Francisco, and other communities in the United States have some form of rent control. Since World War I, rent controls have been widely used in Europe. The rationale for rent controls is to provide an "essential service" that would otherwise be unaffordable by many people at the

Price ceiling

A legally established maximum price a seller can charge.

equilibrium rental price. Let's see why most economists believe that rent controls are counterproductive.

Exhibit 5 is a supply and demand diagram for the quantity of rental units demanded and supplied per month in a hypothetical city. We begin the analysis by assuming no rent controls exist and equilibrium is at point *E*, with a monthly rent of $1,200 per month and 6 million units occupied. Next, assume the city council imposes a rent control (ceiling price) that by law forbids any landlord from renting a unit for more than $800 per month. What does market supply and demand theory predict will happen? At the low rent ceiling of $800, the quantity demanded of rental units will be 8 million, but the quantity supplied will be only 4 million. Consequently, the price ceiling creates a persistent market shortage of 4 million rental units because suppliers cannot raise the rental price without being subjected to legal penalties.

EXHIBIT 5	Rent Control Results in a Shortage of Rental Units

If no rent controls exist, the equilibrium rent for a hypothetical apartment is $1,200 per month at point *E*. However, if the government imposes a rent ceiling of $800 per month, a shortage of 4 million rental units occurs. Because rent cannot rise by law, one outcome is that consumers must search for available units instead of paying a higher rent. Other outcomes include a black market, bribes, discrimination, and other illegal methods of dealing with a shortage of 4 million rental units per month.

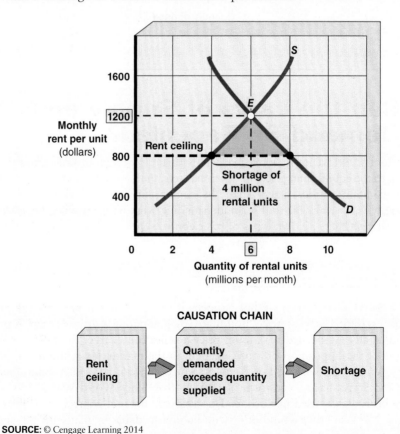

SOURCE: © Cengage Learning 2014

Note that a rent ceiling at or above $1,200 per month would have no effect. If the ceiling is set at the equilibrium rent of $1,200, the quantity of rental units demanded and the quantity of rental units supplied are equal regardless of the rent control. If the rent ceiling is set above the equilibrium rent, the quantity of rental units supplied exceeds the quantity of rental units demanded, and this surplus will cause the market to adjust to the equilibrium rent of $1,200.

What is the impact of rent controls on consumers? First, as a substitute for paying higher prices, consumers must spend more time on waiting lists and searching for housing. This means consumers incur an *opportunity cost* added to the $800 rent set by the government. Second, an illegal market, or *black market*, can arise because of the excess quantity demanded. Because the price of rental units is artificially low, the profit motive encourages tenants to risk breaking the law by subletting their unit to the highest bidder over $800 per month.

From the seller's perspective, rent control encourages two undesirable effects. First, faced with a mandated low rent, landlords may cut maintenance expenses, and housing deterioration will reduce the stock of rental units in the long run. Second, landlords may use discriminatory practices to replace the price system. Once owners realize there is an excess quantity demanded for rentals at the controlled price, they may resort to preferences based on pet ownership or family size to determine how to allocate scarce rental space.

Case 2: Gasoline Price Ceiling   The government placed ceilings on most nonfarm prices during World War II and, to a lesser extent, during the Korean War. In 1971, President Nixon "froze" virtually all wages, prices, and rents until 1973 in an attempt to control inflation. As a result of an oil embargo in late 1973, the government imposed a price ceiling of 55 cents per gallon of gasoline. To deal with the shortage, nonprice rationing schemes were introduced in 1974. Some states used a first-come, first-served system, while other states allowed consumers with even-numbered license plates to buy gas on even-numbered days and those with odd-numbered license plates to buy gas on odd-numbered days. Gas stations were required to close on Friday night and not open until Monday morning. Regardless of the scheme, long waiting lines for gasoline formed, just as the supply and demand model predicts. Finally, in the past, legally imposed price ceilings have been placed on such items as natural gas shipped in interstate commerce and on interest rates for loans. Internationally, as discussed later in the chapter on economies in transition, price ceilings on food and rent were common in the former Soviet Union. Soviet sociologists estimated that members of a typical urban household spent a combined total of 40 hours per week standing in lines to obtain various goods and services.

4-2b PRICE FLOORS

The other side of the price-control coin is a price floor set by government because it fears that the price system might establish a price viewed as "too low." A price floor is a legally established minimum price a seller can be paid. We now turn to two examples of price floors. The first is the minimum wage, and the second is agricultural price supports.

Price floor

A legally established minimum price a seller can be paid.

Case 1: The Minimum Wage Law   In Chapter 1, the second You're the Economist applied *normative* and *positive* reasoning to the issue of the minimum wage. Now you are prepared to apply market supply and demand analysis (positive reasoning) to this debate. Begin by noting that the demand for unskilled labor is the

EXHIBIT 6	A Minimum Wage Results in a Surplus of Labor

When the federal or state government sets a wage-rate floor above the equilibrium wage, a surplus of unskilled labor develops. The supply curve is the number of workers offering their labor services per year at possible wage rates. The demand curve is the number of workers employers are willing and able to hire at various wage rates. Equilibrium wage, W_e, will result if the price system is allowed to operate without government interference. At the minimum wage of W_m, there is a surplus of unemployed workers, $Q_s - Q_d$.

CAUSATION CHAIN

SOURCE: © Cengage Learning 2014

downward-sloping curve shown in Exhibit 6. The wage rate on the vertical axis is the price of unskilled labor, and the amount of unskilled labor employers are willing to hire varies inversely with the wage rate. At a higher wage rate, businesses will hire fewer workers. At a lower wage rate, they will employ a larger quantity of workers.

On the supply side, the wage rate determines the number of unskilled workers willing and able to work per year. At higher wages, workers will give up leisure or schooling to work, and at lower wages, fewer workers will be available for hire. The upward-sloping curve in Exhibit 6 is the supply of labor.

Assuming the freedom to bargain, the price system will establish an equilibrium wage rate of W_e and an equilibrium quantity of labor employed of Q_e. But suppose the government enacts a minimum wage, W_m, which is a price floor above the equilibrium wage, W_e. The intent of the legislation is to "wave a carrot" in front of people who will not work at W_e and to make lower-paid workers better off with a higher wage rate. But consider the undesirable consequences. One result of an artificially high minimum wage is that the number of workers willing to offer their labor increases upward along the supply curve to Q_s, but there are fewer jobs because the number of workers firms are willing to hire decreases to Q_d on the demand curve. The predicted outcome is a labor surplus of unskilled workers, $Q_s - Q_d$, who are unemployed. Moreover, employers are encouraged to substitute machines and skilled labor for the unskilled labor previously employed at equilibrium wage W_e. The minimum wage is therefore considered counterproductive because employers lay off the lowest-skilled workers, who ironically are the type of workers minimum wage legislation intends to help. Also, loss of minimum wage jobs represents a loss of entry-level jobs to those who seek to enter the workforce.

Supporters of the minimum wage are quick to point out that those employed (Q_d) are better off. Even though the minimum wage causes a reduction in employment, some economists argue that a more equal or fairer income distribution is worth the loss of some jobs. Moreover, the shape of the labor demand curve may be much more vertical than shown in Exhibit 6. If this is the case, the unemployment effect of a rise in the minimum wage would be small. In addition, they claim opponents ignore the possibility that unskilled workers lack bargaining power versus employers.

Finally, a minimum wage set at or below the equilibrium wage rate is ineffective. If the minimum wage is set at the equilibrium wage rate of W_e, the quantity of labor demanded and the quantity of labor supplied are equal regardless of the minimum wage. If the minimum wage is set below the equilibrium wage, the forces of supply of and demand for labor establish the equilibrium wage regardless of the minimum wage rate.

Case 2: Agricultural Price Supports   A farm price support is a well-known example of a price floor, which results in government purchases of surplus food and in higher food prices. Agricultural price support programs began in the 1930s as a means of raising the income of farmers, who were suffering from low market prices during the Great Depression. Under these programs, the government guarantees a minimum price above the equilibrium price and agrees to purchase any quantity the farmer is unable to sell at the legal price.

A few of the crops that have received price supports are corn, peanuts, soybeans, wheat, cotton, rice, tobacco, and dairy products. As predicted by market supply and demand analysis, a price support above the equilibrium price causes surpluses. Government warehouses therefore often overflow with such perishable products as butter, cheese, and dry milk purchased with taxpayers' money. The following You're the Economist on the dairy industry examines one of the best-known examples of U.S. government interference with agricultural market prices.

> **CONCLUSION:** *A price ceiling or price floor prevents market adjustment in which competition among buyers and sellers bids the price upward or downward to the equilibrium price.*

Rigging the Market for Milk

Applicable Concept: price supports

Each year the milk industry faces an important question: What does the federal government plan to do about its dairy price support program, which has helped boost farmers' income since 1949? Under the price support program, the federal government agrees to buy storable milk products, such as cheese, butter, and dry milk. If the farmers cannot sell all their products to consumers at a price exceeding the price support level, the federal government will purchase any unsold grade A milk production. Although state-run dairy commissions set their own minimum prices for milk, state price supports closely follow federal levels and are kept within 3 percent of levels in bordering states to reduce interstate milk price competition.

Members of Congress who advocate changes in the price support programs worry that milk surpluses are costing taxpayers too much. Each year the federal government pays billions of dollars to dairy farmers for milk products held in storage at a huge cost. Moreover, the problem is getting worse because the federal government encourages dairy farmers to use ultramodern farming techniques to increase the production per cow. Another concern is that the biggest government price support checks go to the largest farmers, while the number of dairy farmers continues to decline.

Congress is constantly seeking a solution to the milk price support problem. The following are some of the ideas that have been considered:

Shutterstock.com/Matthew Jacques

- Freeze the current price support level. This prospect dismays farmers, who are subject to increasing expenses for feed, electricity, and other resources.
- Eliminate the price supports gradually in yearly increments over the next five years. This would subject the milk market to the price fluctuations of the free market, and farmers would suffer some bad years from low milk prices.
- Have the Department of Agriculture charge dairy farmers a tax of 50 cents for every 100 pounds of milk they produce. The

---

✓ CHECKPOINT

Is There Price Fixing at the Ticket Window?

At sold-out concerts, sports contests, and other events, some ticket holders try to resell their tickets for more than they paid—a practice known as scalping. For scalping to occur, must the original ticket price be legally set by a price floor, at the equilibrium price, or by a price ceiling?

4-2c MARKET FAILURE

In this chapter and the previous chapter, you have gained an understanding of how markets operate. Through the price system, society coordinates economic activity, but markets are not always "Prince Charmings" that achieve *market efficiency*

"I always wondered how the government set milk prices."

Finally, opponents of the dairy price support program argue that the market for milk is inherently a competitive industry and that consumers and taxpayers would be better served without government price supports for milk.

farmers oppose this approach because it would discourage production and run small farmers out of business.

- Have the federal government implement a "whole herd buyout" program. The problem is that using taxpayers' money to get farmers out of the dairy business pushes up the prices of milk products and rewards dairy farmers who own a lot of cows. Besides, what does the government do with the cows after it purchases them?

© Andrew Toos. Reproduction rights obtainable from www.CartoonStock.com

Analyze the Issue

1. Draw a supply and demand graph to illustrate the problem described in the case study and prescribe your own solution.
2. Which proposal do you think best serves the interests of small dairy farmers? Why?
3. Which proposal do you think best serves the interests of consumers? Why?
4. Which proposal do you think best serves the interest of a member of Congress? Why?

Source: © Cengage Learning 2014

---

without a misallocation of resources. It is now time to step back with a critical eye and consider markets that become "ugly frogs" by allocating resources inefficiently. Market failure occurs when market equilibrium results in too few or too many resources being used in the production of a good or service. In this section, you will study four important cases of market failure: lack of competition, externalities, public goods, and income inequality. Market failure is discussed in more detail in the chapter on environmental economics, except for the macroeconomics version of the text.

Market failure

A situation in which market equilibrium results in too few or too many resources being used in the production of a good or service. This inefficiency may justify government intervention.

4-2d LACK OF COMPETITION

There must be competition among both producers and consumers for markets to function properly. But what happens if the producers fail to compete? In *The Wealth of Nations*, Adam Smith stated, "People of the same trade seldom meet together, even for merriment and diversion, but the conversation ends in a

Adam Smith (1723–1790). The father of modern economics, who wrote *The Wealth of Nations* published in 1776.

conspiracy against the public, or in some diversion to raise prices."[1] This famous quotation clearly underscores the fact that in the real world, businesses seek ways to replace consumer sovereignty with "big business sovereignty." What happens when a few firms rig the market and they become the market's boss? By restricting supply through artificial limits on the output of a good, firms can enjoy higher prices and profits. As a result, firms may waste resources and retard technology and innovation.

Exhibit 7 illustrates how IBM, Apple, Gateway, Dell, and other suppliers of personal computers (PCs) could benefit from rigging the market. Without collusive action, the competitive price for PCs is \$1,500, the quantity of 200,000 per month is sold, and efficient equilibrium prevails at point E_1. It is in the best interest of sellers, however, to take steps that would make PCs artificially scarce and raise the price. Graphically, the sellers wish to shift the competitive supply curve, S_1, leftward to the restricted supply curve, S_2. This could happen for a number of reasons, including an agreement among sellers to restrict supply (collusion) and government action. For example, the sellers could lobby the government to pass a law allowing an association of PC suppliers to set production quotas. The proponents might argue this action raises prices and, in turn, profits. Higher profits enable the industry to invest in new capital and become more competitive in world markets.

Opponents of artificially restricted supply argue that although the producers benefit, the lack of competition means the economy loses. The result of restricting supply is that the efficient equilibrium point, E_1, changes to the inefficient equilibrium point, E_2. At point E_2, the higher price of \$2,000 is charged, and the lower equilibrium quantity means that firms devote too few resources to producing PCs and charge an artificially high price. Note that under U.S. antitrust laws, the Justice Department is responsible for prosecuting firms that collude to restrict supply to force higher prices.

4-2e EXTERNALITIES

Externality

A cost or benefit imposed on people other than the consumers and producers of a good or service.

Even when markets are competitive, some markets may still fail because they suffer from the presence of side effects economists call externalities. An externality is a cost or benefit imposed on people other than the consumers and producers of a good or service. Externalities are also called *spillover effects* or *neighborhood effects*. People other than consumers and producers who are affected by these side effects of market exchanges are called *third parties*. Externalities may be either negative or positive; that is, they may be detrimental or beneficial. Suppose you are trying to study and your roommate is listening to Steel Porcupines at full blast on the stereo. The action of your roommate is imposing an unwanted *external cost* or *negative externality* on you and other third parties who are trying to study or sleep. Externalities can also result in an *external benefit* or *positive externality* to nonparticipating parties. When a community proudly displays its neat lawns, gorgeous flowers, and freshly painted homes, visitors are third parties who did none of the work, but enjoy the benefit of the pleasant scenery.

A Graphical Analysis of Pollution   Exhibit 8 provides a graphical analysis of two markets that fail to include externalities in their market prices unless the government takes corrective action. Exhibit 8(a) shows a market for steel in which steel firms burn high-sulfur coal and pollute the environment. Demand curve D and supply curve S_1 establish the inefficient equilibrium, E_1, in the steel market. Not

---

[1]Adam Smith, *An Inquiry into the Nature and Causes of the Wealth of Nations* (1776; reprint, New York: Random House, The Modern Library, 1937), p. 128.

| EXHIBIT 7 | Rigging the PC Market |

At efficient equilibrium point E_1, sellers compete. As a result, the price charged per PC is $1,500, and the quantity of PCs exchanged is 200,000. Suppose suppliers use collusion, government intervention, or other means to restrict the supply of this product. The decrease in supply from S_1 to S_2 establishes inefficient market equilibrium E_2. At E_2, firms charge the higher price of $2,000, and the equilibrium quantity of PCs falls to 150,000. Thus, the outcome of restricted supply is that the market fails because firms use too few resources to produce PCs at an artificially higher price.

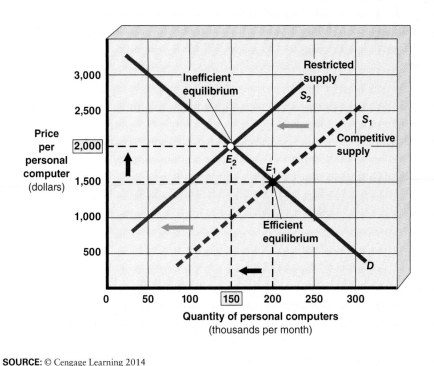

SOURCE: © Cengage Learning 2014

included in S_1 are the *external costs* to the public because the steel firms are not paying for the damage from smoke emissions. If steel firms discharge smoke and ash into the atmosphere, foul air reduces property values, raises health care costs, and generally erodes the quality of life. Because supply curve S_1 does not include these external costs, they are also not included in the price of steel, P_1. In short, the absence of the cost of pollution in the price of steel means the firms produce more steel and pollution than is socially desirable.

S_2 is the supply curve that would exist if the external costs of respiratory illnesses, dirty homes, and other undesirable side effects were included. Once S_2 includes the charges for environmental damage, the equilibrium price rises to P_2, and the equilibrium quantity becomes Q_2. At the efficient equilibrium point, E_2, the steel market achieves allocative efficiency. At E_2, steel firms are paying the full cost and using fewer resources to produce the lower quantity of steel at Q_2.

> **CONCLUSION:** *When the supply curve fails to include external costs, the equilibrium price is artificially low, and the equilibrium quantity is artificially high.*

Regulation and pollution taxes are two ways society can correct the market failure of pollution:

1. **Regulation.** Legislation can set standards that force firms to clean up their emissions as a condition of remaining in business. This means firms must buy, install, and maintain pollution-control equipment. When the extra cost of the pollution equipment is added to the production cost per ton of steel, the initial supply curve, S_1, shifts leftward to supply curve S_2. This means regulation has forced the market equilibrium to change from E_1 to E_2. At point E_2, the firms use fewer resources to produce Q_2 compared to Q_1 output of steel per year, and, therefore, the firms operate efficiently.

2. **Pollution Taxes.** Another approach would be for the government to levy a tax per ton of steel equal to the external cost imposed on society when the firm emits pollution into the air. This action inhibits production by imposing an additional production cost per ton of steel from the pollution taxes and shifts the supply curve leftward from S_1 to S_2. Again, the objective is to change the equilibrium from E_1 to E_2 and eliminate the overuse of resources devoted to steel production and its pollution. The tax revenue could be used to compensate those damaged by the pollution.

A Graphical Analysis of AIDS Vaccinations   As explained above, the supply curve can understate the *external costs* of a product. Now you will see that the demand curve can understate the *external benefits* of a product. Suppose a vaccination is discovered that prevents AIDS. Exhibit 8(b) illustrates the market for immunization against AIDS. Demand curve D_1 reflects the price consumers would pay for shots to receive the benefit of a reduced probability of infection by AIDS. Supply curve S shows the quantities of shots suppliers offer for sale at different prices. At equilibrium point E_1, the market fails to achieve an efficient allocation of resources. The reason is that when buyers are vaccinated, other people who do not purchase AIDS shots (called *free riders*) also benefit because this disease is less likely to spread. Once demand curve D_2 includes external benefits to nonconsumers of AIDS vaccinations (increase in the number of buyers), the efficient equilibrium of E_2 is established. At Q_2, sellers devote greater resources to AIDS vaccinations, and the underallocation of resources is eliminated.

How can society prevent the market failure of AIDS vaccinations? Two approaches follow.

1. **Regulation.** The government can boost consumption and shift the demand curve rightward by requiring all citizens to purchase AIDS shots each year. This approach to capturing external benefits in market demand explains why all school-age children must have polio and other shots before entering school.

2. **Special Subsidies.** Another possible solution would be for the government to increase consumer income by paying consumers for each AIDS vaccination.

| EXHIBIT 8 | Externalities in the Steel and AIDS Vaccination Markets |

In part (a), resources are overallocated at inefficient market equilibrium E_1 because steel firms do not include the cost per ton of pollution in the cost per ton of steel. Supply curve S_2 includes the external costs of pollution. If firms are required to purchase equipment to remove the pollution or to pay a tax on pollution, the economy achieves the efficient equilibrium of E_2.

Part (b) demonstrates that external benefits cause an underallocation of resources. The efficient output at equilibrium point E_2 is obtained if people are required to purchase AIDS shots or if the government pays a subsidy equal to the external benefit per shot.

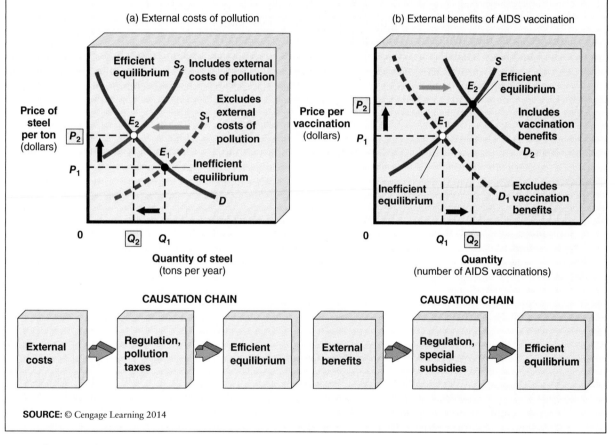

SOURCE: © Cengage Learning 2014

This would mean the government pays each citizen a dollar payment equal to the amount of external benefits per shot purchased. Because the subsidy amount is payable at any price along the demand curve, the demand curve shifts rightward until the efficient equilibrium price and quantity are reached.

CONCLUSION: *When externalities are present, market failure gives incorrect price and quantity signals, and as a result, resources are misallocated. External costs cause the market to overallocate resources, and external benefits cause the market to underallocate resources.*

Can Vouchers Fix Our Schools?

Applicable Concept: public goods versus private goods

In their book, *Free to Choose*, published in 1980, economists Milton Friedman and his wife Rose Friedman proposed a voucher plan for schools.[1] The objective of their proposal was to retain government financing, but give parents greater freedom to choose the schools their children attend. The Friedmans pointed out that under the current system, parents face a strong incentive not to remove their children from the public schools. The reason is because if parents decide to withdraw their children from a public school and send them to a private school, they must pay private tuition in addition to the taxes that finance children enrolled in the public schools.

To remove the financial penalty that limits the freedom of parents to choose schools, the government could give parents a voucher, which is a piece of paper redeemable for a sum of money payable to any approved school. For example, if the government spends $8,000 per year to educate a student, then the voucher could be for this amount. The voucher plan embodies the same principle as the GI Bill that provides educational benefits to military veterans. The veteran receives a voucher good only for educational expenses and is free to choose the school where it is used, provided the school satisfies certain standards.

The Friedmans argue that parents could, and should, be permitted to use the vouchers not only at private schools, but also at other public schools—and not only at schools in their own district, city, or state, but at any school that is willing to accept their child. That option would give every parent a greater opportunity to choose and at the same time would require public schools to charge tuition. The tuition would be competitive because public schools must compete for students both with other public schools and with private schools. It is important to note that this plan relieves no one of the burden of taxation to pay for schooling. It simply gives parents a wider choice as to which competing schools their children can attend, given the amount of funding per student that the community has obligated itself to provide. The plan also does not affect the present standards imposed on private schools to ensure that students attending them satisfy the compulsory attendance laws.

In 1990, Milwaukee began an experiment with school vouchers. The program gave selected children from low-income families taxpayer-funded vouchers to allow them to attend private schools. There has been a continuing heated debate

4-2f PUBLIC GOODS

Public good

A good or service with two properties: (1) users collectively consume benefits, and (2) there is no way to bar people who do not pay (free riders) from consuming the good or service.

Private goods are produced through the price system. In contrast, national defense is an example of a public good provided by the government because of its special characteristics. A public good is a good or service that, once produced, has two properties: (1) users collectively consume benefits, and (2) there is no way to bar people who do not pay (free riders) from consuming the good or service.

To see why the marketplace fails, imagine that Patriot Missiles Inc. offers to sell missile defense systems to people who want private protection against attacks from incoming missiles. First, once the system is operational, everyone in the defense area benefits from increased safety. Second, the *nonexclusive* nature of a public good means it is impossible or very costly for any owner of a Patriot missile defense system to prevent nonowners, the free riders, from reaping the benefits of its protection.

Given the two properties of a public good, why would any private individual purchase a Patriot missile defense system? Why not take a free ride and wait until someone else buys a missile system? Thus, each person wants a Patriot system, but does not want to bear the cost of the system when everyone shares in the benefits. As a result, the market fails to provide Patriot missile defense systems, and everyone among parents, politicians, and educators over the results. In 1998, Wisconsin's highest court ruled in a 4–2 decision that without violating the constitutional separation of church and state, Milwaukee could use public money for vouchers for students who attend religious schools.

A 2002 article in *USA Today* reported:

> Opponents of vouchers have repeatedly argued that they would damage the public schools, draining them of resources and better students. A recent study of the Milwaukee voucher program by Caroline Hoxby, a Harvard economist, suggests just the opposite. She wrote that "schools that faced the most potential competition from vouchers had the best productivity response." No

doubt, the nation's experience with vouchers is limited, yet the evidence cited in a recent Brookings Institution report shows that they do seem to benefit African-American youngsters.[2]

The controversy continues: For example, in a 2002 landmark case, the U.S. Supreme Court ruled that government vouchers for private or parochial schools are constitutional. In 2003, however, a Denver judge struck down Colorado's new school voucher law, ruling that it violated the state's constitution by stripping local school boards of their control over education. In 2006, the Florida Supreme Court ruled that Florida's voucher program for students in the lowest-rated public schools was unconstitutional. Then in 2010, Florida legislated a tax-credit voucher plan for low-income students.

And in 2011, Indiana began the nation's broadest school voucher program.

Analyze the Issue

1. In recent years, school choice has been a hotly debated issue. Explain whether education is a public good. If education is not a public good, why should the government provide it?

2. The Friedmans present a one-sided view of the benefits of a voucher system. Other economists disagree about the potential effectiveness of vouchers. Do you support a voucher system for education? Explain your reasoning.

---

1. Milton Friedman and Rose Friedman, *Free to Choose: A Personal Statement* (New York: Harcourt Brace Jovanovich, 1980), pp. 160–161.
2. Robert J. Bresler, "Vouchers and the Constitution," *USA Today*, May 2002, p. 15.

Source: © Cengage Learning 2014

---

hopes no missile attacks occur before someone finally decides to purchase one. Government can solve this public goods problem by producing Patriot missiles and taxing the public to pay. Unlike a private citizen, the government can use force to collect payments and prevent the free-rider problem. Other examples of public goods include global agreements to reduce emissions, the judicial system, the national emergency warning system, air traffic control, prisons, and traffic lights.

> **CONCLUSION:** *If public goods are available only in the marketplace, people wait for someone else to pay, and the result is an underproduction or zero production of public goods.*

4-2g INCOME INEQUALITY

In the cases of insufficient competition, externalities, and public goods, the marketplace allocates too few or too many resources to producing output. The market may also result in a very unequal distribution of income, thereby raising a very controversial issue. Under the impersonal price system, movie stars earn huge incomes for acting in movies, while homeless people roam the streets penniless. The controversy is therefore over how equal the distribution of income should be and how much government intervention is required to achieve this goal. Some people wish to remove most inequality of income. Others argue for the government to provide a "safety net" minimum income level for all citizens. Still others see high income as an incentive and a "fair" reward for productive resources.

To create a more equal distribution of income, the government uses various programs to transfer money from people with high incomes to those with low incomes. Unemployment compensation and food stamps are examples of such programs. The federal minimum wage is another example of a government attempt to raise the earnings of low-income workers.

✓ CHECKPOINT

Should There Be a War on Drugs?

The U.S. government fights the use of drugs, such as marijuana and cocaine, in a variety of ways, including spraying crops with poisonous chemicals; imposing jail sentences for dealers and users; and confiscating drug-transporting cars, boats, and planes. Which market failure motivates the government to interfere with the market for drugs: lack of competition, externalities, public goods, or income inequality?

Key Concepts

Price ceiling   Market failure   Public good
Price floor   Externality

Summary

- **Price ceilings** and **price floors** are maximum and minimum prices enacted by law, rather than allowing the forces of supply and demand to determine prices. A *price ceiling* is a maximum price mandated by government, and a *price floor,* or *support price* for agricultural products, is a minimum legal price. If a price ceiling is set below the equilibrium price, a shortage will persist. If a price floor is set above the equilibrium price, a surplus will persist.

Price Ceiling

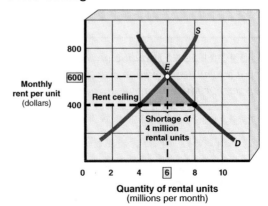

SOURCE: © Cengage Learning 2014

Price Floor

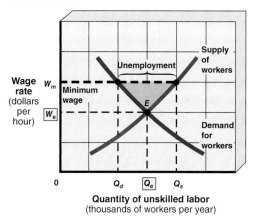

SOURCE: © Cengage Learning 2014

Externalities

(a) External costs of pollution

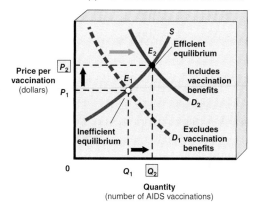

(b) External benefits of AIDS vaccination

SOURCE: © Cengage Learning 2014

- **Market failure** occurs when the market mechanism does not achieve an efficient allocation of resources. Sources of market failure include lack of competition, externalities, public goods, and income inequality. Although controversial, government intervention is a possible way to correct market failure.

- An **externality** is a cost or benefit of a good imposed on people who are not buyers or sellers of that good. Pollution is an example of an *external cost*, which means too many resources are used to produce the product responsible for the pollution. Two basic approaches to solve this market failure are regulation and pollution taxes. Vaccinations provide *external benefits*, which means sellers devote too few resources to produce this product. Two basic solutions to this type of market failure are laws to require consumption of shots and special subsidies.

- **Public goods** are goods that are consumed by all people in a society regardless of whether they pay or not. National defense, air traffic control, and other public goods can benefit many individuals simultaneously and are provided by the government.

Summary of Conclusion Statements

- A price ceiling or price floor prevents market adjustment in which competition among buyers and sellers bids the price upward or downward to the equilibrium price.
- When the supply curve fails to include external costs, the equilibrium price is artificially low, and the equilibrium quantity is artificially high.
- When externalities are present, market failure gives incorrect price and quantity signals, and

as a result, resources are misallocated. External costs cause the market to overallocate resources, and external benefits cause the market to underallocate resources.
- If public goods are available only in the marketplace, people wait for someone else to pay, and the result is an underproduction or zero production of public goods.

Study Questions and Problems

1. Market researchers have studied the market for milk, and their estimates for the supply of and the demand for milk per month are as follows:

Price per gallon	Quantity demanded (millions of gallons)	Quantity supplied (millions of gallons)
$10.00	100	500
8.00	200	400
6.00	300	300
4.00	400	200
2.00	500	100

a. Using the above data, graph the demand for and the supply of milk. Identify the equilibrium point as E, and use dotted lines to connect E to the equilibrium price on the price axis and the equilibrium quantity on the quantity axis.

b. Suppose the government enacts a milk price support of $8 per gallon. Indicate this action on your graph, and explain the effect on the milk market. Why would the government establish such a price support?

c. Now assume the government decides to set a price ceiling of $4 per gallon. Show and explain how this legal price affects your graph of the milk market. What objective could the government be trying to achieve by establishing such a price ceiling?

2. Use a graph to show the impact on the price of Japanese cars sold in the United States if the United States imposes import quotas on Japanese cars. Then draw another graph to show how the change in the price of Japanese cars affects the price of American-made cars in the United States. Explain the market outcome in each graph and the link between the two graphs.

3. Using market supply and demand analysis, explain why labor union leaders are strong advocates of raising the minimum wage above the equilibrium wage.

4. What are the advantages and disadvantages of the price system?

5. Suppose a market is in equilibrium and both demand and supply curves increase. What happens to the equilibrium price if demand increases more than supply?

6. Consider this statement: "Government involvement in markets is inherently inefficient." Do you agree or disagree? Explain.

7. Suppose coal-burning firms are emitting excessive pollution into the air. Suggest two ways the government can deal with this market failure.

8. Explain the impact of external costs and external benefits on resource allocation.

9. Why are public goods not produced in sufficient quantities by private markets?

10. Which of the following are public goods?
    a. Air bags
    b. Pencils
    c. Cycle helmets
    d. City streetlights
    e. Contact lenses

For Online Exercises, go to the Tucker Web site at www.cengage.com/economics/tucker.

✔ CHECKPOINT ANSWERS

Why the Higher Price for Ethanol Fuel?

As shown in Exhibit 9, an increase in demand leads to higher ethanol prices, while an increase in supply leads to lower prices. Because the overall direction of price in the ethanol market was up, the demand increase must have been larger than the supply increase. If you said demand increased by more than supply because consumers reacted more quickly than producers, **YOU ARE CORRECT.**

Is There Price Fixing at the Ticket Window?

Scalpers are evidence of a shortage whereby buyers are unable to find tickets at the official price. As shown in Exhibit 10, scalpers (often illegally) profit from the shortage by selling tickets above the official price. Shortages result when prices are restricted below equilibrium, as is the case when there is a price ceiling. If you said scalping occurs when there is a price ceiling because scalpers charge more than the official maximum price, **YOU ARE CORRECT.**

Should There Be a War on Drugs?

Drug use often affects not only the person using the drugs, but also other members of society. For example, higher crime rates are largely attributable to increased drug usage, and AIDS is often spread when users inject drugs using nonsterile needles. When one person's actions affect others not involved in the decision to buy or sell, the market fails to operate efficiently. If you said the market failure motivating government intervention in the drug market is externalities because drug users impose costs on nonusers, **YOU ARE CORRECT.**

EXHIBIT 9

SOURCE: © Cengage Learning 2014

EXHIBIT 10

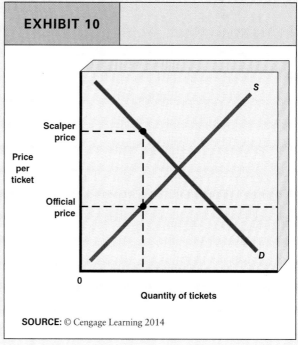

SOURCE: © Cengage Learning 2014

Sample Quiz

For an explanation of the correct answers, visit the Tucker Web site at www.cengage.com/economics/tucker.

1. A decrease in demand with the supply held constant leads to a(an)
   a. increased equilibrium price and an increased equilibrium quantity.
   b. decreased equilibrium price and a decreased equilibrium quantity.
   c. decreased equilibrium price and an increased equilibrium quantity.
   d. increased equilibrium price and a decreased equilibrium quantity.

2. An increased equilibrium price and a decreased equilibrium quantity results from a(an)
   a. decrease in demand.
   b. increase in supply.
   c. decrease in supply.
   d. increase in demand.

3. Assume no price ceiling exists in a market. Then a price ceiling is established below the market equilibrium. What would result?
   a. Shortage
   b. Equilibrium
   c. Surplus
   d. Exchange price

4. Which of the following is *not* an example of market failure?
   a. Lack of competition
   b. Externalities
   c. Efficient equilibrium
   d. Extreme income inequality

5. A cost imposed on people other than the consumers of a good or service is a
   a. price floor.
   b. negative externality.
   c. positive externality.
   d. price ceiling.

6. Suppose X and Y are substitutes. If the price of Y increases, how will this change the market equilibrium for X?
   a. Both equilibrium price and quantity decline.
   b. Both equilibrium price and quantity rise.

c. Equilibrium price declines, and equilibrium quantity rises.
   d. Equilibrium price rises, and equilibrium quantity falls.

7. If the cost of producing a good rises for sellers, how will this affect the market equilibrium for that good?
   a. Price will rise, and quantity will fall.
   b. Price will fall, and quantity will rise.
   c. Both price and quantity will rise.
   d. Both price and quantity will fall.

8. If goods A and B are complements and the price of good B rises, how will this affect the market equilibrium for good A?
   a. Price will rise, and quantity will fall.
   b. Price will fall, and quantity will rise.
   c. Both price and quantity will rise.
   d. Both price and quantity will fall.

9. Suppose Big-Cat and Fat-Cat are rival cat food brands and the price of Fat-Cat is reduced. Following this price drop, is there a shortage or a surplus of Big-Cat at the old price of Big-Cat?
   a. Shortage
   b. Surplus
   c. Neither because equilibrium exists
   d. Neither because a price drop cannot cause a shortage or a surplus

10. Suppose the average equilibrium monthly rental price of apartments and rooms in a college town has been steady at $600, but then the college expands enrollment from 10,000 to 12,000. Suddenly, there is a shortage of rental housing at the prevailing price of $600. Which of the following is *most* likely true?
    a. The shortage occurred because demand increased, and a new market equilibrium will feature higher rental prices and more rental units available on the market.
    b. The shortage occurred because supply increased, and a new market equilibrium will feature lower rental prices and fewer rental units available on the market.
    c. The shortage occurred because demand decreased, and a new market equilibrium

Sample Quiz *continued*

will feature lower rental prices and fewer rental units available on the market.

d. The shortage occurred because demand increased, and a new market equilibrium will feature higher rental prices and fewer rental units available on the market.

11. If a price ceiling is set at $10 and the equilibrium market price is $8, which of the prices below will consumers actually pay?
    a. $10
    b. $8
    c. $18
    d. $2

12. Suppose the state of California imposes a minimum wage of $10 per hour. In the entry-level labor market in California fast-food restaurants, the quantity of labor demanded at $10 per hour is 800,000 and the quantity of labor supplied is 1.2 million. Which of the following is *true*?
    a. There is a shortage of 800,000 workers in the labor market.
    b. There is a surplus of 400,000 workers in the labor market.
    c. There is a shortage of 400,000 workers in the labor market.
    d. There is a surplus of 1.2 million workers in the labor market.

13. Suppose the federal government imposes a price floor (support price) in the milk market at a price of $6 per gallon. If market quantity demanded at $6 is 1 billion gallons, and market quantity supplied is 1.5 billion gallons, which of the following is true?
    a. There is a shortage of 500 million gallons of milk, and the federal government will buy 1 billion gallons to maintain the $6 price.
    b. There is a surplus of 500 million gallons of milk, and the federal government will buy these 500 million gallons to maintain the $6 price.
    c. There is a shortage of 500 million gallons of milk, and the federal government will buy an additional 500 million gallons to maintain the $6 price.

d. There is a surplus of 1 billion gallons of milk, and the federal government will buy 1.5 billion gallons to maintain the $6 price.

14. Suppose the city of Arcata, California, imposes rent control so that rents cannot exceed $1,000 per month on one-bedroom rental units. Suppose $500 had also been the equilibrium rental price in Arcata before a huge new apartment complex was built in the nearby town of McKinleyville, where rents are $800 per month. Which of the following is *most* likely true?
    a. There will be a shortage of rental housing in Arcata at the rent control price of $1,000.
    b. There will be a lasting surplus of rental housing in Arcata after the new apartment complex is built in McKinleyville.
    c. The equilibrium rental price in Arcata will fall below $1,000; thus, rent control will not affect the rental market in Arcata.
    d. The equilibrium price of $1,000 per month in Arcata will not change.

15. Suppose the federal government provides wheat farmers with a price floor above the market equilibrium price of wheat, creating a surplus. Which of the following causes a reduction in the surplus of wheat?
    a. Elimination of the price floor
    b. An increase in the price of wheat
    c. A decrease in the demand for wheat
    d. An increase in the supply of wheat

16. If society allows firms to freely pollute the environment, which of the following is *true*?
    a. Market equilibrium output will be too high relative to the efficient output level.
    b. Market equilibrium output will be too low relative to the efficient output level.
    c. Market equilibrium output will be equivalent to the efficient output level.
    d. The efficient output level can be achieved by giving firms a subsidy for the pollution they generate.

17. If there are external benefits for good X, which of the following is *true*?

Sample Quiz *continued*

a. The socially efficient amount of good X can be achieved if society taxes consumers of good X.

b. The socially efficient amount of good X can be achieved if society subsidizes consumers of good X.

c. The socially efficient amount of good X will be equivalent to the free market equilibrium quantity.

d. The socially efficient amount of good X does not exist.

18. Suppose the federal government imposes a new pollution tax of $0.01 per kilowatt-hour of electricity on coal-fired power producers. Which of the following describes how this tax will affect the market for electricity served by these power plants?

a. Demand for electricity will decrease.

b. Demand for electricity will increase.

c. The supply of electricity will decrease.

d. The supply of electricity will increase.

19. Why don't competitive markets do a good job providing public goods?

a. Because people do not receive benefits from public goods

b. Because firms cannot produce enough goods to satisfy market demand

c. Because public goods generate negative externalities and pollution taxes reduce the incentive for firms to supply public goods

d. Because it is difficult to exclude people from gaining benefits from public goods without paying for them; so market demand does not reflect the benefits to society from the public good

20. Which of the following is *not* an example of market failure?

a. Lack of competition

b. Externalities

c. Efficient equilibrium

d. Extreme income inequality

Applying Supply and Demand Analysis to Health Care

4

One out of every six dollars spent in the United States is spent for health care services. This is a greater percentage than in any other industrialized country.[1] And in 2010, historic health care legislation was enacted to dramatically reform the U.S. system. The topic of health care arouses deep emotions and generates intense media coverage. How can we understand many of the important health care issues? One approach is to listen to the normative statements made by politicians and other concerned citizens. Another approach is to use supply and demand theory to analyze the issue. Here again, the objective is to bring textbook theory to life and use it to provide you with a deeper understanding of third-party health service markets.

4A-1 The Impact of Health Insurance

There is a downward-sloping demand curve for health care services just as there is for other goods and services. Following the same law of demand that applies to cars, clothing, entertainment, and other goods and services, movements along the demand curve for health care occur because consumers respond to changes in the price of health care. As shown in Exhibit A-1, we assume that health care, including doctor visits, medicine, hospital bills, and other medical services, can be measured in units of health care. Without health insurance, consumers buy Q_1 units of health care services per year at a price of P_1 per unit. Assuming supply curve S represents the quantity supplied, the market is in equilibrium at point A. At this point, the total cost of health care can be computed by the price of health care (P_1) times the quantity demanded (Q_1) or represented geometrically by the rectangle $0P_1AQ_1$.

Analysis of the demand curve for health care is complicated by the way health care is financed. About 80 percent of all health care is paid for by *third parties*, including private insurance companies and government programs, such as Medicare and Medicaid. The price of health care services therefore depends on the *copayment rate*, which is the percentage of the cost of services consumers pay out-of-pocket. To understand the impact, it is more realistic to assume consumers are insured and extend the analysis represented in Exhibit A-1. Because patients pay only 20 percent of the bill, the quantity of health care demanded in the figure increases to Q_2 at a lower price of P_2. At point B on the demand curve, insured consumers pay an amount equal to rectangle $0P_2BQ_2$, and insurers pay an amount represented by rectangle P_2P_3CB. Health care providers respond by increasing the quantity supplied from point A to point C on the supply curve S, where the quantity supplied equals the quantity demanded of Q_2. The reason there is no shortage in the health

---

[1]U.S. Census Bureau, *Statistical Abstract of the United States*, 2011, http://www.census.gov/compendia/statab, Table 1301.

EXHIBIT A-1	The Impact of Insurance on the Health Care Market

Without health insurance, the market is in equilibrium at point A, with a price of P_1 and a quantity demanded of Q_1. Total spending is $0P_1AQ_1$. With copayment health insurance, consumers pay the lower price of P_2, and the quantity demanded increases to Q_2. Total health care costs rise to $0P_3CQ_2$, with $0P_2BQ_2$ paid by consumers and P_2P_3CB paid by insurers. As a result, the quantity supplied increases from point A to point C, where it equals the quantity demanded of Q_2.

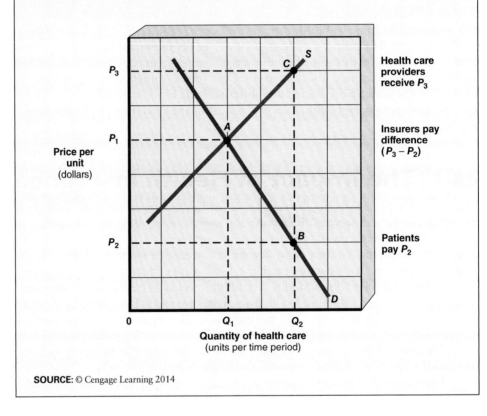

Health care providers receive P_3

Insurers pay difference $(P_3 - P_2)$

Patients pay P_2

Price per unit (dollars)

Quantity of health care (units per time period)

SOURCE: © Cengage Learning 2014

care market is that the combined payments from the insured consumers and insurers equal the total payment required for the movement upward along the supply curve. Stated in terms of rectangles, the total health care payment of $0P_3CQ_2$ equals $0P_2BQ_2$ paid by consumers plus P_2P_3CB paid by insurers.

> **CONCLUSION:** *Compared to a health care market without insurance, the quantity demanded, the quantity supplied, and the total cost of health care are increased by copayment health care insurance.*

Finally, note that Exhibit A-1 represents an overall or general model of the health care market. Individual health care markets are subject to *market failure*. For example, there would be a lack of competition if hospitals, doctors, health maintenance organizations (HMOs), or drug companies conspired to fix prices. Externalities provide another source of market failure, as illustrated previously for vaccinations in Exhibit 8(b). We are also concerned that health care be distributed in a fair way. This concern explains why the government Medicare and Medicaid programs help the elderly and poor afford health care.

4A-2 Shifts in the Demand for Health Care

While changes in the price of health care cause movements along the demand curve, other factors can cause the demand curve to shift. The following are some of the nonprice determinants that can change the demand for health care.

4A-2a NUMBER OF BUYERS

As the population increases, the demand for health care increases. In addition to the total number of people, the distribution of older people in the population is important. As more people move into the 65-and-older age group, the demand for health care services becomes greater because older people have more frequent and prolonged spells of illness. An increase in substance abuse involving alcohol, tobacco, or drugs also increases the demand for health care. For example, if the percentage of babies born into drug-prone families increases, the demand for health care will shift rightward.

4A-2b TASTES AND PREFERENCES

Changes in consumer attitudes toward health care can also change demand. For example, television, movies, magazines, and advertising may be responsible for changes in people's preferences for cosmetic surgery. Moreover, medical science has improved so much that we believe there must be a cure for most ailments. As a result, consumers are willing to buy larger quantities of medical services at each possible price.

Doctors also influence consumer preferences by prescribing treatment. It is often argued that some doctors guard against malpractice suits or boost their incomes by ordering more tests or office visits than are really needed. Some estimates suggest that fraud and abuse account for about 10 percent of total health care spending. These studies reveal that as many as one-third of some procedures are inappropriate.

4A-2c INCOME

Health care is a normal good. Rising inflation-adjusted incomes of consumers in the United States cause the demand curve for health care services to shift to the right. On the other hand, if real median family income remains unchanged, there is no influence on the demand curve.

4A-2d PRICES OF SUBSTITUTES

The prices of medical goods and services that are substitutes can change and, in turn, influence the demand for other medical services. For example, treatment of a back problem by a chiropractor is an alternative for many of the treatments provided by orthopedic doctors. If the price of orthopedic therapy rises, then some people will switch to treatment by a chiropractor. As a result, the demand curve for chiropractic therapy shifts rightward.

4A-3 Shifts in the Supply of Health Care

Changes in the following nonprice factors change the supply of health care.

4A-3a NUMBER OF SELLERS

Sellers of health care include hospitals, nursing homes, physicians in private practice, HMOs, drug companies, chiropractors, psychologists, and a host of other suppliers. To ensure the quality and safety of health care, virtually every facet of the industry is regulated and licensed by the government or controlled by the American Medical Association (AMA). Primarily through medical school accreditation and licensing requirements, the AMA limits the number of people practicing medicine. The federal Food and Drug Administration (FDA) requires testing that delays the introduction of new drugs. Tighter restrictions on the number of sellers shift the health care supply curve leftward, and reduced restrictions shift the supply curve rightward.

4A-3b RESOURCE PRICES

An increase in the costs of resources underlying the supply of health care shifts the supply curve leftward. By far the single most important factor behind increasing health care spending has been technological change. New diagnostic, surgical, and therapeutic equipment is used extensively in the health care industry, and the result is higher costs. Wages, salaries, and other costs, such as the costs of malpractice suits, also influence the supply curve. If hospitals, for example, are paying higher prices for inputs used to produce health care, the supply curve shifts to the left because the same quantities may be supplied only at higher prices.

chapter 5

Price Elasticity of Demand and Supply

Elasticity concerns how *sensitive* changes in quantity are to changes in price. Suppose you are the manager of the Steel Porcupines rock group. You are considering raising your ticket price, and you wonder how the fans will react. You have studied economics and know the law of demand. When the price of a ticket rises, the quantity demanded goes down, ceteris paribus. So you really need to know how many tickets fans will purchase if the band boosts the ticket price. If the lawn seating ticket price for a Steel Porcupines concert is $25, you will sell 20,000 tickets. At $30 per ticket, only 10,000 tickets will be sold. Thus, a $5 increase per ticket cuts the number of tickets sold in half.

Which ticket price should you choose? Is it better to charge a higher ticket price and sell fewer tickets or to charge a lower ticket price and sell more tickets? The answer depends on changes in *total revenue*, or sales, as we move upward along points on the Steel Porcupines' demand curve. At $30 per ticket, sales will be $300,000. If you charge $25, the group will take in $500,000 for a concert. Okay, you say, what happens at $20 per ticket?

This chapter teaches you to calculate the percentage change in the quantity demanded when the price changes by a given percentage. Then you will see how this relates to total revenue. This knowledge of the sensitivity of demand is vital for pricing and targeting markets for goods and services. Next, you will see how changes in consumer income and the prices of related goods affect percentage changes in the quantity demanded. The chapter concludes by relating the concept of price elasticity to supply and the impact of taxation.

In this chapter, you will learn to solve these economics puzzles:

- Can total revenue from a Steel Porcupines concert remain unchanged regardless of changes in the ticket price?
- How sensitive is the quantity of cigarettes demanded to changes in the price of cigarettes?
- What would happen to the sales of Mercedes, BMWs, and Jaguars in the United States if Congress prohibited sales of luxury Japanese cars in this country?
- Can Honda compete with itself?

5-1 Price Elasticity of Demand

In Chapter 3, when you studied the demand curve, the focus was on the law of demand. This law states there is an inverse relationship between the price and the quantity demanded of a good or service. In this chapter, the emphasis is on measuring the *relative size* of changes in the price and the quantity demanded. Now we ask: By *what percentage* does the quantity demanded rise when the price falls by, say, 10 percent?

5-1a THE PRICE ELASTICITY OF DEMAND MIDPOINTS FORMULA

Price elasticity of demand

The ratio of the percentage change in the quantity demanded of a product to a percentage change in its price.

Economists use a price elasticity of demand formula to measure the degree of consumer responsiveness, or sensitivity, to a change in price. Price elasticity of demand is the ratio of the percentage change in the quantity demanded of a product to a percentage change in its price. Price elasticity of demand explains how strongly consumers react to a change in price. Think of quantity demanded as a rubber band. Price elasticity of demand measures how "stretchy" the rubber band is when the price changes. Suppose a university's enrollment drops by 20 percent because tuition rises by 10 percent. Therefore, the price elasticity of demand is 2 (−20 percent/+10 percent). The number 2 means that the quantity demanded (enrollment) changes 2 percent for each 1 percent change in price (tuition). Note there should be a minus sign in front of the 2 because, under the law of demand, price and quantity move in *opposite* directions. However, economists drop the minus sign because we know from the law of demand that quantity demanded and price are inversely related.

The number 2 is an *elasticity coefficient*, which economists use to measure the degree of elasticity. The elasticity formula is

$$E_d = \frac{\text{percentage change in quantity demanded}}{\text{percentage change in price}}$$

where E_d is the elasticity of demand coefficient. Here you must take care. *There is a problem using this formula.* Let's return to the rock group example from the chapter preview. Suppose Steel Porcupines raises its ticket price from $25 to $30 and the number of seats sold falls from 20,000 to 10,000. We can compute the elasticity coefficient as

$$E_d = \frac{\%\Delta Q}{\%\Delta P} = \frac{\dfrac{10,000 - 20,000}{20,000}}{\dfrac{30 - 25}{25}} = \frac{50\%}{20\%} = 2.5$$

Now consider the elasticity coefficient computed between these same points on Steel Porcupines' demand curve when the price is lowered. Starting at $30 per ticket and lowering the ticket price to $25 causes the number of seats sold to rise from 10,000 to 20,000. In this case, the rock group computes a much different elasticity coefficient, as

$$E_d = \frac{\%\Delta Q}{\%\Delta P} = \frac{\dfrac{20,000 - 10,000}{10,000}}{\dfrac{25 - 30}{30}} = \frac{100\%}{17\%} = 5.9$$

There is a reason for the different elasticity coefficients between the same two points on a demand curve (2.5 if price is raised, 5.9 if price is cut). The natural approach is to select the initial point as the base and then compute a percentage change. But price elasticity of demand involves changes between two possible initial base points (P_1, Q_1 or P_2, Q_2). Economists solve this problem of different base points by using the *midpoints* as the base points of changes in prices and quantities demanded. The *midpoints formula* for price elasticity of demand is

$$E_d = \frac{\text{change in quantity}}{\text{sum of quantities}/2} \div \frac{\text{change in price}}{\text{sum of prices}/2}$$

which can be expressed as

$$E_d = \frac{\%\Delta Q}{\%\Delta P} = \frac{\dfrac{Q_2 - Q_1}{Q_1 + Q_2}}{\dfrac{P_2 - P_1}{P_1 + P_2}}$$

where Q_1 represents the first quantity demanded, Q_2 represents the second quantity demanded, and P_1 and P_2 are the first and second prices. Expressed this way, we divide the change in quantity demanded by the *average* quantity demanded. Then this value is divided by the change in the price divided by the *average* price.[1]

It does not matter if Q_1 or P_1 is the first or second number in each term because we are finding averages. Also note that you can drop the 2 as a divisor of both the ($Q_1 + Q_2$) and ($P_1 + P_2$) terms because the 2s in the numerator and the denominator cancel out. Now we can use the midpoints formula to calculate the price elasticity of demand of 3.7 regardless of whether Steel Porcupines raises the ticket price from $25 to $30 or lowers it from $30 to $25.

$$E_d = \frac{\dfrac{Q_2 - Q_1}{Q_1 + Q_2}}{\dfrac{P_2 - P_1}{P_1 + P_2}} = \frac{\dfrac{10,000 - 20,000}{20,000 + 10,000}}{\dfrac{30 - 25}{25 + 30}} = \frac{33\%}{9\%} = 3.7$$

and

---

[1]The midpoints formula is also commonly called the *arc elasticity formula*.

$$E_d = \frac{\dfrac{Q_2 - Q_1}{Q_1 + Q_2}}{\dfrac{P_2 - P_1}{P_1 + P_2}} = \frac{\dfrac{20{,}000 - 10{,}000}{10{,}000 + 20{,}000}}{\dfrac{25 - 30}{30 + 25}} = \frac{33\%}{9\%} = 3.7$$

5-1b THE TOTAL REVENUE TEST OF PRICE ELASTICITY OF DEMAND

As reflected in the midpoints formula, the *responsiveness* of the quantity demanded to a change in price determines the value of the elasticity coefficient. There are three possibilities: (1) the numerator is greater than the denominator, (2) the numerator is less than the denominator, and (3) the numerator equals the denominator. Exhibit 1 presents three cases that the Steel Porcupines rock band may confront.

5-1c ELASTIC DEMAND ($E_D > 1$)

Suppose the Steel Porcupines' demand curve is as depicted in Exhibit 1(a). Using the above midpoints formula, which drops the 2 as a divisor, if the group lowers its ticket price from $30 to $20, the quantity demanded increases from 10,000 to 30,000. Using the midpoints formula, this means that a 20 percent reduction in ticket price brings a 50 percent increase in quantity demanded. Thus, $E_d = 2.5$, and demand is elastic. Elastic demand is a condition in which the percentage change in quantity demanded is greater than the percentage change in price. Demand is elastic when the elasticity coefficient is greater than 1. Because the percentage change in quantity demanded is greater than the percentage change in price, the drop in price causes total revenue (TR) to rise. Total revenue is the total number of dollars a firm earns from the sale of a good or service, which is equal to its price multiplied by the quantity demanded. Perhaps the simplest way to tell whether demand is elastic, unitary elastic, or inelastic is to observe the response of total revenue as the price of a product changes. For example, in Exhibit 1(a), the total revenue at $30 is $300,000. The total revenue at $20 is $600,000. Compare the shaded rectangles under the demand curve, representing total revenue at each price. The gray area is an amount of total revenue unaffected by the price change. Note that the green shaded area gained at $20 per ticket ($400,000) is greater than the red shaded area lost at $30 per ticket ($100,000). This net gain of $300,000 causes the total revenue to increase by this amount when Steel Porcupines lowers the ticket price from $30 to $20.

Elastic demand

A condition in which the percentage change in quantity demanded is greater than the percentage change in price.

Total revenue

The total number of dollars a firm earns from the sale of a good or service, which is equal to its price multiplied by the quantity demanded.

5-1d INELASTIC DEMAND ($E_D < 1$)

The demand curve in Exhibit 1(b) is inelastic. The quantity demanded is less responsive to a change in price. Here a fall in the Steel Porcupines' ticket price from $30 to $20 causes the quantity demanded to increase by just 5,000 tickets (from 20,000 to 25,000 tickets). Using the midpoints formula, a 20 percent fall in the ticket price causes an 11 percent rise in the quantity demanded. This means $E_d = 0.55$ and demand is inelastic. Inelastic demand is a condition in which the percentage change in quantity demanded is less than the percentage change in price. Demand is inelastic when the elasticity coefficient is less than 1. When demand is inelastic, the drop in price causes total revenue to fall from $600,000 to $500,000. Note the net change in the shaded rectangles.

Inelastic demand

A condition in which the percentage change in quantity demanded is less than the percentage change in price.

EXHIBIT 1	The Impact of a Decrease in Price on Total Revenue

These three different demand curve graphs show the relationship between a decrease in concert ticket price and a change in total revenue.

In part (a), the demand curve is elastic between points *A* and *B*. The percentage change in quantity demanded is greater than the percentage change in price, $E_d > 1$. As the ticket price falls from $30 to $20, total revenue increases from $300,000 to $600,000.

Part (b) shows a case in which the demand curve is inelastic between points *C* and *D*. The percentage change in quantity demanded is less than the percentage change in price, $E_d < 1$. As the ticket price decreases over the same range, total revenue falls from $600,000 to $500,000.

Part (c) shows a unitary elastic demand curve. The percentage change in quantity demanded equals the percentage change in price between points *E* and *F*, $E_d = 1$. As the concert ticket price decreases, total revenue remains unchanged at $600,000.

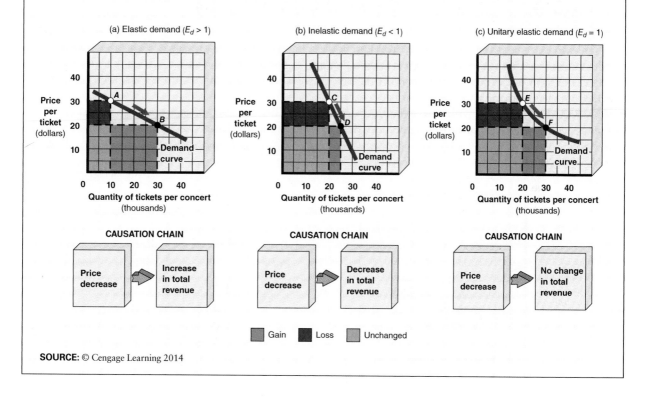

SOURCE: © Cengage Learning 2014

5-1e Unitary Elastic Demand ($E_D = 1$)

An interesting case exists when a demand curve is neither elastic nor inelastic. Exhibit 1(c) shows a demand curve for which any percentage change in price along the curve causes an exact proportional change in quantity demanded. When this situation occurs, the total amount of money spent on a good or service does not vary with changes in price. If Steel Porcupines drops the ticket price from $30 to $20, the quantity demanded rises from 20,000 to 30,000. Therefore, using the midpoints formula, a 20 percent decrease in price brings about a 20 percent

Unitary elastic demand

A condition in which the percentage change in quantity demanded is equal to the percentage change in price.

increase in quantity demanded. If this is the case, demand is unitary elastic ($E_d = 1$), and the total revenue remains unchanged at $600,000. Unitary elastic demand is defined as a condition in which the percentage change in quantity demanded is equal to the percentage change in price. Because the percentage change in price equals the percentage change in quantity, total revenue does not change regardless of changes in price.

5-1f PERFECTLY ELASTIC DEMAND ($E_D = \infty$)

Two extreme cases are shown in Exhibit 2. These represent the limits between which the three demand curves explained above fall. Suppose for the sake of

EXHIBIT 2	Perfectly Elastic and Perfectly Inelastic Demand

Here two extreme demand curves for Steel Porcupines concert tickets are presented. Part (a) shows a demand curve that is a horizontal line. Such a demand curve is perfectly elastic. At $20 per ticket, the Steel Porcupines can sell as many concert tickets as it wishes. At any price above $20, the quantity demanded falls from an infinite number to zero.

Part (b) shows a demand curve that is a vertical line. This demand curve is perfectly inelastic. No matter what the ticket price is, the quantity demanded remains unchanged at 20,000 tickets.

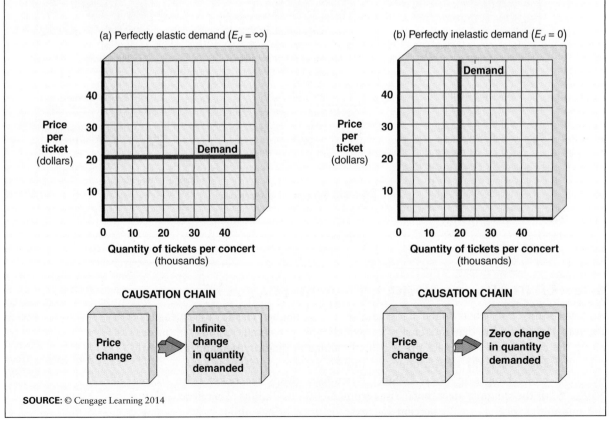

SOURCE: © Cengage Learning 2014

argument that a demand curve is perfectly horizontal, as shown in Exhibit 2(a). At a price of $20, buyers are willing to buy as many tickets as the Steel Porcupines band is willing to offer for sale. At higher prices, buyers buy nothing. For example, at $20.01 per ticket or higher, buyers will buy zero tickets. If so, $E_d = \infty$, and demand is perfectly elastic. Perfectly elastic demand is a condition in which a small percentage change in price brings about an infinite percentage change in quantity demanded.

Perfectly elastic demand

A condition in which a small percentage change in price brings about an infinite percentage change in quantity demanded.

5-1g PERFECTLY INELASTIC DEMAND ($E_D = 0$)

Exhibit 2(b) shows the other extreme case, which is a perfectly vertical demand curve. No matter how high or low the Steel Porcupines' ticket price is, the quantity demanded is 20,000 tickets. Such a demand curve is perfectly inelastic, and $E_d = 0$. Perfectly inelastic demand is a condition in which the quantity demanded does not change as the price changes.

Exhibit 3 summarizes the ranges for price elasticity of demand.

Perfectly inelastic demand

A condition in which the quantity demanded does not change as the price changes.

EXHIBIT 3	Price Elasticity of Demand Terminology		
Elasticity coefficient	**Definition**	**Demand**	**Graph**
$E_d > 1$	Percentage change in quantity demanded is greater than the percentage change in price	Elastic	
$E_d < 1$	Percentage change in quantity demanded is less than the percentage change in price	Inelastic	
$E_d = 1$	Percentage change in quantity demanded is equal to the percentage change in price	Unitary elastic	
$E_d = \infty$	Percentage change in quantity demanded is infinite in relation to the percentage change in price	Perfectly elastic	
$E_d = 0$	Quantity demanded does not change as the price changes	Perfectly inelastic	

SOURCE: © Cengage Learning 2014

5-2 Price Elasticity of Demand Variations along a Demand Curve

The price elasticity of demand for a downward-sloping straight-line demand curve varies as we move along the curve. Look at Exhibit 4, which shows a linear demand curve in part (a) and the corresponding total revenue curve in part (b). Begin at $40 on the demand curve and move down to $35, to $30, to $25, and so on. The table in Exhibit 4 lists variations in the total revenue and the elasticity coefficient (E_d) at different ticket prices. As we move down the upper segment of the demand curve, price elasticity of demand falls, and total revenue rises. For example, measured over the price range of $35 to $30, the price elasticity of demand is 4.33, so this segment of demand is elastic ($E_d > 1$). Between these two prices, total revenue increases from $175,000 to $300,000. At $20, price elasticity is unitary elastic ($E_d = 1$), and total revenue is maximized at $400,000. As we move down the lower segment of the demand curve, price elasticity of demand falls below a value of 1.0, and total revenue falls. Over the price range of $15 to $10, for example, the price elasticity of demand is 0.45, and, therefore, this segment of demand is inelastic ($E_d < 1$). Between these two prices, total revenue decreases from $375,000 to $300,000.

> **CONCLUSION:** *The price elasticity coefficient of demand applies only to a specific range of prices.*

It is no coincidence that the demand curve in Exhibit 4(a) has elastic, unitary elastic, and inelastic segments. In fact, *any downward-sloping straight-line demand curve has ranges of all three of these types of price elasticity of demand.* As we move downward from the top of the demand curve, first there is an elastic range; next a unitary elastic range, and finally an inelastic range. Why? Recall that price elasticity of demand is a ratio of percentage changes. At the upper end of the demand curve, quantities demanded are lower, and prices are higher. A change of 1 unit in quantity demanded is a large percentage change. On the other hand, a $1 price change is a relatively small percentage change. At the lower end of the curve, the situation reverses. A 1-unit change in quantity demanded is a small percentage change. A $1 price change is a relatively larger percentage change. Now pause and refer back to parts (a) and (b) of Exhibit 1. If we examine changes in price along the entire length of these demand curves, we will find elastic, unitary elastic, and inelastic segments.

Exhibit 5 summarizes the relationships between elasticity, price change, and total revenue.

✓ CHECKPOINT

Will Fliers Flock to Low Summer Fares?

US Airways is concerned over low sales and announces special cuts in its fares this summer. The New York to Los Angeles fare, for example, is reduced from $500 to $420. Does US Airways think demand is elastic, unitary elastic, or inelastic?

EXHIBIT 4	The Variation in Elasticity and Total Revenue along a Hypothetical Demand Curve

Part (a) shows a straight-line demand curve and its three elasticity ranges. In the $40–$20 price range, demand is elastic. As price decreases in this range, total revenue increases. At $20, demand is unitary elastic, and total revenue is at its maximum. In the $20–$5 price range, demand is inelastic. As price decreases in this range, total revenue decreases. The total revenue (TR) curve is plotted in part (b) to trace its relationship to price elasticity.

(a) Price elasticity of demand ranges

(b) Total revenue curve

Calculation of Total Revenue and Elasticity along a Hypothetical Demand Curve

Price	Quantity (thousands of tickets)	Total Revenue (thousands of dollars)	Elasticity Coefficient (Ed)	Price Elasticity of Demand
$40	0	$0		
			15.00	Elastic
35	5	175		
			4.33	Elastic
30	10	300		
			2.20	Elastic
25	15	375		
			1.29	Elastic
20	20	400	1.00	Unitary elastic
			0.78	Inelastic
15	25	375		
			0.45	Inelastic
10	30	300		
			0.23	Inelastic
5	35	175		

SOURCE: © Cengage Learning 2014

EXHIBIT 5	Relationships among Elasticity, Price Change, and Total Revenue		
Price elasticity of demand	**Elasticity coefficient**	**Price**	**Total revenue**
Elastic	$E_d > 1$	↑	↓
Elastic	$E_d > 1$	↓	↑
Unitary elastic	$E_d = 1$	↑↓	No change
Inelastic	$E_d < 1$	↑	↑
Inelastic	$E_d < 1$	↓	↓

SOURCE: © Cengage Learning 2014

5-3 Determinants of Price Elasticity of Demand

Economists have estimated price elasticity of demand for various goods and services. Exhibit 6 presents some of these estimates, and as you can see, the elasticity coefficients vary a great deal. For example, the demand for automobiles and for chinaware is elastic. On the other hand, the demand for jewelry and watches and for theater and opera tickets is inelastic. The demand for tires is approximately unitary elastic. Why do the price elasticities of demand for these products vary so much? The following factors cause these differences.

5-3a AVAILABILITY OF SUBSTITUTES

By far, the most important influence on price elasticity of demand is the availability of substitutes. Demand is more elastic for a good or service with close substitutes. If the price of cars rises, consumers can switch to buses, trains, bicycles, and walking. The more public transportation is available, the more responsive quantity demanded is to a change in the price of cars. When consumers have limited alternatives, the demand for a good or service is more price inelastic. If the price of tobacco rises, people addicted to it have few substitutes because not smoking is unappealing to most users.

> **CONCLUSION:** *The price elasticity coefficient of demand is directly related to the availability of good substitutes for a product.*

Price elasticity also depends on the market used to measure demand. For example, studies show the price elasticity of Chevrolets is greater than that of automobiles in general. Chevrolets compete with other cars sold by GM, Ford, Chrysler, Toyota, and other automakers and with buses and trains—all of which are substitutes for Chevrolets. But using the broad class of cars eliminates these specific types of cars as competitors. Instead, substitutes for automobiles include buses and trains,

EXHIBIT 6	Estimated Price Elasticities of Demand	
	Elasticity coefficient	
Item	Short run	Long run
Automobiles	1.87	2.24
Chinaware	1.54	2.55
Movies	0.87	3.67
Tires	0.86	1.19
Commuter rail fares	0.62	1.59
Jewelry and watches	0.41	0.67
Medical care	0.31	0.92
Housing	0.30	1.88
Gasoline	0.20	0.70
Theater and opera tickets	0.18	0.31
Foreign travel	0.14	1.77
Air travel	0.10	2.40

SOURCES: Robert Archibald and Robert Gillingham, "An Analysis of the Short Run Consumer Demand for Gasoline Using Household Survey Data," *Review of Economics and Statistics* 62 (November 1980): 622–628; Hendrik S. Houthakker and Lester D. Taylor, *Consumer Demand in the United States: Analyses and Projections* (Cambridge, MA: Harvard University Press, 1970, pp. 56–149, Richard Voith, "The Long-Run Elasticity of Demand for Commuter Rail Transportation," *Journal of Urban Economics* 30 (November 1991): 360–372.

which are also substitutes for Chevrolets. In short, there are more close substitutes for Chevrolets than there are for all cars.

 CHECKPOINT

Can Trade Sanctions Affect Elasticity of Demand for Cars?

Assume Congress prohibits the sale of Japanese luxury cars, such as Lexus, Acura, and Infiniti, in the United States. How would this affect the price elasticity of demand for Mercedes, BMWs, and Jaguars in the United States?

5-3b SHARE OF BUDGET SPENT ON THE PRODUCT

When the price of salt changes, consumers pay little attention. Why should they notice? The price of salt or matches can double, and this purchase will remain a small percentage of one's budget. If, however, college tuition, the price of dinners at restaurants, or housing prices double, people will look for alternatives. These goods and services account for a large part of people's budgets.

> **CONCLUSION:** *The price elasticity coefficient of demand is directly related to the percentage of one's budget spent for a good or service.*

5-3c ADJUSTMENT TO A PRICE CHANGE OVER TIME

Exhibit 6 separates the elasticity coefficients into short-run and long-run categories. As time passes, buyers can respond fully to a change in the price of a product by finding more substitutes. Consider the demand for gasoline. In the short run, people find it hard to cut back the amount they buy when the price rises sharply. They are accustomed to driving back and forth to work alone in their cars. The typical short-run response is to cut luxury travel and reduce speed on trips. If high prices persist over time, car buyers will find ways to cut back. They can buy cars with better fuel economy (more miles per gallon), form car pools, and ride buses or commuter trains. This explains why the short-run elasticity coefficient of gasoline in the exhibit is more inelastic at 0.2 than the long-run elasticity coefficient of 0.7.

> **CONCLUSION:** *In general, the price elasticity coefficient of demand is higher the longer a price change persists.*

5-4 Other Elasticity Measures

The elasticity concept has other applications beyond calculating the price elasticity of demand. Broadly defined, it is a technique for measuring the response of one variable to changes in some other variable.

5-4a INCOME ELASTICITY OF DEMAND

Income elasticity of demand

The ratio of the percentage change in the quantity demanded of a good or service to a given percentage change in income.

Recall from Chapter 3 that an increase in income can increase demand (shift the demand curve rightward) for a normal good or service and decrease demand (shift the demand curve leftward) for an inferior good or service. To measure exactly how consumption responds to changes in income, economists calculate the income elasticity of demand. Income elasticity of demand is the ratio of the percentage change in the quantity demanded of a good or service to a given percentage change in income. We use a midpoints formula similar to the one we used for calculating price elasticity of demand:

$$E_I = \frac{\text{percentage change in quantity demanded}}{\text{percentage change in income}}$$

$$E_I = \frac{\%\Delta Q}{\%\Delta I} = \frac{\dfrac{Q_2 - Q_1}{Q_1 + Q_2}}{\dfrac{I_2 - I_1}{I_1 + I_2}}$$

Where E_I is the income elasticity of demand coefficient, Q_1 and Q_2 represent quantities demanded before and after the income change, and I_1 and I_2 represent income before and after the income change.

Cigarette Smoking Price Elasticity of Demand

Applicable Concept: price elasticity of demand

Tobacco use is one of the chief preventable causes of death in the world. Since 1964, health warnings have been mandated in the United States on tobacco advertising, including billboards and printed advertising. In 1971, television advertising was prohibited. Most states have banned smoking in state buildings, and the federal government has restricted smoking in federal offices and military facilities. In 1998, the Senate engaged in heated debate over proposed legislation to curb smoking by teenagers. This bill would have raised the price of cigarettes by $1.10 a pack over five years, and the tobacco industry would have paid $369 billion over the next 25 years. Opponents argued that this price increase would be a massive tax on low-income Americans that would generate huge revenues to finance additional government programs and spending. Proponents countered that the bill was not about taxes. Instead, the bill was an attack on the death march of Americans who die early from tobacco-related diseases. Ultimately, the Senate was so divided on the issue that it was impossible, at least for that year, to pass a tobacco bill.

Estimates of the price elasticity of demand for cigarettes in the United States and other high-income countries fall in the inelastic range of 0.62. This means that if prices rise by 10 percent, cigarette consumption will fall by about 6 percent.[1] Moreover, estimates of the price elasticity of demand range significantly across states from 2.00 (Kentucky) to 0.09 (Mississippi).[2] The price elasticity of demand for cigarettes also appears to vary by education. Less educated adults are more responsive to price changes than better-educated adults. This finding supports the theory that less educated people are more present-oriented, or "myopic," than people with more education. Thus, less educated individuals tend to be more influenced by current changes in the price of a pack of cigarettes.[3] Another study in 2000 confirmed that education has strong negative effects on the quantity of cigarettes smoked, especially for high-income individuals. The presence of young children reduces smoking, with the effect most pronounced for women.[4]

A study published in *Health Economics* estimated the relationship between cigarette smoking and price for 34,145 respondents aged 15–29. The price elasticity of smoking was inelastic and varied inversely with age: 0.83 for ages 15–17, 0.52 for ages 18–20, 0.37 for ages 21–23, 0.20 for ages 24–26, and 0.09 for ages 27–29. Thus, younger people were more likely to reduce the number of cigarettes smoked in response to increased prices.[5]

> **Analyze the Issue**
>
> According to the above discussion, what factors influence the price elasticity of demand for cigarettes? What other factors not mentioned in the article might influence the price elasticity of demand for cigarettes?

1. Jon P. Nelson, "Cigarette Demand, Structural Change, and Advertising Bans: International Evidence, 1970–1995," *Contribution to Economic Analysis and Policy* 2, no. 1, 2003, article 10.
2. Craig A. Gallet, "Health Information and Cigarette Consumption: Supply and Spatial Consideration," *Empirica* 33, no. 1, March 2006, pp. 35–47.
3. Frank Chaloupka et al., "Tax, Price and Cigarette Smoking," *Tobacco Control* 11, no. 1, March 2002, pp. 62–73.
4. Joni Hersch, "Gender, Income Levels, and the Demand for Cigarettes," *Journal of Risk and Uncertainty* 21, no. 2–3, November 2000, pp. 263–282.
5. Jeffrey E. Harris and Sandra W. Chan, "The Continuum of Addiction: Cigarette Smoking in Relation to Price among Americans Aged 15–29," *Health Economics* 8, no. 1, February 1999, pp. 81–86.

Source: © Cengage Learning 2014

For a *normal* good or service, the income elasticity of demand is *positive*, $E_I > 0$. Recall that for this type of good, demand and income move in the same direction. Thus, the variables in the numerator and denominator change in the same direction. For an *inferior* good or service, the reverse is true, and the income elasticity of demand is *negative*, $E_I < 0$.

Why is the income elasticity coefficient important? Returning to our rock group example, the Steel Porcupines band needs to know the impact of a recession on ticket sales. During a downturn when consumers' incomes fall, if a rock concert is a *normal good*, the quantity of ticket sales falls. Conversely, if a rock concert is an *inferior good*, the quantity of ticket sales rises. To illustrate, suppose consumers' incomes increase from \$1,000 to \$1,250 per month. As a result, the quantity of tickets demanded increases from 10,000 to 15,000. Based on these data, is a rock concert a normal or an inferior good? We compute as follows:

$$E_I = \frac{\dfrac{Q_2 - Q_1}{Q_1 + Q_2}}{\dfrac{I_2 - I_1}{I_1 + I_2}} = \frac{\dfrac{15,000 - 10,000}{10,000 + 15,000}}{\dfrac{1,250 - 1,000}{1,250 + 1,000}} = \frac{0.20}{0.11} = 1.8$$

The computed income elasticity of demand coefficient of 1.8 summarizes the relationship between changes in rock concert ticket purchases and changes in income. First, E_I is a positive number; therefore, a rock concert is a normal good because people buy more when their incomes rise. Second, ticket purchases are very responsive to changes in income. When income rises by 11 percent, ticket sales increase by more (20 percent).

Exhibit 7 lists estimated income elasticity of demand for selected products.

5-4b CROSS-ELASTICITY OF DEMAND

In Chapter 3, we learned that a change in the price of one good, say, Y, can cause the consumption of another good, say, X, to change (see prices of related goods in Exhibit 5 in Chapter 3). In Exhibit 1(b) in Chapter 4, for example, a sharp

EXHIBIT 7	Estimated Income Elasticities of Demand	
	Elasticity coefficient	
Item	**Short run**	**Long run**
Potatoes	N.A.	0.81
Furniture	2.60	0.53
Dental services	0.38	1.00
Automobiles	5.50	1.07
Physician services	0.28	1.15
Clothing	0.95	1.17
Shoes	0.90	1.50
Gasoline and oil	0.55	1.36
Jewelry and watches	1.00	1.60
Toilet articles	0.25	3.74

SOURCES: Hendrik S. Houthakker and Lester D. Taylor, *Consumer Demand in the United States: Analyses and Projections* (Cambridge, MA: Harvard University Press, 1970); Dale M. Helen, "The Structure of Food Demand: Interrelatedness and Duality," *American Journal of Agricultural Economics* 64, no. 2 (May 1982): 213–221.

rise in the price of gasoline (a complement) causes the number of gas guzzlers purchased to decline. This responsiveness of the quantity demanded to changes in the price of some other good is estimated by the cross-elasticity of demand. Cross-elasticity of demand is the ratio of the percentage change in the quantity demanded of a good or service to a given percentage change in the price of another good or service. Again, we use the midpoints formula as follows to compute the cross-elasticity coefficient of demand:

$$E_c = \frac{\text{percentage change in quantity demanded of one good}}{\text{percentage change in price of another good}}$$

$$E_c = \frac{\%\Delta Q_x}{\%\Delta P_Y} = \frac{\dfrac{Q_{x_2} - Q_{x_1}}{Q_{x_1} + Q_{x_2}}}{\dfrac{P_{Y_2} - P_{Y_1}}{P_{Y_1} + P_{Y_2}}}$$

where E_c is the cross-elasticity coefficient, Q_1 and Q_2 represent quantities before and after the price of another good or service changes, and P_1 and P_2 represent the price of another good or service before and after the price change.

The cross-elasticity coefficient reveals whether a good or service is a *substitute* or a *complement*. For example, suppose Coke increases its price 10 percent, which causes consumers to buy 5 percent more Pepsi. The cross-elasticity of demand for Pepsi is a *positive* 0.50 (+5 percent/+10 percent). Because $E_c > 0$, Coke and Pepsi are *substitutes* because the numerator and denominator variables change in the same direction. The larger the positive coefficient, the greater the substitutability between the two goods.

Now suppose there is a 50 percent increase in the price of motor oil and the quantity demanded of gasoline decreases by 10 percent. The cross-elasticity of demand for gasoline is a *negative* 0.20 (−10 percent/+50 percent). Since $E_c < 0$, these two goods are complements. The larger the negative coefficient, the greater the complementary relationship between the two goods. The variables in the numerator and denominator change in opposite directions.

5-4c PRICE ELASTICITY OF SUPPLY

The price elasticity of supply closely follows the price elasticity of demand concept. Price elasticity of supply is the ratio of the percentage change in the quantity supplied of a product to the percentage change in its price. This elasticity coefficient is calculated using the following formula:

$$E_s = \frac{\text{percentage change in quantity supplied}}{\text{percentage change in price}}$$

where E_s is the price elasticity of supply coefficient. Because price and quantity supplied change in the same direction, the elasticity coefficient is a positive value. Economists use terminology corresponding to that for the elasticity of demand. Supply is *elastic* when $E_s > 1$, *unit elastic* when $E_s = 1$, *inelastic* when $E_s < 1$, *perfectly elastic* when $E_s = \infty$, and *perfectly inelastic* when $E_s = 0$. Exhibit 8 shows three of these cases.

In Chapter 8, we will explain why the time period of analysis is a primary determinant of the shape of the supply curve. More specifically, it will be shown that price elasticity of supply is greater in the long run than in the short run. Thus, the long-run supply curve will be flatter.

Cross-elasticity of demand

The ratio of the percentage change in the quantity demanded of a good or service to a given percentage change in the price of another good or service.

Price elasticity of supply

The ratio of the percentage change in the quantity supplied of a product to the percentage change in its price.

EXHIBIT 8	Price Elasticity of Supply

This figure shows three supply curves. As shown in part (a), a small change in price changes the quantity supplied by an infinite amount: $E_s = \infty$. Part (b) shows the quantity supplied is unaffected by a change in price, $E_s = 0$, and supply is perfectly inelastic. In part (c), the percentage change in quantity supplied is equal to the percentage change in price: $E_s = 1$.

SOURCE: © Cengage Learning 2014

Exhibit 9 gives a summary of the three elasticity concepts presented in this section.

5-4d PRICE ELASTICITY AND THE IMPACT OF TAXATION

Who pays a tax levied on sellers of goods such as gasoline, cigarettes, and alcoholic beverages? One way to answer this question is to say that if the government places a tax on, say, gasoline, the gasoline companies pay the tax. They collect the tax when they sell gas and write the checks to the government for the tax. But this is not the whole story. Instead of looking simply at who writes the checks, economists use the elasticity concept to analyze who "really" pays a tax. Tax incidence is the share of a tax ultimately paid by consumers and sellers. In this section, we show that even though taxes are collected from sellers, buyers do not escape a share of the tax burden. The tax incidence depends on the price elasticities of demand and supply. Let's look at two examples.

Tax incidence

The share of a tax ultimately paid by consumers and sellers.

Suppose the federal government decides to raise the gasoline tax $0.50 per gallon. Exhibit 10 shows the impact of the tax on different demand curves. At E_1 in part (a), the equilibrium price before the tax is $3.00 per gallon and the equilibrium quantity is 30 million gallons per day. The effect of the tax is to shift the supply curve leftward from S_1 to S_2. From the sellers' viewpoint, the cost of each gallon of gasoline increases $0.50 per gallon at any possible selling price. The effect is exactly the same as if the price of crude oil or any resource used to produce gasoline increased.

Sellers would like consumers to pay the entire amount of the tax. This would occur if consumers would pay $3.50 per gallon for the same 30 million gallons per day they purchased before the tax. But the leftward shift in supply establishes a new equilibrium at E_2. The new equilibrium price is $3.25 per gallon, and the equilibrium quantity falls to 25 million gallons per day. At E_2, the entire shaded area

EXHIBIT 9	Summary of Other Elasticity Concepts		
Type	**Definition**	**Elasticity coefficient possibilities**	**Terminology**
Income elasticity of demand	$\dfrac{\text{Percentage change in quantity demanded}}{\text{Percentage change in income}}$	$E_I > 0$	Normal good
		$E_I < 0$	Inferior good
		$E_I > 1$	Income elastic
		$E_I < 1$	Income inelastic
		$E_I = 1$	Income unitary elastic
Cross-elasticity of demand	$\dfrac{\text{Percentage change in quantity demanded of one good}}{\text{Percentage change in price of another good}}$	$E_c < 0$	Complements
		$E_c > 0$	Substitutes
Price elasticity of supply	$\dfrac{\text{Percentage change in quantity supplied}}{\text{Percentage change in price}}$	$E_s > 1$	Elastic
		$E_s = 1$	Unitary elastic
		$E_s < 1$	Inelastic
		$E_s = \infty$	Perfectly elastic
		$E_s = 0$	Perfectly inelastic

SOURCE: © Cengage Learning 2014

represents the tax revenue. The government collects $12.5 million per day, which equals the $0.50 per gallon tax times the 25 million gallons sold each day. The vertical line between points E_2 and T represents the $0.50 tax per gallon. Since consumers now pay $3.25 instead of $3.00 per gallon, they pay one-half of the tax. The sellers pay the remaining half of the tax. Now the sellers send $0.50 to Uncle Sam and keep $2.75 compared to the $3.00 per gallon they kept before the tax.

CONCLUSION: *If the demand curve slopes downward and the supply curve slopes upward, sellers cannot raise the price by the full amount of the tax.*

Part (b) of Exhibit 10 is a special case in which the market price increases by the full amount of the tax per gallon. Here the demand for gasoline is perfectly inelastic. In this case, buyers do not decrease the quantity demanded in response to the decrease in supply caused by the tax. The quantity demanded is 30 million gallons per day before and after the tax. The price, however, increases from E_1 to E_2 by exactly the amount of tax per unit from $3.00 to $3.50 per gallon, and therefore consumers pay the entire burden of the tax. After paying the tax, sellers receive a net price of $3.00 per gallon. The total tax revenue collected by the government is the

EXHIBIT 10	The Tax Incidence of a Tax on Gasoline

In parts (a) and (b), S_1 is the supply curve before the imposition of a tax of $0.50 per gallon on gasoline. The demand curve is not affected by this tax collected from the sellers. The initial equilibrium is E_1. Before the tax, the price is $3.00 per gallon, and 30 million gallons are bought and sold.

In part (a), the equilibrium price rises to $3.25 per gallon at E_2 as a result of the tax. After the tax is paid, sellers receive only $2.75 per gallon (point T) instead of the $3.00 they received before the tax. Thus, buyers pay $0.25 of the tax per gallon, and sellers bear the remaining $0.25. The shaded area is the total tax collected.

As shown in part (b), a tax collected from sellers can be fully shifted to buyers in the unlikely case that demand is perfectly inelastic. Because the quantity of gasoline purchased is unresponsive to a change in price, sellers receive $3.00 per gallon before and after they pay the tax.

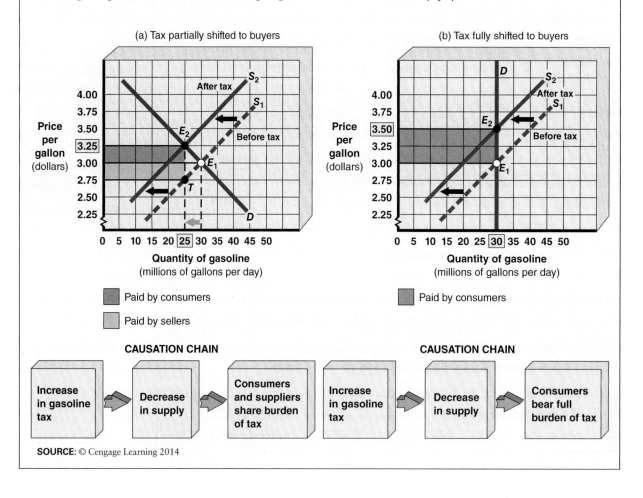

SOURCE: © Cengage Learning 2014

shaded area. Each day $15 million is collected, which equals the $0.50 per gallon tax multiplied by 30 million gallons sold each day.

> **CONCLUSION:** *In the case where demand is perfectly inelastic, sellers can raise the price by the full amount of a tax.*

✔ CHECKPOINT

Can Honda Compete with Itself?

When Honda introduced the Acura to compete with European luxury cars, there was a danger that the new line would take sales away from Honda's Accord. To make Acura more competitive with other luxury cars, suppose Honda cuts the price of Acura while keeping the price of Accord unchanged. If Honda's fear comes true, will it find a negative cross-elasticity of demand, a negative income elasticity of demand, or a positive cross-elasticity of demand?

Key Concepts

Price elasticity of demand
Elastic demand
Total revenue
Inelastic demand

Unitary elastic demand
Perfectly elastic demand
Perfectly inelastic demand
Income elasticity of demand

Cross-elasticity of demand
Price elasticity of supply
Tax incidence

Summary

- **Price elasticity of demand** is a measure of the responsiveness of the quantity demanded to a change in price. Specifically, price elasticity of demand is the ratio of the percentage change in quantity demanded to the percentage change in price.

$$E_d = \frac{\%\Delta Q}{\%\Delta P} = \frac{\dfrac{Q_2 - Q_1}{Q_1 + Q_2}}{\dfrac{P_2 - P_1}{P_1 + P_2}}$$

- **Elastic demand** occurs where there is a change of more than 1 percent in quantity demanded in response to a 1 percent change in price. Demand is elastic when the elasticity coefficient is greater than 1 and *total revenue* (price times quantity) varies inversely with the direction of the price change.

- **Inelastic demand** occurs where there is a change of less than 1 percent in quantity demanded in response to a 1 percent change in price. Demand is inelastic when the elasticity coefficient is less than 1 and total revenue varies directly with the direction of the price change.

- **Unitary elastic demand** occurs where there is a 1 percent change in quantity demanded in response to a 1 percent change in price. Demand is unitary elastic when the elasticity coefficient equals 1 and total revenue remains constant as the price changes.

- **Perfectly elastic demand** occurs when the quantity demanded declines to zero for even the slightest rise or fall in price. This is an extreme case in which the demand curve is horizontal and the elasticity coefficient equals infinity.

- **Perfectly inelastic demand** occurs when the quantity demanded does not change in response to price changes. This is an extreme case in which the demand curve is vertical and the elasticity coefficient equals zero.

- **Determinants of price elasticity of demand** include (a) the availability of substitutes, (b) the percentage of one's budget spent on the product, and (c) the length of time allowed for adjustment. Each of these factors is directly related to the elasticity coefficient.

- **Income elasticity of demand** is the percentage change in quantity demanded divided by the percentage change in income. For a *normal* good or service, income elasticity of demand is positive. For an *inferior* good or service, income elasticity of demand is negative.

- **Cross-elasticity of demand** is the percentage change in the quantity demanded of one product caused by a change in the price of another product. When the cross-elasticity of demand is negative, the two products are complements.

- **Price elasticity of supply** is a measure of the responsiveness of the quantity supplied to a change in price. Price elasticity of supply is the ratio of the percentage change in quantity supplied to the percentage change in price.

- **Tax incidence** is the share of a tax ultimately paid by buyers and sellers. Facing a downward-sloping demand curve and an upward-sloping supply curve, sellers cannot raise the price by the full amount of the tax. If the demand curve is vertical, sellers will raise the price by the full amount of the tax.

Tax Incidence of Gasoline Tax

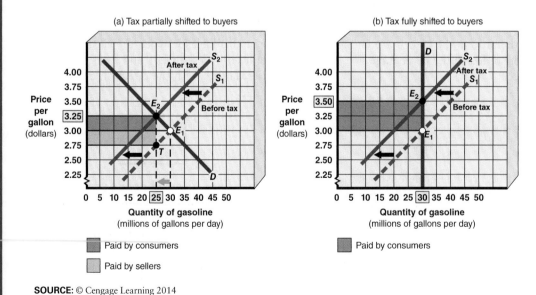

SOURCE: © Cengage Learning 2014

Summary of Conclusion Statements

- The price elasticity coefficient of demand applies only to a specific range of prices.
- The price elasticity coefficient of demand is directly related to the availability of good substitutes for a product.
- The price elasticity coefficient of demand is directly related to the percentage of one's budget spent for a good or service.
- In general, the price elasticity coefficient of demand is higher the longer a price change persists.
- If the demand curve slopes downward and the supply curve slopes upward, sellers cannot raise the price by the full amount of the tax.
- In the case where demand is perfectly inelastic, sellers can raise the price by the full amount of a tax.

Study Questions and Problems

1. If the price of a good or service increases and the total revenue received by the seller declines, is the demand for this good over this segment of the demand curve elastic or inelastic? Explain.

2. Suppose the price elasticity of demand for farm products is inelastic. If the federal government wants to follow a policy of increasing income for farmers, what type of programs will the government enact?

3. Suppose the price elasticity of demand for used cars is estimated to be 3. What does this mean? What will be the effect on the quantity demanded for used cars if the price rises by 10 percent?

4. Consider the following demand schedule:

Price	Quantity demanded	Elasticity coefficient
$25	20	
20	40	_____
15	60	_____
10	80	_____
5	100	_____

What is the price elasticity of demand between
a. $P = \$25$ and $P = \$20$?
b. $P = \$20$ and $P = \$15$?
c. $P = \$15$ and $P = \$10$?
d. $P = \$10$ and $P = \$5$?

5. Suppose a university raises its tuition from $3,000 to $3,500. As a result, student enrollment falls from 5,000 to 4,500. Calculate the price elasticity of demand. Is demand elastic, unitary elastic, or inelastic?

6. Will each of the following changes in price cause total revenue to increase, decrease, or remain unchanged?
a. Price falls, and demand is elastic.
b. Price rises, and demand is elastic.
c. Price falls, and demand is unitary elastic.
d. Price rises, and demand is unitary elastic.
e. Price falls, and demand is inelastic.
f. Price rises, and demand is inelastic.

7. Suppose a movie theater raises the price of popcorn 10 percent, but customers do not buy any less popcorn. What does this tell you about the price elasticity of demand? What will happen to total revenue as a result of the price increase?

8. Charles loves Mello Yello and will spend $10 per week on the product no matter what the price. What is his price elasticity of demand for Mello Yello?

9. Which of the following pairs of goods has the higher price elasticity of demand?
   a. Oranges or Sunkist oranges
   b. Cars or salt
   c. Foreign travel in the short run or foreign travel in the long run

10. The Energizer Bunny that "keeps going and going" has been a very successful ad campaign for batteries. Explain the relationship between this slogan and the firm's price elasticity of demand and total revenue.

11. Suppose the income elasticity of demand for furniture is 3.0 and the income elasticity of demand for physician services is 0.3. Compare the impact on furniture and physician services of a recession that reduces consumers' incomes by 10 percent.

12. How might you determine whether Nike and Reebok are in competition with each other?

13. Assume the cross-elasticity of demand for car tires with respect to the price of cars is −2. What does this tell you about the relationship between car tires and cars when the price of cars rises by 10 percent?

14. Consider the following supply schedule:

Price	Quantity supplied	Elasticity coefficient
$10	50	
8	40	_____
6	30	_____
4	20	_____
2	10	_____
0	0	_____

What is the price elasticity of supply between
   a. $P = \$10$ and $P = \$8$?
   b. $P = \$8$ and $P = \$6$?
   c. $P = \$6$ and $P = \$4$?
   d. $P = \$4$ and $P = \$2$?
   e. $P = \$2$ and $P = \$0$?

15. Why would consumers prefer that the government tax products with elastic, rather than inelastic demand?

16. Opponents of increasing the tax on gasoline argue that the big oil companies just pass the tax along to the consumers. Do you agree or disagree? Explain your answer.

For Online Exercises, go the Tucker Web site at www.cengage.com/economics/tucker.

✓ CHECKPOINT ANSWERS

Will Fliers Flock to Low Summer Fares?

US Airways must believe the quantity of airline tickets demanded during the summer is quite responsive to a price cut. For total revenue to rise with a price cut, the quantity demanded must increase by a larger percentage than the percentage decrease in the price. For this to occur, the price elasticity of demand must exceed 1. If you said US Airways believes demand is elastic, **YOU ARE CORRECT.**

Can Trade Sanctions Affect Elasticity of Demand for Cars?

Because substitutes (Japanese luxury cars) are no longer available to U.S. consumers, the quantity demanded of Mercedes, BMWs, and Jaguars in the United States would be less responsive to changes in the prices for these cars. If you said the price elasticity of demand for Mercedes, BMWs, and Jaguars would become less elastic, **YOU ARE CORRECT.**

Can Honda Compete with Itself?

Determining the effect of cutting the Acura's price on sales of Accords calls for cross-elasticity. Once the price of Acura is cut, Honda would calculate the change in the quantity of Accords demanded. If Acura's decrease in price causes people to buy fewer Accords, Honda is indeed competing with itself. If you said a positive cross-elasticity of demand indicates the two goods are substitutes, **YOU ARE CORRECT.**

Sample Quiz

For an explanation of the correct answers, visit the Tucker Web site at www.cengage.com/economics/tucker.

1. A perfectly elastic demand curve has an elasticity coefficient of
   a. 0.
   b. 1.
   c. less than 1.
   d. infinity.

2. If the percentage change in the quantity demanded of a good is less than the percentage change in price, price elasticity of demand is
   a. elastic.
   b. inelastic.
   c. perfectly inelastic.
   d. unitary elastic.

EXHIBIT 11	Supply and Demand Curves for Good *X*

SOURCE: © Cengage Learning 2014

3. As shown in Exhibit 11, the price elasticity of demand for good *X* between points *E* and *B* is
   a. 3/7 = 0.43.
   b. 7/3 = 2.33.
   c. 1/2 = 0.50.
   d. 1.

4. Which of the following is *true* about the price elasticity of demand on the top part of a linear demand curve?
   a. Demand is inelastic.
   b. Demand is unitary elastic.
   c. Demand is elastic.
   d. It is impossible to tell.

5. Price elasticity of demand tends to be larger in the long run than in the short run. Which of the following is a reason that this statement is *true*?
   a. Over time, people's incomes rise.
   b. If price rises, over time, producers will be able to offer more substitutes.
   c. Over time, the good will become a smaller and smaller share of people's budgets.
   d. People see fewer and fewer substitutes for the good in the long run.

6. If a decrease in the price of movie tickets increases the total revenue of movie theaters, this is evidence that demand is
   a. price elastic.
   b. price inelastic.
   c. unit elastic with respect to price.
   d. perfectly inelastic.

Sample Quiz *continued*

7. Suppose the president of a college argues that a 25 percent tuition increase will raise revenues for the college. It can be concluded that the president thinks that demand to attend this college is
   a. elastic.
   b. inelastic, but not perfectly inelastic.
   c. unitary elastic.
   d. perfectly elastic.

8. The president of Tucker Motors says, "Lowering the price won't sell a single additional Tucker car." The president believes that the price elasticity of demand is
   a. perfectly elastic.
   b. perfectly inelastic.
   c. unitary elastic.
   d. elastic.

9. If a straight-line demand curve slopes down, price elasticity will
   a. remain the same at all points on the demand curve.
   b. change between points along the demand curve.
   c. always be greater than 1.
   d. always equal 1.

10. Along a segment of the demand curve where the price elasticity of demand is less than 1, a decrease in price
    a. is impossible.
    b. will increase total revenue.
    c. will decrease total revenue.
    d. decreases quantity demanded.

11. If Tucker University increases tuition to increase its revenue, it will
    a. not be successful if the demand curve slopes downward.
    b. be successful if demand is elastic.
    c. be successful if demand is inelastic.
    d. be successful if supply is elastic.

12. A demand curve that has constant price elasticity of demand coefficient equal to 1 at *all* points is a (an)
    a. rectangular hyperbola.
    b. downward-sloping straight line.

c. upward-sloping straight line.
d. None of the above answers are correct.

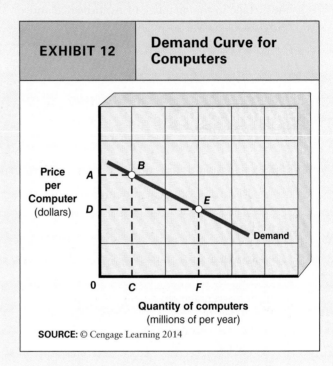

EXHIBIT 12	Demand Curve for Computers

SOURCE: © Cengage Learning 2014

13. In Exhibit 12, if the area 0*ABC* equals the area 0*DEF*, the demand curve is
    a. elastic.
    b. inelastic.
    c. unitary elastic.
    d. nonelastic.

14. In Exhibit 12, the change in total revenue resulting from a change in price from *A* to *D* indicates that the demand curve is
    a. elastic.
    b. inelastic.
    c. unitary elastic.
    d. quasi-elastic.

15. If the price elasticity of demand is elastic, then
    a. $E_d < 1$.
    b. consumers are not very responsive to a price increase.
    c. an increase in the price will increase total revenue.
    d. there are a large number of substitute products available.

Sample Quiz *continued*

16. If the quantity of bread demanded rises 2 percent when the price of bread declines 10 percent, then the price elasticity of demand is
    a. 0.2.
    b. 1.
    c. 2.
    d. 10
    e. cannot be determined

17. Suppose Sally buys exactly five bars of English toffee each week, regardless of whether the toffee bars are regularly priced at $1 or on sale for $0.50. Based on this information, what is Sally's price elasticity of demand for English toffee in this price range?
    a. 0
    b. 1
    c. infinity
    d. cannot be determined.

18. Suppose Bill budgets exactly $50 each month for fresh shrimp regardless of whether shrimp is priced at $10 per pound, or is on sale for $4 per pound. Based on this information, Bill's price elasticity of demand is
    a. 0.
    b. 1.
    c. infinite.
    d. cannot be determined.

19. What is the price elasticity of demand for a vertical demand curve?
    a. Perfectly inelastic
    b. Inelastic but not perfectly inelastic
    c. Unitary elastic
    d. Elastic but not perfectly elastic
    e. Perfectly elastic

20. A perfectly price-elastic demand is consistent with which of the following?
    a. A horizontal demand curve
    b. Few close substitutes
    c. Inferior goods
    d. A low cross-price elasticity of demand.

21. If bus travel is an inferior good, its income elasticity of demand is
    a. strictly greater than 1.
    b. positive.
    c. equal to zero.
    d. negative.

22. If a good is inferior in an economic sense,
    a. it is demand price elastic.
    b. it is demand price inelastic.
    c. the income elasticity of demand is negative.
    d. it is a low-quality good.

23. If automobiles and gasoline are complements, then their cross-elasticity coefficient is
    a. strictly greater than 1.
    b. positive.
    c. equal to zero.
    d. negative.

24. Suppose that when price is $10, quantity supplied is 20 units, and when the price is $6, the quantity supplied is 12 units. What is the price elasticity of supply?
    a. 0.5
    b. 0.8
    c. 1.0
    d. 1.5

25. Using supply and demand analysis, which of the following is *true*, the more elastic the demand curve?
    a. The larger the portion of a sales tax that is passed on to the consumer.
    b. The smaller the portion of a sales tax that is passed on to the consumer.
    c. It does not make any difference how flat the demand curve is; the tax is always split evenly between buyer and seller.
    d. The full tax is always passed on to the consumer no matter how flat the demand curve is.

chapter 6

Consumer Choice Theory

This chapter expands our understanding of demand by investigating more deeply *why* people buy goods and services. In Chapter 3, the law of demand rested on a foundation of common sense and everyday observation. When the price of a Big Mac falls, people *do* buy more, and a price rise causes people to buy less. But there is more to the story.

The focus of this chapter is the logic of consumer behavior. Why does a consumer buy one bundle of goods rather than another? Suppose someone asked why you bought a milkshake and french fries rather than a Coke and a hot dog. You would probably answer that given the money you had to spend, the Coke and hot dog would have given you less satisfaction. In this chapter, you will transform this simple explanation into consumer choice theory and then connect this theory to the law of demand. The chapter ends with another way to explain the demand curve, which involves effects related to income and the prices of other goods.

In this chapter, you will learn to solve these economics puzzles:

- Under what conditions might you be willing to pay $10,000 for a gallon of water and 1 cent for a one-carat diamond?

- When ordering Big Macs, milkshakes, pizza, and other goods, how can you obtain the highest possible satisfaction?

- Do white rats obey the law of demand?

6-1 From Utility to the Law of Demand

The basis of the law of demand is self-interested behavior. Consumers spend their limited budget to satisfy some want, such as listening to a compact disc or driving a new car. The motivation to consume goods and services is to gain utility. Utility is the satisfaction, or pleasure, that people receive from consuming a good or service. Utility is want-satisfying power "in the eye of the beholder." Just as wants differ among people, utility received from consumption varies from person to person. Fred's utility from consuming a BMW will probably differ from Maria's utility. In spite of the subjective nature of utility, this section develops in steps the derivation of a demand curve based on the utility concept.

6-1a TOTAL UTILITY AND MARGINAL UTILITY

Actual measurement of utility is impossible because only you know the satisfaction from consuming, say, four Big Macs in one day. But suppose we could gauge your total utility of consuming four Big Macs in a day. Total utility is the amount of satisfaction received from all the units of a good or service consumed. That is, the utility of the first unit consumed added to that of the second unit and so on. What units can be used to measure total utility? Economists use a mythical unit called a *util*, which allows us to quantify our thinking about consumer behavior.

No one has invented a "utility meter," but assume we could connect such a meter to your brain. Like taking your temperature, we could read the marginal utility each time you eat a Big Mac. Marginal utility is the change in total utility from one additional unit of a good or service. Instead of the total pleasure from eating X number of Big Macs, the question is how much *extra* satisfaction the first, second, or third Big Mac gives you. For example, Exhibit 1(a) shows your marginal utility data for eating four Big Macs in a day. You munch down the first Big Mac. Ah, the util meter hits an 8. You grab another Big Mac and eat it a little more slowly. The util meter hits 4 this time. You're starting to feel full, but you eat a third Big Mac. This one gets a 2. Even though you are pretty full, there is room for one more. You eat the fourth Big Mac very slowly, and it gives you less satisfaction than any of the previous burgers. Your utility meter reads 1. This trend conforms to the law of diminishing marginal utility. The law of diminishing marginal utility is the principle that the extra satisfaction provided by a good or service declines as people consume more in a given period. Economists have found that this is a universal principle of human consumption behavior.

Exhibit 1(a) is a marginal utility, MU, graph. Consistent with the law of diminishing marginal utility, the MU curve slopes downward as you consume more Big Macs. This reflects a steady decline in the utility of each additional Big Mac consumed. If you continue to eat Big Macs, a quantity of Big Macs is eventually reached at which the marginal utility is zero. Here you say to yourself, "If I eat another bite, I'll be sick." Then if you did eat another bite after all, marginal utility would be negative. A rational person never consumes goods when the marginal utility is negative (disutility) unless he or she is paid enough to do so. In our example, we assume you are rational and will not eat a Big Mac

Utility
The satisfaction, or pleasure, that people receive from consuming a good or service.

Total utility
The amount of satisfaction received from all the units of a good or service consumed.

Marginal utility
The change in total utility from one additional unit of a good or service.

Law of diminishing marginal utility
The principle that the extra satisfaction provided by a good or service declines as people consume more in a given period.

EXHIBIT 1	**Diminishing Marginal Utility and Total Utility Curves for Consuming Big Macs**

Part (a) shows that as more Big Macs are consumed per day, the utility from each additional Big Mac declines. The utils are only imaginary because utility cannot be measured. When the marginal utility of each Big Mac consumed is summed, we obtain the total utility curve shown in part (b).

(a) Marginal utility

(b) Total utility

SOURCE: © Cengage Learning 2014

Why Is Water Less Expensive than Diamonds?
Applicable Concepts: total utility and marginal utility

Adam Smith posed a paradox in *The Wealth of Nations*. Water is essential to life and therefore should be of great value. On the other hand, diamonds are not essential to life, so people should value them less than water. Yet, even though water provides more utility, it is cheaper than diamonds. Smith's puzzle came to be known as the diamond-water paradox. Now you can use marginal utility analysis to explain something that baffled the father of economics.

Early economists failed to find the key to the diamond-water puzzle because they did not distinguish between marginal and total utility. Marginal utility theory was not developed until the late nineteenth century. Water is life-giving and does indeed yield much higher total utility than diamonds. However, marginal utility, and not

total utility, determines the price. Water is plentiful in most of the world, so its marginal utility is low. This follows the law of diminishing marginal utility.

Jewelry-quality diamonds, on the other hand, are scarce. Because we have relatively few diamonds, the quantity of diamonds consumed is not large. As a result, the marginal utility of diamonds and the price buyers are willing to pay for them are quite high. Thus, scarcity raises marginal utility and price regardless of the size of total utility.

Exhibit 2 presents a graphical analysis that you can use to unravel the alleged paradox. Part (a) shows the marginal utility per carat you receive from each diamond consumed, and part (b) represents marginal utility per gallon of water consumed. The vertical line, *S*, in each graph is the supply of water or diamonds available per year. Since water is much more plentiful than diamonds,

Denis Vrublevski/Shutterstock.com

the supply curve for water intersects the marginal utility curve at MU_w, which is close to zero. Conversely, the supply curve for diamonds intersects the marginal utility curve at a much higher marginal utility, MU_d. Because of the relative marginal utilities of water and diamonds, you are willing to pay much more for one more carat of a diamond than for one more gallon of water.

EXHIBIT 2	The Diamond-Water Paradox

(a) Marginal utility of diamonds

Marginal utility per carat (utils) — MU_d — *S* — MU

Quantity of diamonds (carats per year)

(b) Marginal utility of water

Marginal utility per gallon (utils) — MU_w — *S* — MU

Quantity of water (gallons per year)

SOURCE: © Cengage Learning 2014

Analyze the Issue

1. Can you imagine a situation in which water would be more expensive than diamonds?
2. Suppose the price per gallon of water is 1 cent and the price per carat of a diamond is $10,000. Is the total utility of diamonds 10,000 times as great as the total utility received from water?

Source: © Cengage Learning 2014

that gives you a negative marginal utility and a stomachache. Also keep in mind that the MU curve for a good is different for different circumstances and individuals. Your MU curve would be much higher if you had not eaten in days. On the other hand, a vegetarian would receive no positive marginal utility from consuming a Big Mac.

Exhibit 1(b) shows how the shape of the total utility, TU, curve varies with marginal utility as you consume more Big Macs each day. The total utility of Big Macs increases steadily because each hamburger provides *additional* satisfaction to the sum of all the Big Macs already consumed. However, the TU curve becomes flatter as the marginal utility diminishes. This is because, as you consume more, the positive pleasure per Big Mac declines, and, in turn, each Big Mac adds less to total utility.

6-1b CONSUMER EQUILIBRIUM

We will now make our example of consumer choice more realistic. Let's examine how Bob Moore, a sophomore at Seaview College, might behave, given a limited budget and the choice between two goods. Suppose Bob goes to McDonald's for lunch with $8 in his pocket to spend for Big Macs and milkshakes. The price of a Big Mac is $2, and the price of a milkshake is also $2. How can Bob enjoy the maximum total utility with his limited money?

Recall from Chapter 2 the concept of *marginal analysis*. This is the method Bob uses to decide how many Big Macs and milkshakes to order. Exhibit 3 shows Bob's marginal utility for each Big Mac and milkshake consumed. The *marginal utility per dollar (MU/P)* is the ratio of the marginal utility of each good to its price. In making purchases, the key consideration is how additional satisfaction relates to price. Using marginal decision making before ordering, Bob compares the marginal utility of one Big Mac to the marginal utility of one milkshake. Being a rational consumer, Bob sees that spending his first $2 on a Big Mac gives more "bang for the buck." The first Big Mac gives him 4 utils per dollar, but the same $2 spent on a milkshake gives him 3 utils per dollar. Next, Bob ponders how to spend his next $2. The best buy now is a milkshake because it gives 3 utils per dollar compared to 2 utils per dollar for a second Big Mac.

EXHIBIT 3	Marginal Utility for Big Macs and Milkshakes (Utils per Day)			
	Big Macs		**Milkshakes**	
Quantity	**MU**	**MU/P**	**MU**	**MU/P**
1	8	4	6	3
2	4	2	4	2
3	2	1	1	1/2
4	1	1/2	0	0

NOTE: The price per Big Mac and per milkshake is $2.
SOURCE: © Cengage Learning 2014

Spending Bob's last $4 is a toss-up. Both the second Big Mac and the second milkshake give the same 2 utils per dollar. So Bob can spend $2 for a second Big Mac and his last $2 for a second milkshake. Or he can spend $2 for a second milkshake and his last $2 for a second Big Mac. The order does not matter. Now that Bob has spent all his income, the marginal utility per dollar of the last Big Mac is equal to the marginal utility per dollar of the last milkshake.

> **CONCLUSION:** *If the marginal utility per last dollar spent on each good is equal and the entire budget is spent, total utility is maximized.*

To convince yourself that two Big Macs and two milkshakes do indeed maximize total utility, consider any other combination Bob could buy with $8. All others yield lower total utility. Suppose Bob were to buy three Big Macs and one milkshake. The third Big Mac adds 2 utils, but giving up the second milkshake subtracts 4 utils. As a result, total utility falls by 2 utils. Or can Bob maximize utility if he were to eat only one Big Mac and drink three milkshakes? The extra utility of the third milkshake is 1 util, but this is less than the 4 utils he would lose by saying no to the second Big Mac. In this case, total utility would fall by 3 utils.

The above example demonstrates the utility-maximizing concept of consumer equilibrium. Consumer equilibrium is a condition in which total utility cannot increase by spending more of a given budget on one good and spending less on another good. Suppose Bob knows not only the exact marginal utility of consuming Big Macs and milkshakes, but also the marginal utility of french fries, pizza, and other goods. To obtain the highest possible satisfaction, Bob allocates his budget so that the last dollar spent on good A, the last on good B, and so on, yield equal MU/P ratios. Consumer equilibrium can be restated algebraically as

Consumer equilibrium

A condition in which total utility cannot increase by spending more of a given budget on one good and spending less on another good.

$$\frac{\text{MU of good } A}{\text{Price of good } A} = \frac{\text{MU of good } B}{\text{Price of good } B} = \frac{\text{MU of good } Z}{\text{Price of good } Z}$$

The letters $A, B, \ldots Z$ indicate all the goods and services purchased by the consumer with a given budget.

6-1c FROM CONSUMER EQUILIBRIUM TO THE LAW OF DEMAND

Understanding the law of diminishing marginal utility and consumer equilibrium provides you with a new set of tools to explore the law of demand. Let's begin with a straightforward link between the law of diminishing marginal utility and the demand curve. Declining marginal utility from consuming more Big Macs and milkshakes means each extra quantity consumed is less important or valuable to the consumer. Therefore, as the quantity consumed increases and the marginal utility falls, Bob is willing to pay less per Big Mac and milkshake. Thus, Bob's individual demand curve conforms to the law of demand and is downward sloping.

A more complete explanation of the law of demand combines diminishing marginal utility and consumer equilibrium. Suppose Bob reaches consumer equilibrium as follows:

$$\frac{\text{MU of Big Mac}}{\text{Price of Big Mac}} = \frac{\text{MU of milkshake}}{\text{Price of milkshake}}$$

$$\frac{4\text{ utils}}{\$2} = \frac{4\text{ utils}}{\$2}$$

Now suppose the price of a Big Mac falls to \$1 and upsets the above equality. This changes the formula to the following:

$$\frac{\text{MU of Big Mac}}{\text{Price of Big Mac}} > \frac{\text{MU of milkshake}}{\text{Price of milkshake}}$$

$$\frac{4\text{ utils}}{\$1} > \frac{4\text{ utils}}{\$2}$$

Now Bob gains more utility per dollar by buying a Big Mac rather than a milkshake. To restore maximum total utility, he spends more on Big Macs. The marginal utility of a Big Mac must fall as he buys more. At the same time, the marginal utility of a milkshake must rise as Bob buys fewer. A fall in the price of Big Macs therefore causes Bob to buy more Big Macs. Voila! The law of demand.

✓ CHECKPOINT

When Dining Out, Do You Eat Smart?

Welcome to Jose's Hacienda! Beside each dish, the menu lists the total utility from each item. If you have \$15 to spend, which meal will you order to achieve consumer equilibrium?

Jose's Hacienda Menu

Tacos \$3 each	Flan* \$2 each	Coke \$1 each
1 taco (99 utils)	1 flan (40 utils)	1 Coke (25 utils)
2 tacos (162 utils)	2 flans (48 utils)	2 Cokes (29 utils)
3 tacos (174 utils)	3 flans (50 utils)	3 Cokes (32 utils)

*Mexican dessert.

6-2 Income and Substitution Effects and the Law of Demand

Since utility is not measurable, it is desirable to have an alternative explanation of demand. Economists offer the following two complementary explanations for the law of demand, which do not rely on utility.

6-2a INCOME EFFECT

One reason people buy more of a good when the price falls is the effect of a price change on real income. The *nominal*, or *money*, amount of your paycheck is simply the number of dollars you earn. On the other hand, price changes alter your *real* income. A rise in prices decreases purchasing power, and a fall in prices increases purchasing power, ceteris paribus.

Suppose your weekly nominal income is $100 and you decide to stock up on Pepsi-Cola (a normal good). If the price per quart is $1, you can afford to buy 100 quarts this week. If the price is instead $0.50 per quart and the prices of other goods remain constant, you are richer because of the rise in purchasing power. As a result, you can buy 200 quarts of Pepsi-Cola without giving up any other goods, or less than 200 quarts and more of other goods. As predicted by the law of demand, the lower price for Pepsi-Cola causes real income to rise and, in turn, causes the quantity demanded to rise. This relationship between changes in real income and your ability to buy goods and services is the income effect. The income effect is the change in quantity demanded of a good or service caused by a change in real income (purchasing power).

Income effect
The change in quantity demanded of a good or service caused by a change in real income (purchasing power).

SOURCE: © Cengage Learning 2014

6-2b SUBSTITUTION EFFECT

There is another reason the change in a good's price causes a change in the quantity demanded. This reason has to do with changing *relative prices*, that is, the price of one good compared to that of another. If the price of Pepsi falls and the price of Coke remains unchanged, Pepsi becomes a better buy. As a result, many consumers will switch from Coke and other beverages and buy Pepsi. Just as the law of demand predicts, this is an increase in quantity demanded. With the price of Pepsi lower than before, the substitution effect causes people to substitute Pepsi for the now relatively more expensive Coke. The substitution effect is the change in quantity demanded of a good or service caused by a change in its price relative to substitutes.

Substitution effect
The change in quantity demanded of a good or service caused by a change in its price relative to substitutes.

SOURCE: © Cengage Learning 2014

Above we discussed the income and the substitution effects separately, but they are complementary explanations for the downward-sloping demand curve.

> **CONCLUSION:** *When the price of a normal good falls, the income effect and the substitution effect combine to cause the quantity demanded to increase.*

Some students express relief that this conclusion has no reference to the untidy word *utility*.

Testing the Law of Demand with White Rats
Applicable Concept: substitution effect

 Economists often envy the controlled laboratory experiments of biologists and other scientists. In the real world, the economist is unable to observe consumer behavior without prices of other goods, expectations, and other factors changing. So it is no wonder that the idea of studying the behavior of white rats to test the law of demand was intriguing. The question was whether the consumer choice of a white rat supports the downward-sloping demand curve.

Standard laboratory rats were placed in experimental cages with two levers. If a rat pressed one lever, nonalcoholic Collins mix was the reward. Pressing the second lever rewarded the rat with root beer. It seems rats are fond of these two beverages. Each rat was given a limited "income" of lever presses per day. After, say, 300 presses, a light above the lever went out, signaling the daily budget was gone. The next day the light was turned on, and the rat was given a new income of lever presses. The "price" of each good corresponded to the number of lever pushes required to obtain 1 milliliter of liquid. For example, if the number of pushes per milliliter for Collins mix released increased by 10 percent, this equaled a 10 percent increase in the price of Collins mix.

The crucial test was to measure the substitution effect resulting from a change in price. As explained in the text, a change in price sets in motion both an income effect and a substitution effect. In the experiment, the price of Collins mix was lowered by decreasing the number of pushes required per milliliter. At the same time, the price of root beer was raised by increasing the number of pushes required per milliliter. To eliminate the income effect, the number of lever presses was raised to compensate for loss of purchasing power. For example, if a rat purchased 4 milliliters of Collins mix per day and 11 milliliters of root beer before the price change, it would be given enough extra pushes after the price change to still purchase these quantities.

In one experiment, a male albino rat was given 300 pushes per day for two weeks, and both liquids were priced at 20 pushes per milliliter. The rat soon settled into a consistent consumption pattern of 4 milliliters of Collins mix and 11 milliliters of root beer per day. Then the experimenters made changes in prices and income. The price (pushes per milliliter) of Collins mix was cut in half, and the price of root beer was doubled. At the same time, the total income of pushes was increased just enough to allow the rat to afford its initial consumption pattern. Stated differently, the income effect was eliminated in order to focus on the substitution effect. After two weeks of decisions under the new conditions, the rat changed its consumption pattern to 17 milliliters of Collins mix and 8 milliliters of root beer per day.

Analyze the Issue
Based on the behavior of the rat described above, what do you conclude about the substitution effect and the slope of the demand curve?

Source: John H. Kagel, Raymond C. Battalio, Howard Rachlin, and Leonard Green, "Demand Curves for Animal Consumers," *Quarterly Journal of Economics* 96 (February 1981): 1–16. Reprinted by permission of Oxford University Press.

✓ CHECKPOINT

Does the Substitution Effect Apply to Buying a Car?

Jenny Tanaka wants to buy a new car, and the annual gasoline expense is a major consideration. Her present car gets 25 miles per gallon (mpg), and she is looking at a new car that gets 40 mpg. Jenny now drives about 12,000 miles per year and pays $3.25 per gallon of gasoline. She therefore calculates an annual gasoline consumption of 480 gallons for her 25 mpg car (12,000 miles/25 mpg) compared to 300 gallons consumed per year for the 40 mpg car (12,000 miles/40 mpg). Because driving the higher-mileage car would use 180 gallons less per year, Jenny estimates the new car will save her $585 in gasoline expense per year (180 gallons × $3.25 per gallon). Suppose Jenny buys the 40 mpg car. Do you predict Jenny will have an annual gasoline savings equal to $585, less than $585, or more than $585?

Key Concepts

Utility
Total utility
Marginal utility

Law of diminishing marginal
utility
Consumer equilibrium

Income effect
Substitution effect

Summary

- **Utility** is the satisfaction or pleasure derived from consumption of a good or service. Actual measurement of utility is impossible, but economists assume it can be measured by a fictitious unit called the *util*.
- **Total utility** is the total level of satisfaction derived from all units of a good or service consumed. *Marginal utility* is the change in total utility from a 1-unit change in the quantity of a good or service consumed.

Relationship between Marginal and Total Utility

(a) Marginal utility

SOURCE: © Cengage Learning 2014

(b) Total utility

Total utility (utils)

16
12
8
4

0   1   2   3   4
Quantity of Big Macs
(number consumed per day)

TU

SOURCE: © Cengage Learning 2014

- The **law of diminishing marginal utility** states that the marginal utility of a good or service eventually declines as consumption increases.

- **Consumer equilibrium** is the condition of reaching the maximum level of satisfaction, given a budget, when the marginal utility per dollar spent on each good purchased is equal. Consumer equilibrium and the law of diminishing marginal utility can be used to derive a downward-sloping demand curve. When the price of a good falls, consumer equilibrium no longer holds because the marginal utility per dollar for the good rises. To restore equilibrium, the consumer must increase consumption. As the quantity demanded increases, the marginal utility falls until equilibrium is again achieved. Thus, the price falls, and the quantity demanded rises, as predicted by the law of demand.

$$\frac{\text{MU of good } A}{\text{price of good } A} = \frac{\text{MU of good } B}{\text{price of good } B} = \frac{\text{MU of good } Z}{\text{price of good } Z}$$

- The **income effect** and **substitution effect** are complementary explanations for the law of demand. When the price changes, these effects work in combination to change the quantity demanded in the opposite direction. As the price falls, real purchasing power increases, causing an increase in the consumer's willingness and ability to purchase a good or service. This is the *income effect*. Also, as the price falls, the consumer substitutes the cheaper good for other goods that are now relatively more expensive. This is the *substitution effect*.

Summary of Conclusion Statements

- If the marginal utility per last dollar spent on each good is equal and the entire budget is spent, total utility is maximized.

- When the price of a normal good falls, the income effect and the substitution effect combine to cause the quantity demanded to increase.

Study Questions and Problems

1. Does a dollar given to a rich person raise the rich person's total utility more than a dollar given to a poor person raises the poor person's total utility?

2. Do you agree with the following statement? "If you like tacos, you should consume as many as you can."

3. This week you have gone to two parties. Assume the total utility you gained from these parties is 100 utils. Then you go to a third party, and your total utility rises to 110 utils. What is the marginal utility of the third party attended per week? Given the law of diminishing marginal utility, what will happen to total utility and marginal utility when you go to a fourth party this week?

4. Suppose your marginal utility for meals at the campus cafeteria this week has fallen to zero. Explain what has happened to your total utility curve derived from consuming these meals. Now explain what will happen to total utility if you eat more meals at the cafeteria this week.

5. Suppose you consume 3 pounds of beef and 5 pounds of pork per month. The price of beef is $1.50 per pound, and pork is $2.00 per pound. Assuming you have studied economics and achieved consumer equilibrium, what is the ratio of the marginal utility of beef to the marginal utility of pork?

6. Suppose the marginal utility of a Coke is 15 utils and its price is $1. The marginal utility of a pizza is 20 utils, and its price is $2. If you buy 1 unit of each good, will you achieve consumer equilibrium? If not, how can greater total utility be obtained?

7. Explain the relationship between the law of diminishing marginal utility and the law of demand.

8. Consider the table below, which lists James's marginal utility schedule for steak and hamburger meals. Given a budget of $45, how many steak and hamburger meals will James buy per month to maximize his total utility? What is the total utility realized?

Steak meals per month	Marginal utility of steak meals	Price per steak meal	Hamburger meals per month	Marginal utility of hamburger meals	Price per hamburger meal
1	20	$10	1	15	$5
2	15	10	2	8	5
3	12	10	3	6	5
4	10	10	4	4	5
5	8	10	5	2	5

9. Using the marginal utility schedule in question 8, begin in consumer equilibrium and assume the price per hamburger meal falls from $5 to $2, all other factors held constant. What is the total utility realized?

10. Suppose the price of a BMW falls. Explain the law of demand based on the income and substitution effects.

For Online Exercises, go to the Tucker Web site at academic.cengage.com/economics/tucker.

✔ CHECKPOINT ANSWERS

When Dining Out, Do You Eat Smart?

Start with one taco (99 marginal utils/$3, or 33 marginal utils/$1). Then order a Coke (25 marginal utils/$1). Next, order another taco (63 marginal utils/$3, or 21 marginal utils/$1). Now treat yourself to a flan (40 marginal utils/$2, or 20 marginal utils/$1). Finish it all with a second flan (4 marginal utils/$1), another Coke (4 marginal utils/$1), and a third taco (4 marginal utils/$1). You have now spent your entire $15 budget. If you said, following the principle of consumer equilibrium, you would order two Cokes, two flans, and three tacos, although not a very nutritious choice, **YOU ARE CORRECT.**

Does the Substitution Effect Apply to Buying a Car?

Buying a higher mpg car will reduce the cost per mile of driving relative to substitutes, such as riding a bus, a train, or an airplane. As the cost of driving falls, the substitution effect predicts Jenny will drive more in the 40 mpg car than the 12,000 miles she now drives per year in the 25 mpg car. The extra cost of gasoline for driving over 12,000 miles per year in the 40 mpg car must be subtracted from the $585 savings that was based on the assumption that Jenny's miles driven per year would remain unchanged when she bought the 40 mpg car. If you said Jenny will save less than $585, **YOU ARE CORRECT.**

Sample Quiz

For an explanation of the correct answers, visit the Tucker Web site at **www.cengage.com/economics/tucker**.

1. The term *utility* refers to the
   a. usefulness of a good in relation to its scarcity.
   b. necessity of a good.
   c. price of a good.
   d. number of goods a consumer has.
   e. pleasure, or satisfaction, a consumer receives upon consuming a good.

2. When total utility is at a maximum, marginal utility is
   a. zero.
   b. positive.
   c. negative.
   d. one.

3. The marginal utilities associated with the first 4 units of consumption of good Y are 10, 12, 9, and 7. What is the total utility associated with the third unit?
   a. 3
   b. 9
   c. 25
   d. 31
   e. The amount cannot be determined from the marginal utilities.

4. Generally speaking, as more of a particular good is purchased, a consumer's marginal utility _____ and total utility _____.
   a. increases; decreases
   b. decreases; increases
   c. increases; increases
   d. decreases; decreases
   e. Generalizations cannot be made.

5. Marginal utility is defined as the
   a. extra satisfaction the consumer receives from an extra $1 of income.
   b. total level of satisfaction a consumer receives upon the consumption of a certain number of goods.
   c. number of hours a consumer would be willing to work to receive a certain product.
   d. extra satisfaction a person derives from consuming an additional unit of a good.

6. The statement "As more of a good is consumed, the utility a person derives from each additional unit diminishes" is known as the
   a. water and diamond paradox.
   b. law of diminishing marginal utility.
   c. law of total utility.
   d. marginal-utility-to-price ratio equalization rule.

7. The law of diminishing marginal utility indicates that the marginal utility curve is
   a. downward sloping.
   b. upward sloping.
   c. U-shaped.
   d. flat.

EXHIBIT 4	Marginal Utility for Data for Clothes and Amusement	
Quantity	Clothes	Amusement
1	15	20
2	13	18
3	10	13
4	8	12
5	6	10

SOURCE: © Cengage Learning 2014

8. Refer to Exhibit 4. Clothes and amusements are priced at $10 each. The marginal utility per dollar for the first unit of amusement is
   a. 0.5.
   b. 1.5.
   c. 2.0.
   d. 5.0.

Sample Quiz *continued*

9. Refer to Exhibit 4. Your budget is $50. The price of amusement goods is $10. If the price of clothes falls to $4, which of the following statements is *true*?
   a. The marginal-utility-to-price ratio for clothes will decrease.
   b. The marginal-utility-to-price ratio for clothes will increase.
   c. The quantity demanded of clothes will decrease.
   d. Both b and c are true.

10. Refer to Exhibit 4. Clothes and amusements are priced at $10 each. If you had a budget of $50, which of the following combinations of goods would you buy?
   a. 4 units of clothes and 1 unit of amusement
   b. 3 units of clothes and 2 units of amusement
   c. 2 units of clothes and 3 units of amusement
   d. 1 unit of clothes and 4 units of amusement

11. Total utility is maximized in the consumption of two goods by equating the
   a. prices of both goods for the last dollar spent on each good.
   b. marginal utilities of both goods for the last dollar spent on each good.
   c. ratios of marginal utility to the price of both goods for the last dollar spent on each good.
   d. marginal utility of one good to the price of the other good.

12. The MU/P equalization principle means consumers will exhaust their expenditure budget so that, in the end, the MU/P ratio is
   a. zero for each good.
   b. higher for goods the consumer wants the most.
   c. maximized for the goods the consumer wants the most.
   d. the same for each good.

13. When the price of a good falls, consumers may increase the quantity consumed because they have greater total purchasing power. Which of the following does this statement describe?
   a. Substitution effect
   b. Income effect
   c. Consumer equilibrium effect
   d. Price effect

14. When the price of a good falls, consumers buy more of the good because it is cheaper relative to competing goods. Which of the following does this statement describe?
   a. Consumer equilibrium effect
   b. Price effect
   c. Income effect
   d. Substitution effect

15. When the price of a normal good falls,
   a. both the income and substitution effects combine to cause the quantity demanded to increase.
   b. the substitution effect will cause people to buy more because the good is relatively less expensive.
   c. the income effect will cause people to buy more because of the increased purchasing power associated with the lower price.
   d. All of the above answers are correct.

16. If utility is *not* maximized,
   a. some change in consumption will increase satisfaction.
   b. no change in consumption will increase utility.
   c. only a change in income will increase utility.
   d. only a change in price will increase utility.

17. A utility-maximizing consumer would never purchase a good if the
   a. MU/P were positive.
   b. marginal utility were positive.
   c. marginal utility were positive.
   d. None of the above answers are correct.

18. Diminishing marginal utility means that as you consume more of a good, other things constant, the
   a. total satisfaction you obtain from consuming this good falls.
   b. total amount produced begins to fall.
   c. marginal product begins to fall.
   d. additional satisfaction you obtain from each additional unit of the good falls.

Sample Quiz *continued*

19. Assume that an individual consumes only hot dogs and colas and that the last hot dog consumed yields 15 utils and the last cola yields 10 utils. If the price of a hot dog is $1.00 and the price of a cola is $0.50, we can conclude that the
    a. consumer should consume more hot dogs and less cola.
    b. price of hot dogs is too high.
    c. consumer should consume fewer hot dogs and more cola.
    d. consumer is in equilibrium.

20. Assume the price of Coca-Cola increases. As a result, your real income decreases and you decrease the quantity of Coca-Cola purchased each month. This is an example of the
    a. income effect.
    b. consumer price effect.
    c. revenue effect.
    d. substitution effect.

21. When the price of a good rises, one effect of this change in price is that some consumers switch to more affordable substitutes, which helps us understand the law of demand. What is this effect called?
    a. Marginal utility effect
    b. Substitution effect
    c. Price effect
    d. Income effect

22. According to the utility model of consumer demand, the demand curve is downward sloping because of the law of
    a. diminishing marginal utility.
    b. diminishing consumer equilibrium.
    c. consumer equilibrium.
    d. diminishing utility maximization.

23. As shown in Exhibit 5, assume that the price of both goods is $1 per unit and you consume 3 units of good X and 3 units of good Y. To maximize total utility without a budget, you should consume
    a. neither X nor Y.
    b. more of X and less of Y.

    c. less of X and more of Y.
    d. more of both X and Y.
    e. less of both X and Y.

EXHIBIT 5	Marginal Utility Data for Goods *X* and *Y*		
Units of good *X*	Marginal utility of good *X*	Units of good *Y*	Marginal utility of good *Y*
1	20	1	14
2	16	2	12
3	12	3	10
4	8	4	8
5	4	5	6

SOURCE: © Cengage Learning 2014

24. As shown in Exhibit 5, assume that the price of both goods is $1 per total unit and your budget is $5. To maximize utility, you should consume
    a. neither X nor Y.
    b. more of X and less of Y.
    c. less of X and more of Y.
    d. more of both X and Y.
    e. less of both X and Y.

25. As shown in Exhibit 5, assume that the price of good X is $2 per unit and the price of good Y is $1 per unit and your budget is $11. If you consume 3 units of good X and 4 units of good Y and maximize utility, you should consume
    a. neither X nor Y.
    b. more of X.
    c. more of Y.
    d. more of both X and Y.
    e. less of both X and Y.

Indifference Curve Analysis

6

This appendix explains another version of consumer choice theory based on indifference curves and budget lines.

6A-1 Constructing an Indifference Curve

Let's begin with an experiment to find out a consumer's consumption preferences for quantities of two goods. The consumer samples a number of pairs of servings with various ounces of lobster tail and steak (surf and turf). Each time the same question is asked: "Would you prefer serving *A* or serving *B*?" After numerous trials, suppose the consumer states indifference between eating choices *A–D* shown in Exhibit A-1. This means the consumer is just as satisfied having either 7 ounces of steak and 4 ounces of lobster (*A*) or 3 ounces of steak and 8 ounces of lobster (*D*) or either of the other two combinations of *B* or *C*. Interpretation of the curve connecting these points is that each of these choices yields the same total utility because no choice is preferred to any other choice. Since, as explained in the chapter, there is no such thing as a utility meter, this approach is actually a method for determining equal levels of satisfaction or total utility for different bundles of goods without an exact measure of utils. The curve derived from this experimental data is called an indifference curve. Note that not only points *A*, *B*, *C*, and *D*, but also all other points on the smooth curve connecting them are equally satisfactory combinations to the consumer.

Indifference Curve

A curve showing the different combinations of two products that yield the same satisfaction or total utility to a consumer.

6A-1a WHY INDIFFERENCE CURVES ARE DOWNWARD SLOPING AND CONVEX

If total utility is the same at all points along the indifference curve, then consuming more of one good must mean less of the other is consumed. Given this condition, movement along the indifference curve generates a curve with a negative slope. Suppose a consumer moves in marginal increments between any two combination points in Exhibit A-1. For instance, say the consumer decides to move from point *A* to point *B* and consume an extra ounce of lobster. To do so, the consumer increases total utility (+MU) by consuming an extra quantity of lobster.

However, because by definition total utility is constant everywhere along the curve, the consumer must give up a quantity of steak (2 ounces) in order to reduce total utility (–MU) by precisely enough to offset the gain in total utility from the extra lobster.

The inverse relationship between goods along the downward-sloping indifference curve means that the absolute value of the slope of an indifference curve equals

---

| EXHIBIT A-1 | A Consumer's Indifference Curve |

Points *A*, *B*, *C*, *D* and each point along the curve represent a combination of steak and lobster that yields equal total utility for a given consumer. Stated differently, the consumer is indifferent between consuming servings having quantities represented by all points composing the indifference curve.

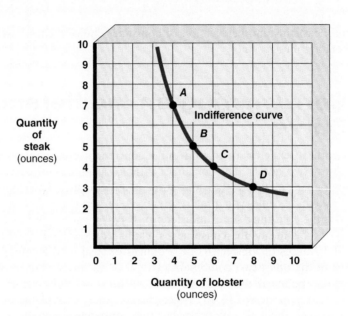

An Indifference Schedule for a Consumer

Choice	Steak (ounces)	Lobster (ounces)
A	7	4
B	5	5
C	4	6
D	3	8

SOURCE: © Cengage Learning 2014

Marginal rate of substitution (MRS)

The rate at which a consumer is willing to substitute one good for another with no change in total utility. The MRS equals the slope of the indifference curve at any point on the curve.

what is called the marginal rate of substitution (MRS). The MRS is the rate at which a consumer is willing to substitute one good for another with no change in total utility. Begin at *A* and move to *B* along the curve. The slope and MRS of the curve is −2/1, or simply 2 when the minus sign is removed to give the absolute value. This is the consumer's subjective willingness to substitute *A* for *B*. At point *A*, the consumer has a substantial amount of steak and relatively little lobster. Therefore, the consumer is willing to forgo or "substitute" 2 ounces of steak to get

1 more ounce of lobster. In other words, the marginal utility of losing each ounce of steak between *A* and *B* is low compared to the marginal utility of gaining each ounce of lobster.

Now suppose the consumer moves from *B* to *C*, and the slope changes to 1/1 (MRS = 1). Between these two points, the consumer is willing to substitute 1 ounce of steak for an equal quantity of lobster. This means that between *B* and *C*, the marginal utility lost per ounce of steak equals the marginal utility gained from each ounce of lobster, while total utility remains constant. Finally, assume the consumer moves from *C* to *D*. Here the slope equals ½ (MRS = ½) because the consumer at point *C* has a substantial amount of lobster and relatively little steak. Consequently, the marginal utility lost from giving up 1 ounce of steak equals twice the marginal utility gained from an additional ounce of lobster.

As we see in this example, as the quantity of lobster increases along the horizontal axis, the marginal utility of additional ounces of lobster decreases. Correspondingly, as the quantity of steak decreases along the vertical axis, its marginal utility increases. So moving down the curve means the consumer is willing to give up smaller and smaller quantities of steak on the vertical axis to obtain each additional ounce of lobster on the horizontal axis.

> **CONCLUSION:** *The slope of the indifference curve is negative and equal to the marginal rate of substitution (MRS), which declines as one moves downward along the curve. The result is a curve with a diminishing slope that is convex (bowed inward) to the origin.*

6A-1b   THE INDIFFERENCE MAP

As explained above, any point selected along an indifference curve gives the same level of satisfaction or total utility. Actually, there are other indifference curves that can be drawn for a consumer. As shown in Exhibit A-2, indifference curves I_1 to I_6 also exist to form an indifference map, which is a selection of a consumer's indifference curves. In fact, if all possible curves were drawn, they would completely fill the space between the axes because there would be so many. And it is important to note that each curve reflects a different level of total utility. Also, each curve moving from the origin in the northeasterly direction from I_1 to I_6 and beyond yields higher total utility. This is reasonable because at each higher indifference curve, the consumer is able to select more of both goods and therefore is better off. To verify this concept, select a combination on one indifference curve in Exhibit A-2 and then select a combination of more of both goods on a higher indifference curve.

Indifference map

A selection of indifference curves with each curve representing a different level of satisfaction or total utility.

> **CONCLUSION:** *Each consumer has a set of indifference curves that form a map. Since consumers wish to achieve the highest possible total utility, they always prefer curves farther from the origin where they can select more quantities of two goods.*

EXHIBIT A-2	**A Consumer's Indifference Map**

An indifference map is a selected set of indifference curves. Along curves farther from the origin, it is possible to select more of both goods compared to indifference curves closer to the origin. Therefore, curves farther from the origin are preferred because they yield higher levels of total utility.

SOURCE: © Cengage Learning 2014

6A-1c THE BUDGET LINE

Having considered the consumer's preferences for steak and lobster in the indifference map, the next step is to see what the consumer can afford. The consumer's ability to purchase steak and lobster is limited, or constrained, by the amount of money (income) the consumer has to spend and the prices of the two goods. Suppose the consumer likes to go to a fine restaurant and budgets $10 per week to dine on surf and turf. The price of steak is $1 per ounce, and the price of lobster is $2 an ounce. If the consumer spends the entire budget on steak, 10 ounces of steak can be purchased. At the other extreme, the whole budget could be spent for lobster, and 5 ounces would be purchased. As shown in Exhibit A-3, and given the consumption possibilities of buying fractions of ounces of steak and lobster, a range of choices can be purchased along the budget line ranging from 10 ounces on the steak axis to 5 ounces on the lobster axis. The table in this exhibit computes selected whole-unit combinations each equaling a $10 total expenditure.

Budget line

A line that shows the different combinations of two goods a consumer can purchase with a given amount of money and prices for the goods.

EXHIBIT A-3	A Consumer's Budget Line

A budget line shows all the possible combinations of goods that can be purchased with a given budget and given prices for these goods.

Selected Whole-Unit Combinations of Steak and Lobster Affordable with a $10 Budget

(1) Choice	(2) Ounces of steak (price = $1/ounce)	(3) Ounces of lobster (price = $2/ounce)	(4) Ounces of lobster (price = $1/ounce)	(5) Total expenditure
A	10	0	0	$10 ($10 + $0)
B	8	1	2	$10 ($8 + $2)
C	4	3	6	$10 ($4 + $6)
D	2	4	8	$10 ($2 + $8)
E	0	5	10	$10 ($0 + $10)

SOURCE: © Cengage Learning 2014

CONCLUSION: *The budget line represents various combinations of goods that a consumer can purchase at given prices with a given budget.*

Computing the slope of the budget line requires some shorthand mathematical notation. Let B represent the amount of money the consumer has to spend on steak and lobster. Also, let P_l and P_s represent the prices of lobster and steak, respectively, and L and S represent the ounces of lobster and steak, respectively. Given this notation, the budget line may be expressed as

$$P_1L + P_sS = B$$

In order to express the equation in slope-intercept form, divide both sides by P_s and get

$$\frac{P_1}{P_s}L + S = \frac{B}{P_s}$$

Solving for S yields

$$S = \frac{B}{P_s} - \frac{P_1}{P_s}L$$

Note that S is a linear function of L with a vertical intercept of B/P_s and a slope of $-P_1/P_s$. Since the price of lobster is \$2 an ounce and the price of steak is \$1 per ounce, the slope of the budget line is -2, or 2 as an absolute value.

CONCLUSION: *The slope of the budget line equals the ratio of the price of good X on the horizontal axis divided by the price of good Y on the vertical axis. Expressed as a formula:*

$$\textbf{slope of budget line} = \textbf{P}_x/\textbf{P}_y$$

6A-1d A CONSUMER EQUILIBRIUM GRAPH

Exhibit A-4 shows the budget line from Exhibit A-3 superimposed on an indifference map. This allows us to easily compare consumer preferences and affordability. The utility-maximizing combination is the equilibrium point X where the budget line is just tangent to the highest attainable indifference curve I_2, and the quantity of steak purchased is 4 ounces and the quantity of lobster is 3 ounces.

As explained in Exhibit A-5 of the appendix to Chapter 1, the slope of a straight line tangent to a curve is equal to the slope of the curve at that point. This mathematical relationship translates into the economic interpretation of the tangency condition in this appendix. At the point of tangency, the MRS equals the slope of the budget line. At point X, the slope is the price ratio $P_1/P_s = 2$ from Exhibit A-3, and, therefore, it follows that MRS $= 2$ at point X on curve I_2 in Exhibit A-4. At any other combination, the MRS will not be equal to the price ratio, and the consumer will reallocate the budget until equilibrium is achieved at point X.

CONCLUSION: *Consumer equilibrium occurs where the budget line is tangent to the highest attainable indifference curve. At this unique point, MRS = slope (price ratio of P_x/P_y).*

EXHIBIT A-4	Consumer Equilibrium

Consumer equilibrium is at point X, where the budget line is tangent to the highest attainable indifference curve, I_2. Only at this point does the marginal rate of substitution (MRS) along I_2 equal the slope of the budget line, which equals the price ratio P_l/P_s. Although point Y is on a higher curve, I_3, and would yield a greater total utility than X, point Y is beyond the budget line and therefore is unattainable by the consumer. Point Z is on a lower indifference curve, but it will not be chosen. The consumer can move upward along the budget line by shifting dollars from purchases of lobster to purchases of steak and reach point X on the higher indifference curve I_2.

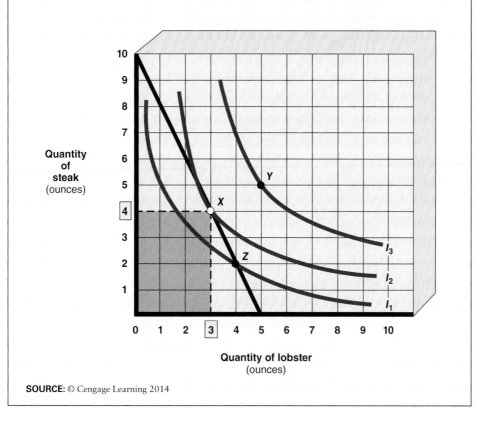

SOURCE: © Cengage Learning 2014

6A-1e DERIVATION OF THE DEMAND CURVE

This appendix concludes with Exhibit A-5, which shows how the demand curve for lobster can be derived from a map of two indifference curves. The table in this exhibit reproduces the table from Exhibit A-3 and adds column (4) with the price of lobster equal to $1 per ounce, rather than $2 per ounce. Now compare columns (3) and (4) in the table. Holding the price of steak constant at $1 per ounce and the budget equal to $10, the consumer can afford to purchase more lobster at each choice except A, where the entire budget is spent on steak. The top graph is drawn from Exhibit A-4, where at point X, the price of lobster is $2 per ounce and the quantity demanded of lobster is 3 ounces. The bottom

EXHIBIT A-5	**Deriving the Demand Curve**

In the top part of this exhibit, the initial budget line intersects the highest attainable indifference curve, I_2, at point X with the price of steak equal to \$1 per ounce and the price of lobster equal to \$2 per ounce. Holding the budget and the price of steak constant at \$10 and \$1, respectively, the price of lobster drops to \$1 per ounce. As a result, the budget line shifts to intersect the higher indifference curve, I_3, at point Y.

The bottom part of the exhibit corresponds points X and Y to points X' and Y', respectively. At \$2 per ounce for lobster, the consumer buys 3 ounces. At \$1 per ounce for lobster, the consumer buys 7 ounces. Connecting these two points results in a downward-sloping demand curve.

Selected Whole-Unit Combinations of Steak and Lobster Affordable with a \$10 Budget

(1) Choice	(2) Ounces of steak (price = \$1/ounce)	(3) Ounces of lobster (price = \$2/ounce)	(4) Ounces of lobster (price = \$1/ounce)	(5) Total expenditure
A	10	0	0	\$10 (\$10 + \$0)
B	8	1	2	\$10 (\$8 + \$2)
C	4	3	6	\$10 (\$4 + \$6)
D	2	4	8	\$10 (\$2 + \$8)
E	0	5	10	\$10 (\$0 + \$10)

SOURCE: © Cengage Learning 2014

graph of Exhibit A-5 shows one point on the demand curve for lobster at X'. To find another point on the demand curve, we decrease the price of lobster to $1 per ounce and trace the new budget line points from column (4) of the table on to the top graph. The budget line swings outward along the horizontal axis, but the original vertical intercept remains unchanged. The reason the vertical axis remains at 10 ounces of steak is because the price of steak is still at $1 per ounce, and if the consumer spends the entire $10 on steak, then the price of lobster is irrelevant to the vertical intercept. However, at a lower price for lobster, the consumer can afford more lobster moving downward along the new budget line with the same $10 budget because lobster is cheaper.

Given the new budget line shown in the top graph in Exhibit A-5, the consumer finds that higher indifference curve I_3 is now attainable. As a result, consumer equilibrium moves from point X to point Y, where 7 ounces of lobster are purchased. This gives the corresponding second point Y' shown in the lower graph. Connecting these two points allows us to draw the consumer's demand curve for lobster. Voila! Consistent with the law of demand, the demand curve is indeed downward sloping.

Key Concepts

Indifference curve   Marginal rate of substitution (MRS)   Indifference map   Budget line

Summary

- An **indifference curve** shows the different quantity combinations of two goods that give the same satisfaction or total utility to a consumer.

- The **marginal rate of substitution (MRS)** is the rate at which a consumer is willing to substitute one good for another with no change in total utility.
- An **indifference map** is a selection of a consumer's indifference curves.

Indifference Curve

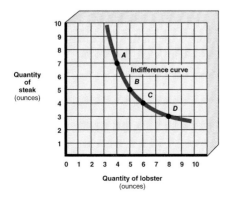

SOURCE: © Cengage Learning 2014

Indifference Map

SOURCE: © Cengage Learning 2014

- The **budget line** gives the different combinations of two goods a consumer can purchase with a given amount of money and relative prices for the goods. The slope of the budget line equals the price of the good on the horizontal axis divided by the price on the vertical axis.

Budget Line

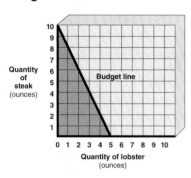

SOURCE: © Cengage Learning 2014

- **Consumer equilibrium** occurs where the budget line is tangent to the highest possible indifference curve, as shown originally at point X. If the price of one good falls, then the consumer

equilibrium changes to point Y on a higher indifference curve. Connecting the two corresponding price-quantity points X' and Y' generates a downward-sloping demand curve.

Consumer Equilibrium

SOURCE: © Cengage Learning 2014

Summary of Conclusion Statements

- The slope of the indifference curve is negative and equal to the marginal rate of substitution (MRS), which declines as one moves downward along the curve. The result is a curve with a diminishing slope that is convex (bowed inward) to the origin.
- Each consumer has a set of indifference curves that form a map. Because consumers wish to achieve the highest possible total utility, they always prefer curves farther from the origin where they can select more quantities of two goods.

- The budget line represents various combinations of goods that a consumer can purchase at given prices with a given budget.
- The slope of the budget line equals the ratio of the price of good X on the horizontal axis divided by the price of good Y on the vertical axis. Expressed as a formula, slope = P_x/P_y.
- Consumer equilibrium occurs where the budget line is tangent to the highest attainable indifference curve. At this unique point, MRS = slope (price ratio of P_x/P_y).

Study Questions and Problems

1. Suppose a consumer's marginal rate of substitution is three slices of pizza for one Coke. If the price of a Coke is $1 and the price of three slices of pizza is $2, would the consumer change his or her consumption combination?

2. Let M represent the quantity of medical services, such as the number of doctor visits, and let O represent the quantity of other goods purchased by a consumer in a given year. Let the budget (B) be in thousands of dollars and

the price of medical services and other goods be in terms of dollars per unit, with $B = 60$, $P_m = 6$, and $P_o = 10$.

a. Graph the budget line and determine the slope.

b. Show the result if the price of medical services (P_o) decreases to $5.

c. Add two indifference curves to the graph that are tangent to the budget line and explain the result.

3. Assume that the data in the following table are an indifference curve for a consumer.

Choice	Units of Y	Units of X
A	10	2
B	6	4
C	4	6
D	2	12

a. Graph this indifference curve and label "Quantity of Y" on the vertical axis and "Quantity of X" on the horizontal axis. Label the points A–D.

b. Assume the consumer's budget is $12 and the prices of X and Y are $1.00 and $1.50, respectively. Draw the budget line in the above graph.

c. What combination of X and Y will the consumer purchase?

d. What is the value of the MRS and the slope (P_x/P_y) at consumer equilibrium?

e. Beginning with the graph drawn in part (a), explain and draw graphs to derive a demand curve for X.

Sample Quiz

For an explanation of the correct answers, visit the Tucker Web site at www.cengage.com/economics/tucker.

1. The slope of an indifference curve is _____, and a movement along the curve causes the loss in marginal utility (MU) of one good to _____ the marginal utility (MU) gained from another good.
   a. zero; maximize
   b. positive; exceed
   c. concave; reduce
   d. negative; equal

2. The _____ is the absolute value of the slope of the indifference curve.
   a. marginal rate of substitution
   b. average rate of transitivity
   c. relative rate of utility
   d. marginal rate of transposition

3. Consumers always _____ indifference curves that are farther from the origin.
   a. reject
   b. cross
   c. prefer
   d. maximize

4. Given the prices of two goods, all quantity combinations inside the budget line are
   a. indifferent.
   b. efficient.
   c. unattainable.
   d. attainable.

5. Consumer equilibrium occurs where the budget line is _____ to the _____ possible indifference curve.
   a. tangent; highest
   b. equal; lowest
   c. marginal; maximum
   d. differential; highest

6. An indifference curve consists of quantity combinations of two goods that yield
   a. equal marginal utilities.
   b. negative marginal utilities.
   c. the same price ratios.
   d. the same total satisfaction.

7. The slope of an indifference curve is equal to the ratio of the _____ of the good on the horizontal axis to the _____ of the good on the vertical axis.
   a. marginal utility (MU); marginal utility (MU)
   b. total utility (TU); total utility (TU)

Sample Quiz *continued*

c. marginal product (MP); marginal product (MP)

d. price (P); total utility (TU)

8. The equation for a budget line for goods X and Y, with P_x being the price of X, P_y being the price of Y, and B being the budget, can be written as
   a. $P_x X + P_y Y = B$.
   b. $P_x X + P_y Y = 1/B$.
   c. $P_x X = B + P_y Y$.
   d. $P_x X / P_y Y = 1 - B$.

9. Given the budget line and indifference curves shown in Exhibit A-6, consumer equilibrium occurs at point
   a. A.
   b. B.
   c. C.
   d. D.
   e. E.

a. marginal utility of one good.

b. total utility of one good.

c. marginal substitution value (MSV).

d. marginal transitivity of one good.

12. The marginal rate of substitution _____ as one moves downward along the indifference curve.
    a. increases
    b. remains constant
    c. decreases
    d. increases and then decreases

13. Assume P_x is the price of good X on the horizontal axis and P_y is the price of good Y on the vertical axis. The slope of the budget line equals
    a. $P_y / P_x Y$.
    b. $P_y Q_y / P_x Q_x$.
    c. $(1 - P_y / P_x)$.
    d. P_x / P_y.

EXHIBIT A-6	Consumer Equilibrium

SOURCE: © Cengage Learning 2014

EXHIBIT A-7	Consumer Equilibrium

SOURCE: © Cengage Learning 2014

---

10. Given the budget line and indifference curves shown in Exhibit A-6, assume the consumer is initially at point C. To maximize total utility, the consumer should
    a. purchase more of good X and less of good Y.
    b. remain at point C.
    c. move to point B and then to point A.
    d. purchase more of good Y and less of good X.

11. An indifference curve has a negative slope because movement along the curve requires the consumer to give up the

14. As shown in Exhibit A-7, the marginal rate of substitution (MRS) at point B is equal to
    a. 0.33.
    b. 2.0.
    c. 0.5.
    d. 3.0.

15. As shown in Exhibit A-7, movement from consumer equilibrium at point A to point B is caused by a(an)
    a. increase in the price of good X.
    b. decrease in the price of good X.
    c. increase in the price of good Y.
    d. decrease in the price of good Y.

chapter 7

Production Costs

Suppose you dream of owning your own company. That's right! You want to be an entrepreneur. You crave the excitement of starting your own firm and making it successful. Instead of working for someone else, you want to be your own boss. You are under no illusions; it is going to take hard work and sacrifice.

You are an electrical engineer who is an expert at designing electronic components for cell phones and similar applications. So you quit your job and invest your nest egg in starting Computech (a mythical company). You lease factory space, hire employees, and purchase raw materials, and soon your company's products begin rolling off the assembly line. And then you find that production cost considerations influence each decision you make in this new business venture.

The purpose of this chapter is to study production and its relationship to various types of costs. Whether your company is new and small or an international giant, understanding costs is essential for success. In this chapter and the next two chapters, you will follow Computech and learn the basic principles of production and the way various types of costs vary with output.

In this chapter, you will learn to solve these economics puzzles:

- Why would an accountant say a firm is making a profit and an economist would say the firm is losing money?

- What is the difference between the short run and the long run?

- How can a company make a profit with a free Web site?

7-1 Costs and Profit

A basic assumption in economics is that the motivation for business decisions is profit maximization. Economists realize that managers of firms sometimes pursue other goals, such as contributing to the United Way or building an empire for the purpose of ego satisfaction. Nevertheless, the profit maximization goal has proved to be the best theory to explain why managers of firms choose a particular level of output or price. To understand profit as a driving force for business firms, we must distinguish between the way economists measure costs and the way accountants measure costs.

7-1a EXPLICIT AND IMPLICIT COSTS

Explicit costs

Payments to nonowners of a firm for their resources.

Implicit costs

The opportunity costs of using resources owned by a firm.

Economists define the total opportunity cost of a business as the sum of *explicit costs* and *implicit costs*. Explicit costs are payments to nonowners of a firm for their resources. In our Computech example, explicit costs include the wages paid to labor, the rental charges for a plant, the cost of electricity, the cost of materials, and the cost of medical insurance. These resources are owned outside the firm and must be purchased with actual payments to these "outsiders."

Implicit costs are the opportunity costs of using resources owned by a firm. These are opportunity costs of resources because the firm makes no actual payments to outsiders. When you started Computech, you gave up the opportunity to earn a salary as an electrical engineer for someone else's firm. When you invested your nest egg in your own enterprise, you gave up the opportunity to earn interest. You also used a building you own to warehouse Computech products. Although you made no payment to anyone, you gave up the opportunity to earn rental payments.

7-1b ECONOMIC AND ACCOUNTING PROFIT

In everyday use, the word *profit* is defined as follows:

$$\text{Profit} = \text{total revenue} - \text{total cost}$$

Economists call this concept *accounting profit*. This popular formula is expressed in economics as

$$\text{Accounting profit} = \text{total revenue} - \text{total explicit cost}$$

Economic profit

Total revenue minus explicit and implicit costs.

Because economic decisions include implicit as well as explicit costs, economists use the concept of economic profit instead of accounting profit. Economic profit is total revenue minus explicit and implicit costs. Economic profit can be positive, zero, or negative (an economic loss). Expressed as an equation:

$$\text{Economic profit} = \text{total revenue} - \text{total opportunity costs}$$

or

$$\text{Economic profit} = \text{total revenue} - (\text{explicit costs} + \text{implicit costs})$$

Exhibit 1 illustrates the importance of the difference between accounting profit and economic profit. Computech must know how well it is doing, so you hire an accounting firm to prepare a financial report. The exhibit shows that Computech earned total revenue of $500,000 in its first year of operation. Explicit

EXHIBIT 1	Computech's Accounting Profit versus Economic Profit	
Item	**Accounting profit**	**Economic profit**
Total revenue	$500,000	$500,000
Less explicit costs:		
Wages and salaries	400,000	400,000
Materials	50,000	50,000
Interest paid	10,000	10,000
Other payments	10,000	10,000
Less implicit costs:		
Forgone salary	0	50,000
Forgone rent	0	10,000
Forgone interest	0	5,000
Equals profit	$30,000	−$35,000

SOURCE: © Cengage Learning 2014

costs for wages, materials, interest, and other payments totaled $470,000. Based on standard accounting procedures, this left an accounting profit of $30,000.

If the analysis ends with accounting profit, Computech is profitable. But accounting practice overstates profit. Because implicit costs are subjective and therefore difficult to measure, accounting profit ignores implicit costs. A few examples will illustrate the importance of implicit costs. Your $50,000-a-year salary as an electrical engineer was forgone in order to spend all your time as owner of Computech. Also forgone were $10,000 in rental income and $5,000 in interest that you would have earned during the year by renting your building and putting your savings in the bank. Subtracting both explicit and implicit costs from total revenue, Computech had an economic loss of $35,000. The firm is failing to cover the opportunity costs of using its resources in the electronics industry. Thus, the firm's resources would earn a higher return if they were used for other alternatives.

How would you interpret a zero economic profit? It's not as bad as it sounds. Economists call this condition normal profit. Normal profit is the minimum profit necessary to keep a firm in operation. Zero economic profit signifies there is just enough total revenue to pay the owners for all explicit and implicit costs. Stated differently, there is no benefit from reallocating resources to another use. For example, assume an owner earns zero economic profit, including an implicit (forfeited) cost of $50,000 per year that could have been earned working for someone else. This means the owner earned as much as would have been earned in the next best employment opportunity.

Normal profit

The minimum profit necessary to keep a firm in operation. A firm that earns normal profits earns total revenue equal to its total opportunity cost.

> **CONCLUSION:** *Since business decision making is based on economic profit, rather than accounting profit, the word* profit *in this text always means economic profit.*

✔ CHECKPOINT

Should the Professor Go or Stay?

Professor Martin is considering leaving the university and opening a consulting business. For her services as a consultant, she would be paid $75,000 a year. To open this business, Professor Martin must convert a house from which she collects rent of $20,000 per year into an office and hire a part-time assistant at a salary of $15,000 per year. The university pays Professor Martin $50,000 a year. Based only on economic decision making, do you predict the professor will leave the university to start a new business?

7-2 Short-Run Production Costs

Having presented the basic definitions of total cost, the next step is to study cost theory. In this section, we explore the relationship between output and cost in the short run. In the next section, the time horizon shifts to the long run.

7-2a SHORT RUN VERSUS LONG RUN

Suppose I asked you, "What is the difference between the short run and the long run?" Your answer might be that the short run is less than a year and the long run is over a year. Good guess, but wrong! Economists do not partition production decisions based on a specific number of days, months, or years. Instead, the distinction depends on the ability to vary the quantity of inputs or resources used in production. There are two types of inputs—*fixed inputs* and *variable inputs*. A fixed input is any resource for which the quantity cannot change during the period of time under consideration. For example, the physical size of a firm's plant and the production capacity of heavy machines cannot easily change within a short period of time. They must remain as fixed amounts while managers decide to vary output. In addition to fixed inputs, the firm uses *variable inputs* in the production process. A variable input is any resource for which the quantity can change during the period of time under consideration. For example, managers can hire fewer or more workers during a given year. They can also change the amount of materials and electricity used in production.

Now we can link the concepts of fixed and variable inputs to the *short run* and the *long run*. The short run is a period of time so short that there is at least one fixed input. For example, the short run is a period of time during which a firm can increase output by hiring more workers (variable input) while the size of the firm's plant (fixed input) remains unchanged. The firm's plant is the most difficult input to change quickly. The long run is a period of time so long that all inputs are variable. In the long run, the firm can build new factories or purchase new machinery. New firms can enter the industry, and existing firms may leave the industry.

Fixed input
Any resource for which the quantity cannot change during the period of time under consideration.

Variable input
Any resource for which the quantity can change during the period of time under consideration.

Short run
A period of time so short that there is at least one fixed input.

Long run
A period of time so long that all inputs are variable.

7-2b THE PRODUCTION FUNCTION

Having defined inputs, we can now describe how these inputs are transferred into outputs using a concept called a production function. A production function is the relationship between the maximum amounts of output a firm can produce and various quantities of inputs. An assumption of the production function model we are about to develop is that the level of technology is fixed. Technological advances would mean more output is possible from a given quantity of inputs.

Exhibit 2(a) presents a short-run production function for Eaglecrest Vineyard. The variable input is the number of workers employed per day, and each worker is presumed to have equal job skills. The acreage, amount of fertilizer, and all other inputs are assumed to be fixed; therefore, our production model is operating in the short run. Employing zero workers produces no bushels of grapes. A single worker can produce 10 bushels per day, but a lot of time is wasted when one worker picks, loads containers, and transports the grapes to the winery. Adding a second worker raises output to 22 bushels per day because the workers divide the tasks and specialize. Adding four more workers raises total product to 50 bushels per day.

Production function
The relationship between the maximum amounts of output a firm can produce and various quantities of inputs.

7-2c MARGINAL PRODUCT

The relationship between changes in total output and changes in labor is called the marginal product of labor. Marginal product is the change in total output produced by adding 1 unit of a variable input, with all other inputs used being held constant. When Eaglecrest increases labor from zero to one worker, output rises from 0 to 10 bushels produced per day. This increase is the result of the addition of one more worker. Therefore, the marginal product so far is 10 bushels per worker. Similar marginal product calculations generate the marginal product curve shown in Exhibit 2(b). Note that marginal product is plotted at the midpoints shown in the table because the change in total output occurs between each additional unit of labor used.

Marginal product
The change in total output produced by adding 1 unit of a variable input, with all other inputs used being held constant.

7-2d THE LAW OF DIMINISHING RETURNS

A long-established economic law called the law of diminishing returns determines the shape of the marginal product curve. The law of diminishing returns states that beyond some point, the marginal product decreases as additional units of a variable factor are added to a fixed factor. Because the law of diminishing returns assumes fixed inputs, this principle is a short-run, rather than a long-run, concept.

This law applies to production of both agricultural and nonagricultural products. Returning to Exhibit 2, we can identify and explain the law of diminishing returns in our Eaglecrest example. Initially, the total output curve rises quite rapidly as this firm hires the first two workers. The marginal product curve reflects the change in the total output curve because marginal product is the slope of the total output curve. As shown in Exhibit 2(b), the range from zero to two workers hired is called *increasing marginal returns*. In this range of output, the last worker hired adds more to total output than does the previous worker.

Diminishing returns begin after the second worker is hired and the marginal product reaches its peak. Beyond two workers, diminishing returns occur, and the marginal product declines. The short-run assumption guarantees this condition. Eventually, marginal product falls because the amount of land per worker falls as

Law of diminishing returns
The principle that states that beyond some point, the marginal product decreases as additional units of a variable factor are added to a fixed factor.

EXHIBIT 2	A Production Function and the Law of Diminishing Returns

Part (a) shows how the total output of bushels of grapes per day increases and the number of workers increases while all other inputs remain constant. This figure is a short-run production function, which relates outputs to a one-variable input while all other inputs are fixed.

Part (b) illustrates the law of diminishing returns. The first worker adds 10 bushels of grapes per day, and marginal product is 10 bushels per day. Adding a second worker adds another 12 bushels of grapes per day to total output. This is the range of increasing marginal returns. After two workers, diminishing marginal returns set in, and marginal product declines continuously.

(a) Total output curve

Short-Run Production Function of Eaglecrest Vineyard

(1) Labor Input (number of workers per day)	(2) Total Output (bushels of grapes per day)	(3) Marginal Product (bushels of grapes per day) [Δ(2)/Δ(1)]
0	0	
		10
1	10	
		12
2	22	
		11
3	33	
		9
4	42	
		6
5	48	
		2
6	50	

(b) Marginal product curve

SOURCE: © Cengage Learning 2014

more workers are added to fixed quantities of land and other inputs used to produce wine. Similar reasoning applies to the Computech example introduced in the chapter preview. Assume Computech operates with a fixed plant size and a fixed number of machines and all other inputs except that the number of workers is fixed. Those in the first group of workers hired divide the most important tasks among themselves, specialize, and achieve increasing returns. Then diminishing returns begin and continue as Computech employs each additional worker. The reason is that as more workers are added, they must share fixed inputs, such as machinery. Some workers are underemployed because they are standing around waiting for a machine to become available. Also, as more workers are hired, there are fewer important tasks to perform. As a result, marginal product declines. In the extreme case, marginal product would be negative. At some number of workers, they must work with such limited floor space, machines, and other fixed inputs that they start stepping on each other's toes. No profit-seeking firm would ever hire workers with zero or negative marginal product. Chapter 11 explains the labor market in more detail and shows how Computech decides exactly how many workers to hire.

7-3 Short-Run Cost Formulas

To make production decisions in either the short run or the long run, a business must determine the costs associated with producing various levels of output. Using Computech, you will study the relationship between two "families" of short-run costs and output: (1) the total cost curves and (2) the average cost curves.

7-3a TOTAL COST CURVES

Total Fixed Cost   As production expands in the short run, costs are divided into two basic categories—*total fixed cost* and *total variable cost*. Total fixed cost (TFC) consists of costs that do not vary as output varies and that must be paid even if output is zero. These are payments that the firm must make in the short run, regardless of the level of output. Even if a firm, such as Computech, produces nothing, it must still pay rent, interest on loans, property taxes, and fire insurance. Fixed costs are therefore beyond management's control in the short run. The total fixed cost for Computech is $100, as shown in column (2) of Exhibit 3.

Total Variable Cost   As the firm expands from zero output, total variable cost is added to total fixed cost. Total variable cost (TVC) consists of costs that are zero when output is zero and vary as output varies. These costs relate to the costs of variable inputs. Examples include wages for hourly workers, electricity, fuel, and raw materials. As a firm uses more input to produce output, its variable costs will increase. Management can control variable costs in the short run by changing the level of output. Exhibit 3 lists the total variable cost for Computech in column (3).

Total Cost   Given total fixed cost and total variable cost, the firm can calculate total cost (TC). Total cost is the sum of total fixed cost and total variable cost at each level of output. As a formula:

$$TC = TFC + TVC$$

Total cost for Computech is shown in column (4) of Exhibit 3. Exhibit 4(a) uses the data in Exhibit 3 to construct graphically the relationships between total cost,

Total fixed cost (TFC)

Costs that do not vary as output varies and that must be paid even if output is zero. These are payments that the firm must make in the short run, regardless of the level of output.

Total variable cost (TVC)

Costs that are zero when output is zero and vary as output varies.

Total cost (TC)

The sum of total fixed cost and total variable cost at each level of output.

total fixed cost, and total variable cost. Note that the TVC curve varies with the level of output and the TFC curve does not. The TC curve is simply the TVC curve plus the vertical distance between the TC and TVC curves, which represents TFC.

7-3b AVERAGE COST CURVES

In addition to total cost, firms are interested in the *per-unit cost*, or *average cost*. Average cost, like product price, is stated on a per-unit basis. The last three columns in Exhibit 3 are *average fixed cost (AFC)*, *average variable cost (AVC)*, and *average total cost (ATC)*. These average, or per-unit, curves are also shown in Exhibit 4(b). These three concepts are defined as follows:

Average fixed cost (AFC)

Total fixed cost divided by the quantity of output produced.

Average Fixed Cost   As output increases, average fixed cost (AFC) falls continuously. Average fixed cost is total fixed cost divided by the quantity of output produced. Written as a formula:

$$AFC = \frac{TFC}{Q}$$

As shown in Exhibit 4(b), the AFC curve approaches the horizontal axis as output expands. This is because larger output numbers divide into TFC and cause AFC to become smaller and smaller.

Average variable cost (AVC)

Total variable cost divided by the quantity of output produced.

Average Variable Cost   The average variable cost (AVC) in our example forms a U-shaped curve. Average variable cost is total variable cost divided by the quantity of output produced. Written as a formula:

$$AVC = \frac{TVC}{Q}$$

The AVC curve is also drawn in Exhibit 4(b). At first, the AVC curve falls, and then after an output of 6 units per hour, the AVC curve rises. Thus, the AVC curve is U-shaped. The explanation for the shape of the AVC curve is given in the next section.

Average total cost (ATC)

Total cost divided by the quantity of output produced.

Average Total Cost   Average total cost (ATC) is sometimes referred to as *per-unit cost*. The average total cost is total cost divided by the quantity of output produced. Written as a formula:

$$ATC = \frac{TC}{Q}$$

or

$$ATC = AFC + AVC$$

Like the AVC curve, the ATC curve is U-shaped, as shown in Exhibit 4(b). At first, the ATC curve falls because its component parts—AVC and AFC—are falling. As output continues to rise, the AVC curve begins to rise, while the AFC curve falls continuously. Beyond the output of 7 units per hour, the rise in the AVC curve is greater than the fall in the AFC curve, which causes the ATC curve to rise in a U-shaped pattern.

Marginal cost (MC)

The change in total cost when one additional unit of output is produced.

Marginal Cost   Marginal analysis asks how much it costs to produce an *additional* unit of output. Column (5) in Exhibit 3 is marginal cost (MC). Marginal cost is the change in total cost when one additional unit of output is produced. Stated

EXHIBIT 3			Short-Run Cost Schedule for Computech				
(1) Total Product (Q)	**(2)** Total Fixed Cost (TFC)	**(3)** Total Variable Cost (TVC)	**(4)** Total Cost (TC)	**(5)** Marginal Cost (MC)	**(6)** Average Fixed Cost (AFC)	**(7)** Average Variable Cost (AVC)	**(8)** Average Total Cost (ATC)
0	$100	$ 0	$100		–	–	–
				$ 50			
1	100	50	150		$100	$50	$150
				34			
2	100	84	184		50	42	92
				24			
3	100	108	208		33	36	69
				19			
4	100	127	227		25	32	57
				23			
5	100	150	250		20	30	50
				30			
6	100	180	280		17	30	47
				38			
7	100	218	318		14	31	45
				48			
8	100	266	366		13	33	46
				59			
9	100	325	425		11	36	47
				75			
10	100	400	500		10	40	50
				95			
11	100	495	595		9	45	54
				117			
12	100	612	712		8	51	59

SOURCE: © Cengage Learning 2014

differently, marginal cost is the ratio of the change in total cost to a 1-unit change in output. Written as a formula:

$$MC = \frac{\text{change in TC}}{\text{change in Q}}$$

Changing output by one unit at a time simplifies the marginal cost calculations in our Computech example. The marginal cost data are listed between output levels to show that marginal cost is the change in total cost as the output level changes.

| EXHIBIT 4 | Short-Run Cost Curves |

The curves in this exhibit are derived by plotting data from Exhibit 3. Part (a) shows that the total cost (TC) at each level of output is the sum of total variable cost (TVC) and total fixed cost (TFC). Because the TFC curve does not vary with output, the shape of the TC curve is determined by the shape of the TVC curve. The vertical distance between the TC and the TVC curves is TFC.

In part (b), the marginal cost (MC) curve decreases at first, then reaches a minimum, and then increases as output increases. The MC curve intersects both the average variable cost (AVC) curve and the average total cost (ATC) curve at the minimum point on each of these cost curves. The average fixed cost (AFC) curve declines continuously as output expands. AFC is also the difference between the ATC and the AVC curves at any quantity of output.

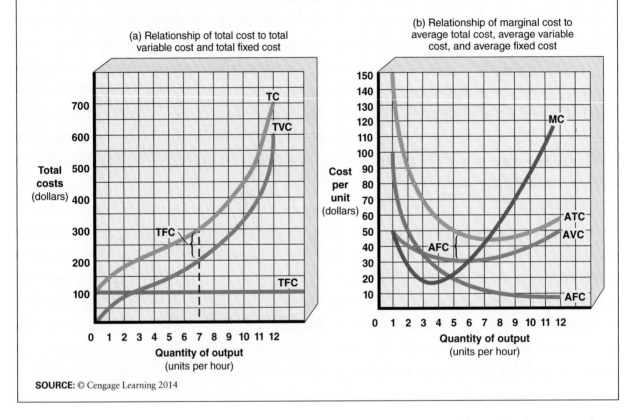

(a) Relationship of total cost to total variable cost and total fixed cost

(b) Relationship of marginal cost to average total cost, average variable cost, and average fixed cost

SOURCE: © Cengage Learning 2014

Exhibit 4(b) shows this marginal cost schedule graphically. In the short run, a firm's marginal cost initially falls as output expands, eventually reaches a minimum, and then rises, forming a J-shaped curve. Note that marginal cost is plotted at the midpoints because the change in cost actually occurs between each additional unit of output.

Exhibit 5 summarizes a firm's short-run cost relationships.

7-4 Marginal Cost Relationships

Part (b) of Exhibit 4 presents two important relationships that require explanation. First, we will explain the rule that links the marginal cost curve to the average cost curves. Second, we will return to the marginal product curve in Exhibit 2(b) and explain its connection to the marginal cost curve.

EXHIBIT 5	Short-Run Cost Formulas	
Cost Concept	**Formula**	**Graph**
Total cost (TC)	$TC = TFC + TVC$	
Marginal cost (MC)	$\dfrac{\text{change in TC}}{\text{change in Q}}$	
Average fixed cost (AFC)	$AFC = \dfrac{TFC}{Q}$	
Average variable cost (AVC)	$AVC = \dfrac{TVC}{Q}$	
Average total cost (ATC)	$ATC = \dfrac{TC}{Q}$	

SOURCE: © Cengage Learning 2014

7-4a THE MARGINAL-AVERAGE RULE

Observe that the MC curve in Exhibit 4(b) intersects both the AVC curve and the ATC curve at their minimum points. This is not accidental. It is a result of a relationship called the marginal-average rule. The marginal-average rule states that when marginal cost is below average cost, average cost falls. When marginal cost is above average cost, average cost rises. When marginal cost equals average cost, average cost is at its minimum point. The marginal-average rule applies to grades, weights, and any average figure.

Perhaps the best way to understand this rule is to apply it to a noneconomic example. Suppose there are 20 students in your class and each student has a grade point average (GPA) of 4.0. The average GPA of the class is therefore 4.0. Now assume another student who has a GPA of 2.0 joins the class. The new average GPA of 21 students in the class falls to 3.9. The average GPA was pulled down because the *marginal* GPA of the additional student was lower than the *average* GPA of the other students. Now suppose we start with a class of 20 students with a

Marginal-average rule

The rule that states when marginal cost is below average cost, average cost falls. When marginal cost is above average cost, average cost rises. When marginal cost equals average cost, average cost is at its minimum point.

2.0 GPA and add a student who has a 4.0 GPA. In this case, the new average GPA of the 21 students rises from 2.0 to 2.1. Thus, the *marginal* GPA of the last student was higher than the *average* GPA of all students in class before the addition of the new student.

Now consider the MC curve in part (b) of Exhibit 4. In the range of output from 0 to 6 units per hour, the MC curve is below the AVC curve, and AVC is falling. Beyond 6 units per hour, the MC curve is above AVC, and AVC is rising. Hence, the relationship between AVC and MC conforms to the marginal-average rule. It follows that the MC curve intersects the AVC curve at its lowest point. This analysis also applies to the relationship between the MC and ATC curves. Initially, the MC curve is lower than the ATC curve until it reaches its minimum, causing the ATC curve to fall. Beginning with 8 units of output, the MC curve exceeds the ATC curve, causing the ATC curve to rise.

✔ CHECKPOINT

Did Michael Jordan Beat the Marginal-Average Rule?

Michael Jordan, formerly of the Chicago Bulls, is one of the finest players in the history of basketball. Suppose he had an average of 33 points per game over the first ten games of the season and then scored 20, 25, 40, 50, and 20 points in the next five games. Did Michael Jordan beat the marginal-average rule?

7-4b MARGINAL COST'S MIRROR IMAGE

Because the MC curve determines the U-shape of the AVC and ATC curves, we must explain the J-shape of the MC curve. Exhibit 6 illustrates that the shape of the MC curve is the mirror reflection of the shape of the marginal product (MP) curve. Comparing parts (a) and (b) of Exhibit 6 gives the following:

> **CONCLUSION:** *The marginal cost declines as the marginal product of a variable input rises if the wage rate is constant. Beginning at the point of diminishing returns, the marginal cost rises as the marginal product of a variable input declines.*

As explained earlier in this chapter, the law of diminishing returns is the declining portion of the MP curve that corresponds to the rising portion of the MC curve. To understand why this relationship exists, we return to the case of Eaglecrest Vineyard presented earlier in Exhibit 2. Now we again assume that labor is the only variable input and add the new important assumption that the wage rate is constant at $100 per day. When Eaglecrest moves from zero labor to hire one worker, its total output rises from 0 to 10 bushels of grapes per day. As explained earlier, the marginal product is also 10 bushels, and the marginal cost is $100/10 = $10 ($\Delta TC/\Delta Q = \Delta TC/MP$). When Eaglecrest hires the second worker, total output rises by 12 bushels per day. Hiring this worker increases the firm's total cost by $100, while the marginal product rises to 12 bushels. The marginal cost of the second worker therefore falls to a minimum at $100/12 = $8.33. At this point, it is noteworthy that the minimum point on the MC curve corresponds to the maximum point on the MP curve. The third worker hired yields only 11 additional bushels of grapes per day, so marginal cost rises to $9.09. Thus, diminishing returns begin with the third worker, and the marginal cost continues to rise as more workers are hired.

SOURCE: © Cengage Learning 2014

7-5 Long-Run Production Costs

As explained earlier in this chapter, the long run is a time period long enough to change the quantity of all fixed inputs. A firm can, for example, build a larger or smaller factory or vary the capacity of its machinery. In this section, we will discuss how varying factory size and *all* other inputs in the long run affect the relationship between production and costs.

7-5a Long-Run Average Cost Curves

Suppose Computech is making its production plans for the future. Taking a long-run view of production means the firm is not locked into a small, medium-sized, or large factory. However, once a factory of a particular size is built, the firm operates in the short run because the plant becomes a fixed input.

> **CONCLUSION:** *A firm operates in the short run when there is insufficient time to alter some fixed input. A firm plans in the long run when all inputs are variable.*

Exhibit 7 illustrates a situation in which there are only three possible factory sizes Computech might select. Short-run cost curves representing these three possible plant sizes are labeled $SRATC_s$, $SRATC_m$, and $SRATC_l$. *SR* is the abbreviation for short run, and *ATC* stands for average total cost. The subscripts *s*, *m*, and *l* represent small, medium, and large plant size, respectively. In the previous sections, there was no need to use SR for short run because we were discussing only short-run cost curves and not long-run cost curves.

Suppose Computech estimates that it will be producing an output level of 6 units per hour for the foreseeable future. Which plant size should the company choose? It will build the plant size represented by $SRATC_s$ because this affords a lower cost of $30 per unit (point A) than the factory size represented by $SRATC_m$, which has a cost of $40 per unit (point B).

EXHIBIT 6	The Inverse Relationship between Marginal Product and Marginal Cost

Part (a) represents the marginal product of labor (MP) curve. At first, each additional worker hired adds more to output than does the previously hired worker, and the MP curve rises until a maximum is reached at two workers hired. At three workers, the law of diminishing returns sets in, and each additional worker hired adds less output than do previously hired workers.

Part (b) shows the marginal cost (MC) curve is a J-shaped curve that is inversely related to the MP curve. Assuming the wage rate remains constant, as the MP curve rises, the MC curve falls. When the MP curve reaches a maximum at two workers, the MC curve is at a minimum. As diminishing returns set in and the MP curve falls, the MC curve rises.

(1) Labor Input (number of workers per day)	(2) Total Output (bushels of grapes per day)	(3) Marginal Product (bushels of grapes per day) [Δ(2)/Δ(1)]	(4) Total Cost per Day [$100 × (1)]	(5) Marginal Cost [Δ(4)/(3)]
0	0		$ 0	
		10		$10.00
1	10		100	
		12		8.33
2	22		200	
		11		9.09
3	33		300	
		9		11.11
4	42		400	
		6		16.66
5	48		500	
		2		50.00
6	50		600	

SOURCE: © Cengage Learning 2014

EXHIBIT 7	The Relationship between Three Factory Sizes and the Long-Run Average Cost Curve

Each of the three short-run ATC curves in the exhibit corresponds to a different plant size. Assuming these are the only three plant-size choices, a firm can choose any one of these plant sizes in the long run. For example, a young firm may operate a small plant represented by the U-shaped short-run average total cost curve $SRATC_s$. As a firm matures and demand for its product expands, it can decide to build a larger factory, corresponding to either $SRATC_m$ or $SRATC_l$. The long-run average cost (LRAC) curve is the green shaded scalloped curve joining the short-run curves below their intersections.

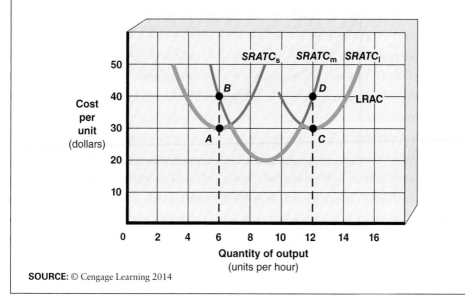

SOURCE: © Cengage Learning 2014

What if production is expected to be 12 units per hour? In this case, the firm will choose the plant size represented by $SRATC_l$. At this plant size, the cost is $30 per unit (point C), which is lower than $40 per unit (point D).

CONCLUSION: *The plant size selected by a firm in the long run depends on the expected level of production.*

Using the three short-run average cost curves shown in Exhibit 7, we can construct the firm's long-run average cost curve (LRAC). The long-run average cost curve traces the lowest cost per unit at which a firm can produce any level of output after the firm can build any desired plant size. The LRAC curve is often called the firm's planning curve. In Exhibit 7, the green curve represents the LRAC curve.

Long-run average cost curve (LRAC)

The curve that traces the lowest cost per unit at which a firm can produce any level of output after the firm can build any desired plant size.

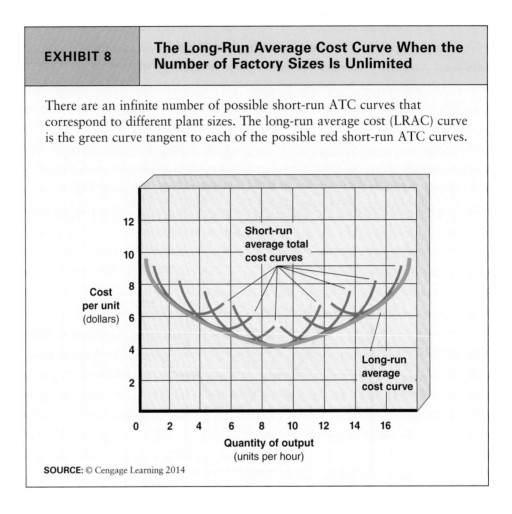

EXHIBIT 8   **The Long-Run Average Cost Curve When the Number of Factory Sizes Is Unlimited**

There are an infinite number of possible short-run ATC curves that correspond to different plant sizes. The long-run average cost (LRAC) curve is the green curve tangent to each of the possible red short-run ATC curves.

Short-run average total cost curves

Long-run average cost curve

Cost per unit (dollars)

Quantity of output (units per hour)

SOURCE: © Cengage Learning 2014

Exhibit 8 shows there are actually an infinite number of possible plant sizes from which managers can choose in the long run. As the intersection points of the short-run ATC curves move closer and closer together, the lumps in the LRAC curve in Exhibit 7 disappear. With a great variety of plant sizes, the corresponding short-run ATC curves trace a smooth LRAC curve in Exhibit 8. When the LRAC curve falls, the tangency points are to the left of the minimum points on the short-run ATC curves. As the LRAC curve rises, the tangency points are to the right of the minimum points on the short-run ATC curves.

7-6 Different Scales of Production

Exhibit 8 depicts long-run average cost as a U-shaped curve. In this section, we will discuss the reasons the LRAC curve falls and then rises when output expands in the long run. In addition, we will learn that the LRAC curve can have a variety of shapes. Note that the law of diminishing returns is not an explanation here because in the long run, there are no fixed inputs.

For simplicity, Exhibit 9 excludes possible short-run ATC curves that touch points along the LRAC curve. Typically, a young firm starts small and builds larger

EXHIBIT 9	A Long-Run Average Cost Curve with Constant Returns to Scale

The long-run average cost (LRAC) curve illustrates a firm that experiences economies of scale until output level Q_1 is reached. Between output levels Q_1 and Q_2, the LRAC curve is flat, and there are constant returns to scale. Beyond output level Q_2, the firm experiences diseconomies of scale, and the LRAC curve rises.

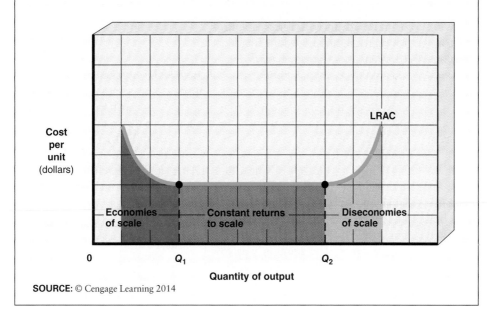

SOURCE: © Cengage Learning 2014

plants as it matures. As the scale of operation expands, the LRAC curve can follow three different patterns. Over the lowest range of output from zero to Q_1, the firm experiences economies of scale. Economies of scale exist when the long-run average cost curve declines as the firm increases output.

There are several reasons for economies of scale. First, a larger firm can increase its *division of labor* and *use of specialization*. Adam Smith noted in *The Wealth of Nations*, published in 1776, that the output of a pin factory is greater when one worker draws the wire, a second straightens it, a third cuts it, a fourth grinds the point, and a fifth makes the head of the pin. As a firm initially expands, having more workers allows managers to break a job into small tasks. Then each worker—including managers—can specialize by mastering narrowly defined tasks rather than trying to be a jack-of-all-trades.[1] The classic example is Henry Ford's assembly line, which greatly reduced the cost of producing automobiles. Today, McDonald's trains its workers at "Hamburger University"; then

Economies of scale

A situation in which the long-run average cost curve declines as the firm increases output.

---

[1] Adam Smith, *An Inquiry into the Nature and Causes of the Wealth of Nations* (1776; reprint, New York: Random House, 1937), pp. 4–6.

Why Is That Web Site You're Using Free?

Applicable Concepts: economies and diseconomies of scale

Pick the best price that you wish to pay for a product. Is zero reserved only for those who believe in Santa Claus? Recall the famous saying by economist Milton Friedman that "there's no such thing as a free lunch." Well, today, more and more Web companies are using digital technology and the principles of *freeconomics* to make profits by giving something away free of charge. And the key to understanding this radical business model is the concept of economies of scale.

How is it possible for companies to cover their production costs with a price of zero? Don't Web businesses have huge fixed costs to buy computer servers and design Web pages? This is true, but once the servers are powered up and the sites are online, the cost of logging in each additional customer is very small. Then as the companies scale expands over time, the cost of servers, bandwidth, and software are spread out over millions of users, and the long-run cost curve declines to almost zero, which is economies of scale.[1]

In the Web land of free payments called *freemiums*, the basic idea is to shift from the view of a market price matching buyers and sellers of a product to a free system with many participants and only a few who exchange cash. After customers get used to the free services, the companies hope that people will pay for more advanced services. Examples of freemiums are Adobe Reader, search engines, blogging platforms, and Skype-to-Skype phone calls. The revenue from the premiums for more powerful services covers the cost of both the premium and free activities. This is the cross-subsidy approach. A legendary example of this marketing strategy is King Gillette, who, in the early 1900s, was having no success selling men on the idea of shaving with disposable thin blades rather than with a straight razor. The solution was to bundle free razors with gum, coffee, marshmallows, and even new bank deposits with the slogan "Shave and Save" attached. The freebie razor without blades was useless, so customers bought the blades and the rest of this success story is history.

Another approach is to use free services to deliver advertising, just like traditional broadcast TV or radio. One company that has very

successfully applied the advertising approach to freemiums is Google. There is no cost to use its search engine, but the results pages feature "Sponsored Links," which are advertisements paid for by Web sites related to the search terms. Google used this model to achieve impressive financial results.

Analyze the Issue

Suppose a hugely successful Web company has used freeconomics, expanded its scale of operations, and spread its long-run costs over larger and larger audiences. After years of profits, the company's profits fell continuously. Using production costs theory, explain why this situation might be occurring.

1. Chris Anderson, "Why $0.00 is the Future of Business," March 2008, http://www.wired.com/images/press/pdf/free.pdf.

Source: © Cengage Learning 2014

some workers prepare food, some specialize in taking orders, and a few workers specialize in the drive-through window operation.

Second, economies of scale result from greater *efficiency of capital*. Suppose machine A costs $1,000 and produces 1,000 units per day. Machine B costs $4,000, but it is technologically more efficient and has a capacity of 8,000 units per day. The low-output firm will find it too costly to purchase machine B, so it uses machine A, and its average cost is $1. The large-scale firm can afford to purchase machine B and produce more efficiently at a per-unit cost of only $0.50.

The LRAC curve may not turn upward and form the U-shaped cost curve shown in Exhibit 8. Between some levels of output, such as Q_1 and Q_2 in Exhibit 9, the LRAC curve no longer declines. In this range of output, the firm increases its plant size, but the LRAC curve remains flat. Economists call this situation constant returns to scale. Constant returns to scale exists when the long-run average cost curve does not change as the firm increases output. Economists believe this is the shape of the LRAC curve in many real-world industries. The scale of operation is important for competitive reasons. Consider a young firm producing less than output Q_1 and competing against a more established firm producing in the constant-returns-to-scale range of output. The LRAC curve shows that the older firm has an average cost advantage.

As a firm becomes large and expands output beyond some level, such as Q_2 in Exhibit 9, it encounters diseconomies of scale. Diseconomies of scale exists when the long-run average cost curve rises as the firm increases output. A very large-scale firm becomes harder to manage. As the firm grows, the chain of command lengthens, and communication becomes more complex. People communicate through forms instead of direct conversation. The firm becomes too bureaucratic, and operations bog down in red tape. Layer upon layer of managers are paid big salaries to shuffle papers that have little or nothing to do with beating the competition by producing output at a lower cost. Consequently, it is no surprise that a firm can become too big, and these management problems can cause the average cost of production to rise.

Steven Jobs, founder of Apple Computer Company, stated:

> When you are growing [too big], you start adding middle management like crazy ... People in the middle have no understanding of the business, and because of that, they screw up communications. To them, it's just a job. The corporation ends up with mediocre people that form a layer of concrete.[2]

Constant returns to scale

A situation in which the long-run average cost curve does not change as the firm increases output.

Diseconomies of scale

A situation in which the long-run average cost curve rises as the firm increases output.

Key Concepts

Explicit costs	Production function	Average total cost (ATC)
Implicit costs	Marginal product	Marginal cost (MC)
Economic profit	Law of diminishing returns	Marginal-average rule
Normal profit	Total fixed cost (TFC)	Long-run average cost curve
Fixed input	Total variable cost (TVC)	(LRAC)
Variable input	Total cost (TC)	Economies of scale
Short run	Average fixed cost (AFC)	Constant returns to scale
Long run	Average variable cost (AVC)	Diseconomies of scale

---

[2]Deborah Wise and Catherine Harris, "Apple's New Crusade," *Business Week*, Nov. 26, 1984, p. 156.

Summary

- **Economic profit** is equal to total revenue minus both *explicit* and *implicit* costs. **Implicit costs** are the opportunity costs of forgone returns to resources owned by a firm. Economic profit is important for decision-making purposes because it includes implicit costs and accounting profit does not. Accounting profit equals total revenue minus explicit costs.
- The **short run** is a time period during which a firm has at least one fixed input, such as its factory size. The **long run** for a firm is defined as a period during which all inputs are variable.
- A **production function** is the relationship between output and inputs. Holding all other factors of production constant, the production function shows that the total output as the amount of one input, such as labor, varies.
- **Marginal product** is the change in total output caused by a 1-unit change in a variable input, such as the number of workers hired. The **law of diminishing returns** states that after some level of output in the short run, each additional unit of the variable input yields less and less marginal product. This range of declining marginal product is the region of diminishing returns.
- **Total fixed cost (TFC)** consists of costs that do not vary with the level of output, such as rent for office space. Total fixed cost is the cost of inputs that do not change as a firm changes output in the short run. **Total variable cost (TVC)** consists of costs that vary with the level of output, such as wages. Total variable cost is the cost of variable inputs used in production. **Total cost (TC)** is the sum of total fixed cost (TFC) and total variable cost (TVC).

Total Cost Curves

Relationship of total cost to total variable cost and total fixed cost

SOURCE: © Cengage Learning 2014

- **Marginal cost (MC)** is the change in total cost associated with one additional unit of output. **Average fixed cost (AFC)** is the total fixed cost divided by total output. **Average variable cost (AVC)** is the total variable cost divided by total output. **Average total cost (ATC)** is the total cost, or the sum of average fixed cost and average variable cost, divided by output.

Average and Marginal Cost Curves

Relationship of marginal cost to average total cost, average variable cost, and average fixed cost

SOURCE: © Cengage Learning 2014

- The **marginal-average rule** explains the relationship between marginal cost and average cost. When marginal cost is less than average cost, average cost falls. When marginal cost is greater than average cost, average cost rises. Following this rule, the marginal cost curve intersects the average variable cost curve and the average total cost curve at their minimum points.
- **Marginal cost (MC)** and **marginal product (MP)** are mirror images of each other. Assuming a constant wage rate, marginal cost equals the wage rate divided by the marginal product. Increasing returns cause marginal cost to fall, and diminishing returns cause marginal cost to rise. This explains the J-shaped marginal cost curve.

Marginal Cost Curve

SOURCE: © Cengage Learning 2014

- The **long-run average cost curve (LRAC)** is a curve drawn tangent to all possible short-run average total cost curves. When the LRAC curve decreases as output increases, a firm experiences **economies of scale**. If the LRAC curve remains unchanged as output increases, a firm experiences **constant returns to scale**. If the LRAC curve increases as output increases, a firm experiences **diseconomies of scale**.

Marginal Product Curve

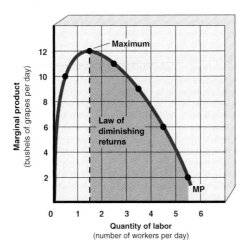

SOURCE: © Cengage Learning 2014

Long-Run Average Cost Curve

SOURCE: © Cengage Learning 2014

Summary of Conclusion Statements

- Because business decision making is based on economic profit, rather than accounting profit, the word *profit* in this text always means economic profit.
- The marginal cost declines as the marginal product of a variable input rises if the wage rate is constant. Beginning at the point of diminishing returns, the marginal cost rises as the marginal product of a variable input declines.
- A firm operates in the short run when there is insufficient time to alter some fixed input. The firm plans in the long run when all inputs are variable.
- The plant size selected by a firm in the long run depends on the expected level of production.

Study Questions and Problems

1. Indicate whether each of the following is an explicit cost or an implicit cost:
   a. A manager's salary
   b. Payments to Dell for computers
   c. A salary forgone by the owner of a firm by operating his or her own company
   d. Interest forgone on a loan an owner makes to his or her own company
   e. Medical insurance payments a company makes for its employees
   f. Income forgone while going to college

2. Suppose you own a video game store. List some of the fixed inputs and variable inputs you would use in operating the store.

3. a. Construct the marginal product schedule for the production function data in the following table.

Labor	Total Output	Marginal Product
0	0	
1	8	
2	18	
3	30	
4	43	
5	55	
6	65	
7	73	
8	79	
9	82	
10	80	

   b. Graph the total output and marginal product curves and identify increasing and diminishing marginal returns.

4. Consider this statement: "Total output starts falling when diminishing returns occur." Do you agree or disagree? Explain.

5. What effect might a decrease in the demand for high definition televisions have on the short-run average total cost curve for this product?

6. a. Construct the cost schedule using the data from the table on the next page for a firm operating in the short run.
   b. Graph the average variable cost, average total cost, and marginal cost curves.

7. Explain why the average total cost curve and the average variable cost curve move closer together as output expands.

8. Ace Manufacturing produces 1,000 hammers per day. The total fixed cost for the plant is $5,000 per day, and the total variable cost is $15,000 per day. Calculate the average fixed cost, average variable cost, average total cost, and total cost at the current output level.

9. An owner of a firm estimates that the average total cost is $6.71 and the marginal cost is $6.71 at the current level of output. Explain the relationship between these marginal cost and average total cost figures.

10. What short-run effect might a decline in the demand for electronic components for automatic teller machines have on Computech's average total cost curve?

11. For mathematically minded students, what is the algebraic relationship between the equation for output and the equation for marginal product in Exhibit 2? Explain the circumstances under which the long-run supply curve for an industry is a horizontal line. Then explain the circumstances under which the long-run supply curve for an industry is an upward-sloping line.

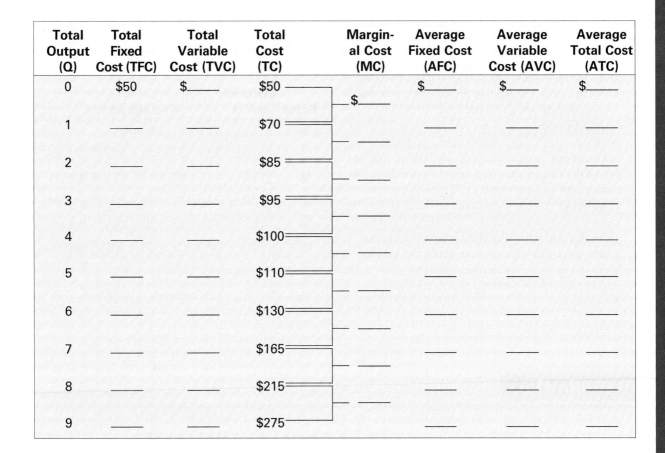

Total Output (Q)	Total Fixed Cost (TFC)	Total Variable Cost (TVC)	Total Cost (TC)	Marginal Cost (MC)	Average Fixed Cost (AFC)	Average Variable Cost (AVC)	Average Total Cost (ATC)
0	$50	$___	$50		$___	$___	$___
				$___			
1	___	___	$70		___	___	___
				___			
2	___	___	$85		___	___	___
				___			
3	___	___	$95		___	___	___
				___			
4	___	___	$100		___	___	___
				___			
5	___	___	$110		___	___	___
				___			
6	___	___	$130		___	___	___
				___			
7	___	___	$165		___	___	___
				___			
8	___	___	$215		___	___	___
				___			
9	___	___	$275		___	___	___

For Online Exercises, go to the Tucker Web site at www.cengage.com/economics/tucker.

✓ CHECKPOINT ANSWERS

Should the Professor Go or Stay?

In the consulting business, the accounting profit is $60,000. An accountant would calculate profit as the annual revenue of $75,000 less the explicit cost of $15,000 per year for the secretary's salary. However, the accountant would neglect implicit costs. Professor Martin's business venture would have implicit costs of $20,000 in forgone rent and $50,000 in forgone earnings. Her economic profit is –$10,000, calculated as the accounting profit of $70,000 less the total implicit costs of $70,000. If you said the professor will pass up the potential accounting profit and stay with the university to avoid an economic loss, **YOU ARE CORRECT.**

Did Michael Jordan Beat the Marginal-Average Rule?

Since Jordan's marginal points in games 11 and 12 were below his average points per game, his average points per game fell from 33 to 31. Games 13 and 14 lifted his average from 31 to 33 points per game because his marginal points in both of these games exceeded his average points per game. Finally, the 20 points in game 15 again reduced his average back to 32 points per game. Thus, when Jordan's marginal points scored in a game were below his season's average points per game, his average fell. When Jordan's marginal points scored in a game were above his season's average points per game, his average rose. If you said even Michael Jordan cannot beat the marginal-average rule, **YOU ARE CORRECT.**

Game	Marginal points	Average points
10		33 over 10 games
11	20	$32 = (33 \times 10 + 20)/11$ games
12	25	$31 = (32 \times 11 + 25)/12$ games
13	40	$32 = (31 \times 12 + 40)/13$ games
14	50	$33 = (32 \times 13 + 50)/14$ games
15	20	$32 = (33 \times 14 + 20)/15$ games

Sample Quiz

For an explanation of the correct answers, visit the Tucker Web site at www.cengage.com/economics/tucker.

1. A firm has $200 million in total revenue and explicit costs of $190 million. Suppose its owners have invested $100 million in the company at an opportunity cost of 10 percent interest per year. What is the firm's economic profit?
   a. $400 million
   b. $100 million
   c. $80 million
   d. zero

2. The units of variable input in a production process are 1, 2, 3, 4, and 5, and the corresponding total outputs are 30, 34, 37, 39, and 40, respectively. What is the marginal product of the fourth unit?
   a. 2
   b. 1
   c. 37
   d. 39

3. The situation in which the marginal product of labor is greater than zero and declining as more labor is hired is called the law of
   a. negative response.
   b. inverse return to labor.
   c. diminishing returns.
   d. demand.

4. Which of the following is *true* if the total variable cost curve is rising?
   a. Average fixed cost is increasing.
   b. Marginal cost is decreasing.
   c. Marginal cost is increasing.
   d. Average fixed cost is constant.

5. If the minimum points of all possible short-run average total cost curves become successively lower as quantity of output increases,
   a. the firm should try to produce less output.
   b. total fixed costs are constant along the LRAC curve.
   c. there are economies of scale.
   d. the firm is probably having significant management problems.

6. A young chef is considering opening his own sushi bar. To do so, he would have to quit his current job, which pays $20,000 a year, and take over a store building that he owns and currently rents to his brother for $6,000 a year. His expenses at the sushi bar would be $50,000 for food and $2,000 for gas and electricity. What are his explicit costs?

Sample Quiz *continued*

a. $26,000
b. $66,000
c. $78,000
d. $52,000

7. An economist left her $100,000-a-year teaching position to work full-time in her own consulting business. In the first year, she had total revenue of $200,000 and business expenses of $150,000. She made an
   a. implicit profit.
   b. economic loss.
   c. economic profit.
   d. accounting loss but not an economic loss.

8. Which of the following *best* describes total fixed cost?
   a. The change in total cost when one additional unit of output is produced
   b. Total cost divided by the quantity of output produced
   c. Total variable cost divided by the quantity of output produced
   d. Total fixed cost divided by the quantity of output produced
   e. Costs that do not vary as output varies

9. A farm can produce 10,000 bushels of wheat per year with five workers and 13,000 bushels with six workers. What is the marginal product of the sixth worker for this farm?
   a. 10,000 bushels
   b. 3,000 bushels
   c. 500 bushels
   d. 23,000 bushels

10. The law of diminishing returns applies to which of the following segments of the marginal product of labor curve?
    a. The entire curve
    b. The downward-sloping segment only
    c. The upward-sloping segment only
    d. The point where labor input is zero

11. Which of the following is *true* at the point where diminishing returns set in?
    a. Both marginal product and marginal cost are at a maximum.
    b. Both marginal product and marginal cost are at a minimum.

c. Marginal product is at a maximum, and marginal cost is at a minimum.
d. Marginal product is at a minimum, and marginal cost is at a maximum.

12. In the long run, total fixed cost
    a. falls.
    b. rises.
    c. is constant.
    d. does not exist.

13. Which of the following is considered a fixed cost of operating an automobile?
    a. Gasoline
    b. Tires
    c. Oil changes
    d. Maintenance
    e. Registration fees

14. Which of the following is an example of a fixed cost for a fishing company?
    a. The cost of hiring a fishing crew
    b. The fuel costs of running the boat
    c. The monthly loan payment on the boat
    d. The supply of nets, hooks, and fishing lines

15. The decreasing portion of a firm's long-run average cost curve is attributable to
    a. increasing marginal cost.
    b. economies of scale.
    c. diseconomies of scale.
    d. constant returns to scale.

16. Diseconomies of scale exist over the range of output for which the long-run average cost curve is
    a. constant.
    b. falling.
    c. rising.
    d. none of the above.

17. Assume both the marginal cost and the average variable cost curves are U-shaped. At the minimum point on the AVC curve, marginal cost must be
    a. greater than the average variable cost.
    b. less than the average variable cost.
    c. equal to the average variable cost.
    d. at its minimum.

18. By filling in the blanks in Exhibit 10, the total cost of producing zero pizzas is shown to be equal to
    a. zero.
    b. $100.

Sample Quiz *continued*

c. $5.
d. $105.
e. $95.

EXHIBIT 10	Costs Schedules for Producing Pizza			
Pizzas	**Fixed cost**	**Variable cost**	**Total cost**	**Marginal cost**
0	$	$	$	$
1		5		
2		13		
3				10
4	100		140	
5				20
6		85		
7			215	

SOURCE: © Cengage Learning 2014

19. By filling in the blanks in Exhibit 10, the fixed cost of producing six pizzas is shown to be equal to
    a. $100.
    b. $150.
    c. $200.
    d. $185.
    e. $85.

20. By filling in the blanks in Exhibit 10, the average variable cost of producing four pizzas is shown to be equal to
    a. $10.
    b. $15.
    c. $20.
    d. $40.
    e. $85.

21. By filling in the blanks in Exhibit 10, the average total cost of producing five pizzas is shown to be equal to
    a. $12.
    b. $15.
    c. $32.
    d. $85.
    e. $160.

22. By filling in the blanks in Exhibit 10, the marginal cost of the fourth pizza is shown to be equal to

a. $10.
b. $15.
c. $17.
d. $23.
e. $40.

EXHIBIT 11	Long-Run Average Cost Curves

SOURCE: © Cengage Learning 2014

23. In Exhibit 11, which firm's long-run average cost curve experiences constant returns to scale?
    a. Firm A
    b. Firm B
    c. Firm C
    d. Firms A and C

24. Which firm in Exhibit 11 displays a long-run average cost curve with diseconomies of scale beginning at 2,000 units of output per week?
    a. Firm A
    b. Firm B
    c. Firm C
    d. Firms A and C

25. Which firm in Exhibit 11 displays a long-run average cost curve with economies of scale throughout the range of output shown?
    a. Firm A
    b. Firm B
    c. Firm C
    d. Firms A and B

Road Map
Microeconomics Fundamentals

part 2

This road map feature helps you tie together material in the part as you travel the Economic Way of Thinking Highway. The following are review questions listed by chapter from the previous part. The key concept in each question is given for emphasis, and each question or set of questions concludes with an interactive game to reinforce the concepts. Go to the Tucker Web site at www.cengage.com/economics/tucker, select the chapter, and play the visual causation chain game designed to make learning fun. Enjoy the cheers when you are correct and suffer the jeers if you miss. The correct answers are given in Appendix C of the text.

CHAPTER 3. MARKET DEMAND AND SUPPLY

1. **Key Concept: Movement along versus shift in demand**
   Which of the following would shift the demand curve for autos to the right?
   a. A fall in the price of autos
   b. A fall in the price of auto insurance
   c. A fall in consumers' incomes
   d. A fall in the price of steel

   Causation Chain Game
   Movement along a Demand Curve versus a Shift in Demand—Exhibit 3

2. **Key Concept: Movement along versus shift in supply**
   Assuming that both soybeans and tobacco can be grown on the same land, a decrease in the price of tobacco, other things being equal, causes a(an)
   a. rightward shift of the supply curve for tobacco.
   b. upward movement along the supply curve for soybeans.
   c. rightward shift in the supply curve for soybeans.
   d. leftward shift in the supply curve for soybeans.

   Causation Chain Game
   Movement along a Supply Curve versus a Shift in Supply—Exhibit 8

3. **Key Concept: Surplus**
   Assume Q_s represents the quantity supplied at a given price and Q_d represents the quantity demanded at the same given price. Which of the following market conditions produce a downward movement of the price?
   a. $Q_s = 1,000$, $Q_d = 750$
   b. $Q_s = 750$, $Q_d = 750$
   c. $Q_s = 750$, $Q_d = 1,000$
   d. $Q_s = 1,000$, $Q_d = 1,000$

4. **Key Concept: Shortage**

Which of the following situations results from a ticket price to a concert set below the equilibrium price?

a. A long line of people wanting to purchase tickets to the concert

b. No line of people wanting to buy tickets to the concert

c. Tickets available at the box office, but no line of people wanting to buy them

d. None of the above

Causation Chain Game

Supply and Demand for Sneakers—Exhibit 12

CHAPTER 4. MARKETS IN ACTION

5. **Key Concept: Change in demand**

A decrease in consumer income decreases the demand for compact discs. As a result of the change to a new equilibrium, there is a(an)

a. leftward shift of the supply curve.

b. rightward shift of the supply curve.

c. upward movement along the supply curve.

d. downward movement along the supply curve.

Causation Chain Game

The Effects of Shifts in Demand on Market Equilibrium—Exhibit 1

6. **Key Concept: Change in supply**

Consider the market for grapes. An increase in the wage paid to grape pickers will cause the

a. demand curve for grapes to shift to the right, resulting in a higher equilibrium price for grapes and a reduction in the quantity consumed.

b. demand curve for grapes to shift to the left, resulting in a lower equilibrium price for grapes and an increase in the quantity consumed.

c. supply curve for grapes to shift to the left, resulting in a lower equilibrium price for grapes and a decrease in the quantity consumed.

d. supply curve for grapes to shift to the left, resulting in a higher equilibrium price for grapes and a decrease in the quantity consumed.

Causation Chain Game

The Effects of Shifts in Supply on Market Equilibrium—Exhibit 2

7. **Key Concept: Rent control**

Rent controls create distortions in the housing market by

a. increasing rents received by landlords.

b. raising property values.

c. encouraging landlords to overspend for maintenance.

d. discouraging new housing construction.

e. increasing the supply of housing in the long run.

Causation Chain Game

Rent Control—Exhibit 5

8. **Key Concept: Minimum wage**
   Which of the following is a good example of a price floor?
   a. Rent controls on apartments in major cities
   b. General admission tickets to concerts
   c. The minimum wage law
   d. Food stamp regulations
   e. Rock concert tickets

 Causation Chain Game
Minimum Wage—Exhibit 6

CHAPTER 5. PRICE ELASTICITY OF DEMAND AND SUPPLY

9. **Key Concept: Price elasticity of demand**
   Suppose Good Food's supermarket raises the price of its steak and finds that its total revenue from steak sales does *not* change. This is evidence that price elasticity of demand for steak is
   a. perfectly elastic.
   b. perfectly inelastic.
   c. unitary elastic.
   d. inelastic.
   e. elastic.

10. **Key Concept: Tax incidence**
    Assuming the demand curve is more elastic (flatter) than the supply curve, which of the following is *true*?
    a. The full tax is always passed on to the consumer no matter how flat (elastic) the demand curve is.
    b. The full tax is always passed on to the seller no matter how flat (elastic) the demand curve is.
    c. The smaller the portion of a sales tax passed on to the consumer.
    d. It does not make any difference how flat (elastic) the demand curve is; the tax is always split evenly between buyer and seller.

 Causation Chain Game
The Incidence of a Tax on Gasoline—Exhibit 10

CHAPTER 6. CONSUMER CHOICE THEORY

11. **Key Concept: Income effect**
    The income effect refers to a change in
    a. income because of changes in the CPI.
    b. the quantity demanded of a good because of a change in the buyer's real income.
    c. the quantity demanded of a good because of a change in the buyer's money income.
    d. none of the above.

Causation Chain Game
Income Effect

12. Key Concept: Substitution effect

Which of the following is the *best* example of the substitution effect?

a. Joe buys fewer apples and more oranges as the result of an increase in the price of apples.

b. Joe buys more apples when his income increases.

c. Joe buys an apple slicer when the price of apples decreases.

d. Joe buys less sugar as the result of an increase in the price of apples.

Causation Chain Game
Substitution Effect

CHAPTER 7. PRODUCTION COSTS

13. Key Concept: Marginal product and marginal cost

Which of the following is true at the point where diminishing returns set in?

a. Both marginal product and marginal cost are at a maximum.

b. Both marginal product and marginal cost are at a minimum.

c. Marginal product is at a maximum, and marginal cost is at a minimum.

d. Marginal product is at a minimum, and marginal cost is at a maximum.

Causation Chain Game
Marginal Product Effects on Marginal Cost

Market Structures

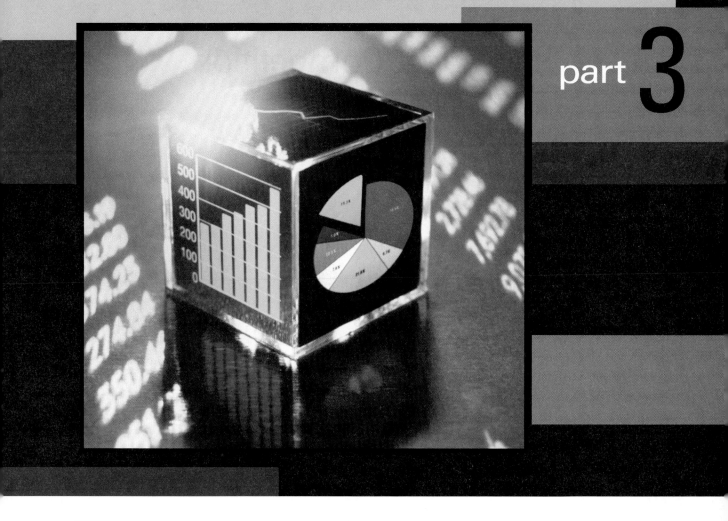

part 3

This part focuses on different types of markets, each defined by a set of characteristics that determines corresponding demand and supply conditions. Chapter 8 describes a highly competitive market consisting of an extremely large number of competing firms, and Chapter 9 explains the theory for a market with only a single seller. Between these extremes, Chapter 10 discusses two markets that have some characteristics of both competition and monopoly. The part concludes by developing labor market theory in Chapter 11.

chapter 8

Perfect Competition

Ostrich farmers in Iowa, Texas, Oklahoma, and other states in the Midwest "stuck their necks out." Many invested millions of dollars converting a portion of their farms into breeding grounds for ostriches. The reason was that mating pairs of ostriches were selling for $75,000 during the late 1990s. Ostrich breeders claimed that ostrich meat would become the low-cholesterol, low-fat health treat, and ostrich prices rose. The high prices for ostriches fueled profit expectations, and many cattle ranchers deserted their cattle and went into the ostrich business.

Adam Smith concluded that competitive forces are like an "invisible hand" that leads people who simply pursue their own interests and, in the process, serve the interests of society. In a competitive market, when the profit potential in the ostrich business looked good, firms entered this market and started raising ostriches. Over time, more and more ostrich farmers flocked to this market, and the population of these big, flightless birds exploded. As a result, the price of a breeding pair plummeted to only a few thousand dollars, profits tumbled, and the number of ostrich farms declined. A decade later, demand increased unexpectedly because mad cow disease plagued Europe, and people bought alternatives to beef. Suppliers could not meet the demand for ostrich burgers, and profits rose again, causing farmers to increase supply by investing in more ostriches.

This chapter combines the demand, cost of production, and marginal analysis concepts from previous chapters to explain how competitive markets determine prices, output, and profits. Here firms are small, like an ostrich ranch or an alligator farm, rather than huge, like Wal-Mart or Microsoft. Other types of markets in which large and powerful firms operate are discussed in the next two chapters.

In this chapter, you will learn to solve these economics puzzles:

- Why is the demand curve horizontal for a firm in a perfectly competitive market?
- Why would a firm stay in business while losing money?
- In the long run, can alligator farms earn an economic profit?

8-1 Perfect Competition

Firms sell goods and services under different market conditions, which economists call market structures. A market structure describes the key traits of a market, including the number of firms, the similarity of the products they sell, and the ease of entry into and exit from the market. Examination of the business sector of our economy reveals firms operating in different market structures. In this chapter and the two chapters that follow, we will study four market structures. The first is perfect competition, to which this entire chapter is devoted. Perfect, or pure, competition is a market structure characterized by (1) a large number of small firms, (2) a homogeneous product, and (3) very easy entry into or exit from the market. Let's discuss each of these characteristics.

8-1a CHARACTERISTICS OF PERFECT COMPETITION

Large Number of Small Firms   How many sellers comprise a large number? And how small is a small firm? Certainly, one, two, or three firms in a market would not be a large number. In fact, the exact number cannot be stated. This condition is fulfilled when each firm in a market has no significant share of total output and, therefore, no ability to affect the product's price. Each firm acts independently, rather than coordinating decisions collectively. For example, there are thousands of independent egg farmers in the United States. If any single egg farmer raises the price, the going market price for eggs is unaffected.

> **CONCLUSION:** *The large-number-of-sellers condition is met when each firm is so small relative to the total market that no single firm can influence the market price.*

Homogeneous Product   In a perfectly competitive market, all firms produce a standardized or homogeneous product. This means the good or service of each firm is identical. Farmer Brown's wheat is identical to Farmer Jones's wheat. Buyers may believe the transportation services of one independent trucker are about the same as another's services. This assumption rules out rivalry among firms in advertising and quality differences.

> **CONCLUSION:** *If a product is homogeneous, buyers are indifferent as to which seller's product they buy.*

Very Easy Entry and Exit   Very easy entry into a market means that a new firm faces no barriers to entry. A barrier to entry is any obstacle that makes it difficult for a new firm to enter a market. Barriers can be financial, technical, or government-imposed barriers such as licenses, permits, and patents. Such barriers

---

Market structure

A classification system for the key traits of a market, including the number of firms, the similarity of the products they sell, and the ease of entry into and exit from the market.

Perfect competition

A market structure characterized by (1) a large number of small firms, (2) a homogeneous product, and (3) very easy entry into or exit from the market. Perfect competition is also referred to as *pure competition.*

Barrier to entry

Any obstacle that makes it difficult for a new firm to enter a market.

do not exist for ostrich farming. Anyone who wants to try his or her hand at raising ostriches needs only a plot of land and feed.

> **CONCLUSION:** *Perfect competition requires that resources be completely mobile to freely enter or exit a market.*

No real-world market exactly fits the three assumptions of perfect competition. The perfectly competitive market structure is a theoretical or ideal model, but some actual markets do approximate the model fairly closely. Examples include farm products markets, the stock market, and the foreign exchange market.

8-1b THE PERFECTLY COMPETITIVE FIRM AS A PRICE TAKER

Price taker

A seller that has no control over the price of the product it sells.

For model-building purposes, suppose a firm operates in a market that conforms to all three of the requirements for perfect competition. This means that the perfectly competitive firm is a price taker. A price taker is a seller that has no control over the price of the product it sells. From the individual firm's perspective, the price of its products is determined by market supply and demand conditions over which the firm has no influence. Look again at the characteristics of a perfectly competitive firm: A small firm that is one among many firms sells a homogeneous product and is exposed to competition from new firms entering the market. These conditions make it impossible for the perfectly competitive firm to have the market power to affect the market price. Instead, the firm must adjust to, or "take," the market price.

Exhibit 1 is a graphical presentation of the relationship between the market supply and demand for electronic components and the demand curve facing a firm in a perfectly competitive market. Here we will assume that the electronic components industry is perfectly competitive, keeping in mind that the real-world market does not exactly fit the model. Exhibit 1(a) shows market supply and demand curves for the quantity of output per hour. The theoretical framework for this model was explained in Chapter 4. The equilibrium price is $70 per unit, and the equilibrium quantity is 60,000 units per hour.

Because the perfectly competitive firm "takes" the equilibrium price, the individual firm's demand curve in Exhibit 1(b) is *perfectly elastic* (horizontal) at the $70 market equilibrium price. (Note the difference between the firm's units per hour and the industry's thousands of units per hour.) Recall from Chapter 5 that when a firm facing a perfectly elastic demand curve tries to raise its price one penny higher than $70, no buyer will purchase its product [Exhibit 2(a) in Chapter 5]. The reason is that many other firms are selling the same product at $70 per unit. Hence, the perfectly competitive firm will not set the price above the prevailing market price and risk selling zero output. Nor will the firm set the price below the market price because a lower price would reduce the firm's revenue, and the firm can sell all it wants to at the going price.

EXHIBIT 1	The Market Price and Demand for the Perfectly Competitive Firm

In part (a), the market equilibrium price is $70 per unit. The perfectly competitive firm in part (b) is a price taker because it is so small relative to the market. At $70, the individual firm faces a horizontal demand curve, D. This means that the firm's demand curve is perfectly elastic. If the firm raises its price even one penny, it will sell zero output.

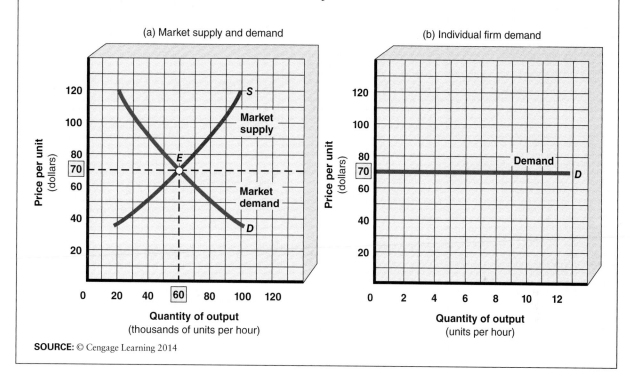

SOURCE: © Cengage Learning 2014

8-2 Short-Run Profit Maximization for a Perfectly Competitive Firm

Since the perfectly competitive firm has no control over price, what does the firm control? The firm makes only one decision—what quantity of output to produce that maximizes profit. This section develops two profit maximization methods that determine the output level for a competitive firm. We begin by examining the total revenue-total cost approach for finding the profit-maximizing level of output. Next, marginal analysis is used to show another method for determining the profit-maximizing level of output. The framework for the analysis is the short run with some fixed input, such as factory size.

8-2a THE TOTAL REVENUE-TOTAL COST METHOD

Exhibit 2 provides hypothetical data on output, total revenue, total cost, and profit for our typical electronic components producer—Computech. Using Computech as our example allows us to extend the data and analysis presented in previous

EXHIBIT 2	Short-Run Profit Maximization Schedule for Computech as a Perfectly Competitive Firm

(1) Output (units per hour) (Q)	(2) Price per Unit (P)	(3) Total Revenue (TR)	(4) Marginal Revenue (MR)	(5) Marginal Cost (MC)	(6) Total Cost (TC)	(7) Average Variable Cost (AVC)	(8) Average Total Cost (ATC)	(9) Profit (+) or Loss (−) [(3) − (6)]
0	$70	$ 0			$100	—	—	−$100
			$70	$50				
1	70	70			150	$50	$150	−80
			70	34				
2	70	140			184	42	92	−44
			70	24				
3	70	210			208	36	69	2
			70	19				
4	70	280			227	32	57	53
			70	23				
5	70	350			250	30	50	100
			70	30				
6	70	420			280	30	47	140
			70	38				
7	70	490			318	31	45	172
			70	48				
8	70	560			366	33	46	194
			70	59				
9	70	630	70	70	425	36	47	205
			70	75				
10	70	700			500	40	50	200
			70	95				
11	70	770			595	45	54	175
			70	117				
12	70	840			712	51	59	128

SOURCE: © Cengage Learning 2014

chapters. The cost figures are taken from Exhibit 3 in Chapter 7. Total fixed cost at zero output is $100. Total revenue is reported in column (3) of Exhibit 2 and is computed as the product price times the quantity. In this case, we assume the market equilibrium price is $70 per unit, as determined in Exhibit 1. Because Computech is a price taker, the total revenue from selling 1 unit is $70, from selling 2 units is $140,

EXHIBIT 3	Short-Run Profit Maximization Using the Total Revenue-Total Cost Method for a Perfectly Competitive Firm

(a) Total revenue and total cost

This exhibit shows the profit-maximizing level of output chosen by a perfectly competitive firm, Computech. Part (a) shows the relationships between total revenue, total cost, and output, given a market price of $70 per unit. The maximum profit is earned by producing 9 units per hour. At this level of output, the vertical distance between the total revenue and the total cost curves is the greatest. At an output level below 3 units per hour, the firm incurs losses.

Profit maximization is also shown in part (b). The maximum profit of $205 per hour corresponds to the profit-maximizing output of 9 units per hour, represented in part (a).

(b) Profit or loss

SOURCE: © Cengage Learning 2014

and so on. Subtracting total cost in column (6) from total revenue in column (3) gives the total profit or loss [column (9)] that the firm earns at each level of output. From 0 to 2 units, the firm incurs losses, and then a *break-even point* (zero economic profit) occurs at about 3 units per hour. Recall from the previous chapter that at zero economic profit, the firm earns only a normal profit, which is the minimum profit necessary to keep a firm in operation. If the firm produces 9 units per hour, it earns the maximum profit of $205 per hour. As output expands between 9 and 12 units of output, the firm's profit diminishes. Exhibit 3 illustrates graphically that the maximum profit occurs where the vertical distance between the total revenue and the total cost curves is at a maximum.

8-2b THE MARGINAL REVENUE EQUALS MARGINAL COST METHOD

A second approach uses *marginal analysis* to determine the profit-maximizing level of output by comparing marginal revenue (marginal benefit) and marginal cost. Recall from the previous chapter that marginal cost is the change in total cost as the output level changes one unit. Also recall that these marginal cost data are listed between the quantity of output line entries because the change in total cost occurs between each additional whole unit of output rather than exactly at each listed output level.

Now we introduce marginal revenue (MR), a concept similar to marginal cost. Marginal revenue is the change in total revenue from the sale of one additional unit of output. Stated another way, marginal revenue is the ratio of the change in total revenue to a change in output.

Mathematically,

Marginal revenue (MR)

The change in total revenue from the sale of one additional unit of output.

$$MR = \frac{\text{change in total revenue}}{\text{one-unit change in output}}$$

As shown in Exhibit 1(b), the perfectly competitive firm faces a perfectly elastic demand curve. Because the competitive firm is a price taker, the sale of each additional unit adds to total revenue an amount equal to the price (average revenue, TR/Q). In our example, Computech adds $70 to its total revenue each time it sells one unit. Therefore, $70 is the marginal revenue for each additional unit of output in column (4) of Exhibit 2. As with MC, MR is also listed between the quantity of output line entries because the change in total revenue occurs between each additional unit of output.

CONCLUSION: *In perfect competition, the firm's marginal revenue equals the price that the firm views as a horizontal demand curve.*

Columns (3) and (6) in Exhibit 2 show that both total revenue and total cost rise as the level of output increases. Now compare marginal revenue and marginal cost in columns (4) and (5). As explained, marginal revenue remains equal to the price, but marginal cost follows the J-shaped pattern introduced in Exhibit 4 of Chapter 7. At first, marginal cost is below marginal revenue, and this means that producing each additional unit adds less to total cost than to total revenue. Economic profit therefore increases as output expands from zero until the output

EXHIBIT 4	Short-Run Profit Maximization Using the Marginal Revenue Equals Marginal Cost Method for a Perfectly Competitive Firm

(a) Price, marginal revenue, and cost per unit

In addition to comparing total revenue and total cost, a firm can find the profit-maximizing level of output by comparing marginal revenue (MR) and marginal cost (MC). As shown in part (a), profit is at a maximum where marginal revenue equals marginal cost at $70 per unit. The intersection of the marginal revenue and marginal cost curves establishes the profit-maximizing output at 9 units per hour.

A profit curve is depicted separately in part (b) to show that the maximum profit occurs when the firm produces at the level of output corresponding to the MR = MC point. Below 3 units per hour output, the firm incurs losses.

(b) Profit or loss

| Price is above ATC where MC = MR | ⟹ | Profit Maximization |

SOURCE: © Cengage Learning 2014

level reaches 9 units per hour. Over this output range, Computech moves from a $100 loss to a $205 profit per hour. Beyond an output level of 9 units per hour, marginal cost exceeds marginal revenue, and profit falls. This is because each additional unit of output raises total cost by more than it raises total revenue. In this case, profit falls from $205 to only $128 per hour as output increases from 9 to 12 units per hour.

Our example leads to this question: How does the firm use its marginal revenue and marginal cost curves to determine the profit-maximizing level of output? The answer is that the firm follows a guideline called the MR = MC rule: *The firm maximizes profit by producing the output where marginal revenue equals marginal cost.* Exhibit 4 relates the marginal revenue curve equals marginal cost curve condition to profit maximization. In Exhibit 4(a), the perfectly elastic demand curve is drawn at the industry-determined price of $70. The average total cost (ATC) and average variable cost (AVC) curves are traced from Exhibit 2. Using marginal analysis, we can relate the MR = MC rule to the same profit data given in Exhibit 2. Between 8 and 9 units of output, the MC curve is below the MR curve ($59 < $70), and the profit curve rises to its peak at $205. Beyond 9 units of output, the MC curve is above the MR curve, and the profit curve falls. For example, between 9 and 10 units of output, marginal cost is $75, and marginal revenue is $70. Therefore, if the firm produces at 9 units of output rather than, say, at 8 or 10 units of output, the MR curve equals the MC curve, and profit is maximized.

You can also calculate profit directly from Exhibit 4(a). At the profit-maximizing level of output of 9 units, the vertical distance between the demand curve and the ATC curve is the *average profit per unit*. Multiplying the average profit per unit times the quantity of output gives the profit [($70 − $47.22) × 9 = $205.02].[1] The shaded rectangle also represents the maximum profit of $205 per hour. Note that we have arrived at the same profit maximization amount ($205) derived by comparing the total revenue and the total cost curves.

8-3 Short-Run Loss Minimization for a Perfectly Competitive Firm

Since the perfectly competitive firm must take the price determined by market supply and demand forces, market conditions can change the prevailing price. When the market price drops, the firm can do nothing but adjust its output to make the best of the situation. Here only the marginal approach is used to predict output decisions of firms. Our model therefore assumes that business managers make their output decisions by comparing the *marginal* effect on profit of a *marginal* change in output.

8-3a A PERFECTLY COMPETITIVE FIRM FACING A SHORT-RUN LOSS

Suppose a decrease in the market demand for electronic components causes the market price to fall to $35. As a result, the firm's horizontal demand curve shifts downward to the new position shown in Exhibit 5(a). In this case, there is no level of output at which the firm earns a profit because any price along the demand curve is below the ATC curve.

Because Computech cannot make a profit, what output level should it choose? The logic of the MR = MC rule given in the profit maximization case applies here as well. At a price of $35, MR = MC at 6 units per hour. Comparing parts (a)

---

[1] In Exhibit 3 in Chapter 7, the average total cost figure at 9 units of output was rounded to $47. It also should be noted that there is often no level of output for which marginal revenue exactly equals marginal cost when dealing with whole units of output.

EXHIBIT 5	Short-Run Loss Minimization Using the Marginal Revenue Equals Marginal Cost Method for a Perfectly Competitive Firm

If the market price is less than the average total cost, the firm will produce a level of output that keeps its loss to a minimum. In part (a), the given price is $35 per unit, and marginal revenue (MR) equals marginal cost (MC) at an output of 6 units per hour.

Part (b) shows that the firm's loss will be greater at any output other than where the marginal revenue and the marginal cost curves intersect. Because the price is above the average variable cost, each unit of output sold pays for the average variable cost and a portion of the average fixed cost.

Price is below ATC where MC = MR ⟹ Loss Minimization

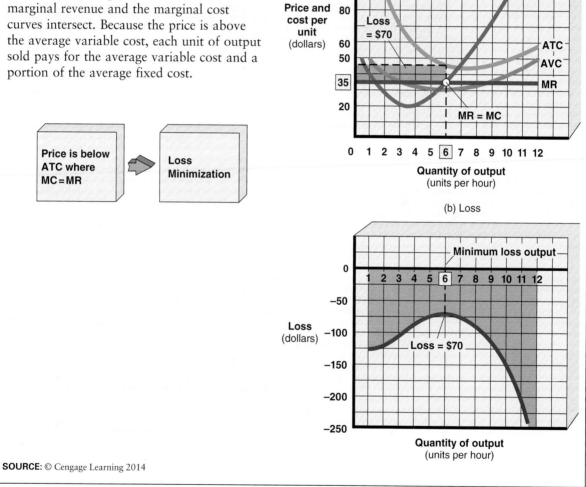

(a) Price, marginal revenue, and cost per unit

(b) Loss

SOURCE: © Cengage Learning 2014

and (b) of Exhibit 5 shows that the firm's loss will be minimized at this level of output. The minimum loss of $70 per hour is equal to the shaded area, which is the *average loss per unit* times the quantity of output [($35 − $46.66) × 6 = −$70].

Note that although the price is not high enough to pay the average total cost, the price is high enough to pay the average variable cost. Each unit sold also contributes to paying a portion of the average fixed cost, which is the vertical distance between the ATC and the AVC curves. This analysis leads us to extend the MR = MC rule: *The firm maximizes profit or minimizes loss by producing the output where marginal revenue equals marginal cost.*

8-3b A PERFECTLY COMPETITIVE FIRM SHUTTING DOWN

What happens if the market price drops below the AVC curve, as shown in Exhibit 6? For example, if the price is $25 per unit, should Computech produce some level of output? The answer is no. The best course of action is for the firm to shut down. *If the price is below the minimum point on the AVC curve, each unit produced would*

EXHIBIT 6	The Short-Run Shutdown Point for a Perfectly Competitive Firm

The shutdown point of $30 per unit is the minimum point on the average variable cost curve (AVC). If the price falls below this price, the firm shuts down. The reason is that operating losses are now greater than total fixed cost. In this exhibit, the price of $25 per unit (MR) is below the AVC curve at any level of output, and the firm would shut down at this price.

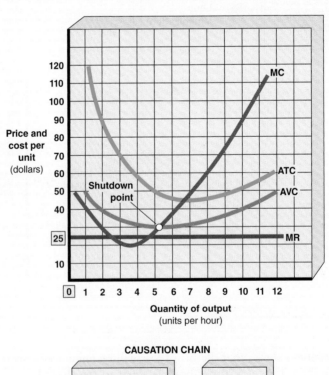

CAUSATION CHAIN

Price (MR) is below minimum average variable cost ➡ Firm will shut down

SOURCE: © Cengage Learning 2014

not cover the variable cost per unit; therefore, operating would increase losses. The firm is better off shutting down and producing zero output. While shut down, the firm might keep its factory, pay fixed costs, and hope for higher prices soon. If the firm does not believe market conditions will improve, it will avoid fixed costs by going out of business.

✔ **CHECKPOINT**

Should Motels Offer Rooms at the Beach for Only $50 a Night?

Myrtle Beach, South Carolina, with its famous Grand Strand and Calabash seafood, is lined with virtually identical motels. Summertime rates run about $200 a night. During the winter, one can find rooms for as little as $50 a night. Assume the average fixed cost of a room per night, including insurance, taxes, and depreciation, is $50. The average guest-related cost for a room each night, including cleaning service and linens, is $45. Would these motels be better off renting rooms for $50 in the off-season or shutting down until summer?

8-4 Short-Run Supply Curves under Perfect Competition

The preceding examples provide a framework for a more complete explanation of the supply curve than was given earlier in Chapter 3. We now develop the short-run supply curve for an individual firm and then derive it for an industry.

8-4a THE PERFECTLY COMPETITIVE FIRM'S SHORT-RUN SUPPLY CURVE

Exhibit 7 reproduces the cost curves from our Computech example. Also represented in the exhibit are three possible demand curves the firm might face—MR_1, MR_2, and MR_3. As the marginal revenue curve moves upward along the marginal cost curve, the MR = MC point changes.

Suppose demand for electronic components begins at a market price close to $30. Point *A* therefore corresponds to a price equal to MR_1, which equals MC at the lowest point on the AVC curve. At any lower price, the firm cuts its loss by shutting down. At a price of about $30, however, the firm produces 5.5 units per hour. Point *A* is therefore the lowest point on the individual firm's short-run supply curve.

If the price rises to $45, represented in the exhibit by MR_2, the firm breaks even and earns a normal profit at point *B* with an output of 7 units per hour. As the marginal revenue curve rises, the firm's supply curve is traced by moving upward along its MC curve. At a price of $90, point *C* is reached. Now MR_3 intersects the MC curve at an output of 10 units per hour, and the firm earns an economic profit. If the price rises higher than $90, the firm will continue to increase the quantity supplied and increase its maximum profit.

EXHIBIT 7	The Perfectly Competitive Firm's Short-Run Supply Curve

This exhibit shows how the short-run supply curve for Computech is derived. When the price is $30, the firm will produce 5.5 units per hour at point *A*. If the price rises to $45, the firm will move upward along its marginal cost curve (MC) to point *B* and produce 7 units per hour. At $90, the firm continues to set price equal to marginal cost, and it produces 10 units per hour. Thus, the firm's short-run supply curve is the MC curve above its AVC curve.

SOURCE: © Cengage Learning 2014

Perfectly competitive firm's short-run supply curve

A firm's marginal cost curve above the minimum point on its average variable cost curve.

Perfectly competitive industry's short-run supply curve

The supply curve derived from horizontal summation of the marginal cost curves of all firms in the industry above the minimum point of each firm's average variable cost curve.

We can now define a perfectly competitive firm's short-run supply curve. The perfectly competitive firm's short-run supply curve is its marginal cost curve above the minimum point on its average variable cost curve.

8-4b THE PERFECTLY COMPETITIVE INDUSTRY'S SHORT-RUN SUPPLY CURVE

Understanding that the firm's short-run supply curve is the segment of its MC curve above its AVC curve sets the stage for derivation of the perfectly competitive industry's short-run supply curve. The perfectly competitive industry's short-run supply curve is the horizontal summation of the marginal cost curves of all firms in the industry above the minimum point of each firm's average variable cost curve.

In Exhibit 7 in Chapter 3, we drew a market supply curve. Now we will reconstruct this market, or industry, supply curve using more precision. Although in perfect competition there are many firms, we suppose for simplicity that the industry has only two firms, Computech and Western Computer Co. Exhibit 8

EXHIBIT 8	Deriving the Industry Short-Run Supply Curve

Assuming input prices remain constant as output expands, the short-run supply curve for an industry is derived by horizontally summing the quantities supplied at each price by all firms in the industry. In this exhibit, we assume there are only two firms in an industry. At $40, Computech supplies 7 units of output, and Western Computer Co. supplies 11 units. The quantity supplied by the industry is therefore 18 units. Other points forming the industry short-run supply curve are obtained similarly.

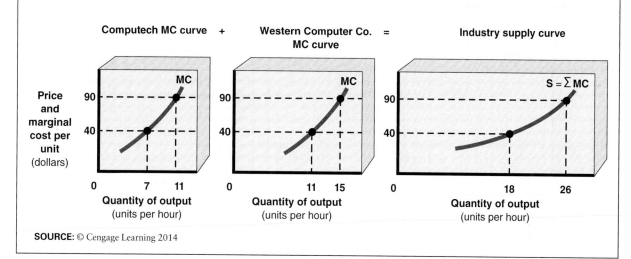

SOURCE: © Cengage Learning 2014

illustrates the MC curves for these two firms. Each firm's MC curve is drawn for prices above the minimum point on the AVC curve. At a price of $40, the quantity supplied by Computech is 7 units, and the quantity supplied by Western Computer Co. is 11 units. Now horizontally add these two quantities and obtain one point on the industry supply curve corresponding to a price of $40 and 18 units. Following this procedure for all prices, we generate the short-run industry supply curve.

Note that the industry supply curve derived above is based on the assumption that input prices remain unchanged as output expands. In the next section, we will learn how changes in input prices affect derivation of the supply curve.

8-4c SHORT-RUN EQUILIBRIUM FOR A PERFECTLY COMPETITIVE FIRM

Exhibit 9 illustrates a condition of short-run equilibrium under perfect competition. Exhibit 9(a) represents the equilibrium price and cost situation for one of the many firms in an industry. As shown in the exhibit, the firm earns an economic profit in the short run by producing 9 units. Exhibit 9(b) depicts short-run equilibrium for the industry. As explained earlier, the industry supply curve is the aggregate of each firm's MC curve above the minimum point on the AVC curve. Including industry demand establishes the equilibrium price of $60 that all firms in the industry must take. The industry's equilibrium quantity supplied is 60,000 units. This state of short-run equilibrium will remain until some factor changes and causes a new equilibrium condition in the industry.

| EXHIBIT 9 | Short-Run Perfectly Competitive Equilibrium |

Short-run equilibrium occurs at point E. The intersection of the industry supply and demand curves shown in part (b) determines the price of $60 facing the firm shown in part (a). Given this equilibrium price, the firm represented in part (a) establishes its profit-maximizing output at 9 units per hour and earns an economic profit shown by the shaded area. Note in part (b) that the short-run industry supply curve is the horizontal summation of the marginal cost (MC) curves of all individual firms above their minimum average variable cost points.

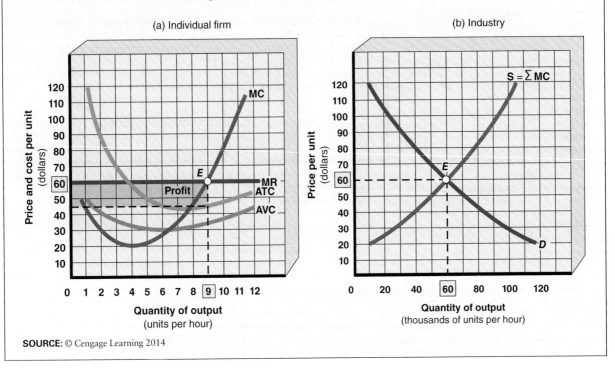

(a) Individual firm

(b) Industry

SOURCE: © Cengage Learning 2014

8-5 Long-Run Supply Curves under Perfect Competition

Recall from Chapter 7 that *all* inputs are variable in the long run. Existing firms in an industry can react to profit opportunities by building larger or smaller plants, buying or selling land and equipment, or varying other inputs that are fixed in the short run. Profits also attract new firms to an industry, while losses cause some existing firms to leave the industry. As you will now see, the free entry and exit characteristic of perfect competition is a crucial determinant of the shape of the long-run supply curve.

8-5a LONG-RUN EQUILIBRIUM FOR A PERFECTLY COMPETITIVE FIRM

As discussed in Chapter 7, in the long run, a firm can change its plant size or any input used to produce a product. This means that an established firm can decide to *leave* an industry if it earns below normal profits (negative economic profits) and that new firms may enter an industry in which earnings of established firms exceed normal profits (positive economic profits). This process of entry and exit of firms is the key to long-run equilibrium. If there are economic profits, new firms enter the industry and shift the short-run industry supply curve to the right. This increase in short-run supply causes the price to fall until economic profits reach zero in the long run. On the other hand, if there are economic losses in an industry, existing firms leave, causing the short-run supply curve to shift to the left, and the price rises. This adjustment continues until economic losses are eliminated and economic profits equal zero in the long run.

Exhibit 10 shows a typical firm in long-run equilibrium. Supply and demand for the market as a whole set the equilibrium price. Thus, in the long run, the firm

EXHIBIT 10	Long-Run Perfectly Competitive Equilibrium

Long-run equilibrium occurs at point *E*. In the long run, the firm earns a normal profit. The firm operates where the price equals the minimum point on its long-run average cost curve (LRAC). At this point, the short-run marginal cost curve (SRMC) intersects both the short-run average total cost curve (SRATC) and the long-run average cost curve (LRAC) at their minimum points.

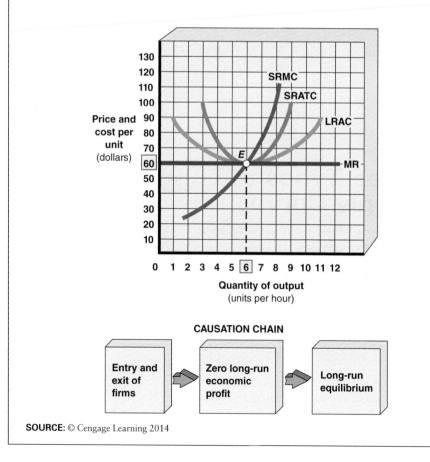

SOURCE: © Cengage Learning 2014

faces an equilibrium price of $60. Following the MR = MC rule, the firm produces an equilibrium output of 6 units per hour. At this output level, the firm earns a normal profit (zero economic profit) because marginal revenue (price) equals the minimum point on both the short-run average total cost curve (SRATC) and the long-run average cost curve (LRAC). Given the U-shaped LRAC curve, the firm is producing with the optimal factory size.

With SRMC representing short-run marginal cost, the conditions for long-run perfectly competitive equilibrium can also be expressed as an equality:

$$P = MR = SRMC = SRATC = LRAC$$

As long as none of the variables in the above formula changes, there is no reason for a perfectly competitive firm to change its output level, factory size, or any aspect of its operation. Everything is just right! Because the typical firm is in a state of equilibrium, the industry is also at rest. Under long-run equilibrium conditions, there are neither positive economic profits to attract new firms to enter the industry nor negative economic profits to force existing firms to leave. In long-run equilibrium, maximum efficiency is achieved. The adjustment process of firms moving into or out of the industry is complete, and the firms charge the lowest possible price to consumers. Next, we will discuss how the firm and industry adjust when market demand changes.

✓ CHECKPOINT

Are You in Business for the Long Run?

You are considering building a Rent Your Own Storage Center. You are trying to decide whether to build 50 storage units at a total economic cost of $200,000, 100 storage units at a total economic cost of $300,000, or 200 storage units at a total economic cost of $700,000. If you wish to survive in the long run, which size will you choose?

Perfectly competitive industry's long-run supply curve

The curve that shows the quantities supplied by the industry at different equilibrium prices after firms complete their entry and exit.

Constant-cost industry

An industry in which the expansion of industry output by the entry of new firms has no effect on the firm's average total cost curve.

8-6 Three Types of Long-Run Supply Curves

There are three possibilities for a perfectly competitive industry's long-run supply curve. The perfectly competitive industry's long-run supply curve shows the quantities supplied by the industry at different equilibrium prices after firms complete their entry and exit. The shape of each of these long-run supply curves depends on the response of input prices as new firms enter the industry. The following sections discuss each of these three cases.

8-6a CONSTANT-COST INDUSTRY

In a constant-cost industry, input prices remain constant as new firms enter or exit the industry. A constant-cost industry is an industry in which the expansion of industry output by the entry of new firms has no effect on the firm's average total cost curve. Exhibit 11(a) reproduces the long-run equilibrium situation from Exhibit 10.

Begin in part (b) of Exhibit 11 at the initial industry equilibrium point E_1 with short-run industry supply curve S_1 and industry demand curve D_1. Now assume the industry demand curve increases from D_1 to D_2. As a result, the industry equilibrium moves temporarily to E_2. Correspondingly, the equilibrium price rises from $60 to $80, and industry output increases from 50,000 to 70,000 units.

The short-run result for the individual firm in the industry happens this way. As shown in part (a) of Exhibit 11, the firm takes the increase in price and adjusts

---

EXHIBIT 11	Long-Run Supply in a Constant-Cost Industry

Part (b) shows an industry in equilibrium at point E_1, producing 50,000 units per hour and selling them for $60 per unit. In part (a), the firm is in equilibrium, producing 6 units per hour and earning a normal profit. Then industry demand increases from D_1 to D_2, and the equilibrium price rises to $80. Industry output rises temporarily to 70,000 units per hour, and the individual firm increases output to 7 units per hour. Firms are now earning an economic profit, which attracts new firms into the industry. In the long run, the entry of these firms causes the short-run supply curve to shift rightward from S_1 to S_2; the price is reestablished at $60; and a new industry equilibrium point, E_3, is established. At E_3, industry output rises to 90,000 units per hour, the SRATC curve remains constant, and the firm's output returns to 6 units per hour. Now the typical firm earns a normal profit, and new firms stop entering the industry. Connecting point E_1 to point E_3 generates the long-run supply curve.

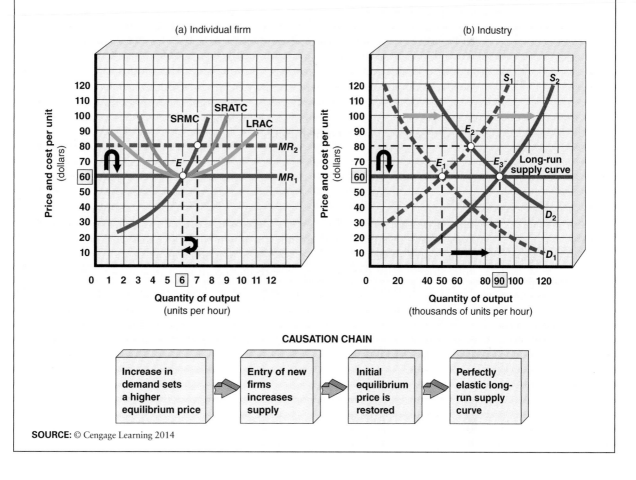

(a) Individual firm

(b) Industry

CAUSATION CHAIN

| Increase in demand sets a higher equilibrium price | ⇨ | Entry of new firms increases supply | ⇨ | Initial equilibrium price is restored | ⇨ | Perfectly elastic long-run supply curve |

SOURCE: © Cengage Learning 2014

its output from 6 to 7 units per hour. At the higher price and output, the firm changes from earning a normal profit to making an economic profit because the new price is above its SRATC curve. All the other firms in the industry make the same adjustment by moving upward along their SRMC curves.

In perfect competition, new firms are free to enter the industry in response to a profit opportunity, and they will do so. The addition of new firms shifts the short-run supply curve rightward from S_1 to S_2. Firms will continue to enter the industry until profit is eliminated. This occurs at equilibrium point E_3, where short-run industry demand curve D_2 intersects short-run supply curve S_2. Thus, the entry of new firms has restored the initial equilibrium price of $60. The firm responds by moving downward along its SRMC curve until it once again produces 6 units and earns a normal profit.

As shown in the exhibit, the path of these changes in industry short-run equilibrium points traces a horizontal line, which is the industry's long-run supply curve.

> **CONCLUSION:** *The long-run supply curve in a perfectly competitive constant-cost industry is perfectly elastic.*

Now we reconsider Exhibit 11 and ask what happens when the demand curve shifts leftward from D_2 to D_1. Beginning in part (b) at point E_3, the decrease in demand causes the price to fall temporarily below $60. As a result, firms incur short-run losses, and some firms leave the industry. The exodus of firms shifts the short-run supply curve leftward from S_2 to S_1, establishing a new equilibrium at point E_1. This decrease in supply restores the equilibrium price to the initial price of $60 per unit. Once equilibrium is reestablished at E_1, there are a smaller number of firms, each earning a normal profit.

8-6b DECREASING-COST INDUSTRY

Decreasing-cost industry

An industry in which the expansion of industry output by the entry of new firms decreases the individual firm's average cost curve (cost curve shifts downward).

Input prices fall as new firms enter a decreasing-cost industry, and output expands. A decreasing-cost industry is an industry in which the expansion of industry output by the entry of new firms decreases each individual firm's cost curve (cost curve shifts downward). For example, as production of electronic components expands, the price of computer chips may decline. The reason is that greater sales volume allows the suppliers to achieve *economies of scale* and lower their input prices to firms in the electronic components industry. Exhibit 12 illustrates the adjustment process of an increase in demand based on the assumption that our example is a decreasing-cost industry.

> **CONCLUSION:** *The long-run supply curve in a perfectly competitive decreasing-cost industry is downward sloping.*

EXHIBIT 12	Long-Run Supply in a Decreasing-Cost Industry

The long-run supply curve for a decreasing-cost industry is downward sloping. The increase in industry demand shown in part (b) causes the price to rise to $80 in the short run. Temporarily, the individual firm illustrated in part (a) earns an economic profit. Higher profits attract new firms, and supply increases. As the industry expands, input prices fall causing the SRATC curve for the firm to shift downward from $SRATC_1$ to $SRATC_2$, and the firm reestablishes long-run equilibrium at the lower price of $50.

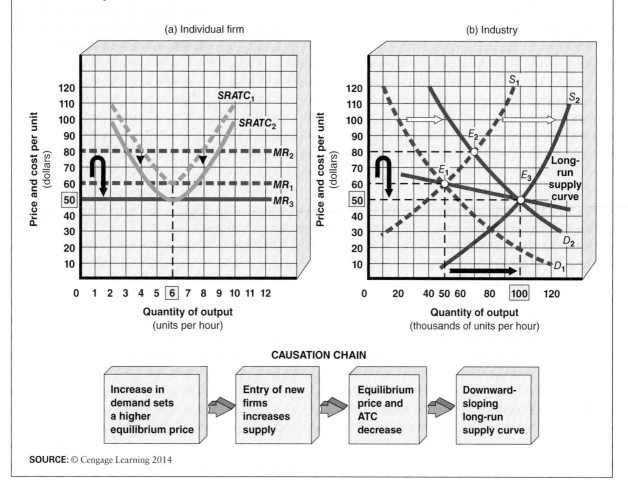

CAUSATION CHAIN

Increase in demand sets a higher equilibrium price	→	Entry of new firms increases supply	→	Equilibrium price and ATC decrease	→	Downward-sloping long-run supply curve

SOURCE: © Cengage Learning 2014

8-6c INCREASING-COST INDUSTRY

In an increasing-cost industry, input prices rise as new firms enter the industry, and output expands. As this type of industry uses more labor and machines, the demand for greater quantities of these inputs drives up input prices. An increasing-cost industry is an industry in which the expansion of industry output by the entry of new firms increases the individual firm's cost curve (cost curve shifts upward). Suppose the electronic component business uses a significant proportion of all electrical engineers in the country. In this case, electrical engineering salaries will rise as firms hire more electrical engineers to expand industry output. In practice, most

Increasing-cost industry

An industry in which the expansion of industry output by the entry of new firms increases the individual firm's average total cost curve (cost curve shifts upward).

Recession Takes a Bite Out of Gator Profits

Applicable Concepts: short-run and long-run competitive equilibrium

In the late 1980s, many farmers who were tired of milking cows, roping steers, and slopping hogs decided to try their hand at a new animal. Anyone feeding this animal, however, could require a gun for protection.

Prior to the late 1970s, alligators were on the endangered species list. Under this protection, their numbers grew so large that wandering alligators became pests in Florida neighborhoods and police were exhausted from chasing them around. Consequently, the ban on hunting was removed, and shrewd entrepreneurs began seeking big profits by turning gators into farm animals. In fact, gator farming became one of Florida's fastest-growing businesses.

The gators spawned several hot industries. The lizard "look"

came back into vogue, and the fashionable sported gator-skin purses, shoes, and belts. Chic didn't come cheap. In New York, gator cowboy boots sold for $1,800, and attaché cases retailed for $4,000. And you could order gator meat at trendy restaurants all along the East Coast. "Why not gator?" asked Red Lobster spokesman Dick Monroe. "Today's two-income households are looking for more variety. And they think it's neat to eat an animal that can eat them."

To meet the demand, Florida doubled the number of its licensed alligator farms compared to the previous four years when they functioned almost entirely as tourist attractions. In 1985, Florida farmers raised 37,000 gators; in 1986, that figure increased by 50 percent. Revenues soared as well. Frank Godwin, owner of Gatorland in Orlando, netted an

estimated $270,000 from the 1,000 animals he harvested annually. Improved technology was applied to gator farming in order to boost profits even higher. Lawler Wells, for example, owner of Hilltop Farms in Avon Park, raised 7,000 gators in darkened hothouses that accelerated their growth.[1]

Seven years later, a 1993 article in *The Washington Post* continued the gator tale: "During the late 1980s, gator ranching was booming, and the industry was being compared to a living gold

industries are increasing-cost industries, and, therefore, the long-run supply curve is upward sloping.

Exhibit 13 shows what happens in an increasing-cost industry when an increase in demand causes output to expand. In part (b), the industry is initially in equilibrium at point E_1. As in the previous case, the demand curve shifts rightward from D_1 to D_2, establishing a new short-run equilibrium at E_2. This movement upward along short-run industry supply curve S_1 raises the price in the short run from $60 to $80, resulting in profit for the typical firm. Once again, new firms enter the industry, and the short-run supply curve shifts rightward from S_1 to S_2. Part (a) of Exhibit 13 shows that the response of the firm's SRATC curve to the industry's expansion differs from the constant-cost industry case. In an increasing-cost industry, the firm's SRATC curve shifts upward from $SRATC_1$ to $SRATC_2$, corresponding to the new short-run equilibrium at point E_3. At this final equilibrium point, the price of $70 is higher than the initial price of $60. Normal profits mine. People rushed into the industry. Some farmers became temporarily rich."[2]

In 1995, a *USA Today* interview with a gator hunter provided evidence of long-run equilibrium: "Armed with a pistol barrel attached to the end of an 8-foot wooden pole, alligator hunter Bill Chaplin fires his 'bankstick' and dispatches a six-footer with a single round of .44 magnum ammunition. What's in it for him? Financially, very little. At $3.50 a pound for the meat and $45 a foot for the hide, an alligator is worth perhaps $100 a foot. After paying for skinning and processing, neither hunter nor landowner gets rich."[3]

A 2000 article in *The Dallas Morning News* provided further evidence: Mark Glass, who began raising gators in 1995 south of Atlanta stated, "I can honestly say I haven't made any money yet, but I hope that's about to change."[4] And a 2003 article from *Knight Ridder/Tribune Business News* gave a pessimistic report for Florida: "Revenue from alligator harvesting has flattened in recent years, despite Florida's efforts to promote the alligator as part of a viable 'aquaculture' industry. It's a tough business."[5] And beginning in 2009, alligator skin bags, belts, shoes, watch straps, and purses were victims of the recession. As a result, many alligator farms were overrun with an unprecedented surplus of unsold alligators and falling prices. Wayne Sagrera, co-owner of Vermillion Gator Farm near Lafayette, Louisiana, stated "We can't invest in eggs if the demand is not there. They're just not selling."[6]

Analyze the Issue

1. Draw short-run firm and industry competitive equilibriums for a perfectly competitive gator-farming industry before the number of alligator farms in Florida doubled. For simplicity, assume the gator farm is earning zero economic profit. Then show the short-run effect of an increase in demand for alligators.

2. Assuming gator farming is perfectly competitive, explain the long-run competitive equilibrium condition for the typical gator farmer and the industry as a whole.

1. Ron Moreau and Penelope Wang, "Gators: Snapping Up Profits," *Newsweek*, Dec. 8, 1986, p. 68.
2. William Booth, "Bag a Gator and Save the Species," *The Washington Post*, Aug. 25, 1993, p. A1.
3. J. Taylor Buckley, "S. Carolina Lets Hunters Go for Gators Again," *USA Today*, Sept. 21, 1995, News Section, p. A1.
4. "More Bite for the Buck," *The Dallas Morning News*, Dec. 6, 2000, p. 2A.
5. Jerry W. Jackson, "Alligators are Growing Part of Florida's Agricultural Landscape," *Knight Ridder/Tribune Business News*, Jan. 26, 2003.
6. Rick Jervis, "Recession Eats into Gator Market," *USA Today*, Oct. 22, 2209, News Section, p. 2A.

Source: © Cengage Learning 2014

are reestablished because profits are squeezed from both the price fall and the rise in the SRATC curve.

The long-run industry supply curve is drawn by connecting the two long-run equilibrium points of E_1 and E_3. Equilibrium point E_2 is not a long-run equilibrium point because it is not established after the entry of new firms has restored normal profits.

CONCLUSION: *The long-run supply curve in a perfectly competitive increasing-cost industry is upward sloping.*

Finally, given the three models presented, you may ask which is the best choice. The answer is that all three versions are possible for any given industry. Only direct observation of the industry can tell which type of industry it is.

EXHIBIT 13	Long-Run Supply in an Increasing-Cost Industry

This pair of graphs derives the long-run supply curve based on the assumption that input prices rise as industry output expands. Part (b) shows that an increase in demand from D_1 to D_2 causes the price to increase in the short run from $60 to $80. The individual firm represented in part (a) earns an economic profit, and new firms enter the industry, causing an increase in industry supply from S_1 to S_2. As output expands, input prices rise and push up the firm's SRATC curve from $SRATC_1$ to $SRATC_2$. As a result, a new long-run equilibrium price is established at $70, which is above the initial equilibrium price. The long-run supply curve for an increasing-cost industry is upward sloping.

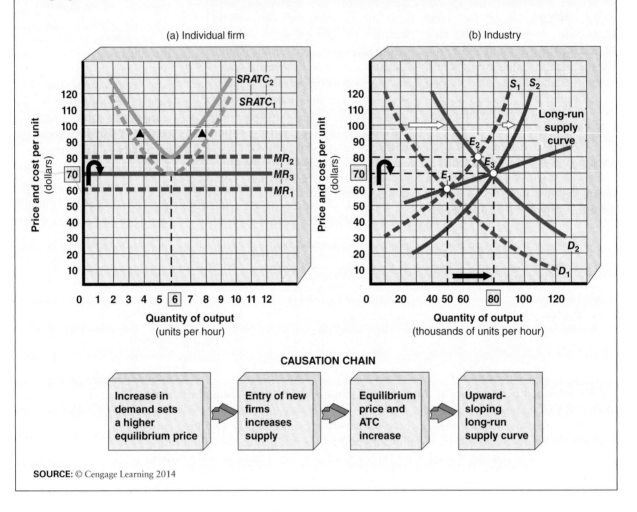

CAUSATION CHAIN

Increase in demand sets a higher equilibrium price ➡ Entry of new firms increases supply ➡ Equilibrium price and ATC increase ➡ Upward-sloping long-run supply curve

SOURCE: © Cengage Learning 2014

Key Concepts

Market structure	Perfectly competitive firm's	long-run supply curve
Perfect competition	short-run supply curve	Constant-cost industry
Barrier to entry	Perfectly competitive industry's	Decreasing-cost industry
Price taker	short-run supply curve	Increasing-cost industry
Marginal revenue (MR)	Perfectly competitive industry's	

Summary

- **Market structure** consists of three market characteristics: (1) the number of sellers, (2) the nature of the product, and (3) the ease of entry into or exit from the market.

- **Perfect competition** is a market structure in which an individual firm cannot affect the price of the product it produces. Each firm in the industry is very small relative to the market as a whole, all the firms sell a homogeneous product, and firms are free to enter and exit the industry.

- A **price-taker** firm in perfect competition faces a perfectly elastic demand curve. It can sell all it wishes at the market-determined price, but it will sell nothing above the given market price. This is because so many competitive firms are willing to sell the same product at the going market price.

- The **total revenue-total cost method** is one way a firm determines the level of output that maximizes profit. Profit reaches a maximum when the vertical difference between the total revenue and the total cost curves is at a maximum.

- The **marginal revenue equals marginal cost method** is a second approach to finding where a firm maximizes profits. **Marginal revenue (MR)** is the change in total revenue from a one-unit change in output. Marginal revenue for a perfectly competitive firm equals the market price. The MR = MC rule states that the firm maximizes profit or minimizes loss by producing the output where marginal revenue equals marginal cost. If the price (average revenue) is below the minimum point on the average variable cost curve, the MR = MC rule does not apply, and the firm shuts down to minimize its losses.

Total Revenue-Total Cost Method

SOURCE: © Cengage Learning 2014

Marginal Revenue Equals Marginal Cost Method

SOURCE: © Cengage Learning 2014

- The **perfectly competitive firm's short-run supply curve** is a curve showing the relationship between the price of a product and the quantity supplied in the short run. The individual firm always produces along its marginal cost curve above its intersection with the average variable cost curve. The **perfectly competitive industry's short-run supply curve** is the horizontal summation of the short-run supply curves of all firms in the industry.

Short-Run Supply Curve

SOURCE: © Cengage Learning 2014

- **Long-run perfectly competitive equilibrium** occurs when a firm earns a normal profit by producing where price equals minimum long-run average cost equals minimum short-run average total cost equals short-run marginal cost.
- In a **constant-cost industry**, total output can be expanded without an increase in the individual

firm's average total cost. Because input prices remain constant, the long-run supply curve in a constant-cost industry is perfectly elastic.

Long-Run Perfectly Competitive Equilibrium

SOURCE: © Cengage Learning 2014

- In a **decreasing-cost industry**, lower input prices result in a downward-sloping industry long-run supply curve. As industry output expands, an individual firm's average total cost curve declines (shifts downward), and the long-run equilibrium market price falls.
- In an **increasing-cost industry**, input prices rise as industry output increases. As a result, an individual firm's average total cost curve rises (shifts upward), and the industry long-run supply curve for an increasing-cost industry is upward sloping.

Summary of Conclusion Statements

- The large-number-of-sellers condition is met when each firm is so small relative to the total market that no single firm can influence the market price.
- If a product is homogeneous, buyers are indifferent as to which seller's product they buy.
- Perfect competition requires that resources be completely mobile to freely enter or exit a market.

- In perfect competition, a firm's marginal revenue equals the price that the firm views as a horizontal demand curve.
- In perfect competition, a firm maximizes profit or minimizes loss by producing the output where marginal revenue equals marginal cost.
- In perfect competition, if the price is below the minimum point on the AVC curve, each unit

produced will not cover the variable cost per unit. Therefore, the firm shuts down.
- The long-run supply curve in a perfectly competitive constant-cost industry is perfectly elastic.
- The long-run supply curve in a perfectly competitive decreasing-cost industry is downward sloping.
- The long-run supply curve in a perfectly competitive increasing-cost industry is upward sloping.

Study Questions and Problems

1. Explain why a perfectly competitive firm would or would not advertise.

2. Does a Kansas wheat farmer fit the perfectly competitive market structure? Explain.

3. Suppose the market equilibrium price of wheat is $2 per bushel in a perfectly competitive industry. Draw the industry supply and demand curves and the demand curve for a single wheat farmer. Explain why the wheat farmer is a price taker.

4. Assuming the market equilibrium price for wheat is $5 per bushel and using the graph above, draw the total revenue and the marginal revenue curves for the typical wheat farmer. Explain how marginal revenue and price are related to the total revenue curve.

5. Consider the following cost data for a perfectly competitive firm in the short run.

If the market price is $150, how many units of output will the firm produce in order to maximize profit in the short run? Specify the amount of economic profit or loss. At what level of output does the firm break even?

6. Consider this statement: "A firm should increase output when it makes a profit." Do you agree or disagree? Explain.

7. Consider this statement: "When marginal revenue equals marginal cost, total cost equals total revenue, and the firm makes zero profit." Do you agree or disagree? Explain.

8. Consider Exhibit 14, which shows the graph of a perfectly competitive firm in the short run.
   a. If the firm's demand curve is MR_3, does the firm earn an economic profit or loss?
   b. Which demand curve(s) indicate(s) the firm incurs a loss?
   c. Which demand curve(s) indicate(s) the firm would shut down?
   d. Identify the firm's short-run supply curve.

Output (Q)	Total Fixed Cost (TFC)	Total Variable Cost (TVC)	Total Cost (TC)	Total Revenue (TR)	Profit
1	$100	$120	$____	$____	$____
2	100	200	____	____	____
3	100	290	____	____	____
4	100	430	____	____	____
5	100	590	____	____	____

| EXHIBIT 14 | A Perfectly Competitive Firm |

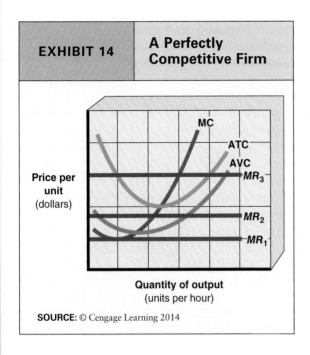

Price per unit (dollars)

Quantity of output (units per hour)

SOURCE: © Cengage Learning 2014

9. Consider this statement: "The perfectly competitive firm will sell all the quantity of output consumers will buy at the prevailing market price." Do you agree or disagree? Explain your answer.

10. Suppose a perfectly competitive firm's demand curve is below its average total cost curve. Explain the conditions under which a firm continues to produce in the short run.

11. Suppose the industry equilibrium price of residential housing construction is $100 per square foot and the minimum average variable cost for a residential construction contractor is $110 per square foot. What would you advise the owner of this firm to do? Explain.

12. Suppose independent truckers operate in a perfectly competitive industry. If these firms are earning positive economic profits, what happens in the long run to the following: the price of trucking services, the industry quantity of output, and the profits of trucking firms? Given these conditions, is the independent trucking industry a constant-cost, increasing-cost, or decreasing-cost industry?

For Online Exercises, go to the Tucker Web site at www.cengage.com/economics/tucker.

✓ CHECKPOINT ANSWERS

Should Motels Offer Rooms at the Beach for Only $50 a Night?

As long as price exceeds average variable cost, the motel is better off operating than shutting down. Because $50 is more than enough to cover the guest-related variable costs of $45 per room, the firm will operate. The $5 remaining after variable costs are covered can be put toward the $50 of fixed costs. Were the motel to shut down, it would make no contribution to these overhead costs. If you said the Myrtle Beach motels should operate during the winter because they can get a price that exceeds their average variable cost, **YOU ARE CORRECT.**

Are You in Business for the Long Run?

In the long run, surviving firms will operate at the minimum of the long-run average cost curve. The average cost of 50 storage units is $4,000 ($200,000/50), the average cost of 100 storage units is $3,000 ($300,000/100), and the average cost of 200 storage units is $3,500 ($700,000/200). Of the three storage-unit quantities given, the one with the lowest average cost is closest to the minimum point on the LRAC curve. If you chose 100 storage units, **YOU ARE CORRECT.**

Sample Quiz

For an explanation of the correct answers, visit the Tucker Web site at www.cengage.com/economics/tucker.

1. As shown in Exhibit 15, suppose the firm's price is OB. The firm's total economic profit at this price is equal to the area of
   a. $CJID$.
   b. $BFHD$.
   c. $AEXD$.
   d. $CGHD$.
   e. zero.

EXHIBIT 15	**Marginal Revenue and Cost per Unit Curves**

SOURCE: © Cengage Learning 2014

2. The firm shown in Exhibit 15 will
   a. produce where marginal cost equals marginal revenue.
   b. be a price taker.
   c. not produce below a price of OA.
   d. All of the above answers are correct.

3. As shown in Exhibit 15, if the price is OD, a perfectly competitive firm maximizes profit at which point on its marginal cost curve?
   a. E
   b. F
   c. I
   d. Between E and I

4. As shown in Exhibit 15, if the price is OB, the firm's total cost of producing at its most profitable level of output is

   a. YF.
   b. XL.
   c. $OYFB$.
   d. $OXEA$.

5. As shown in Exhibit 15, if the price is OD, the firm's total revenue at its most profitable level of output is
   a. $OZID$.
   b. $OYHD$.
   c. $OXLD$.
   d. $OYFB$.

6. As shown in Exhibit 15, suppose the firm's price is OB. The firm's total economic profit at this price is equal to the area of
   a. $CJID$.
   b. $BFHD$.
   c. $AEXD$.
   d. $CGHD$.
   e. zero.

7. As shown in Exhibit 15, if the price is OB, the firm's total cost of producing at its most profitable level of output is
   a. YF.
   b. XL.
   c. $OYFB$.
   d. $OXEA$.

8. The firm shown in Exhibit 15 will
   a. produce where marginal cost equals marginal revenue.
   b. be a price taker.
   c. not produce below a price of OA.
   d. All of the above answers are correct.

9. Perfect competition is defined as market structure in which
   a. there are many small sellers.
   b. the product is homogeneous.
   c. it is very easy for firms to enter or exit the market.
   d. All of the above answers are correct.

10. Under perfect competition, which of the following are the same (equal) at all levels of output?
    a. Price and marginal cost
    b. Price and marginal revenue

Sample Quiz *continued*

c. Marginal cost and marginal revenue
d. All of the above answers are correct.

11. A portrait photographer produces output in packages of 100 photos each. If the output sold increases from 600 to 700 photos, total revenue increases from $1,200 to $1,400. What is the marginal revenue per photo?
    a. $200
    b. $100
    c. $20
    d. $2
    e. $1

12. In the short run, a perfectly competitive firm is producing at a price below average total cost. What is its economic profit?
    a. Positive
    b. Zero
    c. Negative
    d. Normal

13. In Exhibit 16, if output is 200 units per week, economic profit for the firm is
    a. zero.
    b. at its minimum.
    c. at its maximum.
    d. None of the above answers are correct.

EXHIBIT 16	Total Revenue and Total Cost Graph

SOURCE: © Cengage Learning 2014

14. In Exhibit 16, economic profit for the firm is at a maximum when output per week equals

a. 0 units.
b. 100 units.
c. 200 units.
d. 250 units.

15. The point of maximum profit for a business firm is where
    a. $P = AC$.
    b. $TR = TC$.
    c. $MR = AR$.
    d. $MR = MC$.

16. Above the shutdown point, a competitive firm's supply curve coincides with its
    a. marginal revenue curve.
    b. marginal cost curve.
    c. average variable cost curve.
    d. average total cost curve.

17. A perfectly competitive firm's short-run supply curve is the
    a. average total cost curve.
    b. demand curve above the marginal revenue curve.
    c. same as the market supply curve.
    d. marginal cost curve above the average variable cost curve.

18. A perfectly competitive firm's short-run supply curve is
    a. the segment of the marginal cost curve above average fixed cost.
    b. the segment of the marginal cost curve above the minimum level of average variable cost.
    c. the upward-sloping segment of the marginal cost curve.
    d. both a and b.

19. In long-run equilibrium, the perfectly competitive firm sets its price equal to which of the following?
    a. Short-run average total cost
    b. Short-run marginal cost
    c. Long-run average cost
    d. All of the above answers are correct.

20. If there is a permanent increase in demand for the product of a perfectly competitive industry, the process of transition to a new long-run equilibrium will include
    a. the entry of new firms.
    b. temporarily higher profits.
    c. both a and b.
    d. neither a nor b.

chapter 9

Monopoly

Playing the popular board game of Monopoly teaches some of the characteristics of monopoly theory presented in this chapter. In the game version, players win by gaining as much economic power as possible. They strive to own railroads, utilities, Boardwalk, Park Place, and other valuable real estate. Then each player tries to bankrupt opponents by purchasing hotels that charge high prices. A player who rolls the dice and lands on another player's property has no choice—either pay the price or lose the game.

In the last chapter, we studied perfect competition, which may be viewed as the paragon of economic virtue. Why? Under perfect competition, there are many sellers, each lacking any power to influence price. Perfect competition and monopoly are polar extremes. The word *monopoly* is derived from two Greek words meaning "single seller." A monopoly has the market power to set its price and not worry about competitors. Perhaps your college or university has only one bookstore where you can buy textbooks. If so, students are likely to pay higher prices for textbooks than they would if many sellers competed in the campus textbook market.

This chapter explains why firms do not or cannot enter a particular market and compete with a monopolist. Then we explore some of the interesting monopolies around the world. We study how a monopolist determines what price to charge and how much to produce. The chapter ends with a discussion of the pros and cons of monopoly. Most of the analytical tools required here have been introduced in previous chapters.

In this chapter, you will learn to solve these economics puzzles:

- Why doesn't the monopolist gouge consumers by charging the highest possible price?
- How can price discrimination be fair?
- Are medallion cabs in New York City monopolists?

9-1 The Monopoly Market Structure

The model at the opposite extreme from perfect competition is monopoly. Under monopoly, the consumer has a simple choice—either buy the monopolist's product or do without it. Monopoly is a market structure characterized by (1) a single seller, (2) a unique product, and (3) impossible entry into the market. Unlike perfect competition, there are no close substitutes for the monopolist's product. Monopoly, like perfect competition, corresponds only approximately to real-world industries, but it serves as a useful benchmark model. Following are brief descriptions of each monopoly characteristic.

Monopoly

A market structure characterized by (1) a single seller, (2) a unique product, and (3) impossible entry into the market.

9-1a SINGLE SELLER

In perfect competition, many firms make up the industry. In contrast, a monopoly means that a single firm *is* the industry. One firm provides the total supply of a product in a given market. Local monopolies are more common real-world approximations of the model than are national or world market monopolies. For example, a campus bookstore, a cable television company, and an electric power company may be local monopolies. The only gas station, drugstore, or grocery store in Nowhere County, Utah, and a hotdog stand at a football game are also examples of monopolies. Nationally, the U.S. Postal Service monopolizes first-class mail.

9-1b UNIQUE PRODUCT

A unique product means there are *no close substitutes* for the monopolist's product. Thus, the monopolist faces little or no competition. In reality, however, there are few, if any, products that have no close substitutes. Students can buy used text-books from sources other than the campus bookstore, and textbooks can be purchased over the Internet. Satellite television competes with cable television. Natural gas, oil furnaces, and solar energy are substitutes for electric heat. Similarly, the fax machine and email are substitutes for mail service.

9-1c IMPOSSIBLE ENTRY

In perfect competition, there are no constraints to prevent new firms from entering an industry. In the case of monopoly, extremely high barriers make it very difficult or impossible for new firms to enter an industry. Following are the three major barriers that prevent new firms from entering a market and competing with a monopolist.

9-1d OWNERSHIP OF A VITAL RESOURCE

Sole control of the entire supply of a strategic input is one way a monopolist can prevent a newcomer from entering an industry. A famous historical example is Alcoa's monopoly of the U.S. aluminum market from the late 19th century until the end of World War II. The source of Alcoa's monopoly was its control of bauxite ore, which is necessary to produce aluminum. Today, it is very difficult for a new professional sports league to compete with the National Football

League (NFL) or the National Basketball Association (NBA). Why? NFL and NBA teams have contracts with the best players and leases for the best stadiums and arenas.

9-1e LEGAL BARRIERS

The oldest and most effective barriers protecting a firm from potential competitors are the result of government franchises and licenses. The government permits a single firm to provide a certain product and excludes competing firms by law. For example, water and sewer service, natural gas, and cable television operate under monopoly franchises established by state and local governments. In many states, the state government runs monopoly liquor stores and lotteries. The U.S. Postal Service has a government franchise to deliver first-class mail.

Government-granted licenses restrict entry into some industries and occupations. For example, the Federal Communications Commission (FCC) must license radio and television stations. In most states, physicians, lawyers, dentists, nurses, teachers, real estate agents, hairstylists, taxicabs, liquor stores, funeral homes, and other professions and businesses are required to have a license.

Patents and copyrights are another form of government barrier to entry. The government grants patents to inventors, thereby legally prohibiting other firms from selling the patented product for 20 years. Copyrights give creators of literature, art, music, and movies exclusive rights to sell or license their works. The purpose behind granting patents and copyrights is to encourage innovation and new products by guaranteeing exclusive rights to profit from new ideas for a limited period.

9-1f ECONOMIES OF SCALE

Why might competition among firms be unsustainable so that one firm becomes a monopolist? Recall the concept of *economies of scale* from the chapter on production costs. As a result of large-scale production, the long-run average cost (LRAC) of production falls. This means a monopoly can emerge in time *naturally* because of the relationship between average cost and the scale of an operation. As a firm becomes larger, its cost per unit of output is lower compared to a smaller competitor. In the long run, this "survival of the fittest" cost advantage forces smaller firms to leave the industry. Because new firms cannot hope to produce and sell output equal or close to that of the monopolist, thereby achieving the monopolist's low costs, they will not enter the industry. Thus, a monopoly can arise over time and remain dominant in an industry even though the monopolist does not own an essential resource or obtain legal barriers.

Economists call the situation in which one seller emerges in an industry because of economies of scale a natural monopoly. A natural monopoly is an industry in which the long-run average cost of production declines throughout the entire market. As a result, a single firm can supply the entire market demand at a lower cost than two or more smaller firms. Public utilities, such as natural gas, water, and cable television, are examples of natural monopolies. The government grants these industries an exclusive franchise in a geographic area so consumers can benefit from the cost savings that occur when one firm in an industry with significant economies of scale sells a large output. The government then regulates these monopolies through a board of commissioners to prevent exploitation.

Natural monopoly
An industry in which the long-run average cost of production declines throughout the entire market. As a result, a single firm can supply the entire market demand at a lower cost than can two or more smaller firms.

EXHIBIT 1	Minimizing Costs in a Natural Monopoly

In a natural monopoly, a single firm in an industry can produce at a lower cost than two or more firms This condition occurs because the LRAC curve for any firm decreases over the relevant range. For example, one firm can produce 100 units at an average cost of $15 and a total cost of $1,500. Two firms in the industry can produce 100 units of output (50 units each) for a total cost of $2,500, and five firms can produce the same output for a total cost of $3,500.

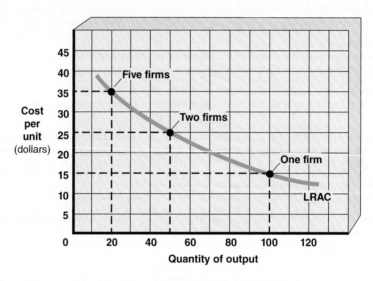

SOURCE: © Cengage Learning 2014

Exhibit 1 depicts the LRAC curve for a natural monopoly. A single firm can produce 100 units at an average cost of $15 and a total cost of $1,500. If two firms each produce 50 units, the total cost rises to $2,500. With five firms producing 20 units each, the total cost rises to $3,500. In the chapter on antitrust and regulation, regulation of a natural monopoly will be explored in greater detail.

CONCLUSION: *Because of economies of scale, a single firm in an industry will produce output at a lower per-unit cost than two or more firms.*

Network good

A good that increases in value to each user as the total number of users increases. As a result, a firm can achieve economies of scale. Examples include Facebook and Match.com.

9-1g NETWORK GOOD

Economies of scale and monopoly power can exist because consumers choose a product that everyone else is using. A network good is a good that increases in value to each user as the total number of users increases. Examples include such Internet products as Facebook and Match.com. People post on Facebook to belong to the same network where everyone posts their profile. Similarly, Match.com is the largest dating service with the largest selections of potential dates.

Monopolies around the World

Applicable Concept: monopoly

Interesting examples of monopolies can be found in other countries. Let's begin with a historical example. In the sixteenth through eighteenth centuries, monarchs granted monopoly rights for a variety of businesses. For example, in 1600, Queen Elizabeth I chartered the British East India Company and gave it a monopoly over England's trade with India. This company was even given the right to coin money and to make peace or war with non-Christian powers. As a result of its monopoly, the company made substantial profits from the trade in Indian cotton goods, silks, and spices. In the late 1700s, the growing power of the company and huge personal fortunes of its officers provoked more and more government control. Finally, in 1858, the company was abolished, ending its trade monopoly, great power, and patronage.

"Diamonds are forever," has been De Beers slogan, but will De Beers be the diamond monopoly forever? De Beers, a South African corporation, was close to being a world monopoly. It owns the world's largest diamond mine, which was discovered in 1866 on a farm in South Africa owned by Johannes De Beer. Through its Central Selling Organization (CSO) headquartered in London, De Beers controlled 80 percent of all the diamonds sold in the world. De Beers controlled the price of jewelry-quality diamonds by requiring suppliers in Russia, Australia, Congo, Botswana, Namibia, and other countries to sell their rough diamonds through De Beers's CSO. Why did suppliers of rough diamonds allow De Beers to set the price and quantity of diamonds sold throughout the world? The answer was that the CSO could put any uncooperative seller out of business. All the CSO had to do was to reach into its huge stockpile of diamonds and flood the market with the type of diamonds being sold by an independent seller. As a result, the price of diamonds would plummet in the competitor's market, and the independent seller would cease to sell diamonds.

In recent years, De Beers lost some of its control of the market. Mines in Australia became more

independent, diamonds were found in Canada, and Russian mines began selling to independents. To deal with the new conditions, De Beers changed its policy in 2001 by closing the CSO and promoting its own brand of diamonds rather than trying to control the world diamond supply. De Beers proclaimed its strategy to be "the diamond supplier of choice." Will this monopoly continue? It is an interesting question.

Genuine caviar, the salty black delicacy, is naturally scarce because it comes from the eggs of sturgeon harvested by fisheries from the Caspian Sea near the mouth of the Volga River. After the Bolshevik revolution in Russia in 1917, a caviar monopoly was established under the control of the Soviet Ministry of Fisheries and the Paris-based Petrosian Company. The Petrosian brothers limited exports of caviar and pushed prices up as high as $1,000 a pound for some varieties. As a result of this worldwide monopoly, both the Soviet government and the Petrosian Company earned handsome profits. It is interesting to note that the vast majority of the tons of caviar harvested each year was consumed at government banquets or sold at bargain prices to top Communist Party officials. With the fall of the Soviet Union, it was impossible for the Ministry of Fisheries to control all exports of caviar. Various former Soviet republics claimed jurisdiction and negotiated independent export contracts. As a result, caviar export prices dropped sharply.

Source: © Cengage Learning 2014

CONCLUSION: *The greater the number of people connected to a network goods system, the more benefits of the product to each person are increased.*

Network goods can result in a firm increasing sales rapidly and thus achieving economies of scale, as illustrated in Exhibit 1. Smaller firms therefore have higher-cost products that cannot compete, and they go out of business.

9-2 Price and Output Decisions for a Monopolist

A major difference between perfect competition and monopoly is the shape of the demand curve, not the shapes of the cost curves. As explained in the previous chapter, a perfectly competitive firm is a *price taker*. In contrast, the next sections explain that a monopolist is a price maker. A price maker is a firm that faces a downward-sloping demand curve. This means a monopolist has the ability to select the product's price. In short, a monopolist can set the price with its corresponding level of output, rather than being a helpless pawn at the mercy of the going industry price. To understand the monopolist, we again apply the marginal approach to our hypothetical electronics company Computech.

Price maker

A firm that faces a downward-sloping demand curve and therefore it can choose among price and output combinations along the demand curve.

9-2a MARGINAL REVENUE, TOTAL REVENUE, AND PRICE ELASTICITY OF DEMAND

Suppose engineers at Computech discover an inexpensive, miraculous electronic device called SAV-U-GAS that anyone can easily attach to a car's engine. Once installed, the device raises gasoline mileage to over 100 miles per gallon. The government grants Computech a patent, and the company becomes a monopolist selling this gas-saver gizmo. Because of this barrier to entry, Computech is the only seller in the industry. Although other firms try to compete with this invention, they create poor substitutes. This means the downward-sloping demand curve for the industry and for the monopolist are identical.

Exhibit 2(a) illustrates the demand and the marginal revenue (MR) curves for a monopolist such as Computech. As the monopolist lowers its price to increase the quantity demanded, changes in both price and quantity affect the firm's total revenue (price times quantity), as shown graphically in Exhibit 2(b). If Computech charges $150, consumers purchase 0 units, and, therefore, total revenue is zero. To sell 1 unit, Computech must lower the price to $138, and total revenue rises from zero to $138. Because the marginal revenue is the increase in total revenue that results from a 1-unit change in output, the MR curve at the first unit of output is $138 ($138 − 0). Thus, the price and the marginal revenue from selling 1 unit are equal at $138. To sell 2 units, the monopolist must lower the price to $125, and total revenue rises to $250. The marginal revenue from selling the second unit is $112 ($250 − $138), which is $13 less than the price received.

EXHIBIT 2	Demand, Marginal Revenue, and Total Revenue for a Monopolist

Part (a) shows the relationship between the demand and the marginal revenue curves. The MR curve is below the demand curve. Between 0 and 6 units of output, MR > 0; at 6 units of output, MR = 0; beyond 6 units of output, MR < 0.

The relationship between demand and total revenue is shown in part (b). When the price is $150, total revenue is zero. When the price is set at zero, total revenue is also zero. Between these two extreme prices, the price of $75 maximizes total revenue. This price corresponds to 6 units of output, which is where the MR curve intersects the quantity axis, halfway between the origin and the intercept of the demand curve.

(a) Demand and marginal revenue curves

Price and marginal revenue (dollars)

Quantity of output (units per hour)

Output per Hour	Price	Total Revenue	Marginal Revenue
0	$150	$0	
			$138
1	138	138	
			112
2	125	250	
			89
3	113	339	
			61
4	100	400	
			40
5	88	440	
			10
6	75	450	
			0
			−9
7	63	441	
			−41
8	50	400	
			−58
9	38	342	
			−92
10	25	250	
			−107
11	13	143	
			−143
12	0	0	

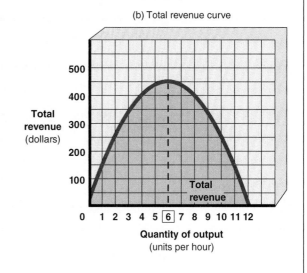

(b) Total revenue curve

Total revenue (dollars)

Quantity of output (units per hour)

SOURCE: © Cengage Learning 2014

As shown in Exhibit 2(a), as the monopolist lowers its price, price is greater than marginal revenue after the first unit of output. Like all marginal measurements, marginal revenue is plotted midway between the quantities.

> **CONCLUSION:** *The demand and marginal revenue curves of the monopolist are downward sloping, in contrast to the horizontal demand and corresponding marginal revenue curves facing the perfectly competitive firm [compare Exhibit 2(a) with Exhibit 1 (b) of the previous chapter].*

Starting from zero output, as the price falls, total revenue rises until it reaches a maximum at 6 units, and then it falls, tracing the "revenue hill" drawn in part (b). The explanation was presented earlier in the discussion of price elasticity of demand in Chapter 5. Recall that a straight-line demand curve has an elastic ($E_d > 1$) segment along the upper half, a unit elastic ($E_d = 1$) segment at the midpoint, and an inelastic ($E_d < 1$) segment along the lower half (see Exhibit 4 in Chapter 5). Recall from Chapter 5 that when $E_d > 1$, total revenue rises as the price drops, and total revenue reaches a maximum where $E_d = 1$. When $E_d < 1$, total revenue falls as the price falls.

As shown in Exhibit 2(b), total revenue for a monopolist is related to marginal revenue. When the MR curve is above the quantity axis (elastic demand), total revenue is increasing. At the intersection of the MR curve and the quantity axis (unit elastic demand), total revenue is at its maximum. When the MR curve is below the quantity axis, total revenue is decreasing (inelastic demand). The monopolist will never operate on the inelastic range of its demand curve that corresponds to a negative marginal revenue. The reason is that, in this inelastic range, the monopolist can increase total revenue by cutting output and raising price. In our example, Computech would not charge a price lower than $75 or produce an output greater than 6 units per hour. Now we turn to the question of what price the monopolist will charge to maximize profit.

In Exhibit 2(a), observe that the MR curve cuts the quantity axis at 6 units, which is half of 12 units. Following an easy rule helps locate the point along the quantity axis where marginal revenue equals zero: *The marginal revenue curve for a straight-line demand curve intersects the quantity axis halfway between the origin and the quantity axis intercept of the demand curve.*

9-2b SHORT-RUN PROFIT MAXIMIZATION FOR A MONOPOLIST USING THE TOTAL REVENUE–TOTAL COST METHOD

Exhibit 3 reproduces the demand, total revenue, and marginal revenue data from Exhibit 2 and adds cost data from the previous two chapters. These data illustrate a situation in which Computech can earn monopoly economic profit in the short run. Subtracting total cost in column 6 from total revenue in column 3 gives the total profit or loss in column 8 that the firm earns at each level of output. From 0 to 1 unit, the monopolist incurs losses, and then a break-even point occurs before 2 units per hour. If the monopolist produces 5 units per hour, it earns the maximum profit of $190 per hour. As output expands between 5 and 8 units of output,

| | EXHIBIT 3 | | Short-Run Profit Maximization Schedule for Computech as a Monopolist | | | | | |

(1) Output per Hour (Q)	(2) Price per Unit (P)	(3) Total Revenue (TR)	(4) Marginal Revenue (MR)	(5) Marginal Cost (MQ)	(6) Total Cost (TC)	(7) Average Total Cost (ATC)	(8) Profit (+) or Loss (−)
0	$150	$ 0			$100	—	−$100
			$138	$50			
1	138	138			150	$150	−12
			112	34			
2	125	250			184	92	66
			89	24			
3	113	339			208	69	131
			61	19			
4	100	400			227	57	173
			40	23			
5	88	440	25	25	250	50	190
			10	30			
6	75	450			280	47	170
			−9	38			
7	63	441			318	45	123
			−41	48			
8	50	400			366	46	34
			−58	59			
9	38	342			425	47	−83
			−92	75			
10	25	250			500	50	−250
			−107	95			
11	13	143			595	54	−452
			−143	117			
12	0	0			712	59	−712

SOURCE: © Cengage Learning 2014

the monopolist's profit diminishes. After 8 units of output, there is a second break-even point, and losses increase as output expands. Exhibit 4 illustrates graphically that where the vertical distance between the total revenue and total cost curves is maximum corresponds to the profit-maximizing output. Note that the total revenue-maximizing output level of 6 units is greater than the profit-maximizing output at 5 units.

EXHIBIT 4	Short-Run Profit Maximization for a Monopolist Using the Total Revenue-Total Cost Method

The profit-maximizing level of output for Computech as a monopolist is shown in this exhibit. Part (a) shows that maximum profit is earned by producing 5 units per hour and charging a price of $88 per unit where the vertical distance between the total revenue and total cost curves is the greatest. In Part (b), the maximum profit of $190 per hour corresponds to the profit-maximizing output of 5 units per hour illustrated in part (a). At output levels below 2 or above 8, the monopolist incurs losses.

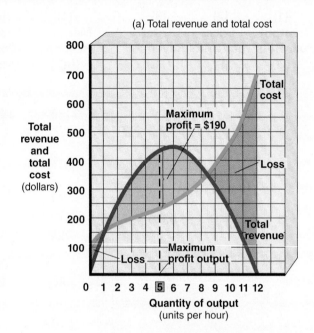

(a) Total revenue and total cost

(b) Profit or loss

SOURCE: © Cengage Learning 2014

9-2c SHORT-RUN PROFIT MAXIMIZATION FOR A MONOPOLIST USING THE MARGINAL REVENUE EQUALS MARGINAL COST METHOD

Exhibit 5 reproduces the demand and cost curves from the table in Exhibit 3. Like the perfectly competitive firm, a monopolist maximizes profit by producing the quantity of output where MR = MC and charging the corresponding price on its demand curve. In this case, 5 units is the quantity at which MR = MC. As represented by point A on the demand curve, the price at 5 units is $88. Point B represents an average total cost (ATC) of $50 at 5 units. Because the price of $88 is above the ATC curve at the MR = MC output, the monopolist earns a profit of $38 per unit. At the hourly output of 5 units, total profit is $190 per hour, as shown by the shaded area ($38 per unit × 5 units).

Observe that a monopolist charges neither the highest possible price nor the total revenue-maximizing price. In Exhibit 5(a), $88 is not the highest possible price. Because Computech is a *price maker*, it could have set a price above $88 and sold less output than 5 units. However, the monopolist does not maximize profit by charging the highest possible price. Any price above $88 does not correspond to the intersection of the MR and MC curves. Now note that 5 units is below the output level where MR intersects the quantity axis and total revenue reaches its peak. Since MR = 0 and $E_d = 1$ when total revenue is maximum at 6 units of output, MC = 0 must also hold to maximize revenue and profit at the same time. A monopolist producing with zero marginal cost is an unlikely case. Hence, the price charged to maximize profit is higher on the demand curve than the price is that maximizes total revenue.

> **CONCLUSION:** *The monopolist always maximizes profit by producing at a price on the elastic segment of its demand curve.*

9-2d A MONOPOLIST FACING A SHORT-RUN LOSS

Having a monopoly does not guarantee profits. A monopolist has no protection against changes in demand or cost conditions. Exhibit 6 shows a situation in which the demand curve is lower at any point than the ATC curve, and total cost therefore exceeds total revenue at any price charged. Because the point where MR = MC at a price of $50 (point A) on the demand curve is above the AVC curve, but below the ATC curve, the best Computech can do is to minimize its loss. This means the monopolist, like the perfectly competitive firm, produces in the short run at a quantity of 5 units per hour where MR = MC. At a price of $50 (point A), the ATC is $70 (point B), and Computech incurs a loss of $100 per hour, represented by the shaded area ($20 × 5 units).

What if MR = MC at a price on the demand curve that is below the AVC for a monopolist? As under perfect competition, the monopolist will shut down. To operate would only add further to its losses.

EXHIBIT 5	Short-Run Profit Maximization for a Monopolist Using the Marginal Revenue Equals Marginal Cost Method

Part (a) illustrates a monopolist electronics firm, Computech, maximizing profit by producing 5 units of output where the marginal revenue (MR) and the marginal cost (MC) curves intersect. The profit-maximizing price the monopolist charges at 5 units of output is $88, which is point A on the demand curve. Because $88 is above the average total cost (ATC) of $50 at point B, the monopolist earns a short-run profit of $190 per hour, represented by the shaded area ($38 profit per unit × 5 units).

At a price of $88 and output of 5 units per hour in part (a), the shaded area in part (b) shows that the profit curve is maximized at $190 per hour. At output levels below 2 or above 8, the monopolist incurs losses.

(a) Price, marginal revenue, and cost per unit

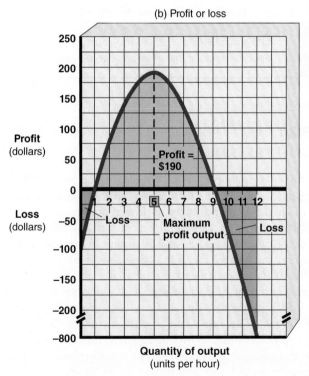

(b) Profit or loss

SOURCE: © Cengage Learning 2014

EXHIBIT 6	**Short-Run Loss Minimization for a Monopolist Using the Marginal Revenue Equals Marginal Cost Method**

In part (a), all points along the demand curve lie below the ATC curve. If the market price charged corresponds to the output where the marginal revenue (MR) and marginal cost (MC) curves intersect, the firm will keep its loss to a minimum. At point *A*, the loss-minimizing price is $50 per unit, and marginal revenue equals marginal cost at an output of 5 units per hour with ATC equal to $70 per unit (point *B*). The short-run loss represented by the shaded area is $100 ($20 loss per unit × 5 units).

Part (b) shows that the firm's short-run loss will be greater at any output other than where the marginal revenue and the marginal cost curves intersect at an output of 5 units per hour. Because the price of $50 is above the average variable cost, each unit of output sold pays for the average variable cost and a portion of the average fixed cost.

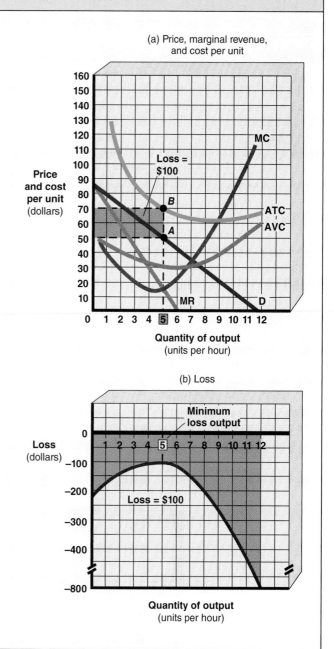

(a) Price, marginal revenue, and cost per unit

(b) Loss

SOURCE: © Cengage Learning 2014

9-2e MONOPOLY IN THE LONG RUN

In perfect competition, economic profits are impossible in the long run. The entry of new firms into the industry drives the product's price down until profits reach zero. Extremely high barriers to entry, however, protect a monopolist.

The Standard Oil Monopoly

Applicable Concept: monopoly

Oil was discovered in western Pennsylvania by Colonel Edwin L. Drake in 1859, and after the Civil War, oil wells sprang up across the landscape. Because oil was plentiful, there was cutthroat competition, and the result was low prices and profits. At this time, John D. Rockefeller, who had grown up selling eggs, was a young Cleveland produce wholesaler in his early twenties. He was doing well in produce, but realized that greater profits could be made in refining oil, where there was less competition than in drilling for oil. So in 1869, Rockefeller borrowed all the money he could and began with two small oil refineries.

To boost his market power, Rockefeller's Standard Oil of Ohio negotiated secret agreements with the railroads. In addition to information on his competitors' shipments, Rockefeller negotiated contracts with the railroads to pay rebates not only

on Standard Oil's oil shipments, but also on its competitors' shipments. Soon Standard Oil was able to buy 21 of its 26 refining competitors in the Cleveland area. As its profits grew, Standard Oil expanded its refining empire by acquiring its own oil fields, railroads, pipelines, and ships. The objective was to control oil from the oil well to the consumer. Over time, Rockefeller came to own a major part of the petroleum industry. Competitors found railroads and pipelines closed to their oil shipments. Rivals that could not be forced out of business were merged with Standard Oil.

In 1870, Standard Oil controlled only 10 percent of the oil industry in the United States. By 1880, Standard Oil controlled over 90 percent of the industry, and its oil was being shipped throughout the world.

The more Standard Oil monopolized the petroleum industry, the higher its profits rose, and the greater its power to eliminate competition became. As competitors dropped out of the industry, Rockefeller became a price maker. He raised prices, and Standard Oil's profits soared. Finally, in 1911, Standard Oil was broken up under the Sherman Antitrust Act of 1890 into competing companies, including companies that eventually became Exxon and Mobil.

Source: © Cengage Learning 2014

CONCLUSION: *If the positions of a monopolist's demand and cost curves give it a profit and nothing disturbs these curves, the monopolist will earn profit in the long run.*

In the long run, the monopolist has great flexibility. The monopolist can alter its plant size to lower cost just as a perfectly competitive firm does. But firms such as Computech will not remain in business in the long run when losses persist—regardless of their monopoly status. Facing long-run losses, the monopolist will transfer its resources to a more profitable industry.

In reality, no monopolist can depend on barriers to protect it fully from competition in the long run. One threat is that entrepreneurs will find innovative ways to compete with a monopoly. For example, Computech must fear that firms will use their ingenuity and new electronic discoveries to develop a better and cheaper gasoline-saving device. To dampen the enthusiasm of potential rivals, one alternative for the monopolist is to sacrifice short-run profits to earn greater profits in the long run. Returning to part (a) of Exhibit 5, the monopolist might wish to charge a price below $88 and produce an output greater than 5 units per hour.

9-3 Price Discrimination

Our discussion so far has assumed the monopolist charges each customer the same price. What if Computech decides to sell identical SAV-U-GAS units for, say, $50 to truckers and $100 to everyone else? Under certain conditions, a monopolist may practice price discrimination to maximize profit. Price discrimination occurs when a seller charges different prices for the same product that are not justified by cost differences.

9-3a CONDITIONS FOR PRICE DISCRIMINATION

All monopolists cannot engage in price discrimination. The following three conditions must exist before a seller can price discriminate:

1. The seller must be a price maker and therefore face a downward-sloping demand curve. This means that monopoly is not the only market structure in which price discrimination may occur.
2. The seller must be able to segment the market by distinguishing between consumers willing to pay different prices. Momentarily, this separation of buyers will be shown to be based on different price elasticities of demand.
3. It must be impossible or too costly for customers to engage in arbitrage. Arbitrage is the practice of earning a profit by buying a good at a low price and reselling the good at a higher price. For example, suppose your campus bookstore tried to boost profits by selling textbooks at a 50 percent discount to seniors. It would not take seniors long to cut the bookstore's profits by buying textbooks at the low price, selling these texts under the list price to all students who are not seniors, and pocketing the difference. In so doing, even without knowing the word *arbitrage*, the seniors would destroy the bookstore's price discrimination scheme.

Although not monopolies, college and university tuition policies meet the conditions for price discrimination. First, lower tuition increases the quantity of openings demanded. Second, applicants' high school grades and SAT scores allow the admissions office to classify "consumers" with different price elasticities of demand. Students with lower grades and SAT scores have fewer substitutes, and their demand curve is less elastic than that of students with higher grades and SAT scores. If the tuition rises at University X, few students with lower grades will be lost because they have few offers of admission from other universities. On the other hand, the loss of students with higher grades and SAT scores is greater because they have more admissions opportunities. Third, the nature of the product prevents arbitrage. A student cannot buy University X admission at one price and sell it to another student for a higher price.

Exhibit 7 illustrates how University X price discriminates. For simplicity, assume the marginal cost of providing education to students is constant and therefore is represented by a horizontal MC curve. To maximize profit, University X follows the MR = MC rule in each market. Given the different price elasticities of demand, the price at which MR = MC differs for average and superior students. As a result, University X sets a higher tuition, T_1, in the average-student market, where demand is less responsive to the higher price. In the superior-student market,

Price discrimination
The practice of a seller charging different prices for the same product that are not justified by cost differences.

Arbitrage
The practice of earning a profit by buying a good at a low price and reselling the good at a higher price.

EXHIBIT 7	Price Discrimination

To maximize profit, University X separates students applying for admission into two markets. The demand curve for admission of average students in part (a) is less elastic than the demand curve for admission of superior students in part (b). Profit maximization occurs when MR = MC in each market. Therefore, University X sets a tuition of T_1 for average students and gives scholarships to superior students, which lowers their tuition to T_2. Using price discrimination, University X earns a greater profit than it would by charging a single tuition to all students.

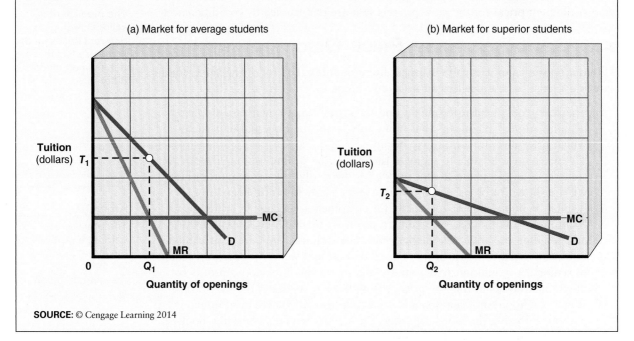

SOURCE: © Cengage Learning 2014

where demand is more responsive, these students receive scholarships, and their tuition is lower at T_2.

9-3b IS PRICE DISCRIMINATION UNFAIR?

Examples of price discrimination abound. Movie theaters offer lower prices for children than for adults. Electric utilities, which are monopolies, charge industrial users of electricity lower rates than residential users. Hotels and restaurants often give discounts to senior citizens, and airlines offer lower fares to vacationers who buy weeks early.

The typical reaction to price discrimination is that it is unfair. From the viewpoint of buyers who pay the higher prices, it is. But look at the other side of price discrimination. First, the seller is pleased because price discrimination increases profits. Second, many buyers benefit from price discrimination by not being excluded from purchasing the product. In Exhibit 7, price discrimination makes it possible for superior students who could not afford to pay a higher tuition to attend University X. Price discrimination also allows retired persons to enjoy hotels and restaurants they could not otherwise afford and enables more children to attend movies.

CHECKPOINT

Why Don't Adults Pay More for Popcorn at the Movies?

At the movies, adults pay a higher ticket price than children do, and each group gets a different-colored ticket. However, when adults and children go to the concession stand, both groups pay the same amount for popcorn and other snacks. Which of the following statements best explains why price discrimination stops at the ticket window? (1) The demand curve for popcorn is perfectly elastic. (2) The theater has no way to divide the buyers of popcorn based on different price elasticities of demand. (3) The theater cannot prevent resale.

9-4 Comparing Monopoly and Perfect Competition

Now that the basics of the two extremes of perfect competition and monopoly have been presented, we can compare and evaluate these market structures. This is an important assessment because the contrast between the disadvantages of monopoly and the advantages of perfect competition is the basis for many government policies, such as antitrust laws. To keep the analysis simple, we assume the monopolist charges a single price, rather than engaging in price discrimination.

9-4a THE MONOPOLIST AS A RESOURCE MISALLOCATOR

Recall the discussion of market efficiency in Chapter 4. This condition exists when a firm charging the equilibrium price uses neither too many nor too few resources to produce a product, so there is no *market failure*. Now you can state this definition of market efficiency in terms of price and marginal cost, as follows: *A perfectly competitive firm that produces the quantity of output at which P = MC achieves an efficient allocation of resources.* This means production reaches the level of output when the price of the last unit produced matches the cost of producing it.

Exhibit 8(a) shows that a perfectly competitive firm produces the quantity of output at which P = MC. The price, P_c (marginal benefit), of the last unit produced equals the marginal cost of the resources used to produce it. In contrast, the monopolist shown in Exhibit 8(b) charges a price, P_m, greater than marginal cost, P > MC. Therefore, consumers are shortchanged because the marginal benefit of the last unit produced exceeds the marginal cost of producing it. Consumers want the monopolist to use more resources and produce additional units, but the monopolist restricts output to maximize profit.

CONCLUSION: *A monopolist is characterized by inefficiency because resources are underallocated to the production of its product.*

| EXHIBIT 8 | Comparing a Perfectly Competitive Firm and a Monopolist |

The perfectly competitive firm in part (a) sets P = MC and produces Q_c output. Therefore, at the last unit of output, the marginal benefit is equal to the marginal cost of resources used to produce it. This condition means perfect competition achieves efficiency.

Part (b) shows that the monopolist produces output Q_m where P > MC. By so doing, consumers are shortchanged because the marginal benefit of the last unit produced exceeds the marginal cost of producing it. Under monopoly, inefficiency occurs because the monopolist underallocates resources to the production of its product. As a result, Q_m is less than Q_c.

(a) Perfectly competitive firm   (b) Monopolist

SOURCE: © Cengage Learning 2014

9-4b PERFECT COMPETITION MEANS MORE OUTPUT FOR LESS

Exhibit 9 presents a comparison of perfect competition and monopoly in the same graph. Suppose the industry begins as perfectly competitive. The market demand curve, D (equal to MR), and the market supply curve, S, establish a perfectly competitive price, P_c, and output, Q_c. Recall from Exhibit 8 in the previous chapter that the competitive industry's supply curve, S, is the horizontal sum of the marginal cost (MC) curves of all the firms in the industry.

Now let's suppose the market structure changes when one firm buys out all the competing firms and the industry becomes a monopoly. Assume further that the demand and cost curves are unaffected by this dramatic change. In a monopoly, the industry demand curve *is* the monopolist's demand curve. Because the single firm is a price maker, the MR curve lies below the demand curve. The industry supply curve now becomes the MC curve for the monopolist. To maximize profit, the monopolist sets MR = MC by restricting the output to Q_m and raising the price to P_m.

> **CONCLUSION:** *Monopoly harms consumers on two fronts. The monopolist charges a higher price and produces a lower output than would result under a perfectly competitive market structure.*

EXHIBIT 9	The Impact of Monopolizing an Industry

Assume an industry is perfectly competitive, with market demand curve D and market supply curve S. The market supply curve is the horizontal summation of all the individual firms' marginal cost curves above their minimum average variable costs. The intersection of market supply and market demand establishes the equilibrium price of P_c and the equilibrium quantity of Q_c. Now assume the industry suddenly changes to a monopoly. The monopolist produces the MR = MC output of Q_m, which is less than Q_c. By restricting output to Q_m, the monopolist is able to charge the higher price of P_m.

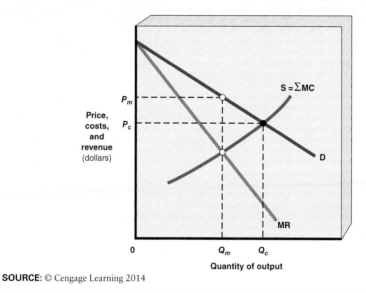

SOURCE: © Cengage Learning 2014

9-5 The Case against and for Monopoly

So far, a strong case has been made against monopoly and in favor of perfect competition. Now it is time to pause and summarize the economist's case against monopoly:

- A monopolist "gouges" consumers by charging a higher price than would be charged under perfect competition.
- Because a monopolist restricts output in order to maximize profit, too few resources are used to produce the product. Stated differently, the monopolist misallocates resources by charging a price greater than marginal cost. In perfectly competitive industries, price is set equal to marginal cost, and the result is an optimal allocation of resources.
- Long-run economic profit for a monopolist exceeds the zero economic profit earned in the long run by a perfectly competitive firm.
- To the extent that the monopolist is a rich John D. Rockefeller, for example, and consumers of oil are poor, monopoly alters the distribution of income in favor of the monopolist.

Not all economists agree that monopoly is bad. Joseph Schumpeter and John Kenneth Galbraith praised monopoly power. They argued that the rate of

New York Taxicabs: Where Have All the Fare Flags Gone?

Applicable Concept: perfect competition versus monopoly

Yellow taxicabs in New York City, which are today one of the most famous icons of the city, are a love and hate relationship. The upside is that you can stick your arm in the air to hail a cab that will take you to your destination. The downside is the traffic jams speckled with yellow cabs that service the city. Flash back to the 1920s, when New York taxicabs were competitive. There was no limit on the number of taxis, and hack licenses were only $10. In addition to a low barrier to entry, taxis engaged in price competition. Cabbies could choose among three different flags to attach to their cars. A red flag cab charged a surcharge for extra passengers. A white flag signaled no surcharge for extra passengers. A green flag meant the cabbie was offering a discount fare. Price wars often erupted, and the vast majority of cabbies flew green flags and charged bargain fares. One strategy was to fly the red flag (high rate) during rush hour and the green flag to offer discounts at off-peak times. Taxi companies also offered a variety of cabs—old, new, big, and small.[1]

As years passed, the system changed because of the concern that competition was causing an overabundance of taxis that congested city streets. The solution was to create a monopoly by law in 1937 designed to limit the number of cabs by requiring all cabs accepting street hails to be painted yellow and possess a medallion on the hood of the taxi. Currently, the Taxi and Limousine Commission (TLC) sets rates and imposes regulations. There are no price wars, and the barrier to entry is high due to the high price of medallions. Today, the aluminum badges that give the right to pick up passengers on the street cost more than $700,000, as determined at infrequent auctions. Because of their high prices, most cabs are owned by investment companies and are leased to the drivers. On the other hand, it is illegal for cabs without medallions

to cruise and pick up passengers who hail them, although the law is often ignored by gypsy cabs. Nonmedallion cabs are authorized to respond only to customers who have ordered the cab in advance by phone or other means. There's no limit on the number of nonmedallion cabs or what the drivers may charge.

Analyze the Issue

Use a graph to compare the price and output of medallion yellow cabs in New York City today with the taxi market before the 1920s.

1. John Tierney, "You'll Wonder Where the Yellow Went," *The New York Times*, July 12, 1998, Section 6, p. 18.

Source: © Cengage Learning 2014

technological change is likely to be greater under monopoly than under perfect competition. In their view, monopoly profits afford giant monopolies the financial strength to invest in the well-equipped laboratories and skilled labor necessary to create technological change.

The counterargument is that monopolists are slow to innovate. Freedom from direct competition means the monopolist is not motivated and therefore tends to stick to the "conventional wisdom." As Nobel laureate Sir John Hicks put it, "The best of all monopoly profit is a quiet life." In short, monopoly offers the opportunity to relax a bit and not worry about the "rat race" of technological change.

What does research on this issue suggest? Not surprisingly, many attempts have been made to verify or refute the effect of market structure on technological change. Unfortunately, the results to date have been inconclusive. For all we know, a mix of large and small firms in an industry may be the optimal mix to create technological change.

Key Concepts

Monopoly
Natural monopoly

Network good
Price maker

Price discrimination
Arbitrage

Summary

- **Monopoly** is a single seller facing the entire industry demand curve because it is the industry. The monopolist sells a unique product, and extremely high barriers to entry protect it from competition.
- **Barriers to entry** that prevent new firms from entering an industry are (1) ownership of an essential resource, (2) legal barriers, and (3) economies of scale. Government franchises, licenses, patents, and copyrights are the most obvious legal barriers to entry.
- A **natural monopoly** arises because of the existence of economies of scale in which the long-run average cost (LRAC) curve falls as production increases. Without government restrictions, economies of scale allow a single firm to produce at a lower cost than any firm producing a smaller output. Thus, smaller firms leave the industry, new firms fear competing with the monopolist, and the result is that a monopoly emerges *naturally*.

Natural Monopoly

SOURCE: © Cengage Learning 2014

- A **network good** is a good that increases in value to each user as the total number of users increases. Examples are Facebook and Match.com.
- A **price-maker** firm faces a downward-sloping demand curve. It therefore searches its demand curve to find the price-output combination that maximizes its profit and minimizes its loss.
- The **marginal revenue** and demand curves are downward sloping for a monopolist. The marginal revenue curve for a monopolist is below the

demand curve, and the total revenue curve reaches its maximum where marginal revenue equals zero.
- **Price elasticity of demand** corresponds to sections of the marginal revenue curve. When MR is positive, price elasticity of demand is elastic, $E_d > 1$. When MR is equal to zero, price elasticity of demand is unit elastic, $E_d = 1$. When MR is negative, price elasticity of demand is inelastic, $E_d < 1$.
- The **short-run profit-maximizing monopolist**, like the perfectly competitive firm, locates the profit-maximizing price by producing the output where the MR and MC curves intersect. If this price is less than the average variable cost (AVC) curve, the monopolist shuts down to minimize losses.

Short-Run Profit Maximizing Monopolist

SOURCE: © Cengage Learning 2014

Short-Run Loss-Minimizing Monopolist

SOURCE: © Cengage Learning 2014

- The **long-run profit-maximizing monopolist** earns a profit because of barriers to entry. If demand and cost conditions prevent the monopolist from earning a profit, the monopolist will leave the industry.
- **Price discrimination** allows the monopolist to increase profits by charging buyers different prices rather than a single price. Three conditions are necessary for price discrimination: (1) the demand curve must be downward sloping, (2) buyers in different markets must have different price elasticities of demand, and (3) buyers must be prevented from reselling the product at a price higher than the purchase price.

- **Monopoly disadvantages** include the following: (1) a monopolist charges a higher price and produces less output than a perfectly competitive firm does, (2) resource allocation is inefficient because the monopolist produces less than if competition existed, (3) monopoly produces higher long-run profits than if competition existed, and (4) monopoly transfers income from consumers to producers to a greater degree than under perfect competition.

Price Discrimination

Monopoly Disadvantages

SOURCE: © Cengage Learning 2014

Summary of Conclusion Statements

- Because of economies of scale, a single firm in an industry will produce output at a lower per-unit cost than two or more firms.
- The greater the number of people connected to a network goods system, the more benefits of the product to each person are increased.

- The demand and marginal revenue curves of the monopolist are downward sloping in contrast to the horizontal demand and corresponding marginal revenue curves facing the perfectly competitive firm.

- The marginal revenue curve for a straight-line demand curve intersects the quantity axis halfway between the origin and the quantity axis intercepts of the demand curve.
- The monopolist always maximizes profit by producing at a price on the elastic segment of its demand curve.
- If the positions of a monopolist's demand and cost curves give it a profit and nothing disturbs

these curves, the monopolist will earn profit in the long run.
- A monopolist is characterized by inefficiency because resources are underallocated to the production of its product.
- Monopoly harms consumers on two fronts. The monopolist charges a higher price and produces a lower output than would result under a perfectly competitive market structure.

Study Questions and Problems

1. Using the three characteristics of monopoly, explain why each of the following is a monopolist:
   a. Local telephone company
   b. San Francisco 49ers football team
   c. U.S. Postal Service

2. Why is the demand curve facing a monopolist downward sloping while the demand curve facing a perfectly competitive firm is horizontal?

3. Suppose an investigator finds that the prices charged for drugs at a hospital are higher than the prices charged for the same products at drugstores in the area served by the hospital. What might explain this situation?

4. Explain why you agree or disagree with the following statements:
   a. "All monopolies are created by the government."

   b. "The monopolist charges the highest possible price."
   c. "The monopolist never takes a loss."

5. Suppose the average cost of producing a kilowatt-hour of electricity is lower for one firm than for another firm serving the same market. Without the government granting a franchise to one of these competing power companies, explain why a single seller is likely to emerge in the long run.

6. Use the above demand schedule for a monopolist to calculate total revenue and marginal revenue. For each price, indicate whether demand is elastic, unit elastic, or inelastic. Using the data from the demand schedule, graph the demand curve, the marginal revenue curve, and the total revenue curve. Identify the elastic, unit elastic, and inelastic segments along the demand curve.

Price	Quantity Demanded (Q)	Total Revenue (TR)	Marginal Revenue (MR)	Price Elasticity of Demand (E_d)
$5.00	0	$_____	$_____	_____
4.50	1	_____	_____	_____
4.00	2	_____	_____	_____
3.50	3	_____	_____	_____
3.00	4	_____	_____	_____
2.50	5	_____	_____	_____
2.00	6	_____	_____	_____
1.50	7	_____	_____	_____
1.00	8	_____	_____	_____
0.50	9	_____	_____	_____
0	10	_____	_____	_____

7. Make the unrealistic assumption that production is costless for the monopolist in question 6. Given the data from the above demand schedule, what price will the monopolist charge, and how much output should the firm produce? How much profit will the firm earn? When marginal cost is above zero, what will be the effect on the price and output of the monopolist?

8. Explain why a monopolist would never produce in the inelastic range of the demand curve.

9. In each of the following cases, state whether the monopolist would increase or decrease output:
   a. Marginal revenue exceeds marginal cost at the output produced.
   b. Marginal cost exceeds marginal revenue at the output produced.

10. Suppose the demand and cost curves for a monopolist are as shown in Exhibit 10 below. Explain what price the monopolist should charge and how much output it should produce.

11. Which of the following constitute price discrimination and which does not?
   a. A department store has a 25 percent off sale.
   b. A publisher sells economics textbooks at a lower price in North Carolina than in New York.
   c. The Japanese sell cars at higher prices in the United States than in Japan.
   d. Your cell phone company charges higher long-distance rates during the day.

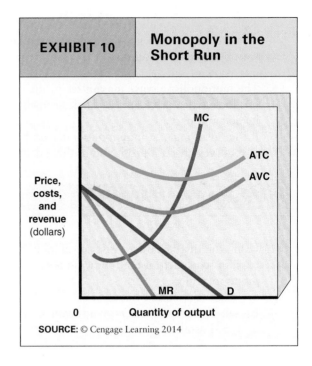

EXHIBIT 10 | **Monopoly in the Short Run**

SOURCE: © Cengage Learning 2014

12. Suppose the candy bar industry approximates a perfectly competitive industry. Suppose also that a single firm buys all the assets of the candy bar firms and establishes a monopoly. Contrast these two market structures with respect to price, output, and allocation of resources. Draw a graph of the market demand and market supply for candy bars before and after the takeover.

For Online Exercises, go to the Tucker Web site at www.cengage.com/economics/tucker.

✓ CHECKPOINT ANSWERS

Why Don't Adults Pay More for Popcorn at the Movies?

First, there are no other popcorn sellers in the lobby, so the theater is a price maker for popcorn and the demand curve slopes downward. Second, the theater could easily set up different lines for adults and children and charge different prices for popcorn. Third, is there a practical way to prevent resale? Does the theater want to try to stop children who resell popcorn to their parents, friends, and other adults? If you said theaters do not practice price discrimination at the concession counter because resale cannot be prevented, **YOU ARE CORRECT.**

Sample Quiz

For an explanation of the correct answers, visit the Tucker Web site at www.cengage.com/economics/tucker.

1. The monopolist faces
   a. a perfectly inelastic demand curve.
   b. a perfectly elastic demand curve.
   c. the entire market demand curve.
   d. All of the answers above are correct.

2. To maximize its profit, a monopoly should choose a price where demand is
   a. elastic.
   b. inelastic.
   c. unitary elastic.
   d. vertical.

3. When marginal revenue is zero for a monopolist facing a downward-sloping straight-line demand curve, the price elasticity of demand is
   a. greater than 1.
   b. equal to 1.
   c. less than 2.
   d. equal to 0.

4. Both a perfectly competitive firm and a monopolist
   a. always earn an economic profit.
   b. maximize profit by setting marginal cost equal to marginal revenue.
   c. maximize profit by setting marginal cost equal to average total cost.
   d. are price takers.

5. Suppose a monopolist's demand curve lies below its average variable cost curve. The firm will
   a. stay in operation in the short run.
   b. earn an economic profit.
   c. earn an economic profit in the long run.
   d. shut down.

6. Which of the following statements *best* describes the price, output, and profit conditions of monopoly?
   a. Price will equal marginal cost at the profit-maximizing level of output, and profits will be positive in the long run.
   b. Price will always equal average variable cost in the short run, and either profits or losses may result in the long run.
   c. In the long run, positive economic profit will be earned.
   d. All of the answers above are correct.

7. Which of the following is *true* for the monopolist?
   a. Marginal revenue is less than the price charged.
   b. Economic profit is possible in the long run.
   c. Profit maximizing or loss minimizing occurs when marginal revenue equals marginal cost.
   d. All of the answers above are correct.

8. Although a monopoly can charge any price it wishes, it chooses
   a. the highest price.
   b. the price equal to marginal cost.
   c. the price that maximizes profit.
   d. competitive prices.
   e. a fair price.

9. As shown in Exhibit 11, the profit-maximizing price for the monopolist is.
   a. OP_1.
   b. OP_2.
   c. OP_3.
   d. OP_4.
   e. OP_5.

10. As shown in Exhibit 11, if the monopolist produces the profit-maximizing output, total revenue is the rectangular area
    a. OQ_1AP_1.
    b. OQ_2BP_2.
    c. OQ_3CP_3.
    d. OQ_2DP_4.

11. As shown in Exhibit 11, the monopolist's total cost is which of the following areas?
    a. P_1AEP_5
    b. P_2BDP_4
    c. P_3CDP_5
    d. P_4DEP_5
    e. None of the answers above are correct.

12. The profit-maximizing output for the monopolist in Exhibit 11 is
    a. zero.
    b. OQ_1.
    c. OQ_2.
    d. OQ_3.

Sample Quiz *continued*

13. As shown in Exhibit 11, if the monopolist produces the profit-maximizing output, total revenue is the rectangular area
    a. $OQAP_1$.
    b. OQ_2BP_2.
    c. OQ_3CP_3.
    d. OQ_2DP_4.

14. As shown in Exhibit 11, the monopolist's profit-maximizing price-quantity point is
    a. *A.*
    b. *B.*
    c. *C.*
    d. *D.*
    e. *E.*

15. Suppose a monopolist charges a price corresponding to the intersection of marginal cost and marginal revenue. If the price is between its average variable cost and average total cost curves, the firm will
    a. earn an economic profit.
    b. stay in operation in the short run, but shut down in the long run if demand remains the same.
    c. shut down.
    d. None of the above answers is correct.

16. The act of buying a commodity in one market at a lower price and selling it in another market at a higher price is known as
    a. buying long.
    b. selling short.
    c. a tariff.
    d. arbitrage.

17. One necessary condition for effective price discrimination is
    a. identical tastes among buyers.
    b. a difference in the price elasticity of demand among buyers.
    c. a single, homogeneous market.
    d. two or more markets with easy resale of products between them.

18. An example of price discrimination is the price charged for
    a. an economics textbook at a campus bookstore.
    b. gasoline.
    c. theater tickets that offer lower prices for children.
    d. a postage stamp.

19. Suppose a monopolist and a perfectly competitive firm have the same cost curves. The monopolistic firm would
    a. charge a lower price than the perfectly competitive firm.
    b. charge a higher price than the perfectly competitive firm.
    c. charge the same price as the perfectly competitive firm.
    d. refuse to operate in the short run unless an economic profit could be made.

20. Suppose there are two markets for football games: (1) rich alumni as fully committed to their alma mater as the lower-income students and (2) students. Based on this information, which market will have the lower elasticity, and thus the higher price, if the university can price-discriminate?
    a. The student market
    b. The alumni market

EXHIBIT 11	Profit Maximizing for a Monopolist

Price, costs, and revenue (dollars)

Quantity of output (units per time period)

SOURCE: © Cengage Learning 2014

chapter 10

Monopolistic Competition and Oligopoly

Suppose your favorite restaurant is Ivan's Oyster Bar. Ivan's does not fit either of the two extreme models studied in the previous two chapters. Instead, Ivan's characteristics are a blend of monopoly and perfect competition. For starters, like a monopolist, Ivan's demand curve is downward sloping. This means Ivan's is a *price maker* because it can charge a higher price for seafood and lose some customers, but many loyal customers will keep coming. The reason is that Ivan's distinguishes its product from that of the competition by advertising, first-rate service, a great salad bar, and other attributes. In short, like a monopolist, Ivan's has a degree of *market power,* which allows it to restrict output and maximize profit. But like a perfectly competitive firm and unlike a monopolist, Ivan's is not the only place to buy a seafood dinner in town. It must share the market with many other restaurants within an hour's drive.

The small Ivan's Oyster Bars and the gigantic Microsofts of the world represent most of the firms with which you deal. These firms compete in two different market structures: *monopolistic competition* or *oligopoly*. Ivan's operates in the former, and Microsoft belongs to the latter. The theories of perfect competition and monopoly from the previous two chapters will help you understand the impact of monopolistic competition and oligopoly market structures on the price and output decisions of real-world firms.

In this chapter, you will learn to solve these economics puzzles:

- Why will Ivan's Oyster Bar make zero economic profit in the long run?

- Why do OPEC and other cartels tend to break down?

- Are Cheerios, Rice Krispies, and other brands sold by firms in the breakfast cereal industry produced under monopolistic competition or oligopoly?

- How does the NCAA Final Four basketball tournament involve imperfect competition?

10-1 The Monopolistic Competition Market Structure

Monopolistic competition

A market structure characterized by (1) many small sellers, (2) a differentiated product, and (3) easy market entry and exit.

Economists define monopolistic competition as a market structure characterized by (1) many small sellers, (2) a differentiated product, and (3) easy market entry and exit. Monopolistic competition fits numerous real-world industries. The following is a brief explanation of each characteristic.

10-1a MANY SMALL SELLERS

Under monopolistic competition, as under perfect competition, the exact number of firms cannot be stated. But in monopolistic competition, the number of sellers is smaller than in perfect competition. In this market structure, consumers have many different varieties of products from which to choose, and prices are competitive. No single seller has a large enough share of the market to control prices. Ivan's Oyster Bar, described in the chapter preview, is an example of a monopolistic competitor. Ivan assumes that his restaurant can set prices slightly higher or improve service *independently* without fear that competitors will react by changing their prices or giving better service. Thus, if any single seafood restaurant raises its price, the going market price for seafood dinners increases by a very small amount.

CONCLUSION: *The many-sellers condition is met when each firm is so small relative to the total market that its pricing decisions have a negligible effect on the market price.*

10-1b DIFFERENTIATED PRODUCT

Product differentiation

The process of creating real or apparent differences between goods and services.

The key feature of monopolistic competition is product differentiation. Product differentiation is the process of creating real or apparent differences between goods and services. A differentiated product has close, but not perfect, substitutes. Although the products of each firm are highly similar, the consumer views them as somewhat different or distinct. There may be 25 seafood restaurants in a given city, but they are not all the same. They differ in location, atmosphere, quality of food, quality of service, and so on.

Product differentiation can be real or imagined. It does not matter which is correct so long as consumers believe such differences exist. For example, many customers think Ivan's has the best seafood in town even though other restaurants offer a similar product. The importance of this viewpoint is that consumers are willing to pay a slightly higher price for Ivan's seafood. This gives Ivan the incentive to appear on local TV cooking shows and to buy ads showing him personally catching the seafood he serves.

CONCLUSION: *When a product is differentiated, buyers are not indifferent as to which seller's product they buy.*

The example of Ivan's restaurant makes it clear that under monopolistic competition, rivalry centers on nonprice competition in addition to price competition. With nonprice competition, a firm competes using advertising, packaging, product development, better quality, and better service, rather than lower prices. Nonprice competition is an important characteristic of monopolistic competition that distinguishes it from perfect competition and monopoly. Under perfect competition, there is no nonprice competition because the product is identical for all firms. Likewise, the monopolist has little incentive to engage in nonprice competition because it sells a unique product.

Nonprice competition

The situation in which a firm competes using advertising, packaging, product development, better quality, and better service, rather than lower prices.

10-1c EASY ENTRY AND EXIT

Unlike a monopoly, firms in a monopolistically competitive market face low barriers to entry. But entry into a monopolistically competitive market is not quite as easy as entry into a perfectly competitive market. Persons who want to enter the seafood restaurant business can get loans, lease space, and start serving seafood without too much trouble. However, these new seafood restaurants may at first have difficulty attracting consumers because of Ivan's established reputation as the best seafood restaurant in town. Ivan's product is therefore differentiated.

Monopolistic competition is by far the most common market structure in the United States. Examples include retail firms, such as grocery stores, hair salons, gas stations, diet centers, and restaurants.

10-2 The Monopolistically Competitive Firm as a Price Maker

Given the characteristics of monopolistic competition, you might think the monopolistic competitor is a *price taker*, but it is not. The primary reason is that its product is differentiated. This gives the monopolistically competitive firm, like the monopolist, limited control over its price. When the price is raised, brand loyalty ensures some customers will remain steadfast. As for a monopolist, the demand curve and the corresponding marginal revenue curve for a monopolistically competitive firm are downward sloping. But the existence of close substitutes causes the demand curve for the monopolistically competitive firm to be more elastic than the demand curve for a monopolist. When Ivan's raises its prices 10 percent, the quantity of seafood dinners demanded declines, say, 30 percent. Instead, if Ivan's had a monopoly, no close substitutes would exist, and consumers would be less sensitive to price changes. As a monopolist, the same 10 percent price hike might lose Ivan's only, say, 15 percent of its quantity of seafood dinners demanded.

> **CONCLUSION:** *The demand curve for a monopolistically competitive firm is less elastic (steeper) than for a perfectly competitive firm and more elastic (flatter) than for a monopolist.*

10-2a ADVERTISING PROS AND CONS

Before presenting the complete graphical models for monopolistic competition, let's pause to examine the topic of advertising further. As explained at the beginning of this chapter, a distinguishing feature of a monopolistically competitive firm is that it engages in nonprice competition by using expensive ads to differentiate its product. Instead of lowering the price, the firm's goal is to convince customers that its product is really different from its rivals' products. Monopolistically competitive firms are frequently running ads that feature lower prices, a higher quality of service, or new products to win customers. Ads proclaim that products make you smarter, better looking, or nicer to be around. Graphically, the firm hopes advertising will make the demand curve less elastic and shift it rightward by changing consumers' tastes in favor of its product. Profit rises when advertising increases the firm's revenue more than the cost of the advertising.

Exhibit 1 illustrates the effect of advertising on the long-run average cost (LRAC) curve for Yummy Frozen Yogurt. Yummy competes with It Can't Be Yogurt and five other stores in the northeastern part of town. Without advertising, the $LRAC_1$ curve represents Yummy's average cost. At the given price charged, the quantity demanded is 6,000 frozen yogurt dishes per month, and the average cost is $2.00 per dish (point A).

To increase profits in the short run, Yummy decides to advertise. Yummy knows, however, that in the long run, new entrants and rising costs will shrink all yogurt stores' economic profits to zero. Then Yummy must come up with some new product to boost sales. But for now, suppose Yummy's advertising campaign is successful and demand increases. Then two short-run effects occur. One is an upward shift in the average cost curve at any level of output from $LRAC_1$ to $LRAC_2$. The vertical distance between these two curves measures the additional average fixed cost of advertising. Another effect is that the quantity demanded increases to 12,000 frozen yogurt dishes per month. Now the average cost is $1.50 at point B on $LRAC_2$.

So far, our story illustrates a social benefit of advertising. Look again at Exhibit 1. The increased volume of sales caused by advertising leads to *economies of scale*, explained in Chapter 7. Without advertising, Yummy operated with a lower output and a higher average cost. With advertising, the benefit to consumers from the reduction in average total cost from A to B outweighs the boost in cost per unit from advertising.

On the other hand, suppose Yummy's advertising campaign is not successful and demand remains unchanged. In this case, the quantity demanded remains at the original 6,000 frozen yogurt dishes per month, but the average total cost rises to $3.00 (point C). Critics of advertising argue this is the typical case and not the reduction from A to B. Instead of economies of scale, advertising is self-canceling. Yummy, It Can't Be Yogurt, and other firms spend large outlays on advertising just to keep their present market share. And in the process, the cost, and therefore the price, of yogurt is increased. Moreover, the additional cost of advertising does not improve the yogurt at all. The only purpose is to persuade or mislead consumers into buying something they do not need. From society's viewpoint, the resources used in advertising could be used for schools, hospitals, bridges, or other more useful purposes.

EXHIBIT 1	The Effect of Advertising on Average Cost

When Yummy Frozen Yogurt increases its advertising costs to sell more yogurt, the firm's average cost curve shifts upward from $LRAC_1$ to $LRAC_2$. If advertising increases the quantity demanded from 6,000 to 12,000 dishes per month, average total cost falls from $2.00 (point A) to $1.50 (point B). However, if the extra cost of advertising fails to increase the quantity demanded, average total cost rises from $2.00 (point A) to $3.00 (point C).

SOURCE: © Cengage Learning 2014

Proponents of advertising counter the argument that advertising is valueless. They argue that ads provide information. Advertising informs consumers of sales, the availability of products, and the advantages of products. Although the product costs a little more, this information saves consumers money and time. Ads also increase price competition among sellers. When Yummy offers discount coupons, other yogurt stores see these ads and respond with lower prices. Finally, consumers are rational and cannot be fooled by advertising. If a product is undesirable, customers will not buy it.

Does monopolistic competition lead to lower prices, greater output, and better-informed consumers? Or does this market structure simply raise prices and annoy customers with useless and often misleading information? This fascinating and ongoing debate is perhaps best analyzed on a case-by-case basis. In a later section, you will learn that advertising to differentiate a product is also a key characteristic of oligopoly.

Social Networking Sites: The New Advertising Game

Applicable Concept: product differentiation

A key characteristic of the market structures discussed in this chapter is that they use advertising to promote product differentiation, which is a form of nonprice competition. The television commercial is considered the most effective method of mass-market advertising. This explains why TV networks charge such high prices for commercial airtime during prominent events, such as the Super Bowl. However, the days when television commercials dominate the advertising world could be fading away. Don't want to be bothered by those advertisements? It's easy: Just press the fast-forward button on the remote of a digital video recorder (DVR). Advertisers are therefore struggling to figure out how to get the attention of consumers by tapping into the popularity of such social networking sites as Facebook, Twitter, Myspace, and YouTube. These sites connect individuals who interact through personal profiles, games, video clips, and more. There are also niche sites focused on very specific activities for

a hyper-targeted audience. For example, Dogster.com is a site for dog lovers and Zappes.com is a popular site for women's and men's shoes. ProductWiki is a resource for shoppers. It gives access to product reviews and lets you compare prices.

The challenge for Web economy entrepreneurs is to earn profits by differentiating their product and creating innovative ways to include advertising. The search engine is a highly successful business model. If someone googles for golf clubs, sponsored links for golf clubs appear on the screen. Social networks provide the prospect of tailoring ads to people's specific interests. Now suppose a golf club company pays Facebook, the crown jewel of social networking, for a page where you and your friends can register and play a game of video golf. What does the company get out of it? A database of tens of thousands of names, all potential customers. However, some ideas are not winners. Facebook implemented a new approach that informed friends whenever a member purchased something from online retailers. Consumers protested this

iStockphoto.com/Nikada

was an invasion of privacy, and the program was abandoned. Now consider this idea: Imagine being at a concert and text messaging a shout-out to your friends. Your message appears during the concert next to the stage on a big screen with a large ad from a company. Is this imposing a negative externality that distracts others in the audience from the performance? And in 2012, GM decided to cancel its advertising because it thought Facebook had little effect on car purchases.

Analyze the Issue

Advertising is tasteless, offensive, and a nuisance that wastes resources. Give three arguments against this idea.

Source: © Cengage Learning 2014

10-3 Price and Output Decisions for a Monopolistically Competitive Firm

Now we are prepared to develop the short-run and long-run graphical models for monopolistic competition. In the short run, you will see that monopolistic competition resembles monopoly. In the long run, however, entry by new firms leads to a more competitive market structure. This section presents a graphical analysis that shows why a monopolistically competitive firm is part perfectly competitive and part monopolistic.

10-3a MONOPOLISTIC COMPETITION IN THE SHORT RUN

Exhibit 2 shows the short-run equilibrium position for Ivan's Oyster Bar—a typical firm under monopolistic competition. As explained earlier, the demand curve slopes downward because customers believe, rightly or wrongly, that Ivan's product is a little better than its competitors' products. Customers like Ivan's family atmosphere, location, and quality of service. These nonprice factors differentiate Ivan's product and allow the restaurant to raise the price of sautéed alligator, shrimp, and oysters at least slightly without losing many sales.

Like the monopolist, the monopolistically competitive firm maximizes short-run profit by following the MR = MC rule. In this case, the marginal cost (MC) and marginal revenue (MR) curves intersect at an output of 600 seafood meals per

EXHIBIT 2	A Monopolistically Competitive Firm in the Short Run

Ivan's Oyster Bar is a monopolistically competitive firm that maximizes short-run profit by producing the output where marginal revenue equals marginal cost. At an output of 600 seafood dinners per week, the price of $18 per dinner is dictated by the firm's demand curve. Given the firm's costs, output, and prices, Ivan's will earn a short-run profit of $1,800 per week.

SOURCE: © Cengage Learning 2014

week. The price per meal of $18 is the point on the demand curve corresponding to this level of output. Because the price exceeds the average total cost (ATC) of $15 per meal, Ivan's earns a short-run economic profit of $1,800 per week. As under monopoly, if the price equals the ATC curve, the firm earns a short-run normal profit. If the price is below the ATC curve, the firm suffers a short-run loss, and if the price is below the average variable cost (AVC) curve, the firm shuts down.

10-3b MONOPOLISTIC COMPETITION IN THE LONG RUN

The monopolistically competitive firm, unlike a monopolist, will not earn an economic profit in the long run. Rather, like a perfect competitor, the monopolistically competitive firm earns only a normal profit (that is, zero economic profit) in the long run. Recall from the chapter on production costs that *normal profit* is the minimum profit necessary to keep a firm in operation. The reason is that short-run profits and easy entry attract new firms into the industry. When Ivan's Oyster Bar earns a short-run profit, as shown in Exhibit 2, two things happen. First, Ivan's demand curve shifts downward as some of each seafood restaurant's market share is taken away by new firms seeking profit. Second, Ivan's, and other seafood restaurants as well, tries to recapture market share by advertising, improving its decor, and utilizing other forms of nonprice competition. As a result, long-run average costs increase, and the firm's LRAC curve shifts upward.

The combination of the leftward shift in the firm's demand curve and the upward shift in its LRAC curve continues in the long run until the monopolistic competitive firm earns zero or normal economic profit. The result is the long-run equilibrium condition shown in Exhibit 3. At a price of $17 per meal, the demand curve is tangent to the LRAC curve at the MR = MC output of 500 meals per week. Once long-run equilibrium is achieved in a monopolistically competitive industry, there is no incentive for new firms to enter or established firms to leave.

10-4 Comparing Monopolistic Competition and Perfect Competition

Some economists argue that the long-run equilibrium condition for a monopolistically competitive firm, as shown in Exhibit 3, results in poor economic performance. Other economists contend that the benefits of a monopolistically competitive industry outweigh the costs. In this section, we again use the standard of perfect competition to understand both sides of this debate.

10-4a THE MONOPOLISTIC COMPETITOR AS A RESOURCE MISALLOCATOR

Like a monopolist, the monopolistically competitive firm fails the efficiency test. As shown in Exhibit 3, under monopolistic competition, Ivan's charges a price that exceeds the marginal cost. Thus, the value to consumers of the last meal produced is greater than the cost of producing it. Ivan's could devote more resources and

EXHIBIT 3	A Monopolistically Competitive Firm in the Long Run

In the long run, the entry of new seafood restaurants decreases the demand for Ivan's seafood. In addition, Ivan's shifts its average cost curve upward by increasing advertising and other expenses in order to compete against new entrants. In the long run, the firm earns zero economic profit at a price of $17 per seafood meal and produces an MR = MC output of 500 meals per week.

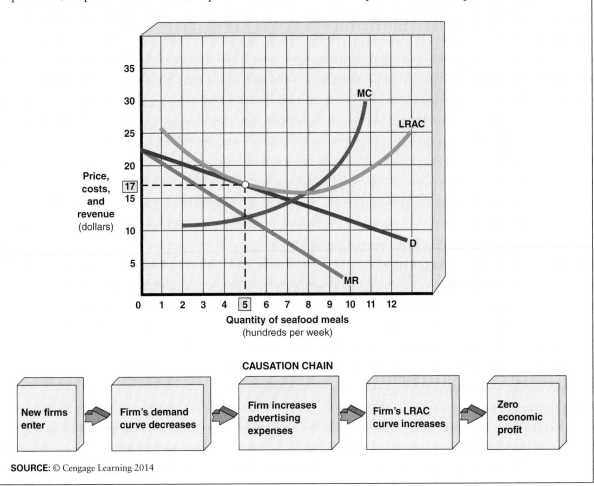

CAUSATION CHAIN

New firms enter ⇒ Firm's demand curve decreases ⇒ Firm increases advertising expenses ⇒ Firm's LRAC curve increases ⇒ Zero economic profit

SOURCE: © Cengage Learning 2014

produce more seafood dinners. To sell this additional output, Ivan's must move downward along its demand curve by reducing the $17 price per meal. As a result, customers would purchase the additional benefits of consuming more seafood meals. However, Ivan's uses less resources and restricts output to 500 seafood meals per week in order to maximize profits where MR = MC.

10-4b MONOPOLISTIC COMPETITION MEANS LESS OUTPUT FOR MORE

Exhibit 4(a) reproduces the long-run condition from Exhibit 3. Exhibit 4(b) assumes that the seafood restaurant market is perfectly competitive. Recall from

EXHIBIT 4	A Comparison of Monopolistic Competition and Perfect Competition in the Long Run

In part (a), Ivan's Oyster Bar is a monopolistically competitive firm that sets its price at $17 per seafood meal and produces 500 meals per week. As a monopolistic competitor, Ivan's earns zero economic profit in the long run and does not produce at the lowest point on its LRAC curve.

Under conditions of perfect competition in part (b), Ivan's becomes a price taker, rather than a price maker. Here the firm faces a flat demand curve at a price of $16 per seafood meal, which is the equilibrium price set by the market demand and supply curves. The output is 800 meals per week, which corresponds to the lowest point on the LRAC curve. Therefore, the price is lower, and the excess capacity of 300 meals per week is utilized when Ivan's operates as a perfectly competitive firm, rather than as a monopolistically competitive firm.

SOURCE: © Cengage Learning 2014

Chapter 8 that the characteristics of perfect competition include the condition that customers perceive seafood meals as *homogeneous* and, as a result, no firms engage in advertising. Because we now assume for the sake of argument that Ivan's product is identical to all other seafood restaurants, Ivan's becomes a *price taker*. In this case, the industry's long-run supply and demand curves set an equilibrium price of $16 per meal. Consequently, Ivan's faces a horizontal demand curve with the price equal to marginal revenue. Also recall from Chapter 8 that long-run equilibrium for a perfectly competitive firm is established by the entry of new firms until the minimum point of $16 per meal on the firm's LRAC curve equals the price, MR and MC. Stated as a formula:

$$P = MR = MC = LRAC$$

A comparison of parts (a) and (b) of Exhibit 4 reveals two important points. First, both the monopolistic competitor and the perfect competitor earn zero economic profit in the long run. Second, the long-run equilibrium output of the monopolistically competitive firm is to the left of the minimum point on the LRAC curve and the price exceeds MC. Like a monopolist, the monopolistically competitive firm therefore charges a higher price and produces less output than a perfectly competitive firm.

In our example, Ivan's would charge $1 less per meal and produce 300 more seafood meals per week in a perfectly competitive market. The extra 300 meals not produced are *excess capacity*, which represents underutilized resources. The criticism of monopolistic competition, then, is that there are too many firms producing too little output at inflated prices and wasting society's resources in the process. For example, on many nights, there are not enough customers for all the restaurants in town. Servers, cooks, tables, and other resources are therefore underutilized. With fewer firms, each would produce a greater output at a lower price and with a lower average cost.

Opinions vary concerning whether the benefits of monopolistic competition exceed the costs. Having many seafood restaurants offers consumers more choice and variety of output. Having Ivan's Oyster Bar and many similar competitors gives consumers extra quality and service options. If you do not like Ivan's sautéed alligator, you may be able to find another restaurant that serves this dish. Also, having many restaurants in a market saves consumers valuable time. Chances are that you will not shed crocodile tears because the travel time required to enjoy an alligator meal is lower.

10-5 Oligopoly—Competition among the Few

Now we turn to oligopoly, an imperfectly competitive market structure in which a few large firms dominate the market. Many manufacturing industries, such as steel, aluminum, automobiles, aircraft, drugs, and tobacco, are best described as oligopolistic. This is the "big business" market structure in which firms aggressively compete by bombarding us with advertising on television and filling our mailboxes with junk mail.

Economists define an oligopoly as a market structure characterized by (1) few large sellers, (2) either a homogeneous or a differentiated product, and (3) difficult market entry. Like monopolistic competition, oligopoly is found in real-world industries. Let's examine each characteristic.

10-5a FEW SELLERS

Oligopoly is competition "among the few." Here we refer to the "Big Three" or "Big Four" to mean that three or four firms dominate an industry. But what does "a few" firms really mean? Does this mean at least two, but less than ten? As with other market structures, the answer is there is no specific number of firms that must dominate an industry before it is an oligopoly. Basically, an oligopoly is a consequence of mutual interdependence. Mutual interdependence is a condition in which an action by one firm may cause a reaction from other firms. Stated another way, a market structure with a few powerful firms makes it easier for oligopolists to collude. The large number of firms under perfect competition or monopolistic competition and the absence of other firms in monopoly rule out mutual interdependence and collusion in these market structures.

Oligopoly

A market structure characterized by (1) few large sellers, (2) either a homogeneous or a differentiated product, and (3) difficult market entry.

Mutual interdependence

A condition in which an action by one firm may cause a reaction from other firms.

When General Motors (GM) considers a price hike or a style change, it must predict how Ford, Chrysler, and Toyota will change their prices and styling in response. Therefore, the decisions under oligopoly are more complex than under perfect competition, monopoly, and monopolistic competition.

> **CONCLUSION:** *The few-sellers condition is met when these few firms are so large relative to the total market that they can affect the market price.*

10-5b HOMOGENEOUS OR DIFFERENTIATED PRODUCT

Under oligopoly, firms can produce either a homogeneous (identical) or a differentiated product. The steel produced by USX is identical to the steel from Republic Steel. The oil sold by Saudi Arabia is identical to the oil from Iran. Similarly, zinc, copper, and aluminum are standardized or homogeneous products. But cars produced by the major automakers are differentiated products. Tires, detergents, and breakfast cereals are also differentiated products sold in oligopolies.

> **CONCLUSION:** *Buyers in an oligopoly may or may not be indifferent as to which seller's product they buy.*

10-5c DIFFICULT ENTRY

Similar to monopoly, formidable barriers to entry in an oligopoly protect firms from new entrants. These barriers include exclusive financial requirements, control over an essential resource, patent rights, and other legal barriers. But the most significant barrier to entry in an oligopoly is *economies of scale*. For example, larger automakers achieve lower average total costs than those incurred by smaller automakers. Consequently, the U.S. auto industry has moved over time from more than 60 firms to only three major U.S.-owned firms.

10-6 Price and Output Decisions for an Oligopolist

Mutual interdependence among firms in an oligopoly makes this market structure more difficult to analyze than perfect competition, monopoly, or monopolistic competition. The price-output decision of an oligopolist is not simply a matter of charging the price where MR = MC. Making price and output decisions in an oligopoly is like playing a game of chess. One player's move depends on the anticipated reactions of the opposing player. One player thinks, "If I move my rook here, my opponent might move her knight there." Likewise, a firm in an oligopoly can have many different possible reactions to the price, nonprice, and output changes of another firm. Consequently, there are different oligopoly models because no single model can cover all cases. The following is a discussion of five well-known oligopoly models: (1) nonprice competition, (2) the kinked demand curve, (3) price leadership, (4) the cartel, and (5) game theory.

10-6a NONPRICE COMPETITION

Major oligopolists often compete using advertising and product differentiation. Instead of "slugging it out" with price cuts, oligopolists may try to capture business from their rivals through better advertising campaigns and improved products. This model of behavior explains why advertising expenditures often are large in the cigarette, soft drink, athletic shoe, and automobile industries. It also explains why the research and development (R&D) function is so important to oligopolists. For example, much engineering effort is aimed largely at developing new products and improving existing products.

Why might oligopolists compete through nonprice competition, rather than price competition? The answer is that each oligopolist perceives that its rival will easily and quickly match any price reduction. In contrast, it is much more difficult to combat a clever and/or important product improvement.

10-6b THE KINKED DEMAND CURVE

Unlike other market structures, different assumptions define different models for any given oligopolistic industry. Over time, the "rules of the game" change, and a new model becomes the best predictor of the behavior of oligopolists. We begin with the kinked demand curve. The strange shape of this curve explains why prices in an oligopolistic market selling cars change far less often than prices in a perfectly competitive market selling wheat.

The kinked demand curve is a demand curve facing an oligopolist that assumes rivals will match a price decrease, but ignore a price increase. Without collusion, the kinked demand curve exists because management tacitly believes that the competition will not be "undersold." On the other hand, a price hike by one firm allows competitors to capture its share of the market. Oligopolistic firms must make pricing decisions, so they are *price makers*, rather than price takers. But as we will soon see in the kinked demand model, the high degree of interdependence among oligopolists restricts their pricing discretion.

In Exhibit 5, a kinked demand curve is drawn for Tucker Motor Company, which we assume competes with GM, Ford, Toyota, and Chrysler in the automobile market. (I suggest you check out the 1988 movie titled *Tucker: The Man and His Dreams*.) The current price per Tucker car is $25,000, and the quantity demanded at this price is 3 million cars per year. Tucker's management assumes that if it raises its price even slightly above $25,000, the other automakers *will not follow* with higher prices. This price gap between the Tucker cars and other cars would drive many of Tucker's customers to its rivals. The segment of the demand curve above $25,000 is therefore relatively flat. Stated differently, above the "kink" in the demand curve, demand is relatively elastic. If Tucker raises the price to, say, $27,250 at point X, this price hike cuts Tucker's quantity demanded to 1.5 million cars per year. Since raising its price is ill-advised, management can consider a price reduction strategy. Suppose Tucker cuts the price of its cars from $25,000 to $22,250 at point Y. The model shows that Tucker gains few customers and the quantity demanded rises only slightly from 3 million to 3.2 million cars per year. The reason for such a small sales boost is that other automakers also cut their prices so that each

Kinked demand curve

A demand curve facing an oligopolist that assumes rivals will match a price decrease, but ignore a price increase.

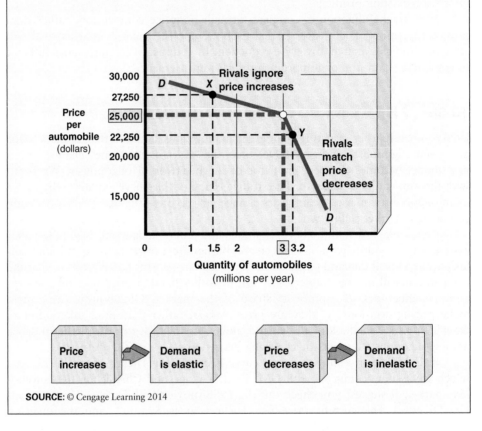

EXHIBIT 5 | **The Kinked Demand Curve**

An oligopolist's demand curve may be kinked. In this graph, an automobile producer believes it faces two demand curves. A price hike from $25,000 to $27,250 per auto causes a sizable reduction in the quantity demanded from 3 million to 1.5 million autos (point X). Demand above the kink is elastic because rivals ignore the firm when it raises the price. Below the kink, the demand curve is less elastic. A price reduction from $25,000 to $22,250 per auto attracts very few new customers, and the quantity demanded increases from 3 million to only 3.2 million autos per year (point Y). Under the kinked demand curve theory, prices will be rigid.

SOURCE: © Cengage Learning 2014

firm can keep its initial market share. However, the lower price does attract some new buyers who could not afford a car at the higher price. The segment of the demand curve below the kink is therefore relatively steep. Here demand is less elastic, meaning the quantity demanded is not very responsive to a price drop.

Given the kinked demand curve facing the oligopolist, management fears the worst and is afraid to raise or lower the price of its product. Under this model of oligopoly, the price established at the kink changes very infrequently. Price rigidity is eliminated only after large cost increases or decreases force a new kinked demand curve with a new higher or lower price at the kink.

Economists continue to debate the importance of the kinked demand model. Critics challenge the theory on theoretical and empirical grounds. On a theoretical level, there is no explanation for how the original price at the kink was determined.

On empirical grounds, studies of certain oligopolistic industries fail to find price stickiness. On the other hand, widespread use of price lists in catalogs that remain fixed for a long time is consistent with kinked demand theory. In any case, the kinked demand theory does not provide a complete explanation of price and output decisions.

10-6c PRICE LEADERSHIP

Without formal agreement, firms can play a game of follow-the-leader that economists call price leadership. Price leadership is a pricing strategy in which a dominant firm sets the price for an industry and the other firms follow. Following this tactic, firms in an industry simply match the price of perhaps, but not necessarily, the biggest firm.

Price leadership is not uncommon. In addition to GM, USX Corporation (steel), Alcoa (aluminum), DuPont (nylon), R. J. Reynolds (cigarettes), and Goodyear Tire & Rubber (tires) are examples of price leaders in U.S. industries.

Price leadership

A pricing strategy in which a dominant firm sets the price for an industry and the other firms follow.

10-6d THE CARTEL

The price leadership model assumes that firms do not collude to avoid price competition. Instead, firms avoid price wars by informally playing by the established pricing rules. Another way to avoid price wars is for oligopolists to agree to a peace treaty. Instead of allowing mutual interdependence to lead to rivalry, firms openly or secretly conspire to form a monopoly called a cartel. A cartel is a group of firms that formally agrees to reduce competition by coordinating the price and output of a product. The goal of a cartel is to reap monopoly profits by replacing competition with cooperation. Cartels are illegal in the United States, but not in other nations. The best-known cartel is the Organization of Petroleum Exporting Countries (OPEC). The members of OPEC divide "black gold" output among themselves according to quotas openly agreed upon at meetings of the OPEC oil ministries. Saudi Arabia is the largest producer and has the largest quota. The Global Economics feature provides a brief summary of some of today's major global cartels.

GLOBAL ECONOMICS

Cartel

A group of firms that formally agree to reduce competition by coordinating the price and output of a product.

Using Exhibit 6, we can demonstrate how a cartel works and why keeping members from cheating is a problem. Our analysis begins before oil-producing firms have formed a cartel. Assume each firm has the same cost curve shown in the exhibit. Price wars have driven each firm to charge $75 a barrel, which is equal to the minimum point on its LRAC curve. Because oil is a standardized product, as under perfect competition, each firm fears raising its price because it will lose all its customers. Thus, the typical firm is in long-run competitive equilibrium at a price of $75 per barrel ($MR_1$), producing 6 million barrels per day. In this condition, economic profits are zero, and the firms decide to organize a meeting of all oil producers to establish a cartel.

Now assume the cartel is formed and each firm agrees to reduce its output to 4 million barrels per day and charge $120 per barrel. If no firms cheat, each firm faces a higher horizontal demand curve, represented by MR_2. At the cartel price, each firm earns an economic profit of $120 million, rather than a normal profit. But what if one firm decides to cheat on the cartel agreement by stepping up its output while other firms stick to their quotas? Output corresponding to the point at which $MR_2 = MC$ is 8 million barrels per day. If a cheating firm expands its output to this level, it can double its profit by earning an extra $120 million. Of course, if all firms cheat and the cartel breaks up, the price and output of each firm return to the initial levels, and economic profit again falls to zero.

Major Cartels in Global Markets
Applicable Concept: cartel

Cartels flourished in Germany and other European countries in the first half of the 20th century. Many had international memberships. After World War II, European countries passed laws against such restrictive trade practices. The following are some of the most important cartels today:

- **Organization of Petroleum Exporting Countries (OPEC).** OPEC was created by Iran, Iraq, Kuwait, Saudi Arabia, and Venezuela in Baghdad in 1960. Today, the Vienna-based OPEC's membership consists of 12 countries that control about 70 percent of the world's oil reserves. Cartels are anticonsumer. OPEC's objective is to set oil production quotas for its members and, in turn, influence global prices of oil and gasoline.

- **International Telecommunications Union (ITU).** Perhaps the world's least-known and most effective cartel of about 140 member nations is based in Geneva, Switzerland. The ITU was founded in 1865 and became an agency of the United Nations in 1947. It is responsible for international regulations and standards governing global telecommunications including satellite communications, Internet access, and radio and TV broadcasting.

- **International Air Transport Association (IATA).** Originally founded in 1919, most of the world's international airlines belong to the IATA. This cartel, headquartered in Montreal, sets international airline ticket prices and safety and security standards for passenger and cargo shipping. It controls access to airports and challenges rules and regulations considered to be unreasonable. The IATA also is concerned with minimizing the impact of air transport on the environment.

Source: © Cengage Learning 2014

10-6e GAME THEORY

Game Theory

A model of the strategic moves and countermoves of rivals.

Game theory is a model of the strategic moves and countermoves of rivals. To illustrate, let's use a noncollusive example of US Airways competing with American Airlines. Each airline independently sets its fare, and Exhibit 7 is a *payoff matrix* that shows profit outcomes for the two airlines resulting from charging either a high fare or a low fare. If both charge the high fare in cell A, they split the market, and each makes a profit of $8 billion. If both decide to charge the low fare in cell D, they also split the market, and the profit for each falls to $5 billion. If one charges the high fare and the other charges the low fare in cell B or cell C, then the low-fare airline attracts most of the customers and earns the maximum possible profit of $10 billion, while the high-fare airline loses $2 billion.

Both rivals in our example are clearly *mutually interdependent* because an action by one firm may cause a reaction from the other firm. Suppose both airlines initially select the most mutually profitable solution and both charge high fares in cell A. This outcome creates an incentive for either airline to charge a lower fare in cell B or cell C and earn the highest possible profit by pulling customers away from its rival. Consequently, assume the next day one airline cuts its fare to gain higher profits. In order to avoid losing customers, this action causes the other airline to counter with an equally low fare. Price competition has therefore forced both airlines to charge the low fare in cell D and earn less than maximum joint profits. Once cell D is reached, neither airline has an incentive to alter the fare either higher or lower because both fear their rival's countermoves. Note that when both firms

EXHIBIT 6	Why a Cartel Member Has an Incentive to Cheat

A representative oil producer operating in a perfectly competitive industry would be in long-run equilibrium at a price of $75 per barrel, producing 6 million barrels per day and making zero economic profit. A cartel can agree to raise the price of oil from $75 to $120 per barrel by restricting the firm to 4 million barrels per day. As a result of this quota, the cartel price is above $90 on the LRAC curve, and the firm earns a daily profit of $120 million. However, if the firm cheats on the cartel agreement, it will set the cartel price equal to the MC curve and earn a total profit of $240 million by adding an additional $120 million. If all firms cheat, the original long-run equilibrium will be reestablished.

Extra profit from cheating = $120 million

Profit without cheating = $120 million

SOURCE: © Cengage Learning 2014

charge the low fare in equilibrium at cell D, consumers benefit from not paying high fares in the other cells.

CONCLUSION: *The payoff matrix demonstrates why a competitive oligopoly tends to result in both rivals using a low-price strategy that does not maximize mutual profits.*

EXHIBIT 7	A Two-Firm Payoff Matrix

Game theory is a method of analyzing the oligopoly puzzle. Two fare options of charging either a high fare or a low fare are given for US Airways and American Airlines. The profit or loss that each earns in cells A–D depends on the pricing decisions of these two rivals. Their collective interest is best served in cell A where each charges the high fare and each makes the maximum profit of $8 billion. But once either airline independently seeks the higher profit of $10 billion by using a low-fare strategy in cell B or C, the other airline counters with a low fare, and both end up charging the low fare in cell D. As a result, mutual profits are $5 billion, rather than $8 billion in cell A. Cell D is the equilibrium outcome because both airlines fear changing the price and causing the other to counter.

		US Airways' options	
		High fare	**Low fare**
American Airlines' options	**High fare**	*A* US Airways' profit = $8 billion American Airlines' profit = $8 billion	*B* US Airways' profit = $10 billion American Airlines' loss = −$2 billion
	Low fare	*C* US Airways' loss = −$2 billion American Airlines' profit = $10 billion	*D* US Airways' profit = $5 billion American Airlines' profit = $5 billion

SOURCE: © Cengage Learning 2014

How can these oligopolists avoid the low-fare outcome in cell D and instead stabilize the more jointly profitable high-fare payoffs in cell A? One possible strategy is called *tit-for-tat*. Under this approach, a player will do whatever the other player did the last time. If one airline defects from cell A by cutting its fare to gain a profit advantage, the other competitor will also cut its fare. After repeated trials, these price-cutting responses serve as a signal that says, "You are not going to get the best of me, so move your fare up!" Once the defector responds by moving back to the high fare, the other airline cooperates and also moves to the high fare. The result is that both players return to cell A without a formal agreement.

Another informal approach is for rivals to coordinate their pricing decisions based on price leadership, as discussed earlier in this chapter. For example, one airline may be much more established or dominant, and the other airline follows whatever price the leader sets. Another approach would be to informally rotate the leadership. Thus, without a formal agreement, the leader sets the profit-maximizing high price in cell A and the other competitor follows. However, this system does not eliminate the threat that the price follower will cheat.

Finally, if cartels were legal in the United States, the airlines could collude and make a formal agreement that each will charge the high fare. However, as explained in the previous section, there is always the incentive for one firm to cheat by moving from cell A to either cell B or cell C, and therefore cartels tend to break down. A remedy might be for the rivals to agree on a penalty for any party that reneges by lowering its fare.

> **CONCLUSION:** *As long as the benefits exceed the costs, cheating can threaten formal or informal agreements among oligopolists to maximize joint profits.*

10-7 An Evaluation of Oligopoly

Oligopoly is much more difficult to evaluate than other market structures. None of the models just presented gives a definite answer to the question of efficiency under oligopoly. Depending on the assumptions made, an oligopolist can behave much like a perfectly competitive firm or more like a monopoly. Nevertheless, let's assume some likely changes that occur if a perfectly competitive industry is suddenly turned into an oligopoly selling a differentiated product.

First, the price charged for the product will be higher than under perfect competition. The smaller the number of firms in an oligopoly and the more difficult it is to enter the industry, the higher the oligopoly price will be in comparison to the perfectly competitive price.

Second, an oligopoly is likely to spend money on advertising, product differentiation, and other forms of nonprice competition. These expenditures can shift the demand curve to the right. As a result, both price and output may be higher under oligopoly than under perfect competition.

Third, in the long run, a perfectly competitive firm earns zero economic profit. The oligopolist, however, can earn a higher profit because it is more difficult for competitors to enter the industry.

✓ CHECKPOINT

Which Model Fits the Cereal Aisle?

As you walk along the cereal aisle, notice the many different cereals on the shelf. For example, you will probably see General Mills' Wheaties, Total, and Cheerios; Kellogg's Corn Flakes, Cracklin' Oat Bran, Frosted Flakes, and Rice Krispies; Quaker Oats' Cap'n Crunch and 100% Natural; and Post's Golden Crisp, to name only a few. There are many different brands of the same product-cereal on the shelves. Each brand is slightly different from the others. Is the breakfast cereal industry's market structure monopolistic competition or oligopoly?

10-8 Review of the Four Market Structures

Now that we have completed the discussion of perfect competition, monopoly, monopolistic competition, and oligopoly, you are prepared to compare these four

How Oligopolists Compete at the Final Four

Applicable Concept: oligopoly

Suppose March Madness included your basketball team making it all the way to the Final Four and you were going to be there. Before leaving, you checked the official Web site and noticed a Coke ad giving a prize to the person who submitted the best video commercial for a new Coke product. But this was only the beginning of the Great Cola Wars. Shortly after leaving the plane at the airport, you encountered a group of students who were giving away huge inflatable plastic hands with index fingers sticking up in the air signaling that your team is number one. The plastic hands were imprinted with the Pepsi-Cola logo and your choice of a Final Four team. And the group was also giving away free ice-cold cans of Pepsi. As you walked along the streets to your hotel, giant inflatable "cans" of Pepsi appeared all over the downtown area on the sidewalks and on top of gas stations. And not to be outdone, the entire side of a prominent three-story building was painted Coca-Cola red and white with the 64 NCAA basketball finalists and all the winners listed bracket by bracket. Following the first-round games, painters were three stories up on scaffolding filling in the Coke sign's brackets for the final two teams, in school colors no less. Inside the arena, the colas continued their battle by scrolling cola ads with other ads under the press rows along either side of the basketball court. This was indeed competition between showboating industry giants worthy of the Final Four competition among the basketball teams.

Many fascinating markets function during the Final Four basketball tournament, including competitive markets that determine prices for parking lots, restaurants, and tickets. (Recall the Checkpoint in Chapter 4 on ticket scalping.) Then there were the hotels surrounding the arena, which joined a centralized booking service. Each hotel had raised its normal price by 75 percent for the weekend.

Analyze the Issue

In this feature, two forms of oligopoly were observed. Identify each of these forms and explain why it is being used by the oligopolists.

market structures. Exhibit 8 summarizes the characteristics and gives examples of each market structure.

EXHIBIT 8	Comparison of Market Structures			
Market structure	Number of sellers	Type of product	Entry condition	Examples
Perfect competition	Large	Homogeneous	Very easy	Agriculture*
Monopoly	One	Unique	Impossible	Public utilities
Monopolistic competition	Many	Differentiated	Easy	Retail trade
Oligopoly	Few	Homogeneous or differentiated	Difficult	Auto, steel, oil

*In the absence of government intervention.
SOURCE: © Cengage Learning 2014

Key Concepts

Monopolistic competition	Oligopoly	Price leadership
Product differentiation	Mutual interdependence	Cartel
Nonprice competition	Kinked demand curve	Game theory

Summary

- **Monopolistic competition** is a market structure characterized by (1) many small sellers, (2) a differentiated product, and (3) easy market entry and exit. Given these characteristics, firms in monopolistic competition have a negligible effect on the market price.
- **Product differentiation** is a key characteristic of monopolistic competition. It is the process of creating real or apparent differences between products.
- **Nonprice competition** includes advertising, packaging, product development, better quality, and better service. Under monopolistic competition and oligopoly, firms may compete using nonprice competition, rather than price competition.

Short-Run Equilibrium for a Monopolistic Competitor

SOURCE: © Cengage Learning 2014

- **Short-run equilibrium for a monopolistic competitor** can yield economic losses, zero economic profits, or economic profits. In the long

run, monopolistic competitors make zero economic profits.

- **Comparing monopolistic competition with perfect competition,** we find that in the long run, the monopolistically competitive firm does not achieve allocative efficiency, charges a higher price, restricts output, and does not produce where average costs are at a minimum.

Comparison of Monopolistic and Perfect Competition

SOURCE: © Cengage Learning 2014

- **Oligopoly** is a market structure characterized by (1) few sellers, (2) either a homogeneous or a differentiated product, and (3) difficult market entry. Oligopolies are **mutually interdependent** because an action by one firm may cause a reaction from other firms.

- The **nonprice competition model** is a theory that might explain oligopolistic behavior. Under this theory, firms use advertising and product differentiation, rather than price reductions, to compete.
- The **kinked demand curve** model explains why prices may be rigid in an oligopoly. The kink occurs because an oligopolist assumes that rivals will match a price decrease, but ignore a price increase.

Kinked Demand Curve

SOURCE: © Cengage Learning 2014

- **Price leadership** is another theory of pricing behavior under oligopoly. When a dominant firm in an industry raises or lowers its price, other firms follow suit.
- A **cartel** is a formal agreement among firms to set prices and output quotas. The goal is to maximize profits, but firms have an incentive to cheat, which is a constant threat to a cartel.

Cartel

Extra profit from cheating = $120 million
Profit without cheating = $120 million

SOURCE: © Cengage Learning 2014

- **Game theory** reveals that (1) oligopolies are mutually interdependent in their pricing policies; (2) without collusion, oligopoly prices and mutual profits are lower; and (3) oligopolists have a temptation to cheat on any collusive agreement.
- **Comparing oligopoly with perfect competition,** we find that the oligopolist allocates resources inefficiently, charges a higher price, and restricts output so that price may exceed average cost.

Summary of Conclusion Statements

- The many-sellers condition is met when each firm is so small relative to the total market that its pricing decisions have a negligible effect on the market price.
- When a product is differentiated, buyers are not indifferent as to which seller's product they buy.
- The demand curve for a monopolistically competitive firm is less elastic (steeper) than for a perfectly competitive firm and more elastic (flatter) than for a monopolist.
- The few-sellers condition is met when these few firms are so large relative to the total market that they can affect the market price.
- Buyers in an oligopoly may or may not be indifferent as to which seller's product they buy.
- The payoff matrix demonstrates why a competitive oligopoly tends to result in both rivals using a low-price strategy that does not maximize mutual profits.
- As long as the benefits exceed the costs, cheating can threaten formal or informal agreements among oligopolists to maximize joint profits.

Study Questions and Problems

1. Compare the monopolistically competitive firm's demand curve to those of a perfect competitor and a monopolist.

2. Suppose the minimum point on the LRAC curve of a soft-drink firm's cola is $1 per liter. Under conditions of monopolistic competition, will the price of a liter bottle of cola in the long run be above $1, equal to $1, less than $1, or impossible to determine?

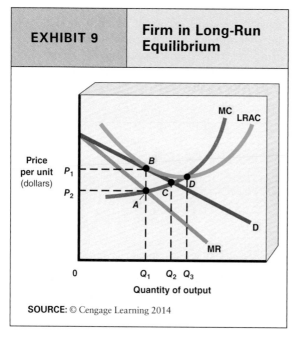

EXHIBIT 9	Firm in Long-Run Equilibrium

SOURCE: © Cengage Learning 2014

3. Exhibit 9 represents a monopolistically competitive firm in long-run equilibrium.
   a. Which price represents the long-run equilibrium price?
   b. Which quantity represents the long-run equilibrium output?
   c. At which quantity is the LRAC curve at its minimum?
   d. Is the long-run equilibrium price greater than, less than, or equal to the marginal cost of producing the equilibrium output?

4. Consider this statement: "Because price equals long-run average cost and profits are zero, a monopolistically competitive firm is efficient." Do you agree or disagree? Explain.

5. Assuming identical long-run cost curves, draw two graphs, and indicate the price and output that result in the long run under monopolistic competition and perfect competition. Evaluate the differences between these two market structures.

6. Draw a graph that shows how advertising affects a firm's ATC curve. Explain how advertising can lead to lower prices in a monopolistically competitive industry.

7. List four goods or services that you have purchased that were produced by an oligopolist. Why are these industries oligopolistic, rather than monopolistically competitive?

8. Why is mutual interdependence important under oligopoly, but not so important under perfect competition, monopoly, or monopolistic competition?

9. Suppose the jeans industry is an oligopoly in which each firm sells its own distinctive brand of jeans. Each firm believes its rivals will not follow its price increases, but will follow its price cuts. Explain the demand curve facing each firm. Does this demand curve mean that firms in the jeans industry do or do not compete against one another?

10. What might be a general distinction between oligopolists that advertise and those that do not?

11. Suppose Canon raised the price of its printers, but Hewlett-Packard (the largest seller) refused to follow. Two years later Canon cut its price, and Hewlett-Packard retaliated with an even deeper price cut, which Canon was forced to match. For the next five years, Hewlett-Packard raised its prices five times, and each time Canon followed suit within 24 hours. Does the pricing behavior of these computer industry firms follow the cartel model or the price leadership model? Why?

12. Evaluate the following statement: "A cartel will put an end to price war, which is a barbaric form of competition that benefits no one."

13. Assume the payoff matrix in Exhibit 7 applies to spending for advertising rather than airline fares. Substitute *Don't Advertise* for *High fare* and *Advertise* for *Low fare*. Assume the same profit and loss figures in each cell, but substitute *Marlboro* for *US Airways* and *Camel* for *American Airlines*. Explain the dynamics of the model and why cigarette companies might be pleased with a government ban on all cigarette advertising.

For Online Exercises, go to the Tucker Web site at www.cengage.com/economics/tucker.

✓ CHECKPOINT ANSWER

Which Model Fits the Cereal Aisle?

The fact that there is a differentiated product does not necessarily mean that many firms are competing along the cereal aisle. The different cereals listed in this example are produced by only four companies: General Mills, Kellogg's, Quaker Oats, and Post. In fact, there are relatively few firms in the cereal industry; so even though they sell a differentiated product, the market structure cannot be monopolistic competition. If you said the cereal industry is an oligopoly, **YOU ARE CORRECT.**

Sample Quiz

For an explanation of the correct answers, visit the Tucker Web site at www.cengage.com/economics/tucker.

1. Clothing stores in cities are an illustration of
   a. perfect competition.
   b. monopoly.
   c. monopolistic competition.
   d. oligopoly.

2. Firms in a monopolistically competitive industry produce
   a. homogeneous goods and services.
   b. differentiated products.
   c. competitive goods only.
   d. consumption goods only.

3. Monopolistic competitive firms in the long run earn
   a. positive economic profits.
   b. zero pure economic profits.
   c. negative economic profits.
   d. None of the above answers are correct.

4. The theory of monopolistic competition predicts that in long-run equilibrium, a monopolistically competitive firm will
   a. produce at the level in which price equals long-run average cost.
   b. operate at minimum long-run average cost.
   c. overutilize its insufficient capacity.
   d. None of the above answers are correct.

5. Which of the following statements *best* describes the price, output, and profit conditions of monopolistic competition?
   a. Price will equal marginal cost at the profit-maximizing level of output; profits will be positive in the long run.
   b. Price will always equal average variable cost in the short run, and either profits or losses may result in the long run.

Sample Quiz *continued*

c. Marginal revenue will equal marginal cost in the short run, profit-maximizing level of output; in the long run, economic profit will be zero.

d. Marginal revenue will equal average total cost in the short run; long-run economic profits will be zero.

6. Entry of new firms will occur in a monopolistic competitive industry until
   a. marginal cost equals zero.
   b. marginal revenue equals zero.
   c. marginal revenue equals marginal cost.
   d. economic profit equals zero.
   e. economic profit is negative.

7. As presented in Exhibit 10, what is the short-run profit-maximizing output for the monopolistic competitive firm?
   a. 0 units per day
   b. 200 units per day
   c. 400 units per day
   d. 600 units per day

EXHIBIT 10	A Monopolistic Competitive Firm

SOURCE: © Cengage Learning 2014

8. As presented in Exhibit l0, what is the short-run profit per unit of output for the monopolistic competitive firm?
   a. Zero
   b. $5

c. $10
d. $15

9. As represented in Exhibit 10, what is the maximum long-run economic profit earned by this monopolistic competitive firm?
   a. Zero
   b. $200 per day
   c. $1,000 per day
   d. $20,000 per day

10. An oligopoly is a market structure in which
    a. one firm has 100 percent of a market.
    b. there are many small firms.
    c. there are many firms with no control over price.
    d. there are few firms selling either a homogeneous or differentiated product.

11. Mutual interdependence among firms in an oligopoly means that
    a. firms never practice price leadership.
    b. firms never form a cartel.
    c. it is difficult to know how firms will react to decisions of rivals.
    d. no formal agreement is possible among firms.

12. A common characteristic of oligopolies is
    a. interdependence in pricing decisions.
    b. independent pricing decisions.
    c. low industry concentration.
    d. few or no plant-level economies of scale.

13. Which of the following *best* describes a cartel?
    a. A group of monopolistically competitive firms that jointly reduces output and raise price in imitation of a monopolist. When entry is very costly, these high prices can persist.
    b. A group of cooperating oligopolists that jointly reduce output and raise price in imitation of a monopolist. When entry is very costly, these high prices can persist.
    c. A monopolist that reduces output and raises price. When entry is very costly, these high prices can persist.
    d. A group of identical noncooperative oligopolists that is able to reproduce a monopoly equilibrium through price rivalry.

Sample Quiz *continued*

14. Which of the following is *true* about an oligopoly equilibrium compared with equilibrium under similar circumstances but with perfect competition?
    a. Output is larger and price is lower than under perfect competition.
    b. Output is larger but price is higher than under perfect competition.
    c. Output is smaller and price is higher than under perfect competition.
    d. Output is smaller and price is lower than under perfect competition.

15. Which of the following market structures describes an industry in which a group of firms formally agrees to control prices and output of a product?
    a. Perfect competition
    b. Monopoly
    c. Oligopoly
    d. Cartel
    e. Monopolistic competition

16. Assume costs are identical for the two firms in Exhibit 11. If both firms were allowed to form a cartel and agree on their prices, equilibrium would be established by
    a. Widget Company charging the low price and Ajax Company charging the high price.
    b. Widget Company charging the high price and Ajax Company charging the low price.

c. Widget Company charging the low price and Ajax Company charging the low price.
d. Widget Company charging the high price and Ajax Company charging the high price.

17. Suppose costs are identical for the two firms in Exhibit 11. If both firms assume the other will compete and charge a lower price, equilibrium will be established by
    a. Widget Company charging the low price and Ajax Company charging the low price.
    b. Widget Company charging the high price and Ajax Company charging the low price.
    c. Widget Company charging the low price and Ajax Company charging the high price.
    d. Widget Company charging the high price and Ajax Company charging the high price.

18. Suppose costs are identical for the two firms in Exhibit 11. Each firm assumes without formal agreement that if it sets the high price, its rival will *not* charge a lower price. Under these "tit-for-tat" conditions, equilibrium will be established by
    a. Widget Company charging the high price and Ajax Company charging the low price.
    b. Widget Company charging the high price and Ajax Company charging the high price.
    c. Widget Company charging the low price and Ajax Company charging the low price.
    d. Widget Company charging the low price and Ajax Company charging the high price.

19. As a result of a kinked demand curve, the price
    a. fluctuates.
    b. falls below the kink.
    c. settles at the kink.
    d. rises above the kink.

20. The "kinked" oligopoly demand curve is a result of the assumption by an oligopolist that
    a. price increases will be matched, but price reductions will not.
    b. price increases will not be matched, but price reductions will.
    c. both price increases and price reductions will be matched.
    d. neither price increases nor price reductions will be matched.

EXHIBIT 11	Two-Firm Payoff Matrix

		Ajax company	
		High price	Low price
Widget company	High price	A $60 billion / $60 billion	B $20 billion / $10 billion
	Low price	C $10 billion / $20 billion	D $20 billion / $20 billion

SOURCE: © Cengage Learning 2014

chapter 11

Labor Markets

In 2011, actor Johnny Depp earned the impressive figure of $50 million, but Oprah Winfrey did even better. She earned $290 million. While one headline reports a sports team signed its star player to a contract paying $10 million annually, another cites a recent survey showing chief executive officers (CEOs) of America's biggest corporations are paid millions of dollars in compensation. The president of the United States is paid $400,000 per year. The worker with a bachelor's degree or more earns an average of over $90,000. The average high school graduate earns less than $40,000, while many others, including college students, toil for the minimum wage.

How are earnings determined? What accounts for the wide differences in earnings? This chapter provides answers by explaining different types of labor markets that determine workers' compensation and the quantity of workers firms hire. Understanding hiring decisions is indeed a key to understanding why some become rich and famous by playing baseball—a kid's game—while other workers might be exploited by firms with labor market power.

The chapter begins with the development of a competitive labor market in which no single buyer or seller can influence the price (wage rate) of labor. The chapter concludes with a discussion of power. As in the product markets, labor market determinations are affected by market power. Power on the side of either unions or employers can alter wage and employment outcomes. For example, the chapter explains how unions affect wages and examines trends in union membership around the world.

In this chapter, you will learn to solve these economics puzzles:

- What determines the wage rate an employer pays?
- How do labor unions influence wages and employment?
- Does the NCAA exploit college athletes?

11-1 The Labor Market under Perfect Competition

In Chapters 8–10, you studied the price and quantity determinations of goods and services produced by firms operating under different market structures—perfect competition, monopoly, oligopoly, and monopolistic competition. As you have learned, market structure affects the price and the quantity of a good or service sold by firms to consumers. Similarly, as this chapter will demonstrate, the price (wage rate) paid to labor and the quantity of labor hired by firms are influenced by whether or not the labor market is competitive.

Recall from Chapter 8 that we assumed the hypothetical firm called Computech produces and sells electronic components in a perfectly competitive market. In this chapter, we also assumed Computech hires workers in a perfectly competitive labor market. In a perfectly competitive labor market, there are many sellers and buyers of labor services. Consequently, wages and salaries are determined by the intersection of the demand for labor and the supply of labor.

11-1a THE DEMAND FOR LABOR

How many workers should Computech hire? To answer this question, Computech must know how much workers contribute to its output. Column (1) of Exhibit 1 lists possible numbers of workers Computech might hire per day, and as discussed

EXHIBIT 1	Computech's Demand for Labor			
Points	(1) Labor Input (workers per day)	(2) Total Output (units per day)	(3) Marginal Product (units per day)	(4) Product Price	(5) Marginal Revenue Product [(3) × (4)]
	0	0		$70	
			5		$350
A	1	5		70	
			4		280
B	2	9		70	
			3		210
C	3	12		70	
			2		140
D	4	14		70	
			1		70
E	5	15		70	

SOURCE: © Cengage Learning 2014

earlier in Chapter 7 on production costs, column (2) shows the total output per day. One worker would produce 5 units per day, 2 workers together would produce 9 units per day, and so on. Note that columns (1) and (2) constitute a *production function,* as represented earlier in Exhibit 2(a) in Chapter 7. Column (3) lists the additional output from hiring each worker. The first worker hired would add 5 units of output per day, the second would produce an additional 4 units (total product of 9 – 5 units produced), and so on. Recall from Chapter 7 that the additional output from hiring another unit of labor is defined as the *marginal product of labor* [see Exhibit 2(b) in Chapter 7]. Consistent with the *law of diminishing returns*, the marginal product falls as the firm hires more workers.[1]

The next step in Computech's hiring decision is to convert marginal product into dollars by calculating the marginal revenue product (MRP), which is the increase in a firm's total revenue resulting from hiring an additional unit of labor or another variable resource. Stated simply, MRP is the dollar value of worker productivity. It is the extra revenue a firm earns from selling the output of an extra worker. Returning to Exhibit 1 in Chapter 8 on perfect competition, suppose the market equilibrium price per unit is $70. Because Computech operates in a perfectly competitive market, the firm can sell any quantity of its product at the $70 market-determined price. Given this situation, the first unit of labor contributes an MRP of $350 per day to revenue ($70 per unit times the 5 units of output). Column (5) of Exhibit 1 lists the MRP of each additional worker hired.

Marginal revenue product (MRP)

The increase in a firm's total revenue resulting from hiring an additional unit of labor or other variable resource.

> **CONCLUSION:** *A perfectly competitive firm's marginal revenue product is equal to the marginal product of its labor times the price of its product. Expressed as a formula:* $MRP = P \times MP$.

Now assuming all other inputs are fixed, Computech can derive its demand curve for labor, which conforms to the law of demand explained in Chapter 3. The demand curve for labor is a curve showing the different quantities of labor employers are willing to hire at different wage rates. It is equal to the MRP of labor. The MRP numbers from Exhibit 1 are duplicated in Exhibit 2. As shown in Exhibit 2, the price of labor in terms of daily wages is measured on the vertical axis. The quantity of workers Computech will hire per day at each wage rate is measured on the horizontal axis. The demand curve for labor is downward sloping: As the wage rate falls, Computech will hire more workers per day. If the wage rate is above $350 (point *A*), Computech will hire no workers because the cost of a worker is more than the dollar value of any worker's contribution to total revenue (MRP). But what happens if Computech pays each worker $280 per day? At point *B*, Computech finds it profitable to hire 2 workers because the MRP of the first worker is greater than the wage rate (extra cost) and the second worker's MRP equals the wage rate. If the wage rate is $140 per day at point *D*, Computech will find it profitable to hire 4 workers. In this case, Computech will not hire the fifth worker. Why? The fifth worker contributes an MRP of $70 to total revenue (point *E*), but this amount is below the wage rate paid of $140. Consequently, Computech cannot maximize profits by hiring the fifth worker because it would be adding more

Demand curve for labor

A curve showing the different quantities of labor employers are willing to hire at different wage rates in a given time period, ceteris paribus. It is equal to the marginal revenue product of labor.

---

[1]Recall from Chapter 7 that at low rates of output, the marginal product may increase with the addition of more labor due to specialization and division of labor. Then, as output expands in the short run, the law of diminishing returns will cause marginal product to decrease.

to costs than to revenue. Specifically, Computech would lose $70 per day by hiring the fifth worker. At a wage rate of $70, however, the fifth worker would be hired.

> **CONCLUSION:** *A firm hires additional workers up to the point where the MRP equals the wage rate.*

EXHIBIT 2	Computech's Demand Curve for Labor

Computech's downward-sloping demand curve for labor is derived from the marginal revenue product (MRP) of labor, which declines as additional workers are hired. The MRP is the change in total revenue that results from hiring one more worker (see Exhibit 1). At point *B*, Computech pays $280 per day and finds it profitable to pay this wage to 2 workers because each worker's MRP equals or exceeds the wage rate. If Computech pays a lower wage rate of $140 per day at point *D*, it is not profitable for the firm to hire the fifth worker because this worker's MRP of $70 is below the wage rate of $140 per day. At a wage rate of $70, the fifth worker would be hired.

CAUSATION CHAIN

Decrease in the wage rate ➡ Increase in the quantity of labor an employer hires

SOURCE: © Cengage Learning 2014

Each firm in the market has a demand for labor based on its MRP data. Summing these individual demand curves for labor provides the market demand curve for labor in the electronic components industry. Another important point must be made. The demand for labor is called derived demand. The derived demand for labor and other factors of production depends on the consumer demand for the final goods and services the factors produce. If consumers are not willing to purchase products requiring electronic components, such as bank teller machines, there is no MRP, and firms will hire no workers to make electronic components for them. On the other hand, if customer demand for bank teller machines soars, the price of units rises, and the MRP of firms in the electronic components industry also rises. The result is a rightward shift in the market demand curve for labor.

Derived demand

The demand for labor and other factors of production that depends on the consumer demand for the final goods and services the factors produce.

11-1b THE SUPPLY OF LABOR

The supply curve of labor is also consistent with the law of supply discussed in Chapter 3. The supply curve of labor shows the different quantities of labor workers are willing to offer employers at different wage rates. Summing the individual supply curves of labor for firms producing electronic units for automated teller machines provides the market supply curve of labor. As shown in Exhibit 3, as the wage rate rises, more workers are willing to supply their labor. Each point indicates the wage rate that must be paid to attract the corresponding number of workers. At point *A*, 20,000 workers offer their services to the industry for $140 per day. At the higher wage rate of $280 per day (point *B*), the quantity of labor supplied is 40,000 workers. More people are willing to work at higher wage rates because the incentive of earning more compensates for the opportunity cost of leisure time. Higher wages also attract workers from other industries that require similar skills, but have lower wage rates.

Ignoring differences in wage scales, why might the supply of less-skilled workers (e.g., carpenters) be greater than that of more-skilled workers (e.g., physicians)? The explanation for this difference is the human capital required to perform various occupations. Human capital is the accumulation of education, training, experience, and health that enables a worker to enter an occupation and be productive. Less human capital is required to be a carpenter than a physician. Therefore, many people are qualified for such work, and the supply of carpenters is larger than the supply of physicians.

Supply curve of labor

A curve showing the different quantities of labor workers are willing to offer employers at different wage rates in a given time period, ceteris paribus.

Human capital

The accumulation of education, training, experience, and health that enables a worker to enter an occupation and be productive.

11-1c THE EQUILIBRIUM WAGE RATE

Wage rates are determined in perfectly competitive markets by the interaction of labor supply and demand. The equilibrium wage rate for the entire electronic components market, shown in Exhibit 4(a), is $210 per day. This wage rate clears the market because the quantity of 30,000 workers demanded equals the quantity of 30,000 workers who are willing to supply their labor services at that wage rate. In a competitive labor market, no single worker can set his or her wage above the equilibrium wage. Such a worker fears not being hired because there are so many workers who will work for $210 per day. Similarly, so many firms are hiring labor that a single firm cannot influence the wage by paying workers more or less than the prevailing wage. Hence, a wage rate above $210 per day would create a surplus of workers seeking employment (unemployment) in the electronic components market, and a wage rate below $210 per day would cause a shortage.

| **EXHIBIT 3** | **The Market Supply Curve of Labor** |

The upward-sloping supply curve of labor for the electronic components industry indicates that a direct relationship exists between the wage rate and the quantity of labor supplied. At point *A*, 20,000 workers are willing to work for $140 per day in this market. If the wage rate rises to $280 per day, 40,000 workers will supply their services to the electronic components labor market.

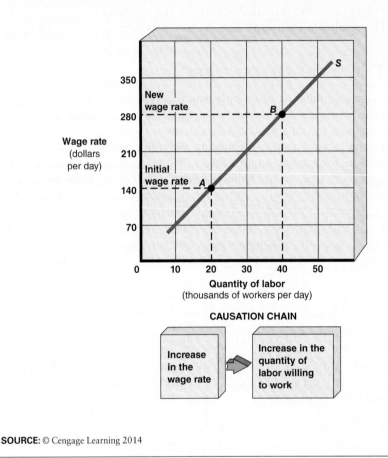

CAUSATION CHAIN

Increase in the wage rate ⇨ Increase in the quantity of labor willing to work

SOURCE: © Cengage Learning 2014

Why does a cardiologist make a much higher hourly wage than a server in a restaurant? As demonstrated in Exhibit 4(a), wage differentials are determined by the demand and supply curves in labor markets for these two occupations. In this case, the equilibrium wage rate for cardiologists greatly exceeds the equilibrium wage rate for servers. In the next chapter, this labor market model is used to explain differences in wages resulting from racial discrimination.

Although the supply curve of labor is upward sloping for the electronic components market, this is not the case for an individual firm, such as Computech, shown in Exhibit 4(b). Because a competitive labor market assumes that each firm is too small to influence the wage rate, Computech is a "wage taker" and therefore pays the market-determined wage rate of $210 per day regardless of the quantity of labor it employs. For this reason, the labor supply to Computech is represented by a horizontal line at the equilibrium wage rate. Given this wage rate of $210 per day,

EXHIBIT 4	A Competitive Labor Market Determines the Firm's Equilibrium Wage

In part (a), the intersection of the supply of labor and the demand for labor curves determines the equilibrium wage rate of $210 per day in the electronic components industry. Part (b) illustrates that a single firm, such as Computech, is a "wage taker." The firm can hire all the workers it wants at this equilibrium wage, so its supply curve, S, is a horizontal line. Computech chooses to hire 3 workers, where the firm's demand curve for labor intersects its supply curve of labor.

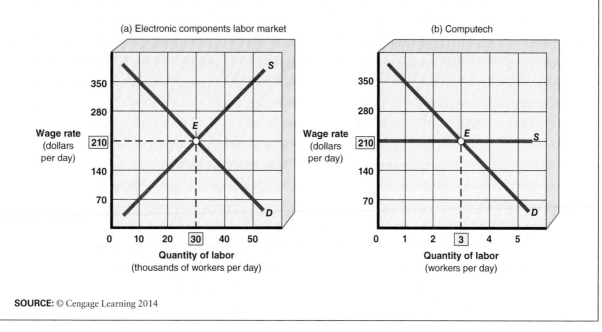

SOURCE: © Cengage Learning 2014

Computech then hires labor up to the equilibrium point, E, where the wage rate equals the third worker's marginal revenue product.

11-2 Labor Unions: Employee Power

The perfectly competitive model does not apply to workers who belong to unions. Unions arose because workers recognized that acting together gave them more bargaining power than acting individually and being at the mercy of their employers. Some of the biggest unions are the Teamsters, United Auto Workers, National Education Association, and American Federation of Government Employees. Two primary objectives of unions are to improve working conditions and raise the wages of union members above the level that would exist in a competitive labor market. To raise wages, unions use three basic strategies: (1) increase the demand for labor, (2) decrease the supply of labor, and (3) exert power to force employers to pay a wage rate above the equilibrium wage rate.

11-2a UNIONS INCREASE THE DEMAND FOR LABOR

Now suppose the workers form a union. One way to increase wages is to use a method called *featherbedding*. This means the union forces firms to hire more workers than are required or to impose work rules that reduce output per worker. For example, contract provisions may prohibit any workers but carpenters from doing even the simplest carpentry work. Another approach is to boost domestic demand for labor by decreasing competition from other nations. For example, the union might lobby Congress to protect the U.S. electronic parts industry against competition from China. Another approach might be to advertise and try to convince the public to "Look for the Union Label." Effective advertising would boost the demand for electronic products with union-made components and, in turn, the demand for union labor because it is *derived demand*.

Exhibit 5 shows how union power can be used to increase the demand curve for labor. This exhibit reproduces the labor market for electronic components

EXHIBIT 5	**A Union Causes an Increase in the Demand Curve for Labor**

A union shifts the demand curve for labor rightward from D_1 to D_2 by featherbedding or other devices. As a result, the equilibrium wage rate increases from \$210 per day at point E_1 to \$280 per day at point E_2, and employment rises from 30,000 to 40,000 workers.

SOURCE: © Cengage Learning 2014

workers from Exhibit 4(a). Begin at equilibrium point E_1, with the wage rate of $210 per day paid to each of 30,000 workers. Then the union causes the demand curve for labor to increase from D_1 to D_2. At the new equilibrium point, E_2, firms hire an additional 10,000 workers and pay each worker an extra $70 per day.

11-2b UNIONS DECREASE THE SUPPLY OF LABOR

Exhibit 6 shows another way unions can use their power to increase the wage rate of their members by restricting the supply of labor. Now suppose the labor market

EXHIBIT 6	A Union Causes a Decrease in the Supply Curve of Labor

A union shifts the supply curve of labor leftward from S_1 to S_2 by restricting union membership or by using other techniques. As a result, the equilibrium wage rate rises from $210 per day at point E_1 to $280 per day at point E_2, and the number of workers hired falls from 40,000 to 30,000.

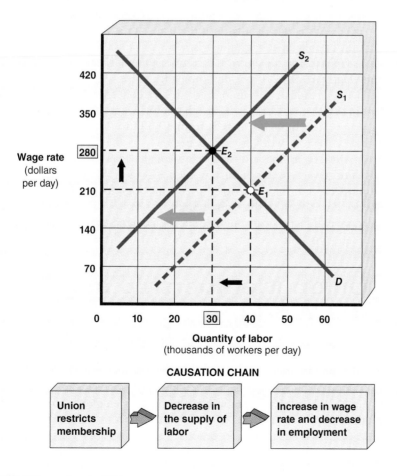

CAUSATION CHAIN

Union restricts membership ⟹ Decrease in the supply of labor ⟹ Increase in wage rate and decrease in employment

SOURCE: © Cengage Learning 2014

is in equilibrium at point E_1, with 40,000 workers making electronic units and earning $210 per day. Then the union uses its power to shift the supply curve of labor leftward from S_1 to S_2 by, say, requiring a longer apprenticeship, charging higher fees, or using some other device designed to reduce union membership. For example, the union might lobby for legislation to reduce immigration or to shorten working hours. As a result of these union actions, the equilibrium wage rate rises to $280 per day at point E_2, and employment is artificially reduced to 30,000 workers. It should be noted that self-serving practices of unions to limit the labor supply and raise wages can be disguised as standards of professionalism, such as those required by the American Medical Association and the American Bar Association, teacher certification requirements, Ph.D. requirements for university faculty, and so on.

11-3 Unions Use Collective Bargaining to Boost Wages

Collective bargaining

The process of negotiating labor contracts between the union and management concerning wages and working conditions.

A third way to raise the wage rate above the equilibrium level is to use collective bargaining. Collective bargaining is the process of negotiating labor contracts between the union and management concerning wages and working conditions. By law, once a union has been certified as the representative of a majority of the workers, employers must deal with the union. If employers deny union demands, the union can strike and reduce profits until the firms agree to a higher wage rate.

The result of collective bargaining is shown in Exhibit 7. Again, we return to the situation depicted for the electronic components market in Exhibit 4(a). At the equilibrium wage rate of $210 per day (point E), there is no surplus or shortage of workers. Then the industry is unionized, and a collective bargaining agreement takes effect in which firms agree to pay the union wage rate of $280 per day. At the higher wage rate, employment falls from 30,000 to 20,000 workers. However, 40,000 workers wish to work for $280 per day, so there is a surplus of 20,000 unemployed workers in the industry. How might firms react to a situation in which they hire fewer workers and pay higher wages? Employers might respond by substituting capital for labor or by transferring operations overseas, where labor costs are lower than in the United States.

Finally, several factors can cause either the demand curve for labor or the supply curve of labor to shift. Exhibit 8 provides a list of these factors.

11-4 Union Membership around the World

How important are unions as measured by the percentage of the labor force that belongs to a union? Let's start during the Great Depression, when millions of people were out of work and union membership was relatively low (see Exhibit 9). To boost employment and earnings, President Franklin D. Roosevelt's National Industrial Recovery Act (NIRA) of 1933 established the right of employees to bargain collectively with their employers, but the act was declared unconstitutional by the Supreme Court in 1935. However, the 1935 National Labor Relations Act (NLRA), known as the Wagner Act, incorporated the labor provisions of the NIRA. The Wagner Act guaranteed workers the right to form unions and to engage in collective bargaining. The combined impact of this legislation and the production demands of World War II created a surge in union membership between 1935 and 1945.

EXHIBIT 7	Union Collective Bargaining Causes a Wage Rate Increase

A union exerts its power through collective bargaining. Instead of the competitive wage rate of $210 at point *E*, firms in the industry avoid a strike by agreeing in a labor contract to $280 per day. The effect is to artificially create a labor surplus (unemployment) of 20,000 workers at the negotiated wage.

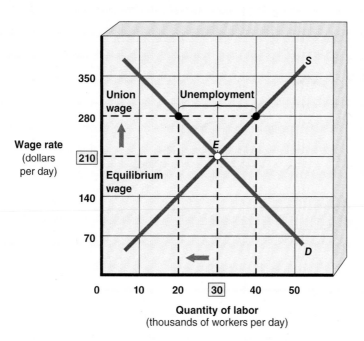

Wage rate (dollars per day)

Quantity of labor (thousands of workers per day)

SOURCE: © Cengage Learning 2014

EXHIBIT 8	Factors Causing Changes in Labor Demand and Labor Supply

Changes in labor demand	Changes in labor supply
1. Unions	1. Unions
2. Prices of substitute inputs	2. Demographic trends
3. Technology	3. Expectations of future income
4. Demand for final products	4. Changes in immigration laws
5. Marginal product of labor	5. Education and training

SOURCE: © Cengage Learning 2014

| EXHIBIT 9 | U.S. Union Membership, 1930–2010 |

As a percentage of nonfarm workers, union membership in the United States grew most rapidly during the decade 1935–1945. Since its peak in 1945, union membership as a percentage of the labor force has fallen to about the level it was in 1935.

SOURCE: *Statistical Abstract of the United States,* 2012, http://www.census.gov/compendia/statab/, Table 663.

Since World War II, union power has declined. Union membership has fallen from about 35 percent of the labor force in 1945 to 12 percent today. Since 1985, union membership of public-sector workers has changed little from 36 percent to 37 percent in 2010. On the other hand, union membership for private-sector workers has declined significantly from 14 percent to 7 percent over the same period of time.

Exhibit 10 shows the unionization rates in other countries. While in Sweden and Denmark nearly all workers belong to a union, union membership in the United States is far below that of other industrialized countries.

11-5 Employer Power

So far labor markets have been explained with employees possessing varying degrees of power to influence wage rates and employment while employers were competitive with no market power. However, significant power can exist on the employer side of the labor market. The extreme case occurs in a monopsony. Monopsony is a labor market in which a single firm hires labor. For example, a single textile mill, mining

Monopsony

A labor market in which a single firm hires labor.

EXHIBIT 10	Union Membership for Selected Countries, 2011

Union membership as a percentage of the civilian labor force in Denmark and Sweden is far above that of the United States. The unionization rates of other industrialized countries, such as Japan, Canada, Germany, the United Kingdom, and Italy, are also higher than the rate in the United States.

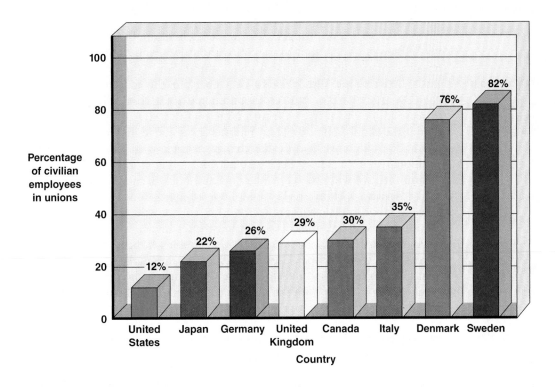

SOURCE: NationMaster.com, *Trade Union Membership by Country,* http://www.nationmaster.com/statistics.

company, or housing contractor might be the only buyer of labor in a particular market. The classical phrase for this situation is the "company town," where for miles around a small town, everyone's livelihood depends on a single employer. The reason for the monopsony is the absence of other firms in the area competing for relatively immobile labor because workers must acquire new skills to find work outside the company town market. Even if a firm doesn't dominate a local labor market, it may have monopsony power over certain types of labor. A hospital, for example, may be the only large employer of nurses in a local market; therefore, it has monopsony power.

11-5a MARGINAL FACTOR COST

This chapter began by assuming Computech operated in a competitive labor market in which no single employer in the electronic components market had any direct influence on the market wage rate. Recall from Exhibit 4 that Computech is a wage taker. More precisely, Computech hires the quantity of labor at the prevailing labor market equilibrium wage rate, which is determined by the point where the firm's downward-sloping MRP curve (demand curve for labor) intersects the horizontal supply curve of labor. The equilibrium wage rate is established by a competitive labor market beyond Computech's power to control.

Now we visit the isolated small town of Plainsville and find General Griffin's, which is a monopsonist producing turkeys. As shown in Exhibit 11, the supply of labor curve facing the monopsonist is upward sloping rather than horizontal. The reason is that General Griffin's is the only firm hiring workers in Plainsville, so it faces the industry, or entire, supply curve of labor in the Plainsville labor market. This situation compares to that of the monopolist, which faces the industry demand curve for a particular product. As a result, the monopolist in a product market cannot sell an additional unit of a good without lowering the price, and the marginal revenue curve falls below the demand curve. For the monopsonist, a distinction exists between the supply curve of labor and the marginal factor cost (MFC) curve. Marginal factor cost is the additional total cost resulting from a one-unit increase in the quantity of a factor. Note that the MFC curve starts above the bottom of the supply curve of labor and then rises above it. The MFC points are plotted at the midpoints because the change in total wage cost occurs between each additional unit of labor. Having made this observation, relax and take a deep breath; then we will proceed to the nuts and bolts of monopsonist theory.

If General Griffin's pays $3 per hour at point A on the upward-sloping supply curve of labor in Plainsville, only 1 worker will be willing to be hired. If the monopsonist wants to hire more labor, it must offer higher wages. If the firm raises its wage offer to $6 per hour for each worker (point B), the quantity of labor supplied increases to 2 workers per hour. In the exhibit, the total wage cost per hour in column (3) is computed by multiplying the wage rate per hour in column (1) times the number of workers per hour in column (2). At point A, the total wage cost per hour is $3, which equals the wage rate. At point B, the total wage cost per hour rises to $12, and MFC is greater than the wage rate of $6 per hour. The explanation is that all workers are assumed to perform the same job. Consequently, the first worker will demand to be paid the same wage rate as the second worker hired at the higher wage rate. Stated differently, General Griffin's must pay a higher wage not only to each additional worker but also to all previously hired workers. If General Griffin's attempts to pay different wage rates for the same job, worker morale will deteriorate, causing labor unrest. Comparing points A through D confirms that MFC is greater than the wage rate for a monopsonist, much like the monopolist's price, which is greater than the marginal revenue.

Marginal factor cost (MFC)

The additional total cost resulting from a one-unit increase in the quantity of a factor.

CONCLUSION: *Because the monopsonist can hire additional workers only by raising the wage rate for all workers, the marginal factor cost exceeds the wage rate.*

11-5b MONOPSONISTIC EQUILIBRIUM

How many workers will General Griffin's hire? To answer this question requires the demand curve for labor that traces labor's marginal revenue product (MRP), explained earlier in this chapter. Recall that MRP reflects the value or contribution of each additional worker because MRP is the increase in total revenue produced by hiring each additional worker. Also, as explained in Chapter 8, the profit-maximizing producer selects the level of output where marginal revenue equals

EXHIBIT 11	A Monopsonist Determines Its Wage Rate

The monopsonist, General Griffin's, faces the industry upward-sloping supply curve of labor in the small town of Plainsville. As the wage rate rises, all workers must be paid the same higher wage. As a result, the change in total wage cost [marginal factor cost in column (4)] exceeds the wage paid to the last worker [column (1)]. The MFC curve therefore lies above the supply curve of labor.

The demand curve for labor is the marginal revenue product (MRP), or the worth to the monopsonist of each worker it hires. The intersection of the MFC and MRP curves at point E determines that General Griffin's hires 2 workers per hour. Because this firm has a monopsony in the Plainsville labor market, it can pay $6 per hour at point B on the supply curve of labor, which is enough to attract 2 workers. However, the worker is exploited because the MRP at point E for the second worker is $12 per hour and the wage rate is only $6. In a competitive labor market, the equilibrium would be at point C, and General Griffin's would pay a higher wage and employ more workers.

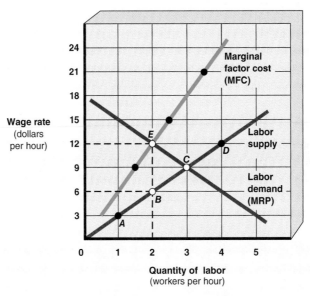

	(1)	(2)	(3)	(4)
		Labor Input	Total Wage Cost	Marginal Factor Cost
	Wage Rate	(workers	(per hour)	(MFC)
Points	(per hour)	per hour)	[(1) × (2)]	[Δ(3)/Δ(2)]
	$ 0	0	$ 0	
				$ 3
A	3	1	3	
				9
B	6	2	12	
				15
C	9	3	27	
				21
D	12	4	48	

SOURCE: © Cengage Learning 2014

marginal cost. Similarly, *the monopsonist in the labor market hires the quantity of labor at which the marginal revenue product of labor equals its marginal factor cost.*

In Exhibit 11, General Griffin's will follow the MRP = MFC rule by hiring 2 workers, determined by the intersection of the MRP and MFC curves at point *E*. But pay special attention to this point: The monopsonist is a "wage maker." It has labor market power and does not have to pay $12 per hour, which equals the contribution of the second worker measured by his or her MRP. Instead of paying workers what their services are worth, the monopsonist follows the supply curve of labor, selects point *B*, and pays $6 per hour rather than $12 per hour. Since $6 per hour is all the firm must pay to attract and hire two workers, the monopsonist can exploit labor by paying less than its marginal revenue product.

One alternative for labor facing a powerful employer is to organize a powerful union and engage in collective bargaining. Totally successful collective bargaining by a labor union could raise the wage rate from $6 per hour at point *B* to $12 per hour at point *E*. General Griffin's will resist the union's demands and offer a lower wage closer to point *B*. Thus, points *B* and *E* represent the boundaries of a potential final settlement. What the negotiated final equilibrium wage rate will be depends on the tactics and resources of the negotiating parties.

Finally, suppose the monopsony is broken up into a large number of small firms. Recall from earlier in this chapter that in competitive labor markets, additional workers are hired to the point where the wage rate is equal to the MRP. In this case, the supply curve of labor intersects the MRP (demand) curve at point *C*, and more workers would be hired with $9 per hour paid to each worker.

> **CONCLUSION:** *A monopsonist hires fewer workers and pays a lower wage than a firm in a competitive labor market.*

✔ CHECKPOINTS

Can the Minimum Wage Create Jobs?

In Chapter 4, Exhibit 5 explained that the effect of the minimum wage in a competitive labor market is to decrease the number of unskilled workers employed. Assume the minimum wage is $9, and consider the effect on the monopsonist represented in Exhibit 11. This means by law the monopsonist cannot hire a worker for a lower wage. In the case of monopsony, contrary to the case of perfect competition, can the minimum wage increase the number of persons working? Explain your answer using Exhibit 11.

If You Don't Like It, Mickey, Take Your Bat and Go Home

Mickey Mantle described his salary negotiations with the Yankees in his autobiography *The Mick*. After winning baseball's Triple Crown in 1955, his salary increased from about $85,000 to $100,000. The next season, he raised his batting average even higher, and the Yankee team owner offered him a pay cut. What is the most likely explanation for the owner's behavior—an increase in the supply of star baseball players, owner monopsony power, or the owner's desire that Mantle find another team?

Should College Athletes Be Paid?

Applicable concept: monopsony

It was perfect football weather on a beautiful autumn Saturday at Nebraska State's stadium. There was a hush in the crowd of 80,000 as the clock showed 5 seconds left in the game and the scoreboard read Home 26, Visitor 30. The Screaming Eagles were playing the Fighting Irish, and the season was on the line. With time running out, the Eagles All-American quarterback Joe Wyoming launched a desperation pass from his 45-yard line. The pass hit the extended fingers of a wide receiver who leaped over three defenders at the Irish 25-yard line and then ran into the end zone all alone. The home crowd roared with joy after staring defeat in the face.

So the season had been in the hands of Joe Wyoming, who received a full scholarship that cost the university more than $40,000 over four years. Because Joe led the Eagles to victory over Notre Dame, the team played in the Sugar Bowl, which paid Nebraska State $5 million for the appearance. In addition, the next year's ticket sales, alumni contributions, and trademark licensing boosted revenues $10 million, while applications for admission to the university increased sharply.

Economist John Leonard argued that college athletes are clearly underpaid because players cannot be paid salaries under National Collegiate Athletic Association (NCAA) rules. His study estimated that a star college football player who is named to an All-American team generates a marginal revenue

Shutterstock.com/Susan Law Cain

product of $100,000 per year for the university. Yet that athlete is paid only a $10,000 scholarship per year.

In Chapter 10, a cartel was explained as a group of firms that use a collusive agreement to act as a monopoly. NCAA regulations serve as a collusive agreement among colleges and universities to act as a monopsony and hire the services of college-bound athletes. Just like an output or sellers' cartel, such as the Organization of Petroleum Exporting Countries (OPEC), the NCAA must enforce the rules against cheaters.

Because this agreement holds players' wages far below their marginal revenue product, the gap creates an incentive for schools to offer "illegal" inducements of cars, money, clothes, and trips to attract good players. Such cheating benefits the college athletes whose wages are raised closer to their marginal revenue products. A school that is not caught benefits by recruiting better players, achieving athletic success, and receiving greater sports

revenue. Schools that follow the rules must depend on the NCAA to punish cheaters by taking away TV appearances, tournament play, bowl invitations, and scholarships.

In 2011, Steve Spurrier, head football coach of the University of South Carolina, proposed a plan to pay football players that would not cost schools or conferences any money. To give players "a piece of the pie," Spurrier proposed that coaches would pay 70 players $300 per game. He acknowledged that his plan probably would not get very far, but it could open the door for future dialogue on this issue. In 2012, the new playoff system sparked discussion of how new television revenue could be shared with players.

Analyze the Issue

Do you favor paying college athletes salaries determined by a competitive labor market rather than by an NCAA agreement? Explain.

Source: © Cengage Learning 2014

Key Concepts

Marginal revenue product (MRP)
Demand curve for labor
Derived demand

Supply curve of labor
Human capital
Collective bargaining

Monopsony
Marginal factor cost (MFC)

Summary

- **Marginal revenue product (MRP)** is determined by a worker's contribution to a firm's total revenue. Algebraically, the marginal revenue product equals the price of the product times the worker's marginal product: $MRP = P \times MP$.
- The **demand curve for labor** shows the quantities of labor a firm is willing to hire at different prices of labor. The marginal revenue product (MRP) of labor curve is the firm's demand curve for labor. Summing individual demand for labor curves gives the market demand curve for labor.

Demand Curve for Labor

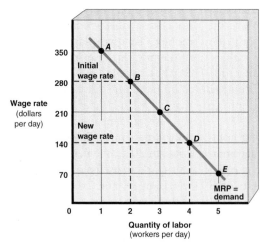

SOURCE: © Cengage Learning 2014

- **Derived demand** means that a firm demands labor because labor is productive. Changes in consumer demand for a product cause changes in the demand for labor and for other resources used to make the product.
- The **supply curve of labor** shows the quantities of workers willing to work at different prices of

labor. The market supply curve of labor is derived by adding the individual supply curves of labor.

Supply Curve of Labor

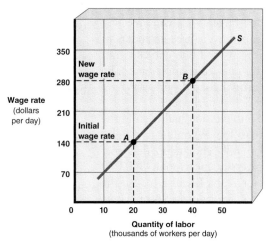

SOURCE: © Cengage Learning 2014

- **Human capital** is the accumulated investment people make in education, training, experience, and health in order to make themselves more productive. One explanation for earnings differences is differences in human capital.
- **Collective bargaining** is the process through which a union and management negotiate a labor contract.
- **Monopsony** is a labor market in which a single firm hires labor. Because the monopsonist faces the industry supply curve of labor and each worker is paid the same wage, changes in total wage cost exceed the wage rate necessary to hire each additional worker. As a result, the **marginal factor cost (MFC)** of labor curve,

which measures changes in total wage cost per worker, lies above the supply curve of labor. The monopsonist's wage rate and quantity of labor are determined where the MFC equals MRP. Since at this point the worker's MRP is greater than the wage paid, the monopsonist exploits workers.

Monopsony

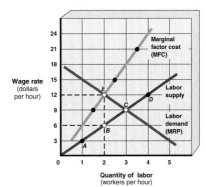

SOURCE: © Cengage Learning 2014

Summary of Conclusion Statements

- A perfectly competitive firm's marginal revenue product is equal to the marginal product of its labor times the price of its product. Expressed as a formula: MRP = P × MP.
- A firm hires additional workers up to the point where the MRP equals the wage rate.

- Because the monopsonist can hire additional workers only by raising the wage rate for all workers, the marginal factor cost exceeds the wage rate.
- A monopsonist hires fewer workers and pays a lower wage than a firm in a competitive labor market.

Study Questions and Problems

1. Consider this statement: "Workers demand jobs, and employers supply jobs." Do you agree or disagree? Explain.

2. The Zippy Paper Company has no control over either the price of paper or the wage it pays its workers. The following table shows the relationship between the number of workers Zippy hires and total output:

Labor input (workers per day)	Total output (boxes of paper per day)
0	0
1	15
2	27
3	36
4	43
5	48
6	51

Assuming the selling price is $10 per box, answer the following questions:
   a. What is the marginal revenue product (MRP) of each worker?
   b. How many workers will Zippy hire if the wage rate is $100 per day?
   c. How many workers will Zippy hire if the wage rate is $75 per day?
   d. Assume the wage rate is $75 per day and the price of a box of paper is $20. How many workers will Zippy hire?

3. Assume the Grand Slam Baseball Store sells $100 worth of baseball cards each day, with 1 employee operating the store. The owner decides to hire a second worker, and the 2 workers together sell $150 worth of baseball cards. What is the second worker's marginal revenue product (MRP)? If the price per card sold is $5, what is the second worker's marginal product (MP)?

4. What is the relationship between the marginal revenue product (MRP) and the demand curve for labor?

5. The market supply curve of labor is upward sloping, but the supply curve of labor for a single firm is horizontal. Explain why.

6. Assume the labor market for loggers is perfectly competitive. How would each of the following events influence the wage rate loggers are paid?
   a. Consumers boycott products made with wood.
   b. Loggers form a union that requires longer apprenticeships, charges high fees, and uses other devices designed to reduce union membership.

7. How does a human capital investment in education increase your lifetime earnings?

8. Suppose states pass laws requiring public school teachers to have a master's degree in order to retain their teaching certificates. What effect would this legislation have on the labor market for teachers?

9. Use the data in question 2, and assume the equilibrium wage rate is $90 per day, determined in a perfectly competitive labor market. Now explain the impact of a union-negotiated collective bargaining agreement that changes the wage rate to $100 per day.

10. Some economists argue that the American Medical Association and the American Bar Association create an effect on labor markets similar to that of a labor union. Do you agree?

11. Assume the Jaguars were in the process of hiring players. Using the following hypothetical table of data, construct a graph to determine the number of quarterbacks the Jaguars hired and the salary paid to each quarterback. Assuming the labor market was competitive, what would be the number of quarterbacks hired and the salary each was paid?

(1) Salary (thousands of dollars)	(2) Number of quarterbacks	(3) Total cost of quarterbacks (thousands of dollars)	(4) Marginal factor cost (MFC) (thousands of dollars)	(5) Marginal revenue product (MRP) (thousands of dollars)
$ 0	0	$ 0	–	–
100	1	100	$100	$700
200	2	400	300	600
300	3	900	500	500
400	4	1,600	700	400
500	5	2,500	900	300

For Online Exercises, go to the Tucker Web site at www.cengage.com/economics/tucker.

✓ CHECKPOINT ANSWERS

Can the Minimum Wage Create Jobs?

The minimum wage of $9 corresponds to point C in Exhibit 11. At this point, the labor supply and labor demand (MRP) curves intersect. Thus, the effect of the minimum wage is to force the monopsonist to operate at the equilibrium that would be established in a competitive labor market. If you said that under monopsony the minimum wage could raise the wage rate and create additional employment, YOU ARE CORRECT.

If You Don't Like It, Mickey, Take Your Bat and Go Home

Baseball players had no free-agent rights in the 1950s. If Mantle did not like the salary offer, his only choice was to go back to his home in Oklahoma. Faced with that alternative, he accepted the salary cut. If you said the team owner achieved monopsony power by prohibiting players from going to another team, YOU ARE CORRECT.

Sample Quiz

For an explanation of the correct answers, visit the Tucker Web site at www.cengage.com/economics/tucker.

1. Alan Jones owns a company that sells life insurance. When he employs 10 salespersons, his firm sells $200,000 worth of contracts per week, and when he employs 11 salespersons, total revenue is $210,000. The marginal revenue product of the 11th salesperson is
   a. $410,000.
   b. $10,000.
   c. $20,000.
   d. $210,000.

2. The demand for labor is
   a. derived demand.
   b. featherbedding demand.
   c. marginal utility demand.
   d. All of the answers above are correct.

3. If product price increases, then
   a. MP will increase.
   b. MFC will increase.
   c. MRP will increase.
   d. MP will decrease.

4. Which of the following statements is *true*?
   a. Derived demand for labor depends on the demand for the product labor produces.
   b. Unions can either increase demand or decrease the supply of labor.
   c. Investment in human capital is expected to increase the demand for those workers.
   d. All the answers above are correct.

5. The optimal hiring rule is to employ labor up to the point where
   a. wage = MFC.
   b. wage = MP.
   c. wage = MR.
   d. wage = MRP.

6. In Exhibit 12, when the marginal revenue product is $20, firms should
   a. continue hiring.
   b. stop hiring.
   c. start firing.
   d. pay a wage above $15 to its workers.

EXHIBIT 12	A Perfectly Competitive Labor Market	
Quantity of labor (thousands)	Marginal revenue product	Total labor cost
5	$25	$ 5
10	20	10
15	15	15
20	10	20
25	5	25

SOURCE: © Cengage Learning 2014

7. In Exhibit 12, how many thousands of workers are the firms willing to hire?
   a. 20
   b. 10
   c. 15
   d. All 25 workers

8. What happens to the MP of labor when the market price of the good produced increases?
   a. Increases proportional to price
   b. Decreases proportional to price
   c. Stays the same
   d. Falls because quantity demanded falls

9. A union can influence the demand for labor by
   a. requiring union fees.
   b. raising union fees.
   c. using effective advertising that convinces customers to buy the "union label."
   d. doing all of the above.

10. A union can influence the equilibrium wage rate by
    a. collective bargaining.
    b. featherbedding.
    c. lobbying for legislation to reduce immigration.
    d. doing all of the above.

Sample Quiz *continued*

11. Which of the following countries has the largest union membership measured as the percentage of civilian employees in unions?
    a. The United States
    b. Japan
    c. The United Kingdom
    d. Sweden

12. Suppose a firm can hire 100 workers at $8.00 per hour but must pay $8.05 per hour to hire 101 workers. Marginal factor cost (MFC) for the 101st worker is approximately equal to
    a. $8.00.
    b. $8.05.
    c. $13.05.
    d. $13.00.

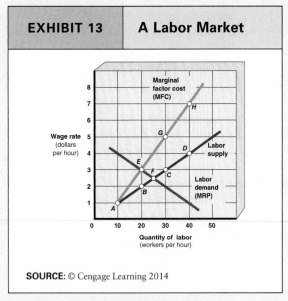

EXHIBIT 13	A Labor Market

SOURCE: © Cengage Learning 2014

13. If the labor market shown in Exhibit 13 is competitive, the wage rate and number of workers employed will be determined at point
    a. *A.*
    b. *B.*
    c. *C.*
    d. *D.*
    e. *F.*

14. If the labor market shown in Exhibit 13 is a monopsony, the wage rate and number of workers employed will be determined at point
    a. *A.*
    b. *B.*
    c. *C.*
    d. *D.*
    e. *F.*

15. Which of the following is *true* for a monopsonist?
    a. wage > TWC
    b. wage > MFC
    c. wage = MFC
    d. wage = MRP
    e. wage < MFC

16. A technological advance that increases the productivity of teachers can be expected to have what effects on the equilibrium labor market for teachers?
    a. Wages will rise, and quantity of labor will fall.
    b. Wages will rise, and quantity of labor will rise.
    c. Wages will fall, and quantity of labor will fall.
    d. Wages will fall, and quantity of labor will rise.
    e. Wages and quantity of labor will remain the same.

17. The optimal number of workers to be hired by a firm operating in a competitive labor market is where
    a. P = MRP.
    b. MP = MRP.
    c. MRP = w.
    d. P = w.

18. A technological advance that increases labor productivity will
    a. lower wages.
    b. decrease the demand for labor as fewer workers are needed.
    c. decrease the supply of labor as fewer workers are needed.
    d. increase the demand for labor as MP rises.
    e. decrease the demand for labor as MP falls.

Sample Quiz *continued*

19. A monopsonist's marginal factor cost (MFC) curve lies above its supply curve because the firm must
    a. lower the factor price to hire more.
    b. increase the price of its product to sell more.
    c. increase the factor price to hire more.
    d. lower the product price to sell more.

20. In Exhibit 14, the marginal factor cost of the eighth employee is
    a. $14.
    b. $13.
    c. $21.
    d. $23.
    e. $112.

EXHIBIT 14	Labor and Wage Rate Data
Labor	Wage
6	$12
7	13
8	14
9	15
10	16

SOURCE: © Cengage Learning 2014

This road map feature helps you tie together material in the part as you travel the Economic Way of Thinking Highway. The following are review questions listed by chapter from the previous part. The key concept in each question is given for emphasis, and each question or set of questions concludes with an interactive game to reinforce the concepts. Go to the Tucker Web site at www.cengage.com/economics/tucker, select the chapter, and play the visual causation chain game designed to make learning fun. Enjoy the cheers when you are correct and suffer the jeers if you miss. The correct answers to the multiple choice questions are given in Appendix C of the text.

CHAPTER **8.** PERFECT COMPETITION

1. **Key Concept: Short-Run Shutdown Point**
   Suppose product price is fixed at $24, MR = MC at Q = 200, AFC = $6, AVC = $25. What do you advise this firm to do?
   a. Increase output.
   b. Decrease output.
   c. Shut down operations.
   d. Stay at the current output; the firm is earning a profit of $1,400.
   e. Stay at the current output; the firm is losing $1,400.

   Causation Chain Game
   The Short-Run Shutdown Point—Exhibit 6

2. **Key Concept: Long-Run Equilibrium**
   Consider a firm operating with the following: price = 10, MR = 10, MC = 10, ATC = 10. This firm is
   a. making an economic profit of 10.
   b. an example of monopolistic competition.
   c. going to go out of business in the long run.
   d. a monopolist for a product with a relatively inelastic demand.
   e. perfectly competitive in long-run equilibrium.

   Causation Chain Game
   Long-Run Perfectly Competitive Equilibrium—Exhibit 10

3. **Key Concept: Constant-Cost Industry**
   Assume the short-run average total cost for a perfectly competitive industry remains constant as the output of the industry expands. In the long run, the industry supply curve will
   a. have a positive slope.
   b. have a negative slope.

c. be perfectly horizontal.
d. be perfectly vertical.

Causation Chain Game
Long-Run Supply in a Constant-Cost Industry—Exhibit 11

4. **Key Concept: Decreasing-Cost Industry**
   Assume the short-run average total cost for a perfectly competitive industry
   decreases as the output of the industry expands. In the long run, the industry
   supply curve will
   a. have a positive slope.
   b. have a negative slope.
   c. be perfectly horizontal.
   d. be perfectly vertical.

Causation Chain Game
Long-Run Supply in Decreasing-Cost Industry—Exhibit 12

5. **Key Concept: Increasing-Cost Industry**
   Suppose that, in the long run, the price of feature films rises as the movie
   production industry expands. We can conclude that movie production is a(an)
   a. increasing-cost industry.
   b. constant-cost industry.
   c. decreasing-cost industry.
   d. marginal-cost industry.

Causation Chain Game
Long-Run Supply in an Increasing-Cost Industry—Exhibit 13

CHAPTER **9.** MONOPOLY

6. **Key Concept: Profit Maximization**
   Assume a monopolist's marginal cost and marginal revenue curves intersect
   and the demand curve passes above its average total cost curve. The firm will
   a. make an economic profit.
   b. stay in operation in the short run, but shut down in the long run.
   c. shut down in the short run.
   d. lower the price.

7. **Key Concept: Loss Minimization**
   Assume a monopolist's marginal cost and marginal revenue curves intersect
   and the demand curve passes above its average total cost curve. The firm will
   a. make an economic profit.
   b. stay in operation in the short run, but shut down in the long run.
   c. shut down in the short run.
   d. lower the price.

Causation Chain Game
Profit Maximization and Loss Minimization—Exhibits 4–5

CHAPTER 10. MONOPOLISTIC COMPETITION AND OLIGOPOLY

8. **Key Concept: Long-Run Monopolistic Competition**
   In the long run, the economic profits of Hoot's Chicken 'n' Ribs, a monopolistic competitor, are
   a. not eliminated, because competition is not perfect.
   b. not eliminated, because the demand curve slopes downward.
   c. eliminated due to firms entering the industry.
   d. eliminated due to firms leaving the industry.
   e. not eliminated, because firms cannot enter the industry.

   Causation Chain Game
   A Monopolistically Competitive Firm in the Long Run—Exhibit 3

CHAPTER 11. LABOR MARKETS

9. **Key Concept: Market Supply Curve of Labor**
   Which of the following statements concerning the supply of labor is *true*?
   a. The supply of labor is determined by the prevailing wage rate.
   b. The labor supply curve is downward sloping.
   c. The wage rate has no effect on the supply of labor.
   d. None of the above are true.

   Causation Chain Game
   The Market Supply Curve of Labor—Exhibit 3

10. **Key Concept: Increase in Demand for Labor**
    Featherbedding allows unions to increase wages by
    a. limiting the supply of labor.
    b. increasing firms' demand for labor.
    c. forcing firms to accept higher-than-equilibrium wages.
    d. reducing labor share of payroll taxes.

    Causation Chain Game
    A Union Causes an Increase in the Demand Curve for Labor—Exhibit 5

11. **Key Concept: Decrease in Supply of Labor**
    Which of the following statements is *true*?
    a. Derived demand for labor depends on the demand for the product labor produces.
    b. Unions can either increase demand or decrease the supply of labor.
    c. Investment in human capital is expected to increase the demand for those workers.
    d. All of the above are true.

    Causation Chain Game
    A Union Causes a Decrease in the Supply Curve of Labor—Exhibit 6

Microeconomics Policy Issues

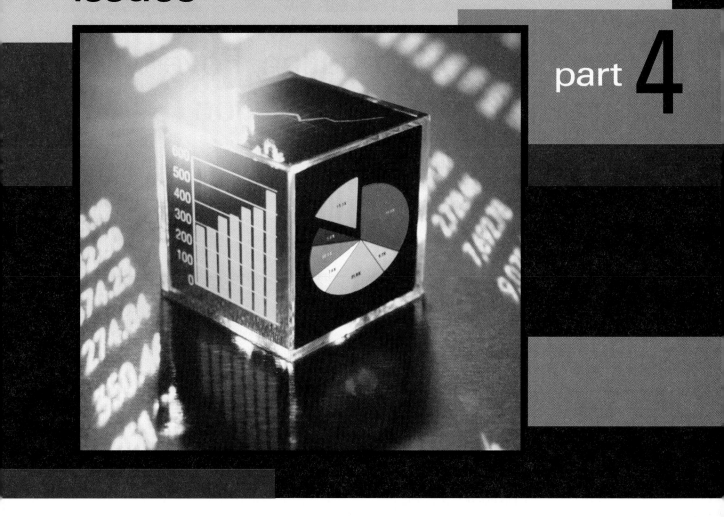

part 4

These three chapters apply micro principles learned in previous chapters to explore policy issues concerning some important economic topics. The first chapter in this part extends the theory of labor markets into an examination of actual data on income and poverty. The second chapter mixes politics and economic theory to discuss such interesting topics as the Microsoft case and the deregulation of energy. The third chapter takes a closer look at ways to deal with externalities, such as pollution permits, which are actually traded on the Chicago Board of Trade.

chapter 12

Income Distribution, Poverty, and Discrimination

The previous chapter examined how variations in wages are determined in competitive and monopsonistic labor markets. These labor supply and demand models do not give the complete picture of labor markets. In this chapter, we turn our attention to the distribution of income, poverty, and discrimination, which are important topics related to labor market wage decisions. The chapter begins by exploring the controversial issue of how the total family income "pie" is cut into various size "slices" or shares for different groups of families. You will examine government data that indicate the trend over the years in the share of income for the richest fifth of the population and the poorest fifth. Here the hotly contested issue of whether the "rich got richer" at the expense of the poor is addressed. In addition, the inequality of income in the United States is compared to that of other countries.

Poverty is an unhappy consequence of an unequal income distribution. Eighteenth-century English poet and essayist Samuel Johnson stated, "A decent provision for the poor is the true test of civilization." One purpose of this chapter is to define poverty and who are the poor. Another objective is to discuss government programs that aid the poor and provide criticisms of these programs. A special feature concerns the important issue of Social Security, past, present, and future.

The chapter concludes with the subject of discrimination, which is one possible explanation for unequal income distribution and poverty. Here you will apply the supply and demand model to explain why women earn less on average than men and African Americans earn less than whites.

In this chapter, you will learn to solve these economics puzzles:

- Could the rich become richer and other income groups also become better off?
- How can a negative income tax solve the welfare controversy?
- Is pay for females fair?

12-1 The Distribution of Income

One function of labor markets is to determine the *distribution of income*—that is, how wages and salaries are divided among members of society. Recall from Chapter 2 that the *For Whom* question is one of the three basic questions that any economic system must answer. Here we study the *For Whom* question in more detail.

12-1a TRENDS IN INCOME DISTRIBUTION

One way to analyze the distribution of income in the United States is illustrated in Exhibit 1. In column 1 of this exhibit, families are divided into six groups according to the percentage of the total annual money income they received. The remaining columns of the table give the percentages of the total money income for each of the six groups in selected years since 1929. These data reveal changes in the distribution of income among families over time. For example, families with income in the top 5 percent in 1929 earned about 9 percent more of the total income pie than they did in 2011. Nonetheless, there is concern that since 1970, the percentage of income received by families in the lowest 20 percent group has fallen, while the income percentages received by the families in the highest fifth and the highest 5 percent have risen.

As shown in Exhibit 1, there is an unequal distribution of income among families. Why didn't each fifth of the families receive 20 percent of the total income? There are many reasons. For example, Exhibit 2 reveals that families headed by a college graduate fare better than those headed by an individual with less education. Recall from the previous chapter that human capital refers to education and skills that increase a worker's productivity. Workers with a greater investment in human capital are likely to be worth more to an employer. Data in this exhibit also indicate that families headed by a male generally earn more than those headed by a female.

EXHIBIT 1	The Division of Total Annual Money Income among Families, 1929–2011					
Percentage of families	**1929**	**1947**	**1970**	**1980**	**1990**	**2011**
Highest 5%	30%	17%	16%	15%	17%	21%
Highest fifth	54	43	41	41	44	49
Second-highest fifth	19	23	24	24	24	23
Middle fifth	14	17	18	18	16	15
Second-lowest fifth	9	12	12	12	11	9
Lowest fifth	4	5	5	5	5	4

SOURCE: U.S. Bureau of the Census, *Historical Income Tables*, http://www.census.gov/hhes/www/income/income.html, Table F-2.

12-1b EQUALITY VERSUS EFFICIENCY

Because the data presented in Exhibits 1 and 2 show that an unequal distribution of income exists in the United States, the normative question to be debated concerns the pros and cons of a more equal income distribution. Those who favor greater equality fear the link between the rich and political power. The wealthy may well use their money to influence national policies that benefit the rich. It is also argued that income inequality results in unequal opportunities for various groups. For example, children of the poor have difficulty obtaining a college education. Consequently, their underutilized productive capacity is a waste of human capital. The poor are also unable to afford health care, and this is a national concern.

Advocates of income inequality pose this question. Suppose you had your choice of living in egalitarian society *A*, where every person earns $40,000 a year, or society *B*, where 20 percent earn $100,000 and 80 percent earn $30,000. You would likely choose society *B* because the incentive to earn more and live better is worth the risk of earning less and living worse. After all, why is the average income higher in society *B*? The answer is that income inequality gives people an incentive to be productive. In contrast, people in society *A* lack such motivation because everyone earns the same income. Those who favor equality of income believe that critics ignore the nonmonetary incentives that can motivate people, such as pride in one's work and nation.

A frequently debated topic concerning income inequality is whether the "rich are getting richer." As we observed earlier, the data in Exhibit 1 reveal that the percentages of total income received by the highest 5 percent and the highest fifth have increased in recent decades, while the percentages received by each of the fifths below the highest decreased slightly.

EXHIBIT 2	Median Money Income of Families, 2011
Characteristic	**Median income***
All families	$60,974
Families headed by a male	43,069
Families headed by a female	30,259
Families with head aged 25–34 years	50,643
Families with head aged 65 years and over	48,538
Families headed by person with less than ninth-grade education	27,815
Families headed by a high school graduate	48,460
Families headed by a person with at least a bachelor's degree	100,096

*Fifty percent of families earn less than the median income, and 50 percent earn more.

SOURCE: U.S. Bureau of the Census, *Historical Income Tables*, http://www.census.gov/hhes/www/income/income.html, Tables F-7, F-11, and F-18.

CONCLUSION: *Measured by distribution of family money income, the richest families have become a little richer and the rest of the family groups, a little poorer in recent decades.*

It is important to note that simply observing changes in income distribution over time does not tell the whole story. Exhibit 3 traces real median family income, adjusted for rising prices, for the period 1980–2011. This measure indicates the trend of the average level of income received by all groups. Generally, the trend for real median income since the 1980s has been upward. This means the size of the income "pie" grew, and, therefore, all of the slices grew larger. However, consistent with the distribution data in Exhibit 1, the relative share of the pie for those with the biggest slice grew slightly larger. In 2000, real median income reached a new high before falling following the recession of 2001 and the Great Recession of 2007–2009.

EXHIBIT 3	Real Median Family Income, 1980–2011

Real median income measures the income adjusted for inflation received by all families in the United States. Fifty percent of families earn less and 50 percent earn more than the median income. The trend of this measure was generally upward until 2000. In 2000, real median income reached a new high before falling following the recession of 2001 and the Great Recession of 2007–2009. In 2011, median family income fell to $60,974.

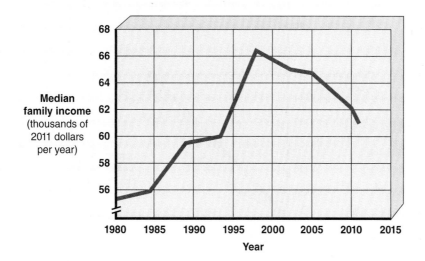

SOURCE: U.S. Bureau of the Census, *Historical Income Tables*, http://www.census.gov/hhes/www/income/income.html, Table F-7.

12-1c THE LORENZ CURVE

Lorenz curve

A graph of the actual cumulative distribution of income compared to a perfectly equal cumulative distribution of income.

The distribution of income data presented in Exhibit 1 can be represented by the Lorenz curve. The Lorenz curve is a graph of the actual cumulative distribution of income compared to a perfectly equal cumulative distribution of income. This curve, is a primary tool for measuring income distribution, developed in 1905 by statistician M. O. Lorenz. Look at the hypothetical Lorenz curve in Exhibit 4. The vertical axis measures the *cumulative* percentage of family income, and the horizontal axis measures the *cumulative* percentage of families from poorest to richest. Starting in the lower left-hand corner on the graph, 0 percent of the families earned 0 percent of the cumulative percentage of money income. At the upper right-hand corner on the graph, 100 percent of the families earned 100 percent of the cumulative percentage of money income. The combination of other total family-total money income points between 0 and 100 percent forms the Lorenz curve.

EXHIBIT 4	A Hypothetical Lorenz Curve

The Lorenz curve shows the cumulative percentage of money income earned from 0 to 100 percent by the cumulative percentage of families, also from 0 to 100 percent. If the income distribution follows the 45-degree perfect equality line, 20 percent of the families earn 20 percent of total money income, 40 percent receive 40 percent of total money income, and so on. The shaded area between the perfect equality line and the Lorenz curve measures the degree of inequality in the distribution of income. The more the Lorenz curve is bowed outward, the more unequal the distribution of income is.

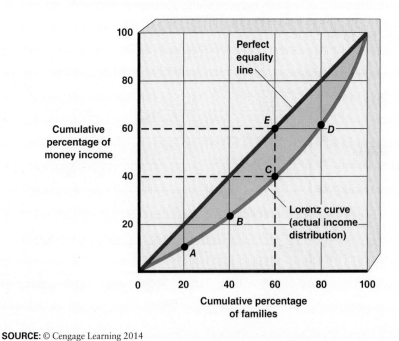

SOURCE: © Cengage Learning 2014

Reading along the horizontal axis, each fifth (20 percent) of the cumulative percentage of families corresponds to its cumulative share of income earned measured along the curve. At point *A*, the lowest 20 percent of families receive 10 percent of total or cumulative income. To read this, go from the 20 percent point on the horizontal axis up to point *A* on the Lorenz curve. Then draw a horizontal line to the vertical axis, and read that it intersects this axis at 10 percent. Point *B* is interpreted as the lowest 40 percent of families earning 10 percent plus 15 percent, which equals a cumulative share of 25 percent. Similarly, point *C* is the cumulative share earned by the lowest 60 percent of families, which equals 40 percent. Finally, point *D* is a bit tricky to interpret. At this point, the lowest 80 percent of families receive about 62 percent of total income. And here is the twist. You must interpret that the richest 20 percent of families earn 38 percent of income (100 percent − 62 percent).

We now turn to the 45-degree line above the Lorenz curve that cuts the box in half. This line represents perfect equality: 20 percent of the families receive 20 percent of total income, 40 percent of the families receive 40 percent of total income, and so on. The distance of the Lorenz curve from the perfect equality line is therefore a measure of unequal income distribution. The gap between points *C* and *E*, for example, indicates that 60 percent of families earn 20 percent less of total income than required for perfect equality. Similar measurements generate the shaded area between the Lorenz curve and the perfect equality line. Thus, the shaded area is a measure of the degree of income inequality for our hypothetical data. A larger shaded area would mean greater income inequality, and the shape of the Lorenz curve would become more bowed outward. A smaller shaded area would represent a more equal income distribution, and the Lorenz curve would be a flatter curve.

It is very important to note that there are limitations associated with using money income statistics. Such data are not adjusted for government-provided food stamps, medical care, housing, or other goods and services. Money income also reflects income before taxes and does not measure unreported income or wealth. Still, used carefully, the Lorenz curve is a convenient tool for visualizing the degree of income inequality.

12-1d INCOME DISTRIBUTION TREND IN THE UNITED STATES

In Exhibit 1, we looked at income distributions for selected years between 1929 and 2011. What can we conclude from these data using the Lorenz curve? Has the overall income distribution become more or less equal? The table in Exhibit 5 restates the income share data for 1929 and 2011 from Exhibit 1, and the cumulative percentage shares of families of quintiles are calculated from the percentage shares.

Exhibit 5 suggests that overall money income distribution has changed little over the period. In the exhibit, there is only a small shaded area between the 1929 and 2011 Lorenz curves. However, the share of income received by the highest fifth of families fell from 54 percent in 1929 to 49 percent in 2011. Note that comparing other years can lead to different conclusions. For example, as shown in Exhibit 1, the distribution of income is less equal since 1970.

EXHIBIT 5	**Lorenz Curves for Family Income Distribution in the United States, 1929 and 2011**

Since 1929, the Lorenz curve has shifted somewhat inward toward the perfect equality line. Thus, there has been a reduction in the inequality of distribution of family money income since 1929.

	1929		2011	
Percentage of families	**Percentage share**	**Cumulative share**	**Percentage share**	**Cumulative share**
Lowest fifth	4%	4%	4%	4%
Second-lowest fifth	9	13	9	13
Middle fifth	14	27	15	28
Second-highest fifth	19	46	23	51
Highest fifth	54	100	49	100

SOURCE: © Cengage Learning 2014

CONCLUSION: *The Lorenz curve has shifted only slightly inward, and therefore closer to the perfect equality line between 1929 and 2011.*

EXHIBIT 6	Lorenz Curves for Selected Countries

Comparing Lorenz curves for the United States, the Czech Republic, and Brazil reveals that income is distributed more equally in the Czech Republic than in the United States and Brazil. As illustrated by the Lorenz curve for Brazil, income inequality is usually greater in less-developed countries.

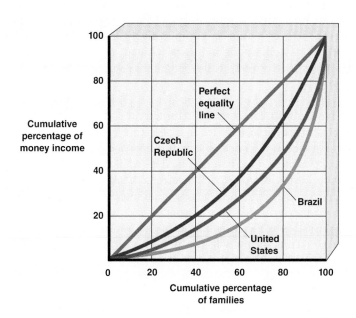

SOURCE: The World Bank Group, http://data.worldbank.org/data-catolog.

12-2 Global Comparisons of Income Distribution

How does the distribution of income in the United States compare with that of other countries? Exhibit 6 presents separate Lorenz curves for the United States, the Czech Republic, and Brazil. This exhibit indicates that the degree of income inequality in the United States exceeds that of the Czech Republic. On the other hand, income distribution is more equal in the United States than in Brazil. In general, the distribution of income in developed nations, such as the United States, Germany, Italy, and Sweden, is more equal than in developing nations, such as Brazil, Mexico, and Zimbabwe.

12-3 Poverty

Having discussed the broader question of how the degree of income distribution inequality is measured, we now turn the spotlight on the fiercely debated issue of poverty. We are all disturbed by homelessness and hungry children. How can poverty exist in a nation of abundance such as the United States? Can economists offer useful ideas to reform and improve our current welfare system? Most of the nation agrees that the welfare system must undergo reforms to reduce poverty, cut welfare dependency, and save taxpayers money. The first step to understanding the problem is to ask this question: Who is poor?

12-3a DEFINING POVERTY

What is poverty? Is it eating Spam when others are eating steak? Or is poverty a family having one car when others have two or more? Is the poverty standard only a matter of normative arguments? Indeed, the term *poverty* is difficult to define. A person whose income is comparatively low in the United States may be viewed as being well off in a less-developed country. Or what we in the United States regard as poverty today might have seemed to be a life of luxury 200 years ago.

There are two views of poverty. One defines poverty in *absolute* terms, and the other defines poverty in *relative* terms. Absolute poverty can be defined as a dollar figure that represents some level of income per year required to purchase some minimum amount of goods and services essential to meeting a person's or a family's basic needs. In contrast, relative poverty might be defined as a level of income that places a person or family in the lowest, say, 20 percent of all persons or families receiving incomes. An unequal distribution of income guarantees that some persons or families will occupy in relative terms the bottom rung of the income ladder. The U.S. government first established an official definition of the poverty line in 1964. The poverty line is the level of income below which a person or a family is considered poor. The poverty line is defined in absolute terms: It is based on the cost of a minimal diet multiplied by three because low-income families spend about one-third of their income on food. In 1964, the poverty income level for a family of four was $3,000 ($1,000 for food × 3). Since 1969, the poverty line figure has been adjusted upward each year for inflation. In 1988, for example, the official poverty income level was $12,092 or below for a family of four. In 2011, a family of four needed an income of $23,201 to clear the poverty threshold.

Exhibit 7(a) shows the percentage of all persons in the U.S. population below the poverty level, beginning with 1959. The poverty rate for all persons was on a downward trend until the early 1980s. After 1980, the percentage remained between 13 and 14 percent until the rate dropped to 11 percent in 2000. This was the lowest level in more than a quarter-century. Following the Great Recession of 2007–2009, the poverty rate rose to 15 percent in 2011. The exhibit also gives an idea of poverty levels by race for selected years. As shown by comparing parts (b) and (c), the percentage of African Americans below the poverty line remained almost three times the percentage of whites between 1970 and 1990. In 2011, the ratio was twice as great.

The poverty rate shown in Exhibit 7 has two major problems. First, this percentage gives no indication of how poor the people included are. A person with an income $1 below the poverty line counts, and so does a person whose income is $5,000 below the threshold. Second, the poverty rate is computed by comparing a family's census cash income from all sources to the poverty line. Cash income includes cash payments from Social Security, unemployment compensation, and Temporary Assistance to Needy Families (TANF). Cash income for the poor does not include noncash transfers, called in-kind transfers. In-kind transfers are government payments in the form of goods and services, rather than cash, including such government programs as food stamps, Medicaid, and housing. These antipoverty programs will be discussed in more detail in the next section.

Poverty line
The level of income below which a person or a family is considered to be poor.

In-kind transfers
Government payments in the form of goods and services, rather than cash, including such government programs as food stamps, Medicaid, and housing.

EXHIBIT 7	Persons below the Poverty Level as a Percentage of the U.S. Population, 1959–2011

In part (a), the official poverty rate for all persons declined sharply between 1959 and the 1970s. After the Great Recession of 2007–2009, the poverty rate rose. Comparison of parts (b) and (c) reveals that the poverty rate for African Americans fell sharply between 1959 and 1970, but since then, it remained almost three times the poverty rate of whites until 1990. In 2011, the ratio was twice as great.

(a) The official poverty rate for all persons

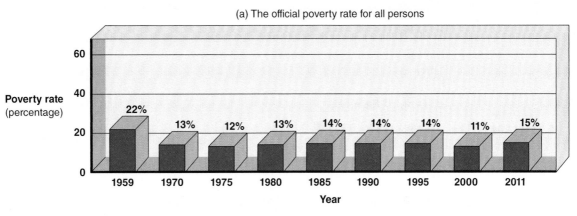

(b) The official poverty rate for African Americans

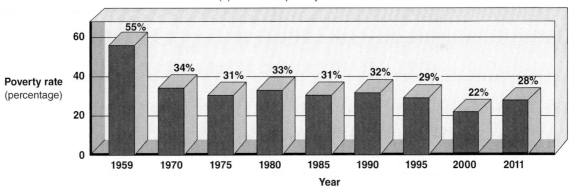

(c) The official poverty rate for whites

SOURCE: U.S. Bureau of the Census, *Income, Poverty, and Health Insurance in the United States: 2011*, http://www.census.gov/index.html, Table 4-1.

EXHIBIT 8	Characteristics of U.S. Persons and Families below the 2011 Poverty Level	
Characteristic		**Percentage below the poverty line**
Region		
South		17%
West		15
Midwest		14
Northeast		13
Type of Family		
Headed by married couple		6
Headed by male, no wife		16
Headed by female, no husband		32
Education of Household Head		
No high school diploma		25
High school diploma, no college		15
Bachelor's degree or more		5

SOURCE: U.S. Bureau of the Census, *Income, Poverty, and Health Insurance in the United States: 2011*, http://www.census.gov/hhes/www/poverty.html, Table 4 and POV29

12-3b WHO ARE THE POOR?

Exhibit 8 lists selected characteristics of families below the poverty level in 2011. Geographically, poor families are most likely to live in the South. An important characteristic of families living below the poverty line in the United States is family structure. The poverty rate was 32 percent for families headed by a female with no husband present and 16 percent for families headed by a male with no female present, compared to only 6 percent for married couples. Finally, poverty is greatly influenced by the lack of educational achievement of the head of household. As shown in the exhibit, 25 percent of families with household heads who have not received a high school diploma are below the poverty line compared to only 5 percent of families whose heads have at least a bachelor's degree.

12-4 Antipoverty Programs

Means test

A requirement that a family's income not exceed a certain level to be eligible for public assistance.

The government has a number of programs specifically designed to aid the poor. The groups eligible for such assistance include disabled persons, elderly persons, and poor families with dependent children. People become eligible for public assistance if their income is below certain levels as measured by a *means test*. A means test is a requirement that a family's income not exceed a certain level to be eligible for public assistance. People who pass the means test may be *entitled* to government assistance. Thus, government welfare programs are often called *entitlement programs*.

Federal programs to assist the poor in the United States are classified into two broad types of programs: *cash* assistance and *in-kind transfers*. As explained previously, the current definition of the poverty threshold excludes in-kind transfers because these programs did not exist when the poverty rate measure was adopted decades ago.

12-4a CASH TRANSFER PROGRAMS

The following are major government programs that alleviate poverty by providing eligible persons with cash payments needed to purchase food, shelter, clothing, and other basic needs.

Social Security (OASDHI) The technical name for our gigantic social insurance program is Old Age, Survivors, Disability, and Health Insurance, or OASDHI. Under the Social Security Act passed in 1935, each worker must pay a payroll tax matched in equal amount by his or her employer. Look at your paycheck, and you will find this deduction under FICA, which stands for Federal Insurance Contribution Act. Most of this money is used on a "pay-as-you-go" basis to pay current benefit recipients, and the remainder goes into the Social Security Trust Fund. Workers may retire between the ages of 65 and 67, depending on year of birth, with full benefits, or at age 62, with reduced benefits. If a wage earner dies, Social Security provides payments to survivors, including spouse and children. In addition, payments are made to disabled workers.

Earned-Income Tax Credit (EITC) This is a refundable federal tax credit based on earned income below a maximum amount provided to low-income wage earners with the purpose of offsetting Social Security payroll taxes paid by the workers. In short, EITC is designed to avoid taxing the working poor further into poverty. Under this program, the tax credit reduces federal income taxes or provides a cash payment if the credit exceeds the tax liability.

Unemployment Compensation Unemployment compensation is a government insurance program that pays income for a limited time period to unemployed workers. This unemployment insurance is financed by a payroll tax on employers, which varies by state and according to the size of the firm's payroll. This means nothing is deducted from employees' paychecks for unemployment compensation. Although the federal government largely collects the taxes and funds this program, it is administered by the states. Any insured worker who becomes unemployed and did not just quit his or her job can become eligible for benefit payments after a short waiting period of usually one week.

Unemployment compensation

The government insurance program that pays income for a short time period to unemployed workers.

Temporary Assistance to Needy Families (TANF) TANF gives states broad discretion to determine eligibility and benefit levels. However, families may not receive benefits for longer than 60 months. Unwed teenage parents must stay in school and live at home, and people convicted of drug-related felonies are banned from receiving TANF or food stamp benefits. In addition, nonworking adults must participate in community service within two months of receiving benefits and must find work within two years. Parents with children under age 1 are exempt from the work requirements (under age 6 if child care is not available).

Social Security: Past, Present, and Future

President Franklin D. Roosevelt signed the Social Security Act in 1935 as a bedrock of the New Deal program to help Americans besieged by the Great Depression. On December 1, 1936, the first official Social Security card was drawn arbitrarily from a stack of applications. The recipient was John D. Sweeney, Jr., who was the son of a wealthy factory owner and had grown up in a 15-room home staffed with servants. Unfortunately, Mr. Sweeney died at the age of 61 without ever receiving any benefits from the Social Security program.

Prior to 2010, the Social Security Trust Fund collected more revenue than it paid out in benefits. The balance was invested exclusively in interest-bearing U.S. Treasury securities. After 2010, revenue fell below benefits. Now the system will begin dipping into the trust fund to make up the difference. In 2037, it is estimated that the trust fund will be depleted. The problem is life expectancy is rising and a larger number of baby boomers born between 1945 and 1964 who are retiring. Excluding increasing the retirement age, the solution to financing a secure retirement program for future generations is to reduce benefits and/or increase revenues.

One idea to restore the trust fund is to allow people to obtain a higher return on their investment by channeling all or some of the money into their own private stock market account because stocks generally outperform U.S. Treasury securities by a significant margin. Unanswered questions of such partial privatization system include: (1) How much money could workers divert from Social Security into their private investment account? (2) What are the transition costs for new government debt required to pay benefits to current retirees not financed by payroll taxes because of money diverted to private accounts? and (3) How should workers be protected if their investments lose money?

Another reform idea is to increase tax revenue by lifting the cap on income subject to Social Security taxes. Currently, employers and employees each pay a fixed percentage payroll tax on worker earnings up to a maximum amount of each employee's salary. However, no tax is paid on the income above that maximum amount, which is currently $106,800. The effect would be to raise revenue by expanding the tax base to include highest-paid employees.

12-4b IN-KIND TRANSFERS

The following are important government in-kind transfer programs that raise the standard of living for the poor.

Medicare   This federal health care program is available to Social Security beneficiaries and persons with certain disabilities. Coverage is provided for hospital care and post-hospital nursing services. It also makes available supplementary low-cost insurance programs that help pay for doctor services and prescription drug expenses. Medicare is financed by payroll taxes on employers and employees.

Medicaid   This is the largest in-kind transfer program. Medicaid provides medical services to eligible poor under age 65 who pass a means test. TANF families qualify for Medicaid in all states. It is financed by general tax revenues.

Supplemental Nutrition Assistance Program (SNAP)   SNAP (formally food stamps) began in 1964 as a federally financed program administered by state governments. The government issues coupons to the poor, who use them like money at the grocery store. The grocer cashes the stamps at a local bank, which redeems them at face value from the government. The cash value of stamps issued varies with the eligible recipient's income and family size. This program has become a major part of the welfare system in the United States.

Housing Assistance   Federal and state governments have a number of different programs to provide affordable housing for poor people. The federal agency overseeing most of these programs is the Department of Housing and Urban Development (HUD). These programs include housing projects owned and operated by the government and subsidies to assist people who rent private housing. In both cases, recipients pay less than the market value for apartments and therefore receive an in-kind transfer.

12-4c WELFARE CRITICISMS

The majority of objections to welfare can be classified into the following major criticisms:

- **Work Disincentives.** Critics have argued that because welfare provides income that is easier to obtain than by working, the poor are often induced to reduce their work effort. In fact, the more a recipient earns from a job, the fewer the benefits he or she receives. Moreover, the taxes to finance welfare payments have some disincentive effects on the work effort of taxpayers. Taxes reduce take-home pay and thus reduce the reward for work.

- **Inefficiencies.** Critics have charged that the huge welfare bureaucracy in Washington, D.C., and throughout the nation results in more money in the pockets of bureaucrats than in the pockets of the poor. This major criticism was expressed by economics professor Thomas Sowell as follows:

    > The amount necessary to lift every man, woman, and child in America above the poverty line has been calculated, and it is one-third of what is in fact spent on poverty programs. Clearly, much of the transfer ends up in the pockets of highly paid administrators, consultants, and staff as well as higher income recipients of benefits from programs advertised as antipoverty efforts.[1]

- **Inequities.** Today, many critics argue that poor persons with equal needs receive different benefits. For example, a needy family in California might receive welfare benefits twice as great as those received by a needy family of the same size in South Carolina. The reason is that benefits under TANF and Medicaid are essentially controlled by the states.

12-5 Reform Proposals

Although there have been numerous proposals for reforming welfare, the various ideas can be classified into two broad approaches. First, the negative income tax offers a major transformation of the entire patchwork of federal, state, and local welfare programs. Second, workfare, which is the cornerstone of TANF, is a departure from the previous welfare system because it is based on work rather than entitlement. However, workfare is not without considerable debate and controversy.

---

[1]Thomas Sowell, *Markets and Minorities* (Basic Books, 1981), p. 122.

12-5a NEGATIVE INCOME TAX

Negative income tax (NIT)

A plan under which families below a certain break-even level of income would receive cash payments that decrease as their incomes increase.

The idea of negative income tax (NIT) was first advanced by the prominent economist Milton Friedman in the early 1960s to reduce work disincentives and welfare bureaucracy while providing for the poor. NIT is a plan under which families below a certain break-even level of income would receive cash payments that decrease as their incomes increase. A NIT system would combine all cash and in-kind transfer welfare programs into a single program administered by a single agency.

Exhibit 9 illustrates how a negative income tax might work. A low-income family of four receives a cash payment until it reaches a *break-even income* at $20,000 per year, where the family neither receives a payment nor pays income taxes. Above $20,000, the family pays income taxes. For example, a family with an income of $30,000 pays $5,000 in taxes, while a family with an income of $10,000 is paid an NIT subsidy of $5,000. A family with zero income receives an NIT payment of $10,000. Thus, the government pays families an amount that varies inversely (negatively) with income.

EXHIBIT 9	A Negative Income Tax Plan

In this example, a family with no earned income receives a $10,000 payment from the government. From $0 to $20,000, payments are reduced by a phase-out rate of $0.50 for each $1.00 of additional income. When income exceeds $20,000, payments fall to zero, and the family pays income taxes. Thus, a family with an income of $30,000 pays $5,000 in taxes.

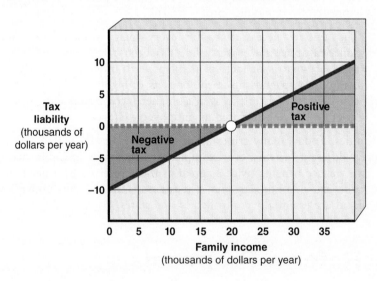

SOURCE: © Cengage Learning 2014

CONCLUSION: *The negative income tax is the reverse of a positive income tax system, in which people pay the government an amount that varies directly with their income.*

The basic idea behind the NIT system is simple: Families with incomes above the break-even income finance payments to families with incomes below the break-even income. Begin at zero income in the exhibit, and assume the income guarantee is set at the poverty income threshold of $10,000. Beyond the guaranteed minimum income of $10,000, government payments are reduced by, say, $0.50 for each $1.00 earned. This rate, called the *phase-out rate*, determines the cash transfers to low-income families until the break-even income is reached.

The NIT system offers several potential advantages. First, bureaucratic costs would be cut because an NIT program could be administered by a single agency. Second, poor people would not suffer the stigma of repeatedly standing in line at the welfare office or using food stamps in the grocery store. The needy would simply file annual, or perhaps quarterly, income returns with the IRS. Third, many economists argue that individuals are rational and know best how to spend their money. Thus, a cash subsidy is preferable to an in-kind transfer.

After years of discussion and study, the NIT has not gained wide support. The NIT system is perceived as a political liability because voters perceive it as a "giveaway" of taxpayers' money. These critics believe in-kind welfare is preferable to cash assistance. When a recipient is given food stamps or a housing subsidy, he or she acquires food and housing, rather than, say, buying drugs and gambling. NIT proponents point out, however, it is known that some food stamps are sold illegally for cash, which is used to buy drugs, alcohol, or whatever. Finally, some critics argue that a generous guaranteed minimum income paid in cash might create a disincentive to work rather than an incentive to work.

✔ CHECKPOINT

Does a Negative Income Tax Discourage Work?

Under a negative income system, people who work receive reduced payments from the government. Even worse, beyond the break-even income, workers must pay taxes. This means there is no basis in an NIT system to argue that the poor will have an incentive to work. Explain why you agree or disagree. (Hint: Construct a table using Exhibit 9, and consider after-tax income.)

12-5b WORKFARE

The 1996 welfare reform bill titled the *Personal Responsibility and Work Opportunity Reconciliation Act* created TANF and gave the states block grants to run welfare programs. To overcome the disincentive to work characteristic of earlier welfare programs based on entitlement, the current approach is to increase the work performed by welfare recipients and encourage their participation in job-training programs. To keep their benefits, welfare recipients must perform some work activities within two years of receiving welfare or risk losing benefits. This idea is called *workfare*. Workfare programs require able-bodied adults to work for the local government or any available private-sector employer in order to be eligible for welfare benefits. The paramount question thus becomes how to create jobs for welfare recipients who often lack basic literacy skills. A large public job plan would be costly and politically unpopular, especially among public employees who fear losing their jobs. Another option is for the government to pay employers to hire welfare

Pulling on the Strings of the Welfare Safety Net

Applicable Concept: welfare reform

Welfare reform appears to be a success: The number of families on welfare has fallen sharply from 4.4 million in 1996 to 1.8 million in 2009.[1] The following is a sampling of articles describing the evolution of welfare under the Personal Responsibility and Work Opportunity Reconciliation Act of 1996.

As reported in *The Washington Post*, Los Angeles County provides a striking contrast of welfare before and after reform in 1996. Prior to 1996, Los Angeles County had a traditional welfare program that provided education and job training without work requirements. After the welfare reform act of 1996, independent researchers found that 43 percent of poor families who were required to participate in

the city's new welfare reform program with work requirements got jobs, while only 32 percent of families randomly selected to remain in the traditional welfare program did. This represented an increase of one-third over the old welfare program. The typical welfare family subject to the new reform initiatives earned $1,286 in the first six months of the program, while "control group" families earned $879, a difference of 46 percent.[2]

A 2002 article in the *Los Angeles Times* concerned the new approach of the federal government providing block grants to states and mandating that the needy find jobs rather than just handing them welfare checks:

Before 1996, when the nation's welfare laws were

radically altered, welfare families might have gotten a monthly welfare check for the rest of their lives. Martha Soria's job would have been mostly to shuffle their paperwork. But with welfare reform came time limits on such benefits and strict new work requirements. And while Soria still shuffles a lot of paperwork, her job as well as the jobs of welfare caseworkers across the state and nation have changed. They have had to master hundreds of new rules and regulations under welfare reform and take on new responsibilities as guidance counselor, job finder, cheerleader, and taskmaster.[3]

recipients. A variation on this idea is for the government to hire personnel firms that would earn a fee for each person placed in a job.

There are potential problems with providing subsidies for companies that hire welfare recipients. One problem is that subsidies can stigmatize welfare recipients and reduce their long-term employment prospects. Another potential problem is that subsidies could be a windfall payment to employers for hiring people who would have been hired without the subsidies. Finally, there is a displacement problem because a subsidized welfare-recipient worker can take the job of an unsubsidized worker who has never received welfare benefits.

12-6 Discrimination

Poverty and discrimination in the workplace are related. Nonwhites and females earn less income when employer prejudice prevents them from receiving job opportunities. Discrimination also occurs when nonwhites and females earn less than, but do basically the same work as, whites and males. Exhibit 10 uses labor market theory to explain how discrimination can cause the equilibrium wage to be lower for nonwhites than for whites.

The following article argues that the states must do more to avoid racial bias:

Under the 1996 law, states have the option to enforce time limits of their choosing. Because of this flexibility, states are left open to discriminate freely. Across the board, race was the determining factor affecting time limit lengths and their application. Observation of the enforcement of time limits shows that states with a higher proportion of African-Americans or Latinos possess shorter time limits than the five-year guideline of the law. Over 20 states have opted to not allow exemptions to these time limits. Over 50 percent of African-American families under welfare are subject to time limits shorter than the federal cutoff, as opposed to 30 percent of whites under welfare.[4]

Reforms continue: A 2008 article in *The Chronicle of Higher Education* reported that a new federal rule would make it easier for some welfare recipients to attend college by counting a year's worth of study, including homework time, as work. The amount of time welfare recipients can spend in basic education and language courses was also expanded. The rule requires colleges to track recipients' class attendance, which some argue stigmatizes these students.[5] And in 2011, Florida passed a law requiring all adult recipients of federal cash benefits from TANF to be drug tested with tests paid by the welfare recipients. Adult welfare recipients who test positive for drugs lose their benefits for a year. A second test failure means loss of benefits for three years. Other states are considering passing similar legislation.

Analyze the Issue

The current approach to welfare reform is to cut the growth of welfare by shifting control from the federal government to the states. The idea is that because state and local officials are closer to the people, welfare programs will improve. Analyze the results presented above based on work disincentives, inefficiencies, and inequities.

1. U.S. Census Bureau, *Statistical Abstract of the United States*, 2012, http://www.census.gov/compendia/statab/, Table 553.
2. Judith Havemann, "Welfare Reform Success Cited in L.A.," *The Washington Post*, Aug. 20, 1998, p. A1.
3. Carla Rivera, "Welfare Reform's Enforcers," *Los Angeles Times*, May 28, 2002, p. A1.
4. Gordon Hurd, "Safety Net Sinking," *Colorlines Magazine*, Summer 2002, p. 17.
5. Elyse Ashburn, "New Federal Rule Could Help Welfare Recipients Stay Longer in College," *The Chronicle of Higher Education*, Feb. 9, 2011, p. A26.

Source: © Cengage Learning 2014

Exhibit 10(a) assumes that employers do not discriminate. This means employers hire workers regardless of race—that is, on the basis of their contribution to revenue (their marginal revenue products, MRPs). Hence, the intersection of the market demand curve, *D*, and the market supply curve, *S*, determines the equilibrium wage rate of $245 per day paid by nondiscriminating employers. The total number of African-American and white workers hired is 14,000 workers.

Now assume for the sake of argument that employers do practice job discrimination against African-American workers. The result, shown in Exhibit 10(b), is two different labor markets—one for whites and one for African Americans. Because discrimination exists, the demand curve for labor for African Americans is to the left of the demand curve for labor for whites, reflecting unjustified restricted employment practices. The supply curve of labor for African Americans is also to the left of the supply curve of labor for white workers because there are fewer African Americans seeking employment than whites.

Given the differences in the labor market demand and supply curves, the equilibrium wage rate for white workers of $280 is higher than the $210 paid to African Americans. Comparison of these wage rates with the labor market equilibrium wage rate of $245 reveals that the effect of discrimination is to change the relative wages of white and African-American workers. Whites earn a higher wage

---

| EXHIBIT 10 | Labor Markets without and with Racial Discrimination |

In part (a), there is no labor market discrimination against African Americans. In this case, the equilibrium wage for all labor is $245 per day. Under discrimination in part (b), the labor demand and labor supply curves for white and African-American workers differ. As a result, the equilibrium wage rate for white workers, $280, is higher than that for African Americans, $210.

SOURCE: © Cengage Learning 2014

---

rate than they would earn in a labor market that did not favor hiring them. Conversely, the African-American wage rate is lower as a result of discrimination.

Comparable worth

The principle that employees who work for the same employer must be paid the same wage when their jobs, even if different, require similar levels of education, training, experience, and responsibility. A nonmarket wage-setting process is used to evaluate and compensate jobs according to point scores assigned to different jobs.

12-6a COMPARABLE WORTH

A controversial public policy aimed at eliminating labor market pay inequities is a concept called comparable worth. Comparable worth is the principle that employees who work for the same employer must be paid the same wages when their jobs, even if different, require similar levels of education, training, experience, and responsibility. Comparable worth is a nonmarket wage-setting remedy to the situation where jobs dominated by women pay less than jobs dominated by men. Because women's work is alleged to be undervalued, the solution is equal pay for jobs evaluated as having "comparable worth" according to point scores assigned to different jobs. In essence, comparable worth replaces labor-market-determined wages with bureaucratic judgments about the valuation of different jobs. For example, compensation paid to an elevator inspector and a nurse can be computed based on quantitative scores in a job-rating scheme. If the jobs' point totals are equal, the average elevator inspector and nurse must be paid equally by law.

Is Pay for Females Fair?

Applicable Concept: comparable worth

Women working full-time earn on average about 20 percent less than men. Discrimination in wages and employment on the basis of sex was made illegal in 1963 by the Equal Pay Act (EPA), which outlawed pay discrimination between men and women doing substantially the same job. This does not mean that unequal pay for the same work cannot exist, but if it does, the differential must be due to factors other than gender.

Proponents of comparable worth argue that the equal-pay-for-equal-work idea has failed. They maintain that women crowd into such female-dominated occupations as secretarial work, nursing, school teaching, and social work because of discrimination against women in male-dominated occupations such as engineering. The increased supply of female labor in female-crowded professions lowers the prevailing wage. If the courts follow the comparable worth principle, they will not consider whether employers intentionally pay less for "women's jobs," but only whether the employers are in compliance with a quantitative rating scheme. The best-known case occurred in the 1980s, when the American Federation of State, County, and Municipal Employees won the first federal court case against the state of Washington. The state was found guilty of wage discrimination against women because it had not followed a comparable worth point system. According to the point system, male-dominated jobs often paid

More than female-dominated jobs even though the female jobs had greater "worth" and therefore "underpaid" female job classes should be raised rather than lowering the "overpaid" male job classes. The court ordered Washington to upgrade nearly 15,000 female employees and award back pay estimated at $377 million. The decision was appealed to higher courts, and the union ultimately lost the case.

Critics of comparable worth argue that it is nearly impossible to measure all of the factors that determine compensation for jobs, and the fact that female occupations earn less than male occupations is not necessarily evidence of discrimination. For example, women often seek occupations more compatible with childrearing. Over the years, it appeared that comparable worth had faded into a golden oldie until the Fair Pay Act of 2007 was introduced by Senator Tom Harkin (D-Iowa) and included then-Senator Barack Obama (D-Illinois) as one of the cosponsors. The premise is that the government has the duty to decide a job's worth. Under its provisions, employers must send the Equal Employment Opportunity Commission (EEOC) annual reports of how pay is determined in any jobs dominated by one gender. The goal is for the EEOC to decide pay for workers in dissimilar but "equivalent" jobs based on criteria established by the EEOC. Such calculations would serve as a basis for workers to sue their employers

based on not being paid the same for "equivalent" work. Although this bill was not enacted, the Lilly Ledbetter Fair Pay Act of 2009 was passed to reset the statute of limitation for pay discrimination.

Finally, the National Equal Pay Task Force was created in 2010 to crack down on violations of equal pay laws. In addition to the Labor Department, members include the Equal Employment Opportunity Commission, the Department of Justice, and the Office of Personnel Management. And in 2012, the "Paycheck Fairness Act" failed in the Senate that would require employers to prove that pay differences between men and women are based on qualifications, education, and other "bona fides."

Analyze the Issue

Suppose the EEOC uses a job-scoring system and determines that the wage rate for a secretary is $50 per hour, while the competitive labor market wage rate is $10 per hour. What would be the effect of such a comparable worth law?

Source: © Cengage Learning 2014

CHECKPOINT

Should the Law Protect Women?

Do you want women mining coal and building skyscrapers? Suppose laws are enacted that protect women by keeping them out of jobs deemed "too strenuous" or "too dangerous." Would the likely effect of such laws be to decrease wages in male-dominated occupations, increase wages in female-intensive occupations, or decrease wages in female-intensive occupations?

Key Concepts

Lorenz curve   Means test   Comparable worth
Poverty line   Unemployment compensation
In-kind transfers   Negative income tax (NIT)

Summary

- The **Lorenz curve** is a measure of inequality of income. Since 1947, the share of money income for each fifth of families ranked according to their income has been quite stable. Also, the degree of income inequality among families in the United States has changed little since 1929. In recent decades, the richest families have become richer; however, the median income of all groups has increased.

Lorenz Curve

SOURCE: © Cengage Learning 2014

- The **poverty line** is a level of cash income below which a family is classified as poor. The poverty income threshold is three times the cost of a minimal diet for a family. Today, about 13 percent of the U.S. population is officially classified as poor.

- **In-kind transfers** are payments to the poor in the form of goods and services, rather than cash. Calculation of the poverty line counts only cash income. In-kind transfers, such as food stamps, Medicaid, and housing, do not count as income for families classified as officially poor. Government cash transfers counted in calculating the poverty line include payments from Social Security, unemployment compensation, and Temporary Assistance to Needy Families.

- **Welfare criticisms** include three major arguments: (1) Welfare reduces the incentive to work for the poor and taxpayers. (2) Welfare is inefficient because much of the money covers administrative costs, rather than providing benefits for the poor. (3) Because many anti-poverty programs are controlled by the state, welfare benefits vary widely.

- The **negative income tax** is a plan to guarantee a certain amount of income for all families. As a low-income family earns income, government payments (negative income tax) are phased out. After reaching a break-even income, families become taxpayers instead of being on the welfare rolls.
- **Comparable worth** is the theory that workers in jobs determined to be of equal value by means of point totals should be paid equally. Instead of allowing labor markets to set wages, independent consultants award points to different jobs on the basis of such criteria as knowledge, experience, and working conditions.

Negative Income Tax

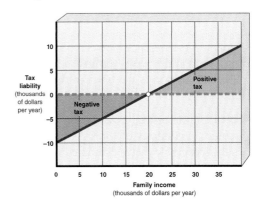

SOURCE: © Cengage Learning 2014

Summary of Conclusion Statements

- Measured by distribution of family money income, the richest families have become a little richer and the rest of the family groups have become a little poorer in recent decades.
- The Lorenz curve has shifted only slightly inward, and therefore closer to the perfect equality line between 1929 and 2011.
- The negative income tax is the reverse of a positive income tax system, in which people pay the government an amount that varies directly with their income.

Study Questions and Problems

1. The following table contains data on the distribution of income in the countries of Alpha and Beta:

| | Alpha | | Beta | |
Percentage of families	Percentage share	Cumulative share	Percentage share	Cumulative share
Lowest fifth	17.7%	—	9.0%	—
Second-lowest fifth	19.9	—	14.2	—
Middle fifth	20.4	—	17.5	—
Second-highest fifth	20.7	—	21.9	—
Highest fifth	21.3	—	37.4	—

a. Compute the cumulative distribution of income for each country.

b. Construct the Lorenz curve for each country.

c. For which country is the distribution of income more equal?

2. Suppose each family in the United States earned an equal money income. What would be the effect?

3. Explain the difference between poverty defined absolutely and poverty defined relatively. Which definition is the basis of the poverty line?

4. Calculate the official poverty threshold annual income for a family of four. Assume the minimally acceptable diet is estimated to be $10 per person per day and the minimum wage is $10 per hour. Will a head of a family of four earn the poverty threshold you have calculated?

5. What are in-kind transfers? Give examples. How are in-kind transfers considered in determining whether a family is below the poverty income threshold?

6. Would free health care reduce poverty, as measured by the government? Would free public housing, day care, and job training for the poor reduce the poverty rate? Explain.

7. What percentage of families in the United States is classified as poor? Which demographic groups have higher poverty rates?

8. List the major government cash assistance and in-kind transfer programs to assist the poor. Which of the programs are not exclusively for the poor?

9. What are three major criticisms of welfare?

10. Assume the government implements a negative income tax plan with a guaranteed minimum income of $5,000 and a phase-out rate for payments of 50 percent. Provide the missing data in the following table:

A Negative Income Tax Plan

Family income	Negative tax	Total after-tax income
$ 0	_____	_____
2,000	_____	_____
4,000	_____	_____
6,000	_____	_____
8,000	_____	_____
10,000	_____	_____

11. Critics of welfare argue that the role of government should be to break down legal barriers to employment rather than use programs that directly provide cash or goods and services. For example, advocates of this approach would remove laws mandating minimum wages, comparable worth, union power, professional licensing, and other restrictive practices. Do you agree or disagree? Why?

For Online Exercises, go to the Tucker Web site at www.cengage.com/economics/tucker.

✓ CHECKPOINT ANSWERS

Does a Negative Income Tax Discourage Work?

The following table is interpreted from Exhibit 9. Even though payments from the government decrease, total after-tax income increases from the combination of the income earned and the negative tax. After the break-even income of $20,000, total after-tax income continues to rise. If you said the NIT system assumes the poor are rational people who are motivated to earn more total after-tax income by working, YOU ARE CORRECT.

Family income	Negative tax	Positive tax	Total after-tax income
$ 0	$10,000	$ 0	$10,000
5,000	7,000	0	12,000
10,000	5,000	0	15,000
15,000	2,500	0	17,500
20,000	0	0	20,000
25,000	0	−2,500	22,500
30,000	0	−5,000	25,000
35,000	0	−7,500	27,500

Should the Law Protect Women?

A law that limits women's access to certain occupations results in their crowding into the remaining occupations. The obstacles facing women in male-dominated occupations artificially restrict competition with men. If you said the increased labor supply in female-intensive occupations decreases their wages, while the decreased labor supply in male-intensive occupations increases wages for males, YOU ARE CORRECT.

Sample Quiz

For an explanation of the correct answers, visit the Tucker Web site at www.cengage.com/economics/tucker.

1. "Dividing the economic pie more equally may reduce the size of the economic pie." This argument is characterized as
   a. untrue.
   b. a form of discrimination.
   c. a conflict between equity and efficiency.
   d. a conflict between full employment and economic growth.

2. The highest fifth of all families receive approximately what percent of the distribution of annual money income among families?
   a. 5 percent
   b. 10 percent
   c. 25 percent
   d. 50 percent

3. Which of the following graphs shows the cumulative shares of income received by a family?
   a. Distribution curve
   b. Lorenz curve
   c. Ricardian curve
   d. Quintile curve

4. As shown in Exhibit 11, the perfect equality line is drawn between points
   a. A and B.
   b. B and D.
   c. A and C along the straight line.
   d. A and C along the curve.

Sample Quiz *continued*

EXHIBIT 11	Lorenz Curve

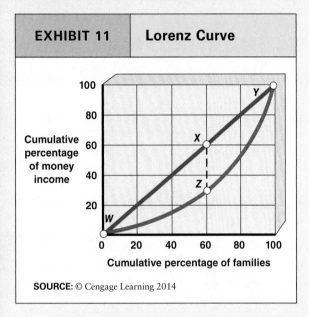

SOURCE: © Cengage Learning 2014

5. As shown in Exhibit 11, 60 percent of families earned a cumulative share of about what percent of income?
   a. 5 percent
   b. 15 percent
   c. 30 percent
   d. 50 percent

6. When the Lorenz curve lies above the diagonal,
   a. the poorest 20 percent of the population receive more than 20 percent of income.
   b. the richest 20 percent of the population receive more than 20 percent of income.
   c. everyone receives the same income.
   d. the curve is wrong because it is impossible for the graph to look like this.

7. The poverty line
   a. separates those on welfare from those not on welfare.
   b. equals three times an economy food budget.
   c. equals the median income level.
   d. includes all of the above answers.

8. Which of the following government programs provides recipients with unrestricted cash payments?
   a. Temporary Assistance to Needy Families (TANF)

b. Medicaid
   c. The food stamp program
   d. Housing assistance programs

9. Medicaid and food stamps are
   a. available only to families.
   b. counterproductive.
   c. forms of in-kind assistance.
   d. forms of cash assistance.

EXHIBIT 12	Negative Income Tax

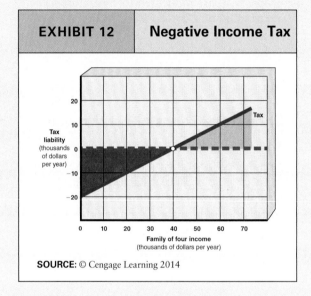

SOURCE: © Cengage Learning 2014

10. As shown in Exhibit 12, a family of four pays income taxes at
    a. an income of $5,000.
    b. any income between zero and $40,000.
    c. all levels of income.
    d. any income above $40,000.

11. As shown in Exhibit 12, a family of four with no earned income receives _____ from the government.
    a. zero payment
    b. the break-even income of $40,000
    c. a $20,000 payment
    d. a $20,000 tax deferment

12. Under the negative income tax scheme in Exhibit 12, families earning between $10,000 and $40,000 would
    a. receive the maximum negative income tax payment of $20,000.

Sample Quiz *continued*

b. receive payments under the negative income tax.

c. pay no income taxes, but receive no payments.

d. do none of the above.

13. Which of the following might increase the supply curve of labor?
    a. Eliminating discrimination against African Americans
    b. Eliminating discrimination against females
    c. Easing licensing requirements
    d. Doing all of the above

14. Consider a law that limits women's access to certain "dangerous" occupations such as coal mining and military combat service. Such a law would likely reduce women's wages because
    a. women would be overqualified for "non-dangerous" jobs.
    b. labor supply in female-intensive occupations would increase.
    c. women would be less likely to obtain college degrees.
    d. comparable worth would no longer exist between men's and women's occupations.

15. Comparable worth is the principle that
    a. goods and services priced the same have about the same worth.
    b. the wage rate equals the value of productivity.
    c. men and women should be paid comparably.
    d. employees who perform comparable jobs should be paid the same wage.

16. Which of the following graphs shows the percentage of the families on one axis and the percentage of income on the other?
    a. Budget-distribution curve
    b. Income-consumption curve
    c. Lorenz curve
    d. Marx curve

17. As shown in Exhibit 4 in the text, when the Lorenz curve lies above the diagonal,
    a. the poorest 20 percent of the population receives more than 20 percent of income.
    b. the richest 20 percent of the population receives more than 20 percent of income.
    c. everyone receives the same income.
    d. the country's income has been rising over time.
    e. the curve is wrong because it is impossible for the graph to look like this.

18. The official U.S. poverty line for a family is calculated by taking 3 times the annual cost of
    a. public housing.
    b. basic medical care.
    c. utilities and transportation.
    d. a minimal diet.

19. Which of the following programs is an example of in-kind assistance to fight poverty in the United States?
    a. Medicaid
    b. unemployment benefits
    c. Temporary Assistance to Needy Families (TANF)
    d. food stamps
    e. both a and d

20. The incentive to work is an ingredient of the negative income tax because
    a. if families work, they will be eliminated from the program.
    b. if families don't work, they will be eliminated from the program.
    c. the more income earned in the workplace, the higher the family's after-tax income.
    d. the more income earned in the workplace, the higher the payment from the government.

chapter 13

Antitrust and Regulation

People of the same trade seldom meet together, even for merriment and diversion, but the conversation ends in a conspiracy against the public, or in some contrivance to raise prices.[1]
—**Adam Smith**

When Microsoft dominated the personal computer software industry, the U.S. government charged the firm and Bill Gates, its founder, with anticompetitive business practices. The media compared the case to John D. Rockefeller's Standard Oil monopoly and the robber barons of the 1890s. In the past, antitrust laws have been successfully used against the nation's largest corporations. This threat of the high legal costs of defending against an antitrust suit serves as a powerful deterrent, discouraging monopolies from engaging in unfair actions intended to eliminate rivals. Here you will explore and form opinions on the Microsoft case, the Standard Oil case, and other major antitrust cases.

When antitrust policy is successful, consumers benefit from lower prices and more output. As you study antitrust policy in this chapter, you will learn that antitrust is somewhat of an art form that blends economic theory and politics—perhaps more politics than economic theory. Interestingly, certain industries and organizations are exempt from antitrust legislation: labor unions, professional baseball teams, public utilities, public transit companies, schools, hospitals, and suppliers of military equipment.

The second half of this chapter turns to government regulation, which affects virtually every business and consumer. Our food is regulated, our environment is regulated, airline safety is regulated, and most industries must deal with some form of regulation. What are the reasons for regulation, and what are its consequences? The explanation begins with a brief survey of regulation in the United States. In the last section, we discuss the rationale for three different types of regulation justified on the basis of market failure.

---

[1]Adam Smith, *An Inquiry into the Nature and Causes of the Wealth of Nations* (1776, reprint, New York: Random House, The Modern Library, 1937), p. 128.

In this chapter, you will learn to solve these economics puzzles:

- Can universities and colleges improve education by engaging in price-fixing?

- Why doesn't the water company or electric company compete?

- Why is market failure an economic rationale for regulation?

13-1 Antitrust

Before the Civil War, industries were populated by small firms, and few economic problems were caused by monopoly. After the Civil War, during the rapid industrialization of the 1870s and 1880s, the railroads and telegraph linked diverse regions of the country and enabled firms to expand into national markets. To gain more control of expanding industries, many competing companies merged or formed a trust. A trust is a combination or cartel consisting of firms that place their assets in the custody of a board of trustees. The trust allows firms that have not actually merged to form a cartel, or a cohesive group of firms that controls an industry in order to charge monopoly prices and earn higher profits. The long list of trusts formed during this period included the iron trust, sugar trust, copper trust, steel trust, coal trust, oil trust, tobacco trust, and even the paper-bag trust. The organizers of many of these trusts became widely known as *robber barons* because they exploited and bullied anyone in their way.

During the last decades of the 19th century, many trusts used various tactics to avoid competition. Recall from Chapter 9 on monopoly that Standard Oil acquired oil fields, railroads, pipelines, and ships and then denied access to rivals. Thus, competing firms had to merge with Standard Oil or go out of business. With the competition eliminated, John D. Rockefeller, the best-known so-called robber baron, raised Standard Oil's prices and limited production, and consumers suffered along with Standard Oil's competitors.

Another anticompetitive strategy used by the industrial giants was predatory pricing. Predatory pricing is the practice of one or more firms temporarily reducing prices in order to eliminate competition and then raising prices. Often trusts would sell a product below cost until their weaker competitors were unable to withstand mounting losses and were forced from the industry. Perhaps even more alarming, some trusts resorted to political corruption. For example, the railroad and petroleum trusts employed corrupt legislators and judges to gain a competitive edge.

By the end of the 19th century, the threat of continuing economic and political abuses created a public opinion quite hostile to big business. Newspapers regularly printed news of the trusts' questionable business practices. The numerous and politically influential farmers blamed the trusts for the high railroad charges that were making farming unprofitable. Consumers and labor unions also raised their voices against monopoly power. The influence of the trusts was discussed constantly in the halls of Congress. In 1888, both major political parties added antimonopoly planks to their campaign platforms. Hatred and distrust of the centralization of economic and political power originated in the Jeffersonian tradition of the United States. Against this background of populist (pro-people) fear of big business and its political power, Congress passed laws aimed at preventing firms from engaging in anticompetitive activities.

Trust

A combination or cartel consisting of firms that place their assets in the custody of a board of trustees.

Predatory pricing

The practice of one or more firms temporarily reducing prices in order to eliminate competition and then raising prices.

The following is a brief description of the major antitrust legislation that constitutes basic antitrust law.

13-1a THE SHERMAN ACT

Sherman Act

The federal antitrust law enacted in 1890 that prohibits monopolization and conspiracies to restrain trade.

The first antitrust law was the Sherman Act. The Sherman Act of 1890 is the federal antitrust law that prohibits monopolization and conspiracies to restrain trade. Today, this act remains the cornerstone of antitrust policy in the United States. It has two main provisions:

Section 1: Every contract, combination in the form of trust or otherwise, or conspiracy in restraint of trade or commerce among the several States, or with foreign nations, is hereby declared to be illegal....

Section 2: Every person who shall monopolize, or attempt to monopolize, or combine or conspire with any other person or persons, to monopolize any part of the trade or commerce among the several States, or with foreign nations, shall be deemed guilty of a misdemeanor, and, on conviction thereof, shall be punished by a fine not exceeding five thousand dollars, or by imprisonment not exceeding one year, or by both said punishments, in the discretion of the court.[2]

In response to the public outcry, Congress intended to craft this law with sweeping language against the trusts. But what does the Sherman Act really say? It is unclear exactly which business practices constitute a "restraint of trade" and therefore a violation of the law. As a result of the extremely vague language, there were numerous court battles, and the act was ineffective for years. For example, the federal government did not win its first notable cases against Standard Oil and American Tobacco until 1911.

The serious consequences of violating the Sherman Act are reflected in the more recent case of Archer Daniels Midland Company (ADM). In 1995, this agribusiness giant pleaded guilty to price-fixing involving lysine and citric acid. It paid a $100 million fine. In 1998, a federal jury convicted three past and present executives of conspiring with competitors to fix the prices of these products. They were sentenced to serve two years in prison and to pay fines of $350,000 each.

13-1b THE CLAYTON ACT

Clayton Act

A 1914 amendment that strengthens the Sherman Act by making it illegal for firms to engage in certain anticompetitive business practices.

As explained above, the Sherman Act initially proved to be little more than a legislative mandate for the courts to spell out the meaning of antitrust laws. To define anticompetitive acts more precisely, Congress passed the Clayton Act. The Clayton Act of 1914 is an amendment that strengthened the Sherman Act by making it illegal for firms to engage in certain anticompetitive business practices. Under this act, the following business practices are illegal, with the important controversial condition that the effect must be to "substantially lessen competition or tend to create a monopoly":

1. **Price Discrimination.** A firm charges different customers different prices for the same product with the price differences not related to cost differences. (Recall the discussion of this topic in the chapter on monopoly.)

---

[2]In 1974, the act was amended so that violations would be treated as felonies.

2. **Exclusive Dealing.** A manufacturer requires a retailer to sign an agreement stipulating the condition that the retailer will not carry any rival products of the manufacturer.

3. **Tying Contracts.** The seller of one product requires the buyer to purchase some other product(s). For example, movie distributors cannot force theaters to purchase projection rights to a blockbuster movie only on the condition that they pay for a bundle of films with much less box office potential.

4. **Stock Acquisition of Competing Companies.** One firm buys the stock of a competing firm.

5. **Interlocking Directorates.** The directors of one company serve on the board of directors of another company in the same industry. Interlocking directorates are illegal, whether or not the effect may be to "substantially lessen competition."

Although more specific than the Sherman Act, the Clayton Act is also vague and leaves a key question unanswered: Exactly when does a situation or action "substantially lessen competition"? To this day, the task of interpreting this ambiguous phrase remains with the courts, and the interpretation changes over time.

13-1c THE FEDERAL TRADE COMMISSION ACT

Since the federal government faced a growing antitrust responsibility in the early 1900s, an agency was needed to investigate alleged anticompetitive practices and reach judgments. The Federal Trade Commission Act was enacted for this purpose. The Federal Trade Commission Act of 1914 established the Federal Trade Commission (FTC) to investigate unfair competitive practices of firms. This act contains perhaps the most general language of any antitrust act. It declares illegal "unfair methods of competition in commerce." The act established a five-member commission appointed by the president to determine the exact meaning of "unfair methods." Today, the FTC is concerned primarily with (1) enforcing consumer protection legislation, (2) prohibiting deceptive advertising, and (3) preventing collusion. When a complaint is filed with the FTC, the commission investigates. If there is a violation, the FTC can negotiate a settlement, issue a cease-and-desist order, or initiate a lawsuit.

Federal Trade Commission Act

The federal act that in 1914 established the Federal Trade Commission (FTC) to investigate unfair competitive practices of firms.

13-1d THE ROBINSON-PATMAN ACT

The Clayton Act has been amended twice. Although price discrimination became illegal under the Clayton Act, that section was not widely enforced at first. This situation changed with the passage of the Robinson-Patman Act. The Robinson-Patman Act of 1936 is an amendment to the Clayton Act that strengthens the Clayton Act's provisions against price discrimination. The Robinson-Patman Act is complex and controversial. Its basic purpose is to prevent large sellers from offering different prices to different buyers where the effect is to harm even a single small firm. In fact, the Robinson-Patman Act is often called the "Chain Store Act" because it was an outgrowth of the competition between small independent sellers and chain stores that developed after World War I.

Robinson-Patman Act

A 1936 amendment to the Clayton Act that strengthens the Clayton Act against price discrimination.

The Robinson-Patman Act encourages lawsuits by small independent firms because it broadens the list of illegal price discrimination practices. This act, for example, makes it illegal for a firm to offer quantity discounts, free advertising, or promotional allowances to one buyer if the firm does not offer the same concessions to all buyers. Be careful to note that the prohibition on price discrimination in the Robinson-Patman Act is limited to situations where the effect is to "substantially lessen competition or tend to create a monopoly." The first You're the Economist offers the opportunity to debate issues concerning this act.

13-1e THE CELLER-KEFAUVER ACT

Celler-Kefauver Act

A 1950 amendment to the Clayton Act that prohibits one firm from merging with a competitor by purchasing its physical assets if the effect is to substantially lessen competition.

Prior to 1950, the U.S. Supreme Court interpreted the Sherman Act as prohibiting mergers between competing firms by stock acquisition, but not prohibiting mergers by the sale of physical assets (plant, equipment, and so on). The Celler-Kefauver Act was the second amendment to the Clayton Act, and it was enacted to address this problem. The Celler-Kefauver Act of 1950 is an amendment to the Clayton Act that prohibits one firm from merging with a competitor by purchasing its physical assets if the effect is to substantially lessen competition. Consequently, this act is sometimes called the "Antimerger Act" because it closed the loophole in the Clayton Act and thereby prohibited anticompetitive mergers, which were the target of the original Clayton Act.

The five major antitrust laws are summarized in Exhibit 1.

EXHIBIT 1	Summary of Major Antitrust Laws
Law (date enacted)	**Key provisions**
Sherman Act (1890)	• Prohibits interstate price fixing and other conspiracies and combinations that restrain trade and attempt to monopolize.
Clayton Act (1914)	• Bolsters and clarifies the Sherman Act by prohibiting specific business practices, including exclusive dealing, tying contracts, stock acquisition of competitors, and interlocking directorates.
Federal Trade Commission Act (1914)	• Established an agency (the FTC) to help enforce antitrust laws by investigating unfair and deceptive business practices.
Robinson-Patman Act (1936)	• Amends the Clayton Act by broadening the list of illegal price discrimination practices to include quantity discounts, free advertising, and promotional allowances offered to large buyers and not to small buyers. The Robinson-Patman Act is often called the "Chain Store Act."
Celler-Kefauver Act (1950)	• Amends the Clayton Act by closing the loophole that permitted a firm to merge by buying assets of a rival, rather than by acquisition of stocks, as outlawed in the original Clayton Act. The Celler-Kefauver Act is often called the "Antimerger Act."

SOURCE: © Cengage Learning 2014

Is Utah Pie's Slice of the Pie Too Small?

Applicable Concept: Robinson-Patman Act

The following is a classic and controversial case: In the 1950s, the market for frozen dessert pies was small, but growing. The Salt Lake City market was supplied by distant plants in California that were owned by Carnation, Continental Baking, and Pet Milk. Until 1957, these three firms accounted for almost all the frozen fruit pies sold in the Salt Lake City market.

The Utah Pie Company had been baking dessert pies in Salt Lake City and selling them fresh for 30 years. This family-owned-and-operated business entered the frozen pie market in 1957. It was immediately successful and grabbed a huge share of the Salt Lake City market. During the relevant years, the market shares of the various competitors were as follows:

Utah Pie's strategy for penetrating the market was to set its prices below those of its competitors.

Due to its immediate success, it built a new plant in 1958. Its local plants gave Utah Pie a locational advantage over its competitors. For most of the time in question, Utah Pie's prices were the lowest in the Salt Lake City market. The incumbent firms, of course, responded to Utah Pie's entry and lower prices by reducing their own prices. As a result, all the larger firms sold frozen pies in Salt Lake City at prices lower than those charged for pies of like grade and quality in other geographic markets considerably closer to their California plants.

Utah Pie sued these three firms, claiming price discrimination. Ultimately, the case was reviewed by the Supreme Court in 1967, which took a dim view of such pricing behavior: "Sellers may not sell like goods to different purchasers at different prices if the result may be to injure competition in either the sellers' or the buyers' market unless such discriminations

are justified as permitted by the Act." Consequently, the Supreme Court found the defendants guilty of price discrimination. Inasmuch as no competitors had been forced from the market, it appears that price discrimination does not have to have an obviously predatory impact to be ruled illegal. All the Court saw in this case was a pattern of falling prices. It feared that such a pattern could result in a lessening of competition if one or more competitors dropped out of the market.

	1958	1959	1960	1961
Utah Pie	67%	34%	46%	45%
Pet	16	36	28	29
Carnation	10	9	12	9
Continental	1	3	2	8
All others	6	18	12	9

Analyze the Issue

Utah Pie sued its three outside competitors under the Robinson-Patman Act. Some have criticized this case because it is an example of the type of bizarre result that can be produced by antitrust policy. Do you agree? Explain.

Source: © Cengage Learning 2014

13-2 Key Antitrust Cases

Antitrust policy can be compared to the rules of baseball or other sports. The House and Senate of the U.S. Congress set the "rules of the game" for antitrust cases, just as the American and National Leagues set the rules of baseball. For example, the rules of baseball say that a player hitting a homer must run from first base to home plate, rather than from third base to home plate. Similarly, the Sherman Act forbids monopolization through predatory pricing by businesses. This brings us to the role of the umpire. After a game, a Little League player asked the first-base umpire, "What do you call when the runner and the ball reach first base at exactly the same time?" The umpire replied, "There's no such thing as a tie. It's always the way I call it." That's how it is with court decisions on antitrust laws, and just like many of the umpire's calls, all the courts' decisions are not "crowd pleasers." With this point in mind, let's look at some important "calls" of courts on antitrust cases.

13-2a THE STANDARD OIL CASE (1911)

President Theodore Roosevelt's administration took action to break up Standard Oil under the Sherman Act. After ten years of litigation, the Supreme Court ruled in 1911 that Standard Oil had achieved its monopoly position in the oil refining industry through illegal business practices. John D. Rockefeller's trust had used railroad rebates, discounts, espionage, control of supplies to rivals, and predatory pricing to gain a monopoly. The remedy was for the Standard Oil Trust to be broken into competing companies: Standard Oil of New York became Mobil, Standard Oil of California became Chevron, Standard Oil of Indiana became Amoco, and Standard Oil of New Jersey became Exxon.

The Standard Oil Trust case established a standard for antitrust rulings. The Supreme Court ruled that (1) Standard Oil was a monopoly with a 90 percent share of the refined-oil market and (2) Standard Oil achieved its monopoly through illegal business behavior intended to exclude rivals. The Court stated that point (2) was critical to its decision and not point (1). This doctrine became known as the rule of reason. The rule of reason is the antitrust doctrine that the existence of monopoly alone is not illegal unless the monopoly engages in illegal business practices. Stated differently, monopoly *per se* is not illegal. Thus, "big is not necessarily bad." Standard Oil and other dominant firms would be broken up not merely because of their dominance, but also because of their abusive behavior.

Between 1911 and 1920, the courts applied the rule of reason in breaking up the American Tobacco Trust and other trusts. In 1920, the Supreme Court also applied the rule of reason when it decided that U.S. Steel was not guilty under the Sherman Act. Although U.S. Steel controlled almost 75 percent of the domestic iron and steel industry, the Supreme Court ruled that it is not *size* that violates the law. Since there was no evidence of unfair pricing practices, U.S. Steel was a "good citizen" not in violation of the Sherman Act.

Rule of reason
The antitrust doctrine that the existence of monopoly alone is not illegal unless the monopoly engages in illegal business practices.

13-2b THE ALCOA CASE (1945)

Thirty-four years after the Standard Oil case, the courts did a "flip-flop" on the rule of reason. In 1940, the Aluminum Company of America (Alcoa) was the only producer of aluminum in the United States. Alcoa's monopoly was primarily the result of its patents and its ownership of a unique resource, bauxite. Moreover, Alcoa kept its prices low to avoid competition and prosecution, behaving as a "good citizen" despite its size. A federal appeals court ruled that Alcoa had violated the Sherman Act and declared:

> Having proved that Alcoa had a monopoly of the domestic ingot market the government had gone far enough…. Congress did not condone "good trusts" and condemn "bad" ones; it forbade all.[3]

With the Alcoa decision, the courts turned from "big is not necessarily bad" to "big is bad." The rule of reason was transformed into the per se rule. The per se rule is the antitrust doctrine that the existence of monopoly alone is illegal, regardless of whether or not the monopoly engages in illegal business practices. Instead of judgments based on the performance of a monopoly, antitrust policy in the United States was switched by the court's interpretation to judgments based solely on the market structure. Interestingly, the court's solution was not to break up Alcoa. Instead, the federal government subsidized Alcoa's competitors. War plants were sold at bargain prices to Reynolds Aluminum and Kaiser Aluminum, and later more rivals entered the aluminum industry.

Per se rule

The antitrust doctrine that the existence of monopoly alone is illegal, regardless of whether or not the monopoly engages in illegal business practices.

13-2c THE IBM CASE (1982)

In 1969, the U.S. Department of Justice brought antitrust action against IBM because of its dominance in the mainframe computer market. The government argued that IBM had a 72 percent share of the electronic digital computing industry. IBM argued that the relevant market was broader and included programmable calculators and other information-processing products. After 13 years of litigation, IBM had spent over $100 million on its defense and had constructed an entire building to store case documents. Finally, in 1982, the government dropped the case. One reason was that Digital Equipment, Apple Computer, and Japanese companies were competing with IBM. Another reason illustrates the mix of politics and antitrust policy. In 1982, Ronald Reagan was president, and he believed in a much less restrictive interpretation of antitrust laws. In any event, the IBM case represented a shift in the general sentiment among those enforcing the antitrust laws from the per se rule back to the rule of reason.

13-2d THE AT&T CASE (1982)

In 1978, the U.S. Department of Justice brought an antitrust suit against AT&T and the Bell System. The issue was complicated. At this time, AT&T was a *natural monopoly* regulated by the government. (Regulation of a natural monopoly will be explained later in this chapter; see Exhibit 4.) The government allowed AT&T to have a monopoly in long-distance and local telephone service and in the production of telephones. The Federal Communications Commission

---

[3]*U.S. v. Aluminum Co. of America*, 148 F.2d 416 (2d Cir. 1945).

(FCC) regulated long-distance rates, and state utility commissioners regulated local rates. What was the objective of giving one company the exclusive right to provide telephone services in the United States? In order to provide everyone with low-cost local services, the regulatory commissions set AT&T's local charges low and its long-distance rates high to cover the lower local rates.

In the 1970s, advances in technology changed the nature of the long-distance telephone industry. Telephone service was no longer a natural monopoly because fiber optics and satellites made cable connections obsolete. Competitors developed, and the government alleged that these rivals were being charged unfairly high fees for access to AT&T's local telephone lines.

On the same day the IBM case ended in 1982, AT&T and the Department of Justice announced this case was settled. AT&T ("Ma Bell") divested itself of 22 local companies ("Baby Bells"), but retained its long-distance telephone service, its research facilities (Bell Laboratories), and its manufacturing facilities (Western Electric Company). As a result, local companies became regulated monopolies in their areas, and local phone rates rose sharply. In nationwide long-distance telephone service, AT&T's competition with MCI and Sprint lowered the price of long-distance telephone service. Moreover, individual customers became responsible for buying their own phones, rather than using only AT&T phones. The result was a highly competitive market, offering a wide range of phone prices and a wide variety of phones.

13-2e THE MIT CASE (1992)

For years, the presidents of many of the nation's top universities—Cornell, Harvard, Yale, Columbia, Brown, Princeton, The University of Pennsylvania, Dartmouth, and MIT—attended annual meetings to discuss tuition, faculty salaries, and financial aid packages. After such meetings, these schools often adjusted tuition charges, salary increases, and even fees for room and board. For example, one year Dartmouth planned to raise faculty salaries by 8.5 percent. The other schools wanted to hold the line at 6.5 percent, so Dartmouth was persuaded to cave in. At other meetings, the group's goal was to make sure each student who applied to more than one of the schools would be offered the same financial aid. At another meeting, Harvard and Yale accused Princeton of offering excessively generous scholarships to top students.

The U.S. Justice Department investigated and charged the eight Ivy League universities and MIT with an illegal conspiracy to fix prices. The Ivy League schools settled the case with a consent decree. This agreement required these schools to cease colluding on tuition, salaries, and financial aid in the future, and in return, none of the schools admitted guilt for a price conspiracy. MIT refused to sign the consent order, and in 1992, a federal district judge ruled that MIT had violated antitrust laws and concluded that students and parents have the right to compare prices when choosing a university. In 1993, an appeals court ordered a new trial and the Justice Department dropped charges with the agreement that MIT would cease comparing financial packages.

✓ CHECKPOINT

Does Price-Fixing Improve Your Education?

Price-fixing agreements are among the monopolistic restraint-of-trade practices prohibited by Section 1 of the Sherman Act. The Supreme Court has concluded that a formal agreement is not necessary to prove conspiracy. Instead, conspiracy may be inferred from the acts of the accused even if the consequences might be considered socially desirable. The presidents of the universities charged with price-fixing in the MIT case defended their business practices with the argument that they openly met to fix prices in order to improve education. With tuition and the amount of financial aid fixed, students and parents will choose their university on the basis of academic quality alone. Consider the discussion of pricing strategies for an oligopoly discussed in Chapter 10. Can you give the presidents a better argument for their defense?

13-2f THE MICROSOFT CASE (2001)

Microsoft Corporation dominated the personal computer (PC) software industry with about a 90 percent share of the PC operating system software and Internet browser markets. And Microsoft had tied its Windows operating systems at zero price (predatory pricing) to its Internet Explorer browser in order to eliminate competition and establish a monopoly in the browser market. The remedies discussed included both conduct and structural remedies. A conduct remedy was a judicial instruction against engaging in specific behavior. For example, Microsoft could be required to include major rival browsers with its browser. Bill Gates likened this proposal to "requiring Coca-Cola to include three cans of Pepsi in every six-pack it sells." Moreover, Microsoft claimed that by integrating Internet Explorer with Windows, it was creating one product and not tying two products. In short, no one using the Windows operating system needed a separate browser.

A structural remedy is a "surgical fix" aimed at permanently altering a company so substantially that further violations are not possible. For example, Microsoft could be split into three companies. One company would have operating systems, such as Windows. A second company could have applications, such as Word, Excel, and PowerPoint. The third company would get Internet Explorer and related Internet business. A major concern with this remedy was that a three-headed monopoly monster might destroy innovation and a seamless transition between Windows and other software applications. Another fear was that prices might rise and software would become much more complicated.

In 2001, a federal appeals court ruled that Microsoft did violate antitrust law to protect a monopoly for its Windows operating system. However, the court ruled the government had failed to prove Microsoft illegally attempted to monopolize the Internet browser market. In response, Microsoft announced that it would allow PC manufacturers to continue adding icons of other technology companies to Microsoft's operating system. In 2002, a federal judge approved most of the provisions of the antitrust settlement reached the previous year with Microsoft.

The major antitrust cases are summarized in Exhibit 2.

EXHIBIT 2	Summary of Major Antitrust Cases
Case (date)	**Key provision**
Standard Oil (1911)	• This case established the rule of reason, allowing a monopoly unless it engages in illegal practices.
Alcoa (1945)	• This case overturned the rule of reason and established the per se rule, under which all monopolies are illegal.
IBM (1982)	• The government dropped its case after 13 years and shifted antitrust policy back to the rule of reason.
AT&T (1982)	• Technology made this government-regulated natural monopoly obsolete, and AT&T was found guilty of anticompetitive pricing.
MIT (1992)	• Eight Ivy League schools agreed to stop colluding to fix prices, and MIT was found guilty of price-fixing while attending open meetings. MIT and the Justice Department reached an agreement after an appeals court ordered a new trial.
Microsoft (2001)	• Microsoft and the government reached a settlement after an appeals court held that the firm illegally protected its Windows monopoly.

SOURCE: © Cengage Learning 2014

13-3 Mergers and Global Antitrust Policy

The decades of the 1980s and 1990s were characterized by a wave of mergers. Mergers are a concern to antitrust regulators because firms can avoid charges of price-fixing by merging into one firm. The antitrust policy toward mergers depends on the type of merger and its likely effect on the relevant market.

13-3a TYPES OF MERGERS

Horizontal merger

A merger of firms that compete in the same market.

Vertical merger

A merger of a firm with its suppliers.

Conglomerate merger

A merger between firms in unrelated markets.

A horizontal merger is a merger of firms that compete in the same market. The mergers of Coca-Cola and PepsiCo, Ford Motor Company and General Motors, and Anheuser Bush and Coors would be hypothetical examples of horizontal mergers. Horizontal mergers raise a red flag because they decrease competition in a market. For example, in 1986, the government blocked the proposed merger between Coca-Cola and Seven Up.

A vertical merger is a merger of a firm with its suppliers. This type of merger occurs between companies at different stages of a production process. Hypothetical examples of vertical mergers would be General Motors merging with a major tire company and Ford Motor Company merging with a large number of car dealerships. Although the government often challenges vertical mergers, global competition has reduced antitrust scrutiny of vertical mergers. If this type of merger lowers costs by eliminating unnecessary supplier charges, U.S. firms will be more competitive in world markets.

A conglomerate merger is a merger between firms in unrelated markets. Suppose an insurance company buys a computer software company or a cigarette company merges with a hotel chain. Actual examples are Philip Morris merging with Miller Brewing Company and General Motors merging with Electronic Data Systems Corporation. No antitrust action was taken to prevent these mergers because the products of the two firms were considered to be unrelated. Conglomerate mergers are generally allowed because they do not significantly decrease competition.

13-3b ANTITRUST POLICIES IN OTHER COUNTRIES

Early antitrust laws were aimed at the domestic economy with little concern for global competitiveness. Because of the internationalization of competition in recent decades, some economists call for a relaxation of antitrust laws to allow firms to merge and compete more effectively in the world economy. Other economists disagree and argue that strong antitrust laws are necessary because small firms create most jobs and innovations.

One reason firms in other countries are so competitive with U.S. firms is that other countries' antitrust laws are weak in comparison to U.S. antitrust laws. For example, no other country breaks up companies for antitrust violations. There are two basic explanations. First, most other countries have smaller populations than the United States. Because other countries have fewer potential customers, they view the global market as the target and design weak antitrust laws accordingly. Stated differently, other countries must sell their products globally in order to achieve economies of scale and be competitive.

Second, other countries have weak antitrust laws based on their culture and history. In the United States, there is a strong belief in Adam Smith's individualistic competition among small firms. This "big is bad" ideology is the foundation of U.S. antitrust laws, but this belief is not prevalent in other countries. In other countries, "big is better," and in countries such as Japan and Germany, government and business work together to compete globally. In contrast, there is a general mistrust of big government working directly with big businesses in the United States.

13-4 Regulation

The same distrust of big business that is the basis of antitrust laws also led to the evolution of regulation and federal regulatory agencies in the United States. The regulatory process in the United States has gone through several phases. In the first phase, from 1887 to the Great Depression, the railroads were the primary target. During the 1930s, the Great Depression created a favorable environment in which regulation spread to the communications, financial, and other industries. After 1970, regulation increased steadily in the areas of health, safety, and the environment until the 1980s, when a deregulation movement began and continued to have momentum in the early 2000s.

13-4a HISTORICAL ORIGINS OF REGULATION

The Early Years The railroads came under regulation in the late 19th century as a result of their unfair pricing practices. At that time in history, railroads faced little competition from other carriers, so there was little to prevent railroads from overcharging. Railroads also practiced price discrimination against isolated rural customers by charging them higher rates for short hauls than they charged city customers for long hauls. In 1887, the Interstate Commerce Commission (ICC) was established to regulate rail prices and to cut the costs of rail transportation by reducing duplicate trains, depots, and tracks. The Food and Drug Administration (FDA) was established in 1906 to oversee the safety of food and drugs.

The Great Depression Era   During the 1930s, regulation was extended to other industries. All surface transportation, including trucks, barges, and oil pipelines, came to be regulated by the ICC. The Civil Aeronautics Board (CAB) was created in 1938 to regulate air travel, and the Federal Communications Commission (FCC) was established in 1934 to regulate telephones, telegraphs, and broadcasting industries. In 1934, as a result of the stock market crash of 1929, the Securities and Exchange Commission (SEC) was created to combat fraud and malpractice in the securities industry.

The Health, Safety, and Environment Era   The Occupational Safety and Health Administration (OSHA) was created in 1970 to reduce the incidence of injury and death in the workplace. This agency cites and fines employers who violate safety and health rules. In the same year, the Environmental Protection Agency (EPA) was established to set and enforce pollution standards. In 1972, the Consumer Product Safety Commission (CPSC) was established to protect the public against injury from unsafe products. The CPSC has the power to ban the sale of hazardous products.

13-4b THE DEREGULATION TREND

Deregulation

The elimination or phasing out of government restrictions on economic activity.

In the 1970s, the higher production costs resulting from regulation generated widespread dissatisfaction with government regulation. The result was a movement toward deregulation in the late 1970s and 1980s. Deregulation is the elimination or phasing out of government restrictions on economic activity. Initially, the major thrust of deregulation was in the transportation and telecommunications industries. The *Airline Deregulation Act of 1978* removed regulated airfares and restrictions against competition in air travel markets. The *Staggers Rail Act of 1980* deregulated the railroads, the *Motor Carrier Act of 1980* deregulated trucking, and the *Bus Regulatory Reform Act of 1982* deregulated bus transportation. The Civil Aeronautics Board (CAB), established in 1938 to regulate airline fares and air routes, was abolished in 1984. The You're the Economist at the end of the chapter examines the effects on the airline industry.

In telecommunications, the most important case was the deregulation and dismantling of AT&T. As explained previously, technological innovations made competition in telecommunications possible, and as a result of an antitrust lawsuit, AT&T was broken up and forced to compete with MCI, Sprint, and other companies for long-distance service. In 1996, Congress passed a telecommunications bill that made additional changes in U.S. telecommunications. This bill deregulated cable television rates, while allowing local and long-distance telephone companies and cable companies to compete. This bill also required television manufacturers to equip new sets with a computer chip to block shows parents do not wish their children to watch.

For nearly 100 years, electricity was a regulated industry in the United States. Privately held utility companies obtained the right to operate a monopoly in exchange for government regulations that set rates and capped profits. In 1992, Congress started the deregulation movement for power companies when it approved the *Energy Policy Act*, which opened competition at the wholesale level. By 2001, 24 states and the District of Columbia had approved deregulation plans, but the California power shortage created a deregulation backlash (see You're the Economist on California electricity deregulation later in the chapter).

EXHIBIT 3	Federal Regulatory Agencies	

Agency	Year created	Function
Interstate Commerce Commission (ICC)	1887*	Regulated interstate ground transportation, including the railroad, trucking, bus, and water carrier industries.
Food and Drug Administration (FDA)	1906	Protects the health of the nation against impure and unsafe foods, drugs, and cosmetics. Develops policy regarding labeling of all drugs.
Securities and Exchange Commission (SEC)	1934	Provides for complete financial disclosure and protects investors in stock and other securities against fraud.
Federal Communications Commission (FCC)	1934	Regulates television, radio, telephone, and telegraph services; satellite transmissions; and cable TV.
Civil Aeronautics Board (CAB)	1938†	Regulated airline fares and routes.
Occupational Safety and Health Administration (OSHA)	1970	Enforces rules in cases involving safety and health violations in the workplace.
Environmental Protection Agency (EPA)	1970	Regulates pollution in the areas of air, water, waste, noise, radiation, and toxic substances.
Consumer Product Safety Commission (CPSC)	1972	Protects the public against unreasonable risks of injury from consumer products.

*Abolished in 1995.
†Abolished in 1984.
SOURCE: © Cengage Learning 2014

The principal functions of the federal regulatory agencies discussed are summarized in Exhibit 3.

13-5 Three Cases for Government Regulation

Government regulation involves political, social, and economic factors, and the general justification for regulation is to protect the public. In this section, we examine three basic situations in which regulation is often imposed: (1) natural monopoly, (2) externalities, and (3) imperfect information. In each of these cases, the argument in favor of regulation is *market failure*. Recall from Chapter 4 that market failure is a situation in which the market operating on its own fails to lead to an efficient allocation of resources.

13-5a NATURAL MONOPOLY

The objective of antitrust policy is to create a level playing field for competing firms. Depending on the case, antitrust policy can result in breaking up a monopoly, preventing formation of a monopoly, and/or punishing anticompetitive business practices of a monopoly. But what happens when it is inefficient for more than one company to operate in a particular market? Stated another way, creation of a level playing field for competitors may not be in the best interest of economic efficiency. This situation exists in a *natural monopoly*. As explained earlier in Exhibit 1 in Chapter 9 on monopoly, a natural monopoly is an industry in which long-run average cost is minimized when only one firm serves the market. Recall that the services of such public utilities as gas, electric, cable TV, and water companies are natural monopolies subject to government regulation. To avoid abuse of this type of monopoly, the prices or rates these public utilities can charge are determined by a federal, state, or local regulatory commission or board.

Exhibit 4 illustrates the demand curve, long-run marginal cost curve (LRMC), and long-run average cost curve (LRAC) for a natural monopoly in the cable TV market—say, a company called Vision Cable. Because of *economies of scale*, the LRAC curve is negatively sloped. Following the *marginal-average rule* explained

EXHIBIT 4	A Regulated Monopoly

If an unregulated monopolist serves the cable TV market, it will set MR = LRMC, charge a price of $150 per month, and provide service to only 40,000 customers (point A). To improve the efficiency of the market by taking advantage of the lower costs of a natural monopoly, government regulators could set the price at $60, which equals long-run marginal cost (point C). This policy is efficient, but losses require public subsidies. The typical solution is to set a "fair-return" price of $90, which allows the monopolist to earn zero economic profit and serve 80,000 customers at point B. This condition does not fully correct the underallocation of resources caused by an unregulated natural monopoly.

SOURCE: © Cengage Learning 2014

in Chapter 7, the LRMC curve is below the falling LRAC curve. Given this condition, the firm's demand curve intersects the LRAC curve at a quantity of 80,000 subscribers and a cost of $90 per month equal to the price (point *B*). Suppose this output is divided equally between Vision Cable and another cable company. As discussed in Exhibit 1 of Chapter 9, the result of competition between cable TV companies is that the cost per subscriber is much higher—and even higher if output is divided among more than two cable companies.

To take advantage of the lower cost, the policy prescription is to create a cable TV market served by only one producer—Vision Cable. The policy problem now is how to keep this unregulated natural monopoly from enjoying a substantial monopoly profit. Instead of providing services for 80,000 customers, Vision Cable will service only 40,000 customers by following the MR = MC rule to maximize profits. The price that corresponds to this output is $150 per month at point *A*. Because the profit-maximizing price exceeds the LRAC curve, monopoly pricing creates too high a price and too small an output. Stated differently, the result is an inefficient cable TV market in which there is an underallocation of resources to produce cable TV service.

For the cable television market to be efficient, regulators must set a price ceiling at $60 per month, which is equal to long-run marginal cost at point *C* on the demand curve. This pricing strategy follows the competitive principle of marginal cost pricing. Marginal cost pricing is a system of pricing in which the price charged equals the marginal cost of the last unit produced. At a price of $60, Vision Cable suffers a loss because although the price covers long-run marginal cost, the price is not high enough to cover long-run average cost. This means the firm can survive in the long run only if the government subsidizes the loss.

What to do? Is there an option that does not require taxpayers' money? Yes! In practice, regulatory commissions have relaxed the objective of efficiency and have focused on establishing a "fair-return" price to be charged by the monopolist. In Exhibit 4, the commission would establish the fair-return price at $90 per month at point *B*, where the demand curve intersects the LRAC curve. Because the price ceiling equals long-run average cost, Vision Cable earns zero economic profit and serves 80,000 customers in the long run. However, remember from the chapter on production costs that in economics, cost includes a normal profit, which is just enough to keep the firm in the cable industry.

Marginal cost pricing

A system of pricing in which the price charged equals the marginal cost of the last unit produced.

> **CONCLUSION:** *Government regulators can achieve efficiency for a natural monopoly by setting a price ceiling equal to the intersection of the demand and the marginal cost curves, but this policy results in losses. An alternative is to set a price ceiling, called the fair-return price, that yields a normal profit, but is somewhat inefficient.*

13-5b EXTERNALITIES

The case of pollution was treated in detail in Exhibit 8(a) in Chapter 4. To refresh your memory, recall that the individual firm in a competitive market has no incentive to eliminate pollution voluntarily. Pollution is an *external cost* imposed on *third parties* who neither produce nor consume a good. Pollution causes polluting

Who Turned Out the Lights in California?

Applicable Concept: price ceiling regulation

In order to keep electricity cheap for its state, the California legislature in 1996 set a retail ceiling price of 10 cents per kilowatt-hour. Moreover, no new power-generating plants were built during the 1990s. The plan was to require utilities to sell their power plants and import electricity as needed from the "spot market" through high-speed transmission lines from other states. In the deregulated wholesale electricity market, a spot market is one in which the price of electricity is determined by supply and demand conditions each hour.

The stage was set for the forces of supply and demand to "turn out the lights." First, demand soared during a heat wave in the summer of 2000 as consumers turned on their air conditioners. Second, there was a leftward shift in supply. High natural gas prices increased the cost of producing electricity in all states. Also, low snowpacks and a drought in the Pacific Northwest reduced the capacity of hydroelectric dams in this region.

Facing shortages from both increased demand and decreased supply, California utilities had no choice but to buy electricity on the spot market as prices soared tenfold over their normal levels. Since customer rates were capped, the price paid by consumers did not cover what the utilities were paying for electricity. The utilities quickly found themselves facing bankruptcy, and this threat caused additional spot rate increases. Duke Power Company of North Carolina, for example, stated that 8 percent of its spot price was a premium to cover the risk of selling to California utilities that might not pay their bills. A subsequent investigation by the Federal Energy Regulatory Commission (FERC) reported evidence that power companies such as Enron developed strategies to drive up prices.

Faced with this crisis, Gray Davis, who was governor of California at the time, called for more price caps. He convinced the FERC to cap wholesale prices in the West during hours of highest demand, combined with a daily regime of rolling blackouts and calls for conservation. In April 2001, Davis abandoned the 1996 price ceiling, thus sharply increasing the retail electricity price.

Analyze the Issue

Draw a graph illustrating California's electricity crisis. Put the label "Price of electricity (cents per kilowatt-hour)" on the vertical axis and "Quantity of electricity (megawatts per hour)" on the horizontal axis. As explained in Chapter 4, draw the changes in demand and supply for electricity in California described above. (Hint: Begin the graph in equilibrium below the price ceiling.)

Source: © Cengage Learning 2014

firms to overproduce, while causing firms that pay the cost of cleaning up the pollution to underproduce. Therefore, expenditures on pollution control would place firms at a competitive disadvantage with respect to firms that do not pay the cost of controlling pollution. If society wants less pollution, this type of market failure justifies government regulation from, say, the EPA. The exact nature of the regulation, however, may take a variety of forms, ranging from direct controls requiring specific pollution-control equipment to taxation.

✓ CHECKPOINT

Why Doesn't the Water Company Compete?

The local water company is considered to be a natural monopoly, and the government prohibits other firms from competing with it. If a natural monopoly can produce water at a lower price than other firms, then why would the government protect the water company from competitors?

Without repeating the explanation given in Exhibit 8(b) in Chapter 4, note that the *external benefits* of a good, such as a vaccination, can lead to underproduction of the good. Again, regulation is necessary if society is to respond to externalities. In this case, the government solution can take various forms, including requiring consumption or providing special subsidies.

13-5c IMPERFECT INFORMATION

In some cases, consumers lack important information about a product, and they cannot make rational decisions. Without complete and reliable information, consumers may be unaware of the dangers of unsafe drugs, hazardous chemicals, and defective products. The source of imperfect information about products may be company errors. Much worse, companies may be able to boost sales by withholding valuable information about a problem with their products.

Let's consider a hypothetical case in which an unsafe Tucker Motors (TM) truck is sold. Suppose the safety defect is a gas tank that is located too close to the side of the truck. As a result, another vehicle can crash into the side of the TM truck and hit the gas tank. Such an accident can cause a deadly explosion. Assume further that TM is aware of this safety problem, but the cost of recalling and fixing the trucks exceeds the estimated cost of lawsuits caused by the defective gas tanks. The market incentive is therefore for TM to withhold knowledge of this defect from uninformed consumers.

Exhibit 5 illustrates this case. With consumers unaware of the defect, the interaction of the supply and demand curves for TM trucks yields an equilibrium at E_1, with 100,000 trucks being sold per year at a price of $30,000 per truck. Next, suppose the Consumer Product Safety Commission (CPSC) exposes the problem, and the media report stories about crash victims who have been severely burned or even killed by flames from the exploding gas tanks in TM trucks. Once the consuming public is aware of the defect, consumers' preferences for TM trucks change, and the demand curve decreases from D_1 to D_2. The result is a new equilibrium at E_2, with 75,000 TM trucks being sold per year at a price of $20,000 per truck. In other words, this case is an application of market supply and demand analysis as presented in Chapter 4.

CONCLUSION: *Deficient information on unsafe products can cause consumers to overconsume a product.*

EXHIBIT 5	The Impact of Imperfect Information on the Market for TM Trucks

An initial equilibrium is established at point E_1, with 100,000 TM trucks purchased each year for $30,000 per truck. This equilibrium is reached without consumers having knowledge of a safety defect. Once consumers are informed of the safety defect, the demand curve shifts leftward from D_1 to D_2. At the new equilibrium point of E_2, 75,000 TM trucks are purchased each year for $20,000 per truck. Thus, imperfect information has resulted in a waste of the resources used to produce 25,000 TM trucks.

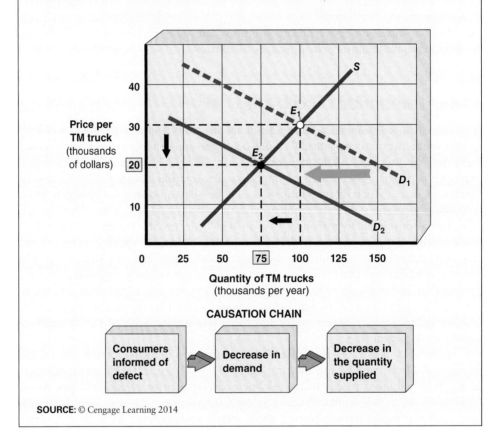

SOURCE: © Cengage Learning 2014

In the TM truck example, resources were used to produce 25,000 trucks that consumers would not purchase when given complete information. These resources were misallocated because they could have been used to produce other goods and services. The solution is for government to prevent companies from making false or deceptive claims by gathering and disseminating accurate information to consumers. This is the rationale for the safety testing of cars, EPA mileage ratings on cars, and warning labels on cigarettes. In extreme cases, a product may be deemed too unsafe, and it is outlawed from sale. Others disagree with this view and argue that the government should only provide information. Once consumers have sufficient information, they should be free to choose.

Does Airline Deregulation Mean Friendlier Skies?

Applicable concept: regulation versus deregulation

A much publicized case of deregulation is the airline industry.

Under regulation by the Civil Aeronautics Board (CAB), airfare competition and the incentive to control costs were reduced or eliminated. The CAB set both fares and routes for carriers. Unable to compete with price, the carriers could compete only with costly nonprice competition, such as advertising. Once the CAB authorized a carrier to provide service between two cities, the frequency of service remained unregulated. When carriers purchased fleets of planes and provided too many flights for their protected routes, profits were squeezed because the percentage of seats filled with passengers (load factor) fell, and the average cost rose. Carriers would then attempt to boost profits by lobbying the CAB for higher fares. In addition to eliminating price competition between established carriers, the CAB restricted entrants into the industry. From 1938 until 1977, the CAB never awarded a major route to any new airline.

Successful deregulation of an industry would be expected to provide the following three results:

- The average price of the service falls.
- The volume and variety of services rise.
- New firms enter the industry, and other firms fail and exit the industry.

The Airline Deregulation Act of 1978 provided these results by changing the structure and business behavior of the airline industry. Although the Federal Aviation Administration (FAA) would still regulate the safety of air service, the CAB was eliminated under this act in 1984, and price competition produced the expected results of lower fares and greater quantity of service. The average passenger price per mile for a flight declined continuously from 1978 to half that rate over the next 25 years on an inflation-adjusted basis, saving consumers billions of dollars in lower fares. Over this same period, the fall in fares contributed to a tripling of passenger miles flown per year.[1]

The airline deregulatory movement is not without criticism. One concern is that lots of airlines went "belly up", and these exits from the industry increased the percentage of all domestic air travel controlled by the industry's largest carriers. Moreover, under the pressure of competition, carriers searched for ways to cut costs, and they created the hub-and-spoke delivery system. This system allows carriers to gather passengers from the "spoke" routes by using smaller, less efficient planes and fly the passengers from the hub in fully occupied, bigger planes at lower cost. Many carriers have gained near monopoly power in "hub" airports. These dominant hub carriers can control access to terminal gates, takeoff time slots, and baggage

Dmitrijs Dmitrijevs/Shutterstock.com

service, and they can charge smaller airlines high rates for using these airport rights.

Today, deregulation continues to exert downward pressure on fares, and old-guard carriers scramble to compete with low-cost carriers such as Southwest and JetBlue. Low-fare tickets, cyberfares, and frequent-flier miles are popular. Should the airlines remain deregulated or return to a government-enforced cartel? Critics point to airlines that are in financial trouble. Defenders of deregulation argue that growth of market concentration and its abuses can be controlled by enforcing antitrust laws and allowing global competition.

Analyze the Issue

Prior to deregulation, critics argued that airline safety would suffer. Instead, although the Federal Aviation Administration's budget was cut following deregulation, the accident rate involving fatalities has fallen. Give a rationale for why the critics' prediction did not come to pass.

---

1. *Statistical Abstract of the United States*, 2008, http://www.census.gov/compendia/statab/ Table 1072.

Source: © Cengage Learning 2014

Key Concepts

Trust
Predatory pricing
Sherman Act of 1890
Clayton Act of 1914
Federal Trade Commission
    Act of 1914

Robinson-Patman Act of 1936
Celler-Kefauver Act of 1950
Rule of reason
Per se rule
Horizontal merger
Vertical merger

Conglomerate merger
Deregulation
Marginal cost pricing

Summary

- A **trust** is a cartel that places the assets of competing companies in the custody of a board of trustees. During the last decades of the 19th century, trusts engaged in anticompetitive strategies, such as *predatory pricing*, to eliminate competition and raise prices.
- The **Sherman Act of 1890** and the **Clayton Act of 1914** are the two most important antitrust laws. The Sherman Act marked the first attempt of the U.S. government to outlaw monopolizing behavior. Because this act was vague, the Clayton Act was passed to define anticompetitive behavior more precisely. The Clayton Act prohibited (1) price discrimination, (2) exclusive dealing, (3) tying contracts, (4) stock acquisition of competing companies, and (5) interlocking directorates.
- The **Federal Trade Commission Act of 1914** established the Federal Trade Commission (FTC) to investigate unfair competitive practices of firms.
- The **Robinson-Patman Act of 1936** strengthened the Clayton Act by prohibiting certain forms of price discrimination. This law is called the "Chain Store Act" because it was aimed at large retail chain stores that were obtaining volume discounts.
- The **Celler-Kefauver Act of 1950** strengthened the Clayton Act by declaring illegal the acquisition of the assets of one firm by another firm if the effect is to lessen competition.
- The **rule of reason** and **per se rule** are the two main doctrines the courts have used in interpreting antitrust law. Under the rule of reason, monopolists were not subject to prosecution unless they acted in an anticompetitive manner. The court decision in the Alcoa case of 1945 replaced the rule of reason with the per se rule, which states that the mere existence of monopoly is illegal. Today, the trend is in favor of dominant firms because of global competition.
- A **horizontal merger** is a merger of two competing firms. A **vertical merger** is a merger of two firms in which one produces an input used by the other firm. A **conglomerate merger** is a merger of two firms producing unrelated products.
- **Deregulation** is a movement that began in the late 1970s and 1980s to eliminate regulations primarily in the transportation and telecommunications industries. Today, the movement to further deregulate electric utilities is being questioned.
- **Marginal cost pricing** is a competitive pricing strategy for a regulated natural monopoly. Using this approach, regulators set the monopolist's price equal to its marginal cost. Another method is for regulators to establish a fair-return price equal to long-run average cost, and the monopolist earns zero economic profit. Regulation of a natural monopoly is justified on the basis of market failure. Two other cases based on market failure include externalities and imperfect information.

Marginal Cost Pricing

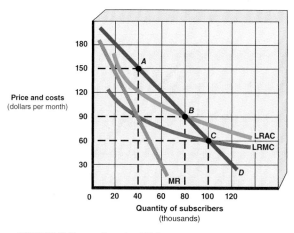

SOURCE: © Cengage Learning 2014

Summary of Conclusion Statements

- Government regulators can achieve efficiency for a natural monopoly by setting a price ceiling equal to the intersection of the demand and the marginal cost curves, but this policy results in losses. An alternative is to set a price ceiling, called the fair-return price, which yields a normal profit, but is somewhat inefficient.
- Deficient information on unsafe products can cause consumers to overconsume a product.

Study Questions and Problems

1. Describe the major provisions of the Sherman Act and the Clayton Act. Who is responsible for enforcing these laws?

2. Two business practices outlawed by the Clayton Act are tying contracts and interlocking directorates. Explain the condition required for these two practices to be a violation of this antitrust law.

3. Distinguish between the Robinson-Patman Act of 1936 and the Celler-Kefauver Act of 1950.

4. Using cases presented in the text, explain the issue in the courts' interpretation of "monopoly versus monopolizing."

5. A controversy in many antitrust court cases involves the definition of the relevant market for a firm's product. How would you argue in the Alcoa case that the government's claim of the firm's high market share was in error?

6. In the MIT case, which students are harmed by the Ivy League schools' coordination of scholarship policy? Professional baseball is exempt from antitrust laws. Should colleges and universities also be exempt from antitrust laws?

7. Based on the antitrust laws, how would you expect the federal government to react to the following situations?
   a. A college bookstore deliberately reduces prices until its only rival is driven out of business. The bookstore then raises its prices.
   b. Real estate firms meet in an open meeting and agree to charge 6 percent commission on sales.

c. Microsoft merges with Apple by a stock acquisition.

d. A small tax preparation company merges with a regional grocery store chain.

8. Based on the cases discussed in the chapter, is the following statement correct? "The antitrust laws in reality deal less with monopolies than with oligopolies."

9. Assume a regulatory agency is given authority over prices and entry conditions for a given industry. Also assume the agency decides to allow new entry, as the CAB did before deregulation, only when it is proven to be "necessary." Would this condition be expected to favor (a) existing regulated firms, (b) new entrants, or (c) consumers? Explain.

10. Exhibit 6 represents a natural monopolist.
    a. If the monopolist is not regulated, what price will it charge, and what quantity will it produce?
    b. If the monopolist is required to use marginal cost pricing, what price will it charge, and what quantity will it produce? Why will the monopolist stay in business?
    c. Assume regulators set a fair-return price at P_b. Why would the monopolist stay in business?

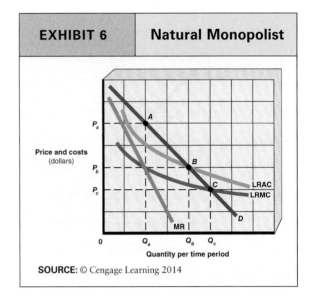

EXHIBIT 6 | **Natural Monopolist**

SOURCE: © Cengage Learning 2014

11. Assume a natural monopolist is required to use marginal cost pricing and a government subsidy covers the loss. What problems might be associated with a public subsidy?

12. Do you agree that "cost does not really matter" as a principle for safety regulation, or do you believe that the cost of a safety device must be justified on the basis of the value of human life protected from a hazard?

For Online Exercises, go to the Tucker Web site at www.cengage.com/economics/tucker.

✓ CHECKPOINT ANSWERS

Does Price-Fixing Improve Your Education?

Accepting the schools' argument that they improve quality by price-fixing makes no more sense than allowing General Motors, Ford, DaimlerChrysler, and Japanese automakers to fix prices in order to improve quality. However, there is often a thin line between price-fixing and price leadership. Price leadership is not illegal as long as the price followers are not coerced. If you said price leadership is defendable and price fixing is not, **YOU ARE CORRECT.**

Why Doesn't the Water Company Compete?

Suppose new firms are allowed to compete with the water company, which is a natural monopolist. The concern is that the rivals will be outcompeted. New water companies must build plants, dig up the streets, and lay new water pipes and duplicate other resources in the same neighborhood. Because the competitors cannot produce water at a lower cost, they will leave the industry, and the resources used to compete with the natural monopolist will be wasted. If you said the government is not protecting the natural monopolist from competition so much as it is protecting against inefficient competitors wasting resources, **YOU ARE CORRECT.**

Sample Quiz

For an explanation of the correct answers, visit the Tucker Web site at www.cengage.com/economics/tucker.

1. The antitrust law that prohibits firms from combining or conspiring to restrain trade in interstate commerce is the
   a. Federal Trade Commission Act.
   b. Clayton Act.
   c. Sherman Antitrust Act.
   d. Robinson-Patman Act

2. Price discrimination that tends to lessen competition is outlawed by the
   a. Sherman Act.
   b. Clayton Act and amended by the Robinson-Patman Act.
   c. Federal Trade Commission Act.
   d. Interstate Commerce Act.

3. If a firm has a tying agreement with a distributor which substantially lessens competition, then it is likely to be in violation of the
   a. Clayton Act.
   b. Robinson-Patman Act.
   c. Sherman Antitrust Act.
   d. Federal Trade Commission Act.

4. For many years, AT&T required customers to rent telephones from AT&T in order to receive phone service. This is an example of
   a. price discrimination.
   b. a tying contract.
   c. an interlocking directorate.
   d. exclusive dealing.

5. Interlocking directorates are illegal under the _____ whether or not the effect may be to substantially lessen competition.
   a. Clayton Act
   b. Robinson-Patman Act
   c. Sherman Antitrust Act
   d. Federal Trade Commission Act

6. Which of the following was *not* illegal under the original Clayton Act?
   a. tying contracts
   b. interlocking directorates
   c. merger by purchase of assets with cash
   d. All of the above were illegal under the original Clayton Act.

7. During this century, court decisions on antitrust have
   a. changed from per se to rule of reason and back to per se.
   b. changed from rule of reason to per se and back to rule of reason.
   c. always emphasized per se.
   d. always emphasized rule of reason.

8. The importance of the Federal Trade Commission Act of 1914 is that it
   a. set up an independent antitrust agency with the power to bring court cases.
   b. strengthened the law against mergers.
   c. strengthened the law against price discrimination.
   d. All of the above answers are correct.

9. The antitrust legislation was designed to help small stores survive competition with large retail chains was the
   a. FTC Act.
   b. Sherman Antitrust Act.
   c. Celler-Kefauver Act.
   d. Robinson-Patman Act.

10. What antitrust legislation made it illegal for a firm to pay cash for a competitor's patents, plant, and equipment?
    a. Sherman Antitrust Act
    b. Celler-Kefauver Act
    c. Robinson-Patman Act
    d. Clayton Act

11. The per se rule was introduced in which case?
    a. Standard Oil
    b. IBM
    c. American Tobacco Trust
    d. Alcoa

12. The Interstate Commerce Commission (ICC) was established in 1887 to regulate
    a. banking.
    b. railroads and all surface transportation.
    c. nationwide advertising.
    d. interstate sales of food and drugs.

Sample Quiz *continued*

13. The Civil Aeronautics Board (CAB) was
    a. established in 1934 and reorganized in 1984.
    b. established in 1938 and eliminated in 1984.
    c. established in 1938 and reorganized in 1991.
    d. never a regulatory agency.

EXHIBIT 7	Public Utility Monopolist

SOURCE: © Cengage Learning 2014

14. As shown in Exhibit 7, an unregulated monopolist would operate at point
    a. W.
    b. Y.
    c. Z.
    d. None of the above answers are correct.

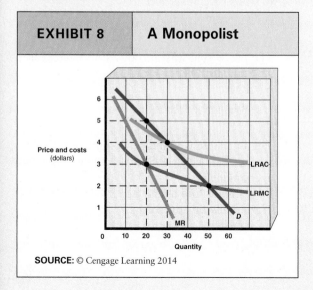

EXHIBIT 8	A Monopolist

SOURCE: © Cengage Learning 2014

15. In Exhibit 8, if this industry is regulated and the regulatory commission wants no excess profits or losses (normal economic profit) to occur, the proper price and output combination to be set is
    a. price = $5; output = 20.
    b. price = $4; output = 30.
    c. price = $3; output = 20.
    d. price = $2; output = 50.

16. In Exhibit 8, if this industry is regulated and the regulatory commission sets price equal to long run marginal cost (LRMC), then
    a. this firm would earn excess profit.
    b. price would equal LRAC.
    c. the firm would suffer losses.
    d. marginal revenue would just be sufficient to cover marginal costs for all units.

17. Under the Clayton Act, which of the following was illegal, even if it was not shown to lessen competition substantially?
    a. price discrimination
    b. tying contracts
    c. horizontal mergers by stock acquisition
    d. interlocking directorates

18. Under the Clayton Act,
    a. the same person can sit on the boards of directors of competing corporations.
    b. mergers are illegal.
    c. monopoly is illegal.
    d. the Sherman Act was repealed.

19. Which of the following is concerned primarily with price discrimination?
    a. Sherman Act
    b. Clayton Act
    c. Robinson-Patman Act
    d. Celler-Kefauver Act

20. Imperfect knowledge about a product can cause
    a. excessive resources devoted to producing a product.
    b. consumers paying too high a price for a product.
    c. overconsumption of a product.
    d. All of the above answers are true.
    e. None of the above answers a.-c. are true.

chapter 14

Environmental Economics

Some years ago, the Nobel Prize-winning economist Milton Friedman and his wife Rose wrote "Free to Choose," in which they put forward the importance of choice in economic as well as personal decisions. Consistent with freedom of economic choices, Americans can select from an almost unlimited number of goods and services. When it comes to transportation, for example, the typical family may drive Minis or Maximas. This same family may own touring bikes, mountain bikes, and hybrid bikes that incorporate features of each. Some U.S. citizens own boats, and others own Jet Skis. Those in colder climates may get around on sleds, snowshoes, or snowmobiles. Some families even own their own planes. The choice of what to buy in the United States is a private decision. I will choose a snowmobile over snowshoes if I want to travel fast and am willing to spend the money. I will choose a Jet Ski over a kayak if I find high-speed travel more exciting than paddling along quietly.

While my choice is private, my decision has consequences for others. My Jet Ski may create waves that threaten to tip your kayak. The noise I make may spoil your desire for peace and quiet. It may also scare wildlife. And the fuel I use to power the Jet Ski not only adds to fuel consumption, but also can contribute to water pollution. Engine exhaust may even make a small contribution to carbon emissions, which may contribute to climate change. Many fear that global warming is causing melting of the polar ice caps, resulting in rising ocean levels and massive flooding of coastal areas throughout the world, as well as climate shifts that could render today's farms tomorrow's deserts.

The other side of the Friedman call for freedom is the damage that is done when these freedoms are limited by government. Up to this point, the competitive market has been shown to be the best engine to generate what consumers want at the lowest possible price. Yet the unbridled use of many of these goods, from Jet Skis and snowmobiles to Coke cans and cigarettes, may not be the best choice for society or the planet. Competitive markets work well when producers and consumers consider all costs in their decisions. But for some goods and services, decision makers fail to include the cost to others of their decision, such as revving the Jet Ski or snowmobile to the detriment of others or throwing the Coke can or cigarette butt out the car window. Although these are local problems, other problems are global in scale, such as carbon emissions from gasoline-burning engines that many believe cause global warming.

This chapter will begin by showing why competitive markets may fail to sufficiently protect the environment and why government intervention may improve our well-being. First, we will see that competitive markets result in market failure by producing "too much pollution." Then we will see how we might correct the market failure, including the possibility of government intervention. Finally, the Friedmans would urge us to recognize that while the government has the potential to improve our well-being, there is also the potential for government failure, where government intervention actually worsens the outcome.

In this chapter, you will learn to solve these economics puzzles:

- Why do competitive markets produce too many hogs and charge too low a price for those hogs?

- How can government legislation, taxes, and permits help society achieve its environmental goals?

- Can government intervention actually reduce environmental quality?

14-1 Competitive Markets and Environmental Efficiency

While society values goods and services produced in markets, it also values air, water, and other environmental amenities. Air and water are shared resources that generally are not priced in the marketplace. The result is that markets often treat these resources as if they were free, resulting in their overuse. Competitive markets, which are the ideal in efficiently allocating many goods and services, fail to achieve preferred levels of output when they treat valuable resources such as air and water as if they were free.

The competitive market has been shown in earlier chapters to achieve *economic efficiency*. This efficiency exists when the price to consumers, reflecting marginal benefit, equals marginal cost. Consumers, such as Jet Ski buyers, consider purchase price, styling, and performance features, such as speed, when comparing models. Producers choose what type of jet ski to make based on profit maximization. Assuming perfect competition, profit maximization occurs where price equals marginal cost.

Private benefits and costs

Benefits and costs to the decision maker, ignoring benefits and costs to third parties. Third parties are people outside the market transaction who are affected by the product.

Buyers and sellers consider only their personal or private benefits and costs. Private benefits and costs are benefits and costs to the decision maker, ignoring benefits and costs to third parties. Third parties are people outside the market transaction who are affected by the product. As explained in Chapter 4, benefits and costs to third parties are known by a variety of names, including third-party effects, spillovers, and most commonly *external benefits and costs* or *externalities*. Recall that externalities are benefits or costs that are not considered by market buyers and sellers. Noise pollution is an externality that affects third parties not powering Jet Skis.

Other externalities that degrade the environment include sulfur emissions from coal-burning electric power plants and the emission of chlorofluorocarbons

(CFCs) associated with aerosol sprays and air conditioners. Sulfur emissions are widely thought to contribute to acid rain, resulting in tree deaths and fish kills. CFCs may be linked to a hole in the atmosphere's ozone layer, which increases the chance of skin cancer from the sun's ultraviolet rays. While CFCs have declined greatly as a result of a worldwide agreement known as the Montreal Protocol, the ozone hole is not expected to disappear before 2050. Automobile emissions contribute to air pollution, which reduces visibility and impairs health. Natural gas prices have fallen to their lowest level in years as a result of a new technology known as hydraulic fracturing, or "frakking," which allows producers to extract more natural gas than they could previously. But with frakking has come reports of contaminated groundwater; flames coming out of faucets; and most recently, small earthquakes that have been attributed to frakking near Youngstown, Ohio.

Everyday externalities include the secondhand effects of cigarette smoke on the health of nonsmokers, as well as cigarette butts tossed out of car windows, farmers' use of pesticides that wash into soil and water with detrimental health effects, and even noise from your next-door neighbor who is having a loud party while you are trying to study for an economics exam. Externalities can be positive as well as negative. You benefit from your classmate's decision to get a flu vaccine.

When externalities are present, competitive markets are not likely to achieve economic efficiency. In competitive markets, price, which reflects marginal private benefit, equals marginal private cost. Efficiency for society requires consideration of both private and social benefits and costs. Social benefits are the sum of benefits to everyone in society, including both private benefits and external benefits. Social costs are the sum of costs to everyone in society, including both private costs and external costs. The condition for economic efficiency occurs when each unit of a good that is produced creates at least as much benefit to society as it does social cost. As a society, we do not want to produce any units of a good that create more in additional social cost than they create in extra social benefit. In other words, we do not want our scarce resources used up on items that will not enhance our collective well-being. A succinct way of stating this condition for maximizing social welfare is to produce units of any good up to the point where

Social benefits and costs

The sum of benefits to everyone in society, including both private benefits and external benefits. Social costs are the sum of costs to everyone in society, including both private costs and external costs.

$$\text{Marginal social benefit} = \text{marginal social cost}$$

Environmental regulations force market participants to include externalities in their decision making. For example, U.S. regulations prohibit the use of CFCs in air conditioners, aerosol cans, and other products. Although regulations such as the ban on CFCs reduce emissions, they are not necessarily the most efficient approach to achieving less pollution. With the dramatic decrease in legal supply, price can rise to the point where some suppliers make the good available illegally. Still, if the side effect is sufficiently dangerous, a ban may be appropriate.

A different approach is that instead of mandating the technology to achieve the goal, the government can specify the goal, but leave the method up to the firm. Suppose businesses wish to expand in areas with high levels of pollution. As an alternative to reducing their own emissions, they can pay another party to reduce its emissions to meet the regulation. For example, a steel company wishing to expand can buy up old cars and retire them as a way of reducing emissions. It may be cheaper for the company to pay someone else to reduce emissions than to achieve an in-house reduction. While the primary purpose of the government's 2009 Cash for Clunkers program was to stimulate car sales, a secondary purpose was to substitute new, high-mileage, low-polluting vehicles in place of old, low-mileage, high-polluting vehicles. We discuss this different approach in more detail later in the chapter in the section on emissions trading.

14-1a PRIVATE AND SOCIAL COSTS

When a producer of Jet Skis or any other product chooses a production method, the producer is motivated by profit maximization. To maximize profit, the firm must choose the most efficient, least costly production method. Production costs include the costs of capital, labor, natural resources (such as land or energy), and entrepreneurship. External costs to others, such as pollution, are not included in production costs because the firm considers only its private costs. Social costs include private costs and external costs.

14-1b COMPETITION AND EXTERNAL COSTS

Suppose large amounts of carbon emissions are produced by gasoline-powered lawn mowers. To reduce pollution, the manufacturer must redesign the engine. Also, suppose there is a lawn mower manufacturer, GreenAcres, that considers social costs. It will choose a different production method for lower emissions lawn mowers. This production method for lower emissions lawn mowers must have a higher cost than the method used by other, more polluting lawn mowers produced by other firms. If this were not the case, other companies would already be using this method.

In a perfectly competitive market, consumers perceive all products as identical. While there may be exceptions, the typical consumer will pay no more for an environmentally friendly GreenAcres mower than for other lawn mowers. In the short run, GreenAcres will earn less than other firms because its costs are higher. In the long run, GreenAcres will lose money and eventually go out of business. Only the lowest-cost firms will survive in the long run. Because price exactly equals minimum private average (and marginal) cost in the long run, average cost for the environmentally conscious company will lie above price, resulting in losses and eventual exit from the industry.

Exhibit 1(a) compares the typical and the "green" lawn mower companies in the short run. Exhibit 1(b) compares the two companies in the long run. The typical company chooses the lowest-cost method of production considering *private cost* only. Its marginal private cost and average private cost are shown as MPC and APC, respectively. The "green" company chooses the production method that has the lowest marginal and average *social cost*, shown as MSC and ASC, respectively. In the short run, MSC lies above MPC, so that the "green" company produces less. In the long run, ASC lies above APC, so the "green" company loses money and eventually exits the industry.

14-1c COMPETITIVE MARKET INEFFICIENCY WHEN EXTERNALITIES EXIST

In competition, only firms that choose the lowest-cost method of production will survive. Firms that choose higher-cost methods will lose money and eventually exit the industry. There is no room for GreenAcres or any other firm that does not minimize cost.

EXHIBIT 1	A Comparison of Costs for Typical and "Green" Firms

A "green" firm has higher costs in both the short run and the long run. The typical firm considers only private costs, as shown by MPC (marginal private cost) in part (a) and APC (average private cost) in part (b). The "green" firm includes both private and external costs, as shown by MSC (marginal social cost) in part (a) and ASC (average social cost) in part (b). These curves reflect social costs. In the short run, price in a competitive industry equals marginal private cost. The "green" firm produces a smaller quantity than the competitive firm. In the long run, price equals minimum long-run average private cost in a competitive industry. Minimum cost for the "green" firm is above price, so the "green" firm loses money and eventually leaves the industry.

(a) Short-run marginal cost   (b) Long-run average cost

SOURCE: © Cengage Learning 2014

Rewarding firms that ignore externalities while punishing firms that recognize externalities is not socially efficient. Efficiency requires that price reflect marginal social benefit and equal marginal social cost. Competition results in a price that reflects marginal private benefit and equals marginal private cost. Efficiency requires that all relevant opportunity costs be included in marginal social cost, while competition forces firms to consider only private costs if they are to survive. If they are allowed to, competitive firms will ignore harmful by-products of their products, such as pollution, climate change, and congestion.

Exhibit 2 shows lawn mower market equilibrium in a competitive market of traditional firms compared to a market of environmentally sensitive "green" firms. Competitive industry supply, S_P, sums the *marginal private costs* of "typical" individual firms that ignore externalities, while "green" industry supply, S_S, sums the *marginal social costs* of GreenAcres and other firms that recognize external costs in their engine design.

When externalities are present, competition leads to a lower price and a larger quantity than the socially efficient point [also see Exhibit 8(a) in Chapter 4] By ignoring external costs, competitive firms produce "too much," and the market

EXHIBIT 2	A Comparison of Equilibriums for Typical Competitive and "Green" Industries

A typical competitive industry operates at price P_c, below the socially efficient price P_s, which would be charged by "green" firms, including all social costs. The competitive industry produces too large a quantity Q_c, compared to the socially efficient quantity Q_s, and charges too low a price, P_c, compared to the socially efficient "green" industry price, P_s.

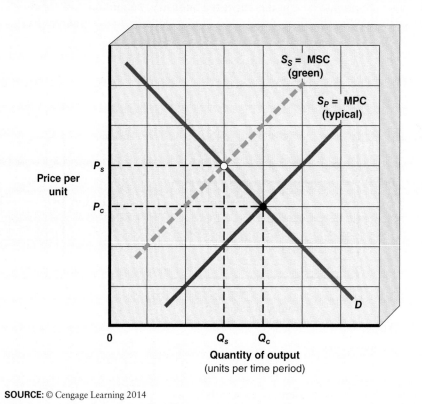

SOURCE: © Cengage Learning 2014

equilibrium price is "too low," compared to a socially efficient industry. Competition leads to too many lawn mowers bought and sold because neither the buyers nor the sellers take into account the external cost of lawn mower engines that release emissions when used for mowing. When there are external costs, the efficient point is at the intersection of the demand curve and the social supply curve, S_S.

From society's point of view, the efficient outcome is an equilibrium quantity of Q_s lawn mowers sold at price P_s. Associated with this outcome is a smaller quantity of pollution than the quantity at the competitive equilibrium. The quantity of pollution associated with quantity Q_s of lawn mowers is the efficient quantity of pollution.

If left to the competitive market, profit-maximizing producers would have no reason to reduce emissions. Emissions reductions, if they occurred at all, would be only an unintended by-product of technological change. For example, if manufacturers substitute a smaller engine so as to reduce lawn mower fuel use, the smaller engine would emit fewer pollutants. The emissions reduction is a by-product of the market reward for a more fuel-efficient mower, which consumers want and are willing to pay for. For emissions reduction to be worthwhile in its own right in a competitive market, it is necessary that consumers be willing to pay for a lower emissions mower.

Why won't consumers offer more for a cleaner mower, just as they might for a more fuel-efficient one? First, consider choosing between two mowers that are identical except that one mower uses one gallon of gas per acre, while the other uses two gallons per acre. You will be willing to pay more for the first mower because you will get to keep the full monetary benefit of reduced fuel purchases.

Now suppose you must choose between two identical mowers except that the "green" mower emits only half as much pollution as the other one. The typical con-sumer will not be willing to pay more for the "green" mower because individually he or she will get only a negligible benefit. Benefits will extend to everyone in the form of cleaner air and reduced global warming. Furthermore, if others buy "green" mowers, you will get the benefits whether or not you purchase a low-emission machine. You are better off being a *free rider*. Recall from the definition of a public good in Chapter 4 that a free rider is someone who enjoys benefits with-out paying the cost. You will get the same benefit of cleaner air whether or not you buy the clean mower. So you will choose to be a free rider and pay nothing for cleaner air, rather than paying extra to get a low-emission machine and still breath-ing the same cleaner air.

The end result is that no one buys a low-emission mower. Each individual chooses to free-ride hoping to benefit from others who choose the "green" model. Once again, competitive markets are unlikely to be efficient.

Free rider
An individual who enjoys benefits without paying the costs.

> **CONCLUSION:** *Unregulated competitive markets will oversupply and underprice products that pollute.*

14-1d EFFICIENT QUANTITY OF POLLUTION

The efficient production level for society is where marginal social benefit equals marginal social cost. The efficient amount of pollution is the amount generated at the socially efficient output level. It is of utmost importance to recognize that the efficient quantity of pollution is not zero. Zero pollution would require zero lawn mowers. Unless society is willing to abandon the American ideal of a neatly trimmed, emerald green lawn, there will continue to be lawn mowers. Nor is it likely that many Americans will return to manual push mowers that do not require fuel, but are slower and take more effort to use than gasoline-engine mowers.

Other alternatives to consider are reduced-emission or emission-free lawn mowers, such as electric mowers. For a parallel situation, consider alternatives to conventional gasoline-engine automobiles. Alternatives include solar and electric vehicles, as well as other transport modes, such as bus, rail, and bicycle. Solar cars, powered by photovoltaic cells, and hydrogen-powered cars are among the vir-tually emission-free alternatives. But a fundamental concept in economics is that there are tradeoffs. Currently, the cost of solar and hydrogen cars is too high given society's unwillingness to pay for reduced emissions. Performance may suffer as well; solar cars, for example, are slower and less able to climb mountainous terrain compared to gasoline-powered cars.

14-2 Achieving Environmental Efficiency

Competitive markets fail to produce the socially efficient quantity when there are externalities. Externalities are a cause of market failure. As explained in Chapter 4, market failure occurs when the private market fails to produce society's preferred outcome.

When there is market failure, we must consider alternatives to the market to achieve efficiency. Government has a potential role when market failure occurs. Just as government can apply antitrust laws when an industry is not competitive, government can apply environmental laws when an industry ignores external costs. Not only are cars required to have catalytic converters, but many states also require annual inspections to make sure the converters are working properly (and to check that consumers have not removed the converters in order to improve gas mileage!).

In the environmental arena, as in other areas of government intervention, there is always the possibility of government failure. Government failure occurs when the government fails to correct market failure. Government officials may fail to achieve an efficient outcome either by doing too little about pollution or by doing too much.

Government officials motivated to keep their jobs may be influenced by large campaign contributors as well as by voter desires. A Michigan legislator is likely to be sympathetic to the concerns of the auto industry and will also be aware of the autoworker layoffs and unemployment that accompany reduced car production. The official may be less motivated by externalities that are borne by third parties who do not vote in Michigan. On the other hand, a New York legislator may support an overly strict emissions standard for automobiles. New York voters benefit from cleaner air and are less concerned about auto-industry job losses.

Much of the effort of environmental economists has gone toward improving the odds that government will help, rather than hinder, attempts to reach environmental goals. Economists generally favor incentive-based regulations over command-and-control regulations. Incentive-based (IB) regulations set an environmental goal, but are flexible as to how buyers and sellers achieve the goal. Incentive-based regulations can make it profitable for firms to reduce emissions. Command-and-control (CAC) regulations set an environmental goal and dictate how the goal will be achieved. Firms unable to meet the goal are penalized, and those that exceed it are not rewarded.

The advantage of IB over CAC regulations is comparable to the advantages of a market system over a command system. Market systems are more efficient because they allow gains from comparative advantage. Businesses can pursue activities with low opportunity costs. Similarly, allowing firms to choose how to achieve environmental goals encourages firms that can improve at low cost to reduce emissions more than firms less able to achieve lower emissions.

More efficiency gains are obtainable from IB regulations than from CAC regulations in both the short run and long run. In the short run, allowing firms to choose how they will reduce emissions is more efficient than prescribing a single approach because firms incur different opportunity costs to lower emissions. In the

Market failure

A situation in which market equilibrium results in too few or too many resources used in the production of a good or service.

Government failure

Government intervention or lack of intervention that fails to correct market failure.

Incentive-based regulations

Government regulations that set an environmental goal, but are flexible as to how buyers and sellers achieve the goal.

Command-and-control regulations

Government regulations that set an environmental goal and dictate how the goal will be achieved.

long run, firms have an incentive to further reduce emissions by improving their technology. It is possible, although unlikely, that CAC regulations will be as efficient as IB regulations in the short run, just as it is possible, although unlikely, that a command system will happen to choose the lowest cost method of production. In the long run, however, command systems do not encourage innovative technology. There is no reward for improving, only a penalty for not meeting the standard. Let's consider how CAC and IB regulations reduce auto emissions.

14-2a COMMAND-AND-CONTROL REGULATIONS

In the 1970s, the U.S. government mandated the use of catalytic converters to reduce auto pollutants. The converter results in reduced hydrocarbon emissions associated with the burning of gasoline. While the catalytic converter undoubtedly reduces pollution, it suffers from several inefficiencies.

First, the requirement that cars have catalytic converters is uniform throughout the country. The marginal car in a high-pollution region, such as Los Angeles, has a much higher external cost than the same car driven across the prairies of Kansas. Efficiency calls for stricter regulations in automobile-intensive regions, such as Los Angeles. Second, there may be other technologies that can achieve the same reduced emissions at a lower cost. Finally, automakers have little incentive to invest in better future technology because the regulations require the firm to meet, but not beat, the standard.

A more subtle inefficiency is that CAC regulations may act as a barrier to entry to other firms, both domestic and international. The U.S. auto industry initially resisted environmental controls, knowing that controls would drive up costs. Foreign manufacturers, such as the Japanese automakers, already met the proposed U.S. standards, but achieved their goal with a different technology. Catalytic converters put the Japanese at a temporary cost disadvantage. Japanese cars were required to have catalytic converters even though they already met the air quality standard.

Another example of CAC regulations is the use of Corporate Average Fuel Economy (CAFE) standards. These oft-discussed standards require each automaker to achieve a minimum number of miles per gallon (mpg) for its fleet. For example, Ford's cars might be required to achieve at least 27 mpg. When this standard was imposed, Ford and other manufacturers invented minivans and sport-utility vehicles (SUVs), which were classified as trucks and therefore not subject to the standard. Until the recent upswing in gas prices, consumers shifted to minivans and SUVs despite their lower fuel efficiency. In the end, Ford met the higher fuel standard, while the average mpg of vehicles actually on the road decreased! By 2025, the standard is scheduled to increase to 54.5 mpg. Only time will tell what ingenuity car companies will display to meet this lofty target.

14-2b INCENTIVE-BASED REGULATIONS

Effluent Taxes   The simplest type of incentive-based (IB) regulation is an effluent tax. An effluent tax is a tax on the pollutant. If car manufacturers face a tax that depends on emissions, they can no longer ignore externalities. They must consider the tax based on emissions in addition to private resource costs. Exhibit 3 shows how an effluent tax can achieve efficiency.

A less direct way of reducing pollutants is a gasoline tax. By increasing the price of gasoline to car owners, the tax results in a smaller quantity demanded of

Effluent tax

A tax on the pollutant.

EXHIBIT 3	Using an Effluent Tax to Achieve Environmental Efficiency

An effluent tax can achieve efficiency. The tax, t, equals marginal external cost, which is the difference between marginal social cost (MSC) and marginal private cost (MPC) at the socially efficient quantity (Q_s). The firm's production costs now include both its private costs and the effluent tax, so it makes production decisions as if it considered marginal social cost.

SOURCE: © Cengage Learning 2014

gasoline and, in turn, lower emissions. Over time, consumers faced with high gas prices seek more fuel-efficient cars, lowering emissions even more.

Taxes can achieve efficiency directly or indirectly and can be placed on buyers or sellers. Although the tax approach may appear simple in theory, some important practical difficulties limit the use of pollution taxes. First, how do we measure external cost? There is no market that buys and sells air pollution or climate change. So the tax is at best an approximation of external cost. Second, studies that have attempted to measure external cost find it to be quite large, requiring a substantial tax. It is widely thought that the price of a gallon of gasoline would have to increase by at least $1 to approximate the external costs of auto emissions, and more if we allow for military costs associated with protecting the oil we obtain from the Middle East. Such a tax, added to the approximately 40 cents in state and federal gasoline taxes that are already imposed to pay for roads, would be unpopular with voters and as a consequence would be unattractive to politicians.

Those who favor the effluent tax approach propose that its revenues could be used for a variety of purposes, one of which could be a reduction in income taxes. If so, this approach is referred to as a *double dividend*. Lower pollution is one dividend, and lower taxes on income is another dividend because lower income taxes encourage work effort. But there is no guarantee that the funds from the effluent tax will be used to reduce income taxes.

Emissions Trading   What if there were a market in which air pollution or climate change could be traded? As a result of the 1990 amendments to the Clean Air Act, markets were established for emissions trading. Emissions trading allows firms to buy and sell the right to pollute. The most active market was for sulfur emissions. Sulfur dioxide causes increased rain acidity. Acid rain can cause damage to lakes, trees, and even cars. It can also contribute to air pollution. The program is widely believed to have reduced the cost of reducing sulfur emissions on the order of 40 percent, as compared to the previous CAC approach. As will be discussed later, the sulfur program is now crippled by a court decision that has essentially reinstituted CAC. As firms must now install prescribed technology, the value of permits has dropped almost to $0.

There are additional markets for air pollution rights. A firm that wishes to build new factories that would add to pollution in an already polluted area may have to find *offsets* before it can relocate. An offset is a reduction in an existing pollution source to counteract pollution from a new source. For example, U.S. Generating Company, an independent power producer, offered in 1992 to buy up automobile "clunkers" in return for permission to expand a coal-fired generating facility that would use the Delaware River and pollute the air. Under this program, the company offered to pay $500 to owners of cars that were at least 16 years old. The factory scraps the old clunkers, thereby offsetting its new source of pollution. The clunker approach makes use of the fact that a small percentage of cars are responsible for a disproportionate share of pollution.

To set up trading for lawn mower or car emissions, the government could require manufacturers to buy permits for each unit of emissions. In the short run, firms would include the cost of permits along with private costs as a component of price. The price would increase most for the dirtiest machines. In the long run, firms would have an incentive to build cleaner products. Firms with the cleanest products would need the fewest permits and might even profit by selling permits to companies that cannot improve as quickly. Whereas GreenAcres lawn mowers would go out of business in an unfettered competitive lawn mower industry, the company would now be in a position to succeed.

Alternatively, emissions trading for cars could be attached to CAFE standards. Auto manufacturers would have to possess permits based on gasoline use. This system would allow manufacturers with more fuel-efficient fleets to sell permits to manufacturers relying on larger, less fuel-efficient cars.

A simple example can demonstrate the cost savings of an IB approach, such as emissions trading, compared to a CAC approach. Suppose two coal-fired electric

Emissions trading
Firms buying and selling the right to pollute.

Offset
A reduction in an existing pollution source to counteract pollution from a new source.

plants each emit 100 tons of sulfur into the air. Plant A can reduce sulfur at a constant cost of $100/ton, while plant B can do so at a cost of $200/ton. The Environmental Protection Agency (EPA) announces that it wishes to cut sulfur emissions in half. Under CAC regulations, each plant will reduce its emissions to 50 tons, a reduction of 100 tons. The cost to plant A is $100/ton × (50 tons) = $5,000. The cost to plant B is $200/ton × (50 tons) = $10,000. The total cost to society of achieving a 100-unit reduction in sulfur emissions is $15,000.

Now suppose the EPA announces that it will give away 100 emissions permits, 50 to plant A and 50 to plant B. Each plant now is allowed to emit 50 units of sulfur. If the two plants do nothing more, each will have to reduce emissions from 100 to 50 tons, and each will do so at the same cost as with CAC regulations. However, there is a lower-cost solution. Plant A is willing to sell its 50 permits at any price above $100/ton because it can reduce its emissions in-house for $100/ton. Plant B is willing to buy emissions permits at any price below $200/ton, the marginal cost of reducing its own emissions. Both plants can gain by plant A selling an additional 50 permits to plant B at a price between $100 and $200.

Suppose they agree to a price of $150/ton. Plant A now finds it profitable to eliminate all its emissions. Its marginal cost of reducing emissions is $100/ton. By reducing its emissions to zero, plant A no longer needs any permits. It can sell its 50 permits for $150/ton, making a profit of $50 per ton by reducing its emissions to zero (at a cost of $100/ton) and selling its permits to plant B (at a gain of $150/ton). In turn, plant B finds it cheaper to buy permits for $150/ton than to reduce emissions at a cost of $200/ton.

In sum, the net cost to reduce emissions by 100 tons for plant A is $100/ton × (100 tons) − $150/ton × (50 tons) = $2,500. The cost to plant B, now that it no longer reduces emissions, is $150/ton × (50 tons) = $7,500. The cost to society of achieving a 100-unit reduction in emissions is $10,000, which is $5,000 less than under the original CAC method.

The real world helps us see problems that textbook theory does not always reveal. Emissions trading has the theoretical potential to achieve environmental goals at the lowest cost, but so far, real-world trading has fallen short of efficiency. There are a number of obstacles to efficient trading, some minor and some major.

New-source bias

Bias that occurs when regulations provide an incentive to keep assets past the efficient point.

Taking the factory and clunker example, one minor problem is a new-source bias. A new-source bias occurs when regulations provide an incentive to keep assets past the efficient point. A firm faced with the need to find offsets if it builds a new factory may stick with an older and dirtier factory rather than pay for offsets. If there were no offset program, it might have been economical to retire the old factory in favor of a less polluting new factory. But if the new factory cannot meet the air quality standard without offsets, the lowest-cost solution becomes extending the life of the old plant. Electric utilities are also finding it worthwhile to continue to operate old coal-fired plants that are exempt from stringent regulations known as New Source Performance Standards that can only be met by newer technology. There also may be a type of free-rider problem. Car owners about to junk their 15-year-old clunkers for $500 may keep them another year if a firm or the government is willing to pay, for example, $4,000 for them. These minor problems are just growing pains of emissions trading, and future emissions markets will find ways to reduce these undesirable outcomes.

Other growing pains include small numbers of buyers or sellers, imperfect information about the value of a permit, and concerns about permit value in the future. Firms will trade actively only if trading is a better alternative than other choices. Some firms may shut down or perhaps relocate in other countries where permits are not needed. Also, emissions may be higher in regions where electric utilities buy permits rather than reduce emissions, known as the hot spot problem. The hot spot problem applies to emissions that do not disperse uniformly, and therefore, emissions may be higher in locations where firms buy permits that allow them to increase emissions. The Tennessee Valley Authority has been a buyer of permits. Not only does Tennessee's air quality suffer, but North Carolina believes its air quality is also compromised as pollution drifts east. The collapse of the sulfur program came about when North Carolina joined other states to challenge the sulfur trading program on the grounds that it did not account for hot spots. Ironically, studies have suggested that the hot spot problem was not widespread.

Nevertheless, emissions trading, increasingly referred to as cap and trade, is increasingly accepted. Europe has established a carbon trading system. Such a system was seriously discussed in the United States, but ultimately did not get through the political process. When new programs are initiated, the government may give away permits according to production or pollution over a designated period, or it may sell permits through an auction to the highest bidders. Naturally, businesses prefer a giveaway, and so governments have typically given away permits to get businesses on board. Buyers of permits may be companies such as electric utilities, or they may be environmentalists. Environmentalists can achieve pollution reduction by outbidding utilities for permits and then refusing to sell them to utilities, thereby forcing the utilities to reduce pollution.

The Chicago Board of Trade, or "Smog" Exchange, allows trading in pollution permits much like trading on the New York Stock Exchange. Companies are required to own a permit for each unit of emissions. Clean companies need fewer permits and offer to sell their extra permits on the exchange. Dirty companies need additional permits and are buyers on the exchange. They will only buy if the permit price is less than what it would cost them to reduce pollution by one more unit. Sellers of permits will charge at least what it costs them to reduce pollution by one more unit. While U.S. companies are not yet required to pay for carbon emissions, some firms have participated in the Chicago exchange in anticipation that controls may be coming.

Exhibit 4 shows the permit price per ton of sulfur dioxide allowances since trading began in 1994. Over the years, the permit price has fluctuated widely from a high of almost $1,600 after a sharp reduction in permits with the passage by the EPA of the Clean Air Interstate Act on March 10, 2005, to its current low of near $0. The EPA has also introduced a market for the trading of nitrogen oxides (NO_x), an emission that contributes to smog. That price has also fluctuated enormously. Initially traded at approximately $800 per ton, it quickly rose to $1,400 but has since fallen to as low as $40.

There is concern that the benefits of emissions trading will be diminished by lack of trading and lingering opposition to the idea of creating a market for pollution rights, especially when permits are given away rather than auctioned, particularly if rights are given away for carbon emissions. There is even a revival of interest in command-and-control regulation. If the government happens to pick the right approach and rewards cleaner technology, some economists favor CAC over the imperfect emissions trading to date. For example, there are supporters of California's approach to reducing auto emissions. California considered a requirement that 10 percent of the cars sold within California must be emissions-free. They anticipated that the mandate would be met with electric vehicles (EVs). However, California then modified the requirement that a similar percentage of cars be hybrids, rather than EVs. It may well be that the requirement will be modified

Hot spot problem
For emissions that do not disperse uniformly, emissions may be higher in locations where firms buy permits that allow them to increase emissions.

| EXHIBIT 4 | Monthly Average Price of Sulfur Dioxide Allowances under the Acid Rain Program |

The Chicago Board of Trade allows trading in pollution permits much like trading on the New York Stock Exchange. This figure shows the sulfur dioxide allowance prices.

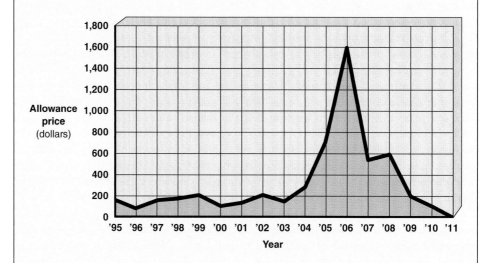

SOURCES: http://www.ferc.gov/market-oversight/othr-mkts/emiss-allow/othr-emns-no-so-pr.pdf and http://www.epa.gov/airmarkets/progress/arp06.html.

further, or eventually abandoned. One of the problems of the CAC approach is trying to second-guess the movements of the market. Just as California assumed electric cars would be a viable alternative, the U.S. government subsidized solar power in the late 1970s. Solar power did not develop as an attractive alternative then, and now lags wind and other alternatives as a renewable source of energy.

Furthermore, critics of the California approach point out that EVs are not emissions-free if they require electricity from a power plant. Certainly, power plants also pollute, although there may be an advantage to transferring pollution away from the most densely populated areas. EVs powered by photovoltaic cells (PVCs) that use solar energy are closer to being emissions free, but there is still pollution in the PVC production process. Perhaps the greatest drawback to EVs is their poor performance to date. They suffer from poor acceleration, limited range, and limited ability to climb hills. Critics maintain that inferior products continue to be the legacy of CAC approaches. In response to rising gas prices, Toyota and other car manufacturers responded with gas-electric hybrid vehicles. Critics suggest that the market has a superior ability to innovate, such as a hybrid vehicle with low emissions, as compared to CAC requiring zero emissions that could not be met by a gas-electric hybrid. However, even hybrid electricity use is not pollution free. Battery production is likely to lead to pollution. If the hybrid is recharged by plugging it in, there is still pollution at the electricity plant where the power is generated. And solar power requires the use of large silicon glass panels, potentially requiring massive amounts of land, as well as silicon waste disposal problems. In 2009, the U.S. government provided a low-cost loan to Solyndra, a manufacturer of solar panels. The company declared bankruptcy in 2011, leading to accusations of government corruption and renewed charges that the government should not pick winners.

There continues to be new programs to promote the use of alternative fuels. Renewable portfolio standards have been adopted by the majority of states that require electric utilities to meet a percentage of their electricity generation using alternative fuels. While not an incentive-based program, it at least allows flexibility in the mix of alternative fuels that can be used. If states could trade, allowing one state to pay another state to help meet a requirement, program efficiency could then be increased. A federal program might be still more efficient and could establish uniformity regarding the definition of alternative fuels. Does wood count? What about energy efficiency? In some states, these sources count, in other states they don't qualify. Feed-in tariffs work in a similar way, requiring utilities to purchase alternative fuels at a relatively high price. These types of rates were actually used in the late 1970s, again to promote solar energy.

> **CONCLUSION:** *Economists generally believe that incentive-based regulations are more efficient than command-and-control regulations.*

Still, much of the public seems more comfortable with controls and rules than with prices and trading. There are a number of possible explanations for the public's view. First, people have difficulty accepting that any pollution is efficient. Nobody wants to think about a higher risk of cancer due to a leak from a nuclear power plant.

Another possible reason for the public's view is a mistrust of experts. People were told by experts that nuclear power would be safe; that hazardous waste disposal sites would not leak; and that people living near Yucca Mountain, Nevada, would accept that location as a safe site for burial of nuclear radioactive wastes. Nevada has since fought off allowing Yucca Mountain to be used as a waste site. The disaster at the Fukushima nuclear plant after the Japanese earthquake and tsunami in March 2011 has been a major setback for nuclear energy, which had been poised for a renaissance by virtue of producing carbon-free electricity. When outcomes differ from what experts promise, the public favors safety over efficiency. No one wants to take a chance on illness or death if the experts are wrong again. And yet would you give up your car or favor a law that set the speed limit at 20 miles per hour? These laws might increase safety, but they would certainly be inefficient.

14-2c   GOVERNMENT AND ENVIRONMENTAL EFFICIENCY

Market failure is likely for products with external costs. To achieve efficiency, buyers and sellers must consider external costs. Government has the power to establish laws, taxes, or permit systems so that market participants pay for external costs.

Although government policy can potentially improve efficiency, there is no guarantee. The countries that emerged from the Soviet Union, where government played a far more dominant role than in the United States, have environmental problems that dwarf those in the United States. In these countries, air and water quality borders on ecocide, with high rates of illness due to environmental degradation. The Chernobyl disaster, in which a nuclear plant malfunctioned and released radioactivity, has caused thousands of premature deaths. In China, another nation where the government plays a major role in the economy, the Beijing weather report frequently calls for "smoky" skies as well as dust storms blowing in from an expanding desert.

In the United States, large numbers of U.S. Department of Defense sites are among the biggest environmental challenges. Hazardous wastes from the production of weapons resulted in toxic burial sites, including Oak Ridge, Tennessee, and Richland, Washington. The U.S. Forest Service frequently permits lumber companies to harvest trees from national forests at subsidized prices. Government environmental officials have even gone to prison for illegally meeting with industry representatives to weaken environmental regulations. And government has tended to ignore the cost to firms of complying with hundreds of thousands of pages of environmental legislation, a set of regulations more voluminous than the U.S. Tax Code. For all these reasons, as well as the widespread dissatisfaction with government in general, there is concern about the effectiveness of government policy in achieving environmental goals. Government officials may pursue self-interest, which could favor polluting industries over societal interests as a whole, especially if industry executives are major campaign contributors.

The Coase Theorem   Ronald Coase, an economist at the University of Chicago and the winner of the 1991 Nobel Prize in Economics, was among the first to caution against the assumption that government intervention in the environmental arena would improve upon private-sector environmental performance. In his famous 1960 paper "The Problem of Social Cost," he even questioned the fundamental assumption of market failure. According to the Coase Theorem, the private sector could achieve social efficiency with minimal government intervention. The role of the government should be limited to the legal establishment of property rights, with environmental disputes resolved with the help of the court. The Coase Theorem is the proposition that private market negotiations can achieve social efficiency regardless of the initial definition of property rights.

As an example of how the Coase Theorem works, consider a train that throws off sparks and occasionally burns a farmer's crops. Exhibit 5 shows railroad profits increasing and farm profits decreasing as more trains run. Each train has an external cost. Emitted sparks can cause fires, which reduce the farmer's crops. If the railroad ignores external cost, it appears that the railroad would choose to run five trains so as to maximize profit, leaving the farmer with no crops. It also appears that to protect the farmer, there should be a law requiring the railroad to find a spark-free technology. Suppose the courts establish a law that farmers have the right to spark-free trains. How could the railroad meet this tougher environmental standard? The railroad could change to a new, higher-cost technology. The cost must be higher, or the railroad would have chosen this environmentally friendly technology in the first place. If the cost is too high, the railroad might go out of business or relocate its tracks away from farms. Alternatively, it may be less expensive to offer the farmer money for any burned crops.

If the trains continue to throw off sparks, the first train will reduce the farmer's profits by $5 and will add $20 to the railroad's profits. The two parties will be

Coase Theorem

The proposition that private market negotiations can achieve social efficiency regardless of the initial definition of property rights.

EXHIBIT 5	Choosing the Efficient Amounts of Spark-Emitting Trains and Farm Crops				
Number of Trains	Total Railroad Profit	Marginal Railroad Profit	Number of Crops	Total Farm Profit	Marginal Farm Profit
0	$ 0		10.5	$105	
		$20			$ −5
1	20		10	100	
		20			−10
2	40		9	90	
		20			−20
3	60		7	70	
		20			−30
4	80		4	40	
		20			−40
5	100		0	0	

SOURCE: © Cengage Learning 2014

able to negotiate a deal, with the farmer receiving a payment of between $5 and $20 from the railroad. What about a second train? This train will add another $20 to railroad profits, but will reduce farm profits by $10. Again, the farmer will permit the railroad to run a second train as long as the railroad pays the farmer at least $10. If a third train runs, marginal social benefit will equal marginal social cost. Society will benefit from more train service, but will lose from fewer crops. The third train will be marginally worthwhile, but additional trains will not run. The fourth train will add $20 to railroad profits, but will reduce farm profit by $30. Thus, the railroad will lose money if it runs the fourth train. By clearly establishing the farmer's right to spark-free trains, the number of trains will be decreased from five to three trains.

Notice that the farmer will be better off if he or she allows sparks as long as the railroad compensates the farmer for damage than if the government requires a spark-free technology. The farmer earns $105 when there are no sparks. With sparks, the farmer will earn at least $105, receiving between $5 and $20 for permitting the first train, at least $10 (and possibly as much as $20) for permitting the second train, and another $20 for the third train. With three trains, the farmer will still earn $70 from crops, in addition to a minimum of $35 for allowing trains, for a total of at least $105.

This outcome is similar to the government solutions examined earlier. Efficiency leads to the efficient amount of pollution, which is typically not zero. No sparks may mean no trains. But Coase asks, Why assume that society is best served by assuming the railroad is the polluter and the farmer the victim? In the 1800s, sparking engines may have been the best available technology, and an occasional fire may have been a natural consequence.

How Should Carbon Emissions Be Reduced: Cap and Trade or Carbon Taxes?

Applicable Concepts: emissions trading and effluent taxes

With the great success that was enjoyed until recently in sulfur dioxide trading and the more modest success of trading in nitrous oxides, we may eventually turn to emissions trading to reduce carbon emissions in the United States. In fact, Europe has already instituted such an exchange. In 2005, the European Union instituted a carbon permit system for electric utilities and other major emitters such as steel companies. However, smaller emitters such as smaller industries and nonpoint sources such as automobiles are not covered.

In some ways, carbon would seem ideally positioned for emissions trading. To the extent that it contributes to global warming, the effect is the same regardless of where that emission takes place. Whether carbon is emitted in France, Spain, or for that matter the United States or China, its effect on the global atmosphere is the same. In this way, carbon is a better candidate for trading than is sulfur, which has a greater impact in the vicinity of its release.

But there is increasing questioning of whether or not carbon trading is preferable to a tax on carbon. One contributing argument is the initial European experience was disappointing. Early projections anticipated that carbon contracts would trade for about $50/ton, given the high cost to industry of

Shutterstock.com/Lane V. Erickson

reducing carbon. By mid-2006, the price of contracts had collapsed to €8/ton (approximately $12). The primary factor for the lower-than-expected price was that numerous national governments had issued enough permits that covered producers did not find it necessary to buy permits. In fact, carbon emissions increased in many countries during the first year of the carbon trading regime.

So consider the outcome if property rights to produce sparks are given to the railroads so that trains are allowed to throw off sparks. If the farmer does nothing, the railroad will run five trains, and the farmer will end up with no crops and no profit. The farmer will increase profit by $40 if only four trains run. Since the fifth train will add only $20 to railroad profit, the farmer can afford to pay as much as $40 (or as little as $20) to stop the fifth train. Similarly, the farmer will gain $30 by stopping the fourth train, more than enough to pay the railroad for forgoing $20 in profit. Once again, negotiations will stop at three trains, the efficient number.

This example demonstrates the Coase Theorem: As long as the courts clearly establish property rights, markets may achieve social efficiency *regardless of the initial assignment of property rights*. Coase's great contribution was to focus attention

Since that time, there have been reforms in the trading system, and prices have risen. While price jumped to €30 by the end of 2007, it is now back down to €6 (US $8). The possibility that an emissions trading system might not reduce carbon emissions has given impetus to those who argue for a carbon tax.

For those who prefer the tax approach, perhaps the most widespread reason is that the tax will raise revenue. The revenue could provide a double dividend, if it is used to reduce taxes that discourage productive activities, such as the income tax. Of course, the revenues could go toward research and development into carbon-reducing technologies or reduction of the national debt. (Or tax opponents would point out it could simply be wasted on pork barrel projects.) While permits could raise revenue if they were auctioned off, rather than given away, the auction would negate one of the main reasons for favoring permits—that industry is willing to support the permit approach because they do not have to pay for the permits.

Other reasons to favor the tax approach include its ability to be more comprehensive, covering all carbon emissions, rather than being limited primarily to large point sources. It could also be fashioned to include other greenhouse gases, such as methane; farmers, for example, would pay a tax based on the number of cows they owned and perhaps on other animals that emit methane.[1] Some prefer the carbon tax on equity grounds. Particularly if coupled with a reduction in income taxes, the tax could offer relief to lower-income households. In contrast, the main beneficiaries of giving away permits are stockholders, which may represent wealthier citizens.[2]

The latest twist is that cap and trade has been spurned by the United States with its opponents calling it a disguised tax that will show up in higher prices for all carbon-emitting goods. In a recent court decision, carbon was declared a pollutant, giving the U.S. Environmental Protection Agency the right to regulate carbon emissions. New regulations aimed at carbon will likely mean the end of new coal-fired electric plants. But existing plants will still pour carbon into the air unless there is a program that imposes a cost on all carbon emissions.

Analyze the Issue

1. What are the advantages and disadvantages of carbon trading, as compared to sulfur dioxide trading?
2. What are the advantages and disadvantages of a tax system, as compared to carbon trading?
3. If a carbon tax is preferable to a trading system on economic grounds, why might we adopt a trading system anyway?

---

1. Jonathan A. Lesser, "Control of Greenhouse Gases Difficult with Cap-and-Trade or Tax-and-Spend," *Natural Gas and Electricity*, December 2007, Wiley Periodicals Inc., http://www3.interscience.wiley.com/cgi-bin/jhome/105559587.
2. Ian W. H. Parry, "Should We Abandon Cap and Trade in Favor of a CO$_2$ Tax?" *Resources*, Summer 2007, 6–10, Resources for the Future, http://www.rff.org/Publications/Resources/Pages/AbandonCapandTrade.aspx

Source: © Cengage Learning 2014

on property rights, a focus that foreshadowed the emissions-trading approach that allows firms to negotiate by buying and selling the right to pollute. But Coase argues for an even more limited role for government. In his view, the government should establish courts and then let markets negotiate.

Some Limitations on the Coase Theorem Coase was instrumental in raising concern about government solutions. It might then seem a simple step to accept his claim that private markets would efficiently resolve environmental problems. In actuality, only a small number of environmental problems readily qualify for Coase Theorem solutions.

First, there are no transactions costs in the Coase Theorem. Transactions costs are the costs of negotiating and enforcing a contract. Turning to the courts

Transactions costs
The costs of negotiating and enforcing a contract.

Why Is the Climate Change Problem So Hard to Solve?

Applicable Concepts: emissions trading and effluent taxes

With much ado, representatives from 192 countries traveled to Copenhagen (or Hopenhagen, as it was referred to) in late 2009, hoping to build upon the Kyoto Conference to reach agreement on steps to reduce carbon emissions, which the participants believed were contributing to global warming. Two weeks later, they came away with little more than a nonbinding agreement brokered between the United States and China that five countries agreed to mitigate their carbon emissions and that the United States would be able to monitor China's compliance with the agreement. In short, the conference produced almost no progress on greenhouse gas emissions.

Why is this problem proving so difficult to solve? There has been widespread, although far from universal, agreement that human activity is contributing to a warming planet, which could lead to flooding, desertification, weather events such as stronger hurricanes, and the spread of tropical diseases to warming countries.

DeoSum/Shutterstock.com

First, consider Copenhagen. Participants came from both developed and developing countries. Developing countries threatened to walk out on the meetings. Kyoto set a precedent that only developed countries would be expected to pay the cost of reducing emissions. Developing countries would be exempt or would expect to receive subsidies or technology transfer from developed countries to reduce emissions. At Copenhagen, developing countries sought millions of dollars to reduce emissions.[1]

Another controversy is over whether countries, developed and developing, should receive credit for offsets. Brazil, for example, wants credit for slowing or reversing the rate at which it is cutting down its rain forest. Trees store carbon. Countries could receive carbon credits for planting trees or possibly for slowing the rate at which trees are being cut down. Brazil and other developing countries want developed countries to pay them, as they claim they are slowing their own development by growing new forests or slowing the conversion of existing forest to agricultural resources.

Further, there is not even agreement over which countries are still developing. At Kyoto, China was still classified as developing, exempt from taking action at its own expense. After growing its gross domestic product (GDP) at nearly a 10 percent annual rate for the last three decades and becoming the world's largest greenhouse gas emitter in the process, is it still a developing country? For purposes of

is a costly process, in terms of both time and money. And dealing with the source of the externality has its own costs. Have you ever tried to negotiate with a noisy neighbor at 2 a.m.? However, there are also transactions costs associated with government solutions. So Coasean negotiations may be preferable to government intervention even when there are substantial private transactions costs.

avoiding the cost of slowing emissions, never mind reducing them; it is advantageous to claim you are still developing. The argument is that developed countries were able to grow and emit greenhouse gases with impunity; it is only fair that developing countries be able to do the same. Developed countries have benefited from industrialization without having to pay for their emissions, so it is fair that they should do so now.

If countries at an international conference do agree to be financially responsible for reducing emissions, they may face problems when they bring those proposals home. First, they face opposition from those who do not accept the argument that human activities contribute to global warming. Recent surveys of the U.S. population showed a decline in those who were convinced that human activities contribute to global warming. And this was even before the incident that has become known as Climategate, whereby intercepted emails of climate change scientists showed the likely suppression of evidence not favorable to their view and obstacles put in the way of those more skeptical of climate science. Some of the intercepted emails had been written by members of the International Panel on Climate Change (IPCC), a Nobel Prize-winning group containing thousands of scientists, including Nobel laureates in Economics. Even more recently, their work was found to have numerous errors, not the least of which was predicting the melting of Himalayan glaciers by 2035, when the actual studies had arrived at a date of 2350.

But perhaps most fundamentally, a solution will have to address the problems of externalities and public goods. Consumers and producers of carbon-emitting products, such as coal-burning power plants and gasoline-burning automobiles, will, in the absence of government intervention, ignore emis-sions. Furthermore, any global agreement to reduce emissions will benefit everyone, whether or not an individual has borne the expense of reducing emissions, a classic example of a public good. Benefits are nonrival and nonexcludable. And agreeing on whether we will actually reduce emissions or simply slow them down will be contentious. Nor is CO_2 the only greenhouse gas. Methane, of which cows are a major emitter, is smaller in volume, but more potent in effect.

So in sum, taking action to slow or stop climate change is one of the most difficult problems humans have faced. There is disagreement on whether humans have contributed to the problem, what countries are responsible for paying for the solution, and how to develop a mechanism that can overcome externalities and public goods problems. In the end, we may find ourselves left to adapt to climate change, abandoning low-lying lands, accepting millions of immigrants from those countries, switching to hot weather crops, and losing flora and fauna that cannot adapt, unless we can develop new approaches to address this challenge.

Analyze the Issue

1. Give an example of an equity (fairness) issue that arises in working toward a global agreement to limit greenhouse gas emissions.

2. Give an example of an efficiency (market failure) issue that arises in working toward a global agreement to limit greenhouse gas emissions.

3. Many countries argue that they should get credit for offsets, such as planting trees. Explain whether the case for offsets is based on efficiency or equity arguments.

---

1. A comprehensive summary of the issues faced by delegates to Copenhagen was contained in a special section of *The Wall Street Journal* entitled "If It Warms Up, Who's Going to Pay," Monday, December 7, 2009.

Source: © Cengage Learning 2014

Second, there are no differences in willingness to pay (WTP) and willingness to accept (WTA) in the Coase Theorem. Many studies have found that people's willingness to pay to acquire a property right, such as an improvement in air quality, is less than the compensation they require to give up a property right, such as accepting lower air quality. If the farmer has the right to spark-free air, he or she may require $50 to allow sparks. Alternatively, if the farmer has to buy that right, he or she may be willing to pay only $20. In other words, people may not view giving up an environmental right you already own as equivalent to buying a right you do not currently own.

Third, Coase assumes there are only two parties in the negotiation. Externalities are typically third-party problems, and there may be many third parties. Do all the farmers get together to negotiate with the railroad, and do all the neighbors get together to reduce noise from the party? With many participants, there is once again a free-rider problem. If noise levels decrease, I get the benefit whether or not I contribute to the negotiations. So why contribute? Stated as a concept, if some individuals benefit while others pay, the free-rider problem is that few will be willing to pay for improvement of the environment or other public goods. As a result, these goods are underproduced.

A related debate is taking place regarding the "Tragedy of the Commons." Tragedy of the Commons occurs when individuals use an open access resource to the point of exhaustion, basing their use on private benefits, while disregarding external costs to others. Ecologist Garrett Hardin maintained that for open access resources, such as fisheries or grazing lands where there are no private property rights, the resources will be overused to the point of collapse. An additional fisher or cattle farmer will consider the private benefit to fishing or grazing, but not the externality of reduced fish or grass to other users of the resource. But political scientist Elinor Ostrom, who was one of the winners of the 2009 Nobel Prize in Economics, finds that private parties will design institutions to sustain the resource. The group will define common property rights, rather than allowing open access, where no one has rights. In some circumstances such as the commons, common property may be preferable to open access or private property rights.

Ecologists and other physical scientists have taken the issue a step further with calls for sustainability. The most common definition is that of the Bruntland Commission (1987) that calls for us to "meet the needs of the present without compromising future needs." Economists have begun to recognize that ecological systems such as the carbon cycle that influences climate must be sustained in order to sustain life. Sustainability is typically a more stringent requirement than social efficiency, as socially efficient solutions are not limited to those that also increase the well-being of future generations. Social efficiency may call for actions to reduce carbon emissions, but sustainability might well call for stronger actions to ensure that future generations are protected from today's decisions. Economists are at the early stages of how to incorporate sustainability into economic analysis.

Free-rider problem

The problem that if some individuals benefit, while others pay, few will be willing to pay for improvement of the environment or other public goods. As a result, these goods are underproduced.

Tragedy of the Commons

Individuals will use an open access resource to the point of exhaustion, basing their use on private benefits while disregarding external costs to others.

Sustainability

Meeting the needs of the present generation without compromising the ability of future generations to meet their needs.

CONCLUSION: *Neither government nor the markets can be asserted to be the best solution to environmental problems. On balance, though, the effort to work toward improved government solutions seems worthwhile, given the outcome for the environment of purely self-interested markets. But alternatives including private ownership and common-property ownership may be preferable where transactions costs are low enough to allow individual or group negotiations over resource use.*

✓ CHECKPOINT

Is It Efficient to Buy Odor-Reducing Technology if You Live Next to a Hog Farm?

You live next door to a hog farm. It is estimated that the smell from the hog farm reduces the value of your home by $7,000. For $5,000, you can purchase technology that reduces the hog smell by half, so your house value would decrease by only $3,500. Assuming the hog farm has the property right to locate next door and that it is not required to reduce the hog smell, what will you do? Will you do nothing or buy the new technology?

Key Concepts

Private benefits and costs
Social benefits and costs
Free rider
Market failure
Government failure
Incentive-based regulations

Command-and-control regulations
Effluent tax
Emissions trading
Offset
New-source bias

Hot spot problem
Coase Theorem
Transactions costs
Free-rider problem
Tragedy of the Commons
Sustainability

Summary

- **Externalities** are benefits or costs that fall on third parties who are neither buyers nor sellers. Pollution is a negative externality or an external cost that is a by-product of many industrial production processes.
- **Market failure** is present when the market produces a socially inefficient outcome (for example, when there are externalities). All firms, including competitive firms, consider private costs, but disregard external costs in making decisions.
- **Government failure** occurs when public-sector actions or lack of actions move us away from desired outcomes, such as efficiency. Government officials seeking campaign contributions and votes may choose environmental measures that favor wealthy contributors over society's best interests.

- **Command-and-control regulations** occur when the government dictates the approach to achieving an environmental goal. Command-and-control regulations are generally inefficient on three grounds: They do not distinguish between high- and low-pollution areas, they do not allow firms to choose lower-cost technologies that could achieve the environmental standard, and they do not encourage investment in improved technology to lower future emissions.
- **Incentive-based regulations** build on markets to achieve environmental efficiency. **Effluent taxes** are taxes that reflect external costs. **Emissions trading** allows firms to buy and sell the "right to pollute."
- The **hot spot problem** applies to emissions that do not disperse uniformly, and therefore,

emissions may be higher in locations where firms buy permits that allow them to increase emissions.

- The **Coase Theorem** maintains that markets can be efficient in the presence of externalities with minimal government intervention. Even in the presence of externalities, markets may produce efficient outcomes so long as property rights are clearly established.

- **Transactions costs, income effects,** and **free-rider problems** are obstacles to achieving environmental efficiency through markets. Transactions costs are the costs of negotiating an agreement, income effects are present when limited income prevents one party from being

able to afford the efficient solution, and free-rider problems are present when participants are better off hiding than revealing their willingness to pay for an environmental improvement.

- **Tragedy of the Commons** predicts that individuals will use fisheries and grazing areas to exhaustion, as they base their use on their private benefits, disregarding the effects of their use on others. The "tragedy" has been questioned by Elinor Ostrom, who finds individuals will establish institutions converting open access property to common property so that the resource can be sustained over time.

Summary of Conclusion Statements

- Unregulated competitive markets will oversupply and underprice products that pollute.
- Economists generally believe that incentive-based regulations are more efficient than command-and-control regulations.
- Neither government nor the markets can be asserted to be the best solution to environmental problems. On balance, though, the

effort to work toward improved government solutions seems worthwhile, given the outcome for the environment of purely self-interested markets. But alternatives including private ownership and common-property ownership may be preferable where transactions costs are low enough to allow individual or group negotiations over resource use.

Study Questions and Problems

1. Compare price and quantity in a competitive industry to those of a "green" industry for a product that generates pollution.

2. Suppose a car sells for $20,000 in a market with no pollution restrictions. Will the car sell for more than $20,000, less than $20,000, or $20,000 when there are pollution restrictions? Explain.

3. You are considering whether to buy one house for $100,000 or another identical house located near high-voltage electric power lines

for $90,000. Assume that it has been established that living near high-voltage lines increases the risk of cancer due to electromagnetic fields (EMFs). If you choose the $90,000 house, is the radiation from EMFs an externality? Explain.

4. Restaurants have observed that large parties (eight or more) leave a lower average tip than smaller parties. Identify the effect, which also makes it more difficult to reach global

environmental agreements, responsible for this phenomenon.

5. Suppose your instructor gives eight homework assignments during the semester. She indicates that anyone who does not turn in all eight assignments will automatically fail the course. Is this an example of a command-and-control or an incentive-based regulation? Explain any inefficiencies of your instructor's approach.

6. Environmentalists in Tennessee brought suit against the Champion Paper Company of North Carolina for polluting the Pigeon River, which flows from North Carolina into eastern Tennessee. Tennessee claimed that the coffee-colored water smelled bad and would not support fishing or swimming. Environmentalists requested that the river be restored to its pristine state, whereby water quality is restored to the level before the coming of industry. The Environmental Protection Agency heard the suit and applied an efficiency standard. Is pristine water an efficiency standard? Explain.

7. Draw a graph to demonstrate your answer to question 6.

8. California once proposed legislation that would have required 10 percent of its car fleet to be nearly emissions-free by the year 2003. This mandate spurred electric vehicle research. Such vehicles could be powered by photovoltaic cells or by batteries that are recharged using an electrical outlet. Would you agree that it is correct to conclude that electric vehicles that use electrical outlets are emissions-free? What about electric vehicles powered by photovoltaic cells?

9. Explain why consumers would not be willing to pay the full costs of a less polluting car in the absence of government regulations.

10. Evaluate the following statement: "When products pollute, government solutions are more efficient than market solutions."

11. Provide an example of a market where you think the Coase Theorem applies. Explain why you think the market satisfies assumptions regarding transactions costs, income effects, and free riders.

12. In a study of ranching laws in the 1800s, an economic researcher found that as these laws restricted the ability of cattle to roam freely, agricultural output increased. Does this researcher's findings support the Coase Theorem? Explain.

13. If we are to take action against global warming, we must reduce carbon emissions. Explain how to reduce carbon emissions by using
    a. command-and-control regulation.
    b. an effluent tax.
    c. emissions trading.

14. A global agreement known as the Montreal Protocol led to the phase-out of chlorofluoro-carbons (CFCs), chemical compounds found in aerosol cans and refrigerants. CFCs may have contributed to the growing hole in the ozone layer. With a diminished ozone layer, there is an increased chance of skin cancer. Explain the effect of this agreement on the price of deodorants and air-conditioning. Also, is a ban on CFCs an efficient approach to the ozone hole problem?

15. Explain the "Tragedy of the Commons" as described by Garrett Hardin. Why does Elinor Ostrom disagree with Hardin's prediction that fisheries and other "commons" will collapse?

16. Distinguish between the concepts of social efficiency and sustainability. Provide an example to demonstrate the distinction.

For Online Exercises, go to the Tucker Web site at www.cengage.com/economics/tucker.

✔ CHECKPOINT ANSWER

Is It Efficient to Buy Odor-Reducing Technology if You Live Next to a Hog Farm?

It is not efficient to purchase the new odor-reducing technology. It would cost $5,000, but would increase your house value by only $3,500. It is not efficient to cut the odor by half if the market will not compensate you sufficiently for reduced hog odors. If your only option is to do nothing or to buy the new technology and you said do nothing, **YOU ARE CORRECT.** (A third option is to pay the hog farm to locate elsewhere. You would be willing to pay up to $7,000 to avoid the $7,000 lost due to the smell of the nearby farm.)

Sample Quiz

For an explanation of the correct answers, visit the Tucker Web site at www.cengage.com/economics/tucker.

1. Private costs are
   a. the full resource costs of an economic activity.
   b. always less than social costs.
   c. the costs of an economic activity borne by the producer.
   d. All of the above answers are correct.

2. When negative externalities such as pollution exist, competition leads to
   a. a socially efficient outcome.
   b. too few goods being bought and sold.
   c. a market equilibrium price that is too high.
   d. more production than would be efficient.

3. From an economic viewpoint, the optimal amount of pollution
   a. is zero because all pollution imposes costs on society.
   b. is that amount firms create when they maximize economic profits by setting their marginal private costs equal to market price.
   c. is that amount where the marginal social costs of producing a good precisely equals the price of the good.
   d. Both answers b. and c. are correct.

4. Which of the following is the best example of a command-and-control regulation?
   a. effluent taxes on pollutants
   b. emissions trading
   c. the requirement that automobiles have catalytic converters
   d. offset programs

EXHIBIT 6	Private and Social Cost

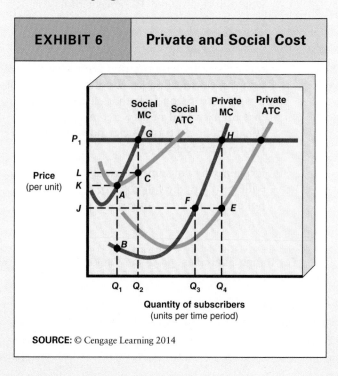

SOURCE: © Cengage Learning 2014

Sample Quiz *continued*

5. The perfectly competitive profit-maximizing firm in Exhibit 6 creates water and air pollution as a consequence of producing its output of pigs. If pollution costs are borne by third parties, the firm will maximize economic profit by choosing to
   a. voluntarily incur costs to reduce its pollution.
   b. produce at output rate Q_3.
   c. produce at output rate Q_2.
   d. produce at output rate Q_4.

6. Use Exhibit 6 to answer the following question. To maximize social welfare, the firm should produce at which of the following output rates?
   a. 0
   b. Q_2
   c. Q_3
   d. Q_4

7. At the efficient level of pollution, the
   a. total social costs and total social benefits of reduction are equal.
   b. marginal social costs and marginal social benefits are equal.
   c. marginal private costs and marginal private benefits are equal.
   d. total private costs and total private benefits are equal.

8. A government policy that charges coal producers a fee per ton of coal produced (an "effluent charge") where the fee is determined by the amount of pollutants discharged into the air or water will lead to a (an)
   a. decrease in the market equilibrium quantity of coal produced
   b. a decrease in the market equilibrium price of coal
   c. increase in the market equilibrium price of coal
   d. Both answers a. and c. are correct.

9. Which of the following is an important lesson from the environmental experience in the former Soviet Union?
   a. Free-market economies are unlikely to have long-run environmental problems.
   b. Government-owned industry tends to be cleaner than privately-owned industry.

   c. Pollution can be worse in a communist system than in a capitalist system.
   d. Pollution can be worse in a capitalist system than in a communist system.

10. According to *most* economists, reducing automobile emissions to zero would be
    a. optimal.
    b. inefficient.
    c. beneficial.
    d. impossible.

11. In a perfectly competitive industry, which of the following is *true*?
    a. The competitive price is higher and the quantity is higher than the socially efficient point.
    b. The competitive price is higher and the quantity is lower than the socially efficient point.
    c. Since the industry is perfectly competitive, price and quantity are at the socially efficient levels.
    d. The competitive price is lower and the quantity is higher than the socially efficient point.

Each time Orville flies over Wilbur's house, the noise reduces the value of Wilbur's house. Exhibit 7 shows the profits to Orville of each flight and the value of Wilbur's house at each flight.

EXHIBIT 7	Impact of Flights on House Value		
Number of flights	Total profits	Marginal profits	Value of Wilbur's house
1	$10,000	$10,000	$100,000
2	18,000	8,000	95,000
3	24,000	6,000	90,000
4	28,000	4,000	85,000
5	30,000	2,000	80,000

SOURCE: © Cengage Learning 2014

Sample Quiz *continued*

12. As shown in Exhibit 7, if Orville has the property right to fly over Wilbur's house but Wilbur is allowed to negotiate with Orville on the number of flights, what will be the number of flights?
    a. 2
    b. 3
    c. 4
    d. 5

13. As shown in Exhibit 7, if Wilbur has the property right to have no planes flying over his house but Orville is allowed to negotiate with Wilbur, what will be the number of flights?
    a. 2
    b. 3
    c. 4
    d. 5

14. As shown in Exhibit 7, at the socially efficient number of flights, what will be the market value of Orville's house?
    a. $100,000
    b. $95,000
    c. $90,000
    d. $85,000

15. According to the Coase Theorem, the private sector can achieve social efficiency if the government
    a. establishes and enforces property rights.
    b. imposes taxes to serve as proxies for external costs.
    c. sets rigorous environmental standards.
    d. encourages competition with antitrust laws.

16. The costs of an economic activity borne by the producers are
    a. always less than social costs.
    b. the full resource costs of an economic activity.
    c. private costs.
    d. All of the above answers are correct.

17. An example of the command-and-control approach to environmental policy is
    a. placing a tax on Freon to reduce its use and the corresponding CFC emissions (which contribute to the ozone hole).
    b. requiring car producers to install new air conditioners that do not use Freon.
    c. allowing coal producers to buy and sell permits to allow CFC emissions.

    d. allowing individuals to sue Freon producers if CFC emissions exceed a government-set standard.

18. If a good is produced up to the point where marginal social benefit equals marginal social cost,
    a. social welfare is maximized.
    b. the good is overproduced and the market is inefficient.
    c. firms are earning zero profits.
    d. all externalities have been eliminated.

Jack enjoys smoking, while Jill fears that secondhand smoke will shorten her life. Exhibit 8 shows the value Jack places on each cigarette he smokes and the value Jill places on her shortened life. Use the table to answer the following questions.

EXHIBIT 8	Cigarette Smoking Data		
Quantity of cigarettes	Total value to Jack of cigarettes	Days of life lost	Total value to Jill of days lost
1	$ 50	1	$ 30
2	90	2	60
3	120	3	90
4	140	4	120
5	150	5	150

SOURCE: © Cengage Learning 2014

19. As shown in Exhibit 8, if smokers have the right to smoke as many cigarettes as they wish and nonsmokers have the right to negotiate, how many cigarettes will Jack smoke?
    a. 1
    b. 3
    c. 5
    d. more than 5

20. As shown in Exhibit 8, what is the socially efficient number of cigarettes?
    a. 0
    b. 1
    c. 3
    d. 5

This road map feature helps you tie together material in the part as you travel the Economic Way of Thinking highway. The following are review questions listed by chapter from the previous part. The key concept in each question is given for emphasis, and each question or set of questions concludes with an interactive game to reinforce the concepts. Go to the Tucker Web site at www.cengage.com/economics/tucker, select the chapter, and play the visual causation chain game designed to make learning fun. Enjoy the cheers when you are correct and suffer the jeers if you miss. The correct answers to the multiple choice questions are given in Appendix C of the text.

CHAPTER 13. ANTITRUST AND REGULATION

1. **Key Concept: Imperfect Information**
   Overconsumption of a product can be caused by:
   a. excessive resources devoted to producing a product.
   b. consumers paying too low a price for a product.
   c. lack of knowledge about a product.
   d. All of the answers above are correct.
   e. None of the answers above are correct.

2. **Key Concept: Imperfect Information**
   Which of the following may be the result of a higher equilibrium price for a product?
   a. Advertising
   b. Expectations
   c. Imperfect information
   d. All of the above
   e. None of the above

3. **Key Concept: Imperfect Information**
   Deficient information on unsafe products can cause:
   a. overconsumption of a product.
   b. waste of resources used to produce a product.
   c. consumers paying a higher price for a product.
   d. All of the answers above are correct.
   e. None of the answers above are correct.

 Causation Chain Game
The Impact of Imperfect Information of the Market—Exhibit 6

CHAPTER 14. ENVIRONMENTAL ECONOMICS

4. Key Concept: Effluent Tax

Which of the following is *true* about incentive-based regulations?

a. They set an environmental goal, but are flexible on how to achieve the goal.
b. They obtain more efficiency gains than is obtainable from CAC regulations.
c. Effluent taxes are an example of incentive-based regulations.
d. All of the above are true.
e. None of the above are true.

5. Key Concept: Effluent Tax

In order to increase society's total welfare (social efficiency), a production process that produces a negative externality should be:

a. taxed.
b. provided by the government.
c. ignored.
d. subsidized.

6. Key Concept: Effluent Tax

A government policy that charges coal producers a fee per ton of coal produced (an "effluent charge"), where the fee is determined by the amount of pollutants discharged into the air or water will lead to a(an)

a. decrease in the market equilibrium quantity of coal produced.
b. decrease in the market equilibrium price of coal.
c. increase in the market equilibrium price of coal.
d. a. and c. are correct.

7. Key Concept: Effluent Tax

In order to achieve efficiency, the size of an effluent tax should be based on

a. the external cost created by the pollutant.
b. people's willingness to pay for a cleaner environment.
c. the expense of installing new "green" equipment.
d. the number of free riders in the industry.

Causation Chain Game
Environmental Efficiency and Effluent Taxes

Macroeconomics Fundamentals

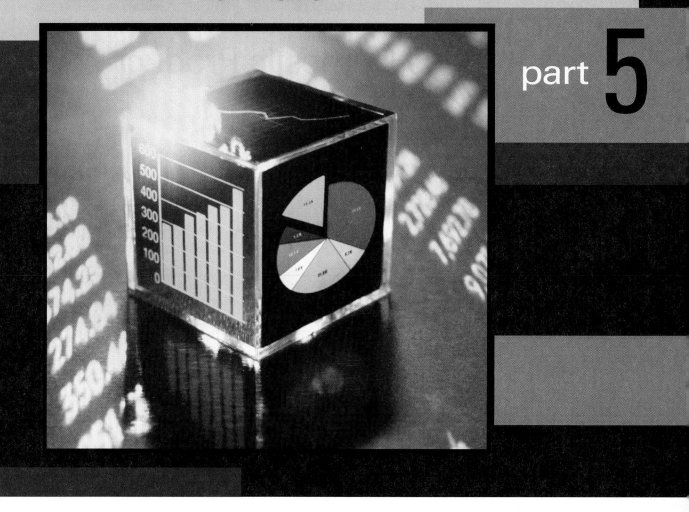

T he three chapters in this part explain key measures of how well the macroeconomy is performing. Knowledge of this material is vital to the discussion of macro theory and policy in the next part. The first chapter in this part explains GDP computation. The next chapter begins by teaching how to measure business cycles and concludes with an examination of unemployment. The final chapter in this part explores the measurement and consequences of inflation.

chapter 15

Gross Domestic Product

Measuring the performance of the economy is an important part of life. Suppose one candidate for president of the United States proclaims that the economy's performance is the best in a generation, and the opposing presidential candidate argues that the economy could perform better. Which statistics would you seek to determine how well the economy is doing? The answer requires understanding some of the nuts and bolts of *national income accounting*. National income accounting is the system used to measure the aggregate income and expenditures for a nation. Despite certain limitations, the national income accounting system provides a valuable indicator of an economy's performance. For example, you can visit the Internet and check the annual *Economic Report of the President* to compare the size or growth of the U.S. economy between years.

Prior to the Great Depression, there were no national accounting procedures for estimating the data required to assess the economy's performance. To provide accounting methodologies for macro data, the late economist Simon Kuznets published a small report in 1934 titled *National Income, 1929–32*. For his pioneering work, Kuznets, the "father of GDP," earned the 1971 Nobel Prize in Economics. Today, thanks in large part to Kuznets, most countries use common national accounting methods. National income accounting serves a nation similar to the manner in which accounting serves a business or household. In each case, accounting methodology is vital for identifying economic problems and formulating plans for achieving goals.

In this chapter, you will learn to solve these economics puzzles:

- Why doesn't economic growth include increases in spending for welfare, Social Security, and unemployment programs?

- Can one newscaster report that the economy grew while another reports that for the same year the economy declined, and both reports be correct?

- How is the calculation of national output affected by environmental damage?

15-1 Gross Domestic Product

The most widely reported measure throughout the world of a nation's economic performance is gross domestic product (GDP), which is the market value of all final goods and services produced in a nation during a period of time, usually a year. GDP therefore excludes production abroad by U.S. businesses. For example, GDP excludes Microsoft's earnings on its foreign operations. On the other hand, GDP includes Toyota's profits from its car plants in the United States. Why is GDP important? It tells a country how well its economy is doing. One advantage of GDP is that it avoids the "apples and oranges" measurement problem. If an economy produces 10 apples one year and 10 oranges the next, can we say that the value of output has changed in any way? To answer this question, we must attach price tags in order to evaluate the relative monetary value of apples and oranges to society. This is the reason GDP measures value using dollars, rather than listing the number of cars, heart transplants, legal cases, toothbrushes, and tanks produced. Instead, the market-determined dollar value establishes the monetary importance of production. In GDP calculations, "money talks." That is, GDP relies on markets to establish the relative value of goods and services.

GDP is compiled by the Bureau of Economic Analysis (BEA), which is an agency of the Department of Commerce. GDP requires that the following two points receive special attention: (1) GDP counts only new domestic production, and (2) it counts only final goods.

> **Gross domestic product (GDP)**
>
> The market value of all final goods and services produced in a nation during a period of time, usually a year.

15-1a GDP COUNTS ONLY NEW DOMESTIC PRODUCTION

National income accountants calculating GDP carefully exclude transactions in two major areas: secondhand transactions and nonproductive financial transactions.

Secondhand Transactions GDP includes only current transactions. It does not include the sale of a used car or the sale of a home constructed some years ago. Such transactions are merely exchanges of previously produced goods and not *current* production of new goods that add to the existing stock of cars and homes. Used items were counted previously in GDP for the year when they were newly produced. However, the sales commission on a used car or a home produced in another GDP period counts in current GDP because the salesperson performed a service during the present period of time.

Nonproductive Financial Transactions GDP does not count purely private or public financial transactions, such as giving private gifts, buying and selling stocks and bonds, and making transfer payments. A transfer payment is a government payment to individuals not in exchange for goods or services currently produced. Welfare, Social Security, veterans' benefits, and unemployment benefits are transfer payments. These transactions are considered nonproductive because they do not represent production of any new or *current* output. Transfer payments are made to people who are entitled to them. The reason could be because of being poor or reaching a certain age. Similarly, stock market transactions represent only the exchange of certificates of ownership (stocks) or indebtedness (bonds) and not actual new production.

> **Transfer payment**
>
> A government payment to individuals not in exchange for goods or services currently produced.

15-1b GDP COUNTS ONLY FINAL GOODS

Final goods

Finished goods and services produced for the ultimate user.

The popular press usually defines GDP as simply "the value of all goods and services produced." This is technically incorrect because GDP counts only final goods, which are finished goods and services produced for the ultimate user. Including all goods and services produced would inflate GDP by *double counting* (counting many items more than once). In order to count only final goods and avoid overstating GDP, national income accountants must take care not to include intermediate goods. Intermediate goods are goods and services used as inputs for the production of final goods. Stated differently, intermediate goods are not produced for consumption by the ultimate user.

Intermediate goods

Goods and services used as inputs for the production of final goods.

Suppose a wholesale distributor sells glass to an automaker. This transaction is not included in GDP. The glass is an intermediate good used in the production of cars. When a customer buys a new car from the car dealer, the value of the glass is included in the car's selling price, which is the value of a final good counted in GDP. Let's consider another example. A wholesale distributor sells glass to a hardware store. GDP does not include this transaction because the hardware store is not the final user. When a customer buys the glass from the hardware store to repair a broken window, the final purchase price of the glass is added to GDP as a consumer expenditure.

15-2 Measuring GDP

GDP is like an enormous puzzle with many pieces to fit together, including markets for products, markets for resources, consumers spending and earning money, and businesses spending and earning money. How can one fit all these puzzle pieces together? One way to understand how all these concepts fit together is to use a simple macroeconomic model called the circular flow model. The circular flow model shows the exchange of money, products, and resources between households and businesses. In exchange for these resources, money payments flow between businesses and households. Exhibit 1 shows the circular flow in a hypothetical economy with no government, no financial markets, and no foreign trade. In this ultra-simple pure market economy, only the households and the businesses make decisions.

Circular flow model

A diagram showing the exchange of money, products, and resources between households and businesses.

15-2a THE CIRCULAR FLOW MODEL

The upper half of the diagram in Exhibit 1 represents *product markets*, in which households exchange money for goods and services produced by firms. The red *supply* arrow in the top loop represents all finished products and the value of services produced, sold, and delivered to consumers. The blue *demand* arrow in the top loop shows why the businesses make this effort to satisfy the consuming households. When consumers decide to buy products, they are actually voting with their dollars. This flow of consumption expenditures from households is sales revenues to businesses and expenses from the viewpoint of households. Notice that the box labeled *product markets* contains a supply and demand graph. This means the forces of supply and demand in individual markets determine the price and quantity of each product exchanged without government interference.

The bottom half of the circular flow diagram consists of the *factor markets*, in which firms *demand* the natural resources, labor, capital, and entrepreneurship needed to produce the goods and services sold in the product markets. Our hypothetical economy is capitalistic, and the model assumes for simplicity that households own the factors of production. Businesses therefore must purchase all their resources from the households. The red *supply* arrow in the bottom loop represents this flow of resources from households to firms, and the blue *demand* arrow is the flow of money payments to households for these resources. These

---

EXHIBIT 1	The Basic Circular Flow Model

In this simple economy, households spend all their income in the upper loop and demand consumer goods and services from businesses. Businesses seek profits by supplying goods and services to households through the product markets. Prices and quantities in individual markets are determined by the market supply and demand model. In the factor markets in the lower loop, resources (land, labor, and capital) are owned by households and supplied to businesses that demand these factors in return for money payments. The forces of supply and demand determine the returns to the factors, for example, wages and the quantity of labor supplied. Overall, goods and services flow clockwise, and the corresponding payments flow counterclockwise.

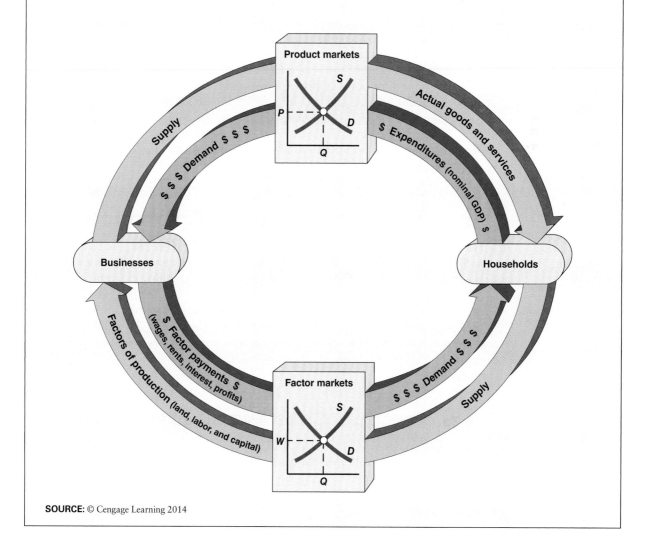

SOURCE: © Cengage Learning 2014

payments are also income earned by households in the form of wages, rents, interest, and profits. As in the product markets, market supply and demand determine the price and quantity of factor payments.

This simple model also assumes all households live from hand to mouth. That is, households spend all the income they earn in the factor markets on products. Households therefore do not save. Likewise, all firms spend all their income earned in the product markets on resources from the factor markets. The simple circular flow model therefore fails to mirror the real world. But it does aid your understanding of the relationships between product markets, factor markets, the flow of money, and the theory behind GDP measurement.

15-2b Flow versus Stock

Flow

A rate of change in a quantity during a given time period, such as dollars per year. For example, income and consumption are flows that occur per week, per month, or per year.

Stock

A quantity measured at one point in time. For example, an inventory of goods or the amount of money in a checking account.

The arrows in Exhibit 1 are flows, rather than stocks. A flow is a rate of change in a quantity during a given time period. Changes in the amount of steel produced per month, the number of computer games purchased per day, the amount of income earned per year, and the number of gallons of water pouring into a bathtub per minute are examples of flows. Flows are always measured in units per time period, such as tons per month, billions of dollars per year, or gallons per hour. A stock is a quantity measured at one point in time. An inventory of goods, the amount of money in a checking account, and the amount of water in a bathtub are examples of stocks. Stocks are measured in tons, dollars, gallons, and so on, at a given point in time.

The important point is this: *All measurements in the circular flow model are rates of change (flows) and tell us nothing about the total amounts (stocks) of goods, services, money, or anything else in the economy.* Consumption expenditures, business production, wages, rents, interest payments, and profits are *flows* of money for newly produced products or resources that affect the level of *stocks* not shown in the model.

15-3 The Expenditure Approach

Expenditure approach

The national income accounting method that measures GDP by adding all the spending for final goods during a period of time.

How does the government actually calculate GDP? One way national income accountants calculate GDP is to use the expenditure approach to measure total spending flowing through product markets in the circular flow diagram. The expenditure approach measures GDP by adding all the spending for final goods during a period of time. Exhibit 2 shows 2011 GDP using the expenditure approach, which breaks down expenditures into four components. The data in this exhibit show that all production in the U.S. economy is ultimately purchased by spending from households, businesses, government, or foreigners. Let's discuss each of these expenditure categories.

15-3a Personal Consumption Expenditures (*C*)

The largest component of GDP in 2011 was $10.7 trillion for the category national income accountants call *personal consumption expenditures*, represented by the letter C. Personal consumption expenditures comprise total spending by households for durable goods, nondurable goods, and services. Durable goods include items such as automobiles, appliances, and furniture because they last longer than three

EXHIBIT 2	Gross Domestic Product Using the Expenditure Approach, 2011		
National income account		**Amount (trillions of dollars)**	**Percentage of GDP**
Personal consumption expenditures (*C*)		$10.7	71%
Durable goods	$1.2		
Nondurable goods	2.4		
Services	7.1		
Gross private domestic investment (*I*)		1.9	12
Fixed investment	1.9		
Change in business inventories	0.04		
Government consumption expenditures and gross investment (*G*)		3.0	20
Federal	1.2		
State and local	1.8		
Net exports of goods and services (*X* − *M*)		−0.5	−3
Exports (X)	2.1		
Imports (M)	2.6		
Gross domestic product (**GDP**)		$15.1	100%

SOURCE: Bureau of Economic Analysis, *National Economic Accounts*, http://www.bea.gov/national/nipaweb/SelectTable.asp?Selected=Y, Table 1.1.5.

years. Food, clothing, soap, and gasoline are examples of nondurables, because they are considered used up or consumed in less than these years. Services, which is the largest category, include recreation, legal advice, medical treatment, education, and any transaction not in the form of a tangible object. This is why the U.S. economy is often referred to as a service economy.

15-3b GROSS PRIVATE DOMESTIC INVESTMENT (*I*)

In 2011, $1.9 trillion was spent for what is officially called *gross private domestic investment* (*I*). This national income account includes "gross" (all) "private" (not government) "domestic" (not foreign) spending by businesses for investment in capital assets that are expected to earn profits in the future. Gross private domestic investment is the sum of two components: (1) *fixed investment* expenditures for newly produced capital goods, such as commercial and residential structures, machinery, equipment, tools, and computers, and (2) change in *business inventories*, which is the net change in spending for unsold finished goods. Note that gross private domestic investment is simply the national income accounting category for "investment," defined in Chapter 2. The only difference is that investment in Exhibit 5 in Chapter 2 was in physical capital, such as manufacturing plants, oil wells, or fast-food restaurants, rather than the dollar value of capital used here.

Now we will take a closer look at gross private domestic investment. Note that national income accountants include the rental value of newly constructed residential housing in the $1.9 trillion spent for fixed investment. A new factory, warehouse, or robot is surely a form of investment, but why include residential housing as business investment rather than consumption by households? The debatable answer is that a new home is considered investment because it provides services in the future that the owner can rent for financial return. For this reason, all newly produced housing is considered investment whether the owner rents or occupies the property.

Finally, the –$121 billion change in business inventories means this amount of net dollar value of unsold finished goods and raw materials was subtracted from the stock of inventories during 2011. A decline in inventories would reduce GDP because households consumed more output than firms produced during this year. When businesses have more on their shelves this year than last, more new production has taken place than has been consumed during this year.

15-3c GOVERNMENT CONSUMPTION EXPENDITURES AND GROSS INVESTMENT (G)

This official category simply called *government spending* includes the value of goods and services government at all levels purchased measured by their costs. For example, spending for police and state university professors enters the GDP accounts at the prices the government pays for them. In addition, the government spends for investment additions to its stock of capital, such as tanks, schools, highways, bridges, and government buildings. In 2011, federal, state, and local government spending (G) totaled $3.0 trillion. As the figures in Exhibit 2 reveal, government purchases by state and local governments far exceeded those of the federal government. It is important to understand that the government spending category of GDP excludes *transfer payments* because, as explained at the beginning of the chapter, they do not represent newly produced goods and services. Instead, transfer payments are paid to those entitled to Social Security benefits, veterans' benefits, welfare, unemployment compensation, and benefits from other programs.

15-3d NET EXPORTS (X − M)

The last GDP account is net exports, expressed in the formula $(X − M)$. Exports (X) are spending by foreigners for U.S. domestically produced goods. Imports (M) are the dollar amount of U.S. purchases of Japanese automobiles, French wine, clothes from China, and other goods produced abroad. The positive sign $(+X)$ means that money flows into the United States from foreigners to pay for our exports. The negative sign $(−M)$ indicates dollars are flowing out of the United States to pay for imports. In 2011, export spending was $2.1 trillion and import spending was −$2.6 trillion. Net exports were therefore −$0.5 trillion. What is the effect of a negative sign for net exports? It means the United States is spending more dollars to purchase foreign products than it is receiving from abroad for U.S. goods. The effect of a negative net exports figure is to reduce U.S. GDP. Stated another way, higher exports (X) relative to imports (M) increases GDP. Prior to the early 1980s, the United States was a consistent net exporter, selling more goods and services to the rest of the world than we purchased from abroad. Since 1983, the United States has been a net importer. International trade is discussed in more detail in the last section of the text.

15-3e A Formula for GDP

Using the expenditure approach, GDP is expressed mathematically in trillions of dollars as

$$GDP = C + I + G + (X - M)$$

For 2011 (see Exhibit 2),

$$\$15.1 = \$10.7 + \$1.9 + \$3.0 + (\$2.1 - \$2.6)$$

This simple equation plays a central role in macroeconomics. It is the basis for analyzing macro problems and formulating macro policy. When economists study the macro economy, they can apply this equation to predict the behavior of the major sectors of the economy: consumption (C) is spending by households, investment (I) is spending by firms, government spending (G) is spending by the government, and net exports (X − M) is net spending by foreigners.

15-4 The Income Approach

The second, somewhat more complex approach to measuring GDP is the income approach. The income approach measures GDP by adding all the incomes earned by households in exchange for the factors of production during a period of time. Both the expenditure approach and the income approach yield identical GDP calculations. As shown in the basic circular flow model, each dollar of expenditure paid by households to businesses in the product markets means a dollar of income flows to households through the factor markets as a payment for the land, labor, and capital required to produce the product. Using the income approach, GDP is expressed as follows:

GDP = compensation of employees + rents + profits + net interest

\+ indirect taxes + depreciation

In practice, it is necessary to add depreciation (capital consumption allowance) to factor payments so that national income equals GDP. Exhibit 3 presents actual 2011 GDP calculated following the income approach, and then each component is discussed in turn.

Income approach

The national income accounting method that measures GDP by adding all incomes, including compensation of employees, rents, net interest, and profits.

15-5 Compensation of Employees

Employees' compensation is the largest of the national income accounts. About 55 percent of GDP in 2011 ($8.3 trillion) was income earned from wages, salaries, and certain supplements paid by firms and government to suppliers of labor. Since labor services play such an important role in production, it is not surprising that employee compensation represents the largest share of the GDP income pie. The supplements consist of employer taxes for Social Security and unemployment

EXHIBIT 3	Gross Domestic Product Using the Income Approach, 2011	
National income account	Amount (trillions of dollars)	Percentage of GDP
Compensation of employees	$8.3	55%
Rental income	0.4	3
Profits	3.0	20
Proprietors' income	1.1	
Corporate profits	1.9	
Net interest	0.5	3
Indirect business taxes	1.2	8
Depreciation	1.7	11
Gross domestic product (GDP)	$15.1	100%

SOURCE: Bureau of Economic Analysis, *National Income Accounts*, http://www.bea.doc/bea.gov/national/nipaweb/SelectTable.asp?Selected=Y, Table 1.7.5.

insurance. Also included are fringe benefits from a variety of private health insurance and pension plans.

15-5a RENTAL INCOME

The smallest source of income is from rent and royalties received by property owners who permit others to use their assets during a time period. For example, this category includes house and apartment rents received by landlords. In 2011, $0.4 trillion was earned in rental income.

15-5b PROFITS

Proprietors' Income   All forms of income earned by unincorporated businesses totaled $1.1 trillion in 2011. Self-employed proprietorships and partnerships simultaneously own their businesses and pay themselves for labor services to their firms.

Corporate Profits   This income category includes all income earned by the stockholders of corporations regardless of whether stockholders receive it. The $1.9 trillion of corporate profits in 2011 was the sum of three sources: (1) dividends, (2) undistributed corporate profits (retained earnings for expanding plant and equipment), and (3) corporate income taxes. Thus, corporate profits using the income approach are "before taxes."

15-5c NET INTEREST

Households both receive and pay interest. Persons who make loans to businesses earn interest income. Suppose you purchase a bond issued by Apple. When Apple pays interest on its bonds, the interest payments are included in the national income accounts. Households also received interest from savings accounts and certificates of deposits (CDs). On the other hand, households borrow money and pay interest on, for example, credit cards, installment loans, and mortgage loans. The net interest of $0.5 trillion in 2011 is the difference between interest income earned and interest payments.

15-5d INDIRECT BUSINESS TAXES

As reported in Exhibit 3, $1.2 trillion was collected by government in the form of indirect business taxes. Why do national income accountants include business taxes in the income approach to GDP competition? Indirect business taxes are levied as a percentage of the prices of goods sold and therefore become part of the revenue received by firms. These taxes include sales taxes, federal excise taxes, license fees, business property taxes, and customs duties. Indirect taxes are not income payments to suppliers of resources. Instead, firms collect indirect taxes and send these funds to the government. Suppose you purchased a new automobile for $20,000, including a $1,000 federal excise tax and state sales tax. These taxes are included in the price, but are income for the government, which represents the public interest of households.

Indirect business taxes

Taxes levied as a percentage of the prices of goods sold and therefore collected as part of the firm's revenue. Firms treat such taxes as production costs. Examples include general sales taxes, excise taxes, and customs duties.

15-5e DEPRECIATION

To reconcile the above income accounts with GDP requires adding the category labeled *consumption of fixed capital*. Consumption of fixed capital is an estimate of the depreciation of capital. This somewhat imposing term is simply an allowance for the portion of capital worn out producing GDP. Over time, capital goods, such as buildings, machines, and equipment, wear out and become less valuable. Depreciation (capital consumption allowance) is therefore a portion of GDP that is not available for income payments. Because it is impossible to measure depreciation accurately, an estimate is entered. In 2011, $1.7 trillion was the estimated amount of GDP attributable to depreciation during the year.

Exhibit 4 presents the conceptual frameworks of the expenditure and income approaches to computing GDP.

✓ CHECKPOINT

How Much Does Mario Add to GDP?

Mario works part-time at Pizza Hut and earns an annual wage plus tips of $15,000. He sold 4,000 pizzas at $15 per pizza during the year. He was unemployed part of the year, so he received unemployment compensation of $3,000. During the past year, Mario bought a used car for $5,000. Using the expenditure approach, how much has Mario contributed to GDP?

EXHIBIT 4	Expenditure and Income Approaches to GDP

Expenditure approach		Income approach
Consumption (*C*) expenditures by households plus		Compensation of employees plus
Investment (*I*) expenditures by businesses plus		Rents plus
Government consumption expenditures and gross investment (*G*) plus	= GDP =	Profits plus
		Net Interest plus
Net exports (*X* – *M*) expenditures by foreign economies		Indirect business taxes plus
		Depreciation

SOURCE: © Cengage Learning 2014

15-6 GDP in Other Countries

Exhibit 5 compares GDP for selected countries in 2011. The United States had the world's highest GDP, and China had the second largest GDP. U.S. GDP, for example, was about twice China's GDP.

15-7 GDP Shortcomings

For various reasons, GDP omits certain measures of overall economic well-being. Because GDP is the basis of government economic policies, there is concern that GDP may be giving us a false impression of the nation's material well-being. GDP is a less-than-perfect measure of the nation's economic pulse because it excludes the following factors.

15-7a NONMARKET TRANSACTIONS

Because GDP counts only market transactions, it excludes certain unpaid activities, such as homemaker production, child rearing, and do-it-yourself home repairs and services. For example, if you take your dirty clothes to the laundry, GDP increases by the amount of the cleaning bill paid. But GDP ignores the value of laundering these same clothes if you wash them yourself at home.

There are two reasons for excluding nonmarket activities from GDP. First, it would be extremely imprecise to attempt to collect data and assign a dollar value to services people provide for themselves or others without compensation. Second, it is difficult to decide which nonmarket activities to exclude and which ones to include. Perhaps repairing your own roof, painting your own house, and repairing your

EXHIBIT 5	An International Comparison of GDPs, 2011

This exhibit shows GDPs in 2011 for selected countries. The United States had the world's highest GDP, and China has the second largest GDP. U.S. GDP, for example, is about twice the size of China's GDP.

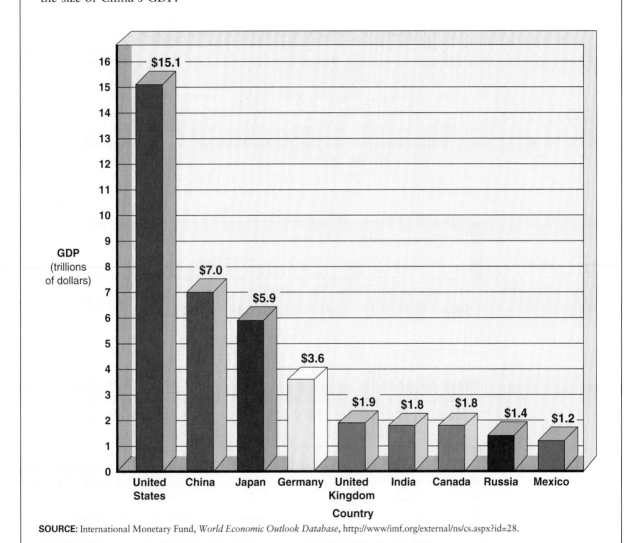

SOURCE: International Monetary Fund, *World Economic Outlook Database*, http://www.imf.org/external/ns/cs.aspx?id=28.

own car should be included. Now consider the value of washing your car. GDP does include the price of cleaning your car if you purchase that service at a car wash, so it could be argued that GDP should include the value of you washing your car at home.

The issue of unpaid do-it-yourself activities affects comparisons of the GDPs of different nations. One reason some less-developed nations have lower GDPs than major industrialized nations is that a greater proportion of people in less-developed nations farm, clean, make repairs, and perform other tasks for their families rather than hire someone else to do the work.

15-7b DISTRIBUTION, KIND, AND QUALITY OF PRODUCTS

GDP is blind to whether a small fraction of the population consumes most of a country's GDP or consumption is evenly divided. GDP also wears a blindfold with respect to the quality and kinds of goods and services that make up a nation's GDP. Consider the fictional economies of Zuba and Econa. Zuba has a GDP of $2,000 billion, and Econa has a GDP of $1,000 billion. At first glance, Zuba appears to possess superior economic well-being. However, Zuba's GDP consists of only military goods, and Econa's products include computers, cell phones, tractors, wheat, milk, houses, and other consumer items. Moreover, assume the majority of the people of Zuba could care less about the output of military goods and would be happier if the country produced more consumer goods. Now consider, for example, the difference in quality between a cell phone purchased today and a cell phone with only few capabilities purchased years ago. Such qualitative improvements are not reflected in GDP.

> **CONCLUSION:** *GDP is a quantitative, rather than a qualitative, measure of the output of goods and services.*

15-7c NEGLECT OF LEISURE TIME

GDP does not directly measure quality-of-life or "happiness" variables such as leisure time. In general, the wealthier a nation becomes, the more leisure time its citizens can afford. Rather than working longer hours, workers often choose to increase their time for recreation and travel. Since 1900, the length of the typical workweek in the United States declined steadily from about 50 hours to about 33 hours in 2011.[1] The last chapter discusses quality-of-life variables in more detail.

> **CONCLUSION:** *It can be argued that GDP understates national well-being because no allowance is made for people working fewer hours than they once did.*

15-7d THE UNDERGROUND ECONOMY

Illegal gambling, prostitution, loan-sharking, illegal guns, and illegal drugs are goods and services that meet all the requirements for GDP. They are final goods with a value determined in "black" markets, but GDP does not include unreported criminal activities because no record is made of these transactions. The "underground" economy also includes tax evasion. One way to avoid paying taxes on a legal activity is to trade or barter goods and services rather than selling them. One person fixes a neighbor's car in return for babysitting services, and the value of the

---

[1] *Economic Report of the President,* 2012, http://www.gpoaccess.gov/eop/, Table B-47.

exchange is unreported. Other individuals and businesses make legal sales for cash and do not report the income earned to the Internal Revenue Service.

Estimates of the size of this subterranean economy vary. Some studies by economists estimate the size of the underground sector is about 9 percent of GDP. This range of estimates is slightly less than the estimated size of the underground economy in most European countries.

> **CONCLUSION:** *If the underground economy is sizable, GDP will understate an economy's performance.*

15-7e ECONOMIC BADS

More production means a larger GDP, regardless of the level of pollution created in the process. Recall from Chapter 4 the discussion of *negative externalities*, such as pollution caused by steel mills, chemical plants, and cigarettes. Air, water, and noise pollution are *economic bads* that impose costs on society not reflected in private market prices and quantities bought and sold. When a polluting company sells its product, this transaction increases GDP. However, critics of GDP argue that it fails to account for the diminished quality of life from the "bads" not reported in GDP.

Stated another way, if production results in pollution and environmental damage, GDP overstates the nation's well-being.

> **CONCLUSION:** *Since the costs of negative by-products are not deducted, GDP overstates the national well-being.*

15-8 Other National Income Accounts

In addition to GDP, the media often report several other national income accounts because they are necessary for studying the macro economy. We now take a brief look at each.

15-8a NATIONAL INCOME (NI)

It can be argued that depreciation should be subtracted from GDP. Recall that GDP is not entirely a measure of newly produced output because it includes an estimated value of capital goods required to replace those worn out in the production process. The measurement designed to correct this deficiency is national income (NI), which is the gross domestic product minus depreciation of the capital worn out in producing output. Stated as a formula

$$\text{NI} = \text{GDP} - \text{depreciation (consumption of fixed capital)}$$

In 2011, $1.7 trillion was the estimated amount of GDP attributable to depreciation during the year. Exhibit 6 shows the actual calculation of NI from GDP in

National income (NI)
The total income earned by resource owners, including wages, rents, interest, and profits. NI is calculated as gross domestic product minus depreciation of the capital worn out in producing output.

Is GDP a False Beacon Steering Us into the Rocks?

Applicable Concept: national income accounting "goods" and "bads"

Suppose a factory in your community has been dumping hazardous wastes into the local water supply and people develop cancer and other illnesses from drinking polluted water. The Environmental Protection Agency (EPA) discovers this pollution and, under the federal "Superfund" law, orders a cleanup and imposes a fine for the damages. The company defends itself against the EPA by hiring lawyers and experts to take the case to court. After years of trial, the company loses the case and has to pay for the cleanup and damages.

In terms of GDP, an amazing "good" result occurs. The primary measure of national economic output, GDP, increases. GDP counts the millions of dollars spent to clean up the water supply. GDP even includes the health care expenses of anyone who develops cancer or other illnesses caused by drinking polluted water. GDP also includes the money spent by the company on lawyers and experts to defend itself against the EPA. And GDP includes the money spent by the EPA to regulate the polluting company.

Now consider what happens when trees are cut down and oil and minerals are used to produce houses, cars, and other goods. The value of the wood, oil, and minerals is an intermediate good implicitly computed in GDP because the value of the final goods is explicitly computed in GDP. Using scarce resources to produce goods and services therefore raises GDP and is considered a "good" result. On the other hand, don't we lose the value of trees, oil, and minerals in the production process, so isn't this a "bad" result?

The Bureau of Economic Analysis (BEA) is an agency of the U.S. Department of Commerce. The BEA is the nation's economic accountant, and it is the source of GDP data cited throughout this text. Critics have called for a new measure designed to estimate the kinds of damage described above. These new accounts would adjust for changes in air and water quality and depletion of oil and minerals. These accounts would also adjust for changes in the stock of renewable natural resources, such as forests and fish stocks. In addition, accounts should be created to measure global warming and destruction of the ozone layer.

As explained in this chapter, a dollar estimate of capital depreciation is subtracted from GDP to compute national income (NI). The argument here is that a dollar estimate of the damage to the

environment should also be subtracted. To ignore measuring such environmental problems, critics argue, threatens future generations. In short, conventional GDP perpetuates a false dichotomy between economic growth and environmental protection.

Critics of this approach argue that assigning a dollar value to environmental damage and resource depletion requires a methodology that is extremely subjective and complex. Nevertheless, national income accountants have not ignored these criticisms, and the National Academy of Sciences has reviewed BEA proposals for ways to account for interactions between the environment and the economy.

Analyze the Issue

Suppose a nuclear power plant disaster occurs. How could GDP be a "false beacon" in this case?

Source: © Cengage Learning 2014

2011. NI measures how much income is *earned* by households that own and supply resources. It includes the total flow of payments to the owners of the factors of production, including wages, rents, interest, and profits. Another way to compute national income is to add compensation of employees, rents, profits, net interest, and indirect business taxes using the income approach demonstrated in Exhibit 3.

EXHIBIT 6	National Income Calculated from Gross Domestic Product, 2011
	Amount (trillions of dollars)
Gross domestic product (GDP)	$15.1
Depreciation	−1.7
National income (NI)	$13.4

SOURCE: Bureau of Economic Analysis, *National Economic Accounts*, http://www.bea.gov/national/nipaweb/SelectTable.asp?Selected=Y, Table 1.7.5.

Exhibit 7 illustrates the transition from GDP to NI and two other measures of the macro economy.[2]

15-8b PERSONAL INCOME (PI)

National income measures the total amount of money *earned*, but determining the amount of income actually *received* by households (not businesses) requires a measurement of personal income (PI). Personal income is the total income received by households that is available for consumption, saving, and payment of personal taxes. Suppose we want to measure the total amount of money individuals receive that they can use to consume products, save, and pay taxes. National income is not the appropriate measure for two reasons. First, NI excludes transfer payments, which constitute unearned income that can be spent, saved, or used to pay taxes. Second, NI includes corporate profits, but stockholders do not receive all these profits. A portion of corporate profits is paid in corporate taxes. Also, retained earnings are not distributed to stockholders, but are channeled back into business operations.

Exhibit 7 illustrates the relationship between personal income and national income, and Exhibit 8 gives the figures for 2011. National income accountants adjust national income by subtracting corporate profits and payroll taxes for Social Security (FICA deductions). Next, *transfer payments* and other income individuals receive from net interest and dividends are added. The net result is the personal income received by households, which in 2011 amounted to $13.0 trillion.

Personal income (PI)

The total income received by households that is available for consumption, saving, and payment of personal taxes.

15-8c DISPOSABLE PERSONAL INCOME (DI)

One final measure of national income is shown at the far right of Exhibit 7. Disposable personal income (DI) is the amount of income that households actually have to spend or save after payment of personal taxes. Disposable, or *after-tax*,

Disposable personal income (DI)

The amount of income that households actually have to spend or save after payment of personal taxes.

[2]As a result of a revision in national income accounting, the only difference between net domestic product (NDP) and national income (NI) is a statistical discrepancy. Because NI is more widely reported in the media, and to simplify, NDP is not calculated here.

EXHIBIT 7	Four Measures of the Macro Economy

The four bars show major measurements of the U.S. macro economy in 2011 in trillions of dollars. Beginning with gross domestic product, depreciation is subtracted to obtain national income. Next, personal income equals national income minus corporate profits and contributions for Social Security insurance (FICA payments) plus transfer payments and other income. Subtracting personal taxes from personal income yields disposable personal income.

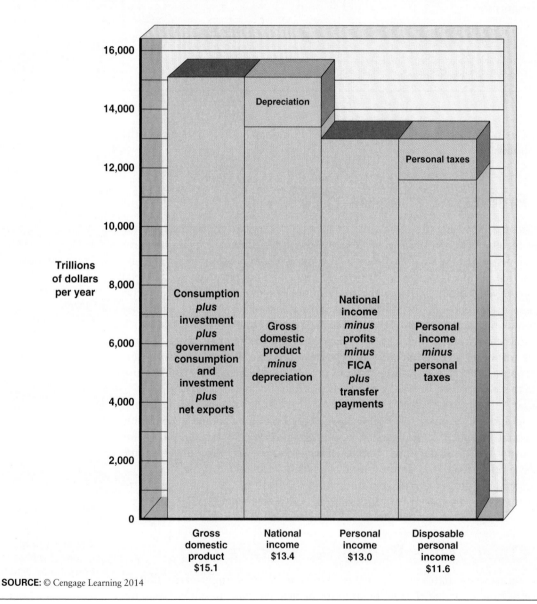

SOURCE: © Cengage Learning 2014

income is equal to personal income minus personal taxes paid to federal, state, and local governments. Personal taxes consist of personal income taxes, personal property taxes, and inheritance taxes. As tabulated in Exhibit 9, disposable personal income in 2011 was $11.6 trillion.

EXHIBIT 8	Personal Income Calculated from National Income, 2011	
		Amount (trillions of dollars)
National income (NI)		$13.4
Corporate profits		−1.9
Contributions for Social Security (FICA)		−0.9
Transfer payments and other income		2.4
Personal income (PI)		$13.0

SOURCE: Bureau of Economic Analysis, *National Economic Accounts*, http://www.bea.gov/national/nipaweb/SelectTable.asp?Selected=Y, Table 1.7.5.

15-9 Changing Nominal GDP to Real GDP

So far, GDP has been expressed as nominal GDP. Nominal GDP is the value of all final goods based on the prices existing during the time period of production. Nominal GDP is also referred to as *current-dollar* or *money GDP*. Nominal GDP grows in three ways. First, output rises and prices remain unchanged. Second, prices rise and output is constant. Third, in the typical case, both output and prices rise. The problem, then, is how to adjust GDP so it reflects only changes in output and not changes in prices. This adjusted GDP allows meaningful comparisons over time when prices are changing.

Changing prices can have a huge impact on how we compare dollar figures. Suppose a newspaper headline reports that a film entitled *The History of Economic Thought* is the biggest box-office sales movie of all time. You ask, How can this be? What about *Gone with the Wind*? Reading the article reveals that this claim is based on the nominal measure of gross box-office receipts. This gives a recent movie with higher ticket prices an advantage over a movie released in 1939 when the average ticket price was about $1. A better measure of popularity would be to compare "real" box-office receipts by multiplying actual attendance figures for each movie by a base year movie price.

Measuring the difference between changes in output and changes in the price level involves making an important distinction between nominal GDP and real GDP. Real GDP is the value of all final goods produced during a given time period based on the prices existing in a selected base year. The U.S. Department of Commerce currently uses 2005 prices as the base year. Real GDP is also referred to as *constant dollar GDP*.

15-9a THE GDP CHAIN PRICE INDEX

The most broadly based measure used to take the changes-in-the-price-level "air" out of the nominal GDP "balloon" and compute real GDP is officially called the GDP chain price index. The GDP chain price index is a measure that compares

Nominal GDP

The value of all final goods based on the prices existing during the time period of production.

Real GDP

The value of all final goods produced during a given time period based on the prices existing in a selected base year.

GDP chain price index

A measure that compares changes in the prices of all final goods during a given year to the prices of those goods in a base year.

EXHIBIT 9	Disposable Personal Income Calculated from Personal Income, 2011	
		Amount (trillions of dollars)
Personal income (PI)		$13.0
Personal taxes		−1.4
Disposable personal income (DI)		$11.6

SOURCE: Bureau of Economic Analysis, *National Economic Accounts*, http://www.bea.gov/national/nipaweb/SelectTable.asp?Selected=Y, Table 2.1.

changes in the prices of all final goods produced during a given time period relative to the prices of those goods in a base year. The GDP chain price index is a broad "deflator" index calculated by a complex chain-weighted geometric series (you are spared the details). It is highly inclusive because it measures not only price changes of consumer goods, but also price changes of business investment, government purchases, exports, and imports. Do not confuse the GDP chain price index with the *consumer price index* (CPI), which is widely reported in the news media. The CPI is a different index, measuring only consumer prices, which we will discuss in the chapter on inflation.

Now it's time to see how the GDP chain price index works. We begin with the following conversion equation:

$$\text{Real GDP} = \frac{\text{nominal GDP}}{\text{GDP chain price index}} \times 100$$

Using 2005 as the base year, suppose you are given the 2011 nominal GDP of $15.1 trillion and the 2011 GDP chain price index of 113.5. To calculate 2011 real GDP, use the above formula as follows:

$$\$13.3 \text{ trillion} = \frac{\$15.1 \text{ trillion}}{113.5} \times 100$$

Exhibit 10 shows actual U.S. nominal GDP, real GDP, and the GDP chain price index for selected years. Column (1) reports nominal GDP, column (2) gives real GDP figures for these years, and column (3) lists corresponding GDP chain price indexes. Notice that the GDP chain price index exceeds 100 in years beyond 2005. This means that prices, on average, have risen since 2005, causing the real purchasing power of the dollar to fall. In years before 2005, the GDP chain price index is less than 100, which means the real purchasing power of the dollar was higher relative to the 2005 base year. At the base year of 2005, nominal and real GDP are identical, and the GDP price index equals 100.

The graph in Exhibit 10 traces real GDP and nominal GDP for the U.S. economy since 1960. Note that nominal GDP usually grows faster than real GDP because inflation is included in the nominal figures. For example, if we calculate the economy's average rate in nominal GDP between 1990 and 2000, we find it was 7.2 percent. If instead we calculate average real GDP growth between the

EXHIBIT 10

Nominal GDP, Real GDP, and the GDP Chain Price Index for Selected Years

Real GDP reflects output valued at 2005 base-year prices, but nominal GDP is annual output valued at prices prevailing during the current year. The intersection of real and nominal GDP occurs in 2005 because in the base year, both nominal GDP and real GDP measure the same output at 2005 prices. Note that the nominal GDP curve has risen more sharply than the real GDP curve as a result of inflation included in the nominal figures.

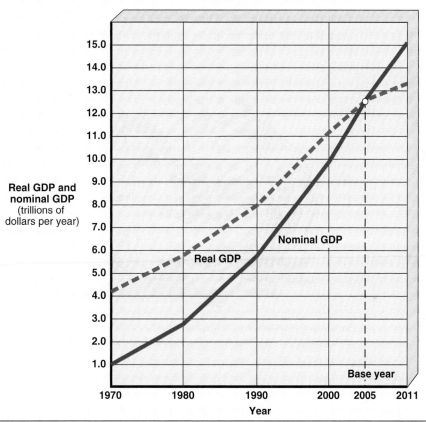

Year	(1) Nominal GDP (trillions of dollars)	(2) Real GDP (trillions of 2005 dollars)	(3) GDP chain price index (2005 = 100)
1970	1.0	4.3	23.3
1980	2.8	5.8	48.3
1990	5.8	8.0	72.5
2000	9.9	11.2	88.4
2005	12.6	12.6	100.0
2011	15.1	13.3	113.5

SOURCE: Bureau of Economic Analysis, *National Economic Accounts*, http://www.bea.gov/national/nipaweb/ SelectTable.aspSelected=Y, Tables 1.1.5, 1.1.6, and *Economic Report of the President*, http://www.gpoaccess.gov/ eop/, Tables B-1, B-2, and B-7.

same years, we find the growth rate was 4.0 percent. You must therefore pay attention to which GDP is being used in an analysis.

✓ CHECKPOINT

Is the Economy Up or Down?

One person reports, "GDP rose this year by 8.5 percent." Another says, "GDP fell by 0.5 percent." Can both reports be right?

"And so, extrapolating from the best figures available, we see that current trends, unless dramatically reversed, will inevitably lead to a situation in which the sky will fall."

© The New Yorker Collection. 1978 Lee Lorenz from www.cartoonbank.com. All rights reserved.

Key Concepts

Gross domestic product (GDP)	Stock	Disposable personal income (DI)
Transfer payment	Expenditure approach	Nominal GDP
Final goods	Income approach	Real GDP
Intermediate goods	Indirect business taxes	GDP chain price index
Circular flow model	National income (NI)	
Flow	Personal income (PI)	

Summary

- **Gross domestic product (GDP)** is the most widely used measure of a nation's economic performance. GDP is the market value of all **final goods** produced in the United States during a period of time, regardless of who owns the factors of production. Secondhand and financial transactions are not counted in GDP. To avoid double counting, GDP also does not include **intermediate goods**. GDP is calculated by either the expenditure approach or the income approach.

- The **circular flow model** is a diagram representing the flow of products and resources between businesses and households in exchange for money payments. **Flows** must be distinguished from **stocks**. Flows are measured in units per time period—for example, dollars per year. Stocks are quantities that exist at a given point in time measured in dollars.

- The **expenditure approach** sums the four major spending components of GDP consumption, investment, government spending, and net exports. Algebraically, $GDP = C + I + G + (X - M)$, where X equals foreign spending for domestic exports and M equals domestic spending for foreign products.

- The **income approach** sums the major income components of GDP, consisting of compensation of employees, rents, profits, net interest, **indirect business taxes**, and depreciation. Indirect business taxes are levied as a percentage of product prices and include sales taxes, excise taxes, and customs duties.

- **National income (NI)** is total income *earned* by households that own and supply resources. It is calculated as GDP minus depreciation.

- **Personal income (PI)** is the total income *received* by households and is calculated as NI minus corporate taxes and Social Security taxes plus transfer payments and other income.

- **Disposable personal income (DI)** is personal income minus personal taxes. DI is the amount of income a household has available to consume or save.

Circular Flow Model

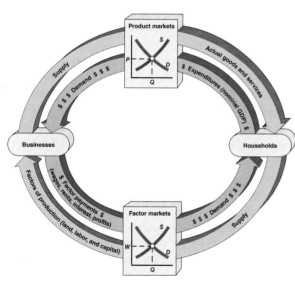

SOURCE: © Cengage Learning 2014

Measures of the Macro Economy

SOURCE: © Cengage Learning 2014

- **Nominal GDP** measures all final goods and services produced in a given time period valued at the prices existing during the time period of production.
- **Real GDP** measures all final goods and services produced in a given time period valued at the prices existing in a base year.
- The **GDP chain price index** is a broad price index used to convert nominal GDP to real

GDP. The GDP chain price index measures changes in the prices of consumer goods, business investment, government spending, exports, and imports. Real GDP is computed by dividing nominal GDP for year X by year X's GDP chain price index and then multiplying the result by 100.

Summary of Conclusion Statements

- GDP is a quantitative, rather than a qualitative, measure of the output of goods and services.
- It can be argued that GDP understates national well-being because no allowance is made for people working fewer hours than they once did.

- If the underground economy is sizable, GDP will understate an economy's performance.
- Because the costs of negative by-products are not deducted, GDP overstates our national well-being.

Study Questions and Problems

1. Which of the following are final goods or services, and which are intermediate goods or services?
   a. A haircut purchased from a hair salon
   b. A new automobile
   c. An oil filter purchased in a new automobile
   d. Crude oil

2. Using the basic circular flow model, explain why the value of businesses' output of goods and services equals the income of households.

3. A small economy produced the following final goods and services during a given month: 3 million pounds of food, 50,000 shirts, 20 houses, 50,000 hours of medical services, 1 automobile plant, and 2 tanks. Calculate the value of this output at the following market prices:
   - $1 per pound of food
   - $20 per shirt
   - $50,000 per house
   - $20 per hour of medical services
   - $1 million per automobile plant
   - $500,000 per tank

4. An economy produces final goods and services with a market value of $5,000 billion in a given year, but only $4,500 billion worth of goods and services is sold to domestic or foreign buyers. Is this nation's GDP $5,000 billion or $4,500 billion? Explain your answer.

5. Explain why a new forklift sold for use in a warehouse is a final good even though it is fixed investment (capital) used to produce other goods. Is there a double-counting problem if this sale is added to GDP?

6. Explain why the government spending (G) component of GDP falls short of actual government expenditures.

7. Explain how net exports affect the U.S. economy. Describe both positive and negative impacts on GDP. Why do national income accountants use net exports to compute GDP, rather than simply adding exports to the other expenditure components of GDP?

8. Suppose the data in Exhibit 11 are for a given year from the annual *Economic Report of the President*. Calculate GDP using the expenditure and income approaches.

EXHIBIT 11	National Income Data
	Amount (billions of dollars)
Corporate profits	$ 305
Depreciation	479
Gross private domestic investment	716
Personal taxes	565
Personal saving	120
Government spending	924
Imports	547
Net interest	337
Compensation of employees	2,648
Rental income	19
Exports	427
Personal consumption expenditures	2,966
Indirect business taxes	370
Contributions for Social Security (FICA)	394
Transfer payments and other income	967
Proprietors' income	328

SOURCE: © Cengage Learning 2014

9. Using the data in Exhibit 11, compute national income (NI) by making the required subtraction from GDP. Explain why NI might be a better measure of economic performance than GDP.

10. Again using the data from Exhibit 11, derive personal income (PI) from national income (NI). Then make the required adjustments to PI to obtain disposable personal income (DI).

11. Suppose U.S. nominal GDP increases from one year to the next year. Can you conclude that these figures present a misleading measure of economic growth? What alternative method would provide a more accurate measure of the rate of growth?

12. Which of the following are counted in this year's GDP? Explain your answer in each case.
    a. Flashy Car Company sold a used car.
    b. Juanita Jones cooked meals for her family.
    c. IBM paid interest on its bonds.
    d. José Suarez purchased 100 shares of Microsoft stock.
    e. Bob Smith received a welfare payment.
    f. Carriage Realty earned a brokerage commission for selling a previously owned house.
    g. The government makes interest payments to persons holding government bonds.
    h. Air and water pollution increase.
    i. Gambling is legalized in all states.
    j. A retired worker receives a Social Security payment.

13. Explain why comparing the GDPs of various nations might not tell you which nations are better off.

For Online Exercises, go to the Tucker Web site at www.cengage.com/economics/tucker.

✓ CHECKPOINT ANSWERS

How Much Does Mario Add to GDP?

Measuring GDP by the expenditure approach, Mario's output production is worth $60,000 because consumers purchased 4,000 pizzas at $15 each. Transfer payments and purchases of goods produced in other years are excluded from GDP. The $3,000 in unemployment compensation received and the $5,000 spent for a used car are therefore not counted in GDP. Mario's income of $15,000 is also not counted using the expenditure approach. If you said using the expenditure approach to measure GDP, Mario contributed $60,000 to GDP, **YOU ARE CORRECT.**

Is the Economy Up or Down?

Between 1973 and 1974, for example, nominal GDP rose from $1,382 to $1,500 billion—an 8.5 percent increase. During the same period, real GDP fell from $4,917 to $4,890 billion—a 0.5 percent decrease. If you said both reports can be correct because of the difference between nominal and real GDP, **YOU ARE CORRECT.**

Sample Quiz

For an explanation of the correct answers, visit the Tucker Web site at www.cengage.com/economics/tucker.

1. Gross domestic product is officially measured by adding together the
   a. quantity of each good and service produced by U.S. residents.
   b. market value of all final goods and services produced within the borders of a nation.
   c. quantity of goods and services produced by companies owned by U.S. citizens.
   d. None of the answers above are correct.

2. Which of the following items is included in the calculation of GDP?
   a. purchase of 100 shares of Microsoft stock
   b. purchase of a used car
   c. the value of a homemaker's services
   d. sale of Gulf War military surplus
   e. None of the above would be included.

3. Which of the following expenditures would *not* be included in GDP?
   a. purchase of a new lawnmower
   b. purchase of a silver cup previously sold new in 1950
   c. purchase of a ticket to the latest movie
   d. All of the above would be counted in GDP.

4. Gross domestic product (GDP) includes
   a. intermediate as well as final goods.
   b. foreign goods as well as domestically produced goods.
   c. used goods sold in the current time period.
   d. only final goods and services.

5. GDP includes
   a. the negative attributes in our quest for more goods and services, such as soil erosion and deforested landscape.
   b. all quality improvements resulting from higher-quality goods replacing inferior goods.
   c. the cleanup expenses associated with pollution.
   d. the value of leisure time.

Sample Quiz *continued*

6. The largest component of GDP is
   a. personal consumption expenditures.
   b. government spending.
   c. durable goods.
   d. net exports.

7. The circular flow of economic activity is a model of the
   a. flow of goods, resources, payments, and expenditures between the sectors of the economy.
   b. influence of government on business behavior.
   c. influence of business on consumers.
   d. role of unions and government in the economy.

8. All final goods and services that make up GDP can be expressed as
   a. $GDP = C + I - G + (X + M)$.
   b. $GDP = C + I + G + (X + M)$.
   c. $GDP = C + I + G + (X - M)$.
   d. $GDP = C + I + (X - M)$.
   e. $GDP = C + I + G$.

9. The expenditure approach for the calculation of GDP includes spending on
   a. consumption, investment, durable goods, and exports.
   b. consumption, gross private domestic investment, government spending for goods and services, and exports.
   c. consumption, gross private domestic investment, government spending for goods and services, and net exports.
   d. consumption, net private domestic investment, government spending for goods and services, and net exports.
   e. consumption, gross private domestic investment, all government spending including transfer payments, and net exports.

10. Which of the following is a shortcoming of GDP?
    a. GDP excludes changes in inventories.
    b. GDP includes an estimate of illegal transactions.
    c. GDP excludes nonmarket transactions.
    d. GDP excludes business investment spending.

11. National income (NI) is calculated by adjusting GDP for
    a. depreciation.
    b. investment and net exports.
    c. Social Security insurance contributions and transfer payments.
    d. corporate and personal income taxes.

12. Which of the following is included in personal income but *not* in national income?
    a. compensation for workers
    b. proprietors' income
    c. corporate profits
    d. Social Security payments

13. Which national income account should be examined to discover trends in the after-tax income that people have to save and spend?
    a. gross domestic product (GDP)
    b. gross national product (GNP)
    c. national income (NI)
    d. disposable personal income (DI)

14. The equation for determining real GDP for year X is
    a. $\dfrac{\text{nominal GDP for year } X}{\text{average nominal GDP}}$.
    b. $\dfrac{\text{nominal GDP for year } X}{\text{GDP for year } X} - 100$.
    c. $\dfrac{\text{nominal GDP for year } X}{\text{GDP chain price index for year } X} \times 100$.
    d. $\dfrac{\text{nominal GDP for year } X}{\text{average family income}} \times 100$.

15. The most broadly based price index is the
    a. real GDP price index.
    b. consumer price index.
    c. producer price index.
    d. GDP chain price index.

16. Which of the following would be counted as a final good for inclusion in GDP?
    a. a piece of glass bought this year by a consumer to fix a broken window
    b. a sheet of glass produced this year by Ford to use for windows in a new car

Sample Quiz *continued*

   c. a tire produced this year and sold to a car maker for a new car sold this year

   d. None of the answers are correct.

17. Based on the circular flow model, money flows from households to businesses in
   a. factor markets.
   b. product markets.
   c. neither factor nor product markets.
   d. both factor and product markets.

18. If the underground economy is sizable, GDP will
   a. understate the economy's performance.
   b. overstate the economy's performance.
   c. fluctuate unpredictably.
   d. accurately reflect this subterranean activity.

19. The income that people earn in resource or factor markets is called
   a. national income.
   b. personal income.
   c. disposable personal income.
   d. transfer payments.
   e. net national product.

20. Increased production, but *not* increased inflation, will result in higher
   a. nominal GDP.
   b. money GDP.
   c. real GDP.
   d. current dollar GDP.

A Four-Sector Circular Flow Model

Sound the trumpets! This exhibit is going to put all the puzzle pieces together. Exhibit A-1 presents a more complex circular flow model by adding three sectors: financial markets, government, and foreign markets. In addition to the spending of households for the output of firms shown in the simplified model in Exhibit A-1, these additions add three *leakages* from the amount of income paid to households. First, part of households' income is saved. Second, part of it is taxed. Third, part of the income is spent on imports. On the other hand, this model includes three sources of spending *injections* for firms' output other than from households. First, firms purchase new plants, equipment, and inventories (investment) from other firms. Second, government consumption purchases are for goods and services from firms. Third, foreigners purchase exports from the firms.

This exhibit presents a circular flow model for an economy, such as the United States, that engages in international trade. The theoretical model includes links between the product and factor markets in the domestic economy and the financial markets, government, and foreign economies. To simplify the model, only dollar payments are shown for the foreign sector.

EXHIBIT A-1 | **The Circular Flow Model of an Open Economy**

SOURCE: © Cengage Learning 2014

chapter 16

Business Cycles and Unemployment

The headline in the morning newspaper reads, "The Economy is in Deep Recession." Later in the day, a radio announcer begins the news by saying, "The unemployment rate rose for the tenth consecutive month." On television, the evening news broadcasts an interview with several economists who predict that the slump will last for another year. Next, a presidential candidate appears on the screen and says, "It's time for change," and the media are abuzz with speculation on the political implications. The growth rate of the economy and the unemployment rate are headline-catching news. Indeed, these measures of macroeconomic instability are important because they affect your future. When real GDP rises and the economy "booms," jobs are more plentiful. A fall in real GDP means a "bust" because the economy forces some firms into bankruptcy and workers lose their jobs. Not being able to find a job when you want one is a painful experience not easily forgotten.

This chapter looks behind the macro economy at a story that touches each of us. It begins by discussing the business cycle. How are the expansions and contractions of business cycles measured? And what causes the business-cycle roller coaster? Finally, you will learn what the types of unemployment are, what "full employment" is, and what the monetary, nonmonetary, and demographic costs of unemployment are.

In this chapter, you will learn to solve these economics puzzles:

- What is the difference between a recession and a depression?
- Is a worker who has given up searching for work counted as unemployed?
- Can an economy produce more output than its potential?

16-1 The Business-Cycle Roller Coaster

A central concern of macroeconomics is the upswings and downswings in the level of real output called the business cycle. The business cycle consists of alternating periods of economic growth and contraction. Business cycles are inherent in market economies. Market-based economies are driven by ever-changing forces of supply and demand. A key measure of cycles is the rise and fall in real GDP, which mirrors changes in employment and other key measures of the macro economy. Recall from the previous chapter that changes in real GDP measure changes in the value of national output, while ignoring changes in the price level.

16-1a THE FOUR PHASES OF THE BUSINESS CYCLE

Exhibit 1(a) illustrates a theoretical business cycle. Although business cycles vary in duration and intensity, each cycle is divided into four phases: *peak*, *recession*, *trough*, and *recovery*. The business cycle looks like a roller coaster. It begins at a peak, drops to a bottom, climbs steeply, and then reaches another peak. Once the trough is reached, the upswing starts again. Although forecasters cannot precisely predict the phases of a cycle, the economy is always operating along one of these phases. Over time, there has been a long-term upward trend with shorter-term cyclical fluctuations around the long-run trend.

Two peaks are illustrated in Exhibit 1(a). At each of these peaks, the economy is close to or at full employment. At a peak, real GDP reaches its maximum. That is, as explained in Chapter 2, the economy is operating near its production possibilities curve, and real GDP is at its highest level relative to recent years. However, a peak is a temporary high point. A macro setback called a recession (or *contraction*) follows each peak. A recession is a downturn in the business cycle during which real GDP declines, business profits fall, the percentage of the workforce without jobs rises, and production capacity is underutilized. A general rule is that a recession consists of at least two consecutive quarters (six months) in which there is a decline in real GDP. Stated differently, during a recession, the economy is functioning inside and farther away from its production possibilities curve.

What is the difference between a *recession* and a *depression*? According to the old saying, "A recession is when your neighbor loses his or her job, and a depression is when you also lose your job!" This one-liner is close to the true distinction between these two concepts. The answer is because no subsequent recession has approached the prolonged severity of the Great Depression from 1929 to 1933, the term *depression* is primarily a historical reference to this extremely deep and long recession. The Great Depression is discussed at the end of this chapter, the chapter on aggregate demand and supply, and the chapter on monetary policy.

The trough is where the level of real GDP "bottoms out." The length of time between the peak and the trough is the duration of the recession. Since the end of World War II, recessions in the United States have averaged 11 months. As shown in Exhibit 2, the last recession, called the Great Recession, lasted 18 months, from December 2007 to June 2009. The percentage decline in real GDP was 4.1 percent, and the national unemployment rate hit a high of 9.7 percent. The Great Recession is the longest recession since the Great Depression, which lasted 43 months.

Business cycle
Alternating periods of economic growth and contraction, which can be measured by changes in real GDP.

Peak
The phase of the business cycle in which real GDP reaches its maximum after rising during a recovery.

Recession
A downturn in the business cycle during which real GDP declines, and the unemployment rate rises. Also called a *contraction*.

Trough
The phase of the business cycle in which real GDP reaches its minimum after falling during a recession.

EXHIBIT 1	**Hypothetical and Actual Business Cycles**

Part (a) illustrates a hypothetical business cycle consisting of four phases: peak, recession, trough, and recovery. These fluctuations of real GDP can be measured by a growth trend line, which shows that over time, real GDP has trended upward. In reality, the fluctuations are not so clearly defined as those in this graph.

Part (b) illustrates actual ups and downs of the business cycle. After a recession in 2001, an upswing continued until the Great Recession began in 2007.

(a) Hypothetical business cycle

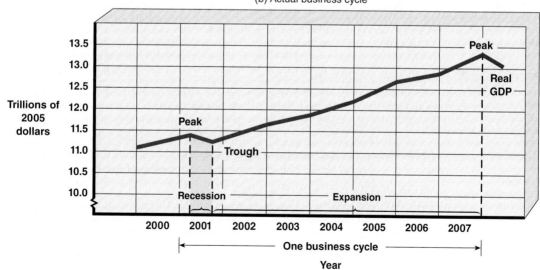

(b) Actual business cycle

SOURCE: Bureau of Economic Analysis, *National Income Accounts*, http://www.bea.gov/national/nipaweb/SelectTable.asp?Selected=Y, Table 1.1.6.

EXHIBIT 2	Severity of Post-World War II Recessions		
Recession dates	Duration (months)	Percentage decline in real GDP	Peak unemployment rate
Nov. 1948–Oct. 1949	11	−1.7%	7.9%
July 1953–May 1954	10	−2.7	5.9
Aug. 1957–Apr. 1958	8	−1.2	7.4
Apr. 1960–Feb. 1961	10	−1.6	6.9
Dec. 1969–Nov. 1970	11	−0.6	5.9
Nov. 1973–Mar. 1975	16	−3.1	8.6
Jan. 1980–July 1980	6	−2.2	7.8
July 1981–Nov. 1982	16	−2.9	10.8
July 1990–Mar. 1991	8	−1.3	6.8
Mar. 2001–Nov. 2001	8	−0.5	5.6
Dec. 2007–June 2009	18	−4.1	9.7
Average	11	−2.8	7.6

SOURCE: National Bureau of Economic Research, *Business Cycle Expansion and Contractions*, http://www.nber.org/cycles/cyclesmain.html. Real GDP and unemployment rate data added by author.

Expansion

An upturn in the business cycle during which real GDP rises. Also called a *recovery*.

The trough is both bad news and good news. It is simultaneously the bottom of the "valley" of the downturn and the foot of the "hill" of improving economic conditions called an expansion or a recovery. An expansion is an upturn in the business cycle during which real GDP rises. During the recovery phase of the cycle, profits generally improve, real GDP increases, and employment moves toward full employment.

Exhibit 1(b) illustrates an actual business cycle by plotting the movement of real GDP in the United States from 2000 to 2007. The economy's initial peak, recession, and trough occurred in 2001, and a strong expansion phase lasted until a second peak in 2007. The National Bureau of Economic Research's Business Cycle Dating Committee determines when the U.S. economy enters a recession and when a recession ends. This committee is composed of six economists who decide on the beginning and ending dates for a recession based on monthly data rather than real GDP because real GDP is measured quarterly and subject to large revisions. Factors that the committee considers in defining a recession include decline in employment, industrial production, income, and sales.

Economic growth

An expansion in national output measured by the annual percentage increase in a nation's real GDP.

16-1b ECONOMIC GROWTH

We will now expand the definition of economic growth given in Chapter 2. In this chapter, recall that an outward shift of the production possibilities curve illustrated economic growth. Also recall that factors such as increases in resources and technological advances were key reasons for economic growth. Here the discussion of economic growth is explained. Economic growth is defined by economists as an expansion in national output measured by the annual percentage increase in a nation's real GDP. The growth trend line in the hypothetical model in Exhibit 1(a) illustrates that over time, our real GDP tends to rise. This general, long-term upward trend in real GDP persists in spite of the peaks, recessions, troughs, and recoveries. As shown by the dashed line in Exhibit 3, since 1930, real GDP in the United States has grown at an average annual rate of 3.5 percent. This annual change may seem small, but about 3 percent annual growth will lead to a doubling of real GDP in only 24 years. The largest expansion in U.S. history occurred over ten years from 1991 to 2001.

> **CONCLUSION:** *We value economic growth as one of our nation's economic goals because it increases our standard of living—it creates a bigger "economic pie."*

EXHIBIT 3	A Historical Record of Business Cycles in the United States, 1929–2011

Real GDP has increased at an average annual growth rate of 3.5 percent since 1930. Above-average annual growth rates have alternated with below-average annual growth rates. Following the Great Depression of 2007, the annual growth rate was a negative 3.5 percent in 2009 and therefore below the zero growth line. In 2011, the growth rate was a below- average 1.7 percent.

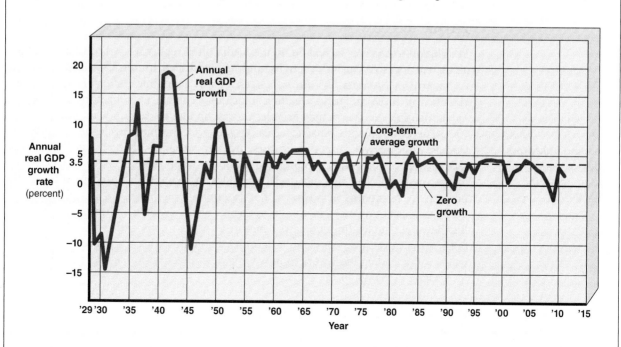

SOURCE: Bureau of Economic Analysis, *National Economic Accounts*, http://www.bea.gov/national/nipaweb/SelectTable.asp?Selected=Y, Table 1.1.6.

Closer examination of Exhibit 3 reveals that the growth path of the U.S. economy over time is not a smooth, rising trend, but instead is a series of year-to-year variations in real GDP. Following the Great Recession beginning in 2007, the growth rate was again a negative 3.5 percent in 2009 before rising to a below-average 1.7 percent in 2011.

✔ CHECKPOINT

Where Are We on the Business-Cycle Roller Coaster?

Suppose the economy is in a recession and everyone is asking when the economy will recover. To find an answer to the state of the economy's health, a television reporter interviews Terrence Carter, a local car dealer. Carter says, "I do not see any recovery. The third quarter of this year we sold more cars than in the second quarter, but sales in these two quarters were far below the first quarter." Is Mr. Carter correct? Are his observations consistent with the peak, recession, trough, or expansion phase of the business cycle?

16-1c REAL GDP GROWTH RATES IN OTHER COUNTRIES

Exhibit 4 presents real GDP growth rates for selected countries in 2011. China and India had the largest rates of growth at 9.5 and 7.8 percent, respectively. The United States and other countries throughout the world had lower growth rates, with Greece having a negative 5 percent rate.

16-1d BUSINESS-CYCLE INDICATORS

In addition to changes in real GDP, the media often report several other macro variables that measure business activity and are published by the U.S. Department of Commerce in *Business Conditions Digest*. These economic *indicator* variables are classified in three categories: leading indicators, coincident indicators, and lagging indicators. Exhibit 5 lists the variables corresponding to each indicator series.

Leading indicators

Variables that change before real GDP changes.

The government's chief forecasting gauge for business cycles is the index of leading indicators. Leading indicators are key variables that change before real GDP changes. This index captures the headlines when there is concern over swings in the economy. The first set of 10 variables in Exhibit 5 is used to forecast the business cycle months in advance. For example, a slump ahead is signaled when declines exceed advances in the components of the leading indicators data series. But beware! The leading indicators may rise for two consecutive months and then fall for the next three consecutive months. Economists are therefore cautious and wait for the leading indicators to move in a new direction for several months before forecasting a change in the cycle.

Is a recession near, or when will a recession end? The Conference Board's Consumer Confidence Index is often reported in the news as a key measure of the economy's health. It is based on a survey of households who are asked their expectations of how well the economy will perform over the next six months. Prolonged consumer pessimism can result in less consumer spending and contribute to

---

EXHIBIT 4	Global Comparison of Real GDP Growth Rates, 2011

The exhibit shows that China and India had the largest rates of growth at 9.5 and 7.5 percent, respectively. In contrast, the United States and other countries had lower growth rates for the year, with Greece the lowest at −5.0 percent.

SOURCE: International Monetary Fund, *World Economic Outlook Database*, http://www.imf.org/external/ns/cs.aspx?id=28.

slowing economic growth. Stated differently, persistent consumer pessimism can result in lower personal consumption expenditures (C) and business investment (I) because businesses reduce investment when consumers' purchases of their products fall.

The second data series of key variables listed in Exhibit 5 are four coincident indicators. Coincident indicators are variables that change at the same time that real GDP changes. For example, as real GDP rises, economists expect employment, personal income, industrial production, and sales to rise.

Coincident indicators

Variables that change at the same time real GDP changes.

EXHIBIT 5	Business-Cycle Indicators

Leading indicators

Average workweek	New building permits
Unemployment claims	Stock prices
New consumer goods orders	Money supply
Delayed deliveries	Interest rates
New orders for plant and equipment	Consumer expectations

Coincident indicators	**Lagging indicators**
Nonagricultural payrolls	Unemployment rate
Personal income minus transfer payments	Duration of unemployment
Industrial production	Labor cost per unit of output
Manufacturing and trade sales	Consumer price index for services
	Commercial and industrial loans
	Consumer credit to personal income ratio
	Prime rate

SOURCE: © Cengage Learning 2014

Lagging indicators

Variables that change after real GDP changes.

The third group of variables listed in Exhibit 5 are lagging indicators. Lagging indicators are seven variables that change after real GDP changes. For example, the duration of unemployment is a lagging indicator. As real GDP increases, the average time workers remain unemployed does not fall until months after the beginning of the expansion.

16-2 Total Spending and the Business Cycle

The uneven historical pattern of economic growth for the U.S. economy gives rise to the following question: What causes business cycles? The theory generally accepted by economists today is that changes in total or aggregate expenditures are the cause of variations in real GDP. Recall from the previous chapter that aggregate expenditures refer to total spending for *final goods* by households, businesses, government, and foreign buyers. Expressed as a formula:

Real GDP = C + I + G + (X − M) → Economic Growth

SOURCE: © Cengage Learning 2014

Why do changes in total spending cause the level of GDP to rise during an expansion? Suppose consumers are optimistic about the economic future. If consumer spending (C) increases, then businesses find it profitable to increase investment (I) in plants and equipment. When firms become more productive, they use more land, labor, and capital. Such increased spending leads to economic growth in output, employment, and incomes. Economic growth occurs when government spending (G) increases. Growth also comes from increases in spending for exports (X) versus imports spending (M). A recession is the result of declines in sectors of real GDP. Now assume consumers become pessimistic about their economic future. If consumer spending (C) decreases, then business profits fall, and businesses decrease investment (I) in plants and equipment. Business becomes less productive and uses fewer resources. Economic growth can also fall if government spending (G) decreases or export spending (X) falls relative to import spending (M).

16-3 Unemployment

Since the abyss of the Great Depression, a major economic goal of the United States has been to achieve a high level of employment. The *Employment Act of 1946* declared it the responsibility of the federal government to use all practical means consistent with free competitive enterprise to create conditions under which all able individuals who are willing to work and seeking work will be afforded useful employment opportunities. Later, Congress amended this act with the *Full Employment and Balanced Growth Act of 1978*, which established specific goals for unemployment and the level of prices.

Each month the Bureau of Labor Statistics (BLS) of the U.S. Department of Labor, in conjunction with the Bureau of the Census, conducts a survey of a random sample of about 60,000 households in the United States. Each member of the household who is 16 years of age or older is asked whether he or she is employed or unemployed. If a person works at least 1 hour per week for pay or at least 15 hours per week as an unpaid worker in a family business, he or she is counted as employed. If the person is not employed, the question then is whether he or she has looked for work in the last month. If so, the person is said to be unemployed. Based on its survey data, the BLS publishes the unemployment rate and other employment-related statistics monthly.

The unemployment rate is the percentage of people in the civilian labor force who are without jobs and are actively seeking jobs. But who is actually counted as an unemployed worker, and which people belong to the labor force? Certainly, all people without jobs are not classified as unemployed. Babies, full-time students, and retired persons are not counted as unemployed. Likewise, individuals who are ill or severely disabled are not included as unemployed. And there are other groups not counted.

Turn to Exhibit 6. The *civilian labor force* is the number of people 16 years of age and over who are either employed or unemployed, excluding members of the armed forces and other groups listed in the "persons not in labor force" category. Based on survey data, the BLS computes the *civilian unemployment rate* using the following formula:

$$\text{Unemployment rate} = \frac{\text{unemployed}}{\text{civilian labor force}} \times 100$$

In 2011, the unemployment rate was

$$8.9\% = \frac{13.7 \text{ million persons}}{153.6 \text{ million persons}} \times 100$$

Unemployment rate

The percentage of people in the civilian labor force who are without jobs and are actively seeking jobs.

Civilian labor force

The number of people 16 years of age and older who are employed or who are actively seeking a job, excluding armed forces, homemakers, discouraged workers, and other persons not in the labor force.

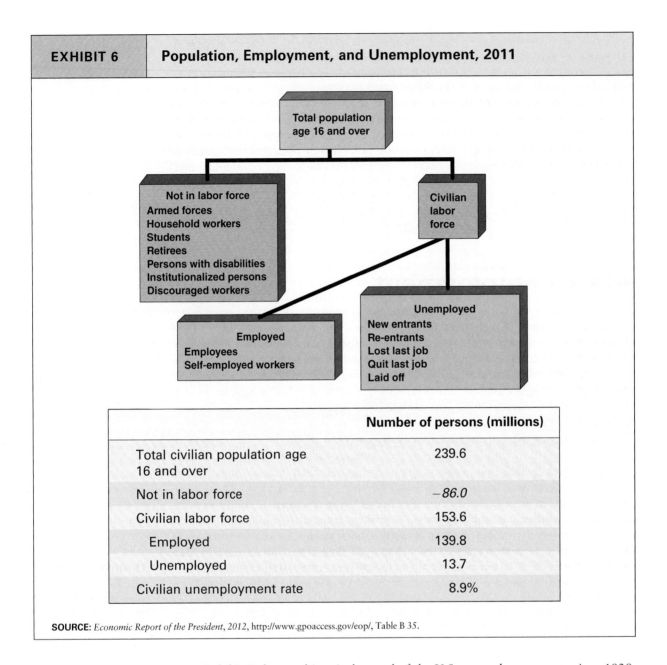

EXHIBIT 6

Population, Employment, and Unemployment, 2011

	Number of persons (millions)
Total civilian population age 16 and over	239.6
Not in labor force	−86.0
Civilian labor force	153.6
Employed	139.8
Unemployed	13.7
Civilian unemployment rate	8.9%

SOURCE: *Economic Report of the President, 2012,* http://www.gpoaccess.gov/eop/, Table B 35.

Exhibit 7 charts a historical record of the U.S. unemployment rate since 1929. Note that the highest unemployment rate was 25 percent in 1933 during the Great Depression. At the other extreme, the lowest unemployment rate we have attained was 1.2 percent in 1944. Following the Great Recession, the unemployment rate surged to 9.6 percent in 2010, which was the highest annual rate since 1983. In 2011, the unemployment rate was 8.9 percent.

16-3a UNEMPLOYMENT IN OTHER COUNTRIES

Exhibit 8 shows unemployment rates for selected countries in 2011. South Africa and Greece had unemployment rates higher than the United States. Other industrialized

EXHIBIT 7	The U.S. Unemployment Rate, 1929–2011

This exhibit shows fluctuations in the civilian unemployment rate since 1929. The unemployment rate reached a high point of 25 percent in 1933 during the Great Depression. The lowest unemployment rate of 1.2 percent was achieved during World War II in 1944. In 2010, the unemployment rate was 9.6 percent, which was the highest annual rate since 1983. In 2011, the unemployment rate was 8.9 percent.

SOURCE: *Economic Report of the President, 2010,* http://www.gpoaccess.gov/eop/, Table B 35.

countries such as Japan and China had unemployment rates much lower than the United States.

16-3b UNEMPLOYMENT RATE CRITICISMS

The unemployment rate is criticized for both understating and overstating the "true" unemployment rate. An example of *overstating* the unemployment rate occurs when respondents to the BLS survey falsely report they are seeking employment. The motivation may be that their eligibility for unemployment compensation or welfare benefits depends on actively pursuing a job. Or possibly an individual is "employed" in illegal activities.

The other side of the coin is that the official definition of unemployment *understates* the unemployment rate by not counting so-called discouraged workers. A discouraged worker is a person who wants to work, but has given up searching

Discouraged worker

A person who wants to work, but who has given up searching for work because he or she believes there will be no job offers.

EXHIBIT 8	Unemployment Rates for Selected Nations, 2011

In 2011, other nations shown had a higher unemployment rate than that of the United States. For example, the unemployment rate of Greece was 7.6 percent higher than the U.S. rate. The United States had an unemployment rate of 8.9 percent, while Canada and Japan had lower rates.

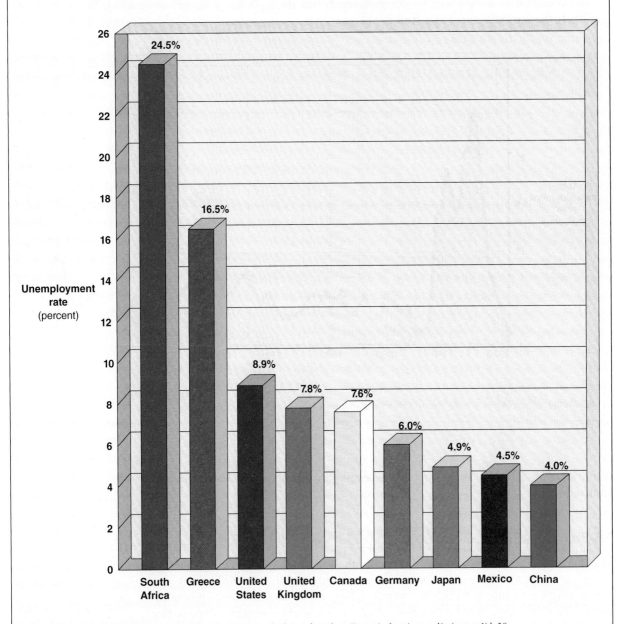

SOURCE: International Monetary Fund, *World Economic Outlook Database*, http://www.imf.org/external/ns/cs.aspx?id=28.

for work because he or she believes there will be no job offers. After repeated rejections, discouraged workers often turn to their families, friends, and public welfare for support. The BLS counts a discouraged worker as anyone who has looked for work within the last 12 months, but is no longer actively looking. The BLS simply includes discouraged workers in the "not in labor force" category listed in Exhibit 6. Because the number of discouraged workers rises during a recession, the underestimation of the official unemployment rate increases during a downturn.

Another example of *understating* the unemployment rate occurs because the official BLS data include all part-time workers as fully employed. These workers are actually partially employed, and many would work full-time if they could find full-time employment. The unemployment rate does not measure *underemployment*. If jobs are scarce and a college graduate takes a job not requiring his or her level of skills, a human resource is underutilized. Or suppose an employer cuts an employee's hours of work from 40 to 20 per week. Such losses of work potential are greater during a recession, but are not reflected in the unemployment rate.

16-4 Types of Unemployment

The unemployment rate is determined by three different types of unemployment: *frictional*, *structural*, and *cyclical*. Understanding these conceptual categories of unemployment aids in understanding and formulating policies to ease the burden of unemployment. In fact, each type of unemployment requires a different policy prescription to reduce it.

16-4a Frictional Unemployment

For some unemployed workers, the absence of a job is only temporary. At any given time, some people with marketable skills are fired, and others voluntarily quit jobs to accept or look for new ones. And there are always young people who leave school and search for their first job. Workers in some industries such as construction experience short periods of unemployment between projects, and temporary layoffs are common. Other workers are "seasonally unemployed." For example, ski resort workers will be employed in the winter, but not in the summer, and certain crops are harvested "in season." Because jobs requiring the skills of these unemployed workers are available, the unemployed workers and the job vacancies are matched and such workers are therefore considered "between jobs." This type of unemployment is called frictional unemployment, and it is not of great concern. Frictional unemployment is temporary unemployment caused by the time required of workers to move from one job to another. Frictional unemployment is unemployment caused by the normal search time required by workers with marketable skills who are changing jobs, initially entering the labor force, or reentering the labor force. The cause of frictional unemployment is either the transition time to a new job or the lack of information required to match a job applicant immediately with a job vacancy. For this reason, frictional unemployment is sometimes called *transitional unemployment* or *search unemployment*.

The fact that job market information is imperfect and operates with "friction" causes frictional unemployment in the economy. Because it takes time to search

Frictional unemployment

Temporary unemployment caused by the time required of workers to move from one job to another.

for the information required to match employer and employees, some workers will always be frictionally unemployed. Frictional unemployment is therefore a normal condition in an economic system permitting freedom of job choice. Improved methods of distributing job information through job listings on the Internet help unemployed workers find jobs more quickly and reduce frictional unemployment.

16-4b STRUCTURAL UNEMPLOYMENT

Structural unemployment

Unemployment caused by a mismatch of the skills of workers out of work and the skills required for existing job opportunities.

Unlike frictional unemployment, structural unemployment is not a short-term situation. Instead, it is long-term, or possibly permanent, unemployment. Structural unemployment is unemployment caused by a mismatch of the skills of workers who are out of work and the skills required for existing job opportunities. Note that changing jobs and lack of job information are *not* problems for structurally unemployed workers. Unlike frictionally unemployed workers who have marketable skills, structurally unemployed workers require additional education or retraining. The following are four causes of structural unemployment.

Lack of Education   Workers may face joblessness because they lack the education or the job-related skills to perform available jobs. This type of structural unemployment particularly affects teenagers and minority groups, but other groups of workers can be affected as well. For example, environmental concerns, such as protecting the spotted owl by restricting trees from being cut, cost some loggers their jobs. Reducing such structural unemployment requires retraining loggers for new jobs as, say, forest rangers.

Changes in Consumer Demand   The consuming public may decide to increase the demand for computer products and decrease the demand for Chevrolet Corvettes. This shift in demand would cause U.S. autoworkers who lose their jobs in Bowling Green, Kentucky, to become structurally unemployed. To regain employment, these unemployed autoworkers must retrain and find job openings in other industries, for example, manufacturing computer printers in North Carolina. Another example involves the reduction in defense spending after a war. This situation creates structural unemployment for discharged military personnel who require retraining after a war for, say, teaching, nursing, or police jobs.

Technological Advances   Implementation of the latest technology may also increase the pool of structural unemployment in a particular industry and region. For example, the U.S. textile industry, located primarily in the South, can fight less expensive foreign textile imports by installing modern machinery. This new capital may replace textile workers. But suppose these unemployed textile workers do not wish to move to a new location where new types of jobs are available. The costs of moving, fear of the unknown, and family ties are understandable reasons for being reluctant to move, and instead, the workers become structurally unemployed until they are retrained for other jobs.

To summarize, there are many causes of structural unemployment, including poor schools, new products, new technology, foreign competition, geographic differences, restricted entry into jobs, and shifts in government priorities. Because of the numerous sources of mismatching between skills and jobs, economists consider a certain level of structural unemployment inevitable. Public and private programs that train employees to fill existing job openings decrease structural unemployment. Conversely, one of the concerns about the minimum wage is that it may contribute to structural unemployment. In Exhibit 6 of Chapter 4, we demonstrated that a minimum wage set by legislation above the equilibrium wage causes unemployment. One approach intended to offset such undesirable effects of the minimum wage is a subminimum wage paid during a training period to give employers an incentive to hire unskilled workers.

Globalization   Certain jobs can be globally resourced, which means they can be performed anywhere in the world. U.S. companies sometimes use outsourcing of U.S. jobs to India, China, and other countries. Outsourcing is the practice of a company having its work done by another company in another country. As a result, U.S. workers can lose their jobs and require retraining for other jobs. It can be argued that outsourcing allows U.S. companies to reduce their costs, lower the prices of U.S. goods, and therefore be more competitive in global markets. In short, jobs are saved from being lost to more efficient competitors, and consumers benefit from lower prices.

A company also has the choice of having a job performed by its own employees in the United States, where the product is sold, or in another country. Offshoring occurs when a U.S. company hires employees from another country to perform jobs once done by the company's American employees. Suppose, for example, a U.S. company hires engineers in India to do jobs once done for this company in the United States. Assume the result is that the average salary paid by the company to these engineers drops $100,000 per year. A benefit is that the company reduces it costs, although some Americans may lose their jobs and must find new jobs.

In conclusion, there will always be mismatching between skills and jobs. Economists therefore consider a level of structural unemployment inevitable.

> **Outsourcing**
> The practice of a company having its work done by another company in another country.

> **Offshoring**
> The practice of work for a company performed by the company's employees located in another country.

16-4c CYCLICAL UNEMPLOYMENT

Cyclical unemployment is directly attributable to the lack of jobs caused by the business cycle. Cyclical unemployment is unemployment caused by the lack of jobs during a recession. When real GDP falls, companies close, jobs disappear, and workers scramble for fewer available jobs. Similar to the game of musical chairs, there are not enough chairs (jobs) for the number of players (workers) in the game.

The Great Depression is a dramatic example of cyclical unemployment. There was a sudden decline in consumption, investment, government spending, and net exports. As a result of this striking fall in real GDP, the unemployment rate rose to about 25 percent (see Exhibit 7). Now notice what happened to the unemployment rate when real GDP rose sharply during World War II. The Great Recession beginning in 2007 is another example of cyclical unemployment. Falling home prices and a plunge in stock prices caused households to cut back on consumption spending and, in combination with a fall in business investment spending, caused a negative growth rate and a sharp rise in the unemployment rate to a high of 9.7 percent at the end of the recession in 2009. To smooth out these swings in unemployment, a focus of macroeconomic policy is to moderate cyclical unemployment.

> **Cyclical unemployment**
> Unemployment caused by the lack of jobs during a recession.

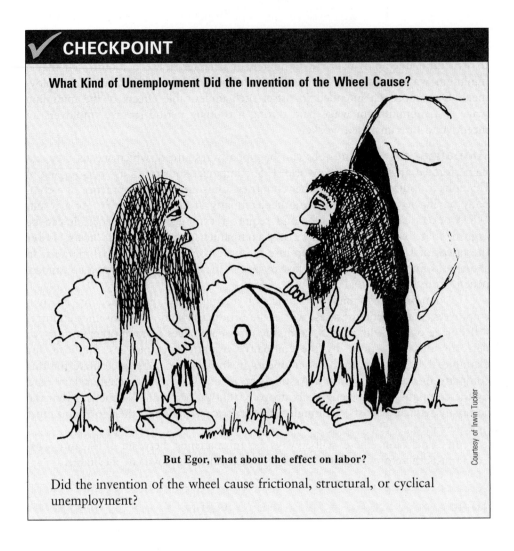

✓ **CHECKPOINT**

What Kind of Unemployment Did the Invention of the Wheel Cause?

But Egor, what about the effect on labor?

Did the invention of the wheel cause frictional, structural, or cyclical unemployment?

Courtesy of Irwin Tucker

16-5 The Goal of Full Employment

Full employment

The situation in which an economy operates at an unemployment rate equal to the sum of the frictional and structural unemployment rates. Also called the *natural rate of unemployment.*

In this section, we take a closer look at the meaning of full employment, also called the *natural rate of unemployment.* Because both frictional and structural unemployment are present in good and bad times, *full employment* does not mean "zero" percent unemployment. Full employment is the situation in which an economy operates at an unemployment rate equal to the sum of the frictional and structural unemployment rates. Full employment therefore is the rate of unemployment that exists without cyclical unemployment.

Unfortunately, economists cannot state with certainty what percentages of the labor force are frictionally and structurally unemployed at any particular point in time. In practice, therefore, full employment is difficult to define. Moreover, the full-employment rate of unemployment, or natural rate of unemployment, changes over time. In the 1960s, 4 percent unemployment was generally considered to represent full employment. In the 1980s, the accepted rate was 6 percent. Currently, the consensus among economists is that the natural rate is close to 5 percent. However, some economists argue that the rate is closer to 7 percent.

What Kind of Unemployment Do Robot Musicians Cause?

Applicable Concept: types of unemployment

The following is a classic article from the late 1980s that illustrates the types of unemployment and describes a recurring labor market situation:

People looking for job security have rarely chosen the music industry. But these days, musicians say, competition from machines has removed what little stability there was. Modern machines can effectively duplicate string sections, drummers, and even horn sections, so with the exception of concerts, the jobs available to live musicians are growing fewer by the day....

It is not the first time that technology has thrown a wrench into musical careers. When talking pictures helped usher in the death of vaudeville, and again, when recorded music replaced live music in radio station studios, the market for musicians took a beating from which it never fully recovered.... The musicians' plight is not getting universal sympathy. Some industry insiders say that the current job problems are an inevitable price of progress, and that musicians should update their skills to deal with the new instruments....

But others insist that more than musicians' livelihood is at stake. Mr. Glasel, [Musicians' Union] Local 802's president, warns that unbridled computerization of music could eventually threaten the quality of music. Jobs for trumpet players, for instance, have dropped precipitously since the synthesizer managed a fair approximation of the trumpet. And without trumpet players, he asked, "where is the next generation going to get its Dizzy Gillespie?"[1]

The threat to musicians' jobs continues: The Toyota Motor Corp. unveiled its instrument-playing humanoid robots at the 2005 World Exposition. The robots played drums and horn instruments, such as trumpets and tubas. And in 2008, a humanoid robot walked on the stage, said, "Hello, everyone," lifted the baton, and conducted the Detroit Symphony Orchestra. Its timing was judged to be impeccable, but the robot conductor lacked any spur-of-the-moment emotions. In 2011 Honda's humanoid robot named ASIMO was displayed at international events. ASIMO is the world's most advanced humanoid robot that can perform complicated tasks, such as playing soccer, dancing, and opening a sealed bottle and pouring a drink in a paper cup.

There is a Robot Hall of Fame at Carnegie Mellon University. The robots fall into two categories—robots from science and robots from science fiction. A panel of experts, each serving a two-year term, chooses robots in each category to be inducted into the Hall of Fame.

Rick Lord/Shutterstock.com

Envelope please! The first winners were the Unimate, the first industrial robot; the Sojourner robot from NASA's Mars Pathfinder mission; R2D2, the "droid" from the Stars Wars films; and HAL-9000, the rogue computer from the film *2001: A Space Odyssey*. And in 2012, robots played a soccer match at the RoboCup in Mexico City.

Analyze the Issue

1. Are the musicians experiencing frictional, structural, or cyclical unemployment? Explain.
2. What solution would you propose for the trumpet players mentioned above?

---

1. James S. Newton, "A Death Knell Sounds for Musical Jobs," *The New York Times*, March 1, 1987, sec. 3, p. 9.

Source: From James S. Newton, "A Death Knell Sounds for Musical Jobs", 'The New York Times', March 1, 1987, sec. 3, p. 9. Copyright © 1987 The New York Times. All rights reserved. Used by permission and protected by the Copyright Laws of the United States. The printing, copying, redistribution, or retransmission of the Material without express written permission is prohibited.

Several reasons are given for why full employment is not fixed. One reason is that between the early 1960s and the early 1980s, the participation of women and teenagers in the labor force increased. This change in the labor force composition increased the full-employment rate of unemployment because both women and young workers (under age 25) typically experience higher unemployment rates than men do. Another frequently cited and controversial reason for the rise in the full-employment rate of unemployment is that larger unemployment compensation payments, food stamps, welfare, and Social Security benefits from the government make unemployment less painful. In the 1990s, the natural rate of unemployment declined somewhat because the entry of females and teenagers into the labor force slowed. Also, the baby boom generation has aged, and middle-aged workers have lower unemployment rates.

16-6 The GDP Gap

GDP gap

The difference between actual real GDP and potential or full-employment real GDP.

When people in an economy are unemployed, society forfeits the production of goods and services. To determine the dollar value of how much society loses if the economy fails to reach the natural rate of unemployment, economists estimate the GDP gap. The GDP gap is the difference between actual real GDP and full-employment real GDP. The level of GDP that could be produced at full employment is also called *potential real GDP*. Expressed as a formula:

$$\text{GDP gap} = \text{actual real GDP} - \text{potential real GDP}$$

The GDP gap can be either positive if actual real GDP exceeds potential real GDP or negative if actual real GDP is less than potential real GDP. Because the GDP gap is calculated on the basis of the difference between GDP at the actual unemployment rate and estimated GDP at the full-employment rate of unemployment, the GDP gap measures the cost of cyclical unemployment. A positive GDP gap measures a boom in the economy when workers are employed overtime, and a negative GDP gap increases during a recession. Exhibit 9 shows the size of the GDP gap (in 2005 prices) from 1997 to 2011, based on potential real GDP and actual real GDP for each of these years. Prior to the 2001 recession, the economy operated above its potential (positive GDP gap). After the 2001 recession, the economy operated below its potential (negative gap) until 2005, when the gap was positive through 2007. Since the Great Recession's beginning in 2007, the U.S. economy has experienced large negative GDP gaps.

> **CONCLUSION:** *The gap between actual and potential real GDP measures the monetary losses of real goods and services to the nation from operating at less than full employment.*

16-6a NONMONETARY AND DEMOGRAPHIC CONSEQUENCES OF UNEMPLOYMENT

The burden of unemployment is more than the loss of potential output measured by the GDP gap. Unemployment also has nonmonetary costs. Some people endure unemployment pretty well because they have substantial savings to draw on, but others sink into despair. Without work, many people lose their feeling of

EXHIBIT 9 | Actual and Potential GDP, 1997–2011

The GDP gap is the difference between actual real GDP and potential real GDP, which is based on the assumption that the economy operates at full employment. A positive GDP gap measures a boom in the economy when workers are employed overtime. Between 1997 and 2000, the U.S. economy experienced a positive GDP gap. The recession in 2001 reversed the GDP gap, and the economy has operated with a negative GDP gap below its potential until 2004, when the gap was positive through 2007. Since the Great Recession beginning in 2007, the U.S. economy has experienced large negative GDP gaps.

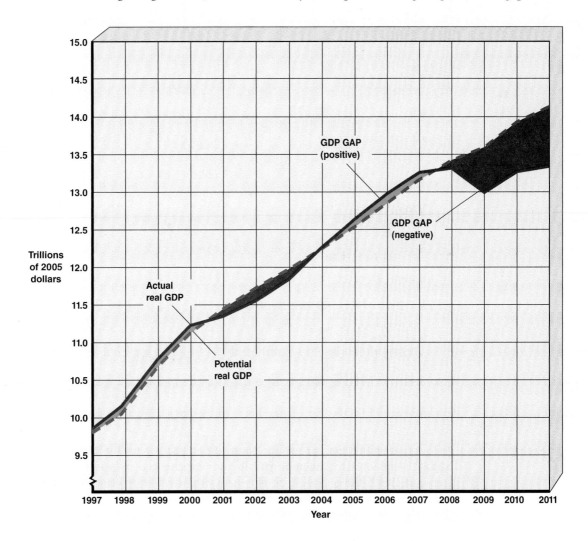

SOURCE: International Monetary Fund, *World Economic Outlook Database*, http://www.imf.org/external/ns/cs.aspx?id=28.

worth. A person's self-image suffers when he or she cannot support a family and be a valuable member of society. Research has associated high unemployment with suicides, crime, mental illness, heart attacks, and other maladies. Moreover, severe unemployment causes despair, family breakups, and political unrest.

EXHIBIT 10	Civilian Unemployment Rates by Selected Demographic Groups, 2011

Demographic Group	Unemployment Rate (percent)
Overall	8.9%
Gender	
Male	9.4
Female	8.5
Race	
White	7.9
Hispanic	11.5
African American	15.8
Teenagers (16–19 years old)	
All	24.4
White	21.7
Hispanics	31.1
African American	41.3
Education (25 years and over)	
Less than high school diploma	14.1
High school graduates	9.4
Bachelor's degree and higher	4.3

SOURCE: Bureau of Labor Statistics, *Current Population Survey*, http://stats.bls.gov/cps/cpsatabs.htm, Table 1-4.

Various labor market groups share the impact of unemployment unequally. Exhibit 10 presents the unemployment rates experienced by selected demographic groups. In 2011, the overall unemployment rate was 8.9 percent, but the figures in the exhibit reveal the unequal burden by gender, race, age, and educational attainment. First, it is interesting to note that the unemployment rate for males was greater than for females. Second, the unemployment rate for African Americans was higher than for whites and Hispanics. Third, teenagers experienced a high unemployment rate because they are new entrants to the workforce who have little employment experience, high quit rates, and little job mobility. Again, race is a strong factor, and the unemployment rate for African-American teenagers was greater than for white teenagers. Among the explanations are discrimination; the concentration of African-Americans in the inner city, where job opportunities for less skilled (blue-collar) workers are inadequate; and the minimum wage law.

Brother Can You Spare a Dime?

Applicable Concept: human costs of unemployment

The unemployment rate does not measure the full impact of unemployment on individuals. Prolonged unemployment not only means lost wages, but it also impairs health and social relationships. The United States fought its most monstrous battle against unemployment during the Great Depression of the 1930s. Return to Exhibit 7 and note that the unemployment rate stayed at 20 percent or more from 1932 through 1935. In 1933, it reached almost 25 percent of the civilian labor force; that is, about one out of every four people who wanted to work could not. This meant 16 million Americans were out of work when our country's population was less than half its present size.[1] For comparison, at the low point of the 1990–1991 recession, about 10 million Americans were officially unemployed.

But these statistics tell only part of the horror story. Millions of workers were "discouraged workers" who had simply given up looking for work because there was no work available, and these people were not counted. People were standing in line for soup kitchens, selling apples on the street, and living in cardboard shacks. "Brother can you spare a dime?" was a common greeting. Some people jumped out of windows, and others roamed the country trying valiantly to survive.

REUTERS/Jason Reed/Landov

John Steinbeck's great novel *The Grapes of Wrath* described millions of midwesterners who drove in caravans to California after being wiped out by drought in what became known as the Dust Bowl.

A 1992 study estimated the frightening impact of sustained unemployment that is not reflected in official unemployment data. Mary Merva, a University of Utah economist, co-authored a study of unemployment in 30 selected big cities from 1976 to 1990. This research found that a 1 percentage point increase in the national unemployment rate resulted in the following:

- 6.7 percent more murders
- 3.1 percent more deaths from stroke
- 5.6 percent more deaths from heart disease
- 3.9 percent increase in suicides[2]

Hard times during the recession of 2007 caused people to cut back on their medical care. According to a survey by the American Heart Association (AHA),

42 percent of the respondents said they trimmed health-related expenses, 32 percent skipped some preventive care, such as a mammogram or an annual physical, and 10 percent stopped or diminished the use of medicine for chronic conditions. And a 2011 article in *The New York Times* reported the finding in a Harvard School of Public Health survey that workers who lost a job through no fault of their own were twice as likely to report developing a new ailment such as high blood pressure, diabetes, or heart disease over the next year and a half, compared with people who were continuously employed.[3]

Although these estimates are subject to statistical qualifications, they underscore the notion that prolonged unemployment poses a real danger to many individuals. As people change their behavior in the face of layoffs, cutbacks, or a sudden drop in net worth, more and more Americans find themselves clinically depressed.

1. U.S. Bureau of the Census, *Historical Statistics of the United States, Colonial Times to 1957* (Washington, D.C.: U.S. Government Printing Office, 1960), Series D46–47, p. 73.
2. Robert Davis, "Recession's Cost: Lives," *USA Today*, Oct. 16, 1992, p. 1A.
3. Roni Caryn Rabin, "Losing Job May Be Hazardous to Health," *The New York Times*, May 9, 2011.

Source: © Cengage Learning 2014

Finally, comparison of the unemployment rates in 2011 by educational attainment reveals the importance of education as an insurance policy against unemployment. Firms are much less likely to lay off a higher-skilled worker with a college education, in whom they have a greater investment in terms of training and salaries, than a worker with only a high school diploma.

Key Concepts

Business cycle	Coincident indicators	Outsourcing
Peak	Lagging indicators	Offshoring
Recession	Unemployment rate	Cyclical unemployment
Trough	Civilian labor force	Full employment
Expansion	Discouraged worker	GDP gap
Economic growth	Frictional unemployment	
Leading indicators	Structural unemployment	

Summary

- **Business cycles** are recurrent rises and falls in real GDP over a period of years. Business cycles vary greatly in duration and intensity. A cycle consists of four phases: peak, recession, trough, and recovery. The generally accepted theory today is that changes in the forces of demand and supply cause business cycles. A **recession** is generally defined as at least two consecutive quarters of real GDP decline. A **trough** is the turning point in national output between recession and recovery. During an **expansion**, there is an upturn in the business cycle, during which real GDP rises. A **peak** occurs when real GDP reaches its maximum level during a recovery.

Hypothetical Business Cycle

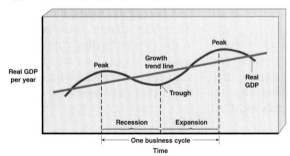

SOURCE: Bureau of Economic Analysis, *National Income Accounts*, http://www.bea.gov/national/nipaweb/SelectTable.asp?Selected=Y, Table 1.1.6.

- **Economic growth** is measured by the annual percentage change in real GDP in a nation. The long-term average annual growth rate since 1930 in the United States has been 3.5 percent.
- **Leading, coincident,** and **lagging indicators** are economic variables that change before, at the same time as, and after changes in real GDP, respectively.
- The **unemployment rate** is the ratio of the number of unemployed to the number in the civilian labor force multiplied by 100. The nation's **civilian labor force** consists of people who are employed plus those who are out of work, but seeking employment.
- **Discouraged workers** are a reason critics say the unemployment rate is *understated*. Discouraged workers are persons who want to work, but have given up searching for work. Another criticism of the unemployment rate is that it *overstates* unemployment because respondents can falsely report they are seeking a job.
- **Frictional, structural,** and **cyclical unemployment** are different types of unemployment. **Frictional unemployment**, including seasonal unemployment, results when workers are

seeking new jobs that exist. The problem is that imperfect information prevents matching the applicants with the available jobs. **Structural unemployment** is long-term unemployment caused by factors in the economy, including lack of education, changes in consumer demand, technological change, and globalization. **Cyclical unemployment** is unemployment resulting from insufficient aggregate demand.

- **Full employment** occurs when the unemployment rate is equal to the total of the frictional and structural unemployment rates. Currently, the full-employment rate of unemployment (natural rate of unemployment) in the United States is considered to be close to 5 percent. At this rate of unemployment, the economy is producing at its maximum potential.

- The **GDP gap** is the difference between actual real GDP and full employment, or potential real GDP. Therefore, the GDP gap measures the loss of output due to cyclical unemployment.

Summary of Conclusion Statements

- We value economic growth as one of our nation's economic goals because it increases our standard of living—it creates a bigger "economic pie."

- The gap between actual and potential real GDP measures the monetary losses of real goods and services to the nation from operating at less than full employment.

Study Questions and Problems

1. What is the basic cause of the business cycle?

2. Following are real GDP figures for 10 quarters:

Quarter	Real GDP (billions of dollars)
1	$ 400
2	500
4	200
5	300
6	500
7	800
8	900
9	1,000
10	500

Plot these data points, and identify the four phases of the business cycle. Give a theory that may explain the cause of the observed business

cycle. What are some of the consequences of a prolonged decline in real GDP? Is the decline in real GDP from $1,000 billion to $500 billion a recession?

3. In a given year, there are 10 million unemployed workers and 120 million employed workers in an economy. Excluding members of the armed forces and persons in institutions and assuming these figures include only civilian workers, calculate the civilian unemployment rate.

4. Describe the relevant criteria that government statisticians use to determine whether a person is "unemployed."

5. How has the official unemployment rate been criticized for overestimating and underestimating unemployment?

6. Why is frictional unemployment inevitable in an economy characterized by imperfect job information?

7. How does structural unemployment differ from cyclical unemployment?

8. Is it reasonable to expect the unemployment rate to fall to zero for an economy? What is the relationship of frictional, structural, and cyclical unemployment to the full-employment rate of unemployment, or natural rate of unemployment?

9. In the 1960s, economists used 4 percent as their approximation for the natural rate of unemployment. Currently, full employment is on the order of 5 percent unemployment. What is the major factor accounting for this rise?

10. Speculate on why teenage unemployment rates exceed those for the overall labor force.

11. Explain the GDP gap.

For Online Exercises, go to the Tucker Web site at www.cengage.com/economics/tucker.

✓ CHECKPOINT ANSWERS

Where Are We on the Business-Cycle Roller Coaster?

The car dealer's sales in the first quarter conformed to the recession phase of the business cycle, and those in the second quarter, to the trough. Then car sales in the third quarter were below those in the first quarter, but the increase over the second quarter indicated a recovery. If you said real GDP during an expansion can be lower than real GDP during a recession, **YOU ARE CORRECT.**

What Kind of Unemployment Did the Invention of the Wheel Cause?

The invention of the wheel represented a new technology for primitive people. Even in the primitive era, many workers who transported goods lost their jobs to the more efficient cart with wheels. If you said the invention of the wheel caused structural unemployment, **YOU ARE CORRECT.**

Sample Quiz

For an explanation of the correct answers, visit the Tucker website at www.cengage.com/economics/tucker.

1. A business cycle is the
   a. period of time in which expansion and contraction of economic activity are equal
   b. period of time in which there are three phases: peak, depression, and expansion
   c. recurring growth and decline in real GDP
   d. period of time in which a business is established and ceases operations

2. A business cycle is the period of time in which
   a. a business is established and ceases operations.
   b. there are four phases: peak, recession, trough, and expansion.
   c. the price level changes.
   d. expansion and contraction of economic activity are equal.

3. The phase of the business cycle follows a recession.
   a. expansion
   b. recession
   c. peak
   d. trough

Sample Quiz *continued*

EXHIBIT 11	Business Cycle

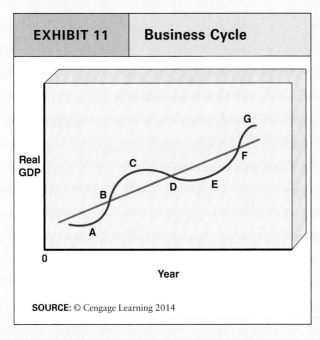

SOURCE: © Cengage Learning 2014

4. In Exhibit 11, the expansion phase of the business cycle is represented by points
   a. *A* and *C*
   b. *B* and *F*
   c. *B* and *D*
   d. *C* and *G*

5. A general rule is that economy is experiencing a recession when
   a. real GDP declines for at least three months.
   b. real GDP declines for at least nine months.
   c. nominal GDP declines for at least nine months.
   d. real GDP declines for at least six months.

6. A person who has given up searching for work is called
   a. frictionally unemployed.
   b. structurally unemployed.
   c. a discouraged worker.
   d. unemployed.

7. John Steinbeck's *Cannery Row* describes a character who takes his own life because of poor job prospects. If he was an unemployed person who gave up looking for work, he would be considered
   a. chronically unemployed.
   b. a discouraged worker.
   c. a member of the labor force.
   d. frictionally unemployed.

8. Unemployment that is of a short duration to allow a person time to find a new job is
   a. structural unemployment.
   b. cyclical unemployment.
   c. frictional unemployment.
   d. durational unemployment.

9. A person who voluntarily quits their job in New York and expects to get a similar job in Los Angeles is an example of
   a. structural unemployment.
   b. cyclical unemployment.
   c. durational unemployment.
   d. frictional unemployment.

10. Frictional unemployment refers to
    a. people who are out of work and have no job skills.
    b. short periods of unemployment needed to match jobs and job seekers.
    c. people who spend relatively long periods out of work.
    d. unemployment related to the ups and downs of the business cycle.

11. Sam is a musician who is out of work because electronic equipment replaced live musicians. This is an example of
    a. frictional unemployment.
    b. cyclical unemployment.
    c. structural unemployment.
    d. involuntary unemployment.

12. Louise is unemployed due to a decrease in the demand for workers with knowledge of a certain word processing language. This is an example of
    a. cyclical unemployment.
    b. frictional unemployment.
    c. involuntary unemployment.
    d. structural unemployment.

Sample Quiz *continued*

13. Consider a broom factory that permanently closes because of foreign competition. If the broom factory's workers cannot find new jobs because their skills are no longer marketable, they are classified as
    a. seasonally unemployed.
    b. frictionally unemployed.
    c. structurally unemployed.
    d. cyclically unemployed.

14. The increase in unemployment associated with a recession is called
    a. structural unemployment.
    b. frictional unemployment.
    c. discouraged unemployment.
    d. cyclical unemployment.

15. Which of the following is *true*?
    a. The GDP gap is the difference between full-employment real GDP and actual real GDP.
    b. We desire economic growth because it increases the nation's standard of living.
    c. Economic growth is measured by the annual percentage increase in a nation's real GDP.
    d. Discouraged workers are a reason critics say the unemployment rate is understated.
    e. All of the above answers are correct.

16. What stage of the business cycle immediately follows the trough?
    a. peak
    b. expansion
    c. recession
    d. depression

17. The government's chief forecasting gauge for business cycles is the
    a. unemployment rate.
    b. real GDP.
    c. personal income index.
    d. index of leading indicators.

18. Which of the following is *not* a lagging indicator?
    a. duration of unemployment
    b. stock prices
    c. commercial and industrial loans
    d. prime rate

19. Suppose the official unemployment rate is 10 percent. We can conclude without question that
    a. the same 10 percent of the people in the economy were out of work for the entire year.
    b. 1 out of every 10 people in the civilian labor force is currently unemployed.
    c. the same 10 percent of the people in the civilian labor force was out of work for the entire year.
    d. every person in the civilian labor force was out of work for 10 percent of the year.

20. Sally lost her job when her company went out of business because of a recession. This is an example of
    a. frictional unemployment.
    b. structural unemployment.
    c. cyclical unemployment.
    d. technological unemployment.

chapter 17

Inflation

In addition to the goals of full employment and economic growth discussed in the previous chapter, keeping prices stable is one of the most important economic goals facing a nation. In the United States, the Great Depression of the 1930s and the Great Recession of 2007 produced profound changes in people's lives from the consequences of unemployment. Similarly, the "Great Inflation" of the 1970s and early 1980s left memories of the miseries of inflation. In fact, every American president since Franklin Roosevelt has resolved to keep the price level stable. Politicians are aware that, as with high unemployment, voters are quick to blame any administration that fails to keep inflation rates under control.

This chapter explains what inflation is: What does it mean when a 50 percent hike in the price of gasoline causes pain at the pump, eggs jump by 35 percent, a gallon of milk is up 23 percent, a loaf of bread climbs 16 percent, and around the world others feel the pinch of higher prices? Here you will study how the government actually measures changes in the price level and computes the rate of inflation. The chapter concludes with a discussion of the consequences and root causes of inflation. It explains who the winners are and who the losers are. For example, you will see what happened in Zimbabwe when the inflation rate reached 231,000,000 percent. After studying this chapter, you will have a much clearer understanding of why inflation is so feared.

In this chapter, you will learn to solve these economics puzzles:

- What is the inflation rate of your college education?
- Can a person's income fall even though he or she received a raise?
- What would Babe Ruth's salary be worth today?
- What is the real price of gasoline?
- Can an interest rate be negative?
- Does inflation harm everyone equally?

17-1 Meaning and Measurement of Inflation

After World War II, a 12-ounce bottle of Pepsi sold for 5 cents. Today, a 12-ounce can of Pepsi sells for more than 20 times that much. This is not inflation. Inflation is an increase in the *general* (average) price level of goods and services in the economy. Inflation's opposite is deflation. Deflation is a decrease in the *general* (average) price level of goods and services in the economy. Note that inflation does not mean that *all* prices of *all* products in the economy rise during a given period of time. For example, the annual percentage change in the average overall price level during the 1970s reached double digits, but the prices of pocket calculators and digital watches actually declined. The reason that the average price level rose in the 1970s was that the rising prices of Pepsi, houses, and other goods outweighed the falling prices of pocket calculators, digital watches, and other goods.

> **CONCLUSION:** *Inflation is an increase in the overall average level of prices and not an increase in the price of any specific product.*

17-1a THE CONSUMER PRICE INDEX

The most widely reported measure of inflation is the consumer price index (CPI), which measures changes in the average prices of consumer goods and services. The CPI is sometimes called the *cost-of-living index*. It includes only consumer goods and services in order to determine how rising prices affect the income of consumers. Unlike the *GDP chain price index* explained in the previous chapter on GDP, the CPI does not consider items purchased by businesses and government.

The Bureau of Labor Statistics (BLS) of the Department of Labor prepares the CPI. Each month the bureau's "price collectors" contact retail stores, homeowners, and tenants in selected cities throughout the United States. Based on these monthly inquiries, the BLS records average prices for a "market basket" of different items purchased by the typical *urban* family. These items are included under the following categories: food, housing, apparel, transportation, medical care, entertainment, and other expenditures. Exhibit 1 presents a more detailed breakdown of these categories and shows the relative importance of each as a percentage of total expenditures. The survey reveals, for example, that 33 cents out of each consumer dollar is spent

Inflation

An increase in the general (average) price level of goods and services in the economy.

Deflation

A decrease in the general (average) price level of goods and services in the economy.

Consumer price index (CPI)

An index that measures changes in the average prices of consumer goods and services.

EXHIBIT 1	Composition of the Consumer Price Index

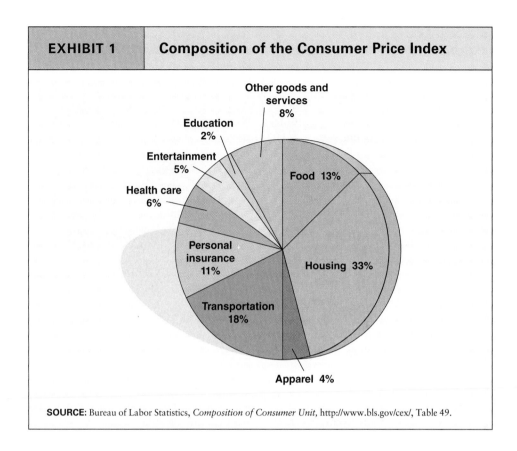

SOURCE: Bureau of Labor Statistics, *Composition of Consumer Unit*, http://www.bls.gov/cex/, Table 49.

for housing and 18 cents for transportation. The composition of the market basket generally remains unchanged from one period to the next, so the CPI is called a *fixed-weight price index*. If 33 percent of consumer spending was on housing during a given base year, the assumption is that 33 percent of spending is still spent on housing in, say, 2011. Over time, particular items in the CPI change. For example, personal computers, digital cameras, and cell phones have been added. The base period is changed periodically.

17-1b HOW THE CPI IS COMPUTED

Exhibit 2 illustrates the basic idea behind the CPI using hypothetical data to show how this price index measures inflation. Suppose, in 1982, a typical family in the United States lived a very meager existence and purchased a market basket of only hamburgers, gasoline, and jeans. Column (1) shows the quantity purchased for each of these items, and column (2) lists the corresponding average selling price. Multiplying the price times the quantity gives the market basket cost in column (3) of each consumer product purchased in 1982. The total cost paid by our typical family for the market basket, based on 1982 prices and quantities purchased, is $245.

Years later it is 2011, and we wish to know the impact of rising prices on consumer purchases. To calculate the CPI, we determine the cost of the *same* market basket, valued at 2011 *current-year prices*, and compare this to the cost at 1982

EXHIBIT 2	A Hypothetical Consumer Price Index for a Simple Economy				
Products in consumers' market basket	(1) 1982 quantity purchased	(2) 1982 price	(3) Market basket cost in 1982 [(1) × (2)]	(4) 2011 price	(5) Market basket cost in 2011 [(1) × (4)]
Hamburgers	50	$ 0.80	$ 40	$ 1.00	$ 50
Gallons of gasoline	250	0.70	175	0.90	225
Jeans	2	15.00	30	30.00	60
			Total 1982 cost = $245		Total 2011 cost = $335

$$2011\ CPI = \frac{2011\ market\ basket\ cost}{1982\ market\ basket\ cost} \times 100$$

$$2011\ CPI = \frac{\$335}{\$245} \times 100 = 136.7$$

SOURCE: © Cengage Learning 2014

Base year

A year chosen as a reference point for comparison with some earlier or later year.

base-year prices. A base year is a year chosen as a reference point for comparison with some earlier or later year. Expressed as a general formula:

$$CPI = \frac{cost\ of\ market\ basket\ of\ products\ at\ current\text{-}year\ (2011)\ prices}{cost\ of\ same\ market\ basket\ of\ products\ at\ base\text{-}year\ (1982)\ prices} \times 100$$

As shown in Exhibit 2, the 2011 cost for our market basket example is calculated by multiplying the 2011 price for each item in column (4) times the 1982 quantity purchased in column (1). Column (5) lists the result for each item in the market basket, and the total market basket cost in 2011 is $335. The CPI value of 136.7 is computed in Exhibit 2 as the ratio of the current 2011 cost of the market basket ($335) to the cost of the same market basket in the 1982 base year ($245) multiplied by 100.

The value of the CPI in the base year is always 100 because the numerator and the denominator of the CPI formula are the same in the base year. Currently, the CPI uses 1982–1984 spending patterns as its base year. Once the BLS selects the base year and uses the market basket technique to generate the CPI numbers, the annual *inflation rate* is computed as the percentage change in the official CPI from one year to the next. Mathematically,

$$Anual\ rate\ of\ inflation = \frac{CPI\ in\ given\ year - CPI\ in\ previous\ year}{CPI\ in\ previous\ year} \times 100$$

Exhibit 3 lists actual CPI for selected years. You can use the above formula and calculate the inflation rate for any given year using the base year of 1982–84 = 100. In 2011, for example, the CPI was 225.0, while in 2010, it was 218.1. The rate of inflation for 2011 is computed as follows:

$$3.2\% = \frac{225.0 - 218.1}{218.1} \times 100$$

EXHIBIT 3	Consumer Price Indexes and Inflation Rates, Selected Years	
Year	CPI	Inflation rate
1931	15.2	—
1932	13.7	−9.9%
1979	72.6	—
1980	82.4	13.5
2000	172.2	—
2001	177.1	2.8
2002	179.9	1.6
2008	215.3	—
2009	214.5	−0.4

SOURCE: Bureau of Labor Statistics, *Consumer Price Index*, http://data.bls.gov/cgi-bin/surveymost?cu.

The negative inflation rate of 9.9 percent for 1932 was deflation, and the 13.5 percent inflation rate for 1980 illustrates a relatively high rate in recent U.S. history. The fall in the inflation rate from 2.8 percent to 1.6 percent between 2001 and 2002 was disinflation. Disinflation is a reduction in the rate of inflation. Disinflation does not mean that prices are falling; rather, it means that the rate of increases in prices is falling. The negative inflation rate of −0.4 percent in 2009 was the first U.S. deflation since 1955.

Disinflation
A reduction in the rate of inflation.

✔ CHECKPOINT

The College Education Price Index

Suppose your *market basket* for a college education consisted of only the four items listed in the following table:

Item	2010	2011
Tuition and fees[1]	$4,500	$5,000
Room and board[2]	6,000	6,200
Books[3]	1,000	1,200
Soft drinks[4]	150	200

[1]Tuition for two semesters.
[2]Payment for nine months.
[3]Ten textbooks.
[4]Two hundred 12-ounce Coca-Colas.

Using 2010 as your base year, what is the percentage change in the college education price index in 2011?

How Much More Does It Cost to Laugh?

Applicable Concept: consumer price index

Are we paying bigger bucks for smaller yuks? Or is it a lower fee for more glee? Is there a bone to pick with the price of rubber chickens? Is the price of Groucho glasses raising eyebrows? The cost of *Mad* magazine driving you mad? Well, you get the idea. Malcolm Kushner, an attorney-turned-humor consultant based in Santa Cruz, California, developed an index based on a compilation of leading humor indicators to measure price changes in things that make us laugh. Kushner created the cost-of-laughing index to track how trends in laughter affect the bottom line. He is a humor consultant who advises corporate leaders on making humor work for business professionals. For example, humor can make executives better public speakers, and laughter reduces stress and can even cure illnesses. Kushner believes humor is America's greatest asset, and his consulting business

gets a lot of publicity from publication of the index. To combat rising humor costs, Kushner has established a Web site at http://www.kushnergroup.com. It organizes links to databases of funny quotes, anecdotes, one-liners, and other material for business speakers and writers.

The exhibit with the Groucho face traces annual percentage changes in the cost of laughing that Kushner has reported to the media. On an annual basis, the inflation rate for laughing remained almost flat as a pancake at about 3 percent from 2000 through 2005. Then in 2006, the humor index took a slippery slide on a banana peel to a disinflation rate of only one-tenth of 1 percent. In 2007, the index rode a roller coaster ride up to 4.7 percent, which was the largest increase since 1999, and then down to −1.4 percent in 2009. This deflation was the first negative percent change in the index history that began in 1987.

Closer examination of the cost-of-laughing index over the years and some other items gives both smiley and sad faces. The good news in 2011 is that the price of a whoopee cushion decreased, but the bad news is that the price of Groucho glasses rose. The major reason for more expensive

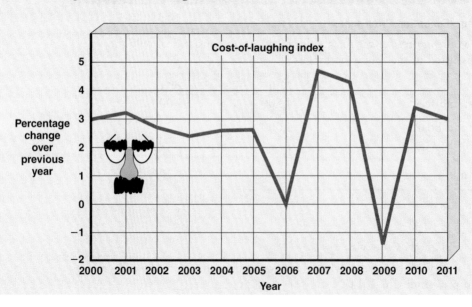

humor is the price of writing a half-hour television situation comedy. Just like the CPI, Kushner's index has been criticized. Note that the fee for writing a TV sitcom dominates the index. Kushner responds to this issue by saying, "Well, I wanted the index to be truly national. The fact that this price dominates the index reflects that TV comedy shows dominate our national culture. If you can laugh for free at a sitcom, you don't need to buy a rubber chicken or go to a comedy club."

Analyze the Issue
No question here. This one is just for fun.

Cost of Laughing Index

Item	2008	2009	2010	2011
Rubber chicken[1]	$51.00	$51.00	$ 72.00	$ 78.00
Groucho glasses[1]	15.00	15.00	21.00	24.00
Whoopee cushion[1]	5.40	5.40	3.00	1.20
Mad magazine[2]	4.99	4.99	5.99	5.99
Singing telegrams[3]				
Pink gorilla	250.00	150.00	185.00	185.00
Dancing chicken	250.00	150.00	185.00	185.00
Fee for writing a TV sitcom[4]	15,482.00	15,482.00	15,946.00	16,437.00
Comedy clubs[5]				
Atlanta: The Punch Line	23.00	20.00	20.00	20.00
Chicago: Second City	25.00	25.00	27.00	27.00
Houston: Laff Stop	25.00	20.00	15.00	15.00
Denver: Comedy Works	25.00	28.00	25.00	25.00
Indianapolis: Crackers Comedy	13.00	15.00	13.00	13.00
Los Angeles: Laugh Factory	20.00	20.00	20.00	20.00
New York: Comic Strip	22.00	25.00	25.00	25.00
Pittsburgh: The Funny Bone	15.00	15.00	15.00	15.00
San Francisco: Punch Line	25.00	21.00	21.00	21.00
Seattle: Comedy Underground	15.00	15.00	15.00	15.00
Total cost of humor basket	$16,266.39	$16,062.39	$16,613.99	$17,112.19
Annual inflation rate	**4.3%**	**−1.4%**	**3.4%**	**3%**

1. One dozen wholesale from Franco-American Novelty Company, Long Island City, New York.
2. April issue.
3. Available from Bellygrams, Manhattan, New York.
4. Minimum fee under Writers Guild of America basic agreement.
5. Admission on Saturday night.

Source: Data provided by Malcolm Kushner.

17-1c HISTORY OF U.S. INFLATION RATES

Exhibit 4 shows how prices have changed in the United States since 1929, as measured by annual changes in the CPI. During the early years of the Great Depression, the nation experienced *deflation*, and the CPI declined at almost a double-digit rate. In contrast, the CPI reached a double-digit inflation rate during and immediately following World War II. After 1950, the inflation rate generally remained below 3 percent until the inflationary pressures from the Vietnam War in the late 1960s. In fact, the average inflation rate between 1950 and 1968 was only 2 percent. Then the inflation rate climbed to more than 10 percent in 1974, 1979, 1980, and 1981, reaching a high of 13.5 percent in 1980. During the 1973–1982 period, the average annual inflation rate was 8.8 percent. Following the 1990–1991 recession, the annual inflation rate moderated, and it averaged 2.5 percent between 1992 and 2010. In 2009 during the Great Recession, the deflation rate was –0.4 percent. In 2011, the inflation rate was 3.2 percent.

EXHIBIT 4	The U.S. Inflation Rate, 1929–2011

During the Great Depression, the economy experienced deflation as prices plunged. During and immediately after World War II, the annual rate of inflation reached the double-digit level. After 1950, the inflation rate was generally below 3 percent until the inflationary pressures from the Vietnam War in the late 1960s. During the 1950–1968 period, the average inflation rate was only 2 percent. In contrast, the inflation rate climbed sharply to an average of 7.6 percent between 1969 and 1982. Between 1992 and 2009, inflation moderated and averaged 2.6 percent annually. In 2009 during the Great Recession, the deflation rate was –0.4 percent. In 2011, the inflation rate was 3.2 percent.

SOURCE: *Economic Report of the President*, 2012, http://www.gpoaccess.gov/eop/, Table B-64.

17-1d CONSUMER PRICE INDEX CRITICISMS

Just as there is criticism of the unemployment rate, the CPI is not a perfect measure of inflation, and it has been the subject of much public debate. There are reasons for this criticism:

1. Changes in the CPI are based on a typical market basket of products that does not match the actual market basket purchased by many consumers. Suppose you spend your nominal annual income entirely on lemonade, hot dogs, and jeans. During this year, the inflation rate is 5 percent, but assume the prices of lemonade, hot dogs, and jeans actually fall. In this case, your real income will rise, and the official inflation rate based on the CPI will *overstate* the impact of inflation on your standard of living. Retired persons, for example, buy a bundle of products that differs from that of the "typical" family. Because retired persons purchase proportionally more medical services than the typical family, the inflation rate may understate the impact of inflation on older persons.

2. The BLS has difficulty adjusting the CPI for changes in *quality*. Compare a TV made in the past with a new TV. The new TV may cost more, but it is much better than the old TV. A portion of the price increase therefore reflects better quality instead of simply a higher price for the same item. If the quality of items improves, increases in the CPI *overstate* inflation. Similarly, deteriorating quality *understates* inflation. The BLS attempts to make adjustments for quality changes in automobiles, electronic equipment, and other products in the market basket, but these adjustments are difficult to determine accurately.

3. The use of a single base-year market basket ignores the law of demand. If the price of a product rises, consumers purchase substitutes, and a smaller quantity is demanded. Suppose orange growers suffer from severe frosts and the supply of oranges decreases. Consequently, the price of oranges increases sharply. According to the *law of demand*, consumers will decrease the quantity demanded of oranges and substitute consumption of, say, apples for oranges. Because the market basket does not automatically change by reducing the percentage or weight of oranges and increasing the percentage of apples, the CPI will *overstate* the impact of higher prices for oranges on the price level. To deal with this *substitution* bias problem, the BLS takes annual surveys to keep up with changing consumption patterns and correct for the fixed market basket limitations of the CPI.

17-2 Consequences of Inflation

We will now turn from measuring inflation to examining its effects on people's income and wealth. Why should inflation cause concern? You will learn in this section that inflation is feared because it can significantly alter one's standard of living. You will see that inflation can create winners, who enjoy a larger slice of the national income pie, and losers, who receive a smaller slice as a result of inflation.

17-2a INFLATION SHRINKS INCOME

Economist Arthur Okun once stated, "This society is built on implicit and explicit contracts.... They are linked to the idea that the dollar means something. If you cannot depend on the value of the dollar, this system is undermined. People will constantly feel they've been fooled and cheated." When prices rise, people worry whether the rise in their income will keep pace with inflation. And the more quickly prices rise, the more people suffer from the stresses of inflation and its uncertainties.

Inflation tends to reduce your standard of living through declines in the purchasing power of money. The greater the rate of inflation, the greater the decline in the quantity of goods we can purchase with a given nominal income, or *money income*. Nominal income is the actual number of dollars received over a period of time. The source of income can be wages, salary, rent, dividends, interest, or pensions.

Nominal income does not measure your real purchasing power. Finding out if you are better or worse off over time requires converting nominal income to real income. Real income is the actual number of dollars received (nominal income) adjusted for changes in the CPI. Real income measures the amount of goods and services that can be purchased with one's nominal income. If the CPI increases and your nominal income remains the same, your real income (purchasing power) falls. In short, if your nominal income fails to keep pace with inflation, your standard of living falls. Suppose your nominal income in Year *1* was $50,000 and the Year *2* CPI value is 207.3. Your real income relative to a base year is

Nominal income

The actual number of dollars received over a period of time.

Real income

The actual number of dollars received (nominal income) adjusted for changes in the CPI.

$$\text{Real income} = \frac{\text{nominal income}}{\text{CPI (as decimal, or CPI/100)}}$$

$$\text{Year } 1 \text{ real income} = \frac{\$50,000}{2.07} = \$24,155$$

Now assume your nominal income rose in the next year (Year 2) by 10 percent, from $50,000 to $55,000, and the CPI increases by 3.8 percent, from 207.3 to 215.3. Thus, you earn more money, but how much better off are you? To answer this question, you must compute your Year *2* real income as follows:

$$\text{Year } 2 \text{ real income} = \frac{\$55,000}{2.15} = \$25,581$$

Using the preceding two computed real-income figures, the percentage change in your real income between Year *1* and Year *2* was 5.9 percent ($1,426/$24,155 × 100). This means that your standard of living has risen because you have an extra $1,426 to spend on entertainment, clothes, or travel. Even though the general price level has risen, your purchasing power has increased because the percentage rise in nominal income more than offsets the rate of inflation. Instead of precisely calculating this relationship, a good approximation can be obtained through the following simple formula:

SOURCE: © Cengage Learning 2014

It should be noted that workers with union contracts are largely unaffected by inflation because their wages automatically increase with increases in the CPI, which is called a *cost-of-living adjustment (COLA)*. For example, under union contracts, an inflation rate of 3 percent in a given year would automatically increase wages by 3 percent.

> **CONCLUSION:** *People whose nominal incomes rise faster than the rate of inflation gain purchasing power, while people whose nominal incomes do not keep pace with inflation lose purchasing power.*

Now suppose someone asks you the following question: In 1932, Babe Ruth, the New York Yankees home run slugger, earned $80,000. How much did he earn in 2011 dollars? Economists convert a past salary into a salary today by using this formula:

$$\text{Salary in given year} = \text{salary in previous year} \times \frac{\text{CPI in given year}}{\text{CPI in previous year}}$$

$$\text{Salary in 2011 dollars} = \$80,000 \times \frac{225.0}{13.7} = \$1,313,868$$

In other words, a salary of $80,000 in 1932 was equivalent to a salary of about $1.3 million today.

Blank Archives/Getty Images

✓ CHECKPOINT

What Is the Real Price of Gasoline?

In 1981, consumers were shocked when the average price for gasoline reached $1.35 per gallon because only a few years previously, gasoline was selling for one-half this price. If the CPI is 1981 was 90.9 and the CPI in 2011 was 225.0, what is the average inflation adjusted price in 2011 dollars?

"I've called the family together to announce that, because of inflation, I'm going to have to let two of you go."

© Joseph Farris/The New Yorker Collection/www.cartoonbank.com

• •

17-2b INFLATION AND WEALTH

Wealth

The value of the stock of assets owned at some point in time.

Income is one measure of economic well-being, and wealth is another. Income is a flow of money earned by selling factors of production. Wealth is the value of the stock of assets owned at some point in time. Wealth includes real estate, stocks, bonds, bank accounts, life insurance policies, cash, and automobiles. A person can have a high income and little wealth or great wealth and little income.

Inflation can benefit holders of wealth because the value of assets tends to increase as prices rise. Consider a home purchased for $200,000 that sells ten years later for $300,000. This 50 percent increase can be largely the result of inflation. People who own forms of wealth that increase in value faster than the inflation rate, such as real estate and stocks, are winners. On the other hand, the impact of inflation on wealth penalizes people without it. Consider younger couples wishing to purchase a home. As prices rise, it becomes more difficult for them to buy a home or acquire other assets.

17-2c INFLATION AND THE REAL INTEREST RATE

Nominal interest rate

The actual rate of interest without adjustment for the inflation rate.

Real interest rate

The nominal rate of interest minus the inflation rate.

Borrowers and savers may be winners or losers, depending on the rate of inflation. Understanding how this might happen requires making a distinction between the nominal interest rate and the real interest rate. The nominal interest rate is the actual rate of interest earned over a period of time. The nominal interest rate, for example, is the interest rate specified on a loan or savings account. If you borrow $10,000 from a bank at a 5 percent annual interest rate for five years, this is more accurately called a 5 percent annual nominal interest rate. Similarly, a $10,000 certificate of deposit that yields 5 percent annual interest is said to have a 5 percent annual nominal interest rate.

The real interest rate is the nominal interest rate minus the inflation rate. The occurrence of inflation means that the real rate of interest will be less than the nominal rate. Suppose the inflation rate during the year is 5 percent. This means that a 5 percent annual nominal interest rate paid on a $10,000 loan amounts to a 2 percent *real interest rate* and a certificate of deposit that yields 5 percent annual nominal interest also earns 2 percent *real interest*.

To understand how inflation can make those who borrow winners, suppose you receive a one-year loan from your parents to start a business. Earning a profit is not your parents' motive, and they know you will repay the loan. Their only concern is that you replace the decline in purchasing power of the money they loaned you. Both you and your parents anticipate the inflation rate will be 2 percent during the year; so the loan is made, and you agree to repay the principal plus the 2 percent to offset inflation. In short, both parties assume payment of a zero real interest rate (the 2 percent nominal interest rate minus the 2 percent rate of inflation). Now consider what happens if the inflation rate is actually 5 percent during the year of the loan. The clear unintentional winner is you, the debtor, because your creditor parents are paid the principal plus 2 percent interest, but their purchasing power still falls by 3 percent because the actual inflation rate is 5 percent. Stated differently, instead of zero, the real interest rate paid on the loan was −3 percent (the 2 percent nominal interest rate minus the 5 percent rate of inflation). In real terms, your parents paid you to borrow from them.

During the late 1970s, the rate of inflation rose frequently. This forced mortgage lenders to protect themselves against declining real interest rates on their loans by offering adjustable-rate mortgages (ARMs) in addition to conventional fixed-rate mortgages. ARMs are home loans that adjust the nominal interest rate to changes in an index, such as rates on Treasury securities. The *subprime loan crisis* resulted from homeowners who were unable to make payments as the interest rate rose on their ARMs. This subject is discussed in more depth in the chapter on monetary policy.

A nest egg in the form of a savings account set aside for a rainy day is also affected by inflation. For example, if the interest rate on a one-year $10,000 certificate of deposit is 5 percent and the inflation rate is zero (5 percent real interest rate), the certificate holder will earn a 5 percent return on his or her savings. If the inflation rate exceeds the nominal rate of interest, the real interest rate is negative, and the saver is hurt because the interest earned does not keep pace with the inflation rate. This is the reason: Suppose, after one year, the saver withdraws the original $10,000 plus the $500 interest earned and the inflation rate during the year has been 10 percent. The real value of $10,500 adjusted for loss of purchasing power is only $9,500 [$10,000 + ($10,000 × −0.05)].

Finally, it is important to note that the nominal interest rate is never negative, but the real interest rate can be either positive or negative.

> **CONCLUSION:** *When the real rate of interest is negative, lenders and savers lose because interest earned does not keep up with the inflation rate.*

> **Adjustable-rate mortgage (ARM)**
>
> A home loan that adjusts the nominal interest rate to changes in an index rate, such as rates on Treasury securities.

17-3 Demand-Pull and Cost-Push Inflation

Economists distinguish between two basic types of inflation, depending on whether it originates from the buyers' or the sellers' side of the market. The analysis presented in this section returns to the cause-and-effect relationship between total spending and the business cycle discussed in the previous chapter.

17-3a DEMAND-PULL INFLATION

Perhaps the most familiar type of inflation is demand-pull inflation, which is a rise in the general price level resulting from an excess of total spending (demand). Demand-pull inflation is often expressed as "too much money chasing too few goods." When sellers are unable to supply all the goods and services buyers demand, sellers respond by raising prices. In short, the general price level in the economy is "pulled up" by the pressure from buyers' total expenditures.

Demand-pull inflation occurs at or close to full employment, when the economy is operating at or near full capacity. Recall that at full employment, all but the frictionally and structurally unemployed are working and earning income. Therefore, total, or aggregate, demand for goods and services is high. Businesses find it profitable to expand their plants and production to meet the buyers' demand, but cannot in the short run. As a result, national output remains fixed, and prices rise as buyers try to outbid one another for the available supply of goods and services. If total spending subsides, so will the pressure on the available supply of products, and prices will not rise as rapidly or may even fall.

> **Demand-pull inflation**
>
> A rise in the general price level resulting from an excess of total spending (demand).

A word of caution: Consumers may not be the only villain in the demand-pull story. Recall that total aggregate spending includes consumer spending (*C*), business investment (*I*), government spending (*G*), and net exports (*X* − *M*). Even foreigners may contribute to inflation by bidding up the price of U.S. exports.

17-3b COST-PUSH INFLATION

An excess of total spending is not the only possible explanation for rising prices. For example, suppose the Organization of Petroleum Exporting Countries (OPEC) sharply increases the price of oil. This action means a significant increase in the cost of producing goods and services. The result could be cost-push inflation. Cost-push inflation is a rise in the general price level resulting from an increase in the cost of production.

Cost-push inflation

An increase in the general price level resulting from an increase in the cost of production.

The source of cost-push inflation is not always such a dramatic event as an OPEC price hike. Any sharp increase in costs to businesses can be a potential source of cost-push inflation. This means that upward pressure on prices can be caused by cost increases for labor, raw materials, construction, equipment, borrowing, and so on. Businesses can also contribute to cost-push inflation by raising prices to increase profits.

The influence of *expectations* on both demand-pull and cost-push inflation is an important consideration. Suppose buyers see prices rise and believe they should purchase that new house or car today before these items cost much more tomorrow. At or near full employment, this demand-pull results in a rise in prices. On the suppliers' side, firms might expect their production costs to rise in the future, so they raise prices in anticipation of the higher costs. The result is cost-push inflation.

Here you should take note of coming attractions. The chapter on aggregate demand and supply develops a modern macro model that you can use to analyze with more precision the factors that determine national output, employment, and the price level. In particular, the last section of this chapter applies the aggregate demand and supply model to the concepts of demand-pull and cost-push inflation. Also, the chapter on monetary policy will discuss the theory that inflation is the result of increases in the money supply in excess of increases in the production of goods and services.

17-4 Inflation in Other Countries

GLOBAL ECONOMICS

Exhibit 5 reveals that inflation rates vary widely among nations. In 2011, Venezuela, Congo, and other countries experienced very high rates of inflation. In contrast, the United States had an inflation rate of 3.2 percent, while Italy and France had lower rates. Ireland and other countries had negative inflation rates.

17-4a INFLATION ON A RAMPAGE

Hyperinflation

An extremely rapid rise in the general price level.

Some people must carry a large stack of money to pay for a chocolate bar because of the disastrous consequences of hyperinflation. Hyperinflation is an extremely rapid rise in the general price level. There is no consensus on when a particular rate of inflation becomes "hyper." However, most economists would agree that an inflation rate of about 100 percent per year or more is hyperinflation. Runaway

EXHIBIT 5   **Annual Inflation Rates in Selected Countries, 2011**

As shown by the bars, inflation was a serious problem in 2011 for Venezuela, Congo, and other countries. The United States experienced an inflation rate of 3.2 percent, while Italy and France had lower rates.

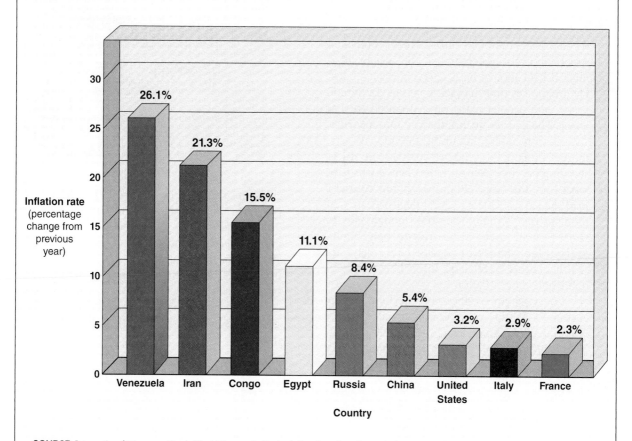

SOURCE: International Monetary Fund, *World Economic Outlook Database*, http://www.imf.org/external/ns/cs.aspx?id=28.

inflation is conducive to rapid and violent social and political change stemming from four causes.

First, individuals and businesses develop an *inflation psychosis*, causing them to buy quickly today in order to avoid paying even more tomorrow. Everyone feels pressure to spend their earnings before their purchasing power deteriorates. Regardless of whether you are paid once, twice, or any number of times per day, you will be eager to spend it immediately.

Second, huge unanticipated inflation jeopardizes debtor-lender contracts, such as credit cards, home mortgages, life insurance policies, pensions, bonds, and other forms of savings. For example, if nominal interest rates rise unexpectedly in response to higher inflation, borrowers find it more difficult to make their monthly payments.

Who Wants to Be a Trillionaire?

Applicable Concept: hyperinflation

The following articles are two historical examples of hyperinflation:

A 1985 *Wall Street Journal* article described hyperinflation in La Paz, Bolivia:

> A courier stumbles into Banco Boliviano Americano, struggling under the weight of a huge bag of money he is carrying on his back. He announces that the sack contains 32 million pesos, and a teller slaps on a notation to that effect. The courier pitches the bag into a corner. "We don't bother counting the money anymore," explains Max Lowes Stah, a loan officer standing nearby. "We take the client's word for what's in the bag." Pointing to the courier's load, he says, "That's a small deposit." At that moment the 32 million pesos—enough bills to stuff a mail sack—were worth only $500. Today, less than two weeks later, they are worth at least $180 less. Life's like that with quadruple-digit inflation....
>
> Prices go up by the day, the hour or the customer. If the pace continues all year it would mean an annual rate of 116,000 percent. The 1,000-peso bill, the most commonly used,

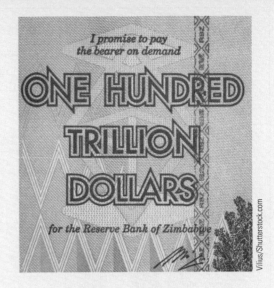

> costs more to print than it purchases. To purchase an average-size television set with 1,000-peso bills, customers have to haul money weighing more than 68 pounds into the showroom. Inflation makes use of credit cards impossible here, and merchants generally can't take checks, either. Restaurant owners often covered their menus with cellophane and changed prices several times daily using a dry-erase marker.[1]

Wage-price spiral

A situation that occurs when increases in nominal wage rates are passed on in higher prices, which, in turn, result in even higher nominal wage rates and prices.

Third, hyperinflation sets a wage-price spiral in motion. A wage-price spiral occurs in a series of steps when increases in nominal wage rates are passed on in higher prices, which, in turn, result in even higher nominal wage rates and prices. A wage-price spiral continues when management believes it can boost prices faster than the rise in labor costs. As the cost of living moves higher, however, labor must again demand even higher wage increases. Each round yields higher and higher prices as wages and prices chase each other in an upward spiral.

Fourth, because the future rate of inflation is difficult or impossible to anticipate, people turn to more speculative investments that might yield higher financial returns. To hedge against the high losses of purchasing power from hyperinflation, funds flow into gold, silver, stamps, jewels, art, antiques, and other currencies, rather than into new factories, machinery, and technological research that expand an economy's production possibilities curve.

A *San Francisco Chronicle* article reported on hyperinflation in Zimbabwe:

> What is happening is no laughing matter. (In 2008, the annual inflation rate was 231 million percent.) For untold numbers of Zimbabweans, bread, margarine, meat and even the morning cup of tea have become unimaginable luxuries. The city suffers rolling electrical blackouts because the state cannot afford parts or technicians to fix broken down power turbines. Mounds of uncollected garbage pile up on the streets of slums. Public-school fees and other ever-rising government surcharges have begun to exceed the monthly incomes of many urban families lucky enough to work. Those with spare cash put it not in banks, but in gilt-edged investments like bags of cornmeal and sugar, guaranteed not to lose their value.[2]

In 2010, Zimbabwe's central bank announced the introduction of new 100 trillion, 50 trillion, 20 trillion, and 10 trillion notes. Want to be a multi-trillionaire?

A *Newsweek* article made the following thoughtful observation:

> Hyperinflation is the worst economic malady that can befall a nation, wiping out the value of money, savings, assets, and thus work. It is worse even than a deep recession. Hyperinflation robs you of what you have now (savings), whereas a recession robs you of what you might have had (higher standards of living if the economy had grown). That's why it so often toppled governments and produced revolution. Recall that it was not the Great Depression that brought the Nazis to power in Germany but rather hyperinflation, which destroyed the middle class of that country by making its savings worthless.[3]

Analyze the Issue

1. Can you relate inflation psychosis to these excerpts? Give an example of a debtor-lender relationship that is jeopardized by hyperinflation.
2. Explain why the workers in Bolivia were striking even though wages rose at an annual rate of 1,500 percent. Do you see any connection between hyperinflation and the political system?

---

1. Sonia L. Nazario, "When Inflation Rate Is 116,000 Percent, Prices Change by the Hour," *The Wall Street Journal*, Feb. 7, 1985, p. 1.
2. Michale Wines, "Zimbabwe: Inflation Capitol," *San Francisco Chronicle*, May 2, 2006, p. A-2.
3. Fareed Zakaria, "Is This the End of Inflation? Turkey's Currency Crisis May Be the Last Battle in the Global War Against Hyperinflation," *Newsweek*, Mar. 19, 2001, p. 38.

History reveals numerous hyperinflation examples. One of the most famous occurred during the 1920s in the German Weimar Republic. Faced with huge World War I reparations payments, the Weimar government simply printed money to pay its bills. By late 1923, the annual inflation rate in Germany had reached 35,000 percent per month. Prices rose frequently, sometimes increasing in minutes, and German currency became so worthless that it was used as kindling for stoves. No one was willing to make new loans, and credit markets collapsed. Wealth was redistributed because those who were heavily in debt easily paid their debts, and people's savings were wiped out.

Finally, hyperinflation is invariably the result of a government's ill-advised decision to increase a country's money supply. Moreover, hyperinflation is not a historical relic, as illustrated in the above Global Economics article.

Key Concepts

Inflation
Deflation
Consumer price index (CPI)
Base year
Disinflation

Nominal income
Real income
Wealth
Nominal interest rate
Real interest rate

Adjustable-rate mortgage (ARM)
Demand-pull inflation
Cost-push inflation
Hyperinflation
Wage-price spiral

Summary

- **Inflation** is an increase in the general (average) price level of goods and services in the economy.
- **Deflation** is a decrease in the general level of prices. During the early years of the Great Depression, there was deflation, and the CPI declined at about a double-digit rate.
- The **consumer price index (CPI)** is the most widely known price-level index. It measures the cost of purchasing a market basket of goods and services by a typical household during a time period relative to the cost of the same bundle during a base year. The annual rate of inflation is computed using the following formula:

$$\text{annual rate of inflation} = \frac{\text{CPI in given year} - \text{CPI in previous year}}{\text{CPI in previous year}} \times 100$$

- **Disinflation** is a reduction in the inflation rate. This does not mean that prices were falling, only that the inflation rate fell.
- The **inflation rate** determined by the CPI is criticized because (1) it is not representative, (2) it has difficulty adjusting for quality changes, and (3) it ignores the relationship between price changes and the importance of items in the market basket.

- **Nominal income** is income measured in actual money amounts. Measuring your purchasing power requires converting nominal income into **real income**, which is nominal income adjusted for inflation.

SOURCE: © Cengage Learning 2014

- The **real interest rate** is the *nominal interest rate* adjusted for inflation. If real interest rates are negative, lenders incur losses.
- An **adjustable-rate mortgage** is a home loan that adjusts the nominal interest rate to changes in an index rate, such as rates on Treasury securities.
- **Demand-pull inflation** is caused by pressure on prices originating from the buyers' side of the market. In contrast, **cost-push inflation** is caused by pressure on prices originating from the sellers' side of the market.
- **Hyperinflation** can seriously disrupt an economy by causing inflation psychosis, credit market collapses, a wage-price spiral, and speculation. A **wage-price spiral** occurs when increases in nominal wages cause higher prices, which, in turn, cause higher wages and prices.

Summary of Conclusion Statements

- Inflation is an increase in the overall average level of prices and not an increase in the price of any specific product.

- People whose nominal incomes rise faster than the rate of inflation gain purchasing power, while people whose nominal incomes do not keep pace with inflation lose purchasing power.

- When the real rate of interest is negative, lenders and savers lose because interest

earned does not keep up with the inflation rate.

Study Questions and Problems

1. Consider this statement: "When the price of a good or service rises, the inflation rate rises." Do you agree or disagree? Explain.

2. Suppose, in the base year, a typical market basket purchased by an urban family cost $250. In Year *1*, the same market basket cost $950. What is the consumer price index (CPI) for Year *1*? If the same market basket cost $1,000 in Year *2*, what is the CPI for Year *2*? What was the Year *2* rate of inflation?

3. What are three criticisms of the CPI?

4. Suppose you earned $100,000 in a given year. Calculate your real income, assuming the CPI is 200 for this year.

5. Explain how a person's purchasing power can decline in a given year even though he or she received a salary increase.

6. Who loses from inflation? Who wins from inflation?

7. Suppose you borrow $100 from a bank at 5 percent interest for one year and the inflation rate that year is 10 percent. Was this loan advantageous to you or to the bank?

8. Suppose the annual nominal rate of interest on a bank certificate of deposit is 12 percent. What would be the effect of an inflation rate of 13 percent?

9. When the economy approaches full employment, why does demand-pull inflation become a problem?

10. How does demand-pull inflation differ from cost-push inflation?

11. Explain this statement: "If everyone expects inflation to occur, it will."

For Online Exercises, go to the Tucker Web site at http://www.cengage.com/economics/tucker.

✓ CHECKPOINT ANSWERS

The College Education Price Index

$$\text{2010 college education price index} = \frac{\text{market basket cost at 2010 prices}}{\text{market basket cost at base-year (2010) prices}} \times 100$$

$$= \frac{\$11,650}{\$11,650} \times 100 = 100$$

$$\text{2011 college education price index} = \frac{\text{market basket cost at 2011 prices}}{\text{market basket cost at base-year (2010) prices}} \times 100$$

$$= \frac{\$12,600}{\$11,650} \times 100 = 108.1$$

$$\text{Percentage change in price level of college education} = \frac{108.1 - 100}{100} \times 100 = 8.1\%$$

If you said the price of a college education increased 8.1 percent in 2011, **YOU ARE CORRECT.**

What s the Real Price of Gasoline?

$$\text{Average gasoline price in 2011 dollars} = \$1.35 \times \frac{225.0}{90.9} = \$3.34$$

If you said the price of $1.35 per gallon for gasoline in 1981 was $3.34 per gallon in 2011 after adjusting for inflation over these years, **YOU ARE CORRECT.**

To update this calculation, click on the CPI Inflation Calculator at http://data.bls.gov/cgi-bin/cpicalc.pl.

Sample Quiz

For an explanation of the correct answers, visit the Tucker Web site at www.cengage.com/economics/tucker.

1. Inflation is defined as an increase in
   a. real wages of workers.
   b. real GDP.
   c. the average price level.
   d. all consumer products.

2. Inflation is measured by an increase in
   a. homes, autos, and basic resources.
   b. prices of all products in the economy.
   c. the consumer price index (CPI).
   d. None of the answsers above is correct.

3. Which one of the following groups benefits from inflation?
   a. borrowers
   b. savers
   c. landlords
   d. lenders

4. Price indexes such as the CPI are calculated using a base year. The term *base year* refers to
   a. the first year that price data are available.
   b. any year in which inflation is higher than 5 percent.
   c. the most recent year in which the business cycle hit the trough.
   d. an arbitrarily chosen reference year.

5. If the consumer price index (CPI) in Year *1* was 200 and the CPI in Year *2* was 215, the rate of inflation is
   a. 215 percent.
   b. 15 percent.
   c. 5 percent.
   d. 7.5 percent.
   e. 8 percent.

6. Which of the following statements is *true*?
   a. Deflation is an increase in the general level of prices.
   b. The consumer price index (CPI) measures changes in the average prices of consumer goods and services.
   c. Disinflation is an increase in the rate of inflation.
   d. Real income is the actual number of dollars received over a period of time.

7. Suppose the price of banana rises over time and consumers respond by buying fewer bananas. This situation contributes to which bias in the consumer price index?
   a. substitution bias
   b. transportation bias
   c. quality bias
   d. indexing bias

Sample Quiz *continued*

8. Deflation means a decrease in
   a. the rate of inflation.
   b. the prices of all products in the economy.
   c. homes, autos, and basic resources.
   d. the general level of prices in the economy.

9. Real income in Year X is equal to
   a. $\dfrac{\text{Year } X \text{ nominal income}}{\text{Year } X \text{ real GDP}} \times 100$.
   b. $\dfrac{\text{Year } X \text{ nominal income}}{\text{Year } X \text{ real output}} \times 100$.
   c. $\dfrac{\text{Year } X \text{ nominal income}}{\text{CPI}/100}$.
   d. Year X nominal income $\times$ CPI.

10. The real interest rate is defined as the
    a. actual interest rate.
    b. fixed rate on consumer loans.
    c. nominal interest rate minus the inflation rate.
    d. expected interest rate minus the inflation rate.

11. If the inflation rate exceeds the nominal rate of interest,
    a. the real interest rate is negative.
    b. lenders lose.
    c. savers lose.
    d. All of the above answers are correct.

12. Suppose you place $10,000 in a retirement fund that earns a nominal interest rate of 8 percent. If you expect inflation to be 5 percent or lower, then you are expecting to earn a real interest rate of at least
    a. 1.6 percent.
    b. 3 percent.
    c. 4 percent.
    d. 5 percent.

13. Which of the following can create demand-pull inflation?
    a. excessive aggregate spending
    b. sharply rising oil prices
    c. higher labor costs
    d. recessions and depressions

14. Which of the following statements is *true*?
    a. Demand-pull inflation is caused by excess total spending.
    b. Cost-push inflation is caused by an increase in resource costs.
    c. If nominal interest rates remain the same and the inflation rate falls, real interest rates increase.
    d. If real interest rates are negative, lenders incur losses.
    e. All of the above answers are correct.

15. Cost-push inflation is due to
    a. labor cost increases.
    b. energy cost increases.
    c. raw material cost increases.
    d. All of the above answers are correct.

16. During periods of hyperinflation, which of the following is the *most* likely response of consumers?
    a. Save as much as possible
    b. Spend money as fast as possible
    c. Invest as much as possible
    d. Lend money

17. The base year in the consumer price index (CPI) is
    a. given a value of zero.
    b. a year chosen as a reference for prices in all other years.
    c. always the first year in the current decade.
    d. established by law.

18. Deflation
    a. was prevalent during the oil shocks of the 1970s.
    b. will cause consumers' purchasing power to shrink under current trends.
    c. has been persistent in the U.S. economy since the Great Depression.
    d. refers to none of the answers above.

19. As the price of gasoline rose during the 1970s, consumers cut back on their use of gasoline relative to other consumer goods. This situation contributed to which bias in the consumer price index?

Sample Quiz *continued*

a. substitution bias
b. transportation bias
c. quality bias
d. indexing bias

20. If the rate of inflation in a given time period turns out to be lower than lenders and borrowers anticipated, then the effect will be a

a. redistribution of wealth from borrowers to lenders.
b. redistribution of wealth from lenders to borrowers.
c. net loss in purchasing power for lenders relative to borrowers.
d. net gain in purchasing power for borrowers relative to lenders.

Road Map
Macroeconomic Fundamentals

This road map feature helps you tie together material in the part as you travel the Economic Way of Thinking highway. The following are review questions listed by chapter from the previous part.

CHAPTER 15. GROSS DOMESTIC PRODUCT

1. **Key Concept: Gross Domestic Product**
   Which of the following items is included in the calculation of GDP?
   a. Purchase of 100 shares of General Motors stock
   b. Purchase of a used car
   c. The value of a homemaker's services
   d. Sale of Gulf War military surplus
   e. None of the above

2. **Key Concept: Expenditure Approach**
   Using the expenditure approach, GDP equals:
   a. $C + I + G + (X - M)$.
   b. $C + I + G + (X + M)$.
   c. $C + I - G + (X - M)$.
   d. $C + I + G - (X - M)$.

3. **Key Concept: GDP Shortcomings**
   If the underground economy is sizable, then GDP will:
   a. understate the economy's performance.
   b. overstate the economy's performance.
   c. fluctuate unpredictably.
   d. accurately reflect this subterranean activity.

4. **Key Concept: Real GDP**
   What is the equation for determining real GDP for year X?
   a. $\dfrac{\text{nominal GDP for year } X}{\text{average nominal GDP}}$
   b. $\dfrac{\text{nominal GDP for year } X}{\text{GDP for year } X} - 100$
   c. $\dfrac{\text{nominal GDP for year } X}{\text{GDP chain price index for year } X} \times 100$
   d. $\dfrac{\text{nominal GDP for year } X}{\text{average family income}} \times 100$

CHAPTER 16. BUSINESS CYCLES AND UNEMPLOYMENT

5. Key Concept: Business Cycle
A business cycle is:
a. the period of time in which expansion and contraction of economic activity are equal.
b. the period of time in which there are three phases: peak, depression, and recovery.
c. recurring growth and decline in real GDP.
d. the period of time in which a business is established and ceases operations.

6. Key Concept: Business Cycle
A business cycle is the period of time in which:
a. a business is established and ceases operations.
b. there are four phases: peak, recession, trough, and recovery.
c. the price level varies with real GDP.
d. expansion and contraction of economic activity are equal.
e. none of the above occur.

7. Key Concept: Unemployment
John Steinbeck's *Cannery Row* describes a character who takes his own life because of poor job prospects. If he was an unemployed person who gave up looking for work, he would be considered:
a. chronically unemployed.
b. a discouraged worker.
c. a member of the labor force.
d. frictionally unemployed.

8. Key Concept: Unemployment
Consider a broom factory that permanently closes because of foreign competition. If the broom factory's workers cannot find new jobs because their skills are no longer marketable, then they are classified as:
a. seasonally unemployed.
b. frictionally unemployed.
c. structurally unemployed.
d. cyclically unemployed.

CHAPTER 17. INFLATION

9. Key Concept: Inflation
Inflation is measured by an increase in:
a. homes, autos, and basic resources.
b. prices of all products in the economy.
c. the consumer price index (CPI).
d. none of the above.

10. **Key Concept: Consumer Price Index Bias**

As the price of gasoline rose during the 1970s, consumers cut back on their use of gasoline relative to other consumer goods. This situation contributed to which bias in the consumer price index?

a. Substitution bias
b. Transportation bias
c. Quality bias
d. Indexing bias

11. **Key Concept: Real Income**

Real income in Year X is equal to:

a. $\dfrac{\text{Year } X \text{ nominal income}}{\text{Year } X \text{ real GDP}} \times 100.$

b. $\dfrac{\text{Year } X \text{ nominal income}}{\text{Year } X \text{ real output}} \times 100.$

c. $\dfrac{\text{Year } X \text{ nominal income}}{\text{CPI}/100}.$

d. Year X nominal income $\times$ CPI.

12. **Key Concept: Cost-Push Inflation**

Cost-push inflation is due to:

a. labor cost increases.
b. energy cost increases.
c. raw material cost increases.
d. all of the above.

Macroeconomic Theory and Policy

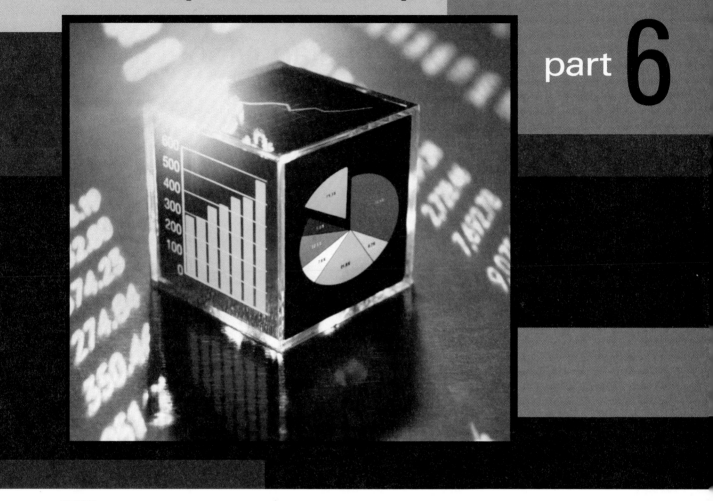

part 6

This part begins with two chapters that present a theoretical model originating in a book published in 1936 by British economist John Maynard Keynes. The purpose of the Keynesian model is to understand the causes and cures of the Great Depression. The next chapter explains another theoretical macro model based on aggregate demand and aggregate supply. The following chapter discusses the federal government's taxing and spending policies, and the next chapter explains actual data measures of government spending and taxation patterns. The part concludes with a chapter on hotly debated topics: federal deficits, surpluses, and the national debt.

chapter 18

The Keynesian Model

In U.S. history, the 1920s are known as the "Roaring 20s." It was a time of optimism and prosperity. The spirit of the times was captivated in the lyrics of a popular song of the day: "Nothing but blue skies do I see." Between 1920 and 1929, real GDP rose by 42 percent. Stock prices soared year after year and made many investors rich. As business boomed, companies invested in new factories, and the U.S. economy was a job-creating machine. People bought fine clothes, had parties, and danced the popular Charleston. Then the business cycle took an abrupt downturn on October 29, 1929, Black Tuesday. The most severe recession in recent U.S. history had begun. During the Great Depression, stock prices fell. Wages fell. Real output fell. Banks failed. Businesses closed their doors, and the unemployment rate soared to 25 percent. Unemployed workers would fight over a job, sell apples on the corner to survive, and walk the streets in bewilderment.

The misery of the Great Depression created a revolution in economic thought. Prior to the Great Depression, economists recognized that over the years, business downturns would interrupt the nation's prosperity, but they believed these episodes were temporary. They argued that in a short time, the price system would automatically restore an economy to full employment without government intervention.

Why didn't the economy self-correct to its 1929 level of real GDP? What went wrong? The stage was set for a new idea offered by British economist **John Maynard Keynes** (pronounced "canes"). Keynes argued that the economy was not self-correcting and therefore could indeed remain below full employment indefinitely because of inadequate aggregate spending. Keynes's work not only explained the crash, but also offered cures requiring the government to play an active rather than a passive role in the economy.

Whether or not economists agree with Keynes's ideas, this famous economist still influences macroeconomics today. This chapter begins with a discussion of classical economic theory before Keynes. Then you will learn what determines the level of consumption and investment expenditures, which are the first two components of Keynes's aggregate expenditures model. In the next chapter, these two components are added to government spending and net exports to form the complete Keynesian aggregate expenditures model.

In this chapter, you will learn to solve these economics puzzles:

- Why did economists believe the Great Depression was impossible?

- According to Keynes, what determines a family's spending for consumption?

- Why did Keynes believe that "animal spirits" and government policy were important to maintain full employment?

18-1 Introducing Classical Theory and the Keynesian Revolution

Prior to the Great Depression of the 1930s, a group of economists known as the classical economists dominated economic thinking.[1] The founder of the classical school of economics was Adam Smith (discussed in the chapter on economies in transition). Macroeconomics had not developed as a separate economic theory, and classical economics was therefore based primarily on microeconomic market equilibrium theory. The classical school of economics was mainstream economics from the 1770s to the Great Depression era. The classical economists believed in the *laissez-faire* "leave it alone" theory that our economy was self-regulating and would correct itself without government interference. The classical economists believed, as you studied in Chapter 4, that the forces of supply and demand naturally achieve full employment in the economy because flexible prices (including wages and interest rates) in competitive markets bring all markets to full-employment equilibrium. After a temporary adjustment period, markets always clear because firms sell all goods and services offered for sale. In short, recessions would naturally cure themselves because the capitalistic price system would automatically restore full employment. The classical model is explained in more detail in the chapter on aggregate demand and supply.

> **CONCLUSION:** *The classical economists believed that a continuing depression is impossible because markets eliminate persistent shortages or surpluses.*

The simple idea known as Say's Law, developed in the early 1800s by *Jean-Baptiste Say*, convinced classical economists that a prolonged depression was impossible. Say's Law is the theory that supply creates its own demand. Say's Law was the cornerstone of classical economics. Simply put, this theory states that long-term underspending is impossible because the production of goods and services (supply) generates an equal amount of total spending (demand) for these goods and services. Recall the circular flow model explained in the chapter on GDP. Suppose a firm produces $1 worth of bread in the product market. This supply decision creates $1 of income to the household sector through the factor markets. In other words, Say's Law is a theory that a glut of unsold products causing workers to lose

John Maynard Keynes

British economist (1883–1946) whose influential work offered an explanation of the Great Depression and suggested, as a cure, that the government should play an active role in the economy.

Classical economists

A group of economists whose theory dominated economic thinking from the 1770s to the Great Depression. They believed recessions would naturally cure themselves because the price system would automatically restore full employment.

Say's Law

The theory that supply creates its own demand.

---

[1]The classical economists included Adam Smith, J. B. Say, David Ricardo, John Stuart Mill, Thomas Malthus, Alfred Marshall, and others.

their jobs is a temporary problem because there is just the right amount of income in the economy to purchase all products produced without layoffs.

> **CONCLUSION:** *In the classical view, unemployment is the result of a short-lived adjustment period in which wages and prices decline or people voluntarily choose not to work. Thus, there is a natural tendency for the economy to restore full employment over time.*

In 1936, seven years after the beginning of the Great Depression and three years before the beginning of World War II, John Maynard Keynes published *The General Theory of Employment, Interest, and Money.*[2] Keynes, a Cambridge University economist, wrote in a time of great uncertainty and instability. His book established macroeconomics as a separate field of economics and challenged the baffled classical economists by turning Say's Law upside down. Keynesian theory argues that "demand creates its own supply." Keynes explained that *aggregate expenditures (demand)* can be forever inadequate for an economy to achieve full employment. Aggregate expenditures are the sum of consumption (C), investment (I), government spending (G), and net exports (X − M). Aggregate expenditures are also known as *aggregate spending* or *aggregate demand*. Recall from the chapter on GDP that C, I, G, and (X − M) are national accounting categories used to calculate GDP following the expenditures approach.

18-1a THE CONSUMPTION FUNCTION

What determines your family's spending for food, clothing, automobiles, education, and other consumer goods and services? According to Keynes, the most important factor is disposable income (personal income to spend after taxes; see Exhibit 9 in the chapter on GDP). Keynes argued it is a fundamental psychological law that if take-home pay increases, consumers will increase their spending and saving. Keynes's focus on the relationship between consumption and real disposable income is represented by the consumption function. The consumption function shows the amount households spend for goods and services at different levels of real disposable income. Recall from Exhibit 2 in the chapter on GDP that consumption is the largest single component of aggregate expenditures.

Exhibit 1 provides data on real disposable income (Y_d) in column (1), consumption (C) in column (2), and saving (S) in column (3) for a hypothetical economy. Since households spend each dollar of real disposable income either for consumption or for saving, the formula for saving is

$$S = Y_d - C$$

From the above equation, it follows that

$$Y_d = C + S$$

Note that if real disposable income is zero, consumption expenditures will be $1 trillion of autonomous consumption. Autonomous consumption is consumption that is independent of the level of real disposable income. It is the amount of

Consumption function

The graph or table that shows the amount households spend for goods and services at different levels of real disposable income.

Autonomous consumption

Consumption that is independent of the level of real disposable income.

---

[2]John Maynard Keynes, *The General Theory of Employment, Interest, and Money* (New York: Harcourt, Brace, and World, 1936).

EXHIBIT 1	The Consumption Function

This exhibit shows the consumption function for a hypothetical economy. The break-even income is $4 trillion real disposable income, where households spend each dollar of real disposable income, $C = Y_d$, and savings are zero. Below $4 trillion, households spend more than their real disposable income by borrowing or withdrawing from past savings. Above the break-even income, households spend less than their real disposable income, and saving occurs. The marginal propensity to consume (MPC) is 0.75 because the slope of the consumption schedule shows that for each dollar increase in income (ΔY_d), consumption increases (ΔC) by 75 cents, and the remaining 25 cents is saved.

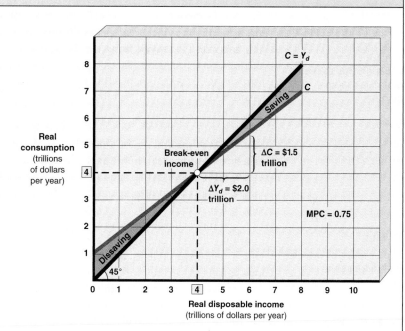

Consumption, Dissaving, Saving, MPC, and MPS Data

(1) Real disposable income (Y_d)	(2) Consumption (C)	(3) Dissaving (−) or Saving (+)	(4) Marginal propensity to consume (MPC) [$\Delta C/\Delta Y_d$ or $\Delta 2/\Delta 1$]	(5) Marginal propensity to save (MPS) [$\Delta S/\Delta Y_d$ or $\Delta 3/\Delta 1$]
$0	$1.00	−$1.00	—	—
1.00	1.75	−0.75	0.75	0.25
2.00	2.50	−0.50	0.75	0.25
3.00	3.25	−0.25	0.75	0.25
4.00	4.00	0	0.75	0.25
5.00	4.75	0.25	0.75	0.25
6.00	5.50	0.50	0.75	0.25
7.00	6.25	0.75	0.75	0.25
8.00	7.00	1.00	0.75	0.25

NOTE: All amounts are in trillions of dollars per year.
SOURCE: © Cengage Learning 2014

Dissaving

The amount by which real personal consumption expenditures exceed real disposable income.

consumption expenditures that occur even when real disposable income is zero. At other low levels of real disposable income, households also spend more on consumer goods and services than they earn in income during the year. If annual real disposable income is any level below $4 trillion, households dissave. Dissaving is the amount by which real personal consumption expenditures exceed real disposable income. Negative saving, or dissaving, is financed by drawing down previously accumulated financial assets, such as savings accounts, stocks, and bonds, or by borrowing. At a real disposable income of $2 trillion per year, for example, families spend $2.5 trillion and thereby dissave $0.5 trillion.

Dissaving is shown in the graph as the vertical distance below the consumption function to the *45-degree line*. The 45-degree line is a geometric construct that represents all points where the value measured on the vertical axis equals the value measured on the horizontal axis. This makes it easier to identify the *break-even, or no-saving income*, which equates real disposable income measured on the horizontal axis and consumption on the vertical axis. In our example, $C = Y_d$ at $4 trillion, where households spend every dollar earned and saving is therefore zero.

Saving

The amount by which real disposable income exceeds real personal consumption expenditures.

At higher levels beyond the break-even income, households earn more income than they wish to spend, and a portion of income is saving. Saving is the amount by which real disposable income exceeds real personal consumption expenditures. Savings can be in various forms, such as funds in a passbook savings account, a certificate of deposit, stocks, or bonds. In Exhibit 1, positive saving is the vertical distance above the consumption function to the 45-degree line. For example, at a real disposable income of $8 trillion, households save $1 trillion.

> **CONCLUSION:** *The 45-degree line is a geometric construct. It indicates all points where real disposable income (measured on the horizontal axis) and real consumption (measured on the vertical axis) are equal. Consequently, the 45-degree line makes it easier to identify the break-even, or no-saving income level.*

18-1b MARGINAL PROPENSITIES TO CONSUME AND SAVE

Marginal propensity to consume (MPC)

The change in consumption resulting from a given change in real disposable income.

Keynes argued that as income grows, so does consumption, but by less than income. This crucial concept is called the marginal propensity to consume (MPC). The marginal propensity to consume is "the change" or "extra" in consumption resulting from a given change in real disposable income. Stated differently, the MPC is the ratio of the change in real consumption (ΔC) to the change in real disposable income (ΔY_d). The Greek letter Δ (delta) means "a change in." Mathematically,

$$\text{MPC} = \frac{\text{change in consumption}}{\text{change in real disposable income}} = \frac{\Delta C}{\Delta Y_d}$$

As shown in column (4) of Exhibit 1, the MPC is 0.75. This means for every dollar increase (decrease) in disposable income (ΔY_d), consumption (ΔC) increases (decreases) 75 cents. In each model developed throughout this text, we assume the MPC is constant for all income levels. In our numerical example, real disposable income rises by $1 trillion between each level of income listed in column (1) of Exhibit 1, and consumption rises by $0.75 trillion. Mathematically,

$$\text{MPC} = \frac{\Delta C}{\Delta Y_d} = \frac{\$0.75 \text{ trillion}}{\$1 \text{ trillion}} = 0.75$$

What do households do with an extra dollar of real disposable income if they do not spend it? There is only one other choice—they save it. The marginal propensity to save (MPS) is the change in saving resulting from a given change in real disposable income. That is, the MPS is the ratio of the change in saving (ΔS) to the change in real disposable income (ΔY_d). Mathematically,

$$\text{MPS} = \frac{\text{change in saving}}{\text{change in real disposable income}} = \frac{\Delta S}{\Delta Y_d}$$

Marginal propensity to save (MPS)

The change in saving resulting from a given change in real disposable income.

The MPS given in column (5) of Exhibit 1 is 0.25. Each dollar increase (decrease) in disposable income (ΔY_d) yields a rise (fall) of 25 cents in the amount of savings (ΔS). Mathematically,

$$\text{MPS} = \frac{\Delta S}{\Delta Y_d} = \frac{\$0.25 \text{ trillion}}{\$1 \text{ trillion}} = 0.25$$

As derived previously, $Y_d = C + S$, so it follows that $\Delta C + \Delta S = \Delta Y_d$. Dividing both sides of this equation by ΔY_d yields

$$\frac{\Delta C}{\Delta Y_d} + \frac{\Delta S}{\Delta Y_d} = \frac{\Delta Y_d}{\Delta Y_d}$$

or

$$\text{MPC} + \text{MPS} = 1$$

In our example, $0.75 + 0.25 = 1$, which means any change in real disposable income is divided between changes in consumption and changes in saving. Hence, if you know the MPC, you can calculate the MPS and vice versa.

18-1c GRAPHICAL ANALYSIS OF MPC

Exhibit 1 shows a graphic representation of the MPC. The consumption function has a positive slope because consumption spending increases with real disposable income. The MPC (slope) of the consumption function, C, for example, between the break-even income of $4 trillion and $6 trillion is measured by dividing $\Delta C = \$1.5$ trillion (the rise) by $\Delta Y_d = \$2.0$ trillion (the run). Since the MPC is constant, the ratio $\Delta C/\Delta Y_d$ between any two levels of real disposable income is 0.75. As a formula:

$$\text{Slope of consumption function} = \frac{\text{rise}}{\text{run}} = \frac{\Delta C}{\Delta Y_d} = \frac{\$1.5 \text{ trillion}}{\$2.0 \text{ trillion}} = 0.75$$

The points along the consumption function, C, in Exhibit 1 can be expressed by the following equation:

$$C = a + bY_d$$

where a is autonomous consumption and b is the MPC, which falls between 0 and 1. Keynes used this basic equation to derive consumption (C), and it is called the Keynesian consumption function.

Using this equation,

$$C = \$1 \text{ trillion} + 0.75\, Y_d$$

For example, at $Y_d = \$4$ trillion,

$$C = \$1 \text{ trillion} + 0.75\, (\$4 \text{ trillion})$$
$$C = \$4 \text{ trillion}$$

To demonstrate how changes in MPC affect the consumption function, Exhibit 2 shows two consumption functions with the same autonomous

EXHIBIT 2	**Consumption Functions for Two Marginal Propensities to Consume**

The MPC is the slope of the consumption function. Here two consumption functions are shown for MPCs of 0.50 and 0.75. The autonomous consumption of $1 trillion is the same for both consumption functions. The higher the MPC, the steeper the consumption function.

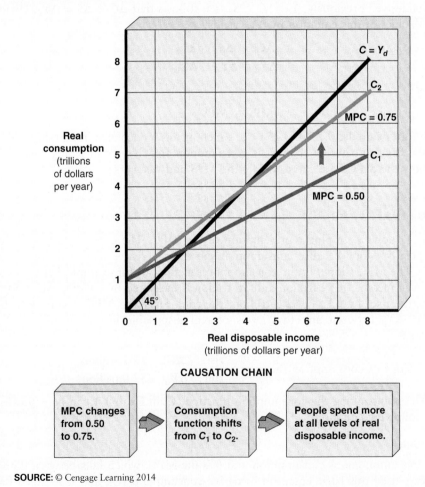

CAUSATION CHAIN

MPC changes from 0.50 to 0.75.	→	Consumption function shifts from C_1 to C_2.	→	People spend more at all levels of real disposable income.

SOURCE: © Cengage Learning 2014

consumption of $1 trillion, but each has a different slope. C_1 has an MPC of 0.50, and C_2 has a larger MPC of 0.75. Thus, the higher the marginal propensity to consume, the steeper the consumption function.

How do changes in taxes cause movements along the consumption function? Suppose there is an income-tax cut. As a result, real disposable income (Y_d) increases and, in turn, induces higher consumption represented by an upward movement along the consumption function. An income-tax hike, on the other hand, reduces real disposable income and causes less consumption shown by a downward movement along the consumption function.

Exhibit 3 provides recent empirical evidence that supports Keynes's theoretical consumption function. Each point in the exhibit represents a pair of values for real personal consumption spending and real disposable income in the United States for years since 2000. Note that the relationship is close to an upward-sloping linear line. As real disposable income rises, real consumption spending also rises.

EXHIBIT 3	U.S. Personal Consumption and Disposable Income, 2000–2011

Keynes argued that a fundamental psychological law exists whereby real disposable income strongly influences real consumption. Actual data on real personal consumption expenditures and real disposable income are consistent with Keynes's theory.

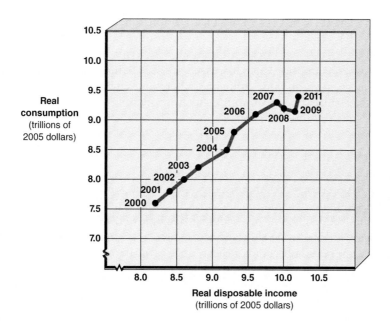

SOURCE: Bureau of Economic Research, *National Economic Accounts*, http://www.bea.gov/national/nipaweb/SelectTable.asp?Selected=Y, Tables 1.1.6 and 2.1.

> **CONCLUSION:** *There is a direct relationship between changes in real disposable income and changes in consumption.*

✔ CHECKPOINT

What's Your MPC?

As your income increases over time, your marginal propensity to consume (MPC) can remain constant, or it can change. Would you expect your MPC to increase, decrease, or remain constant as your income increases throughout your career?

18-2 Reasons the Consumption Function Shifts

Just as nonprice factors in the market supply and demand model, such as consumer tastes and income, shift the demand curve, changes in certain *nonincome* factors cause the consumption function to shift. Exhibit 4 uses hypothetical data to illustrate this difference in terminology. The sole cause of the change in consumption spending from $3 trillion (point *A*) to $4 trillion (point *B*) movement along the stable consumption schedule, C_1, is a $2 trillion change in the level of real disposable income. A change in a nonincome determinant, on the other hand, can cause the consumption schedule to shift upward from $C_1 = a_1 + bY_d$ to $C_2 = a_2 + bY_d$. As a result, households spend an extra $1 trillion ($a_2 - a_1$) at each point along C_2. This means that the level of autonomous consumption has increased by $1 trillion from $1.5 trillion to $2.5 trillion because of some influence other than current Y_d. Nonincome variables that can shift the consumption function include expectations, wealth, the price level, and the interest rate.

18-2a EXPECTATIONS

Consumer expectations are optimistic or pessimistic views of the future that can change consumption spending in the present. Expectations may involve the future inflation rate, the likelihood of becoming unemployed, the likelihood of receiving higher income, or the future shortage of products resulting from a war or other circumstances. Suppose households believe prices will be much higher next year and buy now, rather than paying more in the future. The effect of such expectations would be to trigger current spending at each level of real disposable income and shift the consumption function parallel upward. The anticipation of a recession and fears about losing jobs would make families more tightfisted in their current spending. This means an autonomous decrease in consumption, and the consumption function shifts downward.

EXHIBIT 4	Movement along and Shifts in the Consumption Function

The movement from real consumption spending of $3 trillion (point A) to $4 trillion (point B) along the stable consumption schedule, C_1, is a change in real consumption caused by a $2 trillion change in the level of real disposable income (Y_d). A change in a nonincome determinant causes the consumption function to shift. For example, some nonincome factors may increase autonomous consumption by $1 trillion from a_1 to a_2. As a result, the entire consumption function shifts upward from C_1 to C_2. Nonincome factors include changes in expectations, wealth, the price level, and the interest rate.

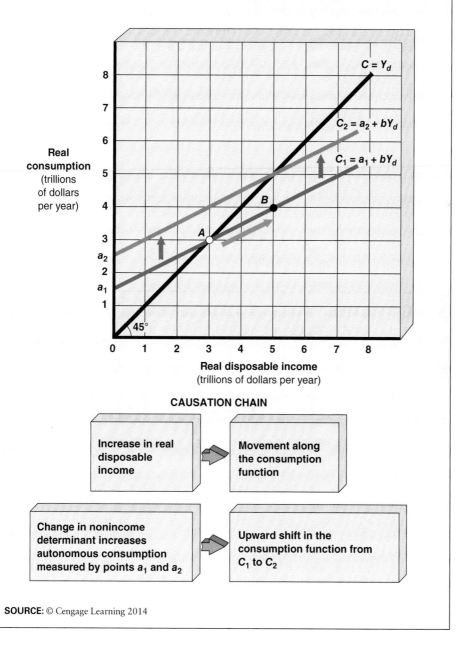

SOURCE: © Cengage Learning 2014

18-2b WEALTH

Holding all other factors constant, the more wealth households accumulate, the more they spend at any level of real disposable income, causing the consumption function to shift upward. Wealth owned by households includes both *real* assets, such as homes, automobiles, and land, and *financial* assets, including cash, savings accounts, stocks, bonds, insurance policies, and pensions. Changes in prices of stocks, real estate, and other assets affect the value of wealth and, in turn, can shift the nation's consumption function. A so-called wealth effect occurred in the 1990s when stock values rose and households increased their spending. And during the financial turmoil in 2008, the fall in stock prices and housing prices was a significant factor in depressing consumption.

Wealth effect

A shift in the consumption function caused by a change in the value of real and financial assets.

18-2c THE PRICE LEVEL

Any change in the general price level shifts the consumption schedule by reducing or enlarging the *purchasing power* of financial assets (wealth) with fixed nominal value. Suppose you own a $100,000 government bond or certificate of deposit. If the price level increases by, say, 10 percent, this same financial asset will buy approximately 10 percent less. Once the real value of financial wealth falls, families are poorer and spend less at any level of real disposable income. As a result, the consumption function shifts downward.

18-2d THE INTEREST RATE

The consumption schedule includes the option of borrowing to finance spending. A lower rate of interest on loans encourages consumers to borrow more, and a higher interest rate discourages consumer indebtedness. If interest rates fall, households may use more credit to finance consumer purchases. The result is a shift upward in the consumption schedule.

> **CONCLUSION:** *A change in real disposable income is the sole cause of a movement along the consumption function. A shift or relocation in the consumption schedule occurs when a factor other than real disposable income changes.*

18-3 Investment Expenditures

According to Keynes, changes in the private-sector components of aggregate expenditures (personal consumption and investment spending) are the major cause of the business cycle. And the more volatile of these two components is investment spending. Personal consumption may be more stable than investment spending because changes in nonincome determinants of personal consumption tend to offset each other. Or maybe people are simply reluctant to change their personal consumption habits. Whatever the reason for the stability of personal consumption, Exhibit 5 demonstrates this point. Over the years, the annual growth rate of real investment has indeed fluctuated much more than real personal consumption. Recall from Exhibit 2 in the chapter on GDP that business investment expenditures (gross private domestic investment) consist of spending on newly produced nonresidential structures, such as factories, equipment,

EXHIBIT 5	A Comparison of the Volatility of Real Investment and Real Consumption, 1965–2011

Real investment spending is highly volatile compared to real personal consumption. The data since 1965 confirm that the annual growth rate of real investment (gross private domestic investment) fluctuates much more than the annual growth rate of real personal consumption.

SOURCE: Bureau of Economic Analysis, *National Economic Accounts*, http://www.bea.gov/national/nipaweb/SelectTable.asp?Selected=Y, Table 1.1.1.

changes in inventories, and residential structures. Note that during the Great Recession (2007–2009), both the consumption and investment growth rates were negative with investment spending dropping sharply to −24 percent.

18-3a THE INVESTMENT DEMAND CURVE

The classical economists believed that the interest rate alone determines the level of investment spending. Keynes disputed this idea. Instead, Keynes argued that expectations of future profits are the primary factor in determining investment, and the interest rate is the financing cost of any investment proposal.

Using a micro example to illustrate the investment decision-making process, suppose a consulting firm plans to purchase a new computer program for $1,000 that will be obsolete in a year. It anticipates that the new software will increase the firm's revenue by $1,100. Thus, assuming no taxes or expenses exist, the expected rate of return or profit is 10 percent. Now consider the impact of the cost of

Investment demand curve

The curve that shows the amount businesses spend for investment goods at different possible rates of interest.

borrowing funds to finance the software investment. If the interest rate is less than 10 percent, the business will earn a profit, so it will make the investment expenditure to buy the computer program. On the other hand, a rate of interest higher than 10 percent means the software investment will be a loss, so this project will not be undertaken.

Understanding a single firm's investment decision from a micro perspective allows us to develop the investment demand curve from the macro vantage point. The investment demand curve shows the amount businesses spend for investment goods at different possible rates of interest. Exhibit 6 expresses the interest rate as annual percentages on the vertical axis. As shown in part (a), changes in the interest rate generate movements along the firm's investment demand curve. If the interest rate falls from, say, 6 percent at point *A* to 4 percent at point *B*, an additional $5 million of real investment spending occurs because *marginal* planned projects become profitable. Stated another way, as a result of this fall in the rate of interest, the firm's real investment increases from $5 million to $10 million.

The relationship among the expected rate of profit, the interest rate, and investment follows this investment rule: *Businesses will undertake all planned investment projects for which the expected rate of profit equals or exceeds the interest rate.*

18-4 Why Investment Demand Is Unstable

Why did Keynes view investment spending as so susceptible to ups and downs? The reason is there are several volatile determinants that cause the investment demand curve to be quite unstable. In short, any factor that changes the expected rate of profit shifts the investment demand curve and thereby changes the investment component of real GDP. As shown in Exhibit 6(b), the initial investment demand curve, I_1, has shifted rightward to I_2, and at an interest rate of 4 percent, $5 million of additional investment spending occurs between points *B* and *C*. The next sections discuss major factors that can shift the investment demand curve.

18-4a EXPECTATIONS

Keynes argued that swings in "animal spirits" cause volatile investment expenditures. Translated this means businesspersons are quite susceptible to moods of optimism and pessimism about future economic conditions. Their expectations about the future translate into estimates of future sales, future costs, and future profitability of investment projects. These forecasts involve a clouded crystal ball, requiring a degree of intuition or normative analysis. There are always many ever-changing factors, such as government spending and tax policies, world events, population growth, and stock market conditions, that make forecasting difficult.

When a wave of pessimism becomes pervasive, businesspeople reduce their expectations for profitability at each rate of interest. Such a pessimistic attitude can become contagious and shift the investment demand curve leftward. This was the case during the Great Depression, when the outlook was dismal. At other times, such as during the 1990s, businesspersons become very optimistic and revise upward their expected rate of profit for investment at each interest rate. If so, the investment demand curve shifts rightward. Thus, Keynes viewed changes in business confidence (expectations) as a major cause of investment spending volatility.

EXHIBIT 6	Movement along and a Shift in a Firm's Investment Demand

Part (a) shows that investment spending by a hypothetical business firm depends on the interest rate. Ceteris paribus, lowering the interest rate from 6 percent at point *A* to 4 percent at point *B* increases the quantity of real investment purchases from $5 million to $10 million during the year.

Keynes argued that investment spending is unstable because a change in volatile factors, such as expectations, technological change, capacity utilization, and business taxes, can shift the location of the investment demand curve. As shown in part (b), the initial investment demand curve, I_1, has shifted rightward to I_2, and at an interest rate of 4 percent, $5 million in additional investment spending occurs between points *B* and *C*.

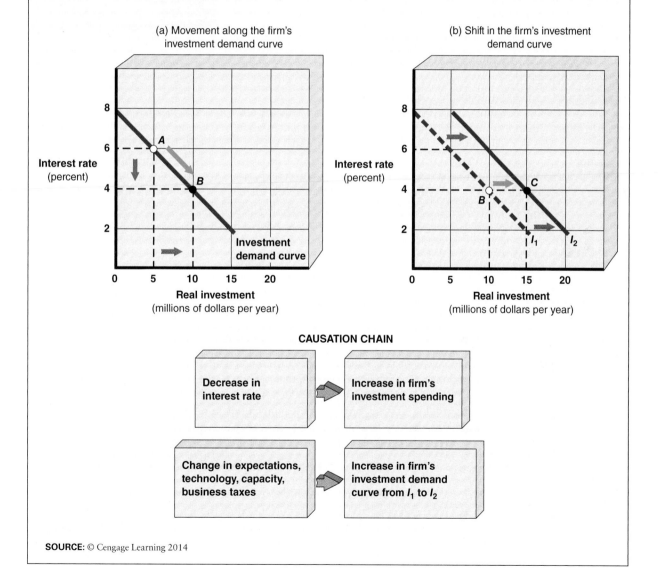

(a) Movement along the firm's investment demand curve

(b) Shift in the firm's investment demand curve

CAUSATION CHAIN

Decrease in interest rate ⟹ Increase in firm's investment spending

Change in expectations, technology, capacity, business taxes ⟹ Increase in firm's investment demand curve from I_1 to I_2

SOURCE: © Cengage Learning 2014

Does a Stock Market Crash Cause Recession?

Applicable Concept: consumption and investment

The stock market soared during the "Roaring 20s." Lavish spending was in style as people-enjoyed their new wealth. Then, on October 29, 1929, Black Tuesday, the stock market crashed. During the Great Depression, banks failed, businesses closed their doors, real GDP plummeted, and unemployment soared. Over the years, much debate has occurred over whether the 1929 stock market crash was merely a symptom or a major cause of the downturn. Evidence exists that the 1929 stock market crash only reflected an economic decline already in progress. For example, months before Black Tuesday, national production had already fallen.

The argument over the impact of a stock market crash on the economy was renewed in 2001. The National Association for Business

Economics (NABE) was holding its annual meeting in the World Trade Center when disaster struck the building on September 11, 2001. "The chandeliers shook, we heard a concussive sound, and as we were herding out, we could see that one tower was burning," said Carl Tannenbaum, the chief economist of LaSalle Bank in Chicago, who was attending the meeting.[1] Just the day before, a panel of NABE economists predicted slow growth for the economy, but no recession. That forecast became obsolete the moment the first plane hit. Analysts predicted a recession, and one reason was that they expected the stock market would dive as profit expectations fell. Indeed, as a result of the September terrorist attacks, the stock market suffered its worst one-week loss since the Great Depression. In the immediate aftermath, equities

losses were estimated to be an extraordinary $1.2 trillion in value.[2]

Prior to the September attacks, the Dow Jones Industrial Average had reached a high of about 11,500 in May, but it had already fallen almost 2,000 points to a low of 9,431 on September 10, 2001. During this period of time, the economy was plagued by the implosion of the dot-com companies and sharp declines in high-tech stocks. After the attacks, the

18-4b TECHNOLOGICAL CHANGE

Technological progress includes the introduction of new products and new ways of doing things. Robots, personal computers, iPhones, the Internet, and similar new inventions provide less costly ways of production. New technologies create a flurry of investment spending as firms buy the latest innovations in order to improve their production capabilities, thereby causing the investment demand curve to shift rightward.

18-4c CAPACITY UTILIZATION

During the Great Depression and the Great Recession, many businesses operated at far less than full capacity. Capacity is defined as the maximum possible output of a firm or an industry. When much of the nation's capital stock stands idle, firms have little incentive to buy more. As a result, the investment demand curve shifts far to the left. Conversely, firms may be operating their plants at a high rate of capacity utilization, and the outlook for sales growth is optimistic. In this case, there is pressure on firms to invest in new investment projects, and the investment demand curve shifts to the right.

stock market closed for the remainder of the week and reopened the following Monday, September 17, 2001, with the famous statue of the Wall Street Bull decorated with American flags and the National Guard patrolling the streets. The result of trading was a huge sell-off and another loss of 1,371 points during the week. Throughout the remainder of the year, the Dow Jones Industrial Average gradually rose toward its pre-September 11 levels, closing at 10,022 on December 31, 2001. Real GDP contracted at a 1.3 percent annual rate in the third quarter of 2001 and then rose in the final three months of 2001 by 1.7 percent, which was a surprisingly strong performance under the circumstances. The six-member panel at the National Bureau of Economic Research (NBER), which is considered the nation's arbiter of U.S. business cycles,

declared in November 2001 that a recession had begun in March and ended eight months later in November of that year.

Stock market plunges are widely reported headline news. One result of these plunges is that many Americans feel poorer because of the threat to their life's savings. In only a few hours, spectacular paper losses reduce the wealth that people are counting on to pay for homes, automobiles, college tuition, or retirement. Although not all U.S. households own stock, everyone fears a steep downhill ride on the Wall Street roller coaster. If a stock market crash leads to a recession, it will cause layoffs and cuts in profit sharing and pension funds. Businesses fear that many families will postpone buying major consumer items in case they need their cash to tide them over the difficult economic times ahead. Reluctance of

consumers to spend lowers aggregate demand, and, in turn, prices and profits fall. Falling sales and anxiety about a recession may lead many business executives to postpone modernization plans. Rather than buying new factories and equipment, businesses continue with used plants and machinery, which means lower private investment spending, employment, output, and income for the overall economy.

> **Analyze the Issue**
>
> Immediately following the attack on the United States on September 11, 2001, the stock market plunged and many observers predicted a recession. Using the consumption and investment functions, explain their predictions.

1. "Worldwide, Hope for Recovery Dims," *Business Week*, Sept. 24, 2001, p. 42.
2. "Economy under Siege," *Fortune*, October 15, 2001, p. 86.

Source: © Cengage Learning 2014

18-4d BUSINESS TAXES

As explained earlier, changes in income taxes on individuals affect disposable income and the level of consumption. Similarly, taxes on business firms can shift the investment demand curve. Business decisions, in reality, depend on the expected *after-tax* rate of profit. An increase in business taxes therefore would lower profitability and shift the investment demand curve to the left. On the other hand, the U.S. government may wish to encourage investment by allowing, say, a *tax credit* for new investment. A 10 percent *investment tax credit* means that if ExxonMobil decides to invest $10 million in a new plant, the corporation's tax bill to the IRS will be cut by $1 million. The effect of this tax policy is that the government increases the profitability of new investment projects by 10 percent and the investment demand curve shifts to the right.

18-4e INVESTMENT AS AN AUTONOMOUS EXPENDITURE

Autonomous expenditure

Spending that does not vary with the level of real disposable income.

Assuming none of the above factors changes in the short run, Keynes argued that investment spending is an autonomous expenditure. An autonomous expenditure is spending that does not vary with the level of real disposable income. Stated simply, autonomous expenditures in the Keynesian model remain a fixed amount, regardless of the level of disposable income. Exhibit 7 shows how the rate of interest determines the aggregate level of autonomous investment for all firms in an economy, regardless of or external to the level of real disposable income. In part (a), at an interest rate of 8 percent, *all* businesses spend $1 trillion for capital goods and inventory. Part (b) shows this $1 trillion is the amount of real investment spending, no matter what the level of real disposable income. If the rate of interest is lower, investment increases, and the horizontal investment demand curve shifts vertically upward. A higher rate of interest discourages investment and shifts the horizontal investment demand curve vertically downward.

EXHIBIT 7	The Aggregate Investment Demand and Autonomous Investment Demand Curves

In part (a), the level of real investment for all firms in an economy is determined by the investment rule that all investment projects for which the expected rate of profit equals or exceeds the interest rate will be undertaken. If the interest rate is 8 percent, real autonomous investment will be $1 trillion, shown as point A on the investment demand curve, I.

In part (b), autonomous real investment expenditures are shown to be independent of the level of real disposable income per year. This means firms will spend $1 trillion regardless of the level of real disposable income per year.

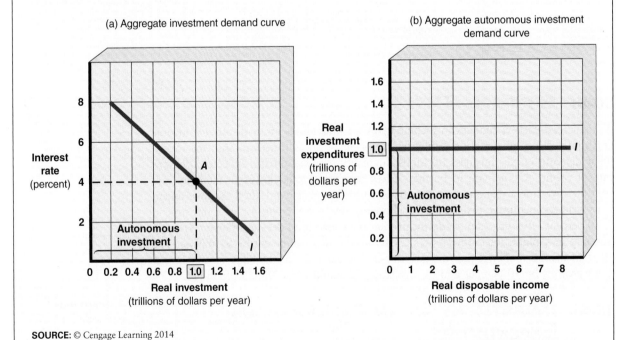

SOURCE: © Cengage Learning 2014

Key Concepts

John Maynard Keynes
Classical economists
Say's Law
Consumption function
autonomous consumption

Dissaving
Saving
Marginal propensity to
  consume (MPC)
Marginal propensity to save (MPS)

Wealth effect
Investment demand curve
Autonomous expenditure

Summary

- **Say's Law** is the classical theory that "supply creates its own demand," and therefore, the Great Depression was impossible. Say's Law is the theory that the value of production generates an equal amount of income and, in turn, total spending. The classical economists rejected the argument that underconsumption is possible because they believed flexible prices, wages, and interest rates would soon establish a balance between supply and demand.

- **John Maynard Keynes** rejected the classical theory that the economy self-corrects in the long run to full employment. The key in Keynesian theory is aggregate demand, rather than the classical economists focus on aggregate supply. Unless aggregate spending is adequate, the economy can experience prolonged and severe unemployment.

- The **consumption function (C)** is determined by changes in the level of real disposable income. **Autonomous consumption** is consumption that occurs even if real disposable income equals zero. Changes in such nonincome determinants as expectations, wealth, the price level, and interest rates can cause shifts in the consumption function.

- The **marginal propensity to consume (MPC)** is the change in consumption associated with a given change in real disposable income. The MPC tells how much of an additional dollar of disposable income households will spend for consumption.

- The **marginal propensity to save (MPS)** is the change in saving associated with a given change

in real disposable income. The MPS measures how much of an additional dollar of disposable income households will save.

Consumption Function

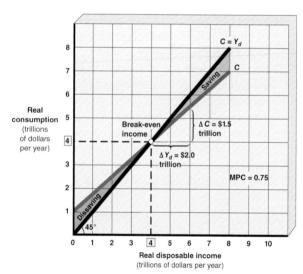

SOURCE: © Cengage Learning 2014

- The **investment demand curve (I)** shows the amount businesses spend for investment goods at different possible rates of interest. The determinants of this schedule are the expected rate of profit and rate of interest. Shifts in the investment demand curve result from changes in expectations, technology, capacity utilization, and business taxes.

Causation Chains

SOURCE: © Cengage Learning 2014

- An **autonomous expenditure** is spending that does not vary with the current level of disposable income. The Keynesian model applies this simplifying assumption to investment. As a result, the investment demand curve is a fixed amount determined by the rate of profit and the interest rate.

Summary of Conclusion Statements

- The classical economists believed that a continuing depression is impossible because markets eliminate persistent shortages or surpluses.
- In the classical view, unemployment is the result of a short-lived adjustment period in which wages and prices decline or people voluntarily choose not to work. Thus, there is a natural tendency for the economy to restore full employment over time.
- The 45-degree line is a geometric construct. It indicates all points where real disposable income (measured on the horizontal axis) and real consumption (measured on the vertical axis) are equal. Consequently, the 45-degree line makes it easier to identify the break-even or no-saving income level.
- There is a direct relationship between changes in real disposable income and changes in consumption.
- A change in real disposable income is the sole cause of a movement along the consumption function. A shift or relocation in the consumption schedule occurs when a factor other than real disposable income changes.
- Businesses will undertake all planned investment projects for which the expected rate of profits equals or exceeds the interest rate.

Study Questions and Problems

1. Explain how the classical economists concluded that Say's Law is valid and long-term unemployment impossible.

2. Use the following consumption function data to answer the questions below.
   a. Calculate the saving schedule.
   b. Determine the marginal propensities to consume (MPC) and save (MPS).
   c. Determine the break-even income.
   d. What is the relationship between the MPC and the MPS?

3. Explain why the MPC and the MPS must always add up to one.

Keynesian Consumption Function (billions of dollars per year)

Real disposable income	Consumption	Saving	MPC	MPS
$100	$150	$___	___	___
200	200	___	___	___
300	250	___	___	___
400	300	___	___	___
500	350	___	___	___

4. How do households "dissave"?

5. Explain how each of the following affects the consumption function:
   a. The expectation is that a prolonged recession will occur in the next year.
   b. Stock prices rise sharply.
   c. The price level rises by 10 percent.
   d. The interest rate on consumer loans rises sharply.
   e. Income taxes increase.

6. Your college is considering investing $6 million to add 10,000 seats to its football stadium. The athletic department forecasts it can sell all these extra seats at each game for a ticket price of $20 per seat, and the team plays six home games per year. If the school can borrow at an interest rate of 14 percent, should the school undertake this project? What would happen if the school expected a losing season and could sell tickets for only half of the 10,000 seats?

7. Why is the investment demand curve less stable than the consumption and saving schedules? What are the basic determinants that can shift the investment demand curve?

8. Suppose most business executives expect a slowdown in the economy. How might this situation affect the economy?

9. The levels of real disposable income and aggregate expenditures for a two-sector economy (consumption and investment) are given in the following table:

Real disposable income (trillions of dollars per year)	Consumption (C) (trillions of dollars per year)
$0	$3.00
1	3.25
2	3.50
3	3.75
4	4.00
5	4.25
6	4.50
7	4.75
8	5.00

a. Construct a graph of the consumption function (C).
b. Determine the autonomous consumption, MPC, and MPS for this hypothetical economy.
c. What is the break-even income consumption of real disposable income?
d. What is the amount of dissavings at $2 trillion real disposable income and the savings at $7 trillion.

For Online Exercises, go to the Tucker Web site at www.cengage.com/economics/tucker.

✓ CHECKPOINT ANSWER

What's Your MPC?

Early in your career when your income is relatively low, you are likely to spend your entire income, and perhaps even dissave, just to afford necessities. During this stage of your life, your MPC will be close to 1. As your income increases and you have purchased the necessities, additional income can go to luxuries. If you become wealthier, you have a higher marginal propensity to save and consequently a lower marginal propensity to consume. If you said your MPC will probably decrease as your income increases, **YOU ARE CORRECT.**

Sample Quiz

For an explanation of the correct answers, visit the Tucker Web site at www.cengage.com/economics/tucker.

1. The popular theory prior to the Great Depression that the economy will automatically adjust to achieve full employment in the long run is
   a. supply-side economics.
   b. Keynesian economics.
   c. classical economics.
   d. mercantilism.

2. The French economist Jean-Baptiste Say transformed the equality of total output and total spending into a law that can be expressed as
   a. unemployment is not possible in the short run.
   b. demand and supply are never equal.
   c. supply creates its own demand.
   d. demand creates its own supply.

3. If the economy is experiencing less than full equilibrium, the Keynesian school recommends that the government
   a. do nothing to stimulate the economy.
   b. undertake fiscal policy to stimulate aggregate demand.
   c. undertake fiscal policy to stimulate aggregate supply.
   d. balance the budget to stimulate aggregate demand.

4. The school of thought that emphasizes the natural tendency for an economy to move toward equilibrium full employment is known as the
   a. Keynesian school.
   b. supply-side school.
   c. noninterventionist school.
   d. classical school.

5. What is the title of the John Maynard Keynes's book published in 1936 that challenged the classical self-correction economic theory?
   a. *In the Long Run, We Are Dead.*
   b. *Classical Economics Revised.*
   c. *General Theory of Employment, Interest, and Money.*
   d. *A Keynesian Approach to Economic Policy.*

6. What is the vertical intercept of the consumption function that represents the portion of consumption expenditure *not* associated with a level of disposable income?
   a. consumption intercept
   b. disposable income intercept
   c. autonomous consumption
   d. automatic consumption line

7. John Maynard Keynes's central proposition that a dollar increase in disposable income would increase consumption, but by less than the increase in disposable income, implies a marginal propensity to consume (MPC) that is
   a. greater than or equal to one.
   b. equal to one.
   c. less than one but greater than zero.
   d. negative.

8. The marginal propensity to consume (MPC) is the slope of the
   a. GDP curve.
   b. disposable income curve.
   c. consumption function.
   d. autonomous consumption curve.

9. The sum of the marginal propensity to consume (MPC) and the marginal propensity to save (MPS) always equals
   a. 1.
   b. 0.
   c. the interest rate.
   d. the marginal propensity to invest (MPI).

10. The relationship between MPC and MPS is
    a. $1 + MPC = MPS$.
    b. $1 - MPC = MPS$.
    c. $1 + MPS = MPC$.
    d. $MPC - MPS = 1$.

11. If the marginal propensity to consume = 0.75, then
    a. the marginal propensity to save = 0.75.
    b. the marginal propensity to save = 1.33.
    c. the marginal propensity to save = 0.20.
    d. the marginal propensity to save = 0.25.

Sample Quiz *continued*

EXHIBIT 8	Consumption Function

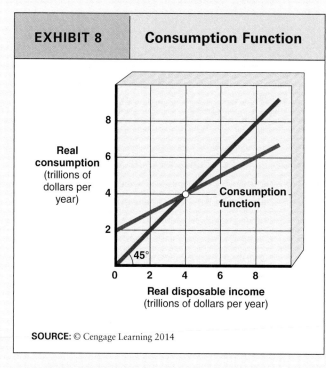

SOURCE: © Cengage Learning 2014

12. As shown in Exhibit 8, autonomous consumption is
    a. 0.
    b. $2 trillion.
    c. $4 trillion.
    d. $6 trillion.
    e. $8 trillion.

13. As shown in Exhibit 8, savings occurs
    a. at 0.
    b. between 0 and $4 trillion.
    c. where disposable income is greater than $4 trillion.
    d. at $2 trillion.

14. As shown in Exhibit 8, dissaving occurs
    a. at $5 trillion.
    b. between 0 and $4 trillion.
    c. where disposable income is greater than $4 trillion.
    d. at $8 trillion.

15. As shown in Exhibit 8, the marginal propensity to consume (MPC) is
    a. 0.33.
    b. 0.50.

c. 0.67.
d. 0.75.

16. As shown in Exhibit 8, the break-even income is
    a. $2 trillion.
    b. $4 trillion.
    c. $6 trillion.
    d. $8 trillion.

17. As shown in Exhibit 8, the 45° line represents
    a. autonomous consumption.
    b. real consumption spending.
    c. real disposable income.
    d. all points where real consumption equals real disposable income.

18. The consumption function is drawn on a graph with disposable income on the horizontal axis. Assume autonomous consumption increases. The effect is
    a. an upward adjustment in the vertical intercept.
    b. no change in the adjustment in the vertical intercept.
    c. an increase in the slope of the consumption function.
    d. a decrease in the slope of the consumption function.

19. The investment demand curve shows the amount businesses spend for investment goods at different possible
    a. price levels.
    b. levels of GDP.
    c. rates of interest.
    d. levels of taxation.

20. A rightward shift of the investment demand curve would be caused by a(an)
    a. increase in the expected rate of return on investment caused by an increase in business confidence.
    b. decrease in the expected rate of return on investment caused by a decrease in business confidence.
    c. increase in the rate of interest.
    d. decrease in the rate of interest.

chapter 19

The Keynesian Model in Action

In 1935, George Bernard Shaw received a letter from John Maynard Keynes, which stated, "I believe myself to be writing a book [*The General Theory*] on economic theory which will largely revolutionize—not, I suppose, at once but in the course of the next ten years—the way the world thinks about economic problems." Indeed, Keynes's macroeconomic theory offered powerful ideas whose time had come during the Great Depression. Building on the foundation of the previous chapter, this chapter describes how Keynes conceived the economy as driven by aggregate demand that can be separated and analyzed under the individual components of consumption (C), investment (I), government spending (G), and net exports (X − M).

You must keep in mind that during the Great Depression era, plants had idle capacity and unemployment was massive. Under these conditions, inflation was not the problem. The Keynesian model therefore generally ignores price level changes and focuses instead on how full-employment output can be achieved by changes in aggregate expenditures.

Like adding icing to a cake, this chapter begins by adding government spending and global trade to the consumption function and autonomous investment demand curve introduced in the previous chapter. The result is the complete aggregate expenditures model. Next, you will learn how the economy gravitates to an equilibrium where aggregate expenditures equal aggregate output (real GDP). And you will look at the link between the equilibrium real GDP and the level of employment in an economy. The analysis will make clear why Keynes argued that there is no self-correction mechanism that eventually moves the nation to the full-employment equilibrium output.

Finally, you will understand one of Keynes's most powerful ideas—the spending multiplier. At the very heart of Keynesian theory is the concept that an initial increase in aggregate spending of $1 in an economy can increase equilibrium output by more than $1. Thus, Keynesian economics offers a cure for an economy in deep recession: government policies that expand aggregate demand, raise national output, create jobs, and restore full employment.

In this chapter, you will learn to solve these economics puzzles:

- Why did Keynes reject the classical theory that "supply creates its own demand"?

- Why did Keynes argue that the government should adopt active policies, rather than allowing the price system to prevail?

- Can the Keynesian model explain an ice cream war?

19-1 Adding Government and Global Trade to the Keynesian Model

In this chapter, we continue our study of the Keynesian model begun in the previous chapter. Consumption and investment are not the only forms of spending. As shown earlier in the chapter on GDP (Exhibit 2), consumption and investment represent 83 percent of total spending, while government spending and net exports account for the remaining 17 percent of GDP.

19-1a GOVERNMENT SPENDING

Government spending is the second largest component of aggregate expenditures in the United States. Like investment, government spending can be considered an autonomous expenditure. The reasoning is that government spending is primarily the result of political decisions made independent of the level of national output.

Exhibit 1(a) shows hypothetical government spending as a horizontal line labeled G at $1 trillion. If government officials increase government spending, the G line shifts vertically upward at each possible level of real GDP to G_1, and reduced government spending shifts the G line vertically downward at each possible level of real GDP to G_2. The amount of the shift is equal to the amount of change in government spending.

Here we must pause to take special note of the change from real disposable income to real GDP on the horizontal axis of the graph. Does it make a difference? No, it makes little difference. In the previous chapter, real disposable income was used following the theory Keynes himself developed. However, it is important to connect aggregate output and income measures. Recall from Exhibit 7 in the chapter on GDP the adjustments required to convert GDP into disposable income (Y_d). As it turns out, real disposable income is a sizable portion of real GDP. Over the last decade, real disposable income, on average, has consistently been about 70 percent of real GDP. If we assume that real disposable income remains the same high proportion of real GDP each year, then we can substitute real GDP for real disposable income in the Keynesian model. Changes in real GDP therefore reflect changes in both real national output and income (real disposable income).

19-1b NET EXPORTS

Like investment and government spending, exports and imports can be treated as autonomous expenditures unaffected by a nation's domestic level of real GDP. Economic conditions in the countries that buy U.S. products affect the level of our exports. On the other hand, the level of imports purchased by U.S. citizens is

GLOBAL ECONOMICS

EXHIBIT 1	Autonomous Government Spending and Net Exports Curves

In part (a), government spending (G) is assumed to be determined by the political decision-making process. The autonomous government spending line, G, is therefore a horizontal line indicating that government spending is independent of the level of real GDP. An increase in government spending shifts G upward to G_1. A decrease shifts G downward to G_2.

Part (b) also shows that net exports are assumed to be independent of the level of GDP. Horizontal line $(X - M)_1$ is negative because imports exceed exports. If exports equal imports, then the net export line shifts upward to $(X - M)$. If exports exceed imports, the net exports line is represented by a positive net exports line, $(X - M)_2$.

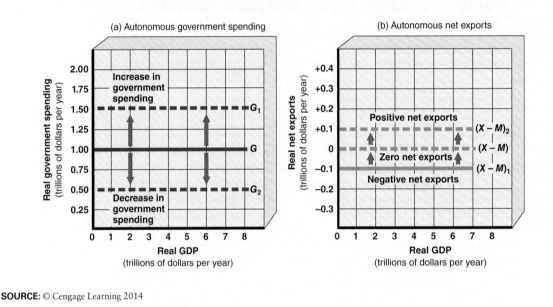

SOURCE: © Cengage Learning 2014

influenced by economic conditions in the United States. As shown in Exhibit 1(b), net exports, $(X - M)$, can be positive, zero, or negative. The level of net exports, or the $(X - M)$ line, is horizontal because net exports are assumed to be independent of the level of real GDP. Since for many years the value of imports we have purchased from foreigners has exceeded the value of exports we have been selling them, the model assumes net exports are negative at line $(X - M)_1$. If exports and imports are equal, the net exports line shifts upward to zero at line $(X - M)$. If exports exceed imports, the positive $(X - M)$ line shifts farther upward to line $(X - M)_2$.

19-2 The Aggregate Expenditures Model

Keynes countered classical theory by developing an alternative theory that explained how a depressed economy can be stuck forever in a below-full-employment equilibrium without adequate aggregate expenditures. In this section, a basic Keynesian model is developed to explain what Keynes meant by his famous saying, "In the long run, we are all dead."

19-2a THE AGGREGATE EXPENDITURES FUNCTION (AE)

A little drum roll please! Now we are ready to tie together concepts and point the spotlight on an important concept called the aggregate expenditures function (AE) necessary to understand Keynes's cure for the Great Depression. The aggregate expenditures function (AE) is the total spending in an economy at different levels of real GDP. The AE function or line is conceptually derived graphically in Exhibit 2 by vertically summing $C + I + G + (X - M)$ at each level of GDP on the horizontal axis. The consumption function (C) explained in the previous chapter begins the AE function with a given level of autonomous consumption spending (a). Next, recall that the consumption function is determined by its slope, which equals the MPC. As

Aggregate expenditures function (AE)

The total spending in an economy at different levels of real GDP.

EXHIBIT 2	**Aggregate Expenditures and Keynesian Equilibrium**

The aggregate expenditures function (AE) begins with the consumption function (C). Then we add investment (I), government spending (G), and net exports ($X - M$). Note that I, G, and ($X - M$) are assumed to be autonomous expenditures and are therefore lines parallel to the C line. The slope of the AE line is determined by the slope of the consumption function, which equals the MPC ($\Delta C/\Delta Y$). At Y^* real GDP, aggregate expenditures equals aggregate income/output (real GDP) along the 45-degree line (AE = Y), and the economy is in equilibrium.

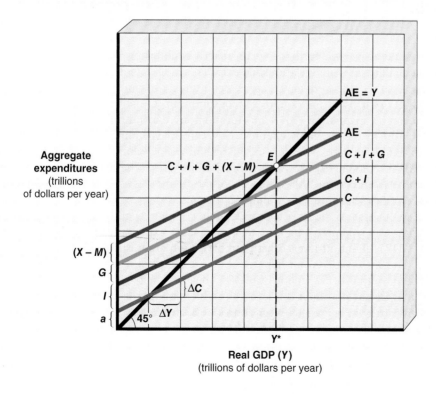

SOURCE: © Cengage Learning 2014

shown in Exhibit 2, MPC is represented by the ratio of the change in consumption to the change in real GDP ($\Delta C/\Delta Y$). Since consumption spending rises by less than real GDP, the MPC is less than 1. Note that it is the slope of the consumption function that gives the entire AE function its upward slope.

The next step in graphing a conceptual AE line is to add expenditures for I, G, and $(X - M)$. To do this, we assume businesses plan to spend a constant amount of investment at all levels of GDP. Therefore, autonomous investment (I) is added parallel to consumption (C) at each level of real GDP. As a result, the AE line shifts vertically upward and consists of $C + I$. Like consumption and investment, government spending and net exports are also assumed to be autonomous spending that remains unchanged regardless of the level of real GDP. Adding government spending (G) results in a parallel upward shift in the AE line to $C + I + G$. The aggregate expenditures function is completed by adding net exports to the $C + I + G$ line, and the AE line shifts parallel upward to $C + I + G (X - M)$. Finally, macro equilibrium is established at point E where aggregate expenditures equal real GDP at Y^* along the 45-degree line.

CONCLUSION: *At the equilibrium level of real GDP, the total value of goods and services produced (real GDP, Y) is precisely equal to the total spending for these goods and services (aggregate expenditures, AE).*

19-2b   TABULAR ANALYSIS OF KEYNESIAN EQUILIBRIUM

In this section, we will further explain macro equilibrium using hypothetical data. Exhibit 3 illustrates the relationship between employment, aggregate output and income (real GDP), and aggregate expenditures for our hypothetical economy. Real GDP (Y) is listed in column (1), consumption (C) is listed in column (2), and investment (I) in column (3) is an autonomous expenditure of $1 trillion from Exhibit 7(b) in the previous chapter. Government spending (G) in column (4) is also an autonomous expenditure of $1 trillion from Exhibit 1(a), and net exports ($X - M$) in column (5) are taken from Exhibit 1(b). The aggregate expenditures function (AE) in column (6) is the sum of the $C + I + G + (X - M)$ components of aggregate expenditures in columns (2) through (5).

Examination of the levels of real GDP in column (1) and the levels of aggregate expenditures in column (6) indicate that an equality exists only at the $5 trillion level of real GDP. All output levels other than $5 trillion are unsustainable macro disequilibrium levels. Consider what happens if businesses employ only enough workers to produce an output of $1 trillion real GDP. Business managers expect total spending to equal aggregate output at this level of production, but this does not happen. At the level of $1 trillion, aggregate expenditures of $3 trillion exceed aggregate output by an *unplanned inventory investment depletion* of $2 trillion, listed in column (7). Firms respond to this happy state of affairs by hiring more workers, expanding output, and generating additional aggregate income. As a result of this process, the economy moves toward the equilibrium of $5 trillion real GDP. Thus, the pressure of empty shelves and warehouses drives our hypothetical economy to create jobs and reduce the unemployment rate (not explicitly shown in the model).

EXHIBIT 3	Equilibrium and Disequilibrium Levels of Employment, Output, and Income						
(1)	(2)	(3)	(4)	(5)	(6)	(7)	(8)
Aggregate Output and Income (real GDP) (*Y*)	Consumption (*C*)	Investment (*I*)	Government (*G*)	Net Exports (*X − M*)	Aggregate Expenditures (AE)	Unplanned Inventory Investment Depletion (−) or Accumulation (+)	Direction of Real GDP and Employment
$ 0	$0.6	$1	$1	$−0.1	$2.5	$−2.S	Increase
1.0	1.1	1	1	−0.1	3.0	−2.0	Increase
2.0	1.6	1	1	−0.1	3.5	−1.5	Increase
3.0	2.1	1	1	−0.1	4.0	−1.0	Increase
4.0	2.6	1	1	−0.1	4.5	−0.5	Increase
5.0	3.1	1	1	−0.1	5.0	0	Equilibrium
6.0	3.6	1	1	−0.1	5.5	+0.5	Decrease
7.0	4.1	1	1	−0.1	6.0	+1.0	Decrease
8.0	4.6	1	1	−0.1	6.5	+1.5	Decrease

NOTE: All amounts are in trillions of dollars per year.
SOURCE: © Cengage Learning 2014

The reverse is true for all levels of real GDP above the $5 trillion equilibrium level. Now suppose firms hire more workers and aggregate output is $7 trillion real GDP. At the real GDP disequilibrium level of $7 trillion, *unplanned inventory investment accumulation* occurs because aggregate expenditures of $6 trillion are insufficient to purchase $7 trillion of output. The result is that unwanted inventories worth $1 trillion remain unsold on the shelves and in the warehouses of business firms. Producers react to this undesirable condition by cutting the rate of output and employment. In this case, real GDP declines toward the equilibrium level of $5 trillion, jobs are lost, and unemployment rises.

CONCLUSION: *Aggregate expenditures in Keynesian economics pull aggregate output either higher or lower toward equilibrium in the economy, as opposed to the classical view that aggregate output generates an equal amount of aggregate spending.*

19-2c GRAPHICAL ANALYSIS OF KEYNESIAN EQUILIBRIUM

Using the data from Exhibit 3, Exhibit 4 presents a graph measuring real aggregate expenditures on the *y*-axis and real GDP on the *x*-axis. Exhibit 4 illustrates the complete aggregate expenditures model. The aggregate expenditures model determines the equilibrium level of real GDP by the intersection of the aggregate

Aggregate expenditures model

The model that determines the equilibrium level of real GDP by the intersection of the aggregate expenditures and aggregate output and income (real GDP) curves.

EXHIBIT 4	The Keynesian Aggregate Expenditures Model

Aggregate expenditures (AE) equal aggregate output (Y) at the equilibrium level of $5 trillion real GDP. Below the equilibrium level of real GDP, an undesired inventory depletion causes businesses to expand production, which pushes the economy toward equilibrium output. Above the equilibrium level of real GDP, an unintended inventory accumulation causes businesses to reduce production, which pushes the economy toward equilibrium output. In Keynesian theory, the full-employment output of $6 trillion real GDP can be reached only by shifting the AE curve upward until the full-capacity output of $6 trillion real GDP is reached.

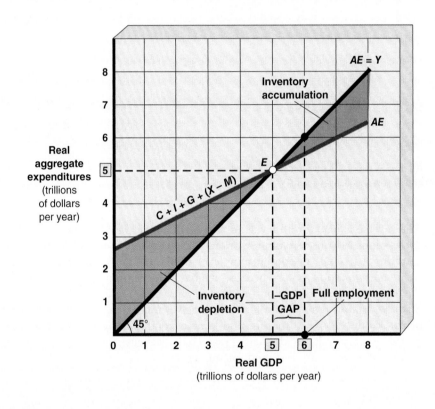

SOURCE: © Cengage Learning 2014

expenditures and aggregate output and income (real GDP) curves. The aggregate expenditure model is sometimes called the *Keynesian Cross*. The 45-degree line now takes on a special significance. Each point along this line is equidistant from the horizontal and vertical axes. Therefore, each point reflects a *possible* equilibrium between real GDP aggregate output (Y) and aggregate expenditures (AE). Note that the AE line indicates aggregate expenditures along a line less steep than the 45-degree line. This is because the slope of the AE line is determined by the marginal propensity to consume (MPC), which is less than 1. Aggregate expenditures equal aggregate output at the $5 trillion real GDP level, and any other level of output is unstable. If businesses produce at some output level that is higher than equilibrium GDP, such as $7 trillion real GDP, the vertical distance between the 45-degree equilibrium line and the AE line measures an undesired inventory accumulation of $1 trillion. This leads businesses to reduce employment, and production drops downward until the economy reaches equilibrium at $5 trillion. You may have already recognized that the difference of $1 trillion between the equilibrium output (actual real GDP) at point E and the full-employment output (potential real GDP) is a negative *GDP gap*, discussed in the chapter on business cycles and unemployment (see Exhibit 9).

Now consider the case in which businesses hire only enough workers to produce aggregate output where the AE line is above the 45-degree equilibrium line. Because aggregate expenditures exceed aggregate output, businesses sell more than they currently produce, which depletes their inventories. Business managers react to this excess aggregate demand condition by hiring more workers and expanding production, causing movement upward along the AE function toward the equilibrium level of $5 trillion real GDP.

Now it's time to pause, take a breath, and appreciate what you have been studying so diligently. It's a powerful idea! Exhibit 4 illustrates the basic explanation offered by Keynes for the Great Depression: *Contrary to classical theory, once an equilibrium is established between aggregate expenditures and aggregate output, there is no tendency for the economy to change, even when equilibrium is well below full employment.* The solution Keynes offered Western economies facing the Great Depression is to shift the AE line upward until the full-employment equilibrium is reached. Otherwise, prolonged unemployment persists indefinitely, and the economy never self-corrects. We now turn to the key idea behind changes in aggregate spending to stabilize the macro economy.

19-3 The Spending Multiplier Effect

Changes in aggregate expenditures in the Keynesian model make things happen. The crux of Keynesian macroeconomic policy depends on a change in aggregate expenditures, which is multiplied or amplified by rounds of spending and respending throughout the economy. Exhibit 5 is an enlarged version of Exhibit 4. Our analysis begins at the initial equilibrium of $5 trillion real GDP (point E), which is below the full-employment output level of $6 trillion real GDP. Now let's assume the government decides to increase government spending by $0.5 trillion. An increase in autonomous government spending of $0.5 trillion per year shifts the aggregate expenditures curve *vertically* upward by this amount from point E on AE_1 to point a on AE_2. This means at the initial output of $5 trillion real GDP, aggregate demand expands by $0.5 trillion to $5.5 trillion. The initial expansion of spending causes inventories (not shown in the graph) to decline by $0.5 trillion because aggregate spending of $5.5 trillion exceeds aggregate output of $5.0 trillion real GDP. Firms respond by stepping up output by $0.5 trillion real GDP per year to replace inventories. The exhibit shows this by the move from point a to point b. Now the marginal propensity to consume enters the picture. Assuming the MPC is 0.50, the expansion of output from $5 trillion to $5.5 trillion puts an extra $500 billion of income into the pockets of workers. Given the MPC of 0.50, these workers increase spending on goods and services by $250 billion (movement from point b to point c). This expansion of consumer spending again causes inventories to decline and output, in turn, to expand by $250 billion,

EXHIBIT 5	**The Spending Multiplier Effect of a Change in Government Spending**

This graph is an enlargement of the spending multiplier process beginning at the point where the economy is in equilibrium at $5 trillion. Then an initial increase of $500 billion in government spending shifts the aggregate expenditures line up vertically from AE_1 to AE_2. After all spending-output-spending rounds are complete, a new equilibrium is restored at point E_1 with a full-employment output of $6 trillion. Thus, the $500 billion initial increase in government spending has caused a $1 trillion increase in real GDP, and the value of the multiplier is 2.

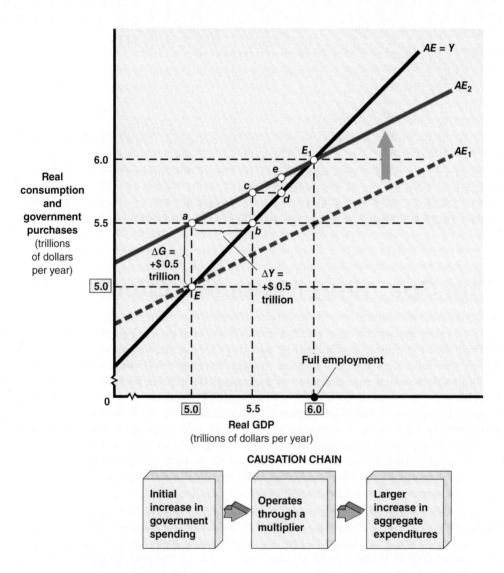

CAUSATION CHAIN

Initial increase in government spending	⇨	Operates through a multiplier	⇨	Larger increase in aggregate expenditures

SOURCE: © Cengage Learning 2014

represented by the distance between point c and point d. This again puts extra income into workers' pockets, of which $125 billion (the distance between points d and e) is spent (MPC × ΔY = 0.50 × $250 billion = $125 billion).

This process of spending-output-spending continues through an infinite number of rounds until output reaches the new equilibrium level of $6 trillion per year at point E_1. Thus, an initial expansion of government spending of $0.5 trillion expands equilibrium output by $1 trillion, which is twice the magnitude of the increase in government spending. Hence, the spending multiplier (SM) is 2. The spending multiplier is the ratio of the change in real GDP to the initial change in any component of aggregate expenditures, including consumption, investment, government spending, and net exports. The formula to compute the amount of change in government spending or other aggregate expenditures required to shift equilibrium aggregate output measured by real GDP is

$$\text{Spending multiplier} = \frac{\text{change in equilibrium real GDP}}{\textit{initial} \text{ change in aggregate expenditures}}$$

In the example presented in Exhibit 5, the spending multiplier is computed as

$$\text{Spending multiplier} = \frac{\Delta Y}{\Delta G} = \frac{\$1,000 \text{ billion}}{\$500 \text{ billion}} = 2$$

Spending multiplier (SM)

The ratio of the change in real GDP to an initial change in any component of aggregate expenditures, including consumption, investment, government spending, and net exports. As a formula, the spending multiplier equals 1/(1 − MPC) or 1/MPS.

19-3a SPENDING MULTIPLIER ARITHMETIC

The graphical presentation of the spending multiplier process should make the basic mechanics clear to you, but we need to be more specific and derive a formula. Therefore, let's pause to tackle the task of explaining in more detail the spending multiplier of 2 used in the above example. Exhibit 6 illustrates numerically the cumulative increase in aggregate expenditures resulting from a $500 billion increase in government spending. In the initial round, the government spends this amount for bridges, national defense, and so forth. Households receive this amount of income. In the second round, these households spend $250 billion (0.50 × $500 billion) on houses, cars, groceries, and other products. In the third round, the incomes of realtors, auto workers, grocers, and others are boosted by $250 billion, and they spend $125 billion (0.50 × $250 billion). These rounds of spending create income for respending in a downward spiral throughout the economy in smaller and smaller amounts until the total level of aggregate expenditures rises by an extra $1,000 billion.

> **CONCLUSION:** *Any initial change in spending by the government, households, or firms creates a chain reaction of further spending, which causes a greater cumulative change in aggregate expenditures.*

You might recognize from algebra that the spending multiplier effect is a process based on an infinite geometric series. The formula for the sum of such a series of numbers is the initial number times 1/(1 − r), where r is the ratio that relates the numbers. Using this formula, the sum (total spending) is calculated as $500 billion ($\Delta G$) × [1/(1 − 0.50)] = $1,000 billion. By simply defining r in the

EXHIBIT 6	Spending Multiplier Effect	
Round	Component of total spending	New consumption spending
1	Government spending	$500
2	Consumption	250
3	Consumption	125
4	Consumption	63
.	.	.
.	.	.
.	.	.
All other rounds	Consumption	62
Total spending		$1,000

NOTE: All amounts are rounded to the nearest billion dollars per year.
SOURCE: © Cengage Learning 2014

infinite series formula as MPC, the spending multiplier for aggregate demand is expressed as

$$\text{Spending multiplier} = \frac{1}{1 - \text{MPC}}$$

Applying this formula to our example:

$$\text{Spending multiplier} = \frac{1}{1 - 0.50} = \frac{1}{0.50} = 2$$

Recall from the previous chapter that MPC + MPS = 1; therefore, MPS = 1 − MPC. Hence, the above multiplier formula can be rewritten as

$$\text{Spending multiplier} = \frac{1}{\text{MPS}}$$

Applying the multiplier formula to our example:

$$\text{Spending multiplier} = \frac{1}{\text{MPS}} = \frac{1}{1 - 0.50} = 2$$

Because MPS and MPC are related, the size of the multiplier depends on the size of the MPC. What will the result be if people spend 80 percent or 33 percent of each dollar of income instead of 50 percent? If the MPC increases (decreases), consumers spend a larger (smaller) share of each additional dollar of output/income in each round, and the size of the multiplier increases (decreases). Exhibit 7 lists the multiplier for different values of MPC and MPS. Economists use real-world macroeconomic data to estimate a more complex multiplier than the simple multiplier formula developed in this chapter. Their estimates of the long-run real-world MPC range from 0.80 to 0.90. An MPC of 0.50 is used in the above examples for simplicity.

EXHIBIT 7	Relationship between MPC, MPS, and the Spending Multiplier	
(1) Marginal propensity to consume (MPC)	(2) Marginal propensity to save (MPS)	(3) Spending multiplier
0.90	0.10	10
0.80	0.20	5
0.75	0.25	4
0.67	0.33	3
0.50	0.50	2
0.33	0.67	1.5

SOURCE: © Cengage Learning 2014

19-4 Recessionary and Inflationary Gaps

The multiplier is important in the Keynesian model because it means that the initial change in aggregate expenditures results in an amplified change in the equilibrium level of real GDP. Such inherent instability can mean bad or good news for an economy. The bad news occurs, for example, when the multiplier amplifies small declines in total spending from, say, consumer and business manager pessimism into downturns in national output, income, and employment. The good news is that, in theory, macroeconomic policy can manage, or manipulate, the economy's performance by a relatively small initial change in aggregate expenditures.

19-4a RECESSIONARY GAP

Using Government Spending to Close a Recessionary Gap
Consider the aggregate expenditures function AE_1 in Exhibit 8. Beginning at point E_1, this hypothetical economy's initial equilibrium level is $4 trillion real GDP. The MPC is 0.50, and the spending multiplier is therefore 2. The full-employment output is $6 trillion real GDP, which means the economy faces a negative GDP gap of $2 trillion. Along the vertical line at the full-employment output level, look at the segment between point a on the initial AE_1 line and point E_2 on the AE_2 line, which is labeled a recessionary gap. A recessionary gap is the amount by which aggregate expenditures fall short of the amount required to achieve full-employment equilibrium. In our example, the recessionary gap is $1 trillion. What is the importance of the recessionary gap? The recessionary gap is the initial increase in autonomous spending required to trigger the multiplier, shift the

Recessionary gap

The amount by which the aggregate expenditures curve must be increased to achieve full-employment equilibrium.

aggregate expenditures function upward from AE_1 to AE_2, and eliminate the positive GDP gap. Stated as an expression,

Initial increase in autonomous expenditures × spending multiplier

= increase in equilibrium output

Using the data in our example,

$1 trillion × 2 = $2 trillion

We now turn to the important question of how to inject an additional $1 trillion spending into the economy, cause AE_1 to shift upward to AE_2, and thereby increase the equilibrium output from $4 trillion to $6 trillion real GDP. Under

EXHIBIT 8	A Recessionary Gap

The hypothetical economy begins in equilibrium at point E_1, with an equilibrium output of $4 trillion real GDP. With aggregate expenditures of AE_1, real GDP will not automatically increase to the $6 trillion full-employment output. The $1 trillion deficiency in total spending required to achieve full employment is the recessionary gap measured by the vertical distance between points a and E_2. Given a multiplier of 2, an initial increase in autonomous expenditures equal to the recessionary gap works through the spending multiplier and causes the economy to move from E_1 to E_2 and achieve full employment.

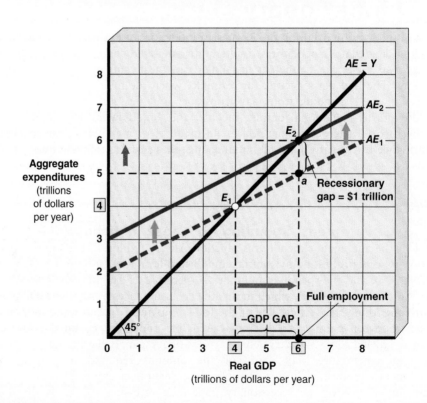

SOURCE: © Cengage Learning 2014

Keynesian theory, when market forces do not automatically do the job, then the central government should take aggressive action and adopt policies that boost autonomous spending [C, I, G, or (X − M)] by an amount equal to the recessionary gap.

Using a Tax Cut to Close a Recessionary Gap

Instead of increasing government spending, let's assume the government decides to cut taxes to close the negative recessionary GDP gap in Exhibit 8. This is an option we have not yet discussed in the context of the aggregate expenditures model, and it requires special consideration. The government may consider changes in two types of taxes: autonomous taxes and income taxes. For simplicity, here the analysis is confined to the simpler concept of autonomous taxes, such as property taxes, which are independent of the levels of real output and income.

Suppose in Exhibit 8 the government reduces autonomous taxes by $800 billion. Would this tax cut be enough to restore full employment? Since real disposable income rises at every level of GDP, so does consumption at all levels of real GDP. As a result, the consumption function and, in turn, the aggregate expenditures function shifts upward, but not by the full amount of the tax cut. Since the MPC is 0.50, this means households spend only $400 billion of the additional $800 billion of disposable income from the tax cut. The remaining $400 billion of the tax cut is added to savings. Hence, after multiplying the tax cut by the MPC, the result of the tax cut is computed as above. That is, in this case, the increase in equilibrium real GDP is $400 billion × 2 = $800 billion. Since GDP would increase only from $4 trillion to $4.8 trillion, the economy would operate below the full-employment real GDP of $6 trillion.

An approach similar to a cut in taxes would be for the government to raise *transfer payments* (welfare, unemployment, and Social Security payments) by $800 billion. This increase in transfer payments, holding taxes constant, increases disposable income dollar for dollar at each level of real GDP. Hence, the consumption and aggregate expenditures lines shift upward by $400 billion. This initial boost in total spending is computed by multiplying the MPC of 0.50 times the increase of $800 billion in transfer payments. The increase in transfer payments has the same effect as an identical cut in taxes, and the equilibrium real GDP increases by $800 billion. Hence, a transfer payment is simply a cut in net taxes.

Another simpler method of calculating the impact of a change in taxes is to use a *tax multiplier*. The tax multiplier is the change in aggregate expenditures (total spending) resulting from an initial change in taxes. Expressed as a formula:

Tax multiplier | The change in aggregate expenditures (total spending) resulting from an initial change in taxes. As a formula, the tax multiplier equals 1 − spending multiplier.

$$\textbf{Tax multiplier} = \textbf{1} - \textbf{spending multiplier}$$

After you calculate the tax multiplier, multiply your answer by the amount of the tax increase or decrease in order to determine the change in aggregate expenditures. Expressed as a formula:

$$\textbf{Change in taxes } (\Delta T) \times \textbf{tax multiplier} = \textbf{change in aggregate expenditures}$$

Returning to the example shown in Exhibit 8, suppose we wish to calculate the tax cut required to increase real GDP by $2 trillion from $4 trillion to $6 trillion and achieve full employment. Using the tax multiplier formula:

$$\textbf{Tax multiplier} = \textbf{1} - \textbf{2} = \textbf{−1}$$
$$\Delta T \times (\textbf{−1}) = \textbf{\$2 trillion}$$
$$\Delta T = \textbf{−\$2 trillion}$$

Therefore, in this hypothetical economy, a $2 trillion tax cut will increase GDP by the $2 trillion required to achieve full employment.

✓ CHECKPOINT

Full-Employment Output, Where Are You?

Suppose the U.S. economy is in equilibrium at $15 trillion real GDP with a recessionary gap. Given an MPC of 0.50, the government estimates that a tax cut of $500 billion is just enough to restore full employment. What is the full-employment real GDP target?

19-4b INFLATIONARY GAP

Inflationary gap

The amount by which the aggregate expenditures curve must be decreased to achieve full-employment equilibrium.

Under other circumstances, an inflationary gap may burden an economy. An inflationary gap is the amount by which aggregate expenditures exceed the amount required to achieve full-employment equilibrium. In Exhibit 9, the inflationary gap of $1 trillion is the vertical distance between point a on the initial AE_1 line and point E_2 on the AE_2 line. Since the economy can produce only $4 trillion in real output, this excess aggregate demand puts upward pressure on prices as buyers compete for this limited real output. If aggregate spending declines from AE_1 to AE_2, the economy moves from an equilibrium of $6 trillion at point E_1 to the full-employment equilibrium of $4 trillion at point E_2, and the inflationary pressure cools.

Again, the Keynesian prescription is for the central government to take aggressive action and adopt policies that reduce autonomous spending [C, I, G, or $(X - M)$] by an amount equal to the inflationary gap. Note from the analysis in the previous section that the government could cut government spending or use a tax hike or a cut in transfer payments to reduce consumption. Stated as an expression,

Initial decrease in autonomous expenditures × spending multiplier
= decrease in equilibrium output

In our example, the MPC is 0.50, so the multiplier is 2. The actual real GDP of $6 trillion is greater than the potential real GDP of $4 trillion, so the negative real GDP gap is –$2 trillion. Hence,

$$-\$1 \text{ trillion} \times 2 = -\$2 \text{ trillion}$$

✓ CHECKPOINT

How Much Spending Must Uncle Sam Cut?

Suppose the U.S. economy is troubled by inflation. The economy is in equilibrium at a real GDP of $15.5 trillion, the MPC is 0.90, and the full-employment output is $15 trillion. If the government decides to eliminate the inflationary gap by cutting government spending, what will be the size of the cut?

EXHIBIT 9	An Inflationary Gap

The hypothetical economy begins in equilibrium at point E_1 with an equilibrium output of $6 trillion real GDP. Given an initial aggregate expenditures function of AE_1, real GDP will not self- correct to the full-employment output of $4 trillion. The $1 trillion excess of total spending over the amount required at full employment is the inflationary gap measured by the vertical distance between points a and E_2. Given a multiplier of 2, an initial decrease in autonomous expenditures of $1 trillion causes the economy to move from point E_1 to E_2, achieve full employment, and cool the upward pressure on prices.

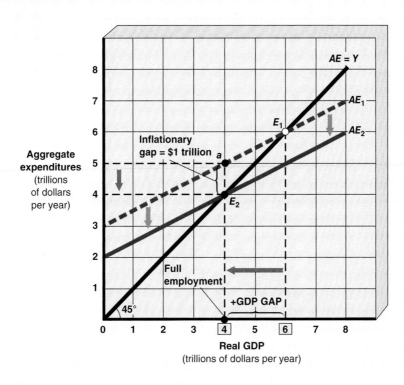

SOURCE: © Cengage Learning 2014

GLOBAL ECONOMICS

The Great Ice Cream War

Applicable concept: aggregate expenditures model

The following article from *The Wall Street Journal* provides a rare insight into the politics of global trade, and the Analyze the Issue connects trade policy to the macro model developed in this chapter:

> While many people relish American-made ice cream with deliberately foreign-sounding names, few people realize that the U.S. government declared war on ice cream imports by restricting them to less than one-tenth of one percent of U.S. consumption. With quotas so low and transportation costs high, few countries bothered to ship any ice cream at all to the United States. For example, in 1988 the United States exported hundreds of thousands of gallons of ice cream to Canada, yet Canadian ice cream was banned from the United States. Only 576 gallons was imported from New Zealand and 12 gallons from Denmark. This was not enough ice cream to stock a large grocery store on a summer Saturday.
>
> The U.S. ice cream quotas dated back to December 31, 1970, when President Nixon decreed that future ice cream imports could not exceed 431,330 gallons a year. Why? That year, according to Deputy Secretary of Agriculture Ann Veneman, testifying before the ITC [U.S. International Trade Commission], the United States was hit with a "flood of imports." This so-called "flood" amounted to barely 1 percent of U.S. ice cream consumption.
>
> How did Mr. Nixon decide to limit imports to exactly 431,330 gallons a year? Section 22 of the Agriculture Adjustment Act allowed the U.S.

wildarrow/Shutterstock.com

> government to protect domestic price-support programs by restricting imports to 50 percent of the annual average imports for a representative period. Ice cream imports did not begin until 1969, so the U.S. government chose 1969 and the two previous years with no ice cream imports in order to calculate a low annual average import quota for this product.

Finally, the article concluded that the U.S. government probably spent more than $1,000 in administrative expenses for each gallon of ice cream imported into the United States. The article's author concluded, "Global trade disputes are rapidly degenerating into a full employment program for government bureaucrats."

Analyze the Issue

Assume the U.S. economy is in an inflationary gap condition. Use the Keynesian aggregate expenditures model to explain why increasing U.S. exports and restricting imports is or is not a desirable policy.

Source: Reprinted from The Wall Street Journal © 1989 Dow Jones & Company. All rights reserved.

Key Concepts

Aggregate expenditures function (AE)
Aggregate expenditures model

Spending multiplier (SM)
Recessionary gap

Tax multiplier
Inflationary gap

Summary

- The **Keynesian theory** argues that the economy is inherently unstable and may require government intervention to control aggregate expenditures and restore full employment. If we assume that real disposable income remains the same high proportion of real GDP, then we can substitute real GDP for real disposable income in the Keynesian model. **Investment, government spending** and **net exports** can be treated as autonomous expenditures. Adding consumption (C), investment (I), government spending (G), and net exports ($X - M$) equals the aggregate expenditures function (AE).

Keynesian Equilibrium

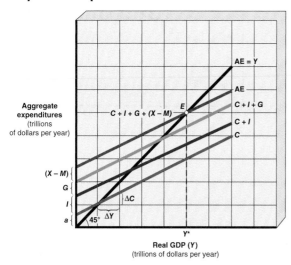

SOURCE: © Cengage Learning 2014

- The **Keynesian aggregate expenditures model** determines the equilibrium level of real GDP by the intersection of the aggregate expenditures and the aggregate output and income curves. Each equilibrium level in the economy is associated with a level of employment and corresponding unemployment rate. Aggregate expenditures and real GDP are equal, graphically, where the $AE = C + I + G + (X - M)$ line intersects the 45-degree line. At any output greater or less than the equilibrium real GDP, unintended inventory investment pressures businesses to alter aggregate output and income until equilibrium at full-employment real GDP is restored.

Keynesian Aggregate Expenditures Model

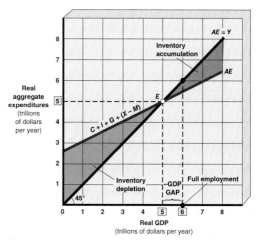

SOURCE: © Cengage Learning 2014

- The **spending multiplier** is the ratio of the change in equilibrium output to the initial change in any of the components of aggregate expenditures. Algebraically, the multiplier is the reciprocal of the marginal propensity to save. The multiplier effect causes the equilibrium level of real GDP to change by several times the initial change in spending.

Spending Multiplier

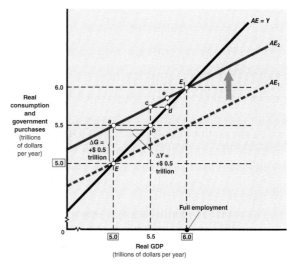

SOURCE: © Cengage Learning 2014

- A **recessionary gap** is the amount by which aggregate expenditures fall short of the amount necessary for the economy to operate at full-employment real GDP. To eliminate a negative GDP gap, the Keynesian solution is to increase autonomous spending by an amount equal to the recessionary gap and operate through the multiplier to increase equilibrium output and income.

Recessionary Gap

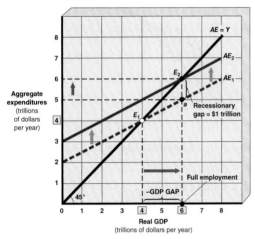

SOURCE: © Cengage Learning 2014

- The **tax multiplier** is the multiplier by which an initial change in taxes changes aggregate demand (total spending) after an infinite number of spending cycles. Expressed as a formula, the tax multiplier = 1 − spending multiplier.

- An **inflationary gap** is the amount by which aggregate expenditures exceed the amount necessary to establish full-employment equilibrium and indicates upward pressure on prices. To eliminate a positive GDP gap, the Keynesian solution is to decrease autonomous spending by an amount equal to the inflationary gap and operate through the multiplier to decrease equilibrium output and income.

Inflationary Gap

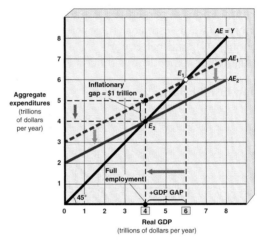

SOURCE: © Cengage Learning 2014

Summary of Conclusion Statements

- At the equilibrium level of real GDP, the total value of goods and services produced (real GDP, Y) is precisely equal to the total spending for these goods and services (aggregate expenditures, AE).
- Aggregate expenditures in Keynesian economics pull aggregate output either higher or lower toward equilibrium in the economy, as opposed to the classical view that aggregate output generates an equal amount of aggregate spending.
- Any initial change in spending by the government, households, or firms creates a chain reaction of further spending, which causes a greater cumulative change in aggregate expenditures.

Study Questions and Problems

1. Assume the level of autonomous investment is $100 billion and aggregate expenditures equal consumption and investment. Based on the following table, answer the questions below.

Employment, Output, Consumption, and Unplanned Inventory

Possible levels of employment (millions of workers)	Real GDP (output) equals disposable income (billions of dollars)	Consumption (billions of dollars)	Unplanned inventory (billions of dollars)
40	$325	$300	$_____
45	375	325	_____
50	425	350	_____
55	475	375	_____
60	525	400	_____
65	575	425	_____
70	625	450	_____

   a. Fill in the unplanned inventory column.
   b. Determine the MPC and MPS.
   c. If this economy employs a labor force of 40 million, what will happen to this level of employment? Explain and identify the equilibrium level of output.

2. Using the data given in question 1, what is the impact of adding net exports? Let imports equal $75 billion, and assume exports equal $50 billion. What is the equilibrium level of employment and output?

3. Explain the determination of equilibrium real GDP by drawing an abstract graph of the aggregate expenditures model. Label the aggregate expenditures line AE and the aggregate output line AO. Explain why the interaction of AE and AO determines the Keynesian equilibrium level of real GDP.

4. Use the aggregate expenditures model to demonstrate the multiplier effect.

5. How are changes in the MPC, changes in the MPS, and the size of the multiplier related? Answer the following questions:
   a. What is the multiplier if the MPC is 0? 0.33? 0.90?
   b. Suppose the equilibrium real GDP is $100 billion and the MPC is 4/5. How much will the equilibrium output change if businesses increase their level of investment by $10 billion?
   c. Using the data given in question 5(b), what will be the change in equilibrium real GDP if the MPC equals 2/3?

6. Assume the MPC is 0.90 and autonomous investment increases by $500 billion. What will be the impact on real GDP?

7. Suppose autonomous investment increases by $100 billion and the MPC is 0.75.
   a. Use the following table to compute four rounds of the spending multiplier effect:

Round	Components of total spending	New consumption spending (billions of dollars)
1	Investment	$_____
2	Consumption	_____
3	Consumption	_____
4	Consumption	_____
	Total spending	_____

   b. Use the spending multiplier formula to compute the final cumulative impact on aggregate spending.

8. First, use the data given in question 1, and assume the level of autonomous investment is $50 billion. If the full-employment level of output is $525 billion, what is the equilibrium level of output and employment? Does a recessionary gap or an inflationary gap exist? Second, assume the level of autonomous

investment is $150 billion. What is the equilibrium level of output and employment? Does a recessionary gap or an inflationary gap exist? Explain the consequences of an inflationary gap using the aggregate expenditures model.

9. Assume an economy is in recession with a MPC of 0.75 and there is a GDP gap of $100 billion. How much must government spending increase to eliminate the gap? Instead of increasing government spending by the amount you calculate, what would be the effect of the government cutting taxes by this amount?

10. Suppose the government wishes to eliminate an inflationary gap of $100 billion and the MPC is 0.50. How much must the government cut its spending? Instead of decreasing government spending by the amount you calculate, what would be the effect of the government increasing taxes by this amount?

For Online Exercises, go to Tucker Web site at www.cengage.com/economics/tucker.

✔ CHECKPOINT ANSWERS

Full-Employment Output, Where Are You?

A tax cut of $500 billion boosts consumer income by this amount. Because the MPC is 0.50, consumers will spend $250 billion of the tax cut and save the remaining $250 billion. To compute the impact of the rise in consumption (ΔC) on real GDP (ΔY), use this formula:

$$\Delta C \times \textbf{multiplier} = \Delta Y$$

where

$$\text{Multiplier} = \frac{1}{\text{MPS}} = \frac{1}{1 - \text{MPC}} = \frac{1}{1 - 0.50} = 2$$

Thus, $250 billion × 2 = $500 billion. The increase in real GDP from the tax cut equals $500 billion, which is added to the initial equilibrium real GDP of $15 trillion to achieve full-employment output. If you said the full-employment real GDP is $15.5 trillion, **YOU ARE CORRECT.**

How Much Spending Must Uncle Sam Cut?

The GDP gap is $500 billion real GDP. To calculate the size of the government spending cut (ΔG) required to decrease real GDP (ΔY) by $500 billion, use this formula:

$$\Delta G \times \textbf{multiplier} = -\Delta Y$$

where

$$\text{Multiplier} = \frac{1}{\text{MPS}} = \frac{1}{1 - \text{MPC}} = \frac{1}{1 - 0.90} = 10$$

Thus,

$$\Delta G = \frac{-\Delta Y}{\text{multiplier}} = \frac{-\$500 \text{ billion}}{10} = -\$50 \text{ billion}$$

If you said the size of the cut in government spending is $50 billion, **YOU ARE CORRECT.**

Sample Quiz

For an explanation of the correct answers, visit the Tucker Web site at www.cengage.com/economics/tucker.

1. Using C to represent consumption, I to represent investment, G to represent government spending, S to represent saving, X to represent exports, and M to represent imports, aggregate expenditures (AE) can be represented by
   a. $C + I + G + (X + M)$.
   b. $(C - S) + G + (X - M)$.
   c. $C + I + G + (X - M)$.
   d. $C + I + G + (X - M) - S$.

2. In the aggregate expenditures model, if aggregate expenditures (AE) are less than GDP, then
   a. inventory is depleted.
   b. inventory is unchanged.
   c. employment decreases.
   d. employment increases.

3. Which of the following are the components of aggregate expenditures?
   a. household consumption, business investment, government spending for goods and services, and net exports
   b. household consumption, business investment, government transfer payments, and net exports
   c. household consumption, business investment, government spending for goods and services, and exports
   d. household consumption, business investment, government spending for goods and services, and saving

4. In the Keynesian model, investment, government spending, and net exports are treated as autonomous expenditures, which means they are independent of
   a. expectations.
   b. the price level.
   c. political processes.
   d. real GDP.

5. As shown in Exhibit 10, equilibrium GDP is
   a. $2 trillion.
   b. $6 trillion.
   c. $10 trillion.
   d. $12 trillion.

EXHIBIT 10   **Keynesian Aggregate Expenditures Model**

SOURCE: © Cengage Learning 2014

6. As shown in Exhibit 10, if GDP is $6 trillion, the economy experiences unplanned inventory
   a. depletion of $2 trillion.
   b. depletion of $6 trillion.
   c. accumulation of $2 trillion.
   d. accumulation of $6 trillion.

7. As shown in Exhibit 10, if GDP is $14 trillion, the economy experiences unplanned inventory
   a. accumulation of $12 trillion.
   b. depletion of $14 trillion.
   c. accumulation of $2 trillion.
   d. depletion of $4 trillion.

8. The ratio of the change in GDP to an initial change in aggregate expenditures (AE) is the
   a. spending multiplier.
   b. permanent income rate.
   c. marginal expenditure rate.
   d. marginal propensity to consume.

9. The formula to compute the spending multiplier is
   a. $1/(MPC + MPS)$.
   b. $1/(1 - MPC)$.
   c. $1/(1 - MPS)$.
   d. $1/(C + I)$.

Sample Quiz *continued*

10. If the marginal propensity to consume (MPC) is 0.80, the value of the spending multiplier is
    a. 2.
    b. 5.
    c. 8.
    d. 10.

11. When households' marginal propensity to consume (MPC) increases, the size of the spending multiplier
    a. also increases.
    b. decreases.
    c. remains unchanged.
    d. reacts unpredictably.

12. Mathematically, the value of the spending multiplier is given by the formula
    a. MPC − 1.
    b. (MPC − 1)/MPC.
    c. 1/MPC.
    d. 1/MPS.

13. Assume the economy is in recession, the MPC is 0.80, and an increase of $200 billion in spending is needed to reach full employment. The target can be reached if government spending is increased by
    a. $20 billion.
    b. $200 billion.
    c. $80 billion.
    d. $40 billion.

14. Using the aggregate expenditures model, assume the aggregate expenditures (AE) line is above the 45-degree line at full-employment GDP. This vertical distance is called a(an)
    a. inflationary gap.
    b. recessionary gap.
    c. negative GDP gap.
    d. marginal propensity to consume gap.

15. Assume that full-employment real GDP is Y = $1,200 billion, the current equilibrium real GDP is Y = $1,600 billion, and the MPC = 0.8. To bring the economy to a full-employment real GDP,
    a. a recessionary gap must be bridged by increasing aggregate expenditures by $80 billion.

    b. an inflationary gap must be bridged by cutting aggregate expenditures by $80 billion.
    c. nothing is needed to bring the economy into full-employment equilibrium.
    d. a recessionary gap must be bridged by increasing aggregate expenditures by $400 billion.
    e. an inflationary gap must be bridged by cutting aggregate expenditures by $400 billion.

16. If the MPC is 0.70, then the spending multiplier is equal to
    a. 0.70.
    b. 0.30.
    c. 0.14.
    d. 3.33.
    e. 5.

17. The equilibrium level of real GDP is $1,000, the target full-employment level of real GDP is $1,500, and the marginal propensity to consume is 0.75. The target can be reached if government spending is
    a. increased by $100 billion.
    b. increased by $125 billion.
    c. increased by $500 billion.
    d. held constant.

EXHIBIT 11   **Keynesian Aggregate Expenditures Model**

SOURCE: © Cengage Learning 2014

Sample Quiz *continued*

18. In Exhibit 11, an increase in aggregate expenditures causes
    a. a movement down the aggregate expenditures curve from equilibrium real GDP of $600 to equilibrium real GDP $1,000.
    b. a movement up the aggregate expenditures curve from equilibrium real GDP of $1,200 to equilibrium real GDP $1,000.
    c. a shift of the aggregate expenditures curve to the right, causing equilibrium real GDP to increase from $600 to $1,000.
    d. a shift of the aggregate expenditures curve to the left, causing equilibrium real GDP to decrease from $1,200 to $1,000.
    e. no change in equilibrium real GDP.

19. In Exhibit 11, the value of the spending multiplier is
    a. 3.
    b. 4.
    c. 5.
    d. 2.
    e. 6.

20. In Exhibit 11, assume the AE_2 line is aggregate expenditures and $1,000 is full-employment real GDP. If the economy operates at a real disposable income of $600, there will be
    a. inventory accumulation of $100.
    b. inventory accumulation of $200.
    c. zero inventory.
    d. inventory depletion of $200.

chapter 20

Aggregate Demand and Supply

Classical economic theory held that the economy would bounce back to full employment as long as prices and wages were flexible. As the unemployment rate soared and remained high during the Great Depression, British economist John Maynard Keynes formulated a new theory with new policy implications. Instead of taking a wait-and-see policy until markets self-correct the economy, Keynes argued that policymakers must take action to influence aggregate spending through changes in government spending. The prescription for the Great Depression was simple: Increase government spending and jobs will be created. Faced with the current financial crisis, Keynesian management of the economy is currently being used to stabilize the U.S. and global economy. Keynes himself would be amazed at the scale and scope of what is happening. The opposition view today is based on the classical model that rejects the federal government stimulus package concept because the economy will self-correct to full employment.

In this chapter, you will use aggregate demand and supply analysis to study the business cycle. The chapter opens with a presentation of the aggregate demand curve and then the aggregate supply curve. Once these concepts are developed, the analysis shows why modern macroeconomics teaches that shifts in aggregate supply or aggregate demand can influence the price level, the equilibrium level of real GDP, and employment. For example, although Keynes was not concerned with the problem of inflation, his theory has implications for fighting demand-pull inflation. In this case, the government must cut spending or increase taxes to reduce aggregate demand. You will probably return to this chapter often because it provides the basic tools with which to organize your thinking about the macro economy.

In this chapter, you will learn to solve these economics puzzles:

- Why does the aggregate supply curve have three different segments?
- Would the greenhouse effect cause inflation, unemployment, or both?
- Was John Maynard Keynes's prescription for the Great Depression right?

20-1 The Aggregate Demand Curve

Here we view the collective demand for *all* goods and services, rather than the *market* demand for a particular good or service. Exhibit 1 shows the aggregate demand curve (AD), which slopes downward and to the right for a given year. The aggregate demand curve shows the level of real GDP purchased by households, businesses, government, and foreigners (net exports) at different possible price levels during a time period, ceteris paribus. Stated differently, the aggregate demand curve shows us the total dollar amount of goods and services that will be demanded in the economy at various price levels. As for the demand curve for an individual market, the lower the economy-wide price level, the greater the aggregate quantity demanded for real goods and services, ceteris paribus.

The downward slope of the aggregate demand curve shows that at a given level of aggregate income, people buy more goods and services at a lower average price level. While the horizontal axis in the market supply and demand model measures

Aggregate demand curve (AD)

The curve that shows the level of real GDP purchased by households, businesses, government, and foreigners (net exports) at different possible price levels during a time period, ceteris paribus.

EXHIBIT 1	The Aggregate Demand Curve

The aggregate demand curve (AD) shows the relationship between the price level and the level of real GDP, other things being equal. The lower the price level, the larger the GDP demanded by households, businesses, government, and foreigners. If the price level is 300 at point A, a real GDP of $8 trillion is demanded. If the price level is 200 at point B, the real GDP demanded increases to $12 trillion.

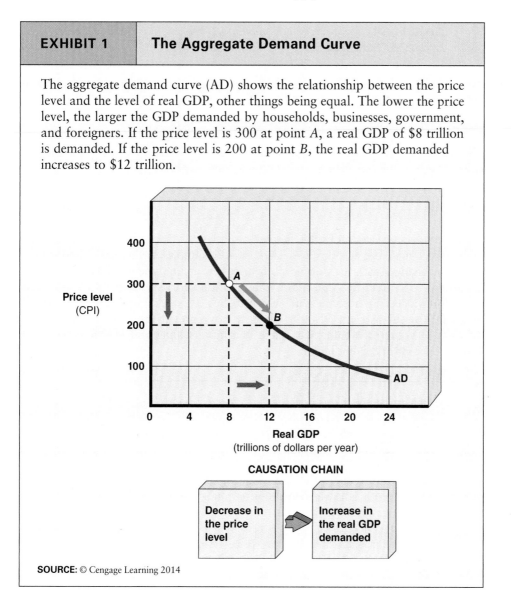

CAUSATION CHAIN

Decrease in the price level → Increase in the real GDP demanded

SOURCE: © Cengage Learning 2014

physical units, such as bushels of wheat, the horizontal axis in the aggregate demand and supply model measures the value of *final* goods and services included in real GDP. Note that the horizontal axis represents the quantity of aggregate production demanded, measured in base-year dollars. The vertical axis is an *index* of the overall price level measured by the consumer price index (CPI), rather than the price per bushel of wheat. As shown in Exhibit 1, if the price level measured by the CPI is 300 at point *A*, a real GDP of $8 trillion is demanded in a given year. If the price level is 200 at point *B*, a real GDP of $12 trillion is demanded. Note that hypothetical data is used throughout this chapter and the next unless otherwise stated.

Although the aggregate demand curve looks like a market demand curve, these concepts are different. As we move along a market demand curve, the price of related goods is assumed to be constant. But when we deal with changes in the general or average price level in an economy, this assumption is meaningless because we are using a market basket measure for *all* goods and services.

> **CONCLUSION:** *The aggregate demand curve and the demand curve are not the same concept.*

20-2 Reasons for the Aggregate Demand Curve's Shape

The reasons for the downward slope of an aggregate demand curve include the *real balances effect*, the *interest-rate effect*, and the *net exports effect*.

20-2a REAL BALANCES EFFECT

Recall from the discussion in the chapter on inflation that cash, checking deposits, savings accounts, and certificates of deposit are examples of financial assets whose real value changes with the price level. If prices are falling, the purchasing power of households rises, and they are more willing and able to spend. Suppose you have $1,000 in a checking account with which to buy 10 weeks' worth of groceries. If prices fall by 20 percent, $1,000 will now buy enough groceries for 12 weeks. This rise in your real wealth may make you more willing and able to purchase a new iPhone out of current income.

> **CONCLUSION:** *Consumers spend more on goods and services when lower prices make their dollars more valuable. Therefore, the real value of money is measured by the quantity of goods and services each dollar buys.*

Real balances effect

The impact on total spending (real GDP) caused by the inverse relationship between the price level and the real value of financial assets with fixed nominal value.

When inflation reduces the real value of fixed-value financial assets held by households, the result is lower consumption, and real GDP falls. The effect of the change in the price level on real consumption spending is called the real balances effect. The real balances effect is the impact on total spending (real GDP) caused by the inverse relationship between the price level and the real value of financial assets with fixed nominal value.

20-2b INTEREST-RATE EFFECT

A second reason why the aggregate demand curve is downward sloping involves the interest-rate effect. The interest-rate effect is the impact on total spending (real GDP) caused by the direct relationship between the price level and the interest rate. A key assumption of the aggregate demand curve is that the supply of money available for borrowing remains fixed. A high price level means people must take more dollars from their wallets and checking accounts in order to purchase goods and services. At a higher price level, the demand for borrowed money to buy products also increases and results in a higher cost of borrowing, that is, higher interest rates. Rising interest rates discourage households from borrowing to purchase homes, cars, and other consumer products. Similarly, at higher interest rates, businesses cut investment projects because the higher cost of borrowing diminishes the profitability of these investments. Thus, assuming fixed credit, an increase in the price level translates through higher interest rates into a lower real GDP.

Interest-rate effect

The impact on total spending (real GDP) caused by the direct relationship between the price level and the interest rate.

20-2c NET EXPORTS EFFECT

Whether American-made goods have lower prices than foreign goods is another important factor in determining the aggregate demand curve. A higher domestic price level tends to make U.S. goods more expensive than foreign goods, and imports rise because consumers substitute imported goods for domestic goods. An increase in the price of U.S. goods in foreign markets also causes U.S. exports to decline. Consequently, a rise in the domestic price level of an economy tends to increase imports, decrease exports, and thereby reduce the net exports component of real GDP. This condition is the net exports effect. The net exports effect is the impact on total spending (real GDP) caused by the inverse relationship between the price level and the net exports of an economy.

Exhibit 2 summarizes the three effects that explain why the aggregate demand curve in Exhibit 1 is downward sloping.

Net exports effect

The impact on total spending (real GDP) caused by the inverse relationship between the price level and the net exports of an economy.

20-3 Nonprice-level Determinants of Aggregate Demand

As was the case with individual demand curves, we must distinguish between *changes in real GDP demanded*, caused by changes in the price level, and *changes in aggregate demand*, caused by changes in one or more of the *nonprice-level determinants*. Once the ceteris paribus assumption is relaxed, changes in variables other than the price level cause a change in the location of the aggregate demand curve. Nonprice-level determinants include the consumption (C), investment (I), government spending (G), and net exports ($X - M$) components of aggregate expenditures explained in the chapter on GDP.

> **CONCLUSION:** *Any change in the individual components of aggregate expenditures shifts the aggregate demand curve.*

EXHIBIT 2	Why the Aggregate Demand Curve Is Downward Sloping
Effect	**Causation chain**
Real balances effect	Price level decreases → Purchasing power rises → Wealth rises → Consumers buy more goods → Real GDP demanded increases
Interest-rate effect	Price level decreases → Purchasing power rises → Demand for fixed supply of credit falls → Interest rates fall → Businesses and households borrow and buy more goods → Real GDP demanded increases
Net exports effect	Price level decreases → U.S. goods become less expensive than foreign goods → Americans and foreigners buy more U.S. goods → Exports rise and imports fall → Real GDP demanded increases

SOURCE: © Cengage Learning 2014

Exhibit 3 illustrates the link between an increase in expenditures and an increase in aggregate demand. Begin at point A on aggregate demand curve AD_1, with a price level of 200 and a real GDP of $12 trillion. Assume the price level remains constant at 200 and the aggregate demand curve increases from AD_1 to AD_2. Consequently, the level of real GDP rises from $12 trillion (point A) to $16 trillion (point B) at the price level of 200. The cause might be that consumers have become more optimistic about the future and their consumption expenditures (C) have risen. Another cause might be that a tax cut increased take-home (disposable income) and consumer purchases increased at each possible price level. Or possibly an increase in business optimism has increased profit expectations, and the level of investment (I) has risen because businesses are spending more for plants and equipment. The same increase in aggregate demand could also have been caused by a boost in government spending (G) or a rise in net exports ($X - M$). A swing to pessimistic expectations by consumers or firms will cause the aggregate demand curve to shift leftward. A leftward shift in the aggregate demand curve may also be caused by a tax increase or a decrease in government spending or net exports.

20-4 The Aggregate Supply Curve

Just as we must distinguish between the aggregate demand and market demand curves, the theory for a market supply curve does not apply directly to the aggregate supply curve. Keeping this condition in mind, we can define the aggregate supply curve (AS) as the curve that shows the level of real GDP produced at different possible price levels during a time period, ceteris paribus. Stated simply, the aggregate supply curve shows us the total dollar amount of goods and services produced in an economy at various price levels. Given this general definition, we must pause to discuss two opposing views—the Keynesian horizontal aggregate supply curve and the classical vertical aggregate supply curve.

Aggregate supply curve (AS)

The curve that shows the level of real GDP produced at different possible price levels during a time period, ceteris paribus.

EXHIBIT 3	A Shift in the Aggregate Demand Curve

At the price level of 200, the real GDP level is \$12 trillion at point *A* on AD_1. An increase in one of the nonprice-level determinants of consumption (*C*), investment (*I*), government spending (*G*), or net exports (*X* – *M*) causes the level of real GDP to rise to \$16 trillion at point *B* on AD_2. Because this effect occurs at any price level, an increase in aggregate expenditures shifts the AD curve rightward. Conversely, a decrease in aggregate expenditures shifts the AD curve leftward.

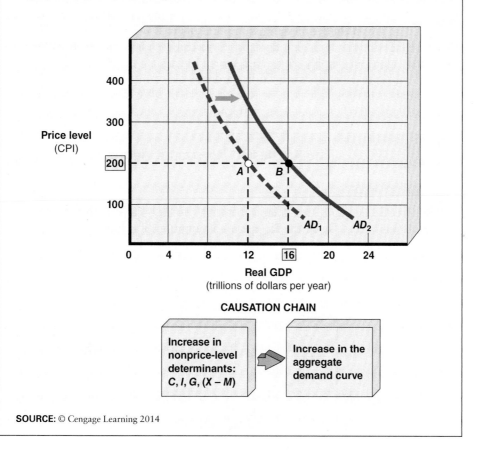

SOURCE: © Cengage Learning 2014

20-4a KEYNESIAN VIEW OF AGGREGATE SUPPLY

Keynes wrote in a time of great uncertainty and instability. In 1936, seven years after the beginning of the Great Depression and three years before the beginning of World War II, John Maynard Keynes published *The General Theory of Employment, Interest, and Money*. In this book, Keynes, a Cambridge University economist, argued that price and wage inflexibility during a recession means that unemployment can be a prolonged affair. Unless an economy trapped in a depression or severe recession is rescued by an increase in aggregate demand, full employment will not be achieved. This Keynesian prediction calls for government to intervene and actively manage aggregate demand to avoid a depression or recession.

Why do Keynesians assume that product prices and wages are fixed? Reasons for upward inflexibility include the following: First, during a deep recession, there are many idle resources in the economy. Consequently, producers are willing to sell at current prices because there are no shortages to put upward pressure on prices. Second, the supply of unemployed workers willing to work for the prevailing wage rate diminishes the power of workers to increase their wages. Reasons for downward inflexibility include: First, union contracts prevent businesses from lowering wage rates. Second, minimum wage laws prevent lower wages. Third, employers believe that cutting wages lowers worker morale and productivity. Therefore, during a recession, employers prefer to freeze wages and lay off or reduce hours for some of their workers until the economy recovers. In fact, the CPI for the last month of each recession since 1948 was at or above the CPI for the first month of the recession. Given the Keynesian assumption of fixed or rigid product prices and wages, changes in the aggregate demand curve cause changes in real GDP along a horizontal aggregate supply curve. In short, Keynesian theory argues that only shifts in aggregate demand can revitalize a depressed economy.

Exhibit 4 portrays the core of Keynesian theory. We begin at equilibrium E_1, with a fixed price level of 200. Given aggregate demand schedule AD_1, the equilibrium

EXHIBIT 4	The Keynesian Horizontal Aggregate Supply Curve

The increase in aggregate demand from AD_1 to AD_2 causes a new equilibrium at E_2. Given the Keynesian assumption of a fixed price level, changes in aggregate demand cause changes in real GDP along the horizontal portion of the aggregate supply curve, AS. Keynesian theory argues that only shifts in aggregate demand possess the ability to restore a depressed economy to the full-employment output.

CAUSATION CHAIN

Government spending (G) increases ⇒ Aggregate demand increases and the economy moves from E_1 to E_2 ⇒ Price level remains constant, while real GDP and employment rise

SOURCE: © Cengage Learning 2014

level of real GDP is $8 trillion. Now government spending (G) increases, causing aggregate demand to rise from AD_1 to AD_2 and equilibrium to shift from E_1 to E_2 along the horizontal aggregate supply curve (AS). At E_2, the economy moves to $12 trillion, which is closer to the full-employment GDP of $16 trillion.

> **CONCLUSION:** *When the aggregate supply curve is horizontal and an economy is in recession below full employment, the only effects of an increase in aggregate demand are increases in real GDP and employment, while the price level does not change. Stated simply, the Keynesian view is that "demand creates its own supply."*

20-4b CLASSICAL VIEW OF AGGREGATE SUPPLY

Prior to the Great Depression of the 1930s, a group of economists known as the *classical economists* dominated economic thinking.[1] The founder of the classical school of economics was Adam Smith (discussed in the chapter on economies in transition). Macroeconomics had not developed as a separate economic theory, and classical economics was therefore based primarily on microeconomic market equilibrium theory. The classical school of economics was mainstream economics from the 1770s to the Great Depression era. The classical economists believed in the *laissez-faire* "leave it alone" theory that the economy was self-regulating and would correct itself over time without government intervention. The classical economists believed, as you studied in Chapter 4, that the forces of supply and demand naturally achieve full employment in the economy because flexible prices (including wages and interest rates) in competitive markets bring all markets to equilibrium. After a temporary adjustment period, markets always clear because firms sell all goods and services offered for sale. In short, recessions naturally cure themselves because the capitalistic price system automatically restores full employment.

Exhibit 5 uses the aggregate demand and supply model to illustrate the classical view that the aggregate supply curve, AS, is a vertical line at the full-employment output of $16 trillion. The vertical shape of the classical aggregate supply curve is based on two assumptions. First, the economy normally operates at its full-employment output level. Second, the price level of products and production costs change by the same percentage, that is, proportionally, in order to maintain a full-employment level of output. This classical theory of flexible prices and wages is at odds with the Keynesian concept of sticky (inflexible) prices and wages.

Exhibit 5 also illustrates why classical economists believe a market economy over time automatically self-corrects without government intervention to full employment. Following the classical scenario, the economy is initially in equilibrium at E_1, the price level is 300, real output is at its full-employment level of $16 trillion, and the aggregate demand curve AD_1 traces total spending. Now suppose private spending falls because households and businesses are pessimistic about economic conditions. This condition causes AD_1 to shift leftward to AD_2. At a price level of 300, the immediate effect is that aggregate output exceeds aggregate spending by $4 trillion ($E_1$ to E'), and unexpected inventory accumulation occurs. To eliminate unsold inventories resulting from the decrease in aggregate demand, business firms temporarily cut back on production and reduce the price level from 300 to 200.

---

[1]The classical economists included Adam Smith, J. B. Say, David Ricardo, John Stuart Mill, Thomas Malthus, Alfred Marshall, and others.

| EXHIBIT 5 | The Classical Vertical Aggregate Supply Curve |

Classical theory teaches that prices and wages adjust to keep the economy operating at its full-employment output of $16 trillion. A decline in aggregate demand from AD_1 to AD_2 will temporarily cause a surplus of $4 trillion, the distance from E' to E_1. Businesses respond by cutting the price level from 300 to 200. As a result, consumers increase their purchases because of the real balances effect, and wages adjust downward. Thus, classical economists predict the economy is self-correcting and will restore full employment at point E_2. E_1 and E_2 therefore represent points along a classical vertical aggregate supply curve, AS.

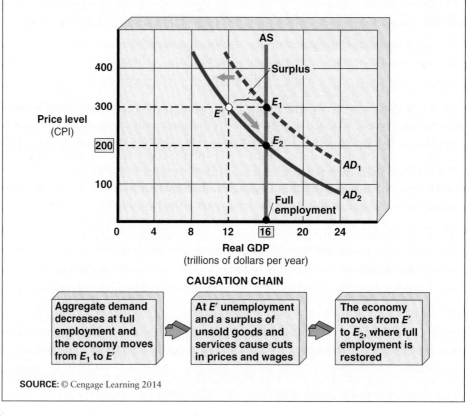

CAUSATION CHAIN

| Aggregate demand decreases at full employment and the economy moves from E_1 to E' | → | At E' unemployment and a surplus of unsold goods and services cause cuts in prices and wages | → | The economy moves from E' to E_2, where full employment is restored |

SOURCE: © Cengage Learning 2014

At E', the decline in aggregate output in response to the surplus also affects prices in the factor markets. As a result of the economy moving from point E_1 to E', there is a decrease in the demand for labor, natural resources, and other inputs used to produce products. This surplus condition in the factor markets means that some workers who are willing to work are laid off and compete with those who still have jobs by reducing their wage demands. Owners of natural resources and capital likewise cut their prices.

How can the classical economists believe that prices and wages are completely flexible? The answer is contained in the *real balances effect*, explained earlier. When businesses reduce the price level from 300 to 200, the cost of living falls by the same proportion. Once the price level falls by 33 percent, a nominal or money wage rate of, say, $21 per hour will purchase 33 percent more groceries after the fall in product prices than it would have before the fall. Workers will therefore accept a pay cut of 33 percent, or $7 per hour. Any worker who refuses the lower wage rate of $14 per hour will be replaced by an unemployed worker willing to accept the going rate.

Exhibit 5 shows an economy-wide proportional fall in prices and wages by the movement downward along AD_2 from E' to a new equilibrium at E_2. At E_2, the economy has self-corrected through downwardly flexible prices and wages to its full-employment level of $16 trillion worth of real GDP at the lower price level of 200. E_1 and E_2 therefore represent points along a classical vertical aggregate supply curve, AS. (The classical model is explained in more detail in the appendix to this chapter.)

> **CONCLUSION:** *When the aggregate supply curve is vertical at the full-employment GDP, the only effect over time of a change in aggregate demand is a change in the price level. Stated simply, the classical view is that "supply creates its own demand."[2]*

Although Keynes himself did not use the AD-AS model, we can use Exhibit 5 to distinguish between Keynes's view and the classical theory of flexible prices and wages. Keynes believed that once the demand curve has shifted from AD_1 to AD_2, the surplus (the distance from E' to E_1) will persist because he rejected price-wage downward flexibility. The economy therefore will remain at the less-than-full-employment output of $12 trillion until the aggregate demand curve shifts rightward and returns to its initial position at AD_1.

> **CONCLUSION:** *Keynesian theory rejects classical theory for an economy in recession because Keynesians argue that during a recession, prices and wages do not adjust downward to restore an economy to full-employment real GDP.*

20-5 Three Ranges of the Aggregate Supply Curve

Having studied the differing theories of the classical economists and Keynes, we will now discuss an eclectic or general view of how the shape of the aggregate supply curve varies as real GDP expands or contracts. The aggregate supply curve, AS, in Exhibit 6 has three distinct ranges or segments, labeled (1) *Keynesian range*, (2) *intermediate range*, and (3) *classical range*.

The Keynesian range is the horizontal segment of the aggregate supply curve, which represents an economy in a severe recession. In Exhibit 6, below real GDP Y_K, the price level remains constant as the level of real GDP rises. Between Y_K and the full-employment output of Y_F, the price level rises as the real GDP level rises. The intermediate range is the rising segment of the aggregate supply curve, which

Keynesian range

The horizontal segment of the aggregate supply curve, which represents an economy in a severe recession.

Intermediate range

The rising segment of the aggregate supply curve, which represents an economy as it approaches full-employment output.

---

[2]This quotation is known as Say's Law, named after the French classical economist Jean-Baptiste Say (1767–1832).

EXHIBIT 6	The Three Ranges of the Aggregate Supply Curve

The aggregate supply curve shows the relationship between the price level and the level of real GDP supplied. It consists of three distinct ranges: (1) a Keynesian range between 0 and Y_K, wherein the price level is constant for an economy in severe recession; (2) an intermediate range between Y_K and Y_F, where both the price level and the level of real GDP vary as an economy approaches full employment; and (3) a classical range, where the price level can vary while the level of real GDP remains constant at the full-employment level of output, Y_F.

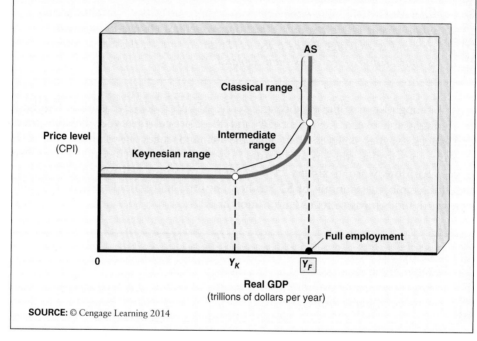

SOURCE: © Cengage Learning 2014

Classical range

The vertical segment of the aggregate supply curve, which represents an economy at full-employment output.

represents an economy approaching full-employment output. Finally, at Y_F, the level of real GDP remains constant, and only the price level rises. The classical range is the vertical segment of the aggregate supply curve, which represents an economy at full-employment output. We will now examine the rationale for each of these three distinct ranges.

20-5a AGGREGATE DEMAND AND AGGREGATE SUPPLY MACROECONOMIC EQUILIBRIUM

In Exhibit 7, the macroeconomic equilibrium level of real GDP corresponding to the point of equality, E, is $8 trillion, and the equilibrium price level is 200. This is the unique combination of price level and output level that equates how much people want to buy with the amount businesses want to produce and sell. Because the entire real GDP value of final products is bought and sold at the price level of 200, there is no upward or downward pressure for the macroeconomic equilibrium

EXHIBIT 7	The Aggregate Demand and Aggregate Supply Model

Macroeconomic equilibrium occurs where the aggregate demand curve, AD, and the aggregate supply curve, AS, intersect. In this case, equilibrium, *E*, is located at the far end of the Keynesian range, where the price level is 200 and the equilibrium output is $8 trillion. In macroeconomic equilibrium, businesses neither overestimate nor underestimate the real GDP demanded at the prevailing price level.

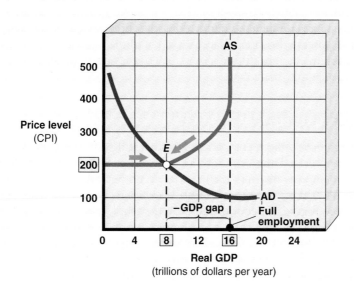

SOURCE: © Cengage Learning 2014

to change. Note that the economy shown in Exhibit 7 is operating on the edge of the Keynesian range, with a negative GDP gap of $8 trillion.

Suppose that in Exhibit 7, the level of output on the AS curve is below $8 trillion and the AD curve remains fixed. At a price level of 200, the real GDP demanded exceeds the real GDP supplied. Under such circumstances, businesses cannot fill orders quickly enough, and inventories are drawn down unexpectedly. Business managers react by hiring more workers and producing more output. Because the economy is operating in the Keynesian range, the price level remains constant at 200. The opposite scenario occurs if the level of real GDP supplied on the AS curve exceeds the real GDP in the intermediate range between $8 trillion and $16 trillion. In this output segment, the price level is between 200 and 400, and businesses face sales that are less than expected. In this case, unintended inventories of unsold goods pile up on the shelves, and management will lay off workers, cut back on production, and reduce prices.

This adjustment process continues until the equilibrium price level and output level are reached at point *E* and there is no upward or downward pressure for the price level to change. Here the production decisions of sellers in the economy equal the total spending decisions of buyers during the given period of time.

> **CONCLUSION:** *At macroeconomic equilibrium, sellers neither overestimate nor underestimate the real GDP demanded at the prevailing price level.*

20-6 Changes in the AD-AS Macroeconomic Equilibrium

One explanation of the business cycle is that the aggregate demand curve moves along a stationary aggregate supply curve. The next step in our analysis therefore is to *shift* the aggregate demand curve along the three ranges of the aggregate supply curve and observe the impact on real GDP and the price level. As the macroeconomic equilibrium changes, the economy experiences more or fewer problems with inflation and unemployment.

20-6a KEYNESIAN RANGE

Keynes's macroeconomic theory offered a powerful solution to the Great Depression. Keynes perceived the economy as being driven by aggregate demand, and Exhibit 8(a) demonstrates this theory with hypothetical data. The range of real GDP below $8 trillion is consistent with Keynesian price and wage inflexibility. Assume the economy is in equilibrium at E_1, with a price level of 200 and a real GDP of $4 trillion. In this case, the economy is in recession far below the full-employment GDP of $16 trillion. The Keynesian prescription for a recession is to increase aggregate demand until the economy achieves full employment. Because the aggregate supply curve is horizontal in the Keynesian range, "demand creates its own supply." Suppose demand shifts rightward from AD_1 to AD_2 and a new equilibrium is established at E_2. Even at the higher real GDP level of $8 trillion, the price level remains at 200. Stated differently, aggregate output can expand throughout this range without raising prices. This is because in the Keynesian range, substantial idle production capacity (including property and unemployed workers competing for available jobs) can be put to work at existing prices.

> **CONCLUSION:** *As aggregate demand increases in the Keynesian range, the price level remains constant as real GDP expands.*

20-6b INTERMEDIATE RANGE

The intermediate range in Exhibit 8(b) is between $8 trillion and $16 trillion worth of real GDP. As output increases in the range of the aggregate supply curve near the full-employment level of output, the considerable slack in the economy disappears. Assume an economy is initially in equilibrium at E_3 and aggregate demand increases from AD_3 to AD_4. As a result, the level of real GDP rises from $8 trillion to $12 trillion, and the price level rises from 200 to 250. In this output range,

EXHIBIT 8	Effects of Increases in Aggregate Demand

The effect of a rightward shift in the aggregate demand curve on the price and output levels depends on the range of the aggregate supply curve in which the shift occurs. In part (a), an increase in aggregate demand causing the equilibrium to change from E_1 to E_2 in the Keynesian range will increase real GDP from $4 trillion to $8 trillion, but the price level will remain unchanged at 200.

In part (b), an increase in aggregate demand causing the equilibrium to change from E_3 to E_4 in the intermediate range will increase real GDP from $8 trillion to $12 trillion, and the price level will rise from 200 to 250.

In part (c), an increase in aggregate demand causing the equilibrium to change from E_5 to E_6 in the classical range will increase the price level from 300 to 400, but real GDP will not increase beyond the full-employment level of $16 trillion.

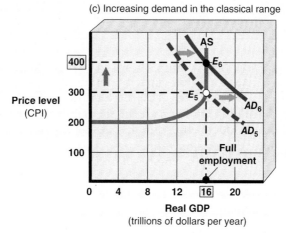

SOURCE: © Cengage Learning 2014

several factors contribute to inflation. First, *bottlenecks* (obstacles to output flow) develop when some firms have no unused capacity and other firms operate below full capacity. Suppose the steel industry is operating at full capacity and cannot fill all its orders for steel. An inadequate supply of one resource, such as steel, can hold up auto production even though the auto industry is operating well below capacity. Consequently, the bottleneck causes firms to raise the price of steel and, in turn, autos. Second, a shortage of certain labor skills while firms are earning higher profits causes businesses to expect that labor will exert its power to obtain sizable wage increases, so businesses raise prices. Wage demands are more difficult to reject when the economy is prospering because businesses fear workers will change jobs or strike. Besides, businesses believe higher prices can be passed on to consumers quite easily because consumers expect higher prices as output expands to near full capacity. Third, as the economy approaches full employment, firms must use less productive workers and less efficient machinery. This inefficiency creates higher production costs, which are passed on to consumers in the form of higher prices.

> **CONCLUSION:** *In the intermediate range, increases in aggregate demand increase both the price level and the real GDP.*

20-6c CLASSICAL RANGE

While inflation resulting from an outward shift in aggregate demand was no problem in the Keynesian range and only a minor problem in the intermediate range, it becomes a serious problem in the classical, or vertical, range.

> **CONCLUSION:** *Once the economy reaches full-employment output in the classical range, additional increases in aggregate demand merely cause inflation, rather than more real GDP.*

Assume the economy shown in Exhibit 8(c) is in equilibrium at E_5, which intersects AS at the full-capacity output. Now suppose aggregate demand shifts rightward from AD_5 to AD_6. Because the aggregate supply curve AS is vertical at \$16 trillion, this increase in the aggregate demand curve boosts the price level from 300 to 400, but it fails to expand real GDP. The explanation is that once the economy operates at capacity, businesses raise their prices in order to ration fully employed resources to those willing to pay the highest prices.

In summary, the AD-AS model presented in this chapter is a combination of the conflicting assumptions of the Keynesian and classical theories separated by an intermediate range, which fits neither extreme precisely. Be forewarned that in later chapters, you will encounter a continuing great controversy over the shape of the aggregate supply curve. Modern-day classical economists believe the entire aggregate supply curve is steep, or vertical. In contrast, Keynesian economists contend that the aggregate supply curve is much flatter, or horizontal.

20-6d THE AD-AS MODEL FOR 2008–2009 DURING THE GREAT RECESSION

Exhibit 9 uses actual data to illustrate the AD-AS model. At E_1, the economy in the third quarter of 2008 was operating at a CPI of 219 and a real GDP of $13.3 trillion, which was below the full-employment real GDP of $13.4 trillion. In 2008, the combination of home prices falling sharply and a plunge in stock prices destroyed household wealth. At the same time, new home construction fell rapidly, which decreased investment spending. Recall from the chapter on gross domestic product that new residential housing is included in investment spending (I). This recessionary condition is illustrated by a movement between E_1 and E_2 caused by the aggregate demand curve decreasing from AD_1 to AD_2 along the intermediate range of the aggregate supply curve AS. At E_2 in the fourth quarter of 2008, the CPI dropped to 212, and real GDP decreased from $13.3 trillion to $13.1 trillion. Next, the aggregate demand curve decreased again from AD_2 to AD_3 in the second

EXHIBIT 9	Effect of Decreases in Aggregate Demand During 2008–2009 of the Great Recession

Beginning in the third quarter of 2008 at E_1, the aggregate demand curve shifted leftward from E_1 to E_2 in the fourth quarter of 2008 along the intermediate range of the aggregate supply curve, AS. The CPI fell from 219 to 212, and real GDP fell from $13.3 trillion to $13.1 trillion. Next, the aggregate demand curve decreased from AD_2 at E_2 to AD_3 at E_3 in the second quarter of 2009 along the Keynesian range of the aggregate supply curve. Here the price level remained constant, and real GDP fell from $13.1 trillion to $12.9 trillion.

SOURCES: Bureau of Economic Analysis, *National Income Accounts*, http://www.bea.gov/national/nipaweb/ SelectTable.asp?Selected=Y, Table 1.1.6 and Bureau of Labor Statistics, *Consumer Price Index*, http://data.bls .gov/cgi-bin/surveymost?cu.

quarter of 2009 along the flat Keynesian range between E_2 and E_3. Here the price level remained approximately constant at 212, while real GDP declined from $13.1 trillion to $12.9 trillion. Although not shown explicitly in the exhibit, the unemployment rate rose during this period from 4.7 percent to 9.5 percent.

20-7 Nonprice-Level Determinants of Aggregate Supply

Our discussion so far has explained changes in real GDP supplied resulting from changes in the aggregate demand curve, given a stationary aggregate supply curve. Now we consider the situation when the aggregate demand curve is stationary and the aggregate supply curve shifts as a result of changes in one or more of the *nonprice-level determinants*. The nonprice-level factors affecting aggregate supply include resource prices (domestic and imported), technological change, taxes, subsidies, and regulations. Note that each of these factors affects production costs. At a given price level, the profit businesses make at any level of real GDP depends on production costs. If costs change, firms respond by changing their output. Lower production costs shift the aggregate supply curve rightward, indicating greater real GDP is supplied at any price level. Conversely, higher production costs shift the aggregate supply curve leftward, meaning less real GDP is supplied at any price level.

Exhibit 10 represents a supply-side explanation of the business cycle, in contrast to the demand-side case presented in Exhibit 8. (Note that for simplicity, the aggregate supply curve can be drawn using only the intermediate segment.) The economy begins in equilibrium at point E_1, with real GDP at $10 trillion and the price level at 175. Then suppose labor unions become less powerful, and their weaker bargaining position causes the wage rate to fall. With lower labor costs per unit of output, businesses seek to increase profits by expanding production at any price level. Hence, the aggregate supply curve shifts rightward from AS_1 to AS_2, and equilibrium changes from E_1 to E_2. As a result, real GDP increases $2 trillion, and the price level decreases from 175 to 150. Changes in other nonprice-level factors also cause an increase in aggregate supply. Lower oil prices, greater entrepreneurship, lower taxes, and reduced government regulation are other examples of conditions that lower production costs and therefore cause a rightward shift of the aggregate supply curve.

What kinds of events might raise production costs and shift the aggregate supply curve leftward? Perhaps there is war in the Persian Gulf or the Organization of Petroleum Exporting Countries (OPEC) disrupts supplies of oil, and higher energy prices spread throughout the economy. Under such a "supply shock," businesses decrease their output at any price level in response to higher production costs per unit. Similarly, larger-than-expected wage increases, higher taxes to protect the environment (see Exhibit 8(a) in Chapter 4), greater government regulation, or firms having to pay higher health insurance premiums would increase production costs and therefore shift the aggregate supply curve leftward. A leftward shift in the aggregate supply curve is discussed further in the next section.

Exhibit 11 summarizes the nonprice-level determinants of aggregate demand and supply for further study and review. In the chapter on monetary policy, you will learn how changes in the supply of money in the economy can also shift the aggregate demand curve and influence macroeconomic performance.

EXHIBIT 10	A Rightward Shift in the Aggregate Supply Curve

Holding the aggregate demand curve constant, the impact on the price level and real GDP depends on whether the aggregate supply curve shifts to the right or the left. A rightward shift of the aggregate supply curve from AS_1 to AS_2 will increase real GDP from $10 trillion to $12 trillion and reduce the price level from 175 to 150.

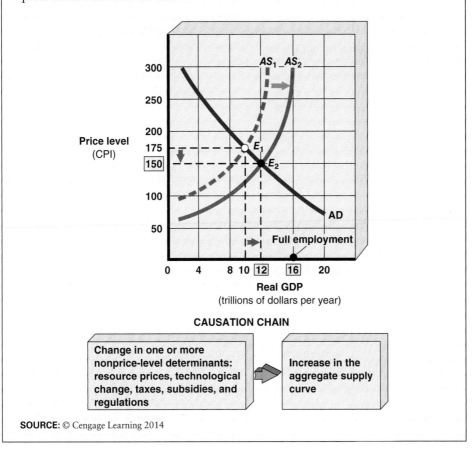

CAUSATION CHAIN

Change in one or more nonprice-level determinants: resource prices, technological change, taxes, subsidies, and regulations	→	Increase in the aggregate supply curve

SOURCE: © Cengage Learning 2014

20-8 Cost-Push and Demand-Pull Inflation Revisited

We now apply the aggregate demand and aggregate supply model to the two types of inflation introduced in the chapter on inflation. This section begins with a historical example of *cost-push inflation* caused by a decrease in the aggregate supply curve. Next, another historical example illustrates *demand-pull inflation*, caused by an increase in the aggregate demand curve.

During the late 1970s and early 1980s, the U.S. economy experienced stagflation. Stagflation is the condition that occurs when an economy experiences the twin maladies of high unemployment and rapid inflation simultaneously.

Stagflation

The condition that occurs when an economy experiences the twin maladies of high unemployment and rapid inflation simultaneously.

EXHIBIT 11	Summary of the Nonprice-Level Determinants of Aggregate Demand and Aggregate Supply
Nonprice-level determinants of aggregate demand (total spending)	**Nonprice-level determinants of aggregate supply**
1. Consumption (*C*)	1. Resource prices (domestic and imported)
2. Investment (*I*)	2. Taxes
3. Government spending (*G*)	3. Technological change
4. Net exports (*X* − *M*)	4. Subsidies
	5. Regulation

SOURCE: © Cengage Learning 2014

Cost-push inflation

An increase in the general price level resulting from an increase in the cost of production that causes the aggregate supply curve to shift leftward.

How could this happen? The dramatic increase in the price of imported oil in 1973–1974 was a villain explained by a *cost-push inflation* scenario. Cost-push inflation, defined in terms of our macro model, is a rise in the price level resulting from a decrease in the aggregate supply curve while the aggregate demand curve remains fixed. As a result of cost-push inflation, real output and employment decrease.

Exhibit 12(a) uses actual data to show how a leftward shift in the supply curve can cause stagflation. In this exhibit, aggregate demand curve *AD* and aggregate supply curve AS_{73} represent the U.S. economy in 1973. Equilibrium was at point E_1, with the price level (CPI) at 44.4 and real GDP at $4,341 billion. Then, in 1974, the impact of a major supply shock shifted the aggregate supply curve leftward from AS_{73} to AS_{74}. The explanation for this shock was the oil embargo instituted by OPEC in retaliation for U.S. support of Israel in its war with the Arabs. Assuming a stable aggregate demand curve between 1973 and 1974, the punch from the energy shock resulted in a new equilibrium at point E_2, with the 1974 CPI at 49.3. The inflation rate for 1973 was 6.2 percent and for 1974 was 11 percent [(49.3 − 44.4)/44.4] × 100. Real GDP fell from $4,341 billion in 1973 to $4,319 billion in 1974, and the unemployment rate (not shown directly in the exhibit) climbed from 4.9 percent to 5.6 percent between these two years.[3]

Demand-pull inflation

A rise in the general price level resulting from an excess of total spending (demand) caused by a rightward shift in the aggregate demand curve.

In contrast, an outward shift in the aggregate demand curve can result in *demand-pull inflation*. Demand-pull inflation, in terms of our macro model, is a rise in the price level resulting from an increase in the aggregate demand curve while the aggregate supply curve remains fixed. Again, we can use aggregate demand and supply analysis and actual data to explain demand-pull inflation. In 1965, when the unemployment rate of 4.5 percent was close to the 4 percent natural rate of unemployment, real government spending increased sharply to fight the Vietnam War without a tax increase (an income tax surcharge was enacted in 1968). The inflation rate jumped sharply from 1.6 percent in 1965 to 2.9 percent in 1966.

---

[3]*Economic Report of the President, 2012*, http://www.gpo.gov/fdsys/pkg/ERP-2012/content-detail.html, Tables B-2, B-42, B-62, and B-64.

EXHIBIT 12	Cost-Push and Demand-Pull Inflation

Parts (a) and (b) illustrate the distinction between cost-push inflation and demand-pull inflation. Cost-push inflation is inflation that results from a decrease in the aggregate supply curve. In part (a), higher oil prices in 1973 caused the aggregate supply curve to shift leftward from AS_{73} to AS_{74}. As a result, real GDP fell from \$4,341 billion to \$4,319 billion, and the price level (CPI) rose from 44.4 to 49.3. This combination of higher price level and lower real output is called stagflation.

As shown in part (b), demand-pull inflation is inflation that results from an increase in aggregate demand beyond the Keynesian range of output. Government spending increased to fight the Vietnam War without a tax increase, causing the aggregate demand curve to shift rightward from AD_{65} to AD_{66}. Consequently, real GDP rose from \$3,191 billion to \$3,399 billion, and the price level (CPI) rose from 31.5 to 32.4.

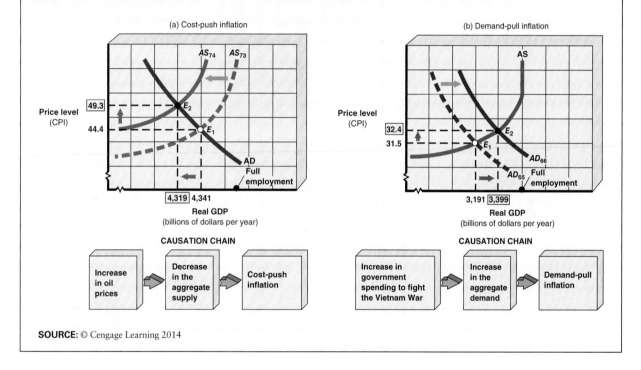

SOURCE: © Cengage Learning 2014

Exhibit 12(b) illustrates what happened to the economy between 1965 and 1966. Suppose the economy was operating in 1965 at E_1, which is in the intermediate output range. The impact of the increase in military spending shifted the aggregate demand curve from AD_{65} to AD_{66}, and the economy moved upward along the aggregate supply curve until it reached E_2. Holding the aggregate supply curve constant, the AD-AS model predicts that increasing aggregate demand at near full employment causes demand-pull inflation. As shown in Exhibit 12(b), real GDP increased from \$3,191 billion in 1963 to \$3,399 billion in 1966, and the CPI rose from 31.5 to 32.4. Thus, the inflation rate for 1966 was 2.9 percent $[(32.4 - 31.5)/31.5] \times 100$. Corresponding to the rise in real output, the unemployment rate of 4.5 percent in 1965 fell to 3.8 percent in 1966.[4]

---

[4]Ibid.

Was John Maynard Keynes Right?

Applicable Concept: aggregate demand and aggregate supply analysis

In *The General Theory of Employment, Interest, and Money,* Keynes wrote:

The ideas of economists and political philosophers, both when they are right and when they are wrong, are more powerful than is commonly understood. Indeed the world is ruled by little else. Practical men, who believe themselves to be quite exempt from any intellectual influences, are usually the slaves of some defunct economist. Madmen in authority, who hear voices in the air, are distilling their frenzy from some academic scribbler of a few years back.... There are not many who are influenced by new theories after they are twenty-five or thirty years of age, so that the ideas which civil servants and politicians and even agitators apply to current events are not likely to be the newest.[1]

Keynes (1883–1946) is regarded as the father of modern macroeconomics. He was the son of an eminent English economist, John Neville Keynes, who was a lecturer in economics and logic at Cambridge University. Keynes was educated at Eton and Cambridge in mathematics and probability theory, but ultimately he selected the field of economics and accepted a lectureship in economics at Cambridge.

Keynes was a many-faceted man who was an honored and supremely successful member of the British academic, financial, and political upper class. He amassed a $2 million personal fortune by speculating in stocks, international currencies, and commodities. (Use CPI index numbers to compute the equivalent amount in today's dollars.) In addition to making a huge fortune for himself, Keynes served as a trustee of King's College and increased its endowment over tenfold.

Keynes was a prolific scholar who is best remembered for *The General Theory,* published in 1936. This work made a convincing attack on the classical theory that capitalism would self-correct from a severe recession. Keynes based his model on the belief that increasing aggregate demand will achieve full employment, while prices and wages remain inflexible. Moreover, his bold policy prescription was for the government to raise its spending and/or reduce taxes in order to increase the economy's aggregate demand curve and put the unemployed back to work.

Price Level, Real GDP, and Unemployment Rate, 1933–1941

Year	CPI	Real GDP (billions of 2000 dollars)	Unemployment rate (percent)
1933	13.0	$ 635	24.9%
1939	13.9	951	17.2
1940	14.0	1,034	14.6
1941	14.7	1,211	9.9

SOURCES: Bureau of Labor Statistics, ftp://ftp.bls.gov/pub/special.requests/cpi/cpiai.txt, Bureau of Economic Analysis, *National Economic Accounts,* http://ww.bea.gov/iTable/iTable.cfm?ReqID=9&step=1, Table 1.1.6 and *Economic Report of the President, 2012,* http://www.gpo.gov/fdsys/pkg/ERP-2012/content-detail.html, Table B-35.

Analyze the Issue

Was Keynes correct? Based on the above data, use the aggregate demand and aggregate supply model to explain Keynes's theory that increases in aggregate demand propel an economy toward full employment.

---

1. J. M. Keynes, *The General Theory of Employment, Interest, and Money* (London: Macmillan, 1936), p. 383.

Sources: © Cengage Learning 2014

In summary, the aggregate supply and aggregate demand curves shift in different directions for various reasons in a given time period. These shifts in the aggregate supply and aggregate demand curves cause upswings and downswings in real GDP—the business cycle. A leftward shift in the aggregate demand curve, for example, can cause a recession. Whereas, a rightward shift of the aggregate demand curve can cause real GDP and employment to rise, and the economy recovers. A leftward shift in the aggregate supply curve can cause a downswing, and a rightward shift might cause an upswing.

> **CONCLUSION:** *The business cycle is a result of shifts in the aggregate demand and aggregate supply curves.*

20-9 Increase in Both Aggregate Demand and Aggregate Supply Curves

Let the trumpets blow! Aggregate demand and supply curves will now edify you by explaining the U.S. economy from the mid-1990s through 2000. Begin in Exhibit 13 at E_1 with real GDP at $8,031 billion and the CPI at 152. As shown in the AD-AS model for 1995, the economy operated below full employment (5.6 percent unemployment rate, not explicitly shown). Over the next five years, the U.S. economy moved to E_2 in 2000 and experienced strong growth in real GDP (from $8,031 billion to $9,817 billion) and mild inflation (the CPI increased from 152 to 172, which is 13.1 percent, or 2.6 percent per year).

The movement from E_1 (below full employment) to E_2 (full employment) was caused by an increase in AD_{95} to AD_{00} and an increase in AS_{95} to AS_{00}. The rightward shift in the AS curve was the result of technological advances, such as the Internet and electronic commerce, which produced larger-than-usual increases in productivity at each possible price level. And as shown earlier in Exhibit 9 of the chapter on business cycles and unemployment, the economy has returned to operating below its full-employment potential real GDP since the recession of 2001, and this negative GDP rose sharply during the recession beginning in 2007.

✔ CHECKPOINT

Would the Greenhouse Effect Cause Inflation, Unemployment, or Both?

You are the chair of the president's Council of Economic Advisers. There has been an extremely hot and dry summer due to a climatic change known as the greenhouse effect. As a result, crop production has fallen drastically. The president calls you to the White House to discuss the impact on the economy. Would you explain to the president that a sharp drop in U.S. crop production would cause inflation, unemployment, or both?

EXHIBIT 13	A Rightward Shift in the Aggregate Demand and Supply Curves

From late 1995 through 2000, the aggregate demand curve increased from AD_{95} to AD_{00}. Significant increases in productivity from technology advances shifted the aggregate supply curve from AS_{95} to AS_{00}. As a result, the U.S economy experienced strong real GDP growth to full employment with mild inflation (the CPI increased from 152 to 172).

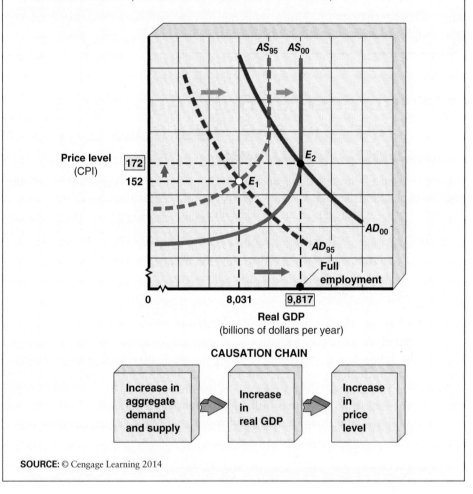

CAUSATION CHAIN

SOURCE: © Cengage Learning 2014

Key Concepts

Aggregate demand curve (AD)
Real balances effect
Interest-rate effect
Net exports effect

Aggregate supply curve (AS)
Keynesian range
Intermediate range
Classical range

Stagflation
Cost-push inflation
Demand-pull inflation

Summary

- The **aggregate demand curve** shows the level of real GDP purchased in the economy at different price levels during a period of time.
- **Reasons why the aggregate demand curve is downward sloping** include the following three effects: (1) The **real balances effect** is the impact on real GDP caused by the inverse relationship between the purchasing power of fixed-value financial assets and inflation, which causes a shift in the consumption schedule. (2) The **interest-rate effect** assumes a fixed money supply; therefore, inflation increases the demand for money. As the demand for money increases, the interest rate rises, causing consumption and investment spending to fall. (3) The **net exports effect** is the impact on real GDP caused by the inverse relationship between net exports and inflation. An increase in the U.S. price level tends to reduce U.S. exports and increase imports, and vice versa.

Shift in the Aggregate Demand Curve

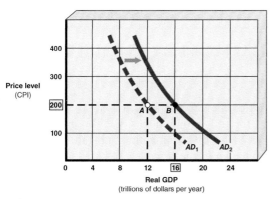

SOURCE: © Cengage Learning 2014

- The **aggregate supply curve** shows the level of real GDP that an economy will produce at different possible price levels. The shape of the aggregate supply curve depends on the flexibility of prices and wages as real GDP expands and contracts. The aggregate supply curve has three ranges: (1) The **Keynesian range** of the curve is horizontal because neither the price level nor production costs will increase or decrease when there is substantial unemployment in the economy. (2) In the **intermediate range**, both prices and costs rise as real GDP rises toward full employment. Prices and production costs rise because of bottlenecks, the stronger bargaining power of labor, and the utilization of less productive workers and capital. (3) The **classical range** is the vertical segment of the aggregate supply curve. It coincides with the full-employment output. Because output is at its maximum, increases in aggregate demand will only cause a rise in the price level.

Aggregate Supply Curve

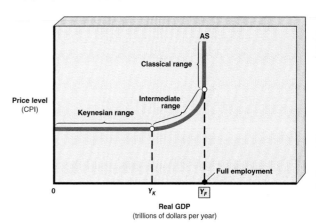

SOURCE: © Cengage Learning 2014

- **Aggregate demand and aggregate supply analysis** determines the equilibrium price level and the equilibrium real GDP by the intersection of the aggregate demand and aggregate supply curves. In macroeconomic equilibrium, businesses neither overestimate nor underestimate the real GDP demanded at the prevailing price level.

Cost-Push Inflation

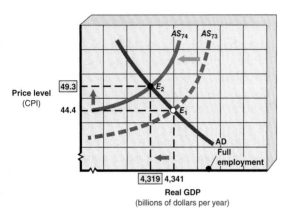

SOURCE: © Cengage Learning 2014

- **Stagflation** exists when an economy experiences inflation and unemployment simultaneously. Holding aggregate demand constant, a decrease in aggregate supply results in the unhealthy condition of a rise in the price level and a fall in real GDP and employment.
- **Cost-push inflation** is inflation that results from a decrease in the aggregate supply curve while the aggregate demand curve remains fixed. Cost-push inflation is undesirable because it is accompanied by declines in both real GDP and employment.
- **Demand-pull inflation** is inflation that results from an increase in the aggregate demand curve in both the classical and the intermediate ranges of the aggregate supply curve, while the aggregate supply curve is fixed.

Demand-Pull Inflation

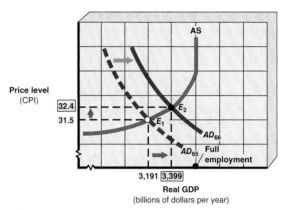

SOURCE: © Cengage Learning 2014

Summary of Conclusion Statements

- The aggregate demand curve and the demand curve are not the same concept.
- Consumers spend more on goods and services when lower prices make their dollars more valuable. Therefore, the real value of money is measured by the quantity of goods and services each dollar buys.
- Any change in the individual components of aggregate expenditures shifts the aggregate demand curve.
- When the aggregate supply curve is horizontal and an economy is in recession below full employment, the only effects of an increase in aggregate demand are increases in real GDP and employment, while the price level does not change. Stated simply, the Keynesian view is that "demand creates its own supply."

- When the aggregate supply curve is vertical at the full-employment GDP, the only effect over time of a change in aggregate demand is a change in the price level. Stated simply, the classical view is that "supply creates its own demand."
- Keynesian theory rejects classical theory for an economy in recession because Keynesians argue that during a recession, prices and wages do not adjust downward to restore an economy to full-employment real GDP.
- At macroeconomic equilibrium, sellers neither overestimate nor underestimate the real GDP demanded at the prevailing price level.
- As aggregate demand increases in the Keynesian range, the price level remains constant as real GDP expands.

- In the intermediate range, increases in aggregate demand increase both the price level and the real GDP.
- Once the economy reaches full-employment output in the classical range, additional increases in aggregate demand merely cause inflation, rather than more real GDP.
- The business cycle is a result of shifts in the aggregate demand and aggregate supply curves.

Study Questions and Problems

1. Explain why the aggregate demand curve is downward sloping. How does your explanation differ from the reasons behind the downward-sloping demand curve for an individual product?

2. Explain the theory of the classical economists that flexible prices and wages ensure that the economy operates at full employment.

3. In which direction would each of the following changes in conditions cause the aggregate demand curve to shift? Explain your answers.
   a. Consumers expect an economic downturn.
   b. A new U.S. president is elected, and the profit expectations of business executives rise.
   c. The federal government increases spending for highways, bridges, and other infrastructure.
   d. The United States increases exports of wheat and other crops to Russia, Ukraine, and other former Soviet republics.

4. Identify the three ranges of the aggregate supply curve. Explain the impact of an increase in the aggregate demand curve in each segment.

5. Consider this statement: "Equilibrium GDP is the same as full employment." Do you agree or disagree? Explain.

6. Assume the aggregate demand and aggregate supply curves intersect at a price level of 100. Explain the effect of a shift in the price level to 120 and to 50.

7. In which direction would each of the following changes in conditions cause the aggregate supply curve to shift? Explain your answers.
   a. The price of gasoline increases because of a catastrophic oil spill.
   b. Labor unions and all other workers agree to a cut in wages to stimulate the economy.
   c. Power companies switch to solar power, and the price of electricity falls.
   d. The federal government increases the excise tax on gasoline in order to finance a deficit.

8. Assume an economy operates in the intermediate range of its aggregate supply curve. State the direction of shift for the aggregate demand or aggregate supply curve for each of the following changes in conditions. What is the effect on the price level? On real GDP? On employment?
   a. The price of crude oil rises significantly.
   b. Spending on national defense doubles.
   c. The costs of imported goods increase.
   d. An improvement in technology raises labor productivity.

9. What shifts in aggregate supply or aggregate demand would cause each of the following conditions for an economy?
   a. The price level rises, and real GDP rises.
   b. The price level falls, and real GDP rises.
   c. The price level falls, and real GDP falls.
   d. The price level rises, and real GDP falls.
   e. The price level falls, and real GDP remains the same.
   f. The price level remains the same, and real GDP rises.

10. Explain cost-push inflation verbally and graphically, using aggregate demand and aggregate supply analysis. Assess the impact on the price level, real GDP, and employment.

11. Explain demand-pull inflation graphically using aggregate demand and supply analysis. Assess the impact on the price level, real GDP, and employment.

For Online Exercises, go to the Tucker Web site at www.cengage.com/economics/tucker.

✓ CHECKPOINT ANSWER

Would the Greenhouse Effect Cause Inflation, Unemployment, or Both?

A drop in food production reduces aggregate supply. The decrease in aggregate supply causes the economy to contract, while prices rise. In addition to the OPEC oil embargo between 1972 and 1974, worldwide weather conditions destroyed crops and contributed to the supply shock that caused stagflation in the U.S. economy. If you said that a severe greenhouse effect would cause both higher unemployment and inflation, **YOU ARE CORRECT.**

Sample Quiz

For an explanation of the correct answers, visit the Tucker Web site at www.cengage.com/economics/tucker.

1. The aggregate demand curve shows how real GDP purchased varies with changes in
   a. unemployment.
   b. output.
   c. the price level.
   d. the interest rate.

2. Which of the following is *not* a component of the aggregate demand curve?
   a. government spending (G)
   b. investment (I)
   c. consumption (C)
   d. net exports (X − M)
   e. saving

3. The real balances effect occurs because a higher price level will reduce the real value of people's
   a. financial assets.
   b. wages.
   c. unpaid debt.
   d. physical investments.

4. The real balance effect is the impact on real GDP caused by the _____ relationship between the price level and the real value of financial assets.
   a. direct
   b. inverse
   c. independent
   d. linear

5. The interest-rate effect is the impact on real GDP caused by the _____ relationship between the price level and the interest rate.
   a. direct
   b. independent
   c. linear
   d. inverse

6. The net exports effect is the _____ relationship between net exports and the price level of an economy.
   a. inverse
   b. independent
   c. direct
   d. linear

7. Which of the following would shift the aggregate demand curve to the left?
   a. an increase in exports
   b. an increase in investment
   c. an increase in government spending
   d. a decrease in government spending

8. Suppose workers become pessimistic about their future employment, which causes them to save more and spend less. If the economy is on the intermediate range of the aggregate supply curve, then
   a. both real GDP and the price level will fall.
   b. real GDP will fall, and the price level will rise.

Sample Quiz *continued*

c. real GDP will rise, and the price level will fall.

d. both real GDP and the price level will rise.

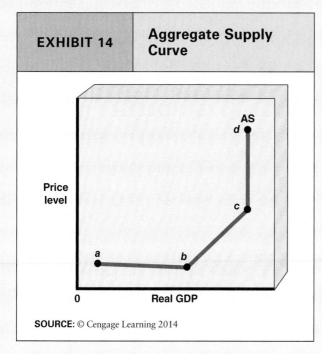

| EXHIBIT 14 | Aggregate Supply Curve |

SOURCE: © Cengage Learning 2014

9. In Exhibit 14, resources are fully employed, and competition among producers for resources will lead to a higher price level in
   a. the segment labeled *ab*.
   b. the segment labeled *bc*.
   c. the segment labeled *cd*.
   d. segments *bc* and *cd*.

10. In Exhibit 14, as production increases, firms resort to offering higher wage rates to attract the dwindling supply of unemployed resources in
    a. the segment labeled *ab*.
    b. the segment labeled *bc*.
    c. the segment labeled *cd*.
    d. segments *bc* and *cd*.

11. An increase in oil prices will shift the aggregate
    a. demand curve leftward.
    b. demand curve rightward.
    c. supply curve leftward.
    d. supply curve rightward.

12. Stagflation is a period of time when the economy is experiencing
    a. inflation and low unemployment.
    b. high unemployment and low levels of inflation at the same time.
    c. high inflation and high unemployment at the same time.
    d. low inflation and low unemployment at the same time.

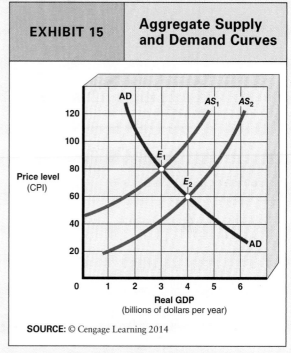

| EXHIBIT 15 | Aggregate Supply and Demand Curves |

SOURCE: © Cengage Learning 2014

13. The shift from AS_1 to AS_2 in Exhibit 15 could be caused by a (an)
    a. sudden increase in the price of oil.
    b. increase in input prices for most firms.
    c. increase in workers' wages.
    d. All of the answers above are correct.

14. As the economy moves to the right in Exhibit 16 along the upward-sloping aggregate supply curve, the
    a. unemployment rate rises.
    b. unemployment rate falls.
    c. inflation rate falls.
    d. None of the above occur.

Sample Quiz *continued*

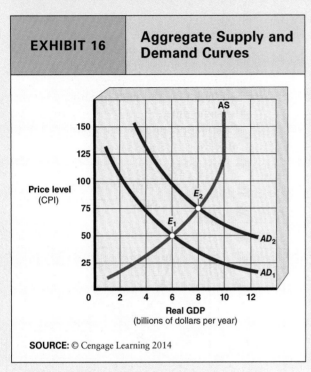

EXHIBIT 16	Aggregate Supply and Demand Curves

SOURCE: © Cengage Learning 2014

15. As the aggregate demand curve shifts from AD_1 to AD_2 in Exhibit 16, the economy experiences
    a. cost-push inflation.
    b. demand-pull inflation.
    c. wage-push inflation.
    d. hyperinflation.

16. The idea that higher prices reduce the purchasing power of financial assets and lead to less consumption and more saving is known as the
    a. real wealth effect.
    b. foreign purchases effect.
    c. income effect.
    d. aggregate demand effect.

17. Which of the following is a belief of classical theory?
    a. long-run full employment
    b. inflexible wages
    c. inflexible prices
    d. All of the above answers are correct

18. In Exhibit 17, if aggregate demand increases from AD_1 to AD_2,
    a. output and prices will increase.
    b. output and prices will decrease.
    c. output alone will increase.
    d. prices alone will decrease.
    e. prices alone will increase.

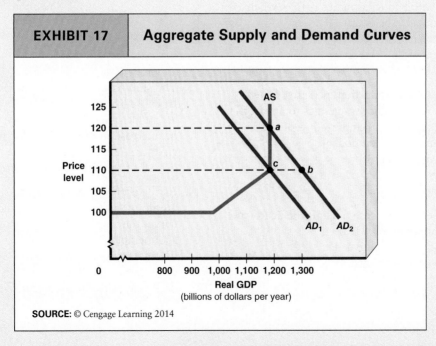

EXHIBIT 17	Aggregate Supply and Demand Curves

SOURCE: © Cengage Learning 2014

Sample Quiz *continued*

19. In Exhibit 17, the aggregate demand and supply curves reflect an economy in which
    a. full employment is at $1,000 billion GDP.
    b. excess aggregate supply is created when there is a shift from AD_1 to AD_2.
    c. excess aggregate demand forces prices up to P = 120.
    d. excess aggregate demand causes prices to stabilize at P = 110.
    e. a new equilibrium is found at point *b*.

20. In Exhibit 17, choosing to operate the economy at GDP = $1,200 billion and P = 110 would be opting for an economy of
    a. no unemployment with inflation.
    b. full employment without inflation.
    c. full employment with inflation.
    d. moderate cyclical unemployment without inflation.

The Self-Correcting Aggregate Demand and Supply Model

It can be argued that the economy is self-regulating. This means that over time, the economy will move itself to full-employment equilibrium. Stated differently, this classical theory is based on the assumption that the economy might ebb and flow around it, but full employment is the normal condition for the economy regardless of gyrations in the price level. To understand this adjustment process, the AD-AS model presented in the chapter must be extended into a more complex model called the self-correcting AD-AS model. First, a distinction will be made between the short-run and long-run aggregate supply curves. Indeed, one of the most controversial areas of macroeconomics is the shape of the aggregate supply curve and the reasons for that shape. Second, we will explain long-run equilibrium using the self-correcting AD-AS model. Third, this appendix concludes by using the self-correcting AD-AS model to explain short-run and long-run adjustments to changes in aggregate demand.

20A-1 Why the Short-Run Aggregate Supply Curve Is Upward Sloping

Short-run aggregate supply curve (SRAS)

The curve that shows the level of real GDP produced at different possible price levels during a time period in which nominal incomes do not change in response to changes in the price level.

Exhibit A-1(a) shows the short-run aggregate supply curve (SRAS), which does not have either the perfectly flat Keynesian segment or the perfectly vertical classical segment developed in Exhibit 6 of this chapter. The short-run supply curve shows the level of real GDP produced at different possible price levels during a time period in which nominal wages and salaries (incomes) do not change in response to changes in the price level. Recall from the chapter on inflation that

$$\text{Real income} = \frac{\text{nominal income}}{\text{CPI (as decimal)}}$$

As explained by this formula, a rise in the price level measured by the CPI decreases real income, and a fall in the price level increases real income. Given the definition of the short-run aggregate supply curve, there are two reasons why one can assume nominal wages and salaries remain fixed in spite of changes in the price level:

1. **Incomplete knowledge.** In a short period of time, workers may be unaware that a change in the price level has changed their real incomes. Consequently, they do not adjust their wage and salary demands according to changes in their real incomes.
2. **Fixed-wage contracts.** Unionized employees, for example, have nominal or money wages stated in their contracts. Also, many professionals receive set

---

EXHIBIT A-1 | Aggregate Supply Curves

The short-run aggregate supply curve (SRAS) in part (a) is based on the assumption that nominal wages and salaries are fixed based on an expected price level of 100 and full-employment real GDP of $8 trillion. An increase in the price level from 100 to 150 increases profits, real GDP, and employment, moving the economy from point *A* to point *B*. A decrease in the price level from 100 to 50 decreases profits, real GDP, and employment, moving the economy from point *A* to point *C*.

The long-run aggregate supply curve (LRAS) in part (b) is vertical at full-employment real GDP. For example, if the price level rises from 100 at point *A* to 150 at point *B*, workers now have enough time to renegotiate higher nominal incomes by a percentage equal to the percentage increase in the price level. This flexible adjustment means that real incomes and profits remain unchanged, and the economy continues to operate at full-employment real GDP.

SOURCE: © Cengage Learning 2014

---

salaries for a year. In these cases, nominal incomes remain constant, or "sticky," for a given time period regardless of changes in the price level.

Given the assumption that changes in the prices of goods and services measured by the CPI do not in a short period of time cause changes in nominal wages, let's examine Exhibit A-1(a) and explain the SRAS curve's upward-sloping shape. Begin at point *A* with a CPI of 100 and observe that the economy is operating at the full-employment real GDP of $8 trillion. Also assume that labor contracts are based on this expected price level. Now suppose the price level unexpectedly increases from 100 to 150 at point *B*. At higher prices for products, firms' revenues increase, and with nominal wages and salaries fixed, profits rise. In response, firms increase output from $8 trillion to $12 trillion, and the economy operates beyond its full-employment output. This occurs because firms increase work hours and train and hire homemakers, retirees, and unemployed workers who were not profitable at or below full-employment real GDP.

Now return to point *A* and assume the CPI falls to 50 at point *C*. In this case, the prices firms receive for their products drop while nominal wages and salaries remain fixed. As a result, firms' revenues and profits fall, and they reduce output from $8 trillion to $4 trillion real GDP. Correspondingly, employment (not shown explicitly in the model) falls below full employment.

> **CONCLUSION:** *The upward-sloping shape of the short-run aggregate supply curve (SRAS) is the result of fixed nominal wages and salaries as the price level changes.*

20A-2 Why the Long-Run Aggregate Supply Curve Is Vertical

Long-run aggregate supply curve (LRAS)

The curve that shows the level of real GDP produced at different possible price levels during a time period in which nominal incomes change by the same percentage as the price level changes.

The long-run aggregate supply curve (LRAS) is presented in Exhibit A-1(b). The long-run aggregate supply curve shows the level of real GDP produced at different possible price levels during a time period in which nominal incomes change by the same percentage as the price level changes. Like the classical vertical segment of the aggregate supply curve developed in Exhibit 6 of the chapter, the long-run aggregate supply curve is vertical at full-employment real GDP.

To understand why the long-run aggregate supply curve is vertical requires the assumption that sufficient time has elapsed for labor contracts to expire, so that nominal wages and salaries can be renegotiated. Stated another way, over a long enough time, workers will calculate changes in their real incomes and obtain increases in their nominal incomes to adjust proportionately to changes in purchasing power. Suppose the CPI is 100 (or as a decimal, 1.0) at point *A* in Exhibit A-1(b) and the average nominal wage is $10 per hour. This means the average real wage is also $10 ($10 nominal wage divided by 1.0). But if the CPI rises to 150 at point *B*, the $10 average real wage falls to $6.67 ($10/1.5). In the long run, workers will demand and receive a new nominal wage of $15, returning their real wage to $10 ($15/1.5). Thus, both the CPI (rise from 100 to 150) and the nominal wage (rise from $10 to $15) changed by the same rate of 50 percent, and the economy moved from point *A* to point *B*, upward along the long-run aggregate supply curve. Note that because both the prices of products measured by the CPI and the nominal wage rise by the same percentage, profit margins remain unchanged in real terms, and firms have no incentive to produce either more or less than the full-employment real GDP of $8 trillion. And because this same adjustment process occurs between any two price levels along LRAS, the curve is vertical, and potential real GDP is independent of the price level. Regardless of rises or falls in the CPI, potential real GDP remains the same.

> **CONCLUSION:** *The vertical shape of the long-run aggregate supply curve (LRAS) is the result of nominal wages and salaries eventually changing by the same percentage as the price level changes.*

EXHIBIT A-2	Self-Correcting AD-AS Model

The short-run aggregate supply curve (SRAS) is based on an expected price level of 100. Point E shows that this equilibrium price level occurs at the intersection of the aggregate demand curve AD, SRAS, and the long-run aggregate supply curve (LRAS).

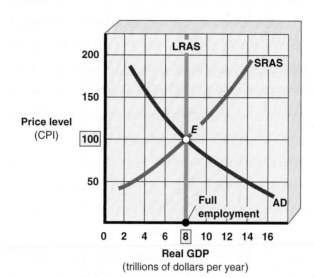

SOURCE: © Cengage Learning 2014

20A-3 Equilibrium in the Self-Correcting AD-AS Model

Exhibit A-2 combines aggregate demand with the short-run and long-run aggregate supply curves from the previous exhibit to form the self-correcting AD-AS model. Equilibrium in the model occurs at point E, where the economy's aggregate demand curve (AD) intersects the vertical long-run aggregate supply curve (LRAS) and the short-run aggregate supply curve (SRAS). In long-run equilibrium, the economy's price level is 100, and full-employment real GDP is $8 trillion.

20A-4 The Impact of an Increase in Aggregate Demand

Now you're ready for some actions and reactions using the model. Suppose that beginning at point E_1 in Exhibit A-3, a change in a nonprice determinant (summarized in Exhibit 11 at the end of the chapter) causes an increase in aggregate demand from AD_1 to AD_2. For example, the shift could be the result of an increase in consumption spending (C), government spending (G), or business investment (I), or greater demand for U.S. exports. Regardless of the cause, the short-run effect is for the economy to move upward along $SRAS_{100}$ to the intersection with AD_2 at the temporary or short-run equilibrium point E_2 with a price level of 150. Recall

EXHIBIT A-3	Adjustments to an Increase in Aggregate Demand Supply Curves

Beginning at long-run equilibrium E_1, the aggregate demand curve increases from AD_1 to AD_2. Because nominal incomes are fixed in the short run, firms raise product prices, earn higher profits, and expand output to short-run equilibrium point E_2. After enough time passes, workers increase their nominal incomes to restore their purchasing power, and the short-run supply curve shifts leftward along AD_2 to a transitional point such as E_3. As the economy moves from E_2 to E_4, profits fall, and firms cut output and employment. Eventually, long-run equilibrium is reached at E_4, with full employment restored by the self-correction process.

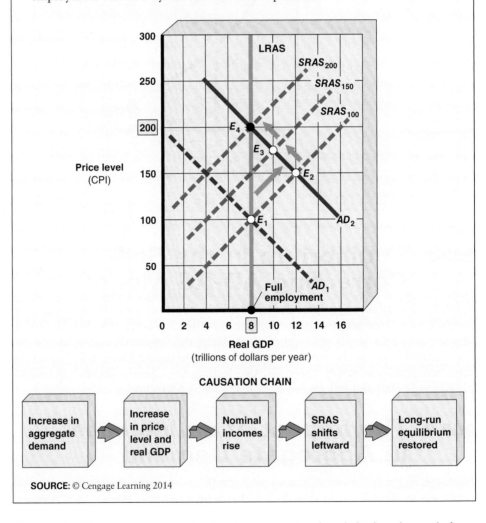

CAUSATION CHAIN

Increase in aggregate demand ⇨ Increase in price level and real GDP ⇨ Nominal incomes rise ⇨ SRAS shifts leftward ⇨ Long-run equilibrium restored

SOURCE: © Cengage Learning 2014

that nominal incomes are fixed in the short run. Faced with higher demand, firms raise prices for products, and because the price of labor remains unchanged, firms earn higher profits and increase employment by hiring workers who were not profitable at full employment. As a result, for a short period of time, real GDP increases above the full-employment real GDP of $8 trillion to $12 trillion. However, the economy cannot produce in excess of full employment forever. What forces are at work to bring real GDP back to full-employment real GDP?

Assume time passes and labor contracts expire. The next step in the transition process at E_2 is that workers begin demanding nominal income increases that will eventually bring their real incomes back to the same real incomes established initially at E_1. Since firms are anxious to maintain their output levels and they are competing for workers, firms meet the wage increase demands of labor. These increases in nominal incomes shift the short-run aggregate supply curve leftward, which causes an upward movement along AD_2. One of the successions of possible intermediate adjustment short-run supply curves along AD_2 is $SRAS_{150}$. This short-run intermediate adjustment is based on an expected price level of 150 determined by the intersection of $SRAS_{150}$ and LRAS. Although the short-run aggregate supply curve $SRAS_{150}$ intersects AD_2 at E_3, the adjustment to the increase in aggregate demand is not yet complete. Workers negotiated increases in nominal incomes based on an expected price level of 150, but the leftward shift of the short-run aggregate supply curve raised the price level to about 175 at E_3. Workers must therefore negotiate another round of higher nominal incomes to restore purchasing power. This process continues until long-run equilibrium is restored at E_4, where the adjustment process ends.

The long-run forecast for the price level at full employment is now 200 at point E_4. $SRAS_{100}$ has shifted leftward to $SRAS_{200}$, which intersects LRAS at point E_4. As a result of the shift in the short-run aggregate supply curve from E_2 to E_4 and the corresponding increase in nominal incomes, firms' profits are cut, and they react by raising product prices, reducing employment, and reducing output. At E_4, the economy has self-adjusted to both short-run and long-run equilibrium at a price level of 200 and full-employment real GDP of $8 trillion. If there are no further shifts in aggregate demand, the economy will remain at E_4 indefinitely. Note that nominal income is higher at point E_4 than it was originally at point E_1, but real wages and salaries remain unchanged, as explained in Exhibit A-1(b).

> **CONCLUSION:** *An increase in aggregate demand in the long run causes the short-run aggregate supply curve to shift leftward because nominal incomes rise and the economy self-corrects to a higher price level at full-employment real GDP.*

20A-5 The Impact of a Decrease in Aggregate Demand

Point E_1 in Exhibit A-4 begins where the sequence of events described in the previous section ends. Now let's see what happens when the aggregate demand curve decreases from AD_1 to AD_2. The reason might be that a wave of pessimism from a stock market crash causes consumers to cut back on their spending and firms postpone buying new factories and equipment. As a result, firms find their sales and profits have declined, and they react by cutting product prices, output, and employment. Workers' nominal incomes remain fixed in the short run with contracts negotiated based on an expected price level of 200. The result of this situation is that the economy moves downward along $SRAS_{200}$ from point E_1 to short-run equilibrium point E_2. Here the price level falls from 200 to 150, and real GDP has fallen from $8 trillion to $4 trillion.

EXHIBIT A-4	Adjustments to a Decrease in Aggregate Demand

Assume the economy is initially at long-run equilibrium point E_1 and aggregate demand decreases from AD_1 to AD_2. Nominal incomes in the short run are fixed based on an expected price level of 200. In response to the fall in aggregate demand, firms' profits decline, and they cut output and employment. As a result, the economy moves downward along $SRAS_{200}$ to temporary equilibrium at E_2. When workers lower their nominal incomes because of competition from unemployed workers, the short-run aggregate supply curve shifts downward to an intermediate point, such as E_3. As workers decrease their nominal incomes based on the new long-run expected price level of 150 at point E_3, profits rise, and firms increase output and employment. In the long run, the short-run aggregate supply curve continues to automatically adjust downward along AD_2 until it again returns to long-run equilibrium at E_4.

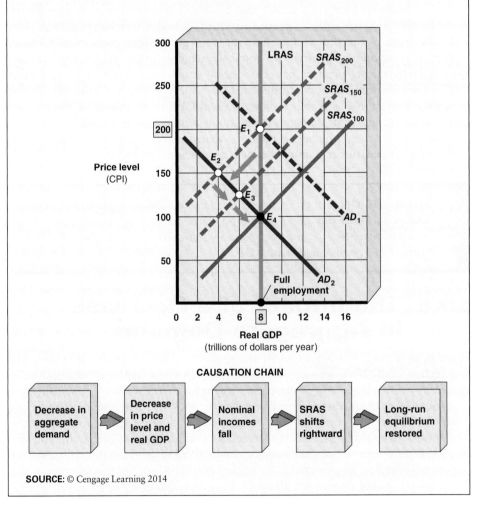

CAUSATION CHAIN

Decrease in aggregate demand ⇒ Decrease in price level and real GDP ⇒ Nominal incomes fall ⇒ SRAS shifts rightward ⇒ Long-run equilibrium restored

SOURCE: © Cengage Learning 2014

At E_2, the economy is in a serious recession, and after, say, a year, workers will accept lower nominal wages and salaries when their contracts are renewed in order to keep their jobs in a time of poor profits and competition from unemployed workers. This willingness to accept lower nominal incomes is made easier by the realization that lower prices for goods means it costs less to maintain the workers' standard of living. As workers make a series of downward adjustments in nominal incomes, the short-run aggregate supply curve moves downward along AD_2 toward E_4. $SRAS_{150}$ illustrates one possible intermediate position corresponding to the long-run expected price level of 150 determined by the intersection of $SRAS_{150}$ and LRAS. However, like E_2, E_3 is not the point of long-run equilibrium. Workers negotiated decreases in nominal increases based on an expected price level of 150, but the rightward shift of the short-run aggregate supply curve has lowered the price level to about 125 at E_3. Under pressure from unemployed workers who will work for still lower real wages and salaries, workers will continue this process of adjusting their nominal incomes lower until $SRAS_{150}$ shifts rightward to point E_4.

Eventually, the long-run expected full-employment price level returns to 100 at point E_4, where the economy has self-corrected to long-run full-employment equilibrium. The result of this adjustment downward along AD_2 between E_2 and E_4 is that lower nominal incomes raise profits and firms respond by lowering prices of products, increasing employment, and increasing output so that real GDP increases from \$4 trillion to \$8 trillion. Unless aggregate demand changes, the economy will be stable at E_4 indefinitely. Finally, observe that average nominal income has decreased by the same percentage between points E_1 and E_4 as the percentage decline in the price level. Therefore, real incomes are unaffected as explained in Exhibit A-1(b).

CONCLUSION: *A decrease in aggregate demand in the long run causes the short-run aggregate supply curve to shift rightward because nominal incomes fall and the economy self-corrects to a lower price level at full-employment real GDP.*

20A-6 Changes in Potential Real GDP

Like the aggregate demand and short-run aggregate supply curves, the long-run aggregate supply curve also changes. As explained in Chapter 2, changes in resources and technology shift the production possibilities curve outward. We now extend this concept of economic growth to the long-run aggregate supply curve as follows:

1. *Changes in resources.* For example, the quantity of land can be increased by reclaiming land from the sea or revitalizing soil. Over time, potential real GDP increases if the full-employment number of workers increases, holding capital and technology constant. Such growth in the labor force can result from population growth. Greater quantities of plants, production lines, computers, and other forms of capital also produce increases in potential real GDP. Capital includes *human capital*, which is the accumulation of education, training, experience, and health of workers.
2. *An advance in technology.* Technological change enables firms to produce more goods from any given amount of inputs. Even with fixed quantities of labor and capital, the latest computer-age machinery increases potential GDP.

EXHIBIT A-5	**Trend of Macro Equilibrium Price Level over Time**

Each hypothetical long-run equilibrium point shows the CPI and real GDP for a given year determined by the intersection of the aggregate demand curve, short-run aggregate supply curve, and long-run aggregate supply curve. Over time, these curves shift, and both the price level and real GDP increase.

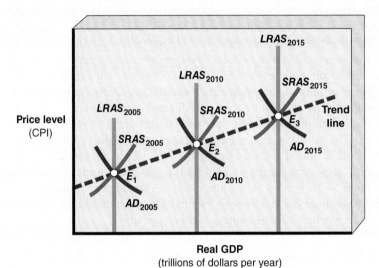

Real GDP
(trillions of dollars per year)

SOURCE: © Cengage Learning 2014

CONCLUSION: *A rightward shift of the long-run aggregate supply curve represents economic growth in potential full-employment real GDP.*

Over time, the U.S. economy typically adds resources and improves technology, and growth occurs in full-employment output. Exhibit A-5 uses basic aggregate demand and supply analysis to explain a hypothetical trend in the price level measured by the CPI between 2005, 2010, and 2015. The trend line connects the macro equilibrium points for each year. The following section uses real-world data to illustrate changes in the long-run aggregate supply curve over time.

20A-7 Increase in the Aggregate Demand and Long-Run Aggregate Supply Curves

The self-correcting AD-AS model shown in Exhibit A-5 revisits Exhibit 13 in the chapter, which illustrated economic growth that occurred between 1995 and 2000 in the U.S. economy. Exhibit A-6, however, uses short-run and long-run aggregate supply curves to expand the analysis. (For simplicity, the real GDP amounts have

EXHIBIT A-6	A Rightward Shift in the Aggregate Demand and Long-Run Aggregate Supply Curves

In 1995, the U.S. economy was operating at \$8.0 trillion below full-employment real GDP of \$8.3 trillion at $LRAS_{95}$. Between 1995 and 2000, the aggregate demand curve increased from AD_{95} to AD_{00}, and the U.S economy moved upward along the short-run aggregate supply curve $SRAS_{95}$ from point E_1 to point E_2. Nominal or money incomes of workers increased, and $SRAS_{95}$ shifted leftward to $SRAS_{00}$, establishing long-run full-employment equilibrium at E_3 on long-run aggregate supply curve $LRAS_{00}$. Technological changes and capital accumulation over these years caused the rightward shift from $LRAS_{95}$ to $LRAS_{00}$, and potential real GDP grew from \$8.3 trillion to \$9.8 trillion.

CAUSATION CHAIN

Increase in aggregate demand and long-run supply ⇒ Increase in price level and real GDP ⇒ Nominal incomes rise ⇒ SRAS shifts leftward ⇒ Long-run equilibrium restored

SOURCE: © Cengage Learning 2014

been rounded.) In 1995, the economy operated at point E_1, with the CPI at 152 and a real GDP of \$8.0 trillion. Since $LRAS_{95}$ at E_1 was estimated to be \$8.3 trillion real GDP, the economy was operating below its full-employment potential with an unemployment rate of 5.6 percent (not explicitly shown in the model). Over the next five years, the U.S. economy moved to full employment at point E_3 in 2000 and experienced growth in real GDP from \$8.0 trillion to \$9.8 trillion. The CPI increased from 152 to 175 (mild inflation), and the unemployment rate fell to 4.0 percent.

During this time period, extraordinary technological change and capital accumulation, particularly in high-tech industries, caused economic growth in potential real GDP, represented by the rightward shift in the vertical long-run supply curve from $LRAS_{95}$ to $LRAS_{00}$. The movement from E_1 below full-employment real GDP was caused by an increase in AD_{95} to AD_{00} and a movement upward along short-run aggregate supply curve $SRAS_{95}$ to point E_2. Over time, the nominal or money wage rate increased, and $SRAS_{95}$ shifted leftward to $SRAS_{00}$. At point E_3, the price level was 175 and equal to potential real GDP of $9.8 trillion.

Key Concepts

Short-run aggregate supply curve (SRAS)   Long-run aggregate supply curve (LRAS)

Summary

- The **upward-sloping shape of the short-run aggregate supply curve (SRAS)** is the result of fixed nominal wages and salaries as the price level changes.
- The **vertical shape of the long-run aggregate supply curve (LRAS)** is the result of nominal wages and salaries eventually changing by the same percentage as the price level changes.
- An **increase in aggregate demand (AD) in the long run** causes the short-run aggregate supply curve (SRAS) to shift leftward because nominal incomes rise and the economy self-corrects

to a higher price level at full-employment real GDP.
- A **decrease in aggregate demand in the long run** causes the short-run aggregate supply curve (SRAS) to shift rightward because nominal incomes fall and the economy self-corrects to a lower price level at full-employment real GDP.
- **Economic growth in potential real GDP** is represented by a rightward shift in the long-run aggregate supply curve (LRAS). Shifts in LRAS are caused by changes in resources and advances in technology.

Study Questions and Problems

1. The economy of Tuckerland has the following aggregate demand and supply schedules, reflecting real GDP in trillions of dollars:
   a. Graph the aggregate demand curve and the short-run aggregate supply curve.
   b. What are short-run equilibrium real GDP and the price level?
   c. If Tuckerland's potential real GDP is $12 trillion, plot the long-run aggregate supply curve (LRAS) in the graph.

Price level (CPI)	Aggregate demand	Short-run aggregate supply
250	$ 4	$16
200	8	12
150	12	8
100	16	4

2. Using the graph from question 1 and assuming long-run equilibrium at $12 trillion, explain the impact of a 10 percent increase in workers' income.

3. Use the graph drawn in question 1 and assume the initial equilibrium is E_1. Next, assume aggregate demand increases by $4 trillion. Draw the effect on short-run equilibrium.

4. Based on the assumptions of question 3, explain verbally the impact of an increase of $4 trillion in aggregate demand on short-run equilibrium.

5. The economy shown in Exhibit A-7 is initially in equilibrium at point E_1, and the aggregate demand curve decreases from AD_1 to AD_2. Explain the long-run adjustment process.

6. In the first quarter of 2001, real GDP was $9.88 trillion, and the price level measured by the GDP chain price index was 101. Real GDP was approximately equal to potential GDP. In the third quarter, aggregate demand decreased to $9.83 trillion, and the price level rose to 103. Draw a graph of this recession.

EXHIBIT A-7	Aggregate Demand and Supply Model

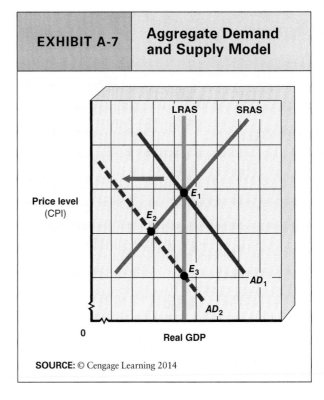

SOURCE: © Cengage Learning 2014

For Online Exercises, go to the Tucker Web site at www.cengage.com/economics/tucker.

Sample Quiz

For an explanation of the correct answers, visit the Tucker Web site at www.cengage.com/economics/tucker.

1. One reason for the short-run aggregate supply curve (SRAS) is
   a. a fixed CPI market basket.
   b. perfect knowledge of workers.
   c. fixed-wage contracts.
   d. the upward-sloping production function.

2. The full-employment level of real GDP is the level that can be produced with
   a. given technology and productive resources.
   b. frictional and structural unemployment equal to zero.
   c. cyclical unemployment equal to zero.
   d. both a and b.
   e. both a and c.

3. Which of the following would cause a decrease in the short-run aggregate supply curve (SRAS)?
   a. an increase in oil prices
   b. an advance in technology
   c. an increase in the CPI
   d. an increase in the long-run aggregate supply curve (LRAS)

4. If nominal wages and salaries are fixed as firms change product prices, the short-run aggregate supply curve (SRAS) is
   a. vertical.
   b. horizontal.
   c. negatively sloped.
   d. positively sloped.

Sample Quiz *continued*

5. Which of the following explains why the short-run aggregate supply curve is upward sloping?
   a. The quantity of real output supplied is inversely related to the aggregate supply curve.
   b. Nominal incomes are fixed.
   c. The capital-output ratio.
   d. An increase in price will increase the supply of money.

6. In an economy where nominal incomes adjust equally to changes in the price level, we would expect the long-run aggregate supply curve to be
   a. vertical.
   b. horizontal.
   c. negatively sloped.
   d. positively sloped.

7. In the AD-AS model, a point where the economy's long-run AS curve, short-run AS curve, and AD curve all intersect at a single point represents a point where
   a. real GDP is equal to its full-employment level.
   b. the conditions of short-run equilibrium are fulfilled.
   c. the conditions of long-run equilibrium are fulfilled.
   d. All of the above answers are correct.
   e. Answers a and c are correct.

8. The intersection between the long-run aggregate supply and aggregate demand curves determines the
   a. level of full-employment real GDP.
   b. average level of prices (CPI).
   c. marginal product.
   d. both a and b.

9. The adjustment of nominal incomes to changes in the price level (CPI) is fixed because of the
   a. volatility of investment spending.
   b. existence of long-term contracts.
   c. complete information possessed by workers.
   d. All of the above answers are correct.

10. In the self-correcting AD-AS model, the economy's short-run equilibrium position is indicated by the intersection of which two curves?
    a. short-run aggregate supply and long-run aggregate supply
    b. short-run aggregate supply and aggregate demand
    c. long-run aggregate supply and aggregate demand
    d. long-run aggregate demand and short-run personal consumption expenditures

11. Which of the following causes a leftward shift in the short-run aggregate supply curve?
    a. an increase of goods prices while nominal incomes are unchanged
    b. an increase in nominal incomes
    c. an increase of full-employment real GDP
    d. an increase of personal consumption expenditures while the price level is unchanged

12. In parts (a) and (b) of Exhibit A-8, the intersection of AD with SRAS indicates
    a. a short-run equilibrium.
    b. a long-run equilibrium.
    c. that the economy needs policies to reduce unemployment.
    d. that the economy is at full employment.

13. In part (a) of Exhibit A-8, suppose the initial equilibrium is at real GDP level Y_1 and price level P_2. At real GDP level Y_1, there is
    a. an inflationary gap.
    b. a recessionary gap.
    c. full employment.
    d. long-run equilibrium.

14. In part (b) of Exhibit A-8, the intersection of SRAS with AD indicates
    a. an economy experiencing a recessionary gap.
    b. an economy experiencing an inflationary gap.
    c. that the economy is in long-run equilibrium.
    d. that the economy has an unemployment rate currently less than the natural rate of unemployment.

Sample Quiz *continued*

15. In part (b) of Exhibit A-8, the intersection of SRAS with LRAS indicates
    a. an economy experiencing a recessionary gap.
    b. long-run equilibrium if the aggregate demand curve (AD) shifts leftward to this point.

    c. that the economy is in long-run equilibrium.
    d. that the economy has an unemployment rate currently greater than the natural rate of unemployment.

16. As shown in Exhibit A-9 and assuming the aggregate demand curve shifts from AD_1 to AD_2, the full-employment level of real GDP is
    a. $10 billion.
    b. $4 billion.
    c. $100 billion.
    d. unable to be determined.

17. Beginning from a point of short-run equilibrium at point E_2 in Exhibit A-9, the economy's movement to a new position of long-run equilibrium from that point would *best* be described as
    a. a movement downward along the AD_2 curve with a shift in the $SRAS_1$ curve to $SRAS_2$.
    b. a movement along the $SRAS_2$ curve with a shift in the AD_2 curve.
    c. a shift in the LRAS curve to an intersection at E_3.
    d. no shift of any kind.

18. Based on Exhibit A-10, when the aggregate demand curve shifts to the position AD_2 and the economy is operating at point E_2, the economy's position of long-run equilibrium corresponds to point
    a. E_1.
    b. E_2.
    c. E_3.
    d. E_1 or E_3.

19. Beginning in Exhibit A-10, from long-run equilibrium at point E_1, the aggregate demand curve shifts to AD_2. The economy's path to a new long-run equilibrium is represented by a movement from
    a. E_3 to E_1 to E_2.
    b. E_1 to E_3 to E_2.
    c. E_2 to E_1 to E_2.
    d. E_1 to E_2 to E_3.

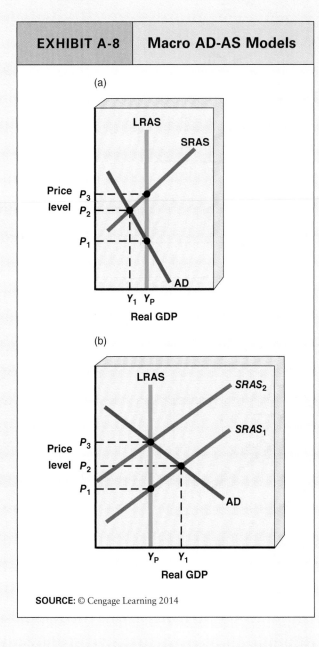

| EXHIBIT A-8 | Macro AD-AS Models |

(a)

(b)

SOURCE: © Cengage Learning 2014

Sample Quiz *continued*

EXHIBIT A-9 | **Aggregate Demand and Supply Model**

SOURCE: © Cengage Learning 2014

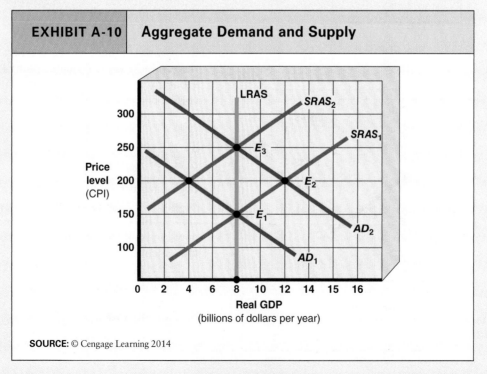

EXHIBIT A-10 | **Aggregate Demand and Supply**

SOURCE: © Cengage Learning 2014

Sample Quiz *continued*

20. Economic growth would be represented in Exhibit A-10 by a(an)
    a. leftward shift in the long-run aggregate supply curve (LRAS).
    b. inward shift of the production possibilities curve.
    c. rightward shift in the long-run aggregate supply curve (LRAS).
    d. movement along the long-run aggregate supply curve (LRAS).

chapter 21

Fiscal Policy

In the early 1980s, under President Ronald Reagan, the federal government reduced personal income tax rates. The goal was to expand aggregate demand and boost real GDP output and employment in order to end the recession of 1980–1981. In the 1990s, a key part of President Bill Clinton's programs was to stimulate economic growth by boosting government spending on long-term investment, including highways, bridges, and education. In 2001, the United States experienced a recession, and during the next two years, President George W. Bush proposed and signed into law tax cuts to stimulate the economy. And in 2008, Americans received a $170 billion tax-rebate stimulus package, followed by another $787 billion federal stimulus package under the Obama administration in 2009 intended to jump-start the economy into recovery from the recession.

Fiscal policy is one of the major issues that touches everyone's life. Fiscal policy is the use of government spending and taxes to influence the nation's output, employment, and price level. Federal government spending policies affect Social Security benefits, price supports for dairy farmers, and employment in the defense industry. Tax policies can change the amount of your paycheck and therefore influence whether you purchase a car or attend college.

Using fiscal policy to influence the performance of the economy has been an important idea since the Keynesian revolution of the 1930s. This chapter removes the political veil and looks at fiscal policy from the viewpoint of two opposing economic theories. First, you will study Keynesian demand-side fiscal policies that "fine-tune" aggregate demand so that the economy grows and achieves full employment with a higher price level. Second, you will study supply-side fiscal policy, which gained prominence during the Reagan administration. Supply-siders view aggregate supply as far more important than aggregate demand. Their fiscal policy prescription is to increase aggregate supply so that the economy grows and achieves full employment with a lower price level.

In this chapter, you will learn to solve these economics puzzles:

- Does an increase in government spending or a tax cut of equal amount provide the greater stimulus to economic growth?

- Can Congress fight a recession without taking any action?

- How could one argue that the federal government can increase tax revenues by cutting taxes?

21-1 Discretionary Fiscal Policy

Here we begin where the previous chapter left off, that is, discussing the use of discretionary fiscal policy, as Keynes advocated, to influence the economy's performance. Discretionary fiscal policy is the deliberate use of changes in government spending or taxes to alter aggregate demand and stabilize the economy. Exhibit 1 lists three basic types of discretionary fiscal policies and the corresponding ways in which the government can pursue each of these options. The first column of the table shows that the government can choose to increase aggregate demand by following an *expansionary* fiscal policy. The second column lists *contractionary* fiscal policy options the government can use to restrain aggregate demand.

Fiscal policy

The use of government spending and taxes to influence the nation's spending, employment, and price level.

Discretionary fiscal policy

The deliberate use of changes in government spending or taxes to alter aggregate demand and stabilize the economy.

21-1a INCREASING GOVERNMENT SPENDING TO COMBAT A RECESSION

Suppose the U.S. economy represented in Exhibit 2 has fallen into recession at equilibrium point E_1, where aggregate demand curve AD_1 intersects the aggregate supply curve, AS, in the near-full-employment range. The price level measured by the CPI is 210, and a real GDP gap of $1 trillion exists below the full-employment output of $14 trillion real GDP. As explained in the previous chapter (Exhibit 5), one approach the president and Congress can follow is provided by classical theory. The classical economists' prescription is to wait because the economy will self-correct to full employment in the long run by adjusting downward along AD_1. But election time is approaching, so there is political pressure to do something about the

EXHIBIT 1	Discretionary Fiscal Policies
Expansionary fiscal policy	**Contractionary fiscal policy**
Increase government spending	Decrease government spending
Decrease taxes	Increase taxes
Increase government spending and taxes equally	Decrease government spending and taxes equally

SOURCE: © Cengage Learning 2014

EXHIBIT 2	**Using Government Spending to Combat a Recession**

The economy in this exhibit is in recession at equilibrium point E_1 on the intermediate range of the aggregate supply curve, AS. The price level is 210, with an output level of $13 trillion real GDP. To reach the full-employment output of $14 trillion in real GDP, the aggregate demand curve must be shifted to the right by $2 trillion real GDP, measured by the horizontal distance between point E_1 on curve AD_1 and point X on curve AD_2. The necessary increase in aggregate demand from AD_1 to AD_2 can be accomplished by increased government spending. Given a spending multiplier of 2, a $1 trillion increase in government spending brings about the required $2 trillion rightward shift in the aggregate demand curve, and equilibrium in the economy changes from E_1 to E_2. Note that the equilibrium real GDP changes by $1 trillion and not by the full amount by which the aggregate demand curve shifts horizontally.

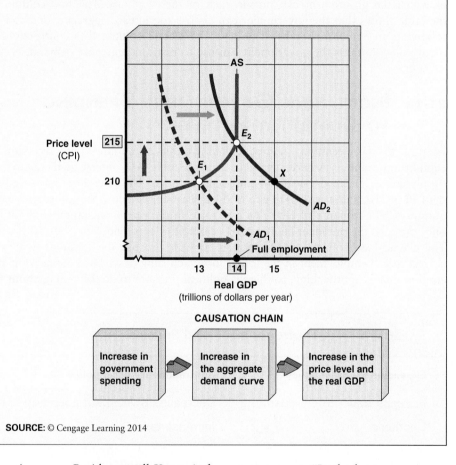

CAUSATION CHAIN

Increase in government spending ⟹ Increase in the aggregate demand curve ⟹ Increase in the price level and the real GDP

SOURCE: © Cengage Learning 2014

recession now. Besides, recall Keynes's famous statement, "In the long run, we are all dead." Hence, policymakers follow Keynesian economics and decide to shift the aggregate demand curve rightward from AD_1 to AD_2 and thereby cure the recession.

How can the federal government do this? In theory, any increase in consumption (C), investment (I), or net exports ($X - M$) can spur aggregate demand. But these spending boosts are not directly under the government's control as is government spending (G). After all, there is always a long wish list of spending proposals for federal highways, health care, education, environmental programs, and so forth. Rather than crossing their fingers and waiting for things to happen in the long run, suppose members of Congress gladly increase government spending to boost employment now.

But just how much new government spending is required? Note that the economy is operating $1 trillion below its full-employment output, but the horizontal distance between AD_1 and AD_2 is $2 trillion. This gap between AD_1 and AD_2 is indicated by the dotted line between points E_1 and X ($15 trillion − $13 trillion). This means that the aggregate demand curve must be shifted to the right by $2 trillion. But it is not necessary to increase government spending by this amount. The following formula can be used to compute the amount of additional government spending required to shift the aggregate demand curve rightward and establish a new full-employment real GDP equilibrium:

Initial change in government spending (ΔG) × spending multiplier

= change in aggregate demand (total spending)

The spending multiplier (SM) in the formula amplifies the amount of new government spending. The spending multiplier is the change in aggregate demand (total spending) resulting from an initial change in any component of aggregate demand, including consumption, investment, government spending, and net exports. Assume the value for the spending multiplier in our example is 2. The next section explains the algebra behind the spending multiplier so that the example can be solved:

$$\Delta G \times 2 = \$2 \text{ trillion}$$

$$\Delta G = \$1 \text{ trillion}$$

Note that the Greek letter Δ (delta) means "a change in." Thus, it takes $1 trillion worth of new government spending to shift the aggregate demand curve to the right by $2 trillion. As described in the previous chapter (Exhibit 6), bottlenecks occur throughout the upward-sloping range of the AS curve. This means prices rise as production increases in response to greater aggregate demand. Returning to Exhibit 2, you can see that $1 trillion worth of new government spending shifts aggregate demand from AD_1 to AD_2. As a result, firms increase output upward along the aggregate supply curve, AS, and total spending moves upward along aggregate demand curve AD_2. This adjustment mechanism moves the economy to a new equilibrium at E_2, with full employment, a higher price level of 215, and a real GDP of $14 trillion per year. At point E_2, the economy experiences *demand-pull inflation*. And here is the important point: Although the aggregate demand curve has increased by $2 trillion, the equilibrium real GDP has increased by only $1 trillion, from $13 to $14 trillion.

Spending multiplier (SM)

The change in aggregate demand (total spending) resulting from initial change in any component of aggregate expenditures, including consumption, investment, government spending, and net exports. As a formula, spending multiplier equals 1/(1 − MPC) or 1/MPS.

> **CONCLUSION:** *In the intermediate segment of the aggregate supply curve, the equilibrium real GDP changes by less than the change in government spending times the spending multiplier.*

21-1b SPENDING MULTIPLIER ARITHMETIC REVISITED[1]

Marginal propensity to consume (MPC)

The change in consumption spending resulting from a given change in income.

Now let's pause to tackle the task of explaining in more detail the spending multiplier of 2 used in the above example. The spending multiplier begins with a concept called the marginal propensity to consume (MPC). The marginal propensity to consume is the change in consumption spending resulting from a given change in income. Algebraically,

$$\text{MPC} = \frac{\text{change in consumption spending}}{\text{change in income}}$$

Exhibit 3 illustrates numerically the cumulative increase in aggregate demand resulting from a $1 trillion increase in government spending. In the initial round, the government spends this amount for bridges, national defense, and so forth. Households receive this amount of income. In the second round, these households spend $500 billion (0.50 × $1 trillion, or $1,000 billion) on houses, cars, groceries, and other products. In the third round, the incomes of realtors, autoworkers, grocers, and others are boosted by $500 billion, and they spend $250 billion (0.50 × $500 billion). Each round of spending creates income for consumption respending in a downward spiral throughout the economy in smaller and smaller amounts until the total level of aggregate demand rises by an extra $2,000 billion ($2 trillion).

EXHIBIT 3	The Spending Multiplier Effect	
Round	**Component of total spending**	**New consumption spending (billions of dollars)**
1	Government spending	$1,000
2	Consumption	500
3	Consumption	250
4	Consumption	125
.	.	.
.	.	.
.	.	.
All other rounds	Consumption	125
	Total spending	$2,000

NOTE: All amounts are rounded to the nearest billion dollars per year.
SOURCE: © Cengage Learning 2014

---

[1]This section duplicates material presented earlier in the chapters titled "The Keynesian Model" and "The Keynesian Model in Action." The reason for repeating this material is that an instructor may choose to skip the Keynesian model presented in these two chapters.

> **CONCLUSION:** *Any initial change in spending by the government, households, or firms creates a chain reaction of further spending, which causes a greater cumulative change in aggregate demand.*

You might recognize from algebra that the spending multiplier effect is a process based on an *infinite geometric series*. The formula for the sum of such a series of numbers is the initial number times $1/(1 - r)$, where r is the ratio that relates the numbers. Using this formula, the sum (total spending) is calculated as $1 trillion $(\Delta G) \times [1/(1 - 0.50)] = \$2$ trillion. By simply defining r in the infinite series formula as MPC, the spending multiplier for aggregate demand is expressed as follows:

$$\text{Spending multiplier} = \frac{1}{1 - \text{MPC}}$$

Applying this formula to our example:

$$\text{Spending multiplier} = \frac{1}{1 - 0.50} = \frac{1}{0.50} = 2$$

If households spend a portion of each extra dollar of income, then the remaining portion of each dollar is saved. The **marginal propensity to save (MPS)** is the change in saving resulting from a given change in income. Therefore,

$$\text{MPC} + \text{MPS} = 1$$

rewritten as

$$\text{MPS} = 1 - \text{MPC}$$

Hence, the above spending multiplier formula can be rewritten as

$$\text{Spending multiplier} = \frac{1}{\text{MPS}}$$

Because MPS and MPC are related, the size of the multiplier depends on the size of the MPC. What will the result be if people spend 80 percent or 33 percent of each dollar of income instead of 50 percent? If the MPC increases (decreases), consumers spend a larger (smaller) share of each additional dollar of output/income in each round, and the size of the multiplier increases (decreases). Exhibit 4 lists the multiplier for different values of MPC and MPS.

Marginal propensity to save (MPS)

The change in saving resulting from a given change in income.

✔ CHECKPOINT

What is the MPC for Uncle Sam's Stimulus Package?

Assume the economy is in a recession, and a stimulus package of $800 billion is passed by the federal government. The administration predicts that this measure will provide a $2,400 billion boost to GDP this year because consumers will spend their extra cash on HD televisions and other items. For this amount of stimulus, what is the established value of MPC used in this forecast?

EXHIBIT 4	Relationship between MPC, MPS, and the Spending Multiplier	
(1) **Marginal propensity to consume (MPC)**	**(2)** **Marginal propensity to save (MPS)**	**(3)** **Spending multiplier**
0.90	0.10	10
0.80	0.20	5
0.75	0.25	4
0.67	0.33	3
0.50	0.50	2
0.33	0.67	1.5

SOURCE: © Cengage Learning 2014

21-1c CUTTING TAXES TO COMBAT A RECESSION

Another expansionary fiscal policy intended to increase aggregate demand and restore full employment calls for the government to cut taxes. Let's return to point E_1 in Exhibit 2. As before, the problem is to shift the aggregate demand curve to the right by $2 trillion. But this time, instead of a $1 trillion increase in government spending, assume Congress votes for a $1 trillion tax cut. How does this cut in taxes affect aggregate demand? First, *disposable personal income* (take-home pay) increases by $1 trillion—the amount of the tax reduction. Second, once again assuming the MPC is 0.50, the increase in disposable personal income induces new consumption spending of $500 billion (0.50 × $1 trillion). Thus, a cut in taxes triggers a multiplier process similar to, but smaller than, the spending multiplier.

Exhibit 5 demonstrates that a tax reduction adds less to aggregate demand than does an equal increase in government spending. Column (1) reproduces the effect of increasing government spending by $1 trillion, and column (2) gives for comparison the effect of lowering taxes by $1 trillion. Note that the only difference between increasing government spending and cutting taxes by the same amount is the impact in the initial round. The reason is that a tax cut injects zero new spending into the economy because the government has purchased no new goods and services. The effect of a tax reduction in round 2 is that people spend a portion of the $1 trillion boost in after-tax income from the tax cut introduced in round 1. Subsequent rounds in the tax multiplier chain generate a cumulative increase in consumption expenditures that totals $1 trillion. Comparing the total changes in aggregate demand in columns (1) and (2) of Exhibit 4 leads to the following:

> **CONCLUSION:** *A tax cut has a smaller multiplier effect on aggregate demand than an equal increase in government spending.*

EXHIBIT 5	Comparison of the Spending and Tax Multipliers		
		Increase in aggregate demand from a	
Round	Component of total spending	(1) $1 trillion increase in government spending $(+\Delta G)$	(2) $1 trillion cut in taxes $(-\Delta T)$
1	Government spending	$1,000	$ 0
2	Consumption	500	500
3	Consumption	250	250
4	Consumption	125	125
.	.	.	.
.	.	.	.
.	.	.	.
All other rounds	Consumption	125	125
	Total spending	$2,000	$1,000

NOTE: All amounts are rounded to the nearest billion dollars per year.
SOURCE: © Cengage Learning 2014

The tax multiplier (TM) can be computed by using a formula and the information from column 2 of Exhibit 5. The tax multiplier is the change in aggregate demand (total spending) resulting from an initial change in taxes. Mathematically, the tax multiplier is given by this formula:

Tax multiplier = 1 − spending multiplier

Returning to Exhibit 2, the tax multiplier formula can be used to calculate the cumulative increase in the aggregate demand from a $1 trillion tax cut. Applying the formula given above and a spending multiplier of 2 yields a tax multiplier of −1. Note that the sign of the tax multiplier is always negative. Thus, a $1 trillion tax cut shifts the aggregate demand curve rightward by only $1 trillion and fails to restore full-employment equilibrium at point E_2. Mathematically,

Change in taxes $(\Delta T) \times$ tax multiplier $(TM) =$ change in aggregate demand (AD)

−$1 trillion $\times$ −1 = $1 trillion

The key to the amount of real GDP growth achieved from a stimulus package depends on the size of the MPC. What proportion of the government spending increase or tax cut is spent for consumption? The answer means the difference between a deeper or milder recession as well as the speed of recovery. What are estimates of real-world multipliers? In Congressional testimony given in July 2008,

Tax multiplier

The change in aggregate demand (total spending) resulting from an initial change in taxes. As a formula, tax multiplier equals 1 − spending multiplier.

Mark Zandi, chief economist for Moody's Economy.com, provided estimates for the one-year multiplier effect for several fiscal policy options. The spending multiplier varied from 1.36 to 1.73 for different federal government spending programs, such as food stamps, extended unemployment insurance benefits, aid to state governments, or bridges and highways. The tax multiplier also varied from 0.27 to 1.29 for different temporary tax cut plans.

21-1d USING FISCAL POLICY TO COMBAT INFLATION

So far, Keynesian expansionary fiscal policy, born of the Great Depression, has been presented as the cure for an economic downturn. Contractionary fiscal policy, on the other hand, can serve in the fight against inflation. Exhibit 6 shows an economy operating at point E_1 on the classical range of the aggregate supply curve, AS. Hence, this economy is producing the full-employment output of $14 trillion real GDP, and the price level is 220. In this situation, any increase in aggregate demand only causes inflation, while real GDP remains unchanged.

Suppose Congress and the president decide to use fiscal policy to reduce the CPI from 220 to 215 because they fear the wrath of voters suffering from the consequences of inflation. Although a fall in consumption, investment, or net exports might do the job, Congress and the president may be unwilling to wait, and they prefer taking direct action by cutting government spending. Given a marginal propensity to consume of 0.50, the spending multiplier is 2. As shown by the horizontal distance between point E_1 on AD_1 and point E' on AD_2 in Exhibit 6, aggregate demand must be decreased by $1 trillion in order to shift the aggregate demand curve from AD_1 to AD_2 and establish equilibrium at E_2, with a price level of 215. Mathematically,

$$\Delta G \times 2 = -\$1 \text{ trillion}$$

$$\Delta G = -\$500 \text{ billion}$$

Using the above formula, a $500 billion cut in real government spending would cause a $1 trillion decrease in the aggregate demand curve from AD_1 to AD_2. The result is a temporary excess aggregate supply of $1 trillion, measured by the distance from E' to E_1. As explained in Exhibit 5 of the previous chapter, the economy follows classical theory and moves downward along AD_2 to a new equilibrium at E_2. Consequently, inflation cools with no change in the full-employment real GDP.

Another approach to the inflation problem would be for Congress and the president to raise taxes. Although tax increases are often considered political suicide, let's suppose Congress calculates just the correct amount of a tax hike required to reduce aggregate demand by $1 trillion.

Assuming a spending multiplier of 2, the tax multiplier is -1. Therefore, a $1 trillion tax hike provides the necessary $1 trillion leftward shift in the aggregate demand curve from AD_1 to AD_2. As a result, the desired equilibrium change from E_1 to E_2 is achieved, and the price level drops from 220 to 215 at the full-employment output of $14 trillion. Mathematically,

$$\Delta T \times -1 = -\$1 \text{ trillion}$$

$$\Delta T = \$1 \text{ trillion}$$

EXHIBIT 6	Using Fiscal Policy to Combat Inflation

The economy in this exhibit is in equilibrium at point E_1 on the classical range of the aggregate supply curve, AS. The price level is 220, and the economy is operating at the full-employment output of $14 trillion real GDP. To reduce the price level to 215, the aggregate demand curve must be shifted to the left by $1 trillion, measured by the horizontal distance between point E_1 on curve AD_1 and point E' on curve AD_2. One way this can be done is by decreasing government spending. With MPC equal to 0.50, and therefore a spending multiplier of 2, a $500 billion decrease in government spending results in the needed $100 billion leftward shift in the aggregate demand curve. As a result, the economy reaches equilibrium at point E_2, and the price level falls from 220 to 215, while real output remains unchanged at full capacity.

An identical decrease in the aggregate demand curve can be obtained by a hike in taxes. A $1 trillion tax increase works through a tax multiplier of -1 and provides the needed $1 trillion decrease in the aggregate demand curve from AD_1 to AD_2.

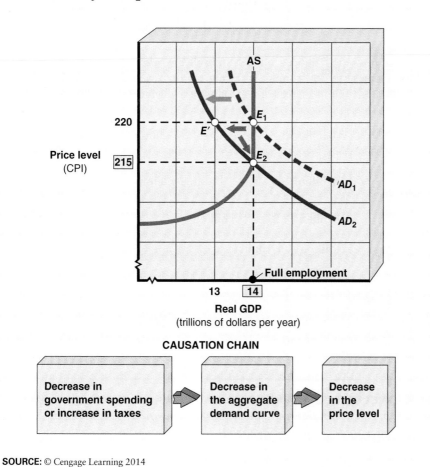

CAUSATION CHAIN

Decrease in government spending or increase in taxes	→	Decrease in the aggregate demand curve	→	Decrease in the price level

SOURCE: © Cengage Learning 2014

21-1e THE BALANCED BUDGET MULTIPLIER

The analysis of Keynesian discretionary fiscal policy presented in the previous section supposes the federal government selects a change in *either* government spending or taxes as a remedy for recession or inflation. However, a controversial fiscal policy requires the government to match, or "balance," any new spending with new taxes. Understanding the impact on the economy of this fiscal policy requires derivation of the balanced budget multiplier. The balanced budget multiplier is an equal change in government spending and taxes, which, as shown below, changes aggregate demand by the amount of the change in government spending. Expressed as a formula,

Balanced budget multiplier

An equal change in government spending and taxes, which changes aggregate demand by the amount of the change in government spending.

Cumulative change in aggregate demand (ΔAD)

= government spending multiplier effect

+ tax multiplier effect

rewritten as

Cumulative change in aggregate demand (ΔAD)

= (initial change in government spending × spending multiplier)

+ (initial change in taxes × tax multiplier)

To see how the balanced budget multiplier works, suppose Congress enacts a $1 billion increase in government spending for highways and it finances these purchases with a $1 billion increase in gasoline taxes. Mathematically,

$$\Delta AD = \left(\$1 \text{ billion} \times \frac{1}{1 - \text{MPC}} \right) + \left(\$1 \text{ billion} \times 1 - \frac{1}{1 - \text{MPC}} \right)$$

$$= \left(\$1 \text{ billion} \times \frac{1}{1 - 0.50} \right) + \left(\$1 \text{ billion} \times 1 - \frac{1}{1 - 0.50} \right)$$

$$= (\$1 \text{ billion} \times 2) + (\$1 \text{ billion} \times -1)$$

$$= \$2 \text{ billion} - \$1 \text{ billion}$$

$$= \$1 \text{ billion}$$

Hence, the balanced budget multiplier is always equal to 1, and the cumulative change in aggregate demand is $1 billion—*the amount of the initial change in government spending.*

> **CONCLUSION:** *Regardless of the MPC, the net effect on the economy of an equal initial increase (decrease) in government spending and taxes is an increase (decrease) in aggregate demand equal to the initial increase (decrease) in government spending.*

✔ **CHECKPOINT**

Walking the Balanced Budget Tightrope

Suppose the president proposes an $800 billion economic stimulus package intended to create jobs. A major criticism of this new spending proposal is that it is not matched by a tax increase. Assume the U.S. economy is below full employment and Congress has passed a law requiring that any increase in spending be matched or balanced by an equal increase in taxes. The MPC is 0.75, and aggregate demand must be increased by $1,000 billion to reach full employment. Will the economy reach full employment if Congress increases spending by $800 billion and increases taxes by the same amount?

21-2 Automatic Stabilizers

Unlike discretionary fiscal policy, automatic stabilizers are policy tools built into the federal budget that help fight unemployment and inflation, while spending and tax laws remain unchanged. Automatic stabilizers are federal expenditures and tax revenues that automatically change levels in order to stabilize an economic expansion or contraction. Automatic stabilizers are sometimes referred to as *nondiscretionary fiscal policy*. Exhibit 7 illustrates the influence of automatic stabilizers on the economy. The downward-sloping line, G, represents federal government expenditures, including such *transfer payments* as unemployment compensation, Medicaid, and welfare. This line falls as real GDP rises. When the economy expands, unemployment falls, and government spending for unemployment compensation, welfare, and other transfer payments decreases. During a downturn, people lose their jobs, and government spending automatically increases because unemployed individuals become eligible for unemployment compensation and other transfer payments.

The direct relationship between tax revenues and real GDP is shown by the upward-sloping line, T. During an expansion, jobs are created, unemployment falls, and workers earn more income and therefore pay more taxes. Thus, income tax collections automatically vary directly with the growth in real GDP.

We begin the analysis of automatic stabilizers with a balanced federal budget. Federal spending, G, is equal to tax collections, T, and the economy is in equilibrium at $14 trillion real GDP. Now assume consumer optimism soars and a spending spree increases the consumption component (C) of total spending. As a result, the economy moves to a new equilibrium at $16 trillion real GDP. The rise in real GDP creates more jobs and higher tax collections. Consequently, taxes rise to $2 trillion on line T. Also, government expenditures fall to $1 trillion because fewer people are collecting transfer payments, such as unemployment compensation and welfare. As a result, the vertical distance between lines T and G represents a federal budget surplus of $1 trillion. A budget surplus occurs when government revenues exceed government expenditures in a given time period.

Automatic stabilizers

Federal expenditures and tax revenues that automatically change levels in order to stabilize an economic expansion or contraction; sometimes referred to as *nondiscretionary fiscal policy*.

Budget surplus

A budget in which government revenues exceed government expenditures in a given time period.

EXHIBIT 7	Automatic Stabilizers

Federal government spending varies inversely with real GDP and is represented by the downward-sloping line, G. Taxes, in contrast, vary directly with real GDP and are represented by the upward-sloping line, T. This means government spending for welfare and other transfer payments declines and tax collections rise as real GDP rises. Thus, if real GDP falls below $14 trillion, the budget deficit rises automatically. The size of the budget deficit is shown by the vertical distance between lines G and T. This budget deficit assists in offsetting a recession because it stimulates aggregate demand. Conversely, when real GDP rises above $14 trillion, a federal budget surplus increases automatically and assists in offsetting inflation.

CAUSATION CHAIN

Increase in real GDP → Tax collections rise and government transfer payments fall → Budget surplus offsets inflation

Decrease in real GDP → Tax collections fall and government transfer payments rise → Budget deficit offsets recession

SOURCE: © Cengage Learning 2014

Now begin again with the economy at $14 trillion in Exhibit 7, and let's change the scenario. Assume that business managers lower their profit expectations. Their revised outlook causes business executives to become pessimistic, so they cut investment spending (I), causing aggregate demand to decline. The corresponding decline in real GDP from $14 trillion to $12 trillion causes tax revenues to fall from $1.5 trillion to $1 trillion on line T. The combined effect of the rise in government spending and the fall in taxes creates a budget deficit. A budget deficit occurs when government expenditures exceed government revenues in a given time period. The vertical distance between lines G and T at $12 trillion real GDP illustrates a federal budget deficit of $1 trillion.

Budget deficit

A budget in which government expenditures exceed government revenues in a given time period.

The key feature of automatic stabilization is that it "leans against the prevailing wind." In short, changes in federal spending and taxes moderate changes in aggregate demand. Stated differently, built-in stabilizers diminish or reduce swings in real GDP. When the economy expands, the fall in government spending for transfer payments and the rise in the level of taxes result in a budget surplus. As the budget surplus grows, people send more money to Washington, which applies braking power against further increases in real GDP. When the economy contracts, the rise in government spending for transfer payments and the fall in the level of taxes yield a budget deficit. As the budget deficit grows, people receive more money from Washington to spend, which slows further decreases in real GDP.

> **CONCLUSION:** *Automatic stabilizers assist in offsetting a recession when real GDP falls and in offsetting inflation when real GDP expands.*

21-3 Supply-Side Fiscal Policy

The focus so far has been on fiscal policy that affects the macro economy solely through the impact of government spending and taxation on aggregate demand. Supply-side economists, whose intellectual roots are in classical economics, argue that *stagflation* in the 1970s was the result of the federal government's failure to follow the theories of supply-side fiscal policy. Supply-side fiscal policy emphasizes government policies that increase aggregate supply in order to achieve long-run growth in real output, full employment, and a lower price level. Supply-side policies became an active economic idea with the election of Ronald Reagan as president in 1980. As discussed in the previous chapter, the U.S. economy in the 1970s experienced high rates of both inflation and unemployment. Stagflation aroused concern about the ability of the U.S. economy to generate long-term advances in the standard of living. This set the stage for a new macroeconomic policy.

Supply-side fiscal policy

A fiscal policy that emphasizes government policies that increase aggregate supply in order to achieve long-run growth in real output, full employment, and a lower price level.

Suppose the economy is initially at E_1 in Exhibit 8(a), with a CPI of 150 and an output of $8 trillion real GDP. The economy is experiencing high unemployment, so the goal is to achieve full employment by increasing real GDP to $12 trillion. As described earlier in this chapter, the federal government might follow Keynesian expansionary fiscal policy and shift the aggregate demand curve

EXHIBIT 8	Keynesian Demand-Side versus Supply-Side Effects

In part (a), assume an economy begins in equilibrium at point E_1, with a price level of 150 and a real GDP of $8 trillion. To boost real output and employment, Keynesian economists prescribe that the federal government raise government spending or cut taxes. By following such demand-side policies, the policymakers work through the multiplier effect and shift the aggregate demand curve from AD_1 to AD_2. As a result, the equilibrium changes to E_2, where real GDP rises to $12 trillion, but the price level also rises to 200. Hence, full employment has been achieved at the expense of higher inflation.

The initial situation for the economy at point E_1 in part (b) is identical to that shown in part (a). However, supply-siders offer a different fiscal policy prescription than the Keynesians. Using some combination of cuts in resource prices, technological advances, tax cuts, subsidies, and regulation reduction, supply-side fiscal policy shifts the aggregate supply curve from AS_1 to AS_2. As a result, the equilibrium in the economy changes to E_2, and real GDP increases to $12 trillion, just as in part (a). The advantage of the supply-side stimulus over the demand-side stimulus is that the price level falls to 100, rather than rising to 200.

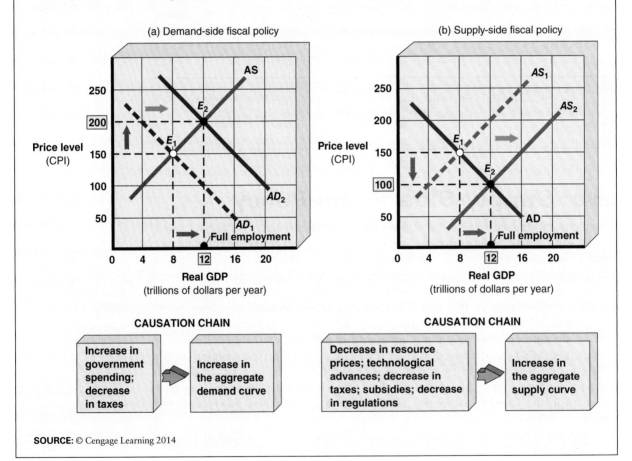

SOURCE: © Cengage Learning 2014

rightward from AD_1 to AD_2. Higher government spending or lower taxes operate through the multiplier effect and cause this increase in aggregate demand. The good news from such a demand-side fiscal policy prescription is that the economy moves toward full employment, but the bad news is that the price level rises. In this case, *demand-pull inflation* would cause the price level to rise from 150 to 200.

Exhibit 8(b) represents the supply-siders' alternative to Keynesian fiscal policy. Again, suppose the economy is initially in equilibrium at E_1. Supply-side economists argue that the federal government should adopt policies that shift the aggregate supply curve rightward from AS_1 to AS_2. An increase in aggregate supply would move the economy to E_2 and achieve the full-employment level of real GDP. Under supply-side theory, there is an additional bonus to full employment. Instead of rising as in Exhibit 8(a), the price level in Exhibit 8(b) falls from 150 to 100. Comparing the two graphs in Exhibit 8, you can see that the supply-siders have a better theoretical case than proponents of demand-side fiscal policy when both inflation and unemployment are concerns.

Note the causation chain under each graph in Exhibit 8. The demand-side fiscal policy options are from column 1 of Exhibit 1 in this chapter, and the supply-side policy alternatives are similar to Exhibit 10 in the previous chapter. For supply-side economics to be effective, the government must implement policies that increase the total output that firms produce at each possible price level. An increase in aggregate supply can be accomplished by some combination of cuts in resource prices, technological advances, subsidies, and reductions in government taxes and government regulations.

Although a laundry list of supply-side policies was advocated during the Reagan administration, the most familiar policy action taken was the tax cuts implemented in 1981. By reducing tax rates on wages and profits, the Reagan administration sought to increase the aggregate supply of goods and services at any price level. However, tax cuts are a Keynesian policy intended to increase aggregate demand, so supply-siders must have a different view of the impact of tax cuts on the economy. To explain these different views of tax cuts, let's begin by stating that both Keynesians and supply-siders agree that tax cuts increase disposable personal income. In Keynesian economics, this boost in disposable personal income works through the *tax multiplier* to increase aggregate demand, as shown earlier in Exhibit 5. Supply-side economists argue instead that changes in disposable income affect the incentive to supply work, save, and invest.

Consider how a supply-side tax cut influences the labor market. Suppose supply and demand in the labor market are initially in equilibrium at point E_1 in Exhibit 9. Before a cut in personal income tax rates, the equilibrium hourly wage rate is W_1, and workers supply L_1 hours of labor per year at this wage rate. When the tax rates are cut, supply-side theory predicts the labor supply curve will shift rightward and establish a new equilibrium at E_2. The rationale is that an increase in the after-tax wage rate gives workers the incentive to work more hours per year. Those in the labor force will want to work longer hours and take fewer vacations. And because Uncle Sam takes a smaller bite out of workers' paychecks, many of those not already in the labor force will now supply their labor. As a result of the increase in the labor supply curve,

EXHIBIT 9 — How Supply-Side Fiscal Policies Affect Labor Markets

Begin with equilibrium in the labor market at point E_1. Here the intersection of the labor supply and demand curves determines a wage rate of W_1 and L_1 hours of labor per year. By lowering tax rates, supply-side fiscal policies increase net after-tax earnings. This extra incentive causes workers to provide additional hours of labor per year. As a result, the labor supply curve increases and establishes a new equilibrium at point E_2. The new wage rate paid by employers falls to W_2, and they use more labor hours per year, L_2.

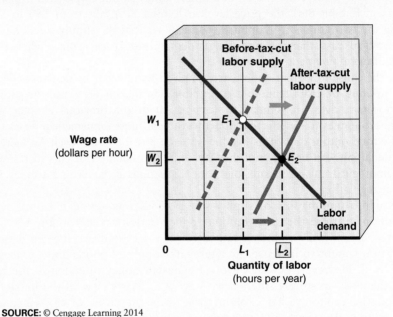

SOURCE: © Cengage Learning 2014

the price of labor falls to W_2 per hour, and the equilibrium number of labor hours increases to L_2.

Supply-side tax cuts of the early 1980s also provided tax breaks that subsidized business investment. Tax credits were available for new equipment and plants and for research and development to encourage technological advances. The idea here was to increase the nation's productive capacity by increasing the quantity and quality of capital. Consequently, the aggregate supply curve would shift rightward because businesses have an extra after-tax profit incentive to invest and produce more at each price level.

The idea of using tax cuts to shift the aggregate supply curve outward is controversial. Despite its logic, the Keynesians argue that the magnitude of any rightward shift in aggregate supply is likely to be small and occur only in the long run. They point out that it takes many years before tax cuts for business generate any change in actual plants and equipment or technological advances. Moreover, individuals can accept tax cuts with a "thank you, Uncle Sam" and not work longer or harder. Meanwhile, unless a reduction in government spending offsets the tax cuts, the effect will be a Keynesian increase in the aggregate demand curve and a higher price level. Exhibit 10 summarizes the important distinction between the supply-side and Keynesian theories on tax cut policy.

Laffer curve

A graph depicting the relationship between tax rates and total tax revenues.

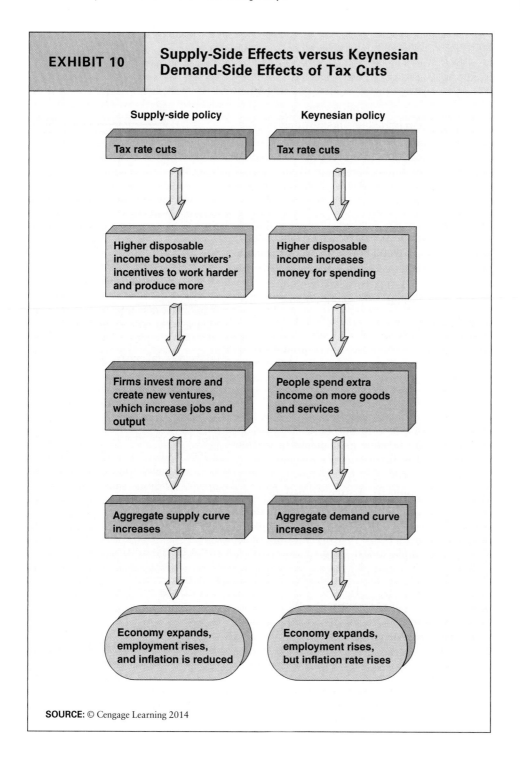

| **EXHIBIT 10** | **Supply-Side Effects versus Keynesian Demand-Side Effects of Tax Cuts** |

Supply-side policy

Tax rate cuts

⬇

Higher disposable income boosts workers' incentives to work harder and produce more

⬇

Firms invest more and create new ventures, which increase jobs and output

⬇

Aggregate supply curve increases

⬇

Economy expands, employment rises, and inflation is reduced

Keynesian policy

Tax rate cuts

⬇

Higher disposable income increases money for spending

⬇

People spend extra income on more goods and services

⬇

Aggregate demand curve increases

⬇

Economy expands, employment rises, but inflation rate rises

SOURCE: © Cengage Learning 2014

The Laffer Curve

Applicable Concept: supply-side fiscal policy

Supply-side economics became popular during the presidential campaign of 1980. This fiscal policy prescription gained prominence after supply-side economist Arthur Laffer, using his pen to draw on a paper napkin, explained what has come to be known as the Laffer curve to an editor of *The Wall Street Journal* at a restaurant in Washington, D.C., in 1974. The Laffer curve is a graph depicting the relationship between tax rates and total tax revenues. As shown in the figure, the hypothetical Laffer curve can be drawn with the federal tax rate on the horizontal axis and tax revenue on the vertical axis. The idea behind this curve is that the federal tax rate affects the incentive for people to work, save, invest, and produce, which in turn influences tax revenue. As the tax rate climbs, Laffer and other supply-siders argue that the erosion of incentives shrinks national income and total tax collections. The editor kept the napkin and published the curve in an editorial in *The Wall Street Journal*. And a theory was born.

Here is how the Laffer curve works. Suppose the federal government sets the federal income tax rate at zero (point A). At a zero income tax rate, people have the maximum incentive to produce, and optimum national income would be earned, but there is zero tax revenue for Uncle Sam. Now assume the federal government sets the income tax rate

at the opposite extreme of 100 percent (point D). At a 100 percent confiscating income tax rate, people have no reason to work, take business risks, produce, and earn income. People seek ways to reduce their tax liabilities by engaging in unreported or underground transactions or by not working at all. As a result, no tax revenue is collected by the Internal Revenue Service. Laffer compared this situation to Robin Hood and his band of merry men (the government) who robbed rich people (taxpayers) traveling through Sherwood Forest to give to the poor. Laffer posed this question, "Do you think that travelers continued to go through Sherwood Forest?" The answer is "no," and Robin Hood's "revenue" would fall.

Because the federal government does not want to collect zero tax revenue, Congress sets the federal income tax rate between zero and 100 percent. Assuming that the income tax rate is related to tax revenue as depicted in the figure, maximum tax revenue, R_{max}, is collected at a tax rate of T_{max} (point B). Laffer argued that the federal income tax rate of T (point C) in 1981 exceeded T_{max} and the result would be tax revenue of R, which is below R_{max}. In Laffer's view, reducing the federal income tax rate leads to an increase in tax revenue because people increase their work effort, saving, and investment and reduce their attempts to avoid paying taxes. Thus, Laffer argued that a cut in federal income

SOURCE: © Cengage Learning 2014

tax rates would unleash economic activity and boost tax revenues needed to reduce the federal budget deficit. President Reagan's belief in the Laffer curve was a major reason why he thought that the federal government could cut personal income tax rates and still balance the federal budget.

The Laffer curve remains a controversial part of supply-side economics. There is still considerable uncertainty about the shape of the Laffer curve and at what point, B, C, or otherwise, along the curve the U.S. economy is operating. There is also no certainty for what tax rate yields maximum tax revenue. And note that below T_{max}, tax rate increases do increase total revenue. Thus, the existence and the usefulness of the Laffer curve are a matter of dispute.

Analyze the Issue

Compare the common perception of how a tax rate cut affects tax revenues with economist Laffer's theory.

Source: © Cengage Learning 2014

Key Concepts

Fiscal policy
Discretionary fiscal policy
Spending multiplier (SM)
Marginal propensity to consume (MPC)

Marginal propensity to save (MPS)
Tax multiplier (TM)
Balanced budget multiplier
Automatic stabilizers
Budget surplus

Budget deficit
Supply-side fiscal policy
Laffer curve

Summary

- **Fiscal policy** is the use of government spending and taxes to stabilize the economy.
- **Discretionary fiscal policy** follows the Keynesian argument that the federal government should manipulate aggregate demand in order to influence the output, employment, and price levels in the economy. Discretionary fiscal policy requires new legislation to change either government spending or taxes in order to stabilize the economy.

Discretionary Fiscal Policies

Expansionary fiscal policy	Contractionary fiscal policy
Increase government spending	Decrease government spending
Decrease taxes	Increase taxes
Increase government spending and taxes equally	Decrease government spending and taxes equally

- The **spending multiplier (SM)** is the multiplier by which an initial change in one component of aggregate demand, for example, government spending, alters aggregate demand (total spending) after an infinite number of spending cycles. Expressed as a formula, the spending multiplier = $1/(1 - MPC)$.
- **Expansionary fiscal policy** is a deliberate increase in government spending, a deliberate decrease in taxes, or some combination of these two options.
- **Contractionary fiscal policy** is a deliberate decrease in government spending, a deliberate

increase in taxes, or some combination of these two options. Using either expansionary or contractionary fiscal policy, the government can shift the aggregate demand curve in order to combat recession, cool inflation, or achieve other macroeconomic goals.
- The **marginal propensity to consume (MPC)** is the change in consumption spending divided by the change in income.
- The **marginal propensity to save (MPS)** is the change in savings divided by the change in income.
- The **tax multiplier** is the change in aggregate demand (total spending) that results from an initial change in taxes after an infinite number of spending cycles. Expressed as a formula, the tax multiplier (TM) = $1 -$ spending multiplier.
- **Combating recession and inflation** can be accomplished by changing government spending or taxes. The total change in aggregate demand from a change in government spending is equal to the change in government spending times the spending multiplier.
- The total change in aggregate demand from a change in taxes is equal to the change in taxes times the tax multiplier.

Combating Recession

SOURCE: © Cengage Learning 2014

Combating Inflation

SOURCE: © Cengage Learning 2014

- The **balanced budget multiplier** is not neutral. A dollar of government spending increases real GDP more than a dollar cut in taxes. Thus, even though the government does not spend more than it collects in taxes, it is still stimulating the economy.
- A **budget surplus** occurs when government revenues exceed government expenditures. A **budget deficit** occurs when government expenditures exceed government revenues.
- **Automatic stabilizers** are changes in taxes and government spending that occur automatically in response to changes in the level of real GDP. The business cycle therefore creates braking power: A *budget surplus* slows an expanding economy; a *budget deficit* reverses a downturn in the economy.

Automatic Stabilizers

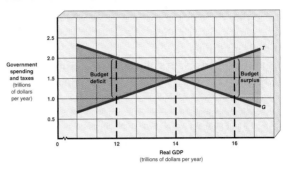

SOURCE: © Cengage Learning 2014

- According to **supply-side fiscal policy,** lower taxes encourage work, saving, and investment, which shift the aggregate supply curve rightward. As a result, output and employment increase without inflation.
- The **Laffer curve** represents the relationship between the income tax rate and the amount of income tax revenue collected by the government.

Summary of Conclusion Statements

- In the intermediate segment of the aggregate supply curve, the equilibrium real GDP changes by less than the change in government spending times the spending multiplier.
- Any initial change in spending by the government, households, or firms creates a chain reaction of further spending, which causes a greater cumulative change in aggregate demand.
- A tax cut has a smaller multiplier effect on aggregate demand than an equal increase in government spending.

- Regardless of the MPC, the net effect on the economy of an equal initial increase (decrease) in government spending and taxes is an increase (decrease) in aggregate demand equal to the initial increase (decrease) in government spending.
- Automatic stabilizers assist in offsetting a recession when real GDP falls and in offsetting inflation when real GDP expands.

Study Questions and Problems

1. Explain how discretionary fiscal policy fights recession and inflation.

2. How does each of the following affect the aggregate demand curve?
   a. Government spending increases.
   b. The amount of taxes collected decreases.

3. In each of the following cases, explain whether the fiscal policy is expansionary, contractionary, or neutral.
   a. The government decreases government spending.
   b. The government increases taxes.
   c. The government increases spending and taxes by an equal amount.

4. Why does a reduction in taxes have a smaller multiplier effect than an increase in government spending of an equal amount?

5. Suppose you are an economic adviser to the president and the economy needs a real GDP increase of $500 billion to reach full-employment equilibrium. If the marginal propensity to consume (MPC) is 0.75 and you are a Keynesian, by how much do you believe Congress must increase government spending to restore the economy to full employment?

6. Consider an economy that is operating at the full-employment level of real GDP. Assuming the MPC is 0.90, predict the effect on the economy of a $50 billion increase in government spending balanced by a $50 billion increase in taxes.

7. Why is a $100 billion increase in government spending for goods and services more expansionary than a $100 billion decrease in taxes?

8. What is the difference between discretionary fiscal policy and automatic stabilizers? How are federal budget surpluses and deficits affected by the business cycle?

9. Assume you are a supply-side economist who is an adviser to the president. If the economy is in recession, what would your fiscal policy prescription be?

10. Suppose Congress enacts a tax reform law and the average federal tax rate drops from 30 percent to 20 percent. Researchers investigate the impact of the tax cut and find that the income subject to the tax increases from $600 billion to $800 billion. The theoretical explanation is that workers have increased their work effort in response to the incentive of lower taxes. Is this a movement along the downward-sloping or the upward-sloping portion of the Laffer curve?

11. Indicate how each of the following would change either the aggregate demand curve or the aggregate supply curve.
    a. Expansionary fiscal policy
    b. Contractionary fiscal policy
    c. Supply-side economics
    d. Demand-pull inflation
    e. Cost-push inflation

For Online Exercises, go to the Tucker Web site at www.cengage.com/economics/tucker.

✔ CHECKPOINT ANSWERS

What is the MPC for Uncle Sam's Stimulus Package?

To calculate the value of the MPC required to increase real GDP (ΔY) by $2,400 billion from an increase in government spending (ΔG) of $800 billion, use this formula:

$$\Delta G \times \text{multiplier} = \Delta Y$$

where

$800 billion × multiplier = $2,400 billion

Thus,

$$\text{Multiplier} = \frac{\$2,400 \text{ billion}}{\$800 \text{ billion}} = 3$$

Using Exhibit 4, if you said that the MPC is 0.67, **YOU ARE CORRECT.**

Walking the Balanced Budget Tightrope

An $800 billion increase in government spending increases aggregate demand by $3,200 billion [government spending increase × spending multiplier, where the spending multiplier = 1/(1 − MPC) = 1/0.25 = 4]. On the other hand, an $800 billion increase in taxes reduces aggregate demand by $2,400 billion (tax cut × tax multiplier, where the tax multiplier = 1 − spending multiplier = 1 − 4 = −3). Thus, the net effect of the spending multiplier and the tax multiplier is an increase in aggregate demand of $800 billion. If you said

Congress has missed its goal of a $1,000 billion boost in aggregate demand by $200 billion and has not restored full employment, **YOU ARE CORRECT.**

Sample Quiz

For an explanation of the correct answers, visit the Tucker Website at academic.cengage.com/economics/tucker.

1. Which of the following is an example of expansionary fiscal policy?
   a. an increase in taxes
   b. a decrease in government spending
   c. an increase in government spending
   d. an increase in taxes and a decrease in government spending equally

2. In the _____ range of the aggregate supply curve, expansionary fiscal policy causes aggregate _____ to increase, which results in a higher price level and a higher equilibrium level of real GDP.
   a. Keynesian, supply
   b. classical, demand
   c. intermediate, demand
   d. intermediate, supply

3. An expansionary fiscal policy may include
   a. increases in government spending.
   b. discretionary increases in transfer payments.
   c. reductions in taxes.
   d. All of the answers above are correct.

4. Suppose the economy in Exhibit 11 is in equilibrium at point E_1 and the marginal propensity to consume (MPC) is 0.80. Following Keynesian economics, to restore full employment, the government should increase its spending by
   a. $200 billion.
   b. $250 billion.

   c. $500 billion.
   d. $1 trillion.

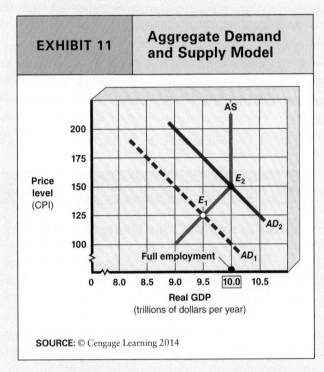

EXHIBIT 11	Aggregate Demand and Supply Model

SOURCE: © Cengage Learning 2014

5. Beginning at equilibrium E_1 in Exhibit 11, when the government increases spending or cuts taxes, the economy will experience
   a. an inflationary recession.
   b. stagflation.

Sample Quiz *continued*

c. cost-push inflation.

d. demand-pull inflation.

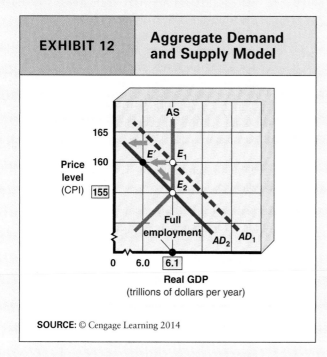

EXHIBIT 12	Aggregate Demand and Supply Model

Price level (CPI)

165

160

155

AS

E'   E₁

E₂

Full employment

AD₂   AD₁

0   6.0   6.1

Real GDP
(trillions of dollars per year)

SOURCE: © Cengage Learning 2014

6. Suppose the economy in Exhibit 12 is in equilibrium at point E_1 and the marginal propensity to consume (MPC) is 0.75. Following Keynesian economics, the federal government can move the economy to point E_2 and reduce inflation by

    a. decreasing government spending by $750 billion.

    b. decreasing government spending by $100 billion.

    c. increasing government spending by $25 billion.

    d. decreasing government spending by $25 billion.

7. Mathematically, the value of the tax multiplier in terms of the marginal propensity to consume (MPC) is given by the formula

    a. $MPC - 1$.

    b. $(MPC - 1)/MPC$.

c. $1/MPC$.

d. $1 - [1/(1 - MPC)]$.

8. A tax multiplier equal to −4.30 would imply that a $100 tax increase would lead to a

    a. $430 decline in real GDP.

    b. $430 increase in real GDP.

    c. 4.3 percent increase in real GDP.

    d. 4.3 percent decrease in real GDP.

    e. 43 percent decrease in real GDP.

9. Equal increases in government spending and taxes will

    a. cancel each other out so that the equilibrium level of real GDP remains unchanged.

    b. lead to an equal decrease in the equilibrium level of real GDP.

    c. lead to an equal increase in the equilibrium level of real GDP.

    d. lead to an increase in the equilibrium level of real GDP output that is larger than the initial change in government spending and taxes.

10. When the economy enters a recession, automatic stabilizers create

    a. higher taxes.

    b. more discretionary spending.

    c. budget deficits.

    d. budget surpluses.

11. Automatic stabilizers "lean against the prevailing wind" of the business cycle because

    a. wages are controlled by the minimum wage law.

    b. federal expenditures and tax revenues change as the level of real GDP changes.

    c. the spending and tax multipliers are constant.

    d. they include the power of special interests.

12. Unemployment compensation payments

    a. rise during a recession and thus reduce the severity of the recession.

    b. rise during a recession and thus increase the severity of the recession.

Sample Quiz *continued*

c. rise during inflationary episodes and thus reduce the severity of the inflation.

d. fall during a recession and thus increase the severity of the recession.

13. According to supply-side fiscal policy, reducing tax rates on wages and profits will
   a. create demand-pull inflation.
   b. lower the price level but may trigger a recession.
   c. result in stagflation.
   d. reduce both unemployment and inflation.

14. Supply-side economics calls for
   a. lower taxes on businesses and individuals.
   b. regulatory reforms to increase productivity.
   c. government subsidies to promote technological advance.
   d. All of the above answers are correct.

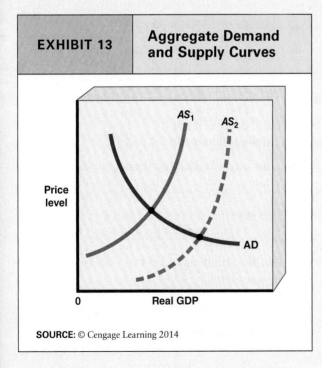

| EXHIBIT 13 | Aggregate Demand and Supply Curves |

SOURCE: © Cengage Learning 2014

15. In Exhibit 13, supply-siders claimed that the shift from AS_1 to AS_2 would occur if the government

   a. increased tax rates and increased the amount of government regulation.
   b. increased tax rates and decreased the amount of government regulation.
   c. decreased tax rates and increased the amount of government regulation.
   d. decreased tax rates and decreased the amount of government regulation.

16. The Laffer curve belongs to which of the following schools of economic thought?
   a. Keynesian
   b. supply-side
   c. demand management
   d. classical

17. According to the Laffer curve, when the tax rate is 100 percent, tax revenue will be
   a. 0.
   b. at the maximum value.
   c. the same as it would be at a 50 percent tax rate.
   d. greater than it would be at a 50 percent tax rate.
   e. the same as it would be at a 20 percent tax rate.

18. Assume the marginal propensity to consume (MPC) is 0.75 and the government increases taxes by $250 billion. The aggregate demand curve will shift to the
   a. left by $1,000 billion.
   b. right by $1,000 billion.
   c. left by $750 billion.
   d. right by $750 billion.

19. When the government levies a $100 million tax on people's income and puts the $100 million back into the economy in the form of a spending program, such as new interstate highway construction, the
   a. tax then generates a $100 million decline in real GDP.
   b. level of real GDP expands by $100 million.
   c. effect on real GDP is uncertain.
   d. tax multiplier overpowers the income multiplier, triggering a rollback in real GDP.

Sample Quiz *continued*

20. Assume the economy is in recession and real GDP is below full employment. The marginal propensity to consume (MPC) is 0.75, and the government follows Keynesian economics by using expansionary fiscal policy to increase aggregate demand (total spending). If an increase of $1,000 billion aggregate demand can restore full employment, the government should
    a. increase spending by $250 billion.
    b. decrease spending by $750 billion.
    c. increase spending by $1,000 billion.
    d. increase spending by $750 billion.

chapter 22

The Public Sector

In the early 1980s, President Ronald Reagan adopted the Laffer curve theory that the federal government could cut tax rates and increase tax revenues. Critics said the result would be lower tax revenues. During the 2000 campaign for the Republican presidential nomination, Steve Forbes continued his attempt to win support for a flat tax, and George W. Bush advocated cutting individual marginal tax rates. However, President Bill Clinton said cutting taxes was not a good idea because ensuring the integrity of Social Security should come first. Between 2001 and 2004, President George W. Bush signed laws that provided for phased-in cuts in the marginal tax rates and increased spending for the war in Iraq and homeland defense. Critics argued that changing the tax structure while increasing spending would worsen the long-term federal budget outlook. And in 2011, grassroots "Tea Parties" were conducted across the nation to protest a too-large federal government that is spending large amounts on economic stimulus packages to deal with the recession.

These events illustrate the persistent real-world controversy surrounding fiscal policy. The previous chapter presented the theory behind fiscal policy. In this chapter, you will examine the practice of fiscal policy. Here the facts of taxation and government expenditures are clearly presented and placed in perspective. You can check, for example, the trend in federal taxes and expenditures during the Obama administration and compare these figures to those of other countries. And you will discover why the government uses different types of taxes and tax rates.

The final section of the chapter challenges the economic role of the public sector. Here you will learn a theory called *public choice*, which examines public sector decisions of politicians, government bureaucrats, voters, and special-interest groups.

In this chapter, you will learn to solve these economics puzzles:

- How does the tax burden in the United States compare to other countries?
- How does the Social Security tax favor the upper-income worker?
- Is a flat tax fair?
- Should we replace the income tax with a national sales tax or a flat tax?

22-1 Government Size and Growth

How big is the public sector in the United States? If we look at Exhibit 1, we see total government expenditures or outlays—including those of federal, state, and local governments—as a percentage of GDP for the 1929–2011 period. When we refer to *government expenditures*, we refer to more than the *government consumption expenditures and investment* (G) account used by national income accountants to calculate GDP (see Exhibit 3 in the chapter on GDP). Government expenditures, or outlays, equal government purchases plus *transfer payments*. Recall from the chapter on GDP that the government national income account (G) includes federal government spending for defense, highways, and education. Transfer payments, not

Government expenditures

Federal, state, and local government outlays for goods and services, including transfer payments.

EXHIBIT 1	The Growth of Government Expenditures as a Percentage of GDP in the United States, 1929–2011

The graph shows the growth of the federal, state, and local governments as measured by government expenditures as a percentage of GDP since 1929. Expenditures rose dramatically during World War II and fell dramatically after the war, but not to previous peacetime levels. Taking account of all government outlays, including transfer payments, the government sector has grown from about one-quarter of GDP in 1950 to about one-third of GDP beginning in 1975 and remained at this level until total government expenditures increased sharply following the Great Recession to 40 percent of GDP in 2009. In 2011, total government expenditures fell slightly to 38 percent.

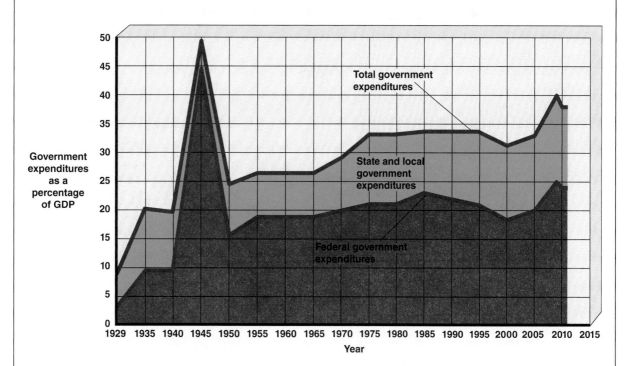

SOURCES: *Economic Report of the President*, 2012, http://www.gpo.gov/fdsys/pkg/ERP-2012/content-detail.htm1, Table B-79; and Bureau of Economic Analysis, *National Income Accounts*, http://www.bea.gov/national/nipaweb/SelectTable.asp?Selected=Y, Tables 1.1.5 and 3.3.

in (*G*), include payments to persons entitled to welfare, Social Security, and unemployment benefits.

As shown in Exhibit 1, total government expenditures skyrocketed as a percentage of GDP during World War II and then took a sharp plunge, but not to previous peacetime levels. Since 1950, total government expenditures grew from about one-quarter of GDP to about one-third beginning in 1975 and remained at this level until total expenditures increased sharply following the Great Recession to a 40 percent of GDP in 2009. In 2011, total government expenditures fell slightly to 38 percent of GDP. The other side of the coin is that today the private sector's share of national output is 62 percent of GDP. Issues concerning federal government spending and financing its debt are discussed in the next chapter.

22-1a GOVERNMENT EXPENDITURES PATTERNS

Exhibit 2 shows program categories for federal government expenditures for 1970 and 2011. The largest category by far in the federal budget for 2011 was a category called *income security*. "Security" means these payments provide income to the elderly or disadvantaged, including Social Security, Medicare, unemployment compensation, public assistance (welfare), federal retirement, and disability benefits. These entitlements are transfer payments in the form of either direct cash payments or in-kind transfers that redistribute income among persons. In 2011, 40 percent of

EXHIBIT 2	Federal Government Expenditures, 1970 and 2011

Between 1970 and 2011, income security became the largest category of federal expenditures. During the same period, national defense declined from the largest spending category to the second largest. Income security and national defense combined accounted for 70 percent of federal outlays in 2011.

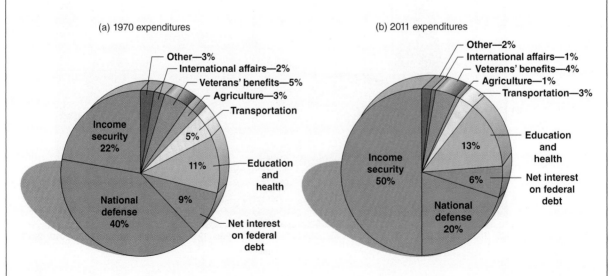

SOURCES: *Economic Report of the President*, 1975, Table C-65, p. 325; and *Economic Report of the President*, 2012, http://www.gpo.gov/fdsys/pkg/ERP-2012/content-detail.htm1, Table B-81.

income security expenditures was spent for Social Security and 28 percent for Medicare.

The second largest category of federal government expenditures in 2011 was national defense. Note that the percentage of the federal budget spent for defense declined from 40 percent in 1970 to 20 percent in 2011, while income security ("safety net") expenditures grew from 22 percent in 1970 to 50 percent in 2011. Hence, the dominant trend in federal government spending between 1970 and 2011 was an increase in the redistribution-of-income role of the federal government and a decrease in the portion of the budget spent for defense.

Federal expenditures for education and health were in third place in 2011, and net interest on the federal debt was in fourth place. Net interest paid is the interest on federal government borrowings minus the interest earned on federal government loans, and in 2011, this category of the budget was 6 percent. Thus, the federal government spent about the same proportion of the budget on financing its debt as on international affairs, veterans' benefits, and agriculture combined.

Finally, you need to be aware that the size and growth of government are measured several ways. We could study *absolute* government spending rather than percentages or compare the growth of spending after adjusting for inflation. Still another technique is to measure the proportion of the population that the public sector employs. Using any of these measurements confirms the following conclusion reached from Exhibits 1 and 2:

> **CONCLUSION:** *The government's share of total economic activity has generally increased since World War II ended in 1945. Most of the growth in combined government expenditures as a percentage of GDP reflects rapidly growing federal government transfer programs.*

22-1b GOVERNMENT EXPENDITURES IN OTHER COUNTRIES

In 2011, U.S. government spending for all levels as a percentage of GDP was lower than that of other advanced industrial countries. As shown in Exhibit 3, the governments of France, Sweden, Germany, and other countries spent a higher percentage of their GDPs than did the federal, state, and local governments of the United States.

22-2 Financing Government Budgets

Where does the federal government obtain the funds to finance its outlays? Exhibit 4 tells the story. We find that the largest revenue source in 2011 was individual income taxes (47 percent), followed closely by social insurance taxes (36 percent), which include payroll taxes paid by employers and employees for Social Security, workers' compensation, and unemployment insurance. The third best revenue collector was corporate income taxes (8 percent). An excise tax is a sales tax on the purchase of a particular good or service. Excise taxes contributed

EXHIBIT 3	Government Expenditures in Other Countries, 2011

In 2011, the U.S. government was less of a spender than other advanced industrial countries. As shown in this exhibit, the governments of France, Sweden, Germany, and other countries spent a higher percentage of their GDPs than did the federal, state, and local governments of the United States.

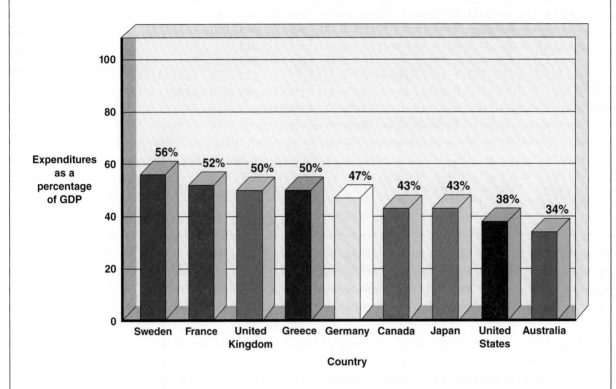

SOURCE: OECD (2011), "*OECD Economic Outlook* No. 90", OECD Economic Outlook: Statistics and Projections (database). http://dx.doi.org/10.1787/data-00588-en

3 percent of total tax receipts. The "Other" category includes receipts from such taxes as customs duties, estate taxes, and gift taxes.

22-2a THE TAX BURDEN IN OTHER COUNTRIES

Before turning our attention in the next section to the criteria for selecting which tax to impose, we must ask how burdensome overall taxation in the United States is. It may surprise you to learn that by international standards, U.S. citizens are among the most lightly taxed people in the industrialized world. Exhibit 5 reveals that in 2011, the tax collector was clearly much more heavy-handed in most other advanced industrial countries based on the fraction of GDP paid in taxes. The French, Swedes, Germans, Greeks, and British, for example, pay far higher taxes as a percentage of GDP than do Americans. It should be noted that countries that tax more heavily also are expected to provide more public services compared to those of the United States.

EXHIBIT 4	Federal Government Receipts, 2011

In 2011, the largest source of revenue for the federal government was individual income taxes, and the second largest source was social insurance taxes.

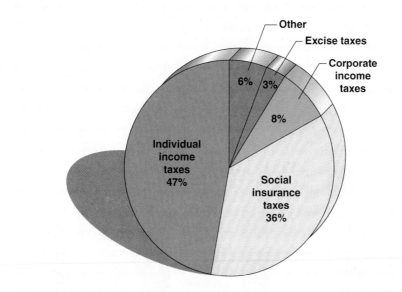

SOURCE: *Economic Report of the President*, 2012, http://www.gpo.gov/fdsys/pkg/ERP-2012/content-detail.html, Table B-81.

Another way to study the burden of taxation in the United States is to observe how it has changed over time. Exhibit 6 charts the growth of taxes as a percentage of GDP in the United States since 1929. Total government taxes, including federal, state, and local taxes, climbed from 11 percent of GDP in 1929 to their highest level of 34 percent in 2000 and then fell to 29 percent in 2011. The exhibit also shows that in 2000, federal taxes as a percentage of GDP rose to a post-World War II high of 21 percent before falling to about 15 percent in 2010 and 2011, which is the lowest percentage since 1950.

22-3 The Art of Taxation

Jean-Baptiste Colbert, finance minister to King Louis XIV of France, once said, "The art of taxation consists of so plucking the goose as to obtain the largest amount of feathers while promoting the smallest amount of hissing." Each year with great zeal, members of Congress and other policymakers debate various ways of raising revenue without causing too much "hissing." As you will learn, the task is difficult because each kind of tax has a different characteristic. Government must decide which tax is "appropriate" based on two basic philosophies of fairness—benefits received and ability-to-pay.

EXHIBIT 5	The Tax Burden in Selected Countries, 2011

Americans were more lightly taxed in 2011 than the citizens of other advanced industrial countries. For example, the Swedes, French, Germans, Greeks, and British pay higher taxes as a percentage of GDP.

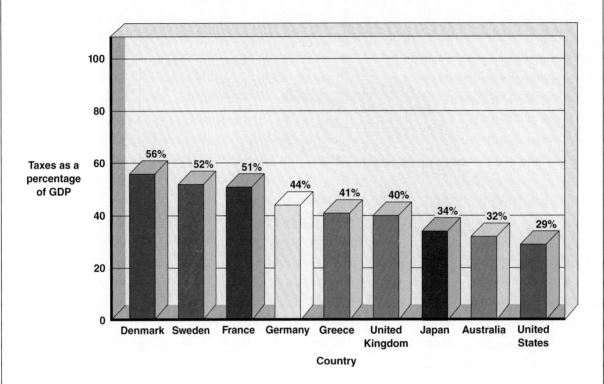

22-3a THE BENEFITS-RECEIVED PRINCIPLE

Benefits-received principle

The concept that those who benefit from government expenditures should pay the taxes that finance their benefits.

What standard or guideline can we use to be sure everyone pays his or her "fair" share of taxes? One possibility is the benefits-received principle of taxation, which is the concept that those who benefit from government expenditures should pay the taxes that finance their benefits. The gasoline tax is an example of a tax that follows the *benefits-received principle*. The number of gallons of gasoline bought is a measure of the amount of highway services used, and the more gallons purchased, the greater the tax paid. Applying benefit-cost analysis, voters will approve additional highways only if the benefits they receive exceed the costs in gasoline taxes they must pay for highway construction and repairs.

Although the benefits-received principle of taxation is applicable to a private good such as gasoline, the nature of *public goods* often makes it impossible to apply this principle. Recall from Chapter 4 that national defense is a public good, which users collectively consume. So how can we separate those who benefit from national defense and make them pay? We cannot, and there are other goods and services for which the benefits-received principle is inconsistent with societal goals.

EXHIBIT 6	The Growth of Taxes as a Percentage of GDP in the United States, 1929–2011

The graph shows the growth in federal, state, and local government taxes as a percentage of GDP since 1929. Total government taxes climbed from about 11 percent of GDP in 1929 to their highest level of 34 percent in 2000 before falling to 29 percent in 2010 and 2011. In 2000, federal taxes as a percentage of GDP reached a post-World War II high of 21 percent before falling to 15 percent in 2010 and 2011, which is the lowest percentage since 1950.

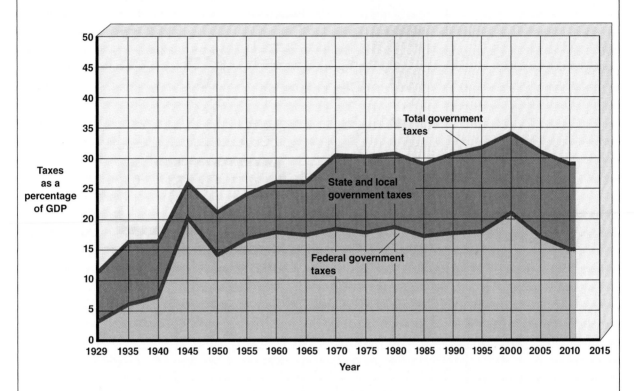

SOURCES: *Economic Report of the President*, 2012, http://www.gpo.gov/fdsys/pkg/ERP-2012/content-detail.htm1, Table B-79; and Bureau of Economic Analysis, *National Income Accounts*, http://www.bea.gov/national/nipaweb/SelectTable.asp?Selected=Y, Tables 1.1.5 and 3.3.

It would be foolish, for example, to ask families receiving food stamps to pay all the taxes required to finance their welfare benefits.

22-3b THE ABILITY-TO-PAY PRINCIPLE

A second popular principle of fairness in taxation sharply contrasts with the benefits-received principle. The ability-to-pay principle of taxation is the concept that those who have higher incomes can afford to pay a greater proportion of their income in taxes, regardless of benefits received. Under this tax philosophy, the rich may send their children to private schools or use private hospitals, but they should bear a heavier tax burden because they are better able to pay. How could there possibly be a problem with such an approach? An individual who earns

Ability-to-pay principle

The concept that those who have higher incomes can afford to pay a greater proportion of their income in taxes, regardless of benefits received.

$200,000 per year should pay X more taxes than an individual who earns only $10,000 per year. The difficulty lies in determining exactly how much more the higher-income individual should pay in taxes to ensure he or she is paying a "fair" amount. Unfortunately, no scientific method can measure precisely what one's "ability" to pay taxes means in dollars or percentage of income. Nevertheless, in the U.S. economy, the ability-to-pay principle dominates the benefits-received principle.

Where is the money I gave you last year?

Courtesy of Irvin Tucker

22-3c PROGRESSIVE, REGRESSIVE, AND PROPORTIONAL TAXES

As we have seen, governments raise revenues from various taxes, such as income taxes, sales taxes, excise taxes, and property taxes. For purposes of analysis, economists classify each of these taxes into three types of taxation—*progressive*, *regressive*, and *proportional*. The focus of these three classifications is the relationship between changes in the tax rates and increases or decreases in income. Income is the tax base because people pay taxes out of income, even though a tax is levied on property, such as land, buildings, automobiles, and furniture.

Progressive Taxes   Following the ability-to-pay principle, individual and corporate income taxes are progressive taxes. A progressive tax charges a higher percentage of income as income rises. For example, if a person earning $10,000 a year pays $1,500 in taxes, the *average* tax rate is 15 percent. If another person earns $100,000 a year and pays $28,000 in taxes, the average tax rate is 28 percent. This tax rate progressivity is the principle behind the federal and state income tax systems. Exhibit 8 illustrates the progressive nature of the federal income tax for a single person filing a 2011 tax return.

Progressive tax

A tax that charges a higher percentage of income as income rises.

EXHIBIT 7	Federal Individual Income Tax Rate Schedule for a Single Taxpayer, 2011					
(1) Taxable income		**(2)**	**(3)** Average tax rate [(2)/(1)]	**(4)** Change in taxable income	**(5)** Change in tax	**(6)** Marginal tax rate [(5)/(4)]
Over	**But not over**	**Tax***				
$ 0	$ 8,500	$ 850	10%	$ 8,500	$ 850	10%
8,500	34,500	4,750	14	26,000	3,900	15
34,500	83,600	17,025	20	49,100	12,275	25
83,600	174,400	42,449	24	90,800	25,424	28
174,400	379,150	110,016	29	204,750	67,567	33
379,150	...	...	...	...	...	35

*Tax calculated at the top of the taxable income brackets.

SOURCE: Internal Revenue Service, Publication 17, *Your Federal Income Tax*, 2012, http://www.irs.gov/publications/index.html, Tax Rate Schedules, p. 274.

Column (1) of Exhibit 7 lists the *taxable income* tax brackets. Taxable income is gross income minus the personal exemption and the standard deduction. The personal exemption and the standard deduction are adjusted each year so inflation does not push taxpayers into higher tax brackets. Column (2) shows the tax bill that a taxpayer at the upper income of each of the five lowest taxable income brackets must pay, and the figures in column (3) are the corresponding average tax rates. The average tax rate is the tax divided by the income:

Average tax rate
The tax divided by the income.

$$\text{Average tax rate} = \frac{\text{total tax due}}{\text{total taxable income}}$$

Thus, at a taxable income of $34,500, the average tax rate is 14 percent ($4,750 divided by $34,500), and at $83,600, it is 20 percent ($17,025 divided by $83,600). A taxable income of over $379,150 is included to represent the upper-income bracket. As these figures indicate, our federal individual income tax is a progressive tax because the average tax rate rises as income increases.

Another key tax rate measure is the marginal tax rate, which is the fraction of additional income paid in taxes. The marginal tax rate formula is expressed as

Marginal tax rate
The fraction of additional income paid in taxes.

$$\text{Marginal tax rate} = \frac{\text{change in taxes due}}{\text{change in taxable income}}$$

Column (6) in Exhibit 7 computes the marginal tax rate for each federal tax bracket in the table. You can comprehend the marginal tax rate by observing in column (1) that when taxable income rises from $8,500 to $34,500 in the second lowest tax bracket, the tax rises from $850 to $4,750 in column (2). Column (4) reports this change in taxable income, and column (5) shows the change in the tax. The marginal tax rate in column (6) is therefore 15 percent ($3,900 divided by $26,000). Apply the same analysis when taxable income increases by $49,100 from $34,500 to $83,600 in the next bracket. An additional $12,275 is added to the $4,750 tax bill, so the marginal tax rate on this extra income is 25 percent ($12,275 divided by $49,100). Similar computations provide the marginal tax rates for the remaining taxable income brackets. The marginal tax rate is important because it determines how much a taxpayer's tax bill changes as his or her income rises or falls within each tax bracket.

Regressive tax

A tax that charges a lower percentage of income as income rises.

Regressive Taxes   A tax can also be a regressive tax. A regressive tax charges a lower percentage of income as income rises. Suppose Mutt, who is earning $10,000 a year, pays a tax of $5,000, and Jeff, who earns $100,000 a year, pays $10,000 in taxes. Although Jeff pays twice the absolute amount, this would be regressive taxation because richer Jeff pays an average tax rate of 10 percent and poorer Mutt suffers a 50 percent tax bite. Such a tax runs afoul of the ability-to-pay principle of taxation.

We will now demonstrate that sales and excise taxes are regressive taxes. Assume that there is a 5 percent sales tax on all purchases and that the Jones family earned $80,000 during the last year, while the Jefferson family earned $20,000. A sales tax is regressive because the richer Jones family will spend a smaller portion of their income to buy food, clothing, and other consumption items. The Joneses, with an $80,000 income, can afford to spend $40,000 on groceries and clothes and save the rest, while the Jeffersons, with a $20,000 income, spend their entire income to feed and clothe their family. Because each family pays a 5 percent sales tax, the lower-income Jeffersons pay sales taxes of $1,000 (0.05 × $20,000). This $1,000 sales tax is 5 percent of their income ($1,000/$20,000). The higher-income Joneses, on the other hand, pay sales taxes of $2,000 (0.05 × $40,000). This $2,000 sales tax is only 2.5 percent of their income ($2,000/$80,000). Although the richer Jones family pays twice the amount of sales tax to the tax collector, the sales tax is regressive because their average tax rate is lower than the Jefferson family's tax rate.

In practice, an example of a regressive tax is the Social Security payroll tax, FICA. The payroll tax is a fixed percentage levied on each worker's earnings and deducted from the worker's paycheck by the employer.

Payroll taxes are regressive for two reasons. First, only wages and salaries are subject to this tax, while other sources of income, such as interest and dividends, are not. Because wealthy individuals typically receive a larger portion of their income from sources other than wages and salaries than do lower-income individuals, the wealthy pay a smaller fraction of their total income in payroll taxes. Second, earnings above a certain level are exempt from the Social Security tax. Thus, the *marginal tax rate* above a given threshold level is zero. In 2011, this level was $110,000 for wage and salary income subject to Social Security tax. Hence, any additional dollars earned above this figure add no additional taxes, and the average tax rate falls. On the other hand, there is no wage base limit for the Medicare tax. It is noteworthy that one idea for reforming Social Security is to adjust or remove the limit on income subject to Social Security tax.

Finally, property taxes are also considered regressive for two reasons. First, property owners add this tax to the rent paid by tenants who generally are lower-income persons. Second, property taxes are a higher percentage of income for poor families than rich families because the poor spend a much greater proportion of their incomes for housing.

| EXHIBIT 8 | The Progressive Income Tax versus a Flat Tax |

The taxable income tax brackets for 2011 are drawn from Exhibit 7. In contrast to the "stair step" tax rates, a flat tax would charge a single rate of, say, 17 percent. This reform proposal is controversial and is discussed in the You're the Economist, "Is It Time to Trash the 1040s?"

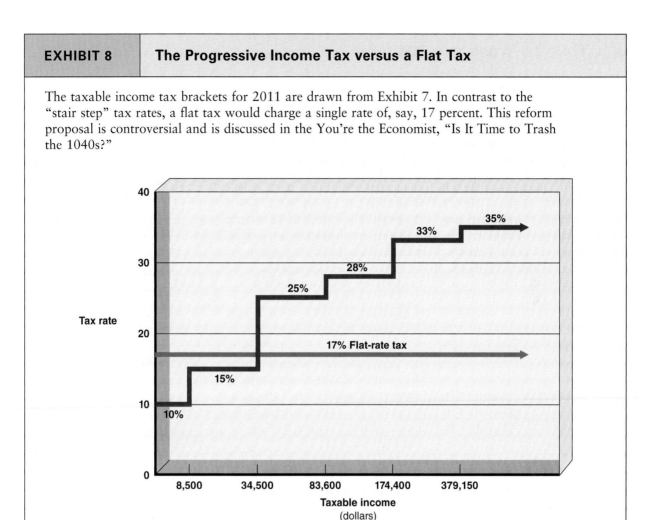

SOURCE: © Cengage Learning 2014

Proportional Taxes   There continues to be considerable interest in simplifying the federal progressive income tax by substituting a proportional tax, also called a *flat tax*. A proportional tax charges the same percentage of income, regardless of the size of income. For example, one way to reform the federal progressive tax rate system would be to eliminate all deductions, exemptions, and loopholes and simply apply the same tax rate, say, 17 percent of income to everyone. Such a reform is illustrated in Exhibit 8. This would avoid the "hissing" from taxpayers who would no longer require legions of accountants and lawyers to file their tax returns. Actually, most flat-tax proposals are not truly proportional because they exempt income below some level and are therefore somewhat progressive. Also, it is debatable that a 17 percent flat tax would raise enough revenue.

Let's look at whether the flat tax satisfies the benefits-received principle and the ability-to-pay principle. First, the flat tax does not necessarily relate to

Proportional tax

A tax that charges the same percentage of income, regardless of the size of income. Also called a *flat-tax rate* or simply a *flat tax*.

Is It Time to Trash the 1040s?

Applicable Concepts: flat tax, national sales tax, and Value Added Tax (VAT)

Two controversial fundamental tax reform ideas are often hot news topics. One proposal is the flat tax discussed earlier in this chapter, and the other is a national sales tax. The flat tax is favored by former presidential candidate and publisher Steve Forbes. It would grant a personal exemption of about $36,000 for a typical family and then tax income above this amount at 17 percent with no deductions. As stated by recent presidential candidate John McCain, the argument for a flat tax is that it would allow people to file their tax returns on a postcard and reduce the number of tax cheats. McCain proposed that the flat tax would be optional to the current tax system.

The flat-tax plan described above creates serious political problems by eliminating taxes on income from dividends, interest, capital gains, and inheritances. Also, eliminating deductions and credits would face strong opposition from the public. For example, eliminating the mortgage interest deduction and exemptions for health care and charity would be a difficult political battle. And there is the fairness question. People at the lower end of the current system of six progressive rates could face a tax increase while upper-income people would get the biggest tax break. The counterargument is that under the current tax system, many millionaires pay nothing because they shelter their income. Under a flat-tax scheme, they would lose deductions and credits.

A national retail sales tax is another tax reform proposal. In 2008, Mike Huckabee, Republican candidate for president, made this

the benefits received from any particular government goods or services. Second, consider a 17 percent tax that collects $17,000 from Ms. "Rich," who is earning $100,000 a year, and $1,700 from Mr. "Poor," who is earning $10,000 a year. Both taxpayers pay the same proportional 17 percent of their incomes, but the $1,700 tax is thought to represent a much greater sacrifice to Mr. Poor than does the $17,000 tax paid by Ms. Rich. After paying her taxes, Ms. Rich can still live comfortably, but Mr. Poor complains that he desperately needed the $1,700 to buy groceries for his family. To be fair, one can argue that the $17,000 paid by Ms. Rich is not enough based on the ability-to-pay principle.

22-3d REFORMING THE TAX SYSTEM

The Supreme Court declared the personal income tax unconstitutional in 1895. This changed in 1913 when the states ratified the Sixteenth Amendment to the Constitution, granting Congress the power to levy taxes on income. The federal income tax was an inconsequential source of revenue until World War II, but since then, it has remained a major source. Currently, 41 states have income taxes, idea, called the Fair Tax, central to his campaign. A consumption tax could eliminate all federal income taxes entirely (personal, corporate, and Social Security) and tax only consumer purchases at a given percentage. Like the flat tax, loopholes would be eliminated, and tax collection would become so simple that the federal government could save billions of dollars by cutting or eliminating the IRS. Taxpayers could save because they would no longer need to hire tax preparers and lawyers to prepare their complicated 1040 tax returns. Also, the tax base would broaden because, while not everyone earns income, almost everyone makes purchases.

Critics of a national sales tax argue that retail businesses would have the added burden of being tax collectors for the federal government, and the IRS would still be required to ensure that taxes are collected on billions of sales transactions. Moreover, huge price increases from the national sales tax would lead to "black market" transactions. The counterargument is that this problem would be no worse than current income tax evasion, and a sales tax indirectly taxes participants in illegal markets when they spend their income in legal markets. Also, a sales tax is regressive because the poor spend a greater share of their income on food, housing, and other necessities. To offset this problem, sales tax advocates propose subsidy checks paid up to some level of income. Critics also point out that retired people who pay little or no federal income tax will not welcome paying a national sales tax.

There are also debates on using a value-added tax (VAT) that is popular in Europe and many other countries. VAT is a consumption tax levied at each stage of production. Suppose a vendor buys apples from a farmer to sell at a market. The vendor's VAT is based on a percentage of the difference (value added) between the cost the vendor paid and the sales price customers pay. Customers who buy the apples bear the VAT cost built in the price of the apples they purchase.

Analyze the Issue

Assume the federal government replaces the federal income tax with a national sales tax on all consumption expenditures. Analyze the impact of this tax change on taxation efficiency and equity. Note that the federal government already collects a nationwide consumption tax through excise taxes on gasoline, liquor, and tobacco.

Source: © Cengage Learning 2014

and personal income taxes may become an increasingly important source of state and local revenues in years to come.

Over the years, Congress has enacted various reforms of the federal tax system. The Tax Reform Act of 1986, for example, marked the first time Congress has completely rewritten the Federal Tax Code since 1954. This law removed millions of households from the tax rolls by roughly doubling the personal exemption allowed for each taxpayer and his or her dependents. Before the tax law changed, there were 15 marginal tax brackets for individuals, ranging from 11 to 50 percent. The Tax Reform Act of 1986 reduced the number of tax brackets to only four. Most taxpayers are in the lower brackets, so the loss in tax revenue that resulted from lowering the individual tax rates was offset by raising taxes on corporations and closing numerous tax loopholes. Consistent with the two key taxation objectives, the intention of this major revision of the federal income tax law was to improve efficiency and make the system fairer by shifting more of the tax burden to corporations. As shown in Exhibits 7 and 8, there are currently six tax brackets, and critics argue that another tax reform act is long overdue. The You're the Economist titled "Is It Time to Trash the 1040s?" discusses ideas to reform the current federal tax system.

22-4 Public Choice Theory

Public choice theory

The analysis of the government's decision-making process for allocating resources.

James Buchanan, who won the 1986 Nobel Prize in economics, is the founder of a body of economic literature called public choice theory. Public choice theory is the analysis of the government's decision-making process for allocating resources. Recall from Chapter 4 that private-market failure is the reason for government intervention in markets. The theory of public choice considers how well the government performs when it replaces or regulates a private market. Rather than operating as the market mechanism to allocate resources, the government is a non-market, political decision-making force. Instead of behaving as private-interest buyers or sellers in the marketplace, actors in the political system have complex incentives in their roles as elected officials, bureaucrats, special-interest lobbyists, and voters.

Buchanan and other public choice theorists raise the fundamental issue of how well a democratic society can make efficient economic decisions. The basic principle of public choice theory is that politicians follow their own self-interest and seek to maximize their reelection chances, rather than promote the best interests of society. Thus, a major contribution of Buchanan has been to link self-interest motivation to government officials just as Adam Smith earlier identified the pursuit of self-interest as the motivation for consumers and producers. In short, individuals within any government agency or institution will act analogously to their private-sector counterparts; they will give first priority to improving their own earnings, working conditions, and status, rather than to being altruistic.

Given this introduction to the subject, let's consider a few public choice theories that explain why the public sector, like the private sector, may also "fail."

22-4a MAJORITY-RULE PROBLEM

Benefit-cost analysis

The comparison of the additional rewards and costs of an economic alternative.

To evaluate choices, economists often use a technique called benefit-cost analysis. Benefit-cost analysis is the comparison of the additional rewards and costs of an economic alternative. If a firm is considering producing a new product, its benefit ("carrots") will be the extra revenue earned from selling the product. The firm's cost ("sticks") is the opportunity cost of using resources to make the product. How many units of the product should the firm manufacture?

> **CONCLUSION:** *Rationally, a profit-maximizing firm follows the marginal rule and produces additional units so long as the marginal benefit exceeds the marginal cost.*

The basic rule of benefit-cost analysis is that undertaking a program whose cost exceeds its benefit is an inefficient waste of resources. In the competitive market system, undertaking projects that yield benefits greater than costs is a sure bet. In the long run, any firm that does not follow the benefit-cost rule will either go out of business or switch to producing products that yield benefits equal to or greater than their costs. Majority-rule voting, however,

EXHIBIT 9	Majority-Rule Benefit-Cost Analysis of Two Park Projects					
	Park Project A			Park Project B		
(1) **Voter**	**(2)** **Marginal cost (taxes)**	**(3)** **Marginal benefit**	**(4)** **Vote**	**(5)** **Marginal cost (taxes)**	**(6)** **Marginal benefit**	**(7)** **Vote**
Bob	$100	$ 0	No	$100	$ 90	No
Juan	100	101	Yes	100	90	No
Theresa	100	101	Yes	100	301	Yes
Total	$300	$202	Passes	$300	$481	Fails

SOURCE: © Cengage Learning 2014

can result in the approval of projects whose costs outweigh their benefits. Exhibit 9 illustrates how an inefficient economic decision can result from the ballot box.

As shown in Exhibit 9, suppose Bob, Juan, and Theresa are the only voters in a mini-society that is considering whether to add two publicly financed park projects, *A* and *B*. The total cost to taxpayers of either park project is $300, and the marginal cost of park *A* or park *B* to each taxpayer is an additional tax of $100 [columns (2) and (5)]. Next, assume each taxpayer determines his or her additional dollar value derived from the benefits of park projects *A* and *B* [columns (3) and (6)]. Assuming each person applies marginal analysis, each will follow the *marginal rule* and vote for a project only if his or her benefit exceeds the cost of the $100 tax. Consider park project *A*. This project is worth $0 to Bob, $101 to Juan, and $101 to Theresa, and this means two Yes votes and one No vote: the majority votes for park *A* [column (4)]. This decision would not happen in the business world. The Walt Disney Company, for example, would rationally reject such a project because the total of all consumers' marginal benefits is only $202, which is less than its $300 marginal cost.

The important point here is that majority-rule voting can make the correct benefit-cost marginal analysis, but it can also lead to a rejection of projects with marginal total benefits that exceed marginal costs. Suppose park project *B* costs $300 as well, and Bob's benefits are $90, Juan's $90, and Theresa's $301 [column (6)]. The total of all marginal benefits from constructing park *B* is $481, and this project would be undertaken in a private-sector market. But because only Theresa's benefits exceed the marginal $100 tax, park project *B* in the political arena receives only one Yes vote against two No votes and fails.

Why is there a distinction between political majority voting and benefit-cost analysis? The reason is that dollars can measure the intensity of voter preferences and "one-person, one-vote" does not. A count of ballots can determine whether a proposal passes or fails, but this count may not be proportional to the dollar strength of benefits among the individual voters.

22-4b SPECIAL-INTEREST GROUP EFFECT

In addition to benefit-cost errors from majority voting, special-interest groups can create government support for programs with costs outweighing their benefits. The *special-interest effect* occurs when the government approves programs that benefit only a small group within society, but society as a whole pays the costs. The influence of special-interest groups is indeed a constant problem for effective government because the benefits of government programs to certain small groups are great and the costs are relatively insignificant to each taxpayer. For example, let's assume the benefits of support prices for dairy farmers are $100 million. Because of the size of these benefits to dairy farmers, this special-interest group can well afford to hire professional lobbyists and donate a million dollars or so to the reelection campaigns of politicians voting for dairy price supports.

In addition to the incentive of financial support from special interests, politicians can also engage in *logrolling*. Logrolling is the political practice of trading votes of support for legislated programs. Politician A says to politician B, "You vote for my dairy price support bill, and I will vote for your tobacco price support bill."

But who pays for these large benefits to special-interest groups? Taxpayers do, of course, but the extra tax burden per taxpayer is very low. Although Congress may enact a $200 million program to favor, say, a few defense contractors, this expenditure costs 100 million taxpayers only $2 per taxpayer. Because in a free society it is relatively easy to organize special-interest constituencies and lobby politicians to spread the cost, it is little wonder that spending programs are popular. Moreover, the small cost of each pet program per taxpayer means there is little reward for a single voter to learn the details of the many special-interest legislation proposals.

22-4c RATIONAL VOTER IGNORANCE

Rational ignorance

The voter's choice to remain uninformed because the marginal cost of obtaining information is higher than the marginal benefit from knowing it.

Politicians, appointed officials, and bureaucrats constitute the supply side of the political marketplace. The demand side of the political market consists of special-interest groups and voters who are subject to what economists call rational ignorance. Rational ignorance is a voter's decision that the benefit of becoming informed about an issue is not worth the cost. A frequent charge in elections is that the candidates are not talking about the issues. One explanation is that the candidates realize that a sizable portion of the voters will make a calculated decision not to judge the candidates based on in-depth knowledge of their positions on a wide range of issues. Instead of going to the trouble of reading position papers and doing research, many voters choose their candidates based simply on party affiliation or on how the candidate appears on television. This approach is rational if the perceived extra effort required to be better informed exceeds the marginal benefit of knowing more about the candidate.

The principle of rational ignorance also explains why eligible voters fail to vote on election day. A popular explanation is that low voter participation results from apathy among potential voters, but the decision can be an exercise in practical benefit-cost analysis. Nonvoters presumably perceive that the opportunity cost of going to the polls outweighs the benefit gained from any of the candidates or issues on the ballot. Moreover, nonvoters perceive that one extra vote is unlikely to change the outcome.

Public choice theorists argue that one reason benefits are difficult to measure is that the voter confronts an *indivisible* public service. In a grocery store, the consumer can decide to spend so much on apples, oranges, and other *divisible* items, but voting involves candidates who take stands on many issues. The point is that voting does not allow the voter to pick and choose among the candidate's good and bad positions. Most voters, in short, must "buy" a confusing mixture of "wants" and "unwants" that are difficult to interpret as a benefit.

22-4d BUREAUCRATIC INEFFICIENCY

The bureaucracy is the body of nonelected officials and administrators who operate government agencies. As government grows, one of the concerns is that the bureaucracy may become more powerful than the executive, legislative, and judicial branches. Public choice theory also considers how bureaucratic behavior affects economic decision making. One principle is that the government bureaucracy tends to be inefficient because of the absence of the profit motive.

What happens when a government agency performs poorly? First, there is no competition from other producers to take away market share. There are no shareholders demanding reform when profits are falling because taxpayers are a poor substitute for stockholder pressure. Second, the typical government response each year is to request a larger budget. Without profits as a measure of performance, the tendency is to use the size of an agency's budget and staff as an indicator of success. In brief, the basic incentive structure of government agencies encourages inefficient management because, unlike the market system, there is a lack of incentive to be cost-conscious or creative. Instead, the hallmark of the bureaucrat is to be extremely cautious and make all decisions "by the book." Such behavior may maximize prestige and security, but it usually fails to minimize costs.

22-4e SHORTSIGHTEDNESS EFFECT

Finally, it can be argued that democracy has a bias toward programs offering clear benefits and hidden costs. The reason is that political officeholders must run for reelection after a relatively short period of two to six years. Given this reality, politicians tend to favor proposals providing immediate benefits, with future generations paying most of the costs. Conversely, they reject programs that have easily identifiable short-run high costs, but offer benefits only after a decade. Hence, the essence of the hidden costs bias, or *shortsightedness effect*, is that both voters and politicians suffer from a short time horizon. Such a myopic view of either future costs or future benefits can cause an irrational acceptance of a program, even though long-run costs exceed short-run benefits, or an irrational rejection of a program with long-run benefits that outweigh short-run costs.

✓ **CHECKPOINT**

What Does Public Choice Say about a Budget Deficit?

In 2002, the situation switched from a few years in which the federal government spent less than it collected in taxes to spending more than tax revenues (discussed in the next chapter). James Buchanan predicted over 30 years ago that growing government deficits would be inevitable. He maintained that government officials would increase spending for their constituents in order to gain votes. Furthermore, politicians would shy away from tax increases for fear of alienating voters. The net effect would be deficits. Was Buchanan's prediction based on the rational ignorance effect, government inefficiency, or the shortsightedness effect?

Key Concepts

Government expenditures
Benefits-received principle
Ability-to-pay principle
Progressive tax

Average tax rate
Marginal tax rate
Regressive tax
Proportional tax or flat tax

Public choice theory
Benefit-cost analysis
Rational ignorance

Summary

- **Government expenditures,** including transfer payments, have grown from about one-quarter of GDP in 1950 to about 40 percent of GDP today.

- **Federal tax revenues** are collected primarily from individual income taxes and social insurance taxes.

Government Expenditures

SOURCES: *Economic Report of the President,* 2012, http://www.gpo.gov/fdsys/pkg/ERP-2012/content-detail.htm1, Table B-79; and Bureau of Economic Analysis, *National Income Accounts,* http://www.bea.gov/national/nipaweb/SelectTable.asp?Selected=Y, Tables 1.1.5 and 3.3.

Federal Tax Revenues

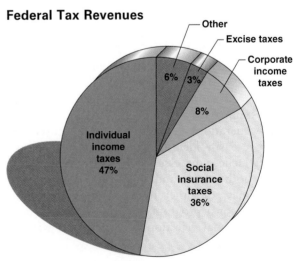

SOURCE: *Economic Report of the President,* 2012, http://www.gpo.gov/fdsys/pkg/ERP-2012/content-detail.htm1, Table B-81.

- The **taxation burden**, measured by taxes as a percentage of GDP, is lighter in the United States than in many other advanced industrial countries.

Taxation Burden

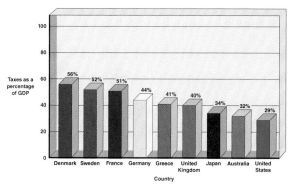

Country

SOURCE: OECD (2011), "*OECD Economic Outlook* No. 90", OECD Economic Outlook: Statistics and Projections (database). http://dx.doi.org/10.1787/data-00588-en

- **Total tax revenues** amounted to about 11 percent of GDP in 1929 and reached the highest level of close to 34 percent in 2000 before falling to 29 percent in 2011. Federal taxes take a larger share of GDP than state and local governments.

Total tax Revenues

SOURCES: *Economic Report of the President*, 2012, http://www.gpo.gov/fdsys/pkg/ERP-2012/content-detail.htm1, Table B-79; and Bureau of Economic Analysis, *National Income Accounts*, http://www.bea.gov/national/nipaweb/SelectTable.asp?Selected=Y, Tables 1.1.5 and 3.3.

- The **benefits-received principle** and the **ability-to-pay principle** are two basic philosophies of taxation fairness. The gasoline tax is a classic example of the benefits-received principle because users of the highways pay the gasoline tax. Progressive income taxes follow the ability-to-pay principle because there is a direct relationship between the average tax rate and income size. Sales, excise, property, and flat-rate taxes violate this principle because each results in a greater burden on the poor than on the rich.
- **Public choice theory** reveals the government's decision-making process. For example, government failure can occur for any of the following reasons: (1) majority voting may not follow benefit-cost analysis; (2) special-interest groups can obtain large benefits and spread their costs over many taxpayers; (3) rational voter ignorance means a sizable portion of the voters will decide not to make informed judgments; (4) bureaucratic behavior may not lead to cost-effective decisions; and (5) politicians suffer from a short time horizon, leading to a bias toward hiding the costs of programs.

Summary of Conclusion Statements

- The government's share of total economic activity has generally increased since World War II ended in 1945. Most of the growth in combined government expenditures as a percentage of GDP reflects rapidly growing federal government transfer programs.

- Rationally, a profit-maximizing firm follows the marginal rule and produces additional units so long as the marginal benefit exceeds the marginal cost.

Study Questions and Problems

1. Explain why federal, state, and local expenditures account for about 40 percent of GDP, but total government spending (G in GDP) is only about 20 percent of GDP.

2. Identify the major differences between federal government outlays and spending by state and local governments.

3. What are the primary tax revenue sources at the federal, state, and local levels of government?

4. Which of the following taxes satisfy the benefits-received principle, and which satisfy the ability-to-pay principle?
   a. Gasoline tax
   b. Federal income tax
   c. Tax on Social Security benefits

5. What is the difference between the marginal tax rate and the average tax rate?

6. Explain why a 5 percent sales tax on gasoline is regressive.

7. Ms. Jones has a taxable income of $30,000, and she must pay $3,000 in taxes. Mr. Smith has a taxable income of $60,000. How much tax must Mr. Smith pay for the tax system to be
   a. progressive?
   b. regressive?
   c. proportional?

8. Explain why each of the following taxes is progressive or regressive.
   a. A $1 per pack federal excise tax on cigarettes
   b. The federal individual income tax
   c. The federal payroll tax

9. Complete the following table, which describes the sales tax paid by individuals at various income levels. Indicate whether the tax is progressive, proportional, or regressive.

Income	Total spending	Sales tax paid	Sales tax paid as a percentage of income
$ 1,000	$ 1,000	$ 100	_____%
5,000	3,500	350	_____
10,000	6,000	600	_____
100,000	40,000	4,000	_____

10. Calculate the average and marginal tax rates in the following table, and indicate whether the tax is progressive, proportional, or regressive. What observation can you make concerning the relationship between marginal and average tax rates?

Income	Tax paid	Average tax rate	Marginal tax rate
$ 0	$ 0	0%	0%
100	10	_____	_____
200	30	_____	_____
300	60	_____	_____
400	100	_____	_____
500	150	_____	_____

11. Compare "dollar voting" in private markets with "majority voting" in the political decision-making system.

For Online Exercises, go to the Tucker Web site at www.cengage.com/economics/tucker.

✓ CHECKPOINT ANSWER

What Does Public Choice Say about a Budget Deficit?

The government uses the deficit to finance clear short-term benefits, paying little attention to long-term consequences. If you said public choice predicts that government officials will emphasize near-term benefits to gain votes (the shortsightedness effect), **YOU ARE CORRECT.**

Sample Quiz

For an explanation of the correct answers, visit the Tucker Web site at www.cengage.com/economics/tucker.

1. Currently, total government expenditures in the United States is approximately
   a. 40 percent of GDP.
   b. 50 percent of GDP.
   c. 75 percent of GDP.
   d. 80 percent of GDP.

2. Which of the following categories accounted for the largest percentage of total federal government expenditures in recent years?
   a. income security
   b. national defense
   c. education and health
   d. interest on the national debt

3. Which of the following taxes contributed the greatest percentage of total federal government tax revenues in recent years?
   a. individual income taxes
   b. corporate income taxes
   c. Social Security taxes
   d. excise taxes

4. How do total taxes as a percentage of GDP in the United States compare to those of Western European countries, such as the United Kingdom, Germany, and Sweden?
   a. U.S. taxation is smaller.
   b. U.S. taxation is about the same.
   c. U.S. taxation is slightly larger.
   d. U.S. taxation is substantially larger.

5. The benefits-received principle of taxation is *most* evident in
   a. progressive tax rates.
   b. excise taxes on gasoline.
   c. the personal income tax.
   d. the corporate income tax.

6. A tax is regressive if it collects a
   a. larger amount as income rises.
   b. constant amount as income rises.
   c. smaller fraction of income as income falls.
   d. smaller fraction of income as income rises.

7. Which of the following is an example of a progressive tax?
   a. the excise tax on cigarettes
   b. the federal tax on gasoline
   c. the federal personal income tax
   d. All of the above answers are correct

8. A tax structured so that people with the same income pay the same percentage of their income in taxes is called a(an)
   a. flat tax.
   b. regressive tax.
   c. progressive tax.
   d. excise tax.

Sample Quiz *continued*

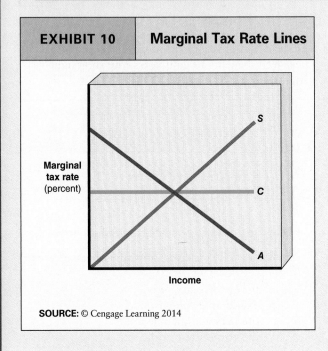

EXHIBIT 10	Marginal Tax Rate Lines

Marginal tax rate (percent)

S

C

A

Income

SOURCE: © Cengage Learning 2014

9. In Exhibit 10, line *A* represents a(an)
   a. regressive tax.
   b. progressive tax.
   c. proportional tax.
   d. ability-to-pay tax.

10. In Exhibit 10, line *B* represents a
    a. regressive tax.
    b. progressive tax.
    c. proportional tax.
    d. flat tax.

11. In Exhibit 10, line *C* represents a
    a. regressive tax.
    b. progressive tax.
    c. proportional tax.
    d. ability-to-pay tax.

12. In Exhibit 10, if *A* represents state and local taxes and *B* represents federal income taxes, what is the result of imposing both types of taxes?
    a. a regressive tax
    b. a progressive tax
    c. a proportional tax
    d. an ability-to-pay tax

13. The study of the decision-making process of government is the study of
    a. Keynesian economics.
    b. public choice theory.
    c. rational expectations theory.
    d. social economics.

14. People who often create benefits for the minority and impose the cost on the majority are called
    a. fair-interest groups.
    b. encounter groups.
    c. laissez-faire groups.
    d. special-interest groups.

15. Voters may choose to remain uninformed about an issue because of
    a. the special-interest effect.
    b. rational ignorance.
    c. bureaucratic inefficiency.
    d. the shortsightedness effect.

16. Which of the following categories accounted for the lowest percentage of total federal government expenditures in recent years?
    a. income security
    b. national defense
    c. education and health
    d. interest on the national debt

17. Since 1929, total government taxes as a percentage of GDP
    a. climbed from 10 percent to about 30 percent.
    b. remained close to 30 percent.
    c. climbed from 30 percent to about 50 percent.
    d. climbed from 15 percent to about 50 percent.

18. "It would be an undue hardship to require people whose income is below $15,000 per year to pay income taxes." This statement reflects which of the following principles for a tax?
    a. benefits-received
    b. inexpensive-to-collect

Sample Quiz *continued*

c. ability-to-pay
d. fairness of contribution

19. If a person is taxed $100 on an income of $1,000, taxed $180 on an income of $2,000, and taxed $220 on an income of $3,000, this person is paying a
a. progressive tax.
b. poll tax.

c. proportional tax.
d. regressive tax.

20. According to the shortsightedness effect, politicians tend to favor projects with
a. short-run benefits and short-run costs.
b. short-run benefits and long-run costs.
c. long-run benefits and short-run costs.
d. long-run benefits and long-run costs.

Federal Deficits, Surpluses, and the National Debt

The U.S. government has been in the red almost continuously since the Revolutionary War forced the Continental Congress to borrow money. The only exception was a brief interlude more than a century and a half ago when our government was debt-free. In December 1834, President Andrew Jackson proudly reported to Congress what he considered to be a major accomplishment of his administration. By New Year's Day 1835, the federal government would succeed in paying off the national debt. It was Jackson's second term as president. Since the close of the War of 1812, the country had experienced tremendous growth, and revenues flowed into the U.S. Treasury from import tariffs and the sale of public land. By early 1836, the nation had been out of debt for two years, and there was a budget surplus of $37 million. The dilemma in those days was how to use the surplus. In 1836, Congress simply decided to divide all but $5 million of the surplus among the states. Then the financial panic of 1837 caused the government to plunge into debt again, where it remains today and for the foreseeable future.

Unlike Andrew Jackson, Abraham Lincoln, in his 1864 Annual Message to Congress, expressed no concern for paying off the national debt. Lincoln stated:

> The great advantage of citizens being creditors as well as debtors, with relation to the public debt, is obvious. Men can readily perceive that they cannot be much oppressed by a debt which they owe to themselves.

As this text is written in 2012, federal government borrowing to cover its budget deficits had accumulated a national debt of about $16 trillion. To the average citizen, this is an incomprehensible amount of money for even the government to owe. Perhaps the best way to picture this sea of red ink is that your individual share is over $50,000 and rising.

In this chapter, you will learn to solve these economics puzzles:

- Can Uncle Sam go bankrupt?

- How does the national debt of the United States compare to the debt of other countries?

- Are we passing the debt burden to our children?

- Who owns the national debt?

23-1 The Federal Budget Balancing Act

What will happen next? Like a high-wire performer swinging one way and then another while the crowd below gazes transfixed, the public in the late 1990s and early 2000s watched the federal budget sway back and forth between deficits and surpluses. As you learned in the preceding chapter on fiscal policy, a federal budget deficit occurs whenever the government spends more than it collects in taxes. The accumulation of these budget deficits over the years is the origin of the national debt. When the federal government has a surplus in its budget, some or all of the surplus can be used to retire the national debt, and it decreases. Here you will take a closer look at the actual budgetary process that creates and finances our national debt.

23-1a THE FEDERAL BUDGETARY PROCESS

In theory, Keynesian discretionary fiscal policy requires that legislation be enacted to change government spending or taxes in order to shift the aggregate demand curve represented in the AD-AS model. In practice, the federal budgetary process, which determines the level of spending and taxation, is not so orderly. The annual "battle of the budget" on Capitol Hill involves political decisions on how much the government plans to spend and where the money will come from to finance these outlays. Wrangling takes place between all sorts of camps: the president versus Congress, Republicans versus Democrats, national security versus economic equality, price stability versus full employment, health care versus tax cuts, and so on. Given the complexities of world events, special-interest groups, volatile public opinion, and political ambitions that complicate the budget process, it is no wonder actual fiscal policy often ignores textbook macroeconomics.

The following brief look at the federal budgetary process shows how Congress and the president make federal spending and tax decisions each year:

Stage 1: Presidential Budget Submission   The president must submit the budget to Congress on or before the first Monday in February of each year. The official title is *The Budget of the United States*. This unveiling of the administration's budget is always big news. Does the president recommend that less money be spent for defense and more for education? Is there an increase in the Social Security payroll tax or the income tax? And how large is the national debt? Is there a budget deficit or a budget surplus?

Stage 2: Budget Resolution   After the president submits the budget in January, Congress takes the lead in the budgetary process. The president's budget now becomes the starting point for congressional consideration. The Congressional Budget Office (CBO) employs a professional staff that advises Congress on the budget. The CBO analyzes the budget by February and reports its evaluation at budget committee hearings in both the House of Representatives and the Senate. After debate, in May, Congress approves an overall budget outline called the *budget resolution*, which sets target levels for spending, tax revenues, and the budget deficit or surplus.

Stage 3: Budget Passed   Throughout the summer and supposedly ending by October 1, Congress and the president debate while congressional committees and subcommittees prepare specific spending and tax law bills. The budget resolution is supposed to guide the spending and revenue decisions of these committees. After Congress passes and the president signs the spending and revenue bills, the federal government has its actual budget for spending and tax collection.

As summarized in Exhibit 1, the budgetary process seems orderly enough, but in practice, it does not work so smoothly. The process can, and often does, go astray. One problem is that Congress does not necessarily follow its own rules. The budget bills are not always passed on time, and when that happens, the fiscal year starts without a budget. Then federal agencies must operate on the basis of *continuing resolutions*, which means each agency operates as it did the previous year until spending bills are approved. In some years, Congress even fails to pass a continuing resolution, and the federal government must shut down and workers stay home until Congress approves the necessary funds.

EXHIBIT 1	**Major Steps in the Federal Budgetary Process**

The first step is the president's transmittal of the administration's budget to Congress. In the second step, Congress passes a budget resolution that sets targets for spending, taxes, and the deficit or surplus. In the third step, Congress passes the budget consisting of specific spending and tax bills. When the president signs the spending and revenue bills, the federal government has its actual budget.

Presidential budget submission February — Budget resolution May — Budget passed and president signs September

SOURCE: © Cengage Learning 2014

23-1b FINANCING THE NATIONAL DEBT

Over the years, the federal government budget experiences imbalances. A budget deficit occurs when federal expenditures, including spending for final goods plus transfer payments, exceed tax revenues collected. A surplus occurs when the government collects more in taxes than it spends. For example, for four years between 1998 and 2001, budget surpluses existed, as discussed in the next You're the Economist feature. As shown in Exhibit 2, deficits returned after the 2001 recession, and following the Great Recession of 2007–2009, deficits reached record highs. In 2009, a record-breaking federal deficit was $1.4 trillion. In 2011, the deficit was $1.3 trillion.

What happens when the government overspends, and the U.S. Treasury must borrow to finance the difference between expenditures and revenues? The answer to that question is the U.S. Treasury borrows by selling Treasury bills (T-bills), notes, and bonds promising to make specified interest payments and to repay the loaned funds on a given date. These government securities are IOUs of the federal government. They are considered a safe haven for idle funds and are purchased by Federal Reserve banks, government agencies, private banks, corporations, individual U.S. citizens, and foreigners. If you own a U.S. government savings bond, for example, you have loaned your funds to the federal government. The stock of these federal government IOUs accumulated over the years is called the *gross public debt*, *federal debt*, or national debt. The national debt is the total amount owed by the federal government to owners of government securities. There are national debt clocks on the Internet and in several cities around the United States that display the amount of money owed by the federal government.

National debt

The total amount owed by the federal government to owners of government securities.

EXHIBIT 2	U.S. Federal Budget Surpluses and Deficits, 1998–2011

During 1998 through 2001, the annual federal government budget was in surplus each year. After the recession of 2001, these surpluses disappeared and deficits appeared, exploding to $1.4 trillion in 2009. In 2011, the deficit was $1.3 trillion.

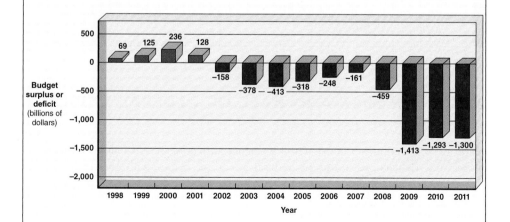

SOURCE: *Economic Report of the President*, 2012, http://www.gpo.gov/fdsys/pkg/ERP-2012/content-detail.html, Table B-78.

Note that the national debt does not include state and local governments' debt. Also, as mentioned above, the national debt does include U.S. Treasury securities purchased by various federal agencies, such as the Social Security trust fund. When the Social Security trust fund collects more in taxes than it pays out in retirement benefits, it lends the extra money to the federal government for spending. This means federal budget deficits would be significantly higher, or budget surpluses would be significantly lower, without federal government borrowing from this trust fund. If we subtract the portion of the national debt held by all government agencies (what the federal government owes to itself), we can compute the net public debt. Beware! Confusion sometimes occurs when the media use the term *public debt* without specifying whether the reference is to "gross" or "net" public debt.

Net public debt

National debt minus all government interagency borrowing.

Before proceeding, let's pause and explain the Social Security trust fund in a little more detail. A misconception is that the Social Security Administration (SSA) collects the annual Social Security surpluses and stacks the cash with reserve cash from previous surpluses in a vault, or special checking account. When the trust fund is in deficit as the baby boomers retire and the ratio of workers paying into the system to people drawing benefits shrinks, the SSA will open the vault and/or write a check to draw on trust fund reserves to pay its obligations.

Here is what really happens to Social Security tax dollars. When excess Social Security taxes are collected by the SSA, these surplus funds must, by law, be immediately withdrawn and given to the Treasury, which, in turn, issues "nonmarketable" interest-bearing Treasury bonds to the SSA. The Treasury then spends this money on welfare, roads, tax cuts, defense, or whatever the federal government decides. On the other hand, if the trust fund cannot pay for retirees' needs, then the SSA will ask the Treasury to redeem its bonds for cash to pay benefits. In this situation, where will the Treasury get the money to repay the SSA? It will either print it, borrow it, levy additional taxes, or cut benefits. In short, the full faith and credit of the U.S. federal government promises to pay itself enough money when needed to pay for Social Security.

CONCLUSION: *The national debt includes the Social Security trust fund, and as a result, federal budget deficits are reduced or budget surpluses are raised.*

23-1c THE RISE AND FALL OF FEDERAL BUDGET SURPLUSES AND DEFICITS

Here we will examine in more detail influences affecting recent federal budget surpluses and deficits. Restraint on federal spending began with the 1990 Budget Enforcement Act (BEA), which set spending caps on broad areas of discretionary spending. The BEA also required that any proposal to increase spending or decrease tax revenues over agreed limits had to be offset by an equal amount of tax revenue increases or new spending cuts. This pay-as-you-go legislation is called a "PayGo" rule. In 1993, Congress passed the Deficit Reduction Act, which increased tax revenues. This act took into account the ability-to-pay principle by increasing the highest marginal tax rate for individuals and raising the corporate income tax rate. It also increased the federal tax on gasoline. A gasoline tax offers the extra benefit of reducing the quantity of energy demanded and conforms to the benefits-received principle. However, a gasoline tax suffers from the problem of being regressive.

The spending caps combined with tax increases and a growing high-employment economy driven by technological advances, for example, the Internet, transformed federal budget deficits into surpluses during the late 1990s. Exhibit 3(a) shows federal expenditures and tax revenues expressed as a percentage of GDP. The difference between these two curves represents the federal deficit or surplus, also expressed as a percentage of GDP. Between 1991 and 2000, federal government expenditures as a percentage of GDP declined from 22 percent to 18 percent of GDP, and federal government tax revenues as a percentage of GDP crept steadily upward from 18 percent to 21 percent of GDP. The result of these changes in tax and spending percentages of GDP was four years of federal surpluses from 1998 to 2001. However, in 2002, the PayGo budget rule expired, and from 2002 through today, the federal budget has returned to red ink deficits.

After the Great Recession beginning in 2007, the deficit surged to historic highs when in 2009, federal expenditures climbed sharply to 25 percent of GDP, while tax revenues plummeted to a record low of only 15 percent of GDP. Recall from the automatic stabilizers explained in the previous chapter that during a recession, government expenditures rise for transfer payments when people lose jobs and tax revenues decline from individuals and companies making less money. Moreover, these unprecedented deficit figures flowed from the Wall Street bailout and economic stimulus bill, which sharply increased federal government spending relative to tax collections. In 2011, expenditures were 25 percent of GDP.

Exhibit 3(b) provides an alternate graph of the federal budget deficit or surplus as a percentage of GDP. During President Reagan's first term in the early 1980s, the combined effect of recession, a military spending buildup, and a cut in income taxes caused a rise in the deficit to 5 percent of GDP. During the 1990–1991 recession, the deficit as a percentage of GDP again reached close to 5 percent. However, during the Great Recession in 2009, the federal deficit soared to a record high since World War II of 10 percent of GDP. In 2011, the deficit fell slightly to 9 percent of GDP.

It is interesting to note that during the Great Depression, federal deficits were unimpressive by today's standards. As a share of GDP, Roosevelt's New Deal deficits (stimulus package) peaked at 6 percent of GDP in 1934. It is also noteworthy that in 2010, President Obama requested and the Senate passed a new PayGo law. But there are 50 programs whose spending is exempt from this law, including Social Security, veterans, trust funds, and emergency spending, such as a jobs bill or unemployment benefits.

23-1d DEBT CEILING

The debt ceiling is a method for curbing the national debt. A debt ceiling is a legislated legal limit on the national debt. This means that the federal government cannot legally allow a budget deficit to raise the national debt beyond the ceiling.

Debt ceiling

A legislated legal limit on the national debt.

| EXHIBIT 3 | Federal Expenditures, Revenues, and Deficits as a Percentage of GDP, 1990–2011 |

Part (a) shows that after the 1990–1991 recession, federal government expenditures as a percentage of GDP declined until 2000, while federal government tax revenues rose steadily. The results were federal surpluses between 1998 and 2001. After the Great Recession beginning in 2007, the deficit reached a record high when expenditures rose to 25 percent of GDP in 2009, and tax revenues plummeted to only 15 percent of GDP. In 2011, expenditures were 24 percent of GDP and taxes were 15 percent.

Part (b) focuses on the federal deficit or surplus as a percentage of GDP. In 1992, the federal deficit as a percentage of GDP was about 5 percent. After reaching a budget surplus peak of 2.4 percent in 2000, the federal budget deficit soared to a historic high of 10 percent of GDP in 2009. In 2011, the deficit was 9 percent of GDP.

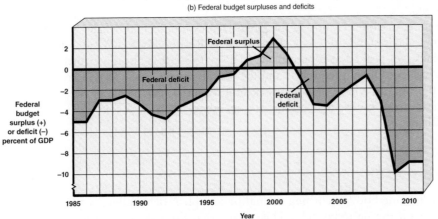

SOURCE: *Economic Report of the President*, 2012, http://www.gpo.gov/fdsys/pkg/ERP-2012/content-detail.htm1, Table B-79.

The Great Federal Budget Surplus Debate
Applicable Concept: federal budget surplus

As unprecedented deficit figures flowed during the Great Recession, it is hard to believe that for four years the federal budget was in surplus. After a one-year small budget surplus in 1969, it took 29 contentious years to eliminate federal budget deficits. And then surpluses occurred between 1998 and 2001, as shown in Exhibits 2 and 3, before becoming today what seems to be a historic relic. These federal budget surpluses aroused as much controversy in their time as deficits do in their years. In short, the hotly contested debate involved whether the surplus should be saved, spent, or devoted to tax cuts. The case for tax cuts and smaller government is based on the view that a surplus is the result of excess tax collections. Proponents of tax cuts pointed out that in 2000, federal tax revenues as a percentage of GDP were the highest since revenues during World War II. Moreover, tax rate cuts would spur the economy and result in higher future tax revenues. The argument for spending a surplus is based on "unmet needs." Instead of tax cuts, the surplus could be used to finance spending for defense, public infrastructure, research and development, and social programs such as education or health care. Also, a large proportion of American households pay no income taxes. Tax cuts therefore do not benefit people who are not prosperous enough to pay taxes.

An alternative to tax cuts and spending increases is paying down the national debt. Former Federal Reserve Chairman Alan Greenspan supported this approach. He said Congress faced the quandary of trying to establish fiscal policy based on long-range forecasts that may prove inaccurate. He stated that if Congress cuts taxes, it also has to be prepared to cut spending significantly in the event that the forecasts on which the cuts were based are proved wrong. On the other hand, using the budget surplus to fund "irrevocable spending programs" would be "the worst of all outcomes." Testifying before the Senate Budget Committee in 2001, Greenspan suggested that the proposed tax cut bill include provisions that would limit the tax cuts if specified future targets for the budget surpluses or debt reduction were not met. These provisions were not included in the 2001 tax bill.

The outcome of the "Great Federal Budget Surplus Debate" was that President George W. Bush signed a $1.35 trillion tax cut bill in 2001 spread over ten years. It was the largest and most widespread tax cut since the 1980s, during Ronald Reagan's presidency. And in spite of the tax cuts, the outlook for surpluses in the future was optimistic. In August 2001, the Office of Management and Budget (OMB) projected continuously growing budget surpluses that would peak at about $400 billion in 2007. The actual federal budget in 2007 was a $161 billion deficit, and the OMB dramatically changed its projections to deficits that exploded to $1.4 trillion in 2009 at the conclusion of the Great Recession. As actual deficit figures become available, check the accuracy of OMB estimates reported here.

Federal budget deficit projections
(billions of dollars)

Source: Office of Management and Budget, http://www.whitehouse.gov/OMB/budget/overview, Summary Table 5.1.

Analyze the Issue

1. Refer to Exhibit 8 in the chapter on fiscal policy. Using demand-side and supply-side fiscal policy theories, explain how a tax cut could either increase or decrease the price level.

2. Using the Laffer curve discussed in the You're the Economist box in the chapter on fiscal policy, explain how proponents could claim that the tax cut would increase tax revenues.

Source: © Cengage Learning 2014

It works like the credit limit on your charge card. When you reach the limit, you cannot charge any more and you must pay cash. When the federal government hits the debt limit, it cannot borrow any more to supplement its cash from taxes and other sources. What usually happens when the budget pushes against the debt ceiling is that the federal government raises its own ceiling to accommodate the budget deficit. Raising the debt ceiling often provokes a fiery political debate over government spending. Failure to raise the debt ceiling means no money for the government to pay its bills, meet its payroll, or pay interest due on the national debt. In 1990, Congress rejected President George H. W. Bush's spending plan, and the government shut down throughout the three-day Columbus Day weekend. Most workers were off for the holiday, and few government agencies were affected. In 2009, a provision of the stimulus bill raised the U.S. debt ceiling in order to allow the record budget deficit described in the previous section.

In 2011 after many months of debate, a bill to raise the debt ceiling was passed just hours before the deadline. The bill raised the debt limit in stages until 2013 while providing dollar-for-dollar spending cuts. Exempt from spending cuts are Social Security, Medicaid, veteran's benefits, military pay, and programs for women, infants, and children. A 12-member bipartisan congressional committee was established to identify future deficit reductions and tax reforms.

23-1e BUDGET SURPLUSES AND DEFICITS IN OTHER COUNTRIES

Exhibit 4 shows numerous countries with government budget deficits as a percentage of GDP in 2011. While Norway had a budget surplus of 13 percent of GDP, Canada, France, and Greece, for example, had deficit percentages lower than the U.S. deficit percentage of 9 percent of GDP. Ireland had a deficit greater than the United States.

23-2 Why Worry over the National Debt?

In 2011, Greece was in financial crisis with a national debt-to-GDP ratio of 165 percent. Fearing default on Greece's debt, creditors have demanded solutions. In response, Greece cut civil service salaries, froze pensions, and enacted new taxes on a long list of items, including fuel, cigarettes, alcohol, jewelry, leather goods, yachts, private jets, and high-end automobiles. Also, Greece accepted international bailout packages, but as this text is written in 2012, there are fears that this crisis could spread.

As shown in Exhibit 5(a), the result of the accumulation of federal deficits in the United States is that the national debt is rising at a rapid rate. The national debt crossed $1 trillion in 1982. And it took 14 years before another $4 trillion was added, reaching the $5 trillion mark in 1996. Fourteen years later in 2010, the national debt accelerated by $9 trillion to $14 trillion. In 2011, the national debt reached $15 trillion.

EXHIBIT 4	A Global Comparison of Government Surpluses and Deficits as a Percentage of GDP, 2011

In 2011, Norway had a budget surplus of 13 percent of GDP. Other nations, such as Canada, France, and Greece, had budget deficits lower than the U.S. deficit of 9 percent of GDP. Ireland had a deficit greater than that of the United States.

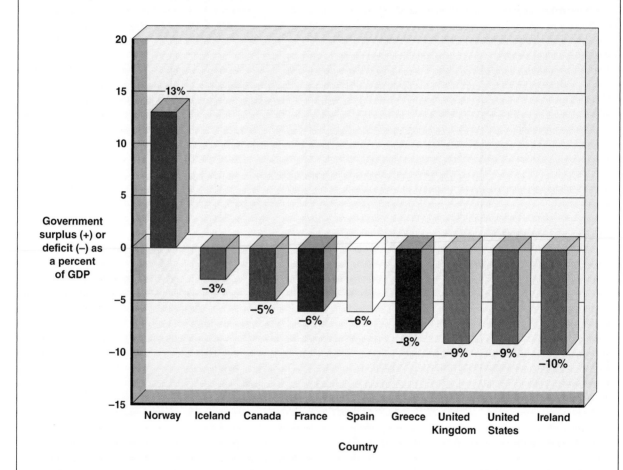

SOURCE: OECD (2011), "OECD Economic Outlook No. 90", OECD Economic Outlook: Statistics and Projections (database). http://dx.doi.org/10.1787/data-00588-en

What are some major causes of the rising national debt? Observe in Exhibit 5(a) the increase in the debt during World War II. In wartime, the government must increase military expenditures sharply and escalate the national debt. Recession also causes the national debt to rise dramatically. Cyclical downturns such as the 1930s, 1974–1975, 1981–1982, 1990–1991, 2001, and 2007–2009 also cause the debt to rise rapidly because a decline in real GDP automatically increases the budget deficit due to lower tax collections and

EXHIBIT 5	The National Debt, 1930–2011

In part (a), we see that the federal debt has skyrocketed since 1980. A concern is that sooner or later the U.S. government will be bankrupt. The counterargument is shown in part (b). The national debt as a percentage of GDP has declined since the end of World War II, when it reached a peak of about 122 percent. After 1980, the federal debt as a percentage of GDP increased and has risen sharply to a historic high since World War II of 99 percent in 2011.

(a) National debt

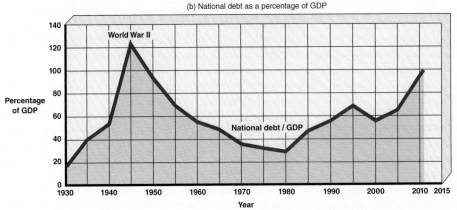

(b) National debt as a percentage of GDP

SOURCES: *Economic Report of the President*, 2012, http://www.gpo.gov/fdsys/pkg/ERP-2012/content-detail.htm1, Table B-79; Tables B-78 and B-79.

greater spending for unemployment compensation and welfare. Currently, as a result of the bailout plans and stimulus spending to boost troubled credit markets, the federal government is financing these plans with government borrowing that has caused a rise in the federal deficit, debt ceiling, and national debt.

Politicians and nonpoliticians alike often speak of the gloom and doom of the national debt. Should we lose sleep over it? To find out, we'll consider three controversial questions:

23-2a   1. CAN UNCLE SAM GO BANKRUPT?

Reasons to Worry   If households and firms persistently operate in the red, as the federal government does, they will go bankrupt sooner or later. How long can a national debt continue to rise before the U.S. government is broke?

Reasons Not to Worry   Whether private or public debt is the issue, debt must be judged relative to the debtor's ability to repay the principal and interest on the debt. Exhibit 5(b) shows that the national debt as a percentage of GDP is lower today than at the end of World War II. In 1945, public debt was about 122 percent of GDP, and by 1980, the ratio of debt to GDP had fallen to 33 percent. This means the debt grew considerably slower than GDP between 1945 and 1980. Since 1980, however, the trend reversed, and the debt has grown faster than GDP. Between 1980 and 2011, the national debt grew from 33 percent to 99 percent of GDP. Still, the United States was not bankrupt in 1945 or 2011. In the future, it can be argued that the debt will again grow slower than the GDP and the ratio will fall again.

There is an even more important point: Uncle Sam never has to pay off the national debt. At the maturity date on a government security, the U.S. Treasury has the constitutional authority to collect taxes levied by Congress, print money, or refinance its obligations. Suppose the government decides not to raise taxes or cause inflation by simply printing money, so it refinances the debt. When a $1 million government bond comes due, as described earlier in this chapter, the U.S. Treasury can simply "roll over" the debt. This financial trade expression means a borrower (here the federal government) pays off its $1 million bond that reaches maturity by issuing a new $1 million bond. In short, the federal government refinances its debt by replacing old bonds with new bonds. This means the federal government never has to pay off the national debt. These debts can be rolled over forever, provided bond buyers have faith in Uncle Sam.

Global Perspective on National Debt   Exhibit 6 provides a global perspective on the national debt. This figure shows the ratio of national debt to GDP for several industrialized nations. Japan, Greece, Italy, and Portugal have a higher debt in relation to GDP than does the United States. The United States, on the other hand, has a national debt-to-GDP ratio about four times as large as Australia's ratio.

EXHIBIT 6	A Global Comparison of National Debt Ratios, 2011

This exhibit shows estimated ratios of national debt to GDP in 2011 for selected industrialized countries. Compared to the United States, Japan, Greece, Italy, and Portugal have higher national debt-to-GDP ratios. On the other hand, the United States has a debt ratio about four times as large as Australia's.

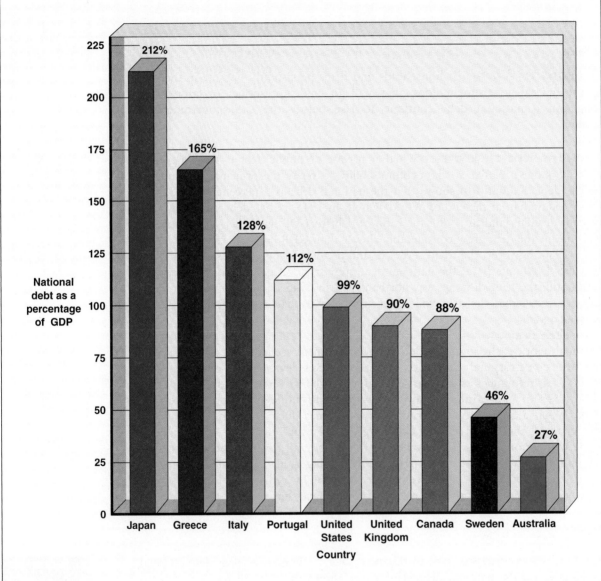

SOURCE: OECD (2011), "OECD Economic Outlook No. 90", OECD Economic Outlook: Statistics and Projections (database). http://dx.doi.org/10.1787/data-00588-en

✔ **CHECKPOINT**

What's Behind the National Debt?

Suppose the federal government has balanced budgets each year and the entire national debt comes due. How could the federal government pay off the national debt without refinancing, raising taxes, or printing money?

23-2b 2. ARE WE PASSING THE DEBT BURDEN TO OUR CHILDREN?

Reasons to Worry   The fear is that interest payments to finance the national debt will swallow an enormous helping of the federal government's budget pie. This means future generations will pay more of their tax dollars to the government's creditors and have less to spend for highways, health care, defense, and other public sector programs. Exhibit 7 shows net interest payments as a percentage of GDP. The net interest payment was only 1.7 percent of GDP right after World War II in 1950, but it increased dramatically after the mid-1970s to more than 3 percent in 1995. Since 1995, the interest payment burden declined to 1.8 percent of GDP in 2011.

Reasons Not to Worry   The burden of the national debt on present and future generations depends on who owns the accumulated national debt. Stated more precisely, the burden of the debt depends on whether it is held internally or externally. The bulk of the public debt is internal national debt. Internal national debt is the portion of the national debt owed to a nation's own citizens. Internal debt financing is viewed as "we owe it to ourselves." One U.S. citizen buys a government security and lends Uncle Sam the money to pay the interest and principal on a maturing government security held by another U.S. citizen. Although this redistribution of income and wealth does indeed favor bondholders, who are typically upper-income individuals, transferring dollars between U.S. citizens does not alter the overall purchasing power in the U.S. economy.

    Those on the "not to worry" side of this issue also concede that an external national debt is a concern. External national debt is the portion of the national debt owed to foreign citizens. Financing the external national debt means interest and principal payments are transfers of money from U.S. citizens to other nations. If foreign governments, banks, corporations, and individual investors hold part of the national debt, the "we owe it to ourselves" argument is weakened. Exhibit 8 shows who owns the securities the U.S. Treasury has issued. In 2011, foreigners owned 31 percent of the total national debt. The largest foreign holder of the debt was China with 8 percent of the total national debt, and next was Japan with 6 percent. Forty-two percent was held by the federal, state, and local governments, primarily by federal agencies such as the U.S. Treasury, the Social Security Administration, and Federal Reserve banks. The Federal Reserve is an independent government agency, as explained in the next chapter. The private sector, consisting

Internal national debt

The portion of the national debt owed to a nation's own citizens.

External national debt

The portion of the national debt owed to foreign citizens.

EXHIBIT 7	Federal Net Interest as a Percentage of GDP, 1940–2011

Some fear that interest payments on the national debt will swallow an enormous portion of the federal budget. The exhibit shows that the net interest payment as a proportion of GDP was only about 1.7 percent right after World War II. In the 1980s and early 1990s, however, the interest rate burden increased dramatically to more than 3 percent in 1995. Since 1995, it declined to 1.8 percent in 2011.

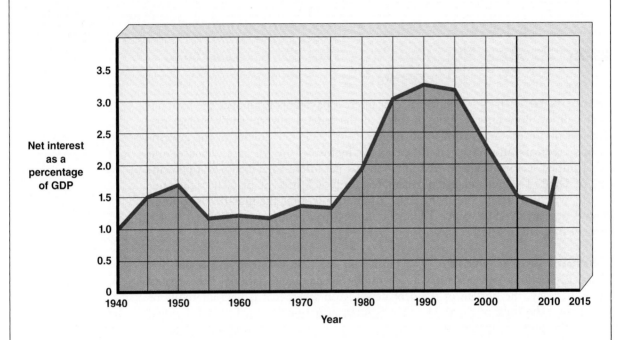

SOURCES: *Economic Report of the President*, 2012, http://www.gpo.gov/fdsys/pkg/ERP-2012/content-detail.html, Tables B 1 and B 80 and Bureau of Economic Analysis, *National Economic Accounts*, http://www.bea.gov/national/nipaweb/SelectTable.asp?Selected=Y, Table 1.1.

of individuals, banks, corporations, and insurance companies, held 27 percent of the national debt. The debt held by the private sector and government entities constitutes the internal national debt.

Although 69 percent of the national debt was internal, the 31 percent of total U.S. debt that is external debt is not necessarily undesirable. Foreign investment in the United States supplements domestic saving. Borrowing from abroad can prevent the higher interest rates that would exist if the U.S. Treasury relied only on domestic savers to purchase federal government securities. A lower interest rate increases U.S. investment and consumer spending, causing the aggregate demand curve to shift rightward.

If we do not need to worry about shifting the burden to future generations, can the current generation escape the debt burden? The answer is *No*. During World War II, for example, the United States operated at full employment along its *production possibilities curve*. As illustrated earlier in Exhibit 2 of

Chapter 2, the people at that time in history were forced to trade off consumer goods production for military goods production. Because massive amounts of resources were diverted to fight World War II, people at that time were forced to give up private consumption of houses, cars, refrigerators, and so on. After the war was over, resources were again devoted to producing more consumer goods and fewer military goods. The same analysis can be used today. At full employment, the burden of the national debt on the current generation is the opportunity cost of private-sector goods and services forgone because land, labor, and capital are used to produce public-sector goods and services.

In other words, the burden of the national debt is incurred when production takes place; it is not postponed until the debt is paid by future generations. When the debt comes due in the future, the government can simply refinance the debt and redistribute money from one group of citizens to another. This redistribution of income does not cause a reallocation of resources away from consumer goods and services in favor of government programs.

EXHIBIT 8	Ownership of the National Debt, 2011

In 2011, 42 percent of the national debt was held by the public sector, including federal, state, and local governments and Federal Reserve banks. The private sector, including individuals, banks, corporations, and insurance companies, held 27 percent, and foreigners owned the remaining 31 percent.

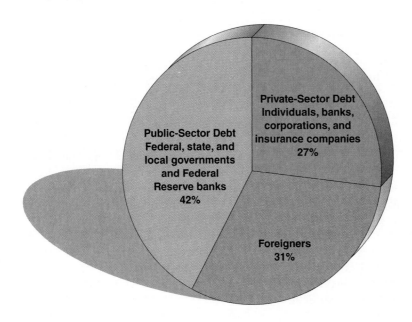

SOURCE: *Economic Report of the President*, 2012, http://www.gpo.gov/fdsys/pkg/ERP-2012/content-detail. html1, Table B-89.

23-2c   3. DOES GOVERNMENT BORROWING CROWD OUT PRIVATE-SECTOR SPENDING?

Crowding-out effect

A reduction in private-sector spending as a result of federal budget deficits financed by U.S. Treasury borrowing. When federal government borrowing increases interest rates, the result is lower consumption by households and lower investment spending by businesses.

Reasons to Worry   Critics of Keynesian fiscal policy believe that government spending financed by borrowing designed to boost aggregate demand has little, if any, effect on growth of real GDP. The reason is that the crowding-out effect dampens the stimulus to aggregate demand from increased federal government spending. The crowding-out effect is a reduction in private-sector spending as a result of higher interest rates caused by U.S. Treasury borrowing (selling securities) to finance government spending. For example, suppose the federal government spends and borrows, rather than collecting taxes, to finance new health care programs. In this case, the size of the national debt rises, and interest rates are pushed up in loan markets. Interest rates rise because the federal government competes with private borrowers for available savings, and less credit is available to consumers and business borrowers. The result of this crowding-out effect is lower consumption $(-\Delta C)$ and business investment $(-\Delta I)$, which offset the boost in aggregate demand $(+\Delta AD)$ from increased government spending $(+\Delta G)$ operating through the spending multiplier.

The crowding-out effect contradicts the theory, explained in the previous Reasons Not to Worry section, that future generations do not bear some of today's debt burden. Recall from Chapter 2 that current investment spending increases living standards in the future by shifting the production possibilities curve outward (Exhibit 5 in Chapter 2). If federal borrowing crowds out private investment in plants and equipment, future generations will have a smaller possible productive capacity.

The AD-AS model will help you understand the crowding-out concept. Exhibit 9 reproduces the situation in which government spending is used to combat a recession, depicted earlier in Exhibit 2 of the chapter on fiscal policy. Begin at E_1, with an equilibrium GDP of $13 trillion, and assume the government increases its spending and uses the spending multiplier to shift the aggregate demand curve rightward from AD_1 to AD_2. Following Keynesian theory, there is zero crowding out, and the economy achieves full employment at equilibrium point E_2, corresponding to real GDP of $14 trillion. Critics of Keynesian theory, however, argue that crowding out occurs. The result of expansionary fiscal policy is not E_2, but some equilibrium point along the AS line between E_1 and E_2. For example, a fall in private expenditures might partially offset the government spending stimulus. With incomplete crowding out, the aggregate demand curve increases only to AD'_2 because of the decline in consumption and investment. The economy therefore moves to E'_2 at a real GDP of $13.5 trillion and does not achieve full employment at E_2. Or crowding out can completely offset the multiplier effect of increased government spending. The fall in private expenditures by consumers and businesses can result in no change in aggregate demand curve AD_1. In this case, the economy remains at E_1, with unemployment unaffected by expansionary policy. Meanwhile, the deficit required to finance extra government spending increases the national debt.

Crowding-in effect

An increase in private-sector spending as a result of federal budget deficits financed by U.S. Treasury borrowing. At less than full employment, consumers hold more Treasury securities and this additional wealth causes them to spend more. Business investment spending increases because of optimistic profit expectations.

Reasons Not to Worry   The crowding-out effect is controversial. Keynesian economists counter critics by saying that any crowding-out effect is small or nonexistent. Instead, at below full-employment real GDP, their counterargument is the crowding-in effect. For example, government capital spending for highways, dams, universities, and infrastructure financed by borrowing might offset any decline in private investment. Another Keynesian argument is that consumers and businesspersons may believe that federal spending is "just what the doctor ordered" for an ailing economy. Federal borrowing incurred to finance the new spending would boost consumption and therefore increase aggregate demand.

EXHIBIT 9	Zero, Partial, and Complete Crowding Out

Beginning at equilibrium E_1, the federal government borrows to finance a deficit created by expansionary fiscal policy. Keynesian theory predicts zero crowding out, which means that an increase in government spending operates through the spending multiplier to shift aggregate demand from AD_1 to AD_2. If crowding out is zero, consumption and investment spending are unaffected by the increase in government spending financed by borrowing. Partial crowding out occurs when a decrease in private spending partially offsets the multiplier effect from an increase in deficit-financed government spending. Partial crowding out results in a shift only from AD_1 to AD'_2 and an equilibrium at E'_2, rather than E_2. If crowding out is complete, a decrease in private spending completely offsets the increase in government spending financed by debt. In this case, the aggregate demand curve remains at AD_1, and the economy remains at E_1.

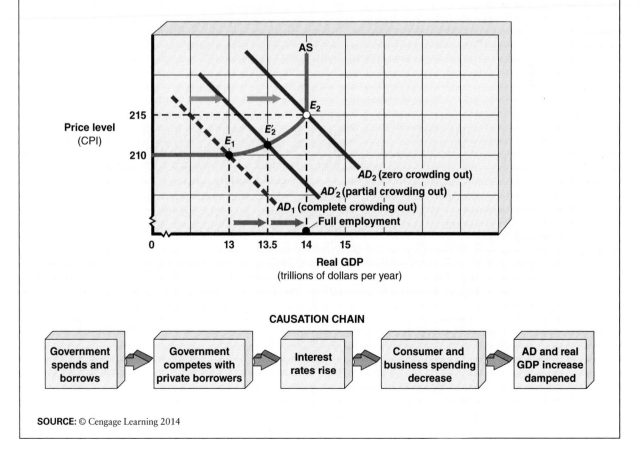

CAUSATION CHAIN

Government spends and borrows → Government competes with private borrowers → Interest rates rise → Consumer and business spending decrease → AD and real GDP increase dampened

SOURCE: © Cengage Learning 2014

How Real Is Uncle Sam's Debt?
Applicable Concepts: national debt and federal deficit

Perhaps the national debt and federal budget deficits are really not so large and threatening. For example, it can be argued that we should use real rather than nominal values to report the national debt—similar to using real GDP to report economic growth. Suppose the national debt rises from $10 trillion to $10.3 trillion and the price level increases by 3 percent in a given year. The nominal value of the national debt therefore has risen by $300 billion because the government must issue $300 billion in newly issued government securities due to higher prices, and real growth in the national debt is therefore zero.

Critics also warn that federal accounting rules are an economic policy disaster. Private businesses, as well as state and local governments, use two budgets. One is the *operating budget*, which includes salaries, interest payments, and other current expenses. The second type of budget, called a *capital budget*, includes spending for investment items, such as machines, buildings, and roads. Expenditures on the capital budget yield benefits over time and may be paid for by long-term borrowing. The federal government does not use a capital

The reason is because holders of Treasury bills, notes, and bonds feel richer. As a result of their greater wealth, consumers spend more now and plan to spend more in the future. Such a blush of optimism may also raise the profit expectations of business managers, and they may increase investment spending. The effect of increased private-sector spending could nullify some or all of the crowding-out effect, which would otherwise offset the boost in aggregate demand from increased government spending. Hence, as explained in the graphical analysis in Exhibit 9, the spending multiplier shifts the aggregate demand curve from AD_1 to AD_2, with zero crowding out.

Finally, both sides of the debate agree that complete crowding out occurs in one situation. Suppose the economy is operating at full employment (point E_2). This is comparable to being on the economy's production possibilities curve. If the government shifts the aggregate demand curve rightward by increasing spending or cutting taxes, the result will be higher prices and a replacement of private sector output with public sector output.

> **CONCLUSION:** *Crowding out is complete if the economy is at full employment, but it is debatable at less than full employment.*

budget. Capital budgeting allows spreading the cost of long-lasting assets over future years. For example, the federal budget makes no distinction between the rental cost of a federal office building and the cost of constructing a new federal office building to replace rented office space. However, payments on borrowing for a new building provide the benefit of a long-lasting asset that offsets rent payments. If a capital budgeting system were used, the public would see that most federal borrowing really finances assets yielding long-term benefits. In short, proponents of a capital budget believe the public's focus should be on the operating budget, which gives a truer measure of the federal deficit. Opponents of changing the accounting rules argue that controversial expenditures would be placed in the capital budget in order to manipulate the size of the deficit or surplus in the operating budget for political reasons.

Finally, some economists argue for other numerical adjustments that show the federal deficit or surplus is really not as it seems. They say it is not the federal deficit or surplus that really matters, but the combined deficits or surpluses of federal, state, and local governments. When state and local governments run budget surpluses, these surpluses are a source of savings in financial markets that adds to federal surpluses or offsets federal borrowing to finance its deficit.

Source: © Cengage Learning 2014

Analyze the Issue

1. Do households make a distinction between spending for current expenses and spending for capital expenses? Compare borrowing $5,000 to take a vacation in Hawaii to borrowing $125,000 to buy a condominium and move out of your rented apartment.
2. Critics of "new accounting" for federal borrowing argue that it does not matter what the government spends the money for. What matters is the total amount that the government spends minus taxes collected. Explain this viewpoint.

Key Concepts

National debt

Net public debt

Debt ceiling

Internal national debt

External national debt

Crowding-out effect

Crowding-in effect

Summary

- The **national debt** is the dollar amount that the federal government owes holders of government securities. It is the cumulative sum of past deficits. The U.S. Treasury issues government securities to finance the deficits. The debt has increased sharply since 1980.

National Debt

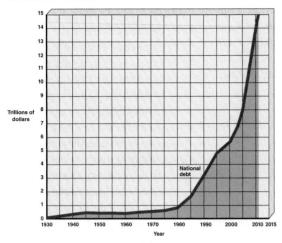

SOURCES: *Economic Report of the President*, 2012, http://www.gpo
.gov/fdsys/pkg/ERP-2012/content-detail.htm1, Table B-79; Tables B-78
and B-79.

- The **net public debt** is the national debt minus all government interagency borrowing (the debt that the federal government owes to itself).
- A **debt ceiling** is a method used to restrict the growth of the national debt.
- **Internal national debt** is the percentage of the national debt a nation owes to its own citizens, including individuals, banks, corporations, insurance companies, and government entities. The "we owe it to ourselves" argument over the debt is that U.S. citizens own the bulk of the U.S. national debt. **External national debt** is a burden because it is the portion of the national debt a nation owes to foreigners. The interest paid on external debt transfers purchasing power to other nations.

Internal and External National Debt

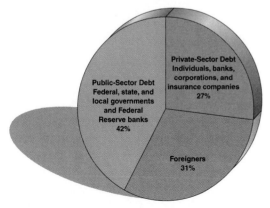

SOURCE: *Economic Report of the President*, 2012, http://www.gpo.gov/
fdsys/pkg/ERP-2012/content-detail.htm1, Table B-89.

- The **burden of the debt debate** involves controversial questions:
  1. **Can Uncle Sam Go Bankrupt?** The U.S. government will not go bankrupt because it never has to pay off its debt. When government securities mature, the U.S. Treasury can refinance, or roll over, the debt by issuing new securities.
  2. **Are We Passing the Debt Burden to Our Children?** One side of this argument is that the burden of the debt falls only on the current generation when the trade-off between public-sector goods and private-sector goods along the production possibilities curve occurs. In short, when resources are used to make missiles today, citizens are forced to give up, say, airplane production in the current period and not later. The counterargument is that there is a sizable external national debt that transfers purchasing power to foreigners.
  3. **Does Government Borrowing Crowd Out Private-Sector Spending?** The **crowding-out effect** is a burden of the national debt that occurs when the government borrows to finance its deficit, causing the interest rate to rise. As the interest rate rises, consumption and business investment fall. If crowding out occurs, reduced private spending completely or partially offsets the multiplier effect of increased government spending. As a result, the expected magnitude of the rightward shift in the aggregate demand curve is partially or completely offset.

     Opponents believe in the **crowding-in effect**. In this view, government capital spending for highways, dams, universities, and infrastructure offsets any decline in business investment from crowding out.

Zero, Partial, and Complete Crowding Out

SOURCE: © Cengage Learning 2014

Summary of Conclusion Statements

- The national debt includes the Social Security trust fund and as a result, federal budget deficits are reduced or budget surpluses are raised.

- Crowding out is complete if the economy is at full employment, but it is debatable at less than full employment.

Study Questions and Problems

1. Explain the relationship between budget deficits and the national debt.

2. Discuss various ways of measuring the size of the national debt.

3. Explain this statement: "The national debt is like taking money out of your left pocket and putting it into your right pocket."

4. Explain this statement: "The most unlikely problem of the national debt is that the government will go bankrupt."

5. Suppose the percentage of the federal debt owned by foreigners increases sharply. Would this trend concern you? Why or why not?

6. Explain the theory that crowding out can weaken or nullify the effect of expansionary fiscal policy financed by federal government borrowing.

7. Suppose the federal government has no national debt and spends $100 billion, while raising only $50 billion in taxes.
   a. What amount of government bonds will the U.S. Treasury issue to finance the deficit?
   b. Next year, assume tax revenues remain at $50 billion. If the government pays a 10 percent rate of interest, add the debt-servicing interest payment to the government's $100 billion expenditure for goods and services the second year.
   c. For the second year, compute the deficit, the amount of new debt issued, and the new national debt.

8. Suppose the media report that the federal deficit this year is $200 billion. The national debt was $5,000 billion last year, and it is $5,200 billion this year. The price level this year is 3 percent higher than it was last year. What is the real deficit?

9. During the presidential campaign of 1932 in the depth of the Great Depression, candidates Herbert Hoover and Franklin D. Roosevelt both advocated reducing the budget deficit using tax hikes and/or expenditure reductions. Evaluate this fiscal policy.

10. Consider this statement: "Our grandchildren may not suffer the entire burden of a federal deficit." Do you agree or disagree? Explain.

11. Suppose you are the economic policy adviser to the president and are asked what should be done to eliminate a federal deficit. What would you recommend?

For Online Exercises, go to the Tucker Web site at www.cengage.com/economics/tucker.

✓ CHECKPOINT ANSWER

What's behind the National Debt?

Every item owned by the federal government, including the White House, office buildings, tanks, and computers, is an asset standing behind the national debt. If you said the assets of the federal government could be sold to pay off the national debt, **YOU ARE CORRECT.**

Sample Quiz

For an explanation of the correct answers, visit the Tucker Web site at www.cengage.com/economics/tucker.

1. Each year, the president must submit a budget proposal to Congress by
   a. February.
   b. April.
   c. July.
   d. October.

2. If the fiscal year begins without a budget and Congress fails to pass continuing resolution, then
   a. the president has the right to raise the debt ceiling.
   b. federal agencies operate on the basis of the previous year's budget.
   c. the interest rate paid on the national debt automatically increases.
   d. the federal government shuts down.

3. Between 1998 and 2001, the federal budget was
   a. never in surplus.
   b. in surplus about as often as it was in deficit.
   c. in surplus.
   d. never in deficit.

4. The sum of past federal budget deficits is the
   a. GDP debt.
   b. trade debt plus GDP.
   c. national debt.
   d. Congressional debt.

5. To finance a federal budget deficit, the U.S. Treasury borrows by selling
   a. Treasury bills.
   b. Treasury notes.

   c. Treasury bonds.
   d. All of the above answers are correct.

6. Most of the U.S. national debt is owed to _____. Thus, a rising national debt implies that there will be a future redistribution of income and wealth in favor of _____.
   a. foreigners, foreigners
   b. other U.S. citizens, bondholders
   c. foreigners, those needing government services
   d. other U.S. citizens, those needing government services

7. Which of the following statements is *false*?
   a. The size of the national debt decreased steadily after World War II.
   b. The national debt increases in size whenever the federal government has a surplus budget.
   c. Currently, the size of the national debt is about the same size as it was during World War II.
   d. All of the answers above are correct.

8. Which of the following statements is *true*?
   a. Currently, the size of the national debt is about the same size as it was during World War II.
   b. The national debt increases in size whenever the federal government has a surplus budget.
   c. The size of the national debt decreased steadily after 1980.

Sample Quiz *continued*

d. The current U.S. national debt is over $15 trillion.

9. Compared to the United Kingdom, the national debt as a percentage of GDP in the United States is
   a. substantially larger.
   b. the same.
   c. slightly larger.
   d. substantially smaller.

10. The national debt is unlikely to cause national bankruptcy because the federal government can
    a. raise taxes.
    b. print money.
    c. refinance its debt.
    d. do all of the above.

11. In recent years, net interest on the national debt paid by the federal government as a percentage of GDP was equal to approximately
    a. 1 percent.
    b. 3 percent.
    c. 6 percent.
    d. 25 percent.

12. Which of the following U.S. Treasury securities represents ownership of the national debt?
    a. bonds owned by the banks and insurance companies
    b. bonds owned by the Social Security Administration
    c. bonds owned by private individuals
    d. All of the above answers are correct.

13. "Crowding out" refers to the situation in which
    a. borrowing by the federal government raises interest rates and causes firms to invest less.
    b. foreigners sell their bonds and purchase U.S. goods and services.
    c. borrowing by the federal government causes state and local governments to lower their taxes.
    d. increased federal taxes to balance the budget cause interest rates to increase and consumer credit to decrease.

14. The crowding-out effect can be
    a. zero.
    b. partial.
    c. complete.
    d. any of the answers are correct.

15. "Crowding in" refers to federal government deficits that
    a. are used for public infrastructure will offset any decline in business investment.
    b. reduce private business and consumption spending.
    c. reduce future rates of economic growth.
    d. all of the answers are correct.

16. If Congress fails to pass a budget before the fiscal year starts, then federal agencies may continue to operate only if Congress has passed a
    a. balanced budget amendment.
    b. deficit reduction plan.
    c. conference resolution.
    d. continuing resolution.

17. With regard to the national debt, to whom does the federal government owe money?
    a. taxpayers
    b. federal government workers
    c. the Federal Reserve system
    d. investors who buy U.S. Treasury bills, bonds, and notes

18. When measured as a percentage of GDP, the U.S. national debt reached its highest levels as a result of
    a. World War II.
    b. the Vietnam War.
    c. the Reagan defense buildup and tax cut.
    d. the Obama economic recovery program.

19. The national debt is unlikely to cause national bankruptcy because the
    a. national debt can be refinanced by issuing new bonds.
    b. interest on the public debt equals GDP.
    c. national debt cannot be shifted to future generations for repayment.
    d. federal government cannot refinance the outstanding national debt.

Sample Quiz *continued*

20. An increase in our federal government's budget deficit will likely
    a. increase the national debt.
    b. increase interest rates.
    c. decrease borrowing by households and businesses.
    d. be less effective in stimulating the economy than the spending multiplier implies because of crowding out.
    e. do all of the above.

Road Map
Macroeconomic Theory and Policy Issues

This road map feature helps you tie together material in the part as you travel the Economic Way of Thinking highway. The following are review questions listed by chapter from the previous part. The key concept in each question is given for emphasis, and each question or set of questions concludes with an interactive game to reinforce the concepts. Go to the Tucker website at www.cengage.com/economics/tucker, select the chapter, and play the visual causation chain game designed to make learning fun. Enjoy the cheers when you are correct and suffer the jeers if you miss. The correct answers for the multiple choice questions are given in Appendix C of the text.

CHAPTER 18. THE KEYNESIAN MODEL

1. **Key Concept: Consumption function**
   The consumption function will shift for all of the following reasons except
   a. a change in a household's real assets.
   b. a change in interest rates.
   c. expectations of price changes.
   d. changes in a household's disposable incomes.
   e. changes in taxation policy.

   Causation Chain Game
   Movement along and Shifts in the Consumption Function—Exhibit 6

2. **Key Concept: Investment demand curve**
   Which of the following will increase investment spending?
   a. More optimistic business expectations
   b. An increase in interest rates
   c. An increase in business taxes
   d. A decrease in capacity utilization
   e. All of the answers above are correct.

   Causation Chain Game
   Movement along and Shifts in a Firm's Investment Demand—Exhibit 8

CHAPTER 19. THE KEYNESIAN MODEL IN ACTION

3. **Key Concept: Spending multiplier**
The ratio of the change in GDP to an initial change in aggregate expenditures (AE) is the
a. spending multiplier.
b. permanent income rate.
c. marginal expenditure rate.
d. marginal propensity to consume.

Causation Chain Game
The Multiplier Effect and Government Spending—Exhibit 4

CHAPTER 20. AGGREGATE DEMAND AND SUPPLY

4. **Key Concept: Aggregate demand curve**
Which of the following is *not* a reason for the downward slope of an aggregate demand curve?
a. real balances or wealth effect
b. real interest-rate effect
c. net exports effect
d. all of the above are reasons

Causation Chain Game
The Aggregate Demand Curve—Exhibit 1

5. **Key Concept: Aggregate demand curve**
Which of the following could *not* be expected to shift the aggregate demand curve?
a. net exports fall
b. consumption spending decreases
c. an increase in government spending
d. a change in real GDP

Causation Chain Game
A Shift in the Aggregate Demand Curve—Exhibit 3

6. **Key Concept: Aggregate supply curve**
The horizontal segment of the aggregate supply curve
a. shows that real GDP can increase only by affecting the economy's price level.
b. shows that real GDP can increase without affecting the economy's price level.
c. depicts a positive relationship between real GDP and the price level.

    d. depicts a negative relationship between real GDP and the price level.

    e. marks the full-employment level of real GDP.

Causation Chain Game

The Keynesian Horizontal Aggregate Supply Curve—Exhibit 4

7. Key Concept: Aggregate supply curve

According to classical theory, if the aggregate demand curve decreased and the economy experienced unemployment, then

    a. the economy would remain in this condition indefinitely.

    b. the government must increase spending to restore full employment.

    c. prices and wages would fall quickly to restore full employment.

    d. the supply of money would increase until the economy returned to full employment.

Causation Chain Game

The Classical Vertical Aggregate Supply Curve—Exhibit 5

8. Key Concept: Aggregate supply curve

If a new method for obtaining oil from dry oil fields is found, then we will see

    a. the AS curve shift to the left.

    b. a movement to the left along the AD curve.

    c. the AD curve shift to the left.

    d. the AD curve shift to the right.

    e. the AS curve shift to the right.

Causation Chain Game

A Rightward Shift in the Aggregate Supply Curve—Exhibit 9

9. Key Concept: Cost-push inflation

Cost-push inflation occurs when the

    a. aggregate demand curve shifts leftward while the aggregate supply curve is fixed.

    b. aggregate supply curve shifts leftward while the aggregate demand curve is fixed.

    c. aggregate demand curve shifts rightward while the aggregate supply curve is fixed.

    d. aggregate supply curve shifts rightward.

Causation Chain Game

Cost-Push and Demand-Pull Inflation—Exhibit 11

10. Key Concept: Demand-pull inflation

Demand-pull inflation is caused by an

    a. increase in aggregate demand.

    b. decrease in aggregate demand.

    c. increase in aggregate supply.

    d. decrease in aggregate supply.

Causation Chain Game

Cost-Push and Demand-Pull Inflation—Exhibit 11

CHAPTER 21. FISCAL POLICY

11. Key Concept: Fiscal policy
Which of the following is an appropriate discretionary fiscal policy to use when the economy is in a recession?
a. increased government spending
b. higher taxes
c. a balanced-budget reduction in both spending and taxes
d. an expansion in the money supply

Causation Chain Game
Using Government Spending to Combat a Recession—Exhibit 2

12. Key Concept: Fiscal policy
If no fiscal policy changes are implemented to fight inflation, suppose the aggregate demand curve will exceed the current aggregate demand curve by $900 billion at any level of prices. Assuming the marginal propensity to consume is 0.90, this increase in aggregate demand could be prevented by
a. increasing government spending by $500 billion.
b. increasing government spending by $140 billion.
c. decreasing taxes by $40 billion.
d. increasing taxes by $100 billion.

Causation Chain Game
Using Fiscal Policy to Combat Inflation—Exhibit 6

13. Key Concept: Automatic stabilizers
Automatic stabilizers "lean against the prevailing wind" of the business cycle because
a. wages are controlled by the minimum wage law.
b. federal expenditures and tax revenues change as the level of real GDP changes.
c. the spending and tax multipliers are constant.
d. they include the power of special interests.

Causation Chain Game
Automatic Stabilizers—Exhibit 7

14. Key Concept: Supply-side economics
An advocate of supply-side fiscal policy would advocate which of the following?
a. subsidies to produce technological advances
b. reduction in regulation
c. reduction in resource prices
d. reduction in taxes
e. All of the answers above are correct.

Causation Chain Game
Keynesian Demand-Side versus Supply-Side Effects—Exhibit 8

CHAPTER 23. FEDERAL DEFICITS, SURPLUSES, AND THE NATIONAL DEBT

15. **Key Concept: Federal budget process**

    If Congress fails to pass a budget before the fiscal year starts, then federal agencies may continue to operate only if Congress has passed a
    a. balanced budget amendment.
    b. deficit reduction plan.
    c. conference resolution.
    d. continuing resolution.

Causation Chain Game

Major Steps in the Federal Budgetary Process—Exhibit 1

Money, Banking, and Monetary Policy

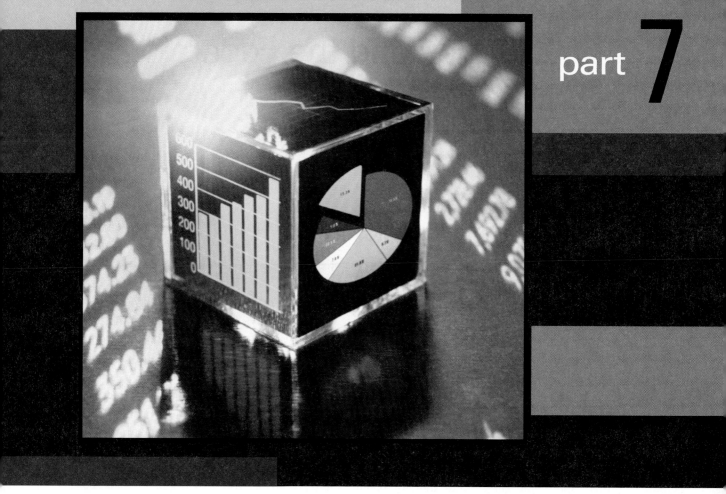

S tudents often find the material in these chapters the most interesting in their principles course because the topic is *money*. The first chapter begins the discussion of money with basic definitions and a description of the Federal Reserve System. Of special interest is a feature on the history of money in the colonies. The next chapter explains how the banking system and the Federal Reserve influence the supply of money. The following chapter compares different macroeconomic theories and concludes with a discussion of monetary policy in the Great Depression and the Great Recession. The final chapter in this part explores additional macro theories based on expectations.

chapter 24

Money and the Federal Reserve System

As the lyrics of the old song go, "Money makes the world go round, the world go round, the world go round." Recall the circular flow model presented in the chapter on GDP. Households exchange *money* for goods and services in the product markets, and firms exchange *money* for resources in the factor markets. In short, money affects the way an economy works. In the chapter on aggregate demand and supply and the chapter on fiscal policy presented earlier in the text, the AD-AS model was developed without explicitly discussing money. In this chapter, and throughout this part, money takes center stage.

Exactly what is money? The answer may surprise you. Imagine yourself on the small South Pacific island of Yap. You are surrounded by exotic fowl, crystal-clear lagoons, delicious fruits, and sunny skies. Now suppose while leisurely strolling along the beach one evening, you suddenly discover a beautiful bamboo hut for sale. As you will discover in this chapter, to pay for your dream hut, you must roll a 5-foot-diameter stone to the area of the island designated as the "bank."

We begin our discussion of money with the three functions money serves. Next, we identify the components of three different definitions of the money supply used in the United States. The remainder of the chapter describes the organization and services of the Federal Reserve System, our nation's central bank. Also, we discuss the Monetary Control Act of 1980 and its relationship to the savings and loan crisis of the 1980s and early 1990s that predated the banking crisis and Great Recession of 2007–2009. Beginning in this chapter and in the next three chapters, you will learn how the Federal Reserve System controls the stock of money in the economy. Then, using the AD-AS model, you will learn how variations in the stock of money in the economy affect total spending, unemployment, and prices.

24-1 What Makes Money *Money*?

Can exchange occur in an economy without money? It certainly can, using a trading system called barter. Barter is the direct exchange of one good or service for another good or service, rather than for money. The problem with barter is that it requires a *coincidence of wants*. Imagine for a moment that dollars and coins are worthless. Farmer Brown needs shoes, so he takes his bushels of wheat to the shoe store and offers to barter wheat for shoes. Unfortunately, the store owner refuses to barter because she wants to trade shoes for pencils, toothpaste, and coffee. Undaunted, Farmer Brown spends more time and effort to find Mr. Jones, who has pencils, toothpaste, and coffee he will trade for bushels of wheat. Although Farmer Brown's luck has improved, he and Mr. Jones must agree on the terms of exchange. Exactly how many pounds of coffee, for example, is a bushel of wheat worth? Assuming this exchange is worked out, Farmer Brown must spend more time returning to the shoe store and negotiating the terms of an exchange of pencils, coffee, and toothpaste for shoes.

Barter

The direct exchange of one good or service for another good or service, rather than for money.

> **CONCLUSION:** *The use of money simplifies and therefore increases market transactions. Money also prevents wasting time that can be devoted to production, thereby promoting economic growth by increasing a nation's production possibilities.*

24-1a THE THREE FUNCTIONS OF MONEY

Suppose citizens of the planet of Starcom want to replace their barter system and must decide what to use for money. Assuming this planet is fortunate enough to have economists, they would explain that anything, regardless of its value, can serve as money if it conforms to the following definition. Money is anything that serves as a medium of exchange, unit of account, and store of value. Money is not limited to dimes, quarters, and dollar bills. Notice that "anything" meeting the three tests is a candidate to serve as money. This explains why precious metals, beaver skins, wampum (shells strung in belts), and cigarettes have all served as money. Let's discuss each of the three functions money serves.

Money

Anything that serves as a medium of exchange, unit of account, and store of value.

Money as a Medium of Exchange In a simple society, barter is a way for participants to exchange goods and services in order to satisfy wants. Barter, however, requires wasting time in the process of exchange that people could use for productive work. If the goal is to increase the volume of transactions and live in a modern economy, the most important function of money is to serve as

659

Medium of exchange

The primary function of money to be widely accepted in exchange for goods and services.

a medium of exchange. Medium of exchange is the primary function of money to be widely accepted in exchange for goods and services. Money removes the problem of coincidence of wants because everyone is willing to accept money in payment, rather than haggling over goods and services. You give up two $20 bills in exchange for a ticket to a rock concert. Because money serves as generalized purchasing power, all in society know that no one will refuse to trade their products for money. In short, money increases trade by providing a much more convenient method of exchange than a cumbersome barter system.

A fascinating question is whether people will find digital cash a more convenient means of payment. Each year more people avoid using checks, paper currency, or coins by transferring funds electronically from their accounts via various Internet-based and other systems. In fact, it is possible that widespread adoption of privately issued digital cash will ultimately replace government-issued currency. Vending and copy machines on many college campuses already accept plastic stored-value cards. Someday vending machines everywhere are likely to have smart card readers that accept electronic money.

Money as a Unit of Account   How does a wheat farmer know whether a bushel of wheat is worth one, two, or more pairs of shoes? How does a family compare its income to expenses or a business know whether it is making a profit? Government must be able to measure tax revenues collected and program expenditures made. And GDP is the *money* value of final goods and services used to compare the national output of the United States to, say, Japan's output. In each of these examples, money serves as a unit of account. Unit of account is the function of money to provide a common measurement of the relative value of goods and services. Without dollars, there is no common denominator. We must therefore decide if one pizza equals a box of pencils, 20 oranges equals one quart of milk, and so forth. Now let's compare the value of two items using money. If the price of one pizza is $20 and the price of a movie ticket is $10, then the value of one pizza equals two movie tickets. In the United States, the monetary unit is the dollar; in Japan, it is the yen; Mexico has its peso; and so on.

Unit of account

The function of money to provide a common measurement of the relative value of goods and services.

Money as a Store of Value   Can you put shrimp under your mattress for months and then exchange them for some product? No! Money, on the other hand, serves as a store of value in exchange for some item in the future. Store of value is the ability of money to hold value over time. You can bury money in your backyard or store it under your mattress for months or years and not worry about it spoiling. This also means you can save money and be confident that you can spend it in the future. However, recall from the chapter on inflation that hyperinflation can destroy money's store-of-value function and, in turn, its medium-of-exchange function.

Store of value

The ability of money to hold value over time.

CONCLUSION: *Money is a useful mechanism for transforming income in the present into future purchases.*

The key property of money is that it is completely *liquid*. This means that money is immediately available to spend in exchange for goods and services without any additional expense. Money is more liquid than real assets (real estate or gold) or paper assets (stocks or bonds). These assets also serve as stores of value, but liquidating (selling) them often involves expenses, such as brokerage fees, and time delays.

> **CONCLUSION:** *Money is the most liquid form of wealth because it can be spent directly in the marketplace.*

24-1b ARE CREDIT CARDS MONEY?

Credit cards, such as Visa, MasterCard, and American Express, are often called "plastic money," but are these cards really money? Let's test credit cards for the three functions of money. First, because credit cards are widely accepted, they serve as a means of payment in an exchange for goods or services.

Second, the credit card statement, and not the card itself, serves as a unit of account. One of the advantages of credit cards is that you receive a statement listing the exact price in dollars paid for each item you charged. Your credit card statement clearly records the dollar amount you spent for gasoline, a dinner, or a trip.

But credit cards clearly fail to meet the store-of-value criterion and are therefore *not* money. The word *credit* means receiving money today to buy products in return for a promise to pay in the future. A credit card represents only a prearranged short-term loan up to a certain limit. If the credit card company goes out of business or for any reason decides not to honor your card, it is worthless. Hence, credit cards do not store value and are *not* money.

✔ CHECKPOINT

Are Debit Cards Money?

Debit cards are used to pay for purchases, and the money is automatically deducted from the user's bank account. Are debit cards money?

24-2 Other Desirable Properties of Money

Once something has passed the three basic requirements to serve as money, there are additional hurdles to clear. First, an important consideration is *scarcity*. Money must be scarce, but not too scarce. Sand, for example, could theoretically serve as money, but sand is a poor choice because people can easily gather a bucketful to pay their bills. A Picasso painting would also be undesirable as money. Because there are so few for circulation, people would have to resort to barter.

Counterfeiting threatens the scarcity of money. Advances in computer graphics, scanners, and color copiers were allowing counterfeiters to win their ongoing battle with the U.S. Secret Service. In response, new bills were issued with a polymer security thread running through them. The larger off-center portraits on the bills allow for a watermark next to the portrait that is visible from both sides against a light.

> **CONCLUSION:** *The supply of money must be great enough to meet ordinary transaction needs, but not be so plentiful that it becomes worthless.*

Why a Loan in Yap Is Hard to Roll Over

Applicable Concept: functions of money

On the tiny South Pacific island of Yap, life is easy, but the currency is hard as a rock. For nearly 2,000 years, the Yapese have used large stone wheels to pay for major purchases, such as land, canoes, and permission to marry. The people of Yap have been using stone money ever since a Yapese warrior named Anagumang used canoes to bring the huge stones over the sea in ancient times from limestone caverns on neighboring Palau. Inspired by the moon, he fashioned the stones into large circles, and the rest is history. The stone's value remained high because of the difficulty and hazards involved in obtaining them over the rough seas.

Yap is a U.S. trust territory, and the dollar is used in grocery stores and gas stations, but reliance on stone money continues. Buying property with stones is "much easier than buying it with U.S. dollars," says John Chodad, who purchased a building lot with a 30-inch stone wheel. "We don't know the value of the U.S. dollar."[1] However, stone wheels don't make good pocket money, so Yapese use other forms of currency, such as beer, for small transactions. Besides stone wheels and beer, the Yapese sometimes spend gaw, consisting of necklaces of stone beads strung together around a whale's tooth. They also buy things with yar, a currency made from large seashells, but these are small change.

Stone disks may change ownership during marriage, transfer of land title, or other exchanges. Yapese lean the stone wheels against their houses or prop up rows of them in village "banks." Most of the stones are smaller in diameter, but some are as much as 12 feet in diameter. Each has a hole in the center so that it can be slipped onto the trunk of a fallen betel-nut tree and carried. It takes 20 men to lift some wheels. Rather than risk a broken stone—or their

© O.D. vande Veer/Alamy

backs—Yapese leave the larger stones where they are and make a mental accounting that the ownership has been transferred. There are some decided advantages to using massive stones for money. They are in short supply, difficult to steal, pose formidable obstacles to counterfeiting, and serve as a tourist attraction.

Analyze the Issue

1. Explain how Yap's large stones pass the three tests in the definition of money.
2. Briefly discuss Yap's large stones in terms of other desirable properties of money.

---

1. Art Pine, "Fixed Assets, Or: Why a Loan in Yap Is Hard to Roll Over," *The Wall Street Journal*, Mar. 29, 1984, p. 1.

Source: © Cengage Learning 2014

Second, money should be *portable* and *divisible*. That is, people should be able to reach into their pockets and make change to buy items at various prices. Statues of George Washington might be attractive money, but they would be difficult to carry and to use to make change. Finally, money must be *uniform*. An ounce of gold is an ounce of gold. The quality differences of beaver skins and seashells, on the other hand, complicate using these items for money. Each exchange would involve the extra trouble of buyers and sellers arguing over which skins or shells are better or worse.

24-3 What Stands behind Our Money?

Historically, early forms of money played two roles. If, for example, a ruler declared beans as money, you could spend them or sell them in the marketplace. Precious metals, tobacco, cows, and other tangible goods are examples of commodity money. Commodity money is anything that serves as money while having market value based on the material from which it is made. This means that money itself has intrinsic worth (the market value of the material). For example, money can be pure gold or silver, both of which are valuable for nonmoney uses, such as making jewelry and serving other industrial purposes.

Today, U.S. paper money and coins are no longer backed by gold or silver. Our paper money was exchangeable for gold or silver until 1934. As a result of the Great Depression, people rapidly tried to get rid of their paper money. The U.S. Treasury's stock of gold dropped so low that Congress passed a law in 1934 that prevented anyone from exchanging gold for $5 and larger bills. Later, in 1963, Congress removed the right to exchange $1 bills for silver. And in the mid-1960s, zinc, copper, and nickel replaced silver in coins.

The important consideration for money is acceptability. The acceptability of a dollar is due in no small degree to the fact that Uncle Sam decrees it to be fiat money. Fiat money is money accepted by law, and not because of its redeemability or intrinsic value. A dollar bill contains only about 3 cents worth of paper, printing inks, and other materials. A quarter contains maybe 10 cents worth of nickel and copper. Pull out a dollar bill and look at it closely. In the upper left corner on the front side is small print that proclaims, "THIS NOTE IS LEGAL TENDER FOR ALL DEBTS, PUBLIC AND PRIVATE." This means that your paper money is fiat money. Also notice that nowhere on the note is there any promise to redeem it for gold, silver, or anything else.

Commodity money

Anything that serves as money while having market value based on the material from which it is made.

Fiat money

Money accepted by law, and not because of its redeemability or intrinsic value.

CONCLUSION: *An item's ability to serve as money does not depend on its own market value or the backing of precious metal.*

24-4 Money Supply Definitions

Now that you understand the basic definition of money, we turn to exactly what constitutes the money supply of the U.S. economy. The following sections examine the two basic methods used to measure the money supply, officially called M1 and M2.

24-4a M1: THE MOST NARROWLY DEFINED MONEY SUPPLY

M1 is the narrowest definition of the money supply. This money definition measures purchasing power immediately available to the public without borrowing or having to give notice. Specifically, M1 measures the currency and checkable

M1

The narrowest definition of the money supply. It includes currency and checkable deposits.

History of Money in the Colonies

The early colonists left behind their well-developed money system in Europe. North American Indians accepted wampum as money, which are beads of polished shells strung in belts. Soon, a group of settlers learned to counterfeit wampum, and it lost its value. As a result, the main method of trading with the Indians was to barter. Later, trade developed with the West Indies, and Spanish coins called "pieces of eight" were circulated widely. Colonists often cut these coins into pieces to make change. Half of a coin became known as "four bits." A quarter part of the coin was referred to as "two bits." The first English colony to mint its own coins was Massachusetts in 1652. A striking pine tree was engraved on these coins called shillings. Other coins such as a six-pence and three-pence were also produced at a mint in

Boston. Several other colonies followed by authorizing their own coin issues.

The first national coin of the United States was issued in 1787 when Congress approved a one-cent copper coin. One side was decorated with a chain of

---

deposits held by the public at a given time, such as a given day, month, or year. Expressed as a formula:

$$M1 = \text{currency} + \text{checkable deposits}$$

Exhibit 1 shows the components of M1 and M2 money supply definitions based on daily averages in 2011.

Currency   Currency includes coins and paper money, officially called Federal Reserve notes, that the public holds for immediate spending. The purpose of currency is to enable us to make small purchases. Currency represents 46 percent of M1.

Currency

Money, including coins and paper money.

Checkable Deposits   Most "big ticket" purchases are paid for with checks or credit cards (which are not money), rather than currency. Checks eliminate trips to the bank, and they are safer than cash. If lost or stolen, checks and credit cards can be replaced at little cost—money cannot. Exhibit 1 shows that a major share of M1 consists of checkable deposits. Checkable deposits are the total money in financial institutions that can be withdrawn "on demand" by writing a check. A checking account balance is a bookkeeping entry, often called a *demand deposit* because it can be converted into cash "on demand." Before the 1980s, only commercial banks could legally provide demand deposits. However, the law changed with the passage of the Depository Institutions Deregulation and Monetary Control Act of 1980. (This act will be discussed later in the chapter.) Today, checking accounts

Checkable deposits

The total money in financial institutions that can be withdrawn by writing a check.

13 links encircling the words "We Are One." The other side had a sundial, the noonday sun, and the Latin word *fugo*, meaning "time flies." Later, this coin became known as the Franklin cent, although there is no evidence that Benjamin Franklin played any role in its design.

In 1792, Congress established a mint in Philadelphia. It manufactured copper cents and half-cents about the size of today's quarters and nickels. In 1794, silver half-dimes and half-dollars increased the variety of available coins. The next year gold eagles ($10) and half-eagles ($5) appeared. The motto "E Pluribus Unum" ("out of many, one") was first used on the half-eagle in 1795. The next year America's first quarters and dimes were issued.

The first paper money in the Americas was printed in 1690. Massachusetts soldiers returned to the colony from fighting the French in Quebec, where they had unsuccessfully laid siege to the city. The colony had no precious metal to pay the soldiers. Hundreds of soldiers threatened mutiny, and the colony decided it must issue bills of credit, which were simply pieces of paper promising to pay the soldiers. Other colonies followed this example and printed their own paper money. Soon paper money was being widely circulated.

In 1775, the need to finance the American Revolution forced the Continental Congress to issue paper money called "continentals," but so much was issued that it rapidly lost its value. George Washington complained, "A wagon load of money will scarcely purchase a wagon load of provisions." This statement is today shortened to the phrase "not worth a continental."

are available from many different financial institutions, such as savings and loan associations, credit unions, and mutual savings banks. For example, many people hold deposits in negotiable order of withdrawal (NOW) accounts or automatic transfer of savings (ATS) accounts, which serve as interest-bearing checking accounts. NOW and ATS accounts permit depositors to spend their deposits without a trip to the bank to withdraw funds. In 2011, 54 percent of M1 was checkable deposits.

24-4b M2: ADDING NEAR MONIES TO M1

M2 is a broader measure of the money supply because it equals M1 plus *near monies*. Many economists consider M1 to be too narrow a measure because it does not include near money accounts that can be used to purchase goods and services. These include passbook savings accounts, money market accounts, mutual fund accounts, and time deposits of less than $100,000. Near monies are interest-bearing deposits easily converted into spendable funds. Written as a formula:

$$M2 = M1 + near\ monies$$

rewritten as

$$M2 = M1 + savings\ deposits + small\ time\ deposits\ of\ less\ than\ \$100,000$$

M2

The definition of the money supply that equals M1 plus near monies, such as savings deposits and small time deposits of less than $100,000.

EXHIBIT 1	Definitions of the Money Supply, 2011

Each of the two pie charts represents the money supply in 2011. M1, the most narrowly defined money supply, is equal to currency (coins and paper money) in circulation plus checkable deposits in financial institutions. M2 is a more broadly defined money supply, equal to M1 plus savings deposits and small time deposits of less than $100,000.

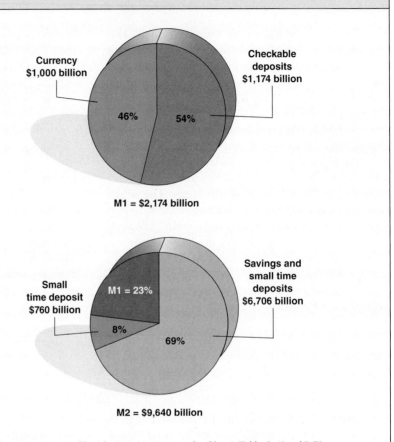

Currency
$1,000 billion

Checkable deposits
$1,174 billion

46%   54%

M1 = $2,174 billion

Small time deposit
$760 billion

Savings and small time deposits
$6,706 billion

M1 = 23%

8%   69%

M2 = $9,640 billion

SOURCE: *Economic Report of the President*, 2012, http://www.gpo.gov/fdsys/pkg/ERP-2012/content-detail.htm1, Tables B-69 and B-70.

Savings Deposits   As shown in Exhibit 1, M1 was 23 percent of M2 in 2011, with savings deposits and small time deposits constituting the remainder of M2. Savings deposits are interest-bearing accounts that can be easily withdrawn. These deposits include passbook savings accounts, money market accounts, mutual fund accounts, and other types of interest-bearing deposits with commercial banks, mutual savings banks, savings and loan associations, and credit unions.

Small Time Deposits   There is a distinction between a *checkable deposit* and a *time deposit*. A time deposit is an interest-bearing account in a financial institution with guaranteed interest for a period of time. Certificates of deposit (CDs), for example, are deposits for a specified time, with a penalty charged for early withdrawal. Where is the line drawn between a small and a large time deposit? The answer is that time deposits of less than $100,000 are "small" and therefore are included in M2. In 2011, 8 percent of M2 was small time deposits.

CONCLUSION: *M1 is more liquid than M2.*

To simplify the discussion throughout the remainder of this text, we will be referring to M1 when we discuss the money supply. However, one can argue that M2, or another measurement of the money supply, may be the best definition. Actually, the boundary lines for any definition of money are somewhat arbitrary.

24-5 The Federal Reserve System

What controls the money supply in the United States? The answer is the Federal Reserve System, popularly called the "Fed." The Fed is the central banker for the nation and provides banking services to commercial banks, other financial institutions, and the federal government. The Fed regulates, supervises, and is responsible for policies concerning money. Congress and the president consult with the Fed to control the size of the money supply and thereby influence the economy's performance.

Other major nations have central banks, such as the Bank of England, the Bank of Japan, and the European Central Bank. The movement in the United States to establish a central banking system gained strength early in the 20th century as a series of bank failures resulted in The Panic of 1907. In that year, stock prices fell, many businesses and banks failed, and millions of depositors lost their savings. The prescription for preventing financial panic was for the government to establish more centralized control over banks. This desire for more safety in banking led to the creation of the Federal Reserve System by the Federal Reserve Act of 1913 during the administration of President Woodrow Wilson. No longer would the supply of money in the economy be determined by individual banks.

24-5a THE FED'S ORGANIZATIONAL CHART

The *Federal Reserve System* is an independent agency of the federal government. Congress is responsible for overseeing the Fed, but does not interfere with its day-to-day decisions. The chairman of the Fed reports to Congress twice each year and often coordinates its actions with the U.S. Treasury and the president. Although the Fed enjoys independent status, its independence can be revoked. If the Fed were to pursue policies contrary to the interests of the nation, Congress could abolish the Fed.

The Federal Reserve System consists of 12 central banks that service banks and other financial institutions within each of the Federal Reserve districts. Each Federal Reserve bank serves as a central banker for the private banks in its region. The United States is the only nation in the world to have 12 separate regional banks instead of a single central bank. In fact, the Fed's structure is the result of a compromise between the traditionalists, who favored a single central bank, and the populists, who distrusted concentration of financial power in the hands of a few. In addition, 25 Federal Reserve branch banks are located throughout the country. The map in Exhibit 2 shows the 12 Federal Reserve districts.

The organizational chart of the Federal Reserve System, given in Exhibit 3, shows that the Board of Governors, located in Washington, D.C., administers the system. The Board of Governors is made up of seven members, appointed by the president and confirmed by the U.S. Senate, who serve for one nonrenewable 14-year term. Their responsibility is to supervise and control the money

Federal Reserve System

The 12 Federal Reserve district banks that service banks and other financial institutions within each of the Federal Reserve districts; popularly called the "Fed."

Board of Governors of the Federal Reserve System

The seven members appointed by the president and confirmed by the U.S. Senate who serve for one nonrenewable 14-year term. Their responsibility is to supervise and control the money supply and the banking system of the United States.

Ben Bernanke, Chairman of the Board of Governors of the Federal Reserve System

EXHIBIT 2	The Twelve Federal Reserve Districts

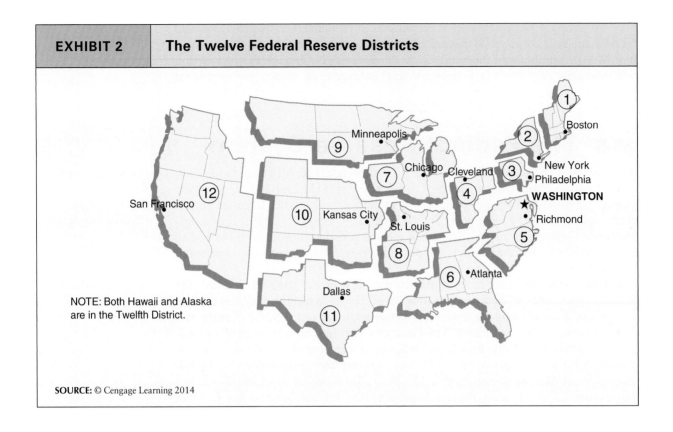

NOTE: Both Hawaii and Alaska are in the Twelfth District.

SOURCE: © Cengage Learning 2014

EXHIBIT 3	The Organization of the Federal Reserve System

The Federal Open Market Committee (FOMC) and the Federal Advisory Council assist the Federal Reserve System's Board of Governors. The 12 regional Federal Reserve district banks and their 25 branches implement broad policies affecting the money supply.

Federal Open Market Committee (FOMC) (Board of Governors, president of New York Federal Reserve Bank, and four additional Federal Reserve district bank presidents)

Federal Advisory Council (12 prominent commercial bankers)

Board of Governors (7 members)

Regional Federal Reserve banks (12 district banks and 25 branch banks)

U.S. banking system (commercial banks, mutual savings banks, savings and loan associations, and credit unions)

SOURCE: © Cengage Learning 2014

supply and the banking system of the United States. Fourteen-year terms for Fed governors create autonomy and insulate the Fed from short-term politics. These terms are staggered so that one term expires every two years. This staggering of terms prevents a president from stacking the board with members favoring the incumbent party's political interests. A president usually makes two appointments in a one-term presidency and four appointments in a two-term presidency. The president designates one member of the Board of Governors to serve as chairman for a four-year term. The chairman is the principal spokesperson for the Fed and has considerable power over policy decisions. In fact, it is often argued that the Fed's chairman is the most powerful individual in the United States next to the president. The current chairman is Ben Bernanke, who was appointed by former President George W. Bush and reappointed by President Barack Obama in 2010.

The Federal Reserve System receives no funding from Congress. This creates financial autonomy for the Fed by removing the fear of congressional review of its budget. Then where does the Fed get funds to operate? Recall from Exhibit 7 of the previous chapter that the Fed holds government securities issued by the U.S. Treasury. The Fed earns interest income from the government securities it holds and the loans it makes to depository institutions. Because the Fed returns any profits to the Treasury, it is motivated to adopt policies to promote the economy's well-being, rather than earning a profit. Moreover, the Board of Governors does not take orders from the president or any other politician. Thus, the Board of Governors is the independent, self-supporting authority of the Federal Reserve System.

On the left side of the organizational chart in Exhibit 3 is the very important Federal Open Market Committee (FOMC). The FOMC directs the buying and selling of U.S. government securities, which are major instruments for controlling the money supply. The FOMC consists of the seven members of the Board of Governors, the president of the New York Federal Reserve Bank, and the presidents of four other Federal Reserve district banks. The FOMC meets to discuss trends in inflation, unemployment, growth rates, and other macro data. FOMC members express their opinions on implementing various monetary policies and then issue policy statements known as *FOMC directives*. A directive, for example, might set the operation of the Fed to stimulate or restrain M1 in order to influence the economy. The next two chapters explain the tools of monetary policy in more detail.

As shown on the right side of the chart, the *Federal Advisory Council* consists of 12 prominent commercial bankers. Each of the 12 Federal Reserve district banks selects one member each year. The council meets periodically to advise the Board of Governors.

Finally, at the bottom of the organizational chart is the remainder of the Federal Reserve System, consisting of only about 3,000 member banks of the approximately 7,000 commercial banks in the United States. Although these 3,000 Fed member banks represent only about 40 percent of U.S. banks, they have about 70 percent of all U.S. bank deposits. A sure sign of Fed membership is the word *National* in a bank's name. The U.S. comptroller of the currency charters national banks, and they are required to be Fed members. Banks that do not have "National" in their title can also be Fed members. States can also charter banks, and these state banks have the option of joining the Federal Reserve. Less than 20 percent of state banks choose to join the Fed. Exhibit 4 shows the top 10 U.S. banks based on their assets.

Federal Open Market Committee (FOMC)

The Federal Reserve's committee that directs the buying and selling of U.S. government securities, which are major instruments for controlling the money supply. The FOMC consists of the seven members of the Federal Reserve's Board of Governors, the president of the New York Federal Reserve Bank, and the presidents of four other Federal Reserve district banks.

| EXHIBIT 4 | Top 10 Banks in the United States, 2011 |

The top 10 banks in the United States include JPMorgan Chase, Bank of America, and Wells Fargo.

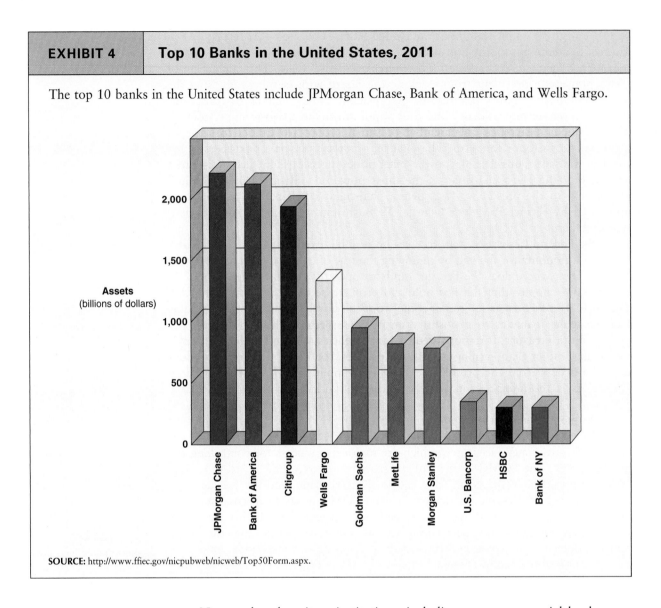

SOURCE: http://www.ffiec.gov/nicpubweb/nicweb/Top50Form.aspx.

Nonmember depository institutions, including many commercial banks, savings and loan associations (S&Ls), savings banks, and credit unions, are not official members of the Fed team. They are, however, influenced by and depend on the Fed for a variety of services, which we will now discuss.

24-6 What a Federal Reserve Bank Does

The typical bank customer never enters the doors of a Federal Reserve district bank or one of its branch banks. The reason is that the Fed does not offer the public checking accounts, savings accounts, or any of the services provided by commercial banks. Instead, the Federal Reserve serves as a "banker's bank." Following are brief descriptions of some of the principal functions of the Federal Reserve.

24-6a CONTROLLING THE MONEY SUPPLY

The primary role of the Fed is to control the nation's money supply. The mechanics of Fed control over the money supply are explained in the next two chapters. To most people, this is a wondrously mysterious process. So that you do not suffer in complete suspense, here is a sneak preview: The Fed has three policy tools, or levers, it can use to change the stock of money in the banking system. The potential macro outcome of changes in the money supply is to affect total spending and therefore real GDP, employment, and the price level.

24-6b CLEARING CHECKS

Because people and businesses use checks to pay for goods and services, check clearing is an important function. Suppose you live in Virginia and have a checking account with a bank in that state. While on vacation in California, you purchase tickets to Disneyland with a check for $200. Disneyland accepts your check and then deposits it in its business checking account in a California bank. This bank must collect payment for your check and does so by sending an electronic copy of your check to the Federal Reserve bank in San Francisco. From there, your check is sent to the Federal Reserve bank in Richmond. At each stop along its journey, the check earns a black stamp mark on the back. Finally, the process ends when $200 is subtracted from your personal checking account. Banks in which checks are deposited have their Fed accounts credited, and banks on which checks are written have their accounts debited. The Fed clearinghouse process is much speedier than depending on the movement of a check between commercial banks.

24-6c SUPERVISING AND REGULATING BANKS

The Fed examines banks' books, sets limits for loans, approves bank mergers, and works with the Federal Deposit Insurance Corporation (FDIC). The FDIC is a government agency established in 1933 that insures commercial bank deposits up to a limit if a bank fails. Congress created the FDIC in response to the huge number of bank failures during the Great Depression and set the insurance limit at $25,000. If the government provides a safety net, people are less likely to panic and withdraw their funds from banks during a period of economic uncertainty. When deposits are insured and a bank fails, the government stands ready to pay depositors or transfer their deposits to a solvent bank. Banks that are members of the Fed are members of the FDIC. State agencies supervise state-chartered banks that are not members of either the Federal Reserve System or the FDIC. To shore up confidence in the U.S. banking system in the wake of bank failures in 2008, the $700 billion U.S. financial industry rescue law raised the FDIC coverage of bank deposits to $250,000 per customer from $100,000.

Federal Deposit Insurance Corporation (FDIC)

A government agency established in 1933 to insure customer deposits up to a limit if a bank fails.

The 1946 film, **It's a Wonderful Life,** is based on a fractional reserve banking system without the FDIC.

24-6d MAINTAINING AND CIRCULATING CURRENCY

Recall that the M1 money supply consists of currency (coins and Federal Reserve notes) and checkable deposits. Note that the Fed does *not* print currency—it *maintains* and *circulates* money. All Federal Reserve notes are printed at the U.S. Bureau of Engraving and Printing's facilities in Washington, D.C., and Fort Worth, Texas. The Treasury mints and issues all coins. Coins are made at U.S. mints located in

Philadelphia and Denver. The bureau and the mints ship new notes and coins to the Federal Reserve banks for circulation. Much of this money is printed or minted simply to replace worn-out bills and coins. Another use of new currency is to meet public demand. Suppose it is the holiday season and banks need more paper money and coins to meet their customers' shopping needs. The Federal Reserve must be ready to ship extra money from its large vaults by armored truck.

24-6e PROTECTING CONSUMERS

Since 1968, the Federal Reserve has played a role in protecting consumers by enforcing statutes enacted by Congress. Perhaps the most important is the *Equal Credit Opportunity Act*, which prohibits discrimination based on race, color, gender, marital status, religion, or national origin in the extension of credit. It also gives married women the right to establish credit histories in their own names. The Federal Reserve receives and tries to resolve consumer complaints against banks.

In 2010, the Consumer Financial Protection Bureau (CFPB) was established. This is an independent bureau within the Federal Reserve that helps consumers make financial decisions. The goal of the CFPB is to promote fairness and make mortgages, credit cards, and other consumer financial services understandable. The objective is to let consumers see clearly the costs and features of loans. As a result, consumers will not be caught by hidden fees or sign loans they cannot afford.

Consumer Financial Protection Bureau (CFPB)

An independent bureau within the Federal Reserve that helps consumers make financial decisions.

24-6f MAINTAINING FEDERAL GOVERNMENT CHECKING ACCOUNTS AND GOLD

The Fed is also Uncle Sam's bank. The U.S. Treasury has the Fed handle its checking account. From this account, the federal government pays for such expenses as federal employees' salaries, Social Security, tax refunds, veterans' benefits, defense, and highways.

Finally, it is interesting to note that the New York Federal Reserve District Bank holds one of the oldest forms of money—*gold*. This gold belongs mainly to foreign governments and is one of the largest accumulations of this precious metal in the world. Viewing a Federal Reserve bank's vault is not something that most tourists typically have on their list of things to do, but I strongly recommend this tour.

The gold vault at the New York Federal Reserve Bank is nearly half the length of a football field and filled with steel and concrete walls several yards thick. Most cells contain the gold of only one nation, and only a few bank employees know the identities of the owners. When trade occurs between two countries, payment between the parties can be made by transferring gold bars from one compartment to another. Note that the Fed and the monetary system of the Yapese have a similarity. Recall from the Global Economics box that in Yap, large stone wheels are not moved; they just change ownership.

24-6g LENDER OF LAST RESORT

The Fed acts as the lender of last resort to prevent a banking crisis. For example, after the terrorist attacks in 2001, the Fed issued billions in loans to banks throughout the United States. And in 2008, several large banks collapsed and others were on the verge. The Fed lent banks enough required reserve balances to meet their obligation to depositors.

24-7 The U.S. Banking Revolution

Prior to the 1980s, the U.S. banking system was simpler. It consisted of many commercial banks authorized by law to offer checking accounts. Then there were the other financial institutions, the so-called thrifts, which included S&Ls, mutual savings banks, and credit unions. The thrifts by law were permitted to accept only savings deposits with no checking privileges. The commercial banks, on the other hand, could not pay interest on checkable deposits. Moreover, a "maximum interest rate allowed by law" limited competition among commercial banks and other financial institutions. As will be explained momentarily, this relatively tranquil U.S. banking structure changed dramatically, and the stage was set for a fascinating banking "horror story."

24-7a THE MONETARY CONTROL ACT OF 1980

A significant law affecting the U.S. banking system is the Depository Institutions Deregulation and Monetary Control Act of 1980, commonly called the Monetary Control Act. This law gave the Federal Reserve System greater control over nonmember banks and made all financial institutions more competitive. The act's four major provisions are the following:

1. *The authority of the Fed over nonmember depository institutions was increased.* Before the Monetary Control Act, less than half the banks in the United States were members of the Fed and subject to its direct control. Under the act's provisions, the Federal Reserve sets uniform reserve requirements for *all* commercial banks, including state and national banks, S&Ls, and credit unions with checking accounts.
2. *All depository institutions are able to borrow loan reserves from Federal Reserve banks.* This practice, called *discounting*, will be explained in the next chapter. Banks also have access to check clearing and other services of the Fed.
3. *The act allows commercial banks, thrifts, money market mutual funds, stock brokerage firms, and retailers to offer a wide variety of banking services.* For example, commercial banks and other financial institutions can pay unrestricted interest rates on checking accounts. Also, S&Ls and other financial institutions can offer checking accounts. Federal credit unions are authorized to make residential real estate loans, and other major corporations can offer traditional banking services.
4. *The act eliminated all interest rate ceilings.* Before this act, S&Ls were allowed to pay depositors a slightly higher interest rate on passbook savings deposits than those paid by commercial banks. The Monetary Control Act removed this advantage of S&Ls over other financial institutions competing for depositors.

Finally, the movement toward deregulation, which blurred the distinctions between financial institutions, continued in 1999 when the *Financial Services Modernization Act* was signed into law. This sweeping measure lifted Depression-era

Monetary Control Act

A law, formally titled the Depository Institutions Deregulation and Monetary Control Act of 1980, that gave the Federal Reserve System greater control over nonmember banks and made all financial institutions more competitive.

The Wreck of Lincoln Savings and Loan

Applicable Concept: deposit insurance

The case of Lincoln Savings and Loan is a classic example of what went wrong during one of the worst financial crises in U.S. history prior to the banking crisis and Great Recession of 2007–2009. In 1984, the Securities and Exchange Commission charged Charles Keating, Jr., with fraud in an Ohio loan scam, but regulators later allowed him to buy Lincoln Savings and Loan in California. Keating hired a staff to carry out his wishes and paid them and his relatives millions. Keating was also generous with politicians in Washington, D.C. Allegedly, five U.S. senators received $1.5 million in campaign contributions from Keating to influence regulators.

Where did Keating's money come from? It came from Lincoln Savings depositors and, ultimately, from taxpayers because the federal government insures deposits of failed S&Ls. When Keating took over Lincoln, it was a healthy S&L with assets of $1.1 billion. But because of deregulation mandated by the Monetary Control Act and other legislation and the lack of enforcement of regulations under the new laws, many S&Ls plunged into high-risk, but potentially highly profitable, ventures. Keating therefore took Lincoln out of sound home mortgage loans and into speculation in Arizona hotels costing $500,000 per room to build, raw land for golf courses, shopping centers, junk bonds, and currency futures.

In 1987, after it was already too late, California regulators became alarmed at the way Lincoln operated and asked the FBI and the FSLIC to take over Lincoln. Keating responded by contacting his friends in Washington, and the regulatory process moved at a snail's pace. Years passed before the government finally closed Lincoln and informed the public that their deposits were not safe in this S&L. During the time regulators were deciding what action to take, it is estimated that Lincoln cost taxpayers another $1 billion. Ultimately, the collapse of Lincoln cost U.S. taxpayers about $3 billion, making it the most expensive S&L failure of all.

Keating and other S&L entrepreneurs say they did nothing wrong. After all, Congress and federal regulators encouraged, or did not discourage, S&Ls to compete by borrowing funds at high interest rates and making risky, but potentially highly profitable, investments. If oil prices and land values fall unexpectedly and loans fail, this is simply the way a market economy works and not the fault of risk-prone wheeler-dealers like Keating.

In 1993, a federal judge sentenced Keating to 12 1/2 years in prison for swindling small investors. The sentence ran concurrently with a 10-year state prison sentence. The judge also ordered Keating to pay $122.4 million in restitution to the government for losses caused by sham property sales. However, the government

Elena Elisseeva/Shutterstock.com

has been unable to locate any significant assets. Keating served four years and nine months.

Analyze the Issue

Critics of federal banking policy argue that deposit insurance is a key reason for banking failures. The banks enjoy a "heads I win, tails the government loses" proposition. Several possible reforms of deposit insurance have been suggested. For example, the limit on insured deposits can be raised, reduced, or eliminated. Do you think a change in deposit insurance would prevent bank failures?

Source: © Cengage Learning 2014

barriers and allows banks, securities firms, and insurance companies to merge and sell each other's products.

24-7b THE SAVINGS AND LOAN CRISIS

Before the recent financial crisis discussed in the chapter on monetary policy, the savings and loan crisis of the 1980s and early 1990s was one of the worst U.S. financial crises since the Great Depression. After the Monetary Control Act removed interest rate ceilings on deposits, competition for customers forced S&Ls to pay higher interest rates on short-term deposits. Unlike the banks, however, S&Ls were earning their income from long-term mortgages at fixed interest rates below the rate required to keep or attract new deposits. The resulting losses enticed the S&Ls to forsake home mortgage loans, which they knew best, and seek high-interest, but riskier, commercial and consumer loans. Unfortunately, these risky higher-interest loans resulted in defaults and more losses. If conditions were not bad enough, lower oil prices depressed the oil-based state economies in Texas, Louisiana, and Oklahoma.

The Federal Savings and Loan Insurance Corporation (FSLIC) was the agency that insured deposits in S&Ls, similar to how the FDIC insures bank deposits. The magnitude of the losses exceeded the insurance fund's ability to pay depositors, and Congress placed the FSLIC's deposit-insurance fund under the FDIC's control. To close or sell ailing S&Ls and protect depositors, Congress enacted the Thrift Bailout Bill in 1989. One provision of this act created the Resolution Trust Corporation (RTC) to carry out a massive federal bailout of failed institutions. The RTC bought the assets and deposits of failed S&Ls and sold them to offset the cost borne by taxpayers. The RTC closed in 1995, and the ultimate cost to taxpayers totaled $125 billion!

Key Concepts

Barter
Money
Medium of exchange
Unit of account
Store of value
Commodity money
Fiat money

M1, M2
Currency
Checkable deposits
Federal Reserve System
Board of Governors of the
    Federal Reserve System

Federal Open Market Committee
    (FOMC)
Federal Deposit Insurance
    Corporation (FDIC)
Consumer Financial Bureau
    (CFPB)
Monetary Control Act

Summary

- **Money** can be anything that meets these three tests. Money must serve as (1) a medium of exchange, (2) a unit of account, and (3) a store of value. Money facilitates more efficient exchange than barter. Other desirable properties of money include scarcity, portability, divisibility, and uniformity.

- **Medium of exchange** is the most important function of money. This means that money is widely accepted in payment for goods and services.

- **Unit of account** is another important function of money. Money is used to measure relative values by serving as a common yardstick for valuing goods and services.
- **Store of value** is the ability of money to hold its value over time. Money is said to be highly *liquid*, which means it is readily usable in exchange.
- **Credit cards** are not money. Credit cards represent a short-term loan and therefore fail as a store of value.
- **Commodity money** is money that has a marketable value, such as gold and silver. Today, the United States uses *fiat money*, which must be accepted by law, but is not convertible into gold, silver, or any commodity.
- **M1** is the narrowest definition of the money supply, which equals currency plus checkable deposits. **M2** is a broader definition of the money supply, which equals M1 plus *near monies*, such as savings deposits and small time deposits.
- The **Federal Reserve System**, our central bank, was established in 1913. The Fed consists of 12 Federal Reserve district banks with 25 branches. The *Board of Governors* is the Fed's governing body. The *Federal Open Market Committee* (FOMC) directs the buying and selling of U.S. government securities, which is a key method of controlling the money supply.
- **Basic Federal Reserve bank functions** are (1) controlling the money supply, (2) clearing checks, (3) supervising and regulating banking, (4) maintaining and circulating currency, (5) protecting consumers, and (6) maintaining the federal government's checking accounts and gold.

Definitions of Money Supply (M1 and M2)

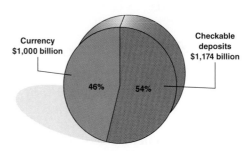

Currency $1,000 billion   46%   54%   Checkable deposits $1,174 billion

M1 = $2,174 billion

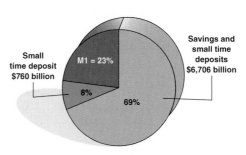

Small time deposit $760 billion   M1 = 23%   8%   69%   Savings and small time deposits $6,706 billion

M2 = $9,640 billion

SOURCE: *Economic Report of the President*, 2012, http://www.gpo.gov/fdsys/pkg/ERP-2012/content-detail.htm1, Tables B-69 and B-70.

- The **Monetary Control Act of 1980** revolutionized U.S. banking by expanding the authority of the Federal Reserve System to all financial institutions. In addition, this law increased competition by blurring the distinctions between commercial banks, thrift institutions, and even nonfinancial institutions.

Summary of Conclusion Statements

- The use of money simplifies and therefore increases market transactions. Money also prevents wasting time that can be devoted to production, thereby promoting economic growth by increasing a nation's production possibilities.
- Money is a useful mechanism for transforming income in the present into future purchases.
- Money is the most liquid form of wealth because it can be spent directly in the marketplace.

- The supply of money must be great enough to meet ordinary transaction needs, but not be so plentiful that it becomes worthless.
- An item's ability to serve as money does not depend on its own market value or the backing of precious metal.
- M1 is more liquid than M2.

Study Questions and Problems

1. Discuss this statement: "A man with a million dollars who is lost in the desert learns the meaning of money."

2. Could each of the following items potentially serve as money? Consider each as (1) a medium of exchange, (2) a unit of account, and (3) a store of value.
   a. Visa credit card
   b. Federal Reserve note
   c. Dog
   d. Beer mug

3. Consider each of the items in question 2 in terms of scarcity, portability, divisibility, and uniformity.

4. What backs the U.S. dollar? Include the distinction between commodity money and fiat money in your answer.

5. What are the components of the most narrowly defined money supply in the United States?

6. Distinguish between M1 and M2. What are near monies?

7. What is the major purpose of the Federal Reserve System? What is the major responsibility of the Board of Governors and the Federal Open Market Committee?

8. Should the Fed be independent or a government agency subordinate to Congress and the president?

9. Which banks must be insured by the FDIC? Which banks can choose not to be insured by the FDIC?

10. Briefly discuss the importance of the Depository Institutions Deregulation and Monetary Control Act of 1980.

For Online Exercises, go to the Tucker Web site at www.cengage.com/economics/tucker.

✔ CHECKPOINT ANSWER

Are Debit Cards Money?

Debit cards serve as a means of payment, and debit card statements serve as a unit of account. Finally, unlike credit cards, debit cards serve as a store of value because they are a means of accessing checkable deposits and not an extension of credit. If you said debit cards are money because they serve all three functions required for money, **YOU ARE CORRECT.**

Sample Quiz

For an explanation of the correct answers, visit the Tucker Web site at www.cengage.com/economics/tucker.

1. Buying a cup of coffee with a dollar bill represents the use of money as a
   a. medium of exchange.
   b. unit of account.
   c. store of value.
   d. All of the above answers are correct.

Sample Quiz *continued*

2. Comparing how many dollars it takes to attend college each year to annual earnings on a job represents the use of money as a
   a. medium of exchange.
   b. unit of account.
   c. store of value.
   d. store of coincidence.

3. Which of the following items does *not* provide a store of value?
   a. currency
   b. checkable deposits
   c. credit cards
   d. All of the above answers are correct.

4. Anything can be money if it acts as a
   a. unit of account.
   b. store of value.
   c. medium of exchange.
   d. All of the above answers must be correct.

5. The ease with which an asset can be converted into a medium of exchange is known as
   a. volatility.
   b. liquidity.
   c. currency.
   d. speculative exchange.

6. Which of the following items is included when computing M1?
   a. coins in circulation
   b. currency in circulation
   c. checking accounting entries
   d. All of the above answers are correct.

7. Which of the following statements is *true*?
   a. Money must be relatively "scarce" if it is to have value.
   b. Money must be divisible and portable.
   c. M1 is the narrowest definition of money.
   d. All of the above answers are correct.

8. M1 money includes all but which of the following?
   a. checkable deposits
   b. savings accounts
   c. paper money
   d. coins

9. Which of the following is counted as part of M2?
   a. currency
   b. checkable deposits at commercial banks
   c. money market funds
   d. All of the above answers are correct.

10. Which definition of the money supply includes credit cards?
    a. M1
    b. M2
    c. Both answers include credit card balances.
    d. Neither answer includes credit card balances.

11. With respect to controlling the money supply, the law requires the Fed to take orders from
    a. the president.
    b. the Speaker of the House.
    c. the Secretary of the Treasury.
    d. no one—the Fed is an independent agency.

12. Which of the following is *not* part of the Federal Reserve System?
    a. Council of Economic Advisors
    b. Board of Governors
    c. Federal Open Market Committee
    d. 12 Federal Reserve District Banks

13. The Fed's principal decision-making body, which directs buying and selling U.S. government securities, is the
    a. Federal Deposit Insurance Corporation.
    b. District Board of Governors.
    c. Federal Open Market Committee.
    d. Reserve Requirement Regulation Conference.

14. The major protection against a sudden mass attempt to withdraw cash from banks is the
    a. Federal Reserve.
    b. Consumer Protection Act.
    c. deposit insurance provided by the FDIC.
    d. gold and silver backing the dollar.

15. The Monetary Control Act of 1980
    a. created less competition among various financial institutions.

Sample Quiz *continued*

b. allowed fewer institutions to offer checking account services.

c. restricted savings and loan associations to long-term loans.

d. did none of the above.

16. Which of the following is a store of value?
   a. federal reserve notes
   b. debit card
   c. passbook savings deposit
   d. Each of the above answers is a store of value.

17. The difference between M1 and M2 is given by which of the following?
   a. M1 includes currency, coins, gold, and silver, whereas M2 does not contain gold and silver.
   b. M1 is made up of currency and checkable deposits, whereas M2 contains M1 plus savings deposits and small time deposits.
   c. M1 is limited to checkable deposits, whereas M2 contains currency.

d. M1 includes only currency, whereas M2 contains M1 plus checkable deposits.

18. Which of the following is a desirable property of money?
   a. scarcity
   b. portability
   c. divisibility
   d. All of the above answers are correct.

19. The Federal Reserve System was founded in
   a. 1913.
   b. 1929.
   c. 1933.
   d. 1935.

20. The Monetary Control Act of 1980 extended the Fed's authority to
   a. impose required reserve ratios on all depository institutions.
   b. control the discount rate.
   c. control the federal funds rate.
   d. All of the above answers are correct.

chapter 25

Money Creation

It has been said that the most important person in Washington, D.C., is the chair of the Federal Reserve because he or she can influence the money supply and therefore the performance of the economy. This chapter builds on your knowledge of money and the Federal Reserve System gained in the previous chapter. You will discover that the Federal Reserve (the Fed) and the banks work together to determine the money supply. The chapter begins with a brief history of the evolution of banking. Then we examine the mechanics of how banks create money in a simplified system during a normal economy. This remarkable process depends on the ability of banks to amplify checkable deposits by generating a spiral of new loans and, in turn, deposits for new spending in the economy. Finally, the Fed's toolkit swings open, and we discuss the three tools used by the Fed to change the money supply.

A common misconception is that banks (including savings and loans and other depository institutions) accept deposits and make loans, and that's about the end of the story. But there is another very important chapter to tell. Banking transactions expand or contract the money supply. Without minting coins or using the printing presses to make paper money, your local bank and other banks can create money; that is, banks can increase the money supply (M1).

The reason people do not understand money creation is that they think the federal government controls the money supply by turning the printing presses on and off. As explained in the previous chapter, this notion is only partly true because money consists largely of bookkeeping entries (checkable deposits). Consequently, writing checks, using an automatic teller machine, and getting a loan affect the size of the checkable deposits component of the money supply.

In this chapter, you will learn to solve these economics puzzles:

- Exactly how is money created in the economy? That is, how does the money supply increase?

- What are the major tools the Federal Reserve uses to control the supply of money?

- Why is there nothing "federal" about the federal funds rate?

25-1 Money Creation Begins

In the Middle Ages, gold was the money of choice in most European nations. One of the problems with gold is that it is a heavy commodity, which makes it difficult to use in transactions or to hide from thieves. The medieval solution was to keep it safely deposited with the people who worked with gold, called *goldsmiths*. This demand for their services inspired goldsmith entrepreneurs to become the founders of modern-day banking.

The goldsmiths sat on their benches with ledgers close by and recorded the amounts of gold placed in their vaults. In fact, the word *bank* is derived from the Italian word for bench, which is *banco*. After assessing the purity of the gold, a goldsmith issued a receipt to the customer for the amount of gold deposited. In return, the goldsmith collected a service charge, just as you pay today for services at your bank. Anyone who possessed the receipt and presented it to the goldsmith could make a withdrawal for the amount of gold written on the receipt.

With these gold receipts in circulation, people began paying their debts with these pieces of paper, rather than actually exchanging gold. Thus, goldsmith receipts became paper money. At first, the goldsmiths were very conservative and issued receipts exactly equal to the amount of gold stored in their vaults. However, some shrewd goldsmiths observed that net withdrawals in any period were only a *fraction* of all the gold "on reserve." This observation produced a powerful idea. Goldsmiths discovered that they could make loans for more gold than they actually held in their vaults. As a result, goldsmiths made extra profit from interest on these loans, and borrowers had more money for spending in their hands.

25-2 How a Single Bank Creates Money

The medieval goldsmiths were the first to practice fractional reserve banking. Modern fractional reserve banking is a system in which banks keep only a percentage of their deposits on reserve as vault cash and deposits at the Fed. In a 100 percent reserve banking system, banks would be unable to create money by making loans. However, as you will learn momentarily, holding less than 100 percent on reserve allows banks to make loans, and in turn, these loans create money in the economy.

Fractional reserve banking

A system in which banks keep only a percentage of their deposits on reserve as vault cash and deposits at the Fed.

25-2a BANKER BOOKKEEPING

We begin our exploration of how the fractional reserve banking system operates in the United States by looking at the balance sheet of a single bank, Typical Bank. A balance sheet is a statement of the assets and liabilities of a bank at a given point in time. Balance sheets are called *T-accounts*. The hypothetical T-account of Typical Bank in Balance Sheet 1 lists only major categories and omits details to keep things simple.

Typical Bank			
Balance Sheet 1			
Assets		**Liabilities**	
Required reserves	$ 5 million	Checkable deposits	$50 million
Excess reserves	0		
Loans	45 million		
Total	$50 million	Total	$50 million

Note: The Fed requires the bank to keep 10 percent of its checkable deposits in reserves. Holding $5 million in required reserves, the bank has zero excess reserves and $45 million in loans to earn profit.

Required reserves

The minimum balance that the Fed requires a bank to hold in vault cash or on deposit with the Fed.

Required reserve ratio

The percentage of deposits that the Fed requires a bank to hold in vault cash or on deposit with the Fed.

On the right side of the balance sheet are the bank's *liabilities*. Liabilities are the amounts the bank owes to others. In our example, the only liabilities are *checkable deposits*, or demand deposits. Note that checkable deposits are assets on the customers' personal balance sheets, but they are debt obligations of Typical Bank. If a depositor writes a check against his or her checking account, the bank must pay this amount. Therefore, checkable deposits are liabilities to the bank.

On the left side of the balance sheet, we see Typical Bank's *assets*. Assets are amounts the bank owns. In our example, these assets consist of required reserves, *excess reserves*, and *loans*. Required reserves are the minimum balance of reserves that the Fed requires a bank to hold in vault cash or on deposit with the Fed. Typical Bank will maximize profits by trying to keep only the minimum amount possible in required reserves.

The required reserve ratio determines the minimum required reserves. The required reserve ratio is the percentage of deposits that the Fed requires a bank to hold in vault cash or on deposit with the Fed rather than being loaned. Here we assume that the Fed's required reserve ratio is 10 percent. Thus, the bank must have required reserves of $5 million (10 percent of $50 million). This leaves Typical Bank with $45 million in loans that provide profit to the bank.

Exhibit 1 shows that the actual required reserve ratio depends on the level of a bank's checkable deposits. Note that the Fed requires a lower percentage for a smaller bank. In the real world, Typical Bank's required reserve ratio would be 3 percent if its checkable deposits were between $11.5 million and $71.0 million.

EXHIBIT 1	**Required Reserve Ratio of the Federal Reserve**
Type of deposit	**Required reserve ratio**
Checkable deposits	
$11.75–$71.0 million	3%
Over $71.0 million	10

SOURCE: Federal Reserve Bank, *Reserve Requirements*, http://www.federalreserve.gov/monetarypolicy/reservereq.htm.

Typical Bank has zero excess reserves so far in our analysis. Excess reserves are potential loan balances of reserves held in vault cash or on deposit with the Fed in excess of required reserves. We will see shortly that excess reserves play a starring role in the banking system's ability to change the money supply. The relationship between reserves accounts can be expressed as follows:

Excess reserves

Potential loan balances held in vault cash or on deposit with the Fed in excess of required reserves.

$$\text{Total reserves} = \text{required reserves} + \text{excess reserves}$$

or

$$\text{Excess reserves} = \text{total reserves} - \text{required reserves}$$

The final entry on the asset side of Typical Bank's balance sheet is loans, which are interest-earning assets of the bank. Loans are bank assets because they represent outstanding credit payable to the bank. In a fractional reserve banking system, the bank uses balances not held in reserves to earn income. In our example, loan officers have written loans totaling $45 million. Finally, note that Typical Bank's assets equal its liabilities. As you will see momentarily, any change on one side of the T-account must be accompanied by an equal amount of change on the other side of the balance sheet.

25-2b STEP ONE: ACCEPTING A NEW DEPOSIT

You are now prepared to see how a bank creates money. Assume the required reserve ratio is 10 percent and one of Best National Bank's depositors, Brad Rich, takes $100,000 in cash from under his mattress and deposits it in his checking account. Balance Sheet 2 records this change by increasing the bank's checkable deposits on the liability side by $100,000. Brad's deposit is a liability of the bank because Brad could change his mind and withdraw his money. On the asset side, Brad's deposit increases assets because the bank has an extra $90,000 to lend after setting aside the proper amount of required reserves. Balance Sheet 2 shows that total reserves are divided between required reserves of $10,000 (10 percent of the deposit) and excess reserves of $90,000 (90 percent of the deposit). Thus, the bank's assets and liabilities remain equal when Brad makes his deposit.

Before proceeding, we must pause to make an important point. Depositing coins or paper currency in a bank has no initial effect on the money supply (M1). Recall from the previous chapter that M1 includes currency in circulation. Therefore, the transfer of $100,000 in cash from the mattress to the bank creates no money because M1 already counts this amount. Moreover, the money supply would *not* have increased had Brad Rich's initial $100,000 deposit been a check written on another bank. In this case, an increase in the assets and liabilities of Best National Bank by $100,000 would simply decrease the assets and liabilities of the other bank by $100,000. Recall that M1 also includes checkable deposits.

> **CONCLUSION:** *Transferring currency to a bank and moving deposits from one bank to another do not affect the money supply (M1).*

Best National Bank

Balance Sheet 2

Assets		Liabilities		Change in M1
Required reserves	+$ 10,000	Brad Rich account	+$100,000	0
Excess reserves	+ 90,000			
Total	$100,000	Total	$100,000	

Step 1: Brad Rich deposits $100,000 in cash, which increases checkable deposits. The Fed requires the bank to keep 10 percent of its new deposit in required reserves, so this account is credited with $10,000. The remaining 90 percent is excess reserves of $90,000. There is no effect on the money supply.

25-2c STEP TWO: MAKING A LOAN

So far, M1 has not changed, as shown in Balance Sheet 2, because Brad has simply taken $100,000 in currency and transferred it to a checkable deposit. Stated differently, the public holds the same $100,000 for spending, and only the form has changed from cash to a checkable deposit. In step two, the actual money creation process occurs. The profit motive provides the incentive for bank officials not to let $90,000 from a new deposit sit languishing in excess reserves. Instead, Best National Bank is eager to make loans and earn a profit by charging interest. Suppose, coincidentally, that Connie Jones walks in with a big smile, asking for a $90,000 loan to purchase equipment for her health spa. Connie has a fine credit record, so the bank accepts Connie's note (IOU) agreeing to repay the loan. Then the bank gives Connie a check for $90,000, which she deposits in her account with the bank. This increases the bank's liabilities by $90,000. As shown in Balance Sheet 3, three entries on the assets side have changed. First, the loan to Connie Jones boosts the loans account to $90,000. Second, the bank must increase required reserves by $9,000 because of the $90,000 increase in checkable deposits on the liabilities side. (Recall that required reserves are 10 percent of checkable deposits.) Required reserves are now $19,000. Third, transferring $9,000 from excess reserves to required reserves reduces the bank's excess reserves from $90,000 to $81,000. Total reserves remain at $100,000 in both Balance Sheet 2 and Balance Sheet 3.

Best National Bank

Balance Sheet 3

Assets		Liabilities		Change in M1
Required reserves	$ 19,000	Brad Rich account	$100,000	
Excess reserves	81,000	Connie Jones account	+90,000	+$90,000
Loans	+90,000			
Total	$190,000	Total	$190,000	

Step 2: The bank loans Connie Jones $90,000 by crediting her checking account with this amount. A corresponding $90,000 balance is added to the loan account. The result is an increase in the money supply of $90,000.

The corresponding entry on the liabilities side of the balance sheet is the bread and butter of money creation. Checkable deposits have increased by $90,000 to $190,000. The reason is that the bank issued a check in Connie's name drawn on a checking account in the bank. Thus, Best National Bank has performed money magic with this transaction. Look what happened to the $100,000 deposited by Brad Rich. It has generated a new $90,000 *loan*, which was added to checkable deposits and therefore increased the money supply by $90,000.

> **CONCLUSION:** *When a bank makes a loan, it creates deposits, and the money supply increases by the amount of the loan because the money supply includes checkable deposits.*

Before proceeding further, you need to pause and take particular notice of the impact of these transactions on the money supply. In step one, Brad's initial deposit did not change M1. But in step two, M1 increased by $90,000 when Best National Bank created money out of thin air by making the loan to Connie Jones. Now Connie has more money in her checking account than she did before, and no one else has less. Connie can now use this money to buy goods and services.

25-2d STEP THREE: CLEARING THE LOAN CHECK

Now Connie Jones can use her new money to purchase equipment for her spa. Suppose Connie buys equipment for her business from Better Health Spa and writes a check for $90,000 drawn on Best National Bank. The owner of Better Health Spa then deposits the check in the firm's account at Yazoo National Bank. Yazoo National will send the check to its Federal Reserve district bank for collection. Recall that each bank maintains required reserves at the Fed. The Fed clears the check by debiting the reserve account of Best National Bank and crediting the reserve account of Yazoo National Bank. The Fed then returns the check to Best National Bank, and this bank reduces Connie Jones's checking account by $90,000. As shown in Balance Sheet 4, Connie Jones's checking account falls to

Best National Bank

Balance Sheet 4

Assets		Liabilities		Change in M1
Required reserves	$ 10,000	Brad Rich account	$100,000	0
Excess reserves	0	Connie Jones account	0	
Loans	90,000			
Total	$100,000	Total	$100,000	

Step 3: Connie Jones pays Better Health Spa with a $90,000 check drawn on Best National Bank. Better Health Spa deposits the check in Yazoo National Bank, which collects from Best National Bank. The result is a debit to Connie's account and to her bank's reserves accounts.

zero, and Best National Bank's liabilities are reduced by $90,000. On the asset side of the balance sheet, required reserves decrease by $9,000, and excess reserves return to zero. Now that all the dust has settled, Best National Bank has required reserves of $10,000 and an IOU for $90,000. Note that this check-clearing process in step three has no effect on M1. The $90,000 increase in M1 created by Best National Bank's loan to Connie remains on deposit at Yazoo National Bank in Better Health Spa's checking account.

Finally, if Brad Rich withdraws $100,000 in cash from Best National Bank, the process described above operates in reverse. The result is a $90,000 decline (destruction) in the money supply.

25-3 Multiplier Expansion of Money by the Banking System

The process of money creation (loans) does not stop at the doors of Best National Bank. Just like the spending multiplier from the chapter on fiscal policy, there is a money multiplier process. Let's continue our story by following the effect on Yazoo National after Better Health Spa deposits $90,000 from Connie Jones. As shown in Balance Sheet 5, Yazoo National's checkable deposits increase by $90,000. Given a required reserve ratio of 10 percent, Yazoo National Bank must keep $9,000 in required reserves, and the remaining $81,000 goes into excess reserves.

Yazoo National Bank			
Balance Sheet 5			
Assets		**Liabilities**	
Required reserves	+$ 9,000	Better Health Spa account	+$90,000
Excess reserves	+ 81,000		
Total	$90,000	Total	$90,000

Note: Given a required reserve ratio of 10 percent, Better Health Spa's deposit of $90,000 from Connie Jones creates $81,000 in additional excess reserves that the bank can lend and thus create additional checkable deposits.

Yazoo National's loan officer now has $81,000 in additional excess reserves to lend and thus create additional checkable deposits, excess reserves, and eventually loans in other banks. Exhibit 2 presents the expansion of the money supply created when Brad Rich makes his initial $100,000 deposit, and then banks make loans that are deposited in other banks.

In Exhibit 2, we see that, lo and behold, an initial deposit of $100,000 in Best National Bank can eventually create a $900,000 increase in the money supply (ΔM1). This is because Brad Rich's initial $100,000 deposit eventually creates total excess reserves of $900,000 in the banking system as a whole. This was created by new loans and, in turn, new deposits in different banks. As this process continues, each bank accepts smaller and smaller increases in checkable deposits because 10 percent of each deposit is held as required reserves. Note that the initial $100,000 was from cash already counted in M1, and so it is not counted in the expansion of the money supply.

EXHIBIT 2	Expansion of the Money Supply			
Round	Bank	Increase in checkable deposits	Increase in required reserves	Increase in excess reserves
1	Best National Bank	$ 100,000	$ 10,000	$ 90,000
2	Yazoo National Bank	90,000	9,000	81,000
3	Bank A	81,000	8,100	72,900
4	Bank B	72,900	7,290	65,610
5	Bank C	65,610	6,561	59,049
6	Bank D	59,049	5,905	53,144
7	Bank E	53,144	5,314	47,830
.	.	.	.	.
.	.	.	.	.
.	.	.	.	.
Total all other banks		478,297	47,830	430,467
Total increase		$1,000,000	$100,000	$900,000 (ΔM1)

Note: A $100,000 cash deposit in Best National Bank creates $900,000 in new deposits in other banks. Each round creates excess reserves, which are loaned to a customer who deposits the loan check in another bank in the next round.

Source: © Cengage Learning 2014

25-3a THE MONEY MULTIPLIER

Fortunately, we do not need to calculate all the individual bank transactions listed in Exhibit 2 in order to derive the change in the money supply initiated by a deposit or withdrawal. Instead, we can use the money multiplier, or *deposit multiplier*. The money multiplier gives the *maximum* change in the money supply (checkable deposits) due to an initial change in the excess reserves held by banks.[1] The money multiplier is equal to 1 divided by the required reserve ratio. Expressed as a formula:

$$\text{Money multiplier (MM)} = \frac{1}{\text{required reserve ratio (RRR)}} = \frac{1}{1/10} = 10$$

The actual change in the money supply is computed by the following formula:

Actual money supply change (ΔM1) = initial change in excess reserves (ER) × money multiplier (MM)

Money multiplier

The maximum change in the money supply (checkable deposits) due to an initial change in the excess reserves banks hold. The money multiplier is equal to 1 divided by the required reserve ratio.

---

[1]The money multiplier (MM) is the sum of the infinite geometric progression $1 + (1 - r) + (1 - r)^2 + (1 - r)^3 + \ldots + (1 - r)^\infty$, where r equals the required reserve ratio.

Symbolically, using the data in Exhibit 2,

$$\Delta M1 = \Delta ER \times MM$$

$$\$900,000 = \$90,000 \times 10$$

25-3b THE REAL-WORLD MONEY MULTIPLIER

In reality, for several reasons, the size of the money multiplier can be considerably smaller than our handy little formula indicates. First, Connie Jones, or any other customer along the money creation process, can decide to put a portion of the loan in her pocket, rather than writing a check to Better Health Spa for the full amount of the loan. Money outside the banking system in someone's wallet or purse or underneath the mattress is a cash leakage, which reduces the value of the money multiplier.

Second, the size of the money multiplier falls when banks do not use all their excess reserves to make loans. Perhaps a financial crisis causes many people to lose confidence in the banking system, and they make large deposit account withdrawals. As a result, banks hold their excess reserves. Or some banks can hold excess reserves because they lack enough "worthy" loan applications. This is the situation under the current credit crunch described in the You're the Economist feature in the next chapter. In short, banks are very cautious to make new loans because they are suffering from holding bad mortgage loans.

> **CONCLUSION:** *When banks decide to retain excess reserves, the money multiplier will be smaller.*

25-4 How Monetary Policy Creates Money

The previous chapter explained that the principal function of the Fed is to control the money supply using three policy tools, or levers. The Fed's use of these tools to influence the economy is more precisely called monetary policy. Monetary policy is the Federal Reserve's use of open market operations, changes in the discount rate, and changes in the required reserve ratio to change the money supply (M1). Using these three tools, or levers, of monetary policy, the Fed can limit or expand deposit creation by the banks and thereby change the money supply.

Monetary policy
The Federal Reserve's use of open market operations, changes in the discount rate, and changes in the required reserve ratio to change the money supply (M1).

25-4a OPEN MARKET OPERATIONS

You have seen how decisions of the public—including those of Brad Rich, Connie Jones, and Better Health Spa—worked through the banking system and increased M1. In this section, you will build on this foundation by learning how the Fed can expand or contract the money supply. We begin with the aggregated Balance Sheet 6 of the 12 Federal Reserve banks of the Federal Reserve System. Total assets of the Fed on June 6, 2012, were $2,854 billion. The majority of these assets ($1,664 billion) were held in U.S. government securities in the form of Treasury bills, Treasury notes, and Treasury bonds, and loans to banks were $5 billion. This contrasts with commercial banks, which hold most of their assets in loans. Finally, the other assets of the Fed include high-grade mortgage-backed securities purchased from banks in order to help stabilize the banking system during the recent financial crisis.

The major liability of the Fed was $1,068 billion worth of Federal Reserve notes—paper currency. This is in contrast to the major liability of commercial banks, which is checkable deposits. As explained in the previous chapter, the Fed issues, but does not actually print, Federal Reserve notes. Instead, the Fed decides how much to issue and then calls the Bureau of Engraving and Printing to order new batches of $10, $20, $50, and $100 bills, which the Fed sends to the banks in armored trucks.

Another important liability of the Fed is the deposits of banks and the U.S. Treasury totaling $1,622. The Fed therefore serves as a bank for these banks and the Treasury. Note that these bank deposits include the required reserve deposits discussed at the beginning of the chapter. Finally, total liabilities and net worth equaled total assets of $2,854 billion. Details of the balance sheet are omitted for simplicity.

Federal Reserve System

Balance Sheet 6

June 6, 2012
(billions of dollars)

Assets		Liabilities	
U.S. government securities	$1,664	Federal Reserve notes	$1,068
Loans to banks	5	Deposits	1,622
Other assets	1,185	Other liabilities and net worth	164
Total assets	$2,854	Total liabilities and net worth	$2,854

Source: Federal Reserve Board, *Factors Affecting Reserve Balances*, http://www.federalreserve.gov/releases/h41/Current/.

Recall the Federal Open Market Committee (FOMC) introduced in the previous chapter. The FOMC, as its name implies, determines the money supply through open market operations. Open market operations are the buying and selling of government securities by the Federal Reserve System. The New York Federal Reserve Bank's trading desk executes these orders. Suppose the FOMC decides to increase the money supply and instructs the New York Fed trading desk to *buy* $100,000 worth of 90-day U.S. Treasury bills (called T-bills).[2] The Fed contacts securities dealers in the private sector for competitive bids. Suppose the Fed accepts the lowest bid, buys $100,000 worth of

Open market operations

The buying and selling of government securities by the Federal Reserve System.

[2]The U.S. Treasury issues T-bills in minimum denominations of $10,000. These marketable obligations of the federal government mature in three months, six months, or one year and are used to finance the budget deficit, as explained in the chapter on this topic. The Treasury sells three-month bills at weekly auctions and six-month and one-year bills less often.

T-bills, and pays the dealer with a check drawn against itself. As shown in Balance Sheet 7, the Fed's assets increase by $100,000 worth of U.S. government IOUs. Once the securities dealer deposits the Fed's check in the firm's account at Best National Bank, the bank will send the $100,000 check back to the Fed. When the Fed receives the check, it will increase Best National's reserves account at the Fed by this amount. The Fed therefore increases its liabilities by $100,000, and M1 increases immediately by $100,000 because the security dealer's checking account increases at Best National Bank. Like a magician waving a magic wand, the Fed has created new money: the initial $100,000 checkable deposit and excess reserves for loans. Given a 10 percent reserve requirement, Best National Bank's required reserves increase by $10,000, and its excess reserves increase by $90,000. Therefore, the money supply will potentially increase by $1 million (the $100,000 initial increase in M1 when the Fed buys the security multiplied by the money multiplier of 10). Note that unlike the example shown previously in Exhibit 2 involving an initial $100,000 cash deposit already counted in M1, here the initial deposit was created by the Fed and therefore not already counted in M1. Expressed as a formula:

$$\text{Actual money supply change} = \text{initial checkable deposit (CD)}$$
$$+ (\text{initial change in excess reserves}$$
$$\times \text{money multiplier})$$
$$\Delta M1 = \Delta CD + (\Delta ER \times MM)$$
$$\$1,000,000 = \$100,000 + (\$90,000 \times 10)$$

Federal Reserve Bank

Balance Sheet 7

Assets	Liabilities	Initial change in M1
U.S. government securities +$100,000	Reserves of Best National Bank +$100,000	+$100,000

Note: To increase the money supply, the Fed conducted open market operations by purchasing $100,000 in government securities. The Fed pays a securities dealer with a Fed check, which the dealer deposits in its bank. The initial change in the money supply is an increase of $100,000.

The process goes into reverse if the FOMC directs the New York Fed trading desk to *sell* U.S. government securities for the Fed's portfolio. As shown in Balance Sheet 8, the goal of the Fed is to decrease the money supply by selling, say, $100,000 in Treasury bonds from the asset side of its balance sheet. In this case, the Fed accepts the best offer from a securities dealer. Again, assume the securities dealer's $100,000 check payable to the Fed is written on the firm's account with Best National Bank. When the Fed accepts the check, it reduces the reserves recorded on the liabilities side of Balance Sheet 8, and Best National Bank reduces the checkable deposits account of the securities dealer. By subtracting $100,000 from Best National Bank's reserves, the Fed decreases M1 initially by $100,000. Again, the Fed has waved its magic wand and extinguished money in the banking system. Given a 10 percent reserve requirement, the money supply can potentially fall by $1 million (the $100,000 initial decrease in M1 when the Fed sells the security multiplied by the money multiplier of 10).

Federal Reserve Bank

Balance Sheet 8

Assets	Liabilities	Initial change in M1
U.S. government securities −$100,000	Reserves of Best National Bank −$100,000	−$100,000

Note: To decrease the money supply, the Fed conducted open market operations by selling $100,000 in government securities. The Fed accepts a securities dealer's check drawn on the dealer's bank. The initial change in the money supply is a decrease of $100,000.

Another way to study open market operations is to look at a typical day at the trading desk located at the Federal Reserve Bank of New York. The manager of the trading desk starts the day by studying estimates of excess reserves in the banking system. If excess reserves are low, few banks have funds to lend. High excess reserves mean many banks can make loans. After collecting this information and other data, the manager looks at the directive from the FOMC and formulates the day's "game plan." Then the manager makes conference calls to several members of the FOMC for approval. With their blessing, the manager has traders in the trading room call dealers who trade in government securities for price quotations. The open market operation has two alternative objectives: purchase or sell government securities.

CONCLUSION: *A purchase of government securities by the Fed injects reserves into the banking system and increases the money supply. A sale of government securities by the Fed reduces reserves in the banking system and decreases the money supply.*

Exhibit 3 illustrates the Federal Reserve's open market operations.

✔ CHECKPOINT

Who Has More Dollar Creation Power?

You find a $1,000 bill hidden beneath the floorboards in your house and decide to deposit it in your checking account. On the same day, the Fed decides to buy $1,000 in government securities from your bank. Assuming a 10 percent reserve requirement, which of these actions creates more money in the economy?

EXHIBIT 3	Open Market Operations

When the Fed buys government securities from dealers, it increases the reserves of the banks. Banks can use these reserves to make loans, which operate through the money multiplier to expand the money supply. When the Fed sells government securities to dealers, it decreases the reserves of the banks. Thus, the banks' capacity to lend diminishes, and as a consequence, the money supply decreases.

SOURCE: © Cengage Learning 2014

25-4b THE DISCOUNT RATE

So far, money creation in the banking system depends on excess reserves acquired from new checkable deposits. Actually, the Fed itself provides another option for banks to obtain reserves through its *discount window*. This is a department within each of the Federal Reserve district banks and not an actual window. Suppose Best National Bank has no excess reserves and

Brad Rich does not walk in with a deposit. Also assume the Fed does not purchase government securities and pay a dealer with a check deposited in Best National Bank. Now enter Connie Jones, who asks for a loan. In this situation, the bank has no money to lend, but it can borrow reserves from the Fed for a short period and pay the discount rate. The discount rate is the interest rate the Fed charges on loans of reserves to banks. All banks and other depository institutions have the privilege of occasionally borrowing at the Fed to cover reserve deficiencies. Changes in the discount rate often signal the Fed's monetary policy direction and therefore can affect the public's expectations about the economy. A lower discount rate encourages banks to borrow reserves and make loans.

Discount rate
The interest rate the Fed charges on loans of reserves to banks.

> **CONCLUSION:** *A higher discount rate discourages banks from borrowing reserves and making loans. If the Fed wants to expand the money supply, it reduces the discount rate. If the objective is to contract the money supply, the Fed raises the discount rate.*

Banks wanting to expand their reserves in order to seek profitable loan opportunities can also turn to the federal funds market. The federal funds market is a private market in which banks lend reserves to each other for less than 24 hours. The word *federal* does not mean it is a government market. It simply means this is an economy-wide or national market. In this market, a bank short of reserves can borrow some reserves from another bank. Using the interbank loan market, Best National Bank can borrow excess reserves from Yazoo National and pay the federal funds rate. The federal funds rate is the interest rate banks charge for overnight loans of reserves to other banks. Reserves borrowed in the federal funds market have no effect on the money supply because such borrowing simply moves reserves from one bank to another. Note that most banks borrow money to meet their reserve requirements primarily through the federal funds market and not the discount window. Also, the federal funds rate is a primary barometer of Fed policy reported in the media. The following You're The Economist provides further explanation of the federal funds rate.

Federal funds market
A private market in which banks lend reserves to each other for less than 24 hours.

Federal funds rate
The interest rate banks charge for overnight loans of reserves to other banks.

25-4c THE REQUIRED RESERVE RATIO

Under the Monetary Control Act of 1980, discussed in the preceding chapter, the Fed can set reserve requirements by law for all banks and savings and loan associations. By changing the required reserve ratio, the Fed can change banks' excess reserves and therefore banks' lending ability. This is potentially a powerful policy lever. Recall that the money multiplier equals 1 divided by the required reserve ratio. Suppose the Fed is concerned about inflation, so it wants to restrain the money supply and thereby dampen aggregate demand in the economy. If the Fed increases the required reserve ratio, the effect is to reduce excess reserves and generate a smaller change in the money supply because the money supply multiplier is smaller. For example, a required reserve ratio of 10 percent yields a money

How Does the FOMC Really Work?

Applicable Concept: monetary policy

The Federal Open Market Committee (FOMC), which is the Fed's most powerful monetary policy-making group, meets eight times a year at the Federal Reserve in Washington, D.C. Often it seems that the whole world is watching for the results. Before the meeting, board members are given three books prepared by the Fed's staff. The "Green Book" forecasts aggregate demand and various prices based on a variety of equations and the assumptions that monetary policy does or does not change. The "Blue Book" might discuss as many as three monetary policy options, the rationale for each option, and the impact of each option on the economy. There is also a "Beige Book," published eight times per year, that gathers anecdotal information on current economic conditions obtained from interviews with key businesspersons, economists, bankers, and other sources.

The meeting begins at precisely 9 a.m. with a discussion of foreign currency operations and domestic open market operations illustrated with colorful graphics. Next, the staff presents their analysis of recent developments and forecasts for the economy laid out in the Green Book. Then each board member around the impressive 27-foot oval mahogany table expresses their views about the analyses, except for the chair, who may choose not to participate in this round. Now it's coffee time and everyone relaxes beneath a 23-foot ceiling with a 1,000-pound chandelier.

After the coffee break, the staff discusses each policy option from the "Blue Book" without recommending a particular option. Generally, three options are presented. Option A is always a decline in interest rates, Option B is always no change in interest rates, and Option C is always an increase. After the staff presentation, board members politely discuss the policy options, but with an important difference. In this policy round, the

multiplier of 10 (1/0.10). If the Fed increases the ratio to 20 percent, the money multiplier falls to 5 (1/0.20).

> **CONCLUSION:** *There is an inverse relationship between the size of the required reserve ratio and the money multiplier.*

Raising the required reserve ratio can sharply reduce the lending power of banks. Consider an initial increase in excess reserves of $10 billion in the banking system when the required reserve ratio is 10 percent. The potential value of loans (deposits) is $100 billion ($10 billion of excess reserves × 10). Now assume the Fed raises the required reserve ratio to 20 percent. The potential value of loans (deposits) falls to $50 billion ($10 billion of excess reserves × 5).

chair goes first. He or she leads the discussion and advocates a policy decision. After other board members express their views, the chair summarizes the consensus and reads a draft of the Directive to be voted on. The Directive gives instructions to the Fed's staff on how to conduct open market operations until the next FOMC meeting. For example, the New York Fed's trading desk may be instructed to increase the money supply in the range of 1 to 5 percent and lower interest rates by buying 90-day U.S. Treasury bills. After discussion, board members vote on the Directive, with the chair voting first and the decision going to the majority. The chair is always expected to be on the winning side. The Directive is sent to the New York Fed's trading desk, and soon about four dozen bond dealers receive the Fed's call. If there is a change in policy, it will be announced at 2:15 that afternoon.

The Fed now communicates its changes in monetary policy by announcing changes in its targets for the federal funds rate. Recall that the Fed does not set this interest rate, but it can influence the rate through open market operations. If the Fed buys bonds, the supply of excess reserves in the banking system increases, and the rate falls. If the Fed sells bonds, the supply of excess reserves in the banking system decreases, and the rate increases. As a result, interest rates in general are influenced. In 2001, the Fed was trying to keep the economy out of recession, and it cut the federal funds rate 11 times, the most since the last recession in 1990–1991. The next chapter explains in more detail the link between changes in the interest rate and changes in other key macro measures. In 2002 and 2003, the Fed again cut the federal funds rate target to support economic recovery. Between 2004 and 2006, the Fed

became concerned about inflation and increased the federal funds rate 17 times. When measuring inflation, the Fed pays closest attention to the *core* CPI—the CPI excluding food and fuel because it is less volatile than the total CPI inflation rate. In 2007, the Fed changed its focus again because it became concerned that a housing slump and credit crunch would slow the economy, and it cut this key rate for the first time in four years. In 2008, the Fed continued cutting the federal funds rate until it reached a record low of almost zero in 2011.

Analyze the Issue

What happened at the last FOMC meeting? Visit http://www.federalreserve.gov/fomc/default.htm. To experience an FOMC meeting, visit http://www.frbsf.org/education/activies/chairman/index.html.

Source: © Cengage Learning 2014

CONCLUSION: *If the Fed wishes to increase the money supply, it decreases the required reserve ratio. If the objective is to decrease the money supply, the Fed increases the required reserve ratio. In reality, changing the required reserve ratio is considered a heavy-handed approach that is an infrequently used tool of monetary policy.*

The Fed used all three of its monetary policy tools to increase the money supply and battle the 1990–1991 recession. In the fall of 1990, the Fed recognized the economy was slipping into a recession, so it purchased federal government securities to inject new reserves into the banking system. The discount rate was lowered eight times between the end of 1990 and early 1992. In early 1992, the reserve requirement on demand deposits was also lowered from 12 percent to 10 percent. In 2002, the Fed responded to the 2001 recession by using open market purchases of securities to increase the money supply, and it decreased the discount rate numerous times. These responses by the Fed eased the negative effects of the terrorist attacks and the recession.

During the Great Recession of 2007–2009, the Fed again followed expansionary monetary policy and used open market purchases to sharply increase the money supply and decrease interest rates by dropping the federal funds rate to a historic low of about zero percent. Moreover, the Fed reduced its reserve requirement and dramatically expanded its scope in response to the loss in confidence among lenders and panic sweeping financial markets that resulted in the flow of credit falling sharply. Using Depression-era emergency powers, the Fed took the radical step of becoming a "lender of last resort" source of short-term loans for a wide range of institutions other than banks. For example, the Fed provided funds to bail out Fannie Mae (the Federal National Mortgage Association) and Freddie Mac (the Federal Home Mortgage Corporation), which backed about half of the nation's mortgage loans, and the Fed provided loans for AIG, the huge insurance firm, because it was simply too large to fail. For more details on monetary policy, read the You're the Economist titled "How Does the FOMC Really Work?"

Exhibit 4 presents a summary of the impact of monetary policy tools.

25-5 Monetary Policy Shortcomings

Monetary policy, like fiscal policy, has its limitations. The Fed's control over the money supply is imperfect for the following reasons.

EXHIBIT 4	The Effect of Monetary Policy Tools on the Money Supply		
Type of monetary policy	Monetary policy action	Mechanism	Change in the money supply
Expansionary	Open market operations purchase	Reserves increase	Increases
Contractionary	Open market operations sale	Reserves decrease	Decreases
Expansionary	Discount rate decreases	Borrowing reserves becomes cheaper	Increases
Contractionary	Discount rate increases	Borrowing reserves becomes costlier	Decreases
Expansionary	Required reserve ratio decreases	Money multiplier increases	Increases
Contractionary	Required reserve ratio increases	Money multiplier decreases	Decreases

SOURCE: © Cengage Learning 2014

25-5a MONEY MULTIPLIER INACCURACY

If the Fed is to manage the money supply, it must know the size of the money multiplier so that it can forecast the increase in the money supply resulting from a change in excess reserves. The value of the money multiplier, however, can be uncertain and subject to decisions independent of the Fed. As explained earlier in the chapter, the public's decision to hold cash and the willingness of banks to make loans affect the total expansion from an initial change in excess reserves. These decisions vary with conditions of prosperity and recession. When the business cycle is in an upturn, banks are very willing to use their excess reserves for making loans, and the money supply expands. During a downturn, bankers are less willing to use their excess reserves for making loans, and the money supply tends to contract.

25-5b WHICH MONEY DEFINITION SHOULD THE FED CONTROL?

As discussed in the previous chapter, there are different definitions of the money supply. What if the Fed masterfully controls M1, but the public transfers more of its deposits to M2? For example, banks can pay higher interest and attract more customers to invest in certificates of deposit. Consequently, the Fed might respond by focusing on M2 instead of M1. In fact, in recent years, the Fed has focused more on M2 than M1 because M2 more closely correlates with changes in GDP.

25-5c LAGS IN MONETARY POLICY VERSUS FISCAL POLICY

Fiscal policy does not happen instantaneously, and neither does monetary policy. Like fiscal policy, monetary policy is subject to time lags. First, an *inside lag* exists between the time a policy change is needed and the time the Fed identifies the problem and decides which policy tool to use. The inside lag is fairly short because financial data are available daily, data on inflation and unemployment monthly, and data on real GDP within three months. Once the Fed has the data, it can quickly decide which policy changes are needed and make appropriate adjustments. The inside lag for monetary policy is shorter than for fiscal policy because fiscal policy is usually the result of a long political budget process.

Second, there is an *outside lag* between the time a policy decision is made and the time the policy change has its effect on the economy. This lag refers to the length of time it takes the money multiplier or spending multiplier to have its full effect on aggregate demand and, in turn, employment, the price level, and real GDP.

Now it's time to answer an important question: Who is the hare and who is the tortoise in the race to the finish line of stabilizing the economy? In the popular version of this story, the hare is much faster, but goofs off along the way and eventually loses to the tortoise at the finish line. In our economics story, however, the Fed is the hare and wins easily over fiscal policy (the tortoise). Although computer model estimates differ widely, the total lag (inside plus outside lags) for monetary policy can be 3 to 12 months. In contrast, the total lag for fiscal policy is not less than a year, and a total lag of three years is quite possible.

Key Concepts

Fractional reserve banking
Required reserves
Required reserve ratio
Excess reserves

Money multiplier
Monetary policy
Open market operations
Discount rate

Federal funds market
Federal funds rate

Summary

- **Fractional reserve banking,** the basis of banking today, originated with the goldsmiths in the Middle Ages. Because depository institutions (banks) are not required to keep all their deposits in vault cash or with the Federal Reserve, banks create money by making loans.

- **Required reserves** are the minimum balance that the Fed requires a bank to hold in vault cash or on deposit with the Fed. The percentage of deposits that must be held as required reserves is called the **required reserve ratio.**

- **Excess reserves** exist when a bank has more reserves than required. Excess reserves allow a bank to create money by exchanging loans for deposits. The money supply is reduced when excess reserves are reduced and loans are repaid.

- The **money multiplier** is used to calculate the maximum change (positive or negative) in checkable deposits (money supply) due to a change in excess reserves. As a formula:

$$\text{Money multiplier} = \frac{1}{\text{required reserve ratio}}$$

The actual change is computed as

Money multiplier

$\times$ **initial change in excess reserves** =

money supply change

- **Monetary policy** is action taken by the Fed to change the money supply. The Fed uses three basic tools: (1) *open market operations,* (2) *changes in the discount rate,* and (3) *changes in the required reserve ratio.*

- **Open market operations** are the buying and selling of government securities by the Fed through its trading desk at the New York Federal Reserve Bank. **Buying government securities** creates extra bank reserves and loans, thereby *expanding* the money supply. **Selling government securities** reduces bank reserves and loans, thereby *contracting* the money supply.

- **Changes in the discount rate** occur when the Fed changes the rate of interest it charges on loans of reserves to banks. Lowering the discount rate makes it easier for banks to borrow reserves from the Fed and expands the money supply. Raising the discount rate discourages banks from borrowing reserves from the Fed and contracts the money supply.

Open Market Operations

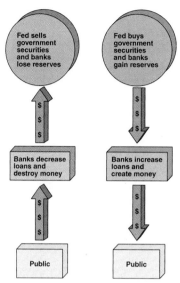

SOURCE: © Cengage Learning 2014

- **Changes in the required reserve ratio** and the size of the money multiplier are *inversely* related. Thus, if the Fed decreases the required reserve ratio, the money multiplier and money supply increase. If the Fed increases the required reserve ratio, the money multiplier and money supply decrease.
- **Monetary policy limitations** include the following: (1) The size or value of the money multiplier can vary. (2) The Fed might control M1, but the public can shift funds to the M2 money supply definition. (3) Time lags occur.

Summary of Conclusion Statements

- Transferring currency to a bank and moving deposits from one bank to another do not affect the money supply (M1).
- When a bank makes a loan, it creates deposits, and the money supply increases by the amount of the loan because the money supply includes checkable deposits.
- When banks decide to retain excess reserves, the money multiplier will be smaller.
- A purchase of government securities by the Fed injects reserves into the banking system and increases the money supply. A sale of government securities by the Fed reduces reserves in the banking system and decreases the money supply.
- A higher discount rate discourages banks from borrowing reserves and making loans. If the Fed wants to expand the money supply, it reduces the discount rate. If the objective is to contract the money supply, the Fed raises the discount rate.
- There is an inverse relationship between the size of the required reserve ratio and the money multiplier.
- If the Fed wishes to increase the money supply, it decreases the required reserve ratio. If the objective is to decrease the money supply, the Fed increases the required reserve ratio. In reality, changing the required reserve ratio is considered a heavy-handed approach, so it is an infrequently used tool of monetary policy.

Study Questions and Problems

1. Relate Shakespeare's admonition "Neither a borrower nor a lender be" to the goldsmiths' evolutionary use of fractional reserve banking.

2. If you deposit a $20 bill into a checking account and your bank has a 10 percent reserve requirement, by how much will the bank's excess reserves rise?

3. Consider this statement: "Banks do not create money because this is the Fed's responsibility." Do you agree or disagree? Explain.

4. In what form does a bank hold its required reserves? Assume the Fed has a 20 percent required reserve ratio. What amount of checkable deposits can be supported by $10 million in required reserves?

5. Suppose you deposit your paycheck drawn on another bank. Explain the impact on the money supply.

6. Suppose you remove $1,000 from under your mattress and deposit it in First National Bank. Using a balance sheet, show the impact of your deposit on the bank's assets and liabilities. If the required reserve ratio is 10 percent, what is the maximum amount the bank can loan from this deposit?

7. Suppose it is the holiday season and you withdraw $1,000 from your account at First National Bank to purchase presents. Using a balance sheet, show the impact on this bank's assets and liabilities. If the required reserve ratio is 20 percent, what is the impact on the bank's loans?

8. Suppose the Federal Reserve's trading desk buys $500,000 in T-bills from a securities dealer who then deposits the Fed's check in Best National Bank. Use a balance sheet to show the impact on the bank's loans. Consider the money multiplier and assume the required reserve ratio is 10 percent. What is the maximum increase in the money supply that can result from this open market transaction?

9. Assume the required reserve ratio is 10 percent and a bank's excess reserves are $50 million. Explain why checkable deposits resulting from new loans based on excess reserves are not likely to generate the maximum of $500 million.

10. Briefly describe the effect on the money supply of the following monetary policies:
    a. The Fed purchases $20 million worth of U.S. Treasury bonds.
    b. The Fed increases the discount rate.
    c. The Fed decreases the discount rate.
    d. The Fed sells $40 million worth of U.S. T-bills.
    e. The Fed decreases the required reserve ratio.

11. What are some problems faced by the Fed in controlling the money supply?

For Online Exercises, go to the Tucker Web site at www.cengage.com/economics/tucker.

✓ CHECKPOINT ANSWER

Who Has More Dollar Creation Power?

Your action adds $1,000 to your bank's liabilities. Also, assets in the form of required reserves increase by $100 (0.10 × $1,000). This means excess reserves increase by $900, allowing the bank to make this amount of new loans. When the Fed buys $1,000 in government securities, the bank again receives $1,000 in reserves. But the Fed's transaction does not change the bank's liabilities; therefore, the full $1,000 can go into loans. Comparing the effect on the total money supply, the money multiplier effect shows a $9,000 addition to the money supply from your action and a $10,000 addition from the Fed's action. If you said the Fed's action creates more money, **YOU ARE CORRECT.**

Sample Quiz

For an explanation of the correct answers, visit the Tucker Web site at www.cengage.com/economics/tucker.

1. European banks began with which of the following?
   a. Monarchs were the first bankers, lending out cash to help the poor learn a craft.
   b. Churches were the first bankers, lending out cash to help the poor learn a craft.
   c. Goldsmiths were the first bankers, and the paper receipts they issued for gold held on deposit became valued as money.
   d. Fishermen were the first bankers, and the paper receipts they issued for fish they stored in the hulls of their ships became valued as money.

2. Which of the following does *not* appear on the asset side of a bank's balance sheet?
   a. required reserves
   b. checkable deposits
   c. loans
   d. excess reserves

3. Which of the following is *not* an interest bearing asset of commercial banks?
   a. required reserves
   b. securities
   c. loans
   d. All of the above are interest bearing assets of commercial banks.

4. Banks would be expected to minimize holding excess reserves because this practice is
   a. illegal.
   b. not profitable.
   c. technically difficult.
   d. subject to a stiff excess reserves tax.

5. Which of the following appears on the asset side of a bank's balance sheet?
   a. excess reserves
   b. loans
   c. required reserves
   d. None of the above answers are correct.
   e. All of the above answers are correct.

6. Assume a simplified banking system in which all banks are subject to a uniform reserve requirement of 20 percent and checkable deposits are the only form of money. A bank that received a new checkable deposit of $10,000 would be able to extend new loans up to a maximum of
   a. $2,000.
   b. $8,000.
   c. $9,000.
   d. $10,000.

7. If the required reserve ratio is a uniform 25 percent on all deposits, the money multiplier will be
   a. 4.00.
   b. 2.50.
   c. 0.40.
   d. 0.25.

8. Assume a simplified banking system subject to a 20 percent required reserve ratio. If there is an initial increase in excess reserves of $100,000, the money supply
   a. increases $100,000.
   b. increases $500,000.
   c. increases $600,000.
   d. decreases $500,000.

9. If the required reserve ratio decreases, the
   a. money multiplier increases.
   b. money multiplier decreases.
   c. amount of excess reserves the bank has decreases.
   d. money multiplier stays the same.

10. Decisions regarding purchases and sales of government securities by the Fed are made by the
    a. Federal Deposit Insurance Commission (FDIC).
    b. Discount Committee (DC).
    c. Federal Open Market Committee (FOMC).
    d. Federal Funds Committee (FFC).

Sample Quiz *continued*

11. The cost to a member bank of borrowing from the Federal Reserve is the
    a. reserve requirement.
    b. price of securities in the open market.
    c. discount rate.
    d. yield on government bonds.

12. Which of the following policy actions by the Fed would cause the money supply to decrease?
    a. an open market purchase of government securities
    b. a decrease in required reserve ratios
    c. an increase in the discount rate
    d. a decrease in the discount rate

13. The rate of interest charged by the Federal Reserve to member banks for reserves borrowed from the Fed is the
    a. federal funds rate.
    b. discount rate.
    c. repurchase rate.
    d. Q ceiling rate.

14. Which of the following actions by the Fed would increase the money supply?
    a. reducing the required reserve ratio
    b. selling government bonds in the open market
    c. increasing the discount rate
    d. None of the above answers are correct.

EXHIBIT 5	**Lower Walloon National Bank**
Assets	**Liabilities**
Reserves $10,000	Checkable $10,000 deposits

SOURCE: © Cengage Learning 2014

15. In Exhibit 5, if the required reserve ratio is 20 percent for all banks and every bank in the banking system loans out all of its excess reserve., then a $10,000 deposit from Mr. Brown in checkable deposits could create for the entire banking system
    a. $8,000 worth of new money.
    b. $2,000 worth of new money.
    c. $10,000 worth of new money.
    d. $40,000 worth of new money.

16. The required reserve ratio for a bank is set by
    a. Congress.
    b. the bank itself.
    c. the Treasury Department.
    d. the banking system.
    e. the Federal Reserve.

17. Assume we have a simplified banking system in balance-sheet equilibrium. Also assume that all banks are subject to a uniform 10 percent reserve requirement and demand deposits are the only form of money. A commercial bank receiving a new demand deposit of $100 would be able to extend new loans in the amount of
    a. $10.
    b. $90.
    c. $100.
    d. $1,000.

18. A bank faces a required reserve ratio of 5 percent. If the bank has $200 million of checkable deposits and $15 million of total reserves, then how large are the bank's excess reserves?
    a. $0
    b. $5 million
    c. $10 million
    d. $15 million

19. A bank currently has checkable deposits of $100,000, reserves of $30,000, and loans of $70,000. If the required reserve ratio is lowered from 20 percent to 15 percent, this bank can increase its loans by
    a. $10,000.
    b. $15,000.
    c. $75,000.
    d. $5,000.
    e. $ 0.

Sample Quiz *continued*

20. When the Fed purchases government securities, it
    a. increases banks' reserves and makes possible an increase in the money supply.
    b. decreases banks' reserves and makes possible a decrease in the money supply.
    c. automatically raises the discount rate.
    d. uses discounting operations to influence margin requirements.
    e. has no effect on either the money supply or the discount rate.

chapter 26

Monetary Policy

Vladimir Lenin, the first communist leader of the Soviet Union, once said the best way to destroy a nation is to destroy its money. Adolf Hitler had the same idea. During World War II, he planned to counterfeit British currency and drop it from planes flying over England. Both cases illustrate that the amount of money in circulation matters. A sudden increase in the quantity of money can render a nation's money valueless. As a consequence, people must resort to barter and waste time making direct exchanges of goods and services, rather than being productive.

The previous two chapters provided the prerequisites for understanding the market for money. You have learned two definitions for the money supply, how the banking system creates money, and how the Fed can control the money supply. Here you will begin by studying the demand for and the supply of money and how they interact to determine the rate of interest. Then we add to this story by linking changes in the money supply to the aggregate demand and aggregate supply model. Using this tool of analysis, you will understand how changes in the demand for money affect interest rates and, in turn, real GDP, employment, and prices.

The first half of this chapter explores how Keynesian economists view the relationship between monetary policy and the economy. The second half of the chapter presents the opposing view of the monetarists. This debate is a clash between two radically different perspectives over the channels through which monetary policy influences the economy. This ideologically charged confrontation is important to the United States' future and is still far from resolved. The chapter concludes with two You're the Economists that allow you to analyze the Keynesian and monetarist views applied to the current financial crisis and the Great Depression.

In this chapter, you will learn to solve these economics puzzles:

- Why do people wish to hold money balances?
- What is a monetary policy transmission mechanism?
- Why would a Nobel laureate economist suggest replacing the Federal Reserve with an intelligent horse?

26-1 The Keynesian View of the Role of Money

26-1a THE DEMAND FOR MONEY

Why do people hold (demand) currency and checkable deposits (M1), rather than put their money to work in stocks, bonds, real estate, or other nonmoney forms of wealth? Because money yields no direct return, people (including businesses) who hold cash or checking account balances incur an *opportunity cost* of forgone interest or profits on the amount of money held. So what are the benefits of holding money? Why would people hold money and thereby forgo earning interest payments? John Maynard Keynes, in his 1936 book *The General Theory of Employment, Interest, and Money*, gave three important motives for doing so: transactions demand, precautionary demand, and speculative demand.

Transactions Demand for Money   The first motive to hold money is the transactions demand. The transactions demand for money is the stock of money people hold to pay everyday predictable expenses. The desire to have "walking around money" to make quick and easy purchases is the principal reason for holding money. Students, for example, have a good idea of how much money they will spend on rent, groceries, utilities, gasoline, and other routine purchases. A business can also predict its payroll, utility bills, supply bills, and other routine expenses. Without enough cash, the public must suffer forgone interest and possibly withdrawal penalties as a result of converting their stocks, bonds, or certificates of deposit into currency or checkable deposits in order to make transactions.

Precautionary Demand for Money   In addition to holding money for ordinary expected purchases, people have a second motive to hold money, called the precautionary demand. The precautionary demand for money is the stock of money people hold to pay unpredictable expenses. This is the "mattress money" people hold to guard against those proverbial rainy days. For example, your car might break down, or your income may drop unexpectedly. Similarly, a business might experience unexpected repair expenses or lower-than-anticipated cash receipts from sales. Because of unforeseen events that could prevent people from paying their bills on time, people hold precautionary balances. This affords the peace of mind that unexpected payments can be made without having to cash in interest-bearing financial assets or to borrow.

Speculative Demand for Money   The third motive for holding money is the speculative demand. The speculative demand for money is the stock of money people hold to take advantage of expected future changes in the price of bonds, stocks, or other nonmoney financial assets. In addition to the transactions and precautionary motives, individuals and businesses demand "betting money" to speculate, or guess, whether the prices of alternative assets will rise or fall. This desire to take advantage of profit-making opportunities when the prices of nonmoney assets fall is the driving force behind the speculative demand. When the interest rate is high, people buy, say, Microsoft 30-year bonds because the opportunity cost of holding money is the high forgone interest earned on these nonmoney assets. When the interest rate is low, people hold more money because there is less opportunity cost in forgone interest earned on investing in bonds. Suppose the interest

Transactions demand for money

The stock of money people hold to pay everyday predictable expenses.

Precautionary demand for money

The stock of money people hold to pay unpredictable expenses.

Speculative demand for money

The stock of money people hold to take advantage of expected future changes in the price of bonds, stocks, or other nonmoney financial assets.

rate on Microsoft 30-year bonds is low. If so, people decide to hold more of their money in the bank and *speculate* that soon the interest rate will climb higher.

> **CONCLUSION:** *As the interest rate falls, the opportunity cost of holding money falls, and people increase their speculative balances.*

Demand for money curve

A curve representing the quantity of money that people hold at different possible interest rates, ceteris paribus.

The Demand for Money Curve   The three motives for holding money combine to create a demand for money curve, which represents the quantity of money people hold at different possible interest rates, ceteris paribus. As shown in Exhibit 1, people increase their money balances when interest rates fall. The reason is that many people move their money out of, for example, money market mutual funds and into checkable deposits (M1).

> **CONCLUSION:** *There is an inverse relationship between the quantity of money demanded and the interest rate.*

What determines the shape of the demand for money curve? Let's start with the transactions and the precautionary demands for money. These money balances are computed as a given proportion of real GDP. Suppose real GDP is $5,000 billion and people wish to hold, say, 10 percent for transactions and precautionary purposes. This means the first $500 billion read along the horizontal axis in Exhibit 1 are held to make purchases and handle unforeseen events.

Now consider the impact of changes in the interest rate on the speculative demand for money. As the interest rate falls, people add larger speculative balances to their transactions and precautionary balances. For example, when the rate is 4 percent per year, the total quantity of money demanded at point A is $1,000 billion, of which $500 billion are speculative balances. If the interest rate is 2 percent, the total quantity of money demanded increases to $1,500 billion at point B, of which $1,000 billion are speculative balances. Therefore, the demand for money curve, labeled "MD," looks much like any other demand curve.

> **CONCLUSION:** *The speculative demand for money at possible interest rates gives the demand for money curve its downward slope.*

26-1b THE EQUILIBRIUM INTEREST RATE

We are now ready to form the money market and determine the equilibrium interest rate by putting the demand for money and the supply of money together. In Exhibit 2, the money demand curve (MD) is identical to that in Exhibit 1. The supply of money curve (MS) is a vertical line because the $1,000 billion quantity of money supplied does not respond to changes in the interest rate. The reason is that our model assumes the Fed has used its tools to set the money supply at this quantity of money regardless of the interest rate.

EXHIBIT 1	The Demand for Money Curve

Assume the level of real GDP is $5,000 billion. Also assume households and businesses demand to hold 10 percent of real GDP ($500 billion) for transactions and precautionary balances. The speculative demand for money varies inversely with the interest rate. At an interest rate of 4 percent, the quantity of money demanded (M1) is $1,000 billion (point *A*), calculated as the sum of transactions and precautionary demand ($500 billion) and speculative demand ($500 billion). At a lower interest rate, a greater total quantity of money is demanded because the opportunity cost of holding money is lower.

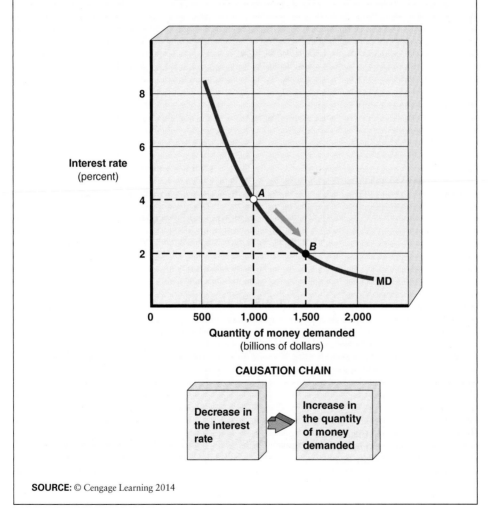

CAUSATION CHAIN

SOURCE: © Cengage Learning 2014

At point *E*, the equilibrium interest rate is 8 percent, determined by the intersection of the demand for money curve and the vertical supply of money curve. People wish to hold exactly the amount of money in circulation, therefore, there is neither upward nor downward pressure on the interest rate.

EXHIBIT 2	The Equilibrium Interest Rate

The money market consists of the demand for and the supply of money. The market demand curve represents the quantity of money people are willing to hold at various interest rates. The money supply curve is a vertical line at $1,000 billion, based on the assumption that this is the quantity of money supplied by the Fed. The equilibrium interest rate is 4 percent and occurs at the intersection of the money demand and money supply curves (point *E*). At any other interest rate, for example, 6 percent or 2 percent, the quantity of money people desire to hold does not equal the quantity available.

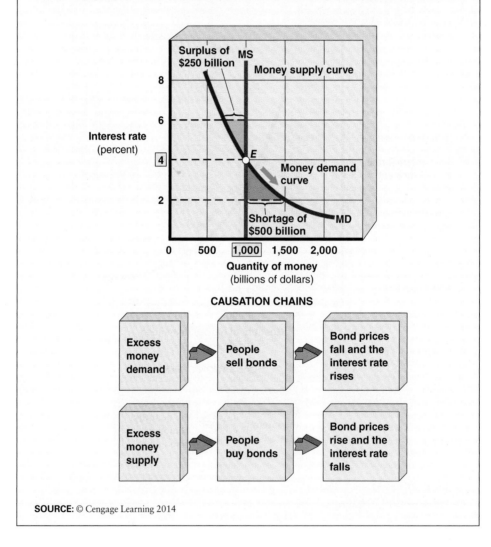

CAUSATION CHAINS

Excess money demand → People sell bonds → Bond prices fall and the interest rate rises

Excess money supply → People buy bonds → Bond prices rise and the interest rate falls

SOURCE: © Cengage Learning 2014

Excess Quantity of Money Demanded   Suppose the interest rate in Exhibit 2 is 2 percent instead of 4 percent. Such a low opportunity cost of money means that people desire to hold a greater quantity of money than the quantity supplied. To eliminate this shortage of $500 billion, individuals and businesses adjust their asset portfolios. They seek more money by selling their bonds or other non-money assets. When many sell or try to sell their bonds, there is an increase in the supply of bonds for sale. Consequently, the price of bonds falls, and the interest rate rises. This rise in the interest rate ceases at the equilibrium interest rate of 4 percent because people are content with their portfolio of money and bonds at point E.

Here we need to pause and look at an example to understand what is happening. Suppose Apple pays 2 percent on its $1,000 30-year bonds. This means Apple pays a bondholder $20 in interest each year and promises to repay the original $1,000 price (face amount) at the end of 30 years. However, a holder of these bonds can sell them before maturity at a market-determined price. If bondholders desire to hold more money than is supplied, they will sell more of these bonds. Then the increase in the supply of bonds causes the price of bonds to fall to, say, $500. As a result, the interest rate rises to 4 percent ($20/$500).

Excess Quantity of Money Supplied   The story reverses for any rate of interest above 4 percent. Let's say the interest rate is 6 percent. In this case, people are holding more money than they wish. Stated differently, they wish to hold less money than is currently in circulation. In this case, the quantity of money demanded is $250 billion less than the quantity supplied. To correct this imbalance, people will move out of cash and checkable deposits by buying bonds. This increase in the demand for bonds will drive up the price of bonds and lower the interest rate. As the interest rate falls, the quantity of money demanded increases as people become more willing to hold money. Finally, the money market reaches equilibrium at point E, and people are content with their mix of money and bonds.

CONCLUSION: *There is an inverse relationship between bond prices and the interest rate that enables the money market to achieve equilibrium.*

26-1c   HOW MONETARY POLICY AFFECTS THE INTEREST RATE

Assuming a stationary demand for money, the equilibrium rate of interest changes in response to changes in monetary policy. As we learned in Exhibit 4 of the previous chapter, the Federal Reserve can alter the money supply through open market operations, changes in the required reserve ratio, or changes in the discount rate. In this section, you will see that the Fed's power to change the money supply can also alter the equilibrium rate of interest.

Increasing the Money Supply   Exhibit 3(a) shows how increasing the money supply will cause the equilibrium rate of interest to fall. Our analysis begins at point E_1, with the money supply at $1,000 billion, which is equal to the quantity of money demanded, and with the equilibrium interest rate at 6 percent. Now suppose the Fed increases the money supply to $1,500 billion by buying government securities in the open market. The impact of the Fed's expansionary monetary policy is to create a $500 billion surplus of money at the prevailing 6 percent interest rate.

How will people react to this excess money in their pockets or checking accounts? Money becomes a "hot potato," and people buy bonds. The rush to purchase bonds drives the price of bonds higher and the interest rate lower. As the

EXHIBIT 3	The Effect of Changes in the Money Supply

In part (a), the Federal Reserve increases the money supply from \$1,000 billion (MS_1) to \$1,500 billion (MS_2). At the initial interest rate of 6 percent (point E_1), there is an excess of \$500 billion beyond the amount people wish to hold. They react by buying bonds, and the interest rate falls until it reaches a new lower equilibrium interest rate at 4 percent (point E_2).

The reverse happens in part (b). The Fed decreases the money supply from \$1,500 billion (MS_1) to \$1,000 billion (MS_2). Beginning at 4 percent (point E_1), people wish to hold \$500 billion more than is available. This shortage disappears when people sell their bonds. As the price of bonds falls, the interest rate rises to the new higher equilibrium interest rate of 6 percent at point E_2.

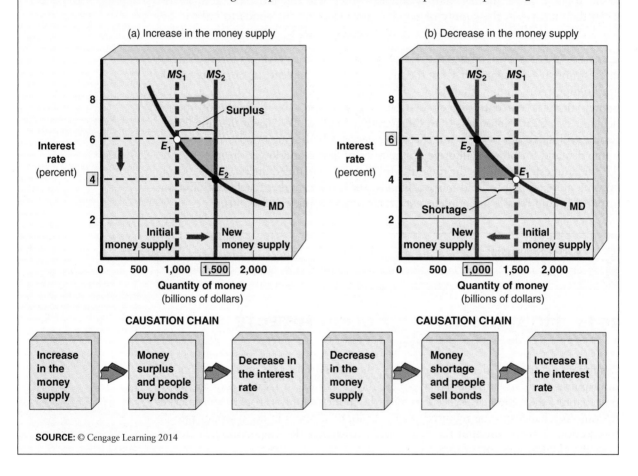

interest rate falls, people are *willing* to hold larger money balances. Or, stated differently, the quantity of money demanded increases until the new equilibrium at E_2 is reached. At the lower interest rate of 8 percent, the opportunity cost of holding money is also lower, and the imbalance between the money demand and money supply curves disappears.

Decreasing the Money Supply   Exhibit 3(b) illustrates how the Fed can put upward pressure on the interest rate with contractionary monetary policy. Beginning at point E_1, the money market is in equilibrium at an interest rate of

4 percent. This time the Fed shrinks the money supply by selling government securities through its trading desk, raising the required reserve ratio, or raising the discount rate. As a result, the money supply decreases from $1,500 billion to $1,000 billion. At the initial equilibrium interest rate of 4 percent, this decrease in the money supply causes a shortage of $500 billion.

Individuals and businesses wish to hold more money than is available. How can the public put more money in their pockets and checking accounts? They can sell their bonds for cash. This selling pressure lowers bond prices, causing the rate of interest to rise. At point E_2, the upward pressure on the interest rate stops. Once the equilibrium interest rate reaches 6 percent, people willingly hold the $1,000 billion money supply.

✓ CHECKPOINT

What Does the Money Supply Curve Look Like When the Fed Targets the Federal Funds Rate?

Suppose the Fed has a policy of adjusting the money supply to achieve interest rate targets. For example, the Fed might set a 6 percent target federal funds rate. If an increase in the demand for money boosts the federal funds rate above 6 percent, the Fed adjusts the money supply until the 6 percent interest rate is restored. Under such a monetary policy, is the supply of money curve vertical, horizontal, or upward sloping with respect to the federal funds rate?

26-1d HOW MONETARY POLICY AFFECTS PRICES, OUTPUT, AND EMPLOYMENT

The next step in our journey is to understand how monetary policy alters the macro economy. Here you should pause and study Exhibit 4. This exhibit illustrates the causation chain linking monetary policy and economic performance.

EXHIBIT 4	The Keynesian Monetary Policy Transmission Mechanism

Keynesians focus on how changes in the money supply affect interest rates and investment spending. In turn, aggregate demand shifts and affects prices, real GDP, and employment.

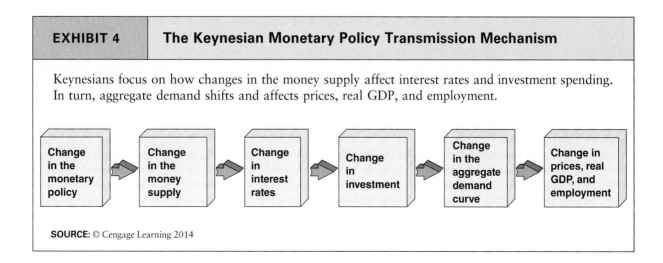

SOURCE: © Cengage Learning 2014

> **CONCLUSION:** *In the Keynesian model, changes in the supply of money affect interest rates. In turn, interest rates affect investment spending, aggregate demand, and, finally, real GDP, employment, and prices.*

The Impact of Monetary Policy Using the AD-AS Model   How do changes in the rate of interest affect aggregate demand? Begin with Exhibit 5(a), which is identical to Exhibit 3(a) and represents the money market. As explained earlier, we assume that the Fed increases the money supply from $1,000 billion ($MS_1$) to $1,500 billion ($MS_2$) and the equilibrium interest rate falls from 6 percent to 4 percent. In part (b), we can see that the falling rate of interest causes an increase in the quantity of investment spending from $800 billion to $850 billion per year. Stated another way, there is a movement downward along the *investment demand curve* (*I*), which you recall from the chapter on GDP is a component of total spending or aggregate demand. The investment demand curve shows the amount businesses spend for investment goods at different possible interest rates.

The classical economists believed that the interest rate alone determines the level of investment spending. Keynes disputed this idea. Instead, Keynes argued that the expectation of future profits is the primary factor determining investment and the interest rate is the financing cost of any investment proposal. Using a micro example to illustrate the investment decision-making process, suppose a consulting firm plans to purchase a new computer program for $1,000 that will be obsolete in a year. The firm anticipates the new software will increase its revenue by $1,100. Thus, assuming no taxes and other expenses, the expected rate of return or profit is 10 percent.

Now consider the impact of the cost of borrowing funds to finance the software investment. If the interest rate is less than 10 percent, the business will earn a profit, and it will make the investment expenditure to obtain the computer program. On the other hand, a rate of interest higher than 10 percent means the software investment will be a loss, so this purchase will not be made. The expected rate of the profit-interest rate-investment relationship follows this rule: *Businesses will undertake all investment projects for which the expected rate of profit equals or exceeds the interest rate.*

Exhibit 5(c) uses the fiscal policy aggregate demand and aggregate supply analysis developed earlier. Begin at point E_1, with a real GDP per year of $13 trillion and a price level of 210. Now consider the link to the change in the money supply. The increase in investment resulting from the fall in the interest rate works through the *spending multiplier* and shifts the aggregate demand curve rightward from AD_1 to AD_2. At the new equilibrium point, E_2, the level of real GDP rises from $13 trillion to $14 trillion, and full employment is achieved. In addition, the price level rises from 210 to 215. Exhibit 5(a) also demonstrates the effect of a contractionary monetary policy. In this case, assume the economy is initially at E_2 and the money supply shifts inward from MS_2 to MS_1, causing the equilibrium rate of interest to rise from 4 percent to 6 percent. The Fed's "tight" money policy causes the level of investment spending to fall from $850 billion to $800 billion, which, in turn, decreases the equilibrium level of real GDP per year from $14 trillion to $13 trillion. As a result, the unemployment rate rises, and the inflation rate falls because the price level falls from 215 to 210.

| EXHIBIT 5 | The Effect of Expansionary Monetary Policy on Aggregate Demand |

In part (a), the money supply is initially MS_1, and the equilibrium rate of interest is 6 percent. The equilibrium point in the money market changes from E_1 to E_2 when the Fed increases the money supply to MS_2. This causes the quantity of money people wish to hold to increase from $1,000 billion to $1,500 billion, and a new lower equilibrium interest rate is established at 4 percent.

The fall in the rate of interest shown in part (b) causes a movement downward along the investment demand curve from point A to point B. Thus, the quantity of investment spending per year increases from $800 billion to $850 billion.

In part (c), the investment component of the aggregate demand curve increases, causing this curve to shift outward from AD_1 to AD_2. As a result, the aggregate demand and supply equilibrium in the product market changes from E_1 to E_2, and the real GDP gap is eliminated. The price level also changes from 210 to 215.

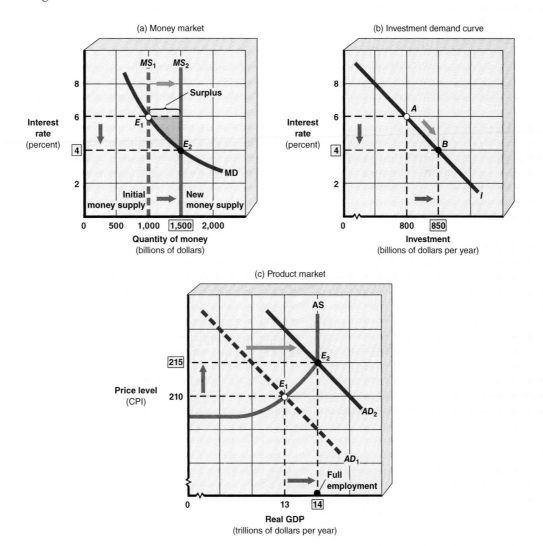

SOURCE: © Cengage Learning 2014

26-2 The Monetarist View of the Role of Money

26-2a THE MONETARIST TRANSMISSION MECHANISM

Monetarism

The theory that changes in the money supply directly determine changes in prices, real GDP, and employment.

Monetarists believe Keynesians suffer from the delusion that monetary policy operates only indirectly, causing changes in the interest rate before affecting aggregate demand and then prices, real GDP, and employment. The opposing school of economic thought, called monetarism, challenges this view. Monetarism is the theory that changes in the money supply directly determine changes in prices, real GDP, and employment. Exhibit 6 illustrates the monetarist transmission mechanism. Comparison of this figure with Exhibit 4 shows that the monetarist model omits the Keynesian interest rate-investment linkage.

The Equation of Exchange Monetarists put the spotlight on the money supply. They argue that to predict the condition of the economy, you simply look at the money supply. If it expands too much, higher rates of inflation will be the forecast. If it contracts too much, unemployment lines will lengthen. Monetarism has its intellectual roots in classical economics, introduced in the chapter on aggregate demand and supply. Monetarists proudly wear *laissez faire* on their sleeves and believe the price system is the macro economy's best friend. To understand monetarism, we begin with the equation of exchange developed by the classical economists in the 19th century. The equation of exchange is an accounting identity that states the money supply times the velocity of money equals total spending. Expressed as a formula, the equation of exchange is written as

Equation of exchange

An accounting identity that states the money supply times the velocity of money equals total spending.

$$MV = PQ$$

Let's begin with the left side of the equation ($M \times V$). M is the money supply (more precisely M1) in circulation, and V represents the velocity of money. The velocity of money is the average number of times per year a dollar of the money supply is spent on final goods and services. Assume you have one crisp $20 bill

Velocity of money

The average number of times per year a dollar of the money supply is spent on final goods and services.

EXHIBIT 6	The Monetarist Monetary Policy Transmission Mechanism

Monetarists believe that changes in the money supply directly cause changes in the aggregate demand curve and thereby changes in prices, real GDP, and employment.

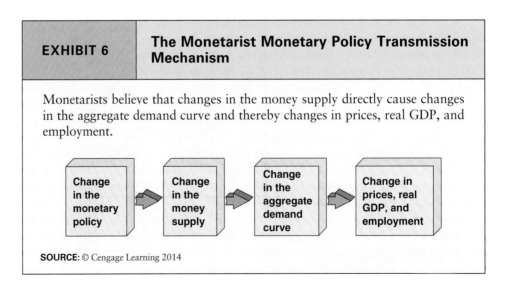

SOURCE: © Cengage Learning 2014

and this is the only money in an ultrasimple economy. Suppose you spend this money on a pizza and soda at Zeno's Pizza Hut. Once Mr. Zeno puts your money in his pocket, he decides to buy an economics book and learn how the views of Keynesians and monetarists differ. And so, Mr. Zeno buys the book at the Wise Professor Book Store for exactly $20. At this point, both Mr. Zeno and Ms. Wise have sold $20 worth of goods. Thus, a single $20 bill has financed $40 worth of total spending. And as long as this $20 bill passes from hand to hand during, say, one year, the value of sales will increase. For example, assume the $20 travels from hand to hand 5 times. This means the velocity of money is 5, and the equation of exchange is expressed as

$$\$20 \times 5 = \$100$$

The equation of exchange is an *identity*—true by definition—that expresses the fact that the value of what people spend is equal to, or exchanged for, what they buy. What people buy is nominal GDP, or ($P \times Q$). Recall that nominal, or money, GDP is equal to the average selling price during the year (P) multiplied by the quantity of actual output of final goods and services (Q). In our simple economy, total spending equals $100. Note that the identity between MV and PQ does not say what happens to either P or Q if MV increases. Although we know by how much the total value of output (PQ) increases, we do not know whether the price level (P) or the quantity of output (Q) or both increase.

Consider a more realistic example. Suppose that nominal GDP last year was $5 trillion and M1 was $1 trillion. How many times did each dollar of the money supply have to be spent to generate this level of total spending in the economy? Using the equation of exchange,

$$M \times V = P \times Q$$
$$\$1 \text{ trillion} \times V = \$5 \text{ trillion}$$
$$V = 5$$

Thus, each dollar was spent an average of 5 times per year.

The Quantity Theory of Money   The equation of exchange is converted from an *identity* to a *theory* by making certain assumptions. The classical economists became the forerunners of modern-day monetarists by arguing that the velocity of money (V) and real output (Q) are fairly constant. The classical economists viewed V as constant because people's habits of holding a certain quantity of money, and therefore the number of times a dollar is spent, are slow to change. Recall from the chapter on aggregate demand and supply that classical economists believed in price and wage flexibility. Hence, they believed the economy would automatically adjust to long-run full-employment output (Q).

Because V and Q are constant by assumption, we have one of the oldest theories of inflation, called the quantity theory of money. The quantity theory of money states that changes in the money supply are directly related to changes in the price level. Monetary policy based on the quantity theory of money therefore directly affects the price level. To illustrate, we will modify the equation of exchange by putting a bar (–) over V and Q to indicate they are fixed or constant in value:

$$M \times \overline{V} = P \times \overline{Q}$$

Quantity theory of money

The theory that changes in the money supply are directly related to changes in the price level.

What if the money supply doubles? The price level also doubles. Or if the Fed cuts the money supply in half, then the price level is also cut in half. Meanwhile, real output of goods and services, Q, remains unchanged.

> **CONCLUSION:** *According to the quantity theory of money, any change in the money supply must lead to a proportional change in the price level.*

In short, monetarists say the cause of inflation is "too much money chasing too few goods." The quantity theory of money denies any role for nonmonetary factors, such as supply shocks from a hike in oil prices, which cause cost-push inflation [see Exhibit 11(a) in the chapter on aggregate demand and supply]. Moreover, this theory ignores the impact of fiscal policy changes in taxation and spending on the price level.

What do the data reveal about the link between changes in the money supply and changes in the rate of inflation? Although the relationship does not exist for all years, the evidence supports the general conclusion that sustained levels of higher growth in the money supply correspond to increases in the inflation rate. For example, when the money supply growth rate was low and averaged 2 percent between 1953 and 1962, the inflation rate averaged 1 percent. During 1973–1982, the money supply grew at a higher average rate of 7 percent, and the average inflation rate rose to 9 percent. More recently, between 1994 and 2007, the money supply increased at a lower average rate of 2 percent, and the average inflation rate dropped to 3 percent. After the Great Recession in 2007 through 2011, the average money supply growth rate increased sharply to 12 percent. If high growth rates of the money supply are sustained, the concern is that the inflation rate will rise.

Modern Monetarism   Today's monetarists have changed the assumptions of the classical quantity theory of money. The evidence indicates that velocity is not constant and the economy does not always operate at full employment. Although M and P are correlated, they do not change proportionally. *Monetarists argue that although velocity is not unchanging, it is nevertheless predictable.* Suppose the predicted velocity of money is 5 and the money supply increases by $100 billion this year. Monetarists would predict that nominal GDP will increase by about $500 billion ($\Delta M \times \widehat{V}$). [The circumflex (^) indicates velocity is predicted.] If the economy is far below full employment, most of the rise in total spending will be in real output. If the economy is near full employment, much of the increase will be in rising prices.

Monetarists refute the Keynesian view that the rate of interest is so important. Instead, the monetarist view is often expressed in the famous single-minded statement that "money does matter." Instead of working through the rate of interest to affect investment and, in turn, the economy, changes in the money supply directly determine economic performance.

> **CONCLUSION:** *To avoid inflation and unemployment, the monetarists' prescription is to be sure that the money supply is at the proper level.*

Fixed Money Target   Monetarism gained credibility in the late 1950s and 1960s, led by Professor Milton Friedman at the University of Chicago. The monetarists have an answer for how to make sure the economy grows at the right rate: Instead of risking policy errors, forget about the rate of interest and follow a steady, predictable monetary policy. Recall from the chapter on money creation that there are limitations on the Fed's ability to control the money supply because of the independent actions of households, firms, banks, and the U.S. Treasury. Monetarists would stop the Fed from tinkering with the money supply, missing the target, and making the economy worse, rather than better. Instead, they say the money supply should expand at the same rate as the potential growth rate in real GDP. That is, it should increase somewhere between 3 percent and 5 percent per year. The Fed should therefore pick a rate and stick to it, even if unexpected changes in velocity cause short periods of inflation or unemployment. This is called following a *monetary rule*. Monetarists argue that their "straitjacket" approach would reduce the intensity and duration of unemployment and inflation by eliminating the monetarists' public enemy number one—the Fed's discretion to change the money supply. A Keynesian once summarized the fixed money supply approach as "Don't do something, just stand there."

> **CONCLUSION:** *Monetarists advocate that the Federal Reserve increase the money supply by a constant percentage each year.*

How Stable Is Velocity?   How stable, or predictable, is the velocity of money? This is a critical question in the Keynesian-monetarist debate. Keynesians do not accept the monetarists' argument that over long periods of time, velocity is stable and predictable. Hence, a change in the money supply can lead to a much larger or smaller change in GDP than the monetarists would predict. As shown in Exhibit 7, Keynesians are quick to point out the turbulent variations in velocity. Velocity gyrated up and down during the 1980s, early 1990s, and years after 2001. Monetarists counter by pointing to the evidence that during the periods of 1960–1981 and 1993–2007, velocity generally rose along a quite predictable or steady annual rate trend line. Since 2007, velocity has declined.

Keynesians focus on short-run variations in V that accompany any long-run velocity growth rate. They therefore argue that following a monetary rule is folly. Suppose the money supply increases at a constant rate, but velocity is greater than expected. This means that total spending (aggregate demand) will be greater than predicted, causing inflation. Lower-than-predicted velocity results in unemployment because total spending is less than expected, which causes the economy to expand too little. The Keynesians believe that the Federal Reserve must be free to change the money supply to offset unexpected changes in velocity. Monetarists counter that the Fed *cannot* predict short-run variations in V, so its "quick-fix" changes in the money supply will often be wrong. This is why monetarists advocate that the Fed follow a monetary rule. Keynesians are willing to accept occasional policy errors and reject this idea in favor of maintaining Fed flexibility to change the money supply in order to affect interest rates, aggregate demand, and the economy.

EXHIBIT 7	The Velocity of Money, 1960–2011

The velocity of money (*V*) equals GDP divided by the supply of money (M1). Keynesians argue that velocity is not stable. During the 1980s, early 1990s, and years after 2001, velocity became quite unpredictable. Monetarists believe velocity is stable over the long term and point to the periods of 1960–1981 and 1993–2000. During these years, velocity rose along a predictable annual rate trend line.

SOURCE: *Economic Report of the President*, 1980 and 2012, http://www.gpo.gov/fdsys/pkg/ERP-2012/content-detail.htm1, Tables B-52, B-1, and B-69.

✔ CHECKPOINT

A Horse of Which Color?

A famous economist once proposed replacing the Fed with an intelligent horse. Each New Year's Day, the horse would stand in front of Fed headquarters to answer monetary policy questions. Reporters would ask, "What is going to happen to the money supply this year?" The horse would tap its hoof four times, and the next day headlines would read "Fed to Once Again Increase the Money Supply 4 Percent." Is this famous economist a Keynesian or a monetarist?

26-3 A Comparison of Macroeconomic Views

By now, your head is probably spinning with dueling schools of economic thought. The debate among the classicals, Keynesians, and monetarists can be quite confusing. This chapter has presented differences in monetary policy between these schools. To refresh your memory and complete the discussion, this section presents a brief review of key differences in fiscal policy introduced in earlier chapters. Exhibit 8 gives a thumbnail summary of the key differences between the three camps. Note the similarity between the classical and the monetarist schools.

26-3a CLASSICAL ECONOMICS

As discussed in the chapter on aggregate demand and supply, the dominant school of economic thought before the Great Depression was classical economics. Classical economics is the theory that free markets will restore full employment without government intervention. The basic theory of the classical economists, introduced by Adam Smith in *The Wealth of Nations* and followed by the 18th- and 19th-century economists, was that a market-directed economy will automatically correct itself to full employment. Consequently, there is no need for fiscal policy designed to restore full employment.

Recall that a key assumption of classical theory is that, given time to adjust, prices and wages will decrease to ensure the economy operates at full employment. A decrease in the aggregate demand curve causes a temporary surplus, which, in turn, causes businesses to cut prices, and, in turn, causes more goods to be purchased because of the real balances effect. As a result, wages adjust downward, and employment rises. Classical economists therefore view the economy as operating in the long run along a vertical aggregate supply curve originating at the full-employment real GDP.

Classical economics
The theory that free markets will restore full employment without government intervention.

26-3b KEYNESIAN ECONOMICS

The Great Depression challenged the classical prescription to wait until markets adjust and full employment is automatically restored. As the unemployment rate rose to 24.9 percent in 1933, people asked how long it would take for the market mechanism to adjust. John Maynard Keynes responded with his famous saying "In the long run we are all dead." Keynes, in his book *The General Theory*, attacked classical theory and in the process revolutionized macroeconomic thought.

As explained in the chapter on fiscal policy, using fiscal policy to affect aggregate demand is a cornerstone of Keynesian economics. Keynesian economics is the theory, first advanced by John Maynard Keynes, that the role of the federal government is to increase or decrease aggregate demand to achieve economic goals. While Keynesians believe monetary policy is often not very powerful, especially during a downturn, they regard fiscal policy as their "top banana." However, Keynesians recognize that one of the potential problems of fiscal policy is the *crowding-out effect*. As shown earlier in Exhibit 9 of the chapter on federal deficits and the national debt, financing a federal deficit by borrowing competes with private borrowers for funds. Given a fixed money supply, the extra demand from the federal government to finance its deficit causes the interest rate to rise. As a result, businesses cut back on investment spending and offset the expected increase in

Keynesian economics
The theory, first advanced by John Maynard Keynes, that the role of the federal government is to increase or decrease aggregate demand to achieve economic goals.

Did the Fed Cause the Great Recession?

Applicable Concept: monetarism

The story of the worst collapse of the housing market and the most serious financial crisis since the Great Depression is filled with villains and no action hero to sweep down from the sky and save the day. It is an Alice in Wonderland story with plenty of blame to go around: homeowners who bought a Trojan horse, rampant speculation, predatory lenders, slick Wall Street operators, greedy CEOs, lax regulators, and debatable Fed policy. Perhaps a phrase by Alan Greenspan, former Fed chairman, called "The Maestro," best described the bust of the housing market bubble when he said, "How do we know when irrational exuberance has unduly escalated asset values?"

The stage was set for the housing crisis by the Fed's response to the recession of 2001. The annual change in the money supply jumped sharply upward from –3.1 percent in 2000 to a 8.7 percent increase in 2001.[1] And, as shown in the above exhibit, the Fed decreased interest rates sharply after 2001 and kept them historically low in order to boost aggregate demand and prevent another recession. Then in 2004, Greenspan addressed the Credit Union Association and said, "American consumers might benefit if lenders provided greater mortgage product alternatives to the traditional fixed rate mortgage." And as if following the Fed chairman's advice, adjustable rate mortgages (ARMs) became the loan of choice for *subprime mortgage loan* borrowers who had poor or less than ideal credit scores. Mailboxes were stuffed with offers to borrow 100 percent or more of a home's value with zero down. Television shows advertised the idea that anyone could make it rich in real estate, and housing became a speculative game. Payments and "teaser" interest rates were held artificially low for the first few years of the loan and then would jump sharply upward. Forget worrying about not affording the home, your income would not be checked, following a "no document" lending practice. In fact, some loans were made to people who were no longer living. Thus,

Source: FRB Federal Open Market Committee, http://www.federalreserve.gov/fomc/fundsrate.htm.

using risky ARMs, banks lent billions of dollars to home buyers who could not pay the bank when the payments and interest rates rose.

Faced with accumulating portfolios of risky debt, banks and mortgage companies sold these risky mortgages to New York investment firms such as Bear Stearns (acquired by JPMorgan Chase with financial backing from the Fed) and Merrill Lynch, who pooled them with other securities. These packages, often called collateralized debt obligations, or CDOs, were sold to customers around

Subprime mortgage loan

A home loan made to borrowers with an above-average risk of default.

aggregate demand. The Keynesian view, however, is that the investment demand curve is not very sensitive to changes in the interest rate, and therefore, only a relatively small amount of investment spending will be crowded out. Thus, the decline in investment only slightly counteracts or offsets an increase in aggregate demand created by a deficit.

> **CONCLUSION:** *Keynesians view the shape of the investment demand curve as rather steep or vertical, so the crowding-out effect is insignificant.*

the world—a process called "securitization." And this securitization occurred with the blessing of ratings agencies such as Standard & Poor's which actually did not know how to evaluate the risk of these securities. With each of these transactions, large fees were collected, and in short, consummation of the deal was the criterion and not validity of the assessment of risk.

Expansion of the housing market bubble was based on an assumption by all the players that the party would never end and real estate prices would always go up. However, beginning in the summer of 2005, subprime foreclosures rose and home prices dropped as people's payments rose under their ARMs. Also, once the value of homes fell below the loan value, people could not refinance loans to get lower payments. When people walked away from their mortgages, Wall Street and foreign investors were stuck with bad loans in their CDOs to write off, CEOs were fired, and many real estate executives were indicted for mortgage fraud. As a result, lenders greatly tightened their lending standards to avoid further risky loans, and a credit crunch made home financing difficult to obtain.

In 2008, the Fed announced that it would allow Wall Street investment firms to receive emergency loans and exchange risky investments for Treasury securities. Also, the Housing and Economic Recovery Act of 2008 was passed that allowed some borrowers to refinance their mortgages with new fixed-rate loans backed by a federal guarantee, and it provided grants for state and local governments in the hardest-hit communities to buy foreclosed property. It also included a tax credit for first-time home buyers who buy housing that is unoccupied. And the Treasury Department was given authority to bail out or take over Fannie Mae and Freddie Mac, the troubled government-created firms that fund the vast majority of mortgage loans in the United States.

In addition, a massive $700 billion bailout plan was enacted in 2008 that gave the Treasury the authority under TARP (Troubled Assets Recovery Program) to buy and resell bad mortgage debt from financial institutions. But TARP changed its original purpose because it was very difficult to determine the price that the government should pay for the risky assets. Consequently, TARP changed its plan and spent over half of its funds to invest government capital into banks by buying preferred stock with a 5 percent rate of return, which is the equivalent of a loan to the bank. Also, the federal government decided to take partial ownership of private U.S. banks until they regain stability and increase lending. Participating banks must curtail executive bonuses and other perks. Meanwhile, the final price tag to the taxpayers for this financial crisis is unknowable.

> **Analyze the Issue**
> In support of the Fed's monetary policy prior to the deflation of the home prices bubble, one can argue that the reality is that increasing the money supply and low-interest rates were required to sustain expansion. Based on the monetarist school of thought, criticize the Fed's policy.

---

1. *Economic Report of the President 2012*, http://www.gpoaccess.gov/eop/, Table B-69.

Source: © Cengage Learning 2014

26-3c MONETARISM

Monetarists are iconoclasts because they attack the belief in the ability of either the Fed or the federal government to stabilize the economy. They argue that fiscal policy is an essentially useless tool that has little or no impact on output or employment because of a total crowding-out effect. Suppose the money supply remains fixed and the federal government borrows to finance its deficit. The intended goal is to increase aggregate demand and restore full employment. According to the monetarists, financing the deficit will drive up the interest rate and crowd out a substantial, not a small, amount of investment spending. The reason is that the

EXHIBIT 8	Comparison of Macroeconomic Theories		
Issue	**Classical**	**Keynesian**	**Monetarist**
	Adam Smith	**John Maynard Keynes**	**Milton Friedman**
Stability of economy	Stable in long run at full employment	Inherently unstable at less than full employment	Stable in long run at full employment
Price-wage flexibility	Yes	No	Yes
Velocity of money	Stable	Unstable	Predictable
Cause of inflation	Excess money supply	Excess aggregate demand	Excess money supply
Causes of unemployment	Short-run price and wage adjustment	Inadequate aggregate demand	Short-run price and wage adjustment
Effect of monetary policy	Changes aggregate demand and prices	Changes interest rate, which changes investment and real GDP	Changes aggregate demand and prices
Effect of fiscal policy	Not necessary	Spending multiplier changes aggregate demand	No effect because of crowding-out effect

Source: © Cengage Learning 2014

monetarists view the investment demand curve as sensitive to changes in the interest rate; therefore, greater amounts of investment spending will be crowded out. As a result, the net effect is no increase in aggregate demand and no reduction in unemployment.

CONCLUSION: *Monetarists view the shape of the investment demand curve as less steep or relatively flat, so the crowding-out effect is significant.*

Monetary Policy during the Great Depression
Applicable Concept: Keynesians versus monetarists

Monetarists and Keynesians still debate the causes of the Great Depression. Monetarists Milton Friedman and Anna Schwartz, in their book *A Monetary History of the United States*, argued that the Great Depression was caused by the decline in the money supply, as shown in Exhibit 9(a).

During the 1920s, the money supply expanded steadily, and prices were generally stable. In response to the great stock market crash of 1929, bank failures, falling real GDP, and rising unemployment, the Fed changed its monetary policy. Through the Great Depression years from 1929 to 1933, M1 declined by 27 percent. Assuming velocity is relatively constant, how will a sharp reduction in the quantity of money in circulation affect the economy? Monetarists predict a reduction in prices, output, and employment. Between 1929 and 1933, the price level declined by 24 percent. In addition to deflation, real GDP was 27 percent lower in 1933 than in

1929. Unemployment rose from 3.2 percent in 1929 to 24.9 percent in 1933. Friedman and Schwartz argued that the ineptness of the Fed's monetary policy during the Great Depression caused the trough in the business cycle to be more severe and sustained.

The Great Depression was indeed not the Fed's finest hour. What should the Fed have done? Friedman and Schwartz argued that the Fed should have used open market operations to increase the money supply. Thus, they concluded that the Fed was to blame for not pursuing an expansionary policy, which would have reduced the severity and duration of the contraction. As shown in part (b), this was not the case for the Great Recession of 2007–2009. From the beginning, the Fed followed an expansionary policy and sharply increased the money supply.

Finally, although the emphasis here is monetary policy, parts (c) and (d) contrast fiscal policy during the two periods using the federal deficit as a percentage of GDP.

During the Great Depression, there was a slight budget surplus until 1931, when the budget turned into a slight budget deficit before reaching a deficit of 5.9 percent of GDP in 1934. In contrast, fiscal policy was more expansionary by running deficits from the beginning of the recession in 2007 to an estimated 10.6 percent of GDP in 2009.

Analyze the Issue

1. Explain why monetarists believe the Fed should have expanded the money supply during the Great Depression.
2. The Keynesians challenge the Friedman-Schwartz monetarists' monetary policy cure for the Great Depression. Use the AD-AS model to explain the Keynesian view. (Hint: Your answer must include the investment demand curve.)

Source: Milton Friedman and Anna J. Schwartz, *A Monetary History of the United States, 1867–1960* (Princeton, N.J.: Princeton University Press, 1963).

Although the monetarists do not trust the Federal Reserve to use discretionary monetary policy, they are quick to point out that only money is important. Changes in the money supply, the basic lever of monetary policy, have a powerful impact. Instead of ineffectual government deficit spending to cure unemployment, an increase in the money supply would definitely stimulate the economy based on the quantity theory of money. In short, changes in the money supply directly result in changes in real GDP.

EXHIBIT 9	The Great Depression Economic Data, 1929–1934 Compared to the Great Recession of 2007–2009

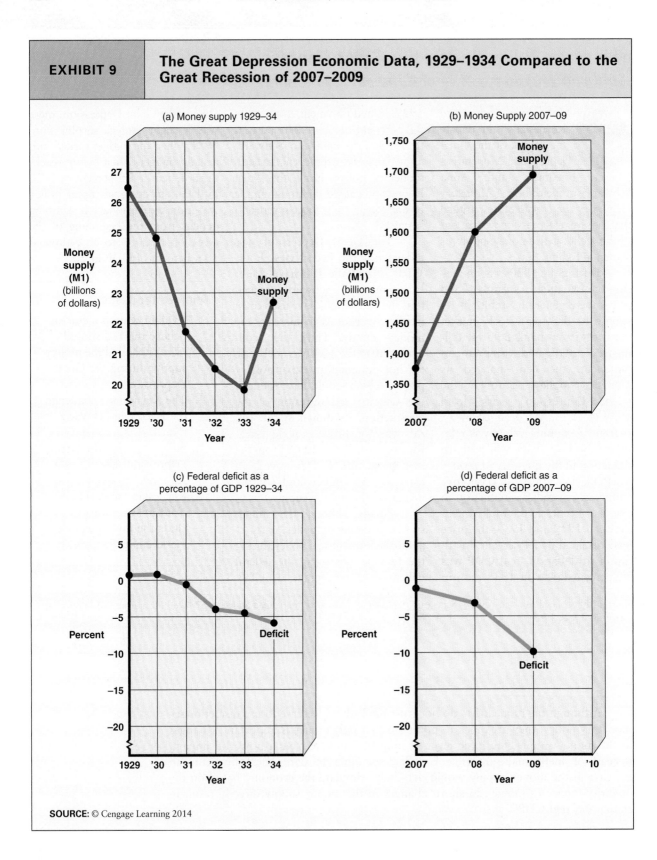

(a) Money supply 1929–34

(b) Money Supply 2007–09

(c) Federal deficit as a percentage of GDP 1929–34

(d) Federal deficit as a percentage of GDP 2007–09

SOURCE: © Cengage Learning 2014

Key Concepts

Transactions demand for money
Precautionary demand for money
Speculative demand for money
Demand for money curve

Monetarism
Keynesian economics
Velocity of money
Quantity theory of money

Subprime mortgage loan
Classical economics
Equation of exchange

Summary

- The **demand for money** in the Keynesian view consists of three reasons why people hold money: (1) **Transactions demand** is money held to pay for everyday predictable expenses. (2) **Precautionary demand** is money held to pay unpredictable expenses. (3) **Speculative demand** is money held to take advantage of price changes in nonmoney assets.
- The **demand for money curve** shows the quantity of money people wish to hold at various rates of interest. As the interest rate rises, the quantity of money demanded is less than when the interest rate is lower.

Demand for Money Curve

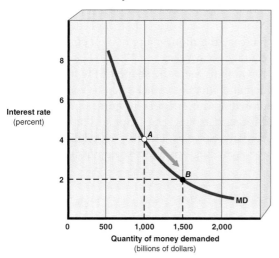

SOURCE: © Cengage Learning 2014

- The **equilibrium interest rate** is determined in the money market by the intersection of the demand for money and the supply of money curves. The money supply (M1), which is determined by the Fed, is represented by a vertical line.

The Equilibrium Interest Rate

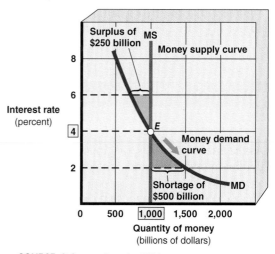

SOURCE: © Cengage Learning 2014

- An **excess quantity of money demanded** causes households and businesses to increase their money balances by selling bonds. This causes the price of bonds to fall, thus driving up the interest rate.
- An **excess quantity of money supplied** causes households and businesses to reduce their money balances by purchasing bonds. The effect is to cause the price of bonds to rise, and thereby, the rate of interest falls.
- The **Keynesian view of the monetary policy transmission mechanism** operates as follows: First, the Fed uses its policy tools to change the money supply. Second, changes in the money supply change the equilibrium interest rate, which affects investment spending. Finally, a change in investment changes aggregate demand and determines the level of prices, real GDP, and employment.
- **Monetarism** is the simpler view that changes in monetary policy directly change aggregate

demand, and thereby prices, real GDP, and employment. Thus, monetarists focus on the money supply, rather than on the rate of interest.

- The **equation of exchange** is an accounting identity that is the foundation of monetarism. The equation ($MV = PQ$) states that the money supply multiplied by the **velocity of money** is equal to the price level multiplied by real output. The velocity of money is the number of times each dollar is spent during a year. Keynesians view velocity as volatile, but monetarists disagree.
- The **quantity theory of money** is a monetarist argument that the velocity of money *(V)* and output *(Q)* variables in the equation of

exchange are relatively constant. Given this assumption, changes in the money supply yield proportional changes in the price level. The monetarist solution to inept Fed tinkering with the money supply that causes inflation or recession is to have the Fed simply pick a rate of growth in the money supply that is consistent with real GDP growth and stick to it.

- **Keynesians' and monetarists' views on fiscal policy** are also different. Keynesians believe the investment demand curve is relatively vertical, and monetarists view it as relatively flat. Monetarists assert that the *crowding-out effect* is large and, therefore, fiscal policy is ineffective. Keynesians argue that the crowding-out effect is small and that fiscal policy is effective.

Summary of Conclusion Statements

- As the interest rate falls, the opportunity cost of holding money falls, and people increase their speculative balances.
- There is an inverse relationship between the quantity of money demanded and the interest rate.
- The speculative demand for money at possible interest rates gives the demand for money curve its downward slope.
- There is an inverse relationship between bond prices and the interest rate that enables the money market to achieve equilibrium.
- In the Keynesian model, changes in the supply of money affect interest rates. In turn, interest rates affect investment spending, aggregate demand, and, finally, real GDP, employment, and prices.

- According to the quantity theory of money, any change in the money supply must lead to a proportional change in the price level.
- To avoid inflation and unemployment, the monetarists' prescription is to be sure that the money supply is at the proper level.
- Monetarists advocate that the Federal Reserve increase the money supply by a constant percentage each year.
- Keynesians view the shape of the investment demand curve as rather steep or vertical, so the crowding-out effect is insignificant.
- Monetarists view the shape of the investment demand curve as less steep or relatively flat, so the crowding-out effect is significant.

Study Questions and Problems

1. How much money do you keep in cash or checkable deposits on a typical day? Under the following conditions, would you increase or decrease your demand for money? Also identify whether the condition affects your transactions demand, precautionary demand, or speculative demand.

   a. Your salary doubles.
   b. The rate of interest on bonds and other assets falls.
   c. An automatic teller machine (ATM) is installed next door, and you have an ATM card.
   d. Bond prices are expected to rise.
   e. You are paid each week instead of monthly.

2. What are the basic motives for the transactions demand, precautionary demand, and speculative demand? Explain how these three demands are combined in a graph to show the total demand for money.

3. Suppose a bond pays annual interest of $80. Compute the interest rate per year that a bondholder can earn if the bond has a face value of $800, $1,000, and $2,000. State the conclusion drawn from your calculations.

EXHIBIT 10	Money Market	
Interest rate (percent)	Demand for money (billions of dollars)	Supply of money (billions of dollars)
8%	$100	$200
6	200	200
4	300	200
2	400	200

Source: © Cengage Learning 2014

4. Using the demand and supply schedule for money shown in Exhibit 10, do the following:
   a. Graph the demand for money and the supply of money curves.
   b. Determine the equilibrium interest rate.
   c. Suppose the Fed increases the money supply by $100 billion. Show the effect in your graph, and describe the money market adjustment process to a new equilibrium interest rate. What is the new equilibrium rate of interest?

5. Assume you are the chair of the Federal Reserve Board of Governors and the condition of the economy is shown in Exhibit 5. Assume you are a Keynesian, and start at point E_1 in the money market and the product market. State the likely direction of change in the price level, real GDP, and employment caused by each of the following monetary policies:
   a. The Fed makes an open market sale of government bonds.
   b. The Fed reduces the required reserve ratio.
   c. The Fed increases the discount rate.

6. "A monetarist investigator might say that the sewer flow of 6,000 gallons an hour consisted of an average of 200 gallons in the sewer at any one time with a complete turnover of the water 30 times every hour."[1] Interpret this statement using the equation of exchange.

7. What is the quantity theory of money, and what does each term in the equation represent?

8. Exhibit 6 shows the monetarist monetary policy transmission mechanism. Assume the economy is in a recession. At each arrow, identify a reason why the transmission process could fail.

9. Explain the difference between the Keynesian and the monetarist views on how an increase in the money supply causes inflation.

10. Based on the quantity theory of money, what would be the impact of increasing the money supply by 25 percent?

11. Suppose the investment demand curve is a vertical line. Would the Keynesian or the monetarist view of the impact of monetary policy on investment spending be correct?

12. Why is the shape of the aggregate supply curve important to the Keynesian-monetarist controversy? (Hint: Review Exhibit 6 in the chapter on aggregate demand and supply.)

For Online Exercises, go to the Tucker Web site at www.cengage.com/economics/tucker.

---

[1]Werner Sichel and Peter Eckstein, *Basic Economic Concepts* (Chicago: Rand McNally, 1974), p. 344.

✓ CHECKPOINT ANSWERS

What Does the Money Supply Curve Look Like When the Fed Targets the Federal Funds Rate?

In Exhibit 11, consider the effect of a shift in the money demand curve from MD_1 to MD_2 when the Fed follows a federal funds rate target of 6 percent. The initial effects are an excess demand for money and upward pressure on the rate. Because the Fed sets the target at 6 percent, it will increase the money supply along the money supply curve, MS, and establish a new equilibrium at E_2. At the new equilibrium, the money supply has increased from $800 billion to $850 billion, and the rate is unchanged at 6 percent. Therefore, the money supply curve is traced by an infinite number of possible equilibrium points along the MS curve. If you said the money supply curve is horizontal when the Fed sets a federal funds rate target, **YOU ARE CORRECT.**

A Horse of Which Color?

The famous economist is Milton Friedman, who favors a monetary rule for the Fed. The horse is a sarcastic way of rejecting Keynesian activist policies that destabilize the economy. Friedman even argues that the Board of Governors of the Federal Reserve System should announce the growth rate for the money supply each year and must resign if the target is missed. If you said the economist is a monetarist, **YOU ARE CORRECT.**

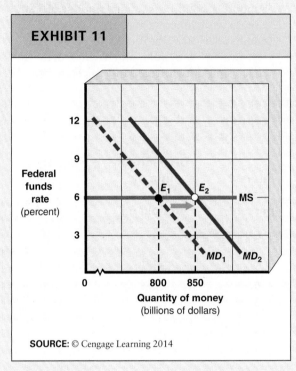

EXHIBIT 11

Federal funds rate (percent)

Quantity of money (billions of dollars)

SOURCE: © Cengage Learning 2014

Sample Quiz

For an explanation of the correct answers, visit the Tucker Web site at www.cengage.com/economics/tucker.

1. The demand for money that households keep for emergency purposes is known as the
   a. precautionary demand.
   b. emergency demand.
   c. speculative demand.
   d. temporary demand.

2. The quantity of money held in response to interest rates is the

   a. transactions motive for holding money.
   b. precautionary motive for holding money.
   c. speculative motive for holding money.
   d. unit-of-account motive for holding money.

3. The speculative demand for money
   a. varies inversely with income.
   b. is only concerned with active money.

Sample Quiz *continued*

c. involves holding money for unexpected problems.

d. varies directly with the transactions demand for money.

e. varies inversely with the interest rate.

4. Other things being equal, the quantity of money that people wish to hold can be expected to
   a. increase as the interest rate increases.
   b. decrease as the interest rate increases.
   c. decrease as real GDP increases.
   d. None of the above answers are correct.

5. A decrease in the interest rate, other things being equal, causes a (an)
   a. upward movement along the demand curve for money.
   b. downward movement along the demand curve for money.
   c. rightward shift of the demand curve for money.
   d. leftward shift of the demand curve for money.

6. Which of the following statements is *true*?
   a. The speculative demand for money at possible interest rates gives the demand for money curve its upward slope.
   b. There is an inverse relationship between the quantity of money demanded and the interest rate.
   c. According to the quantity theory of money, any change in the money supply will have no effect on the price level.
   d. All of the above answers are correct.

7. In Exhibit 12, assume an equilibrium with an interest rate of 15 percent and the money supply at $100 billion. The Fed uses its policy tools to move the economy to a new equilibrium at E_2 with money supply of $150 billion and an interest rate of 10 percent. This change could be the result of a(an)
   a. open market sale of securities by the Fed.
   b. higher discount rate set by the Fed.
   c. higher required reserve ratio set by the Fed.
   d. open market purchase of securities by the Fed.

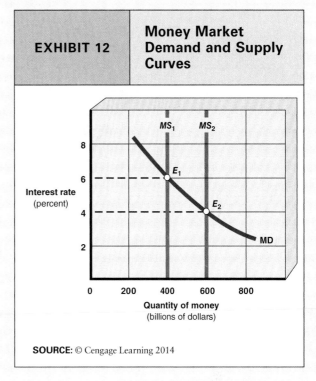

EXHIBIT 12	Money Market Demand and Supply Curves

SOURCE: © Cengage Learning 2014

8. According to Keynesians, an increase in the money supply will
   a. decrease the interest rate, and increase investment, aggregate demand, prices, real GDP, and employment.
   b. decrease the interest rate, and decrease investment, aggregate demand, prices, real GDP, and employment.
   c. increase the interest rate and decrease investment, aggregate demand, prices, real GDP, and employment.
   d. only increase prices.

9. While the classicists believed that both velocity and output are stable, Keynesians believe
   a. velocity is stable, and output is variable.
   b. velocity and output are both variable.
   c. output is stable, and velocity is variable
   d. the same as the classical economists that both output and velocity are stable.

Sample Quiz *continued*

EXHIBIT 13	Money, Investment, and Product Markets

SOURCE: © Cengage Learning 2014

10. In Exhibit 13, when the money supply increases from S_1 to S_2, the equilibrium interest rate
    a. remains unchanged.
    b. increases from i_2 to i_1, increasing investment spending from I_1 to I_2.
    c. increases from i_2 to i_1, decreasing investment spending from I_2 to I_1.
    d. decreases from i_1 to i_2, increasing investment spending from I_1 to I_2.

11. In Exhibit 13, if the interest rate falls from i_1 to i_2, investment spending will
    a. increase, and aggregate demand will shift from AD_1 to AD_2.
    b. decrease, and aggregate demand will shift from AD_2 to AD_1.
    c. remain the same, and aggregate demand will shift from AD_2 to AD_3.
    d. increase, and aggregate demand will shift from AD_2 to AD_1.

12. In Exhibit 13, a shift in aggregate demand from AD_1 to AD_2
    a. cannot raise real GDP because the economy is at full employment.
    b. cannot raise real GDP because the aggregate supply curve is upward sloping at GDP_2.

    c. will raise real GDP because the economy is operating below the full-employment level.
    d. will cause the interest rate to increase from i_2 to i_1.

13. The monetarist transmission mechanism through which monetary policy affects the price level, real GDP, and employment depends on the
    a. indirect impact of changes on the interest rate.
    b. indirect impact of changes on profit expectations.
    c. direct impact of changes in fiscal policy on aggregate demand.
    d. direct impact of changes in the money supply on aggregate demand.

14. The equation of exchange states
    a. $MV = PQ$.
    b. $MP = VQ$.
    c. $MP = V/Q$.
    d. $V = M/PQ$.

15. The quantity theory of money assumes that the velocity of money
    a. is constant.
    b. will rise if the money supply rises and fall if the money supply falls.
    c. will rise if the money supply rises, but will not change if the money supply falls.
    d. will fall if the money supply rises, and will rise if the money supply falls.

16. The transactions demand for money is the demand for money by households for
    a. rainy day spending.
    b. predictable spending purposes.
    c. liquidity purposes.
    d. investing purposes.

17. People react to an excess supply of money by
    a. selling bonds, thus driving up the interest rate.
    b. selling bonds, thus driving down the interest rate.
    c. buying bonds, thus driving up the interest rate.
    d. buying bonds, thus driving down the interest rate.

Sample Quiz *continued*

18. The belief that the velocity of money is *not* constant but is highly predictable is associated with the
    a. classical school.
    b. Keynesian school.
    c. supply-side school.
    d. rational expectations school.
    e. monetarist school.

19. The monetary rule is the view of the
    a. Keynesians that monetary policy is most important.
    b. monetarists that monetary policy is most important.
    c. classical economists that monetary policy is most important.

d. monetarists that the Fed should expand the money supply at a constant rate.

20. Which of the following statements is *true*?
    a. Keynesians advocate increasing the money supply during economic recessions but decreasing the money supply during economic expansions.
    b. Monetarists advocate increasing the money supply by a constant rate year after year.
    c. Keynesians argue that the crowding-out effect is rather insignificant.
    d. Monetarists argue that the crowding-out effect is rather large.
    e. All of the above answers are correct.

26

Policy Disputes Using the Self-Correcting Aggregate Demand and Supply Model

In the appendix to the chapter on aggregate demand and supply, the classical self-correcting aggregate demand and supply model was explained without disagreement. Expansionary and contractionary fiscal policy was discussed in the chapter on fiscal policy, and this chapter explained monetary policy. In this appendix, we combine these topics and examine contrasting fiscal and monetary policies using the self-correcting model.

26A-1 The Classical versus Keynesian Views of Expansionary Policy

The Keynesian activist approach rejects classical nonintervention policy to stabilize the economy using discretionary fiscal policy or activist monetary policy. Exhibit A-1 illustrates opposing theories for restoring an economy in recession to full employment. In both parts (a) and (b), the economy starts with a real GDP of $8 trillion and a price level of 150 at macro equilibrium E_1. Since full-employment real GDP is $12 trillion, the recessionary gap equals $4 trillion. In part (a), the economy closes the gap through the self-correction process. The key classical assumption is that nominal wages are flexible and fall as a result of competition among unemployed workers for jobs. Over time, the result is that the short-term aggregate supply curve ($SRAS_1$) shifts rightward to $SRAS_2$ and the economy automatically adjusts to long-run macro full-employment equilibrium at E_2 with a price level of 100.

Part (b) illustrates the opposing Keynesian theory. This view argues that nominal wages are fixed in the short run. In contrast to the self-correction model, Keynesians advocate using discretionary fiscal policy in which the federal government manages the aggregate demand curve (AD) by increasing government spending or cutting taxes. Both of these policy options work through the multiplier process and increase AD_1 to AD_2. The result is that the economy achieves full employment at macro equilibrium point E_2, where the price level is 200.

Activist monetary policy can also stabilize the economy. The Federal Reserve can increase the money supply, which lowers the interest rate, and in response, business investment spending increases. As a result, AD_1 shifts to AD_2 in part (b) of Exhibit A-1, and full employment is restored at E_2.

Note that both approaches in parts (a) and (b) restore full-employment real GDP; however, the impact on the price level is quite different. If classical theory is correct, the price level falls from 150 to 100. In contrast, if Keynesian theory is correct, the price level rises from 150 to 200, resulting in a higher inflation rate.

EXHIBIT A-1	Opposing Anti-recession Theories

Part (a) illustrates classical theory, which advocates noninterventionist fiscal and monetary policy. The classical assumption is that nominal wages are flexible. At point E_1, unemployed workers compete for jobs, and the wage rate falls, causing the short-run aggregate supply curve to shift from $SRAS_1$ to $SRAS_2$. Full employment is therefore automatically restored at point E_2.

In part (b), Keynesian policy advocates interventionist fiscal and monetary policy. Discretionary fiscal policy increases government spending or cuts taxes to increase the aggregate demand curve from AD_1 to AD_2. Discretionary monetary policy would increase the money supply to increase AD_1 to AD_2.

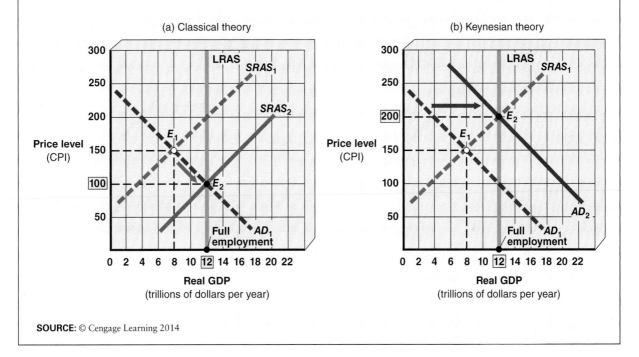

(a) Classical theory

(b) Keynesian theory

SOURCE: © Cengage Learning 2014

CONCLUSION: *The classical approach to a recession is to let market forces shift the short-run aggregate supply curve rightward and restore the economy to full employment. The opposing Keynesian approach to cure a recession is to use discretionary fiscal and monetary policy to increase aggregate demand and achieve full-employment real GDP.*

26A-2 Classical versus Keynesian Views of Contractionary Policy

Exhibit A-2 shows alternative theories for closing an inflationary gap. The classical nonintervention policy relies on competition between firms in response to a shortage of labor. In parts (a) and (b), the economy is at macro equilibrium at point E_1, where the price level is 150 and real GDP is $16 trillion. There is an inflationary gap of $4 trillion greater than the potential real GDP of $12 trillion. In part (a),

| EXHIBIT A-2 | Opposing Anti-inflation Theories |

In part (a), the classical assumption is that at point E_1, firms face a labor shortage and their competition for available workers drives up the nominal wage rate. Under a noninterventionist policy, the short-run aggregate supply curve shifts leftward from $SRAS_1$ to $SRAS_2$, and the economy is automatically restored to full employment at E_2.

Part (b) shows the effect of Keynesian contractionary policy. Discretionary fiscal policy decreases government spending or increases taxes to shift the aggregate demand curve leftward from AD_1 to AD_2. Discretionary monetary policy would decrease the money supply to decrease AD_1 to AD_2.

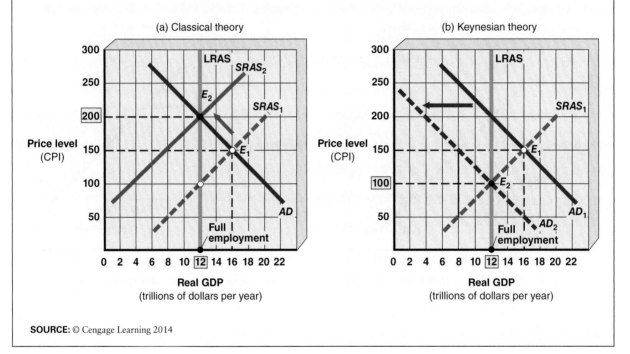

SOURCE: © Cengage Learning 2014

classical theory assumes flexible wages, so nominal wages rise, causing the $SRAS_1$ to shift upward to $SRAS_2$, and the economy reaches full-employment real GDP at point E_2 with a price level of 200.

In part (b), Keynesian contractionary policy aims at decreasing AD_1 to AD_2 using cuts in government spending or tax hikes. Working through the multiplier process, the inflationary gap is eliminated, and the economy moves from point E_1 to E_2, where the price level falls from 150 to 100 and full-employment real GDP of $12 trillion is achieved.

Monetary policy can also be used to shift the aggregate demand curve leftward. In this case, the Federal Reserve could follow a contractionary policy and decrease the money supply, resulting in a higher interest rate, and firms respond by decreasing their investment spending. Consequently, AD_1 decreases to AD_2, and full-employment real GDP is reached at E_2.

As shown in the previous exhibit, opposing theories have different impacts on the price level. In part (a) of Exhibit A-2, the classical approach leads to an increase in the price level from 150 to 200. In contrast, the Keynesian approach yields a decrease in the price level from 150 to 100.

> **CONCLUSION:** *The classical approach to an inflationary gap is to let market forces shift the short-run aggregate supply curve leftward and restore the economy to full employment. The opposing Keynesian approach to cure inflation uses discretionary fiscal and monetary policy to decrease aggregate demand and achieve full-employment real GDP.*

Summary

- The **Keynesian prescription for a recession** rejects the classical assumption that wages are flexible and will fall, causing the short-run aggregate supply curve to shift downward and restore full-employment GDP. Instead, Keynesians support expansionary fiscal and monetary policy to increase aggregate demand and return the economy to the natural rate of unemployment.

- The **Keynesian cure for inflation** also rejects the classical assumption that wages are flexible and will rise, causing the short-run aggregate supply curve to shift upward and restore full-employment GDP. In contrast, Keynesian theory advocates contractionary fiscal and monetary policy to decrease aggregate demand and achieve full-employment macro equilibrium.

Summary of Conclusion Statements

- The classical approach to a recession is to let market forces shift the short-run aggregate supply curve rightward and restore the economy to full employment. The opposing Keynesian approach to cure a recession is to use discretionary fiscal and monetary policy to increase aggregate demand and achieve full-employment real GDP.

- The classical approach to an inflationary gap is to let market forces shift the short-run aggregate supply curve leftward and restore the economy to full employment. The opposing Keynesian approach to cure inflation uses discretionary fiscal and monetary policy to decrease aggregate demand and achieve full-employment real GDP.

Sample Quiz

For an explanation of the correct answers, visit the Tucker Web site at www.cengage.com/economics/tucker.

1. Classical theory advocates _____ policy, and Keynesian theory advocates _____ policy.
   a. nonintervention; intervention
   b. active; nonstabilization
   c. fixed wages; flexible wages
   d. active; passive

2. If the economy is in short-run disequilibrium, an economist following classical theory would advocate that the Federal Reserve make appropriate changes in the
   a. money supply.
   b. reserve requirement.

Sample Quiz *continued*

c. federal funds rate.

d. None of the above answers is correct.

3. Assuming the economy is experiencing a recessionary gap, classical economists predict that
   a. wages will remain fixed.
   b. monetary policy should intervene.
   c. higher wages will shift the short-run aggregate supply curve leftward.
   d. lower wages will shift the short-run aggregate supply curve rightward.

4. Assume the economy is operating at a real GDP above full-employment real GDP. Keynesian economists would prescribe which of the following policies?
   a. nonintervention
   b. passive monetary policy
   c. contractionary
   d. expansionary

5. Assume the economy is experiencing an inflationary gap, Keynesian economists believe that
   a. flexible wages will restore full employment.
   b. the federal government should decrease spending to shift the aggregate demand curve leftward.
   c. the Federal Reserve should lower the interest rate.
   d. the federal government should increase spending to shift the aggregate demand curve rightward.

6. Assume the economy is in short-run equilibrium at a real GDP below its potential real GDP. According to Keynesian theory, which of the following policies should be followed?
   a. The Federal Reserve should increase the money supply.
   b. The federal government should increase spending.
   c. The federal government should do nothing because the economy will self correct to potential real GDP.
   d. All of the above answers are correct.

7. A policy to do nothing and allow the economy to self-correct or adjust without interference from the federal government is also called a (an) _____ policy.
   a. nonintervention
   b. active
   c. stabilization
   d. fixed rule

8. Assume the economy is experiencing a recessionary gap. Keynesian economists would support which of the following policies?
   a. nonstabilization
   b. expansionary
   c. nonintervention
   d. fixed wage

9. Assuming the economy is in a recession, Keynesian economists predict that
   a. wages will remain fixed.
   b. monetary policy will sell government securities.
   c. higher wages will shift the short-run aggregate supply curve leftward.
   d. lower wages will shift the short-run aggregate supply curve rightward.

10. Assume the economy is in short-run equilibrium at a real GDP above its potential real GDP. According to classical theory, which of the following policies should be followed?
    a. The Federal Reserve should use open market operations and buy U.S. government securities.
    b. The Federal Reserve should not follow a fixed rule.
    c. The federal government should cut taxes.
    d. Fiscal policy and monetary policy should *not* be activist.

11. Assume the economy is experiencing an inflationary gap, classical economists believe that
    a. flexible wages will restore full employment.
    b. the federal government should decrease spending to shift the aggregate demand curve leftward.

Sample Quiz *continued*

c. the Federal Reserve should lower the interest rate.

d. the federal government should increase spending to shift the aggregate demand curve rightward.

12. In part (a) of Exhibit A-3, the economy is initially in short-run equilibrium at real GDP level Y_1 and price level P_2. Classical theory argues

a. the federal government must shift AD_1 to AD_2 as shown in part (b).

b. the federal government must shift $SRAS_1$ to $SRAS_2$.

c. $SRAS_1$ will shift to $SRAS_2$ without government intervention.

d. AD_1 will shift to AD_2 without government intervention.

13. Assume that the economy depicted in part (a) of Exhibit A-3 is in short-run equilibrium with AD_1 and $SRAS_1$. If the economy is

left to correct itself according to classical theory

a. wages will fall as long as real GDP is above Y_p.

b. lower wages will result in a shift from $SRAS_1$ to $SRAS_2$.

c. long-run equilibrium will be established at Y_p and P_3.

d. All of the above will take place.

14. In part (b) of Exhibit A-3, the economy is initially in short-run equilibrium at real GDP level Y_1 and price level P_2. If the government decides to intervene, it would

a. increase taxes.

b. decrease the money supply.

c. increase the level of government spending for goods and services.

d. decrease the level of government spending for goods and services.

EXHIBIT A-3	Policy Alternatives

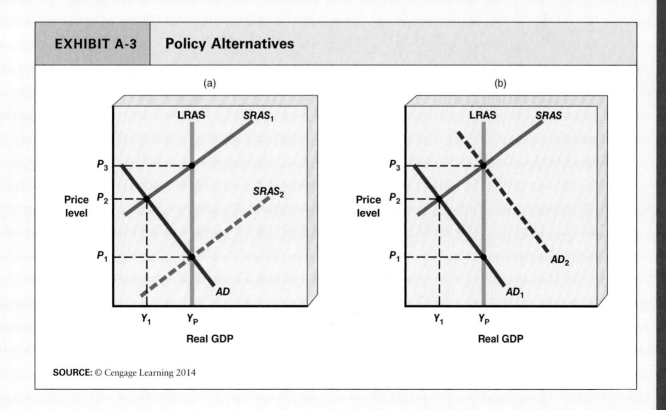

SOURCE: © Cengage Learning 2014

Sample Quiz *continued*

15. Assume that the economy depicted in part (b) of Exhibit A-3 is in short-run equilibrium with AD_1 and $SRAS_1$. Keynesian theory argues
    a. nominal wages will fall as long as employment remains above the natural level of unemployment.
    b. lower wages will result in a shift from $SRAS_1$ to $SRAS_2$.
    c. long-run equilibrium will be established at Y_p and P_1.
    d. government intervention must shift AD_1 to AD_2.

chapter 27

The Phillips Curve and Expectations Theory

This chapter explores the Phillips curve, the expectations theory, and incomes policies (wage and price controls). The Phillips curve traces the relationship between two of the greatest problems of economies everywhere— inflation and unemployment. One of the most fascinating puzzles in economics is whether a stable trade-off exists between these two economic evils. If true, policymakers face a dilemma described by the old saying "Inside each solution there is another problem looking to work its way out." If policymakers reduce the unemployment rate, the inflation rate worsens. Or if they reduce the inflation rate, the unemployment rate rises. In the 1960s, most economists and policymakers thought the way to achieve a particular inflation-unemployment point on the Phillips curve menu was to use Keynesian demand-management policies.

Just as the reality of the Great Depression refuted classical theory, the Great Stagflations of the 1970s and early 1980s challenged the Phillips curve and Keynesian policies. To understand how varying rates of inflation can occur at the same rate of unemployment, we explore two competing ways of thinking called *adaptive expectations* and *rational expectations*. Both of these theories are attacks on the Keynesians who urge the government to interfere with the market economy in order to achieve full employment.

The chapter begins with a discussion of the Phillips curve that explains why both expectations camps believe there is no permanent inflation-unemployment trade-off. In the last part of this chapter, you will see what happens when policymakers fight inflation using policies to control wages and prices (incomes), rather than monetary and fiscal policies.

In this chapter, you will learn to solve these economics puzzles:

- Why might expansionary fiscal and monetary policies be useless in the long run?
- If the Fed is independent, why would the money supply increase before a presidential election?
- Can economic theory explain pop quizzes?
- Can wearing a button reduce inflation?

27-1 The Phillips Curve

In a celebrated article published in 1958, Australian economist A. W. Phillips of the London School of Economics plotted data on unemployment rates and the rate of change in wage rates between 1861 and 1957 in the United Kingdom.[1] Phillips showed there was a remarkably stable inverse relationship between changes in money wages and the unemployment rate. Economists have since extended this concept to the following definition of the Phillips curve. The Phillips curve is a curve showing an inverse relationship between the inflation rate and the unemployment rate. The reason it is acceptable to use the inflation rate, rather than the change in wages, is that wages are the main component of prices. At low rates of unemployment, labor has the market power to push up wages and, in turn, prices. When many workers are pounding the pavement eager for jobs, labor lacks bargaining power to ask for raises. As a result, the upward pressure on prices eases.

Phillips curve

A curve showing an inverse relationship between the inflation rate and the unemployment rate.

27-1a THE PHILLIPS CURVE IN THEORY

Exhibit 1 shows the relationship between the AD-AS model developed earlier and the Phillips curve. In part (a), we assume that the aggregate supply curve, AS, is stationary. Thus, points *A–D* represent possible equilibrium points depending on the location of the aggregate demand curve. As the aggregate demand curve increases from AD_1 to AD_4, real GDP rises from $6.0 trillion to $6.6 trillion, more workers are employed, and the price level (CPI) rises from 100 to 112. The astute reader will recognize from the chapter on aggregate demand and supply that we are discussing *demand-pull inflation*.

The inverse relationship between the price level and unemployment in part (a) determines the shape of the Phillips curve in part (b). Points *A–D* in both figures correspond. If the economy operates at point *A*, the annual rate of inflation is zero, and the unemployment rate is 8 percent. If the economy is at point *B*, the annual rate of inflation is 4 percent, and the unemployment rate is 5 percent. Similarly, points *C* and *D* correspond in both graphs. Note that below point *A*, the price level is below 100 and the economy experiences deflation.

> **CONCLUSION:** *Changes in aggregate demand cause a movement along a stationary Phillips curve.*

27-1b THE PHILLIPS CURVE IN PRACTICE

So far so good. If the world works this way, policymakers must choose from a menu of inflation rate and unemployment rate combinations along the Phillips curve. Do we want *X* percent less unemployment with an opportunity cost of *Y* percent more inflation? Early studies verified the Phillips curve for the U.S. economy in the 1960s. As shown in Exhibit 2, the data fit the Phillips curve very well. Based on this evidence, most economists, including Nobel laureates Paul Samuelson

---

[1]A. W. Phillips, "The Relation between Unemployment and the Rate of Change in Money Wage Rates in the United Kingdom, 1861–1957," *Economica* 25 (November 1958): 283–299.

EXHIBIT 1	The Theoretical Relationship between Changes in Aggregate Demand and the Phillips Curve

In part (a), the aggregate demand curve shifts upward, while the aggregate supply curve remains stationary. The result is a series of equilibrium points *A–D*. As aggregate demand rises along the *AS* curve, the price level (CPI), real GDP, and employment increase. Points *A–D* in parts (a) and (b) correspond. An increase in aggregate demand from AD_1 to AD_4 causes the unemployment rate to fall, but the inflation rate rises. Thus, the increase in aggregate demand results in a movement upward along the Phillips curve.

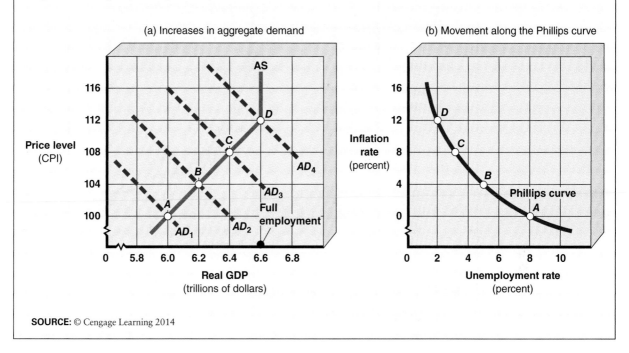

SOURCE: © Cengage Learning 2014

(deceased) and Robert Solow of MIT, believed the Phillips curve was stable. Policymakers might choose low inflation and high unemployment, as in 1961. Or they may prefer higher inflation and lower unemployment, as, for example, in 1969. And the most popular way in the 1960s to reach a particular point on the Phillips curve was to fine-tune the economy using Keynesian demand-management policies.

Then, just as policymakers and economists became comfortable with the Phillips curve, the dream turned into a nightmare. As shown in Exhibit 3, the points for 1970–1990 show the Phillips curve in chaos. The pattern disappeared, and many points moved far above and to the right of the 1960s data. At higher unemployment rates, the corresponding inflation rate was much higher than the Phillips curve predicted. For example, look at 1975, 1979, 1980, and 1981. These data reflect bouts with stagflation, which occurred in the 1970s and early 1980s. Recall from Exhibit 12(a) in the chapter on aggregate demand and supply that *cost-push inflation* is the result of a leftward shift of the aggregate supply curve. In the Great Stagflations of 1973–1974 and 1979–1980, the influence of such "supply shocks" as soaring oil prices pushed up production costs and shifted

EXHIBIT 2	The Phillips Curve for the United States in the 1960s

The figure plots the inflation rate and unemployment rate combinations for the period 1960–1969. A freehand curve drawn through the points conforms very well to the Phillips curve.

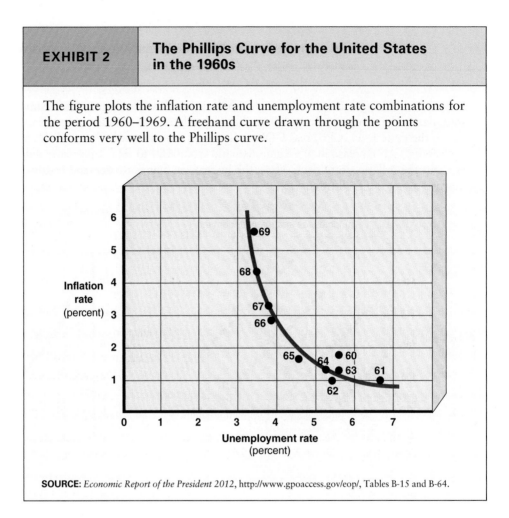

SOURCE: *Economic Report of the President 2012*, http://www.gpoaccess.gov/eop/, Tables B-15 and B-64.

the economy's aggregate supply curve inward. Thus, the Phillips curve theory was in shambles as the nation simultaneously experienced both high inflation and high unemployment. Policymakers therefore turned their focus from the Phillips curve, based on trade-offs, to a "misery index," which added the inflation and unemployment rates.

27-2 The Long-Run Phillips Curve

The simple idea of a stable trade-off between unemployment and inflation was an overnight sensation in the 1960s. By the early 1970s, the Phillips curve was becoming a has-been. Because Keynesian demand-management policies generate the curve, it will come as no surprise that monetarists such as Milton Friedman and Edmund S. Phelps always believed the Phillips curve was just a transitory, short-run relationship. In the mid-1960s, they suggested that the unemployment rate and the rate of inflation are unrelated in the long run. As shown in Exhibit 4, the challengers argued that after a few years, the Phillips curve is a vertical line. As explained below, this monetarist view is also debatable.

EXHIBIT 3	Inflation and Unemployment Rates for the United States, 1970–1990

By 1990, the Phillips curve became unstable. Clearly, many points have been established upward and to the right. The inflation rate therefore can be much higher at any unemployment rate than the Phillips curve of the 1960s predicted.

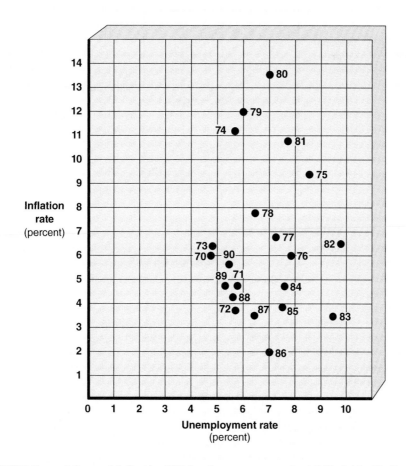

SOURCE: *Economic Report of the President 2012*, http://www.gpoaccess.gov/eop/, Tables B-15 and B-64.

27-2a NATURAL RATE HYPOTHESIS

If the Phillips curve is vertical in the long run, there are profound implications for macroeconomic policy. Expansionary monetary and fiscal policies can, at best, produce a short-lived lowering of unemployment. This is the so-called natural rate hypothesis. The natural rate hypothesis argues that the economy will self-correct to the natural rate of unemployment. The long-run Phillips curve is therefore a vertical line at the natural rate of unemployment. Recall from the chapter on business cycles and unemployment that the natural rate of unemployment, or the full-employment unemployment rate, is equal to the sum of the frictional and structural

Natural rate hypothesis

The hypothesis that argues that the economy will self-correct to the natural rate of unemployment. The long-run Phillips curve is therefore a vertical line at the natural rate of unemployment.

EXHIBIT 4	The Short-Run and Long-Run Phillips Curves

Beginning at point *A*, the economy is operating at the 6 percent natural rate of unemployment. The actual and anticipated inflation rates are 3 percent. An increase in aggregate demand temporarily causes the inflation rate to rise to 6 percent. Under adaptive expectations theory, real wages fall, profits rise, and more workers are employed. The unemployment rate falls to 4 percent, and the economy moves along the short-run Phillips curve PC_1 to point *B*. Over time, workers demand and get nominal wage rate hikes, and profits fall. Workers lose their jobs, and the unemployment rate returns to 6 percent at point *C* on the short-run Phillips curve PC_2. This process will repeat each time expansionary policy attempts to reduce unemployment below the natural rate. The long-run Phillips curve is therefore a vertical line at the natural rate of unemployment. This suggests that Keynesian expansionary policies create only inflation over time.

Under rational expectations theory, workers do not rely only on recent experience. They adjust their nominal wages quickly in proportion to changes in prices. Expansionary policy will move the economy directly upward along the long-run Phillips curve.

CAUSATION CHAINS

Short-run adaptive expectations theory

Aggregate demand increases ⇒ Inflation rate rises, real wages fall, and profits rise ⇒ Unemployment rate falls

Long-run adaptive expectations theory

Inflation rate is constant at higher rate, workers' nominal wage rate rises, and profits fall ⇒ Unemployment rate is restored to full employment

Rational expectations theory

Aggregate demand increases ⇒ Inflation rate rises and nominal wages adjust quickly to equal inflation rate ⇒ Inflation rate rises on vertical line at full employment

SOURCE: © Cengage Learning 2014

unemployment rates. In Exhibit 4, the natural rate of unemployment is 6 percent. Two versions of expectations theory explain the natural rate model. We begin our analysis using *adaptive expectations theory* and then turn to the more recent *rational expectations theory*.

27-2b ADAPTIVE EXPECTATIONS THEORY

To explain the reasoning behind the natural rate hypothesis, let us begin in Exhibit 4 with the economy operating at point *A*, with a 3 percent inflation rate and a 6 percent unemployment rate. Assume the inflation rate has been 3 percent in recent years and this trend is expected to continue. Based on this recent 3 percent rise in the CPI, collective bargaining agreements call for hourly nominal or money wages of $10.00 this year and $10.30 next year. Now suppose an election is approaching and the president and Congress strive to make voters happy by reducing the unemployment rate to 4 percent. Or perhaps policymakers incorrectly believe 4 percent is the natural rate of unemployment. Regardless of the reason for setting this goal, suppose the new expansionary fiscal policy shifts the aggregate demand curve upward along the aggregate supply curve and the economy moves unexpectedly from point *A* this year to point *B* the next year.

Keynesians declare "mission accomplished" when the economy moves up the short-run Phillips curve PC_1 from point *A* to point *B*. This unexpected change brings good news to businesses. Based on an expected inflation rate of 3 percent, employers agreed to pay real wages of $10.00 at point *B*. However, if the inflation rate rises unexpectedly to 6 percent, real wages fall to $9.72 as prices rise.[2] With cheaper labor costs in real terms, profits increase, more workers are hired, real GDP expands, and the unemployment rate drops to 4 percent.

So far, Keynesians and monetarists agree that policymakers and businesses are running the race as though the hare and the workers are acting like the tortoise. But monetarists do not believe workers are caught flat-footed as time passes. Workers soon realize that higher prices have eroded their purchasing power. Consequently, they demand an extra 3 percent raise in the nominal wage rate so that their real wages can be restored to the level prior to the unexpected rise in the inflation rate from 3 to 6 percent. When workers get their raise to offset the higher cost of living, business profits decline, and some workers are laid off until the unemployment rate returns to 6 percent at point *C*. At point *C*, the unemployment rate is right back where it began before the government unsystematically changed its fiscal policy, but the inflation rate has risen from 3 to 6 percent. Keynesians, on the other hand, believe nominal wages are fixed because workers do not demand and get an extra 3 percent rise in nominal wages. In the Keynesian view, demand stimulus reduced unemployment in exchange for the higher inflation rate, and the economy remains at point *B* and does not automatically move in time to point *C*.

Our story describes a *wage-price spiral*, defined in the chapter on inflation, and we need a theory to explain how people form their inflationary expectations. The reason the economy moved from point *A* to point *B* is based on adaptive expectations theory. Adaptive expectations theory is the concept that people believe that the best indicator of the future is recent information. As a result, people

Adaptive expectations theory

The concept that people believe the best indicator of the future is recent information. As a result, people persistently underestimate inflation when it is accelerating and overestimate it while it is slowing down.

---

[2]Assume the price level at point *A* is 100 and the price level rises to 106 at point *B*. The real wage is computed as the nominal wage multiplied by the initial price level divided by the new price level. Thus, the real wage rate at point *B* is equal to $10.30 \times (100/106) = $9.72. If the price level had risen to 103, as expected, the real wage at point *B* would have equaled $10.30 \times (100/103) = $10.00.

persistently underestimate inflation when it is accelerating and overestimate it while it is slowing down. Adaptive expectations theory assumes ignorance of future events, including changes in fiscal and monetary policies. People learn from recent experience and gradually adjust their anticipated inflation rate to the actual inflation rate. This means that at point C, workers expect a higher rate of inflation at any unemployment rate because last year the actual rate of inflation was 6 percent. Unions therefore expect a 6 percent rate of inflation and are no longer satisfied with a contract with less than a 6 percent increase in the nominal wage rate; since anything less would mean a cut in real wages. Thus, workers *adapt* their expectations to 6 percent instead of 3 percent, and the short-run Phillips curve shifts outward from PC_1 to PC_2 in Exhibit 4. In other words, the economy moves from point A to point C on the vertical long-run Phillips curve. If policymakers follow a contractionary policy, adaptive expectations operate in reverse, and the inflation rate declines (see You're the Economist: The Political Business Cycle).

Suppose policymakers figure expansionary policy worked last time, so why not try it again? So they take another stab at creating jobs by stimulating aggregate demand. This time the economy will ride up the new short-run Phillips curve PC_2 from point C to point D, and the whole process will repeat. When the actual inflation rate rises from 6 to 9 percent, nominal wage increases will be a step slow in catching up with price hikes. In time, workers will demand and get a nominal wage hike, which restores their real wage rate, and the economy will reach point E. Faced with the new short-run Phillips curve PC_3, the government will cause an inflation rate of 12 percent at point F if it persists in trying to achieve 4 percent unemployment. Eventually, nominal wages will rise (reducing profits), some workers will lose their jobs, and the economy will move from point F to point G.

> **CONCLUSION:** *According to adaptive expectations theory, expansionary monetary and fiscal policies to reduce the unemployment rate are useless in the long run. After a short-run reduction in unemployment, the economy will self-correct to the natural rate of unemployment, but at a higher inflation rate. Thus, there is no long-run trade-off between inflation and unemployment.*

27-2c THE LONG-RUN PHILLIPS CURVE AND THE LABOR MARKET

We can now give one explanation for the tendency of the inflation-unemployment points shown earlier in Exhibit 3 to shift upward to the right in the 1970s and early 1980s. Demand stimulus policies in the 1960s caught people by surprise, and there was a movement upward along a short-run Phillips curve. As inflation worsened during the 1970s and the early 1980s, adaptive expectations caused the short-run Phillips curves to shift outward. As the inflation rate dropped sharply during the late 1980s, people's inflationary expectations adapted in the downward direction, and the short-run Phillips curve shifted inward. Moreover, as discussed in the chapter on business cycles and unemployment, economists estimated that the *natural rate of unemployment* increased from the 1960s to the 1980s. Recall that the natural rate of unemployment is the full-employment unemployment rate at which the economy operates at capacity

The Political Business Cycle

Applicable Concept: adaptive expectations

The basic ideal of Keynesian economics is that the government uses monetary and fiscal policies to stabilize the economy. On the other hand, the government may be diabolical and deliberately cause business cycles. The political business cycle is therefore Keynesianism in reverse. A political business cycle is a business cycle caused by policymakers to improve politicians' reelection chances.

A basic assumption of the political business cycle model is that democratic government causes business cycles. This theory views politics as, by nature, a short-run game. The rational self-interest goal of politicians is to maximize votes today and worry about tomorrow when tomorrow comes. This means a politician who faces an election must act now and not later. Voters are also short-sighted and want good news now, rather than promises of long-term solutions. If people want jobs, for example, the politicians who seek reelection will use expansionary policies to create jobs. The political process will therefore gladly force a lower unemployment rate now in exchange for a higher inflation rate in the future. The politician who commits the sin of truth and tells the voters a "quick fix" is harmful will probably taste defeat.

Given the realities of politics, politicians may find it easier to let the Fed stimulate the economy. Expansionary fiscal policy requires Congress to approve tax cuts or spending increases. Since members of Congress belong to opposing parties, each side has an incentive to prevent the other party from taking credit for legislation. Even if a bill eventually passes, it may be too late for the election. Fiscal policy takes considerable time to implement and actually affect the economy and, in turn, the voters.

If the Fed is independent, why would the Fed be willing to create political business cycles? Recall that the president appoints the Fed chair and members of the Board of Governors. Thus, the Fed is a semi-separate branch of government that often wishes to avoid conflict with Congress or the president. If the Fed is willing to stimulate aggregate demand before an election, incumbent politicians will benefit at the expense of their opponents. Once the election is over, the Fed will slow down the economy to reduce the inflation rate. Then the concern becomes recession until the next election looms and the Fed stimulates the economy again. Meanwhile, politicians can blame the Fed for driving up prices or starting the downturn.

Pool photo by Newsmakers via Getty Images

Exhibit 5 reveals that the money supply has generally been on the rise before presidential elections. In 1964, 1968, 1972, 1976, 1980 (slight), 1988, 1992, and 2008, the money supply rose before the presidential election and then fell after the presidential election. The 1984, 1996, 2000, and 2004 elections were exceptions. Since this text was written in 2012, the money supply percentage change is not available for the election of 2012.

Analyze the Issue

Based on adaptive expectations theory, assume an expansionary monetary policy has moved the economy to point C in Exhibit 4. Now suppose the election is over and inflation concerns policymakers, so the Fed applies the brakes to monetary policy. Use this diagram to explain the short-run and long-run effects of a contractionary monetary policy.

(potential GDP). This means the vertical long-run Phillips curve intersecting each short-run Phillips curve shifted to the right. The explanation, in part, is because women and teenagers became a larger percentage of the labor force, and these groups of workers often experience higher rates of unemployment. It is also argued that the following measures might reduce the natural rate of unemployment: revising unemployment compensation, changing the minimum wage law, providing

Political business cycle

A business cycle caused by policymakers to improve politicians' reelection chances.

EXHIBIT 5	Money Supply Growth and Presidential Elections, 1960–2008

Since 1960, the money supply has often increased prior to presidential elections. The 1984, 1996, 2000, and 2004 elections were exceptions.

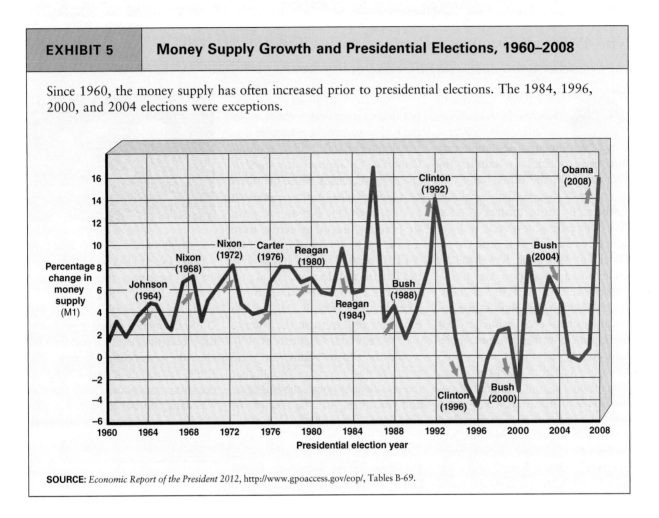

SOURCE: *Economic Report of the President 2012*, http://www.gpoaccess.gov/eop/, Tables B-69.

Rational expectations theory

The belief that people use all available information to predict the future, including the future impact of predictable expansionary monetary and fiscal policies. Predictable expansionary macroeconomic policies can therefore be negated by immediately flexible wages and prices when businesses and workers anticipate the effects of these policies on the economy.

better education and training, improving information on available jobs, removing discrimination, and reducing the monopoly power of unions and businesses.

27-3 The Theory of Rational Expectations

Whether expectations are formed "adaptively" or "rationally" is a hotly contested debate among economists. In the mid-1970s, Robert Lucas of the University of Chicago (1995 Nobel Laureate) is generally credited with introducing rational expectations theory, which is the competing view that adaptive expectations theory is too simplistic. Rational expectations theory is the belief that people use all available information to predict the future, including future monetary and fiscal policies. Hands-on discretionary macroeconomic policies intended to stabilize the economy can therefore be negated when businesses and workers anticipate the effects of these policies on the economy. According to the rational expectations hypothesis, people do not simply think inflation will be about the same next year as last year. Although everyone's crystal ball is clouded, people are intelligent and informed on how the economy works. They not only consider past price changes, but also consider how changes in the federal deficit or money supply will affect inflation next year. Suppose businesses and workers predict that a surge in the money supply or a tax cut will raise the actual inflation rate to, say, 6 percent. They will immediately raise their expectations of the inflation rate to 6 percent even though the most recent rate of inflation was 3 percent. In short, rational expectationists believe that both nominal wages and prices are flexible.

Let's reconsider the case in which the government is trying to reduce the unemployment rate. Begin at point *A* in Exhibit 4 and suppose policymakers strive to reduce unemployment using new expansionary policies to stimulate demand. Under rational expectations theory, workers are not caught napping. Workers will not simply wait until the actual inflation rate exceeds the expected inflation rate at point *B* and then ask for a raise. Although they may lack formal training in forecasting, workers are quite sophisticated in understanding the macro economy. They watch news on television; check economic data on the Internet; and read *The Wall Street Journal*, *Time*, the local newspapers, and AFL-CIO publications for information on government policies and future changes in prices. When new information becomes available, workers revise their expectations.

Because workers wisely use all relevant information to predict future changes, they anticipate that the aggregate demand curve is going to shift rightward, causing a rise in the price level and a fall in real wages. They know that unless they get wage hikes to match the price increases, they will be losers. Consequently, workers rationally raise their nominal wage demands without a time lag so that no gap between the actual and expected rates of inflation occurs. In fact, many collective bargaining agreements contain escalator clauses, providing automatic nominal wage increases as the price level rises. Assuming that workers correctly anticipate the inflation rate, real wages remain unchanged because nominal wages and prices rise proportionately. This means the temporary increase in profits, real GDP, and employment does *not* happen as predicted by adaptive expectationists. In short, rational expectationists refute the short-run Phillips curves drawn in Exhibit 4. There would be, for example, no decrease in unemployment from 6 percent (point *A*) to 4 percent (point *B*). Instead, the only movement in the inflation rate is directly from 3 percent (point *A*) to 6 percent (point *C*). This means higher anticipated inflation is added without delay to current nominal wages and prices, which generates a vertical Phillips curve along such points as *A*, *C*, *E*, and *G*.

CONCLUSION: *According to rational expectations theory, expansionary monetary and fiscal policies used to reduce unemployment are not only useless, but also harmful because the only result is higher inflation.*

On the brighter side, rational expectations theory argues that a credible "stay the course" contractionary fiscal and monetary policy can quickly cool inflation without increasing unemployment. Suppose the economy is at the natural rate of unemployment and the Fed decreases the money supply to lower the rate of inflation. Workers analyze available information on the future impact of the Fed's action from AFL-CIO economists and other sources. They are convinced that policymakers are committed to decreasing aggregate demand until the price level recedes. Armed with this analysis, workers are not surprised, and they reduce their nominal wages as prices fall. In this case, there is no short-run Phillips curve. Contrary to adaptive expectations, inflation can be cured without recession because workers are not caught off guard.

Keynesians reject rational expectations theory because they argue that prices and wages are "sticky" downward (see Exhibit 4 of the chapter on aggregate demand and supply). On the other hand, the classical economists believed that the economy automatically adjusts after short-run delays to full employment in the long run. But in the rational expectations model, not so! There is no short run. Nevertheless, because the theory of rational expectations is similar to the self-correction model of the classical economists, rational expectationists are called *new classical* economists.

> **CONCLUSION:** *According to rational expectations theory, flexible wages and prices adjust immediately to negated predictable monetary and fiscal policy changes, so the economy's self-correction mechanism will restore the natural rate of unemployment. Therefore, discretionary policies should be abandoned, and fixed-rule, stable policies to achieve constant money supply growth and a balanced federal budget are therefore the best way to lower the inflation rate.*

✔ CHECKPOINT

Does Rational Expectations Theory Work in the Classroom?

An economics professor is considering improving class attendance and preparation by giving pop quizzes. Two approaches are being considered: If rational expectations theory operates in the classroom, should the professor (1) give pop quizzes on days when homework is due or (2) keep the pop quizzes a secret and give them randomly?

27-4 Applying the AD-AS Model to the Great Expectations Debate

The distinction between adaptive expectations and rational expectations can be analyzed using the aggregate demand-aggregate supply model presented in Exhibit 6. Assume the economy is currently in equilibrium at point E_1, with a full-employment output of $6 trillion. Now suppose the Fed pursues an expansionary monetary policy designed to create jobs and further reduce unemployment. Hence, the aggregate demand curve shifts rightward from AD_1 to AD_2 along the short-run aggregate supply curve $SRAS_1$. Based on adaptive expectations theory, a monetarist urges the Fed to leave the economy alone. The monetarist's prediction is that the economy will move from equilibrium at E_1 to E_2, causing real GDP to rise from the potential GDP of $6 trillion to the GDP of $6.5 trillion. Recall from Exhibit 9 of the chapter on business cycles and unemployment that this condition in the

EXHIBIT 6	Adaptive Expectations versus Rational Expectations

Suppose policymakers use expansionary policies to increase the aggregate demand curve from AD_1 to AD_2. Adaptive expectations theory argues that labor adjusts nominal wages sluggishly. As a result, the path of the economy is E_1 to E_2 to E_3 with a temporary increase in real GDP to $6.5 trillion and lower unemployment at point E_2. The theory of rational expectations is the competing view that the expansionary policy used to increase the aggregate demand curve from AD_1 to AD_2 is anticipated. Workers anticipate that the price level (CPI) will rise to 110, so they increase their nominal wages without a period of adjustment. As a result, the aggregate supply curve shifts from $SRAS_1$ to $SRAS_2$, causing the economy to move directly from equilibrium point E_1 to point E_3. The result of Keynesian expansionary policies under both theories is that inflation becomes worse and there is no effect on real GDP or employment.

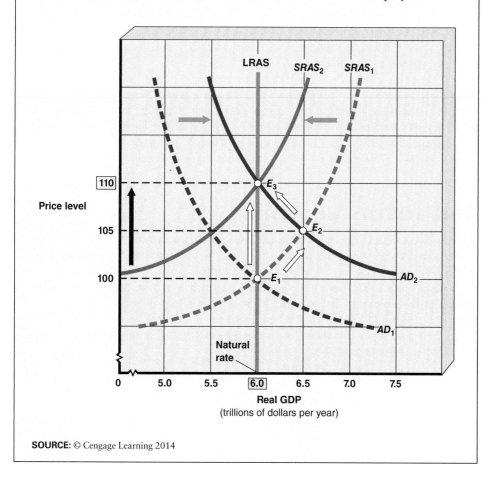

SOURCE: © Cengage Learning 2014

economy is a positive GDP gap of $0.5 trillion. In addition, the price level (CPI) increases from 100 to 105. Eventually, at equilibrium E_2, with unemployment below the natural rate, workers are no longer "caught off guard" and demand higher nominal wages to offset the rise in prices. As a result, production costs rise, causing the short-run aggregate supply curve to shift leftward from $SRAS_1$ to $SRAS_2$; therefore, a new equilibrium is established at E_3. This response drives up the unemployment rate to the natural rate as real output returns to the initial level of $6 trillion. However, Fed activism has not had a neutral effect on the price level because it has risen from the initial level of 100 to 110. The monetarist's prediction is therefore higher inflation and no impact on employment and real GDP in the long run.

A rational expectationist sees events differently. Most people are not "fooled." They are able to rationally predict the consequences of expansionary monetary policies. People anticipate that the economy will move from point E_1 to point E_3, the price level will rise from 100 to 110, and real GDP will not change. Consequently, businesses and workers do not stumble around in the dark, unable to see what the actual inflation rate is going to be. They know, or *anticipate*, that the inflation rate is going to rise 10 percent, and they react immediately by raising prices and wages 10 percent. Because prices and wages increase quickly and proportionately, rational expectations theory predicts a direct path of change in the economy's equilibrium from E_1 to E_3. Stated differently, if firms and workers formulate expectations rationally, any impact of stimulative monetary policy is nullified. Under rational expectations theory, only *unanticipated* or *surprise* policies can influence output and employment. But monetary and fiscal policies based on surprises are not practical.

If workers foresee inflation and prevent erosion of their real wages by demanding and receiving nominal wage raises in advance, aggregate supply is the vertical curve, LRAS. When real wages remain unchanged, there is no incentive for businesses to alter production as prices rise. If rational expectations theory is correct, the economy does not enjoy the short-lived pleasure of lower unemployment at point E_2, as predicted by adaptive expectations theory.

27-5 Incomes Policy

Suppose we accept the power of unions and businesses to raise wages and prices as inevitable. Let's also assume Milton Friedman is correct that discretionary monetary and fiscal policies are useless or counterproductive. Then what approach is left to fight inflation? There is another way, used in the past, which is a collection of regulatory policies called incomes policies. Incomes policies are federal government policies designed to affect the real incomes of workers by controlling nominal wages and prices. Such policies include presidential jawboning, wage-price guidelines, and wage-price controls.

27-5a PRESIDENTIAL JAWBONING

The mildest form of incomes policies is jawboning. Jawboning is oratory intended to pressure unions and businesses to reduce wage and price increases. The government attempts to prevent or roll back wage and price hikes by appealing to labor and business leaders. The most spectacular success with this technique occurred in 1962. President John F. Kennedy called major U.S. steel manufacturers and convinced them to rescind their price increases. But President Kennedy jawboned with a club in hand. He threatened to sell government stockpiles of steel at lower prices.

Incomes policies

Federal government policies designed to affect the real incomes of workers by controlling nominal wages and prices. Such policies include presidential jawboning, wage-price guidelines, and wage-price controls.

Jawboning

Oratory intended to pressure unions and businesses to reduce wage and price increases.

The president also informed the firms that those failing to cooperate would lose government contracts to firms that would lower prices. President Lyndon Johnson followed Kennedy's example and jawboned even more. Then there was the "Blow the Whistle" program under President Richard Nixon. An official agency was established to monitor unwarranted price increases and publicly announce violators of the national interest.

Most economists argue that firms raise prices when changes in demand or cost make it profitable to do so. Jawboning may do a little good for a while, but over time, it is a blunt weapon against inflation.

27-5b WAGE AND PRICE GUIDELINES

A more formal policy to cool down the inflation rate is to establish wage and price guidelines. Wage and price guidelines are voluntary standards set by the government for "permissible" wage and price increases. The Truman and Eisenhower administrations made unsystematic attempts to discourage business and labor from raising prices and wages. But the first systematic wage and price guideline program was initiated during the Kennedy administration, and this approach was also used during the Johnson and Carter administrations. For example, the Carter administration asked labor unions to limit their wage increases to 7 percent. Violators were identified in hopes that adverse publicity would force the unions to comply. Without any enforcement mechanism, the dominant view among economists is that guidelines accomplish little against self-interest.

Wage and price guidelines

Voluntary standards set by the government for "permissible" wage and price increases.

27-5c WAGE AND PRICE CONTROLS

When guidelines have the force of law, the economy moves to a mandatory system of wage and price controls. Wage and price controls are legal restrictions on wage and price increases. Violations can result in fines and imprisonment. Once people believe wages and prices are under control by law, the good news is that they expect lower prices. The bad news is that controls are government interference with market supply and demand.

As discussed in Chapter 4, a ceiling price established below the equilibrium price will cause shortages in markets (see Exhibit 5 in Chapter 4). This usually means rationing of such scarce items as gasoline. When price is not allowed to serve as the rationing device, consumers must incur higher opportunity costs by waiting in long lines for gasoline. This happened in 1979, when the government imposed a price ceiling on gasoline. Another rationing device is government ration coupons that give the right to buy a good. Ration coupons were used for many goods during World War II. Shortages also lead to *black markets*, which are illegal markets for goods at unregulated prices. To enforce the system requires a government bureaucracy at taxpayers' expense.

Long lines for products, ration coupons, and black markets are not popular. This explains why wage and price controls appear primarily during war and rarely in peacetime. The United States has imposed wage and price controls during World War II; the Korean War and the Nixon administration hoped to combat high inflationary expectations built up during the Vietnam War. The inflation rate from 1969 to 1971 averaged 5.2 percent, an alarming rate in those days. The plan was to control inflation and then fight unemployment, which averaged 4.8 percent over the

Wage and price controls

Legal restrictions on wage and price increases. Violations can result in fines and imprisonment.

same period. The first phase of the attack was a 90-day freeze on wages and prices in August 1971. A 15-member Pay Board and a 7-member Price Commission administered the controls. For three months, businesses could not raise prices, wages were frozen, and landlords could not charge higher rents. The intent was to give inflationary expectations a shock treatment. Then the freeze lifted, and wage and price controls were established to limit increases between 1971 and 1974. The bottom line is that in 1971, the inflation rate was 4.4 percent. In 1973, the inflation rate climbed to 6.2 percent. When the experiment with controls ended in 1974, the inflation rate rose to 11 percent. During the same period, the unemployment rate remained between 5 and 6 percent. Obviously, controls did not slay the inflation dragon, although some economists have argued that controls made the dragon less fierce.

In 1968, the Council of Economic Advisors eloquently stated the opinion of most economists on wage and price controls:

> While such controls may be necessary under conditions of an all-out war, it would be folly to consider them as a solution to inflationary pressures that accompany high employment under any other circumstance. ... Although such controls may be unfortunately popular when they are in effect, the appeal quickly disappears once people live under them.[3]

The majority view is that controls destroy the efficient allocation of resources provided by the price system and intrude on economic freedom. Defenders of controls believe this is a small price to pay.

✔ CHECKPOINT

Can Wage and Price Controls Cure Stagflation?

Suppose war in the Persian Gulf destroys much of the world's oil reserves. As a result, the U.S. economy is experiencing a bout of stagflation. You are a member of Congress, and a bill is introduced to fight the problems of high inflation and high unemployment by imposing wage and price controls. Using the AD-AS model, will you vote in favor of controls to cure stagflation by freezing the price level? [Hint: Look at Exhibit 5 of Chapter 4 and Exhibit 12(a) in the chapter on aggregate demand and supply.]

27-6 How Different Macroeconomic Theories Attack Inflation

If incomes policies do not cure an overheated economy during peacetime, policymakers must decide which macroeconomic school "hat" to wear. Exhibit 7 gives a brief description of how four basic macroeconomic models deal with inflation. Recall the monetarist view presented in the previous chapter and supply-side economics explained in the chapter on fiscal policy.

---

[3]*Annual Report of the Council of Economic Advisors* (Washington, D.C.: Government Printing Office, 1968), p. 119.

EXHIBIT 7	How Different Macroeconomic Models Cure Inflation

School of thought
Monetarism

Milton Friedman

Inflation prescription
Monetarists see the cause of inflation as "too much money chasing too few goods," based on the quantity of money theory (MV = PQ). To cure inflation, they would cut the money supply and force the Fed to stick to a fixed money supply growth rate. In the short run, the unemployment rate will rise, but in the long run, it self-corrects to the natural rate.

School of thought
Keynesianism

John Maynard Keynes

Inflation prescription
Keynesians believe in using contractionary fiscal and monetary policies to cool an overheated economy. To decrease aggregate demand, they advocate that the government use tax hikes and/or spending cuts. The Fed should reduce the money supply and cause the rate of interest to rise. The opportunity cost of reducing inflation is greater unemployment. Keynesians also believe that incomes policies are effective.

School of thought
Supply-side economics

Arthur Laffer

Inflation prescription
Supply-siders view the cause of inflation as "not enough goods." Their approach is to increase aggregate supply through cuts in marginal tax rates, government regulations, and import barriers. The effect provides incentives to work, invest, and expand production capacity. Thus, both the inflation rate and the unemployment rate fall.

School of thought
New classical school

Robert Lucas

Inflation prescription
The theory of rational expectations asserts that the public must be convinced that policymakers will stick to restrictive and persistent fiscal and monetary policies. If policymakers have credibility, the inflation rate will be anticipated and will quickly fall without a rise in unemployment.

Source: © Cengage Learning 2014

Ford's Whip Inflation Now (WIN) Button

Applicable Concept: incomes policies

The most interesting historical artifact of the fight against inflation is gathering dust in the White House attic. In October 1974, President Gerald Ford proposed the "WIN" button to a joint session of Congress. The idea was that Americans would wear their "Whip Inflation Now" buttons, and this would break the wage-price spiral. The WIN button represented an appeal to patriotism that would discourage businesses and labor from raising prices and wages.

The logical question is, What circumstances drove the president of the United States to use a button against inflation? We will begin the story in 1971, when the Nixon administration approved wage and price controls to cool inflationary expectations. Beginning in 1972, bad crops caused food prices to soar, and the OPEC oil embargo boosted the price of crude oil. These supply shocks boosted the inflation rate from 3.2 percent in 1972 to 6.2 percent in 1973. Clearly, the wage and price control program was falling apart before controls ended in 1974.

Following the demand-management prescription against inflation, the Fed raised the discount rate in late 1973. Federal Reserve Chair Arthur Burns stated that the Fed must follow a contractionary

monetary policy for years to come. Despite the Fed's restrictive policy, the inflation rate rose to an annual rate of about 14 percent in early 1974. By late 1974, the unemployment rate had risen to 6 percent, but policymakers remained committed to anti-inflation policies. The Fed raised the discount rate again in the fall of 1974, and President Ford called an economic summit meeting. The outcome of the summit was a resolve to stick to the battle plan and beat inflation before turning to the worsening unemployment problem. Aiming for public support, President Ford unveiled the WIN button, accompanied by a tax surcharge and federal spending ceiling proposals. While the fight against inflation preoccupied policymakers, the unemployment rate rose from 5.6 percent in 1974 to 8.5 percent in 1975. The percentage change in real GDP between 1974 and 1975 was –0.6 percent, and recession suddenly replaced inflation as the number one enemy. In response, Congress approved a $22.8 billion tax cut bill in 1975, and the Fed increased the money supply. In 1974, the inflation rate was 11.0 percent, and in 1975, the inflation rate was still at the high rate of 9.1 percent.

What caused this puzzling twist in stabilization policy to deal with stagflation? Many economists

© Bettmann/CORBIS

explain this turn of events by the absence of a conceptual framework to understand the effects of supply shocks on the aggregate supply curve. Instead, policymakers tried to shift the aggregate demand curve back and forth while asking people to wear a WIN button.

Analyze the Issue

Assume the economy is in equilibrium at full employment and the public anticipates restrictive monetary and fiscal policies, including WIN buttons, which decrease aggregate demand in order to combat inflation. Use the AD-AS model depicted in Exhibit 6 to explain the new classical predictions of the impact on the price level, real GDP, and the unemployment rate.

Key Concepts

Phillips curve
Natural rate hypothesis
Adaptive expectations theory

Political business cycle
Rational expectations theory
Incomes policies

Jawboning
Wage and price guidelines
Wage and price controls

Summary

- The **Phillips curve** shows a stable inverse relationship between the inflation rate and the unemployment rate. If policymakers reduce inflation, unemployment increases, and vice versa. During the 1960s, the curve closely fit the inflation and unemployment rates in the United States. Since 1970, the Phillips curve has not conformed to the stable inflation-unemployment trade-off pattern of the 1960s.

The Phillips Curve for the United States in the 1960s

SOURCE: *Economic Report of the President 2012*, http://www.gpoaccess.gov/eop/, Tables B-15 and B-64.

- The **natural rate hypothesis** argues that the economy self-corrects to the natural rate of unemployment. Over time, changes in the rate of inflation are fully anticipated, and prices and wages rise or fall proportionately. As a result, the long-run Phillips curve is a vertical line at the natural rate of unemployment. Thus, Keynesian demand-management policies ultimately cause only higher or lower inflation, and the natural rate of unemployment remains unchanged.

- **Adaptive expectations theory** is the proposition that people base their economic forecasts on recent past information, rather than future information. Once the government causes the inflation rate to rise or fall, people adapt their inflationary expectations to the current inflation rate. The result is a short-run Phillips curve that intersects the vertical long-run Phillips curve. Over time, the economy self-corrects to the natural rate of unemployment.

- The **political business cycle** is created by the incentive for politicians to manipulate the economy to get reelected. Using expansionary policies, officeholders can stimulate the economy before an election. Unemployment falls, and the price level rises. After the election, the strategy is to contract the economy to fight inflation and unemployment rises.

- **Rational expectations theory** argues that it is naive to believe that people change their inflationary expectations based only on the current inflation rate. Rational expectationists belong to the new classical school. Assuming the impact of government policy is predictable, people immediately anticipate higher or lower inflation. Workers quickly change their nominal wages as businesses change prices. Consequently, inflation worsens or improves, and unemployment remains unchanged at the natural rate. Thus, there is no short-run Phillips curve, and the vertical long-run Phillips curve is identical to adaptive expectations theory.

- **Incomes policies** are a variety of federal government programs aimed at directly controlling wages and prices. Incomes policies include jawboning, wage-price guidelines, and wage-price controls. Over time, incomes policies tend to be ineffective.

- **Wage and price controls** are legal restrictions on wages and prices. Most economists do not favor wage and price controls in peacetime.

Such controls are expensive to administer, destroy efficiency, and intrude on economic freedom.

Summary of Conclusion Statements

- Changes in aggregate demand cause a movement along a stationary Phillips curve.
- According to adaptive expectations theory, expansionary monetary and fiscal policies to reduce the unemployment rate are useless in the long run. After a short-run reduction in unemployment, the economy will self-correct to the natural rate of unemployment, but at a higher inflation rate. Thus, there is no long-run trade-off between inflation and unemployment.
- According to rational expectations theory, expansionary monetary and fiscal policies used to reduce unemployment are not only useless,

but also harmful because the only result is higher inflation.
- According to rational expectations theory, flexible wages and prices adjust immediately to negate predictable monetary and fiscal policy changes, so the economy's self-correction mechanism will restore the natural rate of unemployment. Therefore, discretionary policies should be abandoned, and fixed-rule, stable policies to achieve constant money supply growth and a balanced federal budget are the best way to lower the inflation rate.

Study Questions and Problems

1. What is a Phillips curve? Assuming the economy's aggregate supply curve is stable, how would an increase in aggregate demand affect the unemployment rate and the inflation rate?

2. What were the inflation rate and the unemployment rate last year? Do these rates lie on a Phillips curve?

3. What happened in the 1970s and early 1980s to cast doubt on the Phillips curve?

4. Suppose you flipped an honest coin ten times and heads came up eight times. You are about to toss the coin another ten times. Using adaptive expectations, how many heads do you expect? Based on rational expectations, how many heads do you expect?

5. According to adaptive expectations, what happens to the inflation rate and the

unemployment rate in the following situations?
   a. Initially, the economy is operating at the natural rate of 6 percent unemployment. The anticipated rate of inflation is 6 percent, and the actual rate is also 6 percent.
   b. In the next period, there is an unexpected rise in the inflation rate to 10 percent.
   c. In the next period, there is an unexpected rise in the inflation rate to 12 percent.

6. Explain what happens under adaptive expectations theory when monetary and fiscal policymakers use expansionary policy to achieve an unemployment rate below the natural rate.

7. Keynesians believe monetary and fiscal policymakers should stabilize the business cycle. Compare the political business cycle to Keynesian policy objectives.

8. Use Exhibit 8 to answer the questions that follow.
   a. Which points represent the natural unemployment rate?
   b. Which points represent an unemployment rate below the natural unemployment rate?
   c. Which points represent an unemployment rate above the natural unemployment rate?
   d. Explain points A and D on the graph.
   e. Explain points B and C on the graph.
   f. Explain points E and F on the graph.
   g. Why is curve PC_2 to the right of curve PC_1?

9. Based on rational expectations theory, what happens to the inflation rate and the unemployment rate in the following situations?
   a. Initially, the economy is operating at the natural unemployment rate of 4 percent, and the inflation rate is also 4 percent. People correctly anticipate that an increase in the money supply will increase the inflation rate to 6 percent next year.
   b. In the next period, people correctly forecast that a tax cut will cause the inflation rate to rise to 8 percent.
   c. In the next period, they anticipate that the Fed's hike in the discount rate will cause the inflation rate to fall to 4 percent.

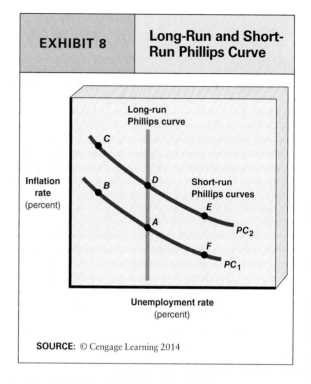

EXHIBIT 8   **Long-Run and Short-Run Phillips Curve**

SOURCE: © Cengage Learning 2014

For Online Exercises, go to the Tucker Web site at www.cengage.com/economics/tucker.

✔ CHECKPOINT ANSWERS

Does Rational Expectations Theory Work in the Classroom?

Under rational expectations, if the students know what is going to happen, they will use this information to negate the policy. If pop quizzes are given on the same day homework is due, the rational students will be certain to attend class on those days and take cuts on other days. If quizzes are random, quiz dates are unknown, so there is always a chance that missing a class may mean missing a quiz. If you said the professor will keep pop quizzes a secret and give them randomly, **YOU ARE CORRECT.**

Can Wage and Price Controls Cure Stagflation?

Assume the economy begins in equilibrium at E_1 in Exhibit 9 and an oil shock causes the economy to move to a new equilibrium at E_2. Without wage and price controls, the price level increases from 150 to 200, and real GDP decreases from $4 trillion to $3 trillion. Now assume laws keep the price level frozen at 150. This means firms cannot raise prices to meet higher costs, so under controls, they are forced to lay off more workers and cut production even further. The economy's equilibrium moves from E_2 to E_3, and real GDP is $2 trillion, rather than $3 trillion, causing unemployment to climb even higher.

Using wage and price controls to fight inflation would cause an even more severe decrease in real GDP; therefore, unemployment is greater than would otherwise be the case. If you voted *no* on the wage and price controls bill because it causes greater shortages and a deeper recession, **YOU ARE CORRECT.**

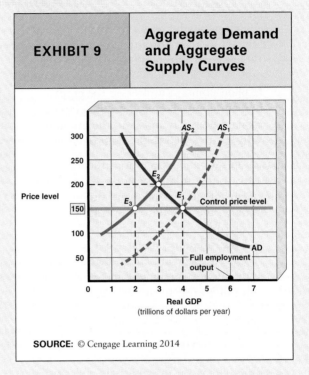

EXHIBIT 9

Aggregate Demand and Aggregate Supply Curves

SOURCE: © Cengage Learning 2014

Sample Quiz

For an explanation of the correct answers, visit the Tucker Web site at www.cengage.com/economics/tucker.

1. The Phillips curve relates the inflation rate to
   a. the unemployment rate.
   b. GDP.
   c. disposable personal income.
   d. the interest rate.

2. On a Phillips curve diagram, an increase in the rate of inflation, other things being equal, is represented by a(an)
   a. upward movement along the Phillips curve.
   b. downward movement along the Phillips curve.
   c. upward shift of the Phillips curve.
   d. downward shift of the Phillips curve.

3. Economists began to lose confidence in the Phillips curve during the
   a. 1930s.
   b. 1960s.
   c. 1970s.
   d. 1980s.

4. The Phillips curve
   a. was relatively well-defined during the 1960s.
   b. demonstrates how to achieve stable economic growth.
   c. shows the trade-off between deficits and inflation.
   d. helps to stimulate entrepreneurial profits.

Sample Quiz *continued*

5. If the long-run Phillips curve is vertical, then any government policy designed to lower
   a. unemployment will not change the unemployment rate and only increase the inflation rate.
   b. unemployment will work, leaving the inflation rate unchanged.
   c. inflation will cause employment to rise.
   d. unemployment will work, causing the inflation rate to fall.

6. The natural rate hypothesis argues that the economy will
   a. self-correct to the natural rate of inflation.
   b. require expansionary fiscal policy to reach the natural rate of unemployment.
   c. self-correct to the natural rate of unemployment.
   d. require expansionary monetary policy to reach the natural rate of unemployment.

7. The long-run Phillips curve is a(an) _____ line at the natural rate of unemployment.
   a. horizontal
   b. vertical
   c. upward-sloping
   d. downward-sloping

8. Under the natural rate hypothesis, expansionary monetary and fiscal policies can at *best* produce a
   a. permanent change in the long-run Phillips curve.
   b. short-run change in the unemployment rate.
   c. long-run change in the unemployment rate.
   d. permanent change in the unemployment rate.

9. The hypothesis that people believe that the *best* indicator of the future is the recent past is
   a. rational expectations.
   b. adaptive expectations.
   c. lagged expectations.
   d. trend expectations.

10. Under adaptive expectations theory, people expect the rate of inflation this year to be
    a. zero, regardless of the rate last year.
    b. the same as last year.

c. the rate based on predictable fiscal policies.
d. All of the answers are correct.

11. According to adaptive expectations theory, expansionary monetary and fiscal policies to reduce the unemployment rate are
    a. useless in the long run.
    b. useless in the short run.
    c. ineffective on the price level.
    d. None of the answers are correct.

12. "Preannounced, stable policies to achieve a low and constant money supply growth and a balanced federal budget are therefore the *best* way to lower the inflation rate." This statement best illustrates
    a. Keynesian theory.
    b. rational expectations theory.
    c. incomes policy.
    d. supply-side theory.

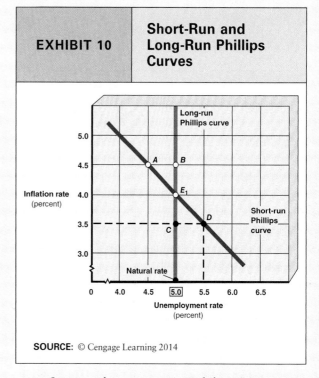

EXHIBIT 10	Short-Run and Long-Run Phillips Curves

SOURCE: © Cengage Learning 2014

13. Suppose the economy in Exhibit 10 is at point E_1, and the Fed increases the money supply. If people have adaptive expectations, then the economy will move

Sample Quiz *continued*

a. to point *A* in the short run and point *B* in the long run.

b. directly to point *B*.

c. to point *C* in the short run and point *D* in the long run.

d. directly to point *D*.

14. Suppose the economy in Exhibit 10 is at point E_1, and the Fed increases the money supply. If people have rational expectations, then the economy will move

a. to point *A* in the short run and point *B* in the long run.

b. directly to point *B*.

c. to point *C* in the short run and point *D* in the long run.

d. directly to point *D*.

15. Which of the following is *not* an example of an incomes policy?

a. presidential jawboning

b. wage and price guidelines

c. wage and price controls

d. All of the above answers are correct.

EXHIBIT 11	Aggregate Demand and Aggregate Supply Curves

SOURCE: © Cengage Learning 2014

16. As shown in Exhibit 11, if people behave according to adaptive expectations theory, an increase in the aggregate demand curve from AD_1 to AD_2 will cause the economy to move

a. directly from E_1 to E_3 and then remain at E_3.

b. directly from E_1 to E_2 and then remain at E_2.

c. from E_1 to E_2 initially and then eventually back to E_1.

d. from E_1 to E_2 initially and then eventually to E_3.

17. As shown in Exhibit 11, if people behave according to adaptive expectations theory, an increase in the aggregate demand curve from AD_1 to AD_2 will cause the price level to move

a. directly from 100 to 110 and then remain at 110.

b. directly from 100 to 105 and then remain at 105.

c. from 100 to 105 initially and then eventually back to 100.

d. from 100 to 105 initially and then eventually to 110.

18. As shown in Exhibit 11, if people behave according to adaptive expectations theory, an increase in the aggregate demand curve from AD_1 to AD_2 will cause

a. labor to adjust nominal wages sluggishly.

b. the aggregate supply curve to shift from $SRAS_1$ to $SRAS_2$.

c. the price level to eventually rise from 100 to 110.

d. All of the above answers are correct.

19. As shown in Exhibit 11, if people behave according to rational expectations theory, an increase in the aggregate demand curve from AD_1 to AD_2 will cause the price level to move

a. directly from 100 to 105 and then remain at 105.

b. directly from 100 to 110 and then remain at 110.

Sample Quiz *continued*

c. from 100 to 105 initially and then eventually back to 100.

d. from 100 to 105 initially and then eventually to 110.

20. As shown in Exhibit 11, if people behave according to rational expectations theory, an increase in the aggregate demand curve from AD_1 to AD_2 will cause the economy to move

a. directly from E_1 to E_3 and then remain at E_3.

b. directly from E_1 to E_2 and then remain at E_2.

c. from E_1 to E_2 initially and then eventually back to E_1.

d. from E_1 to E_2 initially and then eventually to E_3.

Road Map
Money, Banking, and Monetary Policy

This road map feature helps you tie together material in the part as you travel the Economic Way of Thinking highway. The following are review questions listed by chapter from the previous part. The key concept in each question is given for emphasis, and each question or set of questions concludes with an interactive game to reinforce the concepts. Go to the Tucker Web site at www.cengage.com/economics/tucker, select the chapter, and play the visual causation chain game designed to make learning fun. Enjoy the cheers when you are correct and suffer the jeers if you miss. For an explanation of the correct answers, please visit the tutorial at academic.cengage.com/economics/tucker.

CHAPTER 24. MONEY AND THE FEDERAL RESERVE SYSTEM

1. **Key Concept: Money supply definitions**
   Suppose you transfer $1,000 from your checking account to your savings account. How does this action affect the M1 and M2 money supplies?
   a. M1 and M2 are both unchanged.
   b. M1 falls by $1,000, and M2 rises by $1,000.
   c. M1 is unchanged, and M2 rises by $1,000.
   d. M1 falls by $1,000, and M2 is unchanged.

2. **Key Concept: Federal Reserve System**
   Which of the following groups oversees and administers the Federal Reserve System?
   a. House of Representatives
   b. President's Council of Economic Advisors
   c. U.S. Treasury Department
   d. None of the above because the Fed is an independent agency

3. **Key Concept: Monetary Control Act**
   The Monetary Control Act of 1980
   a. allowed savings and loan associations to offer checking accounts.
   b. allowed more institutions to offer checking account services.
   c. created greater competition among various financial institutions.
   d. did all of the above.
   e. did none of the above.

CHAPTER 25. MONEY CREATION

4. Key Concept: Open market operations
When the Fed sells government securities, it
a. lowers the cost of borrowing from the Fed, encouraging banks to make loans to the general public.
b. raises the cost of borrowing from the Fed, discouraging banks from making loans to the general public.
c. increases the amount of excess reserves that banks hold, encouraging them to make loans to the general public.
d. increases the amount of excess reserves that banks hold, discouraging them from making loans to the general public.
e. decreases the amount of excess reserves that banks hold, discouraging them from making loans to the general public.

5. Key Concept: Open market operations
When the Fed buys government securities, it
a. lowers the cost of borrowing from the Fed, encouraging banks to make loans to the general public.
b. raises the cost of borrowing from the Fed, discouraging banks from making loans to the general public.
c. increases the amount of excess reserves that banks hold, encouraging them to make loans to the general public.
d. increases the amount of excess reserves that banks hold, discouraging them from making loans to the general public.
e. decreases the amount of excess reserves that banks hold, discouraging them from making loans to the general public.

CHAPTER 26. MONETARY POLICY

6. Key Concept: Money demand curve
In a two-asset economy with money and T-bills, the quantity of money that people will want to hold, other things being equal, can be expected to
a. decrease as real GDP increases.
b. increase as the interest rate decreases.
c. increase as the interest rate increases.
d. do all of the above.

Causation Chain Game
The Demand for Money Curve—Exhibit 1

7. Key Concept: Equilibrium interest rate
Assume the Fed decreases the money supply and the demand for money curve is fixed. In response, people will
a. sell bonds, thus driving up the interest rate.
b. buy bonds, thus driving down the interest rate.
c. buy bonds, thus driving up the interest rate.
d. sell bonds, thus driving down the interest rate.

8. **Key Concept: Equilibrium interest rate**

   Assume a fixed demand for money curve and the Fed increases the money supply. In response, people will

   a. sell bonds, thus driving up the interest rate.
   b. sell bonds, thus driving down the interest rate.
   c. buy bonds, thus driving up the interest rate.
   d. buy bonds, thus driving down the interest rate.

   Causation Chain Game
   The Equilibrium Interest Rate—Exhibit 2

9. **Key Concept: Change in money supply**

   Assume the demand for money curve is stationary and the Fed increases the money supply. The result is that people

   a. increase the supply of bonds, thus driving up the interest rate.
   b. increase the supply of bonds, thus driving down the interest rate.
   c. increase the demand for bonds, thus driving up the interest rate.
   d. increase the demand for bonds, thus driving down the interest rate.

10. **Key Concept: Change in money supply**

    Assume a fixed demand for money curve and the Fed decreases the money supply. In response, people will

    a. sell bonds, thus driving up the interest rate.
    b. sell bonds, thus driving down the interest rate.
    c. buy bonds, thus driving up the interest rate.
    d. buy bonds, thus driving down the interest rate.

    Causation Chain Game
    The Effect of Changes in the Money Supply—Exhibit 3

11. **Key Concept: Keynesian transmission mechanism**

    The Keynesian cause-and-effect sequence predicts that a decrease in the money supply will cause interest rates to

    a. fall, boosting investment and shifting the AD curve rightward, leading to an increase in real GDP.
    b. fall, boosting investment and shifting the AD curve rightward, leading to a decrease in real GDP.
    c. rise, cutting investment and shifting the AD curve rightward, leading to an increase in real GDP.
    d. rise, boosting investment and shifting the AD curve rightward, leading to an increase in real GDP.
    e. rise, cutting investment and shifting the AD curve leftward, leading to a decrease in real GDP.

    Causation Chain Game
    The Keynesian Monetary Policy Transmission Mechanism—Exhibit 4

12. **Key Concept: Monetarists transmission mechanism**

    Most monetarists favor

    a. frequent changes in the growth rate of the money supply to avoid inflation.

b. placing the Federal Reserve under the Treasury.

c. a steady, gradual shrinkage of the money supply.

d. a constant increase in the money supply year after year equal to the potential annual growth rate in real GDP.

Causation Chain Game

The Monetarist Policy Transmission Mechanism—Exhibit 6

CHAPTER 27. THE PHILLIPS CURVE AND EXPECTATIONS THEORY

13. Key Concept: Adaptive expectations

According to adaptive expectations theory, expansionary monetary and fiscal policies to reduce the unemployment rate are

a. useless in the long run.

b. useless in the short run.

c. ineffective on the price level.

d. none of the above.

14. Key Concept: Rational expectations

The belief that the government can do absolutely nothing in either the short run or the long run to reduce the unemployment rate, because people will anticipate the government's actions, is held by the

a. rational expectations school.

b. neo-Keynesian school.

c. classical school.

d. supply-side school.

e. Keynesian school.

Causation Chain Game

The Short-Run and Long-Run Phillips Curve—Exhibit 4

The International Economy

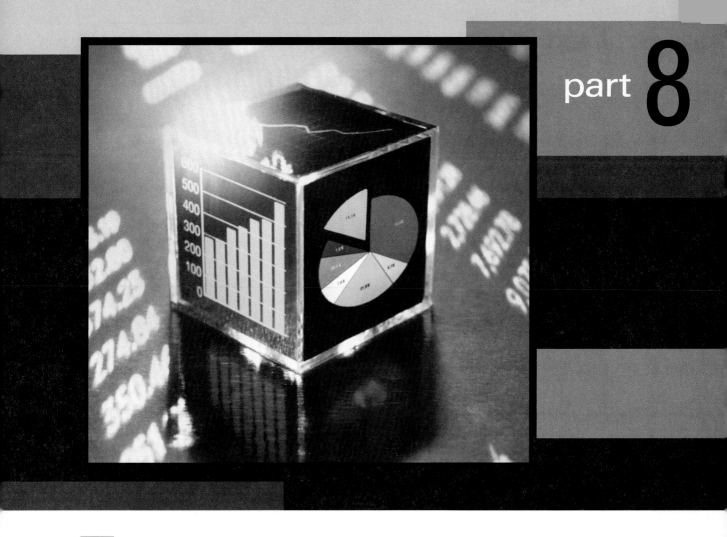

part 8

The final part of this text is devoted to global topics. The first chapter explains the importance of free trade and the mechanics of trade bookkeeping and exchange rates. Here you will find a feature on the birth of the euro. The second chapter takes a historical look at the theoretical debate over capitalism and the transition of Cuba, Russia, and China toward this system. The final chapter provides comparisons of advanced and developing countries. The chapter concludes with the fascinating economic success story of Hong Kong.

chapter 28

International Trade and Finance

Just imagine your life without world trade. For openers, you could not eat bananas from Honduras or chocolate from Nigerian cocoa beans. Nor could you sip French wine, Colombian coffee, or Indian tea. Also forget about driving a Japanese motorcycle or automobile. In addition, you could not buy Italian shoes and most DVDs, televisions, fax machines, and personal computers because they are foreign-made. Taking your vacation in London would also be ruled out if there were no world trade. And the list goes on and on, so the point is clear. World trade is important because it gives consumers more power by expanding their choices. Today, the speed of transportation and communication means producers must compete on a global basis for the favor of consumers.

Trade is often highly controversial. Regardless of whether it is a World Trade Organization (WTO) meeting or a G8 summit meeting, trade talks face protesters in the streets complaining that globalization has triggered a crisis in the world, such as global warming, poverty, soaring oil prices, or food shortages. And in the United States, outsourcing jobs to lower-paid workers overseas continues to be a hotly debated issue.

The first part of this chapter explains the theoretical reason why countries should specialize in producing certain goods and then trade them for imports. Also, you will study arguments for and against the United States protecting itself from "unfair" trade practices by other countries. In the second part of the chapter, you will learn how nations pay each other for world trade. Here you will explore international bookkeeping and discover how supply and demand forces determine that, for example, 1 dollar is worth 100 yen.

In this chapter, you will learn to solve these economics puzzles:

- How does Babe Ruth's decision not to remain a pitcher illustrate an important principle in global trade?
- Is there a valid argument for trade protectionism?
- Should the United States return to the gold standard?

28-1 Why Nations Need Trade

The United States leads the world in imports while also being one of the top exporters in the world. Exhibit 1 reveals which regions are our major trading partners (exports plus imports). Leading the list of nations is Canada, our largest trading partner, followed by China, Mexico, and Japan. Leading U.S. exports are chemicals, machinery, agricultural products, computers, automobiles, and airplanes. Major imports include petroleum, cars, trucks, clothing, and electronics. Why does a nation even bother to trade with the rest of the world? Does it seem strange for the United States to import goods it could produce for itself? Indeed, why doesn't the United States become self-sufficient by growing all its own food, including bananas, sugar, and coffee, making all its own cars, and prohibiting sales of all foreign goods? This section explains why specialization and trade are a nation's keys to a higher standard of living.

28-1a THE PRODUCTION POSSIBILITIES CURVE REVISITED

Consider a world with only two countries—the United States and Japan. To keep the illustration simple, also assume *both* countries produce only two goods—grain and steel. Accordingly, we can construct in Exhibit 2 a *production possibilities*

EXHIBIT 1	U.S. Trading Partners, 2011

In 2011, Canada, China, Mexico, and Japan accounted for over 40 percent of U.S. trade (exports plus imports).

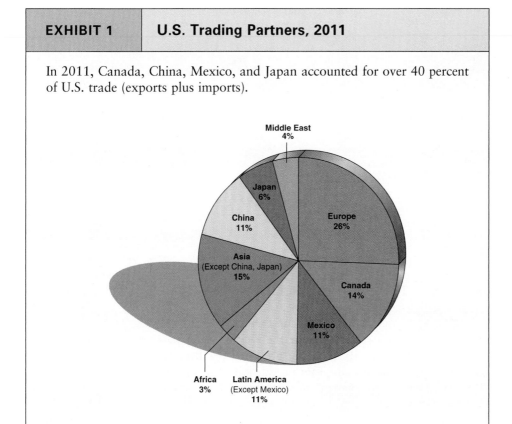

Middle East 4%
Japan 6%
China 11%
Europe 26%
Asia (Except China, Japan) 15%
Canada 14%
Mexico 11%
Africa 3%
Latin America (Except Mexico) 11%

SOURCE: Bureau of Economic Analysis, *U.S. International Transactions by Area*, http://www.bea.gov/international/index.htm, Table 12.

EXHIBIT 2	The Benefits of Specialization and Trade

As shown in part (a), assume the United States chooses point *B* on its production possibilities curve, $PPC_{U.S.}$. Without trade, the United States produces and consumes 60 tons of grain and 20 tons of steel. In part (b), assume Japan also operates along its production possibilities curve, PPC_{Japan}, at point *E*. Without trade, Japan produces and consumes 30 tons of grain and 10 tons of steel.

Now assume the United States specializes in producing grain at point *A* and imports 20 tons of Japanese steel in exchange for 30 tons of grain. Through specialization and trade, the United States moves to consumption possibility point *B'*, outside its production possibilities curve. Japan also moves to a higher standard of living at consumption possibility point *E'*, outside its production possibilities curve.

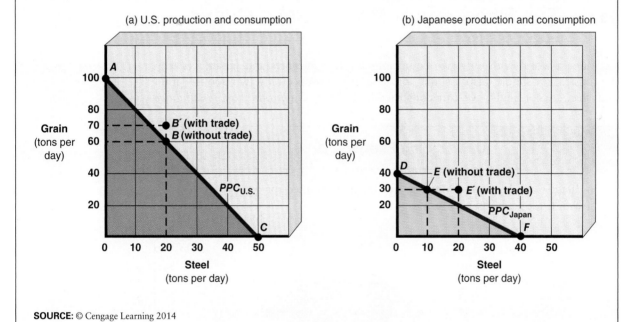

SOURCE: © Cengage Learning 2014

curve for each country. We will also set aside the *law of increasing opportunity costs*, explained in Chapter 2, and assume workers are equally suited to producing grain or steel. This assumption transforms the bowed-out shape of the production possibilities curve into a straight line.

Comparing parts (a) and (b) of Exhibit 2 shows that the United States can produce more grain than Japan. If the United States devotes all its resources to this purpose, 100 tons of grain are produced per day, represented by point *A* in Exhibit 2(a). The maximum grain production of Japan, on the other hand, is only 40 tons per day because Japan has less labor, land, and other factors of production than the United States. This capability is represented by point *D* in Exhibit 2(b).

Now consider the capacities of the two countries for producing steel. If all their respective resources are devoted to this output, the United States produces 50 tons per day (point *C*), and Japan produces only 40 tons per day (point *F*). Again, the greater potential maximum steel output of the United States reflects its greater resources. Both countries are also capable of producing other combinations of grain and steel along their respective production possibilities curves, such as point *B* for the United States and point *E* for Japan.

28-1b SPECIALIZATION WITHOUT TRADE

Assuming no world trade, the production possibilities curve for each country also defines its *consumption possibilities*. Stated another way, we assume that both countries are *self-sufficient* because without imports, they must consume only the combination chosen along their production possibilities curve. Under the assumption of self-sufficiency, suppose the United States prefers to produce and consume 60 tons of grain and 20 tons of steel per day (point *B*). Also assume Japan chooses to produce and consume 30 tons of grain and 10 tons of steel (point *E*). Exhibit 3 lists data corresponding to points *B* and *E* and shows that the total world output is 90 tons of grain and 30 tons of steel.

Now suppose the United States specializes by producing and consuming at point *A*, rather than point *B*. Suppose also that Japan specializes by producing and consuming at point *F*, rather than point *E*. As shown in Exhibit 3, specialization in each country increases total world output per day by 10 tons of grain and 10 tons of steel. Because this extra world output has the potential for making both countries better off, why wouldn't the United States and Japan specialize and produce at points *A* and *F*, respectively? The reason is that although production at these points is clearly possible, neither country wants to consume these combinations of output. The United States prefers to consume less grain and more steel at point *B* compared to point *A*. Japan, on the other hand, prefers to consume more grain and less steel at point *E*, rather than point *F*.

EXHIBIT 3	**Effect of Specialization without Trade on World Output**	
	Grain production (tons per day)	**Steel production (tons per day)**
Before specialization		
United States (at point *B*)	60	20
Japan (at point *E*)	<u>30</u>	<u>10</u>
Total world output	90	30
After specialization		
United States (at point *A*)	100	0
Japan (at point *F*)	<u>0</u>	<u>40</u>
Total world output	100	40

SOURCE: © Cengage Learning 2014

> **CONCLUSION:** *When countries specialize, total world output increases, and therefore, the potential for greater total world consumption also increases.*

28-1c SPECIALIZATION WITH TRADE

Now let's return to Exhibit 2 and demonstrate how world trade benefits countries. Suppose the United States agrees to specialize in grain production at point *A* and to import 20 tons of Japanese steel in exchange for 30 tons of its grain output. Does the United States gain from trade? The answer is Yes. At point *A*, the United States produces 100 tons of grain per day. Subtracting the 30 tons of grain traded to Japan leaves the United States with 70 tons of its own grain production to consume. In return for grain, Japan unloads 20 tons of steel on U.S. shores. Hence, specialization and trade allow the United States to move from point *A* to point *B′*, which is a consumption possibility *outside* its production possibilities curve in Exhibit 2(a). At point *B′*, the United States consumes the same amount of steel and 10 more tons of grain compared to point *B* (without trade).

Japan also has an incentive to specialize by moving its production mix from point *E* to point *F*. With trade, Japan's consumption will be at point *E′*. At point *E′*, Japan has as much grain to consume as it had at point *E*, plus 10 more tons of steel. After trading 20 tons of the 40 tons of steel produced at point *F* for grain, Japan can still consume 20 tons of steel from its production, rather than only 10 tons of steel at point *E*. Thus, point *E′* is a consumption possibility that lies *outside* Japan's production possibilities curve.

> **CONCLUSION:** *Global trade allows a country to consume a combination of goods that exceeds its production possibilities curve.*

28-2 Absolute and Comparative Advantage

Why did the United States decide to produce and export grain instead of steel? Why did Japan choose to produce and export steel rather than grain? Here you study the economic principle that determines specialization and trade. These concepts are absolute advantage and comparative advantage. Absolute advantage is the ability of a country to produce more of a good using the same or fewer resources as another country. Comparative advantage is the ability of a country to produce a good at a lower opportunity cost than another country.

Perhaps a non-economic example will clarify the difference between absolute advantage and comparative advantage. When Babe Ruth played for the New York Yankees, he was the best hitter and the best pitcher not only on the team, but also in all of major league baseball. In fact, before Ruth was traded to the Yankees and switched to the outfield, he was the best left-handed pitcher in the American League for a few seasons with the Boston Red Sox. His final record was 94–46. In other words, he had an *absolute advantage* in both hitting and throwing the baseball. Stated differently, Babe Ruth could produce the same home runs as any

Absolute advantage

The ability of a country to produce a good at a lower opportunity cost than another country.

Comparative advantage

The ability of a country to produce a good at a lower opportunity cost than another country.

other teammate with fewer times at bat. The problem was that if he pitched, he would bat fewer times because pitchers need rest after pitching. The coaches decided that the Babe had a *comparative advantage* in hitting. A few pitchers on the team could pitch almost as well as the Babe, but no one could touch his hitting. In terms of opportunity costs, the Yankees would lose fewer games if the Babe specialized in hitting.

28-2a ABSOLUTE ADVANTAGE

So far in our grain versus steel example, a country's production and trade decisions have not considered how much labor, land, or capital either the United States or Japan uses to produce a ton of grain or steel. For example, Japan might have an absolute advantage in producing *both* grain and steel. In our example, compared to the United States, Japan might use fewer resources per ton to produce grain and steel. Maybe the Japanese work harder or are more skilled. In short, the Japanese may be more productive producers, but their absolute advantage does not matter in specialization and world trade decisions. If Japan has a comparative advantage in steel, it should specialize in steel even if, compared to the United States, it can produce both grain and steel with fewer resources.

> **CONCLUSION:** *Specialization and trade are based on opportunity costs (comparative advantage) and not an absolute advantage.*

28-2b COMPARATIVE ADVANTAGE

Engaging in world trade permits countries to escape the prison of their own production possibilities curves by producing bread, cars, or whatever goods they make best. The decision of the United States to specialize in and export grain and the decision of Japan to specialize in and export steel are based on comparative advantage. Continuing our example from Exhibit 2, we can calculate opportunity costs for the two countries and use comparative advantage to determine which country should specialize in grain and which should specialize in steel. For the United States, the opportunity cost of producing 50 tons of steel is 100 tons of grain not produced, so 1 ton of steel costs 2 tons of grain. For Japan, the opportunity cost of producing 40 tons of steel is 40 tons of grain, so 1 ton of steel costs 1 ton of grain. Japan's steel is therefore cheaper in terms of grain forgone. This means Japan has a comparative advantage in steel production because it must give up less grain to produce steel than the United States. Stated differently, the opportunity cost of steel production is lower in Japan than in the United States.

The other side of the coin is to measure the cost of grain in terms of steel. For the United States, the opportunity cost of producing 100 tons of grain is 50 tons of steel not produced. This means 1 ton of grain costs 1/2 ton of steel. For Japan, the opportunity cost of producing 40 tons of grain is 40 tons of steel, so 1 ton of grain costs 1 ton of steel. The United States has a comparative advantage in grain because its opportunity cost in terms of steel forgone is lower. Thus, the United States should specialize in grain because it is more efficient in grain production. Japan, on the other hand, is relatively more efficient at producing steel and should specialize in this product.

> **CONCLUSION:** *Comparative advantage refers to the relative opportunity costs between different countries of producing the same goods. World output and consumption are maximized when each country specializes in producing and trading goods for which it has a comparative advantage.*

✓ CHECKPOINT

Do Nations with an Advantage Always Trade?

Comparing labor productivity, suppose the United States has an absolute advantage over Costa Rica in the production of calculators and towels. In the United States, a worker can produce 4 calculators or 400 towels in 10 hours. In Costa Rica, a worker can produce 1 calculator or 100 towels in the same amount of time. Under these conditions, are specialization and trade advantageous?

28-3 Free Trade versus Protectionism

Free trade

The flow of goods between countries without restrictions or special taxes.

Protectionism

The government's use of embargoes, tariffs, quotas, and other restrictions to protect domestic producers from foreign competition.

Embargo

A law that bars trade with another country.

Tariff

A tax on an import.

In theory, global trade should be based on comparative advantage and free trade. Free trade is the flow of goods between countries without restrictions or special taxes. In practice, despite the advice of economists, to some degree, every nation protects its own domestic producers from foreign competition. Behind these barriers to trade are special interest groups whose jobs and incomes are threatened, so they clamor to the government for protectionism. Protectionism is the government's use of embargoes, tariffs, quotas, and other restrictions to protect domestic producers from foreign competition.

28-3a EMBARGO

Embargoes are the strongest limit on trade. An embargo is a law that bars trade with another country. For example, the United States and other nations in the world imposed an arms embargo on Iraq in response to its invasion of Kuwait in 1990. The United States also maintains embargoes against Iran, Cuba, and North Korea.

28-3b TARIFF

Tariffs are the most popular and visible measures used to discourage trade. A tariff is a tax on an import. Tariffs are also called customs duties. Suppose the United States imposes a tariff of 2.9 percent on autos. If a foreign car costs $40,000, the amount of the tariff equals $1,160 ($40,000 × 0.029), and the U.S. price, including the tariff, is $41,160. The current U.S. tariff code specifies tariffs on nearly 70 percent of U.S. imports. A tariff can be based on weight, volume, or number of units,

EXHIBIT 4	The Average Tariff Rate, 1930–2011

Under the Smoot-Hawley Act of 1930, the average tariff rate peaked at 20 percent. Since the GATT in 1947 and other trade agreements, tariffs have declined to less than 5 percent.

SOURCES: *Economic Report of the President 1989*, http://www.gpoaccess.gov/eop/, p. 151; United States International Trade Commission, *The Economic Effect of Significant U.S. Import Restraints*, June 2002, p. 146, http://www.USITC.gov/, and *Trade Profiles*, http://stat.wto.org/CountryProfiles/US_e.htm.

or it can be *ad valorem* (figured as a percentage of the price). The average U.S. tariff is less than 5 percent, but individual tariffs vary widely. Tariffs are imposed to reduce imports by raising import prices and to generate revenues for the U.S. Treasury. Exhibit 4 shows the trend of the average tariff rate since 1930.

During the worldwide depression of the 1930s, when one nation raised its tariffs to protect its industries, other nations retaliated by raising their tariffs. Under the Smoot-Hawley tariffs of the 1930s, the average tariff in the United States reached a peak of 20 percent. Durable imports, which were one-third of imports, were subject to an unbelievable tariff rate of 60 percent. In 1947, most of the world's industrialized nations mutually agreed to end the tariff wars by signing the *General Agreement on Tariffs and Trade (GATT)*. Since then, GATT nations have met periodically to negotiate lower tariff rates. GATT agreements have significantly reduced tariffs over the years among member nations. In the 1994 *Uruguay round*, member nations signed a GATT agreement that decreased tariffs and reduced other trade barriers. The most divisive element of this agreement was the creation in 1995 of the Geneva-based World Trade Organization (WTO) to enforce rulings in global trade disputes. The WTO has 155 members and a standing appellate body to render final decisions regarding disputes between WTO members. Critics fear that the WTO might be far more likely to rule in favor of other countries in their trade disputes with the United States. Some people argue that the WTO is unaccountable, and these critics reject free trade and globalization.

To illustrate an interesting case, the United States imposed tariffs in 2002 on steel imports to protect jobs in the struggling U.S. steel industry against foreign

World Trade Organization (WTO)

An international organization of member countries that oversees international trade agreements and rules on trade disputes.

competition. The WTO ruled these tariffs were illegal, and countries in Europe and Asia prepared a list of retaliatory tariffs. These levies targeted products such as citrus fruit grown in Florida and apparel produced in southern states crucial to President Bush's reelection. Meanwhile, U.S. automakers and other steel-consuming industries complained because the tariffs increased their costs. Facing these threats, the United States removed the tariffs on steel imports in 2003. It is interesting to compare this case to the Global Economics feature titled "World Trade Slips on Banana Peel."

28-3c QUOTA

Quota

A limit on the quantity of a good that may be imported in a given time period.

Another way to limit foreign competition is to impose a quota. A quota is a limit on the quantity of a good that may be imported in a given time period. For example, the United States may allow 10 million tons of sugar to be imported over a one-year period. Once this quantity is reached, no more sugar can be imported for the year. About 12 percent of U.S. imports are subject to import quotas. Examples include import quotas on sugar, dairy products, textiles, steel, and even ice cream. Quotas can limit imports from all foreign suppliers or from specific countries. In 2005, for example, global quotas were lifted from Chinese imports. The United States and other European countries demanded quotas to protect their countries from Chinese textiles. Critics argue that, like all barriers to trade, quotas invite nations to retaliate with their own measures to restrict trade, and consumers are harmed by higher prices because of the lack of competition from lower-priced imports. In addition to embargoes, tariffs, and quotas, some nations use subtler measures to discourage trade, such as setting up an overwhelming number of bureaucratic steps that must be taken in order to import a product.

28-4 Arguments for Protection

Free trade provides consumers with lower prices and larger quantities of goods from which to choose. Thus, removing import barriers might save each family a few hundred dollars a year. The problem, however, is that imports could cost some workers their jobs and thousands of dollars per year from lost income. Thus, it is no wonder that in spite of the greater total benefits from free trade to consumers, trade barriers exist. The reason is primarily because workers and owners from import-competing firms have more at stake than consumers, so they go to Washington and lobby for protection. The following are some of the most popular arguments for protection. These arguments have strong political or emotional appeal, but weak support from economists.

28-4a INFANT INDUSTRY ARGUMENT

As the name suggests, the *infant industry argument* is that a new domestic industry needs protection because it is not yet ready to compete with established foreign competitors. An infant industry is in a formative stage and must bear high start-up costs to train an entire workforce, develop new technology, establish marketing channels, and reach economies of scale. With time to grow and protection, an infant industry can reduce costs and "catch up" with established foreign firms.

Economists ask where one draws the arbitrary line between an "infant" and a "grown-up" industry. It is also difficult to make a convincing case for protecting an infant industry in a developed country, such as the United States, where industries are well established. The infant industry argument, however, may have some validity for less-developed countries. Yet, even for these countries, there is a danger. Once protection is granted, the new industry will not experience the competitive pressures necessary to encourage reasonably quick growth and participation in world trade. Also, once an industry is given protection, it is difficult to take it away.

28-4b NATIONAL SECURITY ARGUMENT

Another common argument is that defense-related industries must be protected with embargoes, tariffs, and quotas to ensure national security. By protecting critical defense industries, a nation will not be dependent on foreign countries for the essential defense-related goods it needs to defend protect itself in wartime. The *national defense argument* has been used to protect a long list of industries, including petrochemicals, munitions, steel, and rubber.

This argument gained validity during the War of 1812. Great Britain, the main trading partner of the United States, became an enemy that blockaded our coast. Today, this argument makes less sense for the United States. The government stockpiles missiles, sophisticated electronics, petroleum, and most goods needed in wartime.

28-4c EMPLOYMENT ARGUMENT

The *employment argument* suggests that restricting imports increases domestic jobs in protected industries. According to this protectionist argument, the sale of an imported good comes at the expense of its domestically produced counterpart. Lower domestic output therefore leads to higher domestic unemployment than would otherwise be the case.

It is true that protectionism can increase output and save jobs in some industries at home. Ignored, however, are the higher prices paid by consumers because protectionism reduces competition between domestic goods and imported goods. In addition, there are employment reduction effects to consider. For example, suppose a strict quota is imposed on steel imported into our nation. Reduced foreign competition allows U.S. steelmakers to charge higher prices for their steel. As a result, prices rise and sales fall for cars and other products using steel, causing production and employment to fall in these industries. Thus, the import quota on steel may save jobs in the steel industry, but at the expense of more jobs lost in the steel-consuming industries. Also, by selling U.S. imports, foreigners earn dollars that they can use to buy U.S. exports. Import quotas cause foreigners to have fewer dollars to spend on U.S. exports, resulting in a decrease in employment in U.S. export industries. In short, protectionism may cause a net reduction in the nation's total employment.

28-4d CHEAP FOREIGN LABOR ARGUMENT

Another often heard popular claim is the *cheap labor argument*. It goes something like this: "How can we compete with such unfair competition? Labor costs $10 an hour in the United States, and firms in many developing countries pay only $1 an

World Trade Slips on Banana Peel

Applicable Concept: protectionism

Growing bananas for European markets was a multibillion-dollar bright spot for Latin America's struggling economies. In fact, about half of this region's banana exports traditionally were sold to Europe. Then, in 1993, the European Union (EU) adopted a package of quotas and tariffs aimed at cutting Europe's banana imports from Latin America. The purpose of these restrictions was to give trade preference to 66 banana-growing former colonies of European nations in Africa, the Caribbean, and the Pacific. Ignored was the fact that growers in Latin America grow higher-quality bananas at half the cost of EU-favored growers because of their low labor costs and flat tropical land near port cities.

In 1999, the World Trade Organization (WTO) ruled that the EU was discriminating in favor of European companies importing the fruit and the WTO imposed $191.4 million per year in punitive tariffs on European goods. This was the first time in the four years the WTO had been in existence that such retaliation had been approved and only the second time going back to its predecessor, the General Agreement

on Tariffs and Trade. When the EU failed to comply with the WTO findings, the United States enforced its WTO rights by imposing increased duties on EU imports, including goods ranging from cashmere sweaters and Italian handbags to sheep's milk cheese, British biscuits, and German coffeemakers. The effect of the U.S. sanctions was to double the wholesale prices of these items. Denmark and the Netherlands were exempt from the U.S. tariffs because they were the only nations that voted against the EU banana rules.

hour. Without protection against outsourcing our jobs, U.S. wages will be driven down, and our standard of living will fall."

A major flaw in this argument is that it neglects the reason for the difference in the wage rates between countries. A U.S. worker has more education, training, capital, and access to advanced technology. Therefore, if U.S. workers produce more output per hour than workers in another country, U.S. workers will earn higher wages without a competitive disadvantage. Suppose textile workers in the United States are paid $10 per hour. If a U.S. worker takes 1 hour to produce a rug, the labor cost per rug is $10. Now suppose a worker in India earns $1 per hour, but requires 20 hours to produce a rug on a handloom. In this case, the labor cost per rug is $20. Although the wage rate is 10 times higher in the United States, U.S. productivity is 20 times higher because a U.S. worker can produce 20 rugs in 20 hours, while the worker in India produces only 1 rug in the same amount of time.

Sometimes U.S. companies move their operations to foreign countries where labor is cheaper. Such moves are not always successful because the savings from paying foreign workers a lower wage rate are offset by lower productivity. Other disadvantages of foreign operations include greater transportation costs to U.S. markets and political instability.

Critics charged that the United States was pushing the case for political reasons. American companies, including Chiquita Brands International and Dole Food Company, grow most of their bananas in Latin America. With America's trade deficit running at a record level, U.S. trade experts also argued that the United States had little choice but to act against the EU for failing to abide by the WTO's ruling. Moreover, with increasing voices in the United States questioning the wisdom of globalization, it was important that the WTO prove that it could arbitrate these disputes.

In 2001, it appeared that the banana dispute might be resolved. The EU agreed to increase market access for U.S. banana distributors, and the United States lifted its retaliatory duties on EU products. The agreement also provided that the United States could reimpose the duties if the EU did not complete its phased-in reductions in restrictions on banana imports.

But the banana story just kept "slipping along."

European Union anti-fraud officials say that illegal banana trafficking is proving more lucrative than that in cocaine. A recently exposed scheme saw Italian banana importers use false licenses to pay greatly reduced customs duties on non-quota fruit. The fraud netted smugglers hundreds of millions of euros over a two-year period.

Source: © Cengage Learning 2014

In 2004, Latin American growers again complained that the EU was discriminating against their bananas in favor of producers from African, Caribbean, and Pacific countries. Under the 2001 WTO ruling, the EU was compelled to replace its complex quota and tariff system on bananas with a tariff-only regime. So the EU placed a 176 euro tariff per ton on Latin American suppliers to get into the EU market, while bananas from African and Caribbean countries could export up to 775,000 tons duty-free. The banana war continued in 2008 when a WTO dispute panel ruled for the third time that the EU tariff/quota banana regime was unfair. Finally, the EU initiated a deal agreed to in 2009 that might end this longest trade battle in history. The EU will gradually cut the import tariff on bananas from Latin America in stages until 2017. Also, the banana producing countries from African, Caribbean, and Pacific countries will receive financial aid to help them adjust to stiffer competition.

Analyze the Issue

Make an argument in favor of the European import restrictions. Make an argument against this plan.

28-5 Free Trade Agreements

The trend in recent years has been for nations to negotiate a reduction in trade barriers. In 1993, Congress approved the *North American Free Trade Agreement (NAFTA)*, which linked the United States to its first- and third-largest trading partners, Canada and Mexico. Under NAFTA, which became effective January 1, 1994, tariffs were phased out, and other impediments to trade and investment were eliminated among the three nations. For example, elimination of trade restrictions allows the United States to supply Mexico with more U.S. goods and to boost U.S. jobs. On the other hand, NAFTA was expected to raise Mexico's wages and standard of living by increasing Mexican exports to the United States. Note that NAFTA made no changes in restrictions on labor movement, and workers must enter the United States under a limited immigration quota or illegally. The success of NAFTA remains controversial. At the conclusion of this chapter, we will use data to examine its impact.

The United States and other countries are considering other free trade agreements. In Europe, 27 nations have joined the *European Union (EU)*, which is dedicated to removing all trade barriers within Europe, thereby creating a single European economy almost as large as the U.S. economy. See the Birth of the Euro boxed feature in this chapter.

Birth of the Euro

In 1958, several European nations formed a Common Market to eliminate trade restrictions among member countries. The Common Market called for gradual removal of tariffs and import quotas on goods traded among member nations. Later the name was changed to the *European Economic Community (EEC)*, and it is now called the *European Union (EU)*. This organization established a common system of tariffs for imports from nonmember nations and created common policies for economic matters of joint concern, such as agriculture and transportation. The EU now comprises the 27 nations listed in the following table.

In 1999, 11 European countries, joined later by Greece, followed the United States as an example and united in the *European Economic and Monetary Union (EMU)*. In the United States, 50 states are linked with a common currency, and the Federal Reserve serves as the central bank by conducting monetary policy for the nation. Among the states, trade, labor, and investment enjoy freedom of movement. In 2002, the EMU

Matt Trommer/Shutterstock.com

members replaced their national currencies with a single currency, the euro. The objective was to remove exchange rate fluctuations that impede cross-border transactions. This is why the U.S. Congress created a national currency in 1863 to replace state and private bank currencies.

The EU faces many unanswered questions. Unlike the states of the United States, the EU's member nations do not share a common language or governments. This makes maintaining common macro policies difficult,

The *Asian-Pacific Economic Cooperation (APEC)* was formed in 1989 and today has 21 member nations, including China, Hong Kong, Russia, Japan, and Mexico. This organization is based on a nonbinding agreement to reduce trade barriers between member nations.

In 2003, trade ministers from 34 nations met in Miami to create a plan for the world's largest free-trade area that would tear down trade barriers from Alaska to Argentina. The Free Trade Area of the Americas (FTAA) would span the Western Hemisphere except Cuba. In 2005, the *Central American Free Trade Agreement (CAFTA)* extended the free trade zone to six Central American countries that signed, including Costa Rica, Guatemala, El Salvador, Honduras, Nicaragua, and Dominican Republic. The success or failure of CAFTA will have an impact on future negotiation for FTAA.

Critics are concerned that regional free-trade accords will make global agreements increasingly difficult to achieve. Some fear that trading blocs may erect new barriers, creating "Fortress North America," "Fortress Europe," and similar impediments to the worldwide reduction of trade barriers.

Balance of payments
A bookkeeping record of all the international transactions between a country and other countries during a given period of time.

28-6 The Balance of Payments

When trade occurs between the United States and other nations, many types of financial transactions are recorded in a summary called the balance of payments. The balance of payments is a bookkeeping record of all the international transactions between a country and other countries during a given period of time.

and in recent years, Greece and several other members have experienced financial crises. France, for example, might seek to control inflation, while Germany has reducing unemployment as its highest priority. Coordinating monetary policy among EU nations is also difficult. Although the EU has established the *European Central Bank* headquartered in Frankfurt, Germany, with sole authority over the supply of euros, the central banks of member nations still function. But these national central banks operate similar to the district banks of the Federal Reserve System in the United States. Only time will tell whether EU nations will perform better with a single currency than with separate national currencies. Currently, the United Kingdom, Denmark, and Sweden still use their own currencies.

European Union (EU) Members

Austria	Finland	Latvia	Romania
Belgium	France	Lithuania	Slovenia
Bulgaria	Germany	Luxembourg	Spain
Cyprus	Greece	Malta	Sweden
Czech Republic	Hungary	Netherlands	United Kingdom
Denmark	Ireland	Poland	
Estonia	Italy	Portugal	

This summary is the best way to understand interactions between economies because it records the value of a nation's spending inflows and outflows made by individuals, firms, and governments. Exhibit 5 presents a simplified U.S. balance of payments for 2011.

Note the pluses and minuses in the table. A transaction that is a payment to the United States is entered as a positive amount. A payment by the United States to another country is entered with a minus sign. As our discussion unfolds, you will learn that the balance of payments provides much useful information.

28-6a CURRENT ACCOUNT

The first section of the balance of payments is the *current account*, which includes trade in goods and services. The most widely reported part of the current account is the balance of trade, also called the trade balance. The balance of trade is the value of a nation's imports subtracted from its exports, and it can be expressed in terms of goods, services, or goods and services. The balance of trade most often reported is in terms of goods and services. As shown in lines 1–4, the United States had a *balance of trade deficit* of −$560 billion in 2011. A trade deficit occurs when the value of a country's imports exceeds the value of its exports. When a nation has a trade deficit, it is called an *unfavorable balance of trade* because more is spent for imports than is earned from

Balance of trade

The value of a nation's imports subtracted from its exports. Balance of trade can be expressed in terms of goods, services, or goods and services.

EXHIBIT 5	U.S. Balance of Payments, 2011 (billions of dollars)
Type of transaction	
Current account	
1. Goods exports	$ +1,497
2. Goods imports	−2,236
3. Service exports	+608
4. Service imports	−429
Trade balance (lines 1–4)	−560
5. Investment income (net)	+221
6. Unilateral transfers (net)	−135
Current account balance (lines 1–6)	−474
Capital account	
7. U.S. capital inflow	+784
8. U.S. capital outflow	−396
Capital account balance (lines 7–8)	+388
9. Statistical discrepancy	+86
Net balance (lines 1–9)	0

SOURCE: Bureau of Economic Analysis, click on "Detailed Estimates" for *U.S. International Transactions*, http://www.bea.gov/international/index.htm, Table 1.

exports. Recall that net exports can have a positive (favorable) or negative (unfavorable) effect on GDP = $C + I + G + (X − M)$.

Exhibit 6 charts the annual balance of trade for the United States from 1975 through 2011. Observe that the United States experienced a *balance of trade surplus* in 1975. A trade surplus arises when the value of a country's exports is greater than the value of its imports. This is called a *favorable balance of trade* because the United States earned more from exports than it spent for imports. Since 1975, however, sizable trade deficits have occurred. These trade deficits have attracted much attention because, in part, they reflect the popularity of foreign goods and the lack of competitiveness of goods "Made in U.S.A." Between 2005 and 2008, the U.S. trade deficits reached record-breaking levels of about $700 billion due in part to the rising price of oil imports. During this period, the price per barrel grew steadily until it reached a peak in 2008, and the U.S. trade deficit with OPEC countries doubled while our trade deficit with China tripled. After 2008, oil import prices plunged sharply from a high of $134 per barrel in 2008 to $82 per barrel in 2010, and U. S. trade deficits with OPEC countries fell. Also, U.S. trade deficits with China remained constant at $262 billion between 2008 and 2010. These

EXHIBIT 6	U.S. Balance of Trade, 1975–2011 (billions of dollars)

Since 1975, the United States has experienced trade deficits in which the value of goods and services imports has exceeded the value of goods and services exports. These trade deficits attract much attention because, in part, they reflect the popularity of foreign goods in the United States. During the recession in 2001, the U.S. trade deficit narrowed briefly before continuing an upward trend. The deficit grew to an all-time high of about $700 billion between 2005 and 2008 before declining to $500 billion in 2010 and $560 billion in 2011.

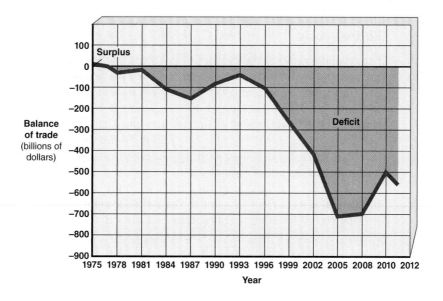

SOURCE: Bureau of Economic Analysis, *International U.S. International Transactions Accounts*, http://www.bea.gov/international/index.htm, Table 1.

factors contributed to the fall in the U.S. balance of trade in 2010. In 2011, the U.S. trade deficit rose again to $560 billion because of higher oil prices and a trade deficit with China.

Lines 3–6 of the current account in Exhibit 5 list ways other than trade of goods that move dollars back and forth between the United States and other countries. Services include insurance, banking, transportation, and tourism. For example, a Japanese tourist who pays a hotel bill in Hawaii buys an export of services, which is a plus, or credit, to our current account (line 3). Similarly, an American visitor to foreign lands buys an import of services, which is a minus, or debit, to our services and therefore a minus to our current account (line 4). Income flowing back from U.S. investments abroad, such as plants, real estate, and securities, is a payment for use of the services of U.S. capital. Foreign countries also receive income flowing from the services of their capital owned in the United States. In 2011, line 5 of the table reports a net investment income flow of $221 billion to the United States.

Finally, we consider line 6, unilateral transfers. This category includes gifts made by our government, charitable organizations, or private individuals to other governments or private parties elsewhere in the world. For example, this item includes U.S. foreign aid to other nations. Similar unilateral transfers into the United States must be subtracted to determine the *net* unilateral transfers. Net unilateral transfers for the United States were −$135 billion in 2011.

Adding lines 1–6 gives the current account balance deficit of −$474 billion in 2011. This deficit means that foreigners sent us more goods, services, investment income, and transfers than we sent to them. Because the current account balance includes more than goods and services, it is a broader measure than the trade balance. Since 1982, the trend in the current account balance has followed the swing into the red shown by the trade balance in Exhibit 6.

28-6b CAPITAL ACCOUNT

The second section of the balance of payments is the *capital account*, which records payment flows for financial capital, such as real estate, corporate stocks, bonds, government securities, and other debt instruments. For example, when Chinese investors buy U.S. Treasury bills or Japanese investors purchase farmland in Hawaii, there is an inflow of dollars into the United States. As Exhibit 5 shows, foreigners made payments of $784 billion to our capital account (line 7). This exceeded the −$396 billion outflow (line 8) from the United States to purchase foreign-owned financial capital.

An important feature of the capital account is that the United States finances any deficit in its current account through this account. The capital account balance in 2011 was $388 billion. This surplus indicates that there was more foreign investment in U.S. assets than U.S. investment in foreign assets during this year.

> **CONCLUSION:** *A current account deficit is financed by a capital account surplus.*

The current account deficit should equal the capital account surplus, but line 9 in the exhibit reveals that the balance of payments is not perfect. The capital account balance does not exactly offset the current account balance. Hence, a credit amount is simply recorded as a statistical discrepancy; therefore, the balance of payments always balances, or equals zero.

28-6c THE INTERNATIONAL DEBT OF THE UNITED STATES

If each nation's balance of payments is always zero, why is there so much talk about a U.S. balance-of-payments problem? The problem is with the *composition* of the balance of payments. Suppose the United States runs a $500 billion deficit in its current account. This means that the current account deficit must be financed by a net annual capital inflow in the capital account of $500 billion. That is, foreign lenders, such as banks and businesses, must purchase U.S. assets and grant loans to the United States that on balance equal $500 billion. For example, a Chinese bank could buy U.S. Treasury bonds. Recall from Exhibit 7 in the chapter on federal deficits and the national debt that the portion of the national debt owed to lenders outside the United States is called *external debt*.

| EXHIBIT 7 | **U.S. Balance of Trade with Selected Countries, 2011 (billions of dollars)** |

The United States has its greatest trade deficits with China, Mexico, and Germany.

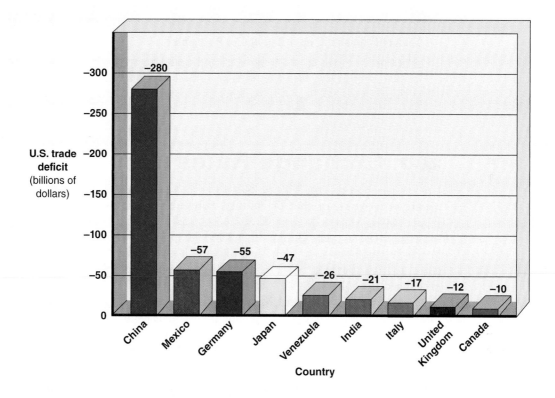

SOURCE: Bureau of Economic Analysis, *U.S. International Transactions by Area*, http://www.bea.gov/international/index.htm, Table 12.

In 1984, the United States became a net debtor for the first time in about 70 years. This means that investments in the United States accumulated by foreigners— stocks, bonds, real estate, and so forth—exceeded the stock of foreign assets owned by the United States. In fact, during the decade of the 1980s, the United States moved from being the world's largest creditor nation to being the largest debtor nation.

Exhibit 7 shows that the United States has its largest trade deficits with China, Mexico, Germany, and Japan, respectively. The concern over continuing trade deficits and the rising international debt that accompanies them is that the United States is artificially enjoying a higher standard of living. When the United States continues to purchase more goods and services abroad than it exports, it might find itself "enjoying now and paying later." Suppose the Chinese and other foreigners decide not to make new U.S. investments and loans. In this case, the United States will be forced to eliminate its trade deficit by bringing exports and imports into balance. In fact, if other countries not only refuse to provide new capital inflows, but also decide to liquidate their investments, the United States would be forced to run a trade surplus. Stated differently, we would be forced to tighten our belts and accept a lower standard of living. How a change in foreign willingness to purchase U.S. assets also affects the international value of the dollar is the topic to which we now turn.

✓ CHECKPOINT

Should Everyone Keep a Balance of Payments?

Nations keep balances of payments and calculate accounts such as their trade deficit or surplus. If nations need these accounts, the 50 states should also maintain balances of payments to manage their economies. Or should they? What about cities?

28-7 Exchange Rates

Each transaction recorded in the balance of payments requires an exchange of one country's currency for that of another. Suppose you buy a Japanese car made in Japan, say, a Mazda. Mazda wants to be paid in yen and not dollars, so dollars must be traded for yen. On the other hand, suppose Pink Panther Airline Company in France purchases an airplane from Boeing in the United States. Pink Panther has euros to pay the bill, but Boeing wants dollars. Consequently, euros must be exchanged for dollars.

Exchange rate

The number of units of one nation's currency that equals one unit of another nation's currency.

The critical question for Mazda, Pink Panther, Boeing, and everyone involved in world trade is, "What is the exchange rate?" The exchange rate is the number of units of one nation's currency that equals one unit of another nation's currency. For example, assume 1.81 dollars can be exchanged for 1 British pound. This means the exchange rate is 1.81 dollars = 1 pound. Alternatively, the exchange rate can be expressed as a reciprocal. Dividing 1 British pound by 1.81 dollars gives 0.552 pounds per dollar. Now suppose you are visiting England and want to buy a T-shirt with a price tag of 10 pounds. Knowing the exchange rate tells you the T-shirt costs $18.10 (10 pounds × $1.81/pound).

CONCLUSION: *An exchange rate can be expressed as a reciprocal.*

28-7a SUPPLY AND DEMAND FOR FOREIGN EXCHANGE

The exchange rate for dollars, or any nation's currency floats, which means it is determined by global forces of supply and demand. For example, consider the exchange rate of yen to dollars, shown in Exhibit 8. Like the price and the quantity of any good traded in markets, the quantity of dollars exchanged is measured on the horizontal axis, and the price per unit is measured on the vertical axis. In this case, the price per unit is the value of the U.S. dollar expressed as the number of yen per dollar.

The demand for dollars in the world currency market comes from Japanese individuals, corporations, and governments that want to buy U.S. exports. Because

EXHIBIT 8	The Supply of and Demand for Dollars

The number of Japanese yen per dollar in the foreign exchange market is determined by the demand for dollars by Japanese citizens and the supply of dollars by U.S. citizens. The equilibrium exchange rate is 100 yen per dollar, and the equilibrium quantity is $300 million per day.

SOURCE: © Cengage Learning 2014

the Japanese buyers must pay for U.S. exports with dollars, they *demand* to exchange their yen for dollars. As expected, the demand curve for dollars or any foreign currency is downward sloping. A decline in the number of yen per dollar means that one yen buys a larger portion of a dollar. This means U.S. goods and investment opportunities are less expensive to Japanese buyers because they must pay fewer yen for each dollar. Thus, as the yen price of dollars decreases, the quantity of dollars demanded by the Japanese to purchase Fords, stocks, land, and other U.S. products and investments increases. For example, suppose a CD recording of the hottest rock group has a $20 price tag. If the exchange rate is 200 yen to the dollar, a Japanese importer would pay 4,000 yen. If the price of dollars to Japanese buyers falls to 100 yen each, the same $20 CD will cost Japanese importers only 2,000 yen. This lower price causes Japanese buyers to increase their orders, which, in turn, increases the quantity of dollars demanded.

The supply curve of dollars is upward sloping. This curve shows the amount of dollars offered for exchange at various yen prices per dollar in the world currency exchange market. Similar to the demand for dollars, the supply of dollars in this market flows from individuals, corporations, and governments in the United States that want to buy Mazdas, stocks, land, and other products and investments from Japan. Because U.S. citizens must pay for the Japanese goods and services in yen, they must exchange dollars for yen. An example will illustrate why the supply curve of dollars slopes upward. Suppose a Nikon camera sells for 100,000 yen in Tokyo and the exchange rate is 100 yen per dollar or 0.01 dollar per yen ($1/100 yen). Therefore, the camera costs an American tourist $1,000. Now assume the exchange rate rises to 250 yen per dollar or 0.004 dollar per yen ($1/250 yen).

The camera will now cost the American buyer only $400. Because the prices of the Nikon camera and other Japanese products fall when the number of yen per dollar rises, Americans respond by purchasing more Japanese imports, which, in turn, increases the quantity of dollars supplied.

The foreign exchange market in Exhibit 8 is in equilibrium at an exchange rate of 100 yen for $1. As you learned in Chapter 3, if the exchange rate is above equilibrium, there will be a surplus of dollars in the world currency market. Citizens of the United States are supplying more dollars than the Japanese demand, and the exchange rate falls. On the other hand, below equilibrium, there will be a shortage of dollars in the world currency market. In this case, the Japanese are demanding more dollars than Americans supply, and the exchange rate rises.

28-7b SHIFTS IN SUPPLY AND DEMAND FOR FOREIGN EXCHANGE

For most of the years between World War II and 1971, currency exchange rates were *fixed*. Exchange rates were based primarily on gold. For example, the German mark was fixed at about 25 cents. The dollar was worth 1/35 of an ounce of gold, and 4 German marks were worth 1/35 of an ounce of gold. Therefore, 1 dollar equaled 4 marks, or 25 cents equaled 1 mark. In 1971, Western nations agreed to stop fixing their exchange rates and to allow their currencies to *float* according to the forces of supply and demand. Exhibit 9 illustrates that these rates can fluctuate widely. For

EXHIBIT 9	Changes in the Yen-per-Dollar Exchange Rate, 1980–2011

Today, most economies are on a system of flexible exchange rates. As the demand and supply curves for currencies change, exchange rates change. In 1980, 1 dollar was worth about 230 Japanese yen. By 2011, the exchange rate had dropped to a post-war low of 80 yen per dollar.

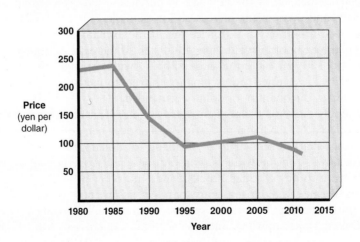

SOURCE: FRED Economic Data, http://research.stlouisfed.org/fred2/series/AEXJUS.

example, in 1980, 1 dollar was worth about 230 Japanese yen. After gyrating up and down over the years, the exchange rate hit a postwar low of 80 yen per dollar in 2011.

Recall from Chapter 3 that the equilibrium price for products changes in response to shifts in the supply and demand curves. The same supply and demand analysis applies to equilibrium exchange rates for foreign currency. There are four important sources of shifts in the supply and demand curves for foreign exchange. Let's consider each in turn.

Tastes and Preferences   Exhibit 10(a) illustrates one important factor that causes the demand for foreign currencies to shift. Suppose the Japanese lose their "taste" for tobacco, U.S. government bonds, and other U.S. products and

EXHIBIT 10	Changes in the Supply and Demand Curves for Dollars

In part (a), U.S. exports become less popular in Japan. This change in tastes for U.S. products and investments decreases the demand for dollars, and the demand curve shifts leftward from D_1 to D_2. As a result, the equilibrium exchange rate falls from 150 yen to the dollar at E_1 to 100 yen to the dollar at E_2.

Part (b) assumes U.S. citizens are influenced by the "Buy American" idea. In this case, our demand for Japanese imports decreases, and U.S. citizens supply fewer dollars to the foreign currency market. The result is that the supply curve shifts leftward from S_1 to S_2, and the equilibrium exchange rate rises from 100 yen per dollar at E_1 to 150 yen per dollar at E_2.

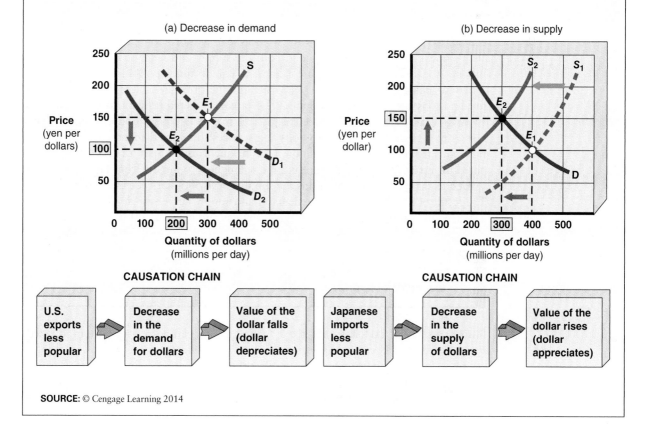

SOURCE: © Cengage Learning 2014

investment opportunities. This decline in the popularity of U.S. products in Japan decreases the demand for dollars at each possible exchange rate, and the demand curve shifts leftward from D_1 to D_2. This change causes the equilibrium exchange rate to fall from 150 yen to the dollar at E_1 to 100 yen to the dollar at E_2. Because the number of yen to the dollar declines, the dollar is said to *depreciate* or become *weaker*. Depreciation of currency is a fall in the price of one currency relative to another.

What happens to the exchange rate if the "Buy American" idea changes our tastes and the demand for Japanese imports decreases? In this case, U.S. citizens supply fewer dollars at any possible exchange rate, and the supply curve in Exhibit 10(b) shifts leftward from S_1 to S_2. As a result, the equilibrium exchange rate rises from 100 yen to the dollar at E_1 to 150 yen to the dollar at E_2. Because the number of yen per dollar rises, the dollar is said to *appreciate* or become *stronger*. Appreciation of currency is a rise in the price of one currency relative to another.

Relative Incomes   Assume income in the United States rises, while income in Japan remains unchanged. As a result, U.S. citizens buy more domestic products and more Japanese imports. The results are a rightward shift in the supply curve for dollars and a decrease in the equilibrium exchange rate. Paradoxically, growth of U.S. income leads to the dollar depreciating, or becoming weaker, against the Japanese yen.

> **CONCLUSION:** *An expansion in relative U.S. income causes a depreciation of the dollar.*

Relative Price Levels   Now we consider a more complex case in which a change in a factor causes a change in both the supply and demand curves for dollars. Assume the foreign exchange rate begins in equilibrium at 100 yen per dollar, as shown at point E_1 in Exhibit 11. Now assume the price level increases in Japan, but remains constant in the United States. The Japanese therefore want to buy more U.S. exports because they have become cheaper relative to Japanese products. This willingness of the Japanese to buy U.S. goods and services shifts the demand curve for dollars rightward from D_1 to D_2. In addition, U.S. products are cheaper for U.S. citizens compared to Japanese imports. As a result, the willingness to import from Japan is reduced at each exchange rate, which means the supply curve of dollars decreases from S_1 to S_2. The result of the shifts in both the demand and supply curves for dollars is to establish a new equilibrium at point E_2, and the exchange rate reaches 200 yen per dollar.

> **CONCLUSION:** *A rise in a trading partner's relative price level causes the dollar to appreciate.*

Relative Real Interest Rates   Changes in relative real (inflation-adjusted) interest rates can have an important effect on the exchange rate. Suppose real interest rates in the United States rise, while those in Japan remain constant. To take advantage of more attractive yields, Japanese investors buy an increased amount of bonds and other interest-bearing securities issued by private and government borrowers in the United States. This change increases the demand for dollars,

---

Depreciation of currency

A fall in the price of one currency relative to another.

Appreciation of currency

A rise in the price of one currency relative to another.

EXHIBIT 11	The Impact of Relative Price Level Changes on Exchange Rates

Begin at E_1, with the exchange rate equal to 100 yen per dollar. Assume prices in Japan rise relative to those in the United States. As a result, the demand for dollars increases, and the supply of dollars decreases. The new equilibrium is at E_2 when the dollar appreciates (rises in value) to 200 yen per dollar.

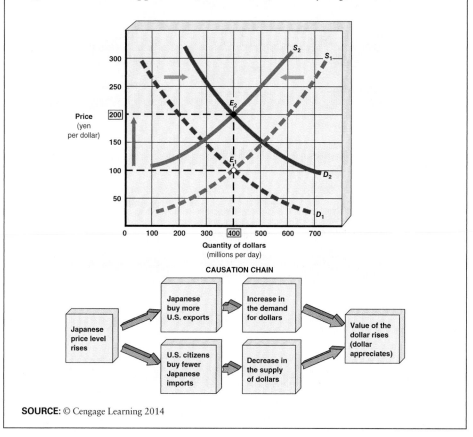

SOURCE: © Cengage Learning 2014

which increases the equilibrium exchange rate of yen to the dollar, causing the dollar to appreciate (or the yen to depreciate).

There can also be an effect on the supply of dollars. When real interest rates rise in the United States, our citizens purchase fewer Japanese securities. Hence, they offer fewer dollars at each possible exchange rate, and the supply curve for dollars shifts leftward. As a result, the equilibrium exchange rate increases, and the dollar appreciates from changes in both the demand for and supply of dollars.

28-7c THE IMPACT OF EXCHANGE RATE FLUCTUATIONS

Now it is time to stop for a minute and draw some important conclusions. As you have just learned, exchange rates between most major currencies are flexible. Instead of being pegged to gold or another fixed standard, their value floats as

EXHIBIT 12	Effects of a Strong or Weak Dollar on U.S. Trade

A strong dollar leads to a decrease in exports and an increase in imports. A weak dollar leads to an increase in exports and a decrease in imports.

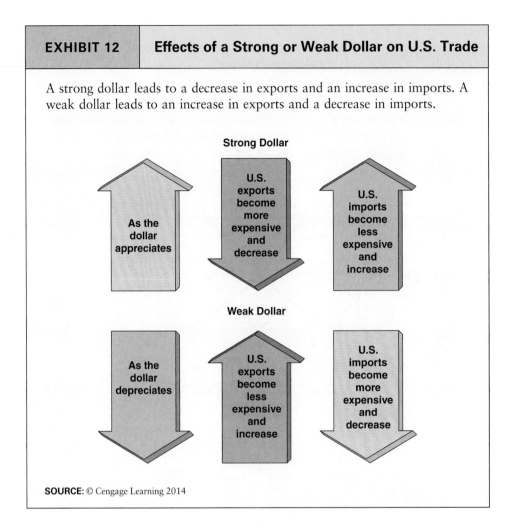

SOURCE: © Cengage Learning 2014

determined by the laws of supply and demand. Consequently, shifts in supply and demand create a weaker or a stronger dollar. But it should be noted that exchange rates do not fluctuate with total freedom. Governments often buy and sell currencies to prevent wide swings in exchange rates. In summary, the strength or weakness of any nation's currency has a profound impact on its economy.

A weak dollar is a "mixed blessing." Ironically, a weak dollar makes U.S. producers happy. Because foreigners pay less of their currency for dollars, this means U.S. producers can sell their less expensive exports to foreign buyers. As export sales rise, jobs are created in the United States. On the other hand, a weak dollar makes foreign producers and domestic consumers unhappy because the prices of Japanese cars, French wine, and Italian shoes are higher. As U.S. imports fall, jobs are lost in foreign countries.

CONCLUSION: *When the dollar is weak, or depreciates, U.S. goods and services cost foreign consumers less, so they buy more U.S. exports. At the same time, a weak dollar means foreign goods and services cost U.S. consumers more, so they buy fewer imports.*

EXHIBIT 13	U.S. Trade Balances with Mexico, 1993–2011			
Year	U.S. Exports to Mexico (billions of dollars)	U.S. Imports from Mexico (billions of dollars)	Exchange Rate (pesos per dollar)	U.S. Trade Surplus (+) or Deficit (−) (billions of dollars)
1993	$ 52	$ 48	3.12	$ +4
1995	55	71	6.45	−16
1997	82	97	7.92	−15
1999	101	120	9.55	−19
2001	118	143	9.34	−25
2003	115	152	10.79	−37
2005	143	188	10.89	−45
2007	161	231	10.93	−70
2009	152	193	13.50	−41
2011	224	281	12.43	−57

SOURCES: Bureau of Economic Analysis, *U.S. International Transactions by Area*, http://www.bea.gov/international.index.htm, Table 12 and FRED Economic Data, http://research.stlouisfed.org/fred2/data/AEXMXUS.txt.

A strong dollar is also a "mixed blessing." A strong dollar makes our major trading partners happy. When U.S. buyers pay fewer dollars for foreign currency, means the prices of Japanese cars, French wine, and Italian shoes are lower. A strong dollar, contrary to the implication of the term, makes U.S. producers unhappy because their exports are more expensive and related jobs decline. Conversely, a strong dollar makes foreign producers happy because the prices of their goods and services are lower, causing U.S. imports to rise. Exhibit 12 summarizes the weak versus strong dollar effects.

> **CONCLUSION:** *When the dollar is strong, or appreciates, U.S. goods and services cost foreign consumers more, so they buy fewer U.S. exports. At the same time, a strong dollar means foreign goods and services cost U.S. consumers less, so they buy more foreign imports.*

Finally, as promised earlier in this chapter, we return to the discussion of NAFTA in order to illustrate the impact of this free trade agreement and the effect of a strong dollar. Recall that in January 1994, NAFTA began a gradual phaseout of tariffs and other trade barriers. Exhibit 13 provides trade data for the United States and Mexico for the years surrounding NAFTA. As the exhibit shows, both exports and imports of goods and services increased sharply after NAFTA. On the

Return to the Yellow Brick Road?

Applicable Concept: exchange rates

Gold is always a fascinating story: *The Wonderful Wizard of Oz* was first published in 1900, and this children's tale has been interpreted as an allegory for political and economic events of the 1890s. For example, the Yellow Brick Road represents the gold standard, Oz in the title is an abbreviation for ounce, Dorothy is the naive public, Emerald City symbolizes Washington, D.C., the Tin Woodman represents the industrial worker, the Scarecrow is the farmer, and the Cyclone is a metaphor for a political revolution. In the end, Dorothy discovers magical powers in her *silver* shoes (changed to ruby in the 1939 film) to find her way home and not the fallacy of the Yellow Brick Road. Although the author of the story, L. Frank Baum, never stated it was his intention, it can be argued that the issue of the story concerns the election of 1896. Democratic presidential nominee William Jennings Bryan (the Cowardly Lion) supported fixing the value of the dollar to both gold and silver (bimetallism), but Republican William McKinley (the Wicked Witch) advocated using only the gold standard. Since McKinley won, the United States remained on the Yellow Brick Road.[1]

The United States adopted the gold standard in 1873, and until the 1930s, most industrial countries were on the gold standard. The gold standard served as an international monetary system in which currencies were defined or pegged in terms of gold. Under the gold standard, a nation with a balance of payments deficit was required to ship gold to other

nations to finance the deficit. Hence, a large excess of imports over exports meant a corresponding outflow of gold from a nation. As a result, that nation's money supply decreased, which, in turn, reduced the aggregate demand for goods and services. Lower domestic demand led to falling prices, lower production, and fewer jobs. In contrast, a nation with a balance of payments surplus would experience an inflow of gold and the opposite effects. In this case, the nation's money supply increased, and its aggregate demand for goods and services rose. Higher aggregate spending, in turn, boosted employment and the price level. In short, the gold standard meant that governments could not control their money supplies and thereby conduct monetary policy.

The gold standard worked fairly well as a fixed exchange rate system so long as nations did not face sudden or severe swings in flows from their stocks of gold. The Great Depression marked the beginning of the end of the gold standard. Nations faced with trade deficits and high unemployment began going off the gold standard, rather than contracting their money supplies by following the gold standard.

In 1933, President Franklin D. Roosevelt took the United States off the gold standard and ordered all 1933 gold double eagle coins already manufactured to be melted down and not circulated. Through a long twisted story worthy of a Sherlock Holmes mystery novel involving the Smithsonian Institution, the former king of Egypt, the Treasury Department,

other hand, a small U.S. trade surplus of $4 billion with Mexico in 1993 turned into a huge trade deficit of $57 billion in 2011.

Before blaming this trade deficit entirely on NAFTA, you must note that the exchange rate rose from 3.12 to 12.43 pesos per dollar. Since 1995, the peso was devalued, and the stronger dollar has put the price of U.S. goods out of reach for many Mexican consumers. This is one reason U.S. exports to Mexico have been lower than they would have been otherwise. At the same time, Mexican goods became less expensive for U.S. consumers, so U.S. imports from Mexico have risen.

the Justice Department, the U.S. Mint, and a long list of intriguing supporting characters, one 1933 double eagle surfaced and was sold for $7.59 million in 2002. This was double the previous record for a coin.

Once the Allies felt certain they would win World War II, the finance ministers of Western nations met in 1944 at Bretton Woods, New Hampshire, to establish a new international monetary system. The new system was based on fixed exchange rates and an international central bank called the *International Monetary Fund (IMF)*. The IMF makes loans to countries faced with short-term balance-of-payments problems. Under this system, nations were expected to maintain fixed exchange rates within a narrow range. In the 1960s and early 1970s, the Bretton Woods system became strained as conditions changed. In the 1960s, inflation rates in the United States rose relative to those in other countries, causing U.S. exports to become more expensive and U.S. imports to become less expensive. This situation increased the supply of dollars abroad and caused an increasing surplus of dollars, thus putting downward pressure on the exchange rate. Monetary authorities in the United States worried that central banks would demand gold for their dollars, the U.S. gold stock would diminish sharply, and the declining money supply would adversely affect the economy.

Something had to give, and it did. In August 1971, President Richard Nixon announced that the United States would no longer honor its obligation to sell gold at $35 an ounce. By 1973, the gold standard was dead, and most of our trading partners were letting the forces of supply and demand determine exchange rates.

Today, some people advocate returning to the gold standard. These gold buffs do not trust the government to control the money supply without the discipline of a gold standard. They argue that if governments have the freedom to print money, political pressures will sooner or later cause them to increase the money supply too much and let inflation rage.

One argument against the gold standard is that no one can control the supply of gold. Big gold discoveries can cause inflation and have done so in the past. On the other hand, slow growth in the stock of mined gold can lead to slow economic growth and a loss of jobs. Governments therefore are unlikely to return to the gold standard because it would mean turning monetary policy over to uncontrollable swings in the stock of gold.

Analyze the Issue

Return to Exhibit 8, and assume the equilibrium exchange rate is 150 yen per dollar and the equilibrium quantity is $300 million. Redraw this figure, and place a horizontal line through the equilibrium exchange rate to represent a fixed exchange rate. Now use this figure to explain why a country would abandon the gold standard.

---

1. Bradley A. Hansen, "The Fable of the Allegory," *Journal of Economic Education*, Summer 2002, pp. 254–264.

Source: © Cengage Learning 2014

Key Concepts

Absolute advantage	Tariff	Balance of trade
Comparative advantage	World Trade Organization	Exchange rate
Free trade	(WTO)	Depreciation of currency
Protectionism	Quota	Appreciation of currency
Embargo	Balance of payments	

Summary

- **Comparative advantage** is a principle that allows nations to gain from trade. Comparative advantage means that each nation *specializes* in a product for which its opportunity cost is lower in terms of the production of another product, and then nations trade. When nations follow this principle, they gain. The reason is that world output increases, and each nation ends up with a higher standard of living by consuming more goods and services than would be possible without specialization and trade.

Comparative Advantage

SOURCE: © Cengage Learning 2014

- **Free trade** benefits a nation as a whole, but individuals may lose jobs and incomes because of the competition from foreign goods and services.
- **Protectionism** is a government's use of embargoes, tariffs, quotas, and other methods to impose barriers intended to both reduce imports and protect particular domestic industries. *Embargoes* prohibit the import or export of particular goods. *Tariffs* discourage imports by making them more expensive. *Quotas* limit the quantity of imports or exports of certain goods. These trade barriers often result primarily from domestic groups that exert political pressure on government in order to gain from these barriers.

- The **balance of payments** is a summary bookkeeping record of all the international transactions a country makes during a year. It is divided into different accounts, including the *current account*, the *capital account*, and the *statistical discrepancy*. The current account summarizes all transactions in currently produced goods and services. The overall balance of payments is always zero after an adjustment for the statistical discrepancy.

- The **balance of trade** measures only goods (not services) that a nation exports and imports. A balance of trade can be in deficit or in surplus. The balance of trade is the most widely reported and largest part of the current account. Since 1975, the United States has experienced balance of trade deficits.

Balance of Trade

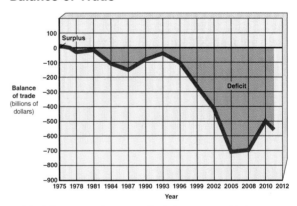

SOURCE: Bureau of Economic Analysis, *International U.S. International Transactions Accounts*, http://www.bea.gov/international/index.htm, Table 1.

- An **exchange rate** is the price of one nation's currency in terms of another nation's currency. Foreigners who wish to purchase U.S. goods, services, and financial assets demand dollars. The supply of dollars reflects the desire of U.S. citizens to purchase foreign goods, services, and financial assets. The intersection of the supply and demand curves for dollars determines the number of units of a foreign currency per dollar.

Exchange Rate

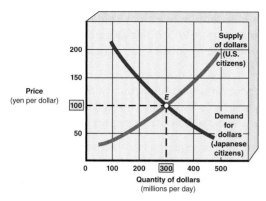

SOURCE: © Cengage Learning 2014

- **Shifts in supply and demand for foreign exchange** result from changes in such factors as tastes, relative price levels, relative real interest rates, and relative income levels.
- **Depreciation of currency** occurs when one currency becomes worth fewer units of another currency. If a currency depreciates, it becomes weaker. Depreciation of a nation's currency increases its exports and decreases its imports.
- **Appreciation of currency** occurs when one currency becomes worth more units of another currency. If a currency appreciates, it becomes stronger. Appreciation of a nation's currency decreases its exports and increases its imports.

Summary of Conclusion Statements

- When countries specialize, total world output increases, and therefore, the potential for greater total world consumption also increases.
- Global trade allows a country to consume a combination of goods that exceeds its production possibilities curve.
- Specialization and trade are based on opportunity costs (comparative advantage) and not on absolute advantage.
- Comparative advantage refers to the relative opportunity costs between different countries of producing the same goods. World output and consumption are maximized when each country specializes in producing and trading goods for which it has a comparative advantage.
- A current account deficit is financed by a capital account surplus.

- An exchange rate can be expressed as a reciprocal.
- An expansion in relative U.S. income causes a depreciation of the dollar.
- A rise in a trading partner's relative price level causes the dollar to appreciate.
- When the dollar is weak, or depreciates, U.S. goods and services cost foreign consumers less, so they buy more U.S. exports. At the same time, a weak dollar means foreign goods and services cost U.S. consumers more, so they buy fewer imports.
- When the dollar is strong, or appreciates, U.S. goods and services cost foreign consumers more, so they buy fewer U.S. exports. At the same time, a strong dollar means foreign goods and services cost U.S. consumers less, so they buy more foreign imports.

Study Questions and Problems

1. The countries of Alpha and Beta produce diamonds and pearls. The production possibilities schedule below describes their potential output in tons per year:

Points on production possibilities curve	Alpha		Beta	
	Diamonds	Pearls	Diamonds	Pearls
A	150	0	90	0
B	100	25	60	60
C	50	50	30	120
D	0	75	0	180

Using the data in the table, answer the following questions:

a. What is the opportunity cost of diamonds for each country?

b. What is the opportunity cost of pearls for each country?

c. In which good does Alpha have a comparative advantage?

d. In which good does Beta have a comparative advantage?

e. Suppose Alpha is producing and consuming at point B on its production possibilities curve and Beta is producing and consuming at point C on its production possibilities curve. Use a table such as Exhibit 3 to explain why both nations would benefit if they specialized.

f. Draw a graph, and use it to explain how Alpha and Beta benefit if they specialize and Alpha agrees to trade 50 tons of diamonds to Beta and Alpha receives 50 tons of pearls in exchange.

2. Bill can paint either two walls or one window frame in one hour. In the same time, Frank can paint either three walls or two window frames. To minimize the time spent painting, who should specialize in painting walls, and who should specialize in painting window frames?

3. Consider this statement: "The principles of specialization and trade according to comparative advantage among nations also apply to states in the United States." Do you agree or disagree? Explain.

4. Would the U.S. government gain any advantage from using tariffs or quotas to restrict imports?

5. Suppose the United States passed a law stating that we would not purchase imports from any country that imposed any trade restrictions on our exports. Who would benefit and who would lose from such retaliation?

6. Now consider question 5 in terms of the law's impact on domestic producers that export goods. Does this policy adversely affect domestic producers that export goods?

7. Consider this statement: "Unrestricted foreign trade costs domestic jobs." Do you agree or disagree? Explain.

8. Do you support a constitutional amendment to prohibit the federal government from imposing any trade barriers, such as tariffs and quotas, except in case of war or national emergency? Why or why not?

9. Discuss this statement: "Because each nation's balance of payments equals zero, it follows that there is actually no significance to a balance of payments deficit or surplus."

10. For each of the following situations, indicate the direction of the shift in the supply curve or the demand curve for dollars, the factor causing the change, and the resulting movement of the equilibrium exchange rate for the dollar in terms of foreign currency:

a. American-made cars become more popular overseas.

b. The United States experiences a recession, while other nations enjoy economic growth.

c. Inflation rates accelerate in the United States, while inflation rates remain constant in other nations.

d. Real interest rates in the United States rise, while real interest rates abroad remain constant.

e. The Japanese put quotas and high tariffs on all imports from the United States.

f. Tourism from the United States increases sharply because of a fare war among airlines.

11. The following table summarizes the supply and the demand for euros:

	U.S. Dollars per Euro				
	$0.05	$0.10	$0.15	$0.20	$0.25
Quantity demanded (per day)	500	400	300	200	100
Quantity supplied (per day)	100	200	300	400	500

Using the above table:
a. Graph the supply and demand curves for euros.
b. Determine the equilibrium exchange rate.
c. Determine what the effect of a fixed exchange rate at $0.10 per euro would be.

For Online Exercises, go to the Tucker Web site at www.cengage.com/economics/tucker.

✓ CHECKPOINT ANSWERS

Do Nations with an Advantage Always Trade?

In the United States, the opportunity cost of producing 1 calculator is 100 towels. In Costa Rica, the opportunity cost of producing 1 calculator is 100 towels. If you said because the opportunity cost is the same for each nation, specialization and trade would not boost total output and therefore Costa Rica would not trade these products, **YOU ARE CORRECT.**

Should Everyone Keep a Balance of Payments?

The principal purpose of the balance of payments is to keep track of payments of national currencies. Because states and cities within the same nation use the same national currency, payments for goods and services traded between these parties do not represent a loss (outflow) or gain (inflow). If you said only nations need to use the balance of payments to account for flows of foreign currency across national boundaries, **YOU ARE CORRECT.**

Sample Quiz

For an explanation of the correct answers, visit the Tucker Web site at www.cengage.com/economics/tucker.

1. The theory of comparative advantage suggests that a (an)
   a. industrialized country should not import.
   b. country that is not competitive should import everything.
   c. country specialize in producing goods or services for which it has a lower opportunity cost.
   d. None of the above answers are correct.

2. Assume the United States can use a given amount of its resources to produce either 20 airplanes or 8 automobiles and Japan can employ the same amount of its resources to

Sample Quiz *continued*

produce either 20 airplanes or 10 automobiles. The United States should specialize in
a. airplanes.
b. automobiles.
c. both goods.
d. neither good.

EXHIBIT 14	Potatoes and Wheat Output (tons per day)	
Country	Potatoes	Wheat
United States	4	2
Ireland	3	1

SOURCE: © Cengage Learning 2014

3. In Exhibit 14, the United States has an absolute advantage in producing
a. potatoes.
b. wheat.
c. both potatoes and wheat.
d. neither potatoes nor wheat.

4. In Exhibit 14, Ireland's opportunity cost of producing one unit of wheat is
a. 1/3 ton of potatoes.
b. 3 tons of potatoes.
c. either a or b.
d. neither a nor b.

5. In Exhibit 14, the United States has a comparative advantage in producing
a. potatoes.
b. wheat.
c. both potatoes and wheat.
d. neither potatoes nor wheat.

6. If each nation in Exhibit 14 specializes in producing the good for which it has a comparative advantage, then
a. Ireland would produce neither potatoes nor wheat.
b. the United States would produce both potatoes and wheat.
c. the United States would produce potatoes.
d. Ireland would produce potatoes.

7. A tariff is a
a. tax on an exported product.
b. limit on the number of goods that can be exported.
c. limit on the number of goods that can be imported.
d. tax on an imported product.
e. subsidy on an imported product.

8. The principal objective of the WTO is to
a. reduce the level of all tariffs.
b. establish fair prices for all goods traded internationally.
c. prevent the trading of services across nations' borders.
d. encourage countries to establish quotas.

9. Which of the following is *not* an argument used in favor of protectionism?
a. to protect an "infant" industry
b. to protect domestic jobs
c. to preserve national security
d. to protect against "unfair" competition because of cheap foreign labor
e. to reduce prices paid by domestic consumers

10. The main explanation for why the cheap foreign labor argument is a poor reason for restricting international trade is that
a. workers who get paid less tend to have lower productivity than those who get paid more.
b. all firms and workers gain when there are no restrictions on international trade.
c. infant industries such as steel and automobiles need to be protected.
d. specialization and free trade usually raise the prices of all the traded goods, so that the workers can get paid more.

11. The account that records a nation's foreign economic transactions is called the
a. trade account.
b. T account.
c. exchange market.
d. balance of payments.

12. Expenditures for services such as tourism, income for foreign investment, and foreign gifts are tabulated in the
a. current account.
b. capital account.

Sample Quiz *continued*

c. official reserve account.

d. goods account.

13. Suppose a German bank purchases a U.S. Treasury bond. This transaction would be recorded in the
    a. capital account.
    b. current account.
    c. goods trade balance.
    d. unilateral transfers.

14. Exhibit 15 shows a situation in which
    a. both the dollar and the pound have depreciated.
    b. both the dollar and the pound have appreciated.
    c. the dollar has depreciated and the pound has appreciated.
    d. the dollar has appreciated and the pound has depreciated.

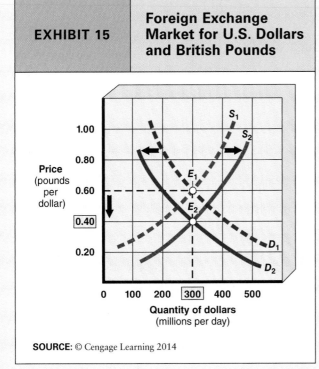

EXHIBIT 15

Foreign Exchange Market for U.S. Dollars and British Pounds

SOURCE: © Cengage Learning 2014

15. Which of the following could cause the dollar-pound exchange rate to change as shown in Exhibit 15?
    a. American goods become more popular in Great Britain.

b. British incomes rise, while U.S. incomes remain unchanged.

c. The U.S. price level rises, while the British price level remains unchanged.

d. The U.S. real interest rate rises, while the British real interest rate remains unchanged.

16. A country that has a lower opportunity cost of producing a good
    a. has a comparative advantage.
    b. can produce the good using fewer resources than another country.
    c. requires fewer labor hours to produce the good.
    d. All of the above answers are correct.

17. If one country can produce a good with fewer resources than another country, this is called
    a. specialization.
    b. geographic advantage.
    c. comparative advantage.
    d. absolute advantage.

18. One big difference between tariffs and quotas is that tariffs
    a. raise the price of a good while quotas lower it.
    b. generate tax revenues while quotas do not.
    c. stimulate international trade while quotas inhibit it.
    d. hurt domestic producers while quotas help them.

19. Which of the following is *not* included in the current account?
    a. exports of goods
    b. imports of goods
    c. U.S. capital inflow and outflow
    d. unilateral transfers

20. A shift of the U.S. demand curve for Mexican pesos to the left and a decrease in the peso price per dollar would result from
    a. an increase in the U.S. inflation rate relative to the rate in Mexico.
    b. a change in U.S. consumers' tastes away from Mexican products and toward products made in South Korea, India, and Taiwan.
    c. U.S. buyers perceiving that domestically-produced products are of a lower quality than products made in Mexico.
    d. All of the above answers are correct.

chapter 29

Economies in Transition

The inherent vice of capitalism is the unequal sharing of blessings. The inherent virtue of communism is the equal sharing of miseries.

—Winston Churchill

The emergence of the market system in Russia, China, and other countries continues while leaders of these countries who were devoted followers of Marxist ideology now say they believe that capitalism, private property, and profit are ideas superior to the communist system. The failure of communism and the transformation toward a market system is personified by the success of McDonald's in Russia and Wal-Mart in China. Today, Russia and other countries continue to experience economic problems during their restructuring, but the commitment to free-market reforms remains. In contrast, in 2009, the media reported the news that the United States was nationalizing banks and General Motors. And in 2011 and 2012, a protest movement called Occupy Wall Street spread across the United States. The anticapitalist slogan of the protests was "We are the 99 percent." The main issues protested were inequity between the wealthiest 1 percent and the rest of the population and corrupt influence of corporations on government. What caused these astonishing turn of events?

To understand how the pieces of the global economic puzzle fit together, this chapter begins with a discussion of the three basic types of economies. Then you will examine the pros and cons of the "isms"—capitalism, socialism, and communism. Here you will explore the worldwide clash between the ideas of Adam Smith and Karl Marx and study their current influence on economic systems. Finally, you will examine economic reforms in Cuba, Russia, and China.

In this chapter, you will learn to solve these economics puzzles:

- Why did drivers in the former Soviet Union remove the windshield wipers and side mirrors whenever they parked their cars?

- What did Adam Smith mean when he said that an "invisible hand" promotes the public interest?

- If the Soviet Union was foolish to run its economy on five-year plans, why do universities, businesses, and governments in a capitalistic economy bother to plan?

29-1 Basic Types of Economic Systems

North Korea and South Korea share the same language and historical background. However, South Korea today is a modern economy and people starve in North Korea. This difference relates to their differing economic systems. An economic system consists of the organizations and methods used to determine what goods and services are produced, how they are produced, and for whom they are produced. As explained earlier in Chapter 2, scarcity forces each economic system to decide what combination of goods to produce, how to produce such goods, and who gets the output once it is produced. The decision-making process involves interaction among many aspects of a nation's culture, such as its laws, form of government, ethics, religions, and customs. Economist Robert L. Heilbroner established a simple way to look at the basic methods society can employ. Each economic system can be classified into one of three basic types: (1) *traditional*, (2) *command*, or (3) *market*.

29-1a THE TRADITIONAL ECONOMY

Why does England have a king or queen? Tradition is the answer. Historically, the traditional economy has been a common system for making economic decisions. The traditional economy is a system that answers the What, How, and For Whom questions the way they have always been answered. People in this type of society learn that copying the previous generation allows them to feel accepted. Anyone who changes ways of doing things asks for trouble from others. This is because people in such a society believe that what was good yesterday, and years ago, must still be a good idea today.

Although most traditional economies have changed to keep pace with modern economic trends, traditional systems are used today, for example, by the Ainu of Canada, the native people of Brazil's rain forest, and the Amish of Pennsylvania. In these societies, the way past generations decided what crops are planted, how they are harvested, and to whom they are distributed remains unchanged over time. People perform their jobs in the manner established by their ancestors. The Amish are well known for rejecting tractors and using horse-drawn plows. Interestingly, the Amish reject Social Security because their society voluntarily redistributes wealth to members who are needy.

29-1b THE TRADITIONAL ECONOMY'S STRENGTHS AND WEAKNESSES

The benefit of the traditional approach is that it minimizes friction among members because relatively little is disputed. Consequently, people in this system may cooperate more freely with one another. In today's industrial world, the Amish and other traditional economies appear very satisfied with their relatively uncomplicated systems. However, critics argue that the traditional system restricts individual initiative and therefore does not lead to the production of advanced goods, new technology, and economic growth.

29-1c THE COMMAND ECONOMY

In a command economy, a dictator or group of central planners makes economic decisions for society. In this system, the What, How, and For Whom questions are answered by a dictator or planners with central authority. The former Soviet Union

---

Economic system

The organizations and methods used to determine what goods and services are produced, how they are produced, and for whom they are produced.

Traditional economy

An economic system that answers the What, How, and For Whom questions the way they have always have been answered.

Command economy

An economic system that answers the What, How, and For Whom questions by a dictator or central authority.

in the past and Cuba and North Korea today are examples of nations with command economies using national economic plans implemented through powerful government committees. Politically selected committees decide on everything, including the number, color, size, quality, and price of autos, brooms, sweaters, and tanks. The state owns the factors of production and dictates answers to the three basic economic questions. The authorities might decide to produce modern weapons instead of schools, or they might decide to devote resources to building huge monuments like the pyramids, built by the rulers of ancient Egypt to honor their dead kings and queens.

In the old Soviet economy, for example, the three basic economic questions were answered by a central planning agency called the *Gosplan*. Following the policies of the political authority (the Politburo), the Gosplan set production quotas and prices for farms, factories, mines, housing construction, medical care, and other producing units. What should the cows be fed? If it is hay, how much land can be used to grow it? How much milk should the cows give? How many people will be dairy farmers? What wages should a dairy farmer earn? Should milk be given to everyone, to a few, or to people chosen by the leaders? If there was a shortage of goods in the shops, then goods would be rationed through queuing. The Gosplan tried to make all these decisions. Today, in Russia and the other former Soviet republics, the Gosplan is a distant memory of the discarded Soviet command system.

The pyramid shown in Exhibit 1 represents the command economy. At the top of the pyramid is a supremely powerful group of central planners, such as the old Soviet Gosplan. That agency established production targets and prices for goods and services. Then the Gosplan transmitted this information to a second layer of specialized state planning agencies. One of these specialized government bureaucracies purchased raw materials, another agency established fashion trends, another set prices, and another government bureaucracy made decisions based on employment and wages.

Production objectives were transmitted from the upper authority layers to the individual producing units, represented by the third layer of the pyramid in Exhibit 1. These producers supplied goods and services to the consumers, as commanded by the central authorities. The bottom portion of the pyramid illustrates the distribution, according to the master plan, of output to consuming units of individuals and households.

29-1d THE COMMAND ECONOMY'S STRENGTHS AND WEAKNESSES

Believe it or not, the command system can be defended. Proponents argue that economic change occurs much faster in a command system than in a traditional economy. This is one reason those dissatisfied with a traditional society might advocate establishment of a command system. The central authorities can ignore custom and order new ways of doing things. Another reason for adopting a command economy is the controversial belief that the government will provide economic security and equity. It is alleged that central authorities ensure that everyone is provided food, clothing, shelter, and medical care regardless of their ability to contribute to society.

The absolute power of central authorities to make right decisions is also the power to be absolutely wrong. Often the planners do not set production goals accurately, and either shortages or surpluses of goods and services are the result. For example, at one point, the planners miscalculated and produced too few windshield wipers and side mirrors for Soviet cars. Faced with shortages of these parts, Soviet drivers removed windshield wipers and side mirrors whenever they parked their cars to prevent theft. On the other hand, the Gosplan allocated some collective

EXHIBIT 1	The Command Economy Pyramid

The principal feature of a command economy is the central planning board at the top, which transmits economic decisions down to the various producing and consuming units below. This process begins with an overall plan from a supreme planning board, such as the old Soviet Gosplan. The Gosplan established production targets and was the ultimate authority over a layer of specialized planning agencies, which authorized capital expansion, raw material purchases, prices, wages, and all other production decisions for individual producing units. Finally, the factories, farms, mines, and other producers distributed the specified output to consumers according to the approved master plan.

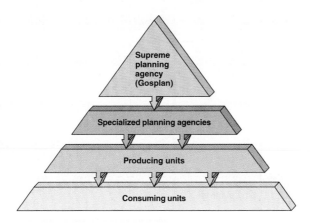

SOURCE: © Cengage Learning 2014

farms far more fertilizer than they could use. To receive the same amount of fertilizer again the next year, farmers simply burned the excess fertilizer. As a result of such decision-making errors, people waited in long lines or stole goods. How does any decision-making group really know how many windshield wipers to produce each year and how much workers making them should earn?

Because profit is not the motive of producers in a command economy, quality and variety of goods also suffer. If the Gosplan ordered a state enterprise to produce 400,000 side mirrors for cars, for example, producers had little incentive to make the extra effort required to create a quality product in a variety of styles. The easiest way to meet the goal was to produce a low-quality product in one style regardless of consumer demand.

Exhibit 2 illustrates how the pricing policy of central planners causes shortages. The demand curve for side mirrors conforms to the law of demand. At lower prices in rubles, the quantity demanded increases. The supply curve is fixed at 400,000 side mirrors because it is set by the central planners and is therefore unresponsive to price variations.

Suppose one of the principal goals of the command economy is to keep the price low. To reach this goal, the central planners set the price of side mirrors at 20 rubles, which is below the equilibrium price of 40 rubles. At 20 rubles, more people can afford a side mirror than at the equilibrium price set by an uncontrolled

EXHIBIT 2	Central Planners Fixing Prices

The central planners' goal is to keep prices low, so they set the price of a side mirror for a car at 20 rubles, which is below the market-determined equilibrium price of 40 rubles. At the set price, however, the quantity demanded is 800,000 side mirrors per year. Also set by the planners, the quantity supplied is 400,000 per year. Thus, the shortage at the government-established price is 400,000 side mirrors per year. As a result, long lines form to buy side mirrors, and black markets appear.

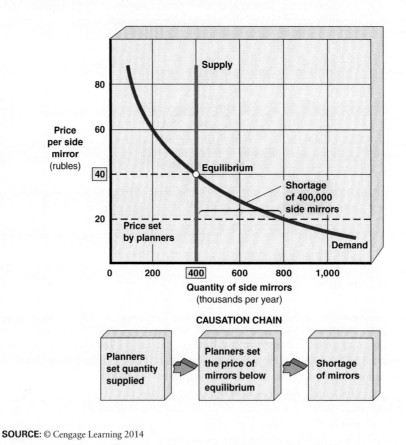

SOURCE: © Cengage Learning 2014

marketplace. The consequence of this lower price set by the planners is a shortage. The quantity demanded at 20 rubles is 800,000 side mirrors, and the quantity supplied is only 400,000 mirrors. Thus, the model explains why side mirrors disappeared from stores long before many who were willing to buy them could do so.

The same graphical analysis applies to centrally planned rental prices for apartments. The central planners in the former Soviet Union set rents below the equilibrium rental prices for apartments. As the model predicts, low rents resulted in a shortage of housing. Meanwhile, the planners promised that improvements in housing would come in time.

> **CONCLUSION:** *When central planners set prices below equilibrium for goods and services, they create shortages, which mean long lines, empty shelves, and black markets.*[1]

29-1e THE MARKET ECONOMY AND THE IDEAS OF ADAM SMITH

In a market economy, neither customs nor a single person or group of central planners answers the three basic economic questions facing society. The market economy is an economic system that answers the What, How, and For Whom questions using prices determined by the interaction of the forces of supply and demand. One of the first people to explain the power of a market economy was the Scottish economist Adam Smith. In the same year that the American colonies declared their political independence in 1776, Smith's *An Inquiry into the Nature and Causes of the Wealth of Nations* presented the blueprint for employing markets to improve economic performance. Smith spent over ten years observing the real world and writing about how nations could best improve their material well-being. He concluded that the answer was to use free markets because this mechanism provides the incentive for everyone to follow his or her *self-interest.*

Adam Smith is the *father of modern economics.* He intended to write a book that would influence popular opinion, and unlike many famous works, his book was an immediate success. The basic philosophy of his book is "the best government is the least government." This belief is known as *laissez-faire,* a French expression meaning "allow to act." As Smith stated, the role of the government should be limited to providing national defense, providing education, maintaining infrastructure, enforcing contracts, and little else. Smith also advocated free trade among nations and rejected the idea that nations should impose trade barriers.

During Smith's lifetime, European nations such as England, France, and Spain intervened to control economic activities. In *The Wealth of Nations,* he argued that economic freedoms are "natural rights" necessary for the dignity of humankind. He believed that free competition among people who follow their self-interest would best benefit society because markets free of government interference produce the greatest output of goods and services possible. As noted above, Smith was an advocate of free international trade and asked the question implied in the full title of his book: Why are some nations richer than others? He explained that the source of any nation's wealth is not really the amount of gold or silver it owns. This was an idea popular during Smith's time called *mercantilism.* Instead, he argued that it is the ability of people to produce products and trade in free markets that creates a nation's wealth.

The importance of markets is that they harness the power of self-interest to answer the What, How, and For Whom questions. Without central planning, markets coordinate the actions of millions of consumers and producers. Smith said that the market economy seemed to be controlled by an invisible hand. The *invisible hand* is a phrase that expresses the belief that the best interests of a society are served when individual consumers and producers compete to achieve their own private interests. Guided by an invisible hand, producers must compete with one another to win consumers'

Market economy

An economic system that answers the What, How, and For Whom questions using prices determined by the interaction of the forces of supply and demand.

Adam Smith (1723–1790) The father of modern economics who wrote *The Wealth of Nations,* published in 1776.

Invisible hand

A phrase that expresses the belief that the best interests of a society are served when individual consumers and producers compete to achieve their own private interests.

Prints & Photographs Division, Library of Congress, LC-USZ62-1740

---

[1]Recall from Exhibit 5 in Chapter 4 that a black market is an illegal market that emerges when a price ceiling is imposed in a free market.

money. The *profit motive* in a competitive marketplace provides profits as a reward for efficient producers, while losses punish inefficient producers. Smith saw profit as the necessary driving force in an individualistic market system. The profit motive leads the butcher, the baker, and other producers to answer the What, How, and For Whom questions at the lowest prices. Consumers also compete with one another to purchase the best goods at the lowest price. Competition automatically regulates the economy and provides more goods and services than a system in which government attempts to accomplish the same task in the *public interest*. In Smith's own words:

> Every individual necessarily labours to render the annual revenue of the society as great as he can. He generally, indeed, neither intends to promote the public interest, nor knows how much he is promoting it. By … directing that industry in such a manner as its produce may be of the greatest value, he intends only his own gain, and he is in this, as in many other cases, led by an invisible hand to promote an end which was no part of his intention. Nor is it always the worse for the society that it was no part of it. By pursuing his own interest he frequently promotes that of the society more effectually than when he really intends to promote it.[2]

29-1f THE MARKET ECONOMY'S STRENGTHS AND WEAKNESSES

In a market system, if consumers want Sudoku puzzles, they can buy them because sellers seek to profit from the sale of Sudoku puzzles. No single person or central planning board makes a formal decision to shift resources and tell firms how to produce what many might view as a frivolous product. Because no central body or set of customs interferes, the market system provides a wide variety of goods and services that buyers and sellers exchange at the lowest prices.

> **CONCLUSION:** *A market economy answers the What to produce and How to produce questions very effectively.*

Those who attack the market economy point out the market failure problems of lack of competition, externalities, public goods, and income inequality, discussed in Chapter 4. For example, critics contend that competition among buyers and sellers results in people who are very wealthy and people who are very poor. In a market economy, output is divided in favor of people who earn higher incomes and own property. Some people will dine on caviar in fine restaurants, while others will wander the streets and beg for food and shelter. Supporters of the market system argue that this inequality of income must exist to give people incentives or rewards for the value of their contributions to others.

29-1g THE MIXED ECONOMY

In the real world, no nation is a pure traditional, command, or market economy. Even primitive tribes employ a few markets in their system. For example, members of a tribe may exchange shells for animal skins. In China, the government allows many private

---

[2]Adam Smith, *An Inquiry into the Nature and Causes of the Wealth of Nations* (1776; reprint, New York: Random House, 1937), p. 423.

shops and farms to operate in free markets. Although the United States is best described as a market economy, it is also a blend of the other two systems. As mentioned earlier, the Amish operate a well-known traditional economy in our nation. The draft during wartime is an example of a command economy in which the government obtains involuntary labor. In addition, taxes "commanded" from taxpayers fund government programs, such as national defense and Social Security. If the economic systems of most nations do not perfectly fit one of the basic definitions, what term best describes their economies? A more appropriate description is that most countries employ a blend of the basic types of economic systems, broadly called a mixed economy. A mixed economy is a system that answers the What, How, and For Whom questions through a mixture of traditional, command, and market systems.

The traditional, command, and market economies can exist in a wide variety of political situations. For instance, the United States and Japan are politically "free" societies in which the market system flourishes. But China uses the market system to a limited degree in spite of its lack of political freedom. Moreover, some of the Western democracies engage in central economic planning. French officials representing government, business, and labor meet annually to discuss economic goals for industry for the next five-year period, but compliance is voluntary. In Japan, a government agency called the *Ministry of Economy, Trade and Industry (METI)* engages in long-term planning. One of the goals of the METI is to encourage exports so that Japan can earn the foreign currencies it needs to pay for oil and other resources.

29-2 The "ISMS"

What type of economic system will a society choose to answer the What, How, and For Whom questions? We could call most economies "mixed," but this would be too imprecise. In the real world, economic systems are labeled with various forms of the popular "isms"—capitalism, socialism, and communism, which are based on the basic types of systems.

29-2a CAPITALISM

The popular term for the market economy discussed previously is capitalism. Capitalism is an economic system characterized by private ownership of resources and markets. *Capitalism* is also called the *free enterprise system*. Regardless of its political system, a capitalist economic system must possess two characteristics: (1) private ownership of resources and (2) decentralized decision making using markets.

Private Ownership   Ownership of resources determines to a great degree who makes the What, How, and For Whom decisions. In a capitalist system, resources are primarily *privately* owned and controlled by individuals and firms, rather than having property rights be *publicly* held by government on behalf of society. In the United States, most capital resources are privately owned, but the term *capitalism* is somewhat confusing because it stresses private ownership of factories, raw materials, farms, and other forms of *capital* even though public ownership of land exists as well.

Decentralized Decision Making   This characteristic of capitalism allows buyers and sellers to exchange goods in markets without government involvement. A capitalist system operates on the principle of consumer sovereignty. Consumer sovereignty is the freedom of consumers to cast their dollar votes to buy, or not to buy, at

---

Mixed economy

An economic system that answers the What, How, and For Whom questions through a mixture of traditional, command, and market systems.

Capitalism

An economic system characterized by private ownership of resources and markets.

Consumer sovereignty

The freedom of consumers to cast their dollar votes to buy, or not to buy, at prices determined in competitive markets.

prices determined in competitive markets. As a result, consumer spending determines what goods and services firms produce. In a capitalist system, most allocative decisions are coordinated by consumers and producers interacting through markets and making their own decisions guided by Adam Smith's "invisible hand." Friedrich Hayek, an Austrian economist who was a 1974 recipient of the Nobel Prize and author of *The Road to Serfdom*, argued that political and economic freedoms are inseparable.

In the real world, many U.S. markets are not perfectly open or free markets with the consumer as sovereign. For example, consumers cannot buy illegal drugs or body organs. In Chapter 4, you learned that the U.S. government sets minimum prices (support prices) for wheat, milk, cheese, and other products. These markets are free only if the market price is above the support price. Similarly, the minimum wage law forces employers to pay a wage above some dollar amount per hour regardless of market conditions.

> **CONCLUSION:** *No nation in the world precisely fits the two criteria for capitalism; however, the United States comes close.*

29-2b CAPITALISM'S STRENGTHS AND WEAKNESSES

One of the major strengths of capitalism is its capacity to achieve *economic efficiency* because competition and the profit motive force production at the lowest cost. Another strength of pure capitalism is *economic freedom* because economic power is widely dispersed. Individual consumers, producers, and workers are free to make decisions based on their own self-interest. Economist Milton Friedman makes a related point: Private ownership limits the power of government to deny goods, services, or jobs to its adversaries.

Critics of capitalism cite several shortcomings. First, capitalism tends toward an unequal distribution of income. This inequality of income among citizens results for several reasons. Private ownership of capital and the other factors of production can cause these factors to become concentrated in the hands of a few individuals or firms. Also, people do not have equal labor skills, and the marketplace rewards those with greater skills. These inequalities may be perpetuated because the rich can provide better education, legal aid, political platforms, and wealth to their heirs. Second, pure capitalism is criticized for its failure to protect the environment. The pursuit of profit and self-interest can take precedence over damage or pollution to the air, rivers, lakes, and streams. Recall the graphical model used in Chapter 4 to illustrate the socially unacceptable impact of producers who pollute the environment.

29-2c SOCIALISM

The idea of socialism has existed for thousands of years. Its basis is the command system. Socialism is an economic system characterized by government ownership of resources and centralized decision making. Socialism is also called *command socialism*. Under a socialist economy, a command system owns and controls in the *public interest* the major industries, such as steel, electricity, and agriculture. However, some free markets can exist in farming, retail trade, and certain service areas. Just as no pure capitalist system exists in the real world, none of the socialist countries in the world today practices pure socialism. In fact, there are as many variants of socialism as there are countries called socialist.

Socialism

An economic system characterized by government ownership of resources and centralized decision making.

Before discussing socialism further, you must realize that socialism is an economic system, and politics should not be confused with economics. Great Britain, France, and Italy have representative democracies, but many of their major industries are or have been nationalized. In the United States, the federal government owns and operates the Tennessee Valley Authority (TVA), the National Aeronautics and Space Administration (NASA), and the U.S. Postal Service, while at the same time allowing private utilities and mail service firms to operate.

29-2d THE IDEAS OF KARL MARX

Despite the transition to capitalism in Russia and Eastern Europe, socialism still prevails in China, Cuba, and many less-developed countries. The theory for socialism and *communism* can be traced to Karl Marx. Marx was a 19th-century German philosopher, revolutionary, and economist. Unlike other economists of the time who followed Adam Smith, Marx rejected the concept of a society operating through private interest and profit.

Karl Marx was born in Germany, the son of a lawyer. In 1841, after receiving a doctorate in philosophy from Berlin University, he turned to journalism and became interested in radical politics. In 1843, Marx married the daughter of a wealthy family and moved to Paris, but his political activities forced him to leave Paris for England. From the age of 31, he lived and wrote his books in London. In London, Marx lived an impoverished life while he and his lifelong friend Friedrich Engels wrote *The Communist Manifesto*, published in 1848. A massive work followed, titled *Das Kapital*, which was published in three volumes between 1867 and 1894. These two works made Karl Marx the most influential economist in the history of socialism. In fact, he devoted his entire life to a revolt against capitalism. As Marx read *The Wealth of Nations*, he saw profits as unjust payments to owners of firms—the capitalists. Marx predicted that the market system would destroy itself because wealthy owners would go too far and exploit workers because unrelenting greed for profits would lead the owners to pay starvation wages. Moreover, the owners would force laborers to work in unsafe conditions, and many would not have a job at all.

Marx believed that private ownership and exploitation would produce a nation driven by a class struggle between a few "haves" and many "have-nots." As he stated in *The Communist Manifesto*, "The history of all existing society is the history of class struggle. Freeman and slave, patrician and plebeian, lord and serf, guildmaster and journeyman, in a word, oppressor and oppressed."[3] In Marx's vision, capitalists were the modern-day oppressors, and the workers were the oppressed proletariat. Someday, Marx predicted, the workers would rise up in a spontaneous bloody revolution against a system benefiting only the owners of capital. Marx believed communism to be the ideal system, which would evolve in stages from capitalism through socialism. Communism is a stateless, classless economic system in which all the factors of production are owned by the workers and people share in production according to their needs. This is the highest form of socialism toward which the revolution should strive.

Under communism, no private property exists to encourage self-interest. There is no struggle between classes of people, and everyone cooperates. In fact, there is no reason to commit crime, and police, lawyers, and courts are unnecessary. Strangely, Marx surpassed Adam Smith in advocating a system with little central government. Marx believed that those who work hard, or are more skilled, will be public spirited. Any "haves" will give voluntarily to "have-nots" until everyone has exactly the same

Karl Marx (1818–1883) His criticism of capitalism advanced communism. He wrote *The Communist Manifesto* and *Das Kapital*.

Communism
A stateless, classless economic system in which all the factors of production are owned by the workers and people share in production according to their needs. In Marx's view, this is the highest form of socialism toward which the revolution should strive.

---

[3]Karl Marx and Friedrich Engels, *The Communist Manifesto* (New York: International Press, 1848), p. 31.

material well-being. In Marx's own words, people would be motivated by the principle "from each according to his ability, to each according to his need." World peace would evolve as nation after nation accepted cooperation and rejected profits and competition. Under the idealized society of communism, there would be no state. No central authority would be necessary to pursue the interests of the people.

Today, we call the economic systems that existed in the former Soviet Union and Eastern Europe, and still exist in Cuba and other countries, *communist*. However, the definition of *socialism* given in this chapter more accurately describes their real-world economic systems. Actually, no nation has achieved the ideal communist society described by Marx, nor has capitalism self-destructed as he predicted. The 1917 communist revolution in Russia did not fit Marx's theory. At that time, Russia was an underdeveloped country, rather than an industrial country filled with greedy capitalists who exploited workers.

29-2e CHARACTERISTICS OF SOCIALISM

Regardless of a society's political system, a socialist economy has two basic characteristics: (1) public ownership and (2) centralized decision making.

Public Ownership Under socialism, the government owns most of the factors of production, including factories, farms, mines, and natural resources. Agriculture in the old Soviet Union illustrates how even this real-world socialist country deviated from total public ownership. In the Soviet Union, there were three rather distinct forms of agriculture: state farms, collective farms, and private plots. In both the state farm and collective farm sectors, central planning authorities determined prices and outputs. In contrast, the government allowed those holding small private plots on peasant farms to operate primarily in free markets that determined price and output levels. Reforms now allow farmers to buy land, tractors, trucks, and other resources from the state. If these reforms continue, they will dramatically end the collectiviation of agriculture begun under Josef Stalin.

Centralized Decision Making Instead of the pursuit of *private interest*, the motivation of pure socialism is the *public interest* of the whole society. For instance, a factory manager cannot decide to raise or lower prices to obtain maximum profits for the factory. Regardless of inventory levels or the opportunity to raise prices, the planners will not permit this action. Instead of exploiting the ups and downs of the market, the goal of the socialist system is to make centralized decisions that protect workers and consumers from decentralized market decisions. Critics argue that the main objective of this centralization is to perpetuate the personal dictatorships of leaders such as Stalin in the old Soviet Union and Fidel Castro in Cuba.

Before the open market reforms, Soviet planners altered earnings to attract workers into certain occupations and achieve planned goals. For example, if space projects needed more engineers, then the state raised the earnings of engineers until the target number of people entered the engineering profession. As shown earlier in Exhibit 2, central planners in the Soviet Union also manipulated consumer prices. If consumers desired more cars than were available, the authorities increased the price of cars. If people wished to purchase less of an item than was available, planners lowered prices. The problem was that this decision process took time. And while the market awaited its orders from the Soviet planners, excess inventories of some items accumulated, and consumers stood in line for cheap products that never seemed to be available. There was an old Soviet saying, "If you see a line, get in it. Whatever it is, it's scarce, and you will not see it tomorrow."

The Soviet factory system did not adhere completely to the command system. The government rewarded successful managers with bonuses that could be substantial. Better apartments, nice vacations, and medals were incentives for outstanding performance. Under economic reforms, plant managers now make decisions based on profitability instead of centralized controls.

✓ **CHECKPOINT**

To Plan or Not to Plan—That Is the Question
You make plans. You planned to go to college. You plan which career to follow. You plan to get married, and so on. Businesses plan. They plan to hire employees, expand their plants, increase profits, and so forth. Because individuals and businesses plan in a market economy, there is really no difference between our system and a command economy. Or is there?

29-2f SOCIALISM'S STRENGTHS AND WEAKNESSES

Proponents of the socialism model argue that this system is superior in achieving an equitable distribution of income. This is because government ownership of capital and other resources prevents a few individuals or groups from acquiring a disproportionate share of the nation's wealth. Also, supporters argue that rapid economic growth is achieved when planners have the power to direct more resources to producing capital goods and fewer resources to producing consumer goods (see Exhibit 5 in Chapter 2).

National goals may seem to be easily formulated and pursued under state directives, but there are problems. For example, proponents of such an economy can claim there is no unemployment because the government assigns all workers a job and allocates resources to complete their production goals. However, economic inefficiency results because the government often uses many workers to perform work requiring only one or two workers. Critics also point out that the absence of the profit motive discourages entrepreneurship and innovation and thus suppresses economic growth.

Socialism is particularly vulnerable to the charge that it ignores the goal of economic freedom and instead creates a privileged class of government bureaucrats who assume the role of "capitalists." Central planners are the key translators of information about consumer preferences and production capabilities flowing to millions of economic units. This complex and cumbersome process is subject to errors and is unresponsive to the wants of the majority of the population. Critics also question whether the distribution of income under socialism is more equitable than under capitalism. In the socialist system, "perks" for government officials, nepotism, and the illegal use of markets create disparities in income.

29-3 Comparing Economic Systems

In reality, all nations operate economic systems that blend capitalism and socialism. Exhibit 3 presents a continuum that attempts to place countries between the two extremes of pure socialism on the left and pure capitalism on the right. Economies characterized by a high degree of both private ownership and market allocation are

EXHIBIT 3	A Classification of Economic Systems

No nation has an economic system that is pure socialism or pure capitalism. All nations mix government ownership and reliance on markets. North Korea and Cuba are closest to pure socialism, while Hong Kong comes closest to pure capitalism. Other real-world economies are placed between these two extremes on the basis of their use of government ownership versus markets.

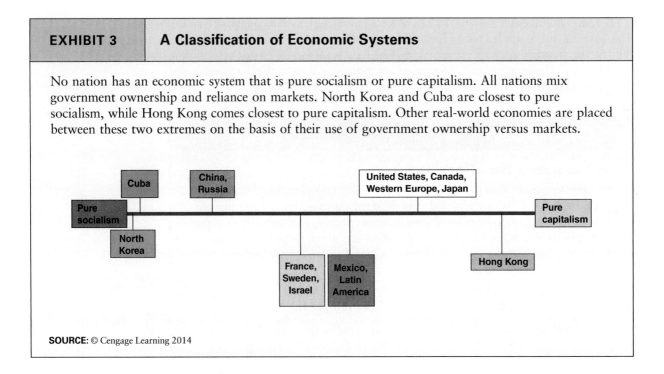

SOURCE: © Cengage Learning 2014

closest to pure capitalism. Hong Kong, Japan, the United States, and Canada fall at the capitalism end of the line. Conversely, economies characterized by much government ownership of resources and central planning are closest to pure socialism. North Korea and Cuba fall close to the pure socialism end of the spectrum, with China and Russia further away from pure socialism.

29-4 Economies in Transition

By the early 1990s, the centrally planned economies in the old Soviet Union and Eastern Europe had collapsed. After more than 70 years in the Soviet Union and over 40 years in Eastern Europe and China, the failed communist economies made a startling switch to embrace capitalism. Faced with severe shortages of food, housing, cars, and other consumer goods, communism could no longer claim better living standards for its citizens. The following is a brief discussion of reforms aimed at introducing market power into the economic systems of Cuba, Russia, and China.

29-4a CUBA

Cuba is a landscape of crumbling once-elegant buildings that often experiences daily power blackouts, fuel shortages, housing shortages, food shortages, and other economic hardships. But regardless of its economics woes, Cuba remains wedded to the communist system. Nevertheless, the collapse of Soviet bloc aid coupled with the effects of the U.S. trade embargo have forced Fidel Castro and the country's new leader, Raul Castro, die-hard Marxists, to reluctantly adopt limited free market reforms. To earn foreign exchange, the dollar has been legalized, and the Cuban government has poured capital into tourism by building several new state-owned hotels and restoring historic sections of Havana. Interestingly, Cuba operates special medical tourist hospitals that treat foreigners and diplomats while excluding Cubans. Cuba has also set up quasi-state enterprises that accept only hard currency. Because few Cubans have dollars or other hard currency, many are earning it by turning to illegal schemes, such as driving gypsy cabs, engaging in prostitution, or selling Cuba's famous cigars and coffee on the black market. Other Cubans have abandoned state jobs and opened small businesses under these new rules. For example, spare rooms in houses can be rented, and artisans can sell their work to tourists. In addition, state farm enterprises have been organized into worker-owned units, and the government allows farmers to sell produce left over after they have met the state's quota. As a result of this free market, some farmers have become venture capitalists, and more food, and a greater variety of food, have become available. In 2008, a series of changes opened access to cell phones, computers, and DVD players. Cubans are now also allowed to patronize tourist hotels. However, such luxuries are prohibitive for most Cubans. And in 2009, to improve its woeful transportation system, Cuban owners of classic American cars were recruited by the government to apply for taxi licenses and set their own fares subject to price floors.

In spite of the private enterprise reforms, Cuba remains essentially a communist system. Workers receive free education, housing, health care, low state salaries in pesos, and rations of staples, such as a monthly allowance of rice, beans, and milk. Profits from hotels and shops go directly into the central bank and help finance Castro's government. The state also discourages private enterprises by taxing them heavily on expected earnings, rather than on actual sales. In addition, there are highly restrictive regulations. For example, restaurants in Havana are limited to 12 seats and cannot expand regardless of demand. And Cuba has halted new licenses for some types of self-employment, including jewelers, mousetrap makers, and magicians or clowns. Currently, Hugo Chavez, president of Venezuela, is using his country's tremendous oil reserves to throw Cuba an economic lifeline, and counter the U.S. embargo against Cuba.

29-4b RUSSIA

In 1991, communist rule ended in Russia. To function efficiently, markets must offer incentives, so workers, the public, and even foreign investors were permitted to buy state property. This meant individuals could own the factors of production and earn profits. Such market incentives were a dagger thrust into the heart of a system previously devoted to rejecting capitalism. A key reform for Russia was to allow supply and demand to set higher prices for basic consumer goods. As shown earlier in Exhibit 2, without central planners, when prices rise to their equilibrium level, the quantity supplied increases and the quantity demanded decreases. At the beginning of 1992, the Russian government removed direct government price controls on most market goods. As the model predicts, average prices rose, leaping 1,735 percent in 1992, and a greater variety of goods started appearing on the shelves. Although workers had to pay more for basic consumer goods, they could at least find goods to buy.

Since 1992, Russia has established an independent central bank and implemented anti-inflationary monetary policies. Cities throughout Russia now have restaurants, megamalls, decent hotels, and streets choked with foreign cars. Russian entrepreneurial spirit and acceptance of it in society is in an embryonic stage, and corruption, including the legal system, is a frequent way of life. Although Russia is far from a successful market economy, the nation is struggling to achieve an amazing economic transition. Russian privatization plans are being implemented, and steps are continuing to create a dynamic economy embracing capitalism. And *Forbes* magazine reports that about 100 billionaires reside in Russia.

China's Quest for Free Market Reform

Applicable Concept: comparative economic systems

For more than 2,000 years, China had a "self-reliance" policy that caused its economy to lag far behind advanced economies. After 1949, the communists under Chairman Mao Zedong abolished private property, executed landlords, and put farmers to work in collectives where members shared equally. These reforms are referred to as *The Great Leap Forward*, which in reality became *The Great Leap Backward*. Without the self-interest motive, communal property created low incentives to work that resulted in widespread famine and millions of deaths. After the death of Mao Zedong in 1976, China adopted new economic reforms that are continuing to transform one of the poorest economies in the world into one of the fastest growing. Under this reform system, households operate in a mixed world of state controls and free markets. A two-track pricing system still exists for some key goods and services, such as coal, petroleum, steel, transportation, and agriculture.

The rural economy is central to China's economic reforms. In the past, when farmers worked collectively in people's communes, the government told the farmers what to produce and how much to produce. They could sell their products only to the state at a price fixed by the government, rather than in markets. A so-called

Gavin Hellier/Getty Images

household contract responsibility system was created as a reform to assign land owned by the state to farmers. The farmers must pay an annual share of their profits to the government, and the state does not cover losses. Farmers, however, have the authority to decide what to produce and the price at which to sell in open markets. As a result, both farmers and consumers are noticeably better off because everyone can find and afford more food.

As farming productivity rose sharply, fewer farmers were needed to work on the land, and this surplus

29-4c THE PEOPLE'S REPUBLIC OF CHINA

Unlike Russia, China has sought economic reform under the direction of its Communist Party. Fundamental economic reforms began in China after the death of Mao Zedong in 1976. Much of this reform was due to the leadership of Deng Xiaoping. Mao was devoted to the egalitarian ideal of communist ideology. Under his rule, thoughts of self-interest were counterrevolutionary, and photographs of Marx, Lenin, and Mao hung on every street corner and in every office and factory. Deng shifted priorities by increasing production of consumer goods and steering China toward becoming a global economic power. And the results have been dramatic. International trade expanded from less than 1 percent of U.S. trade in 1975 to 11 percent in 2011, and the label "Made in China" is common throughout the world. China joined the WTO in 2001 and agreed to open some markets closed to foreigners. China's real GDP growth rate averaged over 10 percent between 2001 and 2011, making it the world's fastest-growing economy.

To make China an industrial power in the 21st century, Chinese planners introduced a two-tier system for industry and agriculture in 1978. Each farm and state enterprise was given a contract to produce a quota. Any amount produced over the quota could be sold in an open market. The Chinese government also encouraged the formation labor moved into emerging township and village non-state enterprises. These enterprises were mostly in light industry and owned collectively by townships or villages. As a result, the composition of rural output has changed. When the reforms began in the late 1970s, farming accounted for 70 percent of the total output and industry for 20 percent. Currently, the structure of the economy has changed dramatically. In 2011, agriculture accounted for only 10 percent of GDP and industry's share had risen to 47 percent.[1]

A 1993 article in *The Boston Globe* provides an interesting observation on China's economic transformation:

> Stuffing the genie back into the bottle might prove difficult. The flood of money has created a bubble, particularly in stocks and property, making some people in China very rich, very fast. The China Daily, China's official English-language newspaper, recently heralded the existence of 1 million millionaires.... These millionaires, many of whom just five years ago were still wearing Mao outfits and following the party's socialist dictates, now sport stylish Western-style suits with the label ostentatiously left on the cuff.[2]

China's controversial womb police have spent decades attempting to control the nation's population according to China's one-child policy. They have succeeded remarkably well, and the country has solved its population problem. China's population will actually decline in 2040, according to U.N. projections.

At the 16th Communist Party Congress in 2003, President Hu Jintao and Communist Party leaders announced another turning point and a new starting point in China's reform process. A key debate concerned reforms that would move China closer to capitalism, including the first-ever guarantee of private property under communist rule. In 2011, Forbes reported that China had over 100 billionaires. And Rupert Hoogewerf, CEO of the *Hurun Report*, says China's recent surge in mega-wealth is "comparable to the U.S. at the end of the 19th century, when you had the Rockefellers and Carnegies."

Analyze the Issue

1. Why would China abandon the goal of income equality and shift from a centrally planned system to a more market-oriented economy?
2. Which groups in China are likely to resist the reforms?

---

1. The World Bank, *Key Development Data & Statistics*, http://web.worldbank.org/.
2. Maggie Farley, "China's Economic Boom Energizing Inflation," *Boston Globe*, Aug. 13, 1993, p. 1A.

Source: © Cengage Learning 2014

of nonstate enterprises owned jointly by managers and their workforces and special economic zones open to foreign investment. In other words, a blend of capitalism and socialism would provide the incentives needed to increase output. As Deng Xiaoping explained, "It doesn't matter whether the cat is black or white as long as it catches mice." These reforms worked, leading to huge increases in farm and industrial output in the 1980s. In fact, some peasant farmers became the wealthiest people in China. After Deng's death in the mid-1990s, leadership of China passed to leaders who continued the policy of free market reforms. Today, forests of glossy skyscrapers, expressways, upscale apartments, and enormous shopping malls in Beijing, Shanghai, and other cities attest to the market-oriented reforms begun years ago. And life in China's fast lane now includes the opportunity of dining at Kentucky Fried Chicken and McDonald's restaurants located in cities throughout the country. Disney is scheduled to open its theme park in 2015, and China is estimated to overtake the United States in total theme park visits by 2020. Also, despite government censorship, China has the largest number of Internet users in the world. (See "Global Economics: China's Quest for Free Market Reform.")

Today, China is a huge nation transforming itself swiftly into a powerful player in the global economy. U.S. exporters are overjoyed at the prospect of selling products to over a billion Chinese consumers. For example, swarms of bicyclists once synonymous with urban China are being pushed off the road by consumers who now can afford cars and trucks. Rolls-Royce and Bentley, the ultra-luxury cars, have expanded into China, and it is estimated that by 2030, China will have more cars on the road than the United States. Also, more Chinese are traveling by air. Consequently, the Chinese are buying more Boeing airplanes and American-made cars. The other side of the coin is the threat of what goods the industrious Chinese workers, with increasing training and foreign investment, might produce and sell abroad. For example, China manufactures most of the world's copiers, microwave ovens, DVD players, and shoes. A ballooning U.S. trade deficit with China is often cited as evidence that China is not playing fair, and the political rhetoric has intensified on both sides of the issue. Other countries fear that China will eliminate their export business with the United States. Moreover, there is concern that lowering trade barriers under free trade agreements will increase Chinese imports into domestic markets and eliminate jobs. In 2007, one Chinese-made product after another was removed from U.S. shelves, for example, lethal pet food, toxic toothpaste, and other contaminated products. This prompted calls for more stringent safety regulations for imports.

Currently, China's leaders are dealing with an economy that is experiencing overheating. Factories suffer electricity shortages, while ports and railways cannot handle all the cargo flowing in and out of the country. China is consuming huge quantities of crude oil, copper, steel, and aluminum. Moreover, there is discontent over labor issues, pollution, and income inequality. While some people dig through trash bins, there are now wealthy private business owners. Despite the unease, China remains a market of great profit and promise and a target for protectionists as it continues its transition from a communist command economy to capitalism. And the debate continues over whether China, a socialist economy, is a strategic trading partner or an emerging economic colossus that will dominate the world economy.

29-5 Privatization versus Nationalization

Privatization

The process of turning a government enterprise into a private enterprise.

Nationalization

The act of transforming a private enterprise's assets into government ownership.

The above discussions of Cuba, Russia, and China provide examples of privatization. Privatization is the process of turning a government enterprise into a private enterprise. It is the opposite of nationalization, which is the act of transforming a private enterprise's assets into government ownership. The motives for nationalization are political as well as economic. Proponents believe that government ownership enables the state on behalf of the people to exercise more effective control and equitable redistribution of wealth and income. Critics argue that government ownership suppresses incentives, entrepreneurship, and private investment that are essential for an enterprise to prosper. During a financial crisis, the argument in favor of nationalization is that a brief period of nationalization is needed to prevent the largest corporations and banks from a downward spiral that affects the entire economy. This is the "too big to fail" argument.

In recent years, Venezuelan president Hugo Chavez has received much press coverage for nationalizing a list of industries, including oil, cement, steel, and ordering the army to take over all rice processing and packaging plants. Chavez stated in a 2007 speech in Caracas, "We're heading toward socialism, and nothing and no one can prevent it."

The United States also has a history of nationalization—most of which was temporary. But one that has endured: Amtrak is a government-owned corporation created in 1971 after railroads had petitioned repeatedly to abandon unprofitable passenger service. As discussed at the conclusion of the chapter on money and the Federal

Reserve System, the Resolution Trust Corporation (RTC) was established in 1989 to take over more than 1,000 failed savings and loans institutions with bad loans and foreclosed homes. After fulfilling its mission to sell the assets of these S&Ls, the RTC was closed in 1995. The recent financial crisis has generated several nationalizations that only in the future will it be known if they are temporary. General Motors provides a prime case. With GM facing bankruptcy in 2009, the U.S. government replaced the CEO and took a 60 percent controlling share, with Canada a 12.5 percent share, the United Auto Workers (UAW) 17.5 percent, and bondholders ending up with the remaining 10 percent. Existing stockholders were given zero shares. Will GM emerge to become successful and nationalization given credit, or will the reverse be the result?

Key Concepts

Economic system

Traditional economy

Command economy

Market economy

Invisible hand

Mixed economy

Capitalism

Consumer sovereignty

Socialism

Communism

Privatization

Nationalization

Summary

- An **economic system** is the set of established procedures by which a society answers the What, How, and For Whom to produce questions.
- **Three basic types of economic systems** are the traditional, command, and market systems. The **traditional system** makes decisions according to custom, and the **command system**, shown in the figure below, answers the three economic questions through some powerful central authority. In contrast, the **market system** uses the impersonal mechanism of the interaction of buyers and sellers in markets to answer the What, How, and For Whom questions.

Command Economy

SOURCE: © Cengage Learning 2014

- **Capitalism** is an economic system in which the factors of production are privately owned and

economic choices are made by consumers and firms in markets. As prescribed by Adam Smith, government plays an extremely limited role, and self-interest is the driving force, held in check, or regulated, by competition.

- **Consumer sovereignty** is the freedom of consumers to determine the types and quantities of products that are produced in an economy by choosing to buy or not to buy.
- **Socialism** is an economic system in which the government owns the factors of production. The central authorities make the myriad of society's economic decisions according to a national plan. The collective good, or public interest, is the intended guiding force behind the central planners' decisions.
- **Communism** is an economic system envisioned by Karl Marx to be an ideal society in which the workers own all the factors of production. Marx believed that workers who work hard will be public spirited and voluntarily redistribute income to those who are less productive. Such a communist nation described by Marx does not exist.
- **Privatization** is the process of turning a government enterprise into a private enterprise. It is the opposite of **nationalization**, which is the act of transforming a private enterprise's assets into government ownership.

Summary of Conclusion Statements

- When central planners set prices below equilibrium for goods and services, they create shortages, which mean long lines, empty shelves, and black markets.

- A market economy answers the What to produce and How to produce questions very effectively.
- No nation in the world precisely fits the two criteria for capitalism; however, the United States comes close.

Study Questions and Problems

1. Give an example of how a nation's culture affects its economic system.
2. Explain the advantages and disadvantages of any two of the three basic types of economic systems.
3. Suppose a national program of free housing for the elderly is paid for by a sizable increase in income taxes. Explain a trade-off that might occur between economic security and efficiency.
4. "The schools are not in the business of pleasing parents and students, and they cannot be allowed to set their own agendas. Their agendas are set by politicians, administrators, and various constituencies that hold the keys to political power. The public system is built to see to it that the schools do what their government wants them to do—that they conform to the higher-order values their governors seek to impose."[4] Relate this statement to Exhibit 1.
5. Suppose you are a farmer. Explain why you would be motivated to work in traditional, command, and market economies.
6. Karl Marx believed the market system was doomed. Why do you think he was right or wrong?
7. If all real-world economies are mixed economies, why is the U.S. economy described as capitalist, while the Cuban economy is described as communist?
8. Suppose you are a factory manager. Describe how you might reach production goals under a system of pure capitalism and under a system of pure socialism.

For Online Exercises, go the Tucker Web site at www.cengage.com/economics/tucker.

✔ CHECKPOINT ANSWER

To Plan or Not to Plan—That Is the Question

When an individual or a business plans in a market economy, other individuals are free to make and follow their own plans. Suppose Hewlett-Packard decides to produce X number of laser printers and sell them at a certain price. The decision does not prohibit IBM from producing Y number of laser printers and selling them for less than Hewlett-Packard's printers. If either firm makes a mistake, only that firm suffers, and other industries are, for the most part, unaffected. Under a command system, a central economic plan would be made for all laser printer manufacturers. If the central planners order the wrong quantity or quality, there could be major harm to other industries and society. If you said there is a major difference between individual planning and central planning for all society, **YOU ARE CORRECT.**

---

[4]John Chubb and Terry More, *Politics, Markets, and the Nation's Public Schools* (Washington, D.C.: Brookings Institution, 1990), p. 38.

Sample Quiz

For an explanation of the correct answers, visit the Tucker Web site at www.cengage.com/economics/tucker.

1. An economic system is the organizations and methods used to determine
   a. what goods and services are produced.
   b. how goods and services are produced.
   c. for whom goods and services are produced.
   d. All of the above answers are correct.

2. In a command economy, the basic economic questions are answered by
   a. central authority.
   b. individual buyers and sellers.
   c. traditional methods.
   d. None of the above answers are correct.

3. Adam Smith was an advocate of
   a. mercantilism.
   b. a nation maximizing its stock of gold.
   c. unrestricted or free trade.
   d. the "visible hand" of public interest.

4. In Adam Smith's competitive market economy, the question of what goods to produce is determined by the
   a. "invisible hand" of the price system.
   b. "invisible hand" of government.
   c. "invisible hand" of public interest.
   d. "visible hand" of laws and regulations.

5. Adam Smith wrote that the
   a. economic problems of 18th-century England were caused by free markets.
   b. government should control the economy.
   c. pursuit of private self-interest promotes the public interest in a market economy.
   d. public or collective interest is not promoted by people pursuing their self-interest.

6. Which of the following is a criticism of capitalism?
   a. unequal distribution of income
   b. failure to protect the environment
   c. exploitation of workers
   d. All of the above answers are correct.

7. Which of the following statements is *true*?
   a. The doctrine of *laissez-faire* advocates an economic system with extensive government intervention and little individual decision making.

   b. In capitalism, income is distributed on the basis of need.
   c. Adam Smith was the father of socialism.
   d. Most real-world economies are mixed economic systems.

8. Which of the following is a strength of a command-based economic system?
   a. Goods can be allocated based on need rather than willingness and ability to pay.
   b. Producers have strong incentives to innovate because successful innovators are rewarded with higher profit.
   c. Consumers can transmit their preference for product quality and variety by way of their "dollar votes" cast in the marketplace.
   d. Because price is freely set based on supply and demand, there are few shortages or surpluses.

9. The term *socialism* refers to which of the following?
   a. a religion centered on community interaction
   b. an economic system characterized by private ownership of resources and decentralized market-price allocation
   c. an economic system characterized by government ownership of resources and centralized allocation
   d. an economic system characterized by voluntary allocation

10. Karl Marx was a (an)
    a. 19th-century German philosopher.
    b. 18th-century Russian economist.
    c. 14th-century Polish banker.
    d. 19th-century Russian journalist.

11. Karl Marx published
    a. *Das Kapital.*
    b. *General Theory of Communism.*
    c. *The Wealth of Nations.*
    d. *The Capitalist Manifesto.*

12. In Marx's ideal communist society, the state
    a. actively promotes income incentives.
    b. follows the doctrine of *laissez-faire.*
    c. owns resources and conducts planning.
    d. does not exist.

Sample Quiz *continued*

13. According to Adam Smith, the "invisible hand" refers to which of the following?
    a. The "best interests of society" (public interest) will occur as an outcome of the market process coordinating the self-interested interactions of buyers and sellers (private interest).
    b. Government interference in markets to prevent greed.
    c. Bribes and graft that interfere with the market process.
    d. The "best interest of society" (public interest) will occur as an outcome of careful guidance by government authorities in allocating scarce good and services according to private interest.

14. A principal feature of a command economy is that _____.
    a. production decisions are made by profit-maximizing firms.
    b. there is a central planning board at the top, which transmits economic decisions down to the various producing and consuming units below.
    c. consumers are allowed to determine that is produced based on their demand for goods and services.
    d. regulatory agencies constrain the most egregious forms of market power in a market system of allocation.

15. Which nation achieved the ideal communist society as described by Marx?
    a. Castro's Cuba
    b. Mao's China
    c. Stalin's Soviet Union
    d. No nation has achieved Marx's vision of a communist society.

16. Adam Smith's book, *The Wealth of Nations*, was published at the time of the
    a. War of 1812.
    b. U.S. Declaration of Independence.
    c. U.S. Civil War.
    d. Great Depression.

17. Which of the following economies is an example of a mixed system?
    a. United States
    b. United Kingdom
    c. Sweden
    d. All of the above answers are correct.

18. Property rights allowing individuals to own goods, services, and factors of production are *most* important in
    a. socialistic economies.
    b. planned economies.
    c. capitalist economies.
    d. command economies.

19. Which of the following is a *correct* characterization of socialism?
    a. Tradition answers the basic economic questions.
    b. Markets are used exclusively to answer the basic economic questions.
    c. Central planning is used to answer the basic economic questions.
    d. Government ownership of many resources and centralized decision-making answers the basic economic questions.

20. Which of the following statements is *true*?
    a. The United States today comes closer to the socialist form of economic organization than it does to capitalism.
    b. When central planners set prices above equilibrium for goods and services, they create shortages.
    c. According to Karl Marx, under capitalism, workers would be exploited and would revolt against the owners of capital.
    d. Adam Smith argued that government's role in society would be to do absolutely nothing.

chapter 30

Growth and the Less-Developed Countries

How would your life be different if you lived in Rwanda or Haiti instead of the United States? It is unlikely that anyone in your family would have a telephone or a car. You surely would not own a personal computer or an iPod. You would not have new clothes or be enrolled in a college or university studying economics. You would not be going out to restaurants or movies. You would be fortunate to have shoes and one full meal each day. You would receive little or no medical care and live in unsanitary surroundings. Hunger, disease, and squalor would engulf you. In fact, the World Bank estimates that over 20 percent of people in developing countries survive on less than $1.25 per day. It is exceedingly difficult for Americans to grasp that one-fifth of the world's population lives at such a meager subsistence level. This chapter's important task is unraveling the secrets of economic growth and development. Why do some countries prosper while others decline?

At different times in history, Egypt, China, Italy, and Greece were highly developed by the standards of their time. On the other hand, at one time, the United States was a struggling, relatively poor country on the path to becoming a rich country. Its growth came in three stages: First, was the agricultural stage. Then came the manufacturing stage when industries such as railroads, steel, and automobiles were driving forces toward economic growth. And, finally, there has been a shift toward service industries. This is the U.S. success story, but it is not the only road countries can follow to lift themselves from the misery of poverty.

In this chapter, you will learn to solve these economics puzzles:

- Is there a difference between economic growth and economic development?
- Why are some countries rich and others poor?
- Is trade a better "engine of growth" than foreign aid and loans?

30-1 Comparing Developed and Less-Developed Countries

Income disparity exists not only among families within the United States, but also among nations. In this section, the great inequality of income between the families of nations will be used to classify nations as rich or poor.

30-1a CLASSIFYING COUNTRIES BY GDP PER CAPITA

GDP per capita

The value of final goods produced (GDP) divided by the total population.

Industrially advanced countries (IACs)

High-income nations that have market economies based on large stocks of technologically advanced capital and well-educated labor. The United States, Canada, Australia, New Zealand, Japan, and most of the countries of Western Europe are IACs.

Less-developed countries (LDCs)

Nations without large stocks of technologically advanced capital and well-educated labor. LDCs are economies based on agriculture, such as most countries of Africa, Asia, and Latin America.

There are about 196 countries in the world. Exhibit 1 shows a ranking of selected countries from high to low GDP per capita. GDP per capita is the value of final goods produced (GDP) divided by the total population. Although any system of defining rich versus poor countries is arbitrary, GDP per capita or average GDP is a fundamental measure of a country's economic well-being. At the top of the income ladder are 27 developed countries called the industrially advanced countries (IACs). Industrially advanced countries are high-income nations that have market economies based on large stocks of technologically advanced capital and well-educated labor. The United States, Canada, Australia, New Zealand, Japan, and most of the countries of Western Europe are IACs. Excluded from the IACs are countries with high incomes whose economies are based on oil under the sand, and not on widespread industrial development. The United Arab Emirates is an example of such a country.

Countries of the world other than IACs are classified as underdeveloped or less-developed countries (LDCs). Less-developed countries are nations without large stocks of technologically advanced capital and well-educated labor. Their economies are based on agriculture, as in most countries of Africa, Asia, and Latin America. Most of the world's population live in LDCs and share widespread poverty.

A closer examination of Exhibit 1 reveals that the differences in living standards between the IACs and LDCs are enormous. For example, the GDP per capita in the United States was $48,387 greater than the average income of $605 in Rwanda. Stated differently, the 2011 average income in the United States was about 80 times larger than the average income in Rwanda. What a difference! Imagine trying to live on only $605 a year in the United States. You probably would not survive.

Exhibit 2 compares GDP per capita for IACs to LDCs by regions of the world for 2011. The average citizen in the IACs enjoyed an income of $48,231, which was 41 times that of the average citizen in Sub-Saharan Africa ($48,231/$1,188). Sub-Saharan Africa includes countries such as Nigeria, Angola, Congo, Sudan, and Zimbabwe. The exhibit also reveals that the greatest concentrations of world poverty are located in the rural areas of East Asia and the Pacific and Sub-Saharan Africa. These regions have many countries characterized by bleak and pervasive poverty, but there are notable exceptions, nicknamed the "Four Tigers" of East Asia—Hong Kong, Singapore, South Korea, and Taiwan. These Pacific Rim countries are newly industrialized economies, which we discuss at the end of this chapter.

EXHIBIT 1	Annual GDP per Capita for Selected Countries, 2011		
Country	**GDP per capita**	**Country**	**GDP per capita**
Industrially Advanced Countries (IACs)			
Luxembourg	$113,533	Japan	45,920
Norway	97,255	France	44,008
Switzerland	81,161	Germany	43,742
Australia	65,477	United Kingdom	38,592
Denmark	59,928	New Zealand	36,648
Sweden	56,956	Spain	36,360
Canada	50,435	Italy	36,267
Netherlands	50,355	Hong Kong	34,049
Austria	49,809	Israel	31,986
Finland	49,350	Greece	27,073
Singapore	49,271	South Korea	22,778
United States	48,387	Portugal	22,413
Ireland	47,531	Taiwan	20,100
Belgium	46,878		
Less-Developed Countries (LDCs)			
Chile	14,278	Iraq	3,513
Russia	12,993	Indonesia	3,509
Brazil	12,789	Georgia	3,210
Venezuela	10,610	Egypt	2,970
Turkey	10,522	India	1,389
Mexico	10,153	Vietnam	1,374
Romania	8,863	Pakistan	1,201
Panama	8,514	Haiti	738
South Africa	8,066	Bangladesh	678
Iran	6,360	Rwanda	605
China	5,414	Mozambique	583
Thailand	5,394	Ethiopia	360
Ukraine	3,621		

SOURCE: International Monetary Fund, *World Economic Outlook Database*, http://www.imf.org/external/ns/cs.aspx?id=28.

EXHIBIT 2	Average GDP per Capita for IACs and LDCs by Region, 2011

This exhibit shows average GDP per capita by regions of the world for 2011. The differences between the rich, industrially advanced countries (IACs) and the poor, less-developed countries (LDCs) in the various regions of the world are enormous. For example, the average citizen in the IACs had an income 41 times that of the average citizen in the LDCs of Sub-Saharan Africa.

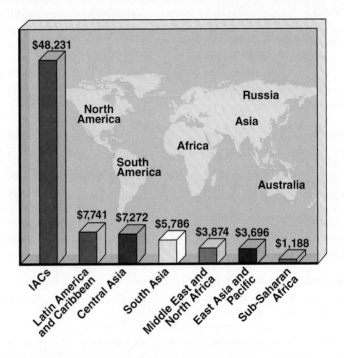

SOURCE: World Bank Group, *Key Development Data & Statistics,* http://data.worldbank.org/country.

30-1b PROBLEMS WITH GDP PER CAPITA COMPARISONS

Several problems are associated with using GDP per capita to compare rich versus poor countries. First, there is a measurement problem because countries tabulate GDP with differing degrees of accuracy. LDCs in general do not use sophisticated methods of gathering and processing GDP and population data. For example, in countries whose economies are based largely on agriculture, a family is more likely to produce goods and services outside the price system. In LDCs, families often grow their own food, make their own clothes, and build their own homes. Estimating the value of this output at market prices is difficult.

CONCLUSION: *LDCs' GDP per capita is subject to greater measurement errors than data for IACs.*

Second, GDP per capita comparisons among countries can be misleading because they ignore the relative income distribution. Some countries have very high per capita incomes, yet most of the income goes to just a few wealthy families. The United Arab Emirates' GDP per capita is higher than that of several IACs. However, the United Arab Emirates earns its income from oil exports, and its income is actually distributed disproportionately to a relatively small number of wealthy families.

> **CONCLUSION:** *GDP per capita comparisons among nations can be misleading because GDP per capita does not measure income distribution.*

Third, GDP per capita comparisons between nations are subject to conversion problems. Making these data comparisons requires converting one nation's currency, say, Japan's yen, into a common currency, the U.S. dollar. Because, as explained in the chapter on international trade and finance, the value of a country's currency can rise or fall for many reasons, the true value of a nation's output can be distorted. For example, during a given year, one government might maintain an artificially high exchange rate and another government might not.

> **CONCLUSION:** *A conversion problem may widen or narrow the GDP per capita gap between nations because the fluctuations in exchange rates do not reflect actual differences in the value of goods and services produced.*

30-1c QUALITY-OF-LIFE MEASURES OF DEVELOPMENT

GDP per capita measures market transactions, but this measure does not give a complete picture of differences in living standards among nations. Exhibit 3 presents other selected socioeconomic indicators of the quality of life. These are variables such as life expectancy at birth, infant mortality rate, literacy rate, per capita energy consumption, and economic freedom ranking. Take a close look at the statistics in Exhibit 3. These data reflect the dimensions of poverty in many of the LDCs. For example, a person born in Japan has a life expectancy that is much longer than a person born in Mozambique, and the infant mortality rate is dramatically higher in Mozambique. Per capita energy consumption measures the use of nonhuman energy to perform work. In IACs, most work is done by machines, and in LDCs, virtually all work is done by people. For example, the average American uses 7,075 kilograms of (oil-equivalent) energy per year, while the average person in Mozambique uses only 416 kilograms. Finally, it is interesting to note that GDP per capita and other quality-of-life indicators are related to the ranking in economic freedom.

How good an indicator of the quality of life is GDP per capita? Exhibit 3 reflects the principle that lower GDP per capita is highly correlated with measures of the quality of life.

> **CONCLUSION:** *In general, GDP per capita is highly correlated with alternative measures of quality of life.*

EXHIBIT 3	Quality-of-Life Indicators for Selected Countries, 2011					
Country	**(1)** **GDP** **per Capita**	**(2)** **Life** **Expectancy** **at Birth** **(years)**	**(3)** **Infant** **Mortality** **Rate**[1]	**(4)** **Literacy** **Rate**[2]	**(5)** **Per Capita** **Energy** **Consumption**[3]	**(6)** **Economic** **Freedom** **Rank**[4]
United States	$48,387	79	8	99%	7,075	10
Japan	45,920	83	3	99	3,713	22
Mexico	10,153	77	17	93	1,646	75
China	5,414	74	18	94	1,598	92
India	1,389	66	63	63	545	94
Bangladesh	678	68	48	56	175	103
Mozambique	583	50	135	55	416	128

[1]Per 1,000 live births.

[2]Percentage age 15 and over who can read and write.

[3]Kilograms of oil equivalent.

[4]The Fraser Institute.

SOURCES: The CIA World Factbook, https://www.cia.gov/library/publications/the-world-factbook/index.html, World Bank Group, *Key Development Data & Statistics*, http://data.worldbank.org/country, The Fraser Institute, http://www.freetheworld.com.

30-2 Economic Growth and Development around the World

Economic growth and development are major goals of IACs and LDCs. People all over the world strive for a higher quality of life for their generation and future generations. However, growth is closer to a life-or-death situation for many LDCs, such as Bangladesh and Mozambique.

Economic growth and economic development are somewhat different, but related, concepts. As shown in Exhibit 4, recall from Chapter 2 that economic growth is the ability of an economy to produce greater levels of output, represented by an outward shift of its production possibilities curve (PPC). Thus, economic growth is defined on a *quantitative* basis using the percentage change in GDP per capita. When a nation's GDP rises more rapidly than its population, GDP per capita rises, and the nation experiences economic growth. Conversely, if GDP expands less than the population of a nation, GDP per capita falls, and the nation experiences negative economic growth.

Economic development is a broader concept that is more *qualitative* in nature. Economic development encompasses improvement in the quality of life, including economic growth in the production of goods and services. In short, continuous economic growth is necessary for economic development, but economic growth is not the only consideration. For example, as explained earlier, GDP per capita does not measure the distribution of income or the political environment that provides the

EXHIBIT 4	Economic Growth

The economy begins with the capacity to produce combinations along production possibilities curve PPC_1. Growth in the resource base or technological advance shifts the production possibilities curve outward from PPC_1 to PPC_2. Points along PPC_2 represent new production possibilities that were previously impossible. The distance that the curve shifts represents an increase in the nation's productive capacity.

CAUSATION CHAIN

Growth in resources or technological advance ⇒ Economic growth

SOURCE: © Cengage Learning 2014

legal, monetary, education, and transportation structures necessary for economic growth.

Economic growth and development involve a complex process that is determined by several interrelated factors. Like the performance of an NBA basketball team, success depends on the joint effort of team players, and one or two weak players can greatly reduce overall performance. However, there is no precise formula for winning. If your team has a player like former NBA great Michael Jordan, it can win even with a few weak players. The remainder of this section examines the key factors, or players, that operate together to produce a nation's economic well-being.

30-2a ENDOWMENT OF NATURAL RESOURCES

Most of the LDCs have comparatively limited bases of natural resources, including mineral deposits and arable land resources. In these countries, most of the available land is used for agricultural production, and clearing tropical forests to obtain more land can cause soil erosion. Also, tropical climates prevail in Central and South America, Africa, the Indian subcontinent, and Southeast Asia. The hot, humid climate in these regions is conducive to weed and insect infestations that plague agriculture.

Although a narrow base of resources does pose a barrier to economic growth and development, no single conclusion can be drawn. For example, how have Hong Kong, Japan, and Israel achieved high standards of living in spite of limited natural resource bases? Each has practically no minerals, little fertile land, and no domestic sources of energy. Nonetheless, these economies have become prosperous. In contrast, Argentina, Venezuela, and Brazil have abundant fertile land and minerals. Yet these and other countries have been growing slowly or not at all. Venezuela, for example, is one of the most oil-rich countries in the world. Ghana, Kenya, and Bolivia are also resource-rich countries that are poor, with little or no economic growth.

> **CONCLUSION:** *Natural resource endowment can promote economic growth, but a country can develop without a large natural resource base.*

30-2b INVESTMENT IN HUMAN RESOURCES

A low level of human capital can also present a barrier to economic growth and development. Recall that human capital is the education, training, experience, and health that improve the knowledge and skills of workers to produce goods and services. In most of the LDCs, investment in human capital is much less than in the IACs. Look back at column (4) in Exhibit 3. Consider how the literacy rate falls for the poorer countries. A country with a lower literacy rate has less ability to educate its labor force and create a basic foundation for economic growth. In fact, often the skills of workers in the poor countries are suited primarily to agriculture, rather than being appropriate for a wide range of industries and economic growth. Further complicating matters is a "brain drain" problem because the best educated and trained workers of poor countries pursue their education in wealthier countries. Column (2) of Exhibit 3 also gives a measure of health among countries with varying levels of GDP per capita. As the GDP per capita falls, the life expectancy at birth falls. Thus, richer countries have the advantage of a better educated and healthier workforce.

> **CONCLUSION:** *Investment in human capital generally results in increases in GDP per capita.*

Thus far, the discussion has been about the quality of labor. We must also talk about the quantity of labor because productivity is related to both the quality and quantity of labor. Overpopulation is a problem for LDCs. In a nutshell, here is why: Other factors held constant, population (labor force) growth can increase a country's GDP. Yet rapid population growth can convert an expanding GDP into a GDP per capita that is stagnant, slow growing, or negative. Stated another way, there is no gain if an increase in output is more than matched by an increase in the number of mouths that must be fed. Suppose the GDP of an LDC grows at, say, 3 percent per year. If there is no growth in population, GDP per capita also grows at 3 percent per year. But what if the population also grows at 3 percent per year? The result is that GDP per capita remains unchanged. If population growth is instead only 1 percent per year, GDP per capita rises 2 percent per year. Obstacles to population control are great and include strong religious and sociocultural arguments against birth control programs.

> **CONCLUSION:** *Rapid population growth combined with low human capital investment explains why many countries are LDCs.*

✔ CHECKPOINT

Does Rapid Growth Mean a Country Is Catching Up?

Suppose country Alpha has a production possibilities curve closer to the origin than the curve for country Beta. Now assume Alpha experiences a 3 percent growth rate in GDP for 10 years and Beta experiences a 6 percent growth rate in GDP for 10 years. At the end of five years, which of the following is the best prediction for the standard of living? (1) Alpha's residents are better off. (2) Beta's residents are better off. (3) Which country's residents are better off cannot be determined.

30-2c ACCUMULATION OF CAPITAL

It did not take long for Robinson Crusoe stranded on a deserted island, to invest in a net in order to catch more fish than he could catch with his hands. Similarly, farmers working with modern tractors can cultivate more acres than farmers working with horse-drawn plows. Recall from Chapter 1 that capital in economics means factories, tractors, trucks, roads, computers, irrigation systems, electricity-generating facilities, and other human-made goods used to produce goods and services.

LDCs suffer from a critical shortage of capital. A family in Somalia owns little in the way of tools except a wooden plow. To make matters worse, roads are terrible, there are few plants generating electricity, and telephone lines are scarce. As shown in Exhibit 5, recall from Chapter 2 that a high-investment country can shift its production possibilities curve outward, but investment in capital goods is not a "free lunch." When more resources are used to produce more factories and machines, there is an opportunity cost of fewer resources available for the production of current consumer goods. This means that LDCs are often caught in a vicious circle of poverty. A vicious circle of poverty is the trap in which countries are poor and cannot afford to save. And low savings translate into low investment. Low investment results in low productivity, which, in turn, keeps incomes low. Any savings that do exist among higher-income persons in poor LDCs are often invested in IACs. This phenomenon is often called "capital flight." These wealthy individuals are afraid to save in their own countries because they fear that their governments may be overthrown and their savings could be lost.

Vicious circle of poverty

The trap in which countries are poor because they cannot afford to save and invest, but they cannot save and invest because they are poor.

EXHIBIT 5	Alpha's and Beta's Present and Future Production Possibilities Curves

In part (a), each year Alpha produces only enough capital (K_a) to replace existing capital that is worn out. Without greater capital and assuming other resources remain fixed, Alpha is unable to shift its production possibilities curve outward. In part (b), each year Beta produces K_b capital, which is more than the amount required to replenish its depreciated capital. In 2010, this expanded capital provides Beta with the extra production capacity to shift its production possibilities curve to the right. If Beta chooses point B on its curve, it has the production capacity to increase the amount of consumer goods from C_b to C_c without producing fewer capital goods.

SOURCE: © Cengage Learning 2014

The United States and other nations have attempted to provide LDCs with foreign aid so that they might grow. These countries desperately need more factories and infrastructure. Infrastructure is capital goods usually provided by the government, including highways, bridges, waste and water systems, and airports. Unfortunately, the amount of capital given to the LDCs is relatively small, and as explained above, workers in the LDCs lack the skills necessary to use the most modern forms of capital. More specifically, LDCs face a major obstacle to capital accumulation because of the lack of entrepreneurs to assume the risks of capital formation.

Infrastructure

Capital goods usually provided by the government, including highways, bridges, waste and water systems, and airports.

> **CONCLUSION:** *There is a significant positive relationship between investment and economic growth and development.*

30-2d TECHNOLOGICAL PROGRESS

As explained earlier in Chapter 2, holding natural resources, labor, and capital constant, advancing the body of knowledge applied to production shifts the production possibilities curve of a country. In fact, technological advances have been at the heart of economic growth and development in recent history. During the last 250 years, brainpower has invented new power-driven machines, advanced communication devices, new energy sources, and countless ways to produce more output with the same resources. How have innovative products improved your productivity? Consider, to name just a few products, the impact of personal computers, word processing software, cell phone photography, the iPhone, and the Internet. In contrast, in many poor countries, waterwheels still bring water to the surface, cloth is woven on handlooms, and oxcarts are the major means of transportation. Consequently, large inputs of human effort are used relative to capital resources.

The United States and other IACs have provided the world with an abundant accumulation of technological knowledge that might be adopted by those LDCs without the resources to undertake the required cost of research and development. However, the results of this transfer process have been mixed. For example, countries such as China, Hong Kong, Singapore, Taiwan, South Korea, and Japan have surely achieved rapid growth in part from the benefit of technological borrowing. Currently, Russia and other Eastern European nations are attempting to apply existing technological knowledge to boost their rates of growth.

The other side of the coin is that much available technology is not suited to LDCs. The old saying "You need to learn to walk before you can run" often applies to the LDCs. For example, small farms of most LDCs are not suited for much of the agricultural technology developed for IACs' large farms. And how many factories in the LDCs are ready to use the most modern robotics in the production process? Stated differently, LDCs need appropriate technology, rather than necessarily the latest technology.

> **CONCLUSION:** *Many LDCs continue to experience low growth rates even though IACs have developed advanced technologies that the world can utilize.*

30-2e POLITICAL ENVIRONMENT

The discussion above leads to the generalization that in order for LDCs to achieve economic growth and development, they must wisely use natural resources, invest in human and physical capital, and adopt advanced technology. This list of policies is not complete. LDC governments must also create a political environment favorable to economic growth. All too often a large part of the problem in poor countries is that resources are wasted as a result of war and political instability. Political leaders must not be corrupt and/or incompetent. Instead of following policies that favor a small elite ruling class, LDC governments must adopt appropriate domestic and international economic policies, discussed under the following three headings of law and order, infrastructure, and international trade.

Law and Order   A basic governmental function is to establish domestic law and order. This function includes many areas, such as a stable legal system, stable money and prices, competitive markets, and private ownership of property. In particular, expropriation of private property rights among LDCs is a barrier to growth. Well-defined private property rights have fostered economic growth in the IACs because this institutional policy has encouraged an entrepreneurial class. Private ownership provides individuals with the incentive to save money and invest in businesses. A stable political environment that ensures private ownership of profits also provides an incentive for individuals in other countries to invest in developing poor countries.

Infrastructure   Assuming an LDC government maintains law and order and the price system is used to allocate goods and services, it is vital that wise decisions be made concerning infrastructure. Indeed, inadequate infrastructure is one of the greatest problems of LDCs. Without such public goods as roads, schools, bridges, and public health and sanitation services, poor countries are unable to generate the substantial external benefits that are an important ingredient in economic growth and development. From the viewpoint of individual firms, government must provide infrastructure because these public goods projects are too costly for a firm to undertake.

International Trade   In general, LDCs can benefit from an expanding volume of trade. This is the theory behind the North American Free Trade Agreement (NAFTA), the General Agreement on Tariffs and Trade (GATT), and the World Trade Organization (WTO) discussed in the chapter on international trade and finance. As explained earlier in this chapter, policies such as tariffs and quotas restrain international trade and thereby inhibit economic growth and development. These trade policies are antigrowth because they restrict the ability of people in one country to trade with people in other countries. Similarly, a country that fixes the exchange rate of its own currency above the market-determined exchange rate makes that country's exports less attractive to foreigners. This means, in turn, that domestic citizens sell less of their goods to foreigners and earn less foreign currency with which to buy imports.

> **CONCLUSION:** *Exchange rate controls artificially set by government above the market exchange rates reduce the volume of both exports and imports (international trade).*

Exhibit 6 summarizes the key factors explained above that determine the economic growth and development of countries. Analysis of this exhibit reveals that economic growth and development are the result of a multidimensional process. This means that it is difficult for countries to break the poverty barrier because they must follow various avenues and improve many factors in order to increase their economic well-being. But it is important to remember that lack of one or more key factors, such as natural resources, does not necessarily keep an LDC in the trap of underdevelopment.

> **CONCLUSION:** *There is no single strategy for economic growth and development.*

EXHIBIT 6	Key Categories That Determine Economic Growth and Development

There are five basic categories that interact to determine the economic growth and development of countries: natural resources, human resources, capital, technological progress, and the political environment. The exhibit also indicates important factors that influence investment in human resources, capital, technological advances, and the political environment. LDCs are faced with a formidable task. Because economic growth and development are multidimensional, LDCs must improve many factors in order to achieve economic progress.

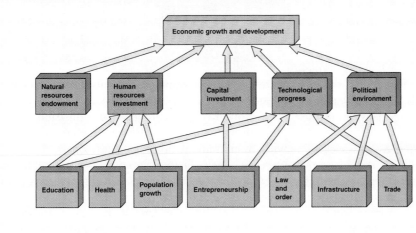

SOURCE: © Cengage Learning 2014

30-3 The Helping Hand of Advanced Countries

How can poor countries escape the vicious circle of poverty? Low GDP per capita leads to low savings and investment, which lead, in turn, to low growth. Although there is no easy way for poor countries to become richer, the United States and other advanced countries can be an instrument of growth. The necessary funds can come from the LDCs' own domestic savings, or it can come from external sources that include foreign private investment, foreign aid, and foreign loans.

Exhibit 7 illustrates how external funds can shift a country's production possibilities curve outward. Here you should look back and review Exhibit 5. Suppose country Alpha is trapped in poverty and produces only enough capital (K_a) to replace the existing capital being worn out. Alpha's consumption level is at C_a, corresponding to point A on production possibilities curve PPC_1. Because C_a is at the subsistence level, Alpha cannot save and invest by substituting

Hong Kong: A Leaping Pacific Rim Tiger

Applicable Concept: newly industrialized economies

As the map shows, the Pacific Rim economies are located along an arc extending from Japan and South Korea in the north to New Zealand in the south. The Four Tigers of East Asia are Hong Kong, Singapore, South Korea, and Taiwan. These "miracle economies" have often experienced higher economic growth rates, lower inflation rates, and lower unemployment rates than many long-established advanced countries.

Hong Kong is a great success story. When Adam Smith published his famous book, *The Wealth of Nations*, in 1776, Hong Kong was little more than a small, barren rock island void of natural resources except fish. Today, Hong Kong is a bustling model of free enterprise in spite of the fact that 7 million inhabitants are crowded into only about 400 square miles—one of the highest population densities in the world.

What is the reason for Hong Kong's success? Following the doctrine of Adam Smith, this economy is a paragon of *laissez-faire*. Hong Kong has among the lowest individual and corporate income tax rates in the world and almost no legal restrictions on business. It has no capital gains tax, no interest tax, no sales tax, and no withholding tax. Hong Kong has become the largest banking center in the Pacific region after Tokyo. International trade is also largely unrestricted, and Hong Kong depends to a large extent on trade through its magnificent harbor for its economic success. Tariffs on imported goods are low, and Hong Kong is known as a safe-haven

warehouse and trading center, with little or no interference from the government.

Hong Kong has proved that industrious people and entrepreneurs working hard on a crowded island with minimum regulations and open trade can improve their living standard without natural resources. Nevertheless, Hong Kong faces economic and political uncertainty. Under a 99-year lease signed in 1898, the United Kingdom transferred Hong Kong to the People's Republic of China in 1997. Will China allow Hong Kong to continue to follow Adam Smith's *laissez-faire* philosophy, resulting in high growth rates, or will Hong Kong change direction? It is anyone's guess. So far, China has not tampered with Hong Kong's *laissez-faire* economy, and its economic freedom ranking is higher than any other country in the world.[1]

capital for current consumption and move upward along PPC_1. This inability to increase capital means Alpha cannot use internal sources of funds to increase its production possibilities curve in the future. There is a way out of the trap using external sources. Now assume Alpha receives an inflow of funds from abroad and buys capital goods that increase its rate of investment from K_a to K_b. At K_b, the rate of capital formation exceeds the value of capital depreciated, and Alpha's production possibilities curve shifts rightward to PPC_2. Economic growth made possible by external investment means Alpha can improve its standard of living by increasing its consumption level from C_a at point A on PPC_1 to C_b at point B on PPC_2.

Recessions in the United States affect the global economy, and Hong Kong is no exception. Hong Kong's GDP growth depends heavily on exports. If, for example, U.S. consumers cut back on purchasing electronic devices, then Hong Kong's growth rate declines. After an 8 percent growth rate in 2000, the falloff in global demand triggered by the 2001 recession in the United States slowed Hong Kong's real GDP growth rate to only 0.5 percent. Between 2004 and 2007, Hong Kong's growth rate recovered to an average of 7.3 percent, and this East Asian tiger was leaping forward and roaring again. However, as a result of the recent financial crisis, Hong Kong slipped into recession in 2011 with a growth rate of –3 percent. But in 2010, Hong Kong became a "leaping Tiger" with a roaring 7 percent growth rate and a 5 percent rate in 2011. The following map compares 2011 data for the Four Tigers of East Asia.

Singapore
GDP per capita: $49,271
GDP growth: 5%
People: 5.3 million
Literacy: 95%

Hong Kong
GDP per capita: $34,049
GDP growth: 6.8%
People: 7.1 million
Literacy: 97%

Taiwan
GDP per capita: $20,100
GDP growth: 4%
People: 23.3 million
Literacy: 96%

South Korea
GDP per capita: $22,778
GDP growth: 4%
People: 48.9 million
Literacy: 99%

Analyze the Issue

One of the keys to Hong Kong's success is its free trade policy. Why is this so important for a developing country? What would be the effect of Hong Kong attempting to protect its domestic industries by raising tariffs and following other protectionist trade policies?

1. Frazer Institute, http://www.freetheworld.com/.

Source: © Cengage Learning 2014

30-3a FOREIGN PRIVATE INVESTMENT

Many countries' development benefits from private-sector foreign investment from private investors. For example, Microsoft might finance construction of a plant in the Philippines to manufacture software, or Bank of America may make loans to the government of Haiti. These large multinational corporations and commercial banks supply scarce capital to the LDCs. A multinational corporation is a firm with headquarters in one country and one or more branch plants in other countries. Multinational firms often seek new investment opportunities in LDCs because these poor countries offer abundant supplies of low-wage labor and raw materials. But the political environment in the LDCs must be conducive to investment. Multinational corporations often become the largest employers, largest taxpayers, and largest exporters in the LDCs.

EXHIBIT 7	The Effect of External Financing on an LDC's Production Possibilities Curve

The poor country of Alpha is initially operating at point A on production possibilities curve PPC_1, with only enough capital (K_a) to replace depreciation. If C_a is the consumption level of subsistence, Alpha's economy cannot grow by reducing consumption. An inflow of external funds from abroad permits the LDC to increase its capital from K_a to K_b and its production possibilities curve shifts outward to PPC_2. At PPC_2, Alpha is able to increase its production of consumer goods from C_a to C_b.

SOURCE: © Cengage Learning 2014

30-3b FOREIGN AID

Foreign aid

The transfer of money or resources from one government to another with no repayment required.

Agency for International Development (AID)

The agency of the U.S. State Department that is in charge of U.S. aid to foreign countries.

About 1 percent of the U.S. federal budget is spent on foreign aid. Foreign aid is the transfer of money or resources from one government to another with no repayment required. These transfers may be made as outright grants, technical assistance, or food supplies. Foreign aid flows from country to country through governments and voluntary agencies, such as the Red Cross, CARE, and Church World Relief. The United States distributes most of its official development assistance through the Agency for International Development (AID), established in 1961. The AID is the agency of the U.S. State Department that is in charge of U.S. aid to foreign countries.

One reason that countries such as the United States provide foreign aid to LDCs is the belief that it is a moral responsibility of richer countries to share their wealth with poorer countries. A second reason is that it is in the best economic interest of the IACs to help the LDCs. When these countries become more prosperous, the IACs have more markets for their exports, and thereby all countries benefit from trade.

The LDCs often complain that foreign aid comes with too many economic and political strings attached. Loans are often offered on a "take it or leave it" basis, tied to policies other than basic trade policies, such as human rights, politics, or the military. Consequently, many LDCs argue for "trade, not aid." If the IACs would simply buy more goods from the LDCs, the LDCs could use their gains in export earnings to purchase more capital and other resources needed for growth. Many people in the United States believe that most foreign aid is a waste of money because it is misused by the recipient countries. This belief has caused Congress to grow increasingly reluctant to send taxpayers' money abroad except in the clearest cases of need or for reasons of national security.

30-3c FOREIGN LOANS

A third source of external funds that can be used to finance LDCs' domestic investment is loans from abroad. Governments, international organizations, and private banks all make loans to LDCs. Like foreign private investment and foreign aid, loans give LDCs the opportunity to shift their production possibilities curves outward. There are various types of loan sources for LDCs. Bilateral loans are made directly from one country to another. The principal agent for official U.S. bilateral loans is the U.S. Agency for International Development, introduced earlier.

One prominent multilateral lending agency is the World Bank. The 188-member World Bank is the lending agency affiliated with the United Nations that makes long-term low-interest loans and provides technical assistance to LDCs. Loans are made only after a planning period lasting a year or more. The World Bank was established in 1944 by major nations meeting in Bretton Woods, New Hampshire. Its first charge was to assist with reconstruction after World War II. Today, the World Bank is located in Washington, D.C., and its main purpose is to channel funds from rich countries to poor countries. Voting shares are in proportion to the money provided by the members. The World Bank makes "last resort" loans to LDCs that are limited to financing basic infrastructure projects, such as schools, health centers, dams, irrigation systems, and transportation facilities, for which private financing is not available. In addition, the World Bank helps LDCs get loans from private lenders by insuring the loans. Thus, the poor countries are able to complete projects and use the economic returns to pay off the lender with interest.

The World Bank is not the only multilateral lending agency making loans to LDCs. The World Bank's partner institution is the International Monetary Fund (IMF). The International Monetary Fund is the lending agency that makes short-term conditional low-interest loans to developing countries. The IMF was also established at Bretton Woods in 1944. Its purpose is to help countries overcome short-run financial difficulties. Typically, the IMF makes conditional loans that require the debtor countries to implement fiscal and monetary policies that will alleviate balance-of-payments deficit problems and promote noninflationary economic growth. The 186-member IMF is not a charitable institution. It operates like a credit union with funding quotas that earn interest on the loans. The United States is the IMF's largest shareholder and thus has effective veto power over IMF decisions.

The IMF has performed a major role in providing short-term loans to developing countries and to economies making the transition to capitalism. In the late 1990s, the IMF provided multibillion-dollar bailouts to Russia, several Asian countries, Brazil, and other countries experiencing economic turmoil. In recent years, the IMF and some of the EU countries made rescue loans to debt-plagued Greece with the condition of deep cutbacks in government spending and tax hikes. Critics argue that as long as governments believe the IMF will bail them out, they will fail to correct their own problems. IMF supporters counter that if the IMF does not intervene, troubled economies will default on outstanding loans and cause a worldwide ripple effect. Critics respond that a flood of low-cost short-term loans from the IMF encourages bad government policies and excessive risk taking by banks. Consequently, a bailout in a crisis generates new financial crises and reduces world economic growth.

World Bank

The lending agency that makes long-term low-interest loans and provides technical assistance to less-developed countries.

International Monetary Fund (IMF)

The lending agency that makes short-term conditional low-interest loans to developing countries.

✓ CHECKPOINT

Is the Minimum Wage an Antipoverty Solution for Poor Countries?

Imagine you are an economic adviser to the president of a poor LDC. The president is seeking policies to promote economic growth and a higher standard of living for citizens of this country. You are asked whether adopting a minimum wage equal to the average of the IACs' average hourly wages would achieve these goals. Recall the discussion of the minimum wage from Chapter 4 and evaluate this policy.

Key Concepts

GDP per capita
Industrially advanced countries
   (IACs)
Less-developed countries
   (LDCs)

Vicious circle of poverty
Infrastructure
Foreign aid
Agency for International
   Development (AID)

World Bank
International Monetary Fund
   (IMF)

Summary

- **GDP per capita** provides a general index of a country's standard of living. Countries with low GDP per capita and slow growth in GDP per capita are less able to satisfy basic needs for food, shelter, clothing, education, and health.
- **Industrially advanced countries (IACs)** are countries with high GDP per capita, and output is produced by technologically advanced capital. Countries that have high incomes without widespread industrial development, such as the oil-rich Arab countries, are not included in the IAC list.
- **Less-developed countries (LDCs)** are countries with low production per person. In these countries, output is produced without large amounts of technologically advanced capital and well-educated labor. The LDCs account for about three-fourths of the world's population.
- The **Four Tigers of the Pacific Rim** are Hong Kong, Singapore, South Korea, and Taiwan. These newly industrialized countries have achieved high growth rates and standards of living.
- **GDP per capita comparisons** are subject to four problems: (1) the accuracy of LDC data is questionable, (2) GDP per capita ignores income distribution, (3) fluctuations in exchange rates affect GDP per capita gaps between countries, and (4) there is no adjustment for cost-of-living differences between countries.
- **Economic growth** and **economic development** are related, but somewhat different concepts. Economic growth is measured quantitatively by GDP per capita, while economic development is a broader concept. In addition to GDP per capita, economic development includes quality-of-life measures, such as life expectancy at birth, adult literacy rate, and per capita energy consumption. Economic growth and development are the result of a complex process that is determined by five major factors: (1) natural resources, (2) human resources, (3) capital, (4) technological progress, and (5) the political environment. There is no single correct strategy for economic development, and a lack of strength in one or more of the five areas does not prevent growth.
- The **vicious circle of poverty** is a trap in which an LDC is too poor to save and therefore it

cannot invest and shift its production possibilities curve outward. As a result, the LDC remains poor. One way for a poor country to

gain savings, invest, and grow is to use funds from external sources such as foreign private investment, foreign aid, and foreign loans.

Summary of Conclusion Statements

- LDCs' GDP per capita is subject to greater measurement errors than data for IACs.
- GDP per capita comparisons among nations can be misleading because GDP per capita does not measure income distribution.
- A conversion problem may widen or narrow the GDP per capita gap between nations because the fluctuations in exchange rates do not reflect actual differences in the value of goods and services produced.
- In general, GDP per capita is highly correlated with alternative measures of quality of life.
- Natural resource endowment can promote economic growth, but a country can develop without a large natural resource base.
- Investment in human capital generally results in increases in GDP per capita.

- Rapid population growth combined with low human capital investment explains why many countries are LDCs.
- There is a significant positive relationship between investment and economic growth and development.
- Many LDCs continue to experience low growth rates even though IACs have developed advanced technologies that the world can utilize.
- Exchange rate controls artificially set by government above the market exchange rates reduce the volume of both exports and imports (international trade).
- There is no single strategy for economic growth and development.

Study Questions and Problems

1. What is the difference between industrially advanced countries (IACs) and less-developed countries (LDCs)? List five IACs and five LDCs.

2. Explain why GDP per capita comparisons among nations are not a perfect measure of differences in economic well-being.

3. Assume you are given the following data for country Alpha and country Beta:

Country	GDP per capita
Alpha	$25,000
Beta	15,000

   a. Based on the GDP per capita data given above, in which country would you prefer to live?
   b. Now assume you are given the following additional quality-of-life data. In which country would you prefer to reside?

Country	Life Expectancy at Birth (years)	Daily per Capita Calorie Supply	Per Capita Energy Consumption*
Alpha	65	2,500	3,000
Beta	70	3,000	4,000

*Kilograms of oil equivalent.

4. What is the difference between economic development and economic growth? Give examples of how each of these concepts can be measured.

5. Do you agree with the argument that the rich nations are getting richer and the poor nations are getting poorer? Is this an oversimplification? Explain.

6. Explain why it is so difficult for poor LDCs to generate investment in capital in order to increase productivity and growth and therefore improve their standard of living.

7. Why is the quest for economic growth and development complicated?

8. Indicate whether each of the following is associated with a high or low level of economic growth and development:

	High	Low
a. Overpopulation	___	___
b. Highly skilled labor	___	___
c. High savings rate	___	___
d. Political stability	___	___
e. Low capital accumulation	___	___
f. Advanced technology	___	___
g. Highly developed infrastructure	___	___
h. High proportion of agriculture	___	___
i. High degree of income inequality	___	___

9. Without external financing from foreign private investment, foreign aid, and foreign loans, poor countries are caught in the vicious circle of poverty. Explain. How does external financing help poor countries achieve economic growth and development?

10. What are some of the problems for LDCs of accepting foreign aid?

11. Why would an LDC argue for "trade, not aid"?

12. Explain the differences among the Agency for International Development (AID), the World Bank, and the International Monetary Fund (IMF).

For Online Exercises, go to the Tucker Web site at www.cengage.com/economics/tucker.

✓ CHECKPOINT ANSWERS

Does Rapid Growth Mean a Country Is Catching Up?

GDP growth alone does not measure the standard of living. You must also consider population. Even though Beta experienced a greater GDP growth rate, its GDP per capita might be less than Alpha's because its population growth rate is greater. Of course, the reverse is also possible, but without population data, we cannot say. If you said which country's people are better off cannot be determined because the GDP must be divided by the population to measure the average standard of living, **YOU ARE CORRECT.**

Is the Minimum Wage an Antipoverty Solution for Poor Countries?

An important source of foreign investment for LDCs is multinational corporations that locate plants and other facilities in these countries. LDCs compete with each other for the economic growth and development benefits that these multinational corporations can provide. For an LDC to win the competition, it must offer political stability, adequate infrastructure, a favorable business climate, and a cheap labor force. If you said you would not support the president's proposal to raise the minimum wage because it would place the LDC at a competitive disadvantage in the labor market, thereby reducing foreign private investment and growth, **YOU ARE CORRECT.**

Sample Quiz

For an explanation of the correct answers, visit the Tucker Web site at www.cengage.com/economics/tucker.

1. Which of the following is a problem when comparing GDP per capita between nations?
   a. GDP per capita fails to measure income distribution.
   b. Fluctuations in exchange rates affect differences in GDP per capita.
   c. GDP per capita is subject to greater measurement errors for LDCs compared to IACs.
   d. All of the above answers are correct.

2. GDP per capita is a relatively good measurement of
   a. the distribution of income.
   b. purchasing power.
   c. household production.
   d. the standard of living.

3. Which of the following is infrastructure?
   a. police
   b. training and education
   c. highways.
   d. All of the answers above answers are correct.

4. Which of the following statements explains the vicious circle of poverty?
   a. By investing in education and infrastructure at the same time, the country can overcome the problems of poverty.
   b. Poverty arises out of the lack of investment, but countries cannot invest because they are poor.
   c. A nation can shift its production possibilities curve inward by shifting more resources into the production of capital goods.
   d. A nation can shift its production possibilities curve outward by shifting more resources into the production of consumer goods.

5. Which of the following is *not* a characteristic of *most* less-developed countries?
   a. inadequate human capital
   b. inadequate capital goods
   c. high population growth rate
   d. inadequate water supplies
   e. high productivity

6. Compared to IACs, LDCs are often characterized by
   a. lower life expectancy.
   b. lower adult literacy.
   c. lower per capita energy consumption.
   d. All of the above answers are correct.

7. Real GDP per capita and other alternative measures of the quality of life are
   a. independent.
   b. directly correlated.
   c. poorly correlated.
   d. inversely related.

8. Economic development encompasses which of the following measures?
   a. economic growth
   b. the political environment
   c. education
   d. All of the above answers are correct.

9. Which of the following is a characteristic of an LDC?
   a. capital flight
   b. vicious circle of poverty
   c. lack of entrepreneurs
   d. All of the above answers are correct.

10. Economic growth and development in LDCs are low because many of them lack
    a. savings.
    b. infrastructure.
    c. a political environment favorable to growth.
    d. All of the above answers are correct.

11. Which of the following is a *true* statement?
    a. The LDC classification is of questionable accuracy.
    b. GDP per capita ignores the degree of income distribution.
    c. GDP per capita is affected by exchange rate changes.
    d. GDP per capita does not account for the difference in the cost of living among nations.
    e. All of the above answers are correct.

Sample Quiz *continued*

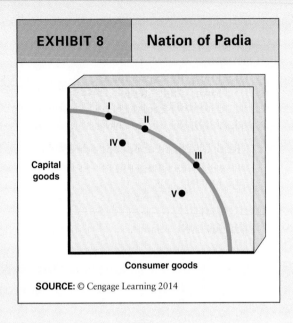

EXHIBIT 8   Nation of Padia

Capital goods

Consumer goods

SOURCE: © Cengage Learning 2014

12. Exhibit 8 shows the production possibilities curve of the nation of Padia. Based only on this information, which point would produce the highest rate of growth?
    a. I
    b. II
    c. III
    d. IV
    e. V

13. Exhibit 8 shows the production possibilities curve of the nation of Padia. Based only on this information, the point which would produce the lowest rate of growth would be
    a. I
    b. II
    c. III
    d. IV
    e. V

14. Which of the following is in charge of U.S. aid to foreign countries?
    a. Agency for International Development (AID)
    b. World Bank
    c. International Monetary Fund (IMF)
    d. New International Economic Order (NIEO)

15. Which of the following makes long-term low-interest loans to LDCs?
    a. Agency for International Development (AID)
    b. World Bank
    c. International Monetary Fund (IMF)
    d. New International Economic Order (NIEO)

16. Which of the following makes short-term conditional low-interest loans to LDCs?
    a. World Bank
    b. Agency for International Development (AID)
    c. Agency for International Finance (AIF)
    d. International Monetary Fund (IMF)

17. Which of the following is *not* an example of a country's infrastructure?
    a. transportation system
    b. communications system
    c. political system
    d. educational system

18. Which of the following *best* defines the vicious circle of poverty?
    a. Countries are poor because they cannot afford to save and invest.
    b. Countries are poor because of high population growth.
    c. Countries are poor because of lack of education and training for workers.
    d. Countries are poor because of poor international credit.

19. If a country's population grows at the same rate as its real GDP, then real per capita GDP
    a. grows at an increasing rate.
    b. grows at a constant rate.
    c. doesn't change.
    d. decreases at a decreasing rate.

20. In order for Ethiopia to increase its future economic growth, it must choose a point that is
    a. below its production possibilities curve.
    b. further along on its production possibilities curve toward the capital goods axis.
    c. further along on its production possibilities curve toward the consumption goods axis.
    d. above its production possibilities curve.

Road Map
The International Economy

part 8

This road map feature helps you tie together material in the part as you travel the Economic Way of Thinking Highway. The following are review questions listed by chapter from the previous part. The key concept in each question is given for emphasis, and each question or set of questions concludes with an interactive game to reinforce the concepts. Go to the Tucker Web site at www.cengage.com/economics/tucker, select the chapter, and play the visual causation chain game designed to make learning fun. Enjoy the cheers when you are correct and suffer the jeers if you miss. The correct answers for the multiple choice questions are given in Appendix C of the text.

CHAPTER 28. INTERNATIONAL TRADE AND FINANCE

1. **Key Concept: Exchange rate changes**
   Which of the following would cause the U.S. demand curve for Japanese yen to shift to the right?
   a. An increase in the U.S. inflation rate compared to the rate in Japan
   b. A higher real rate of interest on investments in Japan than on investments in the United States
   c. The popularity of Japanese products increases in the United States
   d. All of the answers above are correct.

2. **Key Concept: Exchange rate changes**
   Which of the following would cause the supply of dollars curve in the United States to shift to the right?
   a. Japanese imports become less popular.
   b. The value of the dollar falls.
   c. The supply of dollars decreases.
   d. Japanese imports become more popular.

 Causation Chain Game
Changes in the Supply and Demand Curves for Dollars—Exhibit 10

3. **Key Concept: Impact of relative price level changes**
   An increase in inflation in the United States relative to the rate in France would make
   a. U.S. goods relatively less expensive in the United States and in France.
   b. French goods relatively less expensive in the United States, and U.S. goods relatively more expensive in France.
   c. French goods relatively more expensive in the United States and in France.
   d. French goods relatively more expensive in the United States, and U.S. goods relatively less expensive in France.

4. **Key Concept: Impact of relative price level changes**
   If the Japanese price level falls relative to the price level in the United States, then
   a. Japanese buy U.S. exports.
   b. the demand for dollars decreases.
   c. the supply of dollars increases.
   d. the value of the dollar falls.
   e. All of the above are true.

 Causation Chain Game
The Impact of Relative Price Level Changes on Exchange Rates—Exhibit 11

CHAPTER 29. ECONOMIES IN TRANSITION

5. Key Concept: Command economy
Which of the following statements is *true* about a command economy?
a. Shortages occur because of complexities in the planning process.
b. Planners determine what, how many, and for whom goods and services are to be produced.
c. Planners often allocate goods and services using a rationing system.
d. The quality of produced goods and services tends to be inferior.
e. All of the above are true.

6. Key Concept: Command economy
Which of the following statements *best* describes the role played by prices in a command economy such as the former Soviet Union?
a. Prices were used to allocate resources.
b. Prices played the same role as in a market economy.
c. Prices were used to ration final goods and services but not to allocate resources.
d. None of the above statements are true.

Causation Chain Game
Central Planners Fixing Prices—Exhibit 2

CHAPTER 30. GROWTH AND THE LESS-DEVELOPED COUNTRIES

7. Key Concept: Economic growth
An outward shift of an economy's production possibilities curve is caused by an
a. increase in capital.
b. increase in labor.
c. advance in technology.
d. All of the above are true.

8. Key Concept: Economic growth
Which of the following statements is *correct*?
a. Economic development is more quantitative than economic growth.
b. A country cannot achieve economic growth with a limited base of natural resources.
c. Infrastructure is capital provided by the private sector.
d. All of the above are true.
e. All of the above are false.

Causation Chain Game
Economic Growth—Exhibit 4

9. Key Concept: Achieving economic growth
Which of the following can be a barrier to an LDC's economic growth and development?
a. Low population growth
b. A low level of human capital
c. Faster capital accumulation
d. More infrastructure

10. Key Concept: Economic growth and development
To grow and prosper, less-developed countries must *not*
a. invest in human capital.
b. build a strong infrastructure.
c. shift resources out of the production of consumer goods and into the production of capital goods.
d. shift resources out of the production of capital goods and into the production of consumer goods.
e. improve the quality of the water supply.

Causation Chain Game
The Effect of External Financing on an LDC's Production Possibilities Curve—Exhibit 7

Answers to Odd-Numbered Study Questions and Problems[*]

Chapter 1 Introducing the Economic Way of Thinking

1. A poor nation with many people who lack food, clothing, and shelter certainly experiences wants beyond the availability of goods and services to satisfy these unfulfilled wants. On the other hand, no wealthy nation has all the resources necessary to produce everything everyone in the nation wishes to have. Even if you had $1 million and were completely satisfied with your share of goods and services, other desires would be unfulfilled. There is never enough time to accomplish all the things that you can imagine would be worthwhile.

3. Macroeconomics applies an overview perspective to an economy by examining economywide variables, such as inflation, unemployment, and growth of the economy. Microeconomics examines individual economic units, such as the market for corn, gasoline, or ostrich eggs.

5. The real world is full of complexities that make it difficult to understand and predict the relationships between variables. For example, the relationship between changes in the price of gasoline and changes in consumption of gasoline requires abstraction from the reality that such variables as the fuel economy of cars and weather conditions often change at the same time as the price of gasoline.

7. The two events are associated, and the first event (cut in military spending) is the cause of the second event (higher unemployment in the defense industry). The point is that association does not necessarily mean causation, but it might.

Appendix to Chapter 1 Applying Graphs to Economics

1. a. The probability of living is *inversely* related to age. This model could be affected by improvements in diet, better health care, reductions in hazards to health in the workplace, or changes in the speed limit.

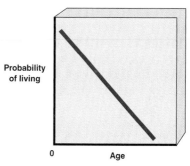

  b. Annual income and years of formal education are *directly* related. This relationship might be influenced by changes in such human characteristics as intelligence, motivation, ability, and family background. An example of an institutional change that could affect this relationship over a number of years is the draft.

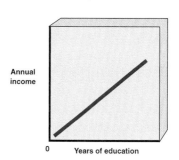

---

[*]Note: Answers to even-numbered questions are in the Instructor's Manual.

c. Inches of snow and sales of bathing suits are *inversely* related. The weather forecast and the price of travel to sunny vacation spots can affect this relationship.

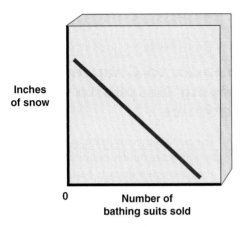

Inches of snow

0   **Number of bathing suits sold**

d. Most alumni and students will argue that the number of football games won is *directly* related to the athletic budget. They reason that winning football games is great advertising and results in increased attendance, contributions, and enrollment that, in turn, increase the athletic budget. Success in football can also be related to other factors, such as school size, age and type of institution, number and income of alumni, and quality of the faculty and administrators.

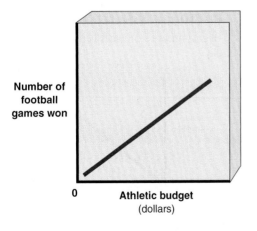

Number of football games won

0   **Athletic budget**
(dollars)

Chapter 2 Production Possibilities, Opportunity Cost, and Economic Growth

1. Because the wants of individuals and society exceed the goods and services available to satisfy these desires, choices must be made. The consumption possibilities of an individual with a fixed income are limited, and as a result, additional consumption of one item necessarily precludes an expenditure on another next-best choice. The forgone alternative is called the opportunity cost, and this concept also applies to societal decisions. If society allocates resources to the production of guns, then those same resources cannot be used at the same time to make butter.

3. Regardless of the price of a lunch, economic resources-land, labor, and capital-are used to produce the lunch. These scarce resources are no longer available to produce other goods and services.

5. Using marginal analysis, students weigh the benefits of attending college against the costs. There is an incentive to attend college when the benefits (improved job opportunities, income, intellectual improvement, social life, and so on) outweigh the opportunity costs.

7.

Flower boxes	Opportunity cost (pies forgone)
0	
1	4 (30 − 26)
2	5 (26 − 21)
3	6 (21 − 15)
4	7 (15 − 8)
5	8 (8 − 0)

9. Movements along the curve are efficient points and conform to the well-known "free lunch" statement. However, inefficient points are exceptions because it is possible to produce more of one output without producing less of another output.

11.

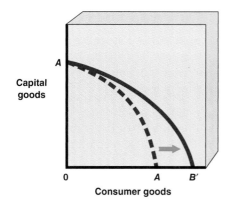

Capital goods / Consumer goods — A, B′, 0, A

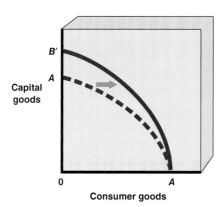

Capital goods / Consumer goods — B′, A, 0, A

Chapter 3 Market Demand and Supply

1. If people buy a good or service because they associate higher quality with higher price, this is a violation of the ceteris paribus assumption. An increase in the quantity demanded results only from a decrease in price. Quality and other nonprice determinants of demand, such as tastes and preferences and the price of related goods, are held constant in the model.

3. a. Demand for cars decreases; oil and cars are *complements*.
   b. Demand for insulation increases; oil and home insulation are *substitutes*.
   c. Demand for coal increases; oil and coal are *substitutes*.
   d. Demand for tires decreases; oil and tires are *complements*.

5. One reason that the demand curve for word processing software shifted to the right might be that people desire new, higher-quality output features. The supply curve can shift to the right when new technology makes it possible to offer more software for sale at different prices.

7. a. Demand shifts to the right.
   b. Supply shifts to the left.
   c. Supply shifts to the right.
   d. Demand shifts to the right.
   e. Demand shifts to the right.
   f. Supply of corn shifts to the left.

9. a. The supply of Blu-ray disc players shifts rightward.
   b. The demand for Blu-ray disc players is unaffected.
   c. The equilibrium price falls, and the equilibrium quantity increases.
   d. The demand for Blu-ray discs increases because of the fall in the price of Blu-ray disc players (a complementary good).

11. The number of seats (quantity supplied) remains constant, but the demand curve shifts because tastes and preferences change according to the importance of each game. Although demand changes, the price is a fixed amount, and to manage a shortage, colleges and universities use amount of contributions, number of years as a contributor, or some other rationing device.

Appendix to Chapter 3 Consumer Surplus, Producer Surplus, and Market Efficiency

1. $50

3.

Price	$30	$15
Consumer surplus	$80	$105
Producer surplus	$25	$5
Total surplus	$105	$110

The lower price results in higher total surplus because in this case the rise in consumer surplus exceeds fall in producer surplus.

Chapter 4 Markets in Action

1.

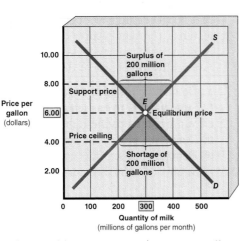

Quantity of milk
(millions of gallons per month)

a. The equilibrium price is $6.00 per gallon, and the equilibrium quantity is 300 million gallons per month. The price system will restore the market's $6.00 per gallon price because either a surplus will drive prices down or a shortage will drive prices up.

b. The support price results in a persistent surplus of 200 million gallons of milk per month, which the government purchases with taxpayers' money. Consequently, taxpayers who do not drink milk are still paying for milk. The purpose of the support price is to bolster the incomes of dairy farmers.

c. The ceiling price will result in a persistent shortage of 200 million gallons of milk per month, but 200 million gallons are purchased by consumers at the low price of $4.00 per gallon. The shortage places a burden on the government to ration milk in order to be fair and to prevent black markets. The government's goal is to keep the price of milk below the equilibrium price of $6.00 per gallon, which would be set by a free market.

3. The labor market can be divided into two separate markets, one for skilled union workers and one for unskilled workers. If the minimum wage is above the equilibrium wage rate and is raised, the effect will be to increase the demand for, and the wage of, skilled union workers because the two groups are substitutes.

5. The equilibrium price rises.

7. The government can reduce emissions by (a) regulations that require smoke-abatement equipment or (b) imposing pollution taxes that shift supply leftward.

9. Pure public goods are not produced in sufficient quantities by private markets because there is no feasible method to exclude free riders.

Chapter 5 Price Elasticity of Demand and Supply

1. Demand is elastic because the percentage change in quantity is greater than the percentage change in price.

3. If the price of used cars is raised 1 percent, the quantity demanded will fall 3 percent. If the price is raised 10 percent, the quantity demanded will fall 30 percent.

5.
$$E_d = \frac{\%\Delta Q}{\%\Delta P} = \frac{\frac{4500 - 5000}{5000 + 4500}}{\frac{3500 - 3000}{3000 + 3500}} = \frac{\frac{1}{19}}{\frac{1}{13}} = 0.68$$

The price elasticity of demand for the university is inelastic.

7. Demand for popcorn is perfectly inelastic, and total revenue will increase.

9. a. Sunkist oranges
   b. Cars
   c. Foreign travel in the long run

11. Furniture sales fall by 30 percent and physician services by only 3 percent. Thus, the demand for physician services is much less responsive to a reduction in income than the demand for furniture.

13. The negative number tells you car tires are complements. If the price of cars rises by 10 percent, the quantity demanded of car tires falls by 20 percent.

15. As the demand for a product becomes more inelastic, the greater the amount of a tax on this product that sellers can pass on to consumers by raising the product's price.

Chapter 6 Consumer Choice Theory

1. Utility is a subjective concept, and, therefore, this statement may or may not be true.

3. Marginal utility is 10 utils. When you attend the fourth party, total utility will increase, but marginal utility will be less than 10 utils.

5. In consumer equilibrium, the marginal utility ratio is 3/4, which is equal to the price ratio.

7. As people consume more of any product, eventually the satisfaction per unit decreases. Since the marginal utility from additional units falls, people will not buy a greater quantity unless the price falls.

9. The initial consumer equilibrium is as follows:

$$\frac{\text{MU of steak meal}}{\text{Price of steak meal}} = \frac{\text{Mu of hamburger meal}}{\text{Price of hamburger meal}}$$

$$\frac{12 \text{ utils}}{\$10} = \frac{6 \text{ utils}}{\$5}$$

The marginal utility per dollar for each good equals 1.2. If the price of a hamburger meal falls to $2, this equality no longer holds. Now the marginal utility per dollar for a hamburger meal becomes higher at 3 (6 utils/$2). James can now increase his total utility by purchasing more hamburger meals per month. Given the law of diminishing returns, the marginal utility of hamburger meals falls until consumer equilibrium is restored.

Appendix to Chapter 6 Indifference Curve Analysis

1. MRS = 3 (3 slices of pizza per Coke), but the ratio of prices is 1/2 ($1.00 per Coke/$2.00 per slice of pizza). Since MRS > slope (the ratio of prices), the consumer is not maximizing total utility. Therefore, the consumer should consume less pizza and more Coke in order to maximize total utility by moving downward along the consumer's indifference curve until consumer equilibrium is achieved where MRS = price ratio = 1/2.

3. a. and b.

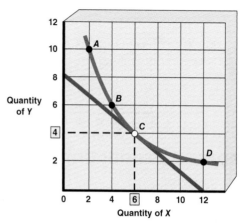

c. Consumer equilibrium occurs at point C with 6 units of X and 4 units of Y purchased.

d. $\quad MRS = P_x/P_y = \dfrac{\$1}{\$1.50} = \dfrac{2}{3}$

e. Hold the price of Y constant at $1.50 and decrease the price of X from $1.00 to $0.50. The new budget line will shift northeastward from the Y axis intercept point of 8 units. Now draw a new indifference curve and determine the new equilibrium point. Finally, draw a graph with various prices of X on the vertical axis and the quantity of X on the horizontal axis. Connecting the two consumer equilibrium points will allow you to draw a downward sloping demand curve.

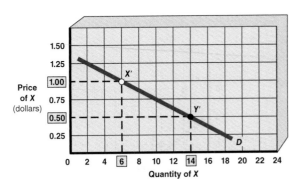

Chapter 7 Production Costs

1. a. explicit cost
    b. explicit cost
    c. implicit cost
    d. implicit cost
    e. explicit cost
    f. implicit cost

3. a.

Labor	Marginal product
1	8
2	10
3	12
4	13
5	12
6	10
7	8
8	6
9	3
10	−2

b.

5. None. The position of a firm's short-run average total cost curve is not related to the demand curve.

7. The ATC and AVC curves converge as output expands because $ATC = AVC + AFC$. As output increases, AFC declines, so most of ATC is therefore AVC.

9. The average total cost-marginal cost rule states that when the marginal cost is below the average total cost, the addition to total cost is below the average total cost, and the average total cost falls. When the marginal cost is greater than the average total cost, the average total cost rises. In this case, the average total cost is at a minimum because it is equal to the marginal cost.

11. The marginal product for any number of workers is the slope of the total output curve. The marginal product is the derivative of the total output curve dTO/dQ, where TO is the total output and Q is the number of workers.

Chapter 8 Perfect Competition

1. A perfectly competitive firm will not advertise. Because all firms in the industry sell the same product, there is no reason for customers to be influenced by ads into buying one firm's product rather than another firm's product.

3.

(a) Wheat market supply and demand

Price per bushel (dollars) — 4.00, 3.00, 2.00, 1.00

Quantity of wheat (thousands of bushels per day) — 0, 2, 4, 6, 8

S — Market supply; Market demand — D

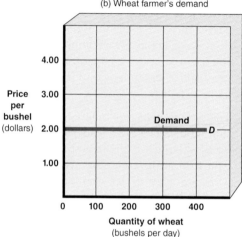

(b) Wheat farmer's demand

Price per bushel (dollars) — 4.00, 3.00, 2.00, 1.00

Demand — D

Quantity of wheat (bushels per day) — 0, 100, 200, 300, 400

A single wheat farmer is a price taker facing a perfectly elastic demand curve because in perfect competition one seller has no control over its price. The reason is that each wheat farmer is one among many, sells a homogeneous product, and must compete with any new farmer entering the wheat market.

5. At a price of $150, the firm produces 4 units and earns an economic profit of $70 ($TR - TC = \$600 - \$530$). The firm breaks even at an output of 2 units.

7. This statement is incorrect. A firm can earn maximum profit (or minimum loss) when marginal revenue equals marginal cost. The confusion is between the "marginal" and the "total" concepts. Marginal cost is the change in total cost from one additional unit of output, and marginal revenue is the change in

total revenue from one additional unit of output.

9. The statement is incorrect. The perfectly competitive firm must consider both its marginal revenue and its marginal cost. Instead of trying to sell all the quantity of output possible, the firm will sell the quantity where $MR = MC$ because beyond this level of output the firm earns less profit.

11. Advise the residential contractor to shut down because the market price exceeds the average variable cost and the firm cannot cover its operating costs.

Chapter 9 Monopoly

1. Each market is served by a single firm providing a unique product. There are no close substitutes for local telephone service, professional football in San Francisco, and first-class mail service. A government franchise imposes a legal barrier to potential competitors in the telephone and first-class mail services. An NFL franchise grants monopoly power to its members in most geographic areas.

3. The reason may be that the hospital has monopoly power because it is the only hospital in the area and patients have no choice. On the other hand, there may be many drugstores competing to sell drugs, and this keeps prices lower than those charged by the hospital.

5. In a natural monopoly, a single seller can produce electricity at a lower cost because the $LRAC$ curve declines. One firm can therefore sell electricity at a cheaper price and drive its competitor out of business over time. Another possibility would be for two competing firms to merge and earn greater profit by lowering cost further.

7. In this special case, sales maximization and profit maximization are the same. The monopolist should charge $2.50 per unit, produce 5 units of output, and earn $12.50 in profit. When the marginal cost curve is not equal to zero, the monopolist's $MR = MC$ output is less than 5 units, the price is higher than $2.50 per unit, and profit is below $12.50.

9. a. increase output
   b. decrease output

11. a. not price discrimination
    b. price discrimination
    c. not price discrimination if justified by a transportation cost difference
    d. price discrimination

Chapter 10 Monopolistic Competition and Oligopoly

1. The monopolistically competitive firm's demand curve is less elastic (steeper) than a perfectly competitive firm's demand curve, but more elastic (flatter) than a monopolist's demand curve.

3. a. P_1
   b. Q_1
   c. Q_3
   d. greater than the marginal cost ($B > A$)

5.

Because $P_{mc} > MC$, the monopolistically competitive firm fails to achieve allocative efficiency. The monopolistically competitive

firm is also inefficient because it charges a higher price and produces less output than under perfect competition. The perfectly competitive firm sets P_{pc} equal to MC and produces a level of output corresponding to the minimum point on the $LRAC$ curve.

7. Answers might include automobiles, airline travel, personal computers, and cigarettes. An oligopoly differs from monopolistic competition by having few sellers, rather than many sellers; either a homogeneous or a differentiated product, rather than all differentiated products; and difficult entry rather than easy entry.

9. Any maverick jeans firm that raises or lowers its price will earn less profits. Therefore, firms in the jeans industry face a kinked demand curve, and prices remain rigid. Although firms do not engage in price competition, they can engage in nonprice competition. Each firm can use advertising and style to market its brand-name product.

11. The pricing behavior follows the price leadership model. The price leader is Hewlett-Packard, which is the largest and most dominant firm in the computer printer industry. After a price war, Cannon followed each of Hewlett-Packard's price hikes.

13. If both firms spend no money advertising, they each earn a profit of $8 billion in cell A. If either firm does not advertise and the other firm does in cell B or cell C, then the advertising firm attracts more customers and earns $10 billion compared to a −$2 billion loss for the rival without ads. This outcome forces both firms to advertise and reduce mutual profits at cell D. As a result of both firms spending large budgets on advertising, their mutual profits are reduced to $5 billion. If the government bans all cigarette advertising, the result is that both firms will move to the mutually high profit cell A.

Chapter 11 Labor Markets

1. This statement is incorrect. Workers supply their labor to employers. Demand refers to the quantity of labor employers hire at various wage rates based on the marginal revenue product of labor.

3. The MRP of the second worker is this person's contribution to total revenue, which is $50 ($150 − $100). Because $MRP = P \times MP$ and $MP = MRP/P$, the second worker's marginal product (MP) is 10 ($50/$5).

5. The firm in a perfectly competitive labor market is a price taker. Because a single firm buys the labor of a relatively small portion of workers in an industry, it can hire additional workers and not drive up the wage rate. For the industry, however, all firms must offer higher wages to attract workers from other industries.

7. Students investing in education are increasing their human capital. A student with greater human capital increases his or her marginal product. At a given product price, the MRP is higher, and firms find it profitable to hire the better-educated worker and pay higher wages.

9. At a wage rate of $90 per day, Zippy Paper Company hires 3 workers because each worker's MRP exceeds or equals the wage rate. Setting the wage rate at $100 per day causes Zippy Paper Company to cut employment from 3 to 2 workers because the third worker's MRP is $10 below the union-caused wage rate of $100 per day.

11. As shown in the exhibit below, for a monopsony, the optimum quantity of labor is 3 quarterbacks, determined at point A, where the MFC curve intersects the MRP curve. However, the team can attract and hire 3 quarterbacks for an annual salary of $300,000 each at point B on the supply of labor curve, rather than paying a quarterback's contribution to the team's revenues (MRP), which is $500,000 per year at point A. In a competitive labor market, the Jacksonville Jaguars hire 4 quarterbacks and pay each $400,000 per year.

Chapter 12 Income Distribution, Poverty, and Discrimination

1. a.

Percentage of families	Alpha		Beta	
	Percent-age share	Cumula-tive share	Percent-age share	Cumula-tive share
Lowest fifth	17.7%	17.7%	9.0%	9.0%
Second-lowest fifth	19.9	37.6	14.2	23.2
Middle fifth	20.4	58.0	17.5	40.7
Second-highest fifth	20.7	78.7	21.9	62.6
Highest fifth	21.3	100.0	37.4	100.0

b.

c. Because the Lorenz curve for Alpha is closest to the perfect equality line, Alpha's distribution of income is more equal compared to Beta.

3. Absolute poverty is defined as a dollar figure that represents some level of income per year required to purchase some minimum amount of goods and services essential to meeting a person's or a family's basic needs. Relative poverty is defined as a level of income required to place a person or family in, say, the lowest 20 percent among all persons or families receiving incomes. The poverty line is based on the absolute definition.

5. In-kind transfers are payments in the form of goods and services rather than cash. Examples

include such government programs as food stamps, Medicaid, and housing. Noncash income is not counted in a family's income to determine whether the family's income is below the poverty line.

7. The percentage of families in the United States classified as poor was about 12 percent. Poor families are more likely to live in the South. The age, race, and education of the head of the family are also important characteristics of poor families.

9. The three major criticisms are that welfare: (1) reduces the work incentive, (2) is inefficient because the programs cost too much to administer, and (3) treats poor persons with the same needs unequally because the states pay different benefits.

11. This is an opinion question. To agree, you assume that markets are perfectly competitive and discrimination is therefore unprofitable. To disagree, you can argue that in reality labor markets will never be perfectly competitive and the government must therefore address the institutional causes of poverty.

Chapter 13 Antitrust and Regulation

1. The Sherman Act outlaws price-fixing or anticompetitive practices designed to eliminate rivals. The Clayton Act clarifies the Sherman Act by outlawing specific business practices, including price discrimination, exclusive dealing, tying contracts, stock acquisition, and interlocking directorates. The U.S. Department of Justice and Federal Trade Commission (FTC) are responsible for enforcing these laws. Private firms can also bring suit against other firms under these laws.

3. Both the Robinson-Patman Act and the Celler-Kefauver Act were amendments to close loopholes in the Clayton Act. The Robinson-Patman Act expanded the list of illegal price discrimination practices to include quantity discounting, free advertising, and promotional allowances offered that "substantially lessen competition or tend to create a monopoly." The Celler-Kefauver Act closed the loophole in the Clayton Act whereby competing firms

could merge by asset acquisition (not outlawed in the Clayton Act), rather than by acquiring stock (outlawed in the Clayton Act).

5. In fact, Alcoa argued that metals such as copper and steel are substitutes for aluminum. Therefore, the relevant industry to compute market share was the metals industry and not the aluminum industry. If the court had chosen the U.S. metals industry as the relevant industry, Alcoa would not have a monopoly.

7. a. The federal government will charge the bookstore with predatory pricing in order to monopolize its college market for books, which is a violation of the Sherman Act.
   b. The federal government will charge the real estate firms with collusion to fix prices, which is a violation of the Sherman Act.
   c. The federal government will charge a violation of the Clayton Act because the combined market share of this horizontal merger would substantially lessen competition in the personal computer market.
   d. The federal government will not charge a violation because this is a conglomerate merger between firms in unrelated industries.

9. The "necessary" condition would be expected to favor existing regulated firms by eliminating or greatly restricting competition and raising prices. The existing regulated firms are better organized politically than either new competitors or consumers. While consumers favor competition and lower prices, regulators would be expected to interpret "necessary" to mean that the service provided by existing firms is sufficient without new firms.

11. Although a public subsidy achieves efficiency, marginal-cost pricing is usually unpopular with voters, who must provide the monopolist with public funds. Moreover, a public subsidy gives the monopolist a disincentive to minimize costs.

Chapter 14 Environmental Economics

1. A competitive industry selling a pollution-generating product will charge a lower price and sell a larger quantity than would be the case for a "green" industry. The competitive

industry has lower costs because it fails to include external costs. Lower costs allow a lower price. A lower price leads to a larger quantity demanded and sold.

3. If you choose the $90,000 house, the EMF radiation is *not* an externality. An externality is a third-party effect, whereby buyers and sellers of a product ignore the spillover effects of their transaction. In this case, the market reflects the risk of cancer, with the seller accepting a lower price and the buyer saving $10,000 to reflect the cancer risk.

   Houses have many characteristics that influence their price, including number of rooms, location, nearby schools, and environmental amenities. If you are willing to buy a house near a nuclear plant, or near EMFs, you, the buyer, bear the consequences, not a third party.

5. An instructor who automatically flunks students who do not turn in all homework assignments is exhibiting command-and-control regulation. She is dictating the production process for achieving knowledge. The inefficiencies are that students may turn in poorly done assignments or may copy assignments and that some students may understand the material without doing the homework or may have an alternative production method, such as the use of computer software, to achieve knowledge. The instructor's method is particularly inefficient if her assignments are busywork and do not really help the students to achieve knowledge.

7.

Paper industry

At Q_p, pollution from paper production leads to coffee-colored rivers. At socially efficient Q_s, there is less pollution, and rivers are less polluted. The rivers are unlikely to be pristine, which requires no production at all.

9. Consumers will share in the benefits of cleaner air if any individual buys a less polluting car. Since they enjoy the same benefit whether they pay extra or their neighbor pays extra for a cleaner car, they will let the neighbor buy the cleaner car. Of course, since their neighbor uses the same reasoning, no one ends up paying extra to buy a cleaner car.

11. Convincing examples should be sent to the author of the text. It is very difficult to find markets where the transaction costs of reaching an agreement are near zero. It is also difficult to find two-party situations, since most pollution spills over to many individuals. With many individuals involved, the free-rider problem arises, as a given individual wants to benefit from pollution agreements, but let others bear the cost. There can often be income effects, as fighting pollution may take a large amount of one's income. Candidates for markets where the Coase Theorem might apply include convincing your neighbor to leash her dog (you might help finance invisible fencing), enforcing laws concerning the fencing of cattle (see question 12 for further discussion), and settling disputes when one builder interferes with the views of existing homes.

13. a. Command-and-control regulation would dictate the use of an alternative technology with lower carbon emissions.
   b. An effluent tax would place a tax on carbon emissions so that firms could no longer ignore these costs. In turn, prices of carbon-emitting products would increase, and quantities would decrease.
   c. Permits would be issued giving the right to emit carbon. The number of permits would equal the socially efficient emissions level. Firms would be allowed to buy or sell these permits. Firms with higher marginal costs of emissions abatement would buy permits, while firms that could reduce emissions at a lower cost would profit from selling permits.

15. According to Garrett Hardin, individuals will use a common property resource as long as their marginal benefits exceed their marginal costs. They will disregard the external costs to others if additional fishing or grazing subtracts from the fish or grass available to others available to others using the common. As all users of the common will behave in this way, the commons will be used beyond the efficient point, and potentially to the point of exhaustion, where the availability of the commons will collapse.

Elinor Ostrom has studied fisheries and other commons and finds that those who are using the resource will attempt to establish institutions that will lead to optimal use. Rather than leave the commons as open access, they will covert it to common property. They will limit who can access the property and limit its use, so that the commons will not be fished or grazed into exhaustion.

Chapter 15 Gross Domestic Product

1. a. final service
   b. final good
   c. intermediate good
   d. intermediate good

3.
3 million pounds of food	
× $1 per pound	= $3 million
50,000 shirts × $20 per shirt	= 1 million
20 houses × $50,000 per house	= 1 million
50,000 hours of medical	
services × $20 per hour	= 1 million
1 automobile plant	
× $1 million per plant	= 1 million
2 tanks × $500,000 per tank	= 1 million
Total value of output	= $8 million

5. Capital is not excluded from being a final good. A final good is a finished good purchased by an ultimate user and not for resale. The ultimate user is the warehouse, so the sale would be included in GDP and there would be no double-counting problem.

7. Using the expenditure approach, net exports are exports minus imports. If the expenditures by foreigners for U.S. products exceed the expenditures by U.S. citizens for foreign products, net exports will be a positive contribution to GDP. If foreigners spend less for U.S. products than U.S. citizens spend for foreign products, GDP is reduced.

9. NI = GDP − depreciation
   $4,007 = $4,486 − $479

   The depreciation charge is not a measure of newly produced output. It is an estimate, subject to error, of the value of capital worn out in the production of final goods and services. Errors in the capital consumption allowance overstate or understate GDP.

11. When the price level is rising, nominal GDP overstates the rate of change between years. Dividing nominal GDP by the GDP chain price index results in real GDP by removing the distortion from inflation. Comparison of real GDP changes between years reflects only changes in the market value of all final products and not changes in the price level.

13. GDP does not tell the mix of output in two nations, say, between military and consumer goods. GDP also does not reveal whether GDP is more equally distributed in one nation compared to another.

Chapter 16 Business Cycles and Unemployment

1. The generally accepted theory of business cycles is that they are the result of changes in the level of total spending, or aggregate demand. Total spending includes spending for final goods by households, businesses, government, and foreign buyers. Expressed as a formula, $GDP = C + I + G + (X − M)$.

3. **Civilian unemployment rate**

$$= \frac{\text{unemployed}}{\text{civilian labor force}} \times 100$$

where the civilian labor force = unemployed + employed. Therefore,

$$8.3\% = \frac{10 \text{ million persons}}{120 \text{ million persons}} \times 100$$

5. The official unemployment rate is overstated when respondents to the BLS falsely report that they are seeking employment. The unemployment rate is understated when

discouraged workers who want to work have given up searching for a job.

7. Structural unemployment occurs when those seeking jobs do not possess the skills necessary to fill the available jobs. Cyclical unemployment is caused by a recession (deficient total spending). In this case, there are not enough available jobs.

9. The increasing participation of women and teenagers in the labor force has increased the rate of unemployment. Women take more time out of the labor force than do men for childbearing and child rearing.

11. The GDP gap is the difference between potential real GDP and actual real GDP. Because potential real GDP is estimated on the basis of the full-employment rate of unemployment, the GDP gap measures the cost of *cyclical* unemployment in terms of real GDP.

Chapter 17 Inflation

1. This statement is incorrect. The price of a single good or service can rise while the average price of all goods and services falls. In short, the inflation rate rises when the average price of consumer goods and services rises.

3. First, the CPI is based on a typical market basket purchased by the urban family. Any group not buying the same market basket, such as retired persons, is not experiencing the price changes measured by changes in the CPI. Second, the CPI fails to adjust for quality changes. Third, the CPI ignores the law of demand and the substitution effect as prices of products change.

5. If the percentage increase in the CPI exceeds the salary increase, a person's purchasing power declines in a given year.

7. The loan is advantageous to you because the real interest rate is −5 percent (5 percent nominal interest rate minus 10 percent inflation). In one year, you must repay $105. If prices rise by 10 percent during the year, the real value of the $105 will be only $95. Therefore, you have borrowed $100 worth of purchasing power and are repaying $95 worth of purchasing power.

9. At full employment, the economy operates at full capacity and produces the maximum output of goods and services. As buyers try to outbid one another for the fixed supply of goods and services, prices rise rapidly.

11. If buyers think prices will be higher tomorrow, they may buy products today and cause demand-pull inflation. If businesses believe prices for inputs will be higher in the future, many will raise prices today and cause cost-push inflation.

Chapter 18 The Keynesian Model

1. Classical economists argued that underconsumption and unemployment could not exist in the long run because of price-wage flexibility. Unsold merchandise would force firms to compete and lower product prices, and unemployed workers would accept a lower wage rate.

3. Consumers have only two options for any extra disposable income they receive. The MPC and MPS must add up to one because the portion of extra income that is not spent must be saved.

5. a. The consumption schedule downshifts, and the saving schedule downshifts.
   b. The consumption schedule upshifts, and the saving schedule downshifts.
   c. The consumption schedule downshifts, and the saving schedule upshifts.
   d. The consumption schedule downshifts, and the saving schedule downshifts.
   e. Both the consumption and the saving schedules downshift.

7. Changes in the nonincome determinants of the consumption and saving schedules tend to offset each other, and people are reluctant to change their consumption and saving habits. On the other hand, Keynes considered the volatility of businesses' decisions to invest as a major cause of the business cycle. The potentially unstable determinants of investment spending include expectations, technological change, the stock of capital goods, and business taxes.

9. a.

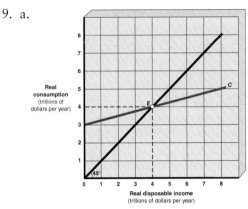

b. The autonomous consumption is $3 trillion where real disposable income is 0. The MPC = 0.25 because each $1 trillion increase in real disposable income results in a $0.25 trillion increase in consumption. Since MPS = (1 − MPC), MPS = (1 − 0.25) = 0.75.

c. The break-even income of real disposable income equals $4 trillion where the C line intersects the 45° line.

d. At $2 trillion real GDP on the 45° line, consumption is $3.5 trillion, so dissavings is $1.5 trillion. At $7 trillion real GDP on the 45° line, consumption is $4.75 trillion, so savings is $2.5 trillion.

Chapter 19 The Keynesian Model in Action

1.

Employment, Output, Consumption, and Unplanned Inventory			
Possible levels of employment (millions)	Real GDP (output) equals disposable income (billions of dollars)	Consumption (billions of dollars)	Unplanned inventory (billions of dollars)
40	325	300	−75
45	375	325	−50
50	425	350	−25
55	475	375	0
60	525	400	25
65	575	425	50
70	625	450	75

a. Answers are given in the above table.

b. $\text{MPC} = \dfrac{\text{change in consumption}}{\text{change in disposable income}}$

$= \dfrac{\$25 \text{ billion}}{\$50 \text{ billion}} = \dfrac{1}{2} = 0.50$

since MPS = 1 − MPC = 1 − 0.50 = 0.50

c. At an employment level of 40 million workers, $75 million in unplanned inventory investment encourages businesses to expand output, and GDP increases toward the equilibrium real GDP of $475 billion.

3.

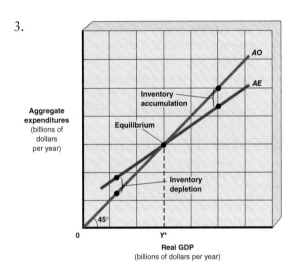

The aggregate expenditures (AE) line intersects the aggregate output (AO) line at the equilibrium level of real GDP, Y*. Below Y*, an unplanned inventory depletion causes businesses to expand output, which pushes the economy toward equilibrium output. Above Y*, an unintended inventory accumulation pushes the economy toward Y* by pressuring businesses to reduce production.

5. $\text{Multiplier} = \dfrac{1}{1 - \text{MPC}} = \dfrac{1}{\text{MPS}}$

The greater the MPC, the smaller the MPS and the greater the size of the multiplier.

a. 1, 1.5, 10

b. Y = M × I = 5 × $10 billion = $50 billion

c. Y = M × I = 3 × $10 billion = $30 billion

7. a.

Round	Component of total spending	New consumption spending (billions of dollars)
1	Investment	$100
2	Consumption	75
3	Consumption	56
4	Consumption	42
	Total spending	$273

b. The spending multiplier is

$$\frac{1}{(1 - MPC)} = \frac{1}{(1 - 0.75)} = \frac{1}{0.25} = 4$$

Therefore, change in investment spending × spending multiplier = change in aggregate spending ($100 billion × 4 = $400 billion). Note: This problem demonstrates how useful the spending multiplier formula is because it avoids working through individual steps in the multiplier process.

9. Spending multiplier

$$= \frac{\text{change in GDP}}{\text{change in government spending}} = \frac{\Delta Y}{\Delta G}$$

Since MPC = 0.75,

$$\text{Spending multiplier} = \frac{1}{(1 - MPC)} = \frac{1}{0.25} = 4$$

rewritten as

$$4 = \frac{\$100 \text{ billion}}{\Delta G}$$

Therefore,

$$\Delta G = \frac{\$100 \text{ billion}}{4} = \$25 \text{ billion}$$

Given that the MPC is 0.75, this means households spend only $18.75 billion of the additional $25 billion of disposable income from the tax cut. Therefore,

$$\Delta C \times \text{spending multiplier} = \text{change in GDP}$$
$$\$18.75 \text{ billion} \times 4 = \$75 \text{ billion}$$

Because GDP must increase by $100 billion, a tax cut of $25 billion would not be enough to restore full-employment GDP.

Chapter 20 Aggregate Demand and Supply

1. There are three reasons why the aggregate demand curve is downward sloping:
   a. The *real balances effect* means that a lower price level increases the purchasing power of money and other financial assets. The result is an increase in consumption, which increases the quantity of real GDP demanded.
   b. The *interest-rate effect* assumes a fixed money supply, and, therefore, a lower price level reduces the demand for borrowing and the interest rate. The lower rate of interest increases spending for consumption and investment.
   c. The *net exports effect* encourages foreign customers to buy more of an economy's domestic exports relative to its domestic purchases of imports when the price level falls. An increase in net exports increases aggregate expenditures.

   Rationales for the downward-sloping demand curve for an individual market are the income effect, the substitution effect, and the law of diminishing marginal utility, which are quite different from the three effects that determine the aggregate demand curve.

3. a. A leftward shift occurs because of a decrease in the consumption schedule.
   b. A rightward shift occurs because of an increase in autonomous investment spending.
   c. A rightward shift occurs because of an increase in government spending.
   d. A rightward shift occurs because of an increase in net exports.

5. This statement may not be correct. The equilibrium GDP is not necessarily the same as the full-employment GDP. Equilibrium GDP refers to the equality between the aggregate demand and the aggregate supply curves, which does not necessarily equal the full capacity of the economy to produce goods and services.

7. a. leftward because of an increase in resource prices
   b. rightward because of a decrease in resource prices
   c. rightward because technological change reduces the cost of production
   d. leftward because an increase in taxes means the price must cover the tax at each possible quantity supplied

9. a. Aggregate demand increases.
   b. Aggregate supply increases.
   c. Aggregate demand decreases.
   d. Aggregate supply decreases.
   e. Aggregate demand decreases along the classical range.
   f. Aggregate demand increases along the Keynesian range.

11. Assuming the aggregate supply curve remains constant, a rightward shift of the aggregate demand curve from AD_1 to AD_2 in the upward-sloping or the vertical range of the aggregate supply curve causes the price level to rise from P_1 to P_2. In addition to demand-pull inflation, the level of real GDP increases from Q_1 to Q_2 and provides the economy with new jobs. In the classical range, inflation is the only undesirable result, and real GDP remains unaffected at Q_2.

Appendix to Chapter 20 The Self-Correcting Aggregate Demand and Supply Model

1. a.–c.

3.

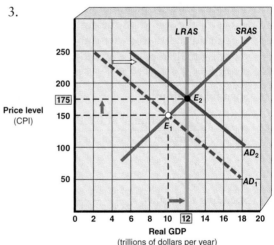

5. Nominal incomes of workers in the short run are fixed. In response to the fall in aggregate demand, firms' profits decline, and they cut output and employment. As a result, the economy moves downward along SRAS to temporary equilibrium at E_2. When workers lower their nominal incomes because of competition from unemployed workers, the

short-run aggregate supply curve shifts right-ward to E_3 and returns to long-run equilibrium. Profits rise and firms increase output and employment while the price level falls.

Chapter 21 Fiscal Policy

1. *Expansionary* fiscal policy refers to increasing government spending and/or decreasing taxes in order to increase aggregate demand and eliminate a GDP gap. *Contractionary* fiscal policy is designed to cool inflation by decreasing aggregate demand. This result is accomplished by decreasing government spending and/or increasing taxes.

3. a. contractionary fiscal policy
   b. contractionary fiscal policy
   c. expansionary fiscal policy

5. The spending multiplier is

$$\frac{1}{1 - \text{MPC}} = \frac{1}{0.25} = \frac{1}{1/4} = 4$$

The spending multiplier (*SM*) times the change in government spending ($\triangle G$) equals the change in aggregate demand ($\triangle AD$). Therefore,

$$\Delta G \times SM = \Delta AD$$
$$\Delta G \times 4 = \$500 \text{ billion}$$
$$\Delta G = \$125 \text{ billion}$$

The government must increase government spending by $125 billion in order to eliminate the GDP gap.

7. The tax multiplier equals the spending multiplier minus 1. Thus, the impact of the expansion in government spending exceeds the impact of an equal amount of tax cut.

9. As a supply-side economist, you would argue that the location of the aggregate supply curve is related to the tax rates. Ceteris paribus, if the tax rates are cut, there will be strong incentives for workers to supply more work, households to save more, and businesses to invest more in capital goods. Thus, cutting tax rates shifts the aggregate supply curve rightward, the level of real GDP rises, and the price level falls.

11. a. rightward shift in the aggregate demand curve
    b. leftward shift in the aggregate demand curve
    c. rightward shift in the aggregate supply curve
    d. rightward shift in the aggregate demand curve
    e. leftward shift in the aggregate supply curve

Chapter 22 The Public Sector

1. Transfer payments account for the difference between total government expenditures, or outlays, and total government spending. Transfers do not "use up" resources; they reallocate purchasing power by collecting taxes from one group and paying benefits to other groups.

3. The primary sources are individual income taxes at the federal level, sales and excise taxes at the state level, and property taxes at the local level.

5. The marginal tax rate is the percentage of additional income paid in taxes. The average tax rate is the amount of taxes paid as a percentage of income.

7. a. more than $6,000
   b. less than $6,000
   c. $6,000

9. Sales tax paid as a percentage of income:
   10%
   7%
   6%
   4%
   Because the sales tax paid as a percentage of income falls as income rises, the tax is regressive.

11. A profit-maximizing firm follows the marginal rule that units will be produced so long as the marginal benefit exceeds or equals the marginal cost. Dollars can measure the intensity of benefits in relation to costs. A "one-person, one-vote" system does not necessarily measure benefits in proportion to the dollar value of benefits among individual voters. Thus, a majority of voters can approve projects for which costs exceed benefits and reject projects for which benefits exceed costs.

Chapter 23 Federal Deficits, Surpluses, and the National Debt

1. The national debt is the sum of past federal budget deficits. When budget deficits are large, the national debt increases at a rapid rate. When budget deficits are small, the national debt increases at a lower rate.

3. The statement makes the argument that most of the debt is internal national debt that one U.S. citizen owes to another U.S. citizen. Suppose the federal government finances a deficit by having the Treasury sell government bonds to one group of U.S. citizens, thereby increasing the national debt. When the bonds mature, the government can pay the interest and principal by issuing new government bonds (rolling over the debt) to another group of U.S. citizens. This argument ignores the income distribution problem that results because interest payments go largely to those who are better off financially.

5. When the government makes interest payments on internally held debt, the money remains in the hands of U.S. citizens. External debt is very different. Repayment of interest and principal to foreigners withdraws purchasing power from U.S. citizens in favor of citizens abroad.

7. a. In year one, the federal deficit begins at $50 billion, and the U.S. Treasury issues $50 billion worth of bonds to finance the deficit.
   b. The next year the federal government must pay interest of $5 billion to service the debt ($50 billion bonds × 0.10 interest rate). Adding the interest payment to the $100 billion spent for goods and services yields a $105 billion expenditure in year two.
   c. For the second year, the deficit is $55 billion ($105 billion in expenditures − $50 billion in taxes), and the U.S. Treasury borrows this amount by issuing new bonds. The new national debt is $105 billion, consisting of the $50 billion in bonds issued in the first year and the $55 billion in bonds issued in the second year.

9. During a depression, tax hikes and/or expenditure cuts would only reduce aggregate demand and, in turn, real GDP, jobs, and income. Because the economy is operating in the Keynesian segment of the aggregate demand curve, this fiscal policy would have no impact on the price level.

11. This answer should be logical and supported by a thoughtful explanation. For example, the federal deficit might be the result of a recession and you argue that the deficit is correct fiscal policy. When the recession ends, the deficit will decline. Other arguments include some combinations of cutting spending or increasing taxes.

Chapter 24 Money and the Federal Reserve System

1. Money is worthless in and of itself. The value of money is to serve as a medium of exchange, a unit of account, and a store of value.

3. a. The quantity of credit cards can be controlled. Credit cards are portable, divisible, and uniform in quality.
   b. The quantity of Federal Reserve notes is controlled by the U.S. government. These notes are portable, divisible, and uniform in quality.
   c. The quantity of dogs is difficult to control. Dogs are not very portable or divisible, and they are certainly not uniform.
   d. The quantity of beer mugs can be controlled. Beer mugs are not very portable or divisible, but they could be made fairly uniform.

5. The narrowest definition of money in the United States is M1. M1 = currency (coins + paper bills) + checkable deposits.

7. The Fed's most important function is to regulate the U.S. money supply. The *Board of Governors* is composed of seven persons who have the responsibility to supervise and control the money supply and the U.S. banking system. The *Federal Open Market Committee (FOMC)* controls the money supply by directing the buying and selling of U.S. government securities.

9. Banks that belong to the Fed must join the FDIC. Banks chartered by the states may affiliate with the FDIC. There are relatively few nonmember, noninsured state banks.

Chapter 25 Money Creation

1. At first, the goldsmiths followed Shakespeare's advice and gave receipts only for gold on deposit in their vaults. They then realized that at any given time new deposits were coming in that could offset old deposits people were drawing down. The conclusion is that banking does not require a 100 percent required reserve ratio. Therefore, loans can be made, which stimulate the economy.

3. Banks can and do create money by granting loans to borrowers. These loans are deposited in customers' checking accounts, and, therefore, banks are participants in the money supply creation process.

5. There is no impact on the money supply. A check deposited in bank *A*, drawn on bank *B*, increases deposits, reserves, and lending at bank *A*. However, bank *B* experiences an equal reduction in deposits, reserves, and lending.

7.

First National Bank

Balance Sheet

Assets		Liabilities	
Reserves	−$1,000	Checkable deposits	−$1,000
Required	−$100		
Excess	−$900		
Total assets	−$1,000	Total liabilities	−$1,000

Negative excess reserves mean that loans must be reduced by $1,000.

9. Some customers may hold cash, rather than writing a check for the full amount of the loan. Some banks may hold excess reserves, rather than using these funds to make loans.

11. The decision of the public to hold cash and the willingness of banks to use excess reserves for loans affect the money multiplier. Variations in the money multiplier can cause unexpected changes in the money supply. Nonbanks can make loans and offer other financial services that are not under the direct control of the Federal Reserve. Finally, the public can decide to transfer funds from M1 to M2 or other definitions of the money supply.

Chapter 26 Monetary Policy

1. a. Transactions and precautionary balances increase.
   b. Speculative balances decrease.
   c. Transactions and precautionary balances decrease.
   d. Speculative balances increase.
   e. Transactions and precautionary balances decrease.

3.

Bond price	Interest rate
$ 800	10%
1,000	8
2,000	44

There is an inverse relationship between the price of a bond and the interest rate.

5. a. The price level declines slightly. Real GDP and employment fall substantially.
   b. The price level, real GDP, and employment rise.
   c. The price level declines slightly. Real GDP and employment fall substantially.

7. In the monetarist view, the velocity of money, V, and the output, Q, variables in the equation of exchange are constant. Therefore, the quantity theory of money is stated as

$$\mathbf{M} \times \mathbf{V} = \mathbf{P} \times \mathbf{Q}$$

Given this equation, changes in the money supply, M1, yield proportionate changes in the price level, P.

9. In the Keynesian view, an increase in the money supply decreases the interest rate and causes investment spending, which increases aggregate demand through the multiplier effect and causes demand-pull inflation. In the monetarist view, money supply growth gives people more money to spend. This direct increase in aggregate demand causes demand-pull inflation.

11. Under such conditions, the Keynesian view is correct. The Fed would have no influence on investment because changes in the interest rate failed to alter the quantity of investment goods demanded.

Chapter 27 The Phillips Curve and Expectations Theory

1. The Phillips curve is an inverse relationship between the inflation rate and the unemployment rate. The increase in aggregate demand would cause the inflation rate to increase and the unemployment rate to decrease.

3. In the 1970s and early 1980s, the economy experienced supply shocks from skyrocketing oil and food prices. The result was a leftward shift in the aggregate supply curve and stagflation.

5. a. The inflation rate is 6 percent, and the unemployment rate is 6 percent.
   b. The inflation rate rises to 10 percent, and the employment rate falls in the short run. In the long run, the unemployment rate returns to 6 percent.
   c. The inflation rate rises to 12 percent, and the unemployment rate falls in the short run. In the long run, the unemployment rate returns to 6 percent.

7. The economy is stimulated prior to an election, and there is a boom. After the election, the strategy is to contract the economy, causing recession until the next election approaches. Thus, political policies are counter to Keynesian policies because political policies cause the business cycle instead of stabilizing it.

9. a. Both prices and nominal wages will rise immediately, causing the inflation rate to rise from 4 percent to 6 percent. The unemployment rate remains unchanged at the 4 percent natural rate.
   b. Both prices and nominal wages will rise immediately, causing the inflation rate to rise from 6 percent to 8 percent. The unemployment rate remains unchanged at the 4 percent natural rate.
   c. Both prices and nominal wages will fall immediately, causing the inflation rate to fall from 8 percent to 4 percent. The unemployment rate remains unchanged at the 4 percent natural rate.

Chapter 28 International Trade and Finance

1. a. In Alpha, the opportunity cost of producing 1 ton of diamonds is 1/2 ton of pearls. In Beta, the opportunity cost of producing 1 ton of diamonds is 2 tons of pearls.
   b. In Alpha, the opportunity cost of producing 1 ton of pearls is 2 tons of diamonds. In Beta, the opportunity cost of producing 1 ton of pearls is 1/2 ton of diamonds.
   c. Because Alpha can produce diamonds at a lower opportunity cost than Beta can, Alpha has a comparative advantage in the production of diamonds.
   d. Because Beta can produce pearls at a lower opportunity cost than Alpha can, Beta has a comparative advantage in the production of pearls.
   e.

	Diamonds (tons per year)	Pearls (tons per year)
Before specialization		
Alpha (at point B)	100	25
Beta (at point C)	30	120
Total output	130	145
After specialization		
Alpha (at point A)	150	0
Beta (at point D)	0	180
Total output	150	180

As shown in the above table, specialization in each country increases total world output per year by 20 tons of diamonds and 35 tons of pearls.

f.

(a) Alpha

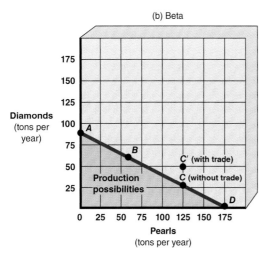

(b) Beta

Diamonds (tons per year)

Pearls (tons per year)

Production possibilities

Without trade, Alpha produces and consumes 100 tons of diamonds and 25 tons of pearls at point B on its production possibilities curve. Without trade, Beta produces and consumes 30 tons of diamonds and 120 tons of pearls (point C). Now assume Alpha specializes in producing diamonds at point A and imports 50 tons of pearls in exchange for 50 tons of diamonds. Through specialization and trade, Alpha moves its consumption possibility to point B′, outside its production possibilities curve.

3. The principle of specialization and trade according to comparative advantage applies to both nations and states in the United States. For example, Florida grows oranges, and Idaho grows potatoes. Trade between these states, just like trade between nations, increases the consumption possibilities.

5. U.S. industries (and their workers) that compete with restricted imports would benefit. Consumers would lose from the reduced supply of imported goods from which to choose and from higher prices for domestic products, resulting from lack of competition from imports.

7. Although some domestic jobs may be lost, new ones are created by international trade. Stated differently, the economy as a whole gains when nations specialize and trade according to the law of comparative advantage, but imports will cost jobs in some specific industries.

9. Although each nation's balance of payments equals zero, its current and capital account balances usually do not equal zero. For example, a current account deficit means a nation purchased more in imports than it sold in exports. On the other hand, this nation's capital account must have a surplus to offset the current account deficit. This means that foreigners are buying more domestic capital (capital inflow) than domestic citizens are buying foreign capital (capital outflow). Thus, net ownership of domestic capital stock is in favor of foreigners.

11. a.

Price (dollars per euro)

Quantity of euros per day (millions)

b. $0.15 per euro

c. An excess quantity of 200 million euros would be demanded.

Chapter 29 Economies in Transition

1. Americans prefer large cars and canned soup. Europeans predominantly buy small cars and dry soup. The role of women and minorities in the workplace is an excellent example of how culture relates to the labor factor of production.

3. Such a program would provide additional economic security for the elderly, but higher taxes could reduce the incentive to work, and economic efficiency might be reduced.

5. In a traditional agricultural system, a benefit would be that members of society would cooperate by helping to build barns, harvest, and so on. Under the command system, worrying about errors and crop failures would be minimized because the state makes the

decisions and everyone in society has a basic income. In a market economy, a bumper crop would mean large profits and the capacity to improve one's standard of living.

7. Because most economies are mixed systems, this term is too broad to be very descriptive. The terms *capitalism* and *communism* are more definitive concerning the role of private ownership, market allocations, and decentralized decision making. Embracing a market-oriented system means a transfer of power from the command bureaucracy to consumers. Markets are incompatible with the principle that socialist citizens are supposed to be concerned with the collective interest.

Chapter 30 Growth and the Less-Developed Countries

1. The difference between IACs and LDCs is based on GDP per capita. This classification is somewhat arbitrary. A country with a high GDP per capita and narrow industrial development based on oil, such as the United Arab Emirates, is excluded from the IAC list. There are 27 economies listed in the text as IACs, including Switzerland, Japan, the United States, Singapore, and Hong Kong. The following countries are considered to be LDCs: Argentina, Mexico, South Africa, Jordan, and Bangladesh.

3. a. Based only on GDP per capita, you would conclude that Alpha is a better place to live because this country produces a greater output of goods and services per person.
   b. Based on the additional evidence, you would change your mind and prefer to live in Beta because the quality-of-life data indicate a higher standard of living in this country.

5. The average growth rate of GDP per capita for IACs exceeds the GDP per capita growth rate for LDCs. This evidence is consistent with the argument. The argument is oversimplified because there is considerable diversity among the LDCs. In a given year, a LDC may have a GDP per capita growth rate greater than many IACs.

7. Economic growth and development are complicated because there is no single prescription that a country can follow. The chapter presents a multidimensional model with five basic categories: natural resources, human resources, capital, technological progress, and political environment. Because an LDC is weak in one or more of the key factors, such as natural resources, does not necessarily mean that the LDC cannot achieve economic success.

9. Because they are poor countries with low GDP per capita, they lack domestic savings to invest in capital; and lacking investment, they remain poor. The rich in these poor countries often put their savings abroad because of the fear of political instability. An inflow of external funds from abroad permits the LDC to increase its capital without reducing its consumption and to shift its production possibilities curve outward.

11. Poor countries are too poor to save enough to finance domestic capital formation. International trade is a way LDCs can generate savings from abroad. Exports provide the LDCs with foreign exchange to pay for imports of capital stock that is necessary for economic growth and development.

Answers to Sample Quizzes

Chapter 1 Introducing the Economic Way of Thinking

1. d   2. c   3. a   4. c   5. b   6. d   7. d   8. d
9. b   10. d   11. a   12. c   13. a   14. b
15. c   16. d   17. d   18. b   19. a   20. d

Appendix 1 Applying Graphs to Economics

1. d   2. d   3. b   4. c   5. a   6. a   7. d
8. c   9. a   10. c   11. d   12. a.   13. b
14. d   15. d   16. c   17. c   18. c   19. d   20. d

Chapter 2 Production Possibilities, Opportunity Cost, and Economic Growth

1. d   2. b   3. a   4. c   5. c   6. e   7. b
8. a   9. c   10. d   11. d   12. b   13. a   14. b
15. a   16. a   17. a   18. d   19. a   20. c

Chapter 3 Market Demand and Supply

1. b   2. a   3. d   4. c   5. d   6. c   7. c
8. d   9. b   10. a   11. b   12. e   13. d
14. a   15. b   16. c   17. b   18. a   19. a
20. b   21. c   22. e   23. d

Appendix 3 Consumer Surplus, Producer Surplus, and Market Efficiency

1. c   2. c   3. c   4. d   5. e   6. d   7. d   8. d
9. a   10. d   11. d   12. d   13. a   14. b
15. d   16. a   17. b   18. d   19. d   20. d

Chapter 4 Markets in Action

1. b   2. c   3. a   4. c   5. b   6. b   7. a
8. d   9. b   10. a   11. b   12. b   13. b
14. c   15. a   16. a   17. b   18. c   19. d
20. c

Chapter 5 Price Elasticity of Demand and Supply

1. d.   2. b   3. a   4. c   5. b   6. a   7. b
8. b   9. b   10. c   11. c   12. a   13. c
14. a   15. d   16. a   17. a   18. b   19. a
20. a   21. d   22. c   23. d   24. c   25. b

Chapter 6 Consumer Choice Theory

1. e   2. a   3. d   4. b   5. d   6. b   7. a
8. c   9. b   10. c   11. c   12. d   13. b
14. d   15. d   16. a   17. c   18. d   19. c
20. a   21. b   22. a   23. d   24. c   25. c

Appendix 6 Indifference Curve Analysis

1. d   2. a   3. c   4. d   5. a   6. d   7. a
8. a   9. d   10. d   11. a   12. c   13. d
14. c   15. b

Chapter 7 Production Costs

1. d   2. a   3. c   4. c   5. c   6. d   7. b
8. e   9. b   10. b   11. c   12. d   13. e
14. c   15. b   16. c   17. c   18. b   19. a
20. a   21. c   22. c   23. b   24. a   25. c

Chapter 8 Perfect Competition

1. e   2. d   3. c   4. c   5. a   6. e   7. c
8. d   9. d   10. b   11. d   12. c   13. a
14. d   15. d   16. b   17. d   18. b   19. d
20. c

Chapter 9 Monopoly

1. c   2. a   3. b   4. b   5. d   6. c   7. d
8. c   9. d   10. d   11. e   12. c   13. d
14. d   15. b   16. d   17. b   18. c   19. b
20. b

Chapter 10 Monopolistic Competition and Oligopoly

1. c   2. b   3. b   4. a   5. c   6. d   7. c
8. b   9. a   10. d   11. c   12. a   13. d   14. c
15. d   16. d   17. a   18. b   19. c   20. b

Chapter 11 Labor Markets

1. b   2. a   3. c   4. d   5. d   6. a   7. c
8. c   9. c   10. d   11. d   12. c   13. e
14. b   15. e   16. b   17. c   18. d   19. c
20. c

Chapter 12 Income Distribution, Poverty, and Discrimination

1. c   2. d   3. b   4. c   5. c   6. d   7. b
8. a   9. c   10. d   11. c   12. b   13. d
14. b   15. d   16. c   17. e   18. d   19. a
20. c

Chapter 13 Antitrust and Regulation

1. c   2. b   3. a   4. b   5. a   6. c   7. b
8. a   9. d   10. b   11. d   12. b   13. b
14. a   15. b   16. c   17. d   18. a   19. c
20. d

Chapter 14 Environmental Economics

1. c   2. d   3. c   4. c   5. d   6. b   7. b
8. d   9. c   10. b   11. d   12. b   13. b
14. c   15. a   16. c   17. b   18. a   19. b
20. c

Chapter 15 Gross Domestic Product

1. b   2. e   3. b   4. d   5. c   6. a   7. a
8. c   9. c   10. c   11. a   12. d   13. d
14. c   15. d   16. a   17. b   18. a   19. a
20. c

Chapter 16 Business Cycles and Unemployment

1. c   2. b   3. d   4. b   5. d   6. c   7. b
8. c   9. d   10. b   11. c   12. d   13. c
14. d   15. e   16. b   17. d   18. b   19. b
20. c

Chapter 17 Inflation

1. c   2. c   3. a   4. d   5. d   6. b   7. a
8. d   9. c   10. c   11. d   12. b   13. a
14. e   15. d   16. b   17. b   18. d   19. a
20. a

Chapter 18 The Keynesian Model

1. c   2. c   3. b   4. d   5. c   6. c   7. c   8. c
9. a   10. b   11. d   12. b   13. c   14. b
15. b   16. b   17. d   18. a   19. c   20. a

Chapter 19 The Keynesian Model in Action

1. c   2. c   3. a   4. d   5. c   6. a   7. c
8. a   9. b   10. b   11. a   12. d   13. d
14. a   15. b   16. d   17. b   18. c   19. d
20. d

Chapter 20 Aggregate Demand and Supply

1. c 2. e 3. a 4. b 5. a 6. a 7. d
8. a 9. c 10. b 11. c 12. c 13. d
14. b 15. b 16. a 17. a 18. e 19. c
20. c

Appendix 20 The Self-Correcting Aggregate Demand and Supply Model

1. c 2. e 3. a 4. d 5. b 6. a 7. d
8. d 9. b 10. b 11. b 12. a 13. b
14. b 15. b 16. a 17. a 18. c 19. d
20. c

Chapter 21 Fiscal Policy

1. c 2. c 3. d 4. a 5. d 6. d 7. d
8. a 9. c 10. c 11. b 12. a 13. d
14. d 15. d 16. b 17. a 18. c 19. b
20. a

Chapter 22 The Public Sector

1. a 2. a 3. a 4. a 5. b 6. d 7. c 8. a
9. a 10. b 11. c 12. c 13. b 14. d
15. b 16. d 17. a 18. c 19. d 20. b

Chapter 23 Federal Deficits, Surpluses, and the National Debt

1. a 2. d 3. c 4. c 5. d 6. b 7. d
8. d 9. c 10. d 11. a 12. d 13. a
14. d 15. a 16. d 17. d 18. a 19. a
20. e

Chapter 24 Money and the Federal Reserve System

1. a 2. b 3. c 4. d 5. b 6. d 7. d
8. b 9. d 10. d 11. d 12. a 13. c

14. c 15. d 16. d 17. b 18. d 19. a
20. a

Chapter 25 Money Creation

1. c 2. b 3. a 4. b 5. e 6. b 7. a
8. b 9. a 10. c 11. c 12. c 13. b
14. a 15. d 16. e 17. b 18. b 19. b
20. a

Chapter 26 Monetary Policy

1. a 2. c 3. e 4. b 5. b 6. b 7. d
8. a 9. b 10. d 11. a 12. c 13. d
14. b 15. a 16. b 17. d 18. e 19. d
20. e

Appendix 26 Policy Disputes Using the Self-Correcting Aggregate Demand and Supply Model

1. a 2. d 3. a 4. c 5. b 6. b 7. a
8. b 9. a 10. d 11. a 12. c 13. b
14. c 15. d

Chapter 27 The Phillips Curve and Expectations Theory

1. a 2. a 3. c 4. a 5. a 6. c 7. b
8. b 9. b 10. b 11. a 12. b 13. a
14. b 15. d 16. d 17. d 18. d 19. b
20. a

Chapter 28 International Trade and Finance

1. c 2. a 3. c 4. b 5. b 6. d 7. d
8. a 9. e 10. a 11. d 12. a 13. a
14. c 15. c 16. a 17. d 18. b 19. c
20. b

Chapter 29 Economies in Transition

1. d   2. a   3. c   4. a   5. c   6. d   7. d
8. a   9. c   10. a   11. a   12. d   13. a
14. b   15. d   16. b   17. d   18. c   19. d   20. c

Chapter 30 Growth and the Less-Developed Countries

1. d   2. d   3. c   4. b   5. e   6. d   7. b   8. d
9. d   10. d   11. e   12. a   13. e   14. a
15. b   16. b   17. c   18. a   19. c   20. b

Answers to Road Map Questions

Part 1

1. e 2. c 3. c 4. d 5. a 6. e 7. d
8. d 9. d 10. b

Part 2

1. b 2. c 3. a 4. a 5. d 6. d 7. d
8. c 9. c 10. c 11. b 12. a 13. c

Part 3

1. c 2. e 3. c 4. b 5. a 6. a 7. b
8. c 9. d 10. b 11. d

Part 4

1. c 2. d 3. d 4. d 5. a 6. d 7. a

Part 5

1. e 2. a 3. a 4. c 5. c 6. b 7. b
8. d 9. a 10. a 11. c 12. d

Part 6

1. d 2. a 3. a 4. d 5. d 6. b 7. c
8. e 9. b 10. a 11. a 12. d 13. b
14. e 15. d

Part 7

1. d 2. d 3. d 4. e 5. c 6. b 7. a
8. d 9. d 10. a 11. e 12. d 13. a
14. a

Part 8

1. d 2. d 3. b 4. e 5. e 6. c 7. d 8. e
9. b 10. d

Appendix

D

U.S. Gross Domestic Product and Related Statistics

U.S. Gross Domestic Product (in billions of dollars) and Related Statistics

	1929	1930	1931	1932	1933	1934	1935	1936	1937	1938
1. Gross domestic product	103.6	91.2	76.5	58.7	56.4	66.0	73.3	83.8	91.9	86.1
2. Personal consumption expenditures	77.4	70.1	60.7	48.7	45.9	51.5	55.9	62.2	66.8	64.3
3. Gross private domestic investment	16.5	10.8	5.9	1.3	1.7	3.7	6.7	8.6	12.2	7.1
4. Government consumption expenditures and gross investment	9.4	10.0	9.9	8.7	8.7	10.5	10.9	13.1	12.8	13.8
5. Net exports	0.4	0.3	0.0	0.0	0.1	0.3	−0.2	−0.1	0.1	1.0
6. National income	93.9	82.9	67.4	51.1	48.8	58.1	66.0	74.7	83.3	76.6
7. Personal income	84.9	76.1	65.2	49.9	46.8	53.7	60.3	68.6	74.1	68.4
8. Disposable personal income	83.2	74.6	64.2	49.1	46.0	52.8	59.3	67.3	72.2	66.5
9. Real gross domestic product (in 2005 dollars)	976.1	892.0	834.2	725.2	715.8	793.7	864.2	977.0	1,027.1	991.8
10. Percent change in real GDP	—	−8.6	−6.5	−13.1	−1.3	10.9	8.9	13.1	5.1	−3.4
11. Consumer price index (1982–84 = 100)	17.1	16.7	15.2	13.7	13.0	13.4	13.7	13.9	14.4	14.1
12. Rate of inflation (percent)	0.0	−2.3	−9.0	−9.9	−5.1	3.1	2.2	1.5	3.6	−2.1
13. Civilian unemployment rate (percent)	3.2	8.7	15.9	23.6	24.9	21.7	20.1	16.9	14.3	19.0
14. Supply of money, M1 (in billions of dollars)	26.4	26.6	21.9	20.4	19.8	23.1	27.0	31.0	29.6	31.8
15. Percent change in M1	—	−0.1	−17.7	−6.8	−2.9	16.7	16.9	14.8	−4.5	7.4
16. Prime rate charged by banks	5.5	1.5	1.5	1.5	1.5	1.5	1.5	1.5	1.5	1.5
17. Federal budget surplus or deficit (in billions of dollars)	0.7	0.7	−0.5	−2.7	−2.6	−3.6	−2.8	−4.3	−2.2	−1.0
18. Federal debt (in billions of dollars)	16.9	16.2	16.8	19.5	22.5	27.1	28.7	33.8	36.4	37.2

(Continued)

U.S. Gross Domestic Product (in billions of dollars) and Related Statistics *(Continued)*

	1939	1940	1941	1942	1943	1944	1945	1946	1947	1948
1. Gross domestic product	92.2	101.4	126.7	161.9	198.6	219.8	223.0	222.2	244.1	269.1
2. Personal consumption expenditures	67.2	71.3	81.1	89.0	99.9	108.7	102.0	144.3	162.0	175.0
3. Gross private domestic investment	9.3	13.6	18.1	10.4	6.1	7.8	10.8	31.1	35.0	48.1
4. Government consumption xpenditures and gross investment	14.8	15.0	26.5	62.7	94.8	105.3	93.0	39.6	36.3	40.5
5. Net exports	0.8	1.5	1.0	−0.3	−2.2	−2.0	−0.8	7.2	10.8	5.5
6. National income	82.0	90.5	115.8	149.5	184.2	198.0	198.3	198.6	216.3	242.6
7. Personal income	72.9	78.4	96.0	123.4	152.1	166.0	171.6	178.6	190.9	209.7
8. Disposable personal income	71.4	76.8	93.7	118.5	135.4	148.3	152.2	161.4	171.1	190.5
9. Real gross domestic product (in 2005 dollars)	1,071.9	1,165.9	1,365.0	1,616.8	1,881.5	2,033.5	2,010.7	1,790.7	1,774.6	1,852.7
10. Percent change in real GDP	8.1	8.8	17.1	18.5	16.4	8.1	−1.1	−10.9	−0.9	4.4
11. Consumer price index (1982–84 = 100)	13.9	14.0	14.7	16.3	17.3	17.6	18.0	19.5	22.3	24.1
12. Rate of inflation (percent)	−1.4	0.7	5.0	10.9	6.1	1.7	2.3	8.3	14.4	8.1
13. Civilian unemployment rate (percent)	17.2	14.6	9.9	4.7	1.9	1.2	1.9	3.9	3.9	3.8
14. Supply of money, M1 (in billions of dollars)	36.2	42.3	48.6	62.9	79.6	90.4	102.3	101.0	113.1	111.5
15. Percent change in M1	13.8	16.9	14.9	29.4	26.6	13.6	13.2	7.5	2.8	−1.4
16. Prime rate charged by banks	1.5	1.5	1.5	1.5	1.5	1.5	1.5	1.5	1.5	1.7
17. Federal budget surplus or deficit (in billions of dollars)	−3.9	−2.9	−4.9	−20.5	−54.6	−47.6	−47.6	−15.9	4.0	11.8
18. Federal debt (in billions of dollars)	48.2	50.7	57.5	79.2	142.6	204.1	260.1	271.0	257.1	252.0

	1949	1950	1951	1952	1953	1954	1955	1956	1957	1958
1. Gross domestic product	267.2	293.7	339.3	358.3	379.3	380.4	414.7	437.4	461.1	467.2
2. Personal consumption expenditures	178.5	192.2	205.5	219.5	233.1	240.0	258.8	271.7	286.9	296.2
3. Gross private domestic investment	36.9	54.1	60.2	54.0	56.4	53.8	69.0	72.0	70.5	64.5
4. Government consumption expenditures and gross investment	46.6	46.7	68.1	83.6	90.5	86.1	86.4	91.4	99.7	106.0
5. Net exports	5.2	0.7	2.5	1.2	−0.7	0.4	0.5	2.4	4.1	0.5
6. National income	237.5	263.9	303.8	321.3	338.6	338.7	372.0	394.9	413.3	415.6
7. Personal income	207.0	228.9	257.9	275.2	291.7	294.3	316.0	339.5	358.5	368.9
8. Disposable personal income	190.2	209.9	230.8	243.2	258.4	264.1	283.1	302.9	319.7	330.4
9. Real gross domestic product (in 2005 dollars)	1,843.1	2,004.2	2,159.3	2,242.0	2,345.2	2,330.4	2,498.2	2,547.6	2,598.8	2,575.4
10. Percent change in real GDP	−0.5	8.7	7.7	3.8	4.6	−0.6	7.2	2.0	2.0	−0.9
11. Consumer price index (1982–84 = 100)	23.8	24.1	26.0	26.5	26.7	26.9	26.8	27.2	28.1	28.9
12. Rate of inflation (percent)	−1.2	1.3	7.9	1.9	0.8	0.7	−0.4	1.5	3.3	2.8
13. Civilian unemployment rate (percent)	5.9	5.3	3.3	3.0	2.9	5.5	4.4	4.1	4.3	6.8
14. Supply of money, M1 (in billions of dollars)	111.2	116.2	122.7	127.4	128.8	132.3	135.2	136.9	135.9	141.1
15. Percent change in M1	−0.3	4.5	5.6	3.8	1.1	2.7	2.2	1.3	−0.7	3.8
16. Prime rate charged by banks	2.0	2.1	2.6	3.0	3.2	3.1	3.2	3.8	4.2	3.8
17. Federal budget surplus or deficit (in billions of dollars)	0.6	−3.1	6.1	−1.5	−6.5	−1.2	−3.0	3.9	3.4	−2.8
18. Federal debt (in billions of dollars)	252.6	256.9	255.3	259.1	266.0	270.8	274.4	272.7	272.3	279.7

(Continued)

U.S. Gross Domestic Product (in billions of dollars) and Related Statistics *(Continued)*

	1959	1960	1961	1962	1963	1964	1965	1966	1967	1968
1. Gross domestic product	506.6	526.4	544.8	585.7	617.8	663.6	719.1	787.7	832.4	909.8
2. Personal consumption expenditures	317.7	331.8	342.2	363.3	382.7	411.5	443.8	480.9	507.8	558.0
3. Gross private domestic investment	78.5	78.9	78.2	88.1	93.8	102.1	118.2	131.3	128.6	141.2
4. Government consumption expenditures and gross investment	110.0	111.5	119.5	130.1	136.4	143.2	151.4	171.6	192.5	209.3
5. Net exports	0.4	4.2	4.9	4.1	4.9	6.9	5.6	3.9	3.6	1.4
6. National income	453.5	473.9	490.7	528.9	559.7	601.4	652.2	701.1	750.4	821.2
7. Personal income	392.3	411.3	428.8	456.4	479.5	514.3	555.5	603.8	648.1	711.7
8. Disposable personal income	350.1	365.2	381.6	404.9	525.0	462.3	497.8	537.4	575.1	624.7
9. Real gross domestic product (in 2005 dollars)	2,760.1	2,828.5	2,894.4	3,069.8	3,204.0	3,389.4	3,607.0	3,842.1	3,939.2	4,129.9
10. Percent change in real GDP	7.2	2.5	2.3	6.1	4.4	5.8	6.4	6.5	2.5	4.8
11. Consumer price index (1982–84 = 100)	29.1	29.6	29.9	30.2	30.6	31.0	31.5	32.4	33.4	34.8
12. Rate of inflation (percent)	0.7	1.7	1.0	1.0	1.3	1.3	1.6	2.9	3.1	4.2
13. Civilian unemployment rate (percent)	5.5	5.5	6.7	5.5	5.7	5.2	4.5	3.8	3.8	3.6
14. Supply of money, M1 (in billions of dollars)	140.0	140.7	145.2	147.8	153.3	160.3	167.9	172.0	183.3	197.4
15. Percent change in M1	−0.8	0.5	3.2	1.8	3.7	4.6	4.7	2.5	6.6	7.7
16. Prime rate charged by banks	4.5	4.8	4.5	4.5	4.5	4.5	4.5	5.6	5.6	6.3
17. Federal budget surplus or deficit (in billions of dollars)	−12.8	0.3	−3.3	−7.1	−4.8	−5.9	−1.4	−3.7	−8.6	−25.2
18. Federal debt (in billions of dollars)	287.5	290.5	292.6	302.9	310.3	316.1	322.3	328.5	340.4	368.7

	1969	1970	1971	1972	1973	1974	1975	1976	1977	1978
1. Gross domestic product	984.4	1,038.3	1,126.8	1,237.9	1,382.3	1,499.5	1,637.7	1,824.6	2,030.1	2,293.8
2. Personal consumption expenditures	605.1	648.3	701.6	770.2	852.0	932.9	1,033.8	1,151.3	1,277.8	1,427.6
3. Gross private domestic investment	156.4	152.4	178.2	207.6	244.5	249.4	230.2	292.0	361.3	438.0
4. Government consumption expenditures and gross investment	221.4	233.7	246.4	263.4	281.7	317.9	357.7	383.0	414.7	453.6
5. Net exports	1.4	4.0	0.6	−3.4	4.1	−0.8	16.0	−1.6	−23.1	−25.4
6. National income	888.5	929.5	1,005.6	1,110.3	1,246.1	1,341.5	1,444.0	1,609.8	1,797.4	2,027.9
7. Personal income	778.3	838.6	903.1	992.6	1,110.5	1,222.7	1,334.9	1,474.7	1,632.5	1,836.7
8. Disposable personal income	673.8	735.5	801.4	869.0	978.1	1,071.7	1,187.3	1,302.3	1,435.0	1,607.3
9. Real gross domestic product (in 2005 dollars)	4,258.2	4,266.3	4,409.5	4,643.8	4,912.8	4,885.7	4,875.4	5,136.9	5,373.1	5,672.8
10. Percent change in real GDP	3.1	0.2	3.4	5.3	5.8	−0.6	−0.2	5.4	4.6	5.6
11. Consumer price index (1982–84 = 100)	36.7	38.8	40.5	41.8	44.4	49.3	53.8	56.9	60.6	65.2
12. Rate of inflation (percent)	5.5	5.7	4.4	3.2	6.2	11.0	9.1	5.8	6.5	7.6
13. Civilian unemployment rate	3.5	4.9	5.9	5.6	4.9	5.6	8.5	7.7	7.1	6.1
14. Supply of money, M1 (in billions of dollars)	203.9	214.4	228.3	249.2	262.9	274.2	287.1	306.2	330.9	357.3
15. Percent change in M1	3.3	5.1	6.5	9.2	5.5	4.3	4.7	6.7	8.1	8.0
16. Prime rate charged by banks	8.0	7.9	5.7	5.3	8.0	10.8	7.9	6.8	6.8	9.1
17. Federal budget surplus or deficit (in billions of dollars)	3.2	−2.8	−23.0	−23.4	−14.9	−6.1	−53.2	−73.7	−53.7	−59.2
18. Federal debt (in billions of dollars)	365.8	380.9	408.2	435.9	466.3	483.9	541.9	629.0	706.4	776.6

(Continued)

U.S. Gross Domestic Product (in billions of dollars) and Related Statistics *(Continued)*

	1979	1980	1981	1982	1983	1984	1985	1986	1987	1988
1. Gross domestic product	2,562.2	2,788.1	3,126.8	3,253.2	3,534.6	3,930.9	4,217.5	4,460.1	4,736.4	5,100.4
2. Personal consumption expenditures	1,591.2	1,755.8	1,939.5	2,075.5	2,288.6	2,501.1	2,717.6	2,896.7	3,097.0	3,350.1
3. Gross private domestic investment	492.9	479.3	572.4	517.2	564.3	735.6	736.2	746.5	785.0	821.6
4. Government consumption expenditures and gross investment	500.7	566.1	627.5	680.4	733.4	796.9	878.9	949.3	999.4	1,038.9
5. Net exports	−22.5	−13.1	−12.5	−20.0	−51.7	−102.7	−115.2	−132.5	−145.0	−110.1
6. National income	2,248.3	2,433.0	2,729.8	2,851.4	3,070.9	3,461.3	3,696.3	3,871.5	4,150.0	4,522.3
7. Personal income	2,059.5	2,301.5	2,582.3	2,766.8	2,952.2	3,268.9	3,496.7	3,696.0	3,924.4	4,231.2
8. Disposable personal income	1,790.9	2,002.7	2,237.1	2,412.7	2,599.8	2,891.5	3,079.3	3,258.8	3,435.3	3,726.3
9. Real gross domestic product (in 2005 dollars)	5,850.1	5,834.0	5,982.1	5,865.9	6,130.9	6,571.5	6,843.4	7,080.5	7,307.0	7,607.4
10. Percent change in real GDP	3.1	−0.3	2.5	−1.9	4.5	7.2	4.1	3.5	3.2	4.1
11. Consumer price index (1982−84 = 100)	72.6	82.4	90.9	96.5	99.6	103.9	107.6	109.6	113.6	118.3
12. Rate of inflation (percent)	11.3	13.5	10.3	6.2	3.2	4.3	3.6	1.9	3.6	4.1
13. Civilian unemployment rate	5.8	7.1	7.6	9.7	9.6	7.5	7.2	7.0	6.2	5.5
14. Supply of money, M1 (in billions of dollars)	381.8	408.5	436.7	474.8	521.4	551.6	619.8	724.7	750.2	786.7
15. Percent change in M1	6.9	7.0	6.9	8.7	9.8	5.8	12.4	16.9	3.5	4.9
16. Prime rate charged by banks	12.7	15.3	18.9	14.9	10.8	12.0	9.9	8.3	8.2	9.3
17. Federal budget surplus or deficit (in billions of dollars)	−40.7	−73.8	−79.0	−128.0	−207.8	−185.4	−212.3	−221.2	−149.7	−155.2
18. Federal debt (in billions of dollars)	829.5	909.1	994.8	1,137.3	1,371.7	1,564.6	1,817.4	2,120.5	2,346.0	2,601.1

	1989	1990	1991	1992	1993	1994	1995	1996	1997	1998
1. Gross domestic product	5,482.1	5,800.5	5,992.1	6,342.3	6,667.4	7,085.2	7,414.7	7,838.5	8,332.4	8,793.5
2. Personal consumption expenditures	3,594.5	3,835.5	3,980.1	4,236.9	4,483.6	4,750.8	4,967.3	5,273.6	5,570.6	5,918.5
3. Gross private domestic investment	874.9	861.0	802.9	864.8	953.3	1,097.3	1,144.0	1,240.2	1,388.7	1,510.8
4. Government consumption expenditures and gross investment	1,100.6	1,181.7	1,236.1	1,273.5	1,294.8	1,329.8	1,374.0	1,421.0	1,474.4	1,526.1
5. Net exports	−87.9	−77.6	−27.0	−32.8	−64.4	−92.7	−90.7	−96.3	−101.4	−161.8
6. National income	4,800.5	5,059.5	5,217.9	5,517.1	5,784.7	6,181.3	6,522.3	6,931.7	7,406.0	7,875.6
7. Personal income	4,557.5	4,846.7	5,031.5	5,347.3	5,568.1	5,874.8	6,200.9	6,591.6	7,000.7	7,525.4
8. Disposable personal income	3,991.4	4,254.0	4,444.9	4,736.7	4,921.6	5,184.3	5,457.0	5,759.6	6,074.6	6,498.9
9. Real gross domestic product (in 2005 dollars)	7,879.2	8,027.1	8,008.3	8,280.0	8,516.2	8,863.1	9,086.0	9,425.8	9,845.9	10,274.7
10. Percent change in real GDP	3.6	1.9	−0.2	3.4	2.9	4.1	2.5	3.7	4.5	4.4
11. Consumer price index (1982–84 = 100)	124.0	130.7	136.2	140.3	144.5	148.2	152.4	156.9	160.5	163.0
12. Rate of inflation (percent)	4.8	5.4	4.2	3.0	3.0	2.6	2.8	3.0	2.3	1.6
13. Civilian unemployment rate	5.3	5.6	6.8	7.5	6.9	6.1	5.6	5.4	4.9	4.5
14. Supply of money, M1 (in billions of dollars)	792.9	824.7	897.0	1,024.9	1,129.8	1,150.8	1,127.5	1,081.4	1,072.5	1,095.7
15. Percent change in M1	0.8	4.0	8.8	14.3	10.2	1.9	−2.0	−4.1	−.08	2.2
16. Prime rate charged by banks	10.9	10.0	8.5	6.3	6.0	7.2	8.8	8.3	8.4	8.4
17. Federal budget surplus or deficit (in billions of dollars)	−152.6	−221.0	−269.2	−290.3	−255.1	−203.2	−164.0	−107.4	−21.9	69.3
18. Federal debt (in billions of dollars)	2,867.8	3,206.3	3,598.2	4,001.8	4,351.0	4,643.3	4,920.6	5,181.5	5,369.2	5,478.2

(Continued)

U.S. Gross Domestic Product (in billions of dollars) and Related Statistics *(Continued)*

	1999	2000	2001	2002	2003	2004	2005	2006
1. Gross domestic product	9,353.5	9,951.5	10,286.2	10,642.3	11,142.2	11,853.3	12,623.0	13,377.2
2. Personal consumption expenditures	6,342.8	6,830.4	7,148.8	7,439.2	7,804.1	8,270.6	8,803.5	9,301.0
3. Gross private domestic investment	1,641.5	1,772.2	1,661.9	1,647.0	1,729.7	1,968.6	2,172.3	2,327.1
4. Government consumption expenditures and gross investment	1,631.3	1,731.0	1,846.4	1,983.3	2,112.6	2,232.8	2,369.9	2,518.4
5. Net exports	−262.1	−382.1	−371.0	−427.2	−504.1	−618.7	−722.7	−769.3
6. National income	8,358.0	8,938.9	9,185.2	9,408.5	9,840.2	10,534.0	11,237.8	12,031.2
7. Personal income	7,910.8	8,559.4	8,883.3	9,060.1	9,378.1	9,9937.2	10,485.9	11,268.1
8. Disposable personal income	6,803.3	7,327.2	7,648.5	8,009.7	8,377.8	8,889.4	9,277.3	9,915.7
9. Real gross domestic product (in 2005 dollars)	10,770.7	11,216.4	11,337.5	11,543.1	11,836.4	12,246.9	12,623.0	12,958.5
10. Percent change in real GDP	4.8	4.1	1.1	1.8	2.5	3.5	3.1	2.7
11. Consumer price index (1982–84 = 100)	166.6	172.2	177.1	179.9	184.0	188.9	195.3	201.6
12. Rate of inflation (percent)	2.2	3.4	2.8	1.6	2.3	2.7	3.4	3.2
13. Civilian unemployment rate	4.2	4.0	4.7	5.8	6.0	5.5	5.1	4.6
14. Supply of money, M1 (in billions of dollars)	1,122.4	1,087.8	1,182.8	1,220.6	1,307.0	1,376.7	1,375.0	1,367.2
15. Percent change in M1	2.4	−3.1	8.7	3.2	7.1	5.3	−0.1	−0.6
16. Prime rate charged by banks	8.0	9.2	6.9	4.7	4.1	4.3	6.2	8.0
17. Federal budget surplus or deficit (in billions of dollars)	125.6	236.2	128.2	−157.8	−377.6	−412.7	−318.3	−248.2
18. Federal debt (in billions of dollars)	5,605.5	5,628.7	5,769.9	6,198.4	6,760.0	7,354.7	7,905.3	8,451.4

	2007	2008	2009	2010	2011
1. Gross domestic product	14,028.7	14,291.5	13,939.0	14,526.5	15,094.0
2. Personal consumption expenditures	9,772.3	10,035.5	9,866.1	10,245.5	10,726.0
3. Gross private domestic investment	2,295.2	2,087.6	1,546.8	1,795.1	1,916.2
4. Government consumption expenditures and gross investment	2,674.2	2,878.1	2,917.5	3,002.8	3,030.6
5. Net exports	−713.1	−709.7	−391.5	−516.9	−578.7
6. National income	12,396.4	12,609.1	12,147.6	12,840.1	13,437.3
7. Personal income	11,912.3	12,460.2	11,930.2	12,373.5	13,005.3
8. Disposable personal income	10,423.6	11,024.5	10,788.8	11,179.7	11,604.9
9. Real gross domestic product (in 2005 dollars)	13,206.4	13,161.9	12,703.1	13,088.0	13,315.1
10. Percentage change in real GDP	1.9	−0.3	−3.5	3.0	1.7
11. Consumer price index (1982–84 = 100)	207.3	215.3	214.5	218.0	224.9
12. Rate of inflation (percent)	2.8	3.8	−0.4	1.6	3.2
13. Civilian unemployment rate	4.6	5.8	9.3	9.6	8.9
14. Supply of money, M1 (in billions of dollars)	1,375.4	1,606.9	1,697.8	1,840.3	2,173.9
15. Percent change in M1	0.6	16.8	5.7	8.4	18.1
16. Prime rate charged by banks	8.1	5.1	3.3	3.3	3.3
17. Federal budget surplus or deficit(in billions of dollars)	−160.7	−458.6	−1,412.7	−1,293.5	−1,299.6
18. Federal debt (in billions)	8,950.7	11,875.9	13,528.8	14,764.2	16,350.9

Glossary

A

Ability-to-pay principle The concept that those who have higher incomes can afford to pay a greater proportion of their income in taxes, regardless of benefits received.

Absolute advantage The ability of a country to produce a good using the same or fewer resources than another country.

Adaptive expectations theory The concept that people believe the best indicator of the future is recent information. As a result, people persistently underestimate inflation when it is accelerating and overestimate it while it is slowing down.

Adjustable-rate mortgage (ARM) A home loan that adjusts the nominal interest rate to changes in an index rate, such as rates on Treasury securities.

Agency for International Development (AID) The agency of the U.S. State Department that is in charge of U.S. aid to foreign countries.

Aggregate demand curve (AD) The curve that shows the level of real gross domestic product (GDP) purchased by households, businesses, government, and foreigners (net exports) at different possible price levels during a time period, ceteris paribus.

Aggregate expenditures function (AE) The function that represents total spending in an economy at a given level of real disposable income.

Aggregate expenditures model The model that determines the equilibrium level of real GDP by the intersection of the aggregate expenditures and aggregate output (and income) curves.

Aggregate supply curve (AS) The curve that shows the level of real GDP produced at different possible price levels during a time period, ceteris paribus.

Appreciation of currency A rise in the price of one currency relative to another.

Arbitrage The practice of earning a profit by buying a good at a low price and reselling the good at a higher price.

Automatic stabilizers Federal expenditures and tax revenues that automatically change levels in order to stabilize an economic expansion or contraction; sometimes referred to as *nondiscretionary fiscal policy*.

Autonomous consumption Consumption that is independent of the level of income (disposable income or real GDP).

Autonomous expenditure Spending that does not vary with the current level of income (disposable income or real GDP).

Average fixed cost (AFC) Total fixed cost divided by the quantity of output produced.

Average tax rate The tax divided by the income.

Average total cost (ATC) Total cost divided by the quantity of output produced.

Average variable cost (AVC) Total variable cost divided by the quantity of output produced.

B

Balance of payments A bookkeeping record of all the international transactions between a country and other countries during a given period of time.

Balance of trade The value of a nation's imports subtracted from its exports. Balance of trade can be expressed in terms of goods, services, or goods and services.

Balanced budget multiplier An equal change in government spending and taxes, which changes aggregate demand by the amount of the change in government spending.

Barrier to entry Any obstacle that makes it difficult for a new firm to enter.

Barter The direct exchange of one good or service for another good or service, rather than for money.

Base year A year chosen as a reference point for comparison with some earlier or later year.

Benefit-cost analysis The comparison of the additional rewards and costs of an economic alternative.

Benefits-received principle The concept that those who benefit from government expenditures should pay the taxes that finance their benefits.

Board of Governors of the Federal Reserve System The seven members appointed by the president and confirmed by the U.S. Senate who serve for one nonrenewable 14-year term. Their responsibility is to supervise and control the money supply and the banking system of the United States.

Budget deficit A budget in which government expenditures exceed government revenues in a given time period.

Budget line A line that represents all combinations of two goods that a consumer can purchase with a fixed amount of money given the price of each good.

Budget surplus A budget in which government revenues exceed government expenditures in a given time period.

Business cycle Alternating periods of economic growth and contraction, which can be measured by changes in real GDP.

C

Capital A human-made good used to produce other goods and services.

Capitalism An economic system characterized by private ownership of resources and markets.

Cartel A group of firms that formally agree to reduce competition by coordinating the price and output of a product.

Celler-Kefauver Act A 1950 amendment to the Clayton Act that prohibits one firm from merging with a competitor by purchasing its physical assets if the effect is to substantially lessen competition.

Ceteris paribus A Latin phrase that means while certain variables change, "all other things remain unchanged."

Change in demand An increase or a decrease in the quantity demanded at each possible price. An increase in demand is a rightward shift in the entire demand curve. A decrease in demand is a leftward shift in the entire demand curve.

Change in quantity demanded A movement between points along a stationary demand curve, ceteris paribus.

Change in quantity supplied A movement between points along a stationary supply curve, ceteris paribus.

Change in supply An increase or a decrease in the quantity supplied at each possible price. An increase in supply is a rightward shift in the entire supply curve. A decrease in supply is a leftward shift in the entire supply curve.

Checkable deposits The total money in financial institutions that can be withdrawn by writing a check.

Circular flow model A diagram showing the exchange of money, products and resources between households and businesses.

Civilian labor force The number of people 16 years of age and older who are employed or who are actively seeking a job, excluding members of the armed forces, homemakers, discouraged workers, and other persons not in the labor force.

Classical economics The theory that free markets will restore full employment without government intervention.

Classical economists A group of economists whose theory dominated economic thinking from the 1770s to the Great Depression. They believed recessions would naturally cure themselves because the price system would automatically restore full employment.

Classical range The vertical segment of the aggregate supply curve, which represents an economy at full-employment output.

Clayton Act A 1914 amendment that strengthens the Sherman Act by making it illegal for firms to engage in certain anticompetitive business practices.

Coase Theorem The proposition that private market negotiations can achieve social efficiency regardless of the initial definition of property rights.

Coincident indicators Variables that change at the same time real GDP changes.

Collective bargaining The process of negotiating labor contracts between the union and management concerning wages and working conditions.

Command economy An economic system that answers the What, How, and For Whom questions by a dictator or central authority.

Command-and-control regulations Government regulations that set an environmental goal and dictate how the goal will be achieved.

Commodity money Anything that serves as money while having market value based on the material from which it is made.

Communism A stateless, classless economic system in which all the factors of production are owned by the workers and people share in production according to their needs. In Marx's view, this is the highest form of socialism toward which the revolution should strive.

Comparable worth The principle that employees who work for the same employer must be paid the same wage when their jobs, even if different, require similar levels of education, training, experience, and responsibility. A nonmarket wage-setting process is used to evaluate and compensate jobs according to point scores assigned to different jobs.

Comparative advantage The ability of a country to produce a good at a lower opportunity cost than another country.

Complementary good A good that is jointly consumed with another good. As a result, there is an inverse relationship between a price change for one good and the demand for its "go together" good.

Conglomerate merger A merger between firms in unrelated markets.

Constant-cost industry An industry in which the expansion of industry output by the entry of new firms has no effect on the individual firm's cost curve.

Constant returns to scale A situation in which the long-run average cost curve does not change as the firm increases output.

Consumer equilibrium A condition in which total utility cannot increase by spending more of a given budget on one good and spending less on another good.

Consumer Financial Protection Bureau (CFPB) An independent bureau within the Federal Reserve that helps consumers make financial decisions.

Consumer price index (CPI) An index that measures changes in the average prices of consumer goods and services.

Consumer sovereignty The freedom of consumers to cast their dollar votes to buy, or not to buy, at prices determined in competitive markets.

Consumer surplus The value of the difference between the price consumers are willing to pay for a product on the demand curve and the price actually paid for it.

Consumption function The graph or table that shows the amount households spend for goods and services at different levels of income (disposable income or real GDP).

Cost-push inflation A rise in the general price level resulting from an increase in the cost of production that causes the aggregate supply curve to shift leftward.

Cross-elasticity of demand The ratio of the percentage change in quantity demanded for a good or service to a given percentage change in the price of another good or service.

Crowding-in effect An increase in private-sector spending as a result of federal budget deficits financed by U.S. Treasury borrowing. At less than full employment, consumers hold more Treasury securities, and this additional wealth causes them to spend more. Business investment spending increases because of optimistic profit expectations.

Crowding-out effect A reduction in private-sector spending as a result of federal budget deficits financed by U.S. Treasury borrowing. When federal government borrowing increases interest rates, the result is lower consumption by households and lower investment spending by businesses.

Currency Money, including coins and paper money.

Cyclical unemployment Unemployment caused by the lack of jobs during a recession.

D

Deadweight loss The net loss of consumer and producer surplus from underproduction or overproduction of a product.

Debt ceiling A legislated legal limit on the national debt.

Decreasing-cost industry An industry in which the expansion of industry output by the entry of new firms decreases the individual firm's cost curves (cost curve shifts downward).

Deflation A decrease in the general (average) price level of goods and services in the economy.

Demand A curve or schedule showing the various quantities of a product consumers are willing to purchase at possible prices during a specified period of time, ceteris paribus.

Demand curve for labor A curve showing the different quantities of labor employers are willing to hire at different wage rates in a given time period, ceteris paribus. It is equal to the marginal revenue product of labor.

Demand for money curve A curve representing the quantity of money that people hold at different possible interest rates, ceteris paribus.

Demand-pull inflation A rise in the general price level resulting from an excess of total spending (demand) caused by a rightward shift in the aggregate demand curve.

Depreciation of currency A fall in the price of one currency relative to another.

Deregulation The elimination or phasing out of government restrictions on economic activity.

Derived demand The demand for labor and other factors of production that depends on the consumer demand for the final goods and services the factors produce.

Direct relationship A positive association between two variables. When one variable increases, the other variable increases, and when one variable decreases, the other variable decreases.

Discount rate The interest rate the Fed charges on loans of reserves to banks.

Discouraged worker A person who wants to work, but who has given up searching for work because he or she believes there will be no job offers.

Discretionary fiscal policy The deliberate use of changes in government spending or taxes to alter aggregate demand and stabilize the economy.

Diseconomies of scale A situation in which the long-run average cost curve rises as the firm increases output.

Disinflation A reduction in the rate of inflation.

Disposable personal income (DI) The amount of income that households actually have to spend or save after payment of personal taxes.

Dissaving The amount by which personal consumption expenditures exceed disposable income.

E

Economic growth The ability of an economy to produce greater levels of output, represented by an outward shift of its production possibilities curve. Also, an expansion in national output measured by the annual percentage increase in a nation's GDP.

Economic profit Total revenue minus explicit and implicit costs.

Economic system The organizations and methods used to determine what goods and services are produced, how they are produced, and for whom they are produced.

Economics The study of how society chooses to allocate its scarce resources to the production of goods and services in order to satisfy unlimited wants.

Economies of scale A situation in which the long-run average cost curve declines as the firm increases output.

Effluent tax A tax on a pollutant.

Elastic demand A condition in which the percentage change in quantity demanded is greater than the percentage change in price.

Embargo A law that bars trade with another country.

Emissions trading Trading that allows firms to buy and sell the right to pollute.

Entrepreneurship The creative ability of individuals to seek profits by taking risks and combining resources to produce innovative products.

Equation of exchange An accounting identity that states the money supply times the velocity of money equals total spending.

Equilibrium A market condition that occurs at any price at which the quantity demanded and the quantity supplied are equal.

Excess reserves Potential loan balances held in vault cash or on deposit with the Fed in excess of required reserves.

Exchange rate The number of units of one nation's currency that equals one unit of another nation's currency.

Expansion An upturn in the business cycle during which real GDP rises. Also called a *recovery*.

Expenditure approach The national income accounting method that measures GDP by adding all the spending for final goods during a period of time.

Explicit costs Payments to nonowners of a firm for their resources.

External national debt The portion of the national debt owed to foreign citizens.

Externality A cost or benefit imposed on people other than the consumers and producers of a good or service.

F

Federal Deposit Insurance Corporation (FDIC) A government agency established in 1933 to insure customer deposits up to a specified limit if a bank fails.

Federal funds market A private market in which banks lend reserves to each other for less than 24 hours.

Federal funds rate The interest rate banks charge for overnight loans of reserves to other banks.

Federal Open Market Committee (FOMC) The Federal Reserve's committee that directs the buying and selling of U.S. government securities, which are major instruments for controlling the money supply. The FOMC consists of the seven members of the Federal Reserve's Board of Governors, the president of the New York Federal Reserve Bank, and the presidents of four other Federal Reserve district banks.

Federal Reserve System The 12 Federal Reserve district banks that service banks and other financial institutions within each of the Federal Reserve districts; popularly called the Fed.

Federal Trade Commission Act The federal act that in 1914 established the Federal Trade Commission (FTC) to investigate unfair competitive practices of firms.

Fiat money Money accepted by law and not because of its tangible value.

Final goods Finished goods and services produced for the ultimate user.

Fiscal policy The use of government spending and taxes to influence the nation's output, employment, and price level.

Fixed input Any resource for which the quantity cannot change during the period of time under consideration.

Flow The rate of change in a quantity during a given period of time, such as dollars per year. For example, income and consumption are flows that occur per week, per month, or per year.

Foreign aid The transfer of money or resources from one government to another with no repayment required.

Fractional reserve banking A system in which banks keep only a percentage of their deposits on reserve as vault cash and deposits at the Fed.

Free trade The flow of goods between countries without restrictions or special taxes.

Free rider An individual who enjoys benefits without paying the costs.

Free-rider problem The problem that if some individuals benefit, while others pay, few will be willing to pay for improvement of the environment or other public goods. As a result, these goods are underproduced.

Frictional unemployment Temporary unemployment caused by the time required of workers to move from one job to another.

Full employment The situation in which an economy operates at an unemployment rate equal to the sum of the frictional and structural unemployment rates. Also called the *natural rate of unemployment*.

G

Game theory A model of the strategic moves and countermoves of rivals.

GDP chain price index A measure that compares changes in the prices of all final goods during a given year to the prices of those goods in a base year.

GDP gap The difference between full-employment real GDP and actual real GDP.

GDP per capita The value of final goods produced (GDP) divided by the total population.

Government expenditures Federal, state, and local government outlays for goods and services, including transfer payments.

Government failure Government intervention or lack of intervention that fails to correct market failure.

Gross domestic product (GDP) The market value of all final goods and services produced in a nation during a period of time, usually a year.

H

Horizontal merger A merger of firms that compete in the same market.

Hot spot problem For emissions that do not disperse uniformly, emissions may be higher in locations where firms buy permits that allow them to increase emissions.

Human capital The accumulation of education, training, experience, and health that enables a worker to enter an occupation and be productive.

Hyperinflation An extremely rapid rise in the general price level.

I

Implicit costs The opportunity costs of using resources owned by a firm.

Incentive-based regulations Government regulations that set an environmental goal, but are flexible as to how buyers and sellers achieve the goal.

Income approach The national income accounting method that measures GDP by adding all incomes, including compensation of employees, rents, net interest, and profits.

Income effect The change in quantity demanded of a good or service caused by a change in real income (purchasing power).

Income elasticity of demand The ratio of the percentage change in quantity demanded for a good or service to a given percentage change in income.

Incomes policies Federal government policies designed to affect the real incomes of workers by controlling nominal wages and prices. Such policies include presidential jawboning, wage-price guidelines, and wage-price controls.

Increasing-cost industry An industry in which the expansion of industry output by the entry of new firms increases the individual firm's cost curves (cost curves shifts upward).

Independent relationship A zero association between two variables. When one variable changes, the other variable remains unchanged.

Indifference curve A curve showing the different quantity combinations of two goods that produce the same satisfaction or total utility to a consumer.

Indifference map A selection of indifference curves with each curve representing a different level of satisfaction or total utility.

Indirect business taxes Taxes levied as a percentage of the prices of goods sold and therefore collected as part of the firm's revenue. Examples include general sales taxes, excise taxes, and customs duties.

Industrially advanced countries (IACs) High-income nations that have market economies based on large stocks of technologically advanced capital and well-educated labor. The United States, Canada, Australia, New Zealand, Japan, and most of the countries of Western Europe are IACs.

Inelastic demand A condition in which the percentage change in quantity demanded is less than the percentage change in price.

Inferior good Any good for which there is an inverse relationship between changes in income and its demand curve.

Inflation An increase in the general (average) price level of goods and services in the economy.

Inflationary gap The amount by which aggregate expenditures exceed the amount required to achieve full-employment equilibrium.

Infrastructure Capital goods usually provided by the government, including highways, bridges, waste and water systems, and airports.

In-kind transfers Government payments in the form of goods and services, rather than cash, including such government programs as food stamps, Medicaid, and housing.

Interest-rate effect The impact on total spending (real GDP) caused by the direct relationship between the price level and the interest rate.

Intermediate goods Goods and services used as inputs for the production of final goods.

Intermediate range The rising segment of the aggregate supply curve, which represents an economy as it approaches full-employment output.

Internal national debt The portion of the national debt owed to a nation's own citizens.

International Monetary Fund (IMF) The lending agency that makes short-term conditional low-interest loans to developing countries.

Inverse relationship A negative association between two variables. When one variable increases, the other variable decreases, and when one variable decreases, the other variable increases.

Investment The accumulation of capital, such as factories, machines, and inventories, that is used to produce goods and services.

Investment demand curve The graph that shows the amount businesses spend for investment goods at different possible rates of interest.

Invisible hand A phrase that expresses the belief that the best interests of a society are served when individual consumers and producers compete to achieve their own private interests.

J

Jawboning Oratory intended to pressure unions and businesses to reduce wage and price increases.

K

Keynes, John Maynard A British economist (1883–1946) whose influential work offered an explanation of the Great Depression and suggested, as a cure, that the government should play an active role in the economy.

Keynesian economics The theory, first advanced by John Maynard Keynes, that the role of the federal government is to increase or decrease aggregate demand to achieve economic goals.

Keynesian range The horizontal segment of the aggregate supply curve, which represents an economy in a severe recession.

Kinked demand curve A demand curve facing an oligopolist that assumes rivals will match a price decrease, but ignore a price increase.

L

Labor The mental and physical capacity of workers to produce goods and services.

Laffer curve A graph depicting the relationship between tax rates and total tax revenues.

Lagging indicators Variables that change after real GDP changes.

Land Any natural resource provided by nature that is used to produce goods and services.

Law of demand The principle that there is an inverse relationship between the price of a good and the quantity buyers are willing to purchase in a defined time period, ceteris paribus.

Law of diminishing marginal utility The principle that the extra satisfaction of a good or service declines as people consume more in a given period.

Law of diminishing returns The principle that beyond some point the marginal product decreases as additional units of a variable factor are added to a fixed factor.

Law of increasing opportunity costs The principle that the opportunity cost increases as production of one output expands.

Law of supply The principle that there is a direct relationship between the price of a good and the quantity sellers are willing and able to offer for sale in a defined time period, ceteris paribus.

Leading indicators Variables that change before real GDP changes.

Less-developed countries (LDCs) Nations without large stocks of technologically advanced capital and well-educated labor. LDCs are economies based on agriculture, such as most countries of Africa, Asia, and Latin America.

Long run A period of time so long that all inputs are variable.

Long-run aggregate supply curve (LRAS) The curve that shows the level of real GDP produced at different possible price levels during a time period in which nominal incomes change by the same percentage as the price level.

Long-run average cost curve (LRAC) The curve that traces the lowest cost per unit at which a firm can produce any level of output when the firm can build a plant of any desired plant size.

Lorenz curve A graph of the actual cumulative distribution of income compared to a perfectly equal cumulative distribution of income.

M

M1 The narrowest definition of the money supply. It includes currency and checkable deposits.

M2 The definition of the money supply that equals M1 plus near monies, such as savings deposits and small time deposits of less than $100,000.

Macroeconomics The branch of economics that studies decision making for the economy as a whole.

Marginal analysis An examination of the effects of additions to or subtractions from a current situation.

Marginal-average rule The rule states that when marginal cost is below average cost, average cost falls. When marginal cost is above average cost, average cost rises. When marginal cost equals average cost, average cost is at its minimum point.

Marginal cost (MC) The change in total cost when one additional unit of output is produced.

Marginal cost pricing A system of pricing in which the price charged equals the marginal cost of the last unit produced.

Marginal factor cost (MFC) The additional total cost resulting from a one-unit increase in the quantity of a factor.

Marginal product The change in total output produced by adding one unit of a variable input, with all other inputs used being held constant.

Marginal propensity to consume (MPC) The change in consumption spending resulting from a given change in income (real disposable income or real GDP).

Marginal propensity to save (MPS) The change in saving resulting from a given change in income (real disposable income or real GDP).

Marginal rate of substitution (MRS) The rate at which the consumer is willing to substitute one good for another good with no change in total utility. The MRS equals the slope of an indifference curve at any point on the curve.

Marginal revenue (MR) The change in total revenue from the sale of one additional unit of output.

Marginal revenue product (MRP) The increase in a firm's total revenue resulting from hiring an additional unit of labor or other variable resource.

Marginal tax rate The fraction of additional income paid in taxes.

Marginal utility The change in total utility from one additional unit of a good or service.

Market Any arrangement in which buyers and sellers interact to determine the price and quantity of goods and services exchanged.

Market economy An economic system that answers the What, How, and For Whom questions using prices determined by the interaction of the forces of supply and demand.

Market failure A situation in which market equilibrium results in too few or too many resources being used in the production of a good or service. This inefficiency may justify government intervention.

Market structure A classification system for the key traits of a market, including the number of firms, the similarity of the products they sell, and the ease of entry into and exit from the market.

Means test A requirement that a family's income not exceed a certain level to be eligible for public assistance.

Medium of exchange The primary function of money to be widely accepted in exchange for goods and services.

Microeconomics The branch of economics that studies decision making by a single individual, household, firm, industry, or level of government.

Mixed economy An economic system than answers the What, How, and For Whom questions through a mixture of traditional, command, and market systems.

Model A simplified description of reality used to understand and predict the relationship between variables.

Monetarism The theory that changes in the money supply directly determine changes in prices, real GDP, and employment.

Monetary Control Act A law, formally titled the Depository Institutions Deregulation and Monetary Control Act of 1980, that gave the Federal Reserve System greater control over nonmember banks and made all financial institutions more competitive.

Monetary policy The Federal Reserve's use of open market operations, changes in the discount rate, and changes in the required reserve ratio to change the money supply (M1).

Money Anything that serves as a medium of exchange, unit of account, and store of value.

Money multiplier The maximum change in the money supply (checkable deposits) due to an initial change in the excess reserves banks hold. The money multiplier is equal to 1 divided by the required reserve ratio.

Monopolistic competition A market structure characterized by (1) many small sellers, (2) a differentiated product, and (3) easy market entry and exit.

Monopoly A market structure characterized by (1) a single seller, (2) a unique product, and (3) impossible entry into the market.

Monopsony A labor market in which a single firm hires labor.

Mutual interdependence A condition in which an action by one firm may cause a reaction from other firms.

N

National debt The total amount owed by the federal government to owners of government securities.

National income (NI) The total income earned by resource owners, including wages, rents, interest, and profits. NI is calculated as GDP minus depreciation of the capital worn out in producing output.

Nationalization The act of transforming a private enterprise's assets to government ownership.

Natural monopoly An industry in which the long-run average cost of production declines throughout the entire market. As a result, a single firm can supply the entire market demand at a lower cost than two or more smaller firms.

Natural rate hypothesis The concept that the economy will self-correct to the natural rate of unemployment. The long-run Phillips curve is therefore a vertical line at the natural rate of unemployment.

Negative income tax (NIT) A plan under which families below a certain break-even level of income would receive cash payments that decrease as their incomes increase.

Net exports effect The impact on total spending (real GDP) caused by the inverse relationship between the price level and the net exports of an economy.

Net public debt National debt minus all government interagency borrowing.

Network good A good that increases in value to each user as the total number of users increases. As a result, a firm can achieve economics of scale. Examples include Facebook and Match.com.

New-source bias Bias that occurs when regulations provide an incentive to keep assets past the efficient point.

Nominal GDP The value of all final goods based on the prices existing during the time period of production.

Nominal income The actual number of dollars received over a period of time.

Nominal interest rate The actual rate of interest without adjustment for the inflation rate.

Nonprice competition The situation in which a firm competes using advertising, packaging, product development, better quality, and better service, rather than lower prices.

Normal good Any good for which there is a direct relationship between changes in income and its demand curve.

Normal profit The minimum profit necessary to keep a firm in operation. A firm that earns normal profit earns total revenue equal to its total opportunity cost.

Normative economics An analysis based on value judgment.

O

Offset Reduction in an existing pollution source to counteract pollution from a new source.

Offshoring Work for a company performed by the company's employees located in another country.

Oligopoly A market structure characterized by (1) few large sellers, (2) either a homogeneous or a differentiated product, and (3) difficult market entry.

Open market operations The buying and selling of government securities by the Federal Reserve System.

Opportunity cost The best alternative sacrificed for a chosen alternative.

Outsourcing The practice of a company having its work done by another company in another country.

P

Peak The phase of the business cycle in which real GDP reaches its maximum after rising during a recovery.

Per se rule The antitrust doctrine that the existence of monopoly alone is illegal, regardless of whether or not the monopoly engages in illegal business practices.

Perfect competition A market structure characterized by (1) a large number of small firms, (2) a homogeneous product, and (3) very easy entry into or exit from the market. Perfect competition is also referred to as *pure competition*.

Perfectly competitive firm's short-run supply curve The firm's marginal cost curve above the minimum point on its average variable cost curve.

Perfectly competitive industry's long-run supply curve The curve that shows the quantities supplied by the industry at different equilibrium prices after firms complete their entry and exit.

Perfectly competitive industry's short-run supply curve The supply curve derived from the horizontal summation of the marginal cost curves of all firms in the industry above the minimum point of each firm's average variable cost curve.

Perfectly elastic demand A condition in which a small percentage change in price brings about an infinite percentage change in quantity demanded.

Perfectly inelastic demand A condition in which the quantity demanded does not change as the price changes.

Personal income (PI) The total income received by households that is available for consumption, saving, and payment of personal taxes.

Phillips curve A curve showing an inverse relationship between the inflation rate and the unemployment rate.

Political business cycle A business cycle caused by policymakers to improve politician's reelection chances.

Positive economics An analysis limited to statements that are verifiable.

Poverty line The level of income below which a person or a family is to be considered poor.

Precautionary demand for money The stock of money people hold to pay unpredictable expenses.

Predatory pricing The practice of one or more firms temporarily reducing prices in order to eliminate competition and then raising prices.

Price ceiling A legally established maximum price a seller can charge.

Price discrimination The practice of a seller charging different prices for the same product that are not justified by cost differences.

Price elasticity of demand The ratio of the percentage change in the quantity demanded of a product to a percentage change in its price.

Price elasticity of supply The ratio of the percentage change in the quantity supplied of a product to the percentage change in its price.

Price floor A legally established minimum price a seller can be paid.

Price leadership A pricing strategy in which a dominant firm sets the price for an industry and the other firms follow.

Price maker A firm that faces a downward-sloping demand curve and therefore it can choose among price and output combinations along the demand curve.

Price system A mechanism that uses the forces of supply and demand to create an equilibrium through rising and falling prices.

Price taker A seller that has no control over the price of the product it sells.

Privatization The process of turning a government enterprise into a private enterprise.

Private benefits and costs Benefits and costs to the decision maker, ignoring benefits and costs to third parties. Third parties are people outside the market transaction who are affected by the product.

Producer surplus The value of the difference between the actual selling price of a product and the price producers are willing to sell it for on the supply curve.

Product differentiation The process of creating real or apparent differences between goods and services.

Production function The relationship between the maximum amounts of output that a firm can produce and various quantities of inputs.

Production possibilities curve A curve that shows the maximum combinations of two outputs an economy can produce in a given period of time with its available resources and technology.

Progressive tax A tax that charges a higher percentage of income as income rises.

Proportional tax A tax that charges the same percentage of income, regardless of the size of income. Also called a *flat-rate tax* or simply a *flat tax*.

Protectionism The government's use of embargoes, tariffs, quotas, and other restrictions to protect domestic producers from foreign competition.

Public choice theory The analysis of the government's decision-making process for allocating resources.

Public good A good or service with two properties: (1) users collectively consume benefits, and (2) there is no way to bar people who do not pay (free riders) from consuming the good or service.

Q

Quantity theory of money The theory that changes in the money supply are directly related to changes in the price level.

Quota A limit on the quantity of a good that may be imported in a given time period.

R

Rational expectations theory The belief that people use all available information to predict the future, including the future impact of predictable monetary and fiscal policies. Predictable expansionary macroeconomic policies can therefore be negated by immediately flexible wages and prices when businesses and workers anticipate the effects of these policies on the economy.

Rational ignorance The voter's choice to remain uninformed because the marginal cost of obtaining information is higher than the marginal benefit from knowing it.

Real balances effect The impact on total spending (real GDP) caused by the inverse relationship between the price level and the real value of financial assets with fixed nominal value.

Real GDP The value of all final goods produced during a given time period based on the prices existing in a selected base year.

Real income The actual number of dollars received (nominal income) adjusted for changes in the CPI.

Real interest rate The nominal rate of interest minus the inflation rate.

Recession A downturn in the business cycle during which real GDP declines. Also called a *contraction*.

Recessionary gap The amount by which aggregate expenditures fall short of the amount required to achieve full-employment equilibrium.

Regressive tax A tax that charges a lower percentage of income as income rises.

Required reserve ratio The percentage of deposits that the Federal Reserve requires a bank to hold in vault cash or on deposit with the Fed.

Required reserves The minimum balance that the Federal Reserve requires a bank to hold in vault cash or on deposit with the Fed.

Resources The basic categories of inputs used to produce goods and services. Resources are also called *factors of production*. Economists divide resources into three categories: land, labor, and capital.

Robinson-Patman Act A 1936 amendment to the Clayton Act that strengthens the Clayton Act against price discrimination.

Rule of reason The antitrust doctrine that the existence of monopoly alone is not illegal unless the monopoly engages in illegal business practices.

S

Saving The part of disposable income households do not spend for consumer goods and services.

Say's Law The theory that supply creates its own demand.

Scarcity The condition in which human wants are forever greater than the available supply of time, goods, and resources.

Sherman Act The federal antitrust law enacted in 1890 that prohibits monopolization and conspiracies to restrain trade.

Short run A period of time so short that there is at least one fixed input.

Short-run aggregate supply curve (SRAS) The curve that shows the level of real GDP produced at different possible price levels during a time period in which nominal incomes do not change in response to changes in the price level.

Shortage A market condition existing at any price where the quantity supplied is less than the quantity demanded.

Slope The ratio of the change in the variable on the vertical axis (the rise or fall) to the change in the variable on the horizontal axis (the run).

Social benefits and costs The sum of benefits to everyone in society, including both private benefits and external benefits. Social costs are the sum of costs to everyone in society, including both private costs and external costs.

Socialism An economic system characterized by government ownership of resources and centralized decision making.

Speculative demand for money The stock of money people hold to take advantage of expected future changes in the price of bonds, stocks, or other nonmoney financial assets.

Spending multiplier (SM) The ratio of the change in aggregate demand (total spending) resulting from an initial change in any component of aggregate expenditures or aggregate demand, including consumption, investment, government spending, and net exports. As a formula, the spending multiplier equals $1/(1 - \text{MPC})$ or $1/\text{MPS}$.

Stagflation The condition that occurs when an economy experiences the twin maladies of high unemployment and rapid inflation simultaneously.

Stock A quantity measured at one point in time. For example, an inventory or the amount of money in a checking account.

Store of value The ability of money to hold value over time.

Structural unemployment Unemployment caused by a mismatch of the skills of workers out of work and the skills required for existing job opportunities.

Subprime mortgage loan A home loan made to borrowers with an above-average risk of default.

Substitute good A good that competes with another good for consumer purchases. As a result, there is a direct relationship between a price change for one good and the demand for its "competitor" good.

Substitution effect The change in quantity demanded of a good or service caused by a change in its price relative to substitutes.

Supply A curve or schedule showing the various quantities of a product sellers are willing to produce and offer for sale at possible prices during a specified period of time, ceteris paribus.

Supply curve of labor A curve showing the different quantities of labor workers are willing to offer employers at different wage rates in a given time period, ceteris paribus.

Supply-side fiscal policy A fiscal policy that emphasizes government policies that increase aggregate supply in order to achieve long-run growth in real output, full employment, and a lower price level.

Surplus A market condition existing at any price where the quantity supplied is greater than the quantity demanded.

Sustainability Meeting the needs of the present generation without compromising the ability of future generations to meet their needs.

T

Tariff A tax on an import.

Tax incidence The share of a tax ultimately paid by consumers and sellers.

Tax multiplier The change in aggregate demand (total spending or total expenditures) resulting from an initial change in taxes. As a formula, the tax multiplier equals 1 − spending multiplier.

Technology The body of knowledge applied to how goods are produced.

Total cost (TC) The sum of total fixed cost and total variable cost at each level of output.

Total fixed cost (TFC) Costs that do not vary as output varies and that must be paid even if output is zero. These are payments that the firm must make in the short run, regardless of the level of output.

Total revenue The total number of dollars a firm earns from the sale of a good or service, which is equal to its price multiplied by the quantity demanded.

Total utility The amount of satisfaction received from all the units of a good or service consumed.

Total variable cost (TVC) Costs that are zero when output is zero and vary as output varies.

Traditional economy An economic system that answers the What, How, and For Whom questions the way they always have been answered.

Tragedy of the Commons Individuals will use an open access resource to the point of exhaustion, basing their use on private benefits while disregarding external costs to others.

Transactions costs The costs of negotiating and enforcing a contract.

Transactions demand for money The stock of money people hold to pay everyday predictable expenses.

Transfer payment A government payment to individuals not in exchange for goods or services currently produced.

Trough The phase of the business cycle in which real GDP reaches its minimum after falling during a recession.

Trust A combination or cartel consisting of firms that place their assets in the custody of a board of trustees.

U

Unemployment compensation The government insurance program that pays income for a short time period to unemployed workers.

Unemployment rate The percentage of people in the civilian labor force who are without jobs and are actively seeking jobs.

Unit of account The function of money to provide a common measurement of the relative value of goods and services.

Unitary elastic demand A condition in which the percentage change in quantity demanded is equal to the percentage change in price.

Utility The satisfaction, or pleasure, that people receive from consuming a good or service.

V

Variable input Any resource for which the quantity can change during the period of time under consideration.

Velocity of money The average number of times per year a dollar of the money supply is spent on final goods and services.

Vertical merger A merger of a firm with its suppliers.

Vicious circle of poverty The trap in which countries are poor because they cannot afford to save and invest, but they cannot save and invest because they are poor.

W

Wage and price controls Legal restrictions on wage and price increases. Violations can result in fines and imprisonment.

Wage and price guidelines Voluntary standards set by the government for "permissible" wage and price increases.

Wage-price spiral A situation that occurs when increases in nominal wage rates are passed on in higher prices, which, in turn, result in even higher nominal wage rates and prices.

Wealth The value of the stock of assets owned at some point in time.

Wealth effect A shift in the consumption function casued by a change in the value of real and financial assets.

World Bank The lending agency that makes long-term low-interest loans and provides technical assistance to less-developed countries.

World Trade Organization (WTO) An international organization of member countries that oversees international trade agreements and rules on trade disputes.

Index

A

Ability-to-pay principle, 609–610, 621
Absolute advantage, 774–775
Accounting profit, 182–183
Acid rain program, 384
Actual real GDP, 513
Adaptive expectations theory
  AD-AS model, 750–752
  definition, 745
  long-run Phillips curve, 744, 757
  political business cycle, 747
Adjustable-rate mortgages (ARM), 469, 474, 720
ADM. *See* Archer Daniels Midland Company
Ad valorem, 777
Advertising
  changes in demand, 101, 300
  deceptive, 349
  economies of scale and, 270
  free, 350
  long-run average cost and, 270, 271
  in monopolistic competition, 270–272
  nonprice competition, 269, 279
  in oligopoly, 277, 279, 285
  social networking, 272
  tobacco, 141
AFC. *See* Average fixed cost
African Americans, 328–329, 337–338
  unemployment and, 450
After-tax income, 417–418
After-tax rate of profit, 499
Agency for International Development
  (AID), 840
Aggregate demand
  automatic stabilizers, 587–589
  decrease in, 571–573, 576
  definition, 486
  demand-pull inflation, 469–470, 548
  discretionary fiscal policy, 577–586
  effect of decreases in during 2008–2009
    recession, 545
  expansionary effect on, 713
  Green Book, 694
  increase in, 537, 543, 569–571, 574–576
  inflationary gap, 520
  Keynes on, 506, 536
  macroeconomic equilibrium, 512,
    540–541
  nonprice-level determinants,
    533–534, 548
  spending multiplier, 513, 515
  supply-side fiscal policy, 589–594
Aggregate demand-aggregate supply model
  (AD-AS). *See also* Self-correcting aggregate
  demand-aggregate supply model
  adaptive expectations *vs.* rational
    expectations, 750–752
  classical range, 540, 544, 553
  crowding-out effect, 642–644, 721
  federal budget and, 627
  intermediate range, 542, 544
  Keynesian range, 542
  Keynes on, 550
  macroeconomic equilibrium, 540–546
  monetary policy, 712
  nonprice-level determinants, 548
  Phillips curve and, 740
  during 2008–2009 recession, 545–546

Aggregate demand curve
  downward sloping, 534
  increase in, 551–552
  interest-rate effect, 533, 534, 553
  macroeconomic equilibrium, 540–541
  net exports effect, 533, 534, 553
  nonprice-level determinants, 533–534
  real balances effect, 532, 534
  shifts in, 535, 552
Aggregate expenditures, 438, 486, 507,
  508–513, 517, 519, 534–535
  Keynesian equilibrium, 509
Aggregate expenditures function,
  499–500, 509–510, 517–518
Aggregate expenditures model, 509–513,
  522, 523
  defined, 511
Aggregate investment demand, 500
Aggregate spending, 470, 486, 513, 520, 537
Aggregate supply
  classical view of, 537–539
  cost-push inflation, 547–549, 551
  demand-pull inflation, 547–549, 551
  discretionary fiscal policy, 584–585
  Keynesian view of, 535–537
  monetary policy, 712
  nonprice-level determinants, 546–547, 548
  supply-side fiscal policy, 589–594
Aggregate supply curve
  classical view of, 537–539
  increase in, 551–552
  Keynesian view of, 535–537
  macroeconomic equilibrium, 540–541
  nonprice-level determinants, 546–547
  ranges of, 539–541
  shift in, 547, 552
  short-run and long-run, 561
Agricultural price supports, 109–110
Agricultural technology, 835
Agriculture Adjustment Act, 522
AHA. *See* American Heart Association
AID. *See* Agency for International Development
AIDS vaccination market, 114–115
Airline Deregulation Act of 1978, 358, 365
Alcoa antitrust case, 352–353, 356, 366
Alligator farming, 232–233
AMA. *See* American Medical Association
American Federation of State, County, and
  Municipal Employees, 339
American Greetings, 11
American Heart Association (AHA), 451
American Medical Association (AMA), 128
American Tobacco Trust, 352
Amish people, 805, 811
Amoco, 352
Amtrak, 820
Antipoverty programs, 330–333, 340
Antitrust
  Alcoa case, 352–353, 356, 366
  AT&T case, 353–354, 356, 358
  IBM case, 353, 356
  internationally, 357
  key cases, 352–356
  laws concerning, 348–350
  mergers, 356–357
  Microsoft Corporation, 346, 355, 356
  Standard Oil, 254, 346, 347, 348, 352, 356
APC. *See* Average private cost
Apple Computer Company, 199, 353

Appreciation of currency, 792, 799
Arbitrage, 255
Arc elasticity formula. *See* Midpoints formula
Archer Daniels Midland Company (ADM), 348
ARM. *See* Adjustable-rate mortgages
ASC. *See* Average social cost
Asia, GDP of, 826, 828, 832, 842
Asian-Pacific Economic Cooperation (APEC),
  782
Assets, 682
  financial, 494
  real, 494
Associated Press, 76
Association *vs.* causation, 10
ATC. *See* Average total cost
ATS. *See* Automatic transfer savings accounts
AT&T antitrust case, 353–354, 356, 358
Australia, 637–638
  government expenditure, 606
  tax burden, 608
Auto emissions, 373, 379, 381, 383
Automatic stabilizers, 587–589, 596
Automatic transfer savings (ATS) accounts, 665
Autonomous consumption, 486, 488, 501
Autonomous expenditure, 499–500, 502
Autonomous government spending, 508
Autonomous investment demand curve, 500
AVC. *See* Average variable cost
Average cost curves, 188–190
Average fixed cost (AFC), 188, 191, 200
Average loss per unit, 221
Average private cost (APC), 374, 375
Average profit per unit, 220
Average social cost (ASC), 374, 375
Average tax rate, 611
Average total cost (ATC), 188, 191, 200, 220
Average variable cost (AVC), 188, 191,
  200, 220

B

Balanced budget multiplier, 586, 596
Balance of payments, 782–788, 798
Balance of trade, 783–785, 787, 798
Banana trade, 780–781
Banco Boliviano Americano, 472
Bangladesh, GDP of, 827, 830
Banker bookkeeping, 681–683
Banking system, 667–669, 671–673, 686–688.
  See also Federal Reserve System
Bank of America, 839
Banks, 667, 669–670. *See also* Federal Reserve
  System
Barriers to entry, 261, 269, 278
Barter, 659
Base year, 460
Baum, L. Frank, 796
BEA. *See* Budget Enforcement Act; Bureau of
  Economic Analysis
Bear Stearns, 720
Benefit-cost analysis, 616
Benefits-received principle, 608–609, 621
Berlin University, 813
Biases, defined, 14
Big Macs, 155–156
"Black gold," 281
"Black" markets, 107, 414, 753

Black Tuesday, 484, 498
BLS. *See* Bureau of Labor Statistics
Board of Governors, 667, 668, 669, 676, 747
Boeing, 788
Boston Globe, 819
Boston Snow Index (BSI), 11
Bottlenecks, 544, 579
"Brain drain," 832
Brazil, 827, 832, 842
    carbon offset reduction, 390
Break-even income, 334, 488
Break-even point, 218
Bruntland Commission, 392
Bryan, William Jennings, 796
BSI. *See* Boston Snow Index
Buchanan, James, 616
Budget deficit, 589, 596
Budget Enforcement Act (BEA), 630
Budget line, 171–173, 177
Budget resolution, 628
Budget surplus, 587, 596
Burden of debt debate, 639–641
Bureaucratic inefficiency, 619
Bureau of Economic Analysis (BEA), 403, 416
Bureau of Labor Statistics (BLS), 439, 458
Bureau of the Census, 439
Burns, Arthur, 756
Bush, George H. W., 14, 634
Bush, George W., 576, 602, 633, 669
Business Conditions Digest, 436
Business Cycle Dating Committee, 434
Business cycles
    described, 452
    indicators, 436–438
    phases of, 432–433, 434
    total spending and, 438–439
    in the United States, 435
Business inventories, 407
Business taxes, 499
Bus Regulatory Reform Act of 1982, 358
Buyers, 63–64, 65, 127

C

CAB. *See* Civil Aeronautics Board
Cable television industry, 358, 361
CAC. *See* Command-and-control regulation
CAFE standards. *See* Corporate Average Fuel
    Economy standards
CAFTA. *See* Central American Free Trade
    Agreement
Canada
    budget, 634, 635
    economic system of, 805, 816
    GDP of, 413, 826–827
    government expenditures, 606
    national debt, 638
    as trading partner, 771
    unemployment, 442
Capacity utilization, 498
Cap and trade, 388–389
Capital
    accumulation of, 569, 833–834
    in circular flow model, 404–405
    costs of, 373
    crowding-in effect, 642–643
    definition, 5
    depreciation, 411, 416
    in developing countries, 841–842
    entrepreneurship, 45
    formation of, 46
    human, 297, 310, 322, 573, 832
    in industrially advanced countries, 826,
        837–838

international debt, 786–787
in national income, 415–417
ownership of, 811–812, 815
physical, 408
price of, 75
production possibilities curve, 45–47
public, 47
Capital account, 786, 798
Capital budget, 644
"Capital flight," 833
Capital formation, 46
Capital gains tax, 838
Capital goods, 38, 45–47, 407
Capitalism, 811–812, 821
Caplan, Arthur, 82
Carbon emissions, 374, 388–389
Carbon taxes, 388–389
CARE (relief agency), 840
Careers in economics, 14–15
Carlson, Chester, 44
Carnation, 351
Cartel(s), 281–282
    definition, 288
    in global markets, 282
Carter, Jimmy, 753
Cash assistance, 331
Cash for Clunkers program, 373–374
Cash transfer programs, 331
Castro, Fidel, 814, 816–817
Castro, Raul, 816
Catalytic converters, 379
Causation *vs.* association, 10
CBO. *See* Congressional Budget Office
CD. *See* Certificates of deposit
CDO. *See* Collateralized debt obligation
Celler-Kefauver Act of 1950, 350, 366
Central American Free Trade Agreement
    (CAFTA), 782
Centralized decision making, 814–815
Central Selling Organization (CSO), 245
CEO. *See* Chief executive officer
Certificates of deposit (CD), 666
Ceteris paribus assumption, 9, 16
CFC emissions. *See* Chlorofluorocarbons
    emissions
Chain price index, 419–422, 424, 458
Chain Store Act. *See* Robinson-Patman Act
Chan, Anthony, 11
Chaplin, Bill, 233
Chavez, Hugo, 817, 820
Cheap foreign labor argument, 779–780
Checkable deposits, 664–665, 666, 673,
    682, 689
Checks clearing, 671, 685–686
Chernobyl nuclear disaster, 386
Chevron, 352
Chicago Board of Trade, 383, 384
Chief executive officer (CEO), 293
China
    economic system of, 810–811, 818–820
    free market reforms, 818–819
    GDP, 413
    global warming, 390
    government efficiency, 386
    inflation rate, 471
    national debt, 639
    quality-of-life measures, 830
    as trading partner, 771, 784–785, 787
    unemployment in, 442
The China Daily (newspaper), 819
Chiquita Brands International, 781
Chlorofluorocarbons (CFC) emissions, 372–373
Chodad, John, 662
Choice, 5–6, 36
Chronicle of Higher Education, 337
Churchill, Winston, 804

Church World Relief, 840
Cigarettes, and price elasticity of demand, 141
Circular flow model, 404–406, 423, 429–430
Civil Aeronautics Board (CAB), 358, 359, 365
Civilian labor force, 439–440, 452
Civilian unemployment rate, 439
Classical economic theory
    consumption function, 486–488, 492–494, 501
    introduction to, 485–486
    investment demand instability, 498–500
    investment expenditures, 494–496
    marginal propensities to consume and save,
        488–491, 501
    monetary policy, 712, 714, 715, 719, 722
    overview of, 719, 722
Classical economists, 485
Classical range, 540, 544, 553
Clayton Act of 1914, 348–349, 350
Clean Air Act, 381
Clean Air Interstate Act, 383
Climate change, 390–391
Climategate, 391
Clinton, Bill, 576, 602
Coase, Ronald, 386
Coase Theorem, 386–392, 394
    described, 386
    example of, 386–389
    limitations of, 389–392
Coca-Cola, 9, 66, 286
Coincidence of wants, 659, 660
Coincident indicators, 437
COLA. *See* Cost-of-living adjustment
Colbert, Jean-Baptiste, 607
Collateralized debt obligation (CDO), 720–721
Collective bargaining, 302, 303, 310
College athletes, 309
Command-and-control regulation (CAC),
    378–379, 393
Command economy, 805–808, 821
Command socialism, 812
Commodity money, 663, 676
Common Market, 782
Communism, 813–814, 821
Communist Manifesto (Marx and Engels), 813
Communist revolution, 814
"Company town," 305
Comparable worth, 338–339, 341
Comparative advantage, 774–775, 798
Competition, lack of, 111–112, 374
Competitive markets, 372–377
Complementary goods, 66, 68, 143, 145
Computers, 76, 112
Conglomerate merger, 356–357, 366
Congo
    inflation rate, 470, 471
Congressional Budget Office (CBO), 628
Constant-cost industry, 228–230, 236
Constant dollar GDP, 419
Constant returns to scale, 199, 201
Consumer choice theory
    consumer equilibrium, 158–159, 164,
        174–175, 178
    income effect, 161, 164
    indifference curve, 170–177
    substitution effect, 161–163, 164, 465
    utility, 155–158, 163
Consumer Confidence Index, 436
Consumer demand, unemployment and, 444
Consumer equilibrium, 158–159, 164,
    174–175, 178
Consumer expectations, 492
Consumer goods, 39
Consumer price index (CPI), 420, 458,
    464–465, 474
    computation of, 458–461
    criticisms, 464–465

Consumer Product Safety Commission (CPSC), 358, 359, 363
Consumer protection, 672
Consumer sovereignty, 811, 821
Consumer surplus, 91, 92, 96
Consumption, 409, 412, 417, 418, 486, 579
Consumption expenditures, 404–409, 437
Consumption function, 486–488, 489–490, 492–494
  movement along, 493
  MPC affect on, 489–490
  shift in, reasons for, 492–494
Consumption of fixed capital, 411, 415
Consumption possibilities, 773
Consumption tax, 617
Continental Baking, 351
Continental Congress, 626
Continuing resolutions, 628
Contraction, economic, 432
Contractionary fiscal policy, 577, 595.
  See also Fiscal policy
Contractionary monetary policy, 696.
  See also Monetary policy
Contractionary policy, 733–734
  classical views of, 733–734
  Keynesian views of, 733–734
Copayment rate, 125
Copenhagen conference, 390
Copyrights, 243
Corporate Average Fuel Economy (CAFE) standards, 379, 381
Corporate profits, 410, 417, 419
Costa Rica, free trade agreements, 782
Cost-of-laughing index, 462–463
Cost-of-living adjustment (COLA), 466
Cost-of-living index, 458
Cost-push inflation, 470, 474, 547–551, 554, 741
Costs. See also Price; Production costs
  profit, and, 182–184, 200
Council of Economic Advisors, 754
Counterfeiting, 661, 662, 704
CPI. See Consumer price index
CPSC. See Consumer Product Safety Commission
Credit cards, 661, 676
Credit Union Association, 720
Cross-elasticity of demand, 142–143, 148
Crowding-in effect, 642
Crowding-out effect, 642–644, 719, 726
  complete, 643–644
  partial, 643
  zero, 643–644
CSO. See Central Selling Organization
Cuba
  command economy and, 806
  economic systems, 816–817
Currency, 664, 671–672, 792.
  See also Exchange rates
Current account, 783–786, 798
Current-dollar GDP, 419
Current-year prices, 460
Curve. See specific curve
Cyclical unemployment, 445, 453
  Great Depression (1929–1933) and, 445
  Great Recession (2007) and, 445

D

Dairy price support program, 111
Dallas Morning News, 233
Das Kapital (Marx), 813
Davis, Gray, 362
Deadweight loss, 94–95, 96
De Beers, 245

Debt ceiling, 631, 634
  national debt and, 631, 634
Debt-to-GDP ratio, 634, 637–638
Decentralized decision making, 811–812
Deceptive advertising, 349
Decreasing-cost industry, 230–231, 236
Deficit Reduction Act, 630
Deflation
  defined, 458, 474
  Great Depression (1929–1933) and, 464
Dell, 76
Demand. See also Market demand; Supply
  changes in, 60–63, 68, 101
  changes in quantity demanded vs. changes in demand, 60–63
  in circular flow model, 404–406
  expectations of buyers, 65, 68
  income, 65, 67
  Keynes on, 486
  law of, 59–60, 83
  market equilibrium, 101, 102, 104
  monopoly and, 247
  nonprice determinants of, 61, 63–68, 76, 84
  number of buyers, 63–64, 67
  for perfectly competitive firm, 215
  prices of related goods, 66, 68
  shifts in for health care, 127–128
  for sneakers, 78–79, 81
  tastes and preferences, 65, 67
Demand curve. See also Supply curve
  definition, 60
  derivation of, 175–177
  kinked, 279–281, 288
  for labor, 294–297, 299–301, 303, 310
  movement along vs. shift in demand, 62
  natural monopoly and, 361
  nonprice determinants, changes in, 67–68
  price elasticity of demand, 136–138
Demand deposit, 664, 682
Demand for money, 706–707, 725
Demand for money curve, 706–707, 725
Demand-pull inflation, 469–470, 474, 547–551, 554, 579, 591, 740
Demand shifters, 61
Deng Xiaoping, 818–819. See also China
Denmark
  tax burden, 608, 621
  union membership and, 305
Department of Commerce, 403, 416, 419
Department of Housing and Urban Development (HUD), 333
Department of Labor, U.S., 439
Deposit insurance, 674
Deposit multiplier, 687
Depository Institutions Monetary Control Act of 1980, 658, 664, 673, 675, 676
Depreciation (capital), 411
Depreciation of currency, 792, 799
Depression, 432. See also Great Depression (1929–1933)
Deregulation, 358, 365
Derived demand, 297, 300, 310
Detroit Symphony Orchestra, 447
Developing nations, 390
DI. See Disposable personal income
Diamond-water paradox, 157
Digital Equipment, 353
Digital video recorder (DVR), 272
Diminishing marginal utility, law of, 155, 164
Diminishing returns, law of, 185–187, 200, 295
Direct relationships, 21–22
Discount rate, 691–693, 698
Discount window, 692
Discouraged workers, 441, 443, 451, 452.
  See also Unemployment

Discretionary fiscal policy, 577–586, 595.
  See also Fiscal policy
  balanced budget multiplier, 586, 596
  expansionary vs. contractionary fiscal policy, 577, 595
  inflation and, 584–585
  spending multiplier (SM), 579–582
  tax cuts, 582–584
Discrimination. See also Racial bias
  in income distributiion/poverty, 336–339, 450
  price. See Price discrimination
Diseconomies of scale, 199, 201
Disequilibrium, 511
Disinflation, 461, 474. See also Inflation
Disney, 819
Disposable personal income (DI), 417–418, 420, 423, 491, 582
Dissaving, 488
Divisibility (money), 662, 675
Division of labor, 197
Dogster.com, 272
Dole Food Company, 781
Dollars, supply and demand for, 788–790.
  See also Currency
Dominican Republic, free trade agreements and, 782
Double counting, 404, 423
Double dividend, 381, 389
Double eagle coins, 796–797
Dow Jones Industrial Average, 498–499
Downward-sloping
  curve, 27
  line, 24
Drake, Edwin L., 254
Duke Power Company, 362
Durable goods, 406–407
DVR. See Digital video recorder

E

Earned-Income Tax Credit (EITC), 331
Economic bads, 415
Economic development, 830–837, 842
Economic efficiency, 372, 812
Economic freedom, 812, 829–830, 838
Economic growth, 42–44, 47, 48–49, 434–435, 830–837, 842
Economic indicators, 11, 436–438
Economic profit, 182–183, 200
Economics
  applying graphs to, 21–29
  careers in, 14–15
  definition, 5–6, 16
  fundamental questions, 35–36, 48
  methodology of, 6–9
  normative vs. positive, 12–14, 16
Economic systems
  command economy, 805–808, 821
  comparison of, 815–816
  definition, 805
  market economy, 809–810
  mixed economy, 810–811
  privatization vs. nationalization, 820–821
  traditional economy, 805
  types of, 805–811, 821
Economic way of thinking
  disagreements, 12
  hazards of, 9–11
  introduction to, 2–16
  methodology, 6–9
  scarce resources and production, 3–5
  scarcity, 3, 16, 36
  scarcity and choice, 5–6

Economies of scale
  advertising and, 270
  in decreasing-cost industry, 230–231
  definition, 196–197, 201
  Internet and, 198
  in monopolies, 243–244
  natural monopoly and, 360–361
  in oligopoly, 278
Education, unemployment and, 444, 450
Educational attainment, 450, 452
EEC. *See* European Economic Community
EEOC. *See* Equal Employment Opportunity
    Commission
Efficiency, economic, 372
Efficiency of capital, 198–199
Efficiency *vs.* equality, 322–323
Efficient points, 40, 48
Effluent taxes, 379–381, 388, 389, 393
Egypt, 825, 827
  inflation rate, 471
Einstein, Albert, 8
Eisenhower, Dwight, 753
EITC. *See* Earned-Income Tax Credit
Elastic demand, 132, 135, 138, 147
Elasticity, defined, 138
Elasticity coefficient, 130, 135, 138, 139
Elastic supply, 143, 145
Electricity, and price ceilings, 362
Electric vehicles (EV), 383–384
Electronic Data Systems Corporation, 357
El Salvador, free trade agreements and, 782
Embargo, 776, 798
Emissions trading, 381–385, 390–391, 393
Employee compensation, 409–411
Employer power, 304–309
Employment, effect of monetary policy on,
    711–712, 723. *See also* Unemployment
Employment Act of 1946, 439
Employment argument, 779
EMU. *See* European Economic and Monetary
    Union
Energy consumption, 829–830
Energy Policy Act, 358
Engels, Friedrich, 813
Enron, 362
Entitlement programs, 331
Entrepreneur, defined, 5
Entrepreneurship, 4–5, 45
Entry, barriers to, 261, 269, 278
Environmental economics
  Coase Theorem, 386–392, 396
  command-and-control regulations, 379, 393
  and competitive markets, 372–377
  competitive markets and environmental effi-
    ciency, 372–377
  effluent taxes, 379–382, 388, 389, 393
  emissions trading, 381–385, 390–391, 393
  environmental efficiency, achieving, 378–392
  government and, 385–392
  incentive-based regulation, 378, 379–385, 393
  trains and farm crops examples, 386–389
Environmental Protection Agency (EPA), 358,
    359, 382, 389, 416
EPA. *See* Environmental Protection Agency;
    Equal Pay Act
Equal Credit Opportunity Act, 672
Equal Employment Opportunity Commission
    (EEOC), 339
Equality, *vs.* efficiency, 322–323
Equal Pay Act (EPA), 339
Equation of exchange, 714–715, 726
Equilibrium
  competitive, 111–112, 232–233
  consumer equilibrium, 158–159, 164,
    174–175, 178
  definition, 79, 85

in employment, output, and income, 511
health care market, 125–126
Keynesian, 510–513
macroeconomic, 540–546
market, 101–105, 375
market failure, 110–111
in monopolistic competition, 287
in monopsony, 306–308
perfectly competitive firm, 214–215,
    225–228, 236
price ceilings, 105–107
price floors, 107–110
price system, 80
in self-correcting AD-AS model, 569
in self-correcting aggregate demand-aggregate
    supply model, 569
for sneakers, 79–80, 81
for typical competitive and "green"
    industries, 376
Equilibrium interest rate, 706–708, 725
Equilibrium prices, 79–80, 91–94, 96,
    104–105, 112
Equilibrium wage rate, 297–299
Essential services, 105
Ethiopia, 827
EU. *See* European Union
Euro, 782
European Central Bank, 783
European Economic and Monetary Union
    (EMU), 782
European Economic Community (EEC), 782
European Union (EU), 780, 781–782, 783
EV. *See* Electric vehicles
Excess capacity, 277
Excess quantity of money supplied and
    demanded, 708–709, 725
Excess reserves, 682–683
Exchange rates, 788–797, 798–799.
    See also Currency
Excise tax, 605
Exclusive dealing, 349
Expansion, 434, 452
Expansionary fiscal policy, 577, 595, 642–643
Expansionary monetary policy, 696
Expansionary policy, 732–733
  classical views of, 732–733
  Keynesian views of, 732–733
Expectations, 75, 78, 470, 492, 496
Expenditure approach, 406–409, 412, 423
Explicit costs, 182, 200
Exports, 407, 408
External benefit, 112, 114, 119, 363, 372
External cost, 112, 113, 119, 361, 372, 374
External debt, 786
Externalities, 112, 119, 359, 361–363,
    372–373, 374–375, 378, 392, 393
External national debt, 639, 646
Exxon, 352

F

FAA. *See* Federal Aviation Administration
Facebook, 82, 272
Factor markets, 404
Fair Labor Standards Act, 13
Fair-return price, 360, 361, 366
Farm crops, as examples of Coase Theorem,
    386–389
Favorable balance of trade, 784
FCC. *See* Federal Communications Commission
FDA. *See* Food and Drug Administration
FDIC. *See* Federal Deposit Insurance
    Corporation
Featherbedding, 299–301

Federal Advisory Council, 668, 669
Federal Aviation Administration (FAA), 365
Federal budget. *See also* National debt
  AD-AS model, 627
  budgetary process, 627–628
  debt ceiling, 631, 634
  surpluses and deficits, 587, 589, 630–634
Federal Communications Commission (FCC),
    243, 358, 359
Federal debt. *See* National debt
Federal Deposit Insurance Corporation
    (FDIC), 671
Federal Energy Regulatory Commission
    (FERC), 362
Federal funds market, 693
Federal funds rate, 693, 695
Federal Insurance Contribution Act (FICA), 331
Federal net interest, 640
Federal Open Market Committee (FOMC), 668,
    669, 676, 689–691, 694–695
Federal Reserve, 633, 639
Federal Reserve Act of 1913, 667
Federal Reserve banks, 629, 639, 641
Federal Reserve System, 820–821
  Board of Governors, 667, 668, 669, 676
  definition, 667
  Federal Open Market Committee (FOMC),
    668, 669, 689–691
  functions of, 670–672
  M1 *vs.* M2, 696–697
  organizational chart, 667–670
Federal Savings and Loan Insurance
    Corporation (FSLIC), 674, 675
Federal Tax Code, 615
Federal tax revenues, 594, 620
Federal Trade Commission (FTC), 349
Federal Trade Commission Act of 1914,
    349, 350, 366
FedEx, 45
FERC. *See* Federal Energy Regulatory
    Commission
Few sellers, 277–278
Fiat money, 663, 676
FICA. *See* Federal Insurance Contribution Act
Final Four, 286
Final goods, 404, 422, 444, 532
Financial assets, 494
Financial capital, 5. *See also* Capital
Financial Services Modernization Act, 673
Fiscal policy, 576–594. *See also* Discretionary
    fiscal policy
  automatic stabilizers, 587–589, 596
  balanced budget multiplier, 586, 596
  definition, 576, 595
  effect of, 721, 722
  expansionary *vs.* contractionary fiscal policy,
    577, 595
  inflation and, 584–585, 595
  Keynesian economic theory, 722, 726
  lags in *vs.* monetary policy, 697–698
  monetarism, 722, 726
  nondiscretionary, 587
  spending multiplier (SM), 579–582
  supply-side, 589–594, 596
  tax cuts, 582–584
Fixed capital, consumption of, 411, 415
Fixed input, 184
Fixed investment, 407
Fixed money target, 717
Fixed resources, 38
Fixed-wage contracts, 560–562
Fixed-weight price index, 458
Flat tax, 602, 613, 614–615
Flows, 406, 423
FOMC. *See* Federal Open Market Committee
FOMC directives, 669

Food and Drug Administration (FDA), 128, 358, 359
Food stamps, 332–333
Forbes, Steve, 602, 614
Forbes magazine, 817, 819
Ford, Gerald, 14, 756
Ford, Henry, 44
Forecasts, 8
Foreign aid, 840–841
Foreign exchange, supply and demand for, 788–793
Foreign investment, 640
Foreign loans, 841–842
Foreign private investment, 839–840
Fractional reserve banking, 681, 698
"Frakking." *See* Hydraulic fracturing
France, 634, 635, 809, 813, 816
   government expenditure, 606
   inflation rate, 470, 471
   tax burden, 608
Franklin, Benjamin, 665
Freeconomics, 198
Free enterprise system, 811
Free market reforms, 816, 818–819
Freemiums, 198
Free-rider problem, 392
Free riders, 116–117, 377
Free to Choose (Friedman and Friedman), 116, 371
Free trade, 776–778, 798
Free trade agreements
   Costa Rica and, 782
   Dominican Republic and, 782
   El Salvador and, 782
   Guatemala and, 782
   Honduras and, 782
   Nicaragua and, 782
Free Trade Area of the Americas (FTAA), 782
Frictional unemployment, 443–444, 452–453
   causes of, 443
   reduce, measures to, 444
Friedman, Milton, 371
   Free to Choose, 116
   on Great Depression (1929–1933), 723
   on inflation, 755
   macroeconomic theory of, 722
   negative income tax, 334
   opportunity cost, 36
   on Phillips curve, 742
   on private ownership, 812
   school vouchers, 116
Friedman, Rose, 116
Frozen dessert pies, 351
FSLIC. *See* Federal Savings and Loan Insurance Corporation
FTC. *See* Federal Trade Commission
Fukushima nuclear plant disaster, 385
Full employment, 446–452, 453
Full Employment and Balanced Growth Act of 1978, 439
Fully employed resources, 38
Future production possibilities curve, 45–47

G

Galbraith, John Kenneth, 259
Game theory, 282–285, 288
Gas-electric hybrid vehicles, 384
Gasoline
   price ceiling, 107
   tax incidence and, 146, 148, 379–380
Gates, Bill, 346, 355
Gator farming, 232–233
Gator profits, 232–233

GATT. *See* General Agreement on Tariffs and Trade
GDP. *See* Gross domestic product
GDP chain price index, 419–422, 424, 458
GDP gap, 448–452
   negative, 513, 517
   positive, 518
GDP per capita, 826–829, 842
General Agreement on Tariffs and Trade (GATT), 777, 836
General Motors, 278, 356, 357, 804, 821
The General Theory of Employment, Interest, and Money (Keynes), 486, 535, 550, 705
Germany, 783, 787
   GDP of, 413
   government expenditure, 606
   inflation rate, 473
   tax burden, 608
   unemployment in, 442
Glass, Mark, 233
Global Economics, 778
Globalization, unemployment and, 445
Global markets (Cartels), 282
Global warming, 390–391
GM. *See* General Motors
Godwin, Frank, 232
Gold, 672, 681
Goldsmiths, 681
Gold standard, 796–797
Gosplan, 806–807
Government. *See also* Federal budget; Government spending; Regulation
   budget financing, 605–607
   consumption expenditures, 407, 408
   consumption expenditures and investment, 603
   environmental efficiency and, 385–392
   expenditures, 603–605, 606, 621, 631, 632, 635, 642
   failure, 378, 393
   receipts, 607
   size and growth of, 603–605
   spending, 408
Government securities, 629, 640, 644
Government spending, 627, 631, 634, 642–643, 644
   to combat recession, 577–579
   crowding-out effect, 642–644
   debt ceiling and, 634
   deficit-financed, 627, 631, 634, 642–643, 644
   Keynesian equilibrium, 510
   in Keynesian model, 507, 508
   private-sector spending and, 642–644, 646
   recessionary gap, 517–520, 523
   spending multiplier effect, 514
GPA. *See* Grade point average
Grade point average (GPA), 191–192
The Grapes of Wrath (Steinbeck), 451
Graphs
   direct relationship, 21–22
   inverse relationships, 23, 24
   slope of a curve, 26–27
   slope of a straight line, 23–25
   study hint for, 29
   three-variable relationship, 27–28
Great Cola Wars, 286
Great Depression (1929-1933), 357, 358, 631
   gold standard and, 796
   inflation and, 464
   monetary policy, 723
   stock prices during, 484, 498
   unemployment, 440, 445, 451, 723
Great Federal Budget Surplus Debate, 633
Great Recession (2007-2009), 329, 658, 674, 716, 720, 723, 724
   AD-AS model, 545–546

business cycles, 433–434, 436
federal deficit and, 629, 631, 632, 633
GDP gap, 448, 449
government expenditures, 604, 631, 632
housing crisis, 720–721
monetary policy, 716, 723
unemployment and, 440, 445
Great Stagflations, 739, 741
Greece
   GDP of, 827
   government expenditure, 606
   national debt, 634–635, 637–638
   tax burden, 608
   unemployment in, 442
Green Book, 694, 696
"Green" firms, 375
"Green" industries, 376
Greenspan, Alan, 633
Greeting card sales, 11
Gross domestic product (GDP), 402–424. *See also* Nominal GDP; Real GDP
   Asia, 826, 828, 832, 842
   Bangladesh, 827, 830
   chain price index, 419–422, 424, 458
   changing nominal GDP to real GDP, 419–422
   definition, 423
   employee compensation, 409–411
   expenditure approach, 406–409, 423
   expenditure *vs.* income approach, 412
   formula for, 409
   Iceland, 635
   income approach, 409, 423
   internationally, 412, 413
   introduction to, 403–404
   Latin America, 828
   measurement of, 404–406
   New Zealand, 826–827
   nominal, 419–422, 424
   Norway, 634, 635
   vs. other measurements, 418
   Pakistan, 827
   vs. potential GDP, 449
   shortcomings of, 412–415
   Singapore, 826–827
   Sub-Saharan Africa, 826, 828
   Taiwan, 826–827
   tax growth as a percentage of, 609
   of United Kingdom, 413
   of United States, 413
Gross investment, 407, 408
Gross private domestic investment, 407–408
Gross public debt. *See* National debt
Guatemala, free trade agreements and, 782

H

Hardin, Garrett, 392
Harkin, Tom, 339
Hayek, Friedrich von, 812
Hazardous waste disposal, 385, 386
Health care, supply and demand analysis of, 125–128
Health Economics, 141
Health insurance, 125–127
Health maintenance organization (HMO), 126–127
Hewlett-Packard, 76
Hicks, John, 260
Hispanics, and unemployment, 450
Hitler, Adolf, 704
HMO. *See* Health maintenance organization
Hogan, Daniel E., 11
Homogeneous products, 213, 278
Honduras, free trade agreements and, 782

Hong Kong
  economic system of, 816
  free trade agreements, 782, 826–827, 835,
    838–839, 842
  GDP of, 827
  as newly industrialized economy, 838, 842
Hoogewerf, Rupert, 819
Horizontal merger, 356, 366
Hot spot problem, 383, 393–394
Housing and Economic Recovery Act of
  2008, 721
Housing assistance, 333
Housing market crisis, 720–721
Hoxby, Caroline, 118
Huckabee, Mike, 614
HUD. *See* Department of Housing and Urban
  Development
Hu Jintao, 819
Human capital, 297, 310, 322, 573, 832
Human resources, 832–833, 837
Hurun Report, 819
Hydraulic fracturing, 373
Hydrogen-powered cars, 377
Hyperinflation, 470–473, 474

I

IAC. *See* Industrially advanced countries
IATA. *See* International Air Transport
  Association
IBM antitrust case, 353, 356
ICC. *See* Interstate Commerce Commission
Ice cream war (trade policy), 522
Iceland, GDP of, 635
Identity, equation of exchange as, 715, 726
If-then statements, 12, 16
Illegal market, 107
IMF. *See* International Monetary Fund
Imperfect information, 359, 363–364
  Tucker Motors trucks and, 364
Implicit costs, 182, 200
Imports, 408
Impossible entry, 242
Incentive-based regulation, 378, 379–385, 393
Income
  after-tax, 417–418
  break-even, 334, 488
  in capitalism, 812
  and demand for health care, 127
  disposable personal, 417–418, 420, 423,
    491, 582
  distribution of, 353–359
  equality *vs.* efficiency, 322–323
  global comparisons of, 327
  inequality, 117–118
  inflation and, 465–467
  Lorenz curve, 324–325, 340
  median money, 322
  money, 465
  national, 415–417, 423
  nominal, 465–466, 474
  as nonprice determinant, 65, 67
  no-saving, 488
  personal, 417, 419, 423
  proprietors', 410
  real, 161, 466, 474
  real median, 323
  rental, 410
  trends in, 321, 325–327
Income approach, 409, 412, 423
Income effect, 161, 164
Income elasticity of demand, 140–142, 145, 148
Income inequality, 117–118
Income security, 604

Incomes policy, 752–754
Income unitary elastic, 145
Incomplete knowledge, 560
Increasing-cost industry, 231–234, 236
Increasing marginal returns, 185
Increasing opportunity costs, law of, 40–42,
  48, 772
Independent relationship, 25
India
  balance of trade with U.S., 787
  GDP of, 413, 827
  life indicators, quality of, 830
Indifference curve
  budget line, 172–174, 178
  construction of, 169–177
  consumer equilibrium, 158–159, 164,
    174–175, 178
  consumer's curve, 170
  definition, 169, 177
  derivation of the demand curve, 175–177
  as downward sloping and convex,
    169–171
  indifference map, 171–172, 177
Indifference map, 171–172, 177
Indirect business taxes, 410, 411, 423
Individual demand curve, 59, 60
Indivisible public service, 619
Industrially advanced countries (IACs), 826,
  827, 828
Inefficient output, 39, 48
Inelastic demand, 132, 135, 138, 147
Inelastic supply, 143, 145
Infant industry argument, 778–779
Infant mortality rate, 829–830
Inferior goods, 65, 67, 141–142, 145, 148
Infinite geometric series, 581
Inflation, 457–474
  comparison of macroeconomic models, 755
  consequences of, 465–469
  cost-push, 470, 474, 547–551, 554, 741
  CPI and, 458, 464–465, 474
  definition, 458, 474
  demand-pull, 469–470, 474, 547–551, 554,
    579, 591, 740
  fiscal policy and, 584–585, 595
  during the Great Depression (1929-1933), 464
  hyperinflation, 470–473, 474
  and income, 459–461
  internationally, 470–473
  Keynes on, 755
  meaning and measurement of, 458–465
  Monetarism on, 755
  and unemployment, 740–747, 756
  and wealth, 468
  in Zimbabwe, 457, 473
Inflationary gap, 520–521, 524
Inflation psychosis, 471
Inflation rate, 460, 461, 474
  China, 471
  Congo, 470, 471
  Egypt, 471
  France, 470, 471
  Germany, 473
  Iran, 477
  Ireland, 470
  Italy, 470, 471
  Russia, 471
  Spain, 471
  United States, 464, 471
  Venezuela, 470, 471
Infrastructure, 834, 836
Injections, spending, 429
In-kind transfers, 330, 331, 332–333, 340
*An Inquiry into the Nature and Causes of the
  Wealth of Nations* (Smith), 809
Inside lag, 697

Intercept, 23
Interest-rate effect, 533, 534, 553
Interest rates
  consumption function, 494
  crowding-out effect, 642–643
  during current recession, 695
  demand for money, 706–707, 725
  as economic indicator, 438
  effect of monetary policy on, 711–712, 725
  equilibrium, 706–709, 725
  inflation and, 468–469, 471
  Keynesian economic theory, 722
  maximum, 107
  and monetary policy, 711–712
  nominal, 468, 474
  real, 468, 474
  relative real, 792–793
  savings and loan crisis, 675
Interlocking directorates, 349
Intermediate goods, 404, 423
Intermediate range, 539–540, 542, 544, 591
Internal debt financing, 639
Internal national debt, 639, 646
International Air Transport Association
  (IATA), 282
International bailout packages, 634
International debt, 786–788
International Monetary Fund (IMF), 797,
  841–842
International Panel on Climate Change
  (IPCC), 391
International Telecommunications Union
  (ITU), 282
International trade and finance, 770–797
  absolute advantage, 774–775
  balance of payments, 782–788, 798
  benefits of, 772, 774, 798
  capital account, 786, 798
  comparative advantage, 774–775, 798
  current account, 783–786, 798
  exchange rates, 788–797
  free trade agreements, 781–782
  free trade *vs.* protectionism, 776–778
  in less-developed countries, 836
  need for, 771–774
  production possibilities curve for,
    771–773
  protectionism arguments, 778–780
  specialization without trade, 773
  specialization with trade, 774
  U.S. international debt, 786–788
Internet Explorer browser, 355
Interstate Commerce Commission (ICC),
  358, 359
Invention, 44
Inventory, 510, 511
Inverse relationships, 23, 24
Investment, 46, 49, 498, 500, 579
Investment demand curve, 495–496, 501,
  712–713
  movement along, 497
Investment demand instability, 496–500
Investment expenditures, 494–496
Investment tax credit, 499
Invisible hand, 212, 809–810, 812
IPCC. *See* International Panel on Climate
  Change
Iran
  inflation rate, 477
Ireland, 634, 635
  inflation rate, 470
Italy, 637–638, 813
  inflation rate, 470, 471
ITU. *See* International Telecommunications
  Union
Ivy League universities, 54

J

Jackson, Andrew, 626
Jagger, Mick, 14
Japan
  economic system of, 816
  GDP, 413
  GDP per capita, 826–827
  government expenditures, 606
  national debt, 637–638, 639
  quality-of-life measures, 829–830
  specialization and trade, benefits of, 772
  tax burden, 608
  as trading partner, 771, 787
  unemployment, 442
Jawboning, 752–753
JetBlue Airways, 365
Jobs, Steven, 199
Johnson, Lyndon, 753
Jordan, Michael, 831
JP Morgan Chase, 720
Justice Department, 797

K

Kaiser Aluminum, 353
Keating, Charles, Jr., 674
Kennedy, John F., 752–753
Kentucky Fried Chicken, 819
Keynes, John Maynard
  on demand, 486
  on expectations, 496
  The General Theory of Employment, Interest, and Money, 535, 550, 705
  on inflation, 755
  introduction to, 484, 485, 501
  on investment demand instability, 496–500
  on investment expenditures, 494, 495
  letter from Shaw, 506
  macroeconomic theory of, 722
  overview of, 722
Keynes, John Neville, 550
Keynesian aggregate
  expenditures model, 509–513, 522, 523
Keynesian economic theory, 506–522, 719–720
  aggregate expenditures model, 509–513
  vs. classical theory, 485–492
  consumption function, 486–488, 492–494
  demand for money, 706–707
  equilibrium, 510–513
  equilibrium interest rate, 706–708
  fiscal policy and, 723, 726
  government spending, 507, 508
  on inflation, 747
  inflationary gap, 520–521, 524
  interest rates, 711
  investment demand, 496–500
  investment expenditures, 494–496
  marginal propensities to consume and save, 488–492
  vs. monetarism, 723
  monetary policy, 709–713
  net exports, 507–508
  overview of, 719–720
  prices, output, and employment, 711–713, 723
  recessionary gap, 517–520, 523
  spending multiplier (SM), 513–520, 523
  vs. supply-side effects of tax cuts, 593
Keynesian equilibrium, 509–513
  aggregate expenditures and, 509
Keynesian monetary policy
  transmission mechanism, 711, 725
Keynesian range, 539, 542, 591
Kinked demand curve, 279–281, 288

Knight Ridder/Tribune Business News, 233
Korean War, 753
Kushner, Malcolm, 462–463
Kuznets, Simon, 402
Kyoto Conference, 390

L

Labor, 4, 107–109, 832–833. *See also* Labor markets
  division of, 197
Laboratory rats, 162
Labor markets
  demand for, 294–297, 299–301, 303, 310
  effect of supply-side fiscal policies on, 592
  employer power, 304–309
  labor unions, 299–304
  and long-run Phillips curve, 746–748
  monopsony, 304–309
  under perfect competition, 294–299
  racial discrimination and, 338
  supply of, 297, 298, 301–302, 303, 310
  union membership, 302–304, 305
Labor unions, 299–304
Laffer, Arthur, 594, 755
Laffer curve, 594, 596, 602
Lagging indicators, 438, 452
Laissez-faire theory, 485, 537, 714, 809, 838
Land, as economic resource, 4
La Puma, John, 82
Latin America
  banana exports, 780–781
  economic system, 816
  GDP of, 828
  trading partner, U. S., 771
Law and order, 835–836
Law of demand, 23, 159–160, 162, 465.
  See also Demand; Demand curve
Law of diminishing marginal utility, 155, 164
Law of diminishing returns, 185–187, 200, 295
Law of increasing opportunity costs, 772
LDC. *See* Less-developed countries
Leading indicators, 436–437, 452
Leakages, household income, 429
Legal barriers, 243
Leisure time, 414
Lender of last resort, 696
Lenin, Vladimir, 704
Leonard, John, 309
Less-developed countries (LDCs)
  aid from advanced countries, 837–842
  capital, accumulation of, 833–834
  compared to developed countries, 826–830
  definition, 826
  economic growth and development, 830–837
  foreign aid, 840–841
  foreign loans, 841–842
  foreign private investment, 839–840
  GDP per capita, 826–828
  human resources, 832–833
  international trade, 836
  natural resources, 831–833
  political environment, 835–836
  private bank lending to, 841
  quality-of-life measures, 829–830
  technological progress, 834–835, 837
Levi Strauss Company, 5
Liabilities, 682
Life expectancy, 829–830, 832
Lilly Ledbetter Fair Pay Act of 2009, 339
Lincoln, Abraham, 626
Lincoln Savings and Loan, 674
Liquidity, 660, 676

Literacy rate, 829–830, 832. *See also* Educational attainment
Loans, 682
Logrolling, 618
London School of Economics, 14, 740
Long run
  defined, 184, 200
  monopolistic competition in, 274, 275
  monopoly in, 253–255
Long-run aggregate supply curve (LRAS), 568, 574–576
Long-run average cost (LRAC)
  advertising and, 270, 271
Long-run average cost (LRAC) curves, 193–196, 201, 227, 243, 261, 360–361
Long-run competitive equilibrium, 232–233
Long-run equilibrium for perfectly competitive firm, 226–228
Long-run marginal cost curve (LRMC), 360–361
Long-run perfectly competitive equilibrium, 236
Long-run Phillips curve, 742–743, 744, 746–748
Long-run production costs, 193–196
Long-run profit maximization, 262
Long-run supply curves
  constant-cost industry, 228–230, 236
  decreasing-cost industry, 230–231, 236
  increasing-cost industry, 231–234, 236
  under perfect competition, 226–228
  for perfectly competitive industry, 228
Lorenz curve, 324–325, 340
  for family income distribution, 326
Los Angeles Times, 336
Loss minimization, 221, 253
LRAC. *See* Long-run average cost curves
LRAS. *See* Long-run aggregate supply curve
LRMC. *See* Long-run marginal cost curve
Lucas, Robert, 748, 755

M

M1, 663–665, 666, 676, 683–688, 690–691, 697, 699, 705–707, 718
M2, 665–667, 676, 697, 699
Macroeconomic equilibrium, 540–546
Macroeconomics, described, 6, 16
Macroeconomic theories, 722. *See also* Classical economic theory; Keynesian economic theory; Monetarism; New classical economists; Supply-side fiscal policy
Macro economy, measures of, 418
Mainframe computer market, 353
Majority-rule problem, 616–617
Mantle, Mickey, 82
Mao Zedong, 818–819
Marginal analysis, 37–38, 48, 158, 218–220
Marginal-average rule, 191–192, 201, 360
Marginal benefit. *See* Marginal revenue
Marginal cost (MC), 188–190, 191, 192–193, 194, 200, 201
Marginal cost pricing, 361, 366
Marginal cost relationships, 190–193
Marginal factor cost (MFC), 305–306, 310–311
Marginal private cost (MPC), 375
Marginal product (MP), 185, 192–193, 194, 200, 201
Marginal product of labor, 295
Marginal propensity to consume (MPC), 488–491, 501, 517, 580, 582, 583, 595
  graphical analysis of, 489–491
  spending multiplier and, 582
Marginal propensity to save (MPS), 488–492, 501, 517, 581–582, 595
  spending multiplier and, 582

Marginal rate of substitution (MRS), 170, 177
Marginal revenue (MR), 218, 235, 246–248, 261
Marginal revenue equals marginal cost method, of loss minimization, 221
Marginal revenue equals marginal cost method, of profit maximization, 218–220, 235, 251, 252, 253
Marginal revenue product (MRP), 295, 307, 310
Marginal rule, 617
Marginal social benefit, 373, 375, 377, 387
Marginal social cost (MSC), 373, 375, 377, 380, 387
Marginal tax rate, 611–617
Marginal utility, 155–158, 163
  curve, 156
Marginal utility per dollar (MU/P), 158
Market, defined, 78
"Market basket," 458
Market demand, 60
Market demand curve, 60, 61, 92
Market economy, 809–810
Market efficiency, 94–96, 110–111
Market equilibrium, 101–105, 375
Market failure, 96, 110–111, 119, 126, 257, 359, 378
Market price, 215
Market structures, 213, 235. See also Monopolistic competition; Monopoly; Oligopoly; Perfect competition
  comparison of, 286
  monopoly, 242–246
Market supply, 70–71
Market supply and demand analysis, 78–80
Market supply curve, 71, 93
Marriage trends, 11
Marshall, Alfred, 80
Marx, Karl, 804, 813–814, 818, 821
Maximum output, 40
Mazda, 788–789
MC. See Marginal cost
McCain, John, 614
McDonald's, 804, 819
MCI, 354, 358
McKinley, William, 796
McRae, Matt, 76
Means test, 330–331
Median money income, 322
Medicaid, 125, 332, 634
Medical tourist hospitals, 816
Medicare, 125, 332
Medium of exchange, 659–660, 675
Mercantilism, 809
Mergers, 356–357, 366
Merrill Lynch, 720
Merva, Mary, 451
Methodology of economics, 6–9
Mexico, 771, 781–782, 787, 795–796
  GDP of, 413
  unemployment in, 442
MFC. See Marginal factor cost
Microeconomics
  definition, 16
  described, 6
Microsoft Corporation, 346, 355, 356, 705–706, 839
Midpoints formula, 130–132
Military goods, 39
Milk, market for, 110, 111
Miller Brewing Company, 357
Minimum wage, 13, 107–109
Ministry of Economy, Trade and Industry (METI), 811
"Misery index," 742
MIT antitrust case, 354
Mixed economy, 810–811
Mobil, 352

Models, 7–8, 16
Monetarism
  definition, 714
  equation of exchange, 714–715, 726
  fiscal policy and, 716, 721, 723, 726
  fixed money target, 717
  on inflation, 755
  vs. Keynesian economic theory, 723
  modern, 716
  monetary policy, 714–724
  overview of, 722, 725–726
  quantity theory of money, 715–716, 726
  on role of money, 714–718
  transmission mechanism, 714–718
  velocity of money, 716, 717–718
Monetarist monetary policy
  transmission mechanism, 714, 725
Monetary Control Act of 1980, 658, 664, 673, 675, 676, 693
A Monetary History of the United States (Friedman and Schwartz), 723
Monetary policy, 704–724
  AD-AS model, 712–713
  classical economic theory, 719, 722
  definition, 688
  discount rate, 692–693, 698
  effect of, 713
  equilibrium interest rate, 706–708, 725
  expansionary, 696
  expansionary effect on aggregate demand, 713
  Federal Open Market Committee (FOMC), 669, 689–691, 694–695
  during the Great Depression (1929–1933), 723
  interest rate, 708–711, 725
  Keynesian economic theory, 705–713, 719–720, 725–726
  Keynesian view of, 705–713, 725–726
  lags in vs. fiscal policy, 697–698
  monetarism, 714
  money creation and, 688–696
  money supply, 686–693, 696–697
  open market operations, 688–689, 692, 698
  prices, output and employment, 711–713, 723
  required reserve ratio, 693–696, 699
  shortcomings of, 696–698
Monetary rule, 717
Money. See also Money creation; Money supply
  commodity vs. fiat, 663, 676
  definition, 659
  demand curve for, 706, 707
  demand for, 705–706, 707, 725
  divisibility, 662, 675
  functions of, 659–660
  history of in American colonies, 664–665
  liquidity, 660, 676
  M1, 705–707, 718
  M1 and M2, 665–667, 676, 697, 699
  as medium of exchange, 659–660, 675
  multiplier expansion of by banking system, 686–688
  portability, 662, 675
  properties of, 661–662
  speculative demand for, 705–706, 725
  as store of value, 660, 676
  as unit of account, 660, 676
Money amount, defined, 161
Money creation
  banker bookkeeping, 681–683
  check clearing, 671, 685–686
  loan making, 684–685
  monetary policy and, 688–696
  money multiplier, 687–688, 697, 698
  multiplier expansion by banking system, 686–688
  new deposit acceptance, 683–684
  by a single bank, 681–683

Money GDP, 419
Money income, 465
Money multiplier, 687–688, 697, 698
Money supply, 663–667, 671, 676, 686–693, 696–697, 709–711, 748
  controlling, 671
  definitions, 663–667, 676
  Federal Open Market Committee (FOMC) and, 669
  Federal Reserve System and, 667
  measuring, methods used for, 663–667
Monopolistic competition, 286
  advertising, 270–272
  characteristics of, 268–269
  definition, 268, 287
  game theory, 282–285, 288
  long run, 274, 275
  market structure, 268–269
  output decisions and, 272–274, 275–277
  vs. perfect competition, 274–277, 287
  price and, 272–274
  as price maker, 269–272
  as resource misallocator, 274–275
  short run, 273–274
Monopoly, 286. See also Antitrust
  characteristics of, 242–246
  critique of, 259–260
  definition, 261
  and demand, 247
  disadvantages, 262
  economies of scale, 243–244
  impact on industry, 259
  international, 245
  long run, 253–255
  long-run profit maximization, 262
  market structure, 242–246
  natural, 243, 353, 359–361
  output decisions, 246–255
  vs. perfect competition, 257–259, 260
  price, 246–255
  price discrimination, 255–257
  regulated, 360
  as resource misallocator, 257–258
  short-run loss minimization, 251, 253
  short-run profit maximization, 248–250, 261
  Standard Oil, 254
Monopsonist, defined, 308
Monopsonistic equilibrium, 306–308
Monopsony, 304–309, 310–311
Monroe, Dick, 232
Montreal Protocol, 373
Moore, Bob, 158
Motor Carrier Act of 1980, 358
Mozambique, 827, 829–830
MP. See Marginal product
MPC. See Marginal private cost; Marginal propensity to consume
MPS. See Marginal propensity to save
MR. See Marginal revenue
MRP. See Marginal revenue product
MRS. See Marginal rate of substitution
MSC. See Marginal social cost
Multinational corporations, 839–840
Multiple expansion of money, 686–688
Musicians, 447
Mutual interdependence, 277, 282, 287–288
MySpace, 272

N

NABE. See National Association for Business Economics
NAFTA. See North American Free Trade Agreement

NASA. *See* National Aeronautics and Space Administration
National Aeronautics and Space Administration (NASA), 813
National Association for Business Economics (NABE), 498
National Bureau of Economic Research (NBER), 434, 499
National Collegiate Athletic Association (NCAA), 309
National debt
  bankruptcy, 637
  budget deficit, 629–630
  budget surplus, 629–630
  burden of debt debate, 639–641
  Canada, 638
  China, 639
  clocks, 629
  crowding-out effect, 642, 644, 719
  definition, 629
  external, 639, 646
  external *vs.* internal, 639–641
  federal deficit and, 644–645
  federal net interest, 640
  financing, 629–630
  global perspective on, 637, 638
  Greece, 634–635, 637–638
  historical record of, 636, 637
  increase in, causes of, 635–636
  internal, 639, 646
  international, 786–788
  Japan, 637–638, 639
  ownership of, in 2011, 641
  passing debt burden to future generations, 639–641
  ratios, 638
National Equal Pay Task Force, 339
National income (NI), 415–417, 423
National Income, 1929–32 (Kuznets), 402
National income accounts, 402, 415–418
National Industrial Recovery Act (NIRA) of 1933, 302
Nationalization, 820–821
National Labor Relations Act (NLRA), 302
National Metal Industries, 11
National sales tax, 614–615
National security argument, for protectionism, 779
National Transplant Organ Act of 1984, 82
Natural monopoly, 243, 261, 353, 359–361
  cost minimizing in, 244
Natural rate hypothesis, 743–745, 757
Natural rate of unemployment, 446, 746–747
Natural resources, 831–833
"Natural rights," 809
NBER. *See* National Bureau of Economic Research
NCAA. *See* National Collegiate Athletic Association
NCAA basketball, 286
Near money, 665
Negative curve, 26
Negative externalities, 112, 415
Negative income tax (NIT), 334–335, 341
  advantages, 335
  criticism of, 335
Negative slope, 23
Negotiable order of withdrawal (NOW) accounts, 665
Neighborhood effects, 112
Net exports, 407, 408–409, 507–508, 510, 523, 579
Net exports effect, 533, 534, 553
Net interest, 410, 411
Net public debt, 630
Net unilateral transfers, 786

Network good, 244, 246, 261
New classical economists, 750
New Deal (Roosevelt's), 631
New deposit acceptance, 683–684
Newly industrialized economies, 826, 838, 842
  Hong Kong as, 838, 842
New-source bias, 382
New Source Performance Standards, 382
Newsweek, 473
New York Federal Reserve Bank, 669, 672
New York Stock Exchange, 383, 384
New York taxicabs, 260
The New York Times, 76, 451
New Zealand
  GDP of, 826–827
NI. *See* National income
Nicaragua, free trade agreements and, 782
NIRA. *See* National Industrial Recovery Act of 1933
NIT. *See* Negative income tax
Nitrogen oxides (NOx), 383
Nixon, Richard, 107, 522, 753, 797
NLRA. *See* National Labor Relations Act
Noise pollution, 372
Nominal amount, 161
Nominal GDP, 419–422, 424. *See also* Gross domestic product (GDP)
Nominal income, 465–466, 474
Nominal interest rate, 468, 474
Nondiscretionary fiscal policy, 587
Nondurable goods, 406
Nonmarket transactions, 412–414
Nonprice competition, 269, 279, 287, 288
Nonprice determinants
  of aggregate demand curve, 533–534, 548
  of demand, 61, 63–68, 76, 84
  of supply, 71, 72–78, 84–85
Nonprice-level determinants, 546–547
Nonproductive financial transactions, 403
Nonrenewable resources, 4
Normal goods, 65, 67, 141–142, 145, 148
Normal profit, 183, 274
Normative economics, 13, 14, 16
North American Free Trade Agreement (NAFTA), 781, 795–796, 836
North Korea
  command economy and, 806
  economic system, 805, 816
Norway
  GDP of, 634, 635
No-saving income, 488
NOW. *See* Negotiable order of withdrawal accounts
Nuclear power, 385

O

Oak Ridge, Tennessee, 386
Obama, Barack, 13, 339, 576, 602, 631
Occupational Safety and Health Administration (OSHA), 358, 359
Occupy Wall Street movement, 804
O'Connor, Sandra Day, 14
Office of Management and Budget (OMB), 633
Office of Personnel Management, 339
Offsets, 381, 382
Offshoring, 445
Oil embargo, 107
Okun, Arthur, 465
Oligopoly, 286. *See also* Market structures
  advertising, 277, 279, 285
  characteristics of, 277–278
  definition, 277, 287–288
  economies of scale, 278

  evaluation of, 285
  in Final Four, 286
  models, 278–285
  output decisions and, 278–285
  vs. perfect competition, 288
  price and, 278–285
OMB. *See* Office of Management and Budget
OPEC. *See* Organization of Petroleum Exporting Countries
OPEC countries, 784, 785
Open market operations, 688–689, 692, 698
Operating budget, 644–645
Opportunity cost, 36–37, 48, 107, 705
Organization of Petroleum Exporting Countries (OPEC), 281, 282, 309, 470, 546
Organ shortage, 82
Origin, defined, 21
OSHA. *See* Occupational Safety and Health Administration
Ostrom, Elinor, 392
Output decisions
  effect of monetary policy on, 711–713
  in monopolistic competition, 272–274, 275–277
  in monopoly, 246–255
  in oligopoly, 278–285
  perfect competition and, 258
Outside lag, 697–698
Outsourcing, defined, 445
Overpopulation, 832
Ownership of vital resource, 242–243

P

Pacific Rim economies, 838
Pakistan, GDP of, 827
Panic of 1907, 667
Patents, 243
Pay-as-you-go legislation, 630
Paycheck Fairness Act, 339
"PayGo" rule, 630, 631
Payoff matrix, 282, 284
Peak (business cycles), 432–433, 452
Peck, Andrew, 76
Pepsi-Cola, 66, 161, 286
Perfect competition, 212–234
  characteristics of, 213–214
  definition, 235
  labor markets under, 294–299
  long-run equilibrium, 236
  long-run supply curves, 226–228
  vs. monopolistic competition, 274–277, 287
  vs. monopoly, 257–259, 260
  vs. oligopoly, 288
  vs. other market structures, 286
  output and, 258
  price takers, 214–215
  short-run loss minimization, 220–223
  short-run profit maximization, 215–220
  short-run supply curves, 223–226, 235–236
Perfectly competitive firm
  demand for, 215
  long-run equilibrium, 226–228
  long-run supply curves, 228
  marginal revenue, 295
  market price, 215
  vs. monopolistic competition, 258
  as price taker, 214–215
  short-run equilibrium, 225–226
  short-run loss minimization, 220–223
  short-run profit maximization, 215–220
  short-run supply curves, 223–226
  shutting down, 222–223

Perfectly competitive industry, short-run supply curves, 224–225, 236
  derivation, 225
Perfectly competitive market, 374
Perfectly elastic demand, 134–135, 148, 214, 215
Perfectly elastic supply, 143, 145
Perfectly inelastic demand, 134, 135, 148
Perfectly inelastic supply, 143, 145
Per se rule, 353, 366
Personal computer software industry, 355
Personal consumption, 491
Personal consumption expenditures, 406
Personal income (PI), 417, 419, 423
Personal Responsibility and Work Opportunity Act of 1996, 335–336
Per-unit cost, 188
Pet Milk, 351
Petrosian Company, 245
Phase-out rate, 335
Phelps, Edmund S., 742
Philip Morris, 357
Phillips, A. W., 740
Phillips curve
  adaptive expectations theory, 744–746
  definition, 740
  long-run, 742–743, 744, 746–748
  long-run, and labor market, 746–748
  natural rate hypothesis, 743–745, 757
  in practice, 740–742
  in theory, 740
Photovoltaic cells (PVC), 377, 384
Physical units, 532
PI. See Personal income
Pink Panther Airline Company, 788
Political business cycle, 747, 757
Political environment, 835–836
Pollution. See also Environmental economics
  acid rain program, 384
  efficient quantity of, 376, 377–378
  emissions trading, 381–385, 390–391, 393
  as externality, 361–362
  graphical analysis of, 112–114
  taxes, 114
Portability (money), 662, 675
Positive curve, 26
Positive economics, 12, 13, 16
Positive externality, 112
Positive slope, 23
Postal Service, U.S., 813
Potential GDP, 449
Potential real GDP, 448, 513, 573–574, 576
Poverty, 327–330, 826, 833, 837. See also Antipoverty programs
Poverty line, 328, 340
  U. S. people below, characteristics of, 330
  U. S. population below, 329
PPC. See Production possibilities curve
Precautionary demand for money, 705
Preconceptions, 14
Predatory pricing, 347, 355
Predictions, 8
Present investment, 45–47
Presidential budget submission, 627
Presidential elections, and money supply, 747, 748
Price. See also Costs
  impact of decrease in on total revenue, 133
  monetary policy, effect of, 711–713
  in monopolistic competition, 272–274
  in monopoly, 246–255
  and nonprice determinants of demand, 64
  and nonprice determinants of supply, 74
  in oligopoly, 278–285
  of other goods firm could produce, 75, 77, 78

of personal computers, 76
of related goods, 66, 68
of substitutes, 127–128
Price ceilings, 105–107, 118, 362
Price change, 138, 140
Price competition, 260
Price discrimination
  conditions for, 255–256
  definition, 262
  fairness of, 256
  laws against, 349–350, 351
Price elasticity, 144–146
Price elasticity of demand
  adjustment to a price change over time, 140
  availability of substitutes, 138–139
  cigarettes and, 141
  cross-elasticity of demand, 142–143, 148
  definition, 147, 261
  demand curve, 136–138
  determinants of, 138–140, 148
  elastic demand, 132, 135, 138, 147
  income elasticity of demand, 140–142, 148
  inelastic demand, 132, 135, 138, 147
  marginal revenue and total revenue, 246–248
  midpoints formula, 130–132
  other measures of, 140–147
  perfectly elastic demand, 134–135, 148, 214, 215
  price elasticity of supply, 143–144, 148
  share of budget spent on the product, 139
  for specific products, 139
  terminology, 135
  total revenue test, 132
  unitary elastic demand, 133–134, 135, 138, 147
  variations along a demand curve, 136–138
Price elasticity of supply, 143–144, 148
Price floors, 107–110, 118–119
Price leadership, 281, 284, 288
Price level, 494, 550
Price maker, 246, 251, 254, 261, 269–272, 279
Price supports, 109–110, 111
Price system, 80, 82, 85
Price taker, 214, 235, 246, 269, 276
Price-wage flexibility, 722
Private benefits and costs, 372, 373, 392
Private goods vs. public goods, 116–117
Private interest, 809, 813, 814
Private ownership, 811
Private property, 813, 818–819
Private-sector spending, 642–644, 646
Privatization, 820–821
Problem identification, 7
"The Problem of Social Cost" (Coase), 386
Producers, expectations of, 75, 78
Producer surplus, 92–94, 96
Product differentiation, 268–269, 272, 278, 287
Production costs, 183–199. See also Costs; Price
  costs and profit, 182–184
  law of diminishing returns, 185–187, 200, 295
  long-run production costs, 193–196
  marginal cost relationships, 190–193, 194
  marginal product, 185
  production function, 185, 186
  scales of production, 196–199
  scarce resources, 3–5
  short-run cost formulas, 187–190, 191
  short-run production costs, 184–187
  short run vs. long run, 184
Production function, 185, 186, 200, 295
Production possibilities curve (PPC)
  for consumer goods, 39
  economic growth and, 830–831

effect of external financing, 837–838, 840
international trade, 771–773
less-developed countries, 837–838, 840
for military goods, 39, 641
outward shift in, 43
overview of, 38–40, 48
present and future, 834
during World War II, 640–641
Product markets, 404
Products, distribution, kind, and quality, 414
ProductWiki, 272
Profit. See also Costs
  accounting, 182–183
  and costs, 182–184
  economic and accounting, 182–183, 200
  in gross domestic product, 410
  maximization of, 215–220, 235, 248–251, 361
  normal, 183
Profit, normal, 274
Profit motive, 810
Progressive taxes, 610–617
Proportional taxes, 613–614
Proprietors' income, 410
Protectionism, 776–781, 798
Public capital, 47
Public choice theory, 602, 616–619, 621
Public goods, 116–117, 119, 391, 608
Public interest, 810, 812, 814
Public ownership, 814
Public sector. See also Government
  government size and growth, 603–605
  public choice theory, 616–619
  taxation, 607–615
Purchasing power, 494
PVC. See Photovoltaic cells

Q

Quality-of-life measures, 829–830
Quantity, and equilibrium price, 79–80
Quantity demanded, changes in, 60–63, 83
Quantity supplied, changes in, 71–72, 84
Quantity theory of money, 715–716, 726
Queen Elizabeth I, 245
Quota, 778, 798

R

Racial bias, 336–338. See also Discrimination
Railroads, regulation and, 357–358
Rational expectations theory, 748–750, 757
Rational voter ignorance, 618–619
Reagan, Ronald
  on antitrust, 353
  federal budget and, 631, 633
  fiscal policy and, 602
  supply-side fiscal policy, 589
  taxes, 576, 589
Real assets, 494
Real balances effect, 532, 534, 538, 553
Real consumption, 495
Real GDP. See also Gross domestic product (GDP)
  internationally, 436–437
  in Keynesian equilibrium, 510
  nominal GDP, 419–422
  price level and unemployment, 550
Real income, 161, 466, 474
Real interest rate, 468, 474
Real investment, 495
Real median income, 323

Recession, 232–233
  government spending, 577–579
  Great Recession of 2007–2009.
    See Great Recession (2007–2009)
  introduction to, 432–433
  post–World War II, 432
  tax cuts, 582–584
Recessionary gap, 517–520, 524
Recovery, 432–433, 434
Red Cross, 840
Regressive taxes, 612
  excise taxes as, 612
  payroll taxes as, 612
  property taxes as, 612
  sales taxes as, 612
Regulation. *See also* Antitrust
  command and control, 379, 393
  vs. deregulation, 358, 365
  externalities, 361–363
  historical origins of, 357–358
  imperfect information, 363–364
  incentive-based, 378, 379–385, 393
  pollution, 114
  price ceilings, 105–107, 118, 362
  situations calling for, 358–365
Regulatory agencies, 357–359
Related goods, prices, 66, 68
Relative incomes, 792
Relative price levels, 792, 793
Relative real interest rates, 792–793
Renewable resources, 4
Rental income, 410
Rent controls, 105–107
Required reserve ratio, 682, 693–696, 698
Required reserves, 682, 698
Research and development (R&D), 279
Resolution Trust Corporation (RTC), 675, 821
Resources, 16
  changes in, 42–44
  definition, 3
  human, 832–833
  misallocation of, 257–258, 274–275, 364
  nonrenewable, 4
  prices of, 75, 77, 128
Revenue hill, 248
Revolutionary War, 626
Reynolds Aluminum, 353
Richland, Washington, 386
Rinehart, James R., 82
The Road to Serfdom (Hayek), 812
"Roaring Twenties," 484, 498
Robber barons, 347
Robinson-Patman Act of 1936, 349–350, 366
Robots, 447
Rockefeller, John D., 254, 259, 346,
  347, 352
Romney, Mitt, 13
Roosevelt, Franklin D., 302, 332, 457, 631, 796
Roosevelt, Theodore, 352
Roosevelt's New Deal, 631
RTC. *See* Resolution Trust Corporation
Russia, 817
  GDP of, 413
  inflation rate, 471
Ruth, Babe, 774

S

Safety defects, 363
Sagrera, Wayne, 233
Salaries, 15
Samuelson, Paul, 740
San Francisco Chronicle, 473
Saving, defined, 488

Savings and loan crisis, 675
Savings deposits, 666
Say, Jean-Baptiste, 485
Say's Law, 485, 501
Scales of production, 196–199
Scarce resources, 3–5
Scarcity, 3, 5–6, 16, 36, 661
School vouchers, 116–117
Schumpeter, Joseph, 259
Schwartz, Anna J., 723
Search unemployment, 443
SEC. *See* Securities and Exchange Commission
Secondhand transactions, 403
Secret Service, U.S., 661
Securities and Exchange Commission (SEC),
  358, 359, 674
Self-correcting aggregate demand-aggregate
    supply model, 598–608, 732–734
  changes in potential real GDP, 573–574
  decrease in aggregate demand, 571–573
  equilibrium in, 569
  increase in aggregate demand, 569–571
  increase in aggregate demand and long-run
    aggregate supply curves, 574–576
  long-run aggregate supply curve
    (LRAS), 568
  short-run aggregate supply curve (SRAS),
    566–568
Self-interest, 809
"Self-reliance" policy, 818
Sellers, 72–73, 77, 128, 277–278
Senate Budget Committee, 633
September 11, 2001, terror attacks, 498
Service industries, 407
Shaw, George Bernard, 12, 506
Sherman Antitrust Act of 1890, 254, 348,
  350, 366
  provisions, 348
Shortage, 79, 85
Short run
  defined, 184, 200
  monopolistic competition in, 273–274
Short-run aggregate supply curve (SRAS),
  566–568, 569, 576
Short-run average total cost (SRATC), 193, 195
Short-run competitive equilibrium, 232–233
Short-run cost curves, 190
Short-run cost formulas, 187–190, 191
Short-run equilibrium, 225–226, 287
Short-run loss, 220–222, 251, 253
Short-run loss minimization, 220–223, 251, 253
Short-run production costs, 184–187
Short-run profit maximization
  marginal revenue equals marginal cost
    method, 218–220, 251, 252
  for monopoly, 248–250, 261
  for perfectly competitive firm, 215–220
  total revenue-total cost method, 215–218,
    235, 248–250
Short-run supply curves, 223–226, 235–236
  perfectly competitive firm, defined, 224
Shortsightedness effect, 619
Shutting down, perfectly competitive firm,
  222–223
Singapore, GDP of, 826–827
Single seller, 242
Slope of a curve, 26–27
Slope of a straight line, 23–25
SM. *See* Spending multiplier
Small sellers, many, 268
Small time deposits, 666–667
Smith, Adam, 616, 838
  as father of modern economics, 809
  founder of classical economic theory,
    485, 537
  invisible hand, 212

macroeconomic theory of, 722
market economy, 809–810
overview of, 722
The Wealth of Nations, 111, 157, 197, 346,
  809, 813
Smith, Frederick W., 45
Smithsonian Institution, 45, 796
Smoot-Hawley Act of 1930, 777
Sneakers, demand for, 78–79, 81
Social benefits and costs, 373, 375
Socialism, 812–813, 814–815, 821
  characteristics of, 814–815
  strengths/weaknesses, 815
Social networking, 272
Social Security, 805, 811
Social Security (OASDHI), 331–333
Social Security Act (1935), 332
Social Security Administration (SSA),
  630, 639
Social Security contributions, 417, 419
Social Security payroll tax, 627
Social Security Trust Fund, 331, 332, 630
Solar cars, 377, 378
Solow, Robert, 741
South Africa
  unemployment in, 442
South Korea, GDP of, 826–827
Southwest Airlines, 365
Soviet factory system, 815
Soviet Gosplan, 806, 807
Soviet Ministry of Fisheries, 245
Soviet Union
  command economy, 805–806
  economic system in, 814
Sowell, Thomas, 333
Spain, 635
  inflation rate, 471
Special-interest group effect, 618
Special-interest groups, 627
Specialization, 197, 772, 773–774
Spending caps, 630–631
Spending multiplier (SM), 513–517, 523,
  579–582, 595, 712
  MPC and, 582
  MPS and, 582
  vs. tax multiplier, 583
Spillover effect, 112
"Spot market," 362
Sprint, 354, 358
SRAS. *See* Short-run aggregate supply curve
SRATC. *See* Short-run average total cost
SSA. *See* Social Security Administration
Stability, economic, 722
Stagflation, 547, 548, 549, 554, 589
Staggers Rail Act of 1980, 358
Stah, Max Lowes, 472
Stalin, Josef, 814
Standard Oil, 346, 347, 348, 352, 356
  monopoly, 254
Standard & Poor's, 721
Standex International Corporation, 11
Steel industry, 115
Steinbeck, John, 451
Stock acquisition of competing companies, 349
Stock market crash, 484, 498–499
Stocks, 406, 423
Store of value, 660, 676
Strauss, Levi, 5
Structural unemployment, 444–445, 453
  causes of, 444–445
  consumer demand, change in, 444
  education, lack of, 444
  globalization, 445
  technological advancement, 444–445
Subprime loan crisis, 469
Sub-Saharan Africa, GDP of, 826, 828

Substitute goods, 66, 68, 138–139, 143, 145, 148
Substitution effect, 161–163, 164, 465
Sudoku puzzles, 810
Sulfur dioxide, 381, 383, 384, 388
Sulfur emissions, 372–373, 381, 382
Super Bowl, 11, 272
"Superfund" law, 416
Supplemental Nutrition Assistance Program (SNAP). See Food stamps
Supply. See also Demand; Market supply
  changes in, 101–104
  changes in quantity supplied vs. changes in supply, 71–72
  in circular flow model, 404–406
  definition, 68
  expectations of producers, 75, 78
  law of, 68–71, 84
  and market equilibrium, 101–104
  nonprice determinants of, 71, 72–78, 84–85
  number of sellers, 72–73, 77, 128
  prices of other goods firm could produce, 75, 77, 78
  resource prices, 75, 77, 128
  shift in vs. movement along supply curve, 73
  shifts in for health care, 128
  for sneakers, 78–79, 81
  taxes and subsidies, 75, 77
  technology, 73–74, 77
Supply curve, 69, 73, 77–78
Supply curve of labor, 297, 298, 310
Supply of money curve, 706–707
Supply shifters, 71
"Supply shock," 546, 741, 756
Supply-side economics, 589, 591, 594, 755
Supply-side fiscal policy, 589–594, 596
Supreme Court, U.S., 614
Surplus, 78–79, 85
Sustainability, 392
Sweden, 638
  government expenditure, 606
  tax burden, 608
Sweeney, John D., Jr., 332

T

T-accounts, 681
Taiwan, GDP of, 826–827
TANF. See Temporary Assistance to Needy Families
Tannenbaum, Carl, 498
Tariff, 776–778
TARP. See Troubled Assets Recovery Program
Tastes and preferences, 65, 67, 127, 791–792
Taxable income, 616
Taxation. See also Tax cuts
  ability-to-pay principle, 609–610
  ad valorem, 777
  average tax rate, 611
  benefits-received principle, 608–609
  bureaucratic inefficiency, 619
  consumption tax, 605
  effluent taxes, 379–381, 388, 389, 393
  excise, 605
  flat tax, 602, 613, 614–615
  growth of as percentage of GDP, 609
  impact of and price elasticity, 144–146
  indirect business tax, 410, 411, 423
  majority-rule problem, 616–617
  marginal tax rate, 611–612
  national sales tax, 614–615
  negative income tax, 334–335, 341
  pollution and, 114
  price elasticity, 144–146

progressive taxes, 610–611
proportional taxes, 613–614
rational voter ignorance, 618–619
reformation of, 614–615
regressive taxes, 612
shortsightedness effect, 619
special-interest group effect, 618
and subsidies, 75, 77, 114–115
tax incidence, 146, 148
value-added tax (VAT), 614–615
Tax burden, 606–607, 621
  Australia, 608
  Denmark, 608
  France, 608
  Germany, 608
  Greece, 608
  Japan, 608
  Sweden, 608
  United Kingdom, 608
  United States, 608
Tax credit, 499
Tax cuts. See also Taxation
  budget surplus and, 630, 633
  to combat recession, 582–584
  discretionary fiscal policy, 582–584
  Reagan and, 576, 589
  recessionary gap, 519–520
  supply-side effects vs. Keynesian demand-side effects, 593
Taxi and Limousine Commission (TLC), 260
Taxicabs, 260
Tax incidence, 146, 148
Tax multiplier (TM), 519, 524, 583–584, 590, 591, 595
  vs. spending multiplier, 583
Tax Reform Act of 1986, 615
T-bills (Treasury bills), 629, 644
TC. See Total cost
"Tea Parties," 602
Technological advances, unemployment and, 444–445
Technological change, 44, 48, 498, 573
Technological knowledge, 835
Technological progress, 834–835
Technology, 38, 73–74, 77
Teenagers, and unemployment, 450
Telephone service, 353–354
Temporary Assistance to Needy Families (TANF), 331
Tennessee Valley Authority (TVA), 383, 813
Terror attacks (September 11, 2001), 498
TFC. See Total fixed cost
Theory, economic, 8. See also Models
Third parties, 112, 125, 361, 372
Three-variable relationship, 27–28
Thrift Bailout Bill, 675
Time deposit, 666
Time magazine, 749
Tit-for-tat strategy, 284
TLC. See Taxi and Limousine Commission
TM. See Tax multiplier; Tucker Motors
Tobacco, 141
Total cost (TC), 187–188, 191, 200
Total cost curves, 187–188
Total fixed cost (TFC), 187, 200
Total revenue (TR), 132, 137, 138, 246–248
Total revenue test, 132
Total revenue-total cost method, of profit maximization, 215–218, 235, 248–250
Total utility, 155–158, 163–164
  curve, 156
Total variable cost (TVC), 187, 200
Toyota Motor Corp., 447
TR. See Total revenue
Trade deficits, 783–785, 787

Trading partners, U.S., 771
Traditional economy, 805
Tragedy of the Commons, 392
Trains, as example of Coase Theorem, 386–389
Transactions costs, 389, 394
Transactions demand for money, 705, 725
Transfer payments, 403, 408, 417, 519, 587, 603
Transitional unemployment, 443
Treasury, U.S., 626, 629–630, 637, 639–640, 642, 644, 663, 667, 669, 671, 672
Treasury bills (T-bills), 629, 644
Treasury Department, 796
Troubled Assets Recovery Program (TARP), 721
Trough, 432–433, 434, 452
Truman, Harry, 12, 753
Trust, 347, 366
Tucker: The Man and His Dreams (movie), 279
Tucker Motors, 280, 363–364
TVA. See Tennessee Valley Authority
TVC. See Total variable cost
Twitter, 272
Tying contracts, 349

U

U. S. Department of Justice, 339
U. S. Forest Service, 386
UAW. See United Auto Workers
Underemployment, 443
Underground economy, 414–415
Unemployment
  causes of, 722
  cyclical, 445, 453
  by demographic groups, 448–450
  discouraged workers, 441, 443, 451, 452
  educational attainment and, 450
  frictional, 443–444, 452–453
  in Germany, 442
  during the Great Depression (1929-1933), 440, 445, 451, 723
  during the Great Recession (2010), 440
  human costs of, 451
  and inflation, 740–747, 756
  internationally, 440–441, 442
  introduction to, 439–440
  natural rate of, 446, 746–747
  nonmonetary and demographic consequences, 448–450
  in South Africa, 442
  structural, 444–445, 453
  teenagers and, 450
  transitional, 443
  types of, 443–445
Unemployment compensation, 331
Unemployment rate
  criticisms of, 441, 443
  historically, 441
  internationally, 442
  introduction to, 439–440
  overstating, 441
  price level and real GDP, 550
  in 1970s, 756
  understating, 443
Unfavorable balance of trade, 783
Uniformity, 662, 675
Union membership, 302–304, 305
Unique product, 242
Unitary elastic demand, 133–134, 135, 138, 147

Unitary elastic supply, 143, 145
United Arab Emirates, 826, 829
United Auto Workers (UAW), 821
United Kingdom
    GDP of, 413
    government expenditure, 606
    tax burden, 608
    unemployment in, 442
United Nations, 819, 841
United States
    balance of trade with India, 787
    business cycles, 435
    GDP of, 413
    government expenditure, 606
    inflation rate, 464, 471
    tax burden, 608
    unemployment, 442
Unit of account, 660, 676
University of Chicago, 748
Unplanned inventory investment,
    510, 511
Upshaw, David L., 11
Upward-sloping
    curve, 26
    line, 23
Uruguay round, 777
U.S. Congress, 626, 627, 628, 630, 633, 634,
    637, 781
U.S. Department of Justice, 353, 354
U.S. House of Representatives, 628
U.S. Mint, 797
U.S. Postal Service, 243, 813
U.S. Secret Service, 661
U.S. Senate, 628, 631, 633
U.S. Steel, 352
U.S. Supreme Court, 117
U.S. Treasury, 332, 626, 629–630, 637,
    639–640, 642, 644, 663, 667, 669,
    671, 672
USA Today, 76, 117, 233
Utah, 351
Utah Pie Company, 351
Utility, 155–158, 163
Utility, marginal, 155–158, 163
Utility companies, 358

V

Value-added tax (VAT), 614–615
Value judgments, 14, 16
Variable input, 184
Variables
    direct relationship, 21–22
    independent relationship, 25
    inverse relationships, 23, 24
    slope of a straight line, 23–25
    three-variable relationship, 27–28
VAT. See Value-added tax
Velocity of money, 716, 717–718, 726
Veneman, Ann, 522
Venezuela
    inflation rates, 470, 471
Vertical merger, 356, 366
Vicious circle of poverty, 833, 842–843
Vietnam War, 464, 753
Vizio, 76

W

Wage and price controls, 753–754, 758
Wage and price guidelines, 753
Wage maker, 308
Wage-price spiral, 472, 745
Wage rates, 306–308
Wagner Act, 302
The Wall Street Journal, 76, 472, 522, 594, 749
Wal-Mart, 804
Wants, coincidence of, 659, 660
War of 1812, 626
Washington, George, 662, 665
The Washington Post, 232, 336
Water-diamond paradox, 157
Wealth, inflation and, 468
Wealth effect, 494
The Wealth of Nations (Smith), 111, 157, 197,
    346, 719, 809, 813, 838
Web sites, 198
Welfare programs, criticisms of, 333
    inefficiencies, 333
    inequities, 333
    work disincentives, 333
Wells, Lawler, 232
Whip Inflation Now (WIN) button, 756
Wikipedia, 76
Willingness to accept (WTA), 391
Willingness to pay (WTP), 391
Winfrey, Oprah, 293
The Wonderful Wizard of Oz
    allegory of exchange rates, 796
Workfare, 335–336
Working poor, 13
World Bank, 841
World Trade Organization (WTO), 770,
    777–778, 780–781, 836
World War II, 631, 633, 635–636, 637, 639,
    640–641, 841
WTA. See Willingness to accept
WTO. See World Trade Organization
WTP. See Willingness to pay
Wyoming, Joe, 309

X

Xerox Corporation, 44

Y

Yap, 658, 662, 672
Yen, 770, 788–793, 797
YouTube, 272
Yucca Mountain, 385

Z

Zandi, Mark, 584
Zappes.com, 272
Zimbabwe
    inflation in, 457, 473